THE ENCYCLOPAEDIA OF EDUCATIONAL MEDIA COMMUNICATIONS AND TECHNOLOGY

The Encyclopaedia of Educational Media Communications and Technology

SECOND EDITION

EDITED BY
DERICK UNWIN AND
RAY McALEESE
Foreword by Geoffrey Hubbard

GREENWOOD PRESS

NEW YORK • WESTPORT, CONNECTICUT • LONDON

Library of Congress Cataloging-in-Publication Data

The Encyclopaedia of educational media communications and technology.

　　Includes bibliographies and index.
　　1. Audio-visual education—Dictionaries.　2. Audio-visual materials—Dictionaries.　3. Educational technology—Dictionaries.　I. Unwin, Derick.
II. McAleese, Ray.
LB1042.5.E52　　　1988　　　371.3′078　　　87–15049
ISBN 0–313–23996–7 (lib. bdg. : alk. paper)

British Library Cataloguing in Publication Data is available.

Copyright © 1988 by Derick Unwin and Ray McAleese

All rights reserved. No portion of this book may be reproduced, by any process or technique, without the express written consent of the publisher.

Library of Congress Catalog Card Number: 87–15049
ISBN: 0–313–23996–7

First published in 1988

Greenwood Press, Inc.
88 Post Road West, Westport, Connecticut 06881

Printed in the United States of America

The paper used in this book complies with the Permanent Paper Standard issued by the National Information Standards Organization (Z39.48–1984).

10　9　8　7　6　5　4　3　2　1

Contents

Contributors	vii
Figures and Tables	xi
Foreword *by Geoffrey Hubbard*	xiii
Preface to the Second Edition	xv
From the Preface to the First Edition	xvii
Macro-Entries	xix
The Encyclopaedia of Educational Media Communications and Technology	1
Index	565

Contributors

JOHN ALEXANDER
Brunel University, London, U.K.

JOHN S. A. ANDERSON
N.I. Department of Education, Belfast, Northern Ireland, U.K.

P. G. BARKER
Department of Computing, University of Durham, Durham, U.K.

F. N. BIRKETT
Department of Mechanical Engineering, Loughborough University of Technology, Loughborough, U.K.

ROBERT BOGNER
Department of Electrical Engineering, University of Adelaide, Adelaide, Australia

ETEINNE BRUNSWIC
Division of Educational Sciences, Contents and Methods of Education, UNESCO, Paris, France

KLAUS BUNG
Recall Training Consultants, London, U.K.

LACHLAN CAMERON
Department of Teacher Education, University of Dublin, Dublin, Eire

R. A. CANNON
Advisory Centre for University Education, University of Adelaide, Adelaide, Australia

GLENN F. CARTWRIGHT
Department of Educational Psychology and Counselling, McGill University, Montreal, Canada

S. CLARK
Scottish Microelectronics Development Project, Glasgow, Scotland, U.K.

JILL COATES
Council for Educational Technology, London, U.K.

RICHARD COTTER
Hawthorn Institute of Education, Melbourne, Australia

GEOFF CRABB
Council for Educational Technology, London, U.K.

F. C. CRIX
Reprographic Services, Open University, Milton Keynes, U.K.

B. CRONIN
Aslib Research Department, London, U.K.

D. DALY
Scottish Council for Educational Technology, Glasgow, Scotland, U.K.

J. S. DANIEL
Laurentian University, Sudbury, Ontario, Canada

CHRISTOPHER DEDE
Education and Futures Research, University of Houston, Houston, Texas, U.S.

ROBERT M. DIAMOND
Center for Instructional Development, Syracuse University, Syracuse, New York, U.S.

NEIL DOHERTY
Queensland Education Department, Brisbane, Australia

JANET DONALD
Center for University Teaching & Learning, McGill University, Montreal, Canada

COLIN DUNNETT
State Education Department, Adelaide, South Australia

A. B. EDINGTON
Media Group Science Technology & Education Division, British Council, London, U.K.

DAN ELLIS
Educational Research & Development Unit, Queensland Institute of Technology, Brisbane, Australia

D. ELY
ERIC Clearinghouse on Information Resources, Syracuse University, Syracuse, New York, U.S.

C. E. ENGEL
Consultant Advisor, Wellcome Tropical Institute, London, U.K.

B. FARRINGTON
Language Laboratory, University of Aberdeen, Aberdeen, Scotland, U.K.

D. J. FOSKETT
Former Librarian, Institute of Education, University of London, London, U.K.

T. W. FYFE
Learning Resources, Dundee College of Education, Scotland, U.K.

GEORGE GEDDES
Jordanhill College of Education, Scotland, U.K.

M. GOLBY
Department of Education, University of Exeter, Exeter, U.K.

EGON G. GUBA
Department of Educational Leadership, Vanderbilt University, Nashville, Tennessee, U.S.

J. HARTLEY
Department of Psychology, University of Keele, Keele, U.K.

D. HAWKRIDGE
Institute of Educational Technology, Open University, Milton Keynes, U.K.

E. U. HEIDT
Fakultat für Padagogik, Universitat Bielefeld, Bielefeld, West Germany

CURTIS P. HO
Educational Communications & Technology, University of Hawaii, U.S.

ANNE HOWE
Middlesex Polytechnic, London, U.K.

JIM HOWE
Department of Artificial Intelligence, University of Edinburgh, Edinburgh, Scotland, U.K.

GEOFFREY HUBBARD
Former Director, Council for Educational Technology, London, U.K.

ZIG KAPELIS
University of Adelaide, Adelaide, Australia

J. M. KELLER
College of Education, Florida State University, Tallahassee, Florida, U.S.

GEORGE R. KLARE
Department of Psychology, Ohio University, Athens, Ohio, U.S.

LORNE E. KOROLUK
University of British Columbia, Vancouver, Canada

GEOFFREY Z. KUCERA
Educational Communications & Technology, University of Hawaii, Honolulu, Hawaii, U.S.

D. G. LANGDON
Corporate Training, Morrison-Knudsen Co., Inc., Boise, Idaho, U.S.

JIM LANGE
Golden West Network, Perth, Western Australia

MILOŠ LÁNSKÝ
Paderborn, West Germany

A. ARVO LEPS
Department of Radio-TV-Film, California State University, Northridge, California, U.S.

YVONNA S. LINCOLN
Department of Educational Leadership, Vanderbilt University, Nashville, Tennessee, U.S.

GRAEME LINDENMAYER
Commercial Development, Telecom Australia, Melbourne, Australia

D. S. LITSTER
Educational Research & Development Unit, Queensland Institute of Technology, Brisbane, Australia

STEPHEN K. LOWER
Department of Chemistry, Simon Fraser University, Burnaby, British Columbia, Canada

RAY McALEESE
University Teaching Centre, University of Aberdeen, Scotland, U.K.

TOM McHALE
State Government Computer Centre, Queensland, Australia

G. R. McNUTT
Faculty of Education, University of New Brunswick, Fredericton, New Brunswick, Canada

J. K. MILLER
Copyright Information Services, Friday Harbor, Washington, U.S.

JOHN NISBET
Department of Education, University of Aberdeen, Aberdeen, Scotland, U.K.

SEYMOUR PAPERT
Department of Mathematics, Massachusetts Institute of Technology, Cambridge, Massachusetts, U.S.

LORNE PARKER
Center for Interactive Programs, University of Wisconsin, Madison, Wisconsin, U.S.

GORDON PASK
Department of Education, Concordia University, Montreal, Canada

P. PEARSON
Peat, Marwick, McLintock, Management Consultants, London, U.K.

S. N. POSTLETHWAIT
Department of Biological Sciences, Purdue University, West Lafayette, Indiana, U.S.

J. M. ROLFE
Ministry of Defense, London, U.K.

N. RUSHBY
Imperial College Computer Centre, London, U.K.

PAUL SAETTLER
Educational Technology & Educational Psychology, California State University, Sacramento, California, U.S.

DEREK SHANKS
Education Department, University of Aberdeen, Aberdeen, Scotland, U.K.

RICHARD SHERRINGTON
Media Department, British Council, London, U.K.

MALCOLM SKILBECK
Deakin University, Geelong, Australia

CONTRIBUTORS

PATRICK SUPPES
  Institute for Mathematical Studies in the Social Sciences, Stanford University, Stanford, California, U.S.

S. JOHN TEAGUE
  Librarian Emeritus, City University, London, U.K.

DAVID C. B. TEATHER
  Armidale College of Advanced Education, Armidale, Australia

MARIELA TOVAR
  Graduate Program in Educational Technology, Concordia University, Montreal, Canada

R. TUCKER
  Scottish Council for Educational Technology, Glasgow, Scotland, U.K.

DERICK UNWIN
  Educational Research & Development Unit, Queensland Institute of Technology, Brisbane, Australia

JESUS VAZQUEZ
  Department of Education, Concordia University, Montreal, Canada

BRUCE WINDOW
  Engineering Department, Australian Broadcasting Commission, Brisbane, Australia

LAURA WINER
  Department of Education, Concordia University, Montreal, Canada

RAYMOND WYMAN
  Professor Emeritus, School of Education, University of Massachusetts, Amherst, Massachusetts, U.S.

VALERIE YULE
  Department of Psychology, University of Aberdeen, Scotland, U.K.

Figures and Tables

FIGURES

1. Flow Chart Showing Audio Media Message Production — 36
2. Triangle Representing the Range of Colors Obtainable from an Addition of Three Primary Colors — 80
3. Signals Corresponding to the Message "Jones Sells Fresh Fruit" — 82
4. Periodic Nature of a Speech Signal, Extracted from "o" in "Jones" — 83
5. Sampling, Quantization, and PCM — 86
6. Description of Signals in Time and in Frequency — 86
7. Multiplexing of Frequency Division and Time Division — 87
8. PCM Signal with Dispersion and Noise — 87
9. Fraction of Transmitted Power Remaining after Passage through 1km of a Typical Coaxial Cable, Showing the Dependence on Frequency — 87
10. Communication Systems with Repeaters in Cascade — 88
11. Use of Light Pen — 90
12. Video Displays — 91
13. Configurations of Communication Systems — 94
14. Communication Satellites — 98
15. The Interrelationship among Models — 132
16. The Comprehensive Model — 133
17. The Classroom/Product Model — 133
18. The Concept of Feedback Circuit Applied to a Thermostatically Controlled Central Heating Process and to a Teaching Process to Show the Similarities/Parallels at a Certain Level of Abstraction — 196
19. Educational Cybernetics as Science or Technology — 198
20. The Didactic Variables — 199
21. State Matrix — 201
22. Communication Model of Information Theory — 202
23. Different Ways of Adjusting Content of Instruction to the Learner — 203
24. Relations — 205
25. Transition Matrix, T — 208
26. Output Matrix, O — 208
27. Merged Matrix ("Automaton Table"), M — 208
28. Automaton Table of the Fierli Automaton — 209
29. Types of Charts — 260
30. Types of Graphs — 263
31. Types of Drawings and Illustrations — 264
32. Poster — 264
33. Cartoon — 264
34. Camera Registration for Graphic Artwork — 270
35. Model of Environment for Learning — 342
36. Grouping and Layout of Lecture Theaters — 351
37. Design of a Theater at Sydney University — 352
38. Alternative Arrangements for Furnishings in Seminar Rooms — 353
39. Grouping of Different Size Learning Spaces — 354
40. Trolley for Audiovisual Equipment — 354

41. Space for Individualized Instruction	354
42. Alternative Arrangements for Rectangular and Trapezium Tables	356
43. A Movable Lecturer's Bench	356
44. The Communication Media	371
45. A Hierarchical Order of Selected Audiovisual Instrumental Media	372
46. Instructional Functions of Various Media	374
47. Media Classified by Encoding versus Duration	375
48. Media Classified by Encoding versus Response Demand	375
49. Media Taxonomy Cube	377
50. The Three Levels of the Stimulus Encoding Dimension	378
51. Identifying Functional Media Attributes	379
52. Microphone Characteristics	395
53. An Extract from a Typical Early Linear Program	452
54. A Typical Frame from a Branching Program on Electronics	453
55. Diagrammatic Representation of Relationship between Simulations and Games: Two Overlapping Sets	478
56. Diagrammatic Representation of Relationship between Simulations, Games, and Contests: Three Overlapping Sets	479
57. Role Pro Forma Used by Players in the Toreside Comprehensive School Simulation-Game	482
58. Examples of Audiovisual Symbols	499

TABLES

1. Channel Requirements of Some Typical Signals	85
2. Major Communication Bearers	92
3. CAI Courses Offered by Computer Curriculum Corporation	108
4. The Strands in Mathematics Skills, Grades 1–8	109
5. The Strands in Language Arts Skills, Grades 3–6	110
6. Mean Time and Cumulative Mean Time for 1979–1980	111
7. Computer Nomenclature	119
8. Comprehensive Models—A Representative Sample	134
9. Support Models—A Representative Sample	134
10. Descriptions of Forms of Charts	262
11. Descriptions of Forms of Graphs	263
12. Modern American Color Associations	266
13. Color Combinations Inappropriate for Color-Deficient Viewers	268
14. Graphic Design Constraints Relative to Display Medium	269
15. Standard Sizes in Graphics for Camera	271
16. Minimum Lettering Height in Graphics	272
17. Some Factors Influencing the Design of Spaces for Audiovisual Media	348
18. The Results of 112 Studies Comparing Programmed with Conventional Instruction	453

Foreword

The Foreword to a wide-ranging conspectus, such as is contained in this volume, is an opportunity to cast an eye both backwards and forwards; to see how far we have come, and to look more keenly at where we might be going. But who are "we"? It is perhaps desirable to start off by saying for whom I write, and who I expect to be the readers of this volume.

The list of contributors is of course deceptive in this regard. They are all highly experienced specialists in their respective fields and, unless the publishers are showing an unusual degree of unworldliness, that is not the class to which they hope to sell: there are not enough of them and they are nearly all on the Contributors list. No, the target audience is much wider and more general; it is all those in teaching and training who are interested in how people learn and how we help them to learn—and that should be all teachers and trainers—and all those whose decisions affect education and training.

The backward look first. Where have we come from and where have we got to? We have come out of the application of audiovisual aids and in many respects we have not, for all the research and all the hard work, got very far. Look, for example, at the place of educational broadcasting today. The quality of the programs generated by the major educational broadcasters is first-class: first-class radio and television and first-class support material for any teacher prepared to take advantage of it. But the extent to which it is used is a continual disappointment. Or, look at the overhead projector—it fits in with the existing teaching style, simply replacing the blackboard with a cleaner and clearer presentational device which enables the expositor to continue to face his audience while pointing to the screen. Yet at two recent international conferences I have seen one presenter put up screens full of typescript which were totally unreadable in the forward rows of the audience, and another turn his back to the audience in order to point with a very long stick at the words on the screen.

There is, however, another aspect of educational technology which I sense has had an impact. It has little to do with equipment; it is the development of ideas about the context in which people learn, the exploration of resource-based and independent learning and of open and distant learning. It seems to me that minds are very much more open to new approaches than they were ten or fifteen years ago, and this of course is infinitely more encouraging than any mere adoption of an aid or technique. It supports the line always taken by the professional educational technologist, that it is only by changing the system that we get significant results; aids prop up existing practices.

This is a matter of some significance when we look to the future. It is now a commonplace to observe that we are in a period of rapid and far-reaching change, resulting from the impact of information technology. It is not just a case of being over-impressed by clever machines; there are characteristics of information technology that make it a most powerful agent of change. First, it is a technology which is miserly in its use of energy, material, and human effort. Second, it is still in its infancy, with the power of devices doubling every two years or so, and costs falling at the same rate. Third, it promises to change our developed economies by making information the most significant traded commodity, and as Anthony Smith has pointed out, information is the only commodity which you still possess after you have sold it to somebody else.

We are, then, embarking on a period of extensive social and economic change, whether planned or adventitious. In looking forward we must ask what needs these times will throw up, what demands will be imposed on the education and training system, and only then how the system can meet those needs and demands. I believe that an effective member of society in the coming decade will be the sort of person we would describe today as the product of a balanced education. He should possess a range of skills in communication and coordination which will enable him to function effectively in a complex environment, have the ability to make moral and aesthetic judgments against internal standards, be self-motivating, a problem solver, yet sensitive, caring, and altruistic. Today, however, we set this paragon up as an ideal, and turn out something rather different. My suspicion is that the future may actually require that we do something about it, and that the social and economic consequences of not so doing may be very serious.

Another factor of some significance is that this very same technology, which is changing society and which offers interesting and powerful methods to education—the ability to make the material really responsive to the student—also extends the capacity of the student to sidestep the institutional system. The electronic systems which will be extended to us so that we may buy goods and services will also enable us to explore extensive sources of information and to take up opportunities to learn; there will be plenty willing to offer the opportunities commercially.

Therefore, if we believe that the professional has something of value to offer, it behooves us to reshape the institutions of education to take advantage of the new technologies and to meet the challenges they pose. That is why it is encouraging that it is ideas that have had an impact rather than equipment. If it seems today that the developments in education are in danger of being equipment-led, we should recognize that this particular demon has already been let loose; it is our world that is being driven by it. Education and training cannot stand aside unless they are prepared to find themselves in a siding. What we have to do is to understand and apply the developments in a sound educational context.

This volume shows that there is plenty of work going on to that end: plenty, but by no means too much. Traditionally, education and training have been conservative, willing to tolerate much in the way of experiment but slow to adopt new methods. In our accelerated modern timescale, we may have to be more adventurous.

Geoffrey Hubbard

Preface to the Second Edition

It is now eight years since the first edition of *EEMCAT* went to press. The march of technology has been more than impressive during this period: nowhere in the first edition was there any suggestion that cheap ubiquitous microcomputers were soon to provide all-purpose adaptive teaching machines, thus belatedly fulfilling one of the cherished dreams of the 1960s teaching machine enthusiasts. Of course it is not the function of *EEMCAT* contributors to devote much space to crystal-balling; the work is intended as a description of what *is*, and only to a modest extent what *might be*. Clearly the educational world as a whole was taken by surprise with regard to the implications of developments in electronics, particularly advances in microprocessor technology and in video storage and retrieval.

Not only are many modern devices inexpensive in real terms, they also offer a magnificent degree of flexibility to educational designers and practitioners. Thus far this has not been an unmixed blessing: the virility of the theory and practice of learning materials design is revealed to be less than adequate for the new situation; educators have long complained of being restrained by the inadequacies of available hardware; we are now finding that a lack of imagination can also be a serious impediment to the evolution of exciting and effective teaching materials.

EEMCAT has been subject to massive changes to accommodate these new thrusts and concerns of education. In addition to major rewriting of all substantial entries found in the first edition, some 34 major entries did not appear the first time around. In nearly every case the omission was because of either nonexistence or minimal importance as perceived in 1977–1978. All these new areas have in turn generated a pervasive jargon of their own, and this is reflected in a radical increase in the number of shorter definition-type "micro-entries" in *EEMCAT2*. No attempt, however, has been made to compete with the various authoritative dictionaries covering such fields as satellite technology, computers, photography, communications, and so on. Rather it has been our policy to identify and include only those terms which are likely to be specifically encountered in an educational context; this of course has not been easy and it is left to the readership to assess how well we have exercised our judgment.

A number of the earlier entries have been omitted on this occasion; for example, virtually all statistical definitions (product-moment correlation, variance, etc.) have been discarded: there is a plethora of readily available texts explaining such items. In spite of this trimming, the micro-entry category now contains around 1,800 entries, as against less than 900 previously.

Probably the most crucial question confronting educators today relates to the fundamental organization of educational systems. The sorts of developments in media and technology that are chronicled in *EEMCAT* suggest with irresistible force that there is no longer a clear and obvious necessity for centralized learning, at least to anything like the extent that we are accustomed to. That is, for much of the formal curriculum it is becoming at best pointless, not to mention economically foolish, to bring students together for institutionalized learning. In fact, changes in education in the coming years will inevitably be dictated by economic and political factors arising out of advancing technology, and these changes are unlikely to be restricted to minor elements of adjustment to existing structures.

Thus this second edition of *EEMCAT* will mark a watershed, dividing the past when media and technology were grafted onto an essentially unchanging pattern of education, from the future wherein learning will chiefly be implemented by new delivery systems owing little to past practice. Educators seem destined, in the words of the old curse, "to live in interesting times."

Derick Unwin
Brisbane, Queensland, Australia
August 1987

From the Preface to the First Edition

The fields embraced by the title of this work are of interest to a very wide range of professional and technical personnel. In the nature of things, few if any workers will have more than a passing acquaintance with the complete range of subjects. That is to say, most of us operate within quite specific operational areas, but nonetheless we frequently need access to information and detail relating to some other topic. The present writer, in the capacity of teacher and researcher, was often reminded of this need, and not infrequently felt irritation at the large number of sources which might have to be consulted to supply the wanted information.

Thus was born the concept of a comprehensive reference book, an encyclopaedia, which could hopefully provide within one volume material which otherwise was widely scattered and consequently difficult to alight upon. This grand design has been gestating for several years, and, as is the way with such worthy intentions, no doubt in its present edition suffers from omissions and shortcomings. It is hoped that the readership will actively communicate with the editorial staff regarding any suggestions for future improvement.

Derick Unwin
April 1977

Macro-Entries

Extended entries are provided on the following topics:

Artificial Intelligence
Assessment
Audio Instruction
Audiovisual Media
Authoring Languages for Computer-Assisted Instruction
Communication Engineering
Communication Satellites
Component Resources
Computer-Assisted Instruction
Copyright (U.K.)
Copyright (U.S.)
Cost-Effectiveness
Course Design
Curriculum Design
Curriculum Theory
Delphi Technique
Developing Countries
Distance Education
Educational Broadcasting
Educational Cybernetics
Educational Innovation
Educational Research Methodology
Evaluation
Evaluation, Naturalistic
Expert Systems
Graphic Design
History of Educational Technology
Holography
Individualization of Instruction
Information Classification and Retrieval
Information Systems for Education

Information Technology
Interactive Video
Language Laboratory
Learning Environment
Media Classification
Medical Education
Microcomputers in Education
Microforms
Military Training
Motivational Design
New Technology and Education
Open University
Orthography
Photocopying and Duplicating
Photography
Programmed Learning
Resource-Based Learning
Simulation and Gaming
Standards in Audiovisual Technology
Symbionics
Teaching Machines
Team Teaching
Telesoftware
Teletext
Television, Educational and Instructional
Textbook Design
Training Technology
UNESCO
Video Recording and Reproduction
Viewdata
Visual Literacy

THE ENCYCLOPAEDIA OF EDUCATIONAL MEDIA COMMUNICATIONS AND TECHNOLOGY

A

AASL. *See* **American Association of School Librarians.**

ABBREVIATIONS. *See* **Acronyms.**

ABC. (1) American Broadcasting Companies: one of the major U.S. broadcasting organizations. (2) *See* **Australian Broadcasting Corporation**.

ABERRATION. A deficiency of lenses which inevitably are imperfect to some degree. The use of multiple elements in a lens can greatly reduce but never eliminate aberrations. The effect of aberration is to degrade the quality of the image.

ABILITY GROUPING. An experimental design technique where subjects are grouped by ability. A program of heterogeneous grouping such that students are selected for educational provision by tests which measure their general or specialized scholastic ability. As only the intellectual aspect of the subjects can be ascertained, there can be wide variation due to external circumstances.

ACADEMIC GAME. Any game that has a specific educational application can be called an academic game. In the terminology of simulation and games a game is distinguished from a simulation by whether it is possible to have winners and losers; that is to say, an academic game has an element of competition not inherent in the real-life situation. Many such games are primarily intended for formal classroom use, but others such as Scrabble can be termed academic games with equal validity.

ACCELERATED MOTION. Means whereby movement in a film takes place at greater speed than it did in reality; opposite of slow motion.

ACCELERATED SPEECH. *See* **Time-Compressed Speech.**

ACCENTUATED CONTRAST. In facsimile, a method of operation whereby all picture elements having a luminance exceeding an intermediate reference level are transmitted as white; those having a luminance level less than the reference are transmitted as black.

ACCESS TIME. In microcomputer hard-disk specifications, the average time it takes for the disk drive to find and read from or write to any selected spot on the disk. Access times vary in the approximate range of 20–100 milliseconds.

More generally, the time that elapses between the instant the control unit calls for a transfer of data to or from a store and the instant this operation is completed. Also the delay encountered when a computer terminal is used for on-line operations as in computer-assisted learning.

ACCUMULATOR. A computer term used to describe a register or a specific storage location in which arithmetic or logical results can be accumulated.

ACE. *See* **American Council on Education.**

ACETATE. Cellulose acetate is a transparent material used for film stock and for overhead transparencies and animation cells. Cellulose nitrate was originally used as a base for movie film, but its highly inflammable nature represented a major fire hazard. With the introduction of the 16mm gauge in 1923 Kodak produced a "safety" film using cellulose acetate. Since 1951 all movie film has been made of cellulose triacetate, which combines noninflammability with the dimensional stability of the nitrate base.

ACHIEVEMENT, ASSESSMENT OF. The technique associated with measuring an individual's achievement against a specific achievement standard (norm), e.g., achievement tests (tests covering areas of academic performance). In experimental programs, it is very difficult to attribute a subject's achievement solely to the experimental variable.

ACHROMATIC. This specialized term is applied to lenses which have been designed with a combination of optical glass types which enable the focal points of different colors of light being transmitted to be brought together in one place, usually the plane of the film being used. Simple lenses do not provide this combining power and are said to suffer from "chromatic aberration." *See* **Apochromat.**

ACOUSTIC COUPLER. A modem-like device which converts data sent from a computer into audible tones which can then be transmitted over normal telephone lines. At the other end of the transmission line another coupler will convert these tones into signals which can be received by a computer or terminal. The coupler is typically the size of a shoe box onto which a conventional telephone handset is mounted. Normally the coupler is used to connect a computer to a computer or a terminal to a computer. In all cases both ends of the transmission line must be equipped with an acoustic coupler.

ACOUSTIC FEEDBACK. *See* **Feedback.**

ACOUSTICS. All those conditions of a given environment which affect the character of sound produced, recorded, or reproduced in it. *See* **Learning Environment.**

ACQUIRED RESPONSES. Behavior primarily learned through experience as distinct from innate responses, which are those primarily associated with inheritance characteristics. Those responses that can be attributed to a certain course of action or sequence of instruction as opposed to responses acquired without the instructional sequence.

ACRONYMS. The list below gives the full form of many acronyms and other abbreviations in the fields of educational media and technology. Many of the items cited will be the subject of entries elsewhere in this volume.

AASL	American Association of School Librarians
ABC	American Broadcasting Companies
ABC	Australian Broadcasting Corporation
ACE	American Council on Education
ACRL	Association of College and Research Libraries
ADCIS	Association for the Development of Computer-Based Instructional Systems
ADP	Automatic Data Processing
AECT	Association for Educational Communications and Technology
AEDS	Association for Educational Data Systems
AERA	American Educational Research Association
AETT	Association for Educational and Training Technology (U.K.)
AFI	American Film Institute
AFIPS	American Federation of Information Processing Sciences
AID	Agency for International Development
AIT	Agency for Instructional Television
ALA	American Library Association
ALISE	Association for Library and Information Science Education
AM	Amplitude Modulation
AMCEE	Association for Media-Based Continuing Education for Engineers
AMEE	Association for Medical Education in Europe
AMTEC	Association for Media and Technology in Education in Canada
ANSI	American National Standards Institute
APA	American Psychological Association
APL	Association for Programmed Learning (now AETT) (U.K.)
APLET	Association for Programmed Learning and Educational Technology (now AETT) (U.K.)
ARL	Association of Research Libraries
ASA	American Standards Association
ASCAP	American Society of Composers, Authors and Publishers
ASCII	American Standard Code for Information Interchange
ASET	Australian Society of Educational Technology
ASFA	American Science Film Association
ASIDIC	Association of Information and Dissemination Centers
ASIS	American Society for Information Science
ASLA	Association of State Library Agencies
ASME	Association for the Study of Medical Education (U.K.)
BACIE	British Association for Commercial and Industrial Education
BASIC	Beginner's All-purpose Symbolic Instructional Code
BBC	British Broadcasting Corporation
BCS	British Computer Society
BCU	Big Close-Up
BERA	British Educational Research Association
BFI	British Film Institute
BISFA	British Industrial and Scientific Film Association
BJET	British Journal of Educational Technology
BLAT	British Life Assurance Trust for Health Education
BPS	British Psychological Society
BUFC	British Universities Film Council (now BUFVC)

Acronym	Definition
BUFVC	British Universities Film & Video Council
CAD	Computer-Aided Design
CADD	Computer-Aided Design and Drafting
CAI	Computer-Assisted/Aided Instruction
CAL	Computer-Assisted/Aided Learning
CATTS	Computer-Assisted Teacher Training System
CATV	Community Antenna Television
CAV	Constant Angular Velocity
CBC	Canadian Broadcasting Corporation
CBE	Computer Based Education
CBS	Columbia Broadcasting System
CCAVAE	Central Committee of Advisers in Audio-Visual Education
CCI	Comité Consultatif International
CCIR	International Consultative Committee for Radio
CCIT	International Consultative Committee for Communications
CCTV	Closed-Circuit Television
CEDO	Centre for Educational Development Overseas (U.K.)
CELP	Colleges of Educational Learning Programmes (U.K.)
CERI	Centre for Educational Research and Innovation (Europe)
CESA	Cooperative Educational Service Agency
CET	Council for Educational Technology (U.K.)
CFI	Canadian Film Institute
CIJE	Current Index to Journals in Education
CIP	Cataloging in Publication
CIT	Commission on Instructional Technology
CLA	Canadian Library Association
CLV	Constant Linear Velocity
CMI	Computer-Managed Instruction
CML	Computer-Managed Learning
COBOL	Common Business Oriented Language
COMSAT	Communications Satellite Corporation
CREDO	Curriculum Renewal and Educational Development Organization (U.K.)
CRT	Cathode-Ray Tube
CTW	Children's Television Workshop
CWP	Communicating Word Processor
DAIR	Dial Access Information Retrieval
DAVI	Division of Audiovisual Instruction (now AECT)
DBS	Direct Broadcasting Satellite
DES	Department of Education and Science (U.K.)
DIN	Deutsche Industries Normen (Europe)
DOS	Disk Operating System
DRAW	Direct Read After Write
EBR	Electron Beam Recording
EBU	European Broadcasting Union
ECTJ	Educational Communication and Technology Journal
EDISED	European Documentation and Information System
EDTV	Extended Definition Television
EFVA	Educational Foundation for Visual Aids (U.K.)
ENG	Electronic News Gathering
ENIAC	Electronic Numerical Integrator and Calculator
EPIE	Educational Products Information Exchange
EPROM	Erasable Programmable Read Only Memory
ERIC	Educational Resources Information Center
ESEA	Elementary and Secondary Education Act
ETA	Educational Television Association (U.K.)
ETV	Educational Television
EUDISED	European Documentation and Information System for Education
EVR	Electronic Video Recording
EWG	Educational Writers Group (U.K.)
FCC	Federal Communications Commission
FIAC	Flanders Interaction Analysis in the Classroom
FIC	Federal Information Center
FM	Frequency Modulation
FOSDIC	Film Optical Sensing Device for Input to Computers
HDTV	High-Definition Television
HEA	Higher Education Act
HERDSA	Higher Education Research & Development Society of Australasia
HeSCA	Health Sciences Communications Association
IBA	Independent Broadcasting Authority (U.K.)
ICAI	Intelligent Computer-Assisted Instruction
ICEM	International Council for Educational Media (Europe)
IEC	International Electro-Technical Committee
IFLA	International Federation of Library Associations
INSITE	Instructional Systems in Teacher Education
INTELSAT	a series of geostationary satellites
ISBD	International Standard Bibliographic Description
ISBN	International Standard Book Number
ISCED	International Standard Classification of Education
ISD	Instructional Systems Development
ISO	International Standards Organization
ISSN	International Standard Serial Number

ITB	Industrial Training Board (U.K.)		OVAC	Overseas Visual Aids Centre (U.K.)
ITFS	Instructional Television Fixed Service		PAL	Phase Alternate Line
ITS	Intelligent Tutoring Systems		PBS	Public Broadcast System
ITV	Instructional Television		PCM	Pulse Code Modulation
kB	Kilobyte		PEACE-SAT	Pan-Pacific Educational and Communication Experiment by Satellite
kHz	Kilohertz		PI	Programmed Instruction
kw	Kilowatts		PICI	Programmed Instruction Centre for Industry (U.K.)
LC	Library of Congress		PL	Programmed Learning
LISP	List Processing		PLATO	Programmed Logic for Automatic Teaching Operations
MARC	Machine-Readable Cataloging		PLET	*Programmed Learning and Educational Technology* (journal) (U.K.)
mB	Megabyte		PROM	Programmable Read Only Memory
MCQ	Multiple-Choice Question		R & D	Research and Development
MDS	Multipoint Distribution System		RAM	Random Access Memory
MEDLAR	Medical Literature Analysis and Retrieval System		RIE	Resources in Education
MEDLINE	Medical Literature Analysis and Retrieval System on Line		ROM	Read Only Memory
MEP	Microelectronics Education Program (U.K.)		SAGSET	Society for Academic Gaming and Simulation in Education and Training (U.K.)
MHz	Megahertz		SAKI	Self-Adaptive Keyboard Instruction
MICR	Magnetic Ink Character Recognition		SCEDSIP	Standing Committee on Educational Development Services in Polytechnics (U.K.)
MPATI	Midwest Program on Airborne Television Instruction		SCET	Scottish Council for Educational Technology
NAC	National Audiovisual Center		SECAM	Séquence à Mémoire
NAEB	National Association of Educational Broadcasters		SFX	Sound Effects
NAVA	National Audiovisual Association		SI	Système International
NBC	National Broadcasting Company		SITE	Satellite Instructional Television Experiment
NCAT	National Center for Audio Tapes		SLR	Single-Lens Reflex Camera
NCAVAE	National Committee for Audiovisual Aids in Education (U.K.)		SMDP	Scottish Microelectronics Development Program (U.K.)
NCET	National Council for Educational Technology (now CET) (U.K.)		SMPTE	Society of Motion Picture and Television Engineers
NDEA	National Defense Education Act		SPG	Synchronous Pulse Generator
NDPCAL	National Development Program in Computer-Assisted Learning (U.K.)		SPSS	Statistical Package for Social Sciences
NEA	National Education Association		SRHE	Society for Research into Higher Education (U.K.)
NECCTA	National Educational Closed Circuit Television Association (now ETA) (U.K.)		SWYG	See What You Get
NET	National Educational Television		TBC	Time-Base Corrector
NICEM	National Information Center for Educational Media		T-COM	Tethered Communications System
NPLC	Network of Programmed Learning Centers (U.K.)		TES	*Times Educational Supplement* (journal) (U.K.)
NSPI	National Society for Performance and Instruction		THES	*Times Higher Educational Supplement* (journal) (U.K.)
NSSE	National Society for the Study of Education		TICCIT	Time-Shared Interactive Computer-Controlled Instructional Television
NTSC	National Television System Committee		TTL	Transistor-Transistor Logic
O & M	Organization and Methods		UBC	Universal Bibliographic Control
OCR	Optical Character Recognition			
OEM	Original Equipment Manufacturer			
OTP	Office of Telecommunications Policy			

UFA	University Film Association
UHF	Ultrahigh Frequency
UNESCO	United Nations Educational Scientific and Cultural Organization
USPEC	User Specification (U.K.)
VCR	VideoCassette Recorder
VDU	Visual Display Unit
VHD	Video High Density
VHF	Very High Frequency
VTR	Vedeo Tape Recorder
WATS	Wide Area Telecommunications Service
WORM	Write Once Read Mostly

ACTINIC. Actinic light is the light to which an emulsion or other light-sensitive material or device is specifically sensitive.

ACTION LEARNING. Learning that takes place as a result of the learner actually taking on a particular role, either in real life or in an arranged or simulated situation.

ACTIVE LINE. *See* **Available Line.**

ACTIVITY SAMPLING. A technique in which a number of instantaneous observations are made of a particular operation or behavior and from which the ratio of observed to nonobserved behavior can be calculated. This technique, which comes from the field of organization and methods, has a lot in common with interaction analysis. The main difference between the two is that the sampling time period in activity sampling need not be constant. A further difference is that in interaction analysis it is usual for the behavior recorded to be that occurring in the previous time period. In activity sampling it is the behavior at the time period. Activity sampling is also known as *work sampling*.

ACUTANCE. The physical assessment of the sharpness of photographic images based on the measurement of minute density differences.

ADAPTIVE PROGRAM. A teaching program that adapts its sequence according to the performance of the learner. In practice, adaptive programming can be achieved only by using a computer to manage the learning operation. The term is generally attributed to Gordon Pask. *See* **Programmed Learning; Self-Adaptive Keyboard Instruction.**

ADCIS. *See* **Association for the Development of Computer-Based Instructional Systems.**

ADDITIVE COLOR. Color that is produced by mixing light of the three primary colors (red, green, and blue). This is the system used in color television and computer displays.

ADDITIVE PRIMARIES. Primary colors which can be mixed to form other colors, but which cannot themselves be produced by mixing other primaries. Red, green, and blue are the primaries in television and when added in various proportions, they produce a wide range of other colors.

ADD-ON CONFERENCE. A PABX facility enabling an extension user to set up calls one by one to a number of extensions and to connect each extension in succession to the conference. Further extensions can be added at any time during the progress of the call.

ADDRESS. A specific location to which a computer sends information. For example, each byte of computer memory (RAM) is identified by a sequential number, say from 1 to 64000. Variables, text, and instructions are broken down into bytes and sent to an address identifiable by one of these numbers. This process is accomplished automatically in the case of high-level languages (BASIC, FORTRAN, etc.). Machine language programming, however, calls for the programmer to specify what goes in what address.

ADJUNCT PROGRAM. A type of instruction wherein programmed learning material is presented to the learner at the end of a text (or a section of a text) in order to reinforce what has been learned. Such programs can be built round text of any type, including textbooks, and can also be appended to practical tasks in a laboratory, workshop, training classroom, etc.

ADULT LITERACY PROJECT. A major BBC project aimed at the adult illiterates in the U.K. The three-year project enjoyed considerable success, utilizing techniques originally developed in *Sesame Street* (Children's Television Workshop).

ADVANCE ORGANIZER. Advance organizers are textual structures that relate potentially meaningful material to be learned to the learner's existing cognitive structure. Such organizers are concepts and propositions that have a superordinate relationship to concepts and specific facts already in the learner's cognitive structure. Material that follows advance organizers is subordinate to the previous material. Advance organizers are central to Ausubel's theory of meaningful learning. Two broad categories of advance organizers are recognizable: expository and comparative. Expository organizers are used with completely new material and serve to provide an anchorage. Comparative organizers are used when the new material is not completely new. Comparative organizers highlight similarities and differences between new and old material.

Ausubel and others have argued that advance organizers facilitate learning, but much doubt has been expressed about this claim. In general, such a preinstructional strategy is found useful. Advance organizers will not raise bad teaching to the level of good teaching: they should be part of the overall teaching strategies that lead to meaningful learning. Advance organizers should not be confused with other preinstructional strategies, for example overviews, pretests, or behavioral objectives.

AECT. *See* **Association for Educational Communications and Technology.**

AEDS. *See* **Association for Educational Data Systems.**

AERIAL. *See* **Antenna.**

AETT. *See* **Association for Educational and Training Technology.**

AFFECTIVE OBJECTIVES. Objectives relating to attitudes, feelings, and emotions. *See* **Bloom's Taxonomy.**

AFI. *See* **American Film Institute.**

A4. *See* **Paper Size.**

AFTER IMAGE. An image which persists after the removal of a visual stimulus. *See* **Persistence.**

AGENCY FOR INSTRUCTIONAL TELEVISION (AIT). An American-Canadian organization whose aim is to strengthen education through television. It aims at coordinating interstate and interprovince agencies.
Box A, Bloomington, Indiana 47401, U.S.

AIDED RECALL. A technique used in interviewing or other forms of research where the interviewer "helps" the interviewee by suggesting associated or related items to that being recalled. *See* **Cue.**

AIMS. A general statement which gives shape and direction to a set of intentions for the future. In practice aims are less clearly defined than behavioral objectives. Loosely speaking, aims are often said to be "broken down into objectives" or "objectives are chosen in the light of aims." Aims are generalizations and starting points, not guidelines.

AIRBRUSH. A precision pen-like spraying device connected by a hose to a compressed air supply which forces light-bodied ink, liquid colors, and paints from a small reservoir cup or bottle. It is used to give soft and even areas of tone or shading in artwork.

AIT. *See* **Agency for Instructional Television.**

ALGORITHM. A step-by-step procedure or set of instructions for solving a problem. Algorithms are composed of checklists, flowcharts, and an action guide to help decision making. In the case of a computer program, the algorithm provides a description of the processes which must be completed before successful execution of the program.

ALGORITHMIC ORIENTED LANGUAGE. A high-level (i.e., not specific to a particular machine) computer language intended mainly for mathematical and scientific applications, e.g., FORTRAN.

ALGORITHMOID. A term closely related to algorithm. L. N. Landa distinguishes algorithmoid from algorithm by suggesting that processes which occur simultaneously or nearly simultaneously are algorithmoid, whereas in algorithms processes occur sequentially. *See* **Educational Cybernetics.**

ALIGN. To set a computer disk drive so that it starts on the outside track at the right position and keeps the head at the right distance and angle. A drive that is misaligned can often read its own disks but may not be able to read disks written on any other drive.

ALIGNMENT. In video reproduction it is important that the video head be accurately aligned with the recorded track on the tape. A tracking adjustment is provided for fine-tuning in this regard.

ALOHA. A remote access computer system, developed as part of the PEACESAT program. Interactive computer users and remote access input-output devices are linked by means of a communications satellite. The main computer is at the University of Hawaii.

ALPHAGEOMETRIC. Videotex graphics that are constructed from basic geometric primitives: arc, point, rectangle, line, polygon.

ALPHAMOSAIC. Videotex graphics that are constructed from small blocks; each alphanumeric character or "letter" is composed of six such blocks, and graphics are a composite of these mosaics.

ALPHANUMERIC. A character set containing both letters and numbers.

AM. *See* **Amplitude Modulation.**

AMBIENT LIGHT. Existing light. Light other than that used for a specific purpose, such as the light that falls on a screen that does not come from the film projector. Whereas excessive ambient light may degrade the image on the screen, some such light may be necessary in a lecture theater for note taking, etc.

AMBIENT NOISE. Natural or background noises, which exist in any situation, that may encroach on sounds that are being recorded. Soundproofing is used to exclude ambient noise from recording studios.

AMBIENT TEMPERATURE. The temperature of the surrounding medium, such as gas or liquid, which comes into contact with equipment. The temperature of the environment.

AMEE. *See* **Association for Medical Education in Europe.**

AMERICAN ASSOCIATION OF SCHOOL LIBRARIANS (AASL). A professional body that represents the interests of all school media personnel.
50 East Huron Street, Chicago, Illinois 60611, U.S.

AMERICAN COUNCIL ON EDUCATION (ACE). An association of higher educational institutions.
1 Dupont Circle, Washington, D.C. 20036, U.S.

AMERICAN FILM INSTITUTE (AFI). An independent organization established in 1967 to "preserve the heritage and advance the art of film and television in America."
John F. Kennedy Center for the Performing Arts, Washington, D.C. 20566, U.S.

AMERICAN LIBRARY ASSOCIATION (ALA). The American Library Association is the major organization for librarians in the United States and Canada. Several committees within the ALA are concerned with the audiovisual field, and a major film preview session is held each year at the annual conference.
50 East Huron Street, Chicago, Illinois 60611, U.S.

AMERICAN NATIONAL STANDARDS INSTITUTE (ANSI). ANSI, like similar bodies in other countries (e.g., the British Standards Institution) is concerned with the establishing of standards or norms for all manner of education hardware.
1430 Broadway, New York, New York 10018, U.S.

AMERICAN SOCIETY FOR INFORMATION SCIENCE (ASIS). A body of professionals who share a common interest in the generation, collection, organization, interpretation, storage, retrieval, dissemination, transformation, and use of information.
1155 16th Street NW, Washington, D.C. 20036, U.S.

AMPEX. The Ampex Corporation introduced the first commerical video tape recorder in 1956. The breakthrough making the storage of video information possible was the concept of the rapidly revolving recording/replay head which permitted adequate bandwidth for video.

AMPLIFIER. A device for increasing the strength of a signal. In audio equipment an amplifier is used to increase the signal strength from tape, disk, or microphone so that it is able to "drive" a loudspeaker.

AMPLITUDE MODULATION (AM). A method whereby the information in an audio signal is carried on the much higher frequency of a radio wave. The envelope of the amplitude of the radio wave in successive cycles is equivalent to the waveform of the initial sound. Historically, AM is the method which was used first, and such transmissions now crowd the short, medium, and long wave bands. This crowding restricts the upper limit of the frequencies which can effectively be broadcast without the transmitter bandwidth overlapping an adjacent channel (the limit is in the region 8–10kHz). The random background of radio noise which a receiver is bound to pick up at all frequencies also appears as minor fluctuations in the amplitude of the carrier wave, and cannot be distinguished electrically from the audio signal. For high-quality transmission, amplitude modulation has largely given way to frequency modulation (FM).

AM RADIO. *See* **Amplitude Modulation.**

AMTEC. *See* **Association for Media and Technology in Education in Canada.**

ANAGLYPH. A method used to reproduce stereoscopic pictures in publications. The two images are superimposed but are printed in complementary colors, usually orange and blue-green. When these images are viewed through a pair of orange and blue-green spectacles, each eye sees a black image of one of the colors and the other disappears. The two images fuse to give a three-dimensional effect.

ANALOG COMPUTER. A computer that performs arithmetical functions upon numbers by using voltages to represent the input variables. An analog computer is able to accept inputs which vary with respect to time, and directly apply these inputs to various devices within the computer which perform the computing operations. The output from the system may be in the form of a graph produced by a plotting pen or a trace on a cathode-ray tube. The output may also be used to control a machine or process, and analog computers therefore have many applications in the automatic control of scientific or industrial processes. Analog computers do not have the ability of digital computers to store data in large quantities, nor are they programmable in the usual sense.

ANALOG SIGNAL. A signal, some characteristic of which is varied continuously (i.e., smoothly as opposed to variation in steps) to convey information. Variations of amplitude and frequency are common.

ANALOG TO DIGITAL CONVERTER. An electronic device for converting an analog (i.e., continuously varying) signal or movement into a digital signal, e.g., for processing by a computer. An example would be the conversion of readings by a voltmeter into digital pulses.

ANALYSIS. The breaking down of complex activities or behavior in order to determine a single solution or range of solutions. It is common to use a variety of mathematical and management analysis techniques in an educational setting. *See* **Algorithm; Skill Analysis; Task Analysis.**

ANALYZING PROJECTOR. A film projector (usually 16mm) which can be run at variable speeds and single frames to enable a film to be analyzed frame by frame or at various speeds of slow motion. Often used in conjunction with high-speed or time-lapse cinephotography to study an exact sequence of events.

ANAMORPHIC LENS. A lens composed of elements which, when used as a "taking" lens, compresses a wide image onto a standard frame of film. When used as a projection lens, it spreads the "squeezed" image out to its proper width. The best-known anamorphic process is CinemaScope.

ANGLE OF VIEW. In film and television the angle subtended by the scene at the camera lens (alternatively expressed in terms of the focal length of a lens covering such an angle). In projection, the angle subtended by the screen to an observer.

ANIK. Canadian domestic satellite series first launched in 1972. The Anik vehicles are used for transcontinental television transmission and also to provide telephone and television facilities to the remote North.

ANIMATED FILM. A film produced by using single-frame or stop-motion techniques where sets of drawings or paintings, or three-dimensional objects such as puppets, are used to create an illusion of movement. In education, animated film is sometimes used to illustrate complex processes that are difficult to visualize in any other way. It is, however, a very expensive and time-consuming technique as one minute of film may require over a thousand different drawings.

ANIMATION. *See* **Animated Film.**

ANIMATION CAMERA. Although it is possible to shoot single frames for animation on an ordinary 16mm camera, it is preferable to use specialist equipment. Particularly desirable is some arrangement to achieve complete precision of film registration. This will ensure that a particular frame of film can always be precisely located in the camera. Various other refinements are to be found in professional animation camera, e.g., a stop motion motor, automatic focus, etc.

ANIMATION STAND. A complex stand that allows an animation camera to be held rigidly above animation drawings and also allows the drawings to be moved in relation to the camera, each other, and the background. Animation stands may have other facilities to allow for special techniques such as combining animation with "real" images.

ANSI. American National Standards Institute. ANSI has established internationally accepted standards in the fields of computing and information technology.

ANSWER PRINT. The finished film offered by the laboratory to the producer for his approval.

ANTENNA (AERIAL). A device that picks up the incoming signal in radio or television. In order to ensure that a strong signal enters the receiver, it is necessary to position an antenna correctly. Height, direction, and configuration in relation to the transmitted signal are important. As signals can be deflected by solid objects, the position of the antenna must be such that as few obstructions come between it and the transmitting source as possible.

ANTICHEAT DEVICES. Devices incorporated into teaching machines that stopped students' manipulating the machines in order to cheat. For example, some machines required the student to make a written response to each question, and these responses disappeared into the machine before the correct answer was communicated to the student.

ANTIOPE. Acquisition Numerique et Televisualisation d'Images Organisées en Pages d'Écritures. The French standard for videotex and teletext.

APERTURE. The opening in a lens through which light passes. Its numerical value is calculated by dividing the actual diameter of the aperture into the focal length of the lens. This gives the f-number. The size of the aperture is controlled by an iris diaphragm which operates over a range of "stops," each one cutting the amount of light passing through the lens by half. Apart from affecting exposure, the size of the aperture also affects depth of focus.

APERTURE CARD. A card which contains an aperture to permit the mounting of microfilm. *See* **Information Classification and Retrieval.**

APL. (1) *See* **Association for Programmed Learning.** (2) An interactive computer language with many features which commend it for computer-aided instruction. However, APL uses very many special symbols, which makes it somewhat impractical with a normal keyboard.

APLET. *See* **Association for Educational and Training Technology.**

APOCHROMAT. A lens (usually a microscope objective or special process lens) which has been corrected for the three primary colors, so that all three are brought to the same plane of focus, as opposed to achromatic lenses, which are corrected for two colors only.

APOGEE. The farthest point from earth reached by a satellite in its elliptical orbit.

APPLE. The first true personal computer to be marketed to the public was the Apple II, conceived by Steve Wozniak, built and sold from Steve Jobs's garage. Launched in 1977, the machine was an instant success and with relatively minor modifications is still on sale today (1987). By 1981 Apple Corporation was spending over $20 million on R&D, resulting in new products such as the Macintosh, LaserWriter, etc. However, the dominant market position enjoyed by Apple in the early 1980s has disappeared under the attack of IBM and IBM-compatible equipment, especially in the business field.

APPLICATION PROGRAM (PACKAGE). A program that puts the resources and capabilities of the computer to use for some specific purpose or task, such as word processing, data base management, graphics, or telecommunications. Users need only supply their own data and parameters. For example, SPSS is a widely used applications package in the field of social science statistics.

ARCHITECTURE. *See* **Learning Environment.**

ARC LIGHT. A type of lamp in which light is produced by a bridge of incandescent particles which carry electric current from one electrode to another. The carbon arc is used for high-power lighting in studios and on location. Modern arc lamps use high-pressure gas-filled quartz tubes to enclose the electrodes. Arc lights are not generally used in educational applications.

AREGON. A telegraphic educational communication system utilizing microcomputers to interactively exchange graphic material between two locations.

ARITHMETIC UNIT. The part of a digital computer where arithmetical and logical operations are performed.

ARRAY (MATRIX). A set of tabulated data such as a table showing the socioeconomic status, IQ, and score on a test, of a set of students. Computers can handle information concerning such arrays very efficiently because each dimension of the array can be assigned to an algebraic variable. Thus if the rows of an array are labeled socioeconomic status, and the columns are headed IQ, any cell of the array can be referred to as $A(i,j)$ where i is the row number and j the column number. The computer can be asked to access, say, $A(3,7)$ which means use the value of A which appears in the third row at the seventh column, which might mean use the test score for professional-class students with IQ in the range 100–109.

ARRAY PROCESSOR. Computer facility which permits parallel processing; i.e., more than one part of a set of instructions can be dealt with at one time. This is a difficult facility to implement, but it provides an enormous increase in the speed of computing.

ARROW DIAGRAM. A representation of a chain of events, each of which depends entirely on the occurrence of the previous event for its existence. *See* **Algorithm.**

ART AID CAMERA. *See* **Process Camera.**

ART AID PROJECTOR. A type of opaque projector which projects opaques, transparencies, and three-dimensional objects onto a drawing-board surface for tracing. It provides complete artwork in one operation without transferring from a tracing, and the size can be manipulated at will.

ART DIRECTOR. Film industry term for the person responsible for the background against which the actors appear. The art director designs all settings both indoors and out and provides every "property" required by the script.

ARTIFICIAL INTELLIGENCE. Artificial Intelligence is an important new approach to the study of intelligent behavior. It is distinguishable from psychology and philosophy, disciplines which also investigate intelligence, through its use of advanced information processing concepts, methods, and techniques to model complex cognitive tasks which are viewed as knowledge-based activities. It shares with education a concern for investigating ways in which knowledge is acquired, represented, and used.

AN OVERVIEW OF ARTIFICIAL INTELLIGENCE

The popular view that a digital computer is a high-speed arithmetic machine appears to be at variance with the proposition that a computer can handle knowledge. Part of the explanation is that a computer is really a big, fast, general-purpose *symbol-manipulating machine*. In recent years, research in artificial intelligence (AI) has stimulated the development of high-level programming languages which are specially designed to carry out operations on *nonnumeric* data, such as characters, words, network structures, formal language statements, or other complex arrangements of symbols. The best-known examples are LISP (McCarthy et al., 1962 EXAMPLE), POP–2 (Burstall et al., 1971 EXAMPLE), and Prolog (Clocksin and Mellish, 1981 EXAMPLE). Using the facilities provided by these languages, investigators have written programs to handle tasks as diverse as understanding sentences written in English and identifying chemical compounds.

From the standpoint of understanding how *we* tackle such tasks, a frequently levied criticism of the AI program is that it does not increase our understanding of our own thinking because the knowledge and knowledge-handling processes that it uses to produce an 'idealized' performance on some task are very different from those which we bring to bear. While much of the early work in the AI field can be criticized on these grounds, process models of human performance are being developed. For additional information, see Newell and Simon (1972 BACKGROUND READING), Boden (1977 BACKGROUND READING), and Mayer (1983 BACKGROUND READING). Despite this activity, during the last ten years or so cross-fertilization between AI and other life sciences has been greatest in the case of education. This interaction is discussed in detail below. The reader who is interested in applications of AI methods to visual processing, natural language interpretation, or robotics should consult Raphael (1976 BACKGROUND READING) for a clearly written introduction to these areas of research.

ARTIFICIAL INTELLIGENCE AND EDUCATIONAL TECHNOLOGY

In the 1960s, many research workers believed that the computer would acquire a *key* role in education through the development and use of programs which would "teach" topics from a wide variety of different subjects. The name given to this enterprise is **computer-assisted instruction** (q.v.) (CAI). CAI sets its roots firmly in the earlier work on programmed instruction (PI): both share a strictly behavioristic educational philosophy. The similarity is best illustrated by the drill-and-practice programs in elementary mathematics and language arts which were developed by Suppes at Stanford University (Suppes and Morningstar, 1970 EXAMPLE). Working with such a program, a child seated at a computer terminal is given a question to answer, such as typing in a number in response to an addition sum or filling in the blanks in a word with appropriate letters. The child's answer is checked, and if it is correct a new question is framed. However, if the answer is wrong, the child is asked to try again. If incorrect a second time, the child is *told* the correct answer before proceeding to a new question. In brief, "learning by being told" is the catch phrase of this brand of education.

One reason why these early CAI programs did not achieve greater popularity was, without doubt, the enormous cost of installing powerful interactive computing facilities to serve all schools, an expenditure beyond even U.S. school budgets at that time. Now, computer hardware costs have dropped by many orders of magnitude due to technological advance; the majority of schools in the Western world are equipped with small microcomputers, and many pupils have access to machines in their homes. But software production costs have not dropped.

Instead, they have increased significantly due to a desire to take maximum advantage of the additional computational power that has become available in the scientific, business, and commercial worlds. In contrast, the majority of educational programs commercially available to schools in the 1980s are based upon the drill-and-practice model because it is cheap to implement on a computer and can be run on even the smallest school machine. But, as Howe and du Boulay (1981 THEORETICAL BACKGROUND) have pointed out, using these programs is tantamount to turning the clock back to an earlier era in education. The major curricular reforms that have been taking place during this second half of the twentieth century are attempting to promote a shift away from a traditional one-sided approach to teaching, using expository methods, to a more interactive style of teaching based on the use of guided discovery and exploration methods. Because the primary objective of the change is to improve pupils' understanding of their schoolwork in the sense that they are better able to apply their knowledge to the solution of a wide range of problems, drill-and-practice is no longer a favored classroom method of working.

The shift to a more learner-centered approach provides the context for an AI contribution because many AI workers share the view that a learner, working in a particular domain, has to build a mental model to represent both the domain-specific knowledge and the related knowledge-handling process. Such knowledge is acquired gradually, being represented in some form of data structure which supports each new activity in the domain and responds by accommodating to and assimilating new knowledge gained in consequence. Notice that knowledge acquisition, i.e., learning, implies activity, physical and/or mental, on the part of the pupil. This approach to learning, "learning by doing," can be sharply contrasted with the expository approach, "learning by being told," and subsumes activities ranging from separating relevant from irrelevant information to altering an explanation to get rid of errors or inconsistencies. With the learner-centered approach, the role of the teacher is to organize situations within which pupils can build their mental representations.

In view of this wide divergence in educational philosophy, it is scarcely surprising that tensions have developed between educational technology and artificial intelligence. Given their associationist model of thinking, the proponents of CAI favor the argument that only technological and financial problems hinder the development of adaptive teaching systems. In contrast, the AI adherents argue that truly individualized teaching systems cannot be built until deep conceptual problems in areas such as knowledge representation, pupil modeling, and language understanding are much better understood. During the last decade, a number of AI research workers have built experimental systems which embody AI methods in an effort to sustain a meaningful interaction between pupil and machine. Their work is outlined in the next two sections. Fuller details can be obtained by consulting Sleeman and Brown (1982 FURTHER DETAIL). The AI influence is also apparent in the innovative work on building learning environments, an activity of increasing importance to education. It is also described below: further information is available from O'Shea and Self (1983 FURTHER DETAIL).

MONITORS: PROGRAMS WHICH GUIDE AND INFORM

A CAI program is an idiot savant: it neither knows nor understands the subject matter being taught. Accordingly, it is not able to make sense of pupils' alternative or interesting answers; it is not able to understand their mistakes, and frequently it is not able to supply them with a useful explanation. Fortunately, the step from frame-based to generative methods for providing the subject materials proved to be a quantum jump in the design of teaching programs. Instead of storing prewritten questions and predicted answers in the computer's memory, the teaching program was equipped with an algorithm for solving problems in the domain of interest. For example, the system built by Uhr (1969 EXAMPLE) generated parameters for its algorithm and compared the pupil's response with the output from the algorithm to check its correctness. However, the real advance lies in subsequent attempts to use an algorithm to evaluate the *process* of achieving an answer, rather than merely to check an answer as a product. In other words, the program is acting as a "monitor," checking the pupil's "working" which in some sense expresses his thinking about a problem, with a view to providing him with help in the form of explanations, hints, or worked examples.

At Stanford University, Goldberg and Suppes devised a program for verifying logical proof procedures. Using an AI technique known as resolution-based theorem proving, their program helped a student to construct a proof by applying to the early lines in the proof sequence rules of inference selected by the student. If his rules could not be applied, the student was given relevant advice. This program was the forerunner of the EXCHECK program which is in regular use, to present complete university level courses in logic, set theory, and proof theory. The fundamental problem was to make the program capable of following proofs, presented in a "natural" manner, i.e., as actually done by practicing mathematicians, instead of requiring that these proofs be expressed as derivations in an elementary system of first order logic (Smith et al., 1975; Smith and Blaine, 1976 EXAMPLE). This was achieved by devising inference procedures that matched natural inferences in strength, degree, and kind.

Another example is the program constructed by Sleeman (1975 EXAMPLE), which helps students solve problems in an area of analytical chemistry. Sleeman takes advantage of work by Feigenbaum and Lederberg at Stanford University. They had constructed a program, called DENDRAL, which, when given a mass spectrogram and the molecular formulae of compounds, hypothesizes molecular formulas which could explain the observed spectrum. DENDRAL contains a theory of molecular structure, a series of rules to explain what types of molecular cleavages take place under mass spectrographic conditions, and a body of heuristic rules which are used to reduce the task of searching the space of possible solutions.

Sleeman's program presents students with a very simple nuclear magnetic resonance spectrum and a molecular formula, and they have to postulate a molecular structure which explains the spectrum, given the constraints of the molecular formula and the various rules which apply in this physical domain. In other words, the interpretation of nuclear magnetic resonance spectra involves specifying the groups which constitute the molecule. But it is not always possible to specify a unique solution, so an arbitrary choice has to be made. If this choice results in violation of a basic constraint, it must be discarded in favor of an alternative, and so on, until all the groups have been specified. This method of making choices, examining the consequences, and discarding the resulting activity sequence when it is incorrect is an AI technique known as "depth first search with backtracking." In operation, the program selects a problem, monitors the student's assertions, and provides lists and summaries on request. Assertions include the equivalent form of the spectrum, the structure of the molecule, and the group forming its head. Corresponding to these assertions are algorithms which build all permissible combinations, given the molecule so far specified, the remaining atoms available, the spectrum still to be explained, and the spectrum corresponding to the molecule built. When the system detects an incorrect assertion, it asks the student to type in an explanation, in English. Using a semantic grammar (Sleeman and Hendley, 1982 DESCRIPTION OF TECHNIQUE), this is parsed into an alternative form so that the student's reasoning can be compared with the operation of the algorithm, and commented upon by the system. This is preferable to a straightforward explanation of an error, which is merely a description of its unsuccessful attempt to complete the depth first search.

The next example is the program constructed by Kimball (1973, 1982 EXAMPLE), which teaches students the techniques of symbolic integration (as opposed to numerical integration). Mastery of this subject requires knowledge of some standard types of integrals, knowledge of a small set of techniques for transforming one integral into another, and an appreciation of whether such a transformation is beneficial or not—the aim being to transform an unknown integral into a combination of standard types. Kimball's program incorporates two well-known AI programs, namely a symbolic integration program, called SAINT (Moses, 1967 DESCRIPTION OF TECHNIQUE), and a program for algebraic simplification, called REDUCE (Hearn, 1970 DESCRIPTION OF TECHNIQUE). These provide knowledge of the subject matter. In operation, it asks the student to provide a problem or it selects a problem from an archive, adjusting the difficulty to conform with its estimate of the student's skill. Then, it checks the correctness of each transformation selected; it queries inappropriate choices and makes suggestions if the student asks for assistance.

While the systems described so far identify mistakes, the BUGGY program (Brown and Burton, 1978 EXAMPLE) provides a mechanism for explaining pupils' mistakes in elementary subtraction sums. Their approach is based upon the assumption that pupils' errors arise, in general, from correctly following incorrect procedures. So they modeled the overall subtraction method as a procedural network, a collection of low-level procedures organized to perform a complete task. If all the procedures in BUGGY's procedural net for subtraction work correctly, then BUGGY will do subtraction sums correctly. On the other hand, replacing correct subprocedures with subprocedures that are faulty will result in systematic errors, typical of the kinds of errors made by novices. A procedural network with one or more faulty subprocedures is called a "diagnostic model," on this account. In operation, BUGGY systematically replaces correct subprocedures with incorrect variants until a consistent diagnostic model is found. There are approximately 70 faulty subprocedures for subtraction. Sometimes a single variant will not explain a pupil's performance: under these circumstances, combinations of two variants are tried. In all, 330 different mistakes, or "bugs," have been identified. The system was tested, using the results of a subtraction test that had been administered to 1,325 pupils, nine to eleven years old. About 40 percent of their errors were modeled successfully, suggesting that they were using nonrandom, though incorrect, procedures.

Promising though this approach is, it is amenable only to problem areas where bugs can be explicated in a more or less complete way; it also requires significant amounts of computing resource on a mainframe machine.

DIALOGUE PROGRAMS: THE COMPUTER AS TUTOR

We turn now to examine attempts to construct programs which in some sense model the teacher as tutor, enjoying an unrestricted dialogue with a pupil. The task is formidable since a dialogue program requires

—an organized, readily accessible store of knowledge about the problem domain

—a capability of making inferences to augment its stored knowledge

—an ability to interpret a pupil's utterances and to generate its own utterances

—a dynamic model of each pupil's knowledge

—an appropriate teaching procedure

None of the AI tutorial programs satisfies these requirements; rather, each focuses on one aspect of the task.

To illustrate the problem of organizing the domain knowledge, we begin with a dialogue teaching program, called SCHOLAR, which was written by Carbonell (1970 EXAMPLE) to teach facts about the geography of South America. Instead of embedding knowledge in prewritten frames, the program was organized around an associative data structure which contained simple geographical information about industries, populations, and capitals. Carbonell's intention was that SCHOLAR should offer a more active form of teaching. Consequently, it was designed to manipulate its data base to construct factual questions, to check unanticipated answers to these questions, and also to answer the pupil's questions. Since Carbonell envisaged that control of the dialogue would be shared between pupil and system, he coined the term "mixed initiative" to highlight the flexibility of the interaction. Before his untimely death, Carbonell had developed SCHOLAR to the stage where it was able to respond to simple questions. This was the most natural direction for the work to take because the program's knowledge of geography is in the form of a network. The nodes of this network are related to each other: each node denotes a concept, which has a name and an attached set of properties. These properties may be facts (e.g., the fact that the language spoken is "Spanish" is attached to the named node "Chile"); they may be pointers to other nodes (e.g., the node "Chile" carries the information that it is a "country," with a pointer to another node, named "Country"), or they may be pointers to procedures for inferring information that is not given explicitly (e.g., it can deduce the products of a place, by retrieving its industries and the products of those industries, using an inference rule, of the form "if place x has industry y and y makes product z then x makes z").

Besides the network representing geographical information, the system has a program that interprets it in the required manner. In operation, SCHOLAR asks questions that provoke simple answers, either words or numbers, frequently selected from lists of alternatives provided by the system. The student's questions are less restricted: an English question or assertion is transformed into a key-word "triple." Next, this triple is compared with the network structure, e.g., "What is the latitude of Brazil?" is transformed into the triple (? latitude Brazil), and a search is made for a node that links "Brazil" and "latitude." SCHOLAR can also respond to the command "Tell me about. . . ." In a semantic network, the distance between two nodes is a measure of relevance. To provide relevant information, it will first mention properties near the mentioned node. A "Tell me more about. . . ." will prompt it to retrieve more distantly related properties, and so on. This also demonstrates one of the weaknesses of this network representation: as the amount of knowledge in the network increases, there will be a rapidly expanding number of false paths associated with general concepts like industry or place, creating a significant search problem.

While SCHOLAR was being developed, in AI interest was already shifting from the use of semantic networks to methods of knowledge representation which offered improved deductive capability. One particular approach, known as the "procedural embedding of knowledge," has provided the basis for a number of illuminating developments. It can be illustrated by taking as example the program, called SHRDLU, which Winograd (1972 EXAMPLE) wrote to test a particular theory of natural language understanding. The popularly held view was that understanding an English sentence is merely a step-by-step process, involving looking up words in a dictionary, recovering the syntactic structure of the sentence, and translating the structure into a form which accesses the system's knowledge. Winograd did not accept this analysis since he took the view that *semantic* knowledge should be used to help disambiguate syntax and syntactic structures. To facilitate the interaction between knowledge about the syntactic form of sentences, knowledge about the meanings of words and phrases, and knowledge about the domain of discourse, throughout his system Winograd uses procedures (small programs) to represent knowledge, rather than static data structures like semantic nets. For example, each word in the dictionary is a little program, and the system checks if a word is being used correctly by executing its program. The advantage of using a homogeneous form of representation is that different pieces of knowledge can be brought to bear more easily in response to the demands imposed by the state of the processing. Thus, the language parser can call semantic programs to find out if the parsing is making sense, and the semantic programs can call deductive programs to check if a particular phrase makes sense in the current context. The success of the kind of procedural representation used in Winograd's program can be seen by watching SHRDLU in action, answering questions, executing commands, accepting information, and asking for clarification, all in "normal" English.

These ideas about knowledge representation are encapsulated in a program called SOPHIE (Brown et al., 1975, 1982 EXAMPLE). SOPHIE is designed to teach students how to trace faults in an electronic apparatus. It operates by presenting students with a circuit diagram of the device, a stabilized low voltage power supply, into which it has introduced a fault of some specific degree of difficulty. The students' task is to trace the fault. After requesting various circuit measurements, students suggest what they think might be wrong, and the program checks that each proposal is consistent with what students should have learned about the behavior of the circuit by making these measurements.

Obviously SOPHIE requires powerful inference-making procedures to enable it to evaluate the student's solution to the problem in the particular context determined by the set of measurements which he has made. The key feature of SOPHIE's inference-making system is that it incorporates a power-supply circuit simulator, modeled by the SPICE circuit simulation system (Nagel and Pederson, 1973 DESCRIPTION OF TECHNIQUE), and a set of "procedural specialists" which transform a given problem into a set of subproblems, each of which can be solved by executing an appropriate model on the simulator, and inferring an answer to the original-problem from the resulting data. For example, if a student suggests that the fault is due to the failure of a particular transistor in a feedback circuit, by making that component fail in the simulator and by running the simulator, a repeat set of measurements is obtained. These hypothetical measurements are compared with those taken by the student, and if disagreement is found, the student is informed about the inconsistencies. Note that the program's task is more than to merely match the values, since it needs to know about values in a working circuit to identify measurements that support the proposed solution from those that are independent of it.

SOPHIE is a very large program, occupying some 300K words of core store on a DECsystem-10 machine. Despite its complexity, which includes the use of a semantic grammer-parsing technique (Burton, 1976 DESCRIPTION OF TECHNIQUE) to interpret questions and statements entered in English, including taking account of their context, Brown and Burton claim that it takes on average only three seconds to respond to an input. While this is a very satisfactory measure of the system's efficiency, we lack evidence about its educational value. Since SOPHIE has no teaching strategy, we must assume that a student using it will have acquired previously some knowledge of the basic electronic principles underlying the design and operation of stabilized DC power supplies. Accordingly, the measurements which the student makes take on meaning in the context of his existing mental model of the power supply, enabling him to put forward a hypothesis. But if his mental model is wrong, the hypothesis will probably be wrong too. Unfortunately, SOPHIE is not sufficiently intelligent to explain why it is wrong. Asking for help will not work very well either since the alternative hypotheses suggested by the program are also based on the assumption that the student's mental model is a sound one.

O'Shea turned his attention to the problem of equipping a program with an explicit teaching strategy which can be altered through experience to facilitate learning (O'Shea, 1979, 1982 EXAMPLE). His system attempts to model a teacher teaching a pupil how to solve quadratic equations, of the form $x^2 + c = b \cdot x$, using the discovery method. It has two main parts: an adaptive teaching program where the teaching strategy is expressed as a production system that proposes changes in the teaching strategy to achieve one of four goals—namely, increase the number of pupils who successfully complete their assignment, increase the average score on a posttest, decrease the amount of pupil time used, and decrease the amount of computer time used—and deduces the possible consequences of the changes. Developed by Newell and Simon (1972 BACKGROUND READING) for investigating human problem solving, in domains such as chess, logic, and cryptarithmetic, a production system is a set of rules which relate actions to prerequisite conditions. That is, each rule is a condition-action statement of the form $C \Rightarrow A$, and means simply that in the circumstances specified by C, the action(s) A will be the result. Obviously, changes may be executed in the condition or action part of a production rule, or in the ordering of the rules associated with a particular goal. Each teaching strategy change made by the deduction system is evaluated by carrying out statistical t-tests to detect significant alterations in the mean scores obtained by a student subsequent to the last experimental change to the production system. While O'Shea's work is an interesting and important development, it is not obvious that it can be applied with the same degree of success to less highly structured problems due to the difficulty of assessing pupils' competence.

The production rule is also a key component in many expert systems, i.e., systems which undertake tasks normally requiring human expertise, such as diagnosing a disease. Usually, an expert system is able to explain its reasoning, if only to reassure human beings that it is reliable. MYCIN, an expert system that diagnoses bacterial blood infections and meningitis and offers antibiotic therapy, has been used as the basis for a tutorial program, called GUIDON (Clancey, 1982 EXAMPLE). MYCIN's expertise is expressed by a few hundred production rules, each consisting of a set of preconditions and a conclusion which is justified if all preconditions are true. To establish a particular conclusion, MYCIN must establish the truth of its preconditions, but each precondition may force a search through the rules, leading to a need to establish preconditions for one or more of these rules, and so on. This method of search is represented as an "and/or tree": an explanation of its reasoning is achieved by expressing the relevant part of the and/or tree in English.

In effect, GUIDON extends MYCIN by adding a teaching strategy and a representation of the student's knowledge of the domain, the latter in the form of an "overlay model" (Carr and Goldstein, 1977 DESCRIPTION OF TECHNIQUE) which treats a student's knowledge as a literal subset of the tutor's knowledge. In operation, the interaction is guided by student-selected cases from MYCIN's repertoire. The intent is for the student to diagnose a case in the same manner, by being given the same initial knowledge and then attempting to duplicate MYCIN's logic, i.e., substantially re-creating MYCIN's and/or tree. The examination is largely directed by GUIDON: it is equipped with about 50 packets of tutorial rules (about 200 total), each packet being concerned with a particular tutorial action. The basic tutorial strategy is opportunistic: advice and assistance is offered during the dialogue: the decisions about when to intervene, and the action to take, are determined by the tutorial rules. As the student works through the case examination, GUIDON tries to assign belief that the student knows each rule in the and/or tree. This constitutes the overlay model, the evidence for belief being based upon background information, answers to questions, and deductions from student hypotheses and conclusions.

While GUIDON attempts to combine all the capabilities of an intelligent tutor in a single system, it too has major weaknesses. In particular, the production rules capture a "black-box" view of the solution process; that is, they describe inputs and outputs but not the reasoning process itself. Hence, when a student learns a rule, the deduction is valid, but the student might not understand why. For example, learning the rule that a particular infection should be treated by a particular drug does not help him to understand why the treatment works. Also, the overlay model is weak: unlike BUGGY, GUIDON does not diagnose bugs in the student's reasoning, so the teaching strategy is also shallow.

BUILDING LEARNING SITUATIONS

Both the AI research worker and the child share a common goal: a desire to solve complex problems. The AI worker is considerably assisted by being given access to powerful computational tools. The AI programming languages, referred to above, are interactive languages, with a modular structure for handling programs built out of parts. In contrast to traditional languages, like BASIC, where the machine has to be provided with a complete list of instructions, in specific order, before it will do any processing, the "incremental" nature of the AI programming languages enables their users to build programs in a piecemeal fashion. This "evolutionary" approach to programming is particularly valuable when tackling complex tasks since the fine detail of the solution might not become obvious until much of the code has been written and tested. Notice, too, that this evolutionary approach is the familiar, natural approach used in everyday problem solving. All this suggests that a child might also be assisted by being given access to powerful computational tools of his own, for modeling his own problem solving.

Howe (1979 THEORETICAL BACKGROUND) likens symbolic model building with the construction of physical models from Meccano parts. Just as the designers of Meccano had to decide what physical components should be provided as a kit of parts, and how they would be combined to form meaningful structures and mechanisms, the designer of a computer-based modeling system has to decide what symbolic instructions should be included in the "kit of symbolic parts," and how they might be related to form symbolic models. While the choice of parts will depend upon the problem domain, they can be fabricated in one of the high-level modular programming languages, such as Logo (Papert, 1980 THEORETICAL BACKGROUND). In the case of Logo, each part is a procedure; parts can be combined as collections of procedures forming a more powerful superprocedure, and so on.

A simple example is the task of teaching a twelve-year-old child some of the mathematical properties of regular plane shapes. Papert has designed turtle geometry for this purpose. In effect, turtle geometry is a kit of commands for moving a pen (the turtle) around a drawing surface, thus providing a learner with facilities for experimenting with the properties of regular plane shapes. The parts are commands like move FORWARD and turn LEFT. They are used as follows. It is assumed that the turtle is at a particular place and that it is facing in a particular direction. To move it forward in the same direction, the learner types the command FORWARD followed by a number which specifies the number of "steps" to be taken. To change the direction, i.e., the heading, he types the command LEFT (or RIGHT) followed by a number which specifies the number of degrees of rotation relative to the *present* heading. Suppose he wants the computer to draw a triangle. Since he must *teach* it how to triangle, he has to construct a new instruction by writing the following procedure which in some sense describes a triangle.

```
BUILD "TRIANGLE"
    FORWARD 150
    LEFT 120
    FORWARD 150
    LEFT 120
    FORWARD 150
    LEFT 120
END
```

The word BUILD alters the computer's state. Because of this, the turtle will not respond directly to each command as it is typed into the machine. Instead, the procedure will be entered into the computer's working memory, line by line, until typing the word END restores the orginal state of the machine. Now, by typing the command TRIANGLE, the child can get the computer to execute the procedure whereupon the turtle will construct an equilateral triangle whose sides are 150 units long. The child can also store the procedure in the computer's permanent memory, retrieving it for subsequent use as and when required. Notice that each procedure created and stored by the child increases the personal nature of the modeling language.

Armed with this modeling system, a child can build a variety of plane shapes, ranging from simple patterns such as squares, triangles, and hexagons to complex patterns reminiscent of the shapes made by Spirograph drawing wheels. One of the strengths of this kit of parts is that the concepts of changing position and changing heading are closely allied to a child's understanding of his own body motion, so he can use existing knowledge to help plan and correct (debug) his drawing procedures.

Instead of teaching about regular shapes, suppose the task is to teach a twelve-year-old child some of the mathematical properties of *irregular* shapes. Turtle geometry is not a suitable representational system for modeling irregularity. Instead, a child would need to be provided with a kit of parts based upon coordinate geometry. But this raises a new issue: the size of the gap between the knowledge that a learner must have to handle some task and the knowledge that he or she actually has. No one could expect an average twelve-year-old child to build coordinate geometry procedures out of more primitive Logo commands since he knows no trigonometry. Instead, the teacher would provide a kit of parts, including instructions like [PLOT x, y] and JOINUP [x, y][x, y]. Of course, the situation would be different if dealing with a mathematically competent sixteen-year-old pupil. Then the teacher might be interested in his ability to understand and build from primitive instructions the kinds of commands supplied to the twelve-year-old.

Model building through the use of procedures has been used in projects as diverse as building data bases, composing tunes, composing poetry, exploring elementary and advanced mathematics, solving elementary motion and balancing problems in physics, investigating engineering control concepts, and constructing and testing simple AC/DC electrical circuits (Eisenstadt, 1978; Bamberger, 1979; Abelson and di Sessa, 1981; Sharples, 1981; Howe et al., 1983; 1984 EXAMPLE; Papert, 1980 THEORETICAL BACKGROUND).

But this is not the only approach to model building. During the last ten years, workers at the Xerox Palo Alto Research Center have developed a new language, called Smalltalk (Goldberg et al., 1982 DESCRIPTION OF TECHNIQUE). It is an object-oriented language; that is to say, a user describes what he wants to model as a collection of objects which communicate with one another by sending and receiving messages. Each object represents either an object-class concept or an instance of an object class. The difference is that an object class contains descriptions of messages and actions whereas the class instances actually do the work, e.g., draw lines, print text, and so on. To take a simple example, in programming an airplane simulator in Smalltalk, Horn (1976 EXAMPLE) defined an object *class* called "instrument" and created instances of that class to draw particular instruments on the display screen. Each instrument had its own position on the screen, its own label, and its own displayed value. Altering one of the airplane's controls caused messages to be exchanged via the object-class concept which located the instances to obtain any values requested or to make alterations to these values. A much more complex example is the use of Smalltalk to build a "laboratory" for modeling such things as a girder bridge under load, so that the user can investigate relationships by adjusting loadings, strengthening girders, or even redesigning the bridge. In this laboratory, called Thinglab (Borning, 1981 EXAMPLE), a device is modeled by describing constraints, that is, relationships that must exist between its parts. Thinglab makes sure that when one part of a system is changed, other parts are updated to resatisfy the constraints. For example, when Centigrade and Fahrenheit temperatures are represented on the screen by graphical scales, changing one temperature will automatically change the other due to the constraint between them. Since the user is responsible for specifying the constraints, but not how they are to be satisfied (that is Thinglab's responsibility), he is able to concentrate fully on the details of the problem.

The designers of Smalltalk argue that object-oriented programming is more natural than procedural programming since it avoids the distinction between procedures for manipulating information and the input of specific information to call these procedures. A somewhat similar argument is made in favor of programming in logic. The notion here is that statements in declarative logic can be interpreted as procedural instructions to the computer (Kowalski, 1979 DESCRIPTION OF TECHNIQUE). This provided the basis for the language Prolog, first implemented by Colmerauer at Marseilles in 1972. A version of the language, Micro-Prolog, is available for microcomputers (Clark et al., 1981 DESCRIPTION OF TECHNIQUE). In Prolog, the user can state facts, such as

Elizabeth is-the-mother-of Charles
Philip is-the-father-of Charles

and rules of inference, for example,

x is-a-parent-of y if x is-the-mother-of y
x is-a-parent-of y if x is-the-father-of y

Then, the user can ask simple questions, such as

Is Elizabeth the mother of Charles?

In Prolog, this is written

Does (Elizabeth is-the-mother-of Charles)

which produces the answer YES.
The question Who are Charles's parents? would be written as

Which (x x-is-a-parent-of Charles)
Answer is Elizabeth
Answer is Philip
No (more) answers

The rule of inference has two roles: first, in this case it defines parenthood, and second, it acts as an instruction about answering questions about parenthood. Prolog is a particularly suitable formalism for building up data bases of facts and rules which can be queried by pupils. Ennals (1983 THEORETICAL BACKGROUND) argues that the real value of logic as a computer language is its contribution to the teaching of logical thinking in all areas of the school curriculum. He sees it as a replacement for traditional school subjects, such as Latin or Euclidean geometry, previously valued for their encouragement of rigorous thinking. At this time, evidence supporting Ennals's view is still awaited.

Regardless of which notation is favored, there is another crucial issue, as yet unresolved, namely, the choice of teaching strategy. Papert (1980 THEORETICAL BACKGROUND) favors open-ended discovery by a pupil, with a minimal amount of intervention by a third party, whereas Howe (Howe et al., 1980; Howe, 1983 THEORETICAL BACKGROUND) argues for a more structured approach, using ordered worksheets. They contain information, exercises which require a learner to type in, run experiments with and make modifications to prewritten programs, and "seeds," suggestions for open-ended program building and/or experimentation using the ideas and techniques exemplified by the prewritten programs. A somewhat similar approach was used by Goldberg (Goldberg and Kay, 1977; Goldberg, 1977, 1979 EXAMPLE) when investigating the applicability of Smalltalk in the classroom. Pupils were presented with model object definitions and were encouraged to explore, modify, and extend them. For example, an illustrated booklet, *The Box Book,* provided a class definition of box, and helped the pupil learn Smalltalk by making boxes "play leapfrog," "dance together," and make designs. Ennals also uses an ordered series of examples in his research into the value of Prolog for schools (Ennals, 1983 THEORETICAL BACKGROUND).

THE WAY AHEAD

Computer education is at a crossroads. Straight ahead is an Orwellian future: a greatly increased classroom penetration by machines that are programmed to tightly control pupils' learning. The motion forward is probably inexorable, impelled by commercial interests and educational and political ideology. The acceleration of interest in advanced information technology, brought about by the Japanese government's fifth-generation computing project, will stimulate further research into the construction of intelligent teaching systems, as professional, industrial, and commercial training aids. But these will be of little interest for schools which lack the computational resources to run them. Institutional funding for research into the design and use of computer-based learning environments has all but ceased both in the United Kingdom and in North America, and shows no signs of being reinvigorated despite the fact that it is probably the only viable alternative. The future for educational computing seems bleak. But it need not be so if due recognition is given to the past, present, and likely future contribution from AI. It is probably too late to turn "right" at these crossroads, but there will be other opportunities.

Jim Howe

REFERENCES

Background Reading

Boden, M. (1977) *Artificial Intelligence and Natural Man.* London: Harvester Press.

Mayer, R. E. (1983) *Thinking, Problem Solving, Cognition.* San Francisco: W. H. Freeman.

Newell, A. and Simon, H. A. (1972) *Human Problem Solving.* Englewood Cliffs, N.J.: Prentice-Hall.

Raphael, B. (1976) *The Thinking Computer: Mind Inside Matter.* San Francisco: W. H. Freeman.

Description of Technique

Burton, R. R. (1976) *Semantic Grammar: An Engineering Technique for Constructing Natural Language Understanding Systems,* Report 3453. Boston: Bolt, Beranek and Newman.

Carr, B. and Goldstein, I. P. (1977) *Overlays: A Theory of Modelling for Computer-assisted Instruction,* AI Memo No. 406. Cambridge, Mass.: Artificial Intelligence Laboratory, MIT.

Clark, K. L., Ennals, J. R., and McCabe, F. G. (1981) *A Micro-PROLOG Primer.* London: Logic Programming Associates.

Goldberg, A., Robson, D., and Ingalls, D. H. H. (1982) *Smalltalk-80: The Interactive Programming Environment.* Reading, Mass.: Addison-Wesley.

Hearn, A. C. (1970) *The Problem of Substitution,* Memo AIM-70. Stanford, Calif.: Artificial Intelligence Laboratory, Stanford University.

Kowalski, R. A. (1979) *Logic for Problem Solving.* Amsterdam: North Holland.

Moses, J. (1967) *Symbolic Integration,* AI Technical Report 47. Cambridge, Mass.: Artificial Intelligence Laboratory, MIT.

Nagel, L. W. and Pederson, D. O. (1973) "Simulation Program with Integrated Circuit Emphasis." In *Proceedings of the Sixteenth Midwest Symposium Circuit Theory.* Waterloo, Canada.

Sleeman, D. H. and Hendley, R. J. (1982) "ACE: A System Which Analyses Complex Explanations." In *Intelligent Tutoring Systems,* ed. D. H. Sleeman and J. S. Brown. London: Academic Press.

Example

Abelson, H. and di Sessa, A. (1981) *Turtle Geometry: The Computer as a Medium for Exploring Mathematics.* Cambridge, Mass.: MIT Press.

Bamberger, J. (1979) *LOGO Music Projects: Experiments in Musical Perception and Design,* LOGO Memo No. 52. Cambridge, Mass.: Artificial Intelligence Laboratory, MIT.

Borning, A. H. (1981) "The Programming Language Aspects of Thinglab, a Constraint-oriented Simulation Laboratory." *ACM Transactions of Programming Languages and Systems* 3: 353–387.

Brown, J. S. and Burton, R. R. (1978) "Diagnostic Models for Procedural Bugs in Basic Mathematical Skills." *Cognitive Science* 2: 155–192.

Brown, J. S., Burton, R. R., and Bell, A. G. (1975) "SOPHIE: A Step Towards Creating a Reactive Learning Environment." *International Journal of Man-Machine Studies* 7: 675–696.

Brown, J. S., Burton, R. R., and de Kleer, J. (1982) "Pedagogical, Natural Language and Knowledge Engineering Techniques in SOPHIE I, II and III." In *Intelligent Tutoring Systems,* ed. D. H. Sleeman and J. S. Brown. London: Academic Press.

Burstall, R. M., Collins, J. S., and Popplestone, R. J. (1971) *Programming in POP-2.* Edinburgh: Edinburgh University Press.

Carbonell, J. R. (1970) "AI in CAI: An Artificial Intelligence Approach to Computer-assisted Instruction." *IEEE Transactions on Man-Machine Systems* MMS-11: 190–202.

Clancey, W. J. (1982) "Tutoring Rules for Guiding a Case Method Dialogue." In *Intelligent Tutoring Systems,* ed. D. H. Sleeman and J. S. Brown. London: Academic Press.

Clocksin, W. F. and Mellish, C. S. (1981) *Programming in Prolog.* Berlin: Springer Verlag.

Eisenstadt, M. (1978) *Artificial Intelligence Project Units 3/4 of Cognitive Psychology: A Third Level Course.* Milton Keynes: Open University Press.

Ennals, J. R. (1983) *Beginning Micro-Prolog.* Chichester: Ellis Horwood.

Goldberg, A. (1977) *Smalltalk in the Classroom,* Report No. SSL 77–2. Palo Alto, Calif.: Xerox Palo Alto Research Center.

———.(1979) "Educational Uses of Dynabook." *Computers and Education* 3: 247–266.

Goldberg, A. and Kay, A. (1977) *Methods for Teaching the Programming Language Smalltalk,* Report No. SSL 77–2. Palo Alto, Calif.: Xerox Palo Alto Research Center.

Horn, B. (1976) "A Smalltalk Airplane Simulator." *Creative Computing* 2: 62–63.

Howe, J.A.M. (1984) *Power for the Pupil,* Research Report. Edinburgh: Department of Artificial Intelligence, University of Edinburgh.

Howe, J.A.M., Ross, P. M., Johnson, K. R., and Inglis, R. (1983) "Model Building, Mathematics and LOGO." In *New Horizons in Educational Computing,* ed. M. Yazdani. Chichester: Ellis Horwood.

Kimball, R. (1982) "A Self-improving Tutor for Symbolic Integration." In *Intelligent Tutoring Systems,* ed. D. H. Sleeman and J. S. Brown. London: Academic Press.

Kimball, R. B. (1973) *Self Optimizing Computer-assisted Tutoring: Theory and Practice,* Technical Report No. 206. Stanford, Calif.: Institute for Mathematical Studies in the Social Sciences, Stanford University.

McCarthy, J., Abrahams, P. W., Edwards, D. J., Hart, J. P., and Levin, M. I. (1962) *LISP 1.5 Programmers' Manual.* Cambridge, Mass.: MIT Press.

O'Shea, T. (1979) *Self-improving Teaching Systems.* Basel: Birkhauser Verlag.

———.(1982) "A Self-improving Quadratic Tutor." In *Intelligent Tutoring Systems,* ed. D. H. Sleeman and J. S. Brown. London: Academic Press.

Sharples, M. (1981) "Microcomputers and Creative Writing." In *Microcomputers in Secondary Education,* ed. J.A.M. Howe and P. M. Ross. London: Kogan Page.

Sleeman, D. H. (1975) "A Problem-solving Monitor for a

Deductive Reasoning Task." *International Journal of Man-Machine Studies* 7: 183–211.

Smith, R. L. and Blaine, L. H. (1976) "A Generalized System for University Mathematics Instruction." *SIGCUE Bulletin* 8: 280–288.

Smith, R. L., Graves, W. H., Blaine, L. H., and Marinov, V. G. (1975) "Computer-assisted Axiomatic Mathematics: Informal Rigor." In *Computers in Education,* ed. R. Lewis and O. Lecarme, Amsterdam: North-Holland.

Suppes, P. and Morningstar, M. (1970) "Four Programs in Computer-assisted Instruction." In *Computer-assisted Instruction, Testing and Guidance,* ed. W. H. Holtzman. New York: Harper and Row.

Uhr, L. (1969) "Teaching Machine Programs That Generate Problems as a Function of Interaction with Students." In *Proceedings of 24th National ACM Conference.* New York: ACM Inc., pp. 125–134.

Winograd, T. (1972) *Understanding Natural Language.* Edinburgh: Edinburgh University Press.

Further Detail

O'Shea, T. and Self, J. (1983) *Learning and Teaching with Computers: Artificial Intelligence in Education.* Sussex: Harvester Press.

Sleeman, D. H. and Brown, J. S. (1982) *Intelligent Tutoring Systems.* London: Academic Press.

Theoretical Background

Ennals, J. R. (1983) *Beginning Micro-PROLOG.* Chichester: Ellis Horwood.

Howe, J.A.M. (1979) "Learning Through Model-building." In *Expert Systems in the Micro-Electronic Age,* ed. D. Michie. Edinburgh: Edinburgh University Press.

———.(1983) Edinburgh LOGO: A Retrospective View." In *An Attitude of Mind,* ed. W. B. Dockrell. Edinburgh: Scottish Council for Research in Education.

Howe, J.A.M. and du Boulay, J.B.H. (1981) "Microprocessor Assisted Learning: Turning the Clock Back?" In *Selected Proceedings in Computer-Based Learning,* ed. N. Rushby. London: Kogan Page.

Howe, J.A.M., O'Shea, T., and Plane, F. (1980) "Teaching Mathematics Through LOGO Programming: An Evaluation Study." In *Computer Assisted Learning: Scope, Progress and Limits,* ed. R. Lewis and E. D. Tagg. Amsterdam: North Holland.

Papert, S. (1980) *Mindstorms: Children, Computers and Powerful Ideas.* Sussex: Harvester Press.

ARTIFICIAL LIGHT. Film, and video camera tubes, are designed to produce the best quality images under particular light conditions. Many indoor films are designed to work best under controlled tungsten lighting. Other films are designed to work best in a range of light conditions close to those of natural outdoor lighting.

Most flash units are designed to produce a range of light suited to daylight-rated film. Filters can be used to approximate a match between one type of film and inappropriate light conditions. Fluorescent and neon lighting pose special problems in achieving good color conditions.

ARTIFICIAL REVERBERATION ("ECHO"). Simulation of the natural die-away of sound that occurs in a room or any other enclosed space (e.g., in a cave, down a well, etc.). Such techniques are used when the available studio acoustics are not reverberant enough. Multimicrophone techniques for music need "echo," as the studios used for this are normally much less reverberant than those used for natural balance. The technique is used to permit different treatment to be applied to each microphone output: after separate control of individual instruments or groups, their sound is fed at appropriate levels to the echo chamber or whatever other device may be used.

ARTWORK. Graphical material prepared for use in audiovisual media and publications. *See* **Graphic Design.**

ASA. Abbreviation for the American Standards Association, but most commonly encountered as a system of rating film emulsion speeds. ASA speeds are usually quoted using an arithmetical scale, e.g., double the speed, double the number. Typical ASA speeds for black-and-white film are between 25 ASA and 500 ASA; for color film between 100 ASA and 1000 ASA. *See* **American National Standards Institute.**

ASCENDING. The order that goes from smallest to largest or first to last; the usual default sort mode in a data base system.

ASCII. An abbreviation for American Standard Code for Information Interchange. This is one of the standard codes used by the computer industry to identify alphabetic (A–Z), numeric (0–9), and special (e.g., symbol, control) characters. These codes facilitate communication between devices such as computers, printers and terminals. There are 128 standard code characters, numbered from 0 to 127.

ASET. *See* **Australian Society of Educational Technology.**

A SIGNAL. In stereo, the signal fed to the left-hand (viewed from in front) loudspeaker of a two-speaker system.

ASIS. *See* **American Society for Information Science.**

ASME (U.K.). *See* **Association for the Study of Medical Education.**

ASPECT RATIO. The numerical ratio of picture width to height. When designing graphics for film, television, slide, or filmstrip programs, it is essential to take into account the ratio of width to height, i.e., aspect ratio, of the final image on the screen. These proportions may only be modified when camera movements (pans, tilts, zooms) or roller titles (film or television titles which move steadily across the screen) are to be used. Before the days of wide-screen cinema systems, the only internationally accepted film aspect ratio was 4:3 (1.33:1). This ratio still persists in 16mm, super-8, and 8mm films. Wide-screen systems may have aspect ratios as high as 2.55:1 although format of about 1.66:1 is now the most common.

The television aspect ratio is 4:3. The shape of the television screen often precludes transmission of the total area of a graphic or caption. There is a lost area known as the cutoff. To be completely safe, all vital information should be contained in the center area of 9 inches by 6 inches on a 12–inch by 9–inch caption card. The British Standard for slides and opaques for television, BS2948, specifies dimensions in detail. The equivalent American standard is PH 22.94–1954, revised in 1960.

Single-frame filmstrips (where the frames are arranged across the filmstrip) have an aspect ratio of 4:3. Double-frame filmstrips (where the frames are aligned along the filmstrip) and slides or transparencies produced by conventional 35mm miniature cameras have an aspect ratio of 3:2.

ASPHERIC LENS. Technically, a lens with nonspherical surfaces. Aspheric lenses are difficult to manufacture and are most often used in projection systems for improved focus and color rendition.

ASSEMBLE. Video editing term for a type of editing wherein sections of recording are put together one after the other. In other words, the program is assembled in sequence, each new section being placed after the preceding one. Contrast this with insert editing, in which new sections are interposed into existing material. *See* **Edit (Video and Film).**

ASSEMBLER LANGUAGE (CODE). A type of computer language which allows a programmer to use symbols and names to define computer instructions (operation codes) and memory addresses. These programs are translated by "assemblers" to produce machine code. Each different model of computer has its own unique machine code and hence assembler language.

ASSESSMENT.

HISTORICAL OVERVIEW

We hear of written competitive examinations for Civil Service posts as early as the Han dynasty in the first century B.C. in China. The procedures became highly refined: by the eleventh century A.D. examination scripts were rewritten by professional copyists to preserve the anonymity of the candidates and there was a system of multiple marking in use. Nevertheless, by the time of the Ming dynasty the examinations were stereotyped, requiring highly specialized literary skills, and almost certainly of little validity (Morris, 1961; Fletcher, 1976).

In Europe at the same time, examinations were predominantly oral and confined to a small number of students. With the growing availability of writing materials and the increasing democratization of entry to education and government service, the written examination, with its greater efficiency in dealing with large numbers of candidates, became prevalent in the nineteenth century. These tests were of the "open-ended" or essay type, and dissatisfaction came to be felt with the consistency of markers (Hartog and Rhodes, 1935, 1956). As a result, interest grew in new methods of testing, such as "objective" tests, which acknowledged only one correct answer for each item. With the growth of interest in equal opportunity, and the realization that educational performance was affected by social background, came an interest in assessing "aptitude," supposedly unaffected by previous learning; these tests were for use particularly in selection for secondary and (especially in the U.S.) third level.

Later developments have been an interest in precision in the definition of educational objectives leading to such taxonomies as that of Bloom (1956), and the more detailed analysis of assessment techniques, using sophisticated statistical methods to define the qualities actually being measured.

There has also been a widening of the areas seen as relevant to educational assessment.

FUNCTIONS OF ASSESSMENT

Assessment may be of individuals, of courses, or of institutions; its functions include provision of diagnostic evidence and selection. One cannot also ignore the incentive function of assessment procedures; the form and content of major examinations will affect the form and content of educational courses and such "backwash" effects must be taken into account when assessment procedures are considered. Where assessment is made with the intention of guiding the further development of the educational process, it is referred to as "formative"; an obvious example might be the traditional school report.

Where the intention is to make a formal assessment at the end of a course, as in traditional school-leaving examinations, the assessment is known as "summative." Formative assessment may thus be seen as forward-looking, summative as backward, although summative tests may be used for selection.

Continuous assessment has particular value for the formative role as the results are available for diagnostic use throughout the course; the end-of-course examination, particularly in the form of a national external examination, traditionally provides little feedback other than an overall grade. Where a course is seen as modular in structure, continuous assessment can be used to provide summative assessment, but if the course is seen as cumulative in effect, then early assessments, however valuable for diagnosis, are irrelevant for summative assessment and the end-of-course examination is appropriate. It should be noted in this context that continuous assessment can use a wide range of techniques including essays and traditional examination forms and in any combination.

RELIABILITY AND VALIDITY

Before dealing in detail with specific methods of assessment, it is necessary to consider the concepts of reliability and validity which are relevant to all.

Reliability may first be considered in terms of marker reliability—the degree to which different markers would agree on the mark for the same work (intermarker) or the consistency with which the same marker would assess the same work on different occasions (intramarker). These are usually assessed simply by calculating product-moment correlation coefficients.

The concept of reliability as applied to a test refers to how consistently a test measures something. The score on a test may be seen as consisting of a "true" score and an error score. Assuming stability in the qualities measured, the true score for an individual sitting the test on different occasions should be constant, but error may vary. This is the basis of the "test-retest" method of measuring reliability where the same individuals sit the test on two different occasions, the scores being correlated to give a "reliability coefficient" (Anastasi, 1968). As candidates might merely remember their answers from the previous occasion, the second sitting must be some weeks after the first. Apart from administrative problems involved, this means that the coefficient measures not only the consistency of the test but the stability over time of the quality being measured. To avoid this problem a parallel test, which can be administered immediately afterwards, is used. There are obvious problems in this "parallel form" (or "alternative forms") method; it is difficult to devise exactly parallel tests, and the most effective items are scattered throughout both tests, making neither of them as effective as a single combined test would be. To avoid two administrations of the test, the "split-half" method is used. Here the test is divided, after being administered, into two halves, usually taking alternate items, and the results on each half correlated as though they were parallel forms. As, within limits set by fatigue, the reliability of a test increases with length, the figure arrived at will be for tests half the length of the original and will therefore underestimate the reliability. This can be corrected by the Spearman-Brown formula (Anastasi, 1968, p. 85).

A slightly different form of reliability is inter-item consistency, which is really a measure of test homogeneity (a test which is not homogeneous may, however, be perfectly reliable in the previous usages). In fact inter-item consistency may be seen as a form of construct validity (see below). The formula known as Kuder-Richardson No. 20 is used for objective-type tests (Nuttall and Willmott, 1972). Mathematically it is the average of all split-half reliability coefficients for the test; as the test is normally split deliberately into equivalent halves for split-half method, the Kuder-Richardson figure will be considerably lower unless the test is homogeneous.

Validity refers to the question of what the test is actually measuring. An unreliable test obviously cannot measure anything consistently, but a very reliable test of, say, geography, may be measuring something totally different (perhaps general intellectual skills). A very simple form of validity is "content" validity, in which the test is examined to ensure that it is sampling the required content and skill areas. In the case of school examinations designed largely to ensure that the term's work has been (or will be) covered, this may be the most appropriate form of validity. A related concept is "face" validity, though not technically a true validity measurement. It refers to whether a test appears relevant, particularly to the candidates, which is obviously important in ensuring their cooperation. Criterion validity is measured by correlating test scores with some outside criterion of the qualities allegedly measured. While this is a highly desirable form of validity, it is often difficult to find a criterion which is itself valid. Such validity may be "concurrent," estimating how well present performance is measured, or "predictive," estimating how well future performance is predicted. Where, for example, school-leaving certificate examination results are used as predictors of university performance, there are two main problems in measuring validity.

1. Only those performing well in the school-leaving examinations are likely to be allowed to enter university. Thus the full range of examination results is not represented. As

the range is narrowed, the correlations will tend to decrease as the relative effect of chance errors is increased.

2. A good criterion is difficult to find. University degree results are usually used, but these may not themselves be particularly valid. Thus a low predictive validity may represent a weakness in the criterion rather than the test.

Where a criterion is difficult to find or when, as assessment is being made of more abstract qualities, no criterion is available, use is made of "construct" validity. This is defined by Mehrens and Lehmann (1975) as "the degree to which the test scores can be accounted for by certain explanatory constructs in a psychological theory." An example might be the validation of intelligence tests by measuring whether test scores increase with age.

Mention has been made of internal consistency. While this determines whether the test measures the same quality throughout, it does not identify which and is therefore not a true test of validity. A similar approach is used in factor analysis in the area of validation. Intercorrelations of different assessments show how far they overlap. By sophisticated computer techniques of factor analysis, these can be developed to extract a relatively small number of factors underlying these tests and the weighting of each test with regard to that factor. Redundant tests (i.e., ones which overlap too much with others) can be therefore eliminated (it should be noted that these tests may not be pedagogically redundant; their inclusion may ensure that parts of the course are studied). The loading of a test with regard to a factor may be seen as its validity in that respect. It should be noted that the factors so produced are statistical artifacts: any meaning given to them is only an assumption based on the evidence available.

Validity is, of course, with reference to particular students and for particular purposes. A test which validly measures understanding of mathematical concepts for eighteen-year-olds may therefore have predictive validity as a university entrance test. The same test applied to twelve-year-olds, being too difficult, might have no validity whatever. Similarly the validity of attainment tests may depend on the candidates' having covered a particular syllabus.

It should be noted that while the concepts of reliability and validity apply to all assessments, many of the techniques are most appropriately applied to objective tests where there are a large number of items and all candidates have to answer all questions. In essay-type examinations the element of choice open to candidates introduces problems (Morrison, 1972). Further aspects of question choice are discussed by Willmott and Hall (1975) and James and Hub (1983).

METHODS OF ASSESSMENT

For its prestige and persistence, pride of place must be given to the essay-type examination, the typical example of the class of "open-ended" test in which "traditionally neither the content nor the style of answer is made explicit to the examinee" (Sheridan, 1974). This style of examination has been persistently criticized for lack of marker reliability, the classic example being the work of Hartog and Rhodes (1935, 1936), but there are other serious failings: the time needed to answer each question means that content sampling is limited, with the resultant effect both on validity and incentive for candidates to cover the whole course; the lack of clear identification of what these tests measure leads to a fear that a generalized writing ability, rather than the nominal subject matter of the test, may be measured. Wiseman (1949) showed higher marker reliability of young (eleven-to twelve-year-old) children, but this is probably because the qualities measured at that level are the more mechanical ones of grammar and punctuation rather than the higher-level skills which defenders of the essay stress.

Two approaches to improving the reliability of the essay may be distinguished. The first is to improve the form of the question; the second is to improve marking techniques.

A distinction is suggested between "extended" and "restricted" response questions. The "restricted response" question, by specifying the form and content of the answers required, decreases ambiguity and the variation due to candidates' interpretation of the question, but perhaps loses the opportunity of testing candidates' ability to organize and synthesize ideas that could be found in the extended responses.

Making all questions compulsory may also decrease the variability due to different candidates' choice of question.

Heywood (1977) has summed up the various options open to improve marking. Multiple marking will increase reliability (possibly at the cost of reducing students to the average), but is obviously time-consuming and impracticable where large numbers of students are involved. In major public examinations, moderation is used to try to maintain some consistency between examiners. Various schemes of analytical marking have been suggested, but Cox (1967) finds they seem to add little to reliability, possibly because even the most detailed criteria can be diversely interpreted by examiners. The scheme of attaching criteria to assignments suggested by MacDonald and Sansom (1979) would seem to increase the information available to students as well as examiners. Model answers to define threshold performances have been used (Thompson and Rentz, 1973) with some claimed success.

The improved training of examiners has been suggested (Heywood, 1977). Branthwaite et al. (1981) suggest that personality factors in examiners may explain inconsistency; how far these are susceptible to training is questionable, but it is reasonable to suppose that attention to avoiding ambiguity and clear identification of the objectives of essay-type questions might improve the quality of these examinations.

There are minor variants of the essay-type examination such as "open-book" examinations where material may be supplied or brought by the student. This reduces the stress on memory work but tends to involve administrative difficulties except in certain specialist areas (e.g., the supply of formulas in statistics tests). Students may be supplied with some or all questions in advance to reduce the examination stress. This technique, known as "prior-notice questions," may obviously limit the students' revision efforts and may lead to attempts to memorize prepared essays. While such variants may be useful, they do not affect the general arguments about the essay; it is defended as the only practicable test of higher-order skills such as integration and organization, but there is little hard evidence to suggest that it measures anything different from selection-type tests (Henderson, 1980).

ORAL, AURAL, AND PRACTICAL ASSESSMENTS

There is a degree of overlap between these categories. Oral examinations may take the form of interviews for selection, viva voce examinations, or language examinations in oral and aural forms which are really practical examinations. These share certain features with practical tests in scientific and technical areas: they tend to be time-consuming and examiner-intensive and therefore expensive; as they often involve ephemeral performances they may not be susceptible to external moderation. This latter problem is of particular importance as oral tests particularly are influenced by the personality interaction of candidate and examiner. To some extent, and at some expense, these problems can be solved by the use of sound and video recording.

Oral examinations and interviews are used particularly in continental Europe, and many studies have shown that they suffer from the same problems of reliability and validity as essays (Ingenkamp, 1977; Trost, 1979). They are, however, defended on the grounds that the oral gives a flexibility not available in the written examination and that interviews can show important personality traits which would not otherwise be recognized. The same recommendations—multiple examiners, training of examiners, and careful structuring of the test—would apply here as in the essay test, although Newble et al. (1980) suggest that consistency in clinical examiners is not susceptible to training.

The practical examination is defended as the only way to determine whether a candidate can actually show (rather than write about) certain skills. Evidence from factor analysis suggests, however, that there may in fact be considerable overlap between the qualities tested in written and practical science exams (Hoste, 1982a). Apart from the problems of subjectivity, there is also the question of limited content sampling as one operation may take up all the available time. The use of the "objective structured practical examination" (Henderson and Cairncross, 1980) can mitigate these problems by providing a selection of subtasks with clearly defined criteria for the examiners.

Objective Tests (q.v.) provide an answer to marker unreliability by allowing only one, predetermined, correct answer. Barring human error, there can be no disagreement between markers, and marking is therefore objective. An element of subjectivity still arises in the choice of items to be included in a test. As items are generally short, a large number can be included in one test, with consequently improved content sampling, and the predetermined answers mean that markers can be unskilled; it is now even possible to have tests machine marked, with obvious advantages where large numbers of candidates are involved. It is also possible to tailor items to test specific objectives where essay tests tend to measure a variety of skills.

As responses are generally supplied for the candidate to choose from, there is obviously a risk of the mark being inflated by guessing. This can be compensated for by a formula, but McIntosh and Morrison (1969) recommend ignoring this factor as irrelevant to final rank order (although Heywood and Youngman [1981] argue that guessers usually guess wrong). A practical disadvantage lies in the construction of such tests, which is a much lengthier process than in an essay-type test; more items are involved and, in the case of multiple-choice questions, several suitable distractors must be prepared for each item. Item banks may be available from which suitable items can be chosen (Wood, 1974). This process is not without problems (Harltey and Grey, 1981).

Objective tests lend themselves particularly to item analysis (though many such techniques can also be used for other forms of assessment). This analysis is usually in terms of "facility," usually expressed as the proportion passing an item, and "discrimination." This latter is a measure of how well any item discriminates between weak and strong candidates and is usually measured for objective test items by a biserial correlation between item performance and total test score; less sophisticated but effective methods based on facility levels in the top and bottom strata are also available.

Facility and discrimination levels are, of course, in the context of particular samples and would be altered if the item were used for older or younger students. The Rasch technique claims to provide a sample-free calibration for item difficulty (Rasch, 1960; Willmott and Fowles, 1974). Fitting items to this scale obviates the needs for discrimination values (though items that are extremely good discriminators might be rejected). The Rasch model demands that "items should fit the model and not that the model should fit the items," as well as making other assumptions such as unidimensionality of measurement, leading to some fear that questions may be chosen and tests completed on the basis of their technical/statistical qualities alone (Goldstein, 1979; Preece, 1980).

The main attack on objective tests is in terms of their ability to measure higher-level skills. Much ingenuity has been shown in devising tests of such skills—Godshalk and associates (1966) demonstrate the use of objective tests in measuring writing abilities—but it is probably true that it is easier to devise items measuring knowledge, comprehension, and application (Vernon, 1964), and there is fear of a backwash effect on educational practice, inhibiting activities of a "creative" type. Tests of "creative ability" have been designed (Getzeis and Jackson, 1962), but as it was realized that the commonly understood concept of creativity involves a number of different processes, the term "divergent thinking," as opposed to the "convergent thinking" involved in traditional objective tests, was used by Hudson (1968). Unfortunately, tests of divergent thinking rarely show high reliability and frequently fail to correlate with each other more highly than with tests of intelligence (Marsh, 1964).

Interest in selection has led to a search for tests of "aptitude," which could be unaffected by social background or experience. This interest in Britain was mainly in selection for second level, while in the U.S. the stress has been on entry to third level. There has been much argument as to how far aptitude can be separated from attainment and how susceptible such tests are to coaching (DerSimonian and Laird, 1983; Jackson, 1980; Powers, 1982; Slack and Porter, 1980), but such tests are still widely used.

Other tests of special aptitudes are used in areas such as guidance both for careers and subject choice within school, where the emphasis is on encouraging self-knowledge rather than providing a precise fit for any particular occupation. Teachers have also always placed affective change high in the list of educational objectives, and school reports have traditionally assessed affective traits in an unsystematic way. Krathwohl et al. (1964) have developed a taxonomy of educational objectives in the affective domain, paralleling Bloom's (1956) cognitive taxonomy, as a basis for systematic classification. Other formal assessment scales can be made on Thurstone-type scales, where the value of responses is graded by judges, or Likert-type scales, where the value is empirically based on the analysis of responses. The Osgood semantic differential technique (Osgood et al., 1957) has also been used; although not basically a rating scale these concepts are rated on a number of bipolar scales. A recent example of this may be found in Hoste (1982b).

An important area for noncognitive assessment is vocational guidance, in measurement of interests and preferences. Assessments in this area may be of empirical construction (by reference to particular, usually occupational, criterion groups), homogenous construction (choice of items being based on factor analysis), or logical construction (items chosen on a basis of logical assessment of the task needs). The last group would require careful validation. Problems in this area involve "response sets," the tendency to answer in a particular direction. "Yea-saying," or the tendency to answer in a positive (or in other individuals, negative) direction can be countered by couching some statements in a negative form. A more subtle problem is the tendency to give socially desirable answers, which can be countered by making the respondent choose one of two or three statements which have been found to be of equal social desirability. This forced-choice technique takes no account of intensity of preference, and as choice of one interest precludes the others, it is not possible to score high on all subscales. These forms are therefore "ipsative" rather than "normative" in that they show the relative preferences for individuals, but they cannot compare one individual with another on the same subscale. Rather than prevent social desirability factors, some forms attempt to measure them with a "lie scale" checking inconsistent or improbably virtuous responses. Nevertheless, where tests are used for selection, it is probably impossible to prevent candidates "faking good"; it is hoped that where tests are used for guidance, the problem will be less marked.

The traditional examination usually measures a variety of skills; the development of factor analysis and the interest in the definition of educational objectives has led to "criterion-referenced" assessments. In the traditional examination, although it is customary to talk vaguely of candidates having reached a certain standard, the marks really show how the candidate stood relative to other candidates; the assessment is "norm-referenced." Criterion-referenced tests measure whether candidates have achieved specific objectives (irrespective of the performance of other students). This has obvious uses with regard to formative assessment and diagnosis of learning problems. With regard to summative assessment, it has been argued that criterion-referenced tests would give a more exact statement of a student's ability than would a global grade. Where such tests are used for selection, however, a global normative assessment may in fact be of more use to the consumer.

Allied to criterion referencing is the concept of mastery learning. Here course objectives are precisely defined: student success is in terms of mastering these objectives rather than scoring a mark which shows skills relative to other students (McGaghie et al., 1978). Competency testing is a very similar concept.

Criterion-referenced tests raise problems of test analyses as many of the conventional measures rely on the spread of scores typical of a normative assessment.

Another development is the process of self-assessment; students' own assessment has been shown largely to coincide with that of teachers (Orpen, 1982). An extension of this is contract grading, where students can decide beforehand the level or grade they aim at. Hassencahl (1979) stresses that the instructor must here ensure the quality as well as the quantity of the work produced.

Where certification is involved, self-assessment may be suspect. Internal school examinations can be used, subject to moderation however, as in the CSE Mode 3 in England. Where continuous assessment is used, it is necessary to provide moderation throughout the course.

REPORTING OF RESULTS

The traditional expression of marks is in terms of single units, often between one and a hundred. This may be felt to express an unrealistic fineness of discrimination, and many public examinations use a system of grades, or bands, usually five or six in number. While misleading discrimination is thus avoided, marginal differences of marks at borderlines are magnified to whole differences of grades.

A score on an assessment measure, or a "raw" score, in itself tells little about performance as it may depend on the difficulty of the paper or the generosity of the marker. Similarly, where marks, possibly from different options on a course, are to be combined, they must be placed on the same footing. In norm-referenced assessments a mark can be expressed relative to others, either in the same group or, in the case of standardized tests, relative to the performance of selected standardization groups.

One method is to use percentile scores, which simply represent the percentage of the way up the total rank order. While simple to interpret, such scales are not suitable for combining scores as, in a normal distribution, a difference between percentile ranks will represent larger difference in raw marks at the extremes of the range than in the middle.

Age and grade norms are generally only used in standardized tests. They put marks in terms of the average scores for particular ages (or grades in school). Among their disadvantages is the fact that nearly half of those in any age group will have a performance age lower than their chronological age and may therefore appear "backward."

The most straightforward method is to translate all scores to a distribution with the same mean and standard deviation. Linear transformation preserves the relationship between raw scores in the original distribution, whereas normalized standard scores convert them to fit a normal curve. Such scores may be expressed in terms of standard deviations above or below the mean, but this produces exotic scores such as 0.75; to provide more familiar scores, the T score is used, which expresses scores on a mean of 50 and standard deviation 10, usually giving scores between 0 and 100.

Stanine scores, used on standardized tests, are similar to normalized standard scores but are based on a scale from 1 to 9.

As these standardized scores essentially show how candidates stand in relation to each other, they are relevant to norm-referenced assessment. There are long-standing fears that standardization techniques based on internal reference, when used for comparison or amalgamation of marks, might obliterate genuine differences in ability between different groups. These fears have been addressed by Vernon (1956); nevertheless, standardization techniques are probably unsafe to use with small groups if there is any good reason to believe that such absolute differences do exist.

With criterion-referenced tests particularly, but not exclusively, interest has grown in providing a "profile" of marks in particular subtests rather than a global assessment. While obviously providing more detailed information, the subtests, being necessarily shorter, will be less reliable than the combined score, and the more complex form of results may prove confusing (Harrison, 1983; Stevenson, 1983).

As the concept of the functions of education widens to include affective as well as cognitive areas, the traditional forms of educational assessment are being seen as inadequate, particularly as a large proportion of pupils are leaving schools in many countries without formal examination qualifications. It is now suggested that certification should be on a basis of profiles not only of examination results but also of attributes of character and personality. A note of caution may be entered here; if assessment is spread over a wider range of attributes, then effectively there is an extension of the area in which control is exercised by the educational system and a contraction of the areas of privacy. This may be compounded by the fact that the techniques of assessment in such areas are less developed and probably less accurate than those in traditional areas.

In summary, developments in educational assessment have been in two main areas; one is the refinement of techniques and increased sophistication of statistical analysis through computerized techniques, the other is a widening of the areas covered by such assessment.

Lachlan Cameron

REFERENCES

Anastasi, A. (1968) *Psychological Testing*. New York: Macmillan.

Black, H. D. and Dockrell, W. B. (1980) "Assessment in the Affective Domain: Do We, Should We?" *British Educational Research Journal* 6 (2): 192–208.

Bloom, B. S., ed. (1956) *Taxonomy of Educational Objectives—The Classification of Educational Goals,* vol.1, *The Cognitive Domain*. London: Longmans.

Branthwaite, E., Trueman, M., and Berrisford, T. (1981) "Unreliability of Marking; Further Evidence and a Possible Explanation." *Educational Review* 33 (1): 41–46.

Brewer, I. M. and Tomlinson, J. D. (1981) "The Use of Learning Profiles in the Assessment and Evaluation of Teachers." *Assessment and Evaluation in Higher Education* 6 (2): 120–164.

Burt, C. (1962) "The Psychology of Creative Ability: A Critical Notice of 'Creativity and Intelligence.' " *British Journal of Educational Psychology* 32: 292–298.

Cox, R. (1967) "Examinations and Higher Education: A Survey of the Literature." *Universities Quarterly* 21 (3): 292–340.

DerSimonian, R. and Laird, N. M. (1983) "Evaluating the Effect of Coaching at SAT Scores: A Meta-analysis." *Harvard Educational Review* 53 (1): 1–15.

Fineman, S. (1981) "Reflections on Peer-Teaching and Peer Assessment—An Undergraduate Experience." *Assessment and Evaluation in Higher Education* 6 (1): 82–93.

Fletcher, R. (1976) *Imperial China*. Harmondsworth: Penguin.

Garrison, D. A. (1979) "Measuring Differences in the Assigning of Grades." *Improving College and University Teaching* 27 (2): 68–71.

Getzels, J. W. and Jackson, P. W. (1962) *Creativity and Intelligence—Explorations in the Gifted Student*. London/New York: Wiley.

Godshalk, F. I., Swinford, F., and Coffman, W. E. (1966) *The Measurement of Writing Ability*. New York: N.Y. College Entrance Examination Board.

Goldstein, M. (1979) "Consequences of Using the Rasch Model for Educational Assessment." *British Educational Research Journal* 5 (2): 211–220.

Harden, R. M. and Cairncross, R. G. (1980) "Assessment of Practical Skills; The Objective Structured Practical Examination." *Studies in Higher Education* 5 (2): 187–196.

Harrison, A. (1983) *Profile Reporting of Examination Results*. London: Methuen/Schools Council.

Hartley, D. and Gray, G. (1981) "Item Banks and School-Based Assessment; The Case of Scottish 'O' Grade Physics." *British Educational Research Journal* 7 (1): 79–90.

Hartog, P. and Rhodes, E. C. (1935) *An Examination of Examiners*. London: Macmillan.

———. (1936) *The Marks of Examiners*. London: Macmillan.

Hassencahl, F. (1979) "Contract Grading in the Classroom." *Improving College and University Teaching* 27 (1): 30–33.

Henderson, E. S. (1980) "The Essay in Continuous Assessment." *Studies in Higher Education* 5 (2): 197–203.

Heywood, J. (1977) *Assessment in Higher Education*. London: Wiley.

Heywood, J. and Youngman, M. B. (1981) "Pupils' Reactions to Multiple Choice Items in Mathematics." *Educational Research* 23 (3): 228–229.

Holdsworth, R. (1981) "Improving the Selective Interview." *Educational and Training* 23 (2): 36–37.

Hoste, R. (1982a) "The Construct Validity of Some Certificate of Secondary Education Biology Examinations: The Evidence from Factor Analysis." *British Educational Research Journal* 8 (1): 31–43.

———. (1982b) "Development of a Semantic Differential Instrument to Quantify Students' Perception of Teaching and Teaching Practice." *Evaluation Newsletter* (SRHE) 6: 13–21.

Hudson, L. (1968) *Contrary Imaginations—A Psychological Study of the English Schoolboy*. London: Methuen.

Ingenkamp, K. (1977) *Educational Assessment*. Windsor: National Foundation for Educational Research.

Jackson, R. (1980) "The Scholastic Aptitude Test: A Response to Slack and Peters' 'Critical Appraisal.' " *Harvard Educational Review* 50 (3): 382–391.

James, C. and Hub, D. R. (1983) "The Effect of Question Choice on the Reliability of an Examination." *International Journal of Electrical Engineering Education* 20 (4): 375–384.

Krathwohl, D. R., ed. (1964) *Taxonomy of Educational Objectives,* vol. 2, *The affective domain*. London: Longmans.

Macdonald, R. and Sansom, D. (1979) "The Use of Assignment Attachments in Assessment." *Assessment in Higher Education* 5 (1): 45–55.

McGaghie, W. C., Miller, G. E., Sasid, A. W., and Telder, T. V. (1978) *Competency Based Curriculum Development in Medical Education: An Introduction*. Geneva: World Health Organization.

McIntosh, H. G. and Morrison, R. B. (1969) *Objective Testing*. London: University of London Press.

Marsh, R. W. (1964) "A Statistical Reappraisal of Getzels and Jackson's Data." *British Journal of Educational Psychology* 34: 91–83.

Mehrens, W. A. and Lehmann, I. J. (1975) *Measurement and Evaluation in Education and Psychology*. New York: Holt, Rhinehart and Winston.

Morris, N. (1961) "An Historian's View of Examinations." In *Examination and English Education,* ed. S. Wiseman. Manchester: Manchester University Press.

Morrison, R. B. (1972) "A Method for Analysing Choice-Type Question Papers." In *British Examinations: Techniques of Analysis,* ed. D. L. Nuttall and A. S. Willmott. Slough: National Foundation for Educational Research.

Newble, D. I., Hoare, J., and Sheldrake, P. F. (1980) "The Selection and Training of Examiners for Clinical Examinations." *Medical Education* 14: 345–349.

Nuttall, D. L. and Willmott, A. S. (1972) *British Examinations; Techniques of Analysis.* Slough: National Foundation for Educational Research.

Orpen, C. (1982) "Student v Lecturer Assessment of Learning: A Research Note." *Higher Education* 11 (5): 567–572.

Osgood, C. E., Suci, G. J. and Tannenbaum, P. H. (1957) *The Measurement of Meaning.* Urbana: University of Illinois Press.

Powers, D. E. (1982) *Estimating the Effects of Various Methods of Preparing for the SAT.* College Board Report No. 82-2. New York: N.Y. College Entrance Examination Board.

Preece, P.F.W. (1980) "On Rashly Rejecting Rasch: A Response to Goldstein." *British Educational Research Journal* 6 (2): 209–210.

Rasch, G. (1960) *Probabilistic Models for Some Intelligence and Attainment Tests.* Copenhagen: Danmarks Paedogiske Institute.

Scottish Education Department. (1982) *The Munn and Dunning Reports—The Government's Development Programme.* Edinburgh: Scottish Education Department.

Sheridan, W. (1974) "Open-Ended Questions." In *Techniques and Problems of Assessment,* ed. H. G. McIntosh. London: Edward Arnold.

Shouksmith, G. (1968) *Assessment through Interviewing.* Oxford: Pergamon.

Slack, W. V. and Porter, D. (1980) "The Scholastic Aptitude Test: A Critical Appraisal." *Harvard Educational Review* 50 (2): 154–175.

Stevenson, M. (1983) "Pupil Profiles—an Alternative to Conventional Examinations?" *British Journal of Educational Studies* 31 (2): 102–116.

Swinton, S. S. and Powers, D. E. (1982) *A Study of the Effects of Special Preparation on GRE Analytical Scores and Item Types,* GRE Board Research Report, No. 78. 2R. Princeton, N.J.: Educational Testing Service.

Thompson, D. J. and Rentz, A. R. (1973) "Large Scale Essay Testing: Implications for Test Construction and Evaluation." The Hague International Symposium on educational testing, quoted in Heywood (1977). Unpublished paper.

Tinari, F. D. (1979) "Item Analysis in Introductory Economics Testing." *Improving College and University Teaching* 27 (2): 61–67.

Trost, G. (1979) "Research in the Federal Republic of Germany with Regard to Interviews for Admission to Higher Education." In *The Use of Tests and Interviews for Admission to Higher Education,* ed. W. Mitter. Windsor: National Foundation for Educational Research.

Vernon, P. E. (1956) *The Measurement of Abilities.* London: University of London Press.

———.(1964) *The Certificate of Secondary Education: An Introduction to Objective-Type Examinations.* London: Her Majesty's Stationery Office.

Willmott, A. S. and Fowles, D. E. (1974) *The Objective Interpretation of Test Performance.* Windsor: National Foundation for Educational Research.

Willmott, A. S. and Hall, C.G.W. (1975) *"O" Level Examined: The Effect of Question Choice.* London: Macmillan.

Wiseman, S. (1949) "The Marking of English Composition in Grammar School Selection." *British Journal of Educational Psychology* 19: 200–209.

Wood, R. (1974) "Question Banking." In *Techniques and Problems in Assessment,* ed. H. G. McIntosh. London: Edward Arnold.

ASSOCIATION FOR EDUCATIONAL AND TRAINING TECHNOLOGY (AETT). AETT (formerly known as APL 1962–1969, and APLET 1969–1979) is an independent voluntary body established in 1962 (as the Association for Programmed Learning) and devoted to "the improvement of education and training through the systematic application of instructional technology. Its main aim is to promote communication between technologists . . . who are interested in the use of educational technology." AETT organizes an international conference each year (ETIC), and from time to time organizes smaller meetings. The conference proceedings are published under the title *Aspects of Educational Technology.* As well as the conference proceedings AETT publishes the journal *Programmed Learning and Educational Technology* (four times a year) and the *International Yearbook of Educational and Instructional Technology* (IYETT). IYETT contains review articles, a worldwide directory of edtech experts, and listings of educational and training materials and equipment.

The Administrator, AETT, BMA House, Tavistock Square, London WC1, U.K.

ASSOCIATION FOR EDUCATIONAL COMMUNICATIONS AND TECHNOLOGY (AECT). The major U.S. professional association concerned with learning and instructional technology. Founded in 1923 as the Department of Visual Instruction (changed in 1947 to the Department of Audiovisual Instruction) of the National Educational Association. The association publishes a number of monographs and two periodicals: *TechTrends* (8 times per year) and *Educational Communication & Technology* (quarterly). The annual conference of the association, held in conjunction with a major exhibition, is an opportunity for educational technologists from around the world to exchange views.

ASSOCIATION FOR EDUCATIONAL DATA SYSTEMS (AEDS). AEDS is a professional association focusing on developments and directions in educational data processing and related computer technology. An annual conference is held and several publications are produced, namely, *AEDS Bulletin, AEDS Journal, AEDS Monitor.*

1201 Sixteenth St. NW, Washington, D.C. 20036, U.S.

ASSOCIATION FOR MEDIA AND TECHNOLOGY IN EDUCATION IN CANADA (AMTEC). The major Canadian body devoted to these topics. Among AMTEC's aims are "to identify and analyze critical issues and developments in educational media and technology and to seek to provide dissemination of valid and useful information." An annual conference is held.

PO Box 174, Station W, Toronto, Ontario, Canada

ASSOCIATION FOR MEDICAL EDUCATION IN EUROPE (AMEE). The association was formed in 1972 with the aim of fostering communication among medical educators and among national associations for medical education. The chief form of membership is the corporate membership of national associations for medical education from countries in the European region of the World Health Organization. Individual members are accepted only from countries without national associations for medical education. The association organizes international meetings and workshops in member countries on subjects of topical interest in medical education. Meetings are open to anyone interested in medical education, and are conducted in English. The association publishes a newsletter twice a year, which goes in bulk to all member associations for distribution to their members. The newsletter contains information about AMEE activities and publications and in addition gives details of other meetings or publications likely to be of interest to European medical educators. Reports of the association's meetings are also published, and a series of Case Studies in Medical Education, each of which consists of an in-depth study of an innovation in the medical education field which has recently taken place in a medical school or institution.

150b Perth Road, Dundee, Scotland, U.K.

ASSOCIATION FOR PROGRAMMED LEARNING (APL). *See* **Association for Educational and Training Technology.**

ASSOCIATION FOR PROGRAMMED LEARNING AND EDUCATIONAL TECHNOLOGY (APLET). *See* **Association for Educational and Training Technology.**

ASSOCIATION FOR THE DEVELOPMENT OF COMPUTER-BASED INSTRUCTIONAL SYSTEMS (ADCIS). ADCIS (formerly known as ADIS) is an international nonprofit organization with members throughout the United States, Canada, and numerous other countries, representing elementary and secondary school systems, colleges and universities, business and industry, as well as military and government agencies.

The purposes of the organization are to (1) advance the investigation and utilization of computer-based instruction (CAI) and/or management (CMI); (2) promote and facilitate the interchange of information, programs, and materials in the best professional and scientific tradition; (3) reduce redundant effort among developers; and (4) specify requirements and priorities for hardware and software development and encourage and facilitate their realization.

A quarterly journal, *Journal of Computer-Based Instruction,* and a bimonthly newsletter are published.

Miller Hall 409, Western Washington University, Bellingham, Washington 98225, U.S.

ASSOCIATION FOR THE STUDY OF MEDICAL EDUCATION (ASME). This British association for medical teachers provides a forum for communication and a focus of ideas for those interested in medical education. It has a variety of activities which are aimed to provide medical teachers with information and interest in medical education. A number of conferences and workshops are arranged each year, covering the teaching of special subjects, the introduction of new teaching techniques, and general questions of policy of relevance to all involved in medical education. A series of medical education booklets is published, designed to give factual information on specific topics of practical importance. The association's journal, *Medical Education,* has an international reputation. It contains articles on the wide range of topics of interest to medical teachers and news and notes on medical education.

ASME is also active in the research field, publishing a register of research, organizing an annual scientific meeting, and becoming involved in research projects. Many overseas visitors contact ASME to obtain help in arranging visits and obtaining advice about medical education in Britain.

The association has two main categories of members, individual and corporate. Corporate membership is held by the majority of medical schools in the U.K. Individual membership is open to anyone with an interest in medical education.

150b Perth Road, Dundee, Scotland, U.K.

ASSUMED BEHAVIOR. The prerequisite skills that the learner must possess or have mastered in order to start on a learning sequence. *See* **Task Analysis.**

ASYNCHRONOUS COMMUNICATION. Communication between computers not requiring exact control of timing. The modem adds a start bit to tell the other computer when a new message is being sent and when it has ended. Asynchronous transmission is the way microcomputers usually communicate.

A TO D CONVERTER. *See* **Analog to Digital Converter.**

ATTENTION SPAN. The length of time over which a learner can give his full attention to a lecture, topic, activity, program, etc. *See* **Microsleep.**

ATTENUATION. A loss of signal strength which occurs along conductors. The degree of attenuation depends on the frequency of the signal and the nature of the conductor. For example, in order for a television signal to travel fairly modest distances without severe loss of signal, the use of coaxial cable is required. In the case of long communication paths, it is usually necessary for there to be amplifying equipment at intervals along the way. Attenuation is expressed as the ratio of the emitted energy level to the received energy level.

ATTENUATOR. A device used to reduce the output of an amplifier or in other situations where it is necessary to lower the amplitude of an electrical signal.

AUDIO. Of or relating to sound and its reproduction. A term used especially to describe the audible as opposed to the visual component of a film, a television program, or any other multimedia presentation.

AUDIO ACTIVE COMPARATIVE LABORATORY. A type of language laboratory configuration, sometimes called "listen-respond-compare," requiring recording facilities for each student so that a response can be checked against a master recording.

AUDIO ACTIVE LABORATORY. A language laboratory, sometimes called "listen-respond" or "audio-passive," which permits the learner to hear his voice by means of headphones, but not to record his voice. *See* **Audio Active Comparative Laboratory; Language Laboratory.**

AUDIOCASSETTE. A plastic cassette containing audiotape, that avoids tedious threading procedures when the tape is placed on a tape recorder. The most common type is the compact cassette introduced in the early sixties by the Philips Company and now universally available. Cassettes containing 60, 90, and 120 minutes of tape (tape speed is 1.875 inches per second) are the most common, but there are other lengths available as well as continuous loop cassettes.

The overwhelming educational advantage of audiocassette equipment as opposed to other audiotape equipment is its simplicity in use. Also, due to a forward-looking licensing policy by Philips when first introducing the format, it is one of the few truly compatible items of audiovisual equipment.

AUDIO CONFERENCING. *See* **Teleconferencing.**

AUDIO INSTRUCTION. Next to the written word, audio is perhaps the second largest distribution medium for instruction. And yet audio, in general, has been more lightly treated for effectiveness than any other medium. The following is meant to provide guidelines and procedures for when to use audio, for what needs, in what formats, and how to produce audio instruction.

BACKGROUND

A casual, or even in-depth, search of the literature will reveal that audio, as a separate medium in and of itself, is given relatively little attention. This is rather surprising considering the wide use of the medium. It may be due to the seeming simplicity of audio. However, audio is not as simple as it might seem at first glance, and it requires as much careful attention in selection, development, and use as any other major medium. To decide initially how to use audio as a purveyor or guidance system to learning will be the first topic of concern.

Often audio instruction is encompassed within the topic of audiovisual. This is not to suggest that audio by itself has not been given some attention, such as its use in language training, which has seen the advent of language laboratories and related hardware. A surge of excitement in the 1960s also prevailed with the advent of the *dial access system* for audio in which the user could *call up* a specific program as needed. More recently, the advent of *variable speech compression* (to be discussed later) has led to much research. Other, more recent investigation has centered on its use for *distant learning* (Parker and Monson, 1980a, 1980b BACKGROUND READING) and as an adjunct to computer-assisted and video instruction (Miller et al., 1983 BACKGROUND READING). However, even with these few areas of interest, little emphasis has been placed on audio compared with the visual media (largely television and film) or the written word (through programmed instruction, etc.). One relatively recent innovation has signaled, probably more than anything else, a first-time concentrated effort in audio instruction, that is, the **audiocassette** (q.v.).

The audiocassette, which was introduced by Philips in the early 1960s, effectively solved three major stumbling blocks to the use of audio on a wide basis. First, audiocassettes made it much easier to distribute audio. Allied to this is the relatively low cost of the cassettes themselves, as well as the relatively low cost of the hardware in which to play back the audio. Cassette recorder/playback units may be found not only at school and work, but in the home and car. Equally important, the audiocassette is easily used by the consumer, and thus not limited, as certain media are, by the complexity of its operation. Millions of audiocassettes are produced and distributed each year. In general, the ease of distribution and low costs associated with audiocassettes removed prior restrictions for both the user and developer.

While the advent of the audiocassette has led to a wider use of, and interest in, audio instruction, it has not necessarily led, in turn, to a similar concentrated effort in proper selection, use, and development. The average producer and user of audio is still apt to select the use of audio for reasons which are the same as its advantages, namely, distribution and convenience of use. While these reasons are sometimes sound, they should not be the only reasons in terms of effective instruction or general communication. Similar lessons have been learned with regard to other media where the hardware has been selected without regard for its best use, time of use, and purposes. Therefore, we will explore these other *first* considerations.

In determining when, where, and for what purpose audio instruction would best be utilized to promote effective and efficient learning, either of two major vantage points may be taken. In the final analysis, it is hoped that both will be applied, and in some instances they both *must* be used:

(a) The *justifications* for audio from successful presentation and promotion of desired learning outcomes, and

(b) The *uses* to which audio is typically applied.

Once the designer has determined what these two vantage points are, he or she will certainly realize that the second of the two is usually applied initially in deciding whether to use audio. In fact, the first vantage point should be applied and then the second. It is then and only then that matters related to structure and method of production should be considered.

JUSTIFICATIONS

With any medium, as with audio, we have an initial tendency to think of the use of a medium in instruction and learning from the standpoint of its *uses*. For example, the use of audio for presenting narrations, role-play, bringing the sounds of the outside world inside the classroom, etc.

While these uses are important, we would do well to first think of when audio, as a medium, is justified because of what audio can do that some other medium cannot do as well. To this end, there are four major areas within which to justify the use of audio.

Objective Needs. The use of a systematic approach to designing and evaluating instruction, called the educational technology approach, shows us that the starting point for selecting any medium is after the instructional need has been established (through needs assessment, or **front-end analysis** [q.v.]), and after the behaviorally defined performance objectives, student characteristics, and learning environment have been specified. The nature of the performance objectives referred to here are as defined by Mager (1962, 1975 AUTHORITY). By contrast, the use of a traditional, nontechnological approach might suggest selecting the medium first. Objectives, however, tell us what *behaviors or performance* the students will be required to perform. Thus, inherent in these statements, or at least implied by them, are indications of what media would best portray, deliver, or provide the opportunity for interaction with the behaviors specified. Some examples of objectives will help to make the point obvious. One should keep in mind the three parts of a **behavioral objective** (q.v.) (conditions, behavioral term, and standards), whether or not all three parts are actually stated; conditions and standards are sometimes implied rather than actually written as part of an objective.

A behavioral objective contains, first of all, a condition or set of conditions. These may be actually written with the objective or they may be implied. The conditions are the circumstances or events which will prompt the performance of the behavior specified in the objectives. Horabin and Lewis (1977 FURTHER DETAIL) label conditions rather well when they refer to them as the "input," while the behavioral term is the "output." It is the conditions which can be looked at as one source to determine if audio (or any other medium) is justified for use. For example, the conditions are italicized in the following objective:

Given the sound of various reed instruments, identify each by name.

Audio instruction would be justified for use in the above objective because the conditions—sounds of the instruments—are necessary in order to perform this objective. The same is true for the conditions of the following objective even though the conditions are implied:

Write a set of notes that distinguish the Main Idea from Supplementary Material.

Conditions for the above objective are implied in either of two forms: a live lecture or a recording. The latter would be more justified from a control and repeated-use standpoint. Thus, in an analysis of objectives for the use of audio, conditions of the objective should be observed whether actually written into the objective or implied.

It is not only the conditions of an objective we have defined for students as the outcomes of their learning that will indicate where audio may be justified. It may also be the behavioral terms themselves. The behavioral terms are the action verbs used in an objective to tell what behavior the student is to perform, i.e., write, identify, choose, select, and so on. Again, Horabin and Lewis appropriately label this the "output." The following objective is a good example of when audio would be justified because of the behavioral term (which has been italicized):

Recite a closing interview to a given policy program, demonstrating at least six of the eight criteria outlined in this course for a successful closing.

Reciting, in the above objective, could be done either live or on tape and perhaps both ways. The latter is preferred for practice and repeated assessment by the student and the one (most likely a teacher) who will evaluate.

Thus, the first major area in which we can look to identify whether audio instruction would be justified for use would be an analysis of the objectives that have been defined as student outcomes of a learning experience. Primarily, the conditions and behavioral terms of objectives are the specific items to analyze. Standards, as a third component of objectives, rarely call for audio needs, although there may be instances where they might.

Facilitating Justification. A second major justification calling for the use of audio instruction is what is called a *facilitating* function. By this is meant instances where the use of audio would greatly aid the student in performance or initial learning because there is a concurrent demand on the student's attention. A simple example will help to illustrate this justification for audio. Consider the following objective for a course:

Using the 1958 CSO table, calculate the probability that any individual of a given age will die in a given year.

One thing you will note about this objective is that neither the condition nor the behavioral term would particularly justify the use of audio instruction. However, have you ever tried to read content describing facts and numbers that are found in a table, graph, or chart? You must have, since it is required of you in almost any textbook, even this encyclopaedia. One thing is obvious about this activity. You cannot read the content and look at the table, graph, or chart at the same time. However, if the content explaining the table were on an audiotape, then you could both listen to and look at the table of information at the same time. This is a facilitative function. The audio facilitates the efficient use of information so that the listener can attune to two functions, listening and looking. There are many instances in learning where audio can be justified for use on a facilitating function basis. Two other good examples of the facilitating function which audio can serve are (1) manipulative, psychomotor skills and (2) as an aid while explaining mathematical calculation, as exemplified in the objective above. Later in this entry a description will be provided of several *instructional designs* that incorporate the use of audio as a facilitator.

Time Control Justification. Thiagarajan (1977 FURTHER DETAIL), in describing his Grouprograms instructional design format (to be discussed later), suggests a particularly interesting justification for the use of audio that is well suited for small group interaction needs. In this design, a stringent time limit is imposed and monitored by the use of an audiotape. Far from being a justification based on the specifications inherent in the objectives outlined for students, this justification is designed to control the efficiency of learning. For example, small groups of students are told (on the audiotape) to engage in the discussion of a topic and to arrive at a decision. The topic is introduced on the audiotape and the tape is left running. The fact that they know exactly how long the tape will run (i.e., 10 minutes) forces the listeners to make efficient use of their time since the tape will continue in the discussion of the topic at hand, whether or not the group is ready to continue listening. Thus, in learning situations where time needs to be controlled efficiently for a variety of reasons, the audiotape provides a convenient means for doing so. This might be important not only in limiting group interaction for discussion and decision-making needs, but also for those learning situations in which the real time of taking action must be simulated, for instance, in the medical field, where a student trainee must ascertain vital signs in an emergency case within a prescribed time limit. In simple terms, the audiotape can be thought of as a clock controlling desirable time limits.

Administrative Justifications. A fourth, and often troublesome, justification for the use of audio instruction is for administrative needs. This is a justification that is quite often used to select audio for use in learning, but also one that is used where it should not necessarily be used. However, administrative uses are worth exploring because they are used to select audio for instruction.

Administrative justifications include such things as ease of distribution, a change of pace for the student, multiuses of a learning package (for instance, on students and subsequently on clients in job situations), a desire to focus in time (such as a review need), and many similar administrative needs. Generally, there is nothing in these justifications which requires audio as against the use of some other medium. Nonetheless, there are times when such reasons may be used. For example, an instructional situation which is predominantly lecture- or printed materials–oriented may well benefit from a change of pace in the use of audio instruction. While we will not dwell on such administrative justifications, one is cautioned to use audio honestly, like any other medium, when and where it can best serve learning.

USES

In addition to viewing audio instruction from a purely justification standpoint of what it should and should not be used for, a more traditional common *uses* standpoint can be taken. It would be hoped that in selecting audio based on its varied uses, one first determines that it has an allied learning justification. For example, the use of audio to accompany visuals—a common use—would be justified because the objectives upon which the visuals themselves are based have conditions or behavioral terms which require audio in the first place. With this in mind, the following will serve as a representative list of uses often given for audio. These are further divided into two categories as they relate to the persons in instruction who would be using the audio.

For the student, audio can have the following uses:

(a) prescribed by a teacher, to present role-play situations prepared in advance or recorded in the classroom;
(b) to present *show and tell* as is often done at primary level;
(c) to present case-study solutions;
(d) to provide narratives to projects completed outside the classroom;
(e) to provide a tape recorder for temporary use by a student as a reward for completion of other activities;
(f) to provide language and speech training and practice;
(g) for independent, self-directed study, with or without supporting materials.

For teachers and instructors, audio can have the following uses:

(a) to bring other experts into the classroom on tape;
(b) to present case situations and problems for solutions, either in fact form or in interview situations;
(c) as narratives to visual or printed materials;
(d) for question-and-answer review and testing;
(e) to bring in the outside world of sounds and work;
(f) as a first-day icebreaker for student introduction and goal setting; evaluated later for areas of specific student interest and postevaluation of course outcomes;
(g) for recording class sessions for subsequent makeup and review by students;
(h) for conducting concurrent activities where audio guides procedures and activities and the teacher is left free to aid individual students;
(i) for self-evaluation by the teacher of his or her instruction;
(j) for lesson plan revisions, with particular attention to questions asked by students which might suggest needed improvement in instruction.

Further details on these uses are given in an article by Langdon and Rahmlow (1977 FURTHER DETAIL) entitled "Instructor Prepared Audio Instruction."

A third viewpoint from which audio has been selected for instruction is from a list of advantages and disadvantages. This viewpoint is not given much weight in that it incorporates the same considerations given previously under the separate headings of justifications and uses. A typical list of advantages, nonetheless, is as follows:

Advantages

(a) Little or no reading ability needed.
(b) Program can be used for group-paced or individualized instruction.
(c) It is easier to spot weakness during developmental testing (students must rewind the tape to review instruction).
(d) Students can look at an illustration as they listen to an explanation. With printed matter they have to flip back and forth from text to illustration.
(e) You can duplicate tapes as you need them. (With printed materials you must duplicate a large number to get costs down.)
(f) You can use music and sound effects to add "color" to an instructional program.
(g) You can conceal the answers from the students more easily when providing interaction requirements.
(h) You can teach some skills more easily (those involving aural discrimination and manipulation of materials).
(i) It probably takes less time to prepare the first draft.
(j) It is easier to simulate the real world.

(k) It is easier to make changes in the program (you simply splice any revision in the master tape).

Disadvantages

(a) Students are locked into a linear presentation (except, as will be noted later, by the use of the Zimdex system).
(b) You need recording equipment.
(c) You need a narrator.
(d) You cannot look ahead and skim (except where time-compressed speech is used).
(e) Students may suffer from listening illiteracy.

AUDIO INSTRUCTION DESIGNS

According to Langdon (1977b AUTHORITY), an instructional design is a "prescription of student learning requirements and events that serves as a guidance function towards specific objectives and to promote desired learning capabilities." A further aspect of this definition specifies "a prescription through which a medium presents and guides instructions." What does an instructional design have to do with audio, or for that matter, any medium, that is selected for instruction?

It could be presupposed, and often is, that once a decision has been made to use audio for instruction, all one needs to do is write a script, make a recording, and distribute the audio as an audiocassette or audio reel-to-reel or record disk. In some instances, this may be all that is necessary. However, in the past two decades, instructional technologists have come to realize that the use of audio as part of an overall instructional design format has greatly aided in its overall effectiveness and efficiency. Often, these instructional designs incorporate the use of audio as the medium for delivery of instruction. The following four designs will typify instructional designs wherein audio is the main delivery system. The reader will find these beneficial as specific formats within which to structure and deliver audio instruction. Before selecting any one of these, or others, it is assumed that the developer has carefully selected audio for the justifications and uses previously specified. It is also assumed that the developer would carefully follow evaluation and validation procedures to assure that audio instruction does, in fact, aid in producing learning.

Audio-tutorial. Apart from audiotapes and audiocassettes that present information or instruction on a purely non-interactive basis (meaning without students responding and subsequent feedback on correctness of responding), possibly the most widely used audio instruction format within a specific instructional design is that of the audio-tutorial.

Originated by Samuel N. Postlethwait (1976 HISTORICAL), currently of Purdue University, the audio-tutorial is, as its name would imply, basically a method of providing a tutorial guidance function for a student without a *live* tutor. The audio part of the total instructional design assumes the role of tutoring: guiding the student through various activities, projects, and other media support systems, and providing interaction through questions and confirming answers (feedback) directed by the tape. A colleague of Postlethwait, and himself the author of a book on the audio-tutorial system, James D. Russell (1977 FURTHER DETAIL) outlines the salient features of the design and the specific role of the audiotape. The following excerpts from Russell's book will provide the reader with some idea of the features and uses:

1. The Audio-tutorial system provides a multi-faceted, multi-media approach to learning which is under the control of the student. It utilises an audiotape as a programming device to tutor the student through the instructional activities and media until he has mastered the objectives of the lesson. The Audio-Tutorial approach is a total instructional system composed of the following three basic components: Independent Study Session, General Assembly Session, and Small Assembly Session.

2. Role of the Audio tape. The Audio-Tutorial approach must not be confused with a "lecture" on tape. Rather, the audiotape is a device for programming each individual student through the learning sequence.

The reader is encouraged to read Russell's book or other sources available for additional details on this design for audio instruction.

Audio-Workbook. Langdon (1977a FURTHER DETAIL), in a book entitled *Audio-Workbook,* suggests three instructional design formats within which audio instruction can be structured to meet varying facilitative and administrative justifications and uses. All three designs link the audiotape (audiocassette) with written "study guide" materials, which the author has determined to be necessary for certain interaction needs between student and subject matter. These three designs include

(a) *Audiocassette Review.* A simplified design in which the audio provides information reviewing a course of study already completed by students. A "response book" contains behavioral objectives by units or assignments, and corresponding questions and feedback either in the book or on the audiotape. This design can also be used for initial learning (rather than subsequent review) in which the predominance of instructional content would be on the audiotape.

(b) *Adjunctive Instruction Design.* Audio instruction is integrated in this design with instruction provided by other media formats (i.e., textbooks). An active responding and feedback mechanism is provided. This design, through the example given (a mathematics course), amply illustrates, in particular, the facilitative function as a justification for the use of audio. Also illustrated is a unique and easy means for indexing the audiocassette to access specific information anywhere on an audiotape. This indexing system, called Zimdex, was devised by Langdon (1972 AUTHORITY; 1976 FURTHER DETAIL) and is reported on later in this entry.

(c) *Update Program*. This instructional design, incorporating a major use of audio to deliver instruction, was originated to fill the needs of students who had completed several courses of instruction and were now functioning in a job situation and needed updating on concepts and knowledge learned previously. A secondary use of the design provides a convenient means for use of the audiocassettes with clients whom the students come into contact with in their job situations. The need to update themselves on specific objectives, rather than necessarily the entire program, leads to specific flexible instructional design characteristics and the use of the previously mentioned Zimdex system. The design may also be used for initial learning in addition to course updating.

Grouprograms. Perhaps the most recent innovative use of audio instruction is the Grouprogram instructional design originated by Sivisailam Thiagarajan, formerly of Indiana University and now a private consultant to business and education.

According to Thiagarajan (1977 FURTHER DETAIL), "The instructional design of Grouprograms provides for small-group learning while maintaining a fairly tight structure. In working through a grouprogram, members of the learning team help each other in their common instructional task and provide individualized instruction of the best variety." This activity is guided by instructions provided on an audiotape of decisions or issues to be resolved by the group.

One of the unique aspects of Grouprograms is that it employs the use of audio on small groups, rather than individuals. Other characteristics include a highly structured and organized (rather than open-ended) learning experience; it is self-contained, permitting leaderless discussions and containing all materials needed; it is group paced, and designed to meet prespecified objectives.

One especially noteworthy feature of Grouprograms is the manner in which the audiotape is used as a control means for *timing*. This justification for the use of audio was mentioned earlier in this discussion of audio instruction.

Rolemaps. Diane Dormant, in her book *Rolemaps* (1980 FURTHER DETAIL), describes a facilitative technique for using audio analogous to the use of audio for Grouprograms. Some additional uses of audio, however, make it worthy of special attention. The audiotape is used to set the role-play situation (scenario), assign and outline individual roles to players, control time perameters for discussion, interject new or additional contingencies, provide transition to additional roles, and provide feedback as appropriate. Those who have experienced difficulty in structuring and delivering role-play needs will find this instructional design particularly noteworthy.

Other Instructional Designs Using Audio. There are, of course, other instructional design formats that use audio instruction either as a part of their overall structure or in combination with other media. While none of the other designs employs audio to the same extent as the three designs discussed above, they are at least worth mentioning for further investigation and study.

The Audiovisual Training Modules design (Stolovitch, 1977 FURTHER DETAIL) employs audio in combination with various media, including slides, print materials, and such.

Instructional Simulation Games (Thiagarajan and Stolovitch, 1977 FURTHER DETAIL) can employ the use of audio for game play.

Audio can also be employed in programmed instruction (Bullock, 1977 FURTHER DETAIL) in general, and in **backward chaining** (q.v.) (Alden, 1977 FURTHER DETAIL) strategies.

The unique considerations given by Parker and Monson (1980b BACKGROUND) in their book *Teletechniques* are worth studying. Of particular note is what they say about humanizing, increasing participation, and handling message style and feedback. In that Teletechniques have to do with all media for telecommunicating, including audio, this instructional design has not been considered separately here.

Of course, beyond these prescribed instructional design strategies are the many noninteractive audio instruction and information programs that are simply "recorded" messages. Indeed, most audio instruction is of a simple narrative form, or audio media messages, such as music, language tapes, etc., that have been "captured" on tape. One could not even begin to evaluate the merits of these straightforward "audio content" messages. Two particular sources to be aware of for finding American audiotapes in general, mostly of the noninteractive form, include the *Index to Educational Audiotapes*, National Information Center for Educational Media, University of Southern California, Los Angeles, California, U.S.; and the catalogue of the National Center for Audiotapes, University of Colorado, Boulder, Colorado, U.S.

DEVELOPMENT

It is curious, and somewhat revealing, that little of substance has been written on how to produce or develop audio instruction that truly addresses itself to the uniqueness of audio. Furthermore, what has been written on the subject is generally in the same context as would be used in describing how to write within the written medium. This includes such things as writing clearly, to the point, to the subject, conversationally, and other such related matters. Or, if procedural approaches have been suggested, they generally relate again to approaches to be followed in writing toward and within any given medium; for example, the use of an instructional technology approach, such as (1) define the objectives, (2) write the criterion questions and answers, (3) define the examples, (4) determine sequence, and so forth. While all of these, and other considerations related to development, are important, it still remains that relatively little has been suggested that is unique to audio itself. There is, perhaps, one exception to this. This is an approach to development suggested by Langdon (1972 AUTHORITY) which calls for producing the audio medium "on its own terms." Incidentally, Langdon also suggests how the same approach may apply as well to developing visual media, although he has not as yet tried the technique. Producing audio messages on their own terms may be summarized as follows. A brief preliminary description will serve to emphasize why this approach is particularly worth considering.

Within the overall context of developing an instructional program in any given medium or mediamix, it is common to begin the development of the written medium by *writing* a manuscript, the audio medium by *writing* a script, and the visual medium by *writing* script (to which visual specifications are made). The key ingredient to note here is that in all three media, or even a mix of media, all begin in the *written* word. Before going any further, we must ask ourselves the question, "Is there any difference between the written word and the spoken word (or visual representation)?" Most would certainly agree (and research is there to back it up) that there are several differences. The differences are particularly apparent between the written word and visual representation, but there is also a difference between the written word and the spoken word. (Allied to this difference is a difference in the degree to which people remember things from the written, spoken, and visual media.) For instance, one of the more obvious differences between the written and spoken word is how *stilted* the written word can sound when recorded; put another way, how freely the spoken word is used in ordinary conversation as opposed to the written word (or audiotape from the written script). The question now becomes "If there is a difference between the spoken and written word, why do we begin and produce the spoken word (in the form of an audiotape) from the written word (script)?" If our intent is to produce the spoken word, then why not begin in the spoken word? Do we not do the same for the written word, that is, begin in the written word? How then would audio instruction be produced *on its own terms?*

The answer to how is very simple. Incorporating the essential step of an instructional technology approach to development, the procedure is briefly outlined in the following flowchart (Figure 1).

The procedure for producing an audio media message on its own terms calls for first defining what the students are to learn in terms of behavioral objectives. Next, questions and answers (or other activity means) for interaction (if provided) are specified. These two items tell us the direction (outcomes) that the audio program must achieve. Beginning in step 3 is the actual procedure to follow in producing the audio instruction through an audio approach. In simple terms, this calls for sitting down with a student (or small group of students), providing the students with an objective or set of objectives, turning on a tape recorder, and having a person who is an expert on the subject of the objectives commence to give an instructional presentation to the objectives. Such an expert (labeled the subject-matter expert, SME) may have some prepared notes to help guide him or her in presenting content, but not a script. This allows for a somewhat structured approach, but more of a free flow of information in a purely audio (spoken word) form. Furthermore, a time limit may be imposed on the SME so as to help avoid too much rambling. All the while, this presentation is being recorded. At an appropriate point or within a specified time limit, the SME will stop and ask the students to answer the questions to the objective. Thus, the SME can check on their having learned or not learned from the presentation on the objective covered. If they have not learned, the SME can ask the students to help clarify. Such exchanges themselves should be recorded. If one wishes, the students might even be allowed to ask questions of their own while the initial presentation is being given.

The above procedure provides the development of an audio program that begins in the audio medium. Thus, what is produced is a closer match to what one intends to end up with—an audio program. This is *producing a media message on its own terms*. The recording that is produced may then be transcribed (verbatim) into a written script and worked on for necessary editing, addition

Figure 1
Flow Chart Showing Audio Media Message Production

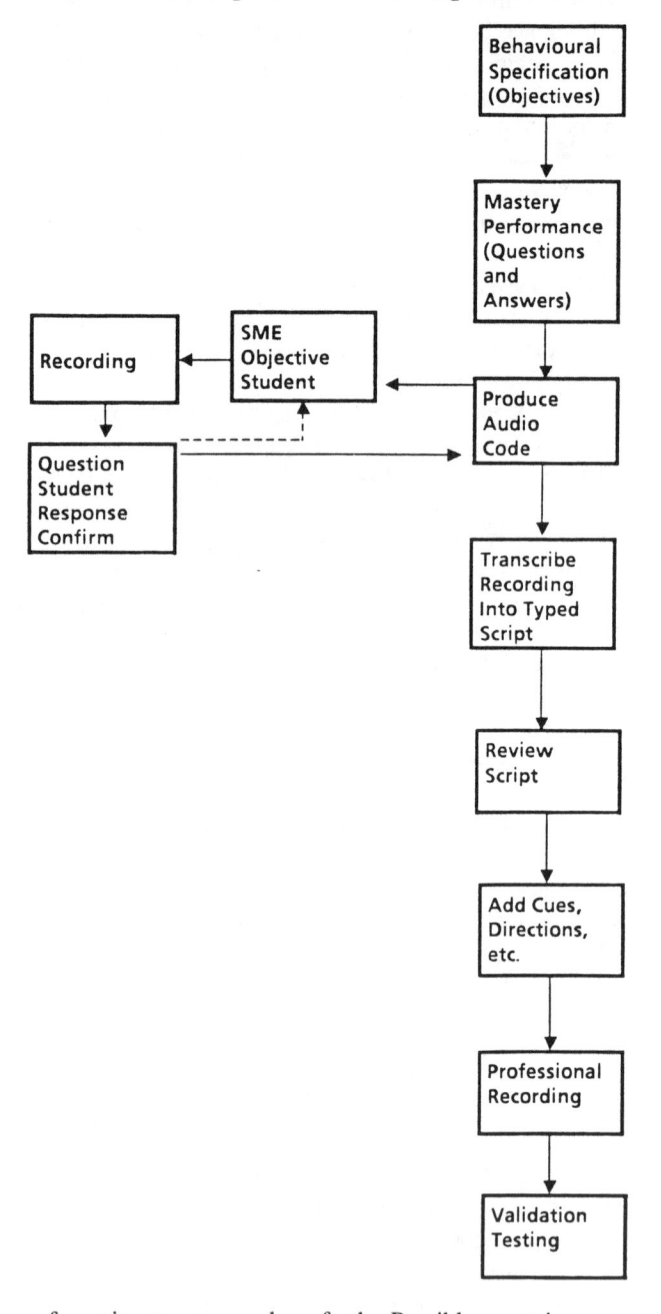

```
Behavioural Specification (Objectives)
        ↓
Mastery Performance (Questions and Answers)
        ↓
Recording ← SME Objective Student → Produce Audio Code
        ↓                              ↑
Question Student Response Confirm -----|
                                       ↓
                              Transcribe Recording Into Typed Script
                                       ↓
                              Review Script
                                       ↓
                              Add Cues, Directions, etc.
                                       ↓
                              Professional Recording
                                       ↓
                              Validation Testing
```

of music, pauses, and so forth. Possibly, certain segments of the original recording can be used in the final product. Due care must be taken in editing not to destroy the *audio* form that originally transpired. The advantages of following such a procedure are several:

(a) The audio produced will be closer to the way we *hear* (as compared to the way we read).
(b) Audio produced in this manner tends to be more free flowing and directive because the producer is in direct contact with a representative(s) of the ultimate user.
(c) The presence of a student(s) will provide firsthand opportunities to clarify learning problems that might surface in what is to be learned.
(d) Within some limits, it takes less time for the expert to produce audio in this manner, because much of the time that would be required of the producer in writing is transferred to clerical personnel in typing from an audiotape, from which the writer then works refinements.

In conclusion, while only limited commentary is possible, the foregoing approach to audio development does represent at least a closer approximation to what audio should ultimately be presented as. There are certainly other considerations to be observed. Several of these and other matters are described in an article by O'Sullivan (1977 FURTHER DETAIL).

SPEECH COMPRESSION AND AUDIO INDEXING

Speech Compression. Speech compression, also labeled time-compressed speech, is a relatively new innovation in audio instruction. While the technology of speech compression has existed for some time, it is only recently that electronic means, allowing lower cost of recording and playback units, have allowed the potential for wider use of the technology.

Essentially, speech compression is a means by which the rate of the recorded message may be speeded up, thus reducing the time required for listening to the audiotape. This is possible without a resulting distraction to the pitch of the recording. In simple terms, one can listen to an audiotape at a faster rate without what is often labeled the "Donald Duck effect." Why is speech compression an important contribution to audio instruction?

First of all, research has shown that most persons can listen and comprehend at rates much higher than the average speaking rate. For instance, the average oral reading rate is around 175 words a minute, and yet the average person can listen at a rate of 300 words per minute.

A related consideration is what happens when the average person listens to an audiotape at normal speed: that is, there is a tendency to be lulled into a lack of attention, particularly if the audio recording is long. Speech compression allows one to vary the rate of listening, so as to, in effect, adjust the listening of an audiotape to what the individual can handle; and thus listener attention is heightened. This might mean increasing the listening rate just slightly to as much as twice the rate of normal speed—again, without a loss in pitch.

Until recently, the cost of producing variable speech-compressed tapes was fairly expensive, due to the hardware needed for recording. Also, the user was locked into listening to a tape at whatever speech-compression rate was made available. User-controlled playback units for varying the speed were not available for general use. Recent new innovations, utilizing electronic means, have resulted in lower cost units, most notably the following three units:

VSC Copycorder, by Magnetic Video Corporation, Farmington, Michigan

VSC A6, by VSC Company, San Francisco, California

Varispeech II, by Lexicon, Waltham, Massachusetts

The above units and others allow the individual user (as opposed to the developer) to set an audiocassette recorded at normal speed to whatever rate he chooses (usually around twice to two and a half times the normal rate). Units are even available for slowing down the rate and may be particularly suited for use in language and speech training. One is cautioned to keep in mind the amount of new information provided in a given time frame. While a hundred new bits of information can be compacted into a minute, how much the average listener can attend to and remember is a critical factor to consider.

In summary, speech compression does offer one more added feature in improving the overall effectiveness and efficiency of audio instruction. An excellent resource for learning and obtaining additional insights into this technology is through the Perceptual Alternatives Laboratory, University of Louisville, Louisville, Kentucky 40208, U.S., through which much of the research and development is currently being coordinated.

Audio Indexing. One of the apparent limitations, from an operational standpoint, of the audiotape (reel or cassette) has been the fact that it must usually be used in a linear fashion. In other words, it is difficult to locate specific information on an audiotape at any given point one might wish, without listening to the entire tape or on a hit-and-miss basis. Attempts at indexing an audiotape have included keying selected segments by the counter number found on certain playback units, keying to the hash marks found on many audiocassettes (on the plastic viewplate) and markings placed on the label that is attached to the cassette. The most accurate indexing system, however, is that which was innovated by Langdon (1976 FURTHER DETAIL) called Zimdex (the title given by the American College, Bryn Mawr, Pennsylvania, U.S.).

Zimdex is a very simple and inexpensive system for indexing an audiocassette for quick and easy access of information at any given point on the tape. It works as follows.

One side (say, Side A) of the audiocassette is reserved for recorded information. For example, suppose Side A is a 30–minute presentation covering six objectives (topics, subtopics); the other side of the tape, Side B, is reserved for a recording of numbers, beginning with 1, with a five-second pause, then 2, and so on until the end, which might be the number 250. We might represent Side A, the information, and Side B, the index numbers, as shown in the chart on page 38. With this chart in mind, the beginning point of each objective can be indicated in a printed table of contents, as for example the following:

Side A Beginning of information on	*Side B* Matching index number heard
Objective 1	1
Objective 2	85
Objective 3	110
Objective 4	185
Objective 5	210

Thus, if a user of the audiocassette wanted to find the beginning point of instruction on the tape for Objective 2, he or she would place the tape on Side B, fast forward or reverse, stop and listen until the number 85 is heard; then stop the tape and turn it over to Side A, and the beginning of the information on Objective 2 would begin. The time required to find the beginning point of instruction is usually 30 seconds or less. Indexing in this manner can be done to specific objectives, topics, words, phrases, or whatever might best be appropriate. Location of specific points on the audiocassette is assured.

SUMMARY

Audio can be a powerful tool for effective and efficient learning. In order to be so, it must be carefully selected, produced, and validated. Audio does have some characteristics that it can accomplish that no other medium alone can. The facilitative function is but one example.

In any decision to use audio by itself or in combination with other media, careful analysis should be given to those factors which justify its use above other media that might also be used. In this regard, there are many uses to which audio can be put, but these uses do not necessarily justify the use of audio itself. When audio is selected because of the needs of objectives that have been defined as learning outcomes, or because it serves a facilitative, time control, or real administrative need, then we are more likely to serve the user as he or she can best be served by audio.

Once audio has been selected because it is needed, other considerations related to instructional format and the process of development should be taken into account. There exist a number of instructional design formats in which audio plays the predominant role as a delivery system of information and control agent of interaction. There are other designs in which audio plays a secondary but important role. Finally, there are audio programs that follow no particular design other than what the individual developer might perceive as the best he or she can produce.

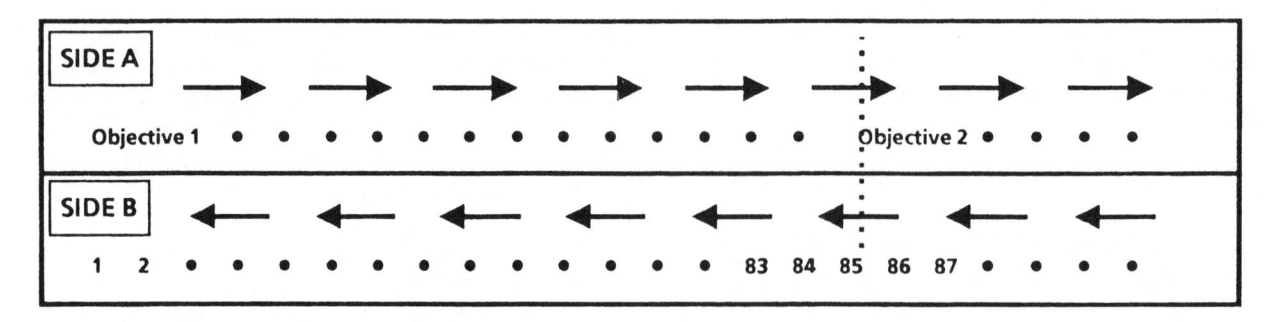

Beyond these things that can be done to select audio for proper use and to produce it at the most effective level (i.e., "on its own terms"), there are certain other recent advancements that have enhanced the use and effectiveness of audio instruction. Most notable in this regard is the advent of compressed speech and accurate means for indexing audiotapes to assure easy and quick access of instruction from any point within the audiotape. Taking these and other considerations in mind should do much to provide students with both effective and efficient audio instruction.

D. G. Langdon

REFERENCES

Authority

Langdon, D. G. (1972) "Media Messages on Their Own Terms." *Educational Technology Magazine* (June): 39–42.

———. (1977b) *Introduction to the Instructional Design Library*. Englewood Cliffs, N.J.: Educational Technology Publications.

Mager, R. F. (1962, 1975) *Preparing Instructional Objectives*. Belmont, Calif.: Fearon Publications.

Background Reading

Miller, K. et al. (1983) "Audio-Enhanced Computer-Assisted Learning and Computer-Controlled Audio Instruction." *Computers and education* 7 (1): 33–54.

Parker, L. A. and Monson, M. K. (1980a) "More Than Meets The Eye: The Effectiveness of Broadcast Audio and Two-Way Audio Instruction for Distant Learning." *University of Wisconsin Review Literature* (Madison) 38: 1–92.

———. (1980b) *Teletechniques: An Instructional Model for Interactive Teleconferencing*. Englewood Cliffs, N.J.: Educational Technology Publications.

Further Detail

Alden, J. (1977) *Backward Chaining*. Englewood Cliffs, N.J.: Educational Technology Publications.

Bullock, D. H. (1977) *Programmed Instruction*. Englewood Cliffs, N.J.: Educational Technology Publications.

Dormant, D. (1980) *Rolemaps*. Englewood Cliffs, N.J.: Educational Technology Publications.

Horabin, I. and Lewis, B. (1977) *Algorithms*. Englewood Cliffs, N.J.: Educational Technology Publications.

Langdon, D. G. (1976) "Zimdex." *Training* (January): 26–27.

———. (1977a) *Audio-Workbook*. Englewood Cliffs, N.J.: Educational Technology Publications.

Langdon, D. G. and Rahmlow, H. F. (1977) "Instructor Prepared Audio Instruction." *Training* (January): 14–16.

Langdon, D. G., Rahmlow, H. F., and Lewis, W. C. (1973) "Audio Indexing for Individualization." *Audiovisual Instruction* (April): 14–15.

O'Sullivan, K. (1977) "Audio for Training and Development: Some Notes about the Medium." *Training and Development Journal* (January): 56–60.

Russell, J. (1977) *Audio Tutorial System*. Englewood Cliffs, N.J.: Educational Technology Publications.

Stolovitch, H. (1977) *Audiovisual Training Modules*. Englewood Cliffs, N.J.: Educational Technology Publications.

Thiagarajan, S. (1977) *Groupprograms*. Englewood Cliffs, N.J.: Educational Technology Publications.

Thiagarajan, S. and Stolovitch, H. (1977) *Instructional Simulation Games*. Englewood Cliffs, N.J.: Educational Technology Publications.

Historical

Postlethwait, S. N. (1976) "Audio Technology: Audio Tape for Programming Instruction." *Educational Broadcasting* (July-August): 17–19.

AUDIO SPECTRUM. The range of sound frequencies to which the human ear is sensitive; usually considered to be 30Hz to 15,000Hz.

AUDIOTAPE. Audiotaping succeeded wire recording and preceded videotaping by many years. Domestic tape recorders using 0.25–inch tape were first marketed in the early 1950s, and it was to be some years before any change in format appeared. However, eventually the Philips cassette (compact cassette) was invented and proceeded to rapidly dominate the market. Compact cassettes use tape 1/8–inch wide, and are suitable for all general purposes; however, the 1/4–inch reel-to-reel format still holds sway for professional purposes, and in commercial recording studios even wider multitrack tape is in use. *See* **Audiocassette.**

AUDIO-TUTORIAL. A term coined by S. N. Postlethwait to describe an individualized and student-centered learning system based on audiotapes and practical experiments. *See* **Individualization of Instruction.**

AUDIOVISUAL. An adjective used originally to describe instructional materials which use a combination of sound and vision, e.g., film. Now a generic term loosely used for all educational communications media including even, for example, realia and audiocassettes.

AUDIOVISUAL COMMUNICATIONS (Journal). Monthly publication containing very practical information, case studies, reviews of equipment, etc.

475 Park Avenue S., New York, New York 10016, U.S.

AUDIOVISUAL INSTRUCTION. *See* **TechTrends.**

AUDIOVISUAL LANGUAGE JOURNAL. A journal devoted to reporting innovations in the use of audiovisual technology in language teaching. Three issues are published per year.

102 Margaret Road, New Barnet, Herts., U.K.

AUDIOVISUAL MEDIA. In 1913, Thomas Edison apparently predicted that film would totally replace the book in New York schools within the decade. Seventy years later that has not happened in New York or anywhere else for that matter. However, the educator—in school, higher education, or industrial training—now has access to a far greater range of audiovisual hardware and software than ever before. The "industrial revolution of education" (Lefranc, 1978 BACKGROUND READING) is continuing, and while some of the developments, such as microcomputing (Megarry et al., 1983 BACKGROUND READING), are outside the scope of this entry, they must be mentioned, partly because they utilize similar hardware (television monitors, etc.) and partly because the technologies appear to be converging (e.g., interactive video).

Surveying the literature indicates that use of audiovisuals is not restricted to one level of education or to any one subject or group of subjects. The amount of published material is substantial and cannot be adequately covered in the scope of this entry. Accordingly, consultation of major indexing and abstracting periodicals such as *Current Index to Journals in Education, British Education Index* and *Dissertation Abstracts International* is recommended both for retrospective searching and for current awareness. Also, although examples in the following text may be drawn from subject-oriented journals, it is not possible to deal with all subject areas, and the subject specialist must look to his own literature and to the guides already mentioned.

Although it is customary to talk of the "new" media, Saettler (1968 HISTORICAL) traces instructional media back to Comenius (1592–1670), a pioneer who stressed the value of pictorial illustrations in teaching and learning. The real boom in audiovisual media as we know them came after World War II in the United States (Hitchens, 1979; Rakow, 1980 HISTORICAL), Britain (Tucker, 1979 HISTORICAL), and Europe generally (Decaigny, 1979 HISTORICAL). Surveys of research are provided by Allen (1971 HISTORICAL), Campeau (1972 HISTORICAL), Coppen (1972 HISTORICAL, updated by Rodwell, 1974, 1975, 1976, 1977), Peterman (1982 BACKGROUND READING), and Razik and Ramroth (1974 HISTORICAL). Many of the sources cited subsequently in this entry include reviews of the literature relevant to the topic.

TERMINOLOGY

"Audiovisual media" is only one description in use in this field: learning resources, educational or instructional media, audiovisual aids, and even sometimes visual aids are often regarded as interchangeable terms. The problem is compounded by the tendency to use a term such as "audiovisual aids" as generic for all teaching and learning media, even those which do not include an audio or visual component in the technical sense, e.g., print-based teaching kits, games and simulations, Jackdaw-type facsimiles. *Nonbook* is a common alternative, but the prefix has negative or inferior connotations. Suggestions such as *metabook* (Enright, 1970 ILLUSTRATION OF A POINT), *materia* (Shifrin, 1973 ILLUSTRATION OF A POINT), and *document* (Butchart, 1977 ILLUSTRATION OF A POINT) have not achieved any currency. The problem is compounded by a tendency to confuse physical form (such as videotape), medium (such as sound recording), and concept (such as game) and to treat them all as "audiovisual media." Wiseman (1979 ILLUSTRATION OF A POINT) outlines these errors of thinking, but she is almost certainly fighting a losing battle against everyday usage.

JUSTIFICATION AND ROLE

Dale (1946 HISTORICAL) suggested that pedagogical experiences could be graded from direct, concrete experience of life to verbal symbols, by way of demonstrations, motion pictures, and so on. Hence it was argued that audiovisual media improved learning by adding concreteness. This view, embodied in his "Cone of experience," was supported by other "Realism theorists," but came under criticism in the 1960s by Travers (1964 HISTORICAL) and others, based on suggestions by

Broadbent (1958 HISTORICAL) that it was difficult to process information from more than one sensory input at a time. Therefore, simple aids could be as successful as, or more successful than, complex ones in generating understanding.

Despite these conflicting views, it sometimes might seem to the observer that the audiovisual bandwagon has rolled on regardless of justification, and that the present danger is that microcomputing will follow a similar course. Not every teacher would agree with Wenger (1983 ILLUSTRATION OF A POINT) that "the appearance of the educational film...was the most significant post-war event in the world of pedagogy."

Moore and Hunt (1980 BACKGROUND READING) identified several reasons for lack of enthusiasm for audiovisual media. These ranged from self-preservation to misunderstanding to a general concern about the impact of the media. A survey by Bennington (1982 BACKGROUND READING) showed that about 30 percent of lecturers questioned were hostile to the use of audiovisuals. Perhaps more significant was the fact that as many as 65 percent had never used them. While it was felt that use of "new" media could allow for closer staff-student contact, there was some degree of concern over a lack of flexibility in such methods. Teather (1978 BACKGROUND READING) suggests that there may be conflict between the "rigid" audiovisual/educational technology approach and the "liberal" university tradition, although the particular course he describes was rated a success.

In general, the educator may be faced with research findings which are inconclusive, contradictory, nongeneralizable, or subject-specific. Many reports of research end by outlining further areas for research rather than presenting firm conclusions. The complexity of factors which interact in the learning situation—learner characteristics, subject matter, media characteristics, and practical considerations—create problems for the teacher, who must also be considered a variable. Mariet (1980 ILLUSTRATION OF A POINT) believes that economic factors and the current fashion in audiovisual media can sometimes lead to choices which are irrational in educational terms. The case for instructional effectiveness as the major consideration in the choice of materials rather than, say, technical factors, is succinctly summarized by Clarke and Angert (1981 ILLUSTRATION OF A POINT): "effective instruction should be more than the result of serendipity."

While hardware, technological innovations and case studies (often "how we do it at our place" in nature) still form part of the literature, there has been a shift in emphasis "from a primary concern with the communications media to a concern with the management of the learning process" (Hitchens, 1979 HISTORICAL). Though Hitchens believes that such a change is a postwar phenomenon, Cambre (1981 HISTORICAL) found that evaluation of media—which implies a concern with the learning process rather than simply the technology—has gone on since the 1920s. Such evaluation was often formative in nature, though predating the term "formative evaluation."

Apart from psychological or pedagogical considerations of their suitability as teaching and learning aids, audiovisual media are carriers of information, in different physical forms. In many cases, the audiovisual item is the prime source (films, television series, photographs) and should find acceptance as such in homes, libraries, and schools. The development of media studies as a school subject may mean that future generations of learners will approach media—recreational, informative, or instructional—with the ability to "read" nonprint forms in the same way as they read print.

VISUAL LITERACY

Whether or not one agrees with Williams (1978 ILLUSTRATION OF A POINT) that the purpose of visual literacy is "to get more and more people able to communicate with each other on a more equal basis," the ability to interpret, respond to, and use visual media—to become visually literate—is important in a society which is increasingly using nonverbal means of communication. The concepts, principles, and research directions of visual literacy are dealt with by Ausburn and Ausburn (1978 BACKGROUND READING), Clayback et al. (1980 BACKGROUND READING), Debes (1978 BACKGROUND READING), Dwyer (1979 BACKGROUND READING), Hitchens (1981 BACKGROUND READING), Levie (1978 BACKGROUND READING), Williams (1978 ILLUSTRATION OF A POINT), and others.

Research indicates that visual literacy is influenced by various factors (Ogden, 1982 BACKGROUND READING). Ahmad (1978 ILLUSTRATION OF A POINT) observed that language and sex were significant influences in picture interpretation, and this is supported by Modiano et al. (1982 ILLUSTRATION OF A POINT), who used textbook illustrations with Mexican-Indian kindergarten children, and found differences in perception between male and female, and between ethnic groups. Comparison of African and Western students' perceptions of visual material led Ajayi-Dopemu (1982 ILLUSTRATION OF A POINT) to similar conclusions regarding the influence of cultural background. Mangan (1978, 1981 ILLUSTRATION OF A POINT) warns that unless such differences are identified beforehand, the use of visuals may be ineffective. He concludes that the ability to interpret images must be learned.

TYPES OF MEDIA

Still Pictures. In instructional media terms, still pictures are among the more traditional aids at the disposal of the educators. Wall charts and similar illustrations are probably the simplest to use, requiring no hardware, but they share certain characteristics with filmstrips, slides, and overhead projector transparencies. These simpler media still have their place, and Schramm (1977 ILLUSTRATION OF A POINT) believes that the expensive "big media" are often used when the simpler, less expensive "little media" would be equally effective.

Are still pictures effective in helping learning? Problems in interpreting pictorial images have already been mentioned, but evidence regarding the efficacy of such images is contradictory. One area which has been studied in some detail is the use of pictures, both in textbooks and separately, in assisting reading. Samuels (1970 ILLUSTRATION OF A POINT) argues that pictures divert the child's attention, but Denberg (1976–1977 ILLUSTRATION OF A POINT) believes that they can be a help or a hindrance depending on the stage of the learner and the type of picture. The latter point is supported by an examination by Higgins (1978 ILLUSTRATION OF A POINT) of the psychological processes involved in picture interpretation, where pictorial content was found to be influential.

Levin and Lesgood (1978 ILLUSTRATION OF A POINT), however, found that the use of pictures to supplement prose increased story recall by 40 percent, though further research was required into the nature of recall as regards central and peripheral information (Levin et al., 1979 ILLUSTRATION OF A POINT). This was also considered by Haring and Fry (1979 ILLUSTRATION OF A POINT) in their work with fourth- and sixth-grade pupils. They found that use of pictures facilitated both immediate and delayed recall, but only of the main ideas of the text. Bernard and Peterson (1983 ILLUSTRATION OF A POINT) also found that recall, and in some cases retention, can be improved when pictures are used. Verbal guidelines can help the learners draw inferences, but do not necessarily improve evaluation of these inferences (Higgins, 1979 ILLUSTRATION OF A POINT).

There appears to have been little investigation of some aspects of the visuals themselves. In the research by Modiano and others (1982 ILLUSTRATION OF A POINT) already discussed, no difference was observed between the effect of paintings and photographs. The importance of placing information within the frame has been studied (Herbener et al., 1979 ILLUSTRATION OF A POINT), but much of the work on the value of color in visuals deals with motion pictures. A color picture may be preferable on aesthetic grounds, but is it more effective in conveying information? According to Rudisill (1952 ILLUSTRATION OF A POINT), children preferred an uncolored illustration to a colored one if the former was more realistic. If the pictures were identical in all other respects, colored pictures were preferred to uncolored. However, Lertchalolarn (1981 ILLUSTRATION OF A POINT) found that while color was preferred to black and white, there was no difference between realistic and nonrealistic pictures in facilitating recognition memory. Comparing combinations of text plus abstract images with text plus realistic images and text alone, Musa (1981 ILLUSTRATION OF A POINT) found that the first category enhanced learning most, and this supports Haynie's conclusions (1978 ILLUSTRATION OF A POINT) regarding line drawings on slides.

Twyman (1972 ILLUSTRATION OF A POINT) investigated the effectiveness of color in illustrated textbooks. Color appeared to aid understanding, but various factors influenced color preference. Katzman and Nyenhuis (1972 ILLUSTRATION OF A POINT) demonstrated that while color increased recall of peripheral material, it made no difference to recall of central material. Language-disordered children need color, according to Straub (1978 ILLUSTRATION OF A POINT), but its effect is less easy to identify with others. The question remains open, and will also be discussed in the context of other media.

Level of detail is also of some importance (Gorman, 1973; Dwyer, 1978 ILLUSTRATION OF A POINT), but again, there appears to be room for further research.

The still picture "freezes" incidents in time, and generally presents all information at a time. Flannel graphs and magnetic boards allow for more flexibility in the gradual assembling of pictorial information in a structured manner, under the control of the teacher. Colborne and Sheppard (1966 ILLUSTRATION OF A POINT) emphasized the importance of sequencing and the necessity of guiding the pupil's observation.

The overhead projector (OHP), of course, permits precisely this sort of sequencing whether by the addition of information on overlays or by felt pen, or by uncovering parts of the transparency. McAlpin (1979 ILLUSTRATION OF A POINT) summarizes the advantages of the OHP as (a) enabling an overview; (b) permitting progressive buildup; (c) permitting analysis (using overlays); and (d) permitting feedback to pupils using the projector. Research by Seymour (1937 ILLUSTRATION OF A POINT) on legibility concluded that dark lettering on a light background was to be preferred to light on dark (e.g., chalk on a blackboard). The value of the white background in OHP work was further supported by Snowberg (1973 ILLUSTRATION OF A POINT), who studied the backgrounds which should be used on projected materials to meet the needs of the viewer. With brightness equalized, he showed that the best colors for legibility were white, yellow, green, red, and blue in decreasing order. Of course, legibility also depends on the lettering used. This topic was investigated by Adams et al., (1965 ILLUSTRATION OF A POINT), resulting in recommendations regarding sizes of lettering to be used.

As regards use of the technique, Chance (1960 BACKGROUND READING) demonstrated that the use of prepared transparencies in a lecture resulted in significant learning gains, an average savings of fifteen minutes per class period, and a general preference among students for this form of presentation. One of the major benefits is the possibility for building up diagrams using the overlay technique. Maddox and Loughran (1977 BACKGROUND READING) found that there was no statistically significant difference among students when material was presented either by prepared complete transparencies or by built-up transparencies. Students preferred the buildup method because, as they explained, they could follow the sequence and had time to copy the material. Cowan (1976 BACKGROUND READING) and Stoane (1980 BACKGROUND READING) combined OHP with audio with some success, and found that the advantages included building up or altering diagrams, without a blank screen (as compared, say, to single-screen tape-slide), the possibility of using overlays, and the opportunity with some OHP systems of incorporating motion.

Research on the effectiveness of slides and filmstrips is also scarce, although when used by McCracken (1965 ILLUSTRATION OF A POINT) to support the teaching of reading at primary school, they were found to improve student interest and stimulate discussion. Colborne (1971 ILLUSTRATION OF A POINT) found slides more effective than a model (Dale's "Cone of experience" would have suggested otherwise), though Weiner and Ganz (1982 ILLUSTRATION OF A POINT) reported little difference in the effect of two- and three-dimensional aids. Haliwell (1962 ILLUSTRATION OF A POINT) compared the value of filmstrip and educational visit, the latter being more successful.

Returning to the topic of color, Winn and Everett (1979 ILLUSTRATION OF A POINT) identify grade level and sex as factors affecting the value of color, but accept that generalization is difficult. Testing with abstract symbols on a colored background, Schecter (1981 ILLUSTRATION OF A POINT) concluded that learner preference was influenced by color, but recognition accuracy was not affected. Marcyes (1981 ILLUSTRATION OF A POINT), though, reports a significant increase in recognition memory scores for colored line illustrations.

Filmstrips from American sources are often captioned (with or without additional teacher's notes), although this practice is not popular in the United Kingdom, possibly because it restricts flexibility and may also cause word-picture confusion. Franzwa (1973 ILLUSTRATION OF A POINT) concluded that in a similar situation, words may attract more attention than pictures. Yet when Bernard and Perri (1982 ILLUSTRATION OF A POINT) added redundant verbal labels to the slides of a two-screen tape-slide presentation, it was more effective. The importance of verbal accompaniment and general method of presentation is brought out in a study made by Hartley and Fuller (1971 ILLUSTRATION OF A POINT) in which they compared blackboards and slides and found that teaching points in a lecture supported by slides were less well remembered than identical points made on a blackboard. A problem in such teaching methods was in fact identified by the students themselves in this investigation, when they pointed out that they needed longer pauses between the slides to assimilate the material. That presentation mode is an important consideration is also demonstrated by Allen (1975 ILLUSTRATION OF A POINT) in his evaluation of students' comparative attitudes to a blackboard presentation and a two-channel slide presentation. Using the latter technique, the lecturer can slowly build up the argument on one screen and then transfer the final visual form to the second screen for holding while the next argument is built up again on the screen. Jonassen (1979 ILLUSTRATION OF A POINT) experimented with two-, three-, and four-screen presentations, previous information being retained on screen, while new information was added. A "significant improvement" in learning was claimed for the multiscreen presentations over single-screen. Similarly, Borman (1981 ILLUSTRATION OF A POINT) found two-, three-, and four-screen presentations effective immediately and in the long term, though single-screen also appeared to be successful on long-term testing.

Still or Moving Pictures. In their review of research Chu and Schramm (1967 BACKGROUND READING) drew some conclusions about the relative effectiveness of still and motion pictures and summarized their findings by stating that there was no consistent evidence that motion pictures enhanced learning more than still pictures did. They also suggested that the beneficial effects of visuals on learning depend ultimately on the nature of the task, familiarity with the concepts being taught, and the test format being used.

Dwyer (1978 ILLUSTRATION OF A POINT) identified numerous studies which showed no significant difference between learning from films or from filmstrips or slides, and some studies which showed the superiority of filmstrips over films. He emphasized the need for great caution when attempting to evaluate research literature as many studies do not give adequate consideration to the inherent capabilities and limitations of the media under consideration. Often, he suggests, it is inappropriate to compare the media; and even those studies where the illustrations displayed through the various media were equivalent (i.e., where slides are made from the frames of the film), they do not convey the same content.

Wells (1970 ILLUSTRATION OF A POINT) compared still photographs, slides, and motion pictures; found no significant differences in the learning gains among botany students taught by the various media; and concluded that the choice of a single medium for presentation of concepts must be based upon its effectiveness in learning, its availability, portability, expense, and study time required. In a further study by Wells et al., (1973 ILLUSTRATION OF A POINT), it was demonstrated that much will depend on the nature of the topic being taught. Media differ in their ability to convey the concepts of time, space, and motion; as one would expect, this study showed that motion pictures are more effective for presenting concepts involving motion, but slides and sequential photographs appear to be more effective than film in presenting concepts involving space. Peri (1978 ILLUSTRATION OF A POINT) found film superior to slides (and a nonmedia control group) regardless of subject, content, cognitive style, or achievement level. In the first year microbiology course described by Noble et al., (1979 ILLUSTRATION OF A POINT), no difference was noted in the efficiency of cine-loop and slide-tape (interestingly, nonnative speakers of English were found to be at a disadvantage even if language was not a component of the item being used). Hines (1981 ILLUSTRATION OF A POINT) measured electroencephalograph reaction to video and tape-slide, and observed no significant difference. However, Jeon and Branson (1981 ILLUSTRATION OF A POINT) compared film, slides with sound, and storyboard. Film learners were seen to perform better in certain motor skills in less time.

In many such comparative media studies, the important factor is found to be not only the type of pictorial presentation used, but also the verbal accompaniment. Thus Laner (1956 ILLUSTRATION OF A POINT) observed that if one is attempting to replace film by pictorial media, the limitations of the visual display cannot be overcome by more realistic presentations; what ultimately controls the degree of understanding and the learning outcomes is the verbal exposition accompanying the pictures.

These findings are consistent with those of Dwyer (1978 ILLUSTRATION OF A POINT), who concludes from his studies of the three media—television, slides, and programmed booklets, and varying types of pictorial detail—that the effectiveness of these forms of visualized instruction depends on a complex interaction of treatment, presentation mode, and educational objectives.

Films and Video. Although films and video are being considered together, there are, of course, many differences between them: costs, techniques, and viewing conditions, for example. There is also some divergence of opinion as to whether or not they are educationally different. Chu and Schramm (1967 BACKGROUND READING), reviewing the literature, found that in many cases films and television were found to be similar. This was supported by Reid and MacLennan (1967 ILLUSTRATION OF A POINT). Mundy (1962 ILLUSTRATION OF A POINT) believed that factors such as commentary and presentation were more important than the medium. Comparing the same item viewed on film and video, Robinson (1981 ILLUSTRATION OF A POINT) found that film viewers understood more and were affected more than video viewers.

Instructional film has been a major teaching and learning aid for a considerable time. Hoban and Van Ormer (1950 HISTORICAL) surveyed 30 years research and derived certain conclusions regarding variable factors in film production: (a) repetition is important; (b) commentary sometimes teaches more than the visuals, but the amount of sound track information needs to be carefully assessed; (c) special effects and optical effects have no teaching value; (d) color has no demonstrable effect on learning; and (e) dramatic sequences also add little. May and Lumsdaine (1958 HISTORICAL) supported many of these conclusions. While Travers (1967 HISTORICAL) examined studies of other media as well as films in the period after 1950, his research does complement Hoban and Van Ormer's work. Again, it was noted that color does not necessarily improve learning and that special effects have little value. One of Traver's conclusions was that single-channel communication (i.e., a silent film with captions) was to be preferred to multichannel. This contrasted with the view of Hartman (1961 HISTORICAL) that visuals could be ambiguous and verbal direction was often necessary, though not always continuously. Conway (1968 ILLUSTRATION OF A POINT) also questioned Travers's assumptions. The work on instructional films at Pennsylvania State College was summarized by Carpenter (1971 HISTORICAL), who noted that the effectiveness of a film depended not only on the film's characteristics but also on its appropriateness to the subject, on the learners, and on the conditions of learning. Other surveys of research and film in teaching and learning are by Berry and Unwin (1975 BACKGROUND READING) and Marchant (1977 BACKGROUND READING), with the latter noting the inconclusiveness of much of the research. He did suggest that repetition and participation were two important factors; both were similarly identified by Hoban and Van Ormer in 1950.

Johnson and Roberson (1979 ILLUSTRATION OF A POINT) tested groups from first grade to adult, and observed no apparent gain in learning due to use of color in films, although color remains an aesthetic factor. Perhaps, of course, widespread exposure to color cinema films and television is one reason for this. Chute (1980 ILLUSTRATION OF A POINT) did find that color helped learning of incidental information, but its effect on task-relevant learning depended on ability level. Further study of the factors influencing learning from a screen is suggested by Metallinos (1979 BACKGROUND READING). Examinations of kinetic structuring by Simmons (1980 ILLUSTRATION OF A POINT) and graphical representations by Napoli (1982 ILLUSTRATION OF A POINT) are examples of this type of research.

One useful presentation technique identified by May and Lumsdaine (1958 HISTORICAL) was the use of narration instead of dialogue. Butler's comparison (1980 ILLUSTRATION OF A POINT) of films using three presentation formats—lecture/demonstration, narrated account, and stills—showed that the narrated version promoted significant gains in cognitive learning. Research by Nugent et al., (1980 ILLUSTRATION OF A POINT), while indicating that production techniques are influential, suggests that it is difficult to provide definitive guidelines. The importance of the teacher's introduction to a film has been largely ignored, but Arwady (1980 ILLUSTRATION OF A POINT) stresses that this must be structured, rather than casual or improvised.

Another factor which seems to affect learning is the environment in which the material is viewed. Wilkinson (1976 ILLUSTRATION OF A POINT) investigated how image size, viewing angle, and contrast affect the performance of students on a visual discrimination task. He reveals that there is a strong interaction between learning outcomes and these variables. Hegarty (1978 BACKGROUND READING) used feature films to examine some determinants of perception. Rich et al., (1966 ILLUSTRATION OF A POINT) compared the effects of a large-screen television presentation with those of a conventional television presentation, and found that there was no significant difference in learning gains between the control and experimental groups. Furthermore, they analyzed some of the other factors which may have been interacting in this situation, such as the viewing angle and distance from the screen, and found that these also had no effect on student outcomes. These results are supported by Dwyer (1978 ILLUSTRATION OF A POINT), who noted that merely increasing the size of the image by projecting onto a larger screen does not improve the effectiveness of the presentation.

Rear-projection screens have two practical advantages in the removal of the noisy and obtrusive projector, and the higher screen brightness which can often be obtained. A British study by Teather (1974 ILLUSTRATION OF A POINT) compared front, rear, and CCTV techniques using material originally designed for CCTV presentations. Results showed that the most effective technique in terms of learning gains was rear projection, but as the researcher admits, an important factor which may have affected these results could be the novelty value of this method. Favorable results from the use of rear projection were also demonstrated by Marchant (1975 ILLUSTRATION OF A POINT), and there would seem to be some justification in assuming that the amount which students learn from film does vary with the projection method used. The consumer's point of view is highlighted by McVey (1979 ILLUSTRATION OF A POINT); the learning environment is important to them, and they are capable of offering an evaluation of it. Unwin's bibliography (1979 BACKGROUND READING) covers the learning environment as well as production variables.

Some recent research suggests that there is still no consensus on the value of film and television. Bird's (1978 ILLUSTRATION OF A POINT) comparison of film with the traditional lecture found film to be no more or less effective than lecture. Hirsh (1979 ILLUSTRATION OF A POINT) argues that the strengths of film can also be its weaknesses, if it is used indiscriminately or as a substitute for teaching. Westervelt and McKinney (1980 ILLUSTRATION OF A POINT) used film in an attempt to influence children's attitudes: the film was insufficient to answer all questions, and the effect was not permanent. At university level, Hult (1980 ILLUSTRATION OF A POINT) noted no improvement in learning when film was used, but in certain circumstances student attitudes were more favorable.

The film loop seems to have declined in popularity, though the evidence of Kenshole (1967 ILLUSTRATION OF A POINT), Pearson and Jepson (1969 ILLUSTRATION OF A POINT), and Smith (1972 ILLUSTRATION OF A POINT) indicated that the loop was effective in terms of educational outcomes, student reactions, and time saving. Much of this research relates to the use of the film loop in teaching manipulative skills, and perusal of software catalogs indicates that commercial productions concentrate on topics in science, sport, and technical education. The short, repetitive format was also useful for "trigger films." These appear to have been paid little attention, but Boud and Pearson (1979 ILLUSTRATION OF A POINT) highlight their value in providing introductory material, in raising general issues, and in stimulating personal responses to a given subject.

Films and video will continue to be used as teaching and learning materials. The increasing attention given to media studies as a school subject may result in learners becoming more film- and video-literate, which may have implications for the educational use of motion pictures. However, Harris and Kirkhope (1979 ILLUSTRATION OF A POINT) noted that students were often unclear as to the relationship of video self-instruction to the rest of their course.

Recorded Sound. The use of sound in teaching and learning can involve commercially produced tapes, in-house recordings, or "off-air" radio programs (live or recorded). Cowan (1982 BACKGROUND READING) stresses the benefits of audiotape as regards the emphasis, inflection, and pace of the human voice, plus cost-effectiveness and storage. Print scores, though, because it can be skimmed and requires no equipment. There can be no direct comparison, Cowan concludes, and both media have advantages and disadvantages. It is worth noting that comparison of audio, a relatively simple method, to other media is not necessarily to the detriment of the former. Daniels (1959 ILLUSTRATION OF A POINT) showed that pupils only listening to the sound track of a physics lesson did not seem to learn less than those watching the original. Presumably the visuals in the case added little to the audio. Schupham (1970 ILLUSTRATION OF A POINT) noted that Danish research comparing print, radio, and television recorded little difference between the three. A more positive outcome was found by Khan (1980 ILLUSTRATION OF A POINT), who examined the use of audio and conventional teaching methods in biology, with students appearing to gain more from the audio-tutorial approach.

In the school situation, Kroll (1974 ILLUSTRATION OF A POINT) studied intermediate grade children and found that higher-ability children did equally well by listening or reading, but lower-ability children did not benefit from audio instruction. For older children, Bligh (1975 ILLUSTRATION OF A POINT) showed that a mixture of lectures, tape, and reading was more effective than any one method used alone.

There are, of course, certain circumstances in which audiotapes have distinct advantages. Distance education is one such area, and McDonald and Knights (1979 ILLUSTRATION OF A POINT) found that audio produced benefits in stimulating work and maintaining student morale, even if print materials were preferred as sources of information. The tapes in this example were either special productions for external use or edited versions of internal student lectures. Another important area is special education. Myers (1978 ILLUSTRATION OF A POINT) used compressed-speech recordings with blind students, and Stone (1983 ILLUSTRATION OF A POINT) reported better results with hearing-impaired pupils when audio was added to visual material.

The audio material must not, however, be taken in isolation. Sheridan (1978 ILLUSTRATION OF A POINT) describes a course for HNC/HND students based on cassettes. There were benefits, but the students could not be expected to cope with a great deal of self-study material and needed guidance. Worksheets served as an aid to immediate recall, according to Brown (1979 ILLUSTRATION OF A POINT), but issue of a set of behavioral objectives was more effective. Use of both did not seem more effective than normal written notes, but resulted in longer recall. Smith (1979 ILLUSTRATION OF A POINT) suggests that audio lessons are best reviewed by either study guides or a summary tape.

Audio recordings, naturally, play a major part in language learning (Willgoss, 1976 BACKGROUND READING). Language laboratories have been widely used, but research on their efficiency is less than conclusive. Lorge (1963 ILLUSTRATION OF A POINT) showed that students using a language laboratory were superior to nonlaboratory groups in speech fluency, intonation, and comprehension; and Freedman (1969 ILLUSTRATION OF A POINT) also noted superiority in teaching a specific grammatical task. On the other hand, studies by Green (1972, 1974 ILLUSTRATION OF A POINT) led him to conclude that teachers and administrators were not justified in assuming that language laboratories were beneficial. Riley (1974 ILLUSTRATION OF A POINT) observed that in a laboratory the normally social activity of language communication was carried out in "solitary confinement." With a change in emphasis from a structural to a functional approach in language teaching, the future place of the language laboratory is unclear (Froehlich, 1982; Salvi, 1982 BACKGROUND READING).

The use of broadcast material is too large a topic to deal with in this entry, but research by Roebuck and McCormick (1973 BACKGROUND READING) on pre-broadcast preparation is worth noting. Hayter (1974 BACKGROUND READING) deals with radio, radio-vision, and television broadcasts, including numerous case studies.

Tape-Slide. The use of tape-slide and tape-filmstrips is common in teaching and learning. In general, both are cheaper than film, have a wide range of commercially produced items available, and offer the option of in-house production. Harding et al. (1981 ILLUSTRATION OF A POINT) compared tape-slide with traditional lectures (as well as a mixture of both) and found student performance to be comparable for both. Costs were similar in the long term, though tape-slide was, understandably, more expensive in the short term. According to Elton et al. (1971 ILLUSTRATION OF A POINT) and Hills (1974 ILLUSTRATION OF A POINT), however, tape-slide is better for self-instruction than as a replacement for lectures. In a comparison with print, Singarella (1981 ILLUSTRATION OF A POINT) found no difference in effectiveness on immediate or delayed testing, and concluded, therefore, that print was more efficient. Haukoos (1982 ILLUSTRATION OF A POINT) looked at the use of tape-slide in biology teaching in four content areas. He reported better grades in one area, better overall grades, and positive student reactions. Certainly, the medium has cost advantages, and though McDonald (1972 ILLUSTRATION OF A POINT) found no significant difference in information gain between tape-slide and video, the former was more cost-effective.

There appears to be a lack of research evidence as to the design and preparation of tape-slide materials. Harden et al. (1968 ILLUSTRATION OF A POINT) recommended a maximum acceptable length of program of 45 minutes; Jones (1976 ILLUSTRATION OF A POINT), the introduction of self-test items. Projection method, automatic or manual, does not seem to matter (Nohavec, 1977 ILLUSTRATION OF A POINT). The introduction into a two-screen presentation of redundant information taken from the sound track was found by Bernard and Perri (1982 ILLUSTRATION OF A POINT) to be more effective than either single-screen tape-slide or two-screen with redundant informaton printed in a booklet. In general, there appears to be little interest in multiscreen presentations for education, although Perrin (1979 ILLUSTRATION OF A POINT) argued that "information density is increased and certain kinds of information are more efficiently learned." Though Trohanis (1975 ILLUSTRATION OF A POINT) observed some initial gains from such a presentation, these gains were not repeated on retesting. Whether or not there are educational advantages in these methods, cost and complexity of operation are likely to be the deciding factors. Multiscreen continues to be used in advertising and promotion, and such presentations continue to grow in size and sophistication.

Other Mixed Media. As an alternative to tape-slide, tape overhead projector transparency has already been mentioned (Cowan, 1976; Stoane, 1980 BACKGROUND READING). Butler (1979 BACKGROUND READING) found that a "visual-tutorial" system was "effective and flexible" in teaching audiovisual media theory and practice. Audiotape plus booklet has been used to replace conventional class instruction (Clarke, 1975 ILLUSTRATION OF A POINT). A combination of tape and colored print is described by Grant (1978 BACKGROUND READING) as a relatively cheap and easy way of introducing laboratory experiments to students. It is perhaps easy to overlook these simpler media when confronted by sophisticated technology. The U.S. journal *Educational Technology* recognized this by devoting an entire issue to "new uses for older media" (1982 BACKGROUND READING).

New Technology. It would be unwise to commit to print, in an entry such as this, any speculation about the future trends of information technology and their relevance to education. It is sufficient, therefore, to note that interest is already being shown in the newest of the "new" media. Dede (1981 BACKGROUND READING), Ramsay (1981 BACKGROUND READING), and Ingle et al. (1983 BACKGROUND READING) have examined the potential of modern developments, as has Rubin (1982 BACKGROUND READING), who calls for research specifically aimed at identifying their educational value. A Delphi study of 56 experts on developments for the remainder of this century (Dayton, 1981 BACKGROUND READING) makes particularly interesting reading.

Computers are one major area of development, but at least two others can be identified, on the basis of their recurrence in the literature. Videotex has attracted some attention (Jackson, 1979; Raggett and Smith, 1979; Anderson, 1980; Daly, 1981; Woolfe, 1981; Newell, 1979 BACKGROUND READING). The videodisc is a potentially important medium for information storage (Horden, 1981; Barrett, 1982 BACKGROUND READING). Interactive video (Laurillard, 1982 BACKGROUND READING) is already available with some commercial discs, and at least one such system also exists using U-matic cassettes. Copeland (1983 BACKGROUND READING) has reported on the CAVIS system at West Sussex Institute of Higher Education, and Wright (1983 BACKGROUND READING) sees possibilities for distance education.

COST-EFFECTIVENESS

In the best of all possible worlds, costs would not matter and educational effectiveness would be the only criterion. However, educators work in a real world governed by real financial constraints, and those who hold the purse strings will examine both costs and effectiveness

(Melmed, 1978 BACKGROUND READING). There is no sign of the review of resources called for by Fielden (1978 BACKGROUND READING), and the best the teacher can hope for is a set of guidelines to assist in decision making (Torrence, 1979; Perry and Perry, 1981 BACKGROUND READING) or case studies of particular experiments with media (Harris and Kirkhope, 1978; Spencer, 1981 BACKGROUND READING).

SELECTION AND USE

To seek guidance in the literature on selection of appropriate media is to risk confusion and indecision. Apart from the question of whether or not research findings are generalizable, the conclusions themselves are often contradictory. For example, Machula (1979 ILLUSTRATION OF A POINT) noted less learning with audio as opposed to video or print, but Kruse (1981 ILLUSTRATION OF A POINT) found no significant difference between the media. Nor did Wager's comparison (1980 ILLUSTRATION OF A POINT) of text or film or live demonstration identify any significant difference. Cohen et al. (1981 ILLUSTRATION OF A POINT) reported that visual-based instruction had no effect on students, course completion, attitudes, or achievement. Brainard (1978 ILLUSTRATION OF A POINT) studied various combinations of print, picture, and sound, concluding that various factors, not only physical form, influenced learning. Even if the use of media produces greater involvement (Franklin and Mabry, 1980 ILLUSTRATION OF A POINT), there seems to be no evidence that user preference influences learning attitudes (Becker, 1963; Miller, 1969; Travers and Alvarado, 1970; Dwyer, 1978 ILLUSTRATION OF A POINT), at least in the short term, although there may be effects in the long term (Palmer, 1975 ILLUSTRATION OF A POINT). Perhaps general guidance such as that offered by Romiszowski (1974 BACKGROUND READING) and Rowntree (1982 BACKGROUND READING) is more valuable than case studies.

Factors governing the successful use of audiovisual media in a teaching or learning situation are complex. They include the learner's age, ability, and knowledge; the nature of the educational message; the physical characteristics of the medium and the environment and the environment in which the medium is used; the participation of the teacher; the policy of the educational establishment and the financial background. There is always a danger that physical and technical factors will outweigh educational considerations; but this is a tendency that should be resisted, because, as Clarke and Angert (1981 ILLUSTRATION OF A POINT) say:

while research to date has taught us woefully little about what to do in terms of resource selection, it has at least taught us what we should not falsely expect physical technology (hardware) to accomplish. Physical technology can neither replace sound intellectual technology nor reduce the necessity for its incorporation into materials and methodologies.

George Geddes

REFERENCES

Background Reading

Anderson, J. (1980) "Exploring Teletext as a Resource." *PLET* 17 (1): 27–35.

Ausburn, L. and Ausburn, F. (1978) "Visual Literacy, Background, Theory and Practice." *PLET* 15 (4): 291–297.

Barrett, R. (1982) *Developments in Optical Disc Technology and Implications for Information Storage and Retrieval*, BL R & D report 5623. London: British Library.

Bennington, M. (1982) "Lecturers' Attitudes to Independent Learning Packages in Higher Education." *PLET* 19 (2): 148–157.

Berry, C. and Unwin, D. (1975) "PLET Monitoring." *PLET* 12 (1): 54–70.

Butler, L. (1979) "Visual Tutorial System for Teaching Media Utilisation." *BJET* 10 (2): 119–128.

Chance, C. W. (1960) *Experimentation in the Adaptation of the Overhead Projector Utilizing 200 Transparencies and 800 Overlays in Teaching Engineering Descriptive Geometry Curricula*. Washington, D.C.: University of Washington.

Chu, G. and Schramm, W. (1967) *Learning for Television: What the Research Says*. Stanford, Calif.: Institute for Communications Research, Stanford University.

Clayback, J. et al. (1980) "Read, Translate, Compare and Evaluate: Visual Language Skills." *Language Arts* 57 (6): 628–634.

Copeland, P. (1983) "An Interactive Video System for Education." In *Aspects of Educational Technology*, 16, ed. A. Trott et al. London: Kogan Page.

Cowan, J. (1976) "Can Tape-Overhead Compete with Tape-Slide?" *Visual Education* (May): 13–14.

———. (1982) "Why Do We Not Just Use Print Materials?" *Educational Technology* 27 (10): 27–28.

Daly, D. W. (1981) "Viewdata in Education." *Educational Media International* 2: 19–22.

Dayton, D. K. (1981) "Future Trends in the Production of Instructional Materials, 1981–2001." *Educational Communications and Technology Journal* 29 (4): 231–249.

Debes, J. L. (1978) "Cultural Symbolism, Visual Literacy and Intellectual Equality." *Educational Media International* 2: 27–31.

Dede, C. (1981) "Educational, Social and Ethical Implications of Technological Innovation." *PLET* 18 (4): 204–213.

Dwyer, F. M. (1979) "The Communicative Potential of Visual Literacy: Research and Implications." *Educational Media International* 2: 19–25.

Educational Technology. (1982) 22 (5). Special issue on mixed media.

Fielden, J. (1978) "The Cost of Innovation and Change in Education." *PLET* 15 (1): 16–25.

Froelich, J. (1982) "The Language Lab: Renaissance or Extinction?" *Die Unterrichtspraxis* 15 (2): 164–169.

Grant, H. M. (1978) "Tape/Pictures in the Laboratory." *BJET* 9 (3): 176–179.

Harris, N.D.C. and Kirkhope, S. (1978) "Costs of Videocartridges as Self Instructional Materials in the Library." *BJET* 9 (2): 94–103.

Hayter, C. G. (1974) *Using Broadcasts in Schools: A Study and Evaluation*. London: BBC/ITV.

Hegarty, S. F. (1978) "Film Perception under Ordinary Viewing Conditions." *BJET* 9 (1): 43–54.

Hitchens, H. (1981) "Discussion of Visual Literacy." *Educational Media International* 1: 6–9.

Horden, A. (1981) *Videoforms: Their Application to Information Storage and Retrieval*. 2d ed. Hertford: National Reprographic Centre for Documentation.

Ingle, H. T. et al. (1983) "Preliminary Report on the New Information Technologies in Education: An International Mail Questionnaire Survey Study." *Educational Media International* 1: 3–7.

Jackson, R. (1979) "Television Text: First Experiences with a New Medium." *BJET* 10 (3): 175–185.

Laurillard, D. M. (1982) "The Potential of Interactive Video." *Journal of Educational Television* 8 (3): 173–180.

Lefranc, R. (1978) "Lessons of Experience in the Use of Media: Problems Created by the Development of the Use of Media in Industrialised Countries." *Educational Media International* 4: 6–16.

Levie, W. H. (1978) "A Prospectus for Instructional Research on Visual Literacy." *Educational Communication and Technology Journal* 26 (1): 25–36.

Maddox, H. and Loughran, R. L. (1977) "Illustrating the Lecture: Prepared Diagrams vs. Built-up Diagrams." *Audiovisual Communication Review* 25: 87–90.

Marchant, H. (1977) "Increasing the Effectiveness of Educational Films: A Selected Review of Research." *BJET* 8 (2): 89–96.

Megarry, J. et al., eds. (1983) *World Yearbook of Education, 1982*. London: Kogan Page.

Melmed, A. (1978) "Economic Analysis of Educational Media." *Educational Media International* 4: 4–6.

Metallinos, N. (1979) "Composition of the TV Picture: Some Hypotheses to Test the Forces Operating within the Television Screen." *Educational Communications and Technology Journal* 27 (3): 205–214.

Moore, D. M. and Hunt, T. C. (1980) "The Nature of Resistance to the Use of Instructional Media." *BJET* 11 (2): 141–148.

Newell, A. F. (1979) "Teletext and Viewdata and Their Relevance to Communication Disorders." *Child: Care, Health and Development* 5 (1): 49–55.

Ogden, D. H. (1982) "Response to Pictures as a Function of Cognitive Style, Sex and Picture Complexity." Ph.D. diss., Indiana University.

Perry, N. N. and Perry, T. (1981) "Media Selection of the Fittest." *Educational Media International* 21 (4): 2307.

Peterman, T. W. (1982) "A Compendium of Selected Research on the Application of Educational Media in the Classroom." Ph.D. diss., Michigan State University.

Raggett, M. and Smith, R. (1979) "Teletext in Education: An Evaluation of Limited Field Trials." *Education in Science* 84: 14–16.

Ramsay, R. D. (1981) "Communications Technology: Its Potential." *PLET* 18 (4): 254–261.

Roebuck, M. and McCormick, J. (1973) "Radio Broadcasts and Resources: (a) Using Programmed Adjuncts." *PLET* 10 (2): 77–81.

Romiszowski, A. J. (1974) *The Selection and Use of Instructional Media*. London: Kogan Page.

Rowntree, D. (1982) *Educational Technology in Curriculum Development*. London: Harper and Row, 1982.

Rubin, A. M. (1982) "The New Media: Potential Uses and Impact of the New Technologies for Children's Learning." *Educational Technology* 22 (12): 5–9.

Salvi, R. (1982) "The Language Laboratory and the Functional Approach: from Pattern Practice to Communication." *Rassegna Italiani di linguistica applicata* 14 (1): 159–169.

Spencer, K. A. (1981) "An Evaluation of the Cost-Effectiveness of Film and Tape-Slide Instructional Presentation for the Mentally Handicapped." *PLET* 18 (1): 23–29.

Stoane, J. A. (1980) "A Technique for OHP/Tape Lesson Packages." In *Aspects of Educational Technology*, 14, ed. R. Winterburn and L. Evans. London: Kogan Page.

Teather, D.C.B. (1978) "Audiovisual Media and Educational Technology in the Traditional University: The Working Compromise or the Grand Design?" *Higher Education* 7 (4): 431–442.

Torrence, D. (1979) "The True Cost of Instructional Media." *Educational Technology* 19 (5): 30–31.

Unwin, D. (1979) "Production and Audience Variables in Film and Television: A Second Selected Bibliography." *PLET* 16 (3): 232–239.

Willgoss, B. C. (1976) "Audiovisual Aids in Foreign Language Learning: The Librarian's Role." *Audiovisual Librarian* 3 (2): 57–64.

Woolfe, R. (1981) "Videotext and Teletext: Similarities, Differences and Prospects." *PLET* 18 (4): 245–253.

Wright, D. (1983) "Interactive Video in Distance Learning." In *Aspects of Educational Technology*, 16, ed. A. Trott et al. London: Kogan Page.

Historical

Allen, W. H. (1971) "Instructional Media Research: Past, Present and Future." *Audiovisual Communications Review* 19: 5–18.

Broadbent, D. C. (1958) *Perception and Communication*. London: Pergamon.

Cambre, M. A. (1981) "Historical Overview of Formative Evaluation of Instructional Media Products." *Educational Communications and Technology Journal*, 29 (1): 3–25.

Campeau, P. L. (1972) *Selective Review of Results of Research on the Use of Audiovisual Media to Teach Adults*. Strasbourg: Council of Europe.

Carpenter, C. R. (1971) "Instructional Film Research: A Brief Review." *BJET* 11 (3): 229–246.

Coppen, H. (1972) *A Survey of British Research in Audio Visual Aids*. London: NCAVAE.

Dale, E. (1946) *Audiovisual Methods in Teaching*. New York: Dryden Press.

Decaigny, T. (1979) "The Long Journey of Audiovisual. . . ." *Educational Media International* 3: 13–16.

Hartman, F. (1961) "Single and Multiple Channel Communication: A Review of Research and a Proposed Model." *Audiovisual Communication Review* 8: 235–262.

Hitchens, H. (1979) "The Evolution of Audiovisual Education in the USA since 1945." *Educational Media International* 3: 6–12.

Hoban, C. F. and Van Ormer, E. B. (1950) *Instructional Film Research, 1918–1950*. Port Washington, N.Y.: U.S. Naval Special Devices Center.

May, M. A. and Lumsdaine, A. A. (1958) *Learning from Films*. New Haven: Yale University Press.

Rakow, J. (1980) "The Audiovisual Myth in America: Filling the Cracks of Educational Technology." *Journal of Education* 162 (4): 34–54.

Razik, R. A. and Romroth, D. M. (1974) *Bibliography of Research on Instructional Media*. Englewood Cliffs, N.J.: Educational Technology Publications.

Rodwell, S. (1974, 1975, 1976, 1977) Supplements 1, 2, 3, 4 to *A Survey of British Research in Audio Visual Aids*. London: NCAVAE.

Saettler, P. (1968) *A History of Instructional Technology*. New York: McGraw-Hill.

Travers, R. M. (1964) *Research and Theory Related to Audiovisual Information Transmission*. Washington, D.C.: U.S. Department of Health, Education and Welfare.

———. (1967) *Research and Theory Related to Audiovisual Information Transmission*. Kalamazoo: Western Michigan University.

Tucker, R. (1979) "Audio Visual Aids in Britain, 1945–80." *Educational Media International* 3: 17–20.

Illustration of a Point

Adams, S. et al. (1965) "Readable Letter Size and Visibility for OHP Transparencies." *Audiovisual Communication Review* 13: 412–417.

Ahmad, M. (1978) "The Effect of Language on the Identification of Pictorial Stimuli." *PLET* 15 (1): 35–41.

Ajayi-Dopemu, Y. (1982) "Visual Aids and the Enhancement of Communication in Africa." *Journal of Educational Television* 8 (3): 203–209.

Allen, P. S. (1975) "A Two Channel Slide Method for Lecture Presentation." *Physics Education* 10 (1): 52–54.

Arwady, J. W. (1980) "The Oral Introduction to the Instructional Film: A Closer Look." *Educational Media International* 20 (3): 18–22.

Becker, S. L. (1963) *The Relationship of Interest and Attention to Retention and Attitude Change*. Iowa City: Iowa University.

Bernard, R. and Perri, D. (1982) "Cross Channel Redundancy: A Strategy to Improve Tape-Slide Design." *PLET* 19 (2): 119–124.

Bernard, R. and Peterson, C. (1983) "Pictures as Retentional Aids to Prose Learning: An Examination of Reiterative Strategies and Contextual Image." In *Aspects of Educational Technology,* 16, ed. A. Trott et al. London: Kogan Page.

Bird, C. M. (1978) "A Comparison of the Effectiveness of Teaching: (1) in the Traditional Classroom Situation, and (2) by Cine Film." In *Aspects of Educational Technology*, 12, ed. D. Brook and R. Race. London: Kogan Page.

Bligh, D. A. (1975) "Are Varied Teaching Methods More Effective?" Ph.D. diss., University of London.

Borman, L. (1981) "A Comparative Study of Multi-Media and Multi-Image." Ph.D. diss., University of Minnesota.

Boud, D. and Pearson, M. (1979) "The Trigger Film: A Stimulus for Affective Learning." *PLET* (1): 52–56.

Brainard, E. K. (1978) "A Study of the Effectiveness of Seven Alternative Media Presentations on the Teaching of Selected Research Skills to Sixth Graders." Ed.D. diss., Rutgers University.

Brown, J. A. (1979) "The Effect of the Use of Behavioral Objectives and Worksheets on Immediate and Delayed Recall in an Audio-cassette Tape Presentation." Ed.D. diss., East Texas State University.

Butchart, I. C. (1977) "Education in the Indexing, Cataloguing and Classification of Non-Book Materials." *Audiovisual Librarian* 3 (4): 129–130.

Butler, R. B. (1980) "A Comparative Analysis of Three Instructional Television Presentation Formats." Ed.D. diss., East Texas State University.

Chute, A. G. (1980) "Effect of Colour and Monochrome Versions of a Film on Incidental and Task-Relevant Learning." *Educational Communications and Technology Journal* 28 (1): 10–18.

Clark, F. E. and Angert, J. F. (1981) "Teacher Commitment to Instructional Design: The Problem of Media Selection and Use." *Educational Technology* 21 (5): 9–15.

Clarke, R. M. (1975) "Replacement of Class Instruction in Histology by Audio-tape and Booklet Self-instruction Sessions." *British Journal of Medical Education"* 9: 34–37.

Cohen, P. A., et al. (1981) "A Meta-analysis of Outcome Studies of Visual-Based Instruction." *Educational Communications and Technology Journal* 29 (1): 26–36.

Colborne, H. V. (1971) *Two Experiments on Methods of Training Children in Road Safety*. Basingstoke, U.K.: Road Research Laboratory.

Colborne, H. V. and Sheppard, D. (1966) "Testing a Poster for Infants." *Safety Education* (Summer): 8–11.

Conway, J. K. (1968) "Differential Memory for Referentially Equivalent Single and Multiple Sign Vehicle Presentations." Ph.D. diss., Indiana University.

Daniels, J. C. (1959) "An Experiment in Television for Schools." *University of Nottingham Institute of Education Bulletin* 31 (January): 1–4.

Denberg, S. O. (1976–1977) "The Interaction of Picture and Print in Reading Instruction." *Reading Research Quarterly* 12: 176–189.

Dwyer, F. M. (1978) *A Guide for Improving Visualized Instruction*. Pennsylvania: State College.

Elton, L.R.B., et al. (1971) "Teaching and Learning Systems in a University Physics Course." *Physics Education* 6 (2): 95–100.

Enright, B. J. (1970) "Non-book/Media Materials and the Library: A Note." *Library Association Record* 72 (12): 369.

Franklin, S. T. and Mabry, N. K. (1980) "Affective Response with Multi-media Teaching of Poetry." *Reading Improvement* 17 (4): 311–312.

Franzwa, D. (1973) "Influence of Meaningfulness, Picture Detail and Presentation Mode on Visual Retention." *Audiovisual Communication Review* 21: 209–224.

Freedman, E. S. (1969) "An Investigation into the Efficacy of the Language Laboratory in Foreign Language Teaching." *AV Language Journal* 7: 75–95.

Gorman, D. A. (1973) "Effects of Varying Pictorial Detail and Presentation Strategy on Concept Formation." *Audiovisual Communication Review* 14: 37–69.

Green, P. S. (1972) "A Study of the Effectiveness of the Language Laboratory in School; Conducted at Archbishop Holgate's Grammar School, York." *International Review of Applied Linguistics in Language Teaching* (August): 283–292.

———. (1974) "A Research into the Effectiveness of Language Laboratories in Schools." In *Commission Interuniversitaire Suisse de Linguistique appliqué: rôle efficacité du laboratoire de langues dans l'enseignement secondaire et universitaire*. Neuchatel: University of Neuchatel.

Haliwell, S. (1962) "An Investigation into the Value of Filmstrip and Educational Visit as Methods of Instruction to Secondary Modern Pupils of 14–15 Years." M.Ed. thesis, University of Manchester.

Harden, R. et al. (1968) "An Audio Visual Technique for Medical Teaching." *Medical and Biological Illustration* 18: 29–31.

Harding, C. M., et al. (1981) "A Comparison of Two Teaching Methods in Mathematical Statistics." *Studies in Higher Education* 6 (2): 139–146.

Haring, M. J. and Fry, M. A. (1979) "Effect of Pictures on Children's Comprehension of Written Text." *Educational Communications and Technology Journal* 27 (3): 185–190.

Harris, N.D.C. and Kirkhope, S. (1979) "Uses of and Students' Reactions to Videocartridges as Self-instructional Materials in the Library." *BJET* 10 (1): 18–31.

Hartley, J. and Fuller, H. C. (1971) "Using Slides in Lectures: An Exploratory Study." *Visual Education* (August): 39–41.

Haukoos, G. D. (1982) "The Influence of Slide-tape Self-instructional Modules on Community College Biology Student Achievement." *Community/Junior College Quarterly of Research and Practice* 7 (1): 31–38.

Haynie, W. J. (1978) "The Instructional Effectiveness of Realism and Enhancement of Illustrations Related to Visual Continuum Theories." Ph.D. diss., Pennsylvania State University.

Herbener, G. F. et al. (1979) "Dynamics of the Frame in Visual Composition." *Educational Communications and Technology Journal* 27 (2): 83–88.

Higgins, L. C. (1978) "A Factor-Analytic Study of Children's Picture Interpretation Behaviour." *Educational Communications and Technology Journal* 26 (3): 215–232.

———. (1979) "Effects of Strategy Orientated Training on Children's Inference Drawing from Pictures." *Educational Communications and Technology Journal* 27 (4): 265–280.

Hills, P. J. (1974) "An Investigation of Some Applications of Self Teaching Systems in the University of Surrey." Ph.D. diss., University of Surrey.

Hines, S. J. (1981) "The Effect of Mode of Visual Presentation (Motion vs. Still) on the Brain Wave Production of College Students." Ed.D. diss., Northern Illinois University.

Hirsh, J. M. (1979) "No Account of the Individual." *British Journal of Physical Education* 10 (1): 10–11.

Hult, R. C. (1980) "The Effectiveness of University Television Instruction and Factors Influencing Student Attitudes." *College Student Journal* 14 (1): 5–7.

Jeon, V. H. and Branson, R. K. (1981) "Performance and Simulated Performance Test Results as a Factor of Instruction by Still and Motion Visuals." *Journal of Educational Technology Systems* 10 (1): 33–34.

Johnson, B. and Roberson, J. (1979) "Color in Instructional Films: Does It Still Make No Difference in Learning Achievement?" *Educational Technology* 19 (1): 32–35.

Jonassen, D. H. (1979) "Implications of Multi-image for Concept Acquisition." *Educational Communications and Technology Journal* 27 (4): 291–302.

Jones, H. C. (1976) "The Value of Self Test Items in Tape-Slide Instruction." *Medical Education* 10: 279–283.

Katzman, N. and Nyenhuis, J. (1972) "Colour vs. Black-and-White Effects on Learning, Opinion and Attention." *Audiovisual Communication Review* 20 (1): 16–28.

Kenshole, G. E. (1967) "An Experiment in University Teaching, Part I and Part II." *Medical and Biological Illustration* 17: 198–200; 18: 24–28.

Khan, A. G. (1980) "Effects of Audiotutorial and Conventional Instructional Techniques on Cognitive Achievements." *Journal of Research in Science Teaching* 17 (1): 47–53.

Kroll, H. M. (1974) "The Relative Effectiveness of Written and Individualised Audio Instruction in the Intermediate Grades." *Audiovisual Communication Review* 22: 247–268.

Kruse, W. D. (1981) "A Comparison of the Effects of Media on Attitude Modification towards the Orthopoedically Handicapped." Ed.D. diss., University of Northern Colorado.

Laner, S. (1965) "An Experimental Study of Pictorial Methods of Instruction." Ph.D. diss., University of Reading.

Lertchalolarn, C. (1981) "The Interactive Effects of Color, Realism, Pictorial Attributes, and Cognitive Style on Pictorial Information Processing." Ph.D. diss., University of Pittsburgh.

Levin, J. R. and Lesgood, A. (1978) "On Pictures in Prose." *Educational Communications and Technology Journal* 26 (3): 233–243.

Levin, J. R. et al. (1979) "Pictures, Imagery and Children's Recall of Central versus Peripheral Sentence Information." *Educational Communications and Technology Journal* 27 (2): 83–95.

Lorge, S. (1963) *The Relative Effectiveness of Four Types of Language Laboratory Experiences*. New York: City Board of Education.

McAlpin, J. (1979) "The Overhead Projector in the Advanced Reading Class." *English Language Teaching Journal* 33 (3): 214–218.

McCracken, G. (1965) "Textfilm Enrichment for Primary Reading Programs." Educational Screen 44 (16–17): 70.

McDonald, R. (1972) *A Comparison of Two Methods of Presenting Occupational Information*. Charleston, W.V.: Appalachia Education Laboratory.

McDonald, R. and Knights, J. (1979) "Learning from Tapes: The Experience of Home-Based Students." *PLET* 16 (1): 46–50.

Machula, R. S. (1979) "Media and Affect: A Comparison of Videotape, Audio-tape and Print." *Journal of Educational Technology Systems* 7 (2): 167–185.

McVey, G. F. (1979) "User Assessment of Media Presentation Rooms." *Educational Communications and Technology Journal* 27 (2): 121–147.

Mangan, J. (1978) "Cultural Conventions of Pictorial Representation: Iconic Literacy and Education." *Educational Communications and Technology Journal* 26 (3): 245–267.

———. (1981) "Learning through Pictures: A Study of Cultural and Cognitive Aspects of Visual Images." Ed.D. diss., University of Massachusetts.

Marchant, H. (1975) "Communicating by Instructional Film: A Presentation Strategy." In *Aspects of Educational Technology*, 8, ed. J. Baggaley et al. London: Pitman.

Marcyes, D. D. (1981) "The Effects of Color and Polarity on Recognition Memory for Projected Positive and Negative Line Stimuli." Ed.D. diss., University of Indiana.

Mariet, F. (1980) "The Social Conditions for a Selection of Instructional Audiovisual Media." *European Journal of Education* 15 (3): 241–249.

Miller, W. C. (1969) "Film Movement and Affective Response and the Effect on Learning and Attitude Formation." *Audiovisual Communication Review* 17: 217–281.

Modiano, N. et al. (1982) "Accurate Perception of Coloured Illustration: Rates of Comprehension in Mexican-Indian Children." *Journal of Cross-Cultural Psychology* 13 (4): 490–495.

Mundy, P. G. (1962) "A Comparison of the Use of Television (BBC) Programmes for Schools and Sound Films as a Teaching Aid." M.A. thesis, University of London.

Musa, M.E.E. (1981) "The Effects of Pictorial Representation on Concept Learning." Ph.D. diss., University of California, Los Angeles.

Myers, J. A. (1978) "Compressed Speech Increases Learning Efficiency." *Education of the Visually Handicapped* 10 (2): 56–64.

Napoli, L. (1982) "Instructional Television: The Effects of Different Types of Graphical Representation, in Color, of Quantitive Data on the Perception of Charts." Ph.D. diss., University of Indiana.

Noble, W. C. et al. (1979) "Comparison of the Efficiency of Slide/Tape and Cine-loop as Teaching Aids for Microbiological Technique." *Journal of Biological Education* 15 (3): 204–206.

Nohavec, R. G. (1977) "Effects of Three Sound Filmstrip Projection Techniques on Information Retention by First Grade Children." Ed.D. diss., University of South Dakota.

Nugent, G. et al. (1980) "Task, Learner and Presentation Interaction in Television Production." *Educational Communications and Technology Journal* 28 (1): 30–38.

Palmer, C. R. (1975) "Attitudes to Learning Method in First Year Chemistry Undergraduates." *BJET* 6 (2): 47–54.

Pearson, S. L. and Jepson, L. (1969) "Short Film Loops in the Teaching of Conservative Dentistry." *Journal of Dental Education* 33: 509–515.

Peri, V. L. (1978) "A Study of the Motion Variable in Relation to Cognitive Style and Achievement Level." Ed.D. diss., University of Southern California.

Perrin, D. G. (1969) "A Theory of Multiple Image Communication." *Audiovisual Communication Review* 17 (4): 368–382.

Reid, J. C. and MacLennan, D. W. (1967) *Research in Instructional TV and Film: Summaries of Studies*. Washington, D.C.: Bureau of Research, U.S. Government Printing Office.

Rich, O. S. et al. (1966) "The Utilization of Large Screen TV to Overcome Shortages of Classroom Space and Teaching Personnel." Ph.D. diss., Brigham Young University, Utah.

Riley, P. (1974) "The Language Laboratory: Implications of the Functional Approach." In *Mélanges pédagogiques*. Nancy: Université de Nancy.

Robinson, R. S. (1981) "Affective Responses to the Literary and Cinematic Elements in an Educational Film: A Descriptive Investigation." Ph.D. diss., University of Wisconsin, Madison.

Rudisill, M. (1952) "Children's Preferences for Color versus Other Qualities in Illustrations." *Elementary School Journal* 52 (8): 444–451.

Samuels, S. R. (1970) "Effects of Pictures on Learning to Read, Comprehension and Attitudes." *Review of Educational Research* 40 (3): 397–407.

Schecter, D. S. (1981) "Learner Preference and Recognition Accuracy Related to Background Color Sequence and Presentation Time of Projected Abstract Symbols." P.E.D. diss., University of Indiana.

Schramm, W. (1977) *Big Media, Little Media: Tools and Technologies for Instruction*. London: Sage Publications.

Schupham, J. (1970) "Broadcasting and the Open University." *Journal of Educational Technology*, 1: 44–51.

Seymour, W. D. (1937) "An Experiment Showing the Superiority of a Light Coloured 'Blackboard.'" *British Journal of Educational Psychology* 7 (3): 259–263.

Sheridan, P. (1978) "A Tape-lecture Course in Chemistry." *Education in Chemistry* 15 (4): 109.

Shifrin, M. (1973) *Information in the School Library*. London: Bingley.

Simmons, E. S. (1980) "The Influence of Kinetic Structure in Films on Biology Students' Achievement and Attitude." *Journal of Research in Science Teaching,* 17 (1): 67–73.

Singarella, T. A. (1981) "The Study of Two Forms of Mediated Instruction." Ph.D. diss., University of Nebraska–Lincoln.

Smith, H. G. (1979) "Investigation of Several Techniques for Reviewing Audio Tutorial Instruction." *Educational Communications and Technology Journal* 27 (3): 155–205.

Smith, J. (1972) "Selection of a Method of Presentation to Aid the Learning of Manipulatory Skills." In *Aspects of Educational Technology,* 6, ed. K. Austwick and N.D.C. Harris. London: Pitman.

Snowberg, R. L. (1973) "Basis for the Selection of Background Colours for Transparencies." *Audiovisual Communication Review* 21 (2): 191–207.

Stone, P. (1983) "Auditory Learning in a School Setting: Procedures and Results." *Volta Review* 85 (1): 7–13.

Straub, J. M. (1978) "A Comparative Study of the Effects of Coloured vs. Black and White Illustrations in the Testing of Language Competence in Children." Ph.D. diss., University of Indiana.

Teather, D.C.B. (1974) "Learning from Film: A Significant Difference between the Effectiveness of Different Projection Methods." *PLET* 11 (6): 328–334.

Travers, R. and Alvarado, V. (1970) "The Design of Pictures for Teaching Children in Elementary School." *Audiovisual Communication Review* 18 (1): 46–64.

Trohanis, P. L. (1975) "Information Learning and Retention with Multiple Images and Audio: A Classroom Experiment." *Audiovisual Communication Review* 23 (4): 395–414.

Twyman, M. (1972) *An Investigation into Some Aspects of the Illustration of Primary School Books*. Reading, Penn.: University of Reading.

Wager, W. (1980) "A Theoretical Framework for Studying Educational Media: A Pilot Study." *Educational Communications and Technology Journal* 28 (1): 19–24.

Weiner, S. and Ganz, S. D. (1982) "Teaching Techniques: A Comparison of the Effect of Two- and Three-dimensional Visual Aids." *Journal of Dental Education* 46 (10): 592–594.

Wells, R. F. (1970) "A Study to Determine Whether General Concepts Which Are Commonly Taught by Motion Pictures Can Be Learned as Effectively by Sequential Still Photographs during Traditional versus Self-based Study Periods." Ph.D. diss., Purdue University, Indiana.

Wells, R. F. et al. (1973) "Effectiveness of Three Visual Media and Two Study Formats in Teaching Concepts Involving Time, Space and Motion." *Audiovisual Communication Review* 21 (2): 233–241.

Wenger, M. (1983) "From Film to Video: Teaching and Communication." *Educational Media International* 2: 3–4.

Westervelt, V. D. and McKinney, J. D. (1980) "Effects of a Film on Non-handicapped Children's Attitudes towards Handicapped Children." *Exceptional Children* 46 (4): 294–296.

Wilkinson, G. L. (1976) "Projection Variables and Performance." *Audiovisual Communication Review"* 24 (4): 413–436.

Williams, C. (1978) "Concept and Purpose of Visual Literacy." *Educational Media International* 3: 26–29.

Winn, W. and Everett, R. T. (1979) "Affective Rating of Color and Black-and-White Pictures." *Educational Communications and Technology Journal* 27 (2): 148–156.

Wiseman, D. (1979) "Audiovisual Materials: The Relationship between Form, Content and Medium." *Audiovisual Librarian* 5 (2): 51–57.

AUDIOVISUAL TECHNOLOGY. The design, function, or working of an audiovisual aid. The term implies and emphasizes the "technical" aspects of educational technology. It is not a synonym for educational technology.

AUSSAT. The first Australian communications satellites were launched in 1985 and christened AUSSAT 1 and 2; the proprietors of the satellites are Aussat Pty. Ltd. Each satellite has an orbiting mass of 655kg and is 6.6m long × 2.2m diameter. Each has 15 transponders, 4 at 30 watts, the rest at 12 watts.

AUSTPAC. Australian packet-switching system, operated by Telecom Australia. *See* **Packet Switching.**

AUSTRALIAN BROADCASTING COMMISSION. *See* **Australian Broadcasting Corporation.**

AUSTRALIAN BROADCASTING CORPORATION (ABC). The national broadcasting service of Australia, also providing an extensive service of radio and television programs and support publications for preschool, school, and certain adult audiences. Until 1983 the organization was called the Australian Broadcasting Commission.

GPO Box 487, Sydney, New South Wales 2001, Australia

AUSTRALIAN SOCIETY OF EDUCATIONAL TECHNOLOGY (ASET). ASET was founded in 1975. Its aims include

1. To provide for a fellowship of persons engaged in and persons interested in educational technology.

2. To provide a forum to exchange, question, or promote ideas or practices within the field of educational technology.

3. To act as a clearinghouse for the dissemination of information, ideas, and research in educational technology.

4. To encourage, or provide for, the publication of materials.

5. To cooperate with international, interstate, or local bodies with similar objects to those of the Society.

An occasional newsletter and a yearbook are published.

Educational Technology Center, 221 Wakefield Street, Adelaide, South Australia 5000

AUTHOR(ING) LANGUAGE. A computer language specially designed to assist the writing of CAL materials. Such languages are usually intended to be used by teachers with limited knowledge of computers, and should therefore be very "friendly." An effective author language will allow for the presentation of text and diagrams, eliciting and checking answers, branching according to several criteria, and so on.

Examples of widely available author languages include COURSEWRITER and PILOT. Some such languages are in wide use, although none of them can claim to fully meet the needs of the inexperienced user. Most personal-computer authoring languages, such as the authoring mode in PILOT, do require some expertise in instructional design and computers.

A variation on the concept of the authoring language is the authoring system: these are specifically designed to help naive users create computer-aided instruction lessons. The more sophisticated systems purport to let users who know nothing about computers apply their expertise about a subject area to create good computerized lessons. See **Authoring Languages for Computer-Assisted Instruction.**

AUTHORING LANGUAGES FOR COMPUTER-ASSISTED INSTRUCTION.

INTRODUCTION AND HISTORICAL PERSPECTIVE

The object of a CAI program of the tutorial type is to engage the student in a dialogue in which each response made by the student is analyzed and used to determine the action to be taken by the program. In principle, a program that accomplishes this can be written in nearly any general-purpose programming language, and over the years this has been done in languages as primitive as BASIC, as elegant as APL, as inappropriate as FORTRAN or COBOL, and as difficult to understand as assembly language. It would likely be easier to list the languages that have *not* been used for CAI!

From the beginning of the first systematic work in CAI in the early 1960s, it has been apparent that the creation of even the simplest kind of CAI dialogue involves a considerable amount of detailed and somewhat repetitive coding that rapidly tends to overwhelm the author by its dullness if not by the manifold opportunities for error in the inevitable GOTO statements that are generally needed to express the various pathways through the program. Even if these barriers can be overcome, the resulting code tends to be difficult for others to understand, and thus almost impossible to maintain or adapt to other purposes. A well-known index of CAI programs contains references to hundreds of instructional programs in this state of limbo, abandoned by the student coder who has long since graduated to more gainful employment, and incapable of resuscitation by anyone else.

It was soon recognized that a specialized authoring language that reflected the general structure of instructional dialogue could both simplify the authoring process and encourage the writing of better programs. Moreover, the programs that were written could be more easily improved and extended as needs changed and experience grew. Given the very high cost of developing courseware (in time and effort, if not in direct monetary terms) and the shortage of authors who are willing and able to design quality instructional programs, the use of anything other than a high-level authoring language for writing CAI materials would seem to be poor utilization of scarce resources.

A large number of such languages were developed in the 1960s, including TUTOR (still used by the PLATO system), three versions of Coursewriter (IBM), PLANIT (developed in the U.S. with support from the National Science Foundation [NSF], but more widely used in Europe), and the CAN series of languages (developed in Canada at the Ontario Institute for Studies in Education). There were (and are) many more, but as is the case with other programming languages, only a small minority ever developed a large group of users.

All of these languages required a large computer system for their implementation, and all except PLANIT (which was written in FORTRAN) were limited to a specific type of computer. This severely impeded the spread of CAI programs between systems of different types, and led to considerable balkanization of effort and "reinvention of the wheel" within largely isolated user groups.

The two languages that have been most successful in terms of hours of usable programming created are Coursewriter III and TUTOR. The former language was of course supported by IBM, which had the advantage of having acquired most of the academic computing market, and was thus able to reach a very wide group of potential users who were in turn able to share programs between different installations. The language had many strengths, and it pioneered a number of features that have continued to influence contemporary CAI languages. Unfortunately, it also had a number of limitations that seriously restricted its application in many areas, particularly in the sciences. By the mid-1970s, when it became evident that IBM was not prepared to overcome these deficiencies and develop the language further, the use of Coursewriter III began to decline; it now exists only in the form of a derivative product that is marketed for industrial training purposes.

The TUTOR language (Sherwood, 1977), in contrast, was developed within the context of the PLATO CAI laboratory at the University of Illinois. Good communication between those responsible for developing and maintaining the language, and the large user group, was an important contributing factor to the evolution and success of TUTOR. (Much of this communication was mediated by the PLATO system itself, which provided interterminal communications and message-forwarding facilities of a kind that other large mainframe systems were not to adopt until fifteen or twenty years later.) The other significant feature of TUTOR was its special adaptation to the graphic display capabilities of the PLATO terminal. Although IBM's Coursewriter II language was also intended for use on a CRT terminal associated with the Model 1500 Instructional System, this language made little provision for nontext graphics. The PLATO terminal embodied the first large-scale use of plasma-discharge technology (again, many years ahead of its time), and was ideally adapted to complex pictorial graphics, animation, and specialized character fonts. Finally, TUTOR was the first CAI authoring language having a modular organization that permitted and indeed encouraged the use of modern structured programming; this is probably the most important single characteristic of the language that gave it so much advantage over its early competitors.

Although the considerable amount of NSF funding was an important element in the success of the PLATO project, it seems fair to say that the TUTOR language, whose richness could not have developed without this continuing funding, served as one of the main vehicles of this success.

The PLATO system is now marketed by the Control Data Corporation. Variants of the TUTOR language are also employed in CAI systems offered by Digital Equipment Corporation (implemented on their VAX minicomputers) and Computer Teaching Corporation (as part of their IBM-PC–based TenCore system).

The other major recipient of NSF funding in the late 1960s and early 1970s was the TICCIT project. TICCIT stands for *Time-Shared Interactive Computer-Controlled Instructional Television;* it was originally developed by the Mitre Corporation, and was an authoring *system* rather than an authoring *language.* In an authoring system, the course designer is interactively polled for such information as the text to be presented, anticipated student responses and actions that should follow, etc. The system then generates the code required to implement the specified sequences. The objection most commonly made to such systems is that they tend to place rather stringent and arbitrary limits on the kinds of dialogue that can be generated, and thus on the instructional strategies that are possible; there is yet one more layer of machine-like inflexibility interposed between the author and the student. TICCIT attempted to overcome this difficulty by providing a variety of strategy formats based on established instructional models. The later development of a companion authoring language (TAL) now allows TICCIT authors as much flexibility as any other major authoring language. TICCIT is presently a commercial product of the Hazeltine Corporation, where it enjoys some success in the industrial training area.

All the authoring languages mentioned thus far were either limited to a single kind of computer or operating system, or required a large computer for their implementation—in most cases, both conditions applied. The authoring languages themselves tended to have large numbers of commands, and considerable training was required before most authors could begin producing usable instructional programs. In the early 1970s, another language appeared that somewhat eased these restrictions. In its original form, PILOT had a very small number of one-character commands, and was so simple (some would say primitive) that it could not only be learned in a few hours but was quite easily implemented as an interpreter on nearly any computer system, including the microcomputers that were soon to appear on the scene.

Since that time, PILOT has become the most democratic of the CAI authoring languages, available at small cost to owners of all of the popular personal microcomputers. As would be expected of a language having a very limited command structure (many of the limitations reflect those of the early microcomputers on whose use the commercial success of PILOT depended), numerous extensions and dialects of PILOT have appeared. In at least one popular version, PILOT statements can be combined with BASIC expressions, permitting considerable computational flexibility. Because PILOT is so easy to learn and is implemented on the cheapest available equipment (i.e., the *only* equipment many schools are able to acquire), this language is now quite widely taught in "computers in education" courses. Unfortunately, "easy to learn" does not necessarily mean "easy to use," particularly in more complex contexts. PILOT lacks the procedures and control structures necessary for modern structured programming, and many versions are severely deficient in computational capability and record-keeping ability.

By 1970, it appeared that the large number of different CAI authoring languages was becoming a major impediment to the sharing and transfer of instructional programs between different institutions. It had already become clear that no single institution would be able to generate all the programs that would be needed to make CAI a viable instructional medium. One possible solution would be to establish a single "standard" authoring language that all users within a large regional or national group would adhere to.

The most well-known effort of this type occurred in Canada. Around 1970, the National Research Council (NRC) of Canada, which had already been involved in CAI development work, proposed that a national authoring language be established. The hope was that all major CAI development work in Canada would use this language, facilitating the exchange of material between institutions in that country, and perhaps even establishing an international standard.

Considerable effort was made to obtain a consensus on the part of potential users for a workable functional standard for such a language, and this document (NRC, 1972) provided the basis for the definition of the language itself, which was done by an outside contractor. The language, which is called NATAL (NRC, 1974; Godfrey, 1984), is procedure-oriented and highly structured. It features a display sublanguage, whose purpose is to enable the use of a wide variety of display devices when executing a given program.

NATAL has been implemented on a variety of computers and is available commercially on the Digital Equipment VAX and the IBM-PC, on which it runs under the Coherent (Unix) operating system.

ELEMENTS OF CAI AUTHORING LANGUAGES

The purpose of this section is to look at some of the kinds of things an authoring language must be able to do. Examples will be given to show how certain languages specify these actions, but no attempt will be made to develop a detailed comparison of different languages.

There exist two fairly comprehensive documents that cover this subject in some detail. The first one, by Zinn (1969), appears to be the earliest attempt to outline authoring language capabilities in an organized way. The second (NRC, 1972) was mentioned previously in connection with NATAL; it was generated by a panel of the National Research Council of Canada.

The treatment that follows is more narrowly focused and makes no attempt to be comprehensive. Emphasis is placed on those aspects of authoring languages that make them different from general-purpose programming languages, and which are essential for the efficient production of high-quality, readily alterable instructional programs.

In order to make these remarks a bit more concrete, examples from several representative authoring languages will be cited. These languages include the following:

DAL   Dimension Authoring Language, a product of Digital Equipment Corporation, implemented on VAX/11 minicomputers. DAL is similar to TUTOR, with the addition of procedure blocks, numerous control structures, and graphics commands.

PILOT   Available in many versions from numerous sources, and generally implemented on microcomputers.

IPS   A procedure-oriented language developed at Simon Fraser University, Canada (Lower, 1980; Barker, 1983). Currently implemented as an interpreter on an IBM mainframe using the MTS operating system.

NATAL   The Canadian "National Authoring Language," developed by the National Research Council of Canada, and available commercially.

TUTOR   The language used by the PLATO CAI system, marketed by Control Data Corporation.

TAL   A component of the TICCIT CAI system, marketed by Hazeltine Corporation.

Organization of Question-Answer Groups. The basic unit of most CAI programs consists of a sequence of operations in which

1. the student is presented with information or a question, and is asked to respond;
2. the system waits for, accepts, and edits the student response;
3. the student response is compared with a series of "anticipated responses"; if a "match" occurs, a specified action is taken.

We will call the code comprising this sequence a *question group,* with the understanding that the term "question" merely refers to that part of the dialogue that immediately precedes the response to be entered by the student. Here is an example of a question group, written in pseudocode as a sequence of procedures:

Q1: DISPLAY(What is the most abundant metallic element in the earth's crust?)
A1: ACCEPT   {prompt for and await student response}
IF (RESPONSE = 'Oxygen') {Wrong answer}
    DISPLAY(Oxygen is the most abundant element, but it's not a metal)
    GOTO(A1)   {jump back to ACCEPT for another try}
IF (RESPONSE = 'aluminum') {see if student entered "aluminum"}

```
DISPLAY(Correct! Aluminum comprises 6% of the atoms
        in the earth's crust)
GOTO(Q2)        {jump forward to next question}
DISPLAY(Sorry, I don't recognize that answer; please try
        again)
GOTO(A1)        {jump back to ACCEPT for another try}
                {begin next question group} Q2:
```

As is outlined above in a rather symbolic way, the major part of the question group specifies comparisons to be made with the student response, and actions to be taken if these comparisons match. Each comparison represents a potential *answer,* and so a comparison command and the "action to be taken" commands that immediately follow it constitute an answer group. We can thus generalize the preceding sequence as follows:

```
DISPLAY(question or instructions to student)
DO WHILE (Done = FALSE)
    ACCEPT  {wait for and accept student response}
        ANSGRP(answer, actions)  {first answer group}
        ANSGRP(answer, actions)  {second answer group}
        ....
        ANSGRP(answer, actions)  {last answer group}
END DO
```

The "actions" associated with each anticipated answer generally include at least the following three:

1. Classify the answer as "right" or "wrong" for scorekeeping purposes.

2. Display text to the student commenting on the answer.

3. Jump to next logical section of program; if the answer was "wrong," this will usually be the previous ACCEPT point; otherwise it may be the following question group, or some other specified part of the course.

In a sense, an answer group can be regarded as an IF-THEN sequence as found in other programming languages:

```
IF (answer matches)
    THEN
        action 1
        action 2
        action 3
    ENDIF
```

Authoring languages that utilize this kind of organization usually have two categories of commands, sometimes called *major* and *minor,* after the nomenclature employed by IBM's early Coursewriter languages.

A major command is one that is executed whenever it is "encountered"; that is, whenever the program is looking for and analyzing student responses. Comparison commands are therefore major commands; as long as program flow continues through a question group, they will be executed. The other class of command, the minor command, can be placed anywhere in the program, but those minor commands immediately preceded by a major (comparison) command will be executed only if that comparison command matched the student response. Thus according to the above scheme, the comparison command establishes the IF-THEN-ENDIF structure, and the minor commands specify the various "actions."

While nearly all authoring languages recognize entities similar to the question group, some separate the response-comparison steps from the code specifying the actions to be taken. This alternative scheme might be represented as follows:

```
BEGIN
DISPLAY(question)
ACCEPT
COMPARE(1, answer)
COMPARE(2, answer)
COMPARE(3, answer)

IF(1, DO.......)
IF(1 and 2, DO.....)
IF(3 and not 2, DO.....)
```

This scheme, seen in the early language PLANIT and more recently in NATAL-74, is of considerable advantage when the anticipated answers have several components, and the actions to be taken depend on what combinations of these components are present.

Modular Structure and Sequencing of Question Groups. Question groups are the main building blocks of most instructional programs. In only very simple and linear programs will these groups be executed in a fixed sequence from the beginning to the end; more commonly, they will be presented in sequences that vary with the requirements and performance of individual students. Also, certain question groups pertaining to a recurring task (such as asking the student to balance an equation) will usually need to appear at several points in the instructional program. In most cases, some sequences of question-response dialogue that form natural groupings will remain more or less immutable, as far as their order of execution is concerned. It is generally desirable to organize these question sequences into higher-order groups that can be invoked from various parts of the instructional program.

One way of achieving this is to include "branching" commands of the GOTO or GOSUB type in the language. The Coursewriter family of languages utilized this approach: a series of label variables, known as return registers, was available for defining the point to which program execution should return once the sequence to which branching occurred was finished. PILOT is an example of a more recent language of this type.

In the wider world of general-purpose programming, this approach to sequence of execution has been long since discredited as leading to programs that are difficult to understand, awkward to revise and change, error prone, and more time-consuming to debug. Above all, it is very difficult to combine the work of several individuals working on different segments of a large program.

Most modern programming languages are designed to facilitate top-down structured programming. As such, they either de-emphasize the use of GOTO statements (PL/I, Pascal, C) or eliminate them completely (Modula-2, FORTH). Instead, the different units are invoked where needed by an appropriate CALL statement. For example, the highest level of a CAI program on punctuation usage might appear as follows:

CALL(Introduction)
CALL(Commas)
CALL(CommaTest)
CALL(Semicolons)
CALL(SemicolonTest)
CALL(Review)
CALL(ReviewTest)

The virtue of this scheme should be obvious; the nature and sequence of the various units is clearly seen, and changes can be made easily and with minimum chance for error. The code for each segment of the course would stand as a largely independent unit, which would itself normally contain similar internal constructs. This kind of organization is usually associated with some form of *block* structure, which means that the user-defined names within each section of code are ordinarily *local* (i.e., "known" only within) that block. It is this feature (which can only be fully appreciated by someone who has done some programming) that is almost essential if independent segments of code are to be combined into a single larger entity.

All of the major authoring languages employ some form of structuring beyond the level of the question group; it could be argued that any language that does not possess such structure is not worthy of serious consideration for any but the most trivial applications. DAL, NATAL-74, and IPS employ procedure-oriented block structures similar to those found in PL/1, Pascal, or C. This means that values can be passed to the called procedures; thus in the statement

CALL ElementDrill ('Na'; 'Sodium'; '11')

the three values shown within the parentheses are passed to three corresponding variables within the procedure. Once the procedure has been written and documented, the CAI author need be concerned only with the details of the CALL statement, and can easily repeat the same instructional strategy using different contents by simply altering the parameters passed to the procedure being called.

In TUTOR, the procedural block structure is somewhat diluted; each question group constitutes a separate *unit* that can be invoked from within a higher-level unit, but earlier versions of the language lacked local variables. More significantly, the sequence of execution is determined in part by a NEXT command that can appear within a unit, and whose operand can vary depending on the student's interaction with that unit. Although this violates part of the dogma of top-down structured programming practice, it provides considerable flexibility and is not too objectionable if it is used carefully and within a fairly narrow context.

TAL is quite rich in organizational components. The basic unit in this language is a *page* (i.e., screen display); successive pages can be overlaid, much as a series of overhead transparencies, building up a larger unit called a *frame*, which might comprise a question group. A series of related frames can then be grouped together to form a *chapter*. Sequence of execution is determined by a series of *branch tables* that can be defined at, and be made local to, the page, frame, and chapter levels. (Variables can also be local to each level.) This freedom in specifying execution sequence would result in chaos if TAL were a stand-alone programming language, but the TAL authoring system provides the prompting required to specify and recall the relations between the units, and there is a *branch table editor* that can be used to examine and alter these relations.

Local Control Structures. As we have seen, one of the major distinguishing features of a CAI authoring language is the existence of structural elements such as the question group, answer group, and units containing related collections of these structures. Even in an authoring language, however, there exists a need for many of the programming capabilities of general-purpose languages. These are made far more valuable when they include local control structures that minimize the need for labels and GOTO commands.

The most common of these is the IF-ENDIF construct. This is available in explicit form in a number of authoring languages, and is used implicitly in Common Pilot and in IPS, where a command can be followed by an expression in square brackets which is evaluated and used to control execution of the rest of the line:

WRITE [SCORE = 10] 'Perfect score!'

The WRITE command is executed only if the statement SCORE = 10 is true. In IPS, this concept is extended to allow selection of alternatives, as in the CASE statement of Pascal:

CALL [WHICH] MOD1 ; MOD2 ; MOD3 ; MOD4

WRITE [?] 'Correct.' ; 'Good' ; 'Right!'

In the first example, the procedure module invoked by the CALL command will depend on whether the value of WHICH is 1, 2, 3, or 4. In the WRITE statement, the text to be displayed on the terminal is randomly selected from the three choices given. Protocols are available which enable the operands of a series of contiguous commands to be selected by one bracketed expression, and an ELSE action can also be specified.

The DAL language possesses an especially rich variety of control structures. In addition to IF-ELSE-ENDIF, DAL offers LOOP-ENDLOOP, FOR-ENDFOR, and TEST-VALUE-ENDTEST. The latter is illustrated by the following example:

TEST   answer
VALUE   "yellow", "red", "blue"
• WRITE You picked a primary color.
VALUE   "green", "violet", "orange"
• WRITE That is a secondary color.
OTHER
• WRITE I don't recognize that color.
ENDTEST

This also illustrates the "dot-indentation" protocol of DAL, which helps organize more complex nested arrangements of control structures.

Answer Analysis. Flexibility in interpreting student responses is an important element in any CAI authoring language. All major authoring languages provide separate means of checking character and numeric answers, and in the latter case, most provide for specification of acceptable ranges of values. These should be expressible in both absolute and relative terms (i.e., as a factor or percentage of the exact value).

In checking for answers in character form, most languages allow the program to search for embedded substrings. This is most commonly done by letting a symbol such as "*" stand for any single character, while "@" represents a string of any length, including zero. Thus the string "mis@i@pi" will be matched by "mississippi," "misisipi," etc. In IPS, the symbol "#" will match numeric quantities, and the substrings matched by all three symbols can be assigned to variables for further analysis.

TUTOR has long had a powerful facility for matching algebraic responses (e.g., "$3Y + 4$"), which are checked for correctness by substituting a random number for the variable and evaluating. One can also specify answers containing both numeric and unit parts, such as "1.3 kg/1", and the system will check both components.

Natural language processing is still beyond the capacity of ordinary CAI systems. However, the need for it can be reduced by careful attention to the design of questions and response prompts. Routines to check for common errors in spelling and "phonetic equivalence" are useful when available.

A separate command is sometimes used to match multiple-choice responses. Thus in IPS, the command

PICK   3

references the third component of a list whose default value is (1, 2, 3, 4, 5 . . .), but which can also be randomly ordered. This greatly simplifies the organization of answer groups based on randomly ordered multiple-choice questions. The same kind of command can be extended to reference light pen, mouse, or touch responses.

Even in languages that are not oriented toward graphics, it is useful to have some way of finding the column location at which the first character of the student response appears. This would permit questions of the form "type an 'x' under the misplaced comma in the following sentence."

Student responses that may contain several different components, all of which must be checked for, are more difficult to analyze and act on, particularly if the correct parts of an incomplete answer are to be retained, so only the missing parts have to be added. The MATCH command of DAL (an extension of the one in TUTOR), combined with DAL's LOOP-ENDLOOP and TEST-VALUE-ENDTEST constructs, provides one of the best ways of implementing this kind of interaction.

Display of Dialogue on the Terminal. With the notable exceptions of PLATO and TICCIT, most of the early CAI systems were first used either with printing terminals or with display terminals having very limited graphics capabilities. It is not surprising, therefore, that most authoring languages, many of which are based on these early models, possess very limited capabilities for composing display screen layouts; displaying subscripts, superscripts, and other symbols not present in the standard character set; defining subscreens; and providing interaction with external devices such as videodiscs and voice input units.

One interesting attempt to provide a degree of device independence, at least for the display of ordinary text, is the "display sublanguage" of NATAL. This provides automatic formatting that adapts text to the line length and other characteristics of the particular terminal.

Specification of text attributes, such as color, reverse

printing, underscoring, etc., is probably best handled by commands included in the text itself, as in the NATAL display sublanguage. This method is also employed in IPS, which uses a protocol similar to that found in the typesetting language T$_E$X:

WRITE "Now look at the \bli{flashing} term in the equation."

WRITE "\yel This whole line will be \unl{yellow} . \~yel"

There are two general methods of organizing the display of text on the student terminal. In the simplest *scrolling* mode, each line is displayed below the previous ones. Cursor addressing and screen erase commands are always available to modify the development of the display, but in their absence, new lines appear at the bottom of the screen as those displayed earlier scroll off the top. In the more controlled *page* method, a complete display screen is specified as a unit, with the student usually in control of the "next page" command. The material seen by the student during display of a given page usually changes in response to the program, but the same identifiable frame of material is in view until the student is ready for the next.

The page display method is probably easier for most authors to manage, particularly with more complex material. In scroll mode the author must give considerable attention to what is disappearing from the screen, as well as what is being added to it. With sufficient care, the two methods can usually be made to give identical results.

TICCIT is strongly page-oriented, and permits the student to flip back and forth between pages as in a book. Both TUTOR and DAL also generally display a page at a time, although student access to pages other than the "next" one must be programmed explicitly.

TICCIT's page-orientation is also reflected in the convenient protocol used by TAL to define windows on the screen display. All the text directed to a given window is automatically formatted to conform to the window's dimensions. In particular, the student's response can be directed to a defined "response box." With this exception, it seems that most authoring languages lack simple and direct commands for defining and using windows.

Interaction with the Student. All authoring languages, almost by definition, possess one or more commands that cause the program to accept input from the student. Most CAI systems also allow the student to enter commands that are not interpreted as answers, but do such things as enter comments about the course, perform calculations, view glossaries, etc. One of the most important of these commands is HELP; there should always be some way for the student to extricate himself from a situation in which the correct answer cannot be found. Most of the major languages have an explicit HELP command that specifies the actions to be taken when this command is encountered.

The "dedicated" CAI terminals such as were originally used by PLATO and TICCIT had special keys for these purposes. TICCIT was especially replete with command option keys, which included functions such as *exit, repeat, back, skip, objective, advice, help, hard, easy, rule, example,* and *practice*. Needless to say, using this wider gamut of options requires more planning by the course designer, who must not only develop the additional dialogue but must integrate its actions into the page display from which it originated.

Now that most general-purpose terminals and microcomputers possess extra keys which are usually programmable, it is practical to include a number of single-keystroke commands in any authoring language.

One important category of student input that has not generally been treated very well at the authoring language level is a positional response as mediated by a light pen, touch panel, mouse, or cursor-control keys. Ideally, one would like the capability of operating in several modes. In one, the "distance," either in character cells or screen coordinates, of the student response from the target location would be retrievable. In another mode, the author would define a screen window or "button" within which a touch indication would associate that window with a multiple-choice index value.

Graphics. CAI is basically a graphics-oriented communication medium; even the simple display of text requires attention to where on the screen the text will appear, how fast it will be presented, and how it will integrate with material already present. Capabilities for doing so existed, in rather rudimentary form, in IBM's early Coursewriter II system, which utilized a video display terminal. It is interesting to note that this same system (and its authoring language) also supported random-access audio and slide projection equipment; these multimedia features have, until recently, not been available in CAI systems capable of implementation on general-purpose computers.

Going beyond simple text, we can recognize several higher levels of graphics capability. First, there is the construction of shapes based on lines, polygons, and circular arcs, generally mediated by corresponding language primitives. These may be used simply to provide a more organized or attractive field in which to present text dialogue, or they can be combined to produce as elaborate a diagram or picture as is needed. If the hardware system permits selective erase and reasonably rapid data transfer, animated motion is possible.

At a still higher level, in terms of both software (fast numeric processing) and hardware (bit-mapped display screens), are presentation of digitized photographic images and interactive manipulation of three-dimensional shapes.

Most authoring languages that support systems capable of graphics have included commands for their creation, usually variants of the primitives for points, lines, and other basic shapes. Historically, these features of languages such as TUTOR predated the availability of similar facilities in non-CAI software and hardware, so it is not surprising that there is little standardization in this area.

Digital Equipment's DAL is a good example of a modern authoring language that integrates graphics commands. In fact, approximately a third of the 70 commands of DAL relate to graphics functions. This rather large number is due partly to the existence of three parallel sets of commands relating to the coordinate systems of the screen, a locally defined graph scale, and relative displacements from an existing location. Also, the graphics command set of DAL is designed to make most of the features of the ReGIS graphics language (see below) available to the author.

There is some question as to how useful a large set of graphics commands can be to the course author. It is generally far easier to define a graphic display by actually creating it interactively, than by using a programming language, in which coordinate positions must be explicitly entered by the author. Graphics editors, computer-aided design systems, and television-based devices are now generally available, and these will certainly be the favored ways of creating and assembling graphical material. Thus the TenCore system can incorporate graphical material created by the popular PC Paintbrush graphics editor.

Perhaps the more useful function of a rich set of graphics commands is to provide a degree of system independence, both at the operational and documentation levels. The importance of doing this is not being overlooked by the commercial computing world, in which interactive graphics is becoming an increasingly major means of user communication with application programs. Here, the trend toward standardization appears to be taking place at a somewhat lower language level.

One such graphics sublanguage is ReGIS, used by Digital Equipment Corporation in its VT240 terminal and its line of personal computers. ReGIS, "Remote Graphics Instruction Set," consists of a set of mnemonic instructions that can be executed by a ROM-resident interpreter built into a terminal. A typical ReGIS command sequence is shown below:

p [300,200] v [, −100] c [+20]

{at the screen position defined by the pixel (x,y = 300,200), draw a line (*v*ector) 100 pixels up (negative y), and at that location draw a *c*ircle with a radius of 20 pixels}

Other ReGIS commands can specify text, character set and character size, writing directions, shading, foreground and background color, blink status, etc. In order to distinguish ReGIS commands from ordinary text to be displayed in the usual way, the commands are preceded by a special "escape sequence," the first character of which is the standard ASCII escape character.

Because ReGIS uses printable ASCII characters, the command strings are easy to write, debug, and alter. Sequences for the construction of more complicated displays can be created by use of an appropriate graphics editor. The main disadvantage of ReGIS is that it is not terminal independent: the numbers in coordinate specifications refer to pixels, so that a line 400 pixels in length might completely fill some terminal screens while it might only be half a screen long on other terminals.

A far more flexible means of specifying graphics is the NAPLPS (North American Presentation-Level Protocol Syntax) standard. This protocol had its origin in the Telidon videotex system developed by the Canadian Department of Communications, and has now been adopted in a somewhat modified form as the standard videotex protocol by AT&T.

The essential feature of the Telidon/NAPLPS protocol is that it is entirely independent of the characteristics of the particular terminal on which the material is to be displayed. Thus x,y coordinate locations are specified as fractions of the available screen dimensions, whatever they might be. If a given display device is incapable of producing the resolution, color, or other features specified, the local decoder attempts the best approximation. This, together with the built-in provision for extensions to the protocol, means that the system should be able to accommodate any display device that may be built in the future. (The maximum resolution that can be specified is 8×10^6 pixels horizontally and vertically; over 10^{13} colors can be specified!) In addition, there are technical features that minimize the amount of code that must be transmitted in order to produce a given display.

As would be expected, the code required to specify a NAPLPS graphic is more complicated than that of ReGIS, and decoding requires far more complex computation. As graphics editors and inexpensive decoders become available in the future, these disadvantages should lose significance in comparison to the very great benefits of system independence and portability. Aside from these considerations, the potential of videotex systems as a means of delivering CAI is a sufficient reason for incorporating a compatible set of graphics commands into an authoring language. A Telidon interface to NATAL has already been demonstrated, and it seems likely that similar capabilities will be demanded in future authoring languages.

Course Generators. Reference has already been made to the TICCIT system, which furnishes ready-made instructional templates (and provides for the creation of new ones) in which the course author is simply prompted for the necessary information pertinent to each dialogue frame, and is thus relieved of the necessity of "programming" in the usual sense of the word. Numerous other systems to accomplish the same general end have been devised; some generate code in a standard authoring language (e.g., TUTOR, TenCore, or PILOT), while others produce output in the form of code or function calls in a general-purpose language such as BASIC or Pascal.

The difficulty with this approach is that most such systems tend to be rather limited; few support such things as random selection of text, complex answer-processing routines, and detailed display layout instructions. But it is just these features whose sensitive use makes the difference between what appears to be a conversation with a teacher and a "programmed instruction" course. Entire courses developed by such means are less likely to convey a sense of immediacy and interest; one would hesitate to construct a textbook chapter or a lecture upon a rigid template, and it hardly seems proper to accept lower quality for CAI.

Still, course generators can justifiably be used to construct parts of a larger course, or to construct a first approximation to a course that can then be extended and modified, and finally "tuned" by ordinary in-line programming.

Courseware Portability. It has long been recognized that one of the primary factors limiting the acceptance of CAI is the very small amount of courseware of acceptable quality that has been developed, is available, and is compatible with a given CAI support system. The latter factor has been particularly exacerbated by the proliferation of authoring languages; the total number of really good instructional programs is small and is dispersed among a number of mutually incompatible systems.

There is no simple answer to this problem, other than the obviously utopian one of getting everyone to use a single standard authoring language. Clearly, the more two different languages resemble each other, the easier it will be to effect a translation. Thus course materials in TUTOR, which represents the largest base of available quality courseware, should be translatable to TenCore or DAL with a minimum of trouble. Generally, the higher level the target language, the easier it is to effect a translation. Also, the easier it is to reproduce the course in the local language simply from what one sees while executing the original course at a terminal.

One interesting approach has been to define a lower-level "CAI assembly language" that would serve as a more easily generated target of a translation program. This low-level language would itself be implemented as an interpreter on any suitable computer. Several experimental efforts have been made along these lines, but no generally useful products have been demonstrated.

Implementation of Authoring Languages. Many of the major CAI authoring languages were developed at about the time that interactive, terminal-oriented systems were first coming into use; in fact, several of the systems supporting these languages (Coursewriter II and III, for example) actually predated the availability of general-purpose terminal systems on the host computers for which the CAI systems were designed. Thus it was not enough to have an authoring language interpreter; an editor of some kind was needed in order to get the material into the system, and a terminal I/O system had to be designed as well. All this meant that a given authoring language was generally quite specific to a particular kind of computer and operating system.

Even today, very few authoring languages except PILOT are implemented on more than one kind of computer. The reasons are partly proprietary, and partly that for efficiency, the CAI system software is usually written in assembly language, which is unique to a particular kind of computer and operating system. Rather than expend several man-years of effort to duplicate an existing language on a new machine, most manufacturers have preferred to implement their own, and presumably better, language, in the hope of making their computer system more attractive to potential users.

An independent software developer, on the other hand, would profit from multiple implementations of the same language on different computers, but this can be economically feasible only if large quantities of each kind of computer are in the hands of potential customers. At present, the educational market appears to be too diffuse for this approach to be generally viable. A contributing factor is the the tendency of budget-starved schools to retain older and less functional equipment that will generally tend to be incompatible with more sophisticated CAI software.

One way of making a CAI system more portable would be to write it in a higher-level language that can be compiled on a wide variety of computer systems. This is the reason that the early PLANIT system was written in FORTRAN. A number of other systems have been written in various other languages, including APL. The IPS language interpreter is written in Spitbol (a compiled version of SNOBOL4), and NATAL-74 is implemented in C. There are several difficulties with this approach; execution efficiency tends to be lower, and there can still be serious incompatibilities in file handling, terminal I/O, and other system-dependent areas.

Since the computer resources needed for designing and testing instructional programs are considerably in excess of those required for the execution of a course by an individual student, it seems reasonable to allocate these two kinds of operations to separate computer systems. The advantage of this separation of function is that the authoring language can be a very powerful one, rather than being constrained by the limited capabilities of a less expensive student station. This has been done for NATAL and for TUTOR, in which the course material developed on a larger and more functional system can be made available in a "compiled" form for execution on student terminals.

A similar approach would be to translate the material, once it has been developed and thoroughly tested on a large mainframe system, into a low-level language such as C, and then recompile this code for the particular microcomputer system of interest. This method (aided by a translation program) is being explored as a means of transporting a large amount of IPS code that was developed on a mainframe system over to microcomputers.

The obvious disadvantage of separating the authoring language from the delivery system is that teachers and others responsible for selecting and using these materials will usually not be able to make any changes to them. Experience has shown that CAI materials almost always do require improving and adapting to local needs, and the ease of doing this is one of the main reasons for advocating the use of a high-level authoring language in the first place. These methods will probably become less necessary as microcomputers become more powerful and the cost of memory decreases.

Stephen K. Lower

REFERENCES

Barker, P. G. and Steele, J. W. (1983) "A Practical Introduction to Authoring for Computer-assisted Instruction. Part 1—IPS." *British Journal of Educational Technology* 14 (1): 26–45.

Godfrey, D. and Brahan, J. (1984) "Computer-Aided Learning Using the NATAL Language." Press Porcepic/Softwords, 560 Johnson Street, Victoria BC V8W 3C6, Canada.

Lower, S. K. (1980) "IPS: A New Authoring Language for Computer-assisted Instruction." *Journal of Computer Based Instruction* 6 (4): 119–124.

National Research Council. (1972) "A Functional Specification of a Programming Language for Computer Aided Learning Applications." Ottawa: National Research Council of Canada, Associate Committee on Instructional Technology.

———. (1974) "National Author Language NATAL-74 Author Guide." Ottawa: National Research Council of Canada, Associate Committee on Instructional Technology.

Sherwood, B. A. (1977) "The TUTOR Language." Minneapolis: Control Data Education Company.

Zinn, K. L. (1969) "A Comparative Study of Languages for Programming Interactive Use of Computers in Instruction. Final Report." Ann Arbor, Mich.: Interuniversity Communications Council (EDUCOM).

AUTOCODE. A specific type of machine code (i.e., not a language) in which a computer program may be written, but which is not a pure machine code. Instructions written in autocode have to be translated before they can be executed.

AUTO-DIAL. Some modems have the capability to be programmed to perform functions automatically. Among other things, this allows them to send and receive data unattended, dial frequently used numbers automatically, redial after a broken connection, etc.

AUTOEXEC.BAT. Start-up file on MS-DOS (PC-DOS). Once the operating system has booted, it looks for a file called autoexec.bat, and if it finds the file, executes it. Items such as clocks, screen attributes, and resident programs can all be loaded automatically in this way, as well as a frequently required applications package such as a word processor or spreadsheet.

AUTOFAX. A facsimile system whereby material may be magnetically stored and later automatically transmitted over the telephone system to the addressees. The system makes it possible for a number of documents to be scanned and stored during the day when the network is busy and tariffs are high, the documents being automatically transmitted to the addressees during the night when network loading and tariffs are low.

AUTOINSTRUCTION. *See* **Self-instruction.**

AUTOMATIC CHANGEOVER. A system which automatically switches one projector off and another on to provide continuous projection with multiple-reel films. In the absence of an automatic changeover device, it may be necessary to interrupt the performance at the end of each reel.

AUTOTUTOR. An early electromechanical multiple-choice teaching machine marketed by US Industries, Inc. The use of 35mm film as program material permitted program length of up to 1,500 frames on a single spool.

A U.S. invention, it achieved considerable success in many countries during the 1960s. The machine was specifically designed to use branching programs constructed according to principles first stated by Norman Crowder. *See* **Teaching Machines.**

AVAILABLE LINE. In facsimile, that part of a scanning line specifically occupied by picture elements. Sometimes known as an *active line*.

AV COMMUNICATION REVIEW. Journal now renamed *Educational Communication and Technology*.

AZIMUTH. The angle a recording or replay head makes with the line along which the tape or film moves. Misalignment causes distortion or loss of signal strength.

B

BACIE. *See* **British Association for Commercial and Industrial Education.**

BACKDROP. The background to a film or television set, either cloth, card, hardboard, or any other material supported on frames.

BACKGROUND LIGHTING. Lighting the background of a scene in order to give it depth and separate the subject from the background.

BACKLIGHT. The term is used in three ways in general photography. When used with other light sources, it can refer to a light placed behind and above the subject, shining slightly toward the camera in order to highlight the top of the subject and provide a separation effect from the background. When used without other major light sources, a backlight pointed to the camera from behind the object can be used to produce either a silhouette or a situation where only the edges of the subject are lit from behind, producing a halo or rim light effect.

The term is also used to refer to a situation where the background is so bright that it will produce a silhouette of the object, e.g., a person standing in front of a white wall. This can be compensated for by opening the aperture enough so that the light reflected from the object will register. This has the effect of overexposing, or washing out, the background. Many automatic cameras provide a backlight compensation control of one or two aperture stops.

BACK PROJECTION (REAR PROJECTION). Projection of a picture on to the back of a translucent screen. Back projection has several applications; in lecture theaters it enables all projection equipment to be positioned behind the screen, and as it gives a brighter image than projection using a reflecting screen, it permits higher levels of ambient light. Alternatively, lower levels of projection light output are acceptable.

In individualized learning devices, such as tape-slide machines, back projection allows the equipment to be self-contained, with a translucent screen on the front. The technique is also used to provide realistic background scenes for film or television although color separation overlay has largely replaced back projection for television when color studio equipment is used. *See* **Projection Screen.**

BACKUP. Term used for a reserve copy of a disk (or tape). Unlike a book or other hardcopy, a small accident (heat, liquid, bending) can destroy all the data on a disk, or at least make it virtually irrecoverable. Thus it is advisable to have a backup for everything of any importance.

BACKUP (HARD DISK). A means of saving a copy of data in case a hardware, program or user error erases the disk. Hard disks can be backed up to floppy disks, but the process is tedious and uses many disks. Better methods include using cassette tape, cartridge tape, or removable hard disks. *See* **Streamer; Streaming Cartridge.**

BACKWARD ANALYSIS. *See* **Critical Path Analysis.**

BACKWARD CHAINING. A concept advocated by Gilbert and closely associated with "mathetics." In chaining, the response to an initial stimulus is in its turn the stimulus to the next response. Gilbert suggested that the learner should complete the last step, in a chain, then the last two and so on until he can perform the whole chain. The technique has the advantage that the learner practices the complete chain once and partially as often as there are steps to the chain. Little empirical evidence exists as to the usefulness of this learning strategy in either motor skills or cognitive skills. Sometimes called "reverse accumulation." *See* **Mathetics.**

BACK WIND. On some cine cameras, the ability to wind the film backwards, so as to expose the same piece of film twice. Back wind may be used for dissolves or trick effects.

BADGE ENGINEERING. The situation in which a company, usually well-known, markets products which are actually manufactured by a different outfit. A well-known educational example was the Bell & Howell microcomputer—in fact, an Apple with a black case and a Bell & Howell badge.

BAND. A range of frequencies between specified limits. The classification adopted internationally is based on numbered bands, each extending from 0.3×10^n Hz to 3×10^n Hz, where n is the band number.

BANDWIDTH. The range of electrical frequencies over which a system or piece of equipment is capable of operating. Commonly used in describing the potential resolution of a television system. The wider the range of frequencies equipment is capable of operating over, the finer the detail it is able to record or transmit. Broadcast television usually operates on a bandwidth of about 5 MHz. With more basic educational equipment the bandwidth may be as little as 2 MHz.

With regard to video displays the bandwidth is the highest frequency signal that a monitor can accept. An ordinary television receiver has a bandwidth of 2–4 MHz, a computer monitor between 5 and 15 MHz, and a high-quality graphics display up to 100 MHz. The limited bandwidth of the receiver will not allow 80 sharp characters on a line. To produce 80 characters, a bandwidth of 5 MHz or more is required.

BANDWIDTH COMPRESSION. In television transmission, a technique enabling the bandwidth normally required for the transmission of a picture of given quality to be reduced by not transmitting redundant information. In a scene in which there is little movement, for example, it is possible to transmit only information relating to those parts of the scene that differ from the previous frame.

BAR CODE. A pattern of lines on grocery products, library books, etc., which uniquely specify the item according to predetermined criteria. Thus a book may be coded according to author, title, publisher, etc., in the same way as a grocery product may be coded according to size, contents, manufacturer, etc. The great benefit of the bar code is that its coded information can be read by a simple optical procedure, such as moving the bar code over a window or passing a pen-reader over the bar code.

BARREL DISTORTION. Distortion of an image whereby straight lines, parallel to the edge of the field, curve inward at their ends.

Pincushion distortion (q.v.) is a related aberration; in both cases the end result of a pronounced distortion is an inferior sharpness of the image.

BASIC. An acronym for Beginners' All-Purpose Symbolic Instruction Code. A very easily learned computer language, generally available on micro (i.e., personal) computers. As a computer language, BASIC suffers from a number of deficiencies: it is relatively unstructured and lacks the sort of text-handling capability which is generally needed for such applications as CAL.

BATCH PROCESSING. A mode of computer usage in which prepared programs and data are loaded into a queue and processed serially. The turnaround time, i.e., the time which elapses between the submission of a job to be placed in the queue and the time when the user gets his results back, is typically of the order of hours. From a computer resource point of view, batch processing is more efficient than time sharing.

BAUD RATE. A technical communications technology term which, strictly speaking, measures rate of change of "states." In practice, the speed at which devices communicate with each other is measured in bauds, and in most cases the baud rate will equal the number of bits per second. For example, a modem which can operate at 1,200 baud will be capable of accepting information at a rate of 1,200 bits per second, i.e., 150 bytes per second (= 150 characters per second): four times as rapidly as one which operates at 300 baud.

BAYONET MOUNT, SOCKET. A push-and-twist type of mounting for a camera lens, lamp, etc. Common in Europe, Australia, etc.

BBC. *See* **British Broadcasting Corporation.**

BBS. Bulletin board systems. Electronic meeting places often operated by individuals using their home computers.

BEADED SCREEN. A type of projection screen where the surface is covered with minute glass beads. Such screens give a very bright image over a relatively narrow angle, but the brightness falls off severely at wide viewing angles.

BEAT. The phenomenon in which two or more periodic quantities having slightly different frequencies combine to produce a resultant frequency having marked periodic variations in amplitude, i.e., beats.

BEHAVIORAL OBJECTIVE. When the terminal behavior required of the learner is stated in terms of observable and testable behaviors, the statement is termed a *behavioral objective*. Of all the characteristics of a systematic approach to educational technology, the writing and testing of behavioral objectives is regarded by some workers as paramount. It is interesting that such a basic position has raised such enormous controversy. Strong feelings both for and against are still evident. The two opposing positions appeared in the early 1960s after the work of Robert Mager. Apart from arguments for and against, there has been consideration of the appropriateness of objectives.

Mager identified three characteristics of a good behavioral objective:

Behavior: specify the behavior that will be accepted as evidence of achievement.

Conditions: specify the conditions under which the behavior must take place.

Standard: specify the conditions under which acceptable performance will be recognized.

Example:

Given an overhead projector, a transparency, and a set of pens, the trainee will be able to make a completed transparency of the given diagram within ten minutes.

Mager emphasized that not all three conditions were needed in every case. They should act simply as guidelines. Other guidelines include the inclusion of action verbs "to state, to put, to write, to list, etc." Ivor Davies has suggested a further and useful condition: "General objective plus action verb."

Example:

The purpose of this lesson is to help you understand Ohm's Law. You will be asked to define V, I, and R, to verify the relationship V = IR, and to identify applications in circuit testing.

Over the years a number of arguments have been advanced with regard to the use and value of behavioral objectives. These are the most commonly expressed:

For

They encourage educators to think and plan in detailed specific terms.

They provide a rational basis for evaluation.

They prescribe the choice of instructional means.

They can be made the basis for units in individualized instruction.

Against

Defining objectives before the event conflicts with discovery.

There are an extremely large number of paths through any body of knowledge, thus reducing the effectiveness of objectives in design.

Trivial objectives are easiest to operationalize.

Lists of behaviors do not reflect the structure of knowledge.

Both arguments for and against are strong; perhaps the fundamental benefit that writing objectives achieves is the clarification of "What am I trying to achieve?"

BELL 103. The AT&T full duplex 300 baud modem standard.

BELL 212A. The AT&T full duplex 1,200 baud modem standard.

BERNOULLI BOX. Mass storage system for microcomputers based on the use of magnetic tape in cartridge form. Advantages claimed over a conventional hard disk include interchangeability (the cartridges can be removed and replaced) and ruggedness (they cannot "crash").

BEST BOY. Senior assistant to the gaffer, i.e., the deputy lighting technician on a film set.

BETA. A videocassette format developed by the Sony Corporation. Beta is one of the two major 0.5 inch formats, VHS being the other. Technically there is little to choose between Beta and VHS, but they are of course quite incompatible.

BETA TESTING. The process of trying out commercial software on a selected group of users. Reports from these "guinea-pigs" are used to eliminate bugs and to improve the convenience and utility of the package.

BFI. *See* **British Film Institute.**

BIAS. A steady voltage used in electrical devices to alter responses. Usually used to describe the voltage applied to a recording head to make it operate near the center of the straight part of the characteristic curve.

BIDIRECTIONAL MICROPHONE. *See* **Microphone Characteristics.**

BIG CLOSE-UP (BCU). Shot taken with the camera nearer to the subject than would be necessary for a close-up; in relation to a human subject, a shot of part of the face only.

BILDSCHIRMTEXT. The West German videotex system.

BINARY. The representation of numbers in terms of powers of two, using the two digits 0 and 1, e.g., the decimal number 5 is 101 in binary ($1 \times 4 + 0 \times 2 + 1 \times 1$).

Binary arithmetic is commonly used in computers because the values of 0 and 1 can easily be represented in physical form, for example, as the presence or absence of current, positive or negative voltage, etc.

BINARY DIGIT. *See* **Bit; Information Theory.**

BINARY SEARCH. A method of searching a file or table by successively dividing the data base in half until you match the desired value or find that it is missing. Binary searches are most effective when the data base is arranged properly and is relatively uniform. Many data base systems use this method for locating items in their indexes.

BINAURAL RECORDING (BINAURAL REPRODUCTION). The terms *binaural* and *stereophonic* are often used synonymously, but strictly speaking, binaural applies to those sound systems with two separate channels from microphones to headphones. Indeed, such a system depends on the use of headphones to ensure that each channel is fed to one ear only.

BIT. An abbreviation for binary digit, i.e., one of the two numbers (0 or 1) used to encode information for a computer. Physically, a bit is represented by a high or low voltage. A good analogy is Morse code, where only two symbols are needed to represent the whole alphabet.

BIT-MAPPED SCREEN. A type of computer display, either cathode-ray tube (i.e., television) or liquid crystal, in which every pixel can be individually addressed. This permits software to generate any desired character or graphic symbol. In BASIC a pixel is brought into play by some such program line as

230 COLOR = 4 : PLOT 171, 83

which would place a point of no. 4 color on the screen on the 83rd line at the 171st position. *See* **High-Resolution Graphics; Pixel.**

BIT PATTERN. A computer term for a sequence of bits representing a specific value such as a character, number, instruction, etc. For example, A may be represented as 00001000; 17 as 00010001; GOTO as 01110010.

BIT PLANE ANIMATION. Procedure in which each sequential animation frame is stored or generated as a separate bit-mapped picture.

BLACK BOX. Electronic device whose internal mechanism is hidden from (or irrelevant to) the user. Also, a term widely used in curriculum evaluation and classroom research referring to a situation where only the inputs and the outputs are considered. The classroom has been described as a ''black box.'' *See* **Curriculum Design; Curriculum Theory; Interaction Analysis.**

BLACK BURST. A video signal containing synchronizing information, but no ''picture'' information. Displayed by a video monitor, a perfectly stable black screen results.

BLACK LEVEL. The level of a video signal corresponding to zero illumination in the scene being transmitted.

In practice it is useful to transmit a signal at black level to monitors on standby so the screen is black until the transmitted picture appears, thus avoiding unwanted visual stimuli.

BLANKING. The process whereby the beam in an image pickup tube is cut off during the retrace period, i.e., while the moving spot returns to the start of its scanning pattern.

BLEED. Where part of the printing area intentionally runs off one or more edges of the page, usually when it is required for an area of color to run right to the edge. Bleeds are generally accomplished after printing by trimming off part of the printed area. *See* **Graphic Design.**

BLIMP. When a cine camera is used in sound filming, it is necessary to put a soundproof cover over it to prevent the noise of the camera mechanism from being picked up by the microphone. A blimp is a soundproof camera box that allows full control of all the functions of the camera.

BLOCK. A group of consecutive words, characters, or bits which are handled as a single unit, particularly with respect to input-output operations.

BLOOM'S TAXONOMY. Benjamin Bloom identified three classes of instructional objectives, referred to as domains: the cognitive domain, the affective domain, and the psychomotor domain. Examples of cognitive objectives would be comprehension, analysis, etc.—the type of intellectual skills normally associated with formal learning. Affective objectives relate to values, emotions, etc.—matters concerned with social and emotional growth. Psychomotor objectives are those associated with motor activity, dexterity, and so on, such as handwriting, driving, swimming.

These three types of objectives will usually require differing methods of teaching and learning. For example, cognitive skills may be achieved through reading and attending lectures, tutorials, etc.; learning to perform well at a sport will involve extensive coaching and practice.

The three domains, with a very detailed analysis of the components of each area, are referred to as Bloom's Taxonomy of Educational Objectives.

BLUEPRINT. Originally, copies of drawings or plans produced by a ferroprussiate process that gives an image on a blue background. The term is now used for all large copies of plans or engineering drawings reproduced by various processes.

BOILERPLATE. Term used in word processing to indicate the construction of all or part of a document by cobbling together previously stored sections. For example, in the preparation of business reports, legal instruments, etc., where various phrases are frequently encountered from day to day.

BOOLEAN ALGEBRA. A mathematical system invented by George Boole (1815–1864) that uses algebraic notation to express logical relationships. The fundamental operation of the digital computer is based on the principles of Boolean algebra.

BOOM. A device for holding something out at a distance, especially a microphone which is dangled by a retractable fishing-rod type apparatus so as to be suspended over the participants.

BOOT. To start up a computer by loading a program into memory from an external storage medium such as a disk. Often accomplished by first loading a small program (the "boot program") whose purpose is to read the larger program into memory. The boot program is said to "pull itself up by its own bootstraps"; hence the term bootstrapping or booting.

BRAINSTORMING. A technique used to generate ideas. A teacher will permit students to originate ideas no matter how wild or seemingly unrelated to the topic under discussion. The technique can be particularly useful in problem-solving situations.

BRANCHING PROGRAM. A sequence in a teaching machine or programmed text which allows the learner to choose an answer and then routes him to the next frame according to the choice which he has made. *See* **Autotutor; Programmed Learning.**

BRANCHING TEACHING MACHINE. A machine which permits the use of branching programs. Such machines, typified by the Autotutor, operated by electromechanical means with the program back-projected from 35mm film. *See* **Programmed Learning; Teaching Machines.**

BRIGHTNESS. The luminous intensity of an object, i.e., photometric brightness. Brightness is also the luminous intensity experienced in visual perception. Important visual effects depend on the relative brightness of various colors; e.g., yellow is brighter than red.

BRIGHTNESS RANGE. The ratio of the lightest to the darkest parts of a scene or image. (More correctly, brightness ratio.)

BRITISH ASSOCIATION FOR COMMERCIAL AND INDUSTRIAL EDUCATION (BACIE). Founded in 1919, BACIE contributes to vocational training through its publications and information services.
16 Park Crest, London WIN 4AP, U.K.

BRITISH BROADCASTING CORPORATION (BBC). One of the two U.K. bodies that provide national schools broadcasts.
Broadcasting House, Portland Place, London W1A 1AA, U.K.
See **Educational Broadcasting; Independent Broadcasting Authority.**

BRITISH COMPUTER SOCIETY (BCS). Professional body for computer personnel. The BCS was founded in 1957.
29 Portland Place, London W1, U.K.

BRITISH COUNCIL. The Media Department comes within the Education and Science Division of the British Council. The division as a whole is concerned with all aspects of educational interchange with countries outside the United Kingdom. The Media Department is responsible for those aspects of this work related to the use of educational technology. The Department is in four units:

1. Consultancies and information

   (a) Provides British specialists for consultancy and training functions overseas.

   (b) Supplies information and advice on many aspects of educational technology in Britian to organizations and individuals overseas, mainly through the council's network of offices in eighty countries.

   (c) Maintains a Resource Center of information on educational media throughout the world.

(d) Publishes a quarterly journal, *Educational Broadcasting International*.

2. Training

(a) Runs courses for staff from educational media institutions overseas, mainly in the Third World. An emphasis is placed upon nonformal education. Courses exist in television production, radio production, scriptwriting, low cost media, utilization and evaluation, and management. Courses are normally three to four months long.

(b) Runs short courses overseas and arranges special short-term training programs for senior overseas staff, involving visits to appropriate institutions throughout the United Kingdom.

3. Production

(a) Produces a range of material on film, slide-tape, and videotape to support training activities in educational media. These may be informational: the SITE experiment, Caribbean Mathematics project, Teachers' Centers; or aids to training: radio training kits, films on English language teaching methods, ETV techniques.

4. Resources

(a) Manages the resources of Tavistock House where the Media Department resides. A broadcast-standard television and radio studio complex; film, graphics, reprographics, a CCTV studio; a range of lecture rooms and workshop areas.

(b) Coordinates the day-to-day scheduling of staff, resources, and activities within the department.

Richard Sherrington

Tavistock House South, Tavistock Square, London WC1, U.K. See **Center for Educational Development Overseas.**

BRITISH FILM INSTITUTE (BFI). An institute set up to administer the National Film Archives and the National Film Theater. The institute's Education Advisory Service provides courses and lectures on film and television. The BFI has two regular publications, *Sight and Sound* and *Monthly Film Bulletin,* and also produces educational pamphlets.

81 Dean Street, London W1, U.K.

BRITISH INDUSTRIAL AND SCIENTIFIC FILM ASSOCIATION (BISFA). An association of companies, organizations, and individuals, mostly in industry, that aims at improving the effective use of media in training.

15 New Bridge Street, Blackfriars, London EC4, U.K.

BRITISH JOURNAL OF EDUCATIONAL TECHNOLOGY. The official journal of the Council for Educational Technology (U.K.). It appears three times a year and contains articles and research papers devoted to all aspects of educational technology.

3 Devonshire Street, London W1, U.K.

BRITISH UNIVERSITIES FILM & VIDEO COUNCIL (BUFVC). The objects of the council are to coordinate and develop the use of film and other audiovisual materials in British institutions of higher education. BUFVC publishes *University Vision,* as well as regular newsletters and catalogs of audiovisual materials. An information service and a film library are also available.

55 Greek Street, London W1, U.K.

BROADBAND. Imprecise term implying operation over a band of frequencies regarded as wide in a given context.

BROADCASTING. *See* **Educational Broadcasting.**

BROADCASTING SATELLITE SERVICE MODE. Programs or other material—e.g., data—sent from a ground station via a satellite are received directly by one-way transmission from the satellite by use of many small "receive-only" earth stations located on the user's premises. *See* **Communication Satellites.**

BROMIDE PRINT. For a long time silver bromide was the main chemical used to produce image-sensitive surfaces on which a photograph could be printed. Bromide printing papers have been replaced for many purposes with resin coated (RC) printing papers, which require less time to process, wash, and dry.

BRUTE. A large spotlight of high power, usually an arc lamp.

BRYNMOR JONES REPORT (U.K.). A committee was set up in the United Kingdom in 1963 by the University Grants Committee (UGC) and other government bodies under the chairmanship of Brynmor Jones, vice-chancellor of the University of Hull, to study the use of audiovisual aids in higher scientific education. The exact terms of reference were "To survey the current use of audiovisual aids in teaching and research in the pure and applied sciences in institutions of higher education in Great Britain and, taking into account their use in similar fields in comparable institutions in selected countries overseas, to assess their potential usefulness and possible lines of development in Great Britain; and to report."

The report was published in 1965 and eventually had far-reaching effects on educational technology in Great Britain. Generally the committee was convinced that audiovisual aids could help to improve the quality of teaching and ease and enrich learning processes.

The main recommendations were that a national center should be established and that central service units should be set up in institutions of higher education. The government of the time was not prepared to provide the financial resources for the national center which the report recommended but the UGC, for its part, adopted the main recommendations, and in 1966 it set up its own subcommittee to implement the report and also decided to offer a strong financial stimulus to those universities which could provide evidence of initiative, and a willingness to assume responsibilities as pathfinders in a new and largely untried field. In all, the UGC encouraged the creation of eight high-activity centers with sufficient financial backing for a wide range of audiovisual media, with particular emphasis on television.

B SIGNAL. In stereo, the signal fed to the right-hand (viewed from in front) loudspeaker of a two-speaker system.

B-TREE. Short for balanced tree, a way of organizing the pointers to information in data bases that allows quick retrieval of any single specified record. So-called B+ or B* trees allow one to list records in sequential order as well.

BUBBLE MEMORY. A type of memory that stores data as patterns of magnetization on tiny crystalline chips. Bubble memories have no mechanical parts and are small and reliable, but are slower than conventional semiconductor memory. Bubble memory retains data even when the power is off.

BUFC. *See* **British Universities Film & Video Council.**

BUFFER STORE. (1) A computer store used to compensate for different speeds of a peripheral device and the central processor when information is being transmitted from one unit to the other. (2) Any device, e.g., a tape recorder, which acts as a temporary store between two pieces of equipment operating at different speeds.

BUFVC. *See* **British Universities Film & Video Council.**

BUG. Computer jargon for a defect in a program, generally one of a subtle nature. Thus debug—to eliminate bugs from a program. Reputedly the term originated when an early computer scientist found a malfunction to be caused by an insect insinuating itself between the contacts of a mechanical relay; she cured the problem by removing the offending item, i.e., "debugging" the computer.

BULK ERASER. A device for erasing an entire reel, cassette, cartridge, etc., of magnetic tape in one operation. It works by exposing the tape to high-frequency alternating current. Better-quality sound recordings can be made if, before using "reclaimed" tape, the reel is passed through a bulk eraser.

BULLETIN. Videotex system offered by ICL, using the Prestel protocol. Mainly used by closed user groups.

BULLETIN BOARD. A flat presentation surface for the display of notices, teaching materials, etc., which are affixed by tacks, pins, or adhesive. Also called a *notice board*.

BULLETIN TYPEWRITER. A device with larger than normal type size. It is ideal for overhead projection transparencies, hecto (spirit) masters, notice boards, etc.

BURN-IN. Image impregnated onto a television camera pickup tube, caused by a bright light, or by the camera being focused on a high-contrast image for too long a period of time.

BUS. (1) A circuit which provides a communication path between two or more devices, such as between a central processor, memory, and peripherals. (2) A computer network arrangement in which all connections branch out from one central line. All signals are available to each station.

BUSINESS GAMES. Academic games or simulations that relate to economics or business. Most business games depend on the use of a computer to rapidly provide and process large quantities of data, and generally operate on a very compressed time scale: a year's activity being compressed into a few days, for example.

BUZZ SESSION. A type of teaching strategy where the class is divided into very small groups which discuss among themselves an assigned problem.

BUZZWORD. A term used to describe jargon, but especially technical terms often used out of context and improperly. Examples: media, accountability, evaluation, etc.

BYTE. A group of eight bits used to encode a single letter, number, or other symbol. Computer memory is commonly expressed in kilobytes (= 1,024 bytes), thus a 64K (= 64 kilobytes) computer can store approximately 64,000 symbols in its random access memory. *See* **Memory (Computer).**

C

C. A computer language which can readily be incorporated into many microcomputers, because in a number of cases compilers exist for this purpose.

CABLE SIZES (VIDEO). *See* **Coaxial Cable.**

CABLE TELEVISION. A widely used method of disseminating television programs by wire directly into the home or institution. There are advantages both to the consumer and to the commercial exploitation of the medium. First, a large number of high-quality channels can be provided (with the introduction of fiber optics it becomes theoretically possible to transmit in excess of 1,000 channels per cable). These signals may originate as broadcast television and be received by high-quality antenna and amplification equipment by the cable company for onward transmission to customers. Alternatively, the company may originate its own channels, live or from tape or film. The customer no longer suffers from the vagaries of reception resulting from climatic conditions and overcrowded air waves.

Second, certain channels can be encoded and made available only by a rented decoder. This is known as "pay-TV," and such channels often offer first-run movies, prestigious live sporting and cultural coverage, etc. The future of cable television is to a large degree dependent on developments in satellite technology, and in particular on the ability of householders to receive satellite transmission via small and cheap earth stations. *See* **Television, Educational and Instructional.**

CACHE. An area of RAM to which parts of the information in a program are copied. Information that is likely to require frequent reading or alteration goes to the cache, where the system can access it more quickly. Caching can significantly speed processing of some programs, especially when using floppy disks for mass storage.

CAD-CAM. Computer-aided design/computer-aided manufacturing. The term covers systems that use computers to help in the design of electronic or mechanical products.

CADD. *See* **Computer-Aided Design and Drafting.**

CAMERA. The basic instrument for recording images. It is a device for making records of the images of objects formed when rays of light pass through a lens and fall onto a light-sensitive surface.

STILL CAMERA

These can be divided into three main groups: miniature, roll film, and large format. The miniature type can be further divided into those using 35 mm film and the so-called subminiature using 16mm (or similar 110 format) film. In education the 35mm camera using a reflex system of viewing and focusing is the most useful, particularly for the production of slides. A wide range of cameras of this type are available, and there is a vast array of accessories which enable them to be adapted for many special uses such as photomicrography, close-up work, copying, etc. Some roll film cameras also have reflex viewing and offer a wide range of accessories, but the increase in cost seldom justifies the use of these cameras for educational work. Large-format cameras are restricted to professional use, e.g., press, graphic arts, etc.

CINE CAMERA

Like still cameras, cine cameras can be divided into groups depending on the size of film they use. The three basic groups are 8mm, 16mm, and 35mm (or larger); the 35mm camera is seldom used for educational work other than in expensive commercial productions. Of the other two formats, the 16mm camera is recognized as being a basic educational tool and represents a truly international format, all 16mm equipment being compatible (a feature rarely found in audiovisual media). So far as 8mm is concerned, the super-8 format introduced in the 1960s proved to have many educational uses, but the advent of cheap and reliable color video systems has resulted in the demise of 8mm film. Especially beneficial with video is the cheapness and long playing time of tape, coupled with instant playback and full sound synchronization.

It seems likely to be only a matter of time before the

16mm format follows 8mm into oblivion, at least in education.

VIDEO CAMERA

Although the sensitive element in a television camera is the surface of an electronic tube (plumbicon or vidicon) rather than a frame of film, this does not affect the optical requirements. The sharpness of the picture will be very dependent on lens quality, and aperture and focusing will have to match the brightness and distance of the subject. However, it is usual for the correct aperture to be selected automatically, and almost always zoom lenses are used to allow moment-to-moment variation of focal length and thus magnification.

As touched on above, the real price of video cameras has steadily decreased over the years, and at the same time the quality and range of facilities have been greatly enhanced. The modern camera provides a really effective and valuable educational tool. *See* **Photography; Television, Educational and Instructional.**

CAMERA ANGLE. The position and direction of a camera relative to the subject it is viewing.

CAMERA CHAIN (OR CHANNEL). A television camera and associated electronic equipment necessary to deliver a complete picture signal. *See* **Television, Educational and Instructional.**

CAMERA CONTROL UNIT (CCU). The equipment in a camera chain which provides the television camera with operating signals and processes the signals from the camera prior to recording or mixing, etc.

CAMERA SPEED. Number of frames exposed per second in a film camera. Normal speed for silent films is 16 fps (i.e., frames per second) and for sound, 24 fps. Film made at higher camera speeds gives slow motion on projection while films made at low camera speeds result in accelerated motion. Extremely low-speed filming is known as time-lapse. Both high-speed and time-lapse filming are used for the analysis of events that are either too fast or too slow to study at normal camera speeds. *See* **Filming Speed.**

CAN. Film and television jargon for a reel of film or videotape. The term "in the can" is commonly used to describe a shot, film, or program that has been satisfactorily taken or completed.

CANADIAN BROADCASTING CORPORATION (CBC). CBC provides national broadcasting service (radio and television, French and English) within Canada as well as Canada's international multilingual shortwave and transcription service.
1500 Bronson Avenue, Ottawa, Ontario, Canada.

CANADIAN FILM INSTITUTE (CFI). The institute concerns itself with the use of both film and television.
75 Albert Street, Ottawa, Ontario, Canada.

CANADIAN LIBRARY ASSOCIATION (CLA). Promotes education, science, and culture within Canada through the library service.
151 Sparks Street, Ottawa, Ontario, Canada.

CANDELA. The standard international unit of luminous intensity. One candela is approximately equal to one candlepower on the old scale.

CAP. Cellular Array Processor. Powerful microprocessor with the potential to vastly increase the power of computers by utilizing VLSI and parallel processing.

CAPACITANCE DISK. A videodisc system in which a stylus touches the surface of the disk to read information encoded in the form of variations in capacitance embedded in the disk. Also known as *Capacitance Electronic Disk* (CED).

CAPSTAN. A device in a tape recorder or similar device for drawing the tape through the head systems at constant speed.

CAPTAIN. Character Pattern Telephone Access Information Network System. The Japanese videotex system, which uses a combination of photographic and mosaic approaches.

CAPTION. Graphic material prepared for television presentation, generally containing lettering. The standard dimension for a caption card is 12″ × 10″ (30.6cm × 25.4cm), the transmitted area being 11 1/4″ × 8 1/2″ (28.5cm × 21.6cm). *See* **Graphic Design.**

CAPTION GENERATOR. Former term for an electronic device for creating alphanumerical captions using a keyboard and feeding them directly into a video signal; this device avoids the need to produce separate artwork for each caption. Now usually known as a *video typewriter*.

CAPTION STAND. A device for holding captions in a convenient position for viewing by a television camera.

CARBON MICROPHONE. A microphone in which vibrations of a diaphragm cause carbon granules to be forced more or less strongly against each other, causing their electrical conductivity to vary. The microphone forms part of an electrical circuit. The carbon microphone is sensitive only to a limited range of middle frequencies and is often used in telephones. The frequency response is unsuitable for music.

CARD. Some microcomputers contain slots into which may be placed printed circuit boards called *cards* or *peripheral cards*. These devices can serve many purposes, including interfacing with printers, provision of extra memory, changes of screen format, provision of timing/clock facilities, and so on.

CARDIOID MICROPHONE. A microphone with a heart-shaped directional characteristic. Very little sound is picked up from behind the microphone, so it is considered to be unidirectional.

CARD PUNCH. (1) An output device on-line to a computer which punches patterns of holes into cards to store data, often for subsequent input to the same or another data-processing system. (2) A keyboard machine operated manually and used to prepare punched cards from source documents for input into a computer.

CARD READER. A machine which senses the data recorded as punched holes in cards and converts it into a form suitable for processing by a computer.

CAROUSEL. A generic term (borrowed from Kodak) for an automatic slide projector with a circular gravity-fed magazine, or for the magazines used with such projectors.

CARREL. A partitioned area or enclosure used for individual study especially in a library. The increased use of audiovisual equipment in libraries and other areas has called for the wider use of carrel systems to prevent sounds and pictures being studied by one student causing a distraction to others. Careful consideration needs be given to the design of carrels to provide sufficient privacy but still avoid making the student feel too isolated. *See* **Learning Environment; Resource-Based Learning.**

CARRIER WAVE. A high-frequency waveform used to carry a lower-frequency signal. *See* **Amplitude Modulation (AM); Frequency Modulation (FM).**

CARTOON FILM. *See* **Animated Film.**

CARTRIDGE. *See* **Cassette.**

CASE STUDY. (1) An illustrative study used in teaching. The study will contain all the relevant information about the subject(s) that the teacher will need to use. (2) A technique widely used in educational research because of its down-to-earth and attention-holding style. The assumption is that a case study forms a natural basis for generalization.

CASSETTE. A container for magnetic tape or film used to simplify the loading of a recorder, camera, or projector. Cassette, cartridge, and magazine all describe systems whereby a container is used to aid the loading of audiovisual devices of one kind or another. In tape recorders, however, the expressions cassette (or compact cassette) and cartridge have specific meanings; cassettes contain two spools within themselves, cartridges only one. Thus, in use, the tape from a cartridge is withdrawn completely into the recorder as play or recording proceeds; while with the cassette only a segment of the tape ever enters the machine.

CATALOG. Microcomputer term for a list of all files stored on a disk; also called a *directory*.

CATHODE-RAY TUBE (CRT). A television picture tube is an example of a CRT. The illumination on the face of the tube is produced by a beam of electrons striking the phosphor coating. In the case of color television three beams (red, green, blue) are in use. The electronic circuits of the receiver vary the strength and direction of the electron beam(s), thus producing the desired series of pictures.

CATTS. *See* **Computer-Assisted Teacher Training System.**

CATV. Community Antenna Television. An early name for cable television. *See* **Cable Television.**

CAV. *See* **Constant Angular Velocity.**

CBS. Columbia Broadcasting System, one of the major U.S. broadcasting organizations.

CCI. *See* **Comité Consultatif International.**

CCIR. International Consultative Committee for Radio. *See* **Standards in Audiovisual Technology.**

CCITT. International Telegraph and Telephone Consultative Committee. The body that formulates recommendations for standardization of such things as data transmission between computers.

CCTV. *See* **Closed-Circuit Television.**

CCU. *See* **Camera Control Unit.**

CD. *See* **Compact Disk.**

CD–I. Compact Disk—Interactive. Mode of usage of compact disks utilizing a rigidly defined set of standards for storage and retrieval of information in an interactive mode.

CD–PROM. *See* **WORM.**

CD–ROM. Compact Disk–Read Only Memory. A 5-inch laser disk which stores up to around 600MB of programs and data. CD–ROM readers are available for connecting to microcomputers in the same way as any other disk drive (although, of course, they cannot be written to), and are expected to become a common means of marketing such items as data-bases, encyclopedias, etc.

CdS METER. An exposure meter that uses a cadmium sulphide cell as a light-sensing agent. *See* **Exposure Meter.**

CED. *See* **Capacitance Disk.**

CEDAR. U.K. advisory service for computer-based education. CEDAR (Computers in Education As a Resource) was established in 1978 with the aim of encouraging and supporting the development of computer-based education (CBE) in Imperial College London. During the period 1973 to 1977 the U.K. government funded a major National Development Programme in Computer-Assisted Learning, and this produced a large quantity of CBE materials, much of it applicable to the work of the college. The initial intention was that CEDAR should work to introduce some of these existing materials into the college rather than develop new ones, thus achieving innovation at low cost.

It soon became clear that a necessary part of the support was the provision of information about CBE. In the course of gathering information from external sources, CEDAR came to be generally regarded as a repository of information, attracting a steady flow of inquiries from other institutions. Inevitably the number of these external requests, and the resources needed to service them, grew, and in 1979 the U.K. Council for Educational Technology provided funding for a full-time information officer. Subsequently, additional funding has been provided by other government organizations, and CEDAR became the central U.K. Information and Advisory Service on the use of computers in education and training.

CEDO. *See* **Center for Educational Development Overseas.**

CEEFAX. *See* **Teletext.**

CELLULOSE ACETATE (CELLULOID). *See* **Acetate.**

CENTER FOR EDUCATIONAL DEVELOPMENT OVERSEAS (CEDO) (U.K.). The Center for Educational Development Overseas comprises an amalgamation of three organizations: the Center for Educational Television Overseas (CETO); the Overseas Visual Aids Center (OVAC); and the Curriculum Renewal and Educational Development Organization (CREDO). CEDO brought these operations together under Ministry of Overseas Development auspices and financing. In 1974, CEDO was amalgamated with the British Council, which receives most of its finance from Ministry of Overseas Development sources. CEDO then ceased to exist, its work being absorbed into the general work of the British Council's Education and Science Division. The educational media functions of CEDO were united in the Division's Media Department.

CENTER FOR EDUCATIONAL RESEARCH AND INNOVATION (CERI) (Europe). An OECD-sponsored organization aimed at stimulating international cooperation in educational innovation and development.

OECD, 2 rue Andre-Pascal, 75016 Paris, France.

CENTER FOR EDUCATIONAL TELEVISION OVERSEAS. *See* **Center for Educational Development Overseas.**

CENTRAL COMMITTEE OF ADVISERS IN AUDIO-VISUAL EDUCATION (CCAAVE). A committee of the (U.K.) National Committee for Audio-Visual Aids in Education.

33 Queen Anne Street, London W1M 0AL, U.K.

CENTRAL PROCESSOR (CP). The "heart" of a computer. It coordinates and controls all on-line devices such as a printer, VDU, etc. All program instructions are held in the CP and all data to be operated on must be fed into it. The CP has three main sections; a memory, an arithmetic unit, and a control unit. Individual computers have CPs that operate in characteristically different ways.

CENTRAL SERVICE UNIT. The name given to an organizational unit providing audiovisual services available to everyone in an institution. When a television service is called a central service unit, it implies that it serves all departments that make up the college or university. There is considerable discussion as to whether central service units are preferable to a collection of autonomous or federal units in different departments. There are many advantages in centralizing services, among which would be economies of scale, unified policy, and coordination of scarce resources. Among the defects would be the remoteness of central service units from the user and their inability to identify with particular groups of users. The Brynmor Jones Committee suggested the setting up of centralized audiovisual units in higher education in the United Kingdom. *See* **Brynmor Jones Report; Tertiary Education.**

CENTRONICS CABLE. A 25–wire cable for connecting a computer to a printer with a Centronics-style wedge-shaped connector used by many printers for parallel operation.

CENTRONICS INTERFACE. A common form of parallel interface for connecting computer terminals to printers and other peripherals. *See* **Parallel Transmission.**

CERI. *See* **Center for Educational Research and Innovation.**

CET (U.K.). *See* **Council for Educational Technology.**

CHAIN. In psychology, a series of simple stages which go to make up a procedure, usually represented by a series of S-R bonds. The pedagogic technique of shaping behavior derives from the concept of chaining. *See* **Backward Chaining; Mathetics.**

CHAINING. *See* **Conversational Chaining.**

CHALKBOARD. Often called a blackboard, even when green. The chalkboard is still, and it looks as if it will remain, one of the teacher's most useful visual aids.

CHANGEOVER CUE. Small spot or other mark made in the top right-hand corner of several frames near the end of a reel of film to give the projectionist a signal for the changeover to the next reel.

CHANNEL. A band of frequencies allocated to a specific use, e.g., a signal television transmitter. Also used to describe the chain of equipment used in conjunction with a television camera to produce a complete television signal.

CHAPTER. A consecutive sequence of frames on a videodisc. The start of a chapter can be directly addressed. This is the only form of addressing available on a CLV disk, whereas a CAV disk can address any individual frame.

CHAPTER STOP. A code embedded in the vertical interval of a videodisc recording that enables videodisc players (usually level one) to locate the beginnings of chapters.

CHARACTER. A letter, digit, punctuation mark, or other written symbol used in transmitting or displaying information. *See* **ASCII.**

CHARACTER GENERATOR. An electronic device used in connection with television productions. Captions consisting of words, numbers, etc., can be produced at a typewriter keyboard and then either directly superimposed onto the screen or stored on magnetic disk for later use. The term *Video Typewriter* is now more generally used, reflecting the greater range of facilities available.

CHARACTERISTIC CURVE. In photography, the graphical representation of the relationship between the exposure to light and the corresponding density produced in photographic emulsions.

CHARACTER RECOGNITION. A computer term that refers to the ability of some computer hardware to recognize patterns. Two main systems operate, OCR (Optical Character Recognition) and MICR (Magnetic Ink Character Recognition).

CHARACTER SET. All the characters available within a system, e.g., the characters on a particular daisy wheel (printer) or available for use on a visual display unit or word processor.

CHECK BIT. *See* **Check Digit.**

CHECK DIGIT. A redundant digit used in an error-detecting procedure such as a parity check. For example, the last digit in a long reference code might be the least significant digit in the sum of all the other digits. Thus, in 200978354278113189 the sum of the actual numbers $(2+0+0+ \ldots +1+8)$ is 69, so 9 is added as a check digit. If an error is introduced during processing, then nine times out of ten the check digit will reveal that an error exists.

CHECKERBOARD CUTTING. The process of preparing a film for A and B roll printing. When roll A carries a scene, roll B carries black film and vice versa. Film edited in this way allows optical effects to be added at the printing stage, and all splices are invisible in the print.

CHECKLIST. A series or list of behaviors that an observer marks off during a period of observation. The observer makes a mark against an item each time it occurs. *See* **Classroom Observation.**

CHILDREN'S TELEVISION WORKSHOP (CTW). Founded in 1968 to produce television for preschool children. The idea of CTW came from Joan Ganz Cooney, a documentary film producer, later to become CTW's president. The first major program was "Sesame Street" in 1969. Subsequent programs include "The Electric Company." Both these programs are very dependent on visual effects to make their points. CTW has a staff of several hundred with eight regional offices in various parts of the United States.

CHIP. A tiny piece of a semiconductor, usually silicon, comprising a complete integrated electrical circuit.

CHROMA. That quality of color which embraces both hue and saturation. White, black, and gray have no chroma.

CHROMA-KEY. The electronic superimposition of part of one picture (e.g., a newsreader) onto another (e.g., film of the current story). The technique is accomplished by separation of saturated colors; i.e., the newsreader can be separated from his background and then inserted into the second picture. *See* **Color Separation Overlay.**

CHROMINANCE. The color information present in an encoded video signal.

CHROMINANCE SIGNAL. That portion of the color television signal which contains the color information.

CIJE. *See* **Current Index to Journals in Education.**

CINEMASCOPE. Trade name of a widely used method of wide-screen presentation. An anamorphic lens is used to obtain the effect, i.e., the squeezing of the image onto standard 35mm film and the subsequent expansion in the projector to achieve the CinemaScope picture which has a width-height ratio of 11:4.

CLAPPER BOARD. A "take" board with a hinged flap that is banged down to make a synchronizing "mark" on both film and sound track. Clapper boards have been largely superseded by electronic devices built into modern cameras and sound recording equipment.

CLASSIFICATION OF MEDIA. *See* **Media Classification.**

CLASSROOM OBSERVATION. Several methods are in use for the systematic observation and recording of activities in the classroom. Most rely to a large degree on the presence of a trained observer who codifies behavior and incidents according to the requirements of the method being used; however, the use of recording devices, particularly television, can provide valuable insights.

This kind of research procedure usually assumes that the presence of the observer and/or the camera has little or no effect on class behavior. The validity of this supposition clearly is fundamental to the usefulness of any subsequent analysis.

CLICK. To press and release the button on a mouse. To click on a selection, you position the mouse-controlled pointer (cursor) on the item and then push the mouse button.

CLIP. A name used to describe a short excerpt of film or videotape. Many argue that when teachers are using television in the classroom, they should punctuate their remarks with short clips of visual or audiovisual material instead of presenting long extracts or complete television programs. The audiovisual clip accentuates or highlights remarks made by the teacher but does not replace him or her.

CLIPBOARD. A temporary memory-storage area where sections of work can be saved for later transfer within files or between documents. A clipboard holds only one item at a time.

CLIP-ON MICROPHONE. A small microphone which can be clipped onto the clothing of a speaker (e.g., onto a tie or lapel) so that it is positioned close to the speaker's mouth. Also known as a *lapel microphone* or *tie microphone*.

CLOSED CAPTIONING. A technique for superimposing subtitles on the bottom of a television picture for the benefit of hearing-impaired viewers. The captions are "closed" because they can only be seen if a special decoder is in use. "Open" captions, visible to all, are not generally acceptable to the average viewer.

CLOSED-CIRCUIT TELEVISION. Term sometimes used for systems where the signal source, camera or video recorder, is physically connected by wire (or rarely by microwave link) to the ultimate receiver(s). This is the usual educational situation.

CLOSED USER GROUPS. Videotex term. Certain nominated frames of information can only be accessed by certain users nominated by the information owner/provider; thus comprising a closed user group.

CLOSE-UP. A shot taken at what appears to be close range as opposed to a medium shot or long shot. In film and television a close-up may be a shot of a face or part of a face. In still photography close-up refers to any picture taken at close range.

Such pictures may require the camera to be too close to the subject to be focused by the normal mechanism built into the lens mount, in which case there are two methods of enabling the image to be brought to focus. These are close-up (supplementary) lenses and extension tubes. Supplementary lenses are particularly applicable to simpler cameras where the lens cannot be removed. They are simple positive lenses that, when placed in front of the camera lens, have the effect of changing the focal length and thus allowing the lens to focus at close range. Extension tubes are attached between the lens and the camera body, increasing the lens-film distance, thereby bringing into focus subjects closer to the lens than normal. *See* **Macrophotography.**

CLOZE TECHNIQUE. A research procedure whereby the difficulty of reading matter is measured by randomly excising words and then determining the success of readers in guessing the missing words. Alternatively, the reading ability of students can be measured by comparing their ability to fill in such gaps with standardized results from skilled readers.

CLUSTER. Term used by MS-DOS (PC-DOS). Disks are divided up into sectors, and data is allocated to sectors for storage. A cluster is the minimum number of sectors which a file can use, and furthermore every file takes up space in whole clusters. Because clusters cannot be split between more than one file, the effective capacity of disks is reduced. This is very noticeable in the case of hard disks where the cluster size may be quite large.

CLV. *See* **Constant Linear Velocity.**

CMOS. Complementary Metal Oxide Semiconductor. CMOS random access memory requires only a minimum of power to remain activated; such RAM is frequently used in portable microcomputers, enabling them to retain data and programs in memory even though the main power switch (and thus the display) is turned off.

C MOUNT. A type of lens fitting commonly used on 16mm cameras and some television cameras.

COAXIAL CABLE. The usual type of cable for video and television applications. The two conductors consist of a central copper wire and an exterior copper braid; separating the conductors is a "dielectric" layer which insulates the conductors from each other. The combination of dimensions and the nature of the dielectric determines the impedance of the cable which for television and video is always 75 ohms. Coaxial cable is particularly good at not picking up extraneous signals, e.g., from nearby electrical sources such as fluorescent lamps.

COBOL. Acronym for the computer language Common Business Oriented Language. Its use is mainly for nonscientific programming or sorting large amounts of data into categories.

CODASYL. An acronym for Conference on Data Systems and Languages, a U.S. government–sponsored industry committee. CODASYL developed standards that led to the COBOL language and many of the more complex types of data bases.

CODE. A system of characters and rules for representing information in language capable of being understood and used by a computer. Code can be in the form of alphanumeric characters or binary data that can be directly executed by a computer.

COGNITIVE OBJECTIVES. *See* **Bloom's Taxonomy.**

COLD START. The process of starting up a microcomputer when the power is first turned on (or as if the power had just been turned on) by loading an operating system into main memory, then loading and running a program. *See* **Warm Start.**

COLLATOR. A machine which sorts or orders sheets or cards into a series of boxes. A collator may be used to put together pages of books in their running order.

COLOPHON. The details of author, title, publisher, date of publication, etc., given at the beginning or end of a document.

COLOR BALANCE. The appearance of an image (e.g., on a television screen) considered in terms of the proportions of its three primary color components.

COLOR BURST. A synchronizing signal used to stabilize the perception and decoding of the chrominance information in a video signal. The burst consists of a few cycles of subcarrier frequency.

COLOR CAST. Color cast or color "shift" in color photography can have many causes, but by far the most common is using film designed to be used in one kind of light under lighting conditions of another color temperature range. For example, using daylight film indoors with incandescent or fluorescent lights. Some color shifts are done deliberately for specific effects. *See* **Artificial Light.**

COLOR ENCODER. A device which produces an NTSC or PAL color signal from separate R, G, and B video inputs.

COLOR SATURATION. The degree to which a color is free of diluting white light.

COLOR SEPARATION OVERLAY. The most common use of the term is in television production where it is often called "chroma-key." Using the appropriate equipment, one camera is focused on a subject in front of a saturated blue background (red or green can be used, but blue is preferred since no saturated blue occurs in human flesh tones). When the system is activated, space is cut into a base picture from a second camera, and the image from the first camera is electronically inserted into that space whose outlines are the borders of the object with none of the blue background. Careful attention to lighting is required. The presence of blue in the base image will also cause problems. The effect is most often used to insert the picture of a person into a background scene.

COLOR TEMPERATURE. Measurement of the color quality of a light source. To avoid color distortion, in color photography and color television, the color temperature of all the lighting must be matched. It must also be matched to the specific requirements of the film or television system. Variations in the color temperature of lamps will result from fluctuations in the voltage supplying them. Some variation will also occur due to the aging of lamps. *See* **Color Cast.**

Figure 2
Triangle Representing the Range of Colors Obtainable from an Addition of Three Primary Colors

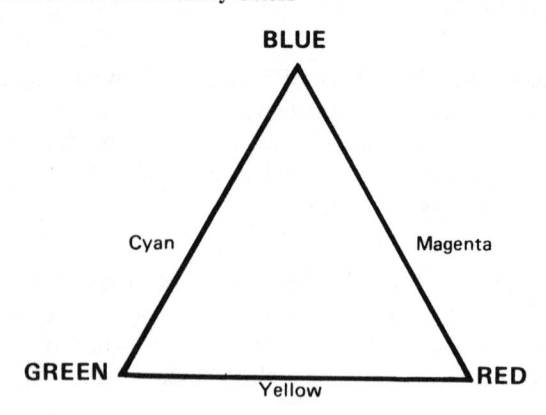

COLOR TRIANGLE. The three primary colors, red, green, and blue, can be mixed together to yield any required hue. In particular, the secondary colors magenta, yellow, and cyan (peacock blue) are obtained by combinations of two primary colors, as demonstrated by Figure 2.

COM. *See* **Computer Output Microfilm.**

COMB BINDING. Method of binding documents that involves using a machine to punch a line of rectangular holes along the left-hand edge of each sheet and then fastening the sheets together using a cylindrical "comb" whose teeth pass through the holes.

COMITÉ CONSULTATIF INTERNATIONAL (CCI). An international body which studies problems of communication and standards. Its work is divided into three sections—telegraphy (CCIT), radio and communication (CCIR), and telephony (CCIF). *See* **Standards in Audiovisual Technology.**

COMMAND. Communication from the user to a computer system (usually typed from the keyboard) directing it to perform some immediate action, i.e., not as part of a program.

COMMISSION ON INSTRUCTIONAL TECHNOLOGY (CIT). A report commissioned in April 1968 to "recommend to the President and the Congress specific actions to provide for the most effective possible application of technology to American Education." The nine-member commission, under the chairmanship of S. M. McMuirin, reported in 1970.

COMMON CARRIER. A medium that is legally required to deliver messages for a fee. Access to the service must be nondiscriminatory and at posted rates. Examples include the U.S. mails, telephone systems, telegraph, etc.

COMMUNICATING WORD PROCESSOR. *See* **Teletex.**

COMMUNICATION ENGINEERING. Communication is necessary for the existence of societies and for mankind's accumulation of knowledge and capability. A feature of great nations in history has been the provision of communication facilities, usually for the use of government, military, and a privileged few. Nowadays powerful communication facilities are available to most people. In many countries the communication authorities are the biggest employers; this fact is partly a response to, and partly a cause of, our dependence on the efficient coordination of resources.

Apart from coordination, communication services provide society with access to vast entertainment and education resources. The way we live and the places we live have been and are being changed by communication facilities. Physical travel to work in choked cities may be replaced by working, studying, and relaxing in outlying centers, or even at home, and accessing data banks, computers, and colleagues by communication facilities.

Communication engineering includes electrical technologies for conveying information from one person or place to another, recording or storing and recovering it, and ensuring its integrity or security.

Other technologies may be involved, such as acoustic, optical, mechanical, and photographic; calligraphy, mail, transportation, and libraries are not normally considered within the scope of communication engineering.

Common examples are radio, telephony, television, telegraphy, data (including computer) communication, tape recording; closely related technologies include remote sensing (including radar and sonar) radio navigation, telemetering (measurement at a distance), telecontrol (control at a distance), object identification, and voice control of machines.

This entry classifies aspects of communication engineering to bring out common, fundamental features, rather than details of specific systems.

COMMUNICATION THEORY

Communication theory (Gabor, 1946; Shannon, 1948) deals with the conversion of the information or messages to be transmitted into a form suitable for the bearer and its reconversion for the receiving terminal interface.

The communication engineer includes in the design such requirements as accuracy (fidelity, noise, error rate) and information rate (bandwidth, resolution, data rate, speed of response, delay) requirements for the messages or information to be transmitted, in conjunction with limiting properties of the bearer or medium (such as interference, noise, fading, distortion, speed of response, bandwidth, delay). In principle, it is possible by the use of suitable encoding or modulation to provide accurate, low-speed performance from inaccurate (noisy, fading, etc.) bearers of sufficient speed. Information theory is a subclass of communication theory which deals with the fundamental limits of what is possible.

Messages, Signals, and Information. These concepts are well illustrated by an example. Mr. Jones set up a shop to sell fresh fruit, and wished to advertise the fact. Thus he set about disseminating the *message* "Jones sells fresh fruit." He did this by painting the words "Jones sells fresh fruit" on the front of his shop, and also by having the message broadcast as a radio commercial and printed in the newspaper.

The corresponding *signals* had quite different forms:

(a) The shop-front notice (colored paint) caused the message to be transmitted as a signal in the form of a pattern of light waves.

(b) In the radio advertisement the announcer's voice was conveyed to the microphone by sound waves. They were changed into electrical waves of a different shape and transmitted as radio waves, which in turn were converted back to sound waves by the radio receiver.

(c) In the newspaper communication the message was transmitted for most of the way as a mechanical signal comprising a pattern of ink and paper.

These and some other examples of *signals* representing the same message are shown in Figure 3.

Thus a given message may be encoded into many different forms, usually chosen to suit the characteristics of the medium. However, whether or not the transmission of a given message conveys *information* is another matter.

The first time Mrs. Brown saw the notice (received the light wave signal) and perceived the message, she thought "That's news. Jones used to sell pianos! Now I can shop conveniently." After receiving the same message many times via the various signals, Mrs. Brown did not take much more notice; it was not informative then. The information associated with a message is related to its surprise value, i.e., its unlikeliness. If Jones had changed the message to "Jones sells baboons," even more notice would have been taken; this message occurs very infrequently and has more novelty value. Other factors, such as its meaning, may contribute to our ideas about the information gained from a particular message,

Figure 3
Signals Corresponding to the Message "Jones Sells Fresh Fruit"

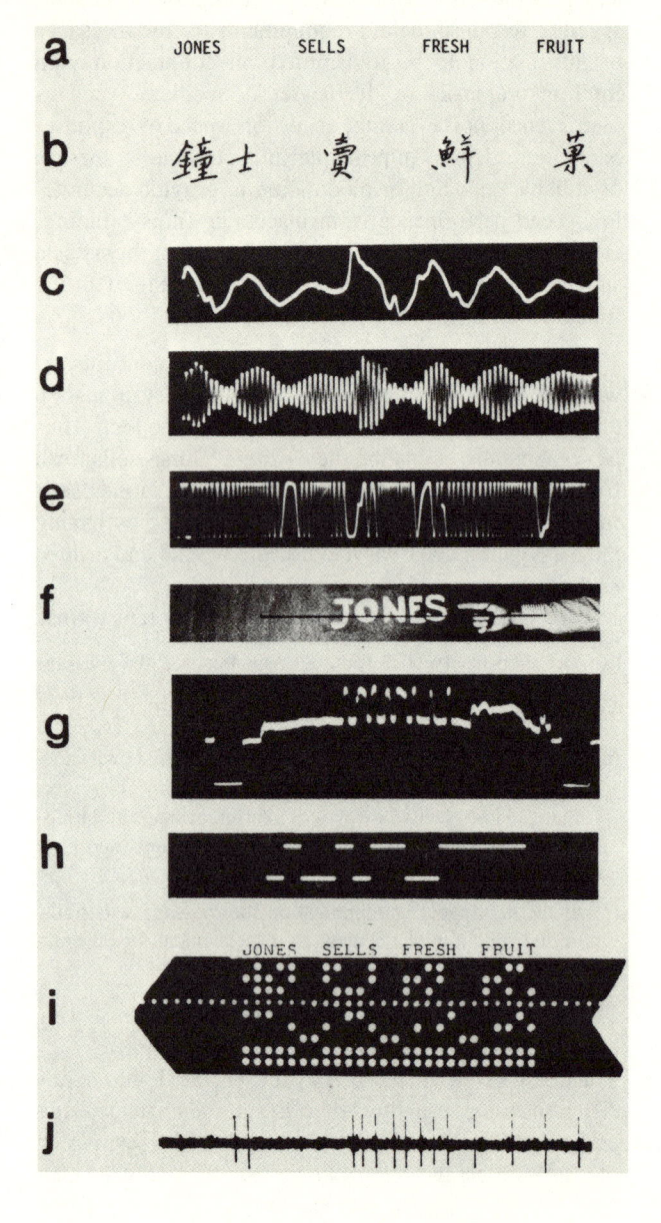

Signals corresponding to the message "Jones sells fresh fruit." (a) Coded for English visual input. (b) Coded for Chinese visual input. (c) Sound pressure waveform corresponding to about 1/50 of the vowel "o" in "Jones." (d) Electrical signal in an amplitude modulated radio transmitter, corresponding to (c). (e) Electrical signal in a frequency modulated radio transmitter, corresponding approximately to (c). The frequency variation is exaggerated. (f) Chalk on blackboard, object for (g). (g) Video (electrical) waveform in a television camera corresponding to the brightness of a line as shown on (f). (h) Teletypewriter electrical waveform corresponding to (f) (including start and stop pulses and a pause). The shortest pulse is of duration 10msec. (i) Punched paper tape as used for storage of Teletypewriter messages. (j) Pulses in a nerve fiber, similar to those used in controlling tongue movement in speaking.

but unlikeliness or surprise value is the most fruitful for studying communication systems. Thus we have a distinction between messages, signals, and information.

Communications engineers are very largely concerned with design and processing of signals required to represent given messages, and information theory (Shannon, 1949) describes fundamental principles concerning the coding of messages to achieve efficient and reliable communication.

Classes of Messages and Their Criteria. Criteria in general will include aspects of economy, reliability, freedom from causing disturbance, and protection from external interference (Cherry, 1957; Freeman, 1981). Extreme examples of reliability requirements are found in automatic guidance systems for aircraft and trains, while broadcast radio receivers are examples of extremely economical communication apparatus. It is desirable that data transmission for credit transactions should be very free of errors through interference, while entertainment television and radio are enjoyable even though frequently subject to interfering effects. Specific information on some criteria in human perception will be found in the section on terminal interfaces and humans. Some examples of classes of messages are the following:

audio: mono and stereo speech, music, and synthetic versions of these, and some audible navigation signals. Criteria may include intelligibility, naturalness, freedom from distortion, dynamic amplitude range, channel separation, privacy, noise immunity;

video: television and related information for direct use by viewing on cathode-ray screens. Criteria include spatial and temporal resolution, faithfulness of tone or contrast and hue, freedom from interference or systematic distortions;

data: patterns representing numbers or symbols, e.g., for remote operation of computers, interrogation of data banks, control of printing machines, automatic credit transactions. Often, other types of messages may be encoded as data. Key criteria in transmission of data are error rate, data rate (e.g., number of characters per second), and delay;

measurement and control: signals representing, e.g., engine temperature, blood pressure, wind velocity, altitude, material stress, luminous intensity, seismic vibrations, time signals. Usually in measurement systems, accuracy, including freedom from perturbations, and speed of response are important criteria;

navigation and guidance: e.g., radio direction finding, distance measurement, position fixing, depth sounding, radar. Criteria are similar to those of measurement communication systems.

Information. The idea of unlikeliness of a message is described precisely by its probability of occurrence, or relative frequency of occurrence. If there were only four messages, a, b, c, d, which could be chosen by a sender and each was chosen with equal probability (i.e., occurred on average an equal number of occasions, in a long time), then the information associated with each choice would be dependent on the number N of possibilities, i.e., four. If the choice is repeated, i.e., a new message is sent on a later occasion, the total number of possibilities is $N \times N = 16$, all equally likely. It is convenient, for computation, to have an information measure that is additive, i.e., the information associated with subsequent choices and transmission adds to that of earlier ones, and the logarithm of N provides this. We say that $I = \log N$ units of information for one choice; $2 \log N$ for two choices, etc. The units depend on the base of the logarithm. Because binary choices are convenient intellectually, and for use with electronic circuits, it is usual to make the base 2, and the units are then called bits (binary digits), i.e.,

$$I = \log_2 N.$$

For example, choice from two equally likely messages yields one bit of information; M choices yield M bits of information. The telegraph signal shown in figure 3(h) could thus convey 15 bits in the interval shown.

If all messages are not of equal probability, the average information associated with a choice is

$$I = \sum_i (-p_i \log_2 p_i)$$

where p_i is the probability that the chosen message is the i'th message; for the case of N equiprobable messages, the value of p_i is $1/N$ for each, i.e., $\log_2 N = -\log_2 1/N = -\log_2 p_i$. The p_i multiplying the logarithm arises from the averaging over all messages. Because of the similarity in reasoning and the formulas appearing in thermodynamics, the information I as defined above is often called "entropy."

An example is the choice of the 27 letters of the English alphabet (including a blank) as messages. If they were equiprobable, the information associated with each would be $\log_2 27 = 4.75$ bits per letter. Taking into account their different frequencies of occurrence, the value obtained from $I = \Sigma (-p_i \log_2 p_i)$ is about 4.1 bits per letter. This shows that prior knowledge reduces the information associated with a choice. Also, we know that choice of a letter in English is not independent of preceding letters. This dependence imposes a set of conditional probabilities on each choice, as a function of the preceding letters. Shannon has shown that the resultant information per letter in normal English is about 1 bit per letter. It may be higher of course in specially prepared texts, e.g., telegrams.

The difference between the possible information per message $\log_2 N$ and that realized after the actual probabilities are taken into account is called "redundancy."

Figure 4
Periodic Nature of a Speech Signal, Extracted from "o" in "Jones"

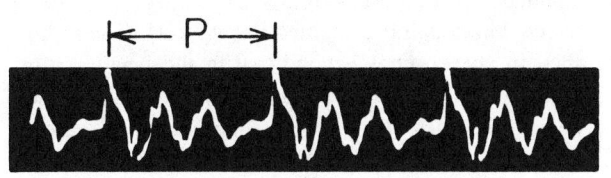

In some cases redundancy in a message source may imply a waste of potential communication. For example, the speech waveform of Figure 4 has a repetitive pattern, and the video waveform (Figure 3[g]) has many constant sections which could contribute much more detail. Likewise, a television picture has correlations between the elements in position and in time so that potential communication capacity is not used.

Much ingenuity has been used to find methods of source encoding to reduce the redundancy presented by a message source.

There is also extraneous information in many messages, i.e., detail which is not redundant but which is irrelevant to the receiver. Source encoding also studies this problem. Examples of source encoding are

(a) A speech waveform such as that in Figure 4 may be encoded by giving full data about one of the periodic sections, plus information about the number of repetitions. More sophisticated coding schemes use more properties of the human voice.

(b) Speech may be encoded by analyzing it to find (about twelve) parameters to resonances and so forth of the human vocal tract, which vary slowly with time as we speak. These are transmitted and used to control a speech synthesizer, i.e., a model which simulates the original speaker's voice mechanism.

(c) In Morse code the more frequently used symbols are encoded as short codes, while less frequently used symbols have longer codes. For example, "e" is encoded as "." while "g" is encoded as "---..". There are now formal procedures for encoding messages or symbols of differing probabilities to obtain optimal efficiency, e.g., the Huffman code.

(d) Television pictures and other pictorial or graphic messages typically include areas in which there is great uniformity or predictability from point to point or from time to time. Because of the great and hence expensive channel capacities required for these messages, many schemes have been proposed for transmitting only data about significant changes, and for taking advantage of the limitations of human visual perception; e.g., fine detail takes longer to notice than large areas, and also errors of shading are not easily seen near the edges of regions of high contrast. A few lines in a cartoon may be just as valuable to a viewer as a complex photographic view.

On the other haxd, redutdancy may be vabuable in 4rotecting a meddage from enrors ib trabsndssion. The redundancy in English permitted the last sentence to be corrected although it contained many errors. The redundancy in speech goes beyond that in the language; redundancy in the acoustical signal (Figure 4) is imposed by the mechanics of the speech mechanism, and is valuable in letting us perceive speech correctly even in the presence of music or loud noise or other irrelevant speech.

Communication engineers often design signals with redundancy to protect them in transmission. Simple examples are

(a) the use of writing as well as numerals on a check to convey the amount to be paid;

(b) the use in a Teletype code (Figure 3[h] and [i]) of "parity" check bits. Only 7 pulse positions or hole positions are needed to specify each character (from up to 128 possibilities), but 8 are used. The extra one may be chosen so that the total number of "ones," i.e., pulses or holes, is even. If an odd number is received, it is known that an error has occurred. Much more complex systems of check bits are used to permit detection and correction of multiple errors. This area of study is called algebraic coding theory.

(c) frequency modulation (FM), commonly used for high-quality broadcasting, uses a signal (Figure 3[e]) in which the frequency and not the amplitude is used for conveying information about the messages. This constraint imposes a pattern of redundancy which indirectly contributes to the low-noise properties of FM. It allows the receiver partially to ignore amplitude variations imposed by interference (e.g., lightning, motor ignitions, electric motors, and thermal agitation of electrons).

Shannon (1948) has shown that provided the channel capacity is at least equal to the information rate of the message source, then error-free transmission is possible, in principle. Achievement of true error-free transmission would require virtually infinite processing time; nevertheless, the existence of the possibility and the description of the required capacity have been immensely stimulating in communication research. Shannon's channel capacity formula is stated as,

$$C = B \log_2 (1 + P_s/P_n)$$

where

C   is the channel capacity in bits per second

B   is the bandwidth in hertz (cycles per second) (see the later sections on signals and noise, and on Medium or Bearer)

P_s is the average power of the signal, in watts, as received

P_n is the average power of disturbing noise at the receiver (it is assumed to have a Gaussian or normal probability density and uniform spectrum)

Derivation and application of this formula are not simple, but it is worth noting that the ratio P_s/P_n gives an indication of the reliability of any single observation of the received signal waveform, and B relates to the number of independent observations available per second.

Table 1 gives typical values of the channel capacity for various bearers. It is interesting to compare these with the channel capacity of human sensory inputs, somewhat less than 50 bits per second (Miller, 1967).

Signals and Noise. Although usually of little interest to the user, signals are what represent his messages inside a communication system, and their properties and design are crucial to its success. In almost all cases a signal in a communication system takes the form of a variation of a quantity with time. For example, the air pressure at the lips of a talker might vary with time as in Figure 3(c). Some other signals are shown in the same figure. These are "time waveforms" and key aspects are the time resolution, i.e., fineness of detail or the shortest element required to specify them, which implies the number of samples (Figure 5[b]) per second required to specify them without significant error. Of course, other aspects such as their statistical descriptions, maximum values, and measures of variation (power) are important in some cases. The speech signal requires some 10,000 samples per second for fairly good quality, the television signal about 10,000,000 per second, and the Teletype signal 50 per second.

Another description of a signal is its frequency spectrum (Figure 6). In this a signal s(t) is considered to be made up or analyzable into the sum of a number of sinusoidal components, i.e., a Fourier series, thus:

$$s(t) = \Sigma_n C_n \sin(2\pi nFt + \phi_n)$$

where

C_n is the magnitude of a component waveform

ϕ_n is the "phase," i.e., a timing parameter of that component

t   is time

F   is a constant (the frequency in hertz or cycles per sec of the lowest frequency component)

n   is a multiplier, yielding nF as the frequency of the general component

Signals described by such a Fourier series are periodic (repeated regularly). The period P is equal to 1/F, i.e., lowest frequency component has one cycle in each period.

Some examples of simple repetitive signals, their components, and spectra are shown in Figure 6. Signals that are not repetitive can be treated as having infinite periods, and hence zero F; i.e., the components are indefinitely

Table 1
Channel Requirements of Some Typical Signals

	Waveform Bandwidth	PCM data rate, bit/sec	Typical compressed form, bit/sec
Speech	3.1 kHz	64,000	10,000
Broadcast audio	15 kHz	—	—
Color TV	6 MHz	50,000,000	10,000,000
Teletypewriter	—	110	—
Facsimile	2 kHz	—	—
Human perception	—	50 max	—

close together and their spectra are thus continuous rather than having discrete lines.

Signals which have fast rates of change or are of short duration tend to have broad spectra; i.e., they need components of high frequency to describe them accurately. In Figure 6(c) and (d) measures of duration ΔT and bandwidth ΔF are shown. Gabor (1946) showed that with a reasonable definition of ΔT and ΔF the product $\Delta T \cdot \Delta F$ cannot be less than about 1/2. This is consistent with the fact that signals with rapid variations in time require large bandwidths.

Often many signals representing different messages are transmitted on the same bearer and separated at the receiving end. Usually such signals are designed so that they may be separated by selecting appropriate time intervals (time division multiplexing) or by selecting by filters parts of the frequency domain (frequency division multiplexing). These principles are illustrated in Figure 7. By either of these multiplexing techniques many hundreds or thousands of telephone channels may be provided on one cable or radio beam or guided light beam (up to many million in this). The most familiar example of a frequency multiplex application is in radio and television broadcasting, where the same bearer carries radio waves from many stations to the same receiver at different frequencies. There the desired station is selected by use of a filtering circuit. *Modulation* is the term used for the conversion of signals to the form needed for transmission.

We have noticed the emphasis on separability of signal waveforms. As efforts are made to increase the quality of information transmitted by a bearer, the pulses such as in Figure 5(k) or the spectra in Figure 7(l) become closer together, and the receiving system has to be very selective to avoid crosstalk, i.e., signals from one channel influencing the output of the receiver selecting the other. Co-channel interference due to inadequate frequency selectivity will be familiar to anyone who has tuned a sensitive radio receiver at night. A similar co-channel interference could be observed if there were an error in the synchronization or timing of the switch which does the selecting of the pulses from the composite signal of Figure 5(k).

However, there is another source of interference between channels in systems that rely on time separation. This is dispersion or smearing of the pulses (Figure 8) and may even include echoes of each pulse delayed by several pulse positions. Sources are nonuniformity in cables, reflections from joints, secondary paths (in a radio system), and electrical properties of a cable such as different characteristics at different frequencies. Usually a cable or wire has increasing attenuation with increase of frequency (Figure 9). Clearly such intersymbol interference from previous pulses can reduce the reliability of detection of a pulse at a given time. Electrical circuits called equalizers are often used to compensate for such effects before pulse detection. Such equalizers are often made to adapt automatically for different transmission characteristics.

Figure 8(d) shows a received pulse signal perturbed by added noise (Figure 8[c]) as well as intersymbol interference. We use the term *noise* to include any disturbance that is not predictable in detail and is not simply related to the signal. The noise waveform of Figure 8(c) is like that produced by thermal motion of the electrons in a wire, by random electronic events in the ionosphere, by steady "corona" discharges from electric power lines, or by the discrete nature of the charge carriers (electrons) in a transistor amplifier. In some critical applications, amplifiers are cooled by liquid nitrogen to reduce thermal noise. Such noise is always present. It is the source of

Figure 5
Sampling, Quantization, and PCM

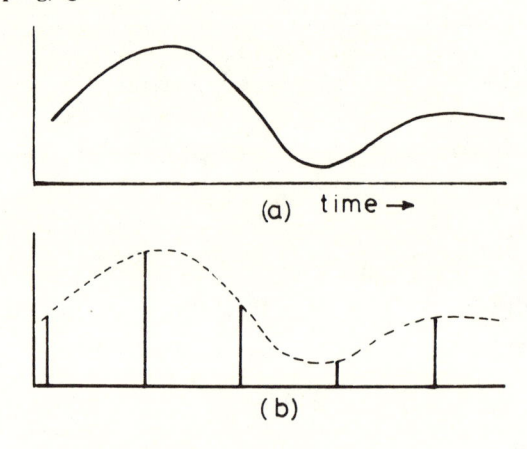

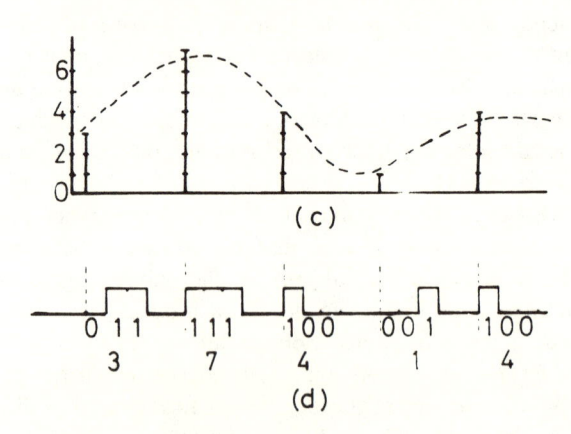

(a) Continuous signal waveform. (b) Instantaneous samples of waveform. (c) Samples quantized to nearest integer. (d) Binary pulse-coded signal representing the quantized samples by 3-bit codes.

the random speckles on a television screen when the set is not tuned to a station, and of the hiss when a radio is detuned. Such noise is composed of the superposition of a very large number of small contributions, and thus has a Gaussian, or normal, distribution of values.

Other sources of noise which may have different characteristics are

(a) impulsive disturbance due to sparking electrical apparatus such as motor vehicle ignitions, electric motors, and dirty electric power line insulators;

(b) lightning discharges, perhaps hundreds of kilometers away;

(c) mechanical vibration and imperfect connections; and

(d) the switching of currents within computers.

Protection from noise includes, of course, making the signals stronger by transmitting at high power (up to

Figure 6
Description of Signals in Time and in Frequency

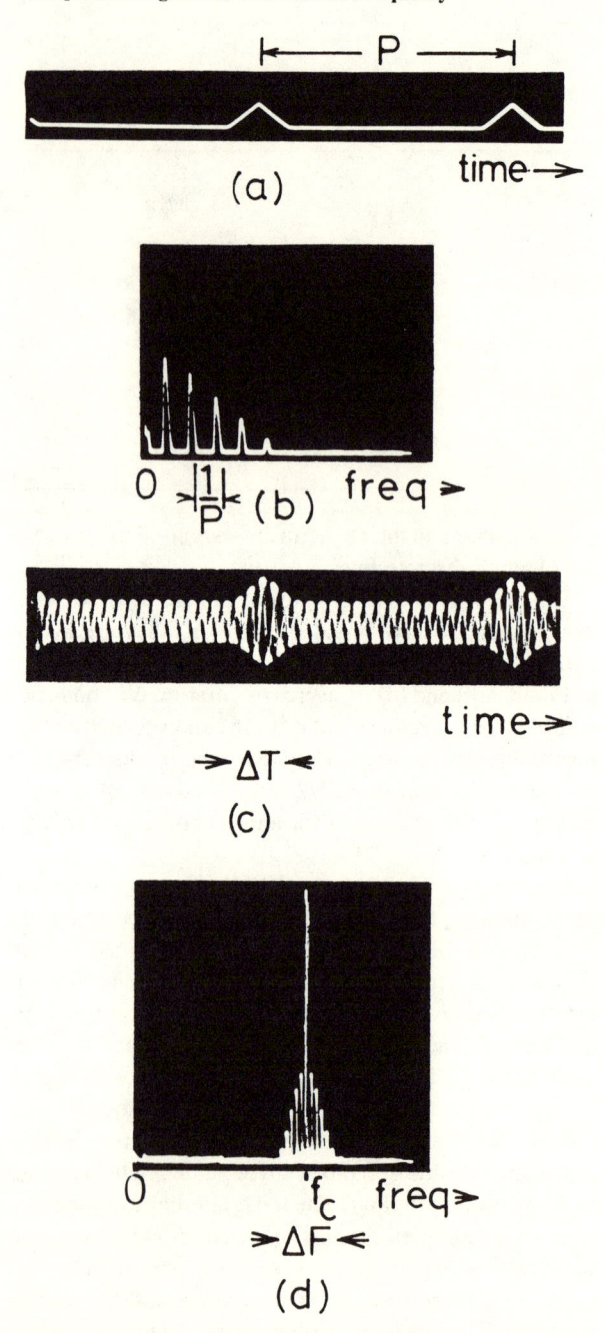

(a) Periodic pulses (period P = 100μsec duration; T = 2.3μsec). (b) Frequency spectrum of pulses of (a). Height of each spike indicates amplitude of sinusoidal component at that frequency. Spacing is the inverse of the period P, i.e., 10,000Hz. (c) Sinusoid of frequency f_c modulated by (a). (d) Spectrum of (c). The scale is different from that of (b).

1,000,000w in some radio transmitters), and reducing the effectiveness of the mechanism producing or introducing the noise, by proper electrical design. However,

Figure 7
Multiplexing of Frequency Division and Time Division

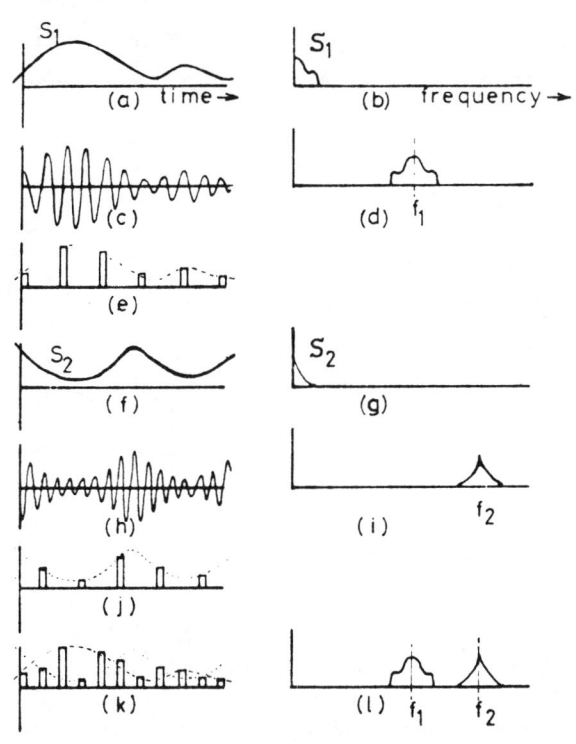

Left column shows time waveforms; right column shows frequency spectra. (a) Modulating signal s₁ or waveform representing message 1. (b) Spectrum S₁ of signal s₁. (c) Sinewave signal (of frequency f₁) amplitude modulated by s₁. (d) Spectrum of modulated signal in (c). (d) Pulses amplitude modulated by signal s₁. (f) Modulating signal s₂ or waveform representing message 2. (g) Spectrum S₂ of signal s₂. (h) Sinewave signal (of frequency f₂) amplitude modulated by s₂. (i) Spectrum of modulated signal in (h). (j) Pulses amplitude modulated by signal s₂. Note that the pulses are placed in between those used for s₁, shown in (e). (k) Sum of (e) and (i), i.e., a composite signal containing the information in s₁ and s₂ time multiplexed, and separable by observation at suitable times. (l) Sum of spectra (d) and (i), corresponding to the sum of signals (c) and (h). The signals may be separated by frequency filtering.

noise is always present, and its effects may be reduced by signal redundancy as noted previously. A particular example of great utility is that of binary (two-state) transmission in which the signal can take only one of two values, e.g., Figure 8(a). It is easier to make a correct binary decision, i.e., "positive or negative" than to choose a correct value from one of many or a continuum. The redundancy in a binary signal consists of a constraint on the permitted values. Of course, large enough noise can still cause errors.

Digital, including binary, signals are often used to represent continuous message waveforms or continuous signals, for example, the speech waveform (Figure 3[c]) and the video (television) waveform (Figure 3[g]). The process (Figure 5) involves sampling and then analog to

Figure 8
PCM Signal with Dispersion and Noise

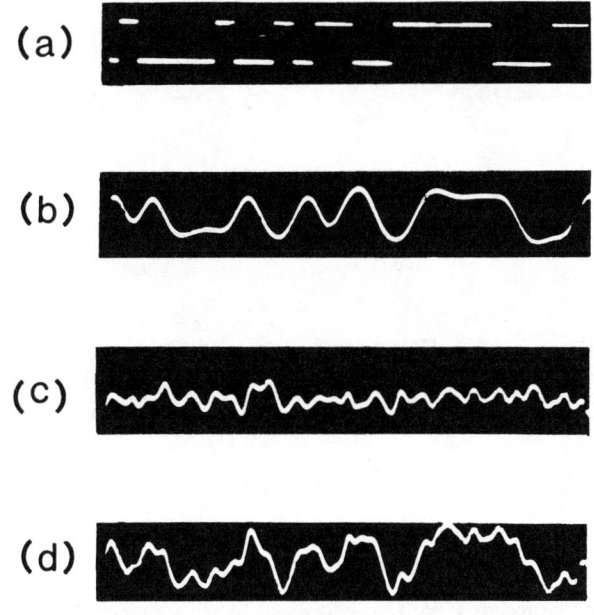

(a) Ideal signal, as transmitted. (b) Signal after distortion by a transmission medium. (c) Random noise. (d) Distorted signal with added noise.

digital conversion to produce, e.g., a binary number corresponding approximately to the value of each sample. This process is called pulse code modulation (pcm).

The differences (Figure 5[c]) between the value that can be represented digitally by a finite number of binary digits and the true value are referred to as "quantizing noise," and usually have effects similar to thermal noise. Telephone applications of pcm usually have 7 or 8 bits per sample, at a rate of 8,000 samples per second, and pcm is widely used for time division multiplex telephone

Figure 9
Fraction of Transmitted Power Remaining after Passage through 1km of a Typical Coaxial Cable, Showing the Dependence on Frequency

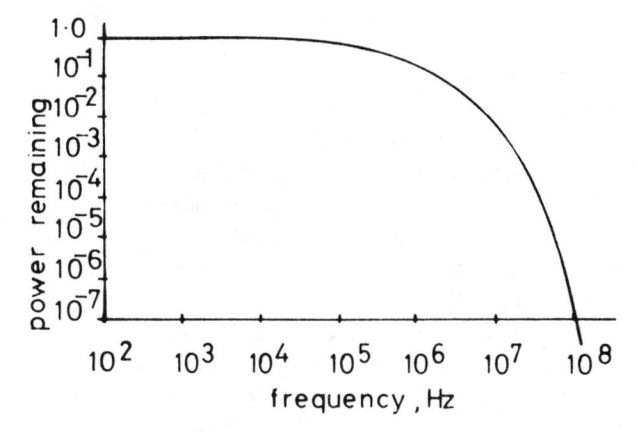

Figure 10
Communication Systems with Repeaters in Cascade

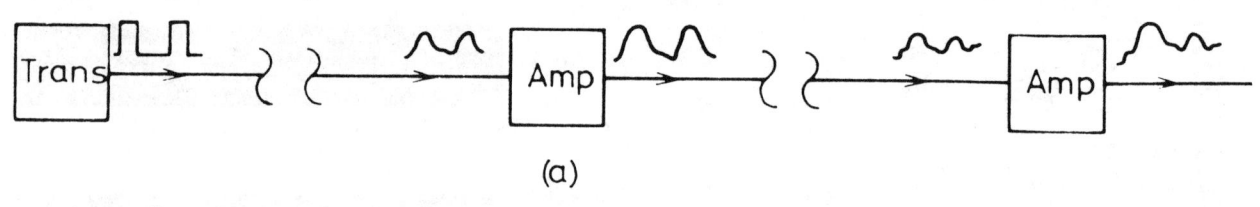

(a)

(b)

(a) Amplifying repeaters. Note progressive deterioration. (b) Regenerative repeaters. Clean signal regenerated at each repeater.

transmissions. Pulses with more than two possible values, up to 256 values, may be used to convey more information per pulse, i.e., to require fewer pulses for a given message. Of course, such pulses are more easily corrupted in transmission than binary pulses.

The world trend is toward digital or pcm representation of all forms of signals in communication systems, largely because of the robustness of this representation, the facility it provides for processing by computer-like exchanges, and the decreasing cost of digital electronics. Substantially all telecommunication authorities are planning toward the "Integrated Services Digital Network" that will serve all classes of use by digitally transmitted signals.

THE TERMINAL INTERFACE AND HUMANS

Many communication systems involve humans as the originators and recipients of the information conveyed. All human-made communication systems have service to humans as their end purpose, although this may be indirect and may even involve intentional disservice to some, as in the case of guided missiles. A key feature, and often the only apparent feature, of many systems is the terminal interface. Examples are telephones, including microphone, receiver, and dial (a control interface); microphones, loudspeakers, and earphones; television cameras and television screens; other video display screens; facsimiles; keyboards; teleprinters; control levers, joysticks, knobs, buttons, and other devices for manual adjustment; indicator lamps; indicating instruments ("meters"); digital displays; electric guitars; tactile sensory inputs; light pens; "mice"; bells; electromyographic and electroencephalographic controls.

These devices play an important part in the effectiveness of a communication system. However, their effectiveness depends on their mode of use and suitability for the task. For example, a loudspeaker is useful for audible messages, a television screen for pictorial messages, and a teleprinter for messages composed of "characters" (letters, numerals, etc.). Many attempts have been made to explore cross-modal uses, e.g., visual and tactile dislays for sounds, audible presentations of environmental data for blind people, speech control of machines, and audible outputs from calculators. Some successes have been demonstrated, but it is clear that our knowledge in this area is in its infancy. Rudimentary control of machines by use of the electrical activity of the brain as observed on the scalp has been demonstrated. Control of limb prostheses by use of the electrical activity of the severed nerve bundles is a fairly well-established technique, although not yet as successful as desired.

There are many factors influencing the success of interfaces. The qualities of the human operator are central; humans are surprisingly adaptable but are subject to psychophysical limitations especially in perception, to limitations of the "language" of the interaction, and by psychological needs (Miller, 1967; Cherry, 1957).

While the nature of many of the devices mentioned above will be familiar, developments and details and use of some are worthy of note. Devices for acoustic inputs, usually called microphones, are activated by variations in air pressure (pressure microphones) or air velocity (velocity microphones) and may be directional, i.e., having higher sensitivity to sound waves from some direction than others. Noise-cancelling microphones are of this class. Improved microphones in future telephones will be advantageous in connection with voice-responding systems, e.g., devices (incorporating computers) for controlling machines by voice using selected limited vocabularies and for verifying the identity of a speaker. Applications will be in telephone access to information services and financial transaction services.

Other applications of voice control are in the control of apparatus requiring visual concentration and hands-free operation. The general-purpose automatic stenographer may never be achieved because of the variability of voices, the ambiguity of spelling, and the need for use of contextual clues and complex linguistic constraints in the transcribing of even simple sentences, although significant progress is being made.

Machine to human communication by synthetic speech has been used for some years in calculators, typewriters for the blind, audio response units for answering inquiries and time services, etc. The utterances are made up from a phonetic (symbolic) description and a set of stored rules for concatenating the control signals driving a simulation of the human vocal mechanism.

Human language is so complex that interfaces such as telephones and teleprinters used for person-to-person communication have not been designed with regard to its structure. However, in the latter devices, the keyboards are arranged so that the keys for the more frequently needed symbols ("characters") are close to the average position of the operator's fingers. The layout is similar to that used on typewriters for a century; higher typing speeds have been demonstrated to be possible with different layouts, but convention is strong. Rarely used symbols are made available by simultaneous operation of the SHIFT key: this provides access to many more symbols than could be provided with one per key only.

Teleprinter machines are often equipped with means for recording messages also on paper or magnetic media, and for retransmitting messages from these media. Many interfaces (terminals) used with computers are made with operational features like typewriters, but with the visual output on a temporary display "soft copy" as opposed to "hard copy," as a printed form is known. Most of these terminals use a large cathode-ray tube as in television receivers; these are called video displays or video terminals. They are often equivalent to a teleprinter as far as the remote equipment is concerned, and thus accept only slow-speed data, or they may accept data at high speed, as from a computer, to build up the displayed picture quickly. Such terminals may be simple displays with no more capability than a typewriter, or they may be "intelligent," incorporating a microcomputer, for example, to permit complex operations on graphic information, the generation of special symbols, or operation of a light pen. This is a device with which the operator can point to part of the display and cause that part to be modified or acted upon in a prearranged way (Figure 11). For example, a menu of options for the next operation may be displayed, in words or symbols, and the light pen used to select the one required. This mode of operation is very suitable for nonexpert users, and permits convenient, reliable dialogue between machines and person; about seven options is the maximum desirable for efficient human performance.

Color displays are valuable for some types of man-machine communication, e.g., in a situation where a three-dimensional object consists of several distinct layers, one behind the other. Graphic representations of such objects are rendered much more comprehensible when the various layers are depicted in different colors. Other techniques available for emphasizing three-dimensional effects in graphic displays are the use of motion, stereoscopic projections, and shading.

Computers are often used via terminals as described above, located remotely and connected either directly by wires, via a "data network," or via a normal telephone line after the relevant number has been dialed. Connection between a terminal and the telephone line, and suitable conversion of the signals is done in a device called a modem (modulator demodulator). This may use acoustic coupling via the normal telephone handset.

Graphic inputs for computers may be made via scanning apparatus related to a television camera in principle, or by a device which senses the position of a stylus, cursor, or light pen used by a person to draw a required figure. Such communication interfaces are widely used in engineering design. Rough sketches input in this way may be refined, modified, repositioned, reoriented, or changed in scale by a computer.

Pictorial information is usually communicated by scanning the original picture, page, or scene with some form of photoelectric sensor. A raster (Figure 12[a]), or system of successive parallel scanning lines, covers the whole picture, and may then be repeated, as in the case of television, to accommodate changes or motion. Figure 3(g) shows the resultant electrical signal produced in a television camera as the word "JONES," Figure 3(f), is scanned on one line near the center. The video signal, after the inclusion of synchronizing pulses for use by the receiver, is transmitted via any convenient bearer with suitable modulation. At the receiver it modulates the intensity of the spot on a cathode-ray tube in sympathy with the light intensity of each corresponding point in the original picture.

Facsimile, or fax, is a similar process used to transmit

	Television (public)	Facsimile
Time for one frame or page	20 msec; also 16 2/3 msec	15 sec
Lines per frame or page	625 (also 405, 525, 819 in some countries)	1,000
Time per line	64 usec	15 msec
Picture elements per line	about 500	2,400
Picture elements per frame or page	about 400,000	about 2,400,000
Bandwidth required	6 MHz	3 kHz (telephone line)

pictures from one office to another. Scanning at transmitter and receiver is often mechanical. Fax usually uses the public telephone network, and its speed is limited by this. Typical data for television and fax are shown in the above table. Newspaper pictures are transmitted in this way.

Various combinations of telephone and two-way television have been explored and used by the public. Conference television, using special studios and television screen arrangements, has been found to be of value in replacing some travel to business conferences.

Special interface needs for handicapped persons are attracting increasing attention as increasingly complex functions can now be carried out automatically. One of

Figure 11
Use of Light Pen

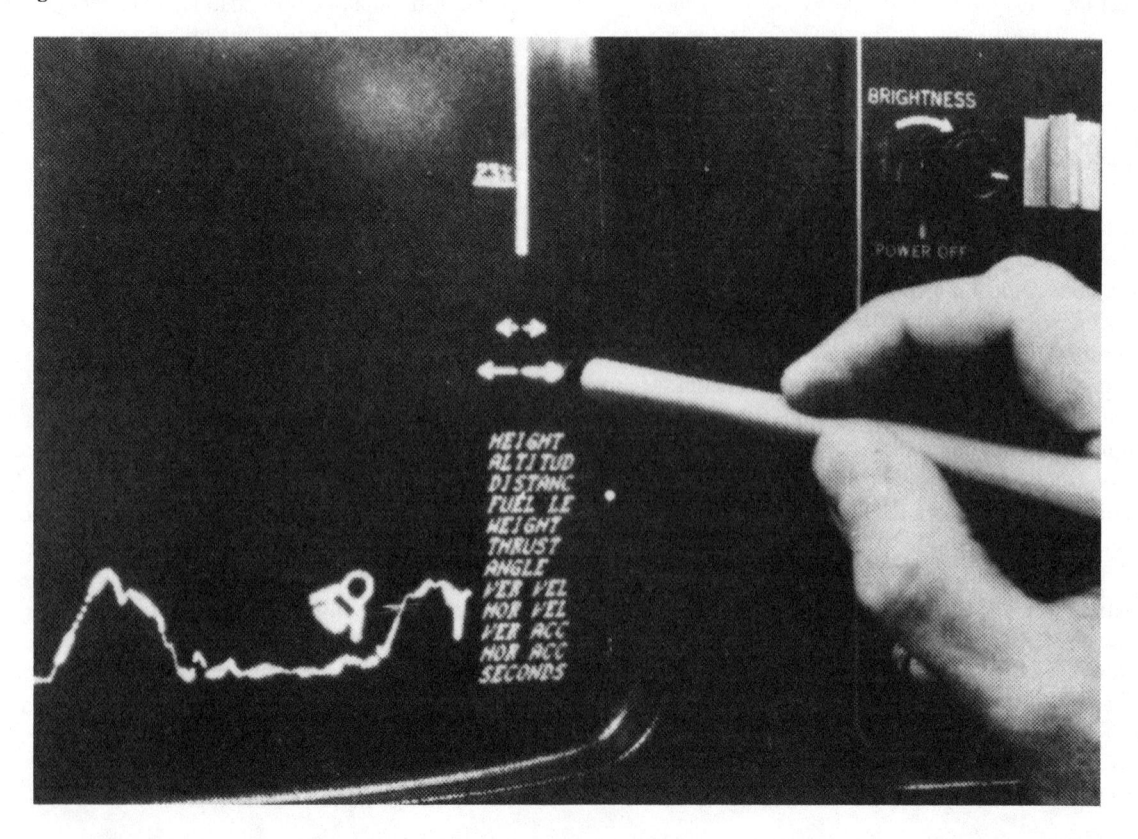

Figure 12
Video Displays

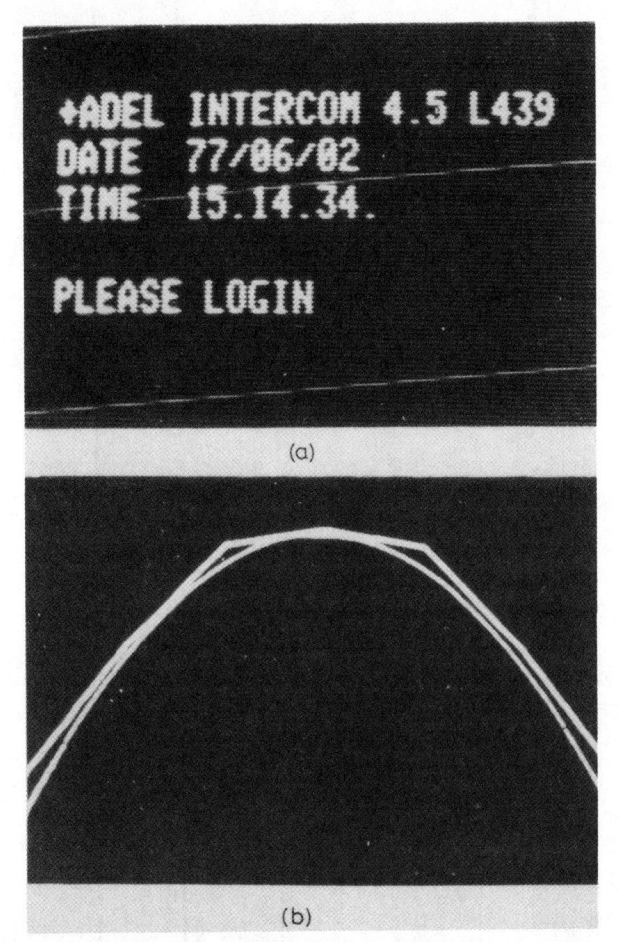

(a) Raster. The background lines are normally invisible. (b) Vector node. Each figure is made up of directed straight lines.

the most interesting examples is the eye gaze communicator in which the direction of gaze of the user is detected photoelectrically without any attachments. The gaze is directed at an element of a menu of choices displayed on a cathode-ray tube, and each choice may cause some function, such as typing a character. Speeds up to two selections per second and typing up to 40 words per minute have been achieved.

Some aspects of the qualities of humans in communication tasks are important in consideration of interfaces. All fundamental limitations, such as those discussed in the section on messages, signals, and information, are operative, but the human may do worse. Despite the vast channel capacities apparently needed for television (e.g., 50,000,000 bits/sec), each human sense cannot handle input information at more than about 25 bits per second, and combinations of the senses provide only slight increases.

Absolute criteria for any particular quality are often of doubtful validity, as the human is adaptable. For example, human visual acuity is such that with bright illumination objects subtending only 30 seconds of arc (about 1 1/4mm apart at 1m distance) may be resolved; in poor light the objects may need to be 50 times as far apart. Contrast of object against background is important, and so is time available. Time and motion are important. Thus, after the scene change in television, it takes up to about one-half second for the eye to appreciate detail. The perceptibility of flicker in a flashing light depends on intensity. In countries where the basic television flicker rate is 50Hz, the flicker becomes objectionable when the intensity is only one quarter of that for systems which use 60Hz rate. Also, perception of light intensity or hue is reduced in regions of a picture with sharp edges or fine detail.

The perception of intensity (e.g., of light, sound) tends to relate logarithmically to the magnitude of stimulus. Thus equal ratios of stimulus magnitude are judged as causing equal changes in sensation. The ranges of intensities (power of stimulus) over which the eye and ear are useful are of the order of 1,000,000 to 1. For time-varying intensities, an averaging over an interval of about 0.1 second is apparent. With the eye there is also spatial averaging, over an area corresponding to about 1/20,000 of the field of vision.

The young human ear is sensitive to signals in the frequency range of about 30Hz to 20kHz; this range is covered by the best hi-fi audio apparatus. Speech requires about 50Hz to 6kHz for faithful reproduction; telephones are often designed for 300Hz to 3,400Hz. Speech powers vary over about 30:1 for one person in a conversation, with another 30:1 variation between people. The ear's frequency resolution is of the order of a few Hz at 1kHz, and intensity changes as small as 10 percent may be noticed. However, in time-varying sounds such as speech and music such small variations are imperceptible.

It seems that the most effective human-to-machine communication to produce a desired machine behavior is by way of modification of machine offerings; this is a common practice in interactive use of computers. How to specify modifications in three, four, or five visual dimensions is an interesting challenge. For example, in computer-aided (or should it be "human-aided"?) circuit layout much of the initial routine work may be done by a computer, but final refinement or modification to include unspecified features often has to be done by human intervention.

When we come to the details of multichoice communication, there are a few principles of man's capacity as a communication channel or receiver that we should bear in mind:

Table 2
Major Communication Bearers

	Appearance		Typical frequency range and capacity	Useable channel capacity bit/sec	Typical range between repeaters (km)	Use	Limitations, notes
Open wire pairs		GUIDED WAVE SYSTEMS	10 140 kHz 15 speech channels each way	6×10^6	100	Telephony, telegraphy in sparsely populated areas. Major historic bearer since inception of telegraph	Lightning interference, crosstalk, reflections
Twisted pair cables (one up to a thousand pairs)			to 250 kHz	2×10^6 per pair	20	Major bearer for telephony and data for short distances less than 20 km	Crosstalk, reflections, dispersion
Coaxial cable (frequently several of these)			4 kHz per pair	4×10^4 per pair; 4800 for practical data	20	For local distribution	
			12 MHz 1000 telephone + 1 TV channel	2×10^8	4	Major bearer for moderately large intensity traffic; high rate data, wired city distribution undersea cables	Attenuation and dispersion
Optical fibre transparent glass fibre		DIRECT WAVE SYSTEMS (BEAMS)	2×10^{14} Hz 500 TV channels or 500,000 telephone channels	10^{11}	10	Major bearer for large intercity routes. Economical bearer for smaller routes and local use	Technology rapidly developing. In use in aircraft because of light weight, and in small commercial systems
High frequency radio			50 kHz at 30 MHz 4 telephone	2×10^5	100	Remote regions; emergency services	Ionospheric interference, and reflections. Electrical apparatus interference
Microwave radio			20 MHz at 4000 MHz 1000 telephone or 4 TV ch.	10^9	30	Major bearer for long routes. Also for short paths, eg. studio to transmitter in TV broadcasting	Interference between systems not adequately separated. Multipath propagation and fading
Satellite radio			as for microwave radio	10^9	15,000	Major bearer for intercontinental distances. Navigation, ship communication, remote communities	Interference with microwave radio. Delay. Thermal and cosmic noise
Broadcasting		NON-DIRECTIONAL	Amplitude modulation broadcasting 0.5-1.5 MHz; 10 MHz and up	10^5 per channel	100 (more at night)	Local amplitude modulation broadcasting	Electrical equipment, thunderstorms, ionospheric reflections
			TV and frequency modulation broadcast 50 mHz-500 mHz	10^8	18,000 80	Internat. broadcasting Local only	As above, but less at higher frequencies. Reflections cause ghosts on TV
Mobile radio			27MHz; 500MHz; 00MHz Several telephone or teletype channels	6×10^4	80	Mobile services - police, ambulance, citizens band	Electrical equipment, congestion, fading
Mobile public telephone			1 mHz at 500 mHz 200 telephones in one system	4×10^4	30	public telephones	Fading due to interference of multiple paths. Thermal and man-made electrical noise

The magical number seven: The number of classes into which we can classify (without recoding) a given dimensional stimulus, e.g., intensity, pitch, colour, the number of items we can recognise without counting, the span of the immediate memory, the number of separate chunks (not bits) of information which we can absorb in one bite; all these numbers are of the order of seven. The similarity of the results in these several cases does not imply that they are different aspects of one common underlying process.

It thus seems in designing a multichoice man-to-machine response facility we should not offer more than about seven choices. At the same time, it appears to be wasteful of a response capability if many less than this are offered. With the limitation of some seven choices, i.e., about three bits of information per choice, we next ask "how often?" As the human's capability is apparently an almost immediate response, the reaction time being about 1/5 second, but exposure to a stimulus needing only about 1/40 second, we could perhaps offer some four choices per second. This is similar to the performance of a skilled typist under optimum conditions, i.e., about twenty-five bits per second. Current computer responses are often considerably slower and interactive computer operation appears satisfactory if the computer delay is not much greater than about a second. As man-machine interaction becomes more fluent, we might expect that its dynamics might be influenced by delay in the same way that delay in telephone circuits can lead to instabilities in conversation when it approaches a second. For this reason telecommunication administrations are careful now to minimise the number of satellite links in a connection to limit the delay. By increasing the number of dimensions to a stimulus, it is possible to increase the number of bits per decision. For six dimensions, 7.2 bits per decision (corresponding to about 150 categories) have been reported. This was for an experiment in which each of six variables in an acoustic stimulus (frequency, intensity, rate of interruption, duration and spatial location) could assume any one of five different values. It seems not surprising that higher dimensioned offerings and responses are more prone to error. Also, it is to be expected that they are more demanding of the human's attention. In such cases attention should be given to making the machine's responses forgiving and to providing a convenient "rub-out" option and preferably a "back-space" one also.

MEDIUM OR BEARER

Examples are wires, cables, radio waves, waveguides, light beams, and acoustic waves. Media for storage include, for example, magnetic tapes, and disks with mechanical encoding (both the recent "compact" discs and the older grooved disks). Bearers represent a large proportion of the efforts of communication engineers and of the cost of many systems. Ideally, the bearer in use is not evident to the user of a communication system. However, physical properties of bearers have a strong influence on their suitability with respect to such factors as reliability, durability, availability, delay, freedom from interference (to and from other systems), mobility and flexibility, environmental considerations, resources needed for their provision and maintenance (especially human skills), and cost.

Most telecommunication systems use electromagnetic wave propagation for conveying the signal from the transmitting terminal to the receiving terminal. Optical communication is in this class because light is composed of electromagnetic waves. It is common for governments to control the provision, and often the ownership, of telecommunication media.

In all electromagnetic propagation systems the energy propagation takes place in space or in an insulating material such as polythene or paper or glass. The waves may be guided directly by wires, etc., indirectly in a beam, or they may be broadcast. Any bearer may be used for any class of message provided sufficient channel capacity is available. Some examples of technologies of greatest practical significance are summarized in Table 2. In this table, the column headed "Usable Channel Capacity, bit/sec" is to give a general indication only and is not necessarily the information theoretic channel capacity; nor is it the rate at which data can be sent by current technology, although in many cases it approximates that rate.

Generally, the guided wave systems are used only for communication between fixed stations (except, e.g., for communication with trains, a special case). Factors limiting guided wave systems are electrical losses in the materials of the cables, which usually become more severe at high frequencies (Figure 9), and irregularities which may cause distortion of the waveforms (Figure 8). Repeaters (amplifiers or regenerative repeaters which analyze the distorted signals and transmit corrected versions) are required at intervals so that signals may be transmitted over long distances, and transatlantic cables have about 100 repeaters.

Optical fibers are the guiding bearers with most promise, and they will be the dominant bearers in the foreseeable future. These are fine rods about 1 to 30 microns in diameter, of specially transparent glass in which light is totally internally reflected so that none is lost through the surface. The glass used is so transparent that less than 10 percent of the light is absorbed in passing 1km through it, and improved materials may permit transatlantic transmission with no amplification. A laser is used to transmit the light into fiber. Optical fibers have advantages of light weight, electrical insulating properties, immense channel capacity, and low cost.

Directed beams of radio waves are often used for economic reasons where cables are too expensive. Reflectors in the form of dishes or horns, or antenna arrays of wires or rods, are used to concentrate the transmitted energy in the needed direction so that the receiver can receive a signal stronger than the inevitable noise. The received energy is inversely proportional to the square of the distance, provided that there are no obstacles or significant reflections or serious absorption of the waves in the air or rain.

Absorption and dispersion limit the range of frequencies that are available for reliable communication, and appear to rule out optical communication via light beams in the open air. Devices that are good at directing narrow beams of radio waves are also good at the receiving terminals, for collecting energy predominantly from the one desired direction. Thus microwave radio links use "dishes" at both ends, and in areas of poor television reception we use "high gain" antennas, aimed in the direction of arrival of the signal waves.

Radio beams are of course convenient and often very economical because there is no need for any construction at all over most of a route. However, they all distribute energy over a much greater area than the receiver and have to be planned carefully to avoid interference between themselves and other radio services. Different frequency ranges are used for adjacent links, and in densely populated areas there are not enough frequency bands to serve all needs. Geographical separation of a few hundred kilometers is usually sufficient because the microwaves, with wavelengths of tens of centimeters down to 1–2 millimeters, travel in fairly straight lines and may be shadowed by the curvature of the earth. Satellites used in communication systems are usually located in geostationary orbits (at about 35,000km over the equator), and each is thus accessible from approximately one-third of the earth's surface.

In broadcasting and in mobile communication the radio medium is invaluable for the freedom it gives in location of terminals. The transmitting antenna is usually designed to give substantially equal radiation in all horizontal directions. Long waves (at low frequencies, below about one MHz) can diffract around hills and buildings, and follow the curvature of the earth (ground waves). However, the total frequency range available with such properties is less than that required for one television channel.

Between about 3 and 30MHz, the waves can usually diffract around local objects, but do not follow the earth's curvature. However, these "high frequency" or "short" waves have been widely used for long-distance communication because they may be reflected by the ionos-

Figure 13
Configurations of Communication Systems

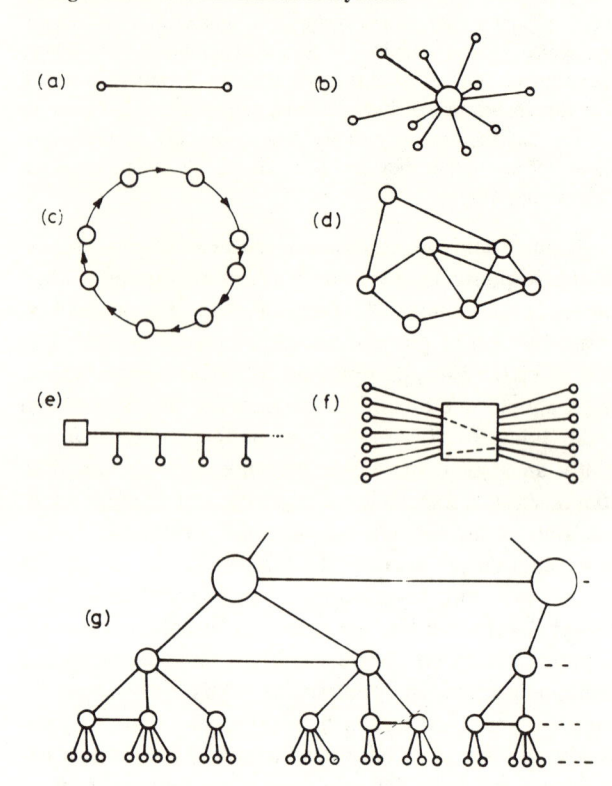

phere, an electrically conducting region of ionized gas 100 to 400km above the earth's surface.

At frequencies greater than about 30MHz radio waves, merely because of the relationship between their lengths (i.e., less than 10m) and the size of objects, tend to behave more like light rays and require line of sight paths. This limits the range of very high frequency (30–300MHz), ultrahigh frequency (300–3,000MHz), and microwave (above 1,000MHz), to less than about 100km because of the curvature of the earth, and causes the poor television reception experienced by people in the shadow of a hill. Consequently, television transmitting antennas are located on towers, on tall buildings, or on mountains.

CONFIGURATION

Figure 13 shows representative examples of the various configurations of communication systems.

Figure 13(a) shows a point-point system. The only degree of freedom available in this system is whether the communication is unidirectional or bidirectional. In the latter case, it may be in only one direction at a time (simplex) or in both directions (duplex).

Figure 13(b) shows a star network. Broadcasting from one radio or television station is an example. Radio control of taxis from a central station is an example of a bidirectional star network. A simple multiple access data bank or computer network could be of this form if there were only one center for providing the service.

Figure 13(c) is a ring network. Any unit on the ring may communicate with any other units simply by transmitting a suitably addressed packet of data. Many addressed packets may be in circulation at once until their destinations have time to receive them. A real network may have many such rings, some touching each other.

Figure 13(d) is a mesh or interconnected network, typical of many telegraph, data, or computer networks used in the packet or message-switched mode. In message-switched or packet-switched networks, messages are transmitted from the source node as strings of bits including a header containing destination address information, and usually other status information such as source, serial number, and urgency. At each intermediate node the header is analyzed, the message is stored and launched when an appropriate outgoing link is free. This mode of operation is called "store and forward." Alternative routing is possible to minimize delays, and a typical network may have information on the traffic in every link held in a computer at every node and updated at one-second intervals. The overall delay may be of the order of milliseconds, which is desirable for human conversations, through a few seconds for interactive computing, or up to several hours in the case of some telegraphs and updating of statistical records.

Figure 13(e) shows a linear network, which may be the configuration of the terminal or customer distribution, connected, for example, to a node of some more complex network. Examples are telephone party lines and multidrop connections of computer terminals. Usually only one terminal can be in communication at one time, but because of the speed at which terminals may be connected and disconnected and data transmitted, it may appear to the operators that many, e.g., 10 or 100, terminals are active at once.

Figure 13(f) shows an extremely simple form of switched network in which terminals are connected together (usually) in pairs for the duration of a dialogue. The most familiar example is the telephone network. The size and complexity of the interconnecting system are of course dependent on the traffic as well as on the total number of terminals. Practical telephone networks are usually hierarchical in structure, as shown in Figure 13(g). In this, the bottom row of circles represents individual terminals, and may include private branch exchanges. There may be as many as several tens of thousands of telephones, or as few as ten, connected to a local exchange, shown by the next row up. One local exchange will usually have links or trunks to other local exchanges in accordance with customers' traffic needs, and it will also be connected to a higher-level trunk exchange. There may be several levels of trunk exchanges, the higher-level ones serving specific geographical regions, culminating in international exchanges. Auxiliary routes not shown are often provided for specific traffic flows between particular exchanges.

The interconnection at exchanges may be effected mechanically or electronically. Essential functions of an exchange, provided by a human operator, mechanical switches, or computer, include determination of the customer's requirements; initiation of a call, identification of the called party, selection of a suitable route, advice to the caller on progress of the call ("ringing," "busy" [including congested routes], "unobtainable"), alerting the called party, detection of termination, charge computation, and accounting.

Many current telephone exchanges use mechanical contacts to connect the telephones. These contacts, which may take several forms, are controlled by a computer, and the term "stored program control" is usually used to denote this form of exchange. Modern exchanges are time-switched; in these, direct electrical connections are replaced by selection of time slots corresponding to the relevant signals. This technique is related to time division multiplex (Figure 7) and the signals are pulse-coded (Figure 5). This form of switching permits the use of electronic logic gates, implemented in economical very large-scale integrated circuits, and the integration of the switching functions with transmission in the form of pulse code modulation.

It is becoming common for networks serving local needs—such as the computer, speech, and data transmission system for one organization—to have the control functions distributed among the terminals, with connections between all terminals. There is then no control center, and communication is controlled by the facilities of the terminals concerned. Linear and ring configurations are often used. Such networks are called **local area networks** (q.v.).

TRAFFIC

Traffic studies are concerned with how many channels are required to satisfy the need for communication between large numbers of potential communicators. For example, two cities each containing one million telephones have a potential demand for one million telephone channels each way between them. Such a demand has never yet occurred, and the statistical behavior of customers shows that only a few hundred channels may be needed, depending of course on many specific factors such as common interests, common languages, and political and economic factors. It is customary to plan for a grade of service such that, for example, only one attempt in 100 is frustrated by congestion or intolerable delay. Also, it is common to share, among several centers, groups of channels, providing communication in similar directions. This practice yields economies because the fluctuations of demand are then less in proportion, and alternative routing becomes possible, giving improved reliability and capability to share capacity for peaks of demand.

Similar considerations apply within cities and even within a single telephone exchange. Data and computer networks, which are currently growing proportionately faster than telephone networks, are relevant to such traffic studies, and have more possibilities because messages may be stored at intermediate points to await availability of a channel.

COMPUTERS AND COMMUNICATION

While many electronic developments have influenced the development of communication systems, the wide capabilities and use of computers are causing great changes, in several ways.

Computers have generated a need for great quantities of data to be communicated. One facet is the use of data banks with computer management and exchange of the data. Familiar examples are airline reservation systems and banking systems. Another facet is the remote access to computing power and the rationalization of computing resources. Both of these communication needs of computers have led to the existence of large commercial and government computer networks, some spanning several continents and incorporating satellite links. A computer user may buy as much computer time and storage as required, just as with telephone service or electricity.

Computers are components of communication systems. For example, in modern telephone exchanges the routing and switching and all other functions are carried out by a computer. This receives the caller's dialed information, interprets it, examines suitable routes for congestion, communicates with a computer in the called party's exchange to cause the ringing, causes the two parties to be connected, monitors the conversation for termination, computes the charge, and updates the account. Current developments are aimed at providing again many of the convenient services that used to be available via human operators, for example, directory services and message taking.

In data or computer networks, some delay (up to a few seconds) is often acceptable. Messages are commonly sent as packets comprising perhaps 1,000 bits including a header which gives the address of the recipient. The packet is examined at each of many intermediate switching centers, or "nodes," checked for accuracy, and perhaps redirected, stored, or referred back for retransmission. Different packets of the same message may go by different routes according to varying traffic. Computers are used at the nodes to check the packets, interpret addresses, optimize routing, and handle queues. Also, the assembly of messages into packets and rearrangement at destination are done by computers.

"Intelligent" terminals—e.g., keyboards, computing cash registers, video displays, teaching machines, and security monitoring systems—contain microcomputers. This application of computers in communication devices has opened up a new scope for telecommunication services.

COMPATIBILITY

The increasing use of remote control computer terminals in business and industry and many other facilities has led to a proliferation of varieties of communication needs. Most telecommunication authorities are involved with planning "integrated services digital networks" that should be compatible with such variety for decades to come. Because of the worldwide interdependence of communication system components and the long service life of telecommunication equipments (typically twenty years), it is important to ensure that they are designed so that future needs will not be prejudiced. Thus, there is great effort expended in designing standards and protocols for interconnection and compatible operation.

At the lowest level there is the description of the forms of coding of signals; for example, what should be the sampling rate and the number of bits per sample in a pcm representation of signals? Then, the method of coding to protect against errors needs to be determined. Signaling standards must incorporate provision for addressing (i.e., transmission of information on the required destination), on class of message, on class of transmitting device, for confirmation of reception, and on status of receiving device (e.g., busy, operational, nonexistent). Because devices in different networks may have to be able to communicate with each other, such signaling standards need to accommodate the requirements for controlling the interfaces between the networks and to provide in a suitable form the information required in the foreign network.

Since 1865 the International Telecommunication Union (ITU) has been the international forum in which telecommunication authorities exchange information and develop standards. It is now an agency of the United Nations and has two major arms, the CCIR (International Radio Consultative Committee) and the CCITT (International Telephony and Telegraphy Consultative Committee), to which most countries of the world contribute through specialized study groups. One of the first acts of the ITU was the adoption of the Morse code as an international standard. Another international organization, the International Standards Organization (OSI), has been a major influence in establishing methodologies and protocols for computer communication via its "open systems integration" (OSI) model.

Robert Bogner

REFERENCES

The literature in communication engineering is voluminous. This selection has been chosen to augment the text article; presentation is best described as Further Reading. This reading will reveal many sources of research, detail theoretical background, and the like.

Abrams, M. and Cotton, I. W., eds. (1984) "Computer Networks: A Tutorial." Los Angeles: IEEE Computer Soc. Press. A collection of reprints of illuminating papers.

Cherry, E. C. (1957). *On Human Communication*. Cambridge, Mass.: MIT Press; new ed., 1966. An exposition of the relationship of communication and information theory to human communication. An exploration of what is communication, at various levels.

Clark, A. P. (1983) *Principles of Digital Data Transmission*. 2d ed. New York: Halstead Press, a division of John Wiley.

Freeman, R. L. (1981) *Telecommunication Transmission Handbook*. New York: John Wiley. Explains the principles, main characteristics, and specifications of the components of telecommunication transmission systems.

Gabor, D. (1946) "Theory of Communication." *Journal of the Institution of Electrical Engineers* 93, pt. 3: 429–457. A milestone in the exposition of time and frequency resolution of signals.

Hills, M. T. (1979) *Telecommunications Switching Principles*. London: Allen and Unwin. A detailed introduction to the principles of interconnection in telecommunication networks, including networks, traffic, and switching technology. While intended for professional engineers, this book introduces each topic clearly, in a manner suitable for nonspecialists.

Inose, H. (1979.) *An Introduction to Digital Integrated Communications Systems*. Tokyo: University of Tokyo Press. Explains in detail all of the key features of digital communication, including switching and transmission, and tells how these features are applied. Intended as a text or reference book for engineers.

Lam, S. S., ed. (1984) *Principles of Communication and Networking Protocols*. Los Angeles: IEEE Computer Soc. Press. A collection of reprints of illuminating papers.

Martin, J. (1979) *Telecommunications and the Computer*. Englewood Cliffs, N.J.: Prentice-Hall. A broad, practical survey of telecommunication principles and practices in a very lucid style. Semitechnical.

———. (1978) *The Wired Society*. Englewood Cliffs, N.J.: Prentice-Hall. Reissued as *The Telematic Society*, 1981. A nontechnical survey of the interaction of modern telecommunications and society, with explanation of each type of service. A perceptive view of possibilities for the future.

Miller, G. A. (1967) *The Psychology of Communication*. New York: Basic Books. A collection of five essays which provide insight into the characteristics of human perception that are important in the design of communication systems.

Monk, A., ed. (1984) *Fundamentals of Human Computer Interaction*. London: Academic Press.

Ronayne, J. (1986) *Introduction to Digital Communication Switching*. London: Pitman.

Shannon, C. E. (1948) "Mathematical Theory of Communication." *Bell System Technical Journal* 27: 379–423, 623–656. Repr. in *The Mathematical Theory of Communication*, ed. C. E. Shannon and W. Weaver. Urbana: University of Illinois Press, 1949. The classical work that laid the foundation of information theory.

Shannon, C. E. and Weaver, W. (1949) *The Mathematical Theory of Communication*. Urbana: University of Illinois Press.

Stallings, W. (1984) *Local Networks. An Introduction*. New York: Macmillan.

Tanenbaum, A. S. (1981) *Computer Networks*. Englewood Cliffs, N.J.: Prentice-Hall.

COMMUNICATION SATELLITES.

INTRODUCTION

Communication satellites are the latest tool to allow educators to get more, higher-quality instruction to more students, regardless of where they live. The major advantages of satellite systems are that they are a distance-insensitive broadcast medium, they go to ten or a hundred points as easily as to one or two, and 3km is the same as 3,000. They are most useful when the network is large, the distances are long, and the amount of traffic needed is high. Educational use of communication satellites is only just beginning, even though trial systems began in the late 1960s and some operational systems have been functioning for a decade or more. These networks have demonstrated the ability to teach double the number of students at half the cost of traditional face-to-face classrooms, without sacrificing educational quality. Indeed, adding telecommunications usually improves the caliber of instruction.

BASIC SATELLITE TECHNOLOGY

Most people have seen a microwave tower (Figure 14a). The two dishes facing in opposite directions suggest the tower's function: to pick up incoming signals from one direction and retransmit them in another. The basic limitation of a microwave system is that the radiation travels in straight lines, or "line of sight" (Figure 14b). Hills

**Figure 14
Communication Satellites**

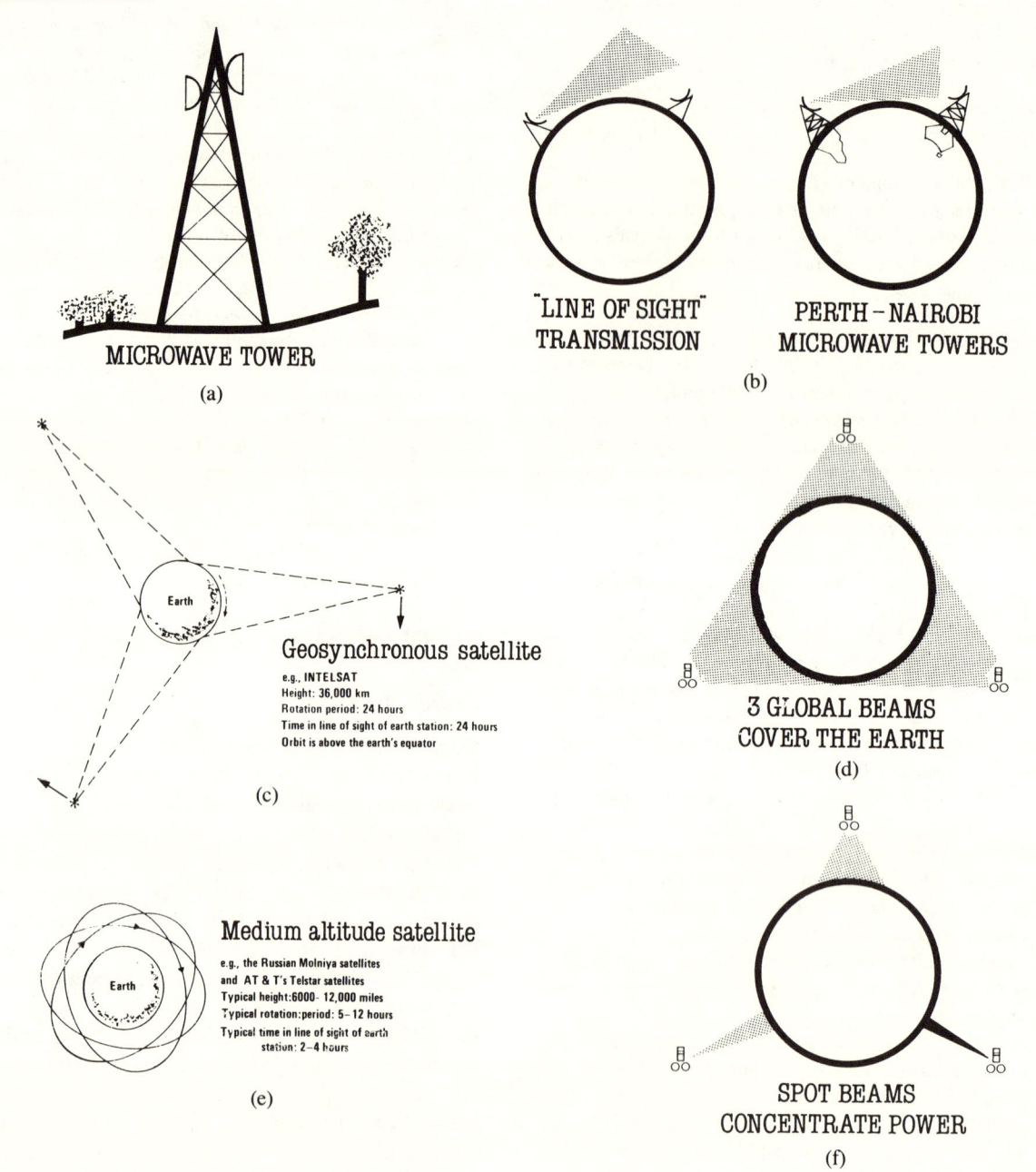

MICROWAVE TOWER
(a)

"LINE OF SIGHT" TRANSMISSION

PERTH – NAIROBI MICROWAVE TOWERS
(b)

Geosynchronous satellite
e.g., INTELSAT
Height: 36,000 km
Rotation period: 24 hours
Time in line of sight of earth station: 24 hours
Orbit is above the earth's equator
(c)

3 GLOBAL BEAMS COVER THE EARTH
(d)

Medium altitude satellite
e.g., the Russian Molniya satellites
and AT & T's Telstar satellites
Typical height: 6000–12,000 miles
Typical rotation period: 5–12 hours
Typical time in line of sight of earth station: 2–4 hours
(e)

SPOT BEAMS CONCENTRATE POWER
(f)

block microwaves, and even if there are no hills in the way, the curvature of the earth requires frequent repeating stations. For example, if we wanted to connect two points without repeater stations, say to across the ocean, from Australia to Africa, we would need to build the towers several hundred miles high.

A communication satellite is simply a microwave tower in the sky. It receives incoming signals from stations on earth and rebroadcasts back to all of the earth that it can "see." From 36,000km a satellite can "see" 40 percent of the earth's surface, which is why Intelsat needs only three satellites to make a worldwide network to carry our overseas telephone calls (3 × 40 = 120 percent; see Figure 14c). Communication satellites are put at 36,000km because at that height a satellite orbits the earth in just 24 hours, precisely the speed at which the earth turns. Thus, it is "geostationary," seeming to be fixed in one place above us (Figure 14d). At any other height, the satellite would seem to move over head, and earth stations would need motors to "track" it, which would make them much more expensive.

Intelsat, which carries much of our overseas telephone traffic, sends its power to the full 40 percent of the earth it can see. In this "global beam," the amount of power that hits any one location is relatively low. But when this energy is focused to hit a smaller area (much as one would focus a spotlight in the theater) the amount of power per location goes up, just as a "key spot" on a single performer at center stage is brighter than one where the focus has been widened to cover the whole cast. Domestic satellites (such as TELSTAR in the United States [Figure 14e], ANIK in Canada, or AUSSAT in Australia) and Regional satellites (such as EUROSAT in Europe or ARABSAT in the Middle East) use such "spot beams" (Figure 14[f]) to focus on single countries or regions. This increases the amount of power that hits the earth, which means that the earth station can be both smaller and cheaper.

Each communication satellite carries a number of "transponders," for transmitter/responder, and each transponder is measured in terms of the amount of the broadcasting band, or bandwidth, it can carry. A typical transponder, with around 50MHz of bandwidth, will carry two television channels or 1,000 telephone channels. Another way to measure communication capacity is in "bit rate," or the number of bits of computer data that it can carry. A television channel requires over 30 *million* bits per second, while a telephone channel can get by with 32 *thousand* bits per second, and most microcomputers communicate at 3 *hundred* bits per second. Thus, satellites can carry an immense number of computer-to-computer conversations.

The major advantage of communication satellites is that they are a broadcast or multipoint system. The satellite can receive a signal from *any* earth station that can see it and retransmit that signal to *all* earth stations that can see it. This means that it is just as easy to connect an earth station to 1,000 other earth stations as it is to connect it to just one other earth station. And it doesn't cost anymore to do so.

The second major advantage is that satellites are "distance insensitive." Since they can see all their earth stations all the time, it makes no difference whether two stations are 3km apart or 3,000km apart. In communication terms, Sydney is as close to San Francisco as San Francisco is to Sausalito. London is as close to Lagos as Lagos is to Lome. Land-based communications (like the telephone) get more expensive as distances get longer, and one must pay separately for each point one wants to connect. Thus, satellites are much cheaper than land-based communication where distances are long or when we want to have more than two points connected together.

SATELLITES AND EDUCATION

Most education is a form of broadcasting: one-to-many transmission of information from teacher to student, with limited feedback from students in the form of questions and examinations. In this traditional lecture approach, teacher-to-student communication is seen as primary, student-to-teacher communication is seen as secondary, and student-to-student communication is usually ignored. In **Distance Education** (q.v.) (correspondence or broadcast schools), the student-to-teacher link is severely limited and student-to-student communication is often prevented altogether. The experience of distance educators, having to cope with the absence of these kinds of communication, has made all educators more aware of their importance to the educational process.

Recent advances in communications technology, such as teleconferencing and electronic mail, have allowed distance educators to greatly improve student-to-teacher feedback and introduce student-to-student communication into distance education systems. At the same time, society has begun to consider constraints beyond distance or physical handicap which might prevent people from taking advantage of traditional, in-classroom education. We have begun to realize that shift workers with irregular work schedules, or parents who are homebound by small children, are also effectively denied a higher education. In a world that is growing ever more complex and competitive, we are beginning to see these people as a resource we cannot afford to waste.

A number of educational systems have been designed around communications technology to begin to tap this pool of unmet demand for higher education. The most famous of these is probably Britain's **Open University** (q.v.), but there are many others—some larger, some smaller, some older, some newer. The successful ones, like the Open University or British Columbia's Knowledge Network or Mexico's Radio Primeria, have demonstrated the ability to teach twice the students at half the cost of in-classroom instruction, while maintaining or improving the quality of teaching and the success rates of the students. The advent of satellite communications has made such success easier.

There are six major ways that satellite communications can improve the quality and reduce the cost of educational enterprise.

Extending the Reach of an Instructor to Hundreds of Students. Traditional classroom instruction is limited by the number of people that can fit into a given location. The maximum number for a simple face-to-face lecture is around 30, if everyone is to have a clear view of the demonstrations or the explanatory material which the instructor puts on the chalkboard. In larger classes, slides and overhead projectors must be added to ensure that all can see. In the larger universities, where a top lecturer may face an auditorium of 300 students, it is quite common to have video cameras focused on the teacher and the chalkboard, with monitor screens scattered around the lecture hall. A broadcast system is merely an extension of this approach, allowing the instruction to be carried to distant classrooms, or even direct to student homes. A telephone return line permits the students to ask questions of the lecturer. Adding a satellite link to such a system means that the instruction can go not just around a city, but around the country or around the world.

Improving Education Quality by Guest Lectures and Team Teaching. A major limiting factor on educational quality is that most classes are taught by a single instructor. No matter how good that instructor may be, his or her knowledge and opinions are necessarily limited. Most instructors overcome this by inviting guest lecturers, whether other teachers or outside experts, to address their classes. Prior to telecommunications systems entering education, the host instructor depended upon local guest speakers who could take the time to come to the class. If a distant expert was required, the cost of travel and accommodation had to be met by the host institution. Naturally, the top experts had far more requests than they could meet. Using a satellite link, a single expert can reach many locations simultaneously, at a fraction of the cost—whether measured in time or in money—of bringing the students from those distant locations to the expert or taking the expert to each location in turn. The same system can be used to allow three or four instructors from different institutions to "team-teach" a course. Students on each of their respective campuses can now have access to a mix of minds, rather than being limited to that of their local instructor.

Improve Quality and Lower Cost of Educational Materials via Exchange. Libraries have long cooperated to ensure that their patrons had access to a wider range of books than a single library could provide, by establishing a system of interlibrary loans. The same can be done with educational materials, given a communication network that makes it easy to determine what resources are available and an inexpensive method of transmitting those resources from one place to another. Dedicated educational satellite networks offer both of those possibilities for the exchange of teaching materials.

Improve Research Productivity by Increasing Scholarly Interaction. The standard lament of a research scientist trying to keep up with the newest developments in the field is that traveling to research conferences is too expensive and waiting for new results to be printed in scientific journals is too slow. Educational communication networks allow scientists to stay in constant touch with each other, sending research papers back and forth at an affordable price via electronic bulletin boards, co-authoring papers via electronic mail, holding brainstorming sessions via audio conference, and attending distant meetings via video conference.

Stimulate Consortia and Ease Coordination of Educational Lobbies. In the United States alone, there are over 200 consortia of higher education institutions. These consortia exist for the purposes of materials exchange, course coordination, joint research projects, or the furtherance of a specific educational goal. The existence of educational communications networks which allow inexpensive and easy conference calls have both stimulated the formation of such consortia around the world and made it easier for them to coordinate their activities.

Provide Communications Savings and Generate Outside Revenue. Many educational institutions that have established satellite communications networks find that they can amortize some of their costs by selling unused time to government agencies and private industry. Since a good portion of an educational institution's telephone bill is to other educational offices and institutions, the establishment of an educational satellite network can reduce existing communication costs.

SUCCESS STORIES

The examples of successful uses of satellite technology abound in all areas of the world, from Europe to South America, from Canada to Australia, from Africa to China. The successful projects use satellite for two-way communication, for radio and television broadcasts, or both, but this is always supplemented with more traditional correspondence materials. There are far too many projects to describe in this short entry, but here is a brief summary of just a few:

Air Force (U.S.) Institute of Technology Tele-teaching Network. A nine-site network that spans four time zones. Established to cope with trainee demand that was too great to be accommodated in the classroom facilities at the old training center, the network found that the savings of travel and per diem expenses for the first 360 students paid for the equipment costs.

California State University at Chico. A combination of satellite and cable systems for distance teaching across the United States. In addition to CSU's own study centers, some businesses have set up facilities at their offices so personnel can take courses without losing any work time in travel.

Indonesian Distance Education Satellite System. Connects thirteen sites (ten universities and three department of higher education offices) for teleteaching, faculty development, administration, and research. Travel costs are down slightly while meetings and faculty productivity are up considerably.

Knowledge Network of the West. Delivers televised school, college, and university programs to remote students of British Columbia, including many two-way discussions between distant students and the on-camera instructors. Cost is one-tenth of traditional campus.

Minerva Madureze (Brazil). Adult primary/secondary school by radio, plus local evening discussions with a monitor, for 177,000 students. Nationwide, the cost of 50 percent of traditional face-to-face system, though the system in Bahia state (8,000 students) cost 1,000 percent more due to overcapitalization and overstaffing. Nationwide, there was no difference in performance compared to face-to-face, but Bahia state students did less well on exams.

National Technological University (U.S.). A consortium of the top engineering schools (MIT, Cal. Tech, etc.) using video and data conferencing to offer higher degrees; began in 1985.

Ontario Tele-Medicine Network. Connects six remote communities to two capital-city teaching hospitals for medical consultation, social therapy, and in-service training. Also handles about 45,000 patient contacts per year.

Television University (China). Television, viewed at work, supplements correspondence. Began in 1979 with 186,000 students—now about 1 million. Detailed cost comparisons not available, but Chinese authorities say it is lower, which is why they expanded the system so rapidly. Urban-based television students do better in exams than their face-to-face counterparts.

University of the South Pacific. Voice and data network connecting the central (Fiji) campus with nine campuses in the other member nations for administration, materials exchange, research, and tele-tutorials. USP-NET began in 1979, and the 1985 failure of the ATS-1 satellite nearly caused a collapse of the university system. Immediate replacement, via Intelsat circuits, was considered vital for institutional survival.

University of the West Indies Distance Teaching Experiment. A satellite audio-conference network connecting five island campuses for teleteaching and administration, beginning in 1983. Operates from 8:00 A.M. to 9:00 P.M. averaging 34 course-hours per week, with administrative meetings fitting in between the courses. Reduces time lost for in-service teacher training by 60 percent.

(U.S.) Veterans Administration (VA) Medical Network. A pilot project connected 32 VA hospitals for in-service training for doctors, nurses, dietitians, and social workers. After seeing the results, VA plans to extend the network to 132 sites.

BARRIERS TO DEVELOPMENT

Although the costs of satellite communications can be quite low, especially when shared among a large number of users, international politics and commerce place a major limitation on the use of satellites for educational networks. Most nations that participate in the Intelsat system have a policy of monopoly carriers for international communications traffic, and domestic satellites are generally prohibited from carrying international traffic. This tends to increase the cost and the complexity of satellite communications by adding a series of middleman companies between the users and the potential network. This monopoly situation is beginning to be broken down in North America and Western Europe, but it may be a long time before this happens in other regions of the world.

In many countries, internal communications are also the property of monopoly carriers, and educational users are further restricted by being prohibited from selling any excess capacity in their satellite system to business users. This makes it difficult for the educational institutions to amortize their costs. These internal monopoly carriers are not sympathetic to educational networks, since they realize that the educators will use their networks in place of making long-distance telephone calls, and hence cut telephone-company revenue. Since the government usually owns the monopoly carriers, this is not an easy barrier to overcome. However, the most important barriers are not economic, but social. The purchase of communications hardware does not guarantee that any use is made of it. Numerous underused educational television and radio studios around the world indicate what can happen if technology is purchased without a commitment to training teachers in its use. These studios are not idle because they are ineffective, nor because they are too costly. They are idle because teachers have not been trained how to use them, and because use of them simply does not count in the performance measures by which teachers are judged for promotion and tenure.

Within a given institution or a given educational system, the most important barriers to progress in educational telecommunications are ignorance, fear, apathy, and lack of encouragement. Most teachers, whether at school, college, or university, have had little contact with satellites and communication technologies during their own education. Their resulting ignorance is a breeding ground for a normal fear in the modern world: that the new technology will somehow take over their jobs. From this fear arises a general opposition to any technological solution to teaching problems. At the same time, most instructors are already working quite hard at their current jobs and have difficulty finding the time to learn about new and possibly frightening things. Putting new technology to use in the classroom has traditionally been a voluntary overload on a few dedicated idealists committed to finding a better way to teach. The majority, seeing this extra effort go completely unrecognized and unrewarded, justifiably consider their own apathy towards satellite communication to be a highly sensible approach.

However, as more and more educational satellite networks prove their worth around the world, we can expect to see more and more support from government and educational administrators. And as this support builds to include recognition and rewards to the successful educational technologists, we will see a concerted effort to deal with the social, economic, and political barriers. In the end, satellite communications will become as normal a part of the education system as did textbooks, calculators, and computers, each in its turn.

Jim Lange

REFERENCES

Bates, A. W. (1975) "Obstacles to Effective use of Communication Media." In *Aspects of Educational Technology 8*. London: Pitman. The new teaching media are underused due to lack of clear teaching objectives, insufficient integration in the curriculum, insufficient recurrent funds, and ignorance of potential benefits.

Commission on Instructional Technology. (1970) *To Improve Learning*. Washington, D.C.: Government Printing Office. U.S. government compilation of research results in instructional technology which is valuable for the number of proven techniques that were known in 1970, but which have yet to be incorporated into educational planning.

Daniel, J., Stroud, M., and Thompson, J. (1982) *Learning at a Distance: A World Perspective*. Edmonton: Athabascan University.

Directors-General of Education. (1981) "Report of Working Party on Educational Use of a Comsat." Canberra: Department of Education. Stresses that technology is only one component in a telecommunications mix, and that use will depend on educator awareness and ownership/control issues. Still no evidence of any planning.

Entwhistle, N. J. (1982) *Styles of Learning and Teaching*. London: John Wiley.

Forsyth, K., and Collins, C. (1983) *British Columbia: Higher Education and New Technology*. Victoria, B.C.: Universities Council of B.C.

Gosling, G.W.H. (1972) *Telecommunication in Education*. Hawthorn: Australian Council for Educational Research. Documents a low level of interest and a lack of planning by educators.

Jamison, D. and McAnany, E. (1978) *Radio for Education and Development*. Beverly Hills, Calif.: Sage Publications.

MacGregor, A. and Mitchel, B. (1984) *Using the Knowledge Network*. Victoria, B.C.: Knowledge Network of the West.

National Science Foundation. (1981) *Learning and Electronic Technology*. Washington, D.C.: Government Printing Office. A more recent U.S. government compilation of the research results about potential benefits. Still no serious consideration of the institutional barriers to adoption.

Parker, L. and Olgren, C. (1984) *The Teleconferencing Resource Book*. Amsterdam: North Holland.

Peraton, H. (1979) *Alternative Routes to Formal Education*. Baltimore: Johns Hopkins University Press.

Ratcliff, J. (1983) "Improving College Curriculum Through Teleconferencing." Dublin: 9th Annual Conference on Improving University Teaching. Iowa State University first used audio-teleconferencing in 1939, but this 45-year-old technology has not caught on in academia, despite the fact that it has been shown to cut costs, save time, and improve faculty productivity, course quality, and off-campus course reliability. The main reason for lack of adoption is that technology requires new skills, new knowledge, and new curricula.

Schramm, W. and Vollan, C. (1982) *A Sampler in Distance Education*. Honolulu: East-West Center.

COMMUNICATION THEORY. See **Communication Engineering; Information Technology.**

COMMUNICATIONS SATELLITE. A vehicle placed in an orbit around the earth and used to relay signals between earth stations. A passive satellite merely reflects signals beamed towards it, whereas an active satellite receives, amplifies, and retransmits such signals. *See* **Geostationary Orbit.**

COMMUNICATIONS SATELLITE CORPORATION (COMSAT). Operates a worldwide communications satellite organization with countries in the International Telecommunications Satellite Consortium.

950 L'enfant Plaza S.W., Washington, D.C. 20024, U.S.

COMOPT. Abbreviation for "combined optical." Optical sound track printed onto a film which also carries pictures.

COMPACT DISK (CD). A small laser-read disk originally used for high-quality digital reproduction of music. However, applications for data storage have become very important: in this mode the disks are referred to as CD–ROM. *See* **CD–ROM.**

COMPANY GAMES. Games where most of the functions of a company are simulated and the players are only concerned with internal operations and consequences of decisions. *See* **Business Games; Simulation and Gaming.**

COMPATIBILITY. The ability of one manufacturer's equipment to work with that of another manufacturer. For example, 16mm film projectors and audiocassette recorders have no compatibility problems, whereas the various competing formats of video recorder and videodisc are completely incompatible.

COMPETENCY-BASED EDUCATION. A form of individualized, self-instructional teaching where the learners are not allowed to progress to the next stage of the learning program until they have demonstrated competency or mastery of the present stage: often the mastery criterion is 100 percent success. An alternative term is **Performance-Based Education** (q.v.).

COMPILER. A computer program that translates high-level computer languages such as COBOL, FORTRAN, and Pascal into computer-specific instructions (machine code).

COMPLEMENTARY COLOR. The color that is left when a primary color is removed from white light. It is thus a combination of the other two primaries. The three complementary colors are magenta (minus green), cyan (minus red), and yellow (minus blue).

COMPONENT RESOURCES. The need to develop a definite strategy to produce resources which will support an educational activity is now considered to be essential. The exclusive use of "chalk-and-talk," albeit sometimes effective, is a damnation of style and dates the user as being old-fashioned. Thus in a new **Training technology** (q.v.) or **educational technology** (q.v.), the creation of support material, aids, and new methods of approach becomes the "core" of any new curriculum. It is in this area of developing resource materials that this strategy is applied, emphasizing the need for that material to be widely available, acceptable to the user *and not highly structured*. Such resources, when produced, will become "components" able to be integrated into many more designs than if they were structured into a complete design at the onset.

That integration into a systems design may well be a nontraditional system such as is involved in a **Distance Education** (q.v.) mode. When involved with distance education it becomes even more important that the resources are components and not tightly bound into the structure of the presentation. If they were tightly linked, then the resources would become the "core" of a remote learning situation as they are material things; this would divert the attention from the interactive control needed by the distance teacher in these non–face-to-face situations.

Thus a strategy must be developed to produce a resource as a component, in its own right. In this way it will be flexible and yet capable of complete curriculum support.

THE STRATEGY OF SEVEN LEVELS

In the development of a resource, there comes a time when a decision has to be made in order for something concrete to be produced. That production decision can be made intuitively, whereby the designer's past experience will be used naturally, or it can be based on some prescription which would lead to a decision capable of being analyzed or discussed.

Many algorithms exist which will assist production. Romiszowski (1968) offers some useful and original algorithms based on sound structure, but the structure and decision-making process involved in their creation is not available to the user and so he is constrained to the algorithmic process itself. In simple terms, when designing or approaching any sequential event, in addition to a precise knowledge of the objective, the design team needs a route guide. This route should itself be dependent on the objective but also be more prescriptive of the means of getting there.

It was with this in mind that seven levels of structure were designed to be considered as seven points on a route to a possible terminal objective (not all objectives will need Level 7). It is essential to the concept of this method that each component or control point is reached and is considered necessary in the achievement of the objective level required. The seven levels are:

Level 1: Jargon and Definitions

Level 2: Component Point Recognition and/or Location

Level 3: Awareness of Purpose or Usage of Component Points

Level 4: An Ability to Practice the Components of Usage or Skill (Groups of Component Points)

Level 5: Awareness of Sequences or Relationships of Groups of Component Points

Level 6: Skill Performance or Application of Relationships in a Sequence

Level 7: Start and Finish Discrimination and Extrapolation

Each level is separately described in more detail.

Jargon and Definitions. This level is of terminology only. It is the level of requirement where knowledge of a word or phrase is present without any necessary accompanying awareness of its full meaning or relationships. It is, however, often necessary where a new word or visual language symbol is present. For example, in geography, the fact that a particular place-name refers to a town and not to a river is necessarily learned before the actual location or other aspects of the concept for which the name is learned. Another way of explaining this is to compare the answers to "Name three rivers of Australia" with "Where is the River Murray?"

Component Point Recognition and/or Location. The components referred to are not necessarily physical; they could be conceptual. It is really a recognition of the meaning of the jargon. The coincident level, involving locating a concept or component, implies looking for it, which is a higher-level skill than recognizing it when it is presented. This is the kind of level required of an apprentice in his first week, or a student at his first lectures, both being presented with all the many components that the lecturer will be dealing with at a later stage. Eventually the lecturer will expect the early components to be recognized and found without being highlighted, presented, or shown.

Awareness of Purpose or Usage of Component Points. This, as an addition to recognizing components, becomes a level in the affective domain (prior to Level 4, which is practical). The purpose of a group of components or events must be realized prior to using that group. Since this is an awareness component, it would very seldom be a terminal objective other than in situations where someone else takes on Level 4 in a later training or education program.

An Ability to Practice the Components of Usage or Skill (Groups of Component Points). This is the achievement or practice of the concept or skill unit or the use of the particular group of components *out of context* from their normal sequence or situation. It is the kind of component that varies enormously in student achievement, and the methods of dealing with it similarly vary from teacher to teacher and trainer to trainer. It is often a psychomotor terminal objective which will be present in any program, whether or not higher levels are to be considered. Typical of this level would be such aims as "the placing of a word in a sentence," "the manipulation of a specific algebraic process," "the performance of a particular group of component skills in a trade" (such as drilling a hole). It should be emphasized that at Level 4 the skill may be performed out of context from a real situation in which it is normally involved. The interrelationship of similar or close components should be avoided until the next level.

Awareness of Sequences or Relationships of Groups of Component Points. This is the level at which the relationship of the components which have been dealt with at the previous level are dealt with as an awareness exercise in order that they may be practiced later. Once an overall awareness has been established, some strategy can be planned for the complete objective. It will be necessary to establish at this level whether or not the skill sequence will be learned by heart, will be directed step by step by a supervisor, or will be clued by some form of checklist. Such a decision will define quite clearly the level of evaluation finally required.

Skill Performance or Application of Relationships in a Sequence. This is where the final skill is to be completed to the level of guidance required as just defined. This guidance in the terminal skill can be in simple or complex form, and definitely stated (e.g., as is required at some stage by a student of parachute jumping, or in a more academic situation, when a lecturer presents closely reasoned arguments to a class).

Start and Finish Discrimination and Extrapolation. This situation is really a review of the whole process, expanding the awareness and ability to a judgment level such as is required by the person receiving training or education in order to teach others. In most cases, if this level of training is required, it will be achieved by practice of the skill and subsequent discussion and review of the activity preceding it. The strategy prescribed by these seven levels provides the skeleton framework on which to base a design or presentation. If the skill is needed to reach any level, it is necessary to have passed through all of the subordinate levels. It is considered whether or not the skill can be achieved. The treatment should not be confused with the taxonomy presented by Bloom (1956), which really defined levels of cognition that could be present in any objective. Such levels will still be present to a greater or lesser extent on each of the levels of treatment outlined in this seven-level strategy. The difficulty of the route through each point or level will depend on the vehicle being used and the "road surface." Bloom's taxonomy really defines route difficulty whereas the "seven-level strategy" gives some descriptive indicators of the route itself.

PRODUCING THE COMPONENT RESOURCES

If a media production requirement is analyzed in terms of the seven levels, the levels themselves can be looked at as offering some form of solution to the form of media requirements. Levels 1, 2, and 3, dealing with component points, will likely be supported by discrete resources for each point; such resources could be called "component resources." Level 4, being a natural skill in its own right, albeit out of context, will be practiced using "realia," or at least exercised by the learner in a classroom situation. Level 5 begins to present an awareness of a sequence of skills or a relationship between concepts. This awareness of the fact of a skill's existence will be mainly in the affective domain and can be presented with what one could call a "complete medium" such as film, tape-slide, or even the teacher by himself. Finally, Levels 6 and 7 are the levels dealing with the complete skill performance and the perfection of that performance.

Level	Description	Resource suggestion
1, 2, 3	Jargon + components	Component resources
4	Skill unit not in context	Actual practice
5	Awareness of sequence	Film, multimedia "complete" package depending on situation
6, 7	Complete skill sequence	Practice depending on situation

One can readily perceive an enormous difference between Levels 1, 2, and 3, and the remainder. Levels 1, 2, and 3 will be included at some stage and in some form, whatever method of approach is chosen. These components are the "core," the "essence" of the whole subject. If materials can be manufactured supporting these core components, then they will be applicable to *all approaches* to the subject in question whether they are used by teachers or students. Thus, component resources allied to the "core" component points will have many component uses and will prove multipurpose or flexible.

The objective continuum dealt with by Morse (1970) suggested a range of objectives. This range had longer-term use and a wide range of application; such a wider range of application is related to the above description of a "core" requirement. The use made of such resources will increase their cost-effectiveness.

ACCEPTABILITY OF SIMPLE RESOURCES

Effectiveness cannot be just a simple judgment of whether a resource works: whether it will be used is usually more important. The availability, acceptability, and awareness of a media solution is just as important as the experimental success level that it achieves in relation to a problem. Today we must consider far more than a discrete media solution to a discrete problem.

When resources are related to a distance education problem, there well may be a need to constrain the whole delivery system to a telephone line, thereby limiting the choice of resources to *still* pictures by **Slow Scan Television** (q.v.) or **Facsimile** (q.v.) or the use of Videotex as in the Tarcoola experiment. The acceptance of such a constraint could bring to the fore the essential nature of a face-to-face visit or demonstration particularly when the seven levels analysis had suggested the content as being a Level 5 or 6.

If a resource is not able to be used due to format or unacceptability, it just won't be used; if this can't be understood, more problems will generate and the objectives will not be attained. The rationale by which one should produce flexible resources is almost a justification after the event. It is only in the production of such components as "visual nouns" that it is possible to realize the enormous shortage of such visuals actually existing in this simple support role.

The term *flexible resources* should perhaps more realistically and more correctly be *essential component resources*. The flexibility of such resources is not just a flexibility of usage by different people for different purposes; it is a flexibility of usage by the same person for different objectives. It must be possible to dispense a prescription of learning aimed at an individual person, or even a small group, which suggests uses of the same resource in a different way to suit their own particular needs. It has long been accepted that the ingredients of a cake in different proportions, put together by different people, are accepted by an enormous variation of consumers. "Flexible resources," then, are resources produced as ingredients or components of a learning objective.

If component resources are flexible resources, they will be used both in face-to-face situations and in distance education by more people, and in practical terms become cost-effective in all situations to which they are carefully applied by selection.

AN EXAMPLE

The Educational Technology Centre of the South Australian Education Department produces resources according to the strategy described above. The particular format is called Pic-a-Pak. The Pic-a-Pak resource materials are designed to be as flexible as possible; they are unstructured, unsequenced, but always based on a given topic. "Designed to be used as support material, background material or even just a collection of raw resource material, based on a specific subject, which could be of assistance in the preparation of lessons or projects." This material was constrained at all design stages to be supportive only up to Level 3 of the strategy, and has been specifically intended to be of flexible usage and of generalized component form.

Many Pic-a-Pak packages contain color transparencies. However, color photographs, overhead projectuals, and even audiocassette tapes may be included. They may contain notes as background or other related supportive material. In order to cross-reference and select components, a reference sheet with black-and-white copies of all the pictures is included as well as a sample library catalog card.

The use of these resources and their choice has also been well reported in the Tarcoola Report as well as the other reports on the communication experiments listed in the references from the South Australian Education Department's Technology Centre. The very existence of the component resources both highlighted the topics and allowed the content of the lesson to be developed totally to the needs of the distance learners. Such a distance use becomes related to the "face-to-face" teaching situation by the resources themselves as the common factor with the objectives.

CONCLUSION

The bridge between the theory of component resources and their use in practice (judged by the sales of and demand for the Pic-a-Pak format) has successfully been traversed, and it must be left for educators to judge the value of, and continuing need for, these "ingredients" as components of learning resources. It is in this way that the creation of our educational resources can be firmly built with simple, precisely defined ingredients or components as their foundation. Even if the building alters shape, the ingredients will remain and can be reused. Such components can support many resource systems for many purposes and could be considered to be visual and/or aural "nouns" for all approaches both from a distance and in face-to-face situations.

Colin Dunnett

REFERENCES

Bloom, B. S. et al. (1956) *Taxonomy of Educational Objectives—Handbook I: Cognitive Domain*. New York: Longman, Green.

Morse, S. L. (1970) "Educational Technology and the Behavioral Objective." In *Aspects of Educational Technology IV*, ed. A. C. Bajpai and J. F. Leedham. London: Pitman.

Romiszowski, A. J. (1968) *The Selection and Use of Teaching Aids*. London: Kogan Page.

South Australian Education Department. (1980) "Communications Experiments for Remote and Isolated Education." Adelaide: Educational Technology Centre, South Australian Education Department.

———. (1981) "Tarcoola Project." Adelaide: Educational Technology Centre, South Australian Education Department.

———. (1983, 1984) "Status Reports." Adelaide: Educational Technology Centre, South Australian Education Department.

Telecom Australia Research Laboratories. (1980) "Teleconferencing Research: Progress Problems & Future Directions." Melbourne: Telecom Australia Research Laboratories.

University of Wisconsin. (1986) *Teleconferencing and Electronic Communications*, vols. 1–6. Madison: University of Wisconsin, Center for Interactive Programs.

———. (1986) *Teleconferencing Directory*. Madison: University of Wisconsin, Center for Interactive Programs.

COMPOSITE VIDEO. Originally this term referred to video signals with picture and sync (timing) information combined in one signal. In current use, it often means standard color video signals that can be connected by a single shielded wire to a monitor. Because the total signal capacity in composite video must split among the picture, color, and timing signals, there is less bandwidth for picture details. Thus, composite video is of inferior quality compared with the equivalent RGB display.

COMPRESSED AUDIO (STILL FRAME AUDIO). A system for providing several seconds of audio to accompany individual frames on a videodisc. This is achieved by digitally encoding the sound.

COMPRESSED SPEECH. *See* **Time-Compressed Speech.**

COMPRESSION. In order to modify a volume range that is too big to be accomodated by a recording system, compression is introduced to reduce the amplitude of the original signal.

COMPUSERVE. U.S. computer information service offering electronic shopping, mail, bulletin board, data, etc., to subscribers via microcomputer and modem.

5000 Arlington Center Blvd., Columbus, Ohio 43220, U.S.

COMPUTER-AIDED DESIGN (CAD) AND DRAFTING (CADD). The use of computers as aids to design and drafting, exploiting computer capabilities of calculation, storing and retrieving data, and of making drawings.

COMPUTER-AIDED LEARNING. Synonym for computer-assisted instruction. From time to time attempts have been made to add precision to the various combinations of words possible in this context, but current usage is very much a matter of individual preference. *See* **Computer Nomenclature.**

COMPUTER-ASSISTED (AIDED) INSTRUCTION (LEARNING) (CAI, CAL). This term usually refers to systems providing on-line direct interactive instruction, testing, and prescription. The dialogue may be based on many different strategies ranging from drill and practice in arithmetic and spelling, through Socratic inquisitory investigations, to "learner-controlled discovery" of scientific or literary truths. *See* **Computer-Assisted Instruction; Computer Nomenclature.**

COMPUTER-ASSISTED INSTRUCTION.

INTRODUCTION

The objective of this entry is to survey current activities in computer-assisted instruction (CAI). In a rapidly developing technology the literature is not as well defined as in the case of more theoretical matters, nor is it in easily accessible journals. Many of the items that I have referenced have appeared only as reports, with limited circulation; in some cases it has been difficult to establish the date the report was issued.

Before discussing the substantive developments in CAI, there is one general issue that is worth elaboration. It is the question of whether or not computers and related forms of high technology constitute a new restraint on individuality and human freedom. There are several points I would like to make about the possible restraints that widespread use of computer technology might impose on education. The first is that the history of education is a history of the introduction of new technologies, which at each stage have been the subject of criticism. Already in Plato's dialogue *Phaedrus,* the use of written records rather than oral methods of instruction was criticized by Socrates and the Sophists. The introduction of books marked a departure from the personalized methods of recitation that were widespread and important for hundreds of years until this century. Mass schooling is perhaps the most important technological change in education in the last one hundred years. It is too easy to forget that as late as 1870 only 2 percent of the high school–age population in the United States completed high school. A large proportion of the society was illiterate; in most other parts of the world the population was even less educated. Moreover, the absence of mass schooling in many parts of the world as late as 1950 is a well-documented fact. The efforts to provide mass schooling and the uniformity of that schooling in its basic structure throughout the world are among the most striking social facts of the twentieth century. It is easy to claim that with this uniform socialization of the primary school, especially, a universal form of indoctrination has been put in place. There is something to this criticism, for the similarity of curriculum and methods of instruction throughout the world is surprising, and no doubt in the process unique features of different cultures have been reduced in importance, if not obliterated.

My second point is that the increasing use of computer technology can provide a new level of uniformity and standardization. Many features of such standardization are of course to be regarded as positive insofar as the level of instruction is raised. There are also opportunities for individualization of instruction that will be discussed more thoroughly in later sections, but my real point is that the new technology does not constitute in any serious sense a new or formidable threat to human individuality and freedom. Over a hundred years ago in his famous essay *On Liberty,* John Stuart Mill described how the source of difficulty is to be found elsewhere, in the lack of concern for freedom by most persons and in the tendencies of the great variety of political institutions to seriously restrain freedom, if not repress it. We do not yet realize the full potential of each individual in our society, but one of the best uses we can make of high technology in the coming decades is to reduce the personal tyranny of one individual over another, especially wherever that tyranny depends upon ignorance. The past record of such tyranny in almost all societies is too easily ignored by many who seem overly anxious about the future.

CAI IN ELEMENTARY AND SECONDARY EDUCATION

In this section, some examples of CAI at the stage of research and development for elementary and secondary schools, and also some examples of commercial products that are fairly widely distributed, are considered. As in the case of the sections that follow, there is no attempt to survey in a detailed way the wide range of activities taking place at many different institutions. It is common knowledge that there is a variety of computer activity in secondary schools throughout the United States and in other parts of the world. A good deal of this activity is not strictly to be classed as computer-assisted instruction, however, but rather as use of the computer in teaching programming, in problem solving, or in elementary courses in data processing oriented toward jobs in industry.

At the public school level the largest number of students participating in CAI are those taking courses offered by Computer Curriculum Corporation (CCC), with which I am associated. At the time this entry was written, more than 400,000 students were using the CCC courses on an essentially daily basis. This usage is spread throughout the United States; most of the students are disadvantaged or handicapped.

The main effort at CCC has been in the development of drill-and-practice courses that supplement regular instruction in the basic skills, especially in reading and mathematics. The courses offered in 1986 by CCC are listed in Table 3, with grade levels shown after each course. The two most widely used curricula are Mathematics Skills, Grades 1–8, and Reading for Comprehension, Grades 3–6.

Strands Strategy. The strands instructional strategy plays a key role in many of these courses, and its explanation is essential to a description of the CCC curricula. A strand represents one content area within a curriculum. For example, a division strand, a decimal strand, and an equation strand are included in the Mathematics Skills curriculum. Each strand is a string of related items whose difficulty progresses from easy to difficult. A computer program keeps records of the student's position and performance separately for every strand. By comparing a student's record of performance on the material in one strand with a preset performance criterion, the program determines whether the student needs more practice at the same level of difficulty within the strand, should move back to an easier level for remedial work, or has mastered the current concept and can move ahead to more difficult work. Then the program automatically adjusts the student's position within the strand. The process of evaluation and adjustment applies to all strands and is continuous throughout each student's interaction with a curriculum.

Evenly spaced gradations in the difficulty of the material allow positions within a strand to be matched to school grade placements by tenths of a year. Grade placement in a specific subject area can then be determined by examining a student's position in the strand representing that area. Since performance in each strand is recorded and evaluated separately, the student may have a different grade placement in every strand of a curriculum. Teacher's reports, available as part of each curriculum, record progress by showing the student's grade placement in each strand at the time of the report.

In a curriculum based on the strands instructional strategy, a normal lesson consists of a mixture of exercises from different strands. Each time an item from a particular curriculum is to be presented, a computer program randomly selects the strand from which it will draw the exercise. Random selection of strands ensures that the

Table 3
CAI Courses Offered by Computer Curriculum Corporation

MATHEMATICS

    Math Concepts, K-3
    Math Skills, 1-8
    Problem Solving, 3-6
    Math Enrichment Modules, 7-Adult
    Introduction to Logic, 7-Adult
    Introduction to Algebra, 9-Adult

READING

    Audio Reading, K-2
    Basic Reading, 2
    Reading, 3-6
    Reading for Comprehension, Revised, 3-6
    Practical Reading Skills, 5-8
    Critical Reading Skills, 7-Adult
    Adult Reading Skills, Adult

LANGUAGE SKILLS

    Spelling Skills, 2-8
    Language Arts Strands, 3-6
    Writing: Process and Skills, 6-9
    Fundamentals of English, 7-Adult
    English as a Second Language, 4-Adult
    Adult Language Skills I, Adult
    Adult Language Skills II, Adult

OTHER

    Survival Skills, 9-Adult
    GED Preparation, 9-Adult
    Keyboard Skills, 4-Adult

COMPUTER EDUCATION

    Computer Literacy, Elementary, 4-6
    Computer Literacy, 7-Adult
    Programming with MICROHOST BASIC, 9-Adult
    Introduction to Computer Science with Pascal, 10-Adult
    Introduction to Data Processing with COBOL, 10-Adult
    Introduction to UNIX Operating Systems, 10-Adult

COURSES BY TELEPHONE

    DIAL-A-DRILL Mental Arithmetic, 1-8
    DIAL-A-DRILL Spelling, 2-8
    DIAL-A-DRILL Reading, 1-4
    DIAL-A-DRILL Practical Reading, 5-Adult

Table 4
The Strands in Mathematics Skills, Grades 1–8

Strand	Name
1	Number Concepts
2	Addition
3	Subtraction
4	Equations
5	Measurement
6	Metric Measurement
7	Applications
8	Multiplication
9	Division
10	Fractions
11	Decimals
12	Problem Solving

student will receive a mixture of different types of items instead of a series of similar items.

Each curriculum also provides for rapid gross adjustment of position in all the strands as the student first begins work in the course. Students who perform very well at their entering grade levels are moved up in half-year steps until they reach more challenging levels. Students who perform poorly are moved down in half-year steps. This adjustment of overall grade level ensures that students are appropriately placed in the curriculum and is in effect only during a student's first ten sessions. I describe briefly three of the courses.

Mathematics Skills, Grades 1–8. This course contains twelve strands, or content areas. Table 4 lists the strands in the mathematics curriculum. The curriculum begins at the first-grade level and extends through grade level 9.0.

Each strand is organized into equivalence classes, or sets of exercises of similar number properties and structure. During each CAI session in mathematics, students receive exercises from all the strands that contain equivalence classes appropriate to their grade levels. Students are not given an equal number of exercises from all strands. The program adjusts the proportion of exercises from each strand to match the proportion of exercises covering that concept in an average textbook.

The curriculum material in Mathematics Skills, Grades 1–8 is not prestored but takes the form of algorithms that use random-number techniques to generate exercises. When a particular equivalence class is selected, a program generates the numerical value used in the exercise, produces the required format information for the presentation of the exercise, and calculates the correct response for comparison with student input. As a result, the arrangement of the lesson and the actual exercises presented differ between students at the same level and between lessons for a student who remains at a constant grade placement for several lessons.

Students are ordinarily at terminals about ten minutes a day, during which time they usually work in excess of 30 exercises. Thus, a student following such a regime for the entire school year of 180 days works more than 5,000 exercises.

Reading for Comprehension, Grades 3–6. This curriculum consists of reading-practice items designed to improve the student's skills in six areas: word attack, vocabulary, literal comprehension of sentence structure, interpretation of written material, passage comprehension, and study skills. It contains material for four years of work at grade levels 3, 4, 5, and 6 as well as supplementary remedial material that extends downward to grade level 2.5.

Special features of the course include the following: optional mouse to select answers, automatic analysis of student spelling or capitalization errors, selected tutorial messages in response to content errors, advanced vocabulary and comprehension exercises at a seventh-grade level, and capability to print out individualized worksheets to provide additional exercises.

Language Arts. This curriculum stresses usage instead of grammar and presents very few grammatical terms. It is divided into two courses, Language Arts Strands and Language Arts Topics. Both courses cover the same general subject areas, but their structures are different. Language Arts Strands uses a strands structure to provide highly individualized mixed drills (Table 5). In Language Arts Topics the entire class receives lessons on a topic assigned by the teacher.

Evaluation. The three curriculums just described have had extensive evaluation by many different evaluation groups, including individual school systems. More than 40 such studies are reported in Macken and Suppes (1976 EVALUATION) and Poulsen and Macken (1978 EVALUATION). A detailed mathematical study of individual student trajectories is found in Suppes, Macken, and Zanotti (1978 EVALUATION).

CAI IN POSTSECONDARY EDUCATION

In this section some salient examples of CAI at universities, community colleges, or other postsecondary institutions are examined to provide a sense of the conceptual variety of the work that is being undertaken. There has

Table 5
The Strands in Language Arts Skills, Grades 3–6

Strand	Content
A	Principal Parts of Verbs
B	Verb Usage
C	Subject-Verb Agreement
D	Pronoun Usage
E	Contractions, Possessives, and Negatives
F	Modifiers
G	Sentence Structure
H	Mechanics

been no attempt to survey the wide range of activities taking place at many different institutions.

Undergraduate Physics at Irvine. Perhaps the best-known current example of the use of computers for instruction in college-level physics is the work done by Alfred Bork and his associates at the University of California–Irvine. Bork has described this activity in a number of publications. In describing the objectives of the kind of work he has done, I draw especially upon Bork (1978 DESCRIPTION OF METHODOLOGY), in which he describes the way in which Physics 3A was taught at Irvine in the fall of 1976 to approximately 300 students. The students had a choice of using a standard textbook or making extensive use of various computer aids. In addition, the course was self-paced; students were urged to make a deliberate choice of a pacing strategy. The course was designed as a mastery-based course along the lines of what is called the **Keller Plan** (q.v.) or PSI **(Personalized System of Instruction** [q.v.]), in which the course is organized into a number of modules. Each module is presumed to be developed around a carefully stated set of objectives, and at the end of each module, students are given a test; until a satisfactory level of performance is achieved, they are not permitted to move to the next module.

Bork describes six different ways in which the computer was used in the course. All students had computer accounts, and during the ten weeks of the term the average student used about 2.5 hours of time per week. Thus the total time involved with the approximately 300 students was about 7,500 hours in the term. Before turning to the various roles of the computer described by Bork, I would like to emphasize that, having had a personal opportunity to see some of his material, I found the use of graphic displays especially impressive and certainly a portent of the way computer graphics will be used in the future for the teaching of physics.

The first role of the computer was simply as a communication device between student and instructor. The instructor, Bork, could send a message to each student in the class, and the students could individually send messages to him. He says that typically he would answer his computer mail once a day, usually in the evening from a terminal at his home.

The second use of the computer was individual programming by the student as an aid to learning physics. The computer language APL was available to the students, and students who chose the computer track spent one of the eight units in learning APL. One reason for the choice of APL was the fact that the computer system at Irvine had available efficient graphic capability within APL.

The third role of the computer was as a tutorial device helping students to learn the basic physics to which they were being exposed. Bork properly emphasizes that tutorial programs are to be contrasted with large lecture courses in which the student must essentially play a passive role. The tutorial programs required ongoing dynamic interaction with the student, and the development of material was tailored to the needs and capacities of the students in a way that is never possible in a large lecture setting.

The fourth role of the computer was as an aid to building physical intuition. In this case, extensive use was made of the graphic capabilities available on the Tektronix terminals used in the course.

The fifth use of the computer was in giving the tests associated with each of the modules. Because of the way PSI courses are organized, alternate forms of each test were required in case the student had to take the test several times before demonstrating mastery of the particular module. During the ten weeks of the course in the fall of 1976, over 10,000 on-line tests were administered. Students perceived this test-giving role as the most significant computer aspect of the course.

The sixth use of the computer was in providing a course management system. As would be expected, all of the results of the on-line tests were recorded; programs were also developed to provide students access to their records and to provide information to the instructor.

Logic at Stanford. Since 1972, the introductory logic course at Stanford has been taught during the regular academic year entirely as a CAI course. Various aspects of the course have been described in a number of publications. Here I draw on Suppes and Sheehan (1981b DESCRIPTION OF METHODOLOGY).

Basic data on the course are given in Table 6. There are 29 lessons that form the core of the course. The number of exercises in each lesson, the mean time to complete the lesson, and the cumulative time are shown, as well as a brief description of the content of each lesson. The cumulative times are shown in parentheses after the times for the individual lessons. The data are for the academic year 1979–1980, but the data for 1985–1986 are similar. It should be emphasized that many of the exercises involve derivations of some complexity, and a strong feature of the program is its ability to accept any derivation falling within the general framework of the rules of inference available at that point in the course. For example, prior to lesson 409, students are required

Table 6
Mean Time and Cumulative Mean Time for 1979–1980

Lesson	Number of exercises	Student's time in hours	Content
401	19	.62 (.62)	Introduction to logic
402	18	.95 (1.57)	Semantics for sentential logic (truth tables)
403	14	.64 (2.21)	Syntax of sentential logic, parentheses
404	14	1.08 (3.29)	Derivations, rules of inference, validity
405	19	3.45 (6.74)	Working premises, dependencies, and conditional proof
406	16	1.71 (8.45)	Further rules of inference
407	12	2.22 (10.67)	New and derived rules of inference
408	23	12.94 (23.61)	Further rules and indirect proof procedure
409	24	2.36 (25.97)	Validity, counterexample, tautology
410	13	.56 (26.53)	Integer arithmetic
411	7	.56 (27.09)	Two rules about equality
412	7	.50 (27.59)	More rules about equality
413	7	.39 (27.98)	The replace equals rules
414	7	.95 (28.93)	Practice using equality in integer arithmetic
415	11	1.90 (30.83)	The commutative axiom for integer arithmetic
416	4	.96 (31.79)	The associative axiom
417	7	2.24 (34.03)	Two axioms and a definition for commutative groups
418	8	1.50 (35.53)	Theorems 1–3 for commutative groups
419	8	1.55 (37.08)	Theorems 4–7 for commutative groups
420	12	1.18 (38.26)	Noncommutative groups
421	8	.68 (38.94)	Finding axioms exercises
422	14	1.94 (40.88)	Symbolizing sentential arguments
423	28	2.98 (43.86)	Symbolizing English sentences in predicate logic
424	31	3.64 (47.50)	Inferences involving quantifiers
425	22	2.90 (50.40)	Quantifiers: restrictions and derived rules
426	21	1.57 (51.97)	Using interpretations to show arguments invalid
427	17	4.28 (56.25)	Quantifiers and interpretation
428	23	6.06 (62.31)	Consistency of premises and independence of axioms
429	40	4.01 (66.32)	The logic of identity (and sorted theories)

Source: P. Suppes and J. Sheehan, "CAI Course in Logic." In *University-Level Computer-Assisted Instruction at Stanford, 1968–1980*, ed. P. Suppes. Stanford, Calif.: Stanford University, Institute for Mathematical Studies in the Social Sciences, 1981, p. 194.

to use particular rules of sentential inference, and only in lesson 409 are they introduced to a general tautological rule of inference. Lesson 410, it may be noted, is devoted to integer arithmetic, which would often not be included in a course in logic. The reason for it in the present context is that this is the theory within which interpretations are given in the course to show that arguments are invalid, premises consistent, or axioms independent. In a non–computer-based course, such interpretations to show invalidity and so forth are ordinarily given informally and without explicit proof of their correctness. In the present framework, the students are asked to prove that their interpretations are correct, and to do this we have fixed upon the domain of integer arithmetic as providing a simple model.

It should be noted that students taking a Pass level require on the average about 75 hours of connect time at a computer terminal, which, at present, may be about the highest of any standard computer-based course in the country. Moreover, for students who go on to take a letter grade of A or B, additional work is required, depending upon the particular sequence of applications they take. For example, those choosing the lesson sequence on social decision theory will require an average of somewhat more than 20 additional hours. Those who take the lesson sequence on Boolean algebra and qualitative foundations of probability will require somewhat less connect time, but they do more proofs that benefit from reflection about strategic lines of attack, which need not necessarily occur while signed on at a terminal.

Also, the number of hours of connect time just discussed does not include the finding-axioms exercises but only the introduction to them in lesson 421. These exercises present the student with a number of statements about a particular theory, for example, statements about elementary properties of betweenness on the line. The student is asked to select not more than a certain number of the statements, for example, five or six, as axioms, and prove the remainder as theorems. This kind of exercise has been advocated by a number of mathematical educators.

Set Theory at Stanford. The curriculum of the course in set theory is classical; it follows closely the content of my earlier book (Suppes, 1960 BACKGROUND READING). The course is based on the Zermelo-Fraenkel axioms for set theory. The first chapter deals with the historical context of the axioms; the next chapter deals with relations and functions. The course then concentrates on finite and infinite sets, the theory of cardinal numbers, the theory of ordinal numbers, and the axiom of choice. Students who take the course for a Pass stop proving theorems at the end of the chapter on the theory of cardinal numbers. Those who go on for a letter grade of A or B must prove theorems in the theory of ordinal numbers and standard results involving the axiom of choice.

Although the conceptual content of the course is classical, the problems we have faced in making it a complete CAI course are not. The logic course just described is in many ways deceptive as a model of how to approach mathematically oriented courses, for the proofs can be formal and the theory of what is required is, although intricate, relatively straightforward compared with the problems of having reasonable rules of proof to match the standard informal style of proofs to be found in courses at the level of difficulty of the one in set theory.

The problems of developing powerful informal mathematical procedures for matching the quality of informal proofs found in textbooks are examined in some detail later and consequently will not be considered further here.

There are about 500 theorems that make up the core of the curriculum. The students are asked to prove a subset of these theorems. The number of students is ordinarily between eight and twelve per term, and therefore individual student lists are easily constructed. Students ordinarily prove between 40 and 50 theorems, depending upon the grade level they are seeking in the course. Details of the course are reported in Suppes and Sheehan (1981a DESCRIPTION OF METHODOLOGY).

Computer Programming. Various international efforts at computer-aided teaching of programming have been documented in the literature. For example, Santos and Millan (1975 BACKGROUND READING) describe such efforts in Brazil; Ballaben and Ercoli (1975 BACKGROUND READING) describe the work of an Italian team; and Su and Emam (1975 BACKGROUND READING) describe a CAI approach to teaching software systems on a minicomputer. Extensive efforts in CAI to teach BASIC have been undertaken by my colleagues at Stanford (Barr, Beard, and Atkinson, 1974, 1975; Lorton and Cole, 1981 BACKGROUND READING). A joint effort at Stanford, undocumented in the literature, was also made to teach the initial portion of the course in LISP by CAI methods. On the other hand, there is a surprisingly small number of courses in computer programming that are taught entirely by CAI and that have anything like the total number of individual student hours at terminals comparable to the logic course described above. The use of CAI for total instruction in computer programming is not nearly as developed as would have been anticipated ten years ago.

Foreign Languages. Work at Stanford in the 1960s began in the teaching of Slavic languages and was conducted primarily by Joseph Van Campen (1981a, 19818b BACKGROUND READING) and his colleague Richard Schupbach (1981 BACKGROUND READING). CAI efforts at Stanford have been devoted to a number of other languages, in particular an extensive effort in French, German, Mandarin Chinese, and Armenian.

CURRENT RESEARCH

In this section I analyze some of the main areas of current research most significant for CAI. The first concerns natural-language processing; the second, the use of digital speech; and the third, informal mathematical procedures.

Natural-Language Processing. Without doubt, the problems of either accepting natural-language input or producing acceptable informal natural-language output constitute some of the most severe constraints on current operational efforts and research in CAI. It is fair to say that there have been no dramatic breakthroughs in the problems of processing English, as either input or output, during the period covered by this entry. Moreover, these problems are not simply a focus of research in CAI but have wider implications for many diverse uses of computers. No doubt the current intensive efforts at developing and marketing sophisticated word processors for office use will have, in the next decade, an impact on the level of natural-language processing that can be implemented efficiently and at reasonable cost in hardware that is just becoming available. All the same, during the period covered by this entry, the difficulties of adequately inputting or outputting natural language by a program run by a computer, no matter how powerful, have become apparent to all who are seriously engaged in thinking about or trying to do something about the problem. From a theoretical standpoint, linguists have come to realize that syntax alone cannot be a satisfactory conceptual basis for language processing, and model-theoretic semanticists represented by logicians and philosophers have come to recognize how far any simple model-theoretic view of the semantics of natural language is from the intricate and subtle details of actual informal usage. In addition, the romantic hope of some computer scientists that the theoretical problems can be bypassed by complicated programs that do not have a well-articulated theoretical basis in syntax and semantics, as well as pragmatics, has also been dashed. Perhaps the most instructive thing that can be said is that we are much more aware of the difficulties now than we were at the beginning of the 1970s.

Uses of Digital Speech. The importance of spoken speech in instruction has been recognized from time immemorial. The earliest articulate and sophisticated advocacy of the importance of spoken dialogue as the highest form of instruction is in Plato's dialogue *Phaedrus,* where Socrates criticizes the impersonal and limited character of written records as a means of instruction. The experiments on the use of audio for CAI at the Institute for Mathematical Studies in the Social Sciences at Stanford are among the most extensive in the world and because of my own close association with them can most easily be reported here. However, I emphasize that the use of audio in CAI is the focus of continued work at other centers as well.

Research on digital speech has been a central and dominant theme of research on CAI in the institute for many years. After several years of attempting to use audiotapes of various design, beginning in the later 1960s the institute concentrated on digital speech, for three good reasons. First, it was too difficult to get adequate reliability from tape devices that were to be used on a round-the-clock basis. Second, it was too difficult to get tape devices that provided sufficiently fast seek times to retrieve any one of a large number of required messages. Third, it was ultimately unsatisfactory to use without exception prestored messages. Ordinary instruction by tutors and teachers does not take place in this fashion. Sentences are constructed on the spot, contingent upon the requirements of the moment. In similar fashion, a really satisfactory computer-driven speech device must be able to synthesize messages as required. No tape devices on the market then or now are able to meet this requirement. Even the promising videodiscs that will be available in the near future will most certainly not have seek times and transfer rates sufficiently fast to permit the synthesis of messages from stored words, syllables, or phonemes.

The technical aspects of the institute's research on digital speech will not be reported here. Twelve articles reporting the work in depth are published in Suppes (1981 AUDIO RESEARCH).

Informal Mathematical Proofs. Since the early 1960s there has been an interest in the development of proof checkers and interactive theorem provers. The initial interest was no doubt simply concern with the question of demonstrating that an application in this area was possible, even if not practical. My own interest in the subject began early in 1963, almost as soon as our work in CAI in the Institute for Mathematical Studies in the Social Sciences began. In order to take account of limited machine capacity, the early work concentrated on developing a logic course for elementary-school students (Suppes, 1972 DESCRIPTION OF METHODOLOGY). In the late 1960s the interest began to focus on more powerful proof checkers that could be used for teaching logic at the college level. Since 1972 the introductory logic course at Stanford has been taught entirely at computer terminals.

Beginning in the early 1970s we had the idea of developing a more powerful interactive theorem prover that could be used for proofs that were not from the standpoint of the use put into explicit logical form. In the development of this theorem prover we concentrated on axiomatic set theory, as a subject close to logic but still one with proofs ordinarily given informally. In fact, it is generally recognized that it would not be practical or feasible to ask students or instructors to produce proofs that satisfied explicit formal criteria. I want to be clear on the point that no one, or practically no one, has ever suggested that the formal proofs characterized explicitly and completely in mathematical logic were ever meant to be a practical approach to the giving of proofs in any nontrivial mathematical domain. The characterization of proofs in this formal way is meant to serve an entirely different purpose, namely, that of providing a setting for studying proofs as mathematical objects.

Since 1974 the undergraduate course in axiomatic set theory at Stanford has been taught entirely at computer-based terminals. The effort at producing the programs, especially the programs embodying the interactive theorem prover in its various versions, has been the result of the extended work of many people. The main improvements on the system since 1975 are the use of more natural and more powerful facilities replacing simply the use of a resolution theorem prover earlier, more student aids such as an extended HELP system, and the use of more informal English in the summarization of proofs.

These new facilities are illustrated by the output of the informal summary of review of a proof for the Hausdorff maximal principle. It is a classical exercise required of students in the course to prove that the Hausdorff maximal principle is equivalent to the axiom of choice. What is given here is the proof of the maximal principle using Zorn's lemma, which has already been derived earlier from the axiom of choice.

Hausdorff Maximal Principle: If A is a family of sets then every chain contained in A is contained in some maximal chain in A.

    Proof:
Assume
    (1) A is a family of sets
Assume
    (2) C is a chain and C $\supseteq$ A
Abbreviate:
    {B: B is a chain and C $\supseteq$ B and B $\supseteq$ A}
by: C!chns

By Zorn's lemma,
    (3) C!chns has a maximal element
Let B be such that
    (4) B is a maximal element of C!chns
Hence,
    (5) B is a chain and C $\supseteq$ B and, B $\supseteq$ A
It follows that,
    (6) B is a maximal chain in A
Therefore,
    (7) C is contained in some maximal chain in A

This summarized proof would not be much shorter written in ordinary textbook fashion. It does not show the use of the more powerful inference procedures, which are deleted in the proof summarization, but the original interactive version generated by the student did make use of these stronger rules.

THE FUTURE

It would be foolhardy to make detailed quantitative predictions about CAI usage in the years ahead. The current developments in computers are moving at too fast a pace to permit a forecast to be made of instructional activities that involve computers ten years from now. However, without attempting a detailed quantitative forecast it is still possible to say some things about the future that are probably correct and that, when not correct, may be interesting because of the kinds of problems they implicitly involve.

1. It is evident that the continued development of more powerful hardware for less money will have a decided impact on usage. It is reasonable to anticipate that by 1990 there will be widespread use of CAI in schools and colleges in the United States, and a rapidly accelerating pattern of development in other parts of the world.

2. By the year 2000 it is reasonable to predict a substantial use of home CAI. Advanced delivery systems will still be in the process of being put in place, but it may well be that stand-alone personal computers will be widely enough distributed and powerful enough by then to support a variety of educational activities in the home. At this point, the technical problems of getting such instructional instrumentation into the home do not seem as complicated and as difficult as organizing the logistical and bureaucratic effort of course production and accreditation procedures. Extensive research on home instruction in the last 50 years shows clearly enough that one of the central problems is providing clear methods of accreditation for the work done. There is, I think, no reason to believe that this situation will change radically because computers are being used for instruction rather

than the simpler means of the past. It will still remain of central importance to the student who is working at home to have well-defined methods of accreditation and a well-defined institutional structure within which to conduct his instructional activities, even though they are centered in the home. There has been a recent increasing movement to offer television courses in community colleges and to reduce drastically the number of times the student is required to come to the campus. There are many reasons to believe that a similar kind of model will be effective in institutionalizing and accrediting home-based instruction of the interactive sort that CAI methods can provide.

3. It is likely that videodiscs or similar devices will offer a variety of programming possibilities that are not yet available for CAI. But if videodisc courses are to have anything like the finished-production qualities of educational films or television, the costs will be substantial, and it is not yet clear how those costs can be recovered. To give some idea of the magnitude of the matter, we may take as a very conservative estimate in 1986 dollars that the production of educational films costs a thousand dollars per minute. This means that the costs of ten courses, each with 50 hours of instruction, would be approximately $30 million. There is as yet no market to encourage investors to consider seriously investing capital funds in these amounts. No doubt, as good, reliable videodisc systems or their technological equivalents become available, courses will be produced, but there will be a continuing problem about the production of high-quality materials because of the high capital costs.

4. Each of the areas reviewed in the Current Research section should have major developments in the next decade. It would indeed be disappointing if by 1995 fairly free natural-language processing in limited areas of knowledge were not possible. By then, the critical question may turn out to be how to do it efficiently rather than the question now of how to do it at all. Also, computers which are mainly silent should begin to be noisily talking "creatures" by 1995 and certainly very much so by 2000. It is true that not all uses of computers have a natural place for spoken speech, but many do, and moreover, as such speech becomes easily available, it is reasonable to anticipate that auxiliary functions at least will depend upon spoken messages. In any case, the central use of spoken language in instruction is scarcely a debatable issue, and it is conservative to predict that computer-generated speech will be one of the significant CAI efforts in the decade ahead.

The matter of informal mathematical procedures, or rich procedures of a more general sort for mathematics and science instruction, is a narrower and more sharply focused topic than that of either natural-language processing or spoken speech, but the implications for teaching of the availability of such procedures are important. By the year 2000, the kind of role that is played by calculators in elementary arithmetical calculations should be played by computers on a very general basis in all kinds of symbolic calculations or in giving the kinds of mathematical proofs now expected of undergraduates in a wide variety of courses. I also predict that the number of people who make use of such symbolic calculations or mathematical proofs will continue to increase dramatically. One way of making such a prediction dramatic would be to hold that the number of people a hundred years from now who use such procedures will stand in relation to the number now as the number who have taken a course in some kind of symbolic mathematics (algebra or geometry, for example) in the 1970s stand in relation to the number who took such a course in the 1870s. The increase will probably not be this dramatic, but it should be quite impressive all the same, as the penetration of science and technology into all phases of our lives, including our intellectual conception of the world we live in, continues.

5. Finally, I come to my last remark about the future. As speech-recognition research, which I have not previously mentioned in this entry, begins to make serious progress of the sort that some of the recent work reported indicates may be possible, we should have by the year 2000, or shortly thereafter, CAI courses that have the features that Socrates thought so desirable so long ago. What is said in Plato's dialogue *Phaedrus* about teaching should be true in the twenty-first century, but now the intimate dialogue between student and tutor will be conducted with a sophisticated computer tutor. The computer tutor will be able to talk to the student at great length and will at least be able to accept and to recognize limited responses by the student.

As Phaedrus says in the dialogue named after him, what we should aspire to is "the living word of knowledge which has a soul, and of which the written word is properly no more than an image."

Patrick Suppes

REFERENCE

Audio Research

Suppes, P., ed. (1981) *University-Level Computer-Assisted Instruction at Stanford: 1968–1980*. Stanford, Calif.: Stanford University, Institute for Mathematical Studies in the Social Sciences.

Background Reading

Ballaben, G. and Ercoli, P. (1975) "Computer-Aided Teaching of Assembler Programming." In *Computers in education,* ed. O. Lecarme and R. Lewis. Amsterdam: IFIP, North-Holland, pp. 217–221.

Barr, A., Beard, M., and Atkinson, R. C. (1974) *A Rationale and Description of the BASIC Instructional Program*, Technical Report 228, Psychology and Education Series. Stanford, Calif.: Stanford University, Institute for Mathematical Studies in the Social Sciences.

———.(1975) "Information Networks for CAI Curriculums." In *Computers in Education*, ed. O. Lecarme and R. Lewis. Amsterdam: IFIP, North-Holland, pp 477–482.

Lorton, P. and Cole, P. (1981) "Computer-Assisted Instruction in Computer Programming: SIMPER, LOGO, and BASIC, 1968–1970." In *University-Level Computer-Assisted Instruction at Stanford: 1968–1980*, ed. P. Suppes. Stanford, Calif.; Stanford University, Institute for Mathematical Studies in the Social Sciences, pp. 841–876.

Santos, S. M. dos and Millan, M. R. (1975) "A System for Teaching Programming by Means of a Brazilian Minicomputer." In *Computers in Education*, ed. O. Lecarme and R. Lewis. Amsterdam: IFIP, North-Holland, pp. 211–216.

Schupbach, R. (1981) "Computer-Assisted Instruction for a Course in the History of the Russian Literary Language." In *University-Level Computer-Assisted Instruction at Stanford: 1968–1980*, ed. P. Suppes. Stanford, Calif.: Stanford University, Institute for Mathematical Studies in the Social Sciences, pp. 657–664.

Su, S.Y.W. and Emam, A. E. (1975) "Teaching Software Systems on a Minicomputer: A CAI Approach." In *Computers in Education*, ed. O. Lecarme and R. Lewis. Amsterdam: IFIP, North-Holland, pp. 223–229.

Suppes, P. (1960) *Axiomatic Set Theory*. New York: Van Nostrand. Slightly rev. ed. New York: Dover, 1972.

Van Campen, J. (1981a) "A Computer-Assisted Course in Russian." In *University-Level Computer-Assisted Instruction at Stanford: 1968–1980*, ed. P. Suppes. Stanford, Calif.: Stanford University, Institute for Mathematical Studies in the Social Sciences, pp. 603–646.

———. (1981b) "Computer-Generated Drills in Second-Language Instruction." In *University-Level Computer-Assisted Instruction at Stanford: 1968–1980*, ed. P. Suppes. Stanford, Calif.: Stanford University, Institute for Mathematical Studies in the Social Sciences, pp. 647–655.

Description of Methodology

Bork, A. (1978) "Computers, Education, and the Future of Educational Institutions." In *Computing in College and University: 1978 and Beyond*. Gerard P. Weeg Memorial Conference. Iowa City: University of Iowa, p. 119.

Suppes, P. (1972) "Computer-Assisted Instruction at Stanford." In *Man and Computer*. Proceedings of international conference, Bordeaux, 1970. Basel: Karger, pp. 298–330.

Suppes, P. and Sheehan, J. (1981a) "CAI Course in Axiomatic Set Theory." In *University-Level Computer-Assisted Instruction at Stanford: 1968–1980*, ed. P. Suppes. Stanford, Calif.; Stanford University, Institute for Mathematical Studies in the Social Sciences, pp. 3–80.

———.(1981b) "CAI Course in Logic." In *University-Level Computer-Assisted Instruction at Stanford: 1968–1980*, ed. P. Suppes. Stanford, Calif.: Stanford University, Institute for Mathematical Studies in the Social Sciences, pp. 193–226.

Evaluation

Macken, E. and Suppes, P. (1976) "Evaluation Studies of CCC Elementary-School Curriculums, 1971–1975." *CCC Educational Studies* 1: 1–37.

Poulsen, G. and Macken, E. (1978) *Evaluation Studies of CCC Elementary Curriculums, 1975–1977*. Palo Alto, Calif.: Computer Curriculum Corporation.

Suppes, P., Macken, E., and Zanotti, M. (1978) "The Role of Global Psychological Models in Instructional Technology." In *Advances in Instructional Psychology*, vol. 1, ed. R. Glaser. Hillsdale, N.J.: Erlbaum, pp. 229–259.

COMPUTER-ASSISTED LEARNING. Synonym for computer-assisted instruction. From time to time attempts have been made to add precision to the various combinations of words possible in this context, but current usage is very much a matter of individual preference. *See* **Computer-Assisted Instruction; Computer Nomenclature.**

COMPUTER-ASSISTED TEACHER TRAINING SYSTEM (CATTS). A computer-based feedback system for training teachers in the Center for Innovation in Teaching the Handicapped, Indiana University. The main advantage of the system is its technical sophistication and its ability to handle complex coding procedures. An observer codes the teacher behavior and, using a coding base, punches data direct into a computer. The computer is programmed to manipulate the data and display a continuous and changing feedback pattern to the teacher via the television monitor. *See* **Interaction Analysis.**

COMPUTER AUDIO. The recognition or generation of sounds by a computer. In some cases all that is involved is random access to prerecorded messages, or comparison of a user's spoken command with commands which he has prerecorded and coded. However, true voice synthesizers, music synthesizers, and true speech recognition systems do exist. These tend to be limited to a selected subset of language, but research and development is very active in this field.

COMPUTER-BASED EDUCATION (CBE). The application of computers to the education process, as distinct from their application to training. Normally, the term *education* is taken to mean formal education, as in schools, colleges, and universities. *See* **Microcomputers in Education.**

COMPUTER-BASED TRAINING (CBT). An instructional method that uses the computer as the principal teaching agent. CBT is the industrial and commercial equivalent of **Computer-Based Education** (q.v.) covering everything from the training of aircrew on flight simulators to training of bank staff in basic clerk procedures.

COMPUTER-GENERATED SOUND. *See* **Computer Audio.**

COMPUTER GRAPHICS. The ability of microcomputers to draw pictures, on screen or on paper, depends on several factors:

Available Memory. Unless large quantities of RAM are available, graphics are restricted to simple diagrams.

Software. Construction of sophisticated graphics calls for advanced software. This is particularly true if fine detail is required, or if movement is involved, as in animation sequences.

Output Hardware. A suitable interface is required to provide an appropriate signal to drive output devices such as enhanced graphic screens.

Displays/Printers/Plotters. The final limiting factors are the resolution, color capabilities, speed, etc., of the chosen output device(s).

To achieve high-quality graphics it is essential to configure a suitable system which may well be a very expensive proposition. It will be necessary to determine the purpose of the graphic output: if the purpose is *representational,* then a lesser degree of accuracy will be acceptable than in the case of, say, CADD (Computer-Aided Design and Drafting) where the computer output must be dimensionally correct.

Early microcomputer graphics, as exemplified by the Apple II, were visibly chunky with a resolution of around 240 × 180 pixels and four colors. By 1986 it was common to have sixteen colors and a resolution of 640 × 350 pixels on an enhanced graphics adapter and screen. Undoubtedly, much higher resolutions will be soon achieved, but practical use of such fine detail will not be realized unless a vast quantity of RAM becomes available. If each pixel is individually controlled as regards color and activity, then one graphic screen of 1000 × 500 pixels (not very different in resolution from a television picture) will need 500K of RAM to construct and store. Quite apart from these RAM requirements, such a picture could not be stored on a standard MS-DOS floppy disk! Additionally, existing hard-copy output devices could not reproduce in such detail.

Thus, the middle ground of graphics can be reasonably accommodated by current technology and short-term changes in memory capability. However, the prospect of cheap television-quality graphics will have to await fairly drastic advances in both available RAM and external storage, together with the development of high-definition drivers screens, and suitable printing/plotting output devices.

COMPUTERIZED ITEM BANKING. The storing in a computer of validated multiple-choice items for inclusion in multiple-choice tests.

COMPUTER LANGUAGE. A language comprehensible to a computer. In essence, a computer operates in a machine code. As it is very difficult for a programmer to write complex instructions in this form, a high-level language is often used. The programmer writes instructions in a language such as Pascal, BASIC, COBOL, or FORTRAN, and the compiler in the computer transforms the instruction into machine code. A computer language can be either high-level (similar to everyday speech, e.g., BASIC uses commands like GOTO, END, PRINT) or low-level.

COMPUTER LITERACY. An ill-defined term concerned with computer familiarity. Problems arise in consideration of exactly what skills and knowledge should be possessed by people who, even though they may not actually work with computers, will be living their daily lives in a society dominated by the use of electronic data processing. Opponents of the concept of computer literacy draw analogies with, for example, the automobile: they argue that one may derive all the normal benefits of personal transportation without any knowledge at all of what is going on under the hood/bonnet. However, it is not unreasonable to suggest that anyone who draws such simplistic analogies demonstrates convincingly the need for computer literacy.

COMPUTER-MANAGED INSTRUCTION (CMI). (1) The use of a computer system to test learners, to prescribe subsequent learning activities, and to keep records and carry out statistical analyses on the progress of learners in an individualized instructional program. (If on-line instruction is added to a CMI system, then it becomes a CAI system.) (2) Using the computer to mark tests, keep an item bank for multiple choice tests; routing students through a course of study on the basis of past attainment or the individual's characteristics; keeping of records of student performance. The computer does not provide the teaching material. (3) A synonym for a diluted form of **Computer-Assisted Instruction** (q.v.). *See* **Computer-Managed Learning.**

COMPUTER-MANAGED LEARNING (CML). The use of computers to manage the learning process, by such means as delivering and marking tests and assignments, recording results, presenting remedial materials to students who fail, and so on. A student can receive feedback on his performance instantaneously, can be given information on areas in which he is weak, can be given remedial assignments, and can be guided through a curriculum with the CML system letting him know what his next piece of work should be.

The CML system can issue reports on student progress, and report on the statistics of each question in a question bank, allowing questions that are too easy, too difficult, or too ill-advised to be identified. CML reduces the time spent by teaching staff on the administrative trivia of keeping grade books, allocating assignments, and marking tests. This releases the teacher to spend more time dealing with students' problems on an individual basis.

COMPUTER MANAGEMENT OF LEARNING (CML). *See* **Computer-Managed Learning.**

COMPUTER NOMENCLATURE. The educational use of computers has become replete with combinatory terms such as CAL, CMI, etc. It is by no means obvious just what is distinguished by these various titles, and indeed some alternatives serve no useful function.

The analysis below evaluates the more common items of nomenclature, and seeks to draw distinctions so far as they in fact exist. Three operational areas of interest are identified: Hardware, Process, and Purpose.

HARDWARE

The computer can be a mainframe (a large computer serving many users simultaneously), mini (a medium-size computer capable of serving several users at one time), or micro (a small, stand-alone computer, now often called a personal computer), either alone or in a network configuration. As the cost:power ratio decreases (i.e., more memory for less money), more variety is found in both educational and training settings.

PROCESS

Aided/Assisted. These terms are synonymous and refer to the use of a computer to achieve the desired result, generally as an adjunct to other instructional procedures.

Managed. In this kind of application the computer is usually perceived as helping teachers and/or administrators more directly than students. In overall instructional management, the computer would carry out testing, routing students through an instructional path, and record-keeping, as well as monitoring, analyzing, and reporting on student work. The student perceives the computer as directing the learning path.

Based. If an activity is said to be computer-based, it involves less direct interaction than in the above categories. Control can rest with either the student or the teacher.

PURPOSE

Instruction. This refers to what are considered the traditional teaching methods of drill-and-practice and tutorial modes. Both are prestructured by the teacher for a given student or group of students and subject matter.

Learning. This is generally used when referring to more adaptive uses of the computer, for example, simulation, modeling, and inquiry.

Training. Training traditionally has a more specific goal-oriented focus than education, often involving specific physical or mental skills that will be required by a job.

(Historically, the difference between the terms *instruction* and *learning* was a geographical one, with *instruction* being the American term and *learning* the British one. Many people now regard them as interchangeable. However, they do still carry overtones of their origins. Because the CAI movement in the United States grew out of the programmed instruction movement, early uses of the computer there were very much in that tradition, hence the more didactic implications of this term today. In the broadest sense, both terms involve using the computer in the teaching process, whether in a primary or adjunct role.)

Testing. The computer can be used in test construction, scoring, evaluation, and analysis. Either batch (delayed input-output, usually using punch cards as the input medium) or interactive (immediate response to user input) mode may be used. The computer can function as an aid to teachers or administrators in both developing and evaluating tests, and recording student achievement on established tests. Tests can be generated which are linear, randomized, or adaptive in nature, and are either general or selective in relation to subject matter.

Table 7 summarizes the common terms and their meanings as used in educational computer nomenclature.

Intelligent Tutoring Systems. Intelligent Tutoring Systems (ITS) is one of the most promising developing areas in educational computing. Known alternatively as Intelligent Computer-Assisted Instruction (ICAI), ITS grew out of adaptive or generative CAI. Common to all ITS is the presence of some form of student modeling which the computer uses in its role of "intelligent" tutor. ITS operate in the following roles: (1) problem-solving mon-

Table 7
Computer Nomenclature

HARDWARE	PROCESS	PURPOSE
Computer • mainframe • mini • micro	**Aided/Assisted** • using the/with the aid of	(prestructured) **Instruction** • traditional teaching methods • drill-and-practice • tutorial
	Managed • monitors, analyzes, reports • overall instructional management, testing planning, record-keeping • directs students • helps teachers and/or administrators	(adaptive) **Learning** • simulation • modelling • inquiry **Training** • directed toward specific goal
	Based • less direct interaction • can be student or teacher controlled	**Testing** • construction and analysis • scoring (batch or interactive) • student evaluation • general or selective • linear, randomized or adaptive

itors; (2) coaches; (3) laboratory instructors; and (4) consultants. ITS also tend to cover relatively limited topic areas (e.g., place value arithmetic) rather than total courses. (There are of course exceptions, and very complex systems exist dealing with such broad areas as medical diagnosis.) ITS generally subscribe to activity-based paradigms; it is therefore unlikely that a computer-based tutor will be able to handle all potential situations. Obviously, the sophistication of these programs will increase with advances in the field of **artificial intelligence** (q.v.).

Laura Winer

COMPUTER OUTPUT MICROFILM (COM). The use of microfilm as a high-density alternative to paper output from computers. Modern COM recorders can produce in under one minute a microfiche containing the equivalent of 400 pages of text or diagrams. This microfiche can then be reproduced by normal photographic means to provide multiple copies.

COMPUTERS IN EDUCATION. See **Computer-Assisted Instruction; Computer-Managed Learning; Computer Nomenclature; Microcomputers in Education; New Technology and Education.**

COMPUTER TYPESETTING. The use of computer hardware to process unjustified "raw" input into justified and hyphenated lines of copy. Elaborate systems allow the processing of input data at speeds of up to many thousands of characters per second.

COMSAT. See **Communications Satellite Corporation.**

CONCATENATE. To unite in a series; to connect together; to chain. For example, the synthesizing or amalgamation of data used by a computer program.

CONDENSER MICROPHONE. A type of microphone where sound waves cause varying changes in the value of a capacitor. Since the capacitor forms part of an electrical circuit, sound energy is thus transformed into a varying electrical voltage. Condenser microphones are classed among the highest-quality studio microphones.

CONDITIONAL JUMP. An instruction causing a program transfer to an instruction location other than the next sequential instruction, provided that a specific condition tested by the instruction is satisfied. If the condition is not satisfied, the next sequential instruction in the program line is executed. For example:

340 IF X=0 THEN GOTO 40000
350 INPUT Y

The program will only follow line 340 by line 350 if X does not equal zero.

CONDITIONING, CLASSICAL. Classical or Pavlovian conditioning refers to the early experimental trials with salivating dogs. If a bell is sounded at the same time as food is introduced, then eventually the sound of the bell will alone produce salivation. Such salivation is referred to as a conditioned reflex. Strictly speaking, the term should be *conditional* after "conditional stimulus." Pavlov called the response conditional to illustrate its dependence on other factors. In translating the original Russian the term *conditioned* has been used. In many senses the original meaning is more accurate.

CONDITIONING, INSTRUMENTAL. A conditioning technique similar to classical conditioning but differing in that the reinforcement occurs after a response has been made.

CONDITIONING, OPERANT. The conditioning or reinforcing of behaviors that lead directly to a predetermined goal. Literally, "related to the response (operant)." In practice, if a subject makes any move or behavior that moves it closer to the goal, i.e., gives a "correct" answer, this is reinforced. All other responses are ignored. B. F. Skinner applied the techniques of operant conditioning to education to produce the concept of linear programmed instruction. *See* **Linear Program.**

CONDUIT. A not-for-profit organization that distributes educational computer software. Inaugurated in 1971 with a grant from the National Science Foundation, CONDUIT is now affiliated with the University of Iowa. CONDUIT packages are subjected to various selection procedures to attempt to ensure suitable standards of conceptual validity, instructional usefulness, program accuracy, and portability.

A biannual magazine, *Pipeline,* is published, as are several monographs concerned with the authoring of CAL materials.

P.O. Box 388, Iowa City, Iowa 52244–0388, U.S.

CONFIGURATION. The hardware (and possibly software) arrangement of a computer system.

CONFRAVISION. U.K. audiovisual conference service. Specially equipped studios in major cities can be linked by audio and video circuits so that participants can see and speak to one another. The service is also available to certain other countries.

CONSOLE. (1) A video display and keyboard together make up the console of a computer. (2) AV term describing any sort of master control center from which operations (audio recording, video recording, dubbing, etc.) can be directed.

CONSTANT ANGULAR VELOCITY (CAV). A videodisc which revolves at a constant speed, one revolution per frame (but two fields per revolution). Each frame of a CAV disk is addressable, which renders it eminently suitable for interactive video purposes.

CONSTANT LINEAR VELOCITY (CLV). The videodisc format used for extended play (e.g., movies). Each frame utilizes a constant length of track, which enables longer playing times but with present technology removes the facility for individual frame addressability. Thus CLV disks are not suitable for interactive video. *See* **Chapter.**

CONSTRUCTED RESPONSE. A response to a question or frame in a program or test which has to be elicited from the student. That is to say, he does not select from a list of alternatives as with multiple-choice responding.

CONSTRUCT LESSON PLAN. A teaching strategy based on three major components: a Diagnostic Pretest, Lesson Plan Cards, and Content Outline. Underlying the strategy is appropriate preparatory study before instruction begins. Students complete a diagnostic test (Testing Pattern or Screening Pattern) after completing preparatory study. Lesson Plan Cards devised by the teacher concentrate on initial objectives not achieved; i.e., instruction is based on material which students have not been able to master. A Content Outline is used to ensure a continuity of instruction. Systematic evaluation of all the procedures is built into the system, and the teacher may make use of a variety of teaching aids, for example, **Response Wheels** (q.v.).

CONTACT PRINTING. Still photograph or motion picture printing in which the processed film being copied is held in contact with the raw film stock or paper during copying, thus producing 1:1 reproduction.

CONTENT ANALYSIS. "Quantitative semantics" (H. D. Haswell). A research technique which describes and quantifies the manifest content of communication. Communicated material, books, lectures, etc., can be analyzed by determining frequencies or ratios of defined categories. Recently computer programs have been written to speed up the process. Content analysis has also been used as an aid to reseach on the structure of language.

CONTINUING EDUCATION. Continuing education programs commonly make use of audiovisual media in reaching a wider audience. Such techniques as **teleconferencing** (q.v.), **slow scan television** (q.v.) etc., have been successfully utilized, as well as more conventional resources such as radio and television. *See* **Distance Education.**

CONTINUOUS CASSETTE. An audiocassette that contains a closed loop of tape. Such cassettes come in a variety of playing times.

CONTINUOUS TONE. A continuous tone visual can reproduce a range of tones from white through gray to black. Photographs and paintings are convenient examples. For a number of technological reasons continuous tone visuals are not suitable for printing press use. Photographs in newspapers, for example, are converted to halftone for printing. *See* **Halftone.**

CONTRACT-BASED LEARNING, TEACHING, TRAINING. Learning, teaching, or training in which an agreed contract of learning expectations, i.e., objectives, is drawn up between the learner and the tutor; the learner is required to fulfill the terms of the contract for assessment purposes.

CONTRAST. The difference in tone between white-and-black areas in a photograph or television picture.

CONTROL CHARACTER. ASCII code includes a number of additional characters accessed by combining a normal key, e.g., C, with a special CONTROL key, giving the ASCII character CONTROL-C. Control characters can be used for many purposes; for example, in the case of Apple II computers, CONTROL-D is a signal that the next instruction refers to the operation of a disk drive.

CONTROLLER. The electronic unit that regulates the operation of a peripheral computer device such as a disk drive. The controller takes general commands from the computer system, converts them into the actual signals for controlling the device, and brings the data and status signals from the device into the computer in the appropriate form.

CONTROL ROOM. A room adjacent to a sound or vision studio in which the actual direction of the programming operation is conducted.

CONVERSATIONAL CHAINING. A type of non-branching program devised by J. A. Barlow in which the desired answer that will fill the blank space in the frame occurs at the same point in frame two where it is emphasized in the text.

CONVERSATIONAL MODE. A computer term that describes a method of operation in which the user is in direct communication with the computer and is able to obtain an immediate response to a command. Also called "On-line mode."

CONVERSATION THEORY. A theory about conversational interactions, the phenomena studied, between "participants" who may be any of the following entities: people, groups of people, coherent (internally interacting) conceptual organizations in one person, coherent systems of shared beliefs (shared concepts). A concept is specified as one or more partially coherent mental operations or "procedures": application of a concept, to recognize, do, or build something which gives rise to a behavior, or an internally perceived image, or both. Hard-valued psychological data are held to be detectable conversational events known as "agreements over an understanding."

This theory has been subjected to more than twenty years of research, initially by Gordon Pask and his colleagues (this work is continuing) and, during the past eleven years, by many other researchers and groups. It is a predictive theory: for example, of fixity of learning strategies, conceptual and learning style, the effects of matching or mismatching teaching and learning strategies, the use of analogies reasoning, insights, and types of creative thinking, including "learning to learn" effects.

Because the definitions are of a homogeneous type, conversation theory has more compactness, as well as generality, then many socio-psychological-educational theories. Thus conversation theory claims to unify the production, stability, and reproduction of concepts and coherent collections of them: the creation of distinctions between universes of discourse (for example, biology, mechanics) and analogical reasoning between such universes. Because of these properties, the theory has conversation principles (of the information transfer of any conversational interaction, of an increase in coherence until insufficient distinction is maintained, of distinction or alternately a parity quality; autonomy or individuality): complementarity principles (of concepts, under application, and behavior; of concepts and the concepts that act productively and reproductively to stabilize them as memorable): exclusion principles (excluding concept constructions that yield insufficient distinction to maintain the coherency they are intended to achieve) and duality (for example, between the application of all concepts in a repertoire and the generation of topics, or shared concepts, and their relation by expressions in a protolanguage or protologic).

Empirical research, in the laboratory and in schools, colleges, and centers for design, has not so far refuted the crucial tenets of this theory. *See* **Entailment Mesh.**
Gordon Pask

CONVERTER. Efficient transmission through **cable television** (q.v.) systems is best achieved by transmitting at the lowest possible frequencies. In order for a conventional television receiver to accept these frequencies, it is necessary to pass the signal through an electronic box called a converter. The converter changes the signal frequencies to those appropriate to the VHF and/or UHF channels of the receiver.

By these means it is possible to have up to 40 or more channels on a cable-TV network.

COPY. (1) To take a selected portion of a screen or document, leaving it intact, and to put a duplicate of that portion onto a clipboard. From the clipboard, it can be pasted into other documents or into a new place in the same document. (2) Typescript or graphic material prior to being typeset or photographed. Material prepared for photographic or more especially photomechanical processes.

COPY CAMERA. In printing or reprography, a camera used to transfer finished copy, artwork, etc., onto a photographic film or photographic plate, together with its ancillary equipment (lighting system, stand, timer, etc.).

COPYING. The process of making photographic reproductions of graphic material, manuscripts, printed matter, paintings, photographs, etc. Although any camera may be used for copying, special copy cameras are available which allow the copy to be held flat and evenly illuminated and the camera to be accurately positioned and focused and held rigidly. *See* **Reprography.**

COPYRIGHT (U.K.). There are very few states which do not have copyright laws, but the form varies from country to country, and in a brief survey it is impractical to attempt to discuss the provisions of each. This entry therefore concentrates on an examination of the principles generally accepted as the basis of copyright legislation and a review of the ways in which copyright influences the adoption of modern educational methods. The principles of copyright may be summarized as the means by which a society confers on works of the intellect the characteristics of ownership which it recognizes in respect of physical property. Some countries, notably those in the Commonwealth, adopt the British approach by granting to the owner of the copyright the sole right to do, or authorize someone else to do, certain acts; and the intention is that in granting authority the owner may make a charge, normally called a royalty, and so be financially rewarded and encouraged to produce more works. Some countries, including France, also confer a "droit moral," a recognition that the creator of a work retains a moral right even after copyright has been completely transferred. This prevents the mutilation or distortion of the work in such a way that the creator's reputation and honor are prejudiced, a privilege unrecognized in British copyright law which takes a more pragmatic and commercial attitude to the matter. Most countries now adhere to either or both the Berne Conventions (1886, 1967) and the Universal Copyright Convention (1952). There are some notable exceptions, in particular China, although it may join the Berne Convention in the near future. These conventions, in general, provide that each member state will extend to the nationals of other member states the same degree of protection as it extends to its own. The conventions apply only to what might be termed the traditional types of material, namely literary, dramatic, musical, and artistic works, together with photographs and cinematograph films. Sound recordings and broadcasts and the rights of performers are not included, although some countries, including the United Kingdom, confer copyright or some other form of protection on these elements, and there are international conventions which relate to them, although few countries have so far ratified them. It may be assumed, therefore, that literary, dramatic, musical and artistic works, photographs and films are protected in most countries irrespective of the country of origin and some countries extend protection to domestic and foreign sound recordings, broadcasts, and performances also.

The period of time during which copyright subsists varies, but 50 years from the death of the author or from first publication is most prevalent and is recommended by the Berne Convention. The Convention specifies that the first owner of a work should be the author (or composer, painter, etc.), but some countries make an exception where the work is produced as part of the duties of the author as an employee. In these cases the first owner is the employer, and this principle is of particular interest to teachers and others who produce original material for inclusion in multimedia packs for use within the institution by which they are employed. The acts which are reserved to the owner of the copyright are, under the Convention, left to the discretion of the member states but they require that, in the Berne terminology, *"reproduction...in any manner or form"* should be an act which, if unauthorized, infringes the copyright. A false assumption which frequently causes confusion is that because, as in the United Kingdom, there may be a single piece of copyright legislation, there is a uniform set of regulations for every category of material protected. This is not the case; the law relating to literary material may differ in significant detail from that provided for, say, artistic works. The differences may be even more significant, as between the traditional types of material and those of the technological era such as sound recordings and films. The logic behind these differences is that the creators or producers of, say, a sound recording, require a different kind of protection from those producing paintings; an obvious example being that while a record company will wish to control, and so financially benefit from, public performances, this is of no interest to a painter since you cannot sing a portrait. A proper appreciation of this theory is of practical importance when considering the copyright status of composite works, those which are made up of a number of different protected works or materials, each separately protected and subject to regulations specific to itself. A sound recording consisting of songs is a simple example, there being at least three distinct copyright elements.

An important element in the application of **educational technology** (q.v.) is the need to provide resource material tailored for individuals or small groups, and although some of this material may be specially produced, much will consist of copies or recordings of or from existing material such as periodicals, textbooks, music, sound recordings, and broadcasts. Bearing in mind the international nature and the extended duration of copyright protection, it is apparent that in most cases such copying and recording will be prohibited unless authority is first obtained. However, the Berne Convention acknowledges the need for concessions to permit the reproduction of works for certain purposes and permits a member state to make appropriate provisions. Many states have made concessions for the benefit of education, but the rapid development of reprographic equipment such as the photocopier and the widespread introduction of tape recorders and video recorders in institutions has created a situation where the need and capability of education to reproduce are often hampered by a copyright law designed to cater to traditional teaching methods. The U.K. Copyright Act of 1956 is a case in point, for although it permits the reproduction of literary, dramatic, musical, and artistic works in schools, it expressly prohibits the use of appliances for making multiple copies and, in addition, does not permit the copying of sound recordings and broadcasts (both protected in the United Kingdom) or films. The failure of the law to keep pace with reality means that a teacher, in order to produce the needed teaching material, must either break the law or undertake the often difficult task of seeking permission each time he or she wishes to copy. The teacher may also be required to pay a royalty. This dilemma faced by teachers in Britain is shared by their colleagues in many other countries and this, together with the growth of copying in the home and in industry and commerce, e.g., the videocassette recorder, has prompted consideration at both the national and international level of ways in which the demand of society to copy on a large scale may be reconciled with the necessity to protect the creator of copyright material from the detrimental effect of reduced sales and royalties which might in the long term lead to a reduction in the amount of new material being produced.

Before going on to consider the ways in which this reconciliation might be achieved, it is important to realize that copyright law does not seek to prohibit a teacher or anyone else from making copies or recordings of protected material. It only requires that, apart from any statutory concessions, the teacher has the permission of the copyright owner. It follows that if the rights owners were willing and able to reach agreement with those using material for teaching purposes, there would be no need for government intervention in the form of new legislation. In essence the present difficulties can be blamed only partly on obsolete laws and primarily on the failure of rights owners and users to make arrangements for their mutual benefit. With few exceptions rights owners have failed to adapt to the changes in their market resulting from the recently acquired ability of their customers to copy. Instead of regarding copying by the user as an opportunity, they have responded in a negative way by treating it as a threat. The theory that the customer is always right is one which any business disregards at its peril, but there are, for example, publishers who resist, even in principle, the perfectly laudable demand of teachers to make copies of extracts from books in order to improve the efficiency of their teaching. Teachers, if using resource-based methods, require not class sets of textbooks but extracts from several books, together with other material specially selected for the purpose. In short, the teacher requires not "books" but "literary works," and publishers, as well as the holders of copyright in other classes of material, might profitably pay more attention to selling the right to copy as a parallel to the selling of materials.

That mutually beneficial progress can be made within the existing law is demonstrated by a licensing scheme negotiated by the **Council for Educational Technology** (q.v.) in 1973, which permits commercial sound recordings and the musical works and performances on them to be copied onto tape for curriculum purposes. The scheme, a model of its kind, allows education authorities and independent institutions to acquire an annual license permitting unrestricted copying of recordings owned by the licensee, who is not required to document the recordings copied. A separate license is available for resource centers which compile programs for distribution to schools, and although this license is subject to certain conditions, they are by no means onerous.

Educational institutions in the United Kingdom also benefit from arrangements made by the broadcasting authorities with rights owners and performers which permit the off-air recording of educational programs for subsequent preview and playback. One condition imposed usually relates to the time the recording can be kept. A more recent development has been the introduction of a licensing scheme for the making of multiple copies of printed matter in schools. This was originally resisted by the local authorities who are responsible for state education but was reluctantly accepted after four of their number had been successfully sued for copyright infringement. The scheme is flawed by the exclusion of such publications as workbooks, maps, and sheet music but even so represents a significant step towards releasing material for class copying.

Failure to reach bilateral arrangements has in some countries resulted in alternatives being forced upon owners and users by way of statutory provisions. Such schemes are based on a principle which undermines the traditional copyright concept that the copyright owner has the sole right to control the use of his material and instead recognizes only that the owner has the right to receive remuneration for a use which he cannot legally prevent. These schemes take various forms. A German version introduced in the early 1970s charged a levy on tape recorders bought for domestic use, the proceeds going to an agency which distributed it to bodies representing composers, authors, record companies, and performers whose interests were likely to be prejudiced by the prevalence of recording records or broadcasts in the home. This approach, although undoubtedly simple to administer, is unfair in that purchasers or recorders have to pay the levy whether they are intending to record protected material or not. Sweden opted for a scheme whereby a lump sum was paid annually by the government to a collecting agency especially set up to receive it, and which permitted schools to make multiple copies of printed material. The scheme included provision for a sampling of copies made, which not only provided information of value to the agency in distributing the revenue but also enabled the annual fee to be adjusted in line with changes in copying volume.

A rather more subtle alternative to the statutory levy or license fee is to extend the principle of "fair dealing" to educational use. Fair dealing is a feature of the copyright law of the United Kingdom and provides that, for certain purposes such as private study, any unauthorized use of copyright material is not an infringement if it can be shown that in the circumstances the use was "fair" to the copyright owner. Fair-dealing provisions tend to encourage copyright owners to issue statements as to what they would consider to be fair, and these statements are very helpful in removing doubt from the minds of potential users and can also be the basis for negotiations on terms for use beyond the agreed limits. It was for this reason that the Council for Educational Technology in its evidence to the Whitford Committee on copyright proposed that the fair-dealing provisions be extended to cover both educational use and the categories of material excluded in the 1956 act, namely, sound recordings, films, and broadcasts. It has to be recognized, though, that a weakness of fair dealing is that statements by copyright owners notwithstanding, a definition of what is fair can only be provided by the courts, a time-consuming and expensive way of getting guidance. If the early court cases interpreted fair dealing in the educational context in a narrow or restrictive way, then it could only be altered by fresh legislation; education could therefore be hindered by unhelpful case law for many years. Whatever procedures are eventually adopted at either the national or international level, it is important that certain principles are understood and accepted if education is to use copyright material in the most effective manner and the livelihood of rights owners is to be protected. These are

1. Teachers must have freedom to copy all types of copyright material to meet their needs and those of their students.

2. In return for this freedom, education must accept the principle of making payment to the rights owners.

3. Rights owners must adapt to the changes brought about by the development of copying appliances and new teaching methods by accepting the need to negotiate for the copying

of material as a subsidiary, and perhaps in the long term a primary, source of revenue.

4. The conditions and regulations under which copying is allowed must be flexible enough to respond to rapidly changing needs; unhampered by arbitrary, confusing, and unenforceable limits on the volume of copying allowed; and linked to a monetary sum which is modest enough to be accepted by users but substantial enough to be worth collecting and distributing.

In short, any new legislation must be so flexible that it will serve the needs of education, and society generally, for the next 30 years, this being the period which we must expect copyright legislation to suffice. No one can foresee that far ahead, but it is certain that technological advances combined with economic and social pressures will have a profound effect on education as on all other aspects of life. New legislation must discard much of the old conventions of copyright and take a fresh look at what is needed.

In the United Kingdom the government has published a white paper which describes plans for new copyright legislation. If passed by Parliament, the legislation will permit off-air recording of radio programs and direct copying of audio material both in the home and in educational establishments. In return the copyright owners will receive the income from a levy on the retail price of blank audiocassettes over 35 minutes duration. Off-air recording of television programs will be permitted in the home free of any levy although there will be a provision to enable the government to impose one on videotapes at a later date if considered desirable. Off-air television recording in educational establishments will be permitted under compulsory licensing schemes, and the new act will include provisions designed to encourage and control voluntary licensing schemes for multiple copying of print.

Geoff Crabb

REFERENCES

Bender, I. R. (1974) "Copyright and Educational Media." In *Educational Media Yearbook 1974*, ed. J. W. Brown. New York: Bowker.

Council for Educational Technology. (1972) *Copyright and Education*. London: CET.

———. (1976) *Copyright and Contract: A Course Work Book*. London: CET.

———. (1976) *Copyright Clearance: A Practical Guide*. London: CET.

PLET. (1977) "Editorial: Copyright a Suitable Case for Exemption." *PLET* 14: 3.

Reform of the Law Relating to Copyright, Designs and Performers Protection (1981) A Consultative Document, Cmnd 8302. London: Her Majesty's Stationery Office.

Whale, R. F. (1967) *Copyright*. London: Longman.

White, T.A.B. and Jacob, R. (1973) *Patents, Trademarks, Copyright and Industrial Designs*. London: Sweet & Maxwell.

Whitford Committee. (1977) *Copyright and Designs Law*, Cmnd 6732. London: Her Majesty's Stationery Office.

United Kingdom Statutes

The Copyright Act 1956
The Performers Protection Act 1958
The Performers Protection Act 1963

Other Conventions

International Convention for the Protection of Performers, Producers of Programs and Broadcasting Organizations (The Rome Convention) 1961

COPYRIGHT (U.S.). In 1976 Congress passed a comprehensive Copyright Revision Act. Few bills have been lobbied so eagerly by so many parties, so the finished product was a series of compromises designed to appease the contending parties. Few are completely satisfied with it, yet it offers a reasonable recognition of the needs of most parties. The law closed several famous loopholes so jukebox owners now must pay annual licenses for each machine and **cable television** (q.v.) operators must pay for "distant signals" they transmit. Educational radio and television stations must pay for certain works which were previously exempt from payments.

Educators' greatest concern centers on Section 107, the fair use section. In its simplest form, it authorizes a small amount of copying not deemed injurious to the copyright proprietors. The courts developed the fair use doctrine but applied it unevenly. The 1976 act gave the doctrine statutory force, with four court-developed criteria supplied to determine whether an action is a fair use: (1) the purpose and character of the use, including whether such use is of a commercial nature or is for nonprofit educational purposes; (2) the nature of the copyrighted work; (3) the amount and substantiality of the portion used in relation to the copyrighted work as a whole; and (4) the effect of the use upon the potential market for or value of the work. These points are difficult to apply, so Section 107 of the Senate and House of Representatives committee reports (hereafter: Reports) explains some of the key points.

The Reports offer five dicta clarifying the first criterion, the purpose and character of the use: (1) The nonprofit element. Teachers in nonprofit schools have greater latitude than individuals working in for-profit organizations. (2) Spontaneity. A teacher "acting individually and at his own volition, makes one or more copies for temporary use by himself for his pupils" enjoys greater latitude in determining whether the act is a fair use. (3) Single and multiple copying. If a teacher makes just enough copies to distribute to a class and the copies are not distributed outside the class, it is probably acceptable if the number of items copied per term is not excessive. (4) Collections and anthologies. If legitimately made copies of one or more works are gathered in an anthology or collection, the action is probably an infringement. (5) Special uses. The Senate report says copying by students as an exercise in shorthand, typing, or foreign language study is a fair use. The Reports indicate it is also a fair use to record a student's musical performances for analysis and criticism. The teacher may retain the recording.

The second criterion is the nature of the copyrighted work. The Reports offer four dicta for applying the criterion to schools: (1) Material intended for performance or public exhibition. Very little copying may be done from drama, music, recorded music, and audiovisual works. (2) Consumable materials. Items designed for single use are rigidly protected from copying. Standard examinations, answer sheets, workbooks, and exercises cannot be copied. (3) Instructional materials. Textbooks and other materials intended for the school market are "less susceptible to reproduction for classroom use than material prepared for general public distribution." (4) Newspapers and news periodicals. The Reports state, "the doctrine of fair use should be liberally applied to allow copying of items of current interest to supplement and update the students' textbooks, but this would not extend to copying from periodicals published primarily for student use." The Reports add, if a work is out of print and copies are not available at a "reasonable cost," there is greater justification for copying.

The third criterion is the amount and substantiality of the material used. In dealing with collections of poems, articles, etc., the Reports suggest it is a fair use to reproduce a single poem or article, but not to reproduce the entire collection or a large part of it. In treating books and periodicals it suggests one may copy a "self-contained" portion of the work; this is understood to permit reproducing an article from a periodical or comparable excerpts from books when the copies "are not substantial in length in proportion to their source." Finally, a work cannot be copied "on a repetitive basis or for continued use." Teachers who want to copy in excess of these limitations must seek the proprietor's permission.

The final criterion is the effect of the copying on the potential market for or value of the work. If copying a work reduces the demand for sales, rentals, or leases, the reproduction is an infringement. Furthermore, if the cumulative effect of repeated copying deprives the proprietor of a sale, rental, or lease, that is also an infringement.

It must be reaffirmed that *all four criteria* (and the various parts of each) must be met in *each* instance of copying if the action is to be a fair use. An unfortunate fallacy has evolved that only one criterion (e.g., the nonprofit character of the use) must be met. Although the courts are not obligated to consider all four criteria in determining an infringement, it is foolhardy to ignore any of them.

Furthermore, the Reports indicate that making a single audio recording or braille copy of an entire work as a free service for the blind is a fair use, and institutions for the deaf may copy programs to reproduce the sound track in captions. The Reports also indicate that it is a fair use for libraries and archives to reproduce films on nitrate stock to preserve them.

The fair use section is oriented to teachers and is silent about the rights of other educational personnel. Representative Robert W. Kastenmeier, chairman of the House Subcommittee on the Courts, Civil Liberties and the Administration of Justice, clarified the matter when he presented the bill for debate in the House: "The committee regards the concept of 'teacher' as broad enough to include instructional specialists working in consultation with actual instructors." When a specialist works in collaboration with a teacher to prepare instructional materials, then the specialist has the same privileges as a teacher. This does not permit administrators to direct teachers to copy certain materials.

The 1976 Copyright Revision Act made major changes in the law, especially as it applies to schools, but it could not resolve every issue. Three issues have been in the news since the act passed: (1) copyright protection for computer programs, (2) videotaping at home, and (3) videotaping for class use. Copyright protection for computer programs was resolved by a 1979 amendment granting full protection for programs, but allowing users to make one copy of a program for archival purposes or to adapt the program for use in their machine. This copy must be retained with the original and destroyed when the user is no longer authorized to use the copyrighted work (Section 117). Subsequent court cases determined the law also applies to programs recorded on ROM and RAM chips. An amendment is under study to provide special protection for the "masks" used to produce microchips. Videotaping off the air for home use was settled in January 1984 by the U.S. Supreme Court. In *Sony v. Universal City Studios* (the Betamax case), the film company sued the manufacturer and others for infringing copyrights by manufacturing and selling the machines and by videotaping off the air. The court determined, in a five to four decision, that videotaping off the air for home use was a fair use and that the manufacturer and sale of the equipment was not a contributory infringement. The film industry is determined to obtain a secondary income from this use of their materials and it is lobbying actively for an amendment that will add a small surcharge to the sale of video tape recorders and blank videotape. The income would be distributed to the copyright owners by the U.S. Copyright Royalty Tribunal.

The issue of videotaping off the air for classroom use is still poorly defined. In 1981, after lengthy negotiation, representatives of the copyright proprietors, the guilds (trade unions), and educators developed the "Guidelines for Off-Air Recording of Broadcast Programming for Educational Purposes," which were published in the *Congressional Record*. The guidelines have been controversial from the beginning. The trade association that negotiated for the proprietors refused to ratify the document, and several major educational film and video distributors specifically repudiated it. Congressional guidelines do not have the force of law, and this one is particularly vulnerable because of the controversy over its adoption. The issue is further clouded by a recent court order in *Encyclopaedia Britannica v. Crooks*, known as the BOCES case. (BOCES derives from the name of the principal defendant, the Erie County New York Board of Cooperative Educational Services.) BOCES operated a sophisticated off-air copying service and built a library of materials copied off the air. Teachers in the twenty-odd school districts served by BOCES could obtain a copy of any program by sending a blank videotape to be copied. Teachers could use the copies indefinitely. BOCES was found guilty and required to pay a substantial sum to compensate the three plaintiffs. As a part of this case, BOCES was enjoined from further copying of the plaintiffs' films. When the case was resolved, BOCES asked to have the injunction lifted and to be allowed to copy under the terms of the guidelines. The court denied the request on the grounds that the films offered by the plaintiffs are readily available for sale, lease, or rental in film and video formats and copying them off the air deprived the vendors of their rights.

J. K. Miller

REFERENCES

Columbia Pictures et al. v. Redd Horne et al. U.S. Dist. Court for the Western Dist. of Pa. No. Civ-83–0016. 1983.

Encyclopaedia Britannica Educational Corp. et al. v. Crooks et al. U.S. Dist. Court for the Western Dist. of N.Y. No. Civ-77–560C. 1983.

"Guidelines for Off-Air Recording of Broadcast Programming for Educational Purposes." (1981) *Congressional Record* October 14: E4751.

Kastenmeier, R. T. (1976) Remarks on the floor of the House of Representatives. *Congressional Record* September 22: H10874–H10875.

Sony Corp. et al. v. Universal City Studios, Inc., et al. U.S. Supreme Court, No. 81–1687. 1984.

U.S. House of Representatives. (1976) *Copyright Law Revision, Report No. 94–1476.*

———. (1976) *General Revision of the Copyright Law ... Conference Report, Report No. 94–1773.*

United States Code, Title 17, "Copyright," Sects. 101, et seq.

U.S. Senate. (1976) *General Revision of the Copyright Law, Report No. 94–473.*

COPYRIGHT SOCIETY OF THE U.S. An association devoted to the protection and study of rights in literature, motion pictures, and other forms of intellectual property.

New York University School of Law, 40 Washington Square S., New York, New York 10012, U.S.

COPY STAND. Ideally, a heavy baseboard with a sturdy vertical column to which a camera is attached. Suitable lights may also be attached to the stand. Material placed on the baseboard is photographed for making slides or subsequent enlargement to the desired format. In education, copy stands are typically used for making slides from illustrations in magazines, newspaper photographs, etc.

CORE. Archaic term for a small piece of magnetic material used as a memory storage medium in computers.

CORRESPONDENCE COURSE. A style of teaching at a distance. Curricular materials are provided for the students and posted from the central office to the remote learner. In essence, the postal service provides the link between the learner and the tutor, but other forms of communication may be possible, e.g., satellite, telephone, television, etc. *See* **Distance Education; Teleconferencing.**

CORRUPT. To damage the data in a data base, intentionally or accidentally. Elaborate precautions must be taken before allowing widespread access to large computing systems by personal computers, in order to guard against corruption of data.

COSFORD CUBE. A simplified form of student feedback. This form of feedback was evolved at the RAF Training Center at Cosford (U.K.) where experiments were carried out to find a cheap method of feedback to the teacher. The Cosford Cube is a 2 1/2–inch (6cm) wooden block painted white, with colored circles on five of the faces, the sixth face being left all white. The edges and corners are rounded so that they fit easily in the hand. In use the cube is held in the hands so that one face is visible to the teacher. The colored faces represent a variety of possible answers. One disadvantage is encountered if students or the teacher is color blind. This can be overcome by using, in addition to colors, numbers or letters. *See* **Feedback Classroom; Response Wheel.**

COST-BENEFIT ANALYSIS. A mathematical technique that equates in monetary terms the costs and benefits accruing to a particular course of action. In general it is very difficult to give accurate monetary values to educational benefits (e.g., innovation, achievement, etc.) but relatively straightforward to do so for costs (e.g., a new audiovisual center). *See* **Cost-Effectiveness.**

COST-EFFECTIVENESS.

INTRODUCTION

In applying the term *cost-effectiveness* to an educational process we are attempting to answer the question: Is the particular process (the subject matter taught, the method of teaching, and the media used) worth the cost involved? In practice, we are not normally considering a particular educational area in isolation, but are essentially comparing one type of process with another.

We might be considering a different method of teaching, such as a modular self-tuition course or a new technical medium such as **computer-assisted learning** (q.v.). In all such cases there is a decision to be made; there is a change, or the possibility of a change, involved; and there are comparisons to be made. We are always seeking the answers to such questions as, Is this method better than that one? Which is the best way of solving this problem? Even where we conclude that things are best left as they are, a decision has been made, change has been contemplated, and alternatives have been compared.

Cost-effectiveness analysis is a methodical procedure for assembling the information required to make such decisions in a well-informed way.

COST-BENEFIT ANALYSIS AND COST-EFFECTIVENESS ANALYSIS

It is as well to draw a distinction between these two approaches as the terms are often used indiscriminately. **Cost-benefit analysis** (q.v.) is an economist's tool which was developed for dealing with investment in the public sector. It is particularly useful in evaluating the scale of costs and benefits, to the nation as a whole, in cases involving major expenditure from public funds to provide services where there is no intention of charging the users of the services with the economic cost of providing them. Such projects can impinge on the private lives of the community in complex ways, and the analysis attempts to take these social effects into account by imputing monetary values to, for example, the "cost" of noise pollution or the "benefit" of being able to make journeys more quickly. A classic example is the Third London Airport study (Commission on the Third London Airport, 1970 EXAMPLE).

With cost-effectiveness analysis, the innovations are often (but not always) on a much smaller scale, involving decisions at a departmental or institutional level. The studies are financially oriented but frequently involve qualitative effects. Monetary values are assigned only to measurable resource effects and not to qualitative effects, which are generally left as the subject of value judgments.

Essentially, the approach looks at alternative policies in one of two ways. In some cases the costs are identical but their outcomes are different; even if the outcomes are not measurable, they can sometimes be confidently ranked in order of preference and thus a clear-cut decision can be reached. In other cases, the costs are different but the outcomes can be assumed to be indistinguishable, and the cheapest alternative can be recommended. In practice, the procedure does not always enable the choice to be made quite so easily as this, but it does assemble all the information in a systematic way and concentrates subjective assessments only on the areas where they are necessary.

COSTS AND OUTCOMES

We have used the term *outcomes* rather than *benefits*. This is partly to avoid confusion with the cost-benefit form of analysis, and partly because the latter term can lead to some predetermined thinking, as it is not always obvious in the initial stages whether some effects are likely to be beneficial or not.

Costs are the resource inputs which are necessary to develop, implement, and operate a proposed change. Outcomes are the results of the change, irrespective of whether they are conventional costs or benefits; thus, there is no need to consider, at the time they are identified, whether they are positive or negative, or indeed unquantifiable. The thing that unifies the outcomes is that they are all the results of which the proposed change in the educational process is the cause.

CLASSIFICATION AND MEASUREMENT OF COSTS AND OUTCOMES

Costs and outcomes can be grouped into those which

—can be measured directly in financial terms,

—can be measured, but not directly in monetary units, and

—are unquantifiable.

Examples of the first type are the purchase of equipment or payments to external staff. The second type would include the use of the time of existing staff, or an effect on students' pass rate or dropout rate. The most common unquantifiable effect is the quality of the learning process itself.

As far as measurement of resource effects is concerned, an important concept is that of "resource units." These are the natural units in which a change in resource usage can be perceived and measured. Only in some cases is money the basic resource unit, and the use of monetary units should, at this stage, be restricted to those resource changes which directly affect the cash flow of the organization concerned.

Measuring resource effects in their basic units, and retaining them in this form, at least until a late stage in the analysis, has the following advantages:

—it inflation-proofs the raw data for further use
—it preserves the options until later in the analysis,
—it gives data which are often more meaningful than notional financial measures: the time of teaching staff is a useful measure to a departmental head, square meters of floor space to an estates officer, and seconds of processing time to a computer manager.

The main criterion for deciding which costs and outcomes to include in the analysis is that they should represent real and discernible effects which are attributable to the change which is being considered. If a new scheme requires extra accommodation, it matters little in the early stages of the study that the organization might have unused space available: there has been a real resource change, even if it is only that there is less unused space than before; it should therefore be identified for consideration later in the analysis. Generally, the only resources which can be ignored are those, such as overheads, which, in normal cost accounting, are derived purely on an allocation basis. The use of these resources will normally not be affected and can be omitted, as in cost-effectiveness studies we are primarily concerned with marginal changes and marginal costs.

Direct financial effects, whether they are costs or outcomes, do not usually present great problems other than time effects (whether to discount cash flows to their present value, or how to treat a large development investment which occurs prior to implementation). These are sufficiently well treated by conventional financial appraisal techniques.

Other measurable effects can often be given a notional monetary value, e.g., the time of existing staff or the use of existing accommodation. However, although a notional value is useful as a starting point, the analyst should consider the true value of the resource to the organization. Is the resource a scarce one? What is its likely opportunity cost, that is, the loss of the best alternative use to which the resource might be put?

THE ANALYSIS

In essence, the approach used in cost-effectiveness analysis is to

—identify the change which is being evaluated, and its objectives
—identify the resource effects and qualitative effects
—decide the basic form of analysis, including time effects, the way in which resources should be measured and treated, and the form of the final output of the analysis
—decide how qualitative effects are to be treated and presented,
—collect resource data in basic units, and other information such as numbers of students and so forth
—assemble all resource data under the headings of basic units for each period (usually a year) of the analysis
—combine data and outcomes as far as possible to give an objective measure of the cost-effectiveness

In the last stage above, the combining of data might involve netting off costs and outcomes measured in the same units against one another; for example, the purchase of equipment which reduces the real financial cost of staff. In other cases, the use of notional monetary values can be used, provided it is made clear in the presentation that they are notional and do not imply true financial effects. As already mentioned, these notional values can frequently be varied by a consideration of opportunity cost principles.

It is thus sometimes possible to reach a firm conclusion where one method is clearly better than another but does not involve any significant difference in cost, or where a cheaper method gives results which are judged subjectively to be at least as good as the alternative. Even where this is not possible, a decision maker will be presented with an orderly analysis of quantitative and qualitative data from which subjectivity has been removed as far as possible.

AN EXAMPLE

An example of a cost-effectiveness study in educational technology (Fielden and Pearson, 1978 EXAMPLE) is summarized briefly here. The study covered the reorganization of a university undergraduate biology teaching laboratory. This involved the replacement of live demonstrations of experiments by videotaped programs. The reasons for the reorganization were, first, to relieve the congestion in the laboratory arising from five simultaneous demonstrations of different experiments to groups of students; and, second, to relieve the pressure on the academic teaching staff and postgraduate demonstrators.

The significant costs were

Financial

Purchase of equipment (£)

Consumables over the 12–year assumed lifetime (£)

Measurable nonfinancial

Development by technicians and AVA staff (man-days)

Development by academic staff (man-days)

Use of AVA studio (studio-days)

The main outcomes were

Financial

Savings in the purchase of animals (£)

Savings from the reduction in recruitment of part-time associate lecturers (£)

Measurable nonfinancial

Saving in academic staff time over the scheme's lifetime (man-days)

Qualitative

Humane considerations of reducing the use of animals for undergraduate teaching

Smooth running of the teaching sessions

Claimed improvement in students' attainment and the quality of the educational process

Two of the resources (money and academic staff time) occur over the twelve years as both costs and outcome savings. These were netted off against each other year by year. Overall, the scheme showed a net cost in financial terms over its lifetime, after discounting the cash flows to their present net value. Although significant, this was relatively small compared with the initial financial outlay for equipment.

Against the net cost could be set the net saving in staff time. In notional monetary units, over all types of staff, this was equivalent to about half of the financial cost, although of course it did not represent a real financial benefit. However, the savings in academic staff time were considered to be particularly valuable as they represented a very scarce resource, whereas the costs in technician and AVA staff time had a very low opportunity cost as, at the time of the development, these resources were overprovided.

Overall, therefore, the scheme was judged (subjectively) to be well worth the relatively small financial cost, particularly when the qualitative outcomes (which included the achievement of one of the scheme's main objectives) were brought into account. This judgment could not have been made with any confidence without a systematic analysis. In particular, it was not obvious beforehand that a large part of the initial cost would be recouped in financial terms apart from the scheme's achieving its stated aims.

P. Pearson

REFERENCES

Background Reading

Dunn, W. and Cumming, C. (1970) "The Application of Cost Effectiveness Techniques to Educational Technology." *Aspects of Educational Technology,* 4. London: Pitman.

Example

Commission on the Third London Airport (1970) Vol. 7. London: Her Majesty's Stationery Office.

Fielden, J. and Pearson, P. K. (1978) *Costing educational practice*. London: Council for Educational Technology, pp. 89–105.

COUNCIL FOR EDUCATIONAL TECHNOLOGY (CET) (U.K.). The council is the central organization in the United Kingdom for promoting the application of educational technology in all sectors of education and training. It was established in October 1973 by the secretary of state for education and science, after consultation with the Scottish and Welsh secretaries of state and with the Department of Education in Northern Ireland. It is not, however, a governmental organization. Legally, it is an educational trust with charitable status, and in practice it is an autonomous body responsible for its own policy.

In 1984–1985 the council underwent a formal review of its functions and activities, as a result of which some changes have been made in the composition of the council itself and in the emphasis placed on various elements of its work.

The three-year forward plan made by the council in 1986 concentrates on "the learning process" as the central focus for the forthcoming work, and sees the following as likely to be its main areas of concern:

(a) the elements of learning

(b) the processes of learning

(c) the variety of learning styles

(d) the methods and strategies that encourage learning to take place

(e) the skills, strategies, and abilities that are needed in order for learning to occur

(f) the skills, systems, and strategies that lead the learner to increasing autonomy

(g) the methods of assessment of personal progress

Full details of the council's program are covered each year in its Annual Report, published in January. *CET News,* published three times a year, aims to keep its readers up-to-date about the progress of projects and other work and to provide contacts for further information.

Jill Coates

COURSE DESIGN. While educators have always been involved in course design, it was not until the late 1960s that a formal procedure for this activity was developed and used. The systems approach, a process for systematically solving a problem, was first developed by the military for use during World War II and then adapted by both industry and, nearly twenty years later, by education.

In two of the earliest publications addressing the use of systems design in education, Banathy (1968 HISTORICAL) defined it as "common sense by design," while Pfeiffer (1968 HISTORICAL) described the concept of a systems model as "a simplified but controllable version of a real world situation." Both saw the systems approach as an efficient and effective way of solving complex educational problems.

EDUCATIONAL APPLICATIONS OF SYSTEMS THEORY

Systems design has been successfully used to help solve many educational problems. These have ranged from long-range planning (Dresch, 1975; Society for College and University Planning, Summer 1981 APPLICATIONS); needs assessment (Kaufman et al., 1981 APPLICATIONS); and teaching conceptual networks (Markle, 1977 APPLICATIONS); to selecting instructional activities (Popham and Baker, 1970 APPLICATIONS); developing instructional materials (Kemp, 1977; Control Data Corporation, 1980 APPLICATIONS); writing behavioral objectives (Briggs, 1970 APPLICATIONS); designing instruction (Kemp, 1985 SYSTEMS MODELS); and the uses of teacher feedback (Gerlach and Ely, 1980 APPLICATIONS). The Open University in England (1977) has used the systems approach to develop independent study courses that used radio, television, and other materials; while Diamond (1975 APPLICATIONS; 1980 SYSTEMS MODELS) developed a model that was used for curriculum and course development.

SIMILARITIES AMONG EDUCATIONAL SYSTEMS USED IN COURSE DESIGN

Hannum and Briggs (1980 LITERATURE REVIEWS), in their analysis of systems design, reported numerous terms used for basically their same general process; systematic instruction (Popham and Baker, 1970; Dick and Carey, 1978 APPLICATIONS), instructional design (Briggs, 1977 SYSTEMS MODELS; Gagné and Briggs, 1979 APPLICATIONS; Briggs and Wager, 1981 SYSTEMS MODELS), instructional systems development (Branson et al., 1975 APPLICATIONS), instructional development (Silber, 1978 LITERATURE REVIEWS), and educational or instructional technology (Armsey and Dahl, 1973; Wittich and Schuller, 1979 HISTORICAL). While each specific approach differed somewhat from the others, Andrews and Goodson (1980 LITERATURE REVIEWS) noted major similarities among them:

(a) The stating of objectives, often based on a formal needs assessment.
(b) Preassessment of students.
(c) The design and implementation of formal instruction.
(d) Revision based on evaluation.
(e) Grading based on the ability to reach desired standards of student performance and criteria rather than by comparing one student with the other.

Knirk and Gustafson (1986 APPLICATIONS) identified several additional common elements, including a procedure for selecting presentation methods and media, field-testing and revision prior to use of newly developed materials and units, and, in most models, the identification of constraints imposed by physical facilities.

SIGNIFICANT DIFFERENCES

While commonalities exist among models, the differences can be significant and will be the result from any of several factors.

Setting. Individuals working at the college or university level tend to have more flexibility in structure and content than do those at the primary and secondary levels or in industry and the military where both goals and time lines are usually firm and prestated and content is often defined in advance. There are also differences in the structure of education in various countries that will either limit or expand the range of options open to the individual teacher or design team. If national or state examinations determine instructional goals, it is more difficult to challenge the assumptions and criteria on which those tests were based.

Who Is Involved. Some models of course design are for use by an individual teacher working on the improvement of his or her own teaching, a course, or a lesson. The majority, however, are structured for use with a team consisting of one or more content experts (teachers) assisted by an instructional designer or developer, an evaluator, and, when appropriate, media experts.

The Author's Perspective. Most models clearly indicate the strength(s) and the biases of their author(s). Systems designed by individuals with instructional technology backgrounds tend to place greater weight on media selection, production, and utilization, while others will stress student characteristics, needs assessment, or perhaps in-depth analysis of the instructional objectives that are to be met. There are also significant differences between models designed by the pragmatist and those designed by the theorist.

SELECTING A MODEL FOR COURSE DESIGN

Andrews and Goodson (1980 LITERATURE REVIEWS), in their article comparing models, identified over 40 with fourteen common elements. Gustafson (1981 LITERATURE REVIEWS) organized the models into four categories and, recognizing that some models exist as subsets of others, felt that no hierarchy could or should be inferred—the Classroom Focused Model, the Product Focused Model, the System Focused Model, and the Organization Focused Model. Davies (1975 APPLICATIONS) identified three basic approaches: the Product Model, the Presumption Model, and the Product-Process Model. To show the significant relationship that exists among models, Diamond (1984 LITERATURE REVIEWS) developed three different classifications: I—Classroom/Product Models; II—Support Models; and III—Comprehensive Models that utilize both of the other categories (see Figures 15, 16, and 17).

The key is selecting that particular model, or combination of models, that most nearly meets the needs, resources, and priorities of a particular project. The most successful course design projects have tended to be those that either used a broad comprehensive model or selected elements from many different approaches. Romiszowski (1981 SYSTEMS MODELS), in presenting a comprehensive model that included the elements of the more specific approaches within it, identified several hundred questions that had to be addressed in defining, analyzing, and successfully solving an instructional design problem.

These models, when used in combination, tend to have the following strengths:

(a) They focus on what and why, as well as how; i.e., basic assumptions about the content and structure of a program tend to be questioned.

(b) While the teacher or faculty member has responsibility for content decisions, others (instructional developers, evaluators, media specialists) have the responsibility for coordination, quality control, and accomplishing certain tasks.

(c) They delay producing a formal statement of instructional objectives until the overall goals of the program are known, the entering competencies and priorities of the students are identified, and the instructional content and sequence determined.

(d) They define and use evaluation in its broadest sense (including both formative and summative evaluation), and rely heavily on data collection and interpretation throughout the process.

(e) They are politically sensitive: an attempt is made to generate support, involvement, and ownership by key decision makers.

This comprehensive approach also reduces significantly those problems common to the classroom/product models:

(a) Many teachers resist stating objectives in a specific behavioral format.

(b) The more significant and long-range educational goals tend to be overlooked as less significant objectives are extensively listed.

(c) Those involved rarely question whether or not the objectives that were developed should have been included in the first place.

(d) The process tends to be insensitive to the politics of change.

Figure 15
The Interrelationship among Models

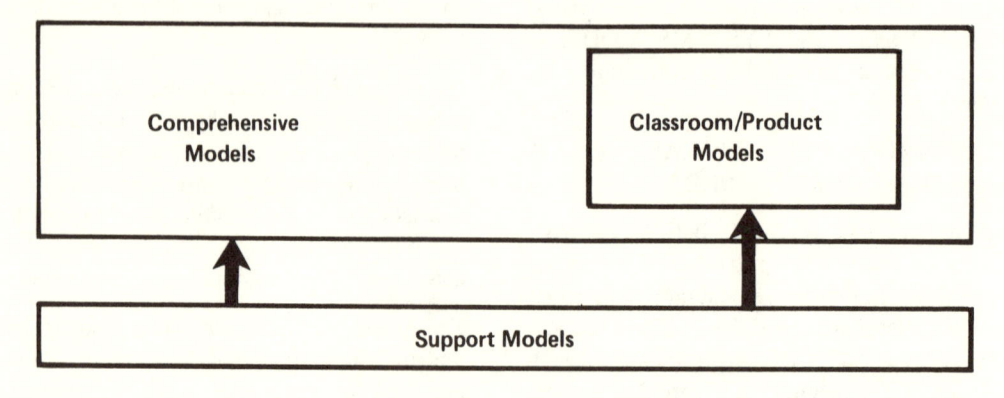

COURSE DESIGN

Figure 16
The Comprehensive Model

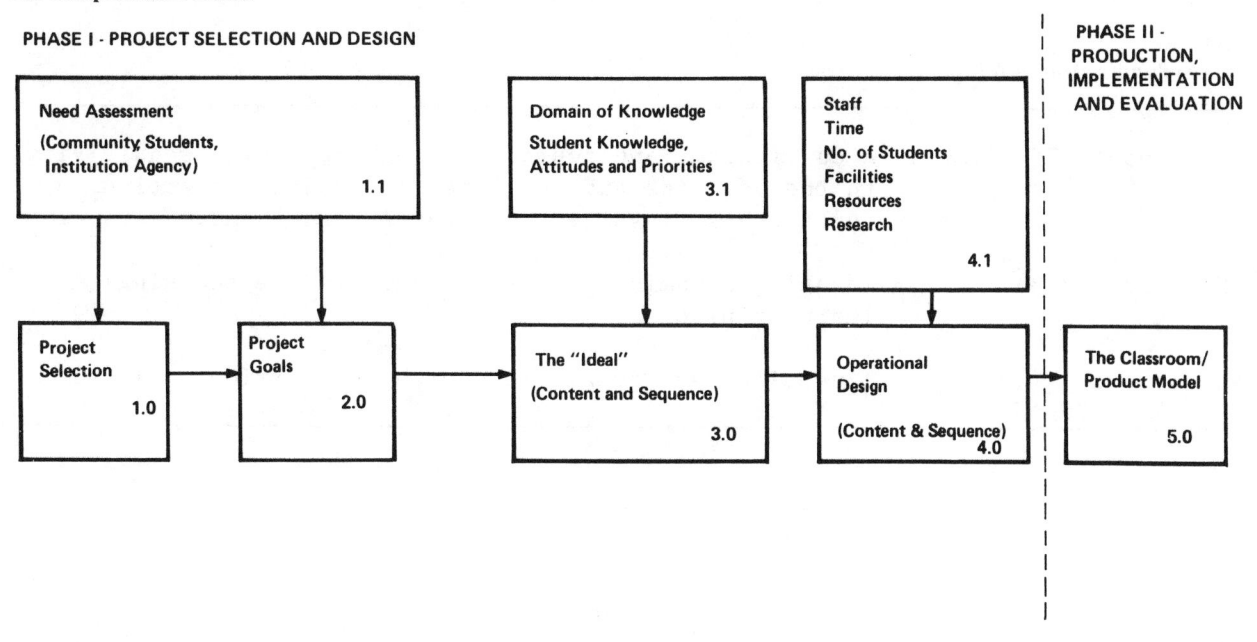

PHASE I - PROJECT SELECTION AND DESIGN | PHASE II - PRODUCTION, IMPLEMENTATION AND EVALUATION

- Need Assessment (Community, Students, Institution Agency) 1.1
- Domain of Knowledge, Student Knowledge, Attitudes and Priorities 3.1
- Staff, Time, No. of Students, Facilities, Resources, Research 4.1
- Project Selection 1.0
- Project Goals 2.0
- The "Ideal" (Content and Sequence) 3.0
- Operational Design (Content & Sequence) 4.0
- The Classroom/Product Model 5.0

Figure 17
The Classroom/Product Model

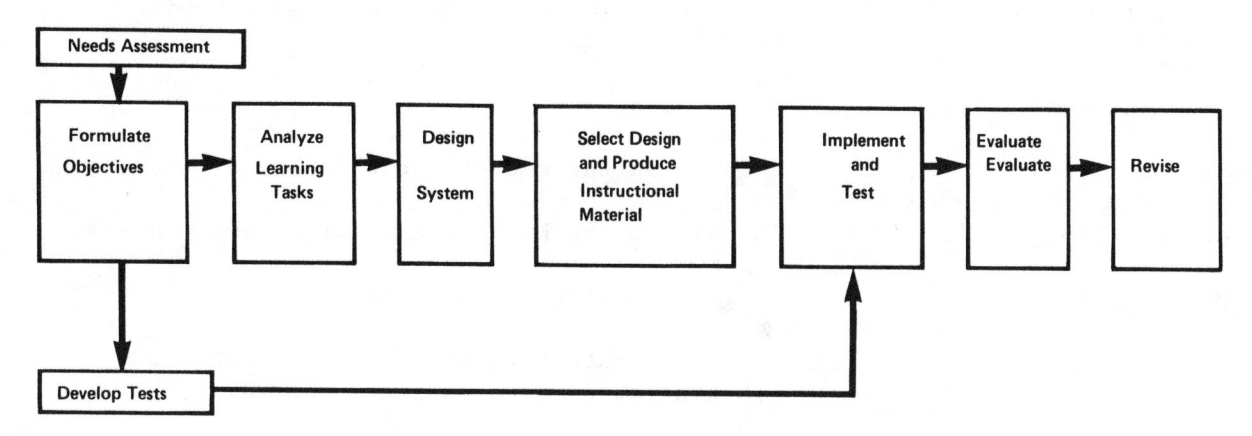

Needs Assessment → Formulate Objectives → Analyze Learning Tasks → Design System → Select Design and Produce Instructional Material → Implement and Test → Evaluate Evaluate → Revise

Formulate Objectives → Develop Tests → Implement and Test

Representative samples of Classroom Product and Comprehensive Models will be found in Tables 8 and 9.

PROJECT SELECTION

Diamond (forthcoming, APPLICATIONS) identified five conditions that should be avoided if a major course or curriculum design project is to be successful:

(a) Projects where content expertise is lacking.
(b) Projects in schools or departments that are undergoing administrative change
(c) Projects involving only one teacher or faculty member (when they leave the project, the project usually dies)
(d) Projects that do not have strong administrative support
(e) Projects where what is expected is unrealistic in terms of time and existing resources

In presenting a sequential process for project selection, he further identified five key areas of consideration:

(a) Needs and priorities (What problems exist? How important are they?)
(b) Administrative considerations (stability, long-term growth potential, etc.)
(c) Potential for success (commitment, quality of faculty, which are realistic goals)

Table 8
Comprehensive Models—A Representative Sample

Diamond (1975, 1980)	A curriculum- and course-focused model with sensitivity to the politics and realities of project selection. Forces those involved to think in the ideal.
Hamreus (1968)	Identifies administrative factors in the teaching/learning process.
Romiszowski (1981)	A detailed and pragmatic course and curriculum model.

Table 9
Support Models—A Representative Sample

Control Data Corporation (1980)	Developing instructional materials to meet training needs.
Kaufman et al. (1981)	Needs assessment
Barson (1965)	Focused on the use of media in higher education
Gagne (1965)	The use of the human component in systems design
Markle (1977)	Teaching conceptual networks
Merrill (1977)	Relating context to learning hierarchies, learning theory, and content analysis
William and Burton (1981)	Integrating learning theory with instructional design
Lent (1979)	Cost-effectiveness
Carey and Carey (1980)	Using formative evaluation in media selection
Keller (1979)	Using motivation in instructional design
Popham and Baker (1970)	Selecting instructional activities

(d) Support agency resources (availability of staff and time)

(e) Political override (importance of the project to the institution, etc.)

CONCLUSION

The systems approach can be an effective tool for helping to improve the quality and effectiveness of an existing course or in designing a new one. The process can assist the teacher in declaring a course that is sensitive to the needs, priorities, and abilities of each student and to the needs of the society and community in which it is offered and that makes maximum use of the available resources. In addition, use of this technique can substantially reduce long-range problems. Course design cannot be left to chance.

Robert M. Diamond

REFERENCES

Applications of Systems Theory

Branson, R. K., Rayner, G. I., Cox, J. L., Furman, J. P., King, F. J., and Hannum, W. H. (1975) *Interservice Procedures for Instructional Systems Development*. Ft. Monroe, Va.: U.S. Army Training and Doctrine Command.

Briggs, L. (1970) *Handbook of Procedures for the Design of Instruction*. Pittsburgh, Penn.: American Institute for Research.

Control Data Corporation. (1980) *Courseware Development Process*. Minneapolis, Minn.

Davies, I. (1975) "Some Aspects of a Theory of Advice: The Management of an Instructional Developer-Client Relationship." *Instructional Science* 3: 351–373.

Diamond, R. M. (forthcoming) *A Systematic Approach to Course and Curriculum Design*. San Francisco: Jossey-Bass.

Dick, W. and Carey, L. (1978) *The Systematic Design of Instruction*. Glenview, Ill.: Scott, Foresman.

Dresch, S. P. (May-June 1975) "A Critique of Planning Model for Postsecondary Education." *Journal of Higher Education* 46 (1): 245–266.

Gagné, R. N. and Briggs, L., (1979) *Principles of Instructional Design*. 2d ed. New York: Holt, Rinehart, and Winston.

Gerlach, V. S. and Ely, D. P. (1980) *Teaching and Media: A Systematic Approach*. 2d ed. Englewood Cliffs, N.J.: Prentice-Hall.

Kaufman, R., Stakinas, R. G., Warner, J. C., and Mayer, H. (Summer 1981) "Relating Needs Assessment, Program Development, Implementation and Evaluation." *Journal of Instructional Development* 4 (4): 17–26.

Kemp, J. E. (1977) *Instructional Design: A Plan for Unit and Course Development*. Belmont, Calif.: Fearon Publishers, pp. 74–81.

Knirk, F. G. and Gustafson, K. L. (1986) *Instructional Technology: A Systematic Approach to Instruction*. New York: Holt, Rinehart & Winston.

Markle, S. M. (Fall 1977) "Teaching Conceptual Networks." *NSPI Journal* 17 (1): 4–7.

Popham, J. and Baker, E. (1970) *Systematic Instruction*. Englewood Cliffs, N.J.: Prentice-Hall.

Society for College and University Planning. (Summer 1981) "Planning for Higher Education," 9 (4).

Historical

Armsey, J. W. and Dahl, N. C. (1973) *An Inquiry into the Uses of Instructional Technology*. New York: Ford Foundation.

Banathy, B. H. (1968) *Instructional Systems*. Palo Alto, Calif.: Fearon.

Pfeiffer, J. (1968) *New Look at Education: Systems Analysis in Our Schools and Colleges*. Poughkeepsie, N.Y.: Odyssey Press.

Wittich, W. and Schuller, C. (1979) *Instructional Technology: Its Nature and Use*. 6th ed. New York: Harper & Row.

Literature Reviews

Andrews, D. H. and Goodson, L. A. (Summer 1980) "A Comparative Analysis of Models of Instructional Design." *Journal of Instructional Development* 3 (4): 2–16.

Diamond, R. M. (1985) "Instructional Design: The Systems Approach." *International Encyclopaedia of Education*. Pergamon Press, pp. 2558–2563.

Gustafson, K. (1981) "Survey of Instructional Development Models." Syracuse, N.Y.: ERIC Clearinghouse on Information Resources, Syracuse University.

Hannum, W. H. and Briggs, L. J. (1980) *How Does Instructional Systems Design Differ from Traditional Instruction?* Chapel Hill, N.C.: University of North Carolina Press.

Silber, K. (1978) "Instructional Development: Deliverance." *Journal of Instructional Development* 2 (1): 2–5.

Systems Models

Briggs, L. (1977) *Instructional Design: Principles and Application*. Englewood Cliffs, N.J.: Educational Technology Publications.

Briggs, L. and Wager, W. W. (1981) *Handbook of Procedures for the Design of Instruction*. 2d ed. Englewood Cliffs, N.J.: Educational Technology Publications.

Diamond, R. M. (1980) "The Syracuse Model for Course and Curriculum Design, Implementation, and Evaluation." *Journal of Instructional Development* 4 (2): 19–22.

Hamreus, D. G. (April 1968) "The Systems Approach to Instructional Development." Monmouth: Teaching Research Division of the Oregon State System of Higher Education.

Instructional Development Institute. (1979) In *Instructional Technology: Its Nature and Use*, by W. Wittich and C. Schuller. 6th ed. New York: Harper and Row: 308–312.

Kemp, J. E. (1985) *The Instructional Design Process*. New York: Harper & Row.

Romiszowski, A. J. (1981) *Designing Instructional Systems*. London: Kogan Page; New York: Nichols Publishing.

Russell, J. D. and Johanningsmeier, K. A. (1981) *Improving Competence Through Modular Instruction*. Dubuque, Iowa: Kendall/Hunt

COURSEWARE. A term used in computer-assisted programs to refer to the textual and computer instructional materials, handbooks, tutorial sheets, multiple-choice questions, the program material itself; but excluding the systems programs, backup manuals, etc. Courseware has been divided into adjunct and mainline, depending on whether it augments or replaces existing instruction. *See* **Authoring Languages for Computer-Assisted Instruction; Computer-Assisted Instruction.**

COVERT RESPONSE. Behavior or a response that cannot be detected by an observer. Such behavior can only be established from observation of further behavior or by introspection on the part of the subject. In **programmed learning** (q.v.), covert responses are often contrasted with overt responses with the former being associated with shorter learning periods.

CP/M. A once widely used operating system for microcomputers (CP/M = Control Program for Micros). CP/M requires a Z-80 microprocessor to be available and thus calls for extra hardware in, for example, the Apple II series. A great deal of business software, e.g., dBase II and Wordstar, was available under CP/M.

CRASH. (1) A situation where a computer program is unable to proceed without being restarted; generally data is lost. A program usually crashes because of a bug or because it lacks sufficient error-trapping routines.(2) To destroy the contents of a hard disk, or the incident that produces such a result. Physical collisions are rare, but a program bug can overwrite files or the directory needed to find the files, making a disk unreadable.

CREDO (U.K.). Curriculum and Renewal and Educational Development Organization. *See* **Center for Educational Development Overseas.**

CRITERION. A characteristic or measurement against which other characteristics are measured. A criterion test is an undisputed test deemed to measure specific performance; thus criterion-referenced scores, etc. Criterion behavior is that expected of a subject after treatment.

CRITERION-REFERENCED TEST. A test which is rigidly bound to predetermined and defined performance standards; a test based on or derived from **behavioral objectives** (q.v.). *See* **Norm-referenced Test.**

CRITICAL PATH ANALYSIS. The determination of the critical path—i.e., a sequence of interconnected events and activities between the start of a project and its completion that requires the shortest time to accomplish. This gives the shortest time in which the project can be completed and is used as a planning aid. Critical path analysis is distinguished from other forms of network analysis by (1) separating planning from scheduling and (2) directly relating time and costs.

CRITICAL PATH PLANNING. *See* **Critical Path Analysis.**

CROP. To indicate changes in the shape or proportion of a visual. The term is used to cover the physical act of trimming a picture, the indication by crop marks or lines where a picture is to be trimmed at a later stage of production, and also for changing the area of the scene included in the viewfinder of the camera while composing the image.

CROSSTALK. If two channels carrying electrical signals are not sufficiently isolated from one another, the interference that one has on the other is known as crosstalk.

CRT. *See* **Cathode-Ray Tube.**

CRYSTAL MICROPHONE. A microphone that uses a piezoelectric crystal as a transducer. Such a crystal generates a small electric current when subjected to a mechanical force. Although inexpensive to manufacture, the frequency response of a crystal microphone is not sufficient for high-quality recording.

CSIRONET. A mainframe computer network connecting a number of tertiary and governmental institutions across Australia. Not readily accessible by microcomputers.

CUE. Another word for "prompt." In one sense it means an action or behavior that starts a chain of events. It also means the significant element(s) in a situation. It may further mean a pedagogic technique used to shape the terminal behavior of a subject. It has again been used in a specific sense of "cue consciousness"—i.e., the ability to detect hints or clues (in relation to examinations or tests).

CUE MARK (CUE DOT). A small mark which appears in the upper right-hand corner of a cine-film print to warn the projectionist that the end of the reel is approaching. The mark, usually a small circle, is on four frames at a point seven seconds from the end of the roll. A second mark appears at one second and gives the cue to start the second projector with the next reel.

CURRENT INDEX TO JOURNALS IN EDUCATION (CIJE). A monthly indexing journal (sister to *Resources in Education*), referring to more than 500 journals by subject descriptors taken from the ERIC Thesaurus of Descriptors.

866 3rd Avenue, New York, New York 10022, U.S.

CURRICULUM DESIGN. The design of the curriculum is central to the processes of planning and evaluating teaching.

THE CURRICULUM

Curriculum is at once one of the most straightforward and most elusive concepts in education. While the term itself, in English, has a long history, it has come into common use relatively recently, mainly as a consequence of the efforts in Western Europe and the United States to develop a systematic or scientific pedagogy in the late nineteenth century. Its literal and narrow meaning is a course to be run. This is a reminder that in education targets are set—courses to be completed—and that there is something akin to a race in the notions of timetable, competitive performance, and prizes to be gained by those who emerge at the head of the field. Curriculum, in the sense of a course of study to be completed, is a readily identified educational concept.

The notion of a definite course to be completed presupposes a particular view about the nature and aims of the educational process. This view is strongly disputed by educational reformers who concern themselves with children's experience, cooperative rather than competitive approaches, and a humane and enlightened pedagogy which brings into question the idea of schooling as a progression through set courses. For these educators, curriculum has other connotations than a course to be run.

A further source of confusion arises from the way the study of curriculum has extended the use of the term *curriculum* and expanded the range of its connotations. Traditionally, it has been the practice to separate curriculum design from those processes which must embody the design. This has been true of design purely through content specification and purely through objectives. More recently, the study of curriculum has increasingly emphasized the understanding of, and skills in handling, personal and social processes within the learning environment, the analysis of the situation in which the curriculum is embedded, and the sociopolitical processes of dissemination. Thus, the term *curriculum* itself comes to be used with very different connotations because of different contextual understandings and background assumptions.

More recently, curriculum research and practice have emphasized the need for curriculum design to incorporate, or even be preceded by, knowledge and experience of the situations in which curriculum is to be implemented. This knowledge and experience is focused, on the one hand, on knowledge by schools and their local hinterlands, and on the other hand, on knowledge of society as a whole in which students will be future citizens. At both levels, knowledge of the milieu is considered essential for curriculum planning. At the national level, Skilbeck (1982a) and Lawton (1983) argue for a broad cultural analysis of the society as essential input for planning a national curriculum framework. At the school level of curriculum planning "situational analysis" should precede any meaningful "goal-formation" (Skilbeck, 1982b), a point supported by Lawton (1983) and Kelly (1982).

It would be misleading to give the impression that there is a separation between national curriculum planning at the broad end of curriculum design and the planning of individual units, courses, and subjects at the sharp end. There are mutual benefits for linking curriculum planning at the national and school level. More will be said about this in the section on school-based curriculum development.

Curriculum theory (q.v.) is characterized by divergent views and rival schools of thought. The aspiration of the followers of Herbart, a German philosopher and educational theorist of the nineteenth century, to establish an agreed science of pedagogy has not been realized, notwithstanding continuing efforts particularly by some learning theorists and educational technologists. Indeed, the dispute goes beyond curriculum and pedagogy, for there is wide disagreement on what constitutes an adequate theory of learning. Curriculum theorists such as Gagné and Bruner have different views on the relationship between instruction and learning and, therefore, on what counts as appropriate curriculum design. This is because they operate with a different view of the learning process, amounting at times to a different vision of the human condition. This may explain to some extent the radical differences and depth of feeling in disputes about curriculum design. However, the study of the curriculum as a species of social inquiry is none the worse for that.

An insight into the divergence of theories is provided by the difficulties encountered in international conferences and meetings when there is a requirement to translate the word *curriculum*. These difficulties are due to the fact that in the relatively short time in which it has featured in educational discourse, curriculum has acquired an immense range of connotations. Not only does the term relate to particular institutional structures and traditions, but educational preferences and values have been attached to it.

A further aspect of usage arises from the circumstances that, since about the mid-1950s, national governments, research and development agencies, foundations, and other bodies have devoted substantial resources to the support of large-scale curriculum development processes. One consequence of this support is that the dominant features of the curriculum development movement have come to be equated by many educators with desirable features of the school curriculum and indeed with the process of course planning and teaching in the classroom. More generally, there has been a tendency to identify the processes of curriculum development with the principal and necessary constituents of curriculum theory. To give one example, the specific, and controversial, curriculum development process of predefining specific planning objectives has frequently been taken as a prescription for the process of curriculum being defined by clear-cut teaching and learning objectives; teachers have frequently been enjoined to teach as if they had clear-cut, precisely defined objectives in mind. Furthermore, it is believed by many educators that the specification of instructional objectives is a first and necessary step in any curriculum design. Following widely publicized critiques by Eisner (1969) in the United States and Stenhouse (1971) in the United Kingdom, there has been a significant challenge to these assumptions.

Much large-scale curriculum development depends for its rationale on a certain view of curriculum design, namely, the objectives-based approach which, in turn, enjoyed support from this large-scale movement especially in its earlier phases. It is an example of a theory being 'selected' because it fitted the purposes of the ultimate decision makers responsible for the large projects. There were other, well-developed views of curriculum design available, but these did not fit the needs of the decision makers. However, some of the challenges to the objectives-based approach have been more reactions than responses and have resulted in antiplanning stances. Both the extreme objectives-based approach and some of the extreme reactions have had distorting effects on balanced curriculum planning. More balanced attempts to refine the objectives model have been made, for example, by giving emphasis to cognitive processes (Bruner, 1966) and to expressive goals (Eisner, 1966), which by their generality and avoidance of a precise prespecification of behavioral outcomes meet some of the criticisms of the original behavioral model.

It is now possible clearly to indicate those types of design which are not predicated on objectives to be achieved and those in which the prespecified objectives model has no place. Nevertheless, it can hardly be said that at the level of theory a clear-cut basis for this distinction has been provided other than by the rather trivial means of differentiating explicit from implicit objectives. The difference appears to rest mainly on the values and preferences of developers and, more fundamentally, on contrasting or conflicting educational ideologies. More will be said on this matter later in this entry.

At its simplest and most orthodox, the term *curriculum* refers to the content of a program or a course of study. This content has been, for centuries, defined in three crucial ways: (a) the structure and content of scholarly texts; (b) the syllabus, or written outline of the topics and themes of a course of study; and (c) examinations. Usually, but not invariably, at the practical level of schooling curriculum discussions include the notion of a timetabled, institutionalized course. Thus arises the idea of curriculum as the "what" of teaching in classrooms. This is the popular, nontechnical concept of curriculum most widely held today. It is also basic to all attempts to frame curriculum theories and to design curricula for educational situations or institutions.

In most national systems of education throughout the world, these three items—the text, the syllabus, and the examination—will provide the definition of curriculum as perceived by teachers, students, parents, employers, and the community at large. The curriculum, according to the popular, orthodox view, has its fullest statement, first, in the text, or texts, which constitute the mainstay of teaching; second, in the syllabus, to which the texts often correspond very closely, providing a framework or outline of required study items; third, in the examination, which tests the students' mastery of the text—and the teachers' adroitness in anticipating the examiners' perception of what is significant in the prescribed course of study. At this level of perception, curriculum design consists of constructing syllabi and examinations according to certain criteria, preparing appropriate texts, and devising units of instruction. Theorizing, inasmuch as this is a critical abstract process, is often regarded as an encumbrance. Hence the popular and misleading pedagogical distinction between "theory" and "practice," theory having in the minds of many practitioners and administrators the uncomfortable character of challenging routines, obscuring apparently straightforward issues, and raising the prospect of impractical alternatives to current routines.

Closer consideration of these three basic elements in curriculum suggests that there are more fundamental factors which must be taken into account in curriculum theory and design. Of these factors, the subject or subject matter to be taught has for centuries been regarded as the most crucial. It was a recognition of the significance of subject matter in learning which led the Greek and

Roman educational theorists from the fifth century B.C. onwards to outline the content of schooling in terms of forms and fields of knowledge, the ancestors of the present-day disciplines of knowledge. The most famous and influential of these formulations, which came to be known in the medieval period as the seven liberal arts, consisted of

music	the quadrivium
arithmetic	
geometry	
astronomy	
grammar	the trivium
dialectic	
rhetoric	

These liberal arts, which were the basis of study in medieval universities, have recurred, until the present time, as the ideal basis of a general education, focused on the formation and development of cognitive skills, but including also an attempt to educate the "whole man."

By derivation, the idea that the school curriculum should largely comprise an induction into fundamental subject disciplines has always exercised a powerful hold on education, even among advocates of highly specialized education at a postschooling stage, e.g., technical education or professional studies in the university. For many, curriculum connotes basic or fundamental knowledge and skills to which are added a variety of enlightening, useful, and socially relevant accomplishments. The relationships between subject disciplines, fundamental forms of knowledge, and the concepts of liberal and general education are of great importance in forming a general theory of the curriculum. The complexity of these relationships is indicated by continuing disputes about the criteria by which disciplines may be defined, these criteria being given greater logical character by philosophers and social and psychological significance by sociologists, historians, and psychologists. Moreover, the work of some theorists, notably Arnaud Reid and Paul Hirst and Philip Phenix, in elucidating a small number of forms of knowledge and experience, e.g., scientific, aesthetic, religious, and so forth, has led many educators to suppose that these forms of knowledge were being proffered as a list of school disciplines which were to form the backbone of the curriculum.

Whether or not the forms of knowledge and the disciplines are capable of yielding an adequate and sufficient content, structure, and methodology of the school curriculum in an age of universal schooling is still one of the major areas of controversy among theorists and practitioners. The balance of opinion challenges the "sufficiency" argument in regard to the disciplines mainly on the grounds of the difficulty of teaching the disciplines progressively to all pupils, the desirability of attempting to do so, and the complexity of contemporary society of which the disciplines of knowledge form only one segment. Whatever standpoint is adopted in relation to this controversy, subject content always features in school curriculum decisions and in efforts to design and develop curriculum.

Subject matter in the school curriculum is still widely treated within or as a direct derivative of discrete disciplines of knowledge. For example, the subject matter of the mathematics textbook may consist of simplified versions of the topics from the discipline of mathematics as practiced and developed over time by academic mathematicians. Alternatively, and this has been the preference of educational reformers from Comenius in the seventeenth century to Dewey in the twentieth, subject matter may be stated with explicit reference to children's views of the world and to selected aspects of contemporary social life, and deliberate attempts may be made to interrelate subject matter from different disciplines. Some writers, notably Dewey (e.g., in *Democracy and Education*), have argued that curriculum making requires that the content of the disciplines of knowledge be analyzed into subject matter that reflects knowledge of both children's learning (psychologizing subject matter) and contemporary social interests and trends (sociologizing subject matter). Such analyses are distinctly pedagogical, and indeed, Dewey's views on these matters have played a crucial part in the emergence of curriculum theory as itself a distinctive field of inquiry and knowledge. Thus, for these theorists, curriculum is not derived through a simplification or reduction of the disciplines of knowledge, nor is teaching merely a process of motivating children to take an interest in subjects that are not of intrinsic interest to them. The starting point for curriculum design, for these theorists, is not a subject or subject matter to be learned, but an analysis of the child, his interests and needs as a learner, and the society with its needs for knowledgeable and trained citizens. Other writers, such as Ausubel, give greater weight to the value of the disciplines as themselves a means of reducing social complexity to manageable concepts. It is generally agreed, however, that any attempt to map out a whole curriculum will involve the utilization of structures, concepts, methodologies, symbols, belief systems, and forms of social organization which are embedded in the disciplines of knowledge as they are practiced in our society. What is mainly in dispute is how these features are to be used in a pedagogical, as distinct from a research, framework and what in addition is required for curriculum making which the disciplines do not or cannot provide.

In educational theory, the emphasis on the content of knowledge as the key element in curriculum has a long and tenacious history. It is an appropriate starting point for a review of the concepts of curriculum development and curriculum design, just because of the force of this idea in educational thought and practice for over two thousand years. However, it is necessary to appreciate that this emphasis represents only one view of the educational process, and it is a view, furthermore, which has been powerfully challenged, especially in modern times, from several sources. By considering these challenges in more detail, we may appreciate something of the range of connotations of the term *curriculum* and the diversity of viewpoints among theorists.

The tradition of academic disciplines of knowledge derived from the liberal arts has come to be increasingly questioned as a sufficient basis for a school curriculum ever since the introduction, in the seventeenth and eighteenth centuries in Western Europe and the American colonies, of compulsory schooling. In the present century, throughout much of the world, schooling has begun to resemble a universal social process, involving whole populations throughout childhood and, increasingly, into adolescence and early adulthood. The modern phenomenon of the whole youth of a nation being schooled has led to criticisms of the academic, specialized, selective, and demanding nature of studies deriving from knowledge disciplines. Subjects which are the staple of communities of specialist scholars in universities and research institutions have been queried as a foundation of mass education, and their relationship to the interests of intellectual and social elites has been offered as a reason for seeking a different kind of knowledge basis for the curriculum of the universal or common school. Defenders of the disciplines have argued for their universality and social relevance, distinguishing their content, structure, and methodology from the enlightened pedagogical processes which, they affirm, are a necessary adjunct to the disciplines. (This distinction has been used by some writers, not very successfully, to differentiate curriculum from instruction.) On the other hand, despite criticism from the field of pedagogy, subject-based curricula have retained much of their strength partly because, not least in developing Third World countries, an education based on the recognized disciplines is understood by parents and students to provide access to positions of status and influence in the new society. In many such countries, the efforts of political elites to transform the content of the European models of schooling they have inherited from the colonial past have been frustrated by the public's reluctance to give up a curriculum which has high social prestige and power to effect social mobility.

While the debates and power struggles continue, schooling is shifting progressively, if slowly, away from subject-defined teaching. It appears that thinkers such as Dewey, who at the beginning of this century argued powerfully against what he regarded as an elitist tradition, were at least a hundred years ahead of their time in that the shift from the subject discipline as the key determinant of school curriculum seems unlikely to occur before the end of the present century.

A second challenge to the subject as the starting point of curriculum analysis arose with the emergence of the science of psychology in the latter half of the nineteenth century. Psychology has had its greatest impact on education in the United States, which is also the country that has made the most extensive use of tests and measurements as an alternative to the traditional kind of written, discursive examination. (But the United States has not abandoned the text and the syllabi, which perhaps are as firmly entrenched in schools there as in any other country in the world.)

As mentioned above, Dewey was one of the early critics of teaching which does not ground itself in an analysis of the characteristics of the learner. As a leading figure in the movement to "psychologize teaching," Dewey in some of his pedagogical writings, such as *The Child and the Curriculum*, argued that subject matter—drawn from whatever source—be brought into a dynamic relationship with defined pupil interests and needs. The difference between this and "subject-centered" teaching may be thought to be mainly one of emphasis, but it is of great significance. In the subject-centered approach, the teachers' major curriculum reference points are their own subject expertise, deriving from their own schooling and college or university training, the textbook, the syllabus, and the examinations. By contrast, in the "learner-centered" approach the teacher acts more as a multidisciplinary diagnoser and designer of learning situations. For this purpose, single texts are of limited value, syllabi cannot be predefined except in very broad outline, and orthodox examinations are frequently irrelevant, at least on educational grounds. Correspondingly, greater emphasis is placed on training the prospective teachers in the psychology of learning, developmental psychology, pedagogy, and educational theory; and less emphasis is given to subject matter learning per se. One of the explanations for the relatively slow change in teacher orientation toward curriculum innovation, which many research studies have noted, is that the influence of the training regimen associated or allied with the content of subjects to be taught prevailed. In several European countries, the secondary schoolteacher still experiences only a minimum of training in pedagogy, receiving the major preparation for teaching through the subject departments of universities.

Since the 1930s, and especially after World War II, the major influences on curriculum theory from the standpoint of children's learning have become very diverse. They include the Swiss "developmental epistemologist" Jean Piaget; the Russian behaviorist I. Pavlov; American behaviorists and learning theorists, including Hull, Skinner, Thorndike, and, more recently, an expanding group of instructional theorists and technologists, such as Gagné, Popham, and Bloom. Much of the work of the latter group attempts to bridge the gap that appeared to be developing between some of the child-centered members of the Piagetian school, who focused on broadly defined phases or stages of human development, and the subject-centered tradition. Other attempts to bridge this gap are to be found in curriculum projects; for example, in the English Science 5–13 project and the Australian Science Education Project, where subject content is organized around a Piagetian model of concept formation.

The third and most powerful challenge to subject-centered curriculum has come from what must be broadly defined as the progressivist movement in pedagogy. This challenge has been of such strength as to have resulted in a redefinition of the term *curriculum* itself. The older and narrower view, which relates curriculum to syllabus and to predefined content to be learned, has had to be abandoned as a consequence of the displacement of one pedagogy by another. This transformation may be indicated, in an oversimplified way, by referring to two models—model A, which will be termed "limited pedagogy," and model B, which will be termed "extended pedagogy."

Model A sees the school as one of many educational agencies. Those other agencies include most conspicuously the family and the church. The school is seen as having a specific role to perform. While this role is not necessarily limited to instruction in predefined subjects, the school is organized and run on the assumption that this instruction is of crucial importance. The curriculum regimen is essentially that of subject-centered teaching. Standards are set (hence the old method of dividing the school into standards 1, 2, 3, etc) and students are instructed in such a way that they are expected or required to meet these standards. The school life may have a strong moral interest ("character building" as an educational value); indeed in some schools, notably the English public and grammar schools of the mid and late nineteenth century, this might be proffered as the chief aim of education.

Nevertheless, the basic categories of the visible curriculum are defined by a succession of subject-defined tasks to be accomplished in classrooms and according to a set timetable. Teachers and many schoolboys knew the fifth theorem of Euclid as the Asinine Bridge—those who failed to master the theorem being the asses, even if their characters were of the strongest mettle! In this model, a distinction is drawn between curricular and extracurricular activities. "Extracurricular" includes pastimes and hobbies, and a wide spectrum of social learning activities which do not feature in the timetable, or at any rate are not given prominence there. The defining characteristics of curriculum, in this model, are that it be subject-related, explicit and visible, timetabled, text-supported, examined, adult-directed, and adult-oriented.

The change in the definition of curriculum introduced through the influence of progressive pedagogy has been profound and complex, and provides the background to an understanding of a very large part of the curriculum development movement since the mid-1950s and of contemporary curriculum theory, even though the change itself commenced in earnest nearly a century ago.

In model B the meaning of curriculum is largely transformed through replacement of one educational ideology by another. Reference has been made already to the views of Dewey. These are of such significance in the whole modern movement in curriculum that an understanding of his pedagogy is a prerequisite to understanding the manner in which the term *curriculum* has become enlarged and changed to the point where many orthodox educators, to say nothing of the public at large, have become almost bemused.

Dewey's central educational concepts were "growth" and "experience." He identified a number of elements which are central in curriculum making. These include the interests and learning capacities of the individual child; the child's life history of experience; a generalized, scientific method of inquiry; different types of subject matter; the social context; and democratic values. While prepared kits of materials, schemes of work, etc., are of value, curriculum making is essentially a task for groups of teachers, in the school setting. Dewey did not develop a particular curriculum design model, although he played a major part in introducing into education such ideas as the project method, learning units based on children's experience, integrated studies, discovery methods, problem-solving techniques, and practical work of various kinds. He was also responsible for challenging many of the traditional tenets of educational theory, including the distinction between liberal and vocational education, separate subject teaching, and authoritarian modes of teaching. Although Dewey was by no means alone, his influence has been a transforming one, at least in American educational theory and in all those theories and practices in different parts of the world where American educational influence has been strong.

The main features of curriculum as redefined by Dewey and his followers are these:

1. Curriculum refers to the totality of student experience insofar as the school or teachers influence and shape that experience.

2. So-called incidental learnings (the term is that of W. H. Kilpatrick, Dewey's chief disciple) are as significant for the teacher and the curriculum designer as are the intended, explicit learnings. "Incidental learnings" are part of the curriculum and include such items as the moral tone of the classroom, the items that students learn from and about each other, and those unintended learning outcomes which may result from ineffective teaching, e.g., lazy study habits.

3. The processes of learning are as important as the content of learning. Covering the ground outlined by a syllabus is less important than learning through problem solving, learning how to make decisions, to select and use sources and resources, learning to evaluate, etc. The modern emphasis on discovery methods, open education, and student experience reflect this interest in learning processes.

4. The design of learning situations is the central curriculum task. This may involve selecting and adapting published materials, creating new situations (e.g., a field trip), etc. Design is a participatory process in which students play an active part, as distinct from a process whereby subject content is predefined for their assimilation.

5. Curriculum making necessarily entails selection and choice from and within a cultural environment. The materials of the curriculum are social artifacts, with a social meaning, and the processes of designing and organizing learning situations are social processes. Hence, curriculum making is a form of social engineering. At a national level, as was argued by the American social reconstructionists (notably, Rugg, Counts, and Brameld) and has been advocated more recently by Third World leaders such as President Nyerere of Tanzania, curriculum design is crucial to social and political change and the curriculum is seen as a key factor in transforming the mentality of a population. Hence, the relationship between curriculum and culture is a central political as well as a pedagogical issue, and participation in curriculum decisions cannot be restricted to professionals and specialists.

6. The requirements of democratic living are argued to be such that there should be elements of common experience in the education of all students regardless of ability, social origins, interest, and likely future careers. Hence the emphasis, in this school of thought, on core curriculum, common learnings, and other ways of promoting the idea of community experience and values.

CURRICULUM DESIGN AND DEVELOPMENT

From the foregoing, it will be apparent that recent and contemporary curriculum theory has brought out very strongly the value or normative dimensions of curriculum making. These value dimensions are varied and reflect the pluralism of modern societies. However, the ideological character of influential curriculum design models has not always been appreciated. Thus, in the curriculum development movement which gained popularity among educators during the 1950s, there was initially a tendency to ignore ideological underpinnings and the movement was widely heralded as a "neutral" application of managerial and design technology to problems of schooling.

The criticisms of writers such as Broudy and Eisner in the United States and Stenhouse in the United Kingdom brought out the ideological basis of managerial-type curriculum designs and they have been followed by numerous attempts to change or broaden this basis. Nevertheless, a prevailing mode of project-based curriculum development emerged during the 1950s and 1960s. Wide use was made of design models incorporating many of the emerging techniques of managed change, including predefined objectives and preplanned dissemination of curriculum products (mainly published materials and hardware).

The modern curriculum development movement received its major impetus in the United States from national-level funding, by both private and governmental agencies, of curriculum renewal projects in mathematics and science. Although large-scale funding had commenced before the late 1950s, the successful Russian launching of Sputnik in 1957 undoubtedly provided the shock to national consciousness that was required to energize and fund substantial projects whose outcome—it was hoped—would enable American high schools to make significant improvements in the quality of their teaching in mathematics, science, and technology. Major legislative programs substantially increasing project funding were introduced, and the idea of the government-funded project as the key item in curriculum renewal emerged in the early sixties.

After making an initial powerful, though not widespread, impact in the United States, the movement spread abroad, first to the United Kingdom then to many other countries, in all continents, which are subject to American influence. For some fifteen years, curriculum development as a planned, national-level educational enterprise, based on specific projects carried out by specially assembled task forces, flourished. By the early

1970s, however, misgivings were being expressed about the results in the schools of these substantial investments of money and human resources. Just as the United States has pioneered the movement, so it was in that country that allegations of the "failure" of curriculum development were most strongly voiced. The major national bodies involved in project funding began to move away from curriculum development project funding. In Britain, the major national agency for supporting curriculum development work, the Schools Council, was under heavy criticism by the mid-1970s, even the prime minister intervening to proclaim publicly the inadequacies of that body. At that time it appeared that much of the original impetus, at any rate, of the modern curriculum development movement was spent. It would be rash, however, to draw the conclusion that project-based development is no longer a major vehicle of curriculum renewal.

While it would be misleading to reduce this whole modern movement to a few general features, there are aspects which are common and widespread, and it is possible to divide these into those that look like enduring and those which are more ephemeral. We should consider first the concept of curriculum development. Ignoring many of the achievements and experiences of the progressive educational movement, including the most important whole-curriculum development program ever undertaken, the American Eight-Year Study of the 1930s, the reformers of the late fifties argued for the desirability of abstracting particular subject areas from their whole school/system context and improving the quality of teaching and learning in these subject areas. The method proposed was, on the face of it, quite simple: a group of scholars and subject specialists would work together, perhaps involving some learning theorists, in mapping out what was both up-to-date and teachable to high school students. The topics and themes thus adduced would be, with the assistance of teachers usually working in summer institutes, expanded into units of subject matter, sometimes combined into a textbook. These units would then be tested by the teachers and perhaps by others, imperfections eliminated and, ultimately, the materials would be prepared for publication. Concurrently and subsequently, other teachers not involved in the original working team would be inducted into the new materials through short, intensive in-service programs.

This development process, and variations of it, was adopted in many of the early mathematics and science projects. As these projects came to fruition, some of them were exported to other countries where teams, instead of starting afresh, set up adaptation groups. Two notable examples were the secondary school Biological Sciences Curriculum Study and the Physical Science Study Committee.

Several significant refinements of the original project team concept emerged during the 1960s, some of them influenced by factors quite outside the educational field. Two of these refinements have had the effect, over a period of years, of bringing into question the whole project-based movement, or at least of so altering its character as to suggest that in the years ahead project-based curriculum development will have a different meaning from what it acquired during the 1950s and 1960s. The first of these refinements is the emergence, in education, of the so-called *research-development-diffusion* model, and the second is the school-based curriculum development movement.

RESEARCH-DEVELOPMENT-DIFFUSION MODEL

The research-development-diffusion model, adopted from agriculture and pharmacy, is directed towards the manufacture, distribution, and utilization of a particular product, to meet some predefined need. It has been promoted by Havelock and his associates at the University of Michigan and by several highly influential international agencies, including the Organization for Economic Cooperation and Development (OECD), which is based in Paris. We shall consider some of the model's main features, its uses and adaptations, and some of the criticisms that have been directed at it. However, it needs to be borne in mind that the model itself, despite its apparently limited success, has had a very powerful influence on contemporary curriculum theory and practice.

The research-development-diffusion approach, in its purest form, requires that research be undertaken ab initio, in relation to a need or a problem which has been very carefully analyzed. Its success depends both on the quality of the analysis and on the existence of agencies or institutions with a sufficiently long life and with adequate investment backing to sustain what may be very long-term programs of research. The monetary problem is a very real one in government-funded agencies and institutions that are subject to political and financial pressures, which frequently mitigate against long-term development planning. Thus the chief reason for the very limited success of the research-development-diffusion approach is, perhaps, that in education, where research has always formed a tiny component of the budget, the conditions required to sustain the analytical research phase of the process do not exist.

One bold attempt to establish applied research centers, the creation in the early 1960s of regional educational laboratories in the United States, has not in fact led to the institutionalizing of the research-development-diffusion model. This is partly because the majority of the laboratories were themselves unable to survive financial, administrative, and political pressures and have collapsed, and partly because the remaining ones have had to demonstrate a capacity to see their products (school and teacher materials) in the educational market place. Generally speaking, they have not been able to undertake lengthy and costly research programs, but have had to concentrate more on materials development and diffusion, and on training.

Another constraining factor in applying the research-development-diffusion model to curriculum making has been the complexity of educational systems, wherein responsibility for the diffusion of educational ideas and materials is widely dispersed. Teacher education institutions are often separate from national ministries or departments; inspectors, who might be regarded as potentially key change agents, have often been seen either as part of the controlling and supervision process or as extraneous to school-level change; research on diffusion has been the responsibility of several agencies and is seldom, if ever, coordinated; diffusion of new materials, at least in Western countries, usually involves commercial publishers who are in competition with one another and, sometimes, with development efforts supported by government or foundations. Finally, the sheer quantitative expansion of most educational systems throughout the world since World War II has meant that the great bulk of material and human resources has had to be allocated to meet quantitative demands, e.g., for school buildings and teachers possessing a minimum of training. In short, the conditions presupposed by successful application of the research-development-diffusion model have been absent.

The research-development-diffusion model has been applied, however, in a more limited way than its proponents envisaged and with a measure of success that many critics have not adequately recognized. Project-based curriculum development may be itself a form of applied research. Before projects on any scale are undertaken, it is usual to spend considerable time and expertise in the analysis of a problem or need. Increasingly, as development funding became more problematic due to economic recession in the early 1970s, this period of analysis became a marked feature of projects. During this phase, and usually also in the early stages of design and development work, research literature is reviewed and an attempt made to extract generalizations, data, or perspectives which may be applicable to the task in hand. Thus, the research component of the research-development-diffusion model, while it is foreshortened and restricted in scope, has not been ignored. Increasingly, also, it has been recognized by developers that their own experience, their inspirational and creative qualities, and their capacity to organize teams of cooperating teachers in materials production and testing, are insufficient for a satisfactory project. What is required, also, is an injection of evaluation data from some quasi-independent source. Thus, project funding now normally includes a budget for "evaluation," or for the systematic reporting of the progress of a project, from the standpoint of an observer who is positioned just a little to one side of the development team itself.

The project model of curriculum-development thus may be seen to incorporate or relate research, in at least the following ways. First, existing, relevant research is analyzed, synthesized, and used as a source of data for project planning. Second, a development project itself aims to test certain hypotheses about teaching and learning, even though these hypotheses may be formulated less as propositions to be tested than as objectives to be achieved (or not). Third, through concurrent evaluation, knowledge about the impact a project is having on its host institution is built up.

The development phase, which is normally the longest and most costly in a project (although some projects of the fifties and sixties can now claim to have fifteen- to twenty-year diffusion phases), involves (a) the design of the project itself; (b) the design of materials, resources, teaching-learning processes, in-service education programs, etc; (c) writing and otherwise producing trial versions of the items listed in (b); (d) field-testing the items listed in (b); and (e) revising and preparing for publication of the materials, resources, etc. Frequently, at this point, which may be between three and six years after the initial funding, the project team breaks up and disperses to other institutions than the one supporting or hosting the project. This dispersion has come to be seen as one of the crucial weaknesses of the project team approach, and its recognition was one of the factors leading to the establishment of permanent or semipermanent curriculum development institutions.

As noted above, the diffusion phase of the research-development-diffusion model has not been susceptible to control in education due to the large and complex structures involved and the lack of articulation of these structures. However, a more basic objection than this has been entered against the research-development-diffusion model. It is that one of the fundamental explanations for the failure of many projects to permeate school systems is that, while the materials they produced may have been of high educational quality, they have not sufficiently engaged at the production phase the ultimate users, teachers and learners. That is to say, the research-development-diffusion model does not seem to have recognized adequately the aspiration of teacher and learner to participate in the development process itself.

Recognition of the aspiration that schoolteachers have to be directly involved in the determination of what they are to teach and how they are to teach it was poor in the early stages of the curriculum development movement, which were dominated, in the United States at least, by academics, scholars, and researchers. Similarly, the research-development-diffusion model gave scant recognition to what might be termed school culture: the ways schools organize themselves; the values, interests, and aspirations of teachers; the symbolic and other meaning systems that are at work in schools; the nature of classroom life; the modes of approach adopted by students; the ambitions of parents, etc. Instead, the model addressed itself primarily to the design, manufacture, and distribution of quality products, relying too heavily on untested assumptions, drawn from the learning sciences, about design criteria and from the commercial sphere, about how the "market" could be permeated.

The development of the research-development-diffusion model, from the 1960s and into the 1980s, was closely connected with the work of the national centers or central agencies of curriculum research and development. These agencies included the Schools Council for Curriculum and Examinations for England and Wales, the Australian Curriculum Development Centre, and the American Regional Laboratories and the University Research and Development Centers, as well as UNESCO sponsorship of international programs. During that period there was heavy criticism of the research-development-diffusion model, and other more decentralized forms of curriculum development, relying on participant involvement, existed alongside the research-development-diffusion model. However, national centers learned to make use of participant involvement and the research-development-diffusion model itself underwent extensive change (Skilbeck, 1984b). The work of the Schools Council in Britain showed this kind of development. In recent times, central agencies have developed sophisticated strategies of both exploiting and promoting participant involvement and local difference.

SCHOOL-BASED CURRICULUM DEVELOPMENT

The movement to which this criticism of the research-development-diffusion model has led, and the second of the refinements noted above, is school-based curriculum development, whose roots lie in the progressivist ideology and its concern for teacher-pupil-parent initiation and sponsorship of learning processes. It is important to draw a distinction between the school as the focus of participatory curriculum decisions, on the one hand, and the school as the center of a materials production effort on the other. Among the agencies required to support school-based curriculum development are local, regional, and national centers for resource and materials production and for certain forms of in-service teacher education.

Research-development-diffusion models were one, not fully satisfactory, attempt to give structure and a permanent dynamic to the projects-based movement which mushroomed during the early 1960s. Another attempt was made through the insertion into educational development planning of the procedures of management by objectives.

Since the challenges to the large-scale curriculum projects in the late sixties—challenges which documented the problematic nature of the research-development-diffusion model of curriculum development and the Center-Periphery model of dissemination—there has been a growing advocacy of school-based curriculum development. Unlike the large-scale projects, school-based curriculum development does not isolate specific elements (or subjects) of the curriculum for development. Instead the focus is on whole-curriculum planning requiring the addressing of such curricular issues as balance, breadth, and appropriate kinds and levels of specialization. To facilitate this, a comprehensive educational support system (including preservice and in-service teacher education) needs to promote teachers' professional development in understanding the significance of the relevant research of the central agencies, and more importantly, in developing the skills and confidence to conduct their own action research.

Curriculum research and development at both levels can be of considerable mutual benefit. School-based curriculum development provides an important model of action research and could provide the necessary feedback from the tacit, intuitive world of the teacher, the lack of which has been so much criticized in the challenges to the research-development-diffusion model of curriculum design. Links need to be established between these two levels of curriculum development which would require radical structural reforms within educational systems. Individuals need more varied and flexible career experience.

In moving towards a more favorable environment for school-based curriculum development, changes need to be holistic in two important ways. First, systemic reform is required if teachers are realistically to be expected to engage in school-based curriculum development. While school-based curriculum development has long been inspired by a progressivist philosophy, it has more recently found favor with those who want to reduce expenditure in education and withdraw funds from central government agencies of curriculum development. Thus in America, Australia, and the United Kingdom, such agencies have either been closed down or allowed to wither through lack of funds. Teachers are expected to engage in school-based curriculum development, in addition to what they are already doing, without the kind of systemic support already mentioned. An important role in supporting school-based curriculum development remains for central agencies in terms of consultancy, guidance on broad national curriculum frameworks, assistance to local curriculum developers, centrally collating and then publicizing local action research and curriculum development, materials production and appropriate large-scale curriculum research and development.

Second, changes to the curriculum itself need to be conceptualized and implemented within a holistic framework. This makes professional demands on teachers well beyond knowledge of their subjects and associated teaching methodologies. Certain understandings from the foundation disciplines, as well as a range of social and "organizational" skills, are essential if teachers are to engage in whole-curriculum decision making and planning. Traditionally, teachers' status has been strongly tied to competence within a subject or field of knowledge. The status of teachers tends to increase as the level moves toward more senior classes *because* subject knowledge is emphasized. Being expert in a subject or specialized field is an important factor in a teacher's sense of professionalism. However, although subject competence should continue to be valued and valued highly, teachers' knowledge must be extended into areas of philosophy, and more broadly into the human and social sciences, if they are to be equipped to engage in genuine school-based curriculum development. Whole-curriculum planning at the school level depends on systemic support mentioned above, especially in in-service education.

MANAGEMENT BY OBJECTIVES

The development project lent itself to objectives planning since the project was designed to solve certain problems, through a task force approach, in a specified time period. It appeared to its progenitors that the whole task was self-contained and that, through a sufficiently precise and concrete statement of what ought to be achieved, resources could be effectively and efficiently marshalled to achieve those predefined ends.

One source of this kind of thinking was the management-by-objectives movement in business and the military. Another was Ralph Tyler's book *Basic Principles of Curriculum and Instruction* which, after a period of relative obscurity following its publication in 1949 as a text for Tyler's curriculum theory course at the University of Chicago, became an educational best-seller in many countries during the 1960s. It is of interest that Tyler had been, as evaluator of the prewar Eight Year Study, a leading figure in the progressive education movement, yet his *Basic Principles* seemed to draw little on the progressivist ideology. The book, popularly known as the Tyler rationale, consists essentially of a step-by-step analysis of what is involved in designing a curriculum. The first step proposed by Tyler is the formulation of objectives. He asks "What educational purposes should the school seek to attain?" and goes on to elaborate the other steps by asking "What educational experiences can be provided that are likely to attain these purposes? How can these experiences be effectively organized? How can we determine whether these purposes are being attained?" (p. 1). His rationale may be shown diagrammatically as follows:

Selection of educational purposes	Selection of learning experiences	Organization of learning experiences	Evaluation of learning experiences

Although the Tyler rationale has been extensively criticized, notably by Kliebard, it remains the most lucid and convincing account of the means-ends approach to curriculum planning: define the ends, specify them in the form of clear-cut, concrete objectives, and then adduce the means required to achieve them.

Despite its power and persuasiveness, the Tyler rationale is basically only a framework for analysis and action. For detailed development work to be done using the means-end model, a much more elaborate framework for defining objectives was required. This was provided, in the mid to late fifties, by a team sponsored by the American Psychological Society, under the overall direction of Benjamin Bloom who, like Tyler, was a professor at the University of Chicago. The task Bloom and his associates set themselves was to produce a taxonomy for classifying the learning processes and outcomes that examiners seek to elicit when they set tests. They sought to meet the long-standing criticism that examiners, especially those preparing objective-type tests, encourage lower-level cognitive processes such as factual recall. The question they set themselves, and then proceeded to answer, was what other, higher-level, cognitive processes should examiners, and teachers, seek to elicit and to what learning processes other than cognition might they give attention? Bloom and his associates produced two taxonomies under the title of *Taxonomy of Educational Objectives* (Handbook 1, *The Cognitive Domain;* Handbook 2, *The Affective Domain.*) They envisaged a third handbook on the psychomotor domain, and several versions of it ultimately appeared. Although designed basically for examiners, to enable and encourage them to produce a wider range of test items than were then commonly used, the handbooks were quickly seized upon by curriculum developers who saw the taxonomies of objectives as guides to the construction of objectives which would foster the learning that educational critics found lacking in much of contemporary schooling.

As the movement for developing curriculum at the center gathered momentum in the 1960s, larger claims were made for the power of objectives as organizing tools. The objectives approach to curriculum design was considerably tightened by Mager (1962): not only were objectives to be prespecified in behavioral terms but also achievement criteria and background conditions of performance. This moves towards not only predefining the content of learning but also controlling (certain aspects of) the learning environment itself. Glaser (1963) led the movement toward criterion-referenced testing, based on discrete, itemized objectives, a movement strongly linked to **programmed learning** (q.v.) and what is termed "individualized instruction." However, "individualized" is used in the special sense that students work by themselves and "at their own pace." Students experiencing individualized instruction work through the same preset learning pathways; these may contain "loops" and "forks" but for all that remain standardized, programmed "packages." This stress on the individual should not be confused with that which characterizes pupil-centered curriculum. In the latter case, the emphasis on the individual is different in two important respects. First, the learning is not standardized, packaged, and thus made transportable from the developer's laboratory to certain prespecified and therefore (in some respects) standardized learning environments. Second, the stress on the individual is not meant to isolate the individual; is not meant to be at the expense of the community, but through engagement with the community.

In its earlier stages the objectives approach to curriculum design emphasized *quantitative* aspects of learning. Thus, Glaser (1970) outlines an approach to learning which advocates measurement of the "entering behavior of the learner" and continuous assessment leading to measurement of the learning increase as a result of the instructional process. An assumption underlying this position is that any learning increase is as a result of instruction and not any concurrent experiences of the student. The desire to measure learning precisely leads to both a narrow conception of learning and a preemptive limitation of the boundaries of the learning environment.

Some of the strongest advocates of the objectives approach have softened their views. Thus, Popham (1972) admits that "there are some important goals, which we have for our children, which are *currently* unassessable. To the extent that such goals are extremely meritorious they are *worth the risk* of our pursuing them even if we cannot reliably discern whether they have been accomplished." In the sixties, Lee Cronbach and Robert Stake, originally committed to measurement by objectives-based assessment, became advocates of more qualitative evaluation and, by implication, curriculum design which transcends prespecified behavioral objectives. The recent work of Guba represents a more recent softening of the hard line on objectives (Guba and Lincoln, 1981).

Nevertheless, the objectives movement remains strong in the United States; in technical and vocational education it remains widespread in other parts of the world. The tradition of job analysis going back to F. W. Taylor tends to generate specific syllabus objectives in much vocational curriculum. Debate in this area, first, is concerned with whether it is economically practical or even possible to prespecify vast and structured minutiae of technological learning when technology is changing so rapidly. Second, there is the question whether this provides a suitable learning environment for the development of flexibility and openness, which are required for social and technological change. The structural design of much vocational curriculum assumes that items of knowledge and skill can be routinized and are noninteractive. The great mistake occurs when it is assumed that all learning is of this sort and that routines need not be embedded in some wider context.

The extreme view of planning by objectives has led to an equally extreme rejection of any notion of objectives. For example, Kelly (1982) rejects the notion of curriculum aims because they lead to a hierarchical organization of objectives. Other educators have been led to adopt an antiplanning attitude altogether. This has had unfortunate consequences for curriculum development, leading to situations caricatured by "what shall we do today, sir?"

It is the reductionist misuse of objectives, in which curriculum planning is reduced to the writing of objectives, that needs to be isolated for criticism. Ivor Davies (1976) provides a balanced and comprehensive approach to the use of objectives in curriculum planning: objectives need to be justified both in terms of an analysis of a situation and a commitment to a philosophy. Davies sees objectives as means—but as means in a dynamic relationship with ends; objectives represent a commitment to the process of education and cannot be decontextualized from their origins. M. MacDonald-Ross (1973) provides a powerful critique of the misuse of objectives without rejecting them: the linear, "feed-forward" misuse of objectives oversimplifies the complex and difficult task of curriculum planning.

Debate about objectives is notoriously plagued by semantic differences. What we mean by "objective" can vary both in degree of specificity and the way it attached to a particular environment. Some objectives of centrally developed curriculum are highly specific in content and are independent of particular learning environments. Such objectives are developed independently of particular learning environments (or generalized across learning environments) and are presented to teachers without any justification. Such connotations of "objective" are very different from those in which objectives arise out of the learning environment itself and the experience of the teachers in it. Much of the difficulty with objectives can be resolved in school-based curriculum development where objectives are not imposed on the learning environment but grow out of the experience of the environment itself. Such objectives are likely to be responsive to needs, open to revision, interactive with each other and more general aims, and generated by the tacit knowledge of the classroom which discourages an over-logicized, rational approach to curriculum design.

The educational potential of objectives depends very much on who constructs the objectives. Teacher (and student) participation in the process of developing objectives would be a valuable development of the objectives model and help to locate objectives within the actual processes of teaching and learning. This process would promote the emergence of cognitive objectives (Bruner, 1966) in which outcomes are not important per se and do not define objectives but are more the embodiment of student understanding and discovery, which are the real objectives. In addition, teacher (and student) participation in developing objectives would also facilitate the development of expressive objectives (Eisner, 1979) which apply to those activities, especially the arts, whose success necessarily depends on personal expression and where the activity has no further aim than the expression of certain qualities intrinsic to itself. Furthermore, the qualities intrinsic to the activity are those which are conceived by the agent.

TECHNIQUES AND CONTEXT FAVORABLE TO INNOVATION

By the early 1960s, therefore, the curriculum development movement appeared to be well provided for, at least with an apparatus of techniques and a context in which innovation was welcomed. The context and the techniques included

—a political and social climate favoring increased investment in educational research and development designed to promote change in current school practice

—an expanding fiscal base, providing public and private resources for research and development efforts beyond the capacity and interest of any classroom, school, or even school system

—the active involvement in school reform of distinguished scholars and teachers prepared to give time and creative effort to curriculum renewal

—practical experience of task force–type projects operating on a three- to six-year time scale and directed towards producing marketable school materials

—a model of research, development, and diffusion suggesting modes of action on which successful changes in schooling could be predicted

—a basic framework for designing new curriculum, the Tyler rationale

—a schematization of educational objectives, the Bloom-Krathwohl taxonomy the establishment of imminent establishment of national, regional and local institutions for resource and materials development

—an expanding base of teacher education and educational study in universities capable of producing trained teachers, researchers, and developers

Yet during the 1960s and into the 1970s, the curriculum development movement became increasingly complex, self-critical, and exposed to substantial educational and public criticism. As often happens in education, the early aspirations were too simple and naive, the claims too ambitious; and the procedures, models, and techniques available or proposed for use were inadequate to the task. What has happened is that, in coming of age, the curriculum development movement has had to reduce its claims and accept that change in education is both slow and sui generis, not simply a variant of change in other spheres. The concept of curriculum innovation has, as a consequence, become more subtle and sophisticated, while the rate of change in practice has come to be accepted as much slower than the reformers of the 1950s and 1960s realized.

It has been accepted that, while it is quite possible to design and implement projects according to certain prespecified objectives, all projects have as well both tacit objectives and unintended outcomes. These may not correspond at all closely with, and may run counter to, the explicit objectives and intended outcomes. Furthermore, closer analysis of teaching-learning processes and of school situations have revealed a condition of very unequal readiness to receive and assimilate the innovative mentality which has been an essential part of the modern curriculum development movement. It is, perhaps, only a relatively small proportion of schools and teachers that can play the demanding roles that participation in sustained curriculum change requires.

The most interesting thing about the curriculum development movement from the late 1960s onwards is not the so-called failure of sponsored projects to effect changes in schools, but the increasing recognition by educators that curriculum development is a much more complex activity than was earlier recognized by the project enthusiasts. This point had long been understood by some theorists. For example, in 1951 Benne and Muntyan in their book *Human Relations and Curriculum Change* correctly pointed out that a change in the curriculum means a change in the social system of the school. One of the weaknesses of the scholar-teacher project teams of the 1960s was that, doing much of their work outside the school and concentrating on the materials produced as the outcome of their efforts, they paid insufficient attention to the problems associated with changing schools as living social organisms.

However, a major change in the socioeconomic and political climate since the early to mid-1970s (depending on the particular country) had led to cuts in education budgets and an unfavorable climate for funding curriculum development. The negative results have included the severe curtailment of the work of central agencies and the expectation that teachers will add curriculum development to their other functions without any easing of teaching loads. With falling rolls in some countries or some sectors of education and the consequent staff losses, there has been a narrowing of the curriculum. However, some positive aspects have emerged in that the changed situation has led schools to examine their general aims and priorities, and with less scope for specialist subject teaching, teachers have been encouraged to look at the whole curriculum. In addition, in the United Kingdom there are pressures from national ministries on schools to review, evaluate, and develop curriculum. (*Department of Education and Science*, 1981; Circulars 6/81 and 9/83). The social and economic difficulties have also had the effect of making schools look at how the curriculum helps pupils cope with life beyond the school. The phenomenon of massive youth unemployment has forced teachers to rethink curriculum aims with regard to the upper secondary students. In Britain, curriculum for the 16–19 age group has become a specialized area of curriculum with new emphases on life skills, work experience, and practical activities. While the negative effects of education cuts cannot be underestimated, teachers are responding to curriculum development and improvement at the school level more independently than in the days of the large-scale project. Schools themselves are beginning to develop their own solutions to curriculum problems.

THE CURRICULUM CHANGE PROCESS

Just as school-based curriculum development has emerged from a recognition of the limitations of curriculum packages produced outside schools for insertion into them, so has it been recognized that without associated processes of change, curriculum change in and of itself is likely to be only partially effective.

Associated changes of at least two kinds are required. First, planned organizational changes at the school and school system level are a necessary adjunct of significant curriculum change. The organizational changes will normally involve staff roles, relationships and groupings, timetable, overall balance of studies, classroom organization, and some aspects of school administration. Second, and this was accepted by the first generation of curriculum developers in the 1950s, teacher in-service education is essential not only for the first generation of teachers working with the new curriculum but on a continuing basis.

The costs and difficulties of organizing in-service education on the very large scale required have been a deterrent to most educational authorities. Increasingly, developers of new materials are building into the development process itself a teacher induction component and some projects, notably the American Man: A Course of Study (MACOS) and, to a lesser extent, the English Humanities Curriculum Project (HCP), have always required prospective users to participate in a training program as a condition of use. Such requirements are rare and barely enforceable. Until there is a closer coordination, nationally, of agencies responsible for development and those responsible for the whole spectrum of teacher education, there cannot be a fully effective linkage established between curriculum renewal and one of its vital support systems, teacher education. Such coordination is being attempted in a major new Australian project, the Social Education Materials Project (SEMP), and it is worthy of note that this process of establishing linkage will take at least as long as the materials design development, testing, and publication phase.

CURRICULUM EVALUATION

Reference has been made above to some of the relationships between curriculum development and evaluation. **Evaluation** (q.v.) is a separate topic in this volume. Suffice it to say here that as there has been a dramatic change in the meaning of the term *curriculum* during the middle years of the century, and a remarkable upsurge of interest in sponsored development in place of more haphazard change processes, so evaluation objectives and procedures have been transformed, as evaluators have endeavored to meet the requirements of evaluating the new curricula.

Broadly speaking, there have been five phases of curriculum evaluation since the mid 1950s. First, there was the classic experimental period, when evaluators attempted to apply to curriculum change the controlled experimental procedures of educational psychology. This phase changed, partly following the criticism of Cronbach, who correctly pointed out that new curricula involved not only procedures (which, in principle at any rate, might be compared under controlled conditions with existing procedures), but new ends, and were more appropriately evaluated in relation to these ends according to their efficiency and effectiveness in achieving them. The design of the taxonomies of educational objectives provided a powerful new tool for this purpose. Thus, in the second, means-ends phase evaluators sought to assess the extent to which the objectives, specified by the developers, were being achieved. Criticism leveled at this approach included the point that there are many factors requiring evaluation apart from the intentions of developers. Also, evaluators began to take an interest in the school context in which curriculum changes were being introduced. In the third phase, evaluators addressed themselves to the question, What are the diverse meanings and uses of evaluation data?

Evaluation data produced at the conclusion of a project may be of historical interest and have utility for accountability purposes but by its nature and timing cannot affect the course of the project itself. A distinction was drawn by Scriven in 1967 between summative (end point) evaluation and formative evaluation which, carried on throughout the life of a project, is able to influence its direction. The fourth phase of evaluation has witnessed a blossoming of theories and schools and may be thought of as an eclectic period which has followed naturally on the broadening of inquiries and research in education to cover subjective viewpoints of participants in learning situations, the culture of the school, and the social and political climates effecting educational change.

The fifth and current phase is characterized by a greater rigor in evaluation studies and a result in part of the use of evaluation for purposes of accountability, and hence the sponsors' demands for more precision about outcomes and effects. Perhaps more crucial than this is the recognition, within the evaluation profession itself, that the previously polarized "quantitative" and "naturalistic" styles may be interrelated in various ways. There is now a strengthened relationship, in the curriculum field, between the processes of review (observation and reflective inquiry into practices), evaluation, (entailing more extended analysis and judgment), and development (modification or change in policy and practice). Evaluation has thus come to occupy a more integral position in curriculum planning and design.

House (1980) identified eight approaches to evaluation that characterize current practice. They are not identified necessarily as discrete methodologies but as "idealizations" of evaluation approaches. House lists these approaches as (1) systems analysis, (2) behavioral objectives, (3) decision making, (4) goal-free, (5) art criticism, (6) professional review, (7) quasi-legal, and (8) cast study.

CONCLUSION

These eight approaches, together with subsequent additions and variations, indicate the catholicity of current curriculum evaluation thought and practice. Administrators, project sponsors, teachers, and the wider community are offered a choice of approaches which by their very eclecticism starkly challenge the mounting public demands that educational processes in general and curriculum changes in particular account for themselves in terms of measurable benefit. It is no longer possible to quantify this benefit in a way that indicates clearly which changes are "working" and which are not.

Indeed, if there is any distinguishing characteristic of the modern curriculum movement, it is the doubt that it has cast upon the whole notion of definable educational outcomes. The modern period has been one of experimentation, challenge to orthodoxies of all kinds, and inventiveness with respect both to ends and means in curriculum making. Basically, the same processes are at work in curriculum theory, the design and development of projects, evaluation, and a growing body of curriculum practice in schools. These processes derive from many sources, including uncertainty about or repudiation of traditional values and beliefs regarding educational outcomes, a willingness and a resource to innovate and to adapt thought and practice to changing social and cultural circumstances, and a greater flexibility of thought regarding the kinds of experiences students can appropriately undergo in schools. Moreover, during the modern phase, curriculum theory and design have been characterized by a remarkable injection of critical and creative energy, without parallel in any previous period. A field of curriculum theory, research study, and practice has been established, a language created, and communication mechanisms brought into operation. While the effect of this on teaching and learning in schools is still very limited and partial, it is a reasonable prediction that during the next twenty years there will be a mutual enrichment of theory and practice which will have transforming effects on both.

Malcolm Skilbeck and Richard Cotter

REFERENCES

Ausubel, D. P. (1968) *Educational Psychology: A Cognitive View*. New York: Holt, Rinehart and Winston.

Bellack, A. A. and Kliebard, H. A. (1977) *Curriculum and Evaluation*. Berkeley, Calif.: McCutchan.

Benne, K. D. and Muntyan, B., eds. (1951) *Human Relations in Curriculum Change*. New York: Dryden. Repr. in Biological Sciences Curriculum Study series. Washington: American Institute of Biological Sciences, 1959.

Bloom, B. S. et al. (1956) *Taxonomy of Education Objectives,* Handbook 1, *The Cognitive Domain;* Handbook 2, *The Affective Domain*. New York: David McKay.

Brameld, T. (1957) *Cultural Foundations of Education: An Interdisciplinary Exploration*. New York: Harper.

Broudy, H. S. (1970) "The Philosophical Foundations of Educational Objectives." *Educational Theory* 20 (1): 3–21.

Bruner, J. S. (1966) *Towards a Theory of Instruction*. Cambridge, Mass.: Harvard University Press.

Counts, G. S. (1932) *Dare the School Build a New Social Order?* New York: John Day.

Cronbach, L. J. (1963) "Evaluation for Course Improvement." In *New Curricula,* ed. R. Heath. London: Harper & Row.

Cronbach, L. J., and associates. (1981) *Towards Reform of Program Evaluation*. San Francisco: Jossey-Bass.

Davies, I. K. (1976) *Objectives*. Maidenhead, Berkshire, England: McGraw-Hill.

Department of Education and Science. (1981) *The School Curriculum*. London: Her Majesty's Stationery Office.

Dewey, J. (1902) *The Child and the Curriculum*. Chicago: University of Chicago Press.

———. (1916) *Democracy and Education*. New York: Macmillan.

Eisner, E. (1979) *The Educational Imagination*. New York: Macmillan.

Eisner, E. W. (1969) "Instructional and Expressive Objectives: Their Formulation and Use in Curriculum." In *Instructional Objectives,* by W. J. Popham et al. American Educational Research Association Monograph Series on Curriculum Evaluation. Chicago: Rand McNally.

Gagné, R. M. and Briggs, L. J. (1974) *Principles of Instructional Design*. New York: Holt, Rinehart and Winston.

Glaser, R. (1963) "Instructional technology and the measurement of learning outcomes." *American Psychologist* 18: 519–521.

———. (1970) "Evaluation of instruction and changing educational models." In *The Evaluation of Instruction: Issues and Problems,* ed. M. C. Wittrock and D. E. Wiley. New York: Holt, Rinehart & Winston.

Guba, E. G. and Lincoln, Y. (1981) *Effective Evaluation*. San Francisco: Jossey-Bass.

Havelock, R. G. (1970) "The Utilisation of Educational Research and Development," *BJET* 2 (2): 84–98.

Hirst, P. H. (1974) *Knowledge and the Curriculum*. London: Routledge & Kegan Paul.

House, E. R. (1980) *Evaluating with Validity*. Beverly Hills, Calif.: Sage Publications.

Kelly, A. V. (1982) *The Curriculum: Theory and Practice*. 2d ed. London: Harper & Row.

Kilpatrick, W. H. (1929) *Foundations of Method*. New York: Macmillan.

Lawton, D. (1983) *Curriculum Studies and Educational Planning*. London: Hodder and Stoughton.

MacDonald-Ross, M. (1973) "Behavioural objectives—a critical review." *Instructional Science* 2 (1):1–52.

Mager, R. F. (1962) *Preparing Objectives for Programmed Instruction*. San Francisco: Fearon.

OECD/CERI (1978) *School-based Curriculum Development*. Paris: OECD.

Popham, W. J. (1972) "Must all objectives be behavioural?" *Educational Leadership* 29 (7): 605–608.

Reid, L. A. (1961) *Ways of Knowledge and Experience*. London: Allen & Unwin.

Rugg, H., ed. (1926) *NSE Yearbook 26,* Part 1: *The Foundations and Technique of Curriculum Construction*. Bloomington, Ill.: Public School Publishing.

Scriven, M. (1967) "The Methodology of Evaluation." In *Perspectives in Curriculum Evaluation,* by R. W. Taylor, R. M. Gagné, and M. Scriven. American Educational Research Association Monograph Series on Curriculum Evaluation, no. 1. Chicago: Rand McNally, pp. 39–83.

Skilbeck, M. (1982a) *A Core Curriculum for the Common School*. London: University of London Institute of Education.

———. (1982b) "School-based Curriculum Development." In *Planning in the Curriculum,* ed. V. Lee and D. Zeldin. London: Hodder and Stoughton.

———. (1984a) "Curriculum Development—R.D.D. to Review, Evaluate, Develop (RED)." *World Yearbook of Education*. London: Kogan Page.

———. (1984b) *Readings in School-Based Currriculum Development*. London: Harper & Row.

———. (1984c) *School-based Curriculum Development*. London: Harper & Row.

Stake, R. E. (1967) "The Countenance of Educational Evaluation." *Teachers' College Record* 68 (7): 523–540.

Stenhouse, L. (1971) "Some Limitations of the Use of Objectives in Curriculum Research and Planning." *Paedagogica Europaea* 6: 73–83.

Tyler, R. W. (1949) *Basic Principles of Curriculum and Instruction*. Chicago: University of Chicago Press.

Tyler, R. W., Gagné, R. M., and Scriven, M. (1967) *Perspectives of Curriculum Evaluation*. American Educational Research Association Monograph Series on Curriculum Evaluation No. 1. Chicago: Rand McNally.

CURRICULUM THEORY. The term *curriculum* has accumulated a very wide range of meanings. These have now settled to a broader rather than a narrower definition so that discussions on curriculum are now apt to include not only the content of instruction but also the methods employed, the delineation of objectives, evaluation procedures, and even the structure of research into the entire process. Thus the first of the terms which concern us here attracts a miscellany of considerations only loosely connected together. Second, the term *theory* has a long and slippery history in educational discourse. The sense in which studies and research in education are theoretical in relation to the practice of schoolteachers and others remains largely a conundrum. So it is that the conjunction of our two key terms amounts to a philosophical problem of great depth and results in a great difficulty for anyone attempting an analysis. It has been a feature of recent years to relate together the rapidly developing interests of academics, principally teacher trainers, with growing public debate on the control, content, and scope of the curriculum provided in primary and secondary schools.

CONCEPTS

Much curriculum theory has centered upon what Schwab (1969) called "the unstable but usable arts of the practitioner." It must be noted, however, that study and inquiry of the school curriculum need not be confined to the interests of practicing teachers. Social scientists may take a purely empirical interest in the process of schooling, particularly perhaps when they wish to test claims made by educational policymakers for the impact of educational initiatives on declining economies. This concern may be predicted as a likely emphasis in the latter part of the eighties when innovations such as the Technical and Vocational Education Initiative in England and Wales came to fruition. The aim of economic regeneration promises to supplant the sociological interest of twenty years before in the egalitarian possibilities for investment in comprehensive schooling.

In Britain curriculum theory has been historically a product of teacher training institutions. Courses in curriculum theory are virtually restricted to teacher training institutions, where they have a considerable vogue. Most students in initial training will study curriculum theory in some guise or other as part of their education course. Experienced teachers will encounter curriculum theory in in-service programs.

The aspiration to be practical, in the senses of providing professional skill and informing professional decision making, raises questions familiar in the history of teacher training. There is considerable speculation and controversy about the relationship between the study of education and practical competence. Education as a subject has attained a unity through the presentation of courses, the accumulation of literature and examinations, and the existence of a body of scholars. Nevertheless, its claim to epistemological status as a discipline in its own right remains unproven. Instead, education is still conceived as an undefined amalgam of contributing disciplines (Tibble, 1966). Curriculum became a new arrival in the 1960s alongside the established disciplines of philosophy, sociology, psychology, and history. In many courses curriculum became either a fifth option or, perhaps more defensibly, a core course attempting to relate the others together in (mainly) B.Ed. degrees. In such arrangements assumptions are necessarily made about the relationships, on the one hand, between the contributing studies themselves and, on the other hand, between those studies taken together and practical activity. Curriculum has claimed a special intermediary role closer to practice than education theory, yet reflective and relevant. Such claims must, however, remain unguaranteed since they have not obtained anything like universal assent. Indeed, there remain critics who regard the study of curriculum as a fraudulent charade. In order to examine such claims a definition of the field will be necessary, together with some understanding of its historical evolution and the contending traditions now represented in it.

Curriculum theory is no narrow study of pedagogy. To elucidate the range of considerations relevant to decisions on the design of learning systems; to explore the means of justifying the selection of content, the adoption of particular methods, and the evaluation of effectiveness—this is the agenda for curriculum theory. The framing questions for the development of such a theory are

1. What ought to be learned?
2. How ought it to be learned?

3. What measures ought to be taken to evaluate the learning provided for in the curriculum?
4. What principles ought to be stipulated to guide decisions on (1), (2) and (3) above?

These framing questions for curriculum theory are in the normative form, thus making plain at the start that curriculum study is irreducibly evaluative. Any curriculum theory must contain both evaluative and empirical aspects. The questions are also phrased impersonally, so as not to suggest that they are questions reserved to any one interest group, especially teachers. In this conception of curriculum theory, which is admittedly *itself* stipulative, the school curriculum is seen as potentially the legitimate concern of parties other than teachers, for example, parents, employers, learned societies, and trade unions. Curriculum theory thus has the widened responsibility of providing a language in which discussion can be conducted among and between these various interest groups.

It cannot be pretended that such a theory is yet available in any form that gains more than minority assent. There are rather a number of contending traditions in the field representing different and sometimes conflicting intellectual and cultural heritages. Just as the curriculum itself can be seen as an arena for the contest between rival views of the worthwhile, so curriculum theory in turn seeks to encompass the sometimes incompatible, sometimes uneasily coexisting, visions of educational reality held by different intellectual and social groups. Any attempt to arbitrate between such contending perspectives on the curriculum will be a deeply problematic exercise.

Perhaps the limits of our present knowledge allow us only to identify three influential traditions in the field of curriculum theory, suggesting the main features of each and recommending readers to their own pursuit of the resolution between them. The traditions I identify may be dubbed the "technocratic," the "liberal humanist," and the "anthropological relativist."

THE TECHNOCRATIC TRADITION

Curriculum theory is conducted against the pervasive influence of this line of thinking, whose prime exemplars are Bobbitt and Tyler (Bobbitt, 1918, 1924; Tyler, 1949). The idea that decisions about design for learning can be achieved by recourse to a means-end model of human action is fundamental here. If we are clear about what we wish to teach and the reasons why, curriculum decisions are to be reached through the specification of clear objectives and the choice of technically apt methods for the achievement of those objectives. Clear objectives entail the specification of outcomes in terms of the learners' abilities at the end of the course or item of instruction. Preferably, these outcomes should be stated behaviorally; that is, they should be statements open to no or little interpretation, being value-neutral statements containing verbs of learner behavior which can be observed to be present. Success in curriculum is to be measured in terms of the learners' status in relation to these behavioral measures. Evaluation likewise consists in checks of the *achievement* of the learners against the objectives prescribed for them.

There are a number of significant objections to this account of curriculum theory. First, it rests on an assumption as to fundamental agreement on the aims and objectives of the program. In itself it does not provide a means of debating the desirability of the aims and objectives that are to be the starting points for the program. On the contrary, these are taken as read, and curriculum planning is cast as the technical exercise of designing learning to prespecified ends.

Second, it makes the assumption that all learning can be reduced to statements of learner behavior. Against this, there is the commonsense view that learning, being a mental process, goes on covertly in the mind. Neither of these two extremes is defensible. If there is to be no evidence of learning, it is hard to see that we can ever be justified in ascribing the achievement of learning to someone. However, to take definite and specific evidence of learning to be always prespecifiable is to miss the point that an indefinite range of evidence may be appropriate to claims that a learner has had success. This is particularly the case where learning is of an order other than merely physical performance—where statements of behavior are not only *evidence for* but also *constitutive of* any objective you could specify (Hirst, 1974). In higher-order learning, whether cognitive or affective in character, finite lists of behavior are inappropriate because the achievements are so complex that they can only be adjudicated contextually by one who has knowledge both of the area of achievement under consideration and of the learner's relation to it. What is true, however, is that teachers and evaluators must make such judgments and that they do so on the basis of learner performance. The technocratic tradition makes the mistake of misrepresenting educational performance by reducing the range of evidence for it.

Third, it adopts a version of teaching as molding a learner to a predetermined shape. This view of teaching is not current in all traditions of schooling. It has its home in industrial and military training situations. In other traditions this conception of the teacher's task is broadened to acknowledge the possibility, even the desirability, of learners' transcending the teacher's knowledge during the teaching-learning transaction. The likelihood of this broadening of conception of the teaching task increases as subject matter itself becomes more problematic. Thus, in military drill situations, for example, it is assumed that conformity to behaviorally specified performances is all that is required. There, prespecified behavioral objectives are entirely suitable descriptions of what is looked for. If we consider physical education, however, it becomes apparent that what is sought is not exhaustively described in physical terms. Qualities of control in movement and attributes such as imagination in movement quickly evade behavioral description. Considering intellectual achievements and achievement in personal, social, aesthetic, emotional, and moral education, we find that descriptions of relevant achievements are highly elaborate, couched in terms peculiar to those several areas and, when they are manifested, discernible only to those already initiated in the field. That this is so negates one of the major claims for the technocratic tradition, namely, that it permits systematic technical evaluation of learning programs, thereby opening them up to the scrutiny of a public not itself initiated into the forms of understanding underlying the aims, content, and methodology of the program.

Fourth, the technocratic tradition casts the subject matter of the curriculum into a subsidiary relationship to the objectives of the curriculum (Stenhouse, 1970). There is here the objection that educational planning demands attention to the logic of subject matter in order to identify what is educationally worthwhile. We can, moreover, acknowledge that this is so without at the same time adopting the fully fledged version of taking a means to an end that the tradition demands. Educational value, critics such as R. S. Peters have insisted, is implicit in worthwhile activities. Such activities are to be pursued as educational for the procedural principles inherent in them. They are not to be deemed educative only provisionally upon the observable results they happen to bring about in learners. However poorly mastered, they exemplify public traditions of rationality which are entailed in the concept of education itself (Peters, 1966).

That there is some use in the techniques of "rational curriculum planning" propounded in the technocratic tradition is undoubted. Historically, the movement offered a clear prescription for planners in a situation where there were no clear models. Planners were offered clear guidance on the specification of knowledge (Bloom et al., 1956). For learners it offered descriptions of their tasks which were in many ways helpful to them and in some cases formed the basis for contractual arrangements between teacher and learner. The clarity of planning model also provided a language of criticism for the public at large. This is not a trifling consideration, bearing in mind the enormous sums the public votes for education. It is in the United States that the movement has had its greatest influence. There, business, industrial, and academic work ethics are more closely aligned than in Europe. As an ideological position on the curriculum, it is not surprising that the technocratic tradition has held sway where a means-end model of human action is so influential in closely related spheres of social life. In European cultures there has been a historically more distant relationship between the worlds of commerce and industry and education. For that reason, when the theory of the curriculum in its technocratic form crossed the Atlantic it met with considerable resistance.

J. F. Kerr's collection *Changing the Curriculum* (1968) is a representative early attempt to translate the mainly American technocratic tradition into an English idiom. It was paralleled by a number of similar books (Wheeler, 1967; Nicholls and Nicholls, 1972; Taylor, 1970; Wiseman and Pidgeon, 1972). The key feature of these transplants is their emphasis on model building as a technique for planning. The orientation is practical curriculum planning and reform based on the principles of rational curriculum planning. It will be instructive to review Kerr's model and to base our discussion upon it. We should first note, however, a number of important points about model building in general. Models, particularly when diagrammatically presented, have a power to beguile with their simplicity. This simplicity is a necessary feature, for model making is essentially an attempt to filter out significant from trivial features of a situation. The criteria for significance cannot themselves be represented in models, as they are presuppositions going toward their construction. In the case of Kerr's model, there is a presupposition that the model is not merely a *description* of curriculum reality but is designed to assist decision making. It is thus a model *for* the curriculum rather than a model *of* the curriculum, an important distinction made by Maccia (1962). It is prescriptive as well as descriptive, and the relationship between the two aspects is obscure. This is so because of a confusion that often vitiates curriculum theory, namely, a confusion between curriculum as *plan* and curriculum as *process*. A model for planning will clearly differ, though it must be premised upon, a model for process. A model of the processes of the curriculum would be an attempt to chart the significant occurrences and transactions in schooling; a model for planning must have an implicit theory about how these processes are to be modified. Kerr's model reveals a vacillation between these two conceptions, and it shares this defect with many other such model building exercises.

THE LIBERAL HUMANIST TRADITION

Kerr's book can be seen as the superimposition of a conceptual apparatus and package of planning recommendations upon an existing set of doctrines about curriculum planning. It is noteworthy that the model specifies "knowledge" as a major section of the curriculum reflecting a traditionally naive acceptance of contemporary school knowledge as "given" in the curriculum. Moreover, the model goes on to indicate that school knowledge has some tight relationship with "disciplines," although "pupils" and "society" are given apparently equal status as sources for objectives.

What is significant is an implicit compromise with the dominant view of curriculum as initiation into a settled body of high-status subjects, without reflection on what validates these subjects singly and what relationships they have together as contributions to the educational experience of the young. Curriculum theory, as taught before the impact of work such as Kerr's, did not bear that title. It consisted in the pedagogy of received subjects against a justificatory ideology of education that stressed the inherent value of theoretical activities such as have their home in university and research contexts. The key text here is Paul Hirst's *Liberal Education and the Nature of Knowledge* (1965).

Hirst argues that the knowledge of which mind is "constituted" consists of a range of "forms of thought," each of which represents a unique way of experiencing and understanding the world. By "a form of knowledge" is meant a distinct way in which our experience becomes structured round the use of accepted public symbols. The symbols thus having public meaning, their use is in some way testable against experience, and there is the progressive development of series of tested symbolic expressions. In this way experience has been probed further and further by extending and elaborating the use of the symbols, and by means of these, it has become possible for the personal experience of individuals to become more fully structured, more fully understood. The various forms of knowledge can be seen in low-level developments within the common area of our knowledge of the everyday world. From this there branch out the developed forms which, taking certain elements in our common knowledge as a basis, have grown in distinctive ways. In the developed forms of knowledge the following related distinguishing features can be seen:

1. They each involve certain central concepts that are peculiar in character to the form. For example, those of gravity, acceleration, hydrogen, and photosynthesis characteristic of the sciences; number, integral, and matrix in mathematics; God, sin, and predestination in religion; ought, good, and wrong in moral knowledge.

2. In a given form of knowledge these and other concepts that denote, if perhaps in a very complex way, certain aspects of experience form a network of possible relationships in which experience can be understood. As a result the form has a distinctive logical structure.

3. The form, by virtue of its particular terms and logic, has expressions or statements (possibly answering a distinctive type of question) that in some way or other, however indirect it may be, are testable against experience. This is the case in scientific knowledge, moral knowledge, and in the arts, though in the arts no questions are explicit and the criteria for the tests are only partially expressible in words. Each form, then, has distinctive expressions that are testable against experience in accordance with particular criteria that are peculiar to the form.

4. The forms have developed particular techniques and skills for exploring experience and testing their distinctive expressions, for instance, the techniques of the sciences and those of the various literary arts. The result has been the amassing of all the symbolically expressed knowledge that we now have in the arts and the sciences.

For Hirst, a liberal education must minimally involve the pupil being initiated into all the "forms of thought." Thus he advocates a knowledge-centered curriculum, though not necessarily a curriculum based upon any particular division of knowledge into "subjects." For example, he recognizes that "fields of knowledge" also exist, examples of which are theoretical and practical areas of activity such as agriculture, medicine, or education itself. Other theorists in this camp are King and Brownell (1966), who conceive an academic discipline as a "community of discourse," a group of scholars with a sense of shared concerns, publications, and shared identity, and Phenix (1964), who bases his recommendation on a logical analysis of what can be meaningfully said. In Britain writers such as Whitfield (1971) paralleled the Americans Bruner (1960, 1966) and Ford and Pugho (1964) in drawing attention to the importance of structure in subject matter. Structure renders mere information meaningful, provides for readier learning, promotes transfer, and reduces the gap between elementary and advanced knowledge in a field.

Pedagogically, a long-standing model of teaching in which a learner is conceived as a postulant to be initiated into the mysteries of a subject by working at it alongside a "master" (very much a model of traditional university teaching) was developed in the new emphasis on fundamentals of a subject. Oakeshott (1974) expresses the pedagogic point thus:

All actual conduct, all specific activity springs up within an already existing idiom of activity. And by "idiom of activity" I mean a knowledge of how to behave appropriately in the circumstances. Scientific activity is the exploration of the knowledge scientists have of how to go about asking and answering scientific questions; moral activity is the exploration of the knowledge we have of how to behave well. And we come to penetrate an idiom of activity in no other way than by practising the activity; for it is only in the practice of an activity that we can acquire the knowledge of how to practise it.

Liberal humanism as represented by these modern writers is not without challenge. Some doubt that the intellectual demands of such a knowledge-based curriculum could be made accessible to all pupils. Bantock (1971), for example, suggests that the contemporary watered-down academic education offered to the mass of children is unsatisfactory and argues, against Hirst, that the basis of the curriculum for the mass of unacademic children should be more concrete, more practical, and "affective-artistic" in orientation. Bantock's view is based on a romantic conception of working-class culture and is, of course, a form of academic elitism. Other critics of the liberal humanist ideology are found among those who advocate a "socially relevant" curriculum, particularly in areas of urban decay (Midwinter, 1972). Such a view can be called into question as potentially socially divisive in offering a school experience directly related only to local conditions and not to cosomopolitan problems (Merson and Campbell, 1974).

Perhaps more significantly, the liberal humanist tradition is opposed by a longer-standing protest movement, namely, child-centered progressivism. If the liberal humanist takes the structure of knowledge as his starting point for curriculum planning, the progressivist takes subject matter into consideration only insofar as it illuminates the child's world. Growth is the central metaphor. Malcolm Skilbeck (1976a) outlines some of the major tenets of the Romantic movement that underlie progressivism thus:

(a) The movement is a fundamental challenge to Enlightenment confidence in rationality, objectivity, universalism, causality, abstract analysis, and urbanity. It emphasizes "human inwardness," private subjective meanings and symbols, states of consciousness, feeling states, and complex personal motives.

(b) Knowledge is yielded by direct experience, intuition, reverie, and by communication in full encounter with persons and things; it is "wrenched from nature," but not by cold science.

(c) Man is a spiritual entity who is nevertheless, in Cervantes's phrase, the "son of his works," discovering and fulfilling himself through his energetic, active impingement on the external world. He is not a "factor" in nature, but a free, responsible moral agent.

(d) Sincerity, wholeheartedness, self-sacrifice, indomitable will in pursuit of some self-fulfilling cause are all worthwhile; compromise and the "sellout" are crimes.

(e) Society is organic, plant- or animal-like, interacting with environment and varying in time and place; it is not a clockwork mechanism following universal laws; history is not "universal" but a succession of unique, varied particulars; culture and society are diverse, not reducible to a single ideal type; man's cultural life is a life of struggle and conflict.

(f) Man's "natural habitat" is the remote, the colorful, the wild, the elemental countryside, woodlands, distant islands, unexplored territories; urban, industrial society is vicious, depraving, distorting.

(g) God, if He exists, is reachable through emotional ritual, or mystical exercise, including communing with nature. By some romantics He is seen to exist as the enemy of mankind, a giant torturer.

(h) Art is authentic inasmuch as it expresses the passions and deepest experience of the individual artist; art is communication between persons and groups within a culture and in historical time. But art is not undisciplined; the task is "to keep one's head in the course of the storm and to direct one's troops."

(i) The child is father of the man, his own "best philosopher"; childhood experience is authentic, direct, vivid, penetrating, rich, and fleeting; childhood is a state worthy in itself and not merely as a prelude to adulthood.

For the progressive, pedagogy is opportunistic, sustained by intimate knowledge of the individual child in a framework of organized resources. The teacher is seen as expert on child development, learning, and classroom organization. Planning is the provision of opportunities for the following of interests in a secure emotional framework or "benign environment" (Fisher, 1972).

The technocratic import of rational planning does not fit well into the liberal humanist ideology. **Behavioral objectives** (q.v.) are inappropriate for cognitive achievement if it is intended thereby that value-neutral checklists should be used to evaluate teaching by assessors not themselves initiated into the complex norms of understanding being developed. This is not to say, however, that there are *no* objectives in liberal humanist teaching; only that objectives are complex, of a high order, and as yet little researched (Hirst, 1965).

Furthermore, the experience of teachers in Britain in attempting to work with rational planning models has not been satisfactory, and the technique has been much modified in practice (Schools Council, 1972, 1973; Taylor, 1970). The explanation for such difficulties, however they are lamented by advocates of the technocratic model, lies both in the adverse ideologies of education described above and in the autonomy of schools in Britain. This autonomy has enabled schools to develop traditions of educational practice that do not seek to account for themselves to outsiders.

THE ANTHROPOLOGICAL RELATIVIST TRADITION

It is in appreciation of the deficiencies of the technocratic and liberal humanist approaches to curriculum that attention has most recently returned to a view of curriculum as a cultural artifact.

What are the sources, and what priorities exist among them, for objectives in rational planning? The technique itself can give no clue to that question. What justifies the central position accorded knowledge, and the particular selection of all knowledge that is school knowledge, against its sociological critics? Such critics have pointed to the historical and class contexts that have produced the academic school curriculum and have criticized the mechanisms whereby that curriculum acts as uneven distributors of life chances and power (Young, 1971; Keddie, 1973; Holly, 1971, 1973).

So it is that the first Open University course in curriculum contained a substantial section devoted to a systems approach that stemmed from the technocratic tradition (Open University, 1972a). The fundamental disagreements within the team producing the course *The Curriculum: Context, Design and Development* for the Open University were well publicized in the U.K. educational press. The succeeding course, designed to replace the original Open University offering (Open University, 1976), by contrast promotes a view of curriculum as a cultural transaction among generations, interest groups, and institutions. The third-generation curriculum course from the Open University, *Purpose and Planning in the Curriculum,* has developed this view and promises to sustain the interest in a cultural analysis approach to curriculum planning. Lawton's most recent book, *Curriculum Studies and Educational Planning* (1983), is also characterized by its emphasis upon a broad conception of the curriculum in line with the tradition we are here discussing.

In such a conception of curriculum the value of an objectives-based approach and the status of traditional subjects wait upon a "cultural analysis." That is to say, the school curriculum is seen as the meeting place of a large number of legitimate interests, for example, those of pupils, teachers, parents, employers, trade unions. The curriculum needs to accomodate as many such interests as possible. The central problem of curriculum is, therefore, to develop mechanisms for the expression of those interests and clearer conceptions of the rights and duties of the parties concerned. The spirit of this approach is seen in practice in the Schools Council's Working Paper 53, *The Whole Curriculum 13–16,* in which an "educational covenant" is suggested between interested parties (Schools Council, 1975). The pivotal position of teachers in this dispensation is obvious. It is also obvious that teachers are ill-equipped for the task of mediating conflict, setting up dialogue at an ideological level (for questions of curriculum design are ultimately profoundly ideological), and developing curricula that are more than uneasy compromises, having a coherent design that identifies shared values and makes room for legitimate dissent.

To trace the heritage of this view of curriculum as ideology in action, and to recognize that this view is itself ideological in that it takes a definite line on the role of school in relation to cultural and political structures, we have to return to American sources. Dewey saw school knowledge as validated by its contribution, pragmatically, to democratic cultural development (Dewey, 1899). Smith, Stanley, and Shores (1950) summarize and epitomize a long line of thinking that takes the school as a socializing institution, whose function is to transmit to the next generation those things within the culture that are most valued, including ideas, ideals, beliefs, skills, tools, aesthetic discernment, methods of thinking, and institutions. School is thus an institution concerned to centralize experience around what is valued universally. What is more, a society that respects minorities will expect school also to represent subcultures in its curriculum. Determining what is most generally valued, what are the identifiable subcultures in a pluralistic society, how cultural universals and cultural specialities are to be educationally mediated (Linton, 1936), becomes the focal problem for curriculum design. With the observation that there is a developing literature taking a cultural approach to curriculum study, notably Lawton (1973, 1975, 1983), Stenhouse (1967, 1975), Reynolds and Skilbeck (1976), we may best conclude by discussing the two most important and contentious centers of interest of the late seventies, the core curriculum and evaluation.

THE POLITICAL DEBATE

If the origins of curriculum theory lay in the American interest in systems management and the British interest among teacher trainers, its future must lie in its response to a political climate on both sides of the Atlantic calling in question some of the fundamentals of schools in democratic, even postindustrial, societies. The first intimations of this coming crisis occurred with the political debates ensuing from the developing economic recession of the 1970s. In Great Britain a so-called Great Debate drew education to the center of the political stage. For the first time a prime minister made a speech concerned only with educational issues. James Callaghan's Ruskin College speech (October 1976) drew particular attention to the possibility of a core or protected part of the curriculum in schools and also expressed the traditional concern for standards. Ensuing events have resulted in a closer audit of schoolwork through a mechanism of accountability to governing bodies. At the same time the membership of governing bodies of schools has been widened, to some extent democratized, and made generally less mysterious to the public. In this situation teachers require a supervised yet intelligible way of expressing their educational values. These have to be in terms which make sense to a public and parental opinion which has now the courage to ask abrasive questions. In such dialogues the language of systems management and the esoteric language of cultural anthropologists may not find a sympathetic response. The future of curriculum theory must lie in bringing the sometimes arcane aspirations of teachers, with their visions of intrinsic educational values, to bear upon an increasingly materialistic and utilitarian political culture.

Political events since the Great Debate have precipitated new focuses for theoretical and practical interest. Whether there should be a "common learnings" curriculum for all pupils, irrespective of age, sex, ability, social class, or school attended, is the first of these questions, referred to as the "core curriculum" debate. There has been some cross-fertilization of ideas between the liberal thinkers on the theoretical side and those more directly concerned with implementation such as Her Majesty's Inspectors. HMI's Red Book is a collection of papers from an important professional body urging a coherent curriculum based upon a view of knowledge as differentiated into Hirstian forms.

Notwithstanding these developments, the device of exposing all children to a de facto core made up of traditional academic disciplines has been, if not discredited in principle, insufficiently justified. Traditional "subjects" have not received adequate theoretical attention for their educational value. Broudy, Smith, and Burnett (1964) argue for the curriculum as a kind of "cultural map" and arrive at five groupings of curriculum content designed to enable a student to find his way about a culture. Jenkins (1976) describes these groupings as follows:

1. Bodies of knowledge that serve as symbolic tools of thinking, communication, and learning. These include the language of ordinary discourse, of logic, of quantity, and of art.
2. Bodies of knowledge that systematize basic facts and their relations. These disciplines (the basic sciences) give us a way of speaking and thinking about the world and everything in it; a way structured by the conceptual system that characterizes each discipline.
3. Bodies of knowledge that organize information along the routes of cultural development. History, biography, and evolutionary studies serve this purpose by giving some kind of order to the past.
4. Bodies of knowledge that project future problems and attempt to regulate the activities of the social order. Agriculture, medicine, technology, and national defense are examples of the former. Political science, jurisprudence, economics, and management are examples of the latter. We have also developed sciences to guide dissemination of knowledge, e.g., education, mass communication, journalism, library science, custodianships of records and relics.
5. Integrative and inspirational disciplines which create syntheses or value schema in the form of philosophies, theologies, and works of art.

For the fifth category Broudy recommends the "examplar approach: a careful study of a small number of examples of great books, great works of art, and systems of ideas."

The resulting "schema for schooling" was premised on the assumption that knowledge is applied interpretively in making sense of the world. Pupils need to find their way around. The task of the curriculum is to give them "cognitive and evaluative maps."

Phenix (1964) generates six possible "realms of meaning" developed from the notion that human beings are essentially creatures who have the power to express and experience meanings. General education for Phenix is the process of engendering "essential meanings." Phenix's patterns of meanings are

1. *symbolics,* comprising "ordinary language, mathematics and various types of non-discursive symbolic forms such as gestures, rituals, rhythmic patterns, and the like."

2. *empirics,* including "the sciences of the physical world, of living things and of man."
3. *aesthetics,* containing "the various arts, such as music, the visual arts, the arts of movement, and literature."
4. *synnoetics,* signifying the "personal knowledge" of Michael Polanyi, "relational insight" or "direct awareness" of oneself or others.
5. *ethics,* including "moral meanings," and moral conduct.
6. *synoptics,* referring "to meanings that are comprehensively integrative" and including history, religion, and philosophy.

The suggestions of Broudy, Smith and Burnett, and Phenix appear defective as bases for the core curriculum. Any such proposals must be clear about what they *exclude* in a situation where values are pluralistic and not monolithic. Additionally, of course, they do not indicate an actual curricular organization, which has to be arrived at in a particular school situation.

A problem-oriented approach to the core is suggested by Kluckhohn and Strodtbeck (1961), who postulate five major problems "confronting all people at all times." These are: (1) the character of human nature; (2) the relationship of man to nature; (3) man's view of time; (4) his relationship to activity; (5) his relationship to other men.

A cultural approach to the core would be to say that these considerations are manifested in all societies at all times, and school should represent the current range of views about them. Having treated these universals, schools would then be free to develop their own curricula in relation to the particularities of their own local environment. This would include the exploration of a role in developing and interpreting local cultures, whether regionally, ethnically, or social-class based (Chanan and Gilchrist, 1974). Skilbeck (1976b) presents a model for school-based curriculum development in which such an analysis could be conducted.

It must be noted that the above analysis is premised unreservedly upon a particular view of the relationship between schools and society. There are those who would challenge such a view, and the second political question that has come into focus emphasizes this point. The evaluation is not a straightforward matter of checking students' performance against prespecified goals unless an assumption is made about the background political framework within which such measurements are taken. For the technocratic tradition as identified above, evaluation is a simple matter. For the liberal humanist, examinations provide a gold standard of evaluation. In both cases evaluation is achieved through the assessment of students. A culturally based curriculum design, however, must seek an evaluation process fully cognizant of the meanings imported into the educational process by participants. It would also require the stiffening of a political theory. It cannot be pretended that either of these requirements has been satisfactorily realized. The movement to control schools from the above has produced a spirited counter in the form of school self-evaluation. Various methodologies have been vigorously developed particularly in local areas where the responsible education authority has taken a particularly zealous view of its responsibilities to monitor its curriculum and report to central government.

In this situation new paradigms of evaluation activity have recently been developed. A new emphasis on understanding the curriculum as a set of processes has given rise to a conception of evaluation, not as the measurement of outcomes, but as "illumination" of the whole scene (Parlett and Hamilton, 1972; Stake, 1967). Such portrayals of the curriculum attempt to present a record of an anthropological kind. They are not infrequently neutral as between competing prescriptions for reform or contending interest groups within the curriculum. The aspiration is to give a faithful portrayal of things as they are, while recognizing that all descriptions are formulated from a point of view. The question "what happened" is answerable from many differing prespectives and yields surprisingly diverse responses. It is only with the development of much more sensitive measuring instruments, which basically means much more sensitive fieldworkers, that curriculum development as a securely based intervention in cultural development can proceed. Evaluation is at one with the curriculum it serves, for conceptions of evaluation are intimately tied in with overarching conceptions of the curriculum itself. Key questions necessary to delimit evaluation are: Who is to evaluate? What is he to look for? What methods are to be employed? To whom is the evaluator to report? To what use are his findings to be put? By defining evaluation against these questions, we simultaneously define the curriculum field. It is to be expected that curriculum theory, having now a firm base in the academic world, will contribute in a muscular way to the contest for educational evaluation being fought out in the 1980s.

M. Golby

REFERENCES

Bantock, G. H. (1971) "Towards a Theory of Popular Education." *Times Educational Supplement,* 12 and 19 March.

Bloom, B. S. et al. (1956) *Taxonomy of Educational Objec-*

tives, *Handbook 1: The Cognitive Domain*. London: Longman.
Bobbitt, F. (1918) *The Curriculum*. Boston: Houghton Mifflin.
———. (1924) *How To Make a Curriculum*. Boston: Houghton Mifflin.
Broudy, A. S., Smith, B. O., and Burnett, J. R. (1964) *Democracy and Excellence in American Secondary Education*. Chicago: Rand McNally.
Bruner, J. (1960) *The Process of Education*. Cambridge, Mass.: Harvard University Press.
———. (1966) *Towards a Theory of Instruction*. Cambridge, Mass.: The Belknap Press of Harvard University Press.
Chanan, G. and Gilchrist, L. (1974) *What School Is For*. London: Methuen.
Dewey, J. (1899) *The School and Society*. Chicago: University of Chicago Press.
Fisher, R. J. (1972) *Learning How To Learn: The English Primary School and American Education*. New York: Harcourt Brace Jovanovich.
Ford, G. W. and Pugho, L., eds. (1964) *The Structure of Knowledge and the Curriculum*. Chicago: Rand McNally.
Her Majesty's Inspectors. (1979) *Curriculum 11–16*. London: Her Majesty's Stationery Office.
Hirst, P. H. (1965) "Liberal Education and the Nature of Knowledge." In *Philosophical Analysis and Education*, ed. R. D. Archanbauld. London: Routledge & Kegan Paul.
———. (1974) *Knowledge and the Curriculum*. London: Routledge & Kegan Paul.
Holly, D. (1971) *Schools, Society and Humanity*. London: MacGibbon & Kee.
———. (1973) *Beyond Curriculum*. London: Hart-Davis/MacGibbon.
Jenkins, D. R. (1976) *Curriculum: An Introduction*. London: Open Books.
Keddie, N., ed. (1973) *Tinker, Tailor: The Myth of Cultural Deprivation*. Harmondsworth: Penguin Books.
Kerr, J. F., ed. (1968) *Changing the Curriculum*. London: University of London Press.
King, A. R. and Brownell, J. R. (1966) *The Curriculum and the Disciplines of Knowledge*. New York: Wiley.
Kluckholn, F. L. and Strodtbeck, B. (1961) *Variations on Value Orientations*. Evanston, Ill.: Row Peterson.
Lawton, D. (1973) *Social Class, Educational Theory and Curriculum Planning*. London: Routledge & Kegan Paul.
———. (1975) *Class, Culture and the Curriculum*. London: Routledge & Kegan Paul.
———. (1983) *Curriculum Studies and Educational Planning*. London: Hodder & Stoughton.
Linton, R. (1936) *The Study of Man*. New York: Appleton-Century-Crofts.
Maccia, E. (1962) *The Conceptions of Model in Educational Theorizing*. Columbus: Bureau of Research and Service, Ohio State University.
Merson, M. W. and Campbell, R. J. (1974) "Community Education: Instruction for Inequality." *Education for Teaching*. Spring: 43–49.
Midwinter, E. (1972) *Projections: An Educational Priority Area at Work*. London: Ward Lock Educational.
Nicholls, A. and Nicholls, H. (1972) *Developing a Curriculum: A Practical Guide*. London: Allen & Unwin.
Oakeshott, M. (1974) *Rationalism in Politics and Other Essays*. London: Methuen.
O'Connor, D. J. (1957) *Introduction to the Philosophy of Education*. London: Routledge & Kegan Paul.
Open University. (1972a) *Course E283. The Curriculum: Context, Design and Development*. Milton Keynes: Open University Press.
———. (1972b) *Course E283: Unit 9. Teaching Strategies*. Milton Keynes: Open University Press.
———. (1976) *Course E203. Curriculum Design and Development*. Milton Keynes: Open University Press.
Parlett, M. and Hamilton, D. (1971) *Evaluation as Illumination: A New Approach to the Study of Innovatory Programs*. Edinburgh: Centre for Research in the Educational Sciences, University of Edinburgh.
Peters, R. S. (1966) *Ethics and Education*. London: Allen & Unwin.
Phenix, P. (1964) *Realms of Meaning: A Philosophy of the Curriculum for General Education*. New York: McGraw-Hill.
Reynolds, J. and Skilbeck, M. (1976) *Culture and the Classroom*. London: Open Books.
Schools Council. (1972) *With Objectives in Mind: Guide to Science 5–13*. London: Macdonald Educational.
———. (1973) *Evaluation in Curriculum Development: Twelve Case Studies*. London: Macmillan/Schools Council.
———. (1975) *The Whole Curriculum 13–16*. London: Evans/Methuen Educational.
Schwab, J. J. (1969) "The Practical: A Language for Curriculum." *School Review* 78 (1): 1–24.
Skilbeck, M. (1976a) *Culture, Ideology and Knowledge, Open University Course E203, Unit 3*. Milton Keynes: Open University Press.
———. (1976b) "School-based Curriculum Development and Teacher Education." In *Open University Course E203, Unit 7 (Appendix)*. Milton Keynes: Open University Press.
Smith, B. O., Stanley, W. O., and Shores, J. H. (1950) *Fundamentals of Curriculum Development*. New York: Harcourt, Brace & World.
Stake, R. E. (1967) "The Countenance of Curriculum Evaluation." *Teachers College Record* 68: 523–540.
Stenhouse, L. A. (1967) *Culture and Education*. London: Nelson.
———. (1970) "Some Limitations of the Use of Objectives in Curriculum Research and Planning." *Pedagogica Europaea* 6: 73–83.
———. (1975) *An Introduction to Curriculum Research and Development*. London: Heinemann.
Taylor, P. H. (1970) *How Teachers Plan Their Courses*. Slough: National Foundation for Educational Research.

Tibble, J. W. (1966) *The Study of Education*. London: Routledge & Kegan Paul.

Tyler, R. W. (1949) *Basic Principles of Curriculum and Instruction*. Chicago: University of Chicago Press.

Wheeler, D. K. (1967) *Curriculum Process*. London: University of London Press.

Whitfield, R. (1971) *Disciplines of the Curriculum*. Maidenhead: McGraw-Hill.

Wiseman, S. and Pidgeon, D. (1972) *Curriculum Evaluation*. Slough: National Foundation for Educational Research.

Young, M.F.D., ed. (1971) *Knowledge and Control*. London: Collier-Macmillan.

CURSOR. A symbol (often flashing) of some kind used on VDUs to indicate the position at which the next symbol typed will be placed.

CUT. (1) To take a selected portion of a screen or document, remove it from its current location, and put it on the clipboard. From the clipboard, it can be pasted into other documents or into a new place in the same document. (2) To abruptly replace one shot by another, e.g., "Cut from camera 2 to camera 1." (3) Command to stop action, usually given to the floor manager or camera operator.

CUT AND PASTE. Word processing techniques in which sections of text are removed ("cut") and/or inserted ("pasted"). The terms are a direct parallel with the physical method of assembling artwork for printing.

CUT FILM. Single pieces of film for use one at a time in some larger camera formats are referred to as cut or sheet films. This contrasts with more common cameras which use a film format where a number of exposures are made on a strip or "roll" of film.

CUTTING COPY. A print of a cine film master that is used for editing purposes and then as a guide when finally cutting the master.

CWP. Communicating Word Processor. *See* **Teletex.**

CYBERNETICS. *See* **Conversation Theory; Educational Cybernetics; Entailment Mesh.**

CYBERTEL. A private videotex system operated by Control Data Pty. Ltd.

CYCLOPS. A telewriter/teleconferencing system formerly in use at the Open University, U.K. The facility offered good graphics and other advantages including the availability of sound (e.g., the teacher's voice) and ease of creation of materials; no programming skills were needed.

CYCLORAMA. Circular or curving neutral backdrop commonly found in television studios. It may be made of cloth or some more rigid material.

D

DAD. *See* **Digital Audio Disc.**

DAISY WHEEL. A print head for a typewriter or a printer. The device, which basically is similar in operation to a "thimble" or to a "golf-ball," consists of plastic fingers carrying the various letters, numbers, etc., and which are impressed against the ribbon at the time of printing. These fingers are arranged in a circular pattern around a central disk, thus looking rather like the flower of a daisy. The wheels are interchangeable, giving a wide choice of type styles.

DALTON PLAN. An individualized teaching plan that originated at Dalton High School, Dalton, Massachusetts (U.S.), around 1920. It requires pupils to carry out regular assignments, their progress being recorded on job cards, and requires a combination of individual and group work supported by regular pupil-teacher conferences.

DARKROOM. A room from which all external light is excluded so that light-sensitive photographic materials can be safely used. Appropriate safelights are provided according to the type of materials to be used.

A darkroom usually contains one or more enlargers for color and/or monochrome enlargement, and will generally incorporate a wet area with sinks and so forth for processing and rinsing.

DARK SLIDE. Originally a light-proof film holder for use with plate or cut film cameras, the term is also used for an opaque insert in a series of programmed slides which produces a black screen between color slides which is held for some length of time for a particular purpose.

DATA. In computer terms *data* is all, or any selection of, the operands and results involved in any operation or set of operations. More generally, a collection or set of information.

DATA BANK. *See* **Data base.**

DATA BASE. Essentially a store or bank of information on a particular topic or group of topics. ERIC, for example, is an educational data base. However, the term is usually restricted to a computer store which permits searching on the basis of key words (descriptors). Thus an ERIC search requires the client to find (from the ERIC thesaurus) sufficient key words to adequately delineate his interest. For example, a search for documents based on the descriptors Simulation and Social Sciences might turn up literally thousands of documents. Clearly the search must be narrowed down by the use of additional descriptors such as Grade 7, Educationally Disadvantaged, and so on.

Microcomputer software exists which allows easy compilation of personal data bases. A research worker may convert several thousand index cards to a few floppy disks, which permit very fast and accurate searching. A school library catalog, a slide collection, any sort of inventory, all lend themselves to implementation as data bases. It is essential, however, to spend time on a preliminary analysis of the purposes of the data base, so as to ensure that cataloging, amending, and searching can all be performed in a convenient manner. For example, most data bases will extend to more than one disk; it will be helpful if the allocation to disks is done in such a manner as to ensure that the most suitable disk is chosen first when updating, searching, etc.

In summary, the storage and retrieval of information is one of the activities that computers are best suited for. The establishment and use of data bases has many worthwhile educational applications, and will lead to substantial gains in convenience and efficiency. Additionally, of course, the existence of large data bases such as ERIC is of inestimable value to the research worker. *See* **Information Classification and Retrieval.**

DATA BASE MANAGEMENT SYSTEM. A program that provides a framework for creating collections of data for use by different programs and that serves as the interface between the programs and the data. The data base management system (DBMS) can also include a query facility for making individual requests for information from the data base and a reporting facility for producing a formatted list of selected data.

DATA LINK. Dedicated wiring used in computing for transmitting and receiving data between two remote terminals, or a remote terminal and a central processor, or two central processors.

DATA PREPARATION. The process of selecting data from source documents and recording it in a form suitable for input to a computer.

DATA PROCESSING. The process in computing of carrying out a systematic sequence of operations on data with the object of extracting or revising information.

DATA TERMINAL EQUIPMENT (DTE). Computer terminal specifically designed for the transmission and reception of data from remote computers, for example, by using the Austpac packet switching network.

DATEL. Data transmission service provided by Telecom Australia which uses conventional undedicated telephone lines as communication channels.

DAYLIGHT PROJECTION. A projection system that in one way or another gives a screen bright enough to be used in high levels of ambient light. Generally, back projection is used, but front projection is possible using screens with special highly directional qualities.

DAYLIGHT SCREEN. A projection screen constructed so that clear images from a slide or other projector can be seen in an undarkened room; examples of daylight screens are the beaded screen, lenticular screen, and slivered screen.

DBMS. *See* **Data base Management System.**

DB-9. The common name for a type of connector used for making serial connections between modems, computers, and some types of printers and networks. It has a D-shaped shell containing nine pins or sockets in two rows.

DBS. *See* **Direct Broadcasting Satellite.**

DEAD ACOUSTIC. One in which a substantial loss is introduced at every reflection. For studio work this is the nearest approximation to an outdoor acoustic (in which little or no sound is reflected).

DEBUG. *See* **Bug.**

DECAY CHARACTERISTIC (OF STUDIO). The curve which indicates how the sound intensity falls after a steady note is cut off. Plotted in decibels against time, decay should roughly follow a single straight line.

DECIBEL. One tenth of a bel. The unit used to measure signal gain or loss in a circuit, but most commonly used to express intensities of sound. The scale is logarithmic, so that a sound of intensity 90 decibels is ten times the intensity of a sound measuring 80 decibels.

DECISION DYNAMIC TRAINING. A management-training technique developed at Strathclyde University (U.K.). Simulation exercises and video recordings are used to examine the dynamics of a decision-making group.

DECISION THEORY. A mathematical technique for forecasting unpredictable events and errors in variables. Decision analysis is a technique in identifying the most appropriate organization for a company. *See* **Game Theory.**

DECISION TREE. A type of flowchart that summarizes various alternatives in decision-making processes. The object is not to find a critical path or an optimum solution, but to display the range of alternatives available.

DECK. A tape-transporting mechanism or record-playing device. The term is used to describe the mechanical equipment required for playing tapes or records as opposed to the electronic components.

DECODER. The circuity in a color television receiver which transforms the detected color signals into a form suitable to operate the color tube.

DEDICATED COMPUTER. Computer or computer system designed to fulfill one particular task (or related group of tasks). Examples include library circulation systems, some word processors, on-board computers in airplanes, etc.

DEFAULT. A value, action, or setting that is automatically assumed by a computer system or program when no other explicit information has been given. For example, a word processing program may assume a pitch of ten characters to the inch unless specifically instructed otherwise.

DEFINITION. A term used to indicate the fineness of detail an image recording system is able to record. It is affected by the lens used, the recording medium, and the reproducing system. *See* **Resolving Power.**

DEGAUSS (DE-FLUX). The process of demagnetizing the metallic parts of a tape recorder which come into contact with the tape. Regular degaussing is important if quality of reproducing is to be maintained.

DELPHI TECHNIQUE. The Delphi technique was developed in the 1950s by Olaf Helmer and associates of the Rand Corporation. The initial purpose for which this forecasting technique was used was to obtain opinions about defense problems and to collect opinions of the future occurrence of social and technological advances. In its original form, the Delphi technique could be described as a forecasting method in which the participants are asked to generate ideas on future possibilities in a given field and to make predictions on the likely date of occurrence of these possibilities. A specific feature of the Delphi technique is the opportunity for participants to modify earlier judgments by providing them with additional information generated within the participant group. The aim of this modification procedure is to develop consensus within the group on the issues which are being considered. The process of modification is iterative and may be used until consensus or no change in opinion is reached.

Since its inception. the Delphi technique has undergone a number of modifications and a number of variants may be used. The basic procedure is generally as follows:

(a) Members of a selected panel of experts are asked to respond individually to an open-ended questionnaire. The purpose of the questionnaire is to allow the participants to generate ideas on future directions within their area of expertise. These ideas form the basis of the second questionnaire.

(b) The second questionnaire consists of items developed from the ideas in the first round. Participants are asked to rate these items in terms of various criteria which may include possible time of occurrence, desirability, priority, nature of possible interventions, and the degree of impact any future change may make.

(c) Analysis of the results of the second questionnaire is usually provided in the form of median response and interquartile range for each item. Participants whose responses lie outside the interquartile range are asked to provide reasons for their extreme position.

(d) In the light of the statistical evidence and information provided by participants adopting extreme positions on issues, participants are asked to rate the questionnaire items once again and to change their ratings if they should desire.

(e) This process may be continued until no change is discerned in responses (i.e., until consensus is reached or no change in polarization occurs). Studies indicate that 99 percent of change of opinion occurs by the time step (d) is completed. The features of the Delphi technique have been summarized by Weatherman and Swenson (1974):

(1) the strength of informed judgment by a panel of experts in a given field

(2) the anonymity of the participants, which reduces undesirable effects of group interaction

(3) provision of statistical data and additional information which allows consensus to be reached without asking a group to arrive at a common opinion

(4) ability of the director of the study, by selection of items and feedback, to reduce irrelevancies in the exercise

Assumptions which are made in using the Delphi technique as a forecasting method may be grouped into two areas:

(a) Assumptions relating to the panel of experts. It is assumed that the panel is large enough to be a representative sample of experts in the field under investigation and that the participants will seriously reconsider their original opinions in the light of additional information.

(b) Assumptions relating to procedures. It is assumed that the meaning of questionnaire items is clear to the respondents and that there is no effect on the results of the questionnaire by participants who fail to respond after the first or subsequent questionnaires.

EDUCATIONAL APPLICATIONS

Weaver (1972) distinguishes between exploratory and normative uses of the Delphi technique. Exploratory Delphi studies are those which develop a picture of the future as respondents expect it to be. Normative Delphi studies are designed to establish a plan of the future as desired by the respondents. It is considered that most Delphi studies in education are normative. Judd (1978) analyzed publications of Delphi studies in education and categorized them into three groups: studies on goals and objectives, studies on curriculum problems, and studies on administration changes.

Two studies which are considered to be useful as examples of the Delphi technique applied to education are the study in changes in postsecondary education by the National Center for Higher Education Management Systems, Colorado (Huckfeldt, 1972), and a study to identify problems related to general education in Alberta in the next thirty years (Berghofer, 1970, 1971). The first study is seen as a good example of a large-scale Delphi study; the second, as an example of the selection of respondents and the use of modified feedback procedure.

D. S. Litster

REFERENCES

Battersley, D. (1984) "Delphi Technique: Its Methodology and Application in Higher Education." In *Research and De-*

velopment in Higher Education, vol. 5, ed. I. R. Dunn. Higher Education Research and Development Society of Australasia, pp. 249–262.

Berghofer, D. E. (1970) *General Education in Post-secondary Non-university Educational Institutions in Alberta. Research Studies in Post-Secondary Education no. 9.* Edmonton, Canada: Alberta Colleges Commission.

———. (1971) "An Application of the Delphi Technique to Educational Planning." *Canadian Administrator* 10: 25–28.

Huckfeldt, V. (1972) *A Forecast of Changes in Post-secondary Education.* Boulder, Colo.: Western Interstate Commission for Higher Education.

Judd, R. C. (1978) "Delphi in Higher Education Revisited." *International Journal of Institutional Management in Higher Education* 2: 31–45.

Linstone, H. A. (1978) "The Delphi Technique." In *Handbook of Futures Research,* ed. J. Fowles. London: Greenwood Press.

Linstone, H. A. and Turoff, M., eds. (1975) *Delphi Method: Techniques and Applications.* Woburn, Mass.: Addison-Wesley.

McGaw, B., Browne, R. K., and Rees, P. (1976) "Delphi in Education: Review and Assessment." *Australian Journal of Education* 20: 59–76.

Weatherman, R. and Swenson, K. (1974) "Delphi Technique." In *Futurism in Education: Methodologies.* ed. S. P. Heneley and J. R. Yates. Berkeley, Calif.: McCutchan.

Weaver, W. T. (1972) *Delphi: A Critical Review.* Educational Policy Research Center Report RR7. New York: State University of New York.

DENSITOMETER. A device that measures with a high degree of accuracy the density of photographic images. It is used to assess photographic negatives particularly for contrast and exposure.

DENSITY. In photography, exposure of a film followed by processing, produces blackening which is quantitatively measured as density.

DEPENDENT VARIABLE. A variable which is studied or measured in an experimental procedure, as opposed to one that is under the direct control of the experimenter. *See* **Independent Variable.**

DEPTH OF FIELD. The zone of sharpness extending in front of and beyond the point at which a camera lens is focused. Depth of field depends on the focal length of the lens and the aperture at which it is set, and is not to be confused with depth of focus.

DEPTH OF FOCUS. The range of movement through which a camera lens may be adjusted while the image remains sharp.

DESCENDERS. The lower parts of lowercase letters like "g" and "y" that fall below the x-height of a typeface.

DESCRIPTOR. (1) In documentation, a term that is used loosely as a synonym for a key word. (2) In data storage, a broad subject heading that stands for a particular idea or concept and is used to facilitate retrieval of relevant information.

DESKTOP PUBLISHING. The advent of laser printers with printing resolutions of 300 dots per inch (dpi) transformed microcomputer printed output. Most dot-matrix printers are incapable of bettering 75–120 dpi with consequent chunky graphics and only average text, so the concept of producing brochures, newsletters, manuals, etc., with a professional appearance could not be realized before the laser printer.

Print quality alone would not be enough to spawn a new industry; the complementary element was the ability of a microcomputer, using suitable software, to show on the screen what the printed product would look like. Beyond a doubt, the combination of the Macintosh and the Apple Laser Printer which appeared around 1985 inaugurated desktop publishing. Many publishing software packages have since appeared for the different brands of microcomputer. They all have in common such features as:

1. Word processing facilities for inputting text, including features such as columns, pagination, and a variety of fonts and sizes.

2. The ability to construct (and to retrieve from other sources) graphics, and to size and place them anywhere in the text.

3. SWYG: the screen shows a realistic representation of what the printed page will look like.

It should be noted that such features as listed above are not enough in themselves to comprise a good publishing program; probably the most significant aspect for many users is speed. It is vital that a user can make a change, say on page one, such as editing out a few words, have the screen redrawn, and be ready to continue work within a few seconds.

Other components contributing to a versatile desktop publishing system would be a scanner to capture original material such as photographs and drawings for use within the system, and a library of clip art. It must be emphasized that the current (1987) resolution of laser printers (300 dpi) does not approach that of phototypesetting—typically over 1,000 dpi. However, for many purposes the lower resolution is quite adequate, and the possibility also exists for the output from some packages to be directly used by a phototypesetting agency.

Forecasts have repeatedly been made for the growth of desktop publishing to lead to a multibillion dollar industry. Only time will show if this is so, but it is clear that developments will be largely dependent on the quality, especially ease of use, of available software.

DETENT. A switch or other controlling element which is mechanically or electronically biased in favor of some default position; e.g., as in a joystick, which takes up a central position unless otherwise moved.

DEVELOPER. A developer converts the latent image formed during exposure of a film into a visible form. It does this by changing into black metallic silver the silver salt compounds in the emulsion that have been affected by light.

DEVELOPING COUNTRIES.

EDUCATIONAL PROBLEMS

What is a developing country? This is an emotive question with no single standard, clear-cut (or internationally agreed) definition. In its role as arbiter of such matters, the World Bank in its *World Development Report 1983* classified the countries of the world into three main groups: developing countries, industrial market economies, and East European nonmarket economies. The developing countries were further subdivided into least-developed countries (LDCs) and middle-income developing countries. Those countries designated as LDCs had a 1981 GNP per person of less than $410. Included in this group of 35 countries are those with few or no natural resources. Often landlocked, with population problems (either of very high or very low population density), and inhospitable terrains and climates; these countries have suffered even more than most from the fluctuations in recent world trading systems and patterns. Countries of large populations like Bangladesh, or large geographical areas such as the Sudan, share these problems equally with small countries such as Nepal or Rwanda. The World Bank list of least-developed countries includes Afghanistan, Bangladesh, Benin, Bhutan, Botswana, Burundi, Cape Verde, Central African Republic, Chad, Comoros, Djibouti, Equatorial Guinea, Ethiopia, The Gambia, Guinea, Guinea Bissau, Laos, Lesotho, Malawi, Maldives, Mali, Nepal, Niger, Rwanda, Samoa, Sao Tome and Principe, Sierra Leone, Somalia, Sudan, Tanzania, Togo, Uganda, Upper Volta, Yemen Arab Republic, and the People's Democratic Republic of Yemen.

Middle-income developing countries, i.e., those with an income of more than $410 GNP per person, are further divided by the World Bank into oil exporters and oil importers. Middle-income oil exporters comprise Algeria, Angola, Congo, Ecuador, Egypt, Gabon, Indonesia, Islamic Republic of Iran, Iraq, Malaysia, Mexico, Nigeria, Peru, Syria, Trinidad and Tobago, Tunisia, and Venezuela. Middle-income oil importers comprise all other middle-income developing countries not classified as oil exporters.

High-income oil exporters, which are not included in developing countries, include Bahrain, Brunei, Kuwait, Libya, Oman, Qatar, Saudi Arabia, and the United Arab Emirates.

It is in the middle-income developing countries that can be found many examples of countries that can genuinely be described as "developing." During the 1970s there was a marked and distinct positive movement of the indexes which are used by social economists to denote development. Health is improving, paid employment is increasing, and educational opportunity particularly is increasing. Progress may be slow—but it is perceptible.

These categories make it immediately apparent that the application of a purely financial yardstick gives no real guidance to the general level of development—far less educational development—in any one country. As Harbison (1973) and others have shown, high per capita GNP is no measure of educational development. From an educational point of view, indexes such as adult literacy rates, percentage of GNP devoted to education, primary school enrollment ratio and dropout rates are much more sensitive in measuring development. During the period from 1972 to 1981, the adult illiteracy rate in Africa dropped from around 74 percent to 50 percent, in Asia from 47 percent to 25 percent, and in Latin America from 24 percent to 17 percent.

Bare statistics do not, however, describe all of the educational problems facing the countries in the developing world. An educational planner in almost any of the 90 or so countries in the poorest categories of the World Bank classification would be certain to have to face some or all of the following problems: an increase in school enrollment as a result of growing public demand for education; an increase in the numbers of school (and possibly even university) leavers who cannot find employment in the monetary sector; a high percentage of illiteracy in the adult and working populations; severe shortages of trained, qualified, and experienced manpower at all levels of the educational system; syllabi and curricula which are often irrelevant to the needs, if not the aspirations, of the learners; and severe shortages of money.

Not all educationally developing countries have money problems, however. The oil revenues of a number of countries have enabled them to adopt a wealth-based strategy for their development. Not for them a slow, planned, and phased buildup of their educational and training systems. Their present level of income, although high, is a finite asset which is being invested with a minimum of delay. This investment is in training a skilled and competent work force which will enable industrial progress to be maintained once the oil resources are depleted. For these countries "training" has become the prime function of their education system. This emphasis on systems which can produce large numbers of trained people in as short a time as possible has inevitably led those countries to consider the educational methods, machines, and materials being used and marketed in the countries of Europe and North America.

One of the major problems facing those who have to make the political decisions concerning the educational system in most of the developing world is that the uncertain present economic growth rates have brought little benefits to the poorest members of their communities. New education and training systems need to be designed to enable the masses which have been unable to participate in the modern sector to be more productive. Wide variations of opportunity exist at present between urban and rural sectors. In Colombia, according to the World Bank (1976), the number of primary school students who successfully complete their course is ten times larger in urban schools than in rural schools. Dropouts in the latter are the main reason.

Although money is short in absolute terms in many developing countries, the percentage of national budgets spent on education is staggeringly high. The Philippines, the Dominican Republic, Senegal, Mali, and Upper Volta all spend more than twice that spent on education in the United Kingdom. Thirty percent is not uncommon. Despite this, educational systems in most developing countries are considered by the World Bank (1976) to be inefficient in their use of resources.

EDUCATIONAL TECHNOLOGY

Coombs and Ahmed (1974) commented that "The heavy reliance on face-to-face oral instruction has absorbed the bulk of resources in staff costs . . . leaving little or nothing for other aids to learning . . . and caused them to become the main bottleneck to expanding learning opportunities." This situation has changed little, if at all, since then. The total spending in all forms of teaching and learning aids—including the most basic classroom equipment of blackboard, paint, chalk, and desks—is often much less than 5 percent of the total expenditure on education. The design, production, and use of local educational materials do not always have the priority which they deserve. Coombs and Ahmed go on to say—and this is an issue which has relevance to the application of all educational technology everywhere, not just in developing countries—"It has also wasted the greatest educational resource of all . . . the extraordinary capacity of motivated people to learn on their own when given easy access to the stuff of learning."

Pre-1960. Almost all of the countries in the developing world came under the influence of the metropolitan countries of Europe, either as colonies or protectorates. Those which did not, such as Afghanistan, Ethiopia, Nepal, and Thailand, have attracted massive external multilateral assistance and influence over the past three decades. The historical associations have produced profound and lasting effects on the educational systems of the countries concerned, although not always just as mere reflections of the colonizing power. In Britain, formal education is, and always has been, very decentralized. This is not so in most of the Commonwealth countries nor most other developing countries. Ministries of Education, which have evolved from colonial Departments of Education, usually have total and absolute control of their systems, curricula standards, materials, staff, and so on.

The biggest element in terms of expense and size was then, and still is, the classroom teacher, or more specifically, the primary classroom teacher. Earning extremely low wages, seldom having much more education than the pupils they taught, no professional training, no supervision or in-service training, no access to or support from educational materials and resources, little motivation in terms of promotion or salary and often—in rural areas—little status, primary schoolteachers provided an unstable foundation for the educational pyramid.

It was against this kind of background that educational planners and administrators in developing countries eagerly listened to, and were convinced by, those from the developed countries who, reacting against the sterility of the "chalk-and-talk" approach to education, were enthusiastically advocating the use of visual aids. In the 1950s—and indeed even today—almost all of the education and training taking place throughout the world, especially the developing world, was based on a teacher, a textbook, a blackboard and chalk, and writing materials for the learners. The use of visual aids, particularly the simple varieties such as posters, charts, flannel graphs, and models which could be made by the teachers themselves from local low-cost materials, was welcomed as a major breakthrough. This period coincided with an expansionist phase of the world economy, which in turn had enabled a major growth in the use of films, filmstrips, and slides in schools in America, Canada, and much of Europe.

At this time, as was so often to be repeated in the future, a transfer of technology from developed to developing countries took place. Not perhaps a fully considered, carefully planned transfer from which both the givers and the receivers expected the same results. Audiovisual centers and services were created in many developing countries. Whether by reluctant bureaucrats at the insistence of an eager group of teachers, or by those with a missionary zeal to improve education or by external aid agencies, they came into being. Often it seemed their main purpose was their existence.

It was this phase of exuberant, inexperienced enthusiasm which gave rise to so many of the harshly critical but usually unpublished reports of the time. These reports—as opposed to the public statements from donors and recipients—highlighted the unsuitability of much of the equipment, the inability of local staff to maintain and service it, and the complete lack of suitable software. Whenever a single fault occurred anywhere, the total system broke down. The equipment was consigned to a storeroom to await review and condemnation by another visiting expert. Audiovisual aids had overtaken the capacity of the users to make use of them. They become discredited as "white elephants," as irrelevant intrusions on the serious business of education. It will be instructive for future analysts of the development of educational technology to compare and contrast this, and later phases, with the introduction of microprocessors (1983) into educational system—local, regional, national, and international.

Concurrently with this, there had been a quiet, unspectacular, but nevertheless very significant expansion of a mass medium of major importance: radio. Educational radio was something of an orphan in the developing world. Formal educational broadcasting was first started in the United Kingdom in 1924. By 1927, when the British Broadcasting Corporation (BBC) came into being, broadcasters had quite firmly adopted a responsibility for schools broadcasting. In the colonies and dominions broadcasting services were set up along lines and patterns similar in structure, style, and methods to the BBC. Each of these broadcasting systems sooner or later set up a "schools broadcasting unit." In 1938 India had a schools broadcasting service operated by the broadcasting authorities. By the early 1950s several developing countries had broadcasting services which were putting out programs for schools.

Not much was written or recorded about these early initiatives. The most likely reason for this was the lack of success they achieved. The developing countries had strongly centralized, strongly controlled educational systems. They also had strongly centralized, strongly controlled broadcasting systems. These national broadcasting systems invariably assumed responsibility for educational broadcasting. But often this responsibility ended with the transmission of the programs. Responsibility for providing receivers and for organizing the classroom use of the programs and their follow-up was left to the education authorities. These education authorities, who often had not been—or felt that they had not been—involved in the decision-making processes relating to the broadcasts, were less than enthusiastic in directing or encouraging their teachers to use radio. A conflict of control and responsibility occurred.

This issue of control of educational broadcasting posed less of a problem in those parts of the world where the control of broadcasting itself was less severe and more decentralized. In 1947 in Colombia the Popular Cultural Action of Radio Sutatenza (ACPO) was set up with the backing of the Church to provide a national system of adult basic education using radio. This service, which still puts out almost twenty hours of programming each day, and which is relayed through three other stations in Colombia, has become the country's largest radio network.

In the World Bank publication (1976) on the use of radio for education it is interesting to note that South American countries tend to dominate the case studies: Nicaragua, Mexico, the Dominican Republic, and Honduras. For the rest of the developing world, only in Tanzania is there an example of a study in which radio has been the major medium of instruction. It is salutary to relate that for reasons largely political, no significant activity is still continuing in these major projects.

Where the lines of control were clear and unequivocal problems did not arise, some strong, spirited, small-scale projects did demonstrate the ability of radio to be an effective force in development. The success of the "saucepan special" radio receiver was a spin-off from the expansion of the Central African Broadcasting Service in the late 1940s. This showed that comparatively cheap and easy access to radio programs was eagerly sought by a large local population, which at that time was estimated to own fewer than 100 radio receivers. In 1949, and only with considerable reluctance, a British battery manufacturer produced a low-cost, simple, battery-operated shortwave radio receiver for use in Central Africa. One of the earliest models used as its housing what had been originally produced as a 9-inch round aluminium pot. Within three months of their introduction, 1,500 "saucepan specials" had been sold, and within the next few years sales rose to over 50,000.

Although more and more developing countries were making moves to establish some form of educational radio service in the 1950s, these efforts were often to be overtaken by two, all-powerful, international forces. The famous "wind of change" brought independence to more than fifty different states and territories during the late 1950s and early 1960s. Television had established itself, at least in the developed world, as a genuine medium. The potential influence which television could exert, and the sense of national status which it conferred, were readily appreciated by those concerned with the establishment of the new countries. Where ready finance was not available, loans were negotiated or aid was procured and national television services came into being. Although these services were often equipped with rudimentary studio equipment, had limited signal coverage (not always even covering the capital city), and frequently transmitted to fewer than 1,000 receivers, nevertheless official statements were made that television had been introduced for purposes of "national development." "National development" was frequently used as a synonym for "education," and so the introduction of television was justified on the grounds of it being a means of providing mass education quickly and efficiently.

Even more so than in the case of radio, educational television created severe tensions and conflicts of control. In one West African country the permanent secretary of the Ministry of Education only learned from the daily press that his country was to have educational television for schools. The broadcasting authorities had been given the official mandate to introduce schools television.

1960–1970. No decade—including the present one—had a greater *expansion* of the use of media in developing countries. The trends which has been established in the late 1950s followed through into a multitude of specific, but usually small, projects in the 1960s. Audiovisual aids—and educational radio—were still "imported" into developing countries despite little qualitative improvement. Educational television services were set up at a furious pace.

The mid-1960s saw another major innovation in education in the Western world. It is now generally accepted that the launching of the first communication satellite, Sputnik, by the Russians in 1957 led to the major programs of curriculum renewal and development in the United States which were felt to be worthy of exporting to developing countries. Almost simultaneously in the United Kingdom, with the support of the forward-looking Nuffield Foundation, a serious rethinking of the whole philosophy and purpose of the teaching of two of what were seen as the most vitally significant subjects for development—science and mathematics—was underway. This new approach was adopted in the belief that science and mathematics could best be learned by doing rather than by listening. Learning should not be solely teacher-centered but should become learner-centered. Activity-based learning should become the main element in any "new" school syllabus. This fundamental shift of emphasis was of major significance to the use of the mass media within formal educational systems. Curriculum renewal and development, as proposed by the Nuffield approach, is incompatible and in conflict with the use of both radio and television as mass, centralized instructional media.

These deeply divisive philosophical conflicts were reflected throughout the developing world during most of the 1960s and 1970s. The reality of independence had forced governments in the developing world to consider the two most basic issues of education—quantity and quality. Quantity seemed to have a solution in the use of the mass media. Quality seemed to have a solution in creation and evolution of educational curricula which were relevant and indigenous to the needs of the country itself. Most of the smaller educational development projects of that time seemed to concentrate on either one or the other. There were exceptions, however. These exceptions form some of the best known—and most heavily documented—projects of media use in developing countries.

A retrospective consideration in the USAID Commission Study, *Educational Technology and the Developing Countries* (1972), showed that "Simply by what has happened so far, we must reach the simple pragmatic conclusion that the most impressive current uses of educational technology in the developing world... are those that use television." These "impressive uses," however, were limited to a handful of countries, all of which were geographically small: Samoa, El Salvador, and Hong Kong. Other well-publicized projects in Niger, Sierra Leone, Ethiopia, India, and Sudan attracted only deserved skepticism because of their pretensions to be regarded as national projects. No schools more than a few miles outside Niamey, Freetown, Addis Ababa, Delhi, or Khartoum were able to receive television signals, even had they wished to do so. A special case was American Samoa, a small territory of political importance to the United States.

In the early 1960s, with the strong personal support of the governor of Samoa and with hefty financial support from Washington, a decision was taken to use television as the core element in "an explosive upgrading" educational development program. It was decided to create a system which would cover the entire school population at all levels and in all subjects. Four studios were set up and six channels were opened in order to produce the 6,000 television lessons which were felt to be necessary. This massive output caused major problems at the production level. Low standards of writing, directing, and visualization eventually forced a reduction in output. The low quality of programming in turn produced a marked decline of interest among viewers, especially at the upper levels in the educational system.

Later research has shown that perhaps the most significant impact of ETV in Samoa has been its deleterious effects on Samoan society. The ETV project has been seen as an attempt to use American expertise and culture to assist Samoan society to achieve standards to which the society had never reasonably expected to aspire. It has been concluded (Arnove, 1976): "The compulsory pervasiveness of TV education dominated by American cultural values, languages and ideas, may have severely damaged Samoan cultural integrity and social equilibrium."

Like many other projects being supported by international finance, the use of television in El Salvador was initially seen as one element in a national scheme for educational improvement. The biggest problem for El Salvador, the smallest and the most densely populated mainland country in the Western hemisphere, was identified in the mid-1960s as being the lack of middle-level technical manpower. The then government produced a major Educational Reform Program to create a system which would produce people able to move El Salvador from an agrarian economy, based on coffee, to a mixed industrial economy. Television was seen as the catalytic agent for speeding up and spreading the needed changes. Although there was a quantifiable overall improvement in student educational performance produced by the Educational Reform Program which made heavy use of television, nevertheless little observable or measurable improvement has taken place in job opportunities. Educational reform may have taken place; but for what purpose?

There were marked (and related) similarities in the ways in which Singapore and Hong Kong (small densely populated city-states which are themselves heavily dependent on modern electronic technology) made eager and effective use of educational television to contribute to their educational development. ETV was seen by both territories as one element in an educational strategy to improve educational quality at both primary and secondary levels. From their own Ministry of Education studios both services provided programs for multiple transmission to the schools. Both are now producing materials other than ETV lessons, and the mode of distribution has moved away from being exclusively by broadcast transmission.

There have of course been failures. With the support of eager and well-meaning external agencies, very many developing countries committed themselves to projects using the new media which, far from being successful, can only be described as expensive failures. The reasons for these failures are various and complex and very often involve important personalities as well as policies. It would be far less than fair to suggest that there was any single, simple reason responsible for the failures; lack of planning, lack of trained manpower, lack of relevance, lack of continuing support, the work of consultants from international agencies—they all feature as major reasons. The issue of control is also important. Because television is a comparatively expensive and sophisticated medium requiring trained and skilled manpower, the arguments for concentrating all such resources and expertise in one organization in a developing country are powerful. The national broadcasting service is frequently the only rational choice.

Broadcasters, by influence or by tradition, are, or should be, creative. The constraints of syllabi lesson guides, and speed and pacing of programs to suit the needs of the classroom audience, have caused irritation and even resentment in the production staff of many services. Educational broadcasting was seen as a training ground, a second-best—or even worse, as a reject store for production and technical staff who were not involved in general broadcasting.

1970s–Present. Six major trends are distinctly discernible in the use of media in the developing countries during this period.

Television. Most countries which have committed themselves to using television for educational purposes had done so by 1970. The initial euphoria and enthusiasm then started to wear off. Most projects—particularly the bigger and more publicized projects like those in Samoa and El Salvador—were put under close scrutiny, and their weaknesses highlighted. The estimated cost of the Samoan project was $157 per pupil per year in 1973. This is more than the total annual per student cost of education in most LDCs, and more than the average per capita GNP for a few of them. Despite this high level of expenditure, the project never achieved its objectives.

It had been assumed earlier that television by itself could be the main agent for producing educational change, but by the early 1970s it became abundantly clear that where television was not fully related to or integrated with the educational and communication fabric of the society of its users, it was not likely to be effective. By 1972 the World Bank was warning its potential borrowers of the danger that "the hardware installation will precede the programme planning and production, organisation and teacher training and equipment maintenance which are essential to the effective utilisation of hardware...."

A gradual appreciation of the value of the strategic or systems approach to educational problems was developing. Television no longer occupied pride of place purely because of its glamour or expense. Broadcast television ceased to be the only form in which the medium was used for instructional purposes. The evolution of the ETV service in Singapore into a much more broadly based Educational Media Service reflected this trend of television being just one element in a larger strategy. An important development in the evolution of educational television was the advent of the low-cost (or comparatively low-cost) videocassette recorder (VCR). This was seen as being able to end the inflexibility of the timetable, to overcome the weakness of the transitory nature of the medium, and above all, to overcome teacher resistance to the use of television.

Radio. In sheer volume of output and size of audience, radio has become the most universal mass medium of communication. Although UNESCO estimated that in 1972 there were over 10,000 radio transmitters broadcasting to over 650,000,000 radio receivers in almost 200 different countries and territories, the systematic use of radio for educational purposes has not yet been fully developed. During the 1970s and into the 1980s, more and more use is being made of radio. In Nicaragua and Mexico there were major projects. Ethiopia, despite a protracted period of internal upheaval, pushed ahead with plans for a nationwide educational radio network run by the Ministry of Education. Thailand obtained World Bank support for the creation of a separate national radio network devoted to educational broadcasting. One of the first decisions of the newly independent government of Zimbabwe was to open a new radio channel to be specifically concerned with educational broadcasting.

Radio features more and more in the plans of LDCs to involve, and by involvement, to encourage their rural populations to participate in the development process. Present evidence suggests that radio, as a mass medium, has its greatest impact as a sensitizing and stimulating agent among adult listeners rather than as a pure didactic medium for children in classrooms.

Satellite Broadcasting. Confronted with the massive problems of enormous numbers and vast distances, compounded by intense political pressures, many of the larger developing countries became involved in preparatory studies using satellites to relay educational broadcasts as far back as the late 1960s and early 1970s. Here was a solution to many potential problems. Brazil, Indonesia, the countries of the Arab World, the Andean Consortium, etc., were all eager seekers of information and support.

It was India, through its SITE Project (Satellite for Instructional Television Experiment), which in 1975–1976 demonstrated some of the potential of using such systems. This experimental project selected 2,400 villages in six different states as receptors. The vast quantity of evaluation data is being used as India moves towards using its indigenous satellite from 1984 onwards.

It is only in the developing world that such an experiment has taken place on such a scale, and it is only in the developing world that such a follow-up is in hand.

Community Media. A complete contrast to the macro approach of the satellite is the development of community media. Here, typically, a variety of different channels of communication are made available to members of a group or community to enable them actively to participate in the decision-making and developmental problems which face them. Small-format, low-cost technologies such as portable video systems, low-powered transmitters, simple audio cassette systems, 8mm or super-8mm film and basic reprographic equipment are the most common tools of the community media trade.

Tanzania experimented with this approach in the mid-1970s. Again, an educational success but an economic or cost-benefit failure. Kenya is considering its use; agricultural extension services in Morocco and support services for a major groundwater irrigation project in Indonesia have used this kind of equipment in order to involve the local farmers. Major social issues such as family planning and community resettlement are showing themselves to be more susceptible to this approach, if not treatment, by a locally based low-cost, contact-media approach.

Distance Education. The United Kingdom Open University (UKOU) started its teaching activities in 1971. The operational success of this national distance-education institution led to a major, and continuing, interest in the techniques which it pioneered. Since that time analogues in both the developing and the developed world have been considered, formulated, and brought into being or are in the process of growth.

By 1975 Costa Rica, Iran, Venezuela, Pakistan, Sri Lanka, Jordan, Egypt, Mexico, Thailand, Ecuador, Colombia, Tanzania, India, and Kenya were just a sample of those developing countries which had declared an intention to set up some form of distance-education institution. Not all of these countries were considering setting up a tertiary-level institution, but they were considering using the attractively cost-effective techniques of self-instructional correspondence education linked to radio, television, and face-to-face instruction. By the early 1980s, major distance-education institutions in LDCs were operating in Pakistan, Sri Lanka, Thailand, Venezuela, and Costa Rica.

No global consideration of distance education could be complete without mentioning what is currently being planned in China. As part of its developmental program, the Chinese government has established plans to develop, with World Bank assistance, a major project to reinforce its Central Television University and its network of 28 Provincial Television Universities. The prime function of this project is to create a system (working with an enhanced polytechnic system) which will produce a higher quantity and quality of vocationally and technically qualified manpower.

Computers and Microprocessors. As the 1950s produced audiovisual aids, as the 1960s produced educational television, the 1970s integrated systems and distance education, so history will record that the 1980s was the time when the computer revolution started to make an impact on European education systems. It may be tempting to suggest that exactly the same aspirations will be held, the same delusions delivered—indeed the same, almost standard, process of the introduction of any new technology to any educational system—will follow.

In engineering terms, the transistor development of the 1960s became the solid-state evolution, and then revolution, of the late 1970s and 1980s. The technology is now better, it is cheaper, it is accessible and (in the jargon) user-friendly. Evidence suggests it can be used; it is a tool of the young not an instrument of the teacher; it interfaces with the big media; it is at home with small media.

There is no doubt a bandwagon is rolling. An assessment of where it has reached and what it has achieved in the developing countries of the world will be an interesting assignment to undertake in 1990.

ROLE OF EXTERNAL AGENCIES AND DONORS

No consideration of educational technology in the developing world is complete without taking into account the major influences which have been exerted by external agencies and donors. Up till now there has been little or no evidence that the developing world has decided to follow its own independent method of using educational media. Notable exceptions to this are Singapore, Cuba, China, Zimbabwe, Iran, and Tanzania. In preindependence days the metropolitan powers created systems which they felt were appropriate to the needs of their dependent territories. With independence these systems were invariably helped and reinforced by the provision of equipment, materials, training, and personnel on a bilateral basis.

In the early 1960s a new, vigorous, well-financed, and well-intentioned source of aid was provided through the United States Agency for International Development (USAID). The American approach, in contrast to the British method, was to make available considerable quantities of equipment, materials, training, and personnel on short, intensive crash programs. In northern Nigeria in the early 1960s—where, despite the most obvious planning weaknesses, ETV had been introduced by the government—USAID provided experts and materials to support a project for which the American experience had little background or understanding.

The British role has been that of supporter rather than controller or even major partner. With the exception of a small, ill-fated ETV project in Sierra Leone in 1968, the United Kingdom has never funded an educational media project as such. One exception has been that from 1976, the Overseas Development Administration (ODA) of the government of the United Kingdom has given support, in phases, to the Allama Iqbal Open University of Pakistan. Strong and sustained support has been given to other projects by providing training courses, short-term secondment of personnel, and limited quantities of equipment. Some consideration has been made recently of the role of educational consultants, in particular the role of consultants supported by U.K. agencies (McAleese, 1977, 1978).

In their dealings with their ex-territories the French had a more direct approach. On a bilateral basis, they provided the entire financial and manpower support for the project which introduced ETV into what was one of the least developed and poorest countries in the world—Niger. This well-documented experimental project, which never expanded as had originally been planned, has been succinctly described by one of its French experts as "a pedagogic success but an economic fiasco." The West Germans have typified their assistance to media projects in Ghana, Brazil, Zambia, Singapore, and Kenya by providing large quantities of equipment together with personnel and finance for basic running costs.

Coming after these bilateral developments, the U.N. network superimposed a vast system of educational assistance to the developing countries. In Senegal, in Kenya, in Thailand, in Malaysia, in India—in fact, in almost every country which had expressed an interest in educational media—a program of some type was set up, usually involving UNESCO as the executive agents on behalf of the U.N. Development Program.

By the 1970s the World Bank and its associated ILAs, such as the Asian Development Bank (ADB) and the IADB (the Inter-American Development Bank), became the major source of finance for educational assistance to the developing world. Educational technology projects had in general become much more specific, much better planned, and also much bigger. The large-scale Ivory Coast national ETV project received World Bank support as well as the combined donor support of the members of the Club d'Abdijan—a consortium of aid agencies working in cooperation. The project was a rare example of international assistance.

Other major donors were the large philanthropic foundations. The Ford Foundation (and to a lesser extent during the 1960s, the Nuffield Foundation of the United

Kingdom) provided funds for pioneering work in the use of educational media in developing countries. The Delhi ETV project was set up and funded for ten years by the Ford Foundation.

The voluntary agencies, charities, and the churches are also active in providing funds, training, and assistance for media work, especially in the adult and nonformal field.

HOW SUCCESSFUL HAS IT BEEN, OR WILL IT BE?

Despite the rhetoric of the supporters of educational technology and the enthusiasm of many of its practitioners, critical comments and conclusions have been advanced over the years about the effectiveness of educational technology in the developing world. The first major international study of educational technology in the developing world was conducted by a team led by Wilbur Schramm on behalf of UNESCO and the International Institute for Educational Planning in 1967. This study concluded in its final analysis: "The fact is that most uses of the educational media throughout the world are quite insignificant parts of the total educational effort . . . their full potential has never been tested" (Schramm et al., 1967). Five years later, in 1972, a USAID-funded study concluded: "Educational technology is still in a primitive state everywhere in the world. Its history to date has been marked with false starts, inflated expectations and assorted misunderstandings."

In 1973, the Ford Foundation, one of the most powerful private supporters of educational innovation, published the results of an inquiry into the uses of instructional technology (Armsey and Dahl, 1973). The first sentence of the concluding chapter begins, "The conditions of success and the use of the things of learning are many, varied, imprecise, changeable and changing." The report recognized that although success was an altogether more elusive characteristic than failure, it could be categorized by the necessary existence of certain essential and basic conditions. The first and most fundamental of these nine conditions was that "a recognized and generally agreed need must exist before educational technology can be introduced and be effective."

Many, often expensive, attempts to apply educational media to the solution of educational problems in the Commonwealth led to a study being commissioned in the member countries. The purpose of this study was an attempt to isolate those conditions which contributed to—or indeed were essential to—the success of educational media projects (CEDO, 1974). In common with a few earlier studies and several subsequently, the CEDO study identified a range of factors and conditions which were consistently present in successful projects. Without the presence of these factors, success had never been achieved nor could the presence of these factors guarantee success. All that could be said with certainty is that in the absence of even one of these criteria, the success of an entire project would almost certainly be at risk.

All these earlier studies were broad-ranging and had looked at several media. In 1976 Arnove produced a very uncompromising analysis of the future expectations and possibilities for educational television in developing countries. The final paragraph of his conclusion is worth quoting in full: "In reviewing the past experiences of many countries with ETV the authors tend to be skeptical about the probability of long lasting educational improvement taking place through this medium—unless many of the provisos they raise in the subsequent chapters are taken into account by planners." The recent decade with its economic and other uncertainties has given glimpses of the potential of both micro and macro applications of educational technology. The applications of microcomputers to educational systems may well be leading to a major revolution.

Despite the trenchant and usually justifiable comments, other studies have shown that educational media can be—and have been—used effectively for a wide range of educational and instructional purposes in developing countries. From primary school to tertiary level, in nonformal education and across almost the full range of subjects, the new media have been used. Generalizations about past effectiveness are difficult. Results of media application must be assessed within the system in which they are achieved, no matter how imperfect that system may be. This is and will remain the real test of the effectiveness of any educational medium, whether in a developed or a developing country.

A. B. Edington

REFERENCES

Academy for Educational Development. (1972) *Educational Technology and the Developing Countries*. Washington, D.C.: Academy for Educational Development.

Armsey, J. and Dahl, N. (1973) *An Enquiry into the Uses of Instructional Technology*. New York: Ford Foundation.

Arnove, R., ed. (1976) *Educational Television: Policy Critique and Guide for Developing Countries*. New York: Praeger.

CEDO. (1974) *New Media and Education in the Commonwealth*. London: Commonwealth Secretariat/CEDO.

Coombs, P. H. and Ahmed, H. (1974) *Attacking Rural Poverty*. Baltimore, Md.: Johns Hopkins University Press.

Harbison, F. H. (1973) *Educational Sector Planning for Development of Nationwide Learning Systems*. Washington, D.C.: Overseas Liaison Committee, American Council on Education.

Lyle, J. (1982) "Since 1967—The Original Case Studies Reviewed." In *Organizing Educational Broadcasting*, ed. D. Hawkridge and J. Robinson. London: Croom Helm; Paris: UNESCO.

McAleese, R. (1977) "The Role of the Media Consultant." *Educational Broadcasting International*, 10 (4): 182–184.

———. (1978) "The Role of the Educational Consultant and Developing Countries." In *Aspects of Educational Technology*, 2d ed. P. Race and J. Hanson. London: Kogan Page.

Schramm, W., Coombs, P., Kahnert, F., and Lyle, J. (1967) *The New Media: A Memo to Educational Planners*. Paris: UNESCO.

World Bank. (1976) *Radio for Education and Development. Case Studies*. Washington, D.C.: World Bank.

———. (1983) *World Development Report 1983*. London: Oxford University Press.

DEVICE DRIVER. A special computer program that translates the general commands from an operating system or user program into the exact instructions a specific peripheral device needs. Often, device drivers for a few standard peripherals are built into the operating system, but others must be added during installation procedures.

DIAL ACCESS INFORMATION RETRIEVAL (DAIR). A somewhat arcane method of providing student access to resources. At one time (circa 1965) DAIR seemed to be a promising concept, but more recent developments in equipment and organization have made it obsolescent.

The fully automated DAIR system comprised a vast central store of information, some in combined video-audio form, some in audio only. This information is stored on tapes held semi-permanently on master high-speed recorders. The student, having found the appropriate dial code from a directory, dials for his lesson. His booth is automatically assigned a buffer tape recorder in a bank of such instruments, and his required lesson is passed from the master tape to the tape on the buffer recorder at high speed. The contents of the tape are then relayed to the booth at normal speed.

DAIR obviously had much in common with the centralized television distribution systems once favored in many higher education institutions. It is possible that DAIR will experience a resurgence in the new location of the home, using the telephone line connected via modem to a microcomputer.

DIAPOSITIVE. A positive picture on a transparent base intended for viewing by transmitted light, e.g., 35mm slides.

DIAZO PROCESS. An imaging system that uses diazonium salt. The action of light on these substances causes decomposition, and so a positive image is produced. Diazo films are available in a variety of forms and a wide range of well-saturated colors. They are used among other things for producing overhead transparencies and slides. Production of diazo transparencies involves contact printing a high-contrast negative with the diazo film using ultraviolet light; the film is then developed in ammonia vapor.

DIDACTOGRAM. A diagram that shows how students perform in **programmed learning** (q.v.). Such diagrams use shorthand notation for frames and branches. Didactograms are part of a program analysis devised by A. Bjerstedt. Graphic aids such as the didactogram are very useful in analyzing programs during their development. *See* **Didule**.

DIDULE. The fundamental instructional unit in **programmed learning** (q.v.), according to A. Bjerstedt. A didule is similar to a frame in that a frame is both instructional unit and presentation unit. A didule has three components: stimule (information component), respule (response request), and feedback.

DIFFERENTIAL FOCUS. Arranging a shot so that a subject stands out against an out-of-focus background or foreground.

DIFFICULTY INDEX. The difficulty level of a test item in relation to the proportion of a sample successfully solving it. *See* **Item Analysis; Multiple-Choice Question**.

DIF FILES. DIF stands for "data interchange format" and is a particular standard for data files. It is used by many programs and allows files created on one software package to be read by another software package. DIF files may not be interchangeable between different machines because although the files are compatible, the disks may be formatted differently for different machines. Programs using DIF files include VisiCalc, Symphony, Lotus 1–2–3, etc.

DIFFUSION TRANSFER PROCESS. A photographic process that involves the passage of unexposed silver salts from an exposed negative sheet to a positive sheet while the two are squeezed together with a suitable developing agent between them. The positive sheet contains chemicals that blacken the silver salts, thus producing a positive image. When the transfer is complete, the two sheets are peeled apart and the negative is usually discarded. This is a process similar to that used in Polaroid cameras.

DIGITAL AUDIO DISK (DAD). High-quality storage and retrieval system for music, using a laser disk to carry digitized sound information.

DIGITAL RECORDING. A method of coding and storing information in the form of a series of uniform pulses. It is used in television as a method of processing video signals, and increasingly for high-quality sound recording.

DIGITIZE. To translate an image into a list of coordinates.

DIGITIZER. A device which is able to convert information or measurements into a form which can be conveniently read by a computer.

DIN. Abbreviation for Deutsche Industries Normen, the German standards association. DIN standards apply to a wide range of products including items of equipment such as plugs and sockets, and to photographic film. *See* **Standards in Audiovisual Technology.**

DIN CONNECTOR. A round connector used in computer applications, as well as on many tape records and home video cameras. It is a common European-style connector, made according to German industry (DIN) standards.

DIOPTER. A measure of lens power or magnification: power of a lens in diopters is equal to the reciprocal of its focal length in meters.

DIORAMA. A three-dimensional representation created by placing figures and other objects in front of a flat painted background. The use of special lighting, hanging mobiles, etc., can be used to improve the illusion of depth.

DIRECT BROADCASTING SATELLITE (DBS). A high-powered satellite which beams signals down over a wide area to small inexpensive earth stations. Satellites are of course commonly used to transmit television signals direct to earth stations, but up to the mid-1980s the receivers were so large and costly that they had little domestic application.

DBSs will be operating over the U.S., Europe, and Japan by the late 1980s.

DIRECTOR. Originally the person responsible for the creative side of film production. In television the term is used more loosely, and many refer to someone in charge of a subsidiary stage of production.

DIRECTORY. A list of all files stored on a disk; alternatively called a catalog.

DIRECT READ AFTER WRITE (DRAW). An optical disk system which allows very large quantities of data to be recorded (once only) and read.

DIRECT RETRIEVAL. Accessing data on a disk or in memory by looking up a key value in an index and then using the associated pointer to find where to read or write the required data. It is quicker than sequential access, where each record in the file is read or written to in turn.

DISCOVERY METHOD. A heuristic teaching strategy based on the proposition that learning is more effective and enjoyable if the students ''discover'' facts and relationships for themselves. Many recent instructional schemes, especially in science and mathematics, have utilized this method. However, the implementation of discovery learning makes very considerable demands on the teacher's time and skill. *See* **Resource-Based Learning.**

DISCRIMINATION INDEX. A measure of the ability of an item in a multiple-choice test to discriminate between ''good'' and ''bad'' students. Different methods have been suggested for computing such an index. Most common is the Point Biserial Correlation Coefficient between individual responses and total marks. A simpler approach is to calculate the Johnson Index.

$D = (H - L)/M$

H = the number of correct responses given by the top 27 percent of candidates

L = the number of correct responses given by the bottom 27 percent of candidates

M = the maximum possible difference (i.e., the number in a 27 percent group)

If $D = 0.4$ it shows a good degree of discrimination. For the Point Biserial Coefficient a value of 0.3 is required. The Johnson Index is useful where there are a large number of candidates. In practice, **item analysis** (q.v.) will allow the tester to identify those items that have low discrimination indexes and to eliminate these from the test.

DISK. *See* **Floppy Disk; Hard Disk; Videodisk.**

DISK DRIVE. Device for reading from and writing to computer disks. Analogous to an audio or video tape recorder in that the information is stored in magnetic form. However, an extremely important feature is the ability to very rapidly search for particular information; that is, disk drives are random access devices. In this regard disks are markedly superior to tapes as storage media for data. *See* **Disk Operating System.**

DISK OPERATING SYSTEM. A program or set of programs used to supervise a sequence of programs in the computer. Specifically, programs which facilitate the storage, retrieval, or copying of information (files) from the disk storage system of the computer. A disk operating system (DOS) provides a standardized method of archiving data and programs so that they may be transported from system to system.

DISK SERVER. A hard-disk drive that each station on a network can use to store and retrieve files. Unlike the more complex file server, a disk server does not allow network stations to share files.

DISPLAY. Information exhibited on the screen of a display device, such as a video monitor; alternatively, the display device itself.

DISPLAY DEVICE. A device that exhibits information visually, such as a television set, video monitor, or liquid crystal panel.

DISSOLVE. A visual screen effect where one image slowly fades out while another slowly fades in to replace it. The term was first used as "lap dissolve" in film production to indicate a change of scene or time. The term is applied to television production, where the effect is often called a "mix" because more than one camera is involved.

Dissolves are common effects in multiprojector slide presentations where a device controls the projectors. The speed of the dissolve can be changed for effect. Many super-8 and small-format video cameras can achieve a similar effect by rewinding the film or tape and reexposing part of the image with the special settings provided.

DISTANCE EDUCATION. Distance education is the generic term for formal processes of instruction in which teacher and learner carry out their essential tasks apart. It is currently the fastest growing form of education, particularly at the postcompulsory level. Many countries have established open or distance universities since 1970, and some of these institutions count their enrollments in the hundreds of thousands.

DEFINITION

The term *distance education* came into common use in English only in the 1970s although it has a longer history in French, German, and Spanish. In 1982 the International Council for Correspondence Education, a UNESCO affiliate with members in 50 countries, changed its name to the International Council for Distance Education. This change signified a broad international consensus about the meaning and use of the term although older expressions continue to be used within particular countries, e.g., external studies (Australia, New Zealand); home study, independent study (U.S.); correspondence education (U.K., India). The term *open* has frequently been used since the late 1960s to refer to institutions that both operate at a distance and have eliminated academic prerequisites for admission.

Distance education has six key characteristics:

1. The separation of teacher and learner, which distinguishes it from classroom-based instruction.
2. A relationship between the student and an institution, which distinguishes it from private study.
3. The use of media, including of course print, for communication between the institution and the learner.
4. The provision of means for two-way communication between the institution and the learner.
5. The possibility of occasional face-to-face meetings.
6. The opportunity for achieving economies of scale since the marginal costs of teaching additional students are low once there is a critical mass of enrollments.

Some examples of educational processes with these characteristics are the Australian Schools of the Air and government correspondence branches in North America offering primary- and secondary-level education; private/commercial/military correspondence colleges; multimedia open universities; broadcast telecourses with local support; modular self-instructional packages for use by on-campus students; independent study divisions of universities and colleges; instructional teleconferencing and telecommunications networks; satellite education projects with local instructional support; community development/education projects where local group leaders base their work on centrally produced teaching materials. These very diverse educational settings share the common challenges of distance education; namely, the preparation of instructional materials, the organization of two-way communication and support to students learning in different places at different times, and, usually, the obligation to operate more cost-effectively than conventional educational institutions.

HISTORICAL DEVELOPMENT

The didactic letters of St. Paul and their use by the individuals and groups who constituted the early Christian churches created a process which had most of the features of distance education. However, significant developments in correspondence education, which was the earliest form of distance education, had to wait until the introduction of regular mail services. Once postal services were available, correspondence education grew rapidly, sometimes in conjunction with newspapers. A certain A. Mueller advertised instruction in English composition "through the medium of the Post" in 1833 in a Swedish weekly. In 1840, after the introduction of uniform penny postage in England, Isaac Pitman offered a correspondence course in shorthand. Later in the nineteenth century, correspondence education took root in the United States with a newspaper course in mining safety in Scranton, Pennsylvania. The resulting enterprise, International Correspondence Schools, is now among the world's largest correspondence institutions.

The early twentieth century saw the steady growth of correspondence education and, in particular, the setting up of government correspondence schools in Australia, Canada, and the United States to facilitate the primary and secondary education of children in remote areas. In 1938 representatives from seven countries met in Victoria, British Columbia, and founded the International Council for Correspondence Education (ICCE).

Although the first half of the twentieth century also saw the growth of film, radio, and the telephone, it was not until the 1960s that serious attention was paid to the use of these media to enrich and expand correspondence education. Chicago's TV College was an early example of multimedia higher education and an important milestone was passed in 1964 when the British politician Harold Wilson made the creation of a "University of the Air" a major goal of his future government. The result, after a planning committee had visited existing examples of university distance education in Australia, South Africa, and the United States, was the granting of a Royal Charter to the Open University in 1969. This institution, which became the largest U.K. university within two years of admitting its first students in 1971, captured the imagination of the British public by its use of broadcast radio and television and rapidly won the admiration of educators the world over.

Since the early 1970s distance universities have been established in many other countries, including Costa Rica, Spain, Venezuela, Pakistan, Israel, Holland, Nigeria, Japan, Thailand, China, and India. Particularly strong growth has taken place in Asia where, in 1983, three institutions (Central China TV University, Sukhothai Thammithirat Open University, and the Korea Air and Correspondence University) had a combined enrollment of over one million.

In the early 1980s the strategy for developing distance education moved away from the creation of new, autonomous institutions to the networking of existing institutions. Examples of this new trend are the Norsk Fjernundervisning (Norway), which is a small office established to promote collaboration between private correspondence schools, state media agencies, and the voluntary sector; the Knowledge Network of the West (Canada), which runs a satellite network for existing institutions; and the ambitious plans to extend distance education in Colombia (South America). It is too early to assess the success of these projects. However, securing cooperation and innovation within existing educational institutions is of interest to governments all over the world that no longer have the inclination or the funds to create distance education institutions from scratch. A new interest is being taken in institutions, notably in Australia, New Zealand, and the United States, which have offered both on-campus programs and distance education for many years.

WORLDWIDE APPLICATIONS

Distance education takes a variety of forms in the different countries of the world. The activities of commercial, private, or nonprofit correspondence colleges account for the largest numbers of distance students in North America and Western Europe. Some colleges, such as International Correspondence Schools, Rapid Results College, and LiberHermods, offer courses over a wide range of general and professional subjects while others specialize in a single subject (e.g., motor transport, genealogy). In North America there is also a tradition of correspondence education at the secondary level organized by the educational authorities of some U.S. states and Canadian provinces. However, recent trends have seen a decrease in the number of school-age children taking these courses, but a significant increase in the number of adults continuing their secondary education by this route. There is also a trend to use correspondence courses as learning packages to enrich the programs offered by some smaller schools.

In North America most distance education at the university level is provided through the independent study units that are part of a large number of universities. The list of the correspondence courses available from U.S. universities runs to over 100 pages. With only a few exceptions such as Athabasca University, Alberta, and the Open Learning Institute, British Columbia, North America has not followed the trend of creating open universities. This can be explained by the extensive network of postsecondary institutions already in place before 1970 and the constitutional attribution of responsibility for education to the states and provinces which, in general, have rather small populations.

In Western Europe several countries with unitary constitutional structures and large populations have funded separate distance education institutions from the public purse. France's Centre National d'Enseignement par Correspondance enrolls over 200,000 students, while Britain, Spain and the Netherlands have distance teaching universities. A similar institution at a more local level exists in West Germany's North Rhine Westphalia (Fernuniversität) and is proposed for Italy's Calabria.

Distance education in the Soviet bloc goes back 50 years and is closely integrated to both conventional education and employment. Many students in these countries combine classroom education (on both a full-time and a part-time basis) and distance education during the course of their studies. Since employers are obliged to give time off for day release and residential sessions, Soviet bloc distance education includes a more significant face-to-face teaching component than is normally found elsewhere. Distance education is offered through some fourteen universities and involves over two million students.

The Middle East has not yet seen any very extensive developments in distance education. Many Arab countries have small populations and substantial oil revenues to finance the expansion of the conventional education system. A distance university that had been created in Iran under the Shah was closed when the regime fell. However, distance education methods are the basis for Israel's Everyman's University, the UNRWA/UNESCO project for training Palestinian teachers, and some activities of the Arab literacy organization.

Asia presents a very different picture. In India there exists an Open School, a variety of private institutions, and correspondence branches in twenty universities. The universities alone enroll over 130,000 correspondence students, and a further impetus to distance education at this level was the establishment in 1982 of an open university in the state of Andhra Pradesh. It seems likely that some other states will follow suit. In Pakistan Allama Iqbal Open University was founded in 1975 and has already enrolled over 200,000 students in a system that uses some broadcasting in addition to correspondence teaching. In the Far East developments are occurring very rapidly indeed. In the People's Republic the Central China TV University and its 28 affiliates enrolled over 750,000 students in 1983. In Thailand the Sukhothai Thammithirat Open University grew from 120,000 to 180,000 enrollments in this period. Similar figures are found at the Korea Air and Correspondence University, while the Japan University of the Air opened in 1983 after some fourteen years of planning. These university institutions complement distance education at other levels, and one of the effects of their creation has been to increase the overall prestige and impact of all forms of distance teaching at all levels.

Australia and New Zealand have a very long tradition of distance education. The first state correspondence school in the English-speaking world was established in the state of Victoria in 1914, and by 1922 there were similar schools serving children in six Australian states. In 1951 the first School of the Air was set up in Alice Springs, and now twelve of these schools cooperate closely with the correspondence schools so that children benefit from both the daily radio link and the courses prepared in the state capitals. At the postsecondary level distance education is conducted by institutions that also teach on-campus students. The best-known examples are Massey University in New Zealand and the University of New England in New South Wales. Australia has rejected the idea of creating a separate open university although it is concerned to rationalize the distance education offerings of the five universities and twenty other postsecondary institutions that are active in external studies.

The University of the South Pacific (USP) is a good example of the use of distance education in particularly challenging circumstances. It serves a region consisting of hundreds of islands in an area of ocean the size of Australia. The people of the region speak many different languages. By using satellite links for tutorials, USP serves students throughout the region with courses in English.

Distance education is undergoing rapid development in Latin America. There are open universities in Costa Rica and Venezuela and a major national effort is in progress in Colombia to ensure that existing institutions expand opportunities for studying at a distance. Elsewhere in the region some thirty universities have offered distance courses although many of these initiatives seem rather fragile. At the secondary-school level, distance education methods have been used both for in-school projects, in which the media substitute for skill in labor, and out-of-school projects where the bulk of the work is done by the students alone. The best-documented projects are those in Brazil, Mexico, Nicaragua, and the Dominican Republic. Finally, there are well over a hundred commercial vocational correspondence schools operating in the region in Spanish, Portuguese, or English.

There is a widespread realization that distance education will have a major role in the continuing development of education in Africa since the resources are not available to build conventional schools and colleges on the scale that would be required. Private-sector correspondence colleges such as Rapid Results, Wolsey Hall, International Correspondence Schools, and the Central African Correspondence College have reached hundreds of thousands of students, including many current African leaders. More recently there has been steady growth of government-sponsored distance teaching agencies both for formal schooling and community development. Africa has one of the oldest distance teaching universities (the University of South Africa) and one of the newest (the Nigerian Open University, founded in 1982). In general, African distance education has concentrated on education below university level although several universities have provided expertise and support for programs focusing on school-age students (e.g., the Zimbabwe Science [ZIMSCI] project to upgrade science teaching in the secondary schools; the University of Nairobi's contribution to programs aimed at bringing high-school dropouts into the rural labor market).

This brief summary of worldwide applications reveals the diversity of distance education. Even estimating the total numbers of students learning at a distance around the globe is extremely difficult since data are not available in a systematic fashion. From the figures that are available an estimate of ten million is likely to be conservative. One useful by-product of the increasing visibility and importance of distance education has been a greater attention to researching and documenting the phenomenon. The creation in 1983 of an International Information and Documentation Centre on Distance Education at the U.K. Open University under the joint sponsorship of the United Nations University and the International Council for Distance Education is an encouraging sign.

COMPONENTS OF DISTANCE EDUCATION SYSTEMS

It is convenient to examine distance education systems in terms of their four main subsystems:

— the courses subsystem, concerned with the creation, production, and distribution of learning materials
— the student subsystem, concerned with enrollment, support, and assessment of students and their learning needs
— the logistical subsystem
— the decision-making and control subsystem.

Any distance education system will have a set of general educational, social, and economic objectives which achieve their most concrete expression in a curriculum made up of courses. The course creation process takes the objectives of a particular part of the curriculum and converts academic ideas and instructional strategies, through appropriate media, into a prototype for achieving these objectives.

There is no single teaching model for distance education. Strategies currently in use borrow from a number of models and theories of learning. From his own experience and research on correspondence education in Sweden, Holmberg developed a theory of distance education as a method of guided didactic conversation. This approach stresses the use of friendly conversational forms, the development of feelings of personal relation between teaching and learning parties, the use of up-to-date knowledge of didactics, and the need for organization and guidance from the teaching institution. Others have stressed the need to achieve balance between learning activities carried out by the student independently and those which involve a relation of give and take with staff and fellow students. A common feature of most theories of distance education is an emphasis on learning rather than teaching. Since the students are at a distance, it is essential for institutional strategies to center on them. There appears to be a direct link between academic success and students' perceptions that the distance education institution has a personal interest in each one of them.

While it is essential to operate from a sound basis of instructional principles, practical considerations and the local context in fact determine many key instructional features of distance education systems. An important decision, for example, is whether to design a paced course in which students move as a batch from a fixed starting date toward a common final exam or to leave the system unpaced and allow students to enroll when they please and move at the pace each individual finds appropriate. While this choice could be the subject of a long theoretical and philosophical debate, it is usually made very early in the development of each system on purely practical grounds. A paced system may be chosen in order to be like conventional institutions or to facilitate the use of broadcasting. An unpaced system may be chosen so that courses may be phased in as they become available and revised on a continuous basis.

Another aspect of course design in which context has more influence than theory is the choice of media. Each distance education system normally establishes an instructional framework which applies with relatively minor variations to all its courses. Commercial distance education colleges use media such as print, filmstrips, records, audiocassettes, and experimental kits that do not involve agencies other than the college and the student. Publicly funded systems often include the use of open-circuit broadcasts and/or local study centers through arrangements with other public agencies or institutions. A commitment to the use of television, in particular, was an important part of the political agenda behind the creation of public distance education institutions in the 1970s. In the event, television has played a smaller role than anticipated, even in those institutions, such as the U.K. Open University, which have used it with success. The reasons for the relative neglect of television vary from country to country and include, as well as academic conservatism and the difficulty of producing good instructional programs, weaknesses in the system of television distribution/coverage, cost, and the importance of the written word in university-level study.

In the 1980s the trend is for all institutions to follow the private sector, concentrating on those media that can be directly controlled by the student. In the industrial countries these will soon include videocassettes and programs for microcomputers. The challenge for course designers is not to choose media but to use well those media already adopted by their particular distance education system. This still leaves great scope for creativity. Designing instructional audiocassettes for use with a course package is not the same as producing a radio program. Similarly, videocassettes that the student can stop, rewind, and replay, have richer instructional possibilities than broadcast television.

While the overall design of distance courses varies from country to country as a function of prevailing educational philosophies and the resources available, the design is almost always more systematic than in conventional classroom courses. This is especially true in those distance education systems that use teams of staff to prepare each course. Explicit objectives, breakdown of course content into units, and a direct relation between objectives, content, and student assessment are a feature of such courses. Special emphasis is placed on designing activities for the learner and including frequent feedback both from self-assessment and on assignments submitted to the institution.

Once a prototype course has been designed, the materials must be produced in quantity and made available to students. Although computerized word processing and composition technology is rapidly changing the economics of printing, it is still true that the cost of sophisticated visual design using color and artwork needs to be amortized on long print runs. The complexity of the media mix, the number of students taking each course, and the length of time between revisions of the materials are key elements in the economics of distance education. Since a distance education course involves much higher investment costs than a classroom course, its economic viability depends on achieving low variable costs, i.e., low marginal costs per additional student once a critical mass of enrollments is reached.

Methods for the distribution of course materials will depend on the communications infrastructure of the country in which the course is offered. Some countries still have reliable postal services, and mailings can be made to individual students. In Latin America registered mail is often used, partly in order to ensure that undelivered materials are returned to the institution in countries where it is customary to change accommodation regularly. In West Africa course materials are sent by beer trucks to local distribution points. In Thailand examinations are distributed under police escort.

Simplicity of distribution is one of the major advantages of the broadcast media. Making television programs available on a variety of cable networks or in study centers involves more complicated logistics.

Before examining the student subsystem it will be useful to describe some of the key characteristics of distance students. The earlier survey of worldwide applications reported that some children study at a distance. However, the great majority of distance students are adults between 20 and 40 years of age. Research evidence shows that the maturity and motivation which facilitate independent study at a distance tend not to be acquired before age 25. In the industrial countries, where distance education is used primarily to provide a second chance for adults or an alternative form of continuing education, students are generally over 25. However, much of the current rapid growth of distance education, particularly in the Far East, involves young school leavers who cannot be accommodated in conventional postsecondary institutions. These young students need strong support from the system until they develop good study habits and skills in time management.

In general, distance students are more heterogeneous in age and educational background than those in conventional institutions. They are usually not from the wealthier strata of society and, since they combine education with employment, have to study part-time and at home. Contrary to popular belief, urban areas often produce a higher than average proportion of distance students, presumably attracted by a system that allows flexibility as to time and place of study. The balance between male and female students varies widely around the world. For example, while women form the majority of Canadian university distance education students, men account for most of the student body in systems where the courses are directly job-related. However, distance education provides important opportunities for women in countries where emancipation is in progress but the provision of places for women in conventional institutions has not kept pace.

The student subsystem in distance education exists to provide service to students. While the separation of teacher and learner is the essence of distance education, a further challenge is the separation of the learner from the administrative services of the institution. In conventional education, services are within walking distance of the classrooms and the student can be referred from one office to another for different needs. Furthermore, classmates and teachers are a ready source of information about the academic policies and mores of the institution. In distance education all the administrative functions must be made explicit and blended into a system which ensures that the right action is taken without the student having to make separate requests for each service. This implies a large number of small-scale interrelated modules rich in human interfaces and dependent on the efficient flow of information.

The three phases of student administration are (1) admission/registration; (2) support during study; and (3) assessment/certification. Phase 1 includes advertising the institution's offerings, providing guidance to potential applicants by phone or in person, receiving applications, informing the applicant of acceptance or rejection, registering students and receiving fees, and initiating the processes necessary to mail materials and provide tutorial support.

The key to this phase and to those that follow is the creation and maintenance of a student file that drives a complex series of operations. The instruction to ship course materials to the student interfaces with a warehousing system that must keep track of stocks and returnable materials. The allocation of a student to any residential session included in the course triggers another set of operations and may well generate inquiries arising from the student's special requirements. Since distance education attracts many handicapped students, the system must "remember" the special needs of each. Tutors and counselors depend for their effectiveness on information about the student, and they themselves must keep the institution informed of the student's progress.

The formal assessment of student achievement is of particular importance since society depends on the validity of qualifications awarded by educational institutions. Distance education usually involves both continuous assessment and final examinations, both of which rely on effective file maintenance. Conventional institutions need only post the time and place of exams. The distance education system must set up a nationwide examination system and tell each student which center to attend. The problem of ensuring examination security is commensurately greater.

Finally, once the student has completed the necessary courses successfully, a qualification is awarded. Here again the file plays an essential role in enabling the institution to ensure that all the requirements have been met.

Given that the essential aim of student support is to personalize education, this emphasis on administrative systems may seem excessive. In distance education, however, personalization and efficient information flow are inseparable.

Personal support to distant students is provided in a variety of ways. Some institutions provide face-to-face contact at, e.g., weekend schools, tutorials, study groups or self-help groups, and social events. Less direct human contact may be maintained by written or audiocassette correspondence with a tutor, telephone calls and teleconferences, or computer communications. Such interactive activities are a vital element of distance education and distinguish it from purely private study. A common reaction to perceived system weaknesses (e.g., high attrition rates) is to increase the quantity of such activities. However, since the costs of interactive activities, unlike the costs of materials for independent study, rise in direct proportion to student numbers, this solution quickly runs into financial constraints. Furthermore, those interactive activities based on face-to-face contact also require the student to travel, thereby reducing the flexibility that is an important attraction of distance education.

The separation of teacher and learner, as well as the large numbers involved, has obliged distance education institutions to develop highly systematic methods of student assessment. Indeed, the creation of these institutions has significantly advanced the state of the art of assessment for the benefit of all forms of education. The basic dilemma of distance education is that the adult students it attracts are particularly fearful of examinations, whereas the institutions, often relatively new, have to be particularly careful of their academic reputations. There is a continued tension between what is educationally desirable and what is administratively necessary. Although distance education has done much to expand the usefulness of objective tests, questions requiring short answers or essays also feature in most assessment systems. Here the key problem, once appropriate questions have been formulated, is to ensure that common standards are applied in marking very large numbers of scripts. The markets are numerous and may never meet. As well as providing the best possible marking guidelines, the institution must monitor its markers continuously. In large systems this is really only possible by using the computer. Just as computer analyses of results can identify the poor items in an objective test, they can also identify markers who are too severe or too easygoing so that the institution can alert these individuals.

The third of the four main distance education subsystems is concerned with logistics. Distance education shares many of the features of enterprises that manufacture, distribute, and service products. Indeed, with warehouses, print shops, and loading bays, the buildings that house distance education are more reminiscent of light industry than of conventional schools or colleges. Like industry, a distance education system has to operate and maintain specialized equipment; contract for services; purchase, store, and distribute consumables; and maintain a competent staff. Techniques for these logistic activities can be adapted from the existing body of industrial know-how once the distance education institution has identified its specific needs.

Identifying and responding to needs is the task of the fourth subsystem: decision making and control. Here there are major differences between conventional and distance education. In conventional education the locus of management of the learning process is the teacher in the classroom. Power is diffused through a cellular management structure. In distance education it is the institution as a whole, rather than any individual teacher, that must manage the learning process. Given the complexity of that process and the degree of coordination it imposes on the many components of the distance education system, the management functions of planning, organization, leadership, and evaluation are of crucial importance.

While planning is essential during an institution's initial growth, which is often phenomenally rapid in distance education, it is equally necessary later on. Institutions are expected to take advantage of their flexibility and speed of response to meet new educational needs as they arise. Both the purpose of the institution (what business are we in?) and the means of achieving it must be constantly reviewed. Although distance education has to wait until new technologies are widely available to students before incorporating them in teaching strategies, changeover from one medium to another (e.g., from broadcasting to cassette distribution) requires planning, as does the use of a new medium such as the personal microcomputer.

The main organizational problems in distance education are experienced by institutions operating at the university level since the need for an efficient hierarchical executive structure conflicts with academic traditions of governance. The line between policy formulation and its executive implementation is hard to draw even when a unicameral governing board is used instead of the bicameral structure (board and senate) found in conventional universities. It is also difficult to draw a clear line between academic and nonacademic staff since distance education requires both a higher proportion and a greater diversity of professional staff, as distinct from discipline specialists, than does conventional education.

These tensions make special demands on the leaders of distance education institutions. Such people must combine, to an unusual degree, the ability to structure the system successfully for its production function and the skill of motivating people to give of their best in a demanding environment that may at first seem alien to some of the staff. Distance education has been fortunate in its leaders over the years. In the 1970s individuals such as Lord Walter Perry (U.K.) and Wichit Srisa-an (Thailand) continued this leadership tradition and made great personal contributions to the development of education at a distance worldwide.

Evaluation, which should permeate all management activities, consists of measuring, comparing, and correcting. Each presents special problems in distance education. Measurement is complicated by distance. Comparisons are difficult since standards (e.g., on staffing ratios) from conventional education are usually inappropriate, and the contexts in which other distance education systems operate vary widely. Before taking corrective action on the basis of evaluative data, management should ensure that it is indeed the operation, rather than the measurements or the standards, that requires modification.

CURRENT ISSUES

The decade of the 1970s established that distance education is a credible cost-effective way of improving access, providing a second chance, or retraining large numbers of people. Its use is expanding in many countries for a variety of purposes. Naturally, the particular challenges distance education faces in the 1980s vary according to the type of application and the local context.

In North America and Europe the two major issues are the integration of home electronics, especially videocassette players and microcomputers, into teaching strategies and the development of techniques for networking conventional institutions, publishers, software developers, and cable operators/broadcasters into the distance education endeavor.

In the developing countries of Asia, simply handling the explosive growth of distance education while maintaining an acceptable level of academic quality and administrative efficiency will be a huge challenge. The distance universities in China and Thailand will be operating on a scale that has never been attempted before, even by the biggest of the private and military correspondence colleges.

Australia has the opposite challenge, namely, operating distance education on a small scale from a large number of institutions that also teach on-campus. Greater cooperation between institutions will be required in order to expand offerings in specialized subjects. The recent move by Deakin University to administer distance education from individual academic departments, rather than from a central unit, will be watched with interest.

In Latin America the main brake on the development of distance education has been the lack of political and administrative continuity both at the national level and in the institutions. Now the level of interest is increasing sharply, and particularly determined steps to expand distance education are being made in Colombia. However, the financial problems faced by several of the major countries in the region will no doubt affect the involvement of governments in new projects.

Distance education in Africa is also greatly affected by the political and financial stability of individual nations. The private correspondence colleges have a central role in African distance education. Educational opportunity in several African countries could be sharply reduced if the activities of these colleges are cut back, whether for ideological reasons or for lack of foreign exchange.

In summary, distance education aims to expand educational opportunity and improve the quality of learning by using mass media, two-way communication, and the principles of educational technology in situations where teacher and learner cannot get together. Its development in the 1970s was an important phenomenon in education. While some of the novelty has since worn off, distance education continues to expand at a rapid pace and is bringing to millions the autonomy and intellectual self-confidence that comes from this combination of independent learning and personal contact.

J. S. Daniel

REFERENCES

Background Viewing

Educating Rita, Acorn Pictures, a Lewis Gilbert film with Michael Caine and Julie Walters.

Background Reading

Daniel, J. S., Stroud, M. A., and Thompson, J. R. (1982) *Learning at a Distance: A World Perspective.* Edmonton, Alberta, Canada: Athabasca University/ICCE. The diversity of distance education is illustrated by over 100 contributions from more than twenty countries.

Holmberg, B. (1981) *Status and Trends of Distance Education.* London: Kogan Page. A unified approach by a leading scholar in the field.

Kaye, A. and Rumble, G. (1981) *Distance Teaching for Higher and Adult Education.* London: Croom Helm. A systematic analysis of distance teaching systems.

Neil, M. W. (1981) *Education of Adults at a Distance.* London: Kogan Page. Report of a conference held at the U.K. Open University in 1979.

Sewart, D., Keegan, D., and Holmberg, B. (1983) *Distance Education: International Perspectives.* London: Croom Helm. Reprint of 24 articles published since 1975 covering, inter alia, theory, societal role, students, media, course development, student support, economics.

Historical

Baath, J. A. (1980) *Postal Two-Way Communication in Correspondence Education.* Malmo, Sweden: LiberHermods, 11–46.

Journals/Periodicals

Bulletin of the International Council for Distance Education. Secretary, ICDE, Athabasca University, Edmonton, Alberta, Canada T5V 1G9.

Distance Education. I. Mitchell, SACAE, Salisbury Campus, 5109 Australia.

Teaching at a Distance. RTS, Open University, Milton Keynes, MK7 6AA, U.K.

Never Too Far. Sukhothai Thammithirat Open University, Bangkok, Thailand.

DITHERING. Mechanism of putting two colors so close together on a computer screen that the eye interprets the resulting effect as being a third color.

DITTO MACHINE. *See* **Hectograph.**

DOCUMENTARY. A film that shows a real situation as opposed to one based on fictional or contrived situations. The term is derived from the French word for travel films, *documentaire.* The word *documentary* was first used by John Grierson, a pioneer Scottish film maker, who defined it as "creative treatment of actuality."

The use of film in education owes much to the techniques developed by documentary filmmakers.

DOCUMENT READER. A computer device which can read printed documents. The high-speed reading of typescript by optical scanning is a recent and important innovation. *See* **Magnetic Ink Character Recognition; Optical Character Recognition.**

DOCUMENTATION. Documentation describes a collection of documents which enables one to operate, maintain, and modify courseware or software. In general, computer programs contain many peculiarities and particularities, associated with their authors and with the current state of the particular computer they were written for. If these particulars are not all carefully documented, it is impossible to "repair" or adapt the programs once the original programmer has forgotten what he did, or is no longer available. Another sort of documentation is required to specify the population of learners for which courseware was developed, and the instructional objectives and levels of performance which were achieved.

DOLBY NOISE REDUCTION SYSTEM. Special electronic circuitry invented by R. Dolby (of video tape recorder fame; *see* **Ampex**) and used in high-quality sound reproducing systems that enables the signal-to-noise ratio to be greatly improved. It works by introducing selective compression to the incoming signal which is processed through a matching network to reconstitute the original sound on replay. Dolby sound is particularly important in hi-fi cassette recorders which are prone to unacceptable hiss otherwise.

DOLLY. A wheeled trolley for carrying a film or television camera.

DOLLY SHOT. A shot in a film or television program in which the camera moves in or out on a stationary object and in the process changes the relative size of the object. The camera is said to "dolly" in and out. It may also "dolly" up and down, such as from the trunk of a tree to its highest branch.

DOS. *See* **Disk Operating System.**

DOS 3.3. A disk operating system for the Apple II.

DOT MATRIX. A common type of printer for connection to a microcomputer. The actual printing comprises a grid of dots which renders the process unsuitable for enlargement, but for normal purposes the output from a dot matrix printer is adequate. Such printers are economically priced and can print considerably faster than ones using a daisy wheel or thimble.

DOUBLE BAND PROJECTOR. A film projector that has, in addition to the normal film channel, a sound recording channel that uses sprocketted tape. The two channels, usually one on each side of the projector, are mechanically coupled so there is no possibility of picture and sound being out of synchronization. Double band projectors are particularly useful for adding commentaries to films in small-scale production units. After the sound track is recorded it can be transferred to an edge magnetic stripe on the film or sent away for optical transfer and printing.

DOUBLE-CLICK. To allow a single button on a mouse to indicate more than one type of operation, some software interprets two clicks in rapid succession (a double-click) as a different command from two separate clicks.

DOUBLE DENSITY. Term applied to floppy disks which are of superior quality and capable of storing information on a greater number of tracks (typically 80) than can a single-density disk (typically 40 tracks), giving twice the storage capacity. Naturally, a suitable disk drive and operating system are needed.

DOUBLE PROJECTION. A technique whereby two slide projectors are coupled by an electronic device to enable one slide to be dissolved into the next and also to avoid any black interval between slides.

DOUBLE SYSTEM SOUND. The separate recording of sound and vision in cine photography. Usually the sound recording is accomplished on a tape recorder which is synchronized with the camera by electronic means. *See* **Synchronized Sound.**

DOWNLEG. Downlink.

DOWNLINK. The communications link from a satellite to an earth station.

DOWNLOAD. To transfer data from one computer to another, generally from a larger system to a smaller one. For example, centrally stored programs can be downloaded on demand to a home computer via telephone line.

DOWNSTREAM KEYER. A device used in television production which superimposes captions onto the output from a vision mixer (switcher), with the result that the caption is not affected by the mixer controls.

DOWN TIME. Period during which a computer system (or any other equipment) is not operating on account of maintenance or other technical reasons.

DRAW. *See* **Direct Read After Write.**

DRILL AND PRACTICE. An educational approach that has the student work through many examples of the same type of problem. Computers are held to be particularly good at presenting this type of lesson because of their infinite patience and accuracy. If the expected answer involves concepts that can be phrased in various ways, the software must be capable of recognizing alternate formulations.

DRIVE. *See* **Disk Drive.**

DRIVER. The software interface between a computer and a peripheral such as a printer. In this case the driver provides the appropriate signals to indicate, for example, boldface, pitch, super up or down, carriage return, and so on. Most word processors provide drivers for the more popular printers. Note that the driver does not take the place of the series or parallel hardware interface which is essential for communication to modems, printers, etc.

DROPOUT. Loss of signal due to a fault, usually caused by wear, in a videotape coating.

DRY MOUNTING. The technique of fixing photographs or other flat items to cardboard mounts using thin sheets of tissue coated on both sides with shellac. The shellac melts when exposed to heat in a dry mounting press.

DRY TRANSFER PROCESS. A process used by graphic artists where a preprinted letter, number, symbol, color, etc., is transferred from a transparent or translucent carrier sheet to any dry surface by rubbing the image down with a pencil, ballpoint pen, or burnisher. Dry transfer lettering allows high-quality lettering to be added to artwork quickly and easily. *See* **Graphic Design.**

DTE. An abbreviation for data terminal equipment, the term used as part of the RS-232 standard for serial connections to terminals, computers, and other equipment that might connect to a modem.

DUBBING. The act of transferring audio and/or video from one tape to another. The term is also used more specifically to refer to that part of the editing process when the various sounds, pictures, etc., to be used are combined, by mixing, onto a single track. Also used to describe the process whereby a new sound track is made for a foreign language film or video.

DUMP. To print out or save on a permanent storage medium (usually a printer) the contents of a particular section of the computer memory. Alternatively a dump may consist of sending the entire contents of the computer's memory to a peripheral. *See* **Screen Dump.**

DUPE. Short term for duplicate or copy of a slide or film, either negative or positive. Quickly produced dupes are often used for editing where the final choices of shots can be more carefully reproduced later. In audio or video work a copy is called a "dub," and copying sound or vision is called "dubbing."

DUPING. The act of making additional copies of a film or slide.

DUPLEX. *See* **Full Duplex; Half Duplex.**

DUPLICATING. *See* **Photocopying and Duplicating.**

DVORAK KEYBOARD. Alternative layout for typewriter and computer keyboards, with the commonly used keys positioned to improve typing speed and accuracy. Some microcomputer hardware and software allows the user to opt for a Dvorak layout. However, the entrenched QWERTY arrangement will be hard to displace.

DYNAMIC MICROPHONE. A generic term for microphones which work on electrodynamic principles, i.e., moving coil and ribbon. *See* **Microphone Characteristics.**

DYNAMIC RANGE. In sound recording, the range between the loudest sound and the quietest. When the dynamic range is too big to be accommodated by a recording system, compression is introduced.

E

EARLIEST EVENT TIME. A term used in **critical path analysis** (q.v.) to denote the earliest time at which a given event or operation can occur. The earliest finish is the earliest start plus the duration of the activity.

EARLY BIRD. Transatlantic satellite put into service in 1965. Early Bird was the very first geosynchronous communications satellite, and permitted the transmission of live programs between the continents as well as greatly enhancing telephone capabilities.

EARPHONES. *See* **Headset.**

EARTH STATION. A facility which can transmit and/or receive signals from a satellite. Generally, the earth station will require a large dish antenna to capture the signals in sufficient strength, but in practice a 2.5m dish is adequate for many small-scale applications, e.g., individual reception of distance education programs. The advent of **direct broadcasting satellites** (q.v.) with their much greater broadcasting strength permits smaller and cheaper antennas.

EBCDIC. An acronym for extended binary-coded decimal interchange code, the code that IBM uses for representing characters and control values on large computers. EBCDIC uses the 256 possible 8–bit patterns to represent a selection of graphic (printing) and nongraphic (control) codes.

Although the code values are different, ASCII and EBCDIC have very similar graphic (printing) characters, so it is relatively easy to translate from one to the other for simple text. Many of the control codes are different, however.

ECHO. (1) A broadcast television signal which has been reflected during transmission with sufficient magnitude and time difference to be detected as a signal distinct from that of the primary signal. Echoes appear as reflections or "ghosts." (2) Computer term for the duplication of output to more than one destination, as when program commands are not only acted upon by the processor but also appear on the screen.

EDGE STRIPE. Narrow magnetic stripe applied between the perforation holes and edge of cine film on which a sound track may be recorded.

EDIT (COMPUTER). To change or modify; for example, to insert, remove, replace, or move text in a word-processed document.

EDIT (VIDEO AND FILM). The act of rearranging material into its final form, either by physically cutting and splicing (film) or by electronic means (video). *See* **Film Editing; Moviola; Pause Edit; Video Editing.**

EDTV. *See* **Extended Definition Television.**

EDUCATIONAL ACCESS CHANNEL. A cable television channel reserved for free use by educational agencies.

EDUCATIONAL BROADCASTING. Educational broadcasting—instructional broadcasting in the U.S.—is broadcasting designed to teach its audience, or to motivate its audience to learn. It is usually produced by specialist educational departments within larger broadcasting organizations, or by specialist educational companies or stations, and programs are usually grouped into series which cumulatively and sequentially build listeners' and viewers' skills, knowledge, or awareness. Patterns of educational broadcasting vary considerably throughout the world and are the results of different histories of development.

EDUCATIONAL AND EDUCATIVE BROADCASTING—DIFFICULTIES OF DEFINITION

Often the distinctions between educational broadcasting and *educative* broadcasting from the broadcasters' general services may be difficult to detect; the self-imposed goals of many broadcasting organizations—to inform, educate, and entertain—imply that many a general output broadcaster will sometimes share the same purposes and goals for his programs that the educational broadcaster espouses. A producer who seeks through general-output programs to make his viewers or listeners more effective consumers, or to alert them to social or political issues, or to explain the workings of some new scientific or technical device, may make a program indistinguishable in style and effectiveness from that which an educational broadcaster makes. Sometimes the general-output producer may achieve educational goals more effectively than the educational broadcaster can, because he may have far higher budgets and resources at his disposal than his overtly educational counterpart. For example, who would doubt the effectiveness of the televising of Alex Haley's *Roots* in bringing to the American people a better understanding of the history and nature of slavery and racial prejudice; or of the effectiveness of the BBC's historical costume dramas in making viewers around the world aware of otherwise unfamiliar and inaccessible ideas, events, and attitudes. Neither the BBC's historical costume dramas nor *Roots* set out to be "educational." These series were not produced by an educational broadcasting department or company, yet they were highly educative for their viewers. What, then, constitutes the difference between educative and educational broadcasting?

Any convention or conference on educational broadcasting makes possible some distinction between the two forms. The conference of educational broadcasters will usually contain groups with specific interests in preschool, school, or adult and continuing educational broadcasting. Educational broadcasters work closely with educators, often having claims in their own right to educational expertise, and they produce programs and series which are often geared to particular publics within the overall audience. Their series aim to engage listeners' or viewers' emotions and intellects and to stimulate their publics to further work or learning or other activity. That their product may at times be indistinguishable in its effects from the best of general-output programming is a tribute to the latter and by no means diminishes the value or importance of purposeful—and often highly expert and challenging—educational broadcasting.

THE DEVELOPMENT OF EDUCATIONAL BROADCASTING

Britain. When the British Broadcasting Company was formed in 1922, education formed from the start a part of its policy and output. When, in 1927, the British Broadcasting Corporation was granted its first charter, this enshrined the triple aims of education, information, and entertainment, and these three principles have been upheld in all subsequent charters. From the outset the BBC provided talks by experts in the arts and sciences with the deliberate aim of raising the level of cultural and cognitive awareness of its listeners. That this may sound a patronizing attitude to the modern-day ear is perhaps not surprising; it reflects the attitude and policy of J.C.W. Reith, who personally, and by his choice of staff, put a serious, if not elitist, stamp on early British broadcasting. A reason for his ability to follow this policy was the system by which the BBC was, and still is, funded. The corporation's income is from a license fee levied on all who use the service. (Nowadays BBC license fees are levied only on households possessing television sets.) It was the absence of competition or commercial pressure which enabled the BBC from the outset to offer the public a mix of programs designed to inform and broaden popular taste. Without doubt, Reith enabled many people for the first time to gain ready access to the thoughts, the ideas, and the products of some of the great minds of the age.

The BBC established a school radio service in 1924, and this provision has grown and continued to the present day. In 1957 television services from BBC and also from the then newly established Independent Television service (ITV) were introduced.

From the outset the BBC had established a council of distinguished educators to guide program provision for schools. The school Broadcasting Council for the United Kingdom, and its associated national regional councils continue to provide policy for BBC school series at the present time. ITV series policy is guided by the various ITV companies' own Educational Advisory Councils and by the Educational Advisory Council of the Independent Broadcasting Authority (IBA), the body which supervises the operation of ITV and which grants and reviews the franchises under which the ITV companies operate. Over the past ten years both BBC and independent local radio stations have opened, and in varying degrees and in different ways have produced output directly intended for school use.

Adult education programs were commenced in the earliest days by the BBC, and although the continuity of provision has not been as clear-cut as that for schools, nevertheless there has been a regular and sizable output first of radio and then of television designed specifically for adult educational purposes. ITV has a consistent and regular provision of adult education. The newly established independent Channel Four has significant adult educational material.

ITV, including Channel Four, is commercial, reliant for income on advertising. The mix of BBC and ITV services, with their different systems of funding, has led to competition for audiences for peak-time entertainment viewing but has not placed insuperable pressures on the continuation of educational broadcasting services. This is because the act of Parliament which established commercial broadcasting in Britain contains a requirement that the ITV companies produce educational output, and has vested the IBA with the requirement and the powers to ensure that this responsibility is discharged. Channel Four does not identify or specifically label its educational output as such, on the grounds that the distinction between educational and educative broadcasting, discussed above, is an artificial one.

An important development in educational broadcasting at the higher educational level has been the use of radio and television programs as teaching media within Open University (OU) courses. Radio and television have taught perhaps 5 percent of the content of OU courses and their cost has been in the order of 20 percent of the OU budget. But the existence of OU broadcasts has had a value over and above its straightforward teaching role: broadcasts have alerted the public to the existence of the OU and the educational opportunities it has opened up; the broadcasts have acted as "markers," offering students studying at home a check on the timetable of their progress through the correspondence texts; and, perhaps most important of all, the programs have given many people confidence that they could deal with university-level study and, therefore, the impetus to apply for an Open University place.

Basically, educational broadcasting in Britain is in excellent health. It is produced by well-established departments within the U.K. broadcasting organizations, is well funded, has access to excellent educational advice, and in production terms draws on the same facilities and expertise that are available for general-output broadcasting.

United States. The aspirations and visions for educational broadcasting within a general public broadcasting service that were espoused in Britain by Lord Reith were shared by D. Sarnoff and other pioneers of broadcasting in the United States. However, in the United States the thrust of commercial development in broadcasting left little room for education. Stations were commercial and devoted to gaining mass popular patronage by listeners. Though there was some attempt at control and intervention at federal government level through the actions of the Federal Communications Commission, this did not lead either to a consistent or coherent national provision of educational radio services or to any significant demand for national services from school or adult educators.

The chief developments in educational radio in the early days occurred in major cities like Chicago and New York, which developed radio stations offering a full service for schools, and in some areas in the midwest in which services were developed by the universities, most notably Wisconsin. Professor C. A. Siepmann argued at the time for the establishing of central tape libraries containing recorded programs which could be borrowed and used in the classroom as an alternative to their broadcast transmission (Siepmann, 1958). In 1952 the Federal Communications Commission allocated 242 channels for public service programs. The first ETV station opened in 1953, and by 1959 there were 45 stations which were community-owned, university-owned, or were part of network groups of school systems. They transmitted for in-school or credit-course use, children's viewing out of school, and for adult viewing at home. Though by the standards of commercial television the audiences for the programs were low, by the standards of education the audiences were enormous. (For a national overview of the state of development of instructional broadcasting in the United States in the late 1950s, see Schramm, 1960).

The number of stations in operation in North America has continued to grow. Often the funding for developments in educational television has been by donations from private foundations. The Ford Foundation established the Fund for the Advancement of Education to encourage institutions to adopt technological means to overcome their problems (Murphy and Gross, 1966). The most ambitious project which the fund supported was the National Program for the Use of TV in the Public Schools. Although the scheme was not without its detractors, it did establish firmly that television was a significant tool of enrichment for teaching. At the adult education level the Fund for the Advancement of Education supported another successful and innovative project, the Chicago City College. This scheme produced a two-year course for home-based learners who could not find places in the colleges.

Another celebrated and successful sponsored project was the Hagerstown Project. The U.S. Electronic Industries Association and the Ford Foundation supported this project jointly; it provided a closed-circuit system for the schools and the junior college of Washington County, Maryland. The scheme provided television teaching at all grades plus in-service education for teachers. Interim evaluation of the project concluded that "TV is best used as a specialized kind of learning experience or as an aid to classroom instruction" (Brish, 1964). The project demonstrated that broadcasting was especially useful in supporting teachers in those curriculum areas where they were personally least well-equipped; in areas like art, music, and science television could provide valuable expert input which in turn would be mediated to pupils by generalist teachers. The Hagerstown project was never fully analyzed; it fell victim to a survey of dubious validity revealing disillusion with ETV. This was especially unfortunate as the project had provided pointers to effective use of broadcasting which prompted emulation throughout the world.

A further example of innovation in educational broadcasting in the United States has been provided by the Children's Television Workshop (CTW) through its use of formative research in developing series. The series "Sesame Street," made chiefly for home viewing by children, set out to win an audience of youngsters including those whose home backgrounds were not supportive of the ethos or aims of schools. The programs were educational, but it was recognized from the outset that they would also have to be attractive and engaging enough to win an audience against the enormous competition provided by all other available television services. The Children's Television Workshop engaged in what was probably the most extensive and costly formative process ever undertaken in preparing an educational series. Thorough investigation of the content and approaches appropriate to the needs, interests, and attitudes of the target children was carried out, and the series was developed in the light of evaluation of pilot sequences (these investigations are summarized in articles in Bates and Robinson, 1977). "Sesame Street," and "The Electric Company" for an older age range, have been transmitted in many countries of the world and have been of seminal influence on the style of educational broadcasting in many nations.

Other Industrialized Countries. Educational broadcasting has developed in most of the industrialized countries of the world as an adjunct to existing general broadcasting services. Usually the impetus for particular emphasis and development in educational broadcasting has been educational crisis of one sort or another in the particular countries.

In many countries school television services were developed as a response to teacher shortages and/or as a means of updating or improving teachers' skills. Most European countries developed school series in the 1950s, and by the mid-1960s all West European countries were provided. Television services in France started in 1951, and in Italy in 1958 (these are described in Cassirer, 1960). The impetus for the development of Telescuola in Italy was the need to provide education for eleven- to fourteen-year-olds in regions where there were no schools for pupils beyond the primary years. The Telescuola scheme involved a network of coordinators to mediate televised lessons and to conduct associated follow-up work with supporting textbooks.

This use of television to reach otherwise unreachable audiences was emulated in other European countries, with adult audiences. French services were provided for viewing in "teleclubs" in villages and were designed to provide material which would be developed by *animateurs*. Topics dealt with in these services included information about agriculture (Dumazedier, 1956). Similar work was carried out in Japan (UNESCO, 1960).

The Scandinavian countries have very well-established broadcasting services with a long history, experience, and a justifiably high reputation. In Sweden broadcasts have long been valued by, and are excellently integrated into the work of, schools. Area resource centers keep recordings of radio and television programs for distribution to schools by regular delivery and collection services so that programs from past output may be utilized alongside programs currently on transmission. Production values are high. Adult education broadcasts are provided which bring innovative and motivating material to highly dispersed populations in areas of low population density. Adult education broadcasting is seen as part of a partnership with institutions of further and higher education; the participation rate in adult education in various forms in Sweden is extraordinarily high, at nearly 50 percent of the adult population. Finland, Norway, and Denmark have similar long traditions of school and adult education and enjoy similarly high reputations.

In Germany educational broadcasting is provided both by the national service and also by the regional stations. It is strongly supported by money from the national government, which also provides generous support for school publications.

In France much work has been undertaken on the theoretical basis for the relationship between broadcasting and the national educational curriculum. Broadcast services are provided, but the level of program production is lower than in Scandinavia, Germany, or Britain.

In Eire there has been a history of innovative and valuable broadcasting. It is unfortunate that due to economic stringencies educational production from Telefisearan is now almost at a standstill.

In Canada there has been a history of educational broadcasting as distinguished as in the United States. Like their counterparts in the United States, Canadian broadcasters have employed technical devices an electronic generation ahead of their counterparts in Europe; TV Ontario is currently using satellite transmissions and transmission of computer software as a regular feature of educational broadcasting. The station has managed to exist and its services to grow in competition with a plethora of commercial channels and in partnership with other educational agencies and networks.

Australia has a strong tradition of educational broadcasting in part modeled on the British system. The Australian Broadcasting Corporation (ABC) took a form and shape not dissimilar from that of the BBC. ABC has a strong educational broadcasting department which has close and positive links with the various state educational authorities. It has over time naturally developed its own special services and characteristics. The thin spread of population in parts of that vast country has led to much "teaching at a distance," with radio and television services being transmitted to widely dispersed home learners of school age and in adult education. Some broadcast teaching is now interactive, with teachers and pupils linked for certain times of the day by telephone or radio transmitters/receivers.

The Developing Countries. The problems of providing adequate educational opportunity in the developed world have been, and remain, considerable. Broadly, however, the infrastructure of skilled and literate populations in the developed world has meant that broadcasting has been used as an adjunct to other means of education; broadcasting has been either mediated through teachers or co-ordinators or provided as a stimulus for learners to make use of other existing educational provision. Where broadcasts have been aimed at home learners in the developed countries, the target population has in most cases been literate, possessing experience of formal education to a postprimary level and possessing some skill in autonomous learning.

In the developing countries the infrastructure of a well-funded education system and a generally literate population cannot be taken for granted. Over the past twenty years and more, many major national initiatives have been undertaken to use educational broadcasting as a primary tool of education and instruction.

A short list of certain of these major initiatives would include formal adult/youth education in Cuba (1962); formal school education in Samoa, (1964) and Niger (1964); formal primary school education in Colombia (1964); extension school studies in Mexico (1966), El Salvador (1968), the Ivory Coast (1971), and Korea (1974). Educational broadcasting by satellite transmission has been conducted in India (the SITE project, 1975) and Indonesia (1976). (Articles on all these initiatives may be found in Bates and Robinson, 1977.)

Many of these operations have been costly, requiring funding from the World Bank or from the overseas development agencies of the industrialized countries. Studies of the effectiveness of large-scale educational broadcasting projects in developing countries have shown that definition of audiences; learning goals; program styles; relationships between program makers, educators, and audiences; and awareness of barriers to the acceptance of the material being broadcast must be taken into account if the projects are to be successful.

Many, perhaps most, of the *successful* projects have started as pilot projects, the pilot projects being evaluated and the evaluations used as part of formative research for the major projects. The World Bank and other major funding agencies for educational broadcasting projects in the developing world have, over the past five or more years, viewed more rigorously and critically requests for loans for development projects using educational broadcasting than was the case in the 1960s and the early 1970s.

USING EDUCATIONAL BROADCASTING

It is generally accepted that broadcasts for schools should support the curriculum, rather than overtly lead it. In countries where there is a national curriculum this poses fewer problems for the broadcasters than in those countries where considerable freedom and autonomy are granted to individual teachers to determine their own syllabi and objectives. (In Britain, for example, although there is effective agreement about the skills and knowledge that children should possess at various stages of development, and although there is a system of public examinations at 16+ and 18+, teachers have very considerable freedom to devise different approaches which will achieve desired educational objectives.)

Appropriate educational broadcasting can nevertheless assist considerably in schools, no matter what the educational system. In the primary years broadcasting can assist generalist teachers by providing specialist subject material for them to mediate. In Britain few primary teachers would feel competent to teach music to their pupils; yet radio music broadcasts, which are taken in the majority of schools in the country, ensure that singing, ensemble playing with melodic and pitched percussion instruments, and music appreciation remain a lively part of school education. Nonspecialist teachers make similar use of highly expert and motivating material on primary science, history, and geography.

It is not simply in curriculum areas in which teachers lack specialist skills that broadcasting can play a valuable role. Broadcasting provides motivation, for example, to children to *want* to read; it can make books exciting and attractive, motivating the normally unmotivated child to go to a book in the expectation that the book will be rewarding. Television series which use animation to bring books to life often do more than any other medium—including the unaided teacher—could possibly do to make books attractive. Broadcasting has developed many such valuable roles.

In the secondary years educational broadcasts are generally produced for mediation by specialist subject teachers. The role of educational broadcasts for specialist use is in providing resources otherwise unobtainable by the teachers. The television production team can gain access to people, places, objects, events, and processes which are beyond the reach or scope of the class teacher, and make these phenomena accessible; can show expensive scientific equipment that is never found in schools; can bring a map to life by showing ground and aerial views of distant places; can show and explain the latest Landsat photograph, etc. Radio can bring together the best of actors and the best directors to bring a text to life, or to make accessible the distant age; radio documentary can show the viewpoint of a member of another community, country, religion, or political persuasion.

Educational broadcasting is not restricted to improving cognitive awareness. Drama, documentaries, and magazine programs can do much valuable work in the *affective* domain; they can help adolescents to understand the physical and emotional changes that at their ages they experience, or help pupils to see adult viewpoints, or encourage pupils to grapple with issues of authority, responsibility, and concern for others, with a directness and force not otherwise available.

A measure of the value which teachers place on educational broadcasting may be gathered by a brief summary of statistics. In 1979–1980 in Britain 99 percent of all primary schools and over 90 percent of all secondary schools used a selection of BBC school series. This level of use represents a *daily* audience of 2.5 million pupils for radio programs and 2.4 million pupils for television programs. Over 6 million items of printed material—pupil's and teacher's workbooks and notes—were sold to schools. The use of ITV school series in Britain—not too greatly behind that for BBC Television—is additional to the above figures.

Although school programs are supportive of the activities and curricular objectives practiced in Britain, the series often spread, or speed, the dissemination of new ideas and curriculum development. Educational producers have educational expertise themselves; they also have opportunities before making programs to consult with experts and curriculum developers throughout the countries in which they broadcast. In practice the results of their consultations are shown in the synthesis of ideas that they incorporate in programs. Although programs do not run ahead of teachers' needs, broadcasts often make developments in curriculum thinking accessible to hard-pressed specialist teachers whose own thinking on curriculum development is limited by the day-to-day tasks of classroom teaching. One of the main instruments of curriculum development in the United Kingdom until recently, the Schools Council (now being reformulated by government as two councils, one for examinations and the other for curriculum) recently conducted a survey of the means by which its innovative materials had been disseminated. School television was found to be *the* most potent means of dissemination of ideas and approaches from Schools Council curriculum materials.

In adult education, or continuing education, broadcasting has shifted in emphasis, especially over the past ten years or so, away from being a self-contained medium of education or instruction and towards ever greater partnerships with other educational agencies. Although it retains a commitment to the individual learner at home, for example, through provision of courses in foreign languages, the fact that many, perhaps most educational broadcasting services *are* national means that broadcasters can become associated with national schemes and campaigns. Like school broadcasts, adult and continuing education broadcasts can motivate the normally unmotivated and provide support for both cognitive and affective learning.

The great strength of broadcasting is that it gets into the homes of people whose own experience of formal education was unsuccessful. It can motivate people to learn who, without its stimulus, would never enroll at an evening institute or college offering evening classes. Broadcasting is increasingly seen as a motivating agent, able to penetrate into people's houses, and thereby to trawl a "catch" of viewers who will come forward for further study outside their homes. A good example of this partnership is provided by the BBC's Adult Literacy Campaign.

The Adult Literacy Campaign involved regular, short, motivational programs at peak viewing hours designed to encourage adult illiterates to come forward for help in learning to read. The programs were light in style, frequently very funny, and based on the dramatic device of recounting the experiences of two lorry drivers, one of whom played the part of an illiterate. He was portrayed as a man who was very far from stupid, but whose ability to profit from his own school days had been negligible. The series not only provided encouragement for illiterates to "try again" with learning to read and write, but also produced a sympathetic and sometimes admiring reaction from literate viewers; the devices which illiterates in a literate society adopt to hide their illiteracy are often highly ingenious. The whole scheme operated in partnership with libraries, evening institutes, a telephone referral service, and the use of many thousands of individual volunteers who came forward for training courses and then provided one-to-one instruction to illiterate neighbors, using specially prepared materials. Partnership, funding, and coordination for the project took considerable time to establish before the programs were made. Formative evaluation of a number of program styles was conducted. The campaign helped 200,000 people in Britain to overcome their illiteracy.

Adult and continuing education broadcasts have, again

in partnership with other agencies, addressed and provided invaluable resources for other major issues of our time. Health education in many forms—giving up smoking, healthy eating, exercise, bringing up children—has been an area of considerable success for broadcasting. So too has the whole area of helping understanding of the roles and uses of new technologies. Encouraging understanding of and positive attitudes toward living in a multicultural society has been a further role for broadcasting. Educational broadcasting has a distinguished history of programs in, and a continuing and vigorous concern for, most of the major issues of our time.

THE FUTURE OF EDUCATIONAL BROADCASTING

In its 60 years of evolution educational broadcasting has changed and developed as part of the changing world. Will it survive another 60 years, and if so, how will it further evolve and develop? It is obvious that educational broadcasting, if it is to have a future, must evolve both within an evolving education service and also as part of the overall broadcasting services. Continuation and development of educational broadcasting is assured if it can be consonant with the needs of education and the determinants of overall broadcasting policy.

Some of the signs of healthy evolution and development are evident. Educational broadcasting has done much, around the world in many different initiatives, to spread awareness of computers, their use, and the changes they will bring to societies. Broadcasters are moving into new technologies: the transmission of telesoftware, i.e., computer software transmitted by **teletext** (q.v.), should be in service before 1984 in Britain and shortly afterwards in several other countries; in North America videodiscs are being compiled to offer access to combinations of moving and still pictures, text, and computer software on a branching programmed-learning basis; experiments with new means of distribution of broadcasts, for example, by a "mixed economy" of broadcasting and cassette distribution. All these and other initiatives show broadcasters moving with the tide and in reasonable control of their futures.

Not all educational broadcasting is in such good shape. The virtual cessation of educational broadcasting in Eire is an indication, perhaps a warning, that in times of financial difficulty education can be lost more readily, and to less public outcry, than other broadcasting services.

Where countries operate both school radio and television services, the trends are for audiences for the former to be reducing, and for television to be stable or rising. This is not true for each individual series on radio, but it is generally the case around the world that secondary schools are using less radio but more television than was the case ten years ago. It may be that, for the secondary school age range, it will prove impossible for broadcasters to provide a radio service which is consonant both with the needs of schools and the ethos of radio services. Popular radio is moving more and more into "sequence" broadcasting—fairly rapidly changing topics, interspersed with music—designed often for "background" listening. It may be that it will prove impossible to persuade pupils willingly to listen to more concentrated types of radio, and that teachers will reject sequence radio as a vehicle for a wide range of school subjects. Few areas of broadcasting need greater effort, probably through formative research, than that of revitalizing the contemporary idioms for secondary school radio program making.

What is the context within which educational broadcasting will operate in the next decade? Over the next ten years or so, there will be an expansion in the range and number of broadcast services available in Europe. Rather on the American pattern, a plethora of competing television channels will spring up, based on satellite and cable transmission as well as conventional terrestrial transmissions. All this at a time when it is likely that audiences for broadcasting will in general be diminishing, the reasons for this decline being the number of feature films available for hire on videocassettes, and the increasing number of home computer owners who will use their television set as a video display unit rather than as a means of receiving the broadcasters' signals. If, therefore, there are to be more broadcasters chasing a declining audience, then the patronage for any particular channel is likely to become smaller. In Britain, for example, the ownership of a franchise for a commercial television station, even over an affluent region, is no longer a license to print money. When the profits become even more slender, the question must be raised whether or not commercial television will ask to be released from its current obligations to provide educational broadcasting. If the BBC finds that it cannot command a large enough share of the total U.K. audience, then it will have difficulty in establishing its right to license fee increases in pace with or in excess of the rate of inflation. Where financial pressures occur, the likelihood of educational broadcasting being relegated to the third division of importance, or indeed discontinued, cannot be discounted. It will be surprising if all of the national educational broadcasting services currently operating in Europe are still in business at the end of the 1980s.

Trends from successful stations are already becoming clear. In many countries of Europe there is, in spite of the wide range of satellite and cable channels which are promised, a shortage of air space. A recent straw poll among broadcasters at a conference indicated that perhaps a third of the countries represented were having, or could foresee, problems of access to suitable airtime placings. The "mixed economy" of transmission, and subsequently of distribution of *recordings* of broadcasts, will almost certainly become a fairly common pattern. There are also sound educational reasons for adopting this distribution pattern; it is possible to give a new order and sequence to television broadcasts when they are distributed on videocassette or videodisc—indeed, a new format becomes desirable. The ease with which broadcasts may now be recorded, especially on television, has led to a major increase in the level of recorded use over the last few years. Once the majority of use becomes recorded, then it ceases to be meaningful to think of broadcasts as complete programs of ten, twenty, or fifteen minutes with beginnings, middles, and ends: it starts to become important to think of the broadcast resources as underlying resource *material* made for a range of kinds of mediation by the teacher, and for a range of different means of access. The videodisc player could become a revolutionary tool of information distribution and retrieval, and its potential as a vehicle for handling the visual resources of the broadcasters is immense. It remains to be seen whether or not the videodisc becomes a common educational tool. It is difficult to see how, if it can be released onto the market at a reasonable level of cost, it can fail to make a major impact on education and the whole business of data storage and retrieval.

Educational broadcasters, like the wider family of broadcasters of which they form a part, have a high survival value. Educational broadcasting in some shape or form will certainly survive into the future, if only because it has so firmly established its value at the present. It will be fascinating over the next years and decades to see just how it accommodates to and forms part of the range of teaching and learning resources side by side with computers, data base, and the new information techniques and systems developed for education over the next generation.

John Alexander

REFERENCES

Bates, A. and Robinson, J., eds. (1977) *Evaluating Educational Television and Radio*. Milton Keynes: Open University Press.

Brish, W. M. (1964) *Washington County Closed Circuit Television Report*. Hagerstown, Maryland.

Cassirer, H. H. (1960) *Television Teaching Today*. Paris: UNESCO.

Dumazedier, J. (1956) *Television and Rural Adult Education*. Paris: UNESCO.

Murphy, J. and Gross, R. (1966) *Learning by Television*. New York: Fund for the Advancement of Learning.

Schramm, W., ed. (1960) *The Impact of Educational Television*. Urbana: University of Illinois Press.

Siepmann, C. A. (1958) *TV and Our School Crisis*. New York: Dodd, Mead.

UNESCO. (1960) *Rural Television in Japan*. Paris: UNESCO.

EDUCATIONAL BUILDINGS. For many years the design and construction of educational buildings inevitably reflected the traditional view of instruction: the teacher confronting a group of students. For reasons of convenience this has resulted in the typical classroom or lecture hall being a rectangular box with some sort of lectern and display apparatus (e.g., chalkboard) at one of the short ends. Unfortunately, many educational innovations, whether of an organizational or a methodological kind, are ill-adapted to such conservative surrounds.

In recent times architects have come to accept the overwhelming requirement for *flexibility* in educational buildings, and this has led to imaginative constructions which greatly facilitate the effective use of modern communications media. Thus we find efficient arrangements for various forms of projection, appropriate sound-amplifying provision in larger auditoria, and especially spaces and movement areas which are capable of transformation into alternative environments as the need arises.

As education comes to be seen more as facilitation of information transfer, designers will face new and major challenges to cope with the technical demands of ubiquitous display devices, and the interconnection of educational facilities between home, institution, workplace, etc. Schools and universities designed for the 1990s will bear little resemblance to those generally found today.
See **Learning Environment; New Technology and Education.**

EDUCATIONAL CINEMA. *See* **Audiovisual Media.**

EDUCATIONAL COMMUNICATION. *See* **Communication Engineering; Educational Cybernetics; Information Technology.**

EDUCATIONAL COMMUNICATION AND TECHNOLOGY JOURNAL. Formerly known as the *AV Communication Review*, this is the official journal of the Association for Educational Communications and Technology, published four times per year since 1953. The articles carried are generally theory- or research-oriented.

School of Education, Indiana University, Bloomington, IN 47405, U.S.

EDUCATIONAL CYBERNETICS.

INTRODUCTION

Educational cybernetics is a field of science and technology in which the concepts, insights, methods, and products of general cybernetics are applied to teaching and training processes. It is important to education because

1. the generality of its concepts allows model building, which enables us

    (a) to place the many separated results of educational research and development into one coherent framework,

    (b) to make comparisons between theories, assertions, and approaches which do not at first sight appear to be comparable, and

    (c) to pinpoint assertions which, at first sight, appear to be distinct, but on closer analysis turn out to be identical or overlapping

2. its methods enable us to carry out scientific research into learning processes applied to subject matters of substantial bulk and complexity and over extended periods of time (''realistic'' learning tasks)

3. its mathematical methods and models permit us not only to record past events but also to make testable quantitative predictions of educational hypotheses

4. its methods enable us not only to use computers to present teaching materials to learners and to control their progress in various ways but also to help in the *construction* of teaching programs and other teaching materials

5. its methods help in the development of multipurpose and single-purpose teaching machines including specialized computers and adaptive teaching systems which closely simulate selected features of the behavior of good teachers.

SYSTEMS: THE BASIC CONCEPT OF GENERAL CYBERNETICS

Cybernetics as a science studies objects, phenomena, and processes of many different kinds. It can do so because it approaches them at a fairly high level of abstraction. It ignores (abstracts from) certain features and concentrates on others which the objects under study have in common.

If we ignore the obvious differences between plants, animals, and human beings, we can refer to all of them as organisms. They are opposed to groups of organisms (societies) and to man-made objects. If we go further and ignore the differences between organisms, societies, inanimate and man-made objects, we can refer to all and each of them as systems. Organisms and objects have at least one feature in common: both are tangible. Societies are somewhat more abstract: their members are tangible, but they are not tangible as a whole. We can also imagine or create totally abstract systems which are characterized only by their ability to receive some inputs and react to them, thereby producing certain outputs and simultaneously changing their states. The input/output signals will, on this abstract level, be called signs.

We are interested in the behavior of a system, i.e.,

1. Which signs can it distinguish/accept? Each such sign is called *input letter*. The set of input letters is called *input alphabet*.

2. Which signs/responses can it emit? Each sign is called *output letter*. The set of output letters is called *output alphabet*.

3. Which/how many states may it assume? The set of states is called the *state alphabet*.

When the system receives an input letter, it responds by moving to a new state (which may be identical with the previous state) and emits an output letter. There may be occasions when it does not emit an output letter. We then say that it has emitted the ''empty letter'' (Glushkov, 1966). We know/understand the behavior of a system if we can predict how it will respond to a specific input letter when it is in a specific state.

Systems may be connected with one another in various ways so that one system receives input letters from another system and transmits its output letters to another system. The chains (strings) of letters going from one system to the other are called *information*. Sets of systems which thus interact with one another can themselves be regarded as systems (or supersystems). It is also possible that the output of a system directly or, more frequently, indirectly affects the input to the same system (is fed back to the same system). Such an arrangement of systems is called a *feedback circuit*. Systems with feedback circuits are often set up in order to enable the system to maintain a certain state (example: thermostat) or to reach a certain goal (example: teaching process). The behavior of such systems can often be described by means of algorithms.

Norbert Wiener, in 1948, recognized that such feedback control circuits can be used to describe the behavior of animate and inanimate systems (Figure 18) and thus, with his book *Cybernetics* (Wiener, 1961), gave rise to the new discipline we are discussing here.

As an introduction to the concept of ''system,'' see Beishon, 1971; Ashby, 1965; Klír and Valach, 1967; Rubin, 1971.

CYBERNETICS AND ITS RELEVANCE TO EDUCATION

Cybernetics is a field of science and technology. As a science, it is concerned with the accumulation of knowledge about its object of study. As a technology, it is concerned with the construction of devices which simulate the processes which it studies. While other sciences study *material* objects and processes, cybernetics studies the transfer, storage, and processing of *information* (Frank, 1966). Since education, training, teaching, and learning are, at least partly, concerned with the transfer, storage, and processing of information, they are a po-

Figure 18
The Concept of Feedback Circuit Applied to a Thermostatically Controlled Central Heating Process and to a Teaching Process to Show the Similarities/Parallels at a Certain Level of Abstraction

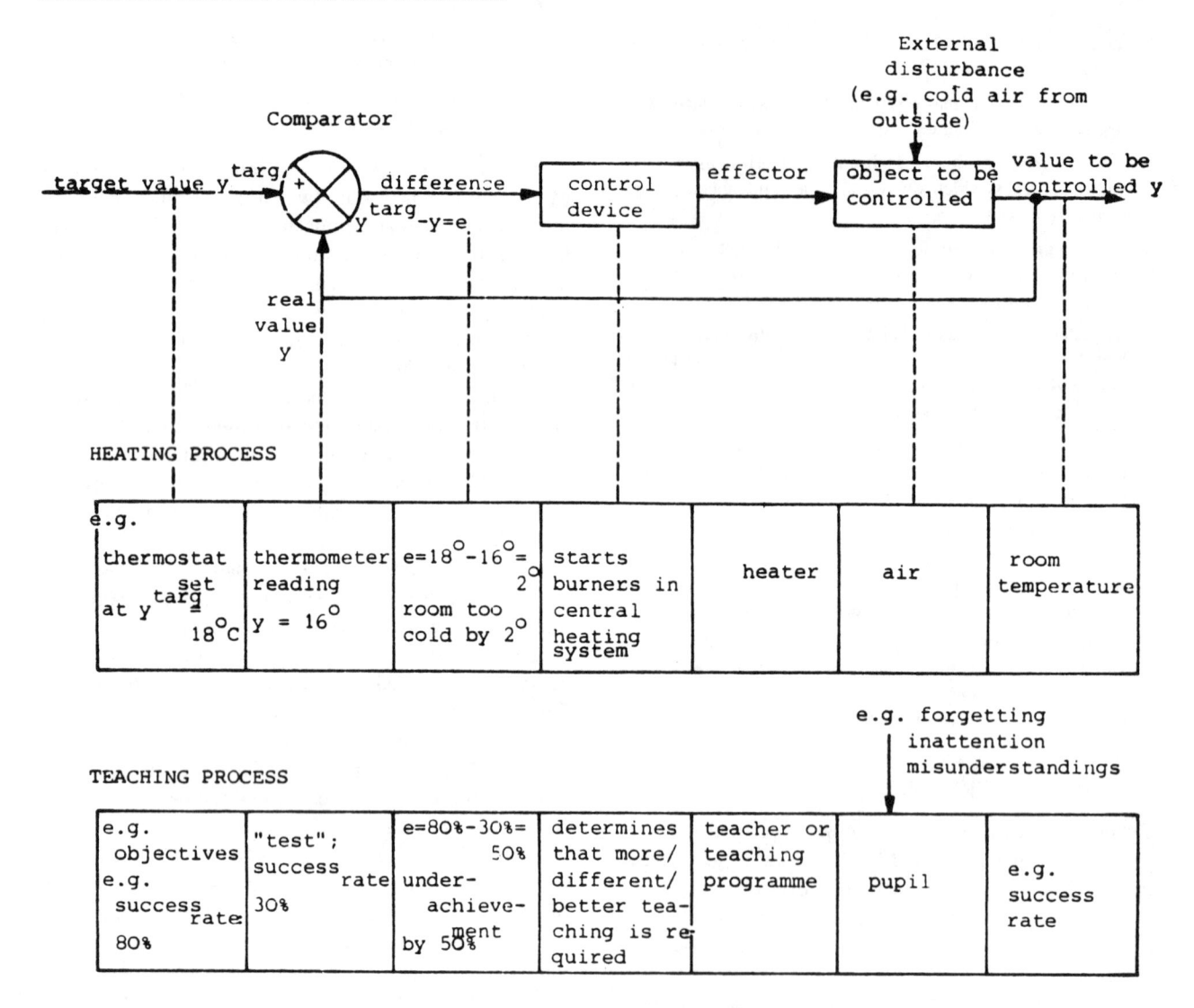

[Diagram: Feedback circuit with Comparator receiving target value y_{targ} (+) and real value y (−), producing difference $y_{targ} - y = e$, feeding into control device → effector → object to be controlled (subject to External disturbance, e.g. cold air from outside) → value to be controlled y (with feedback to comparator).]

HEATING PROCESS

| e.g. thermostat set at $y_{targ} = 18°C$ | thermometer reading $y = 16°$ | $e = 18° - 16° = 2°$ room too cold by 2° | starts burners in central heating system | heater | air | room temperature |

TEACHING PROCESS

external disturbance: e.g. forgetting, inattention, misunderstandings

| e.g. objectives e.g. success rate 80% | "test"; success rate 30% | $e = 80\% - 30\% = 50\%$ under-achievement by 50% | determines that more/ different/ better teaching is required | teacher or teaching programme | pupil | e.g. success rate |

tential field of study for cybernetics. This potential has been realized since about 1962 (Frank, 1962).

At the high level of abstraction at which cybernetics studies the role of information, striking similarities become apparent between organisms (biological systems: plants, animals, humans) and man-made systems (machines and other devices). When studying biological systems, cybernetics is not satisfied with gaining "insight" into the role of information in the system but tries to construct a man-made system which simulates the behavior of the biological system. The degree to which the man-made system is successful in its task is regarded as an indication of the extent to which the cybernetician has "understood" the organism he was trying to simulate. Instead of saying that the cybernetician tries to simulate the behavior of the organism he studies, we can also say that he "transfers the functions of the organism to a technical system" or that he tries to "objectivate" the functions of the organism. The technical system created for this purpose is then called the *objectivation* of the organism (Frank, 1966a, 1971). The behavior of organisms can be objectivated through special-purpose machines and/or through fairly general machines. The most general of these are computers. Objectivation in computers is successful to the extent to which the cybernetician succeeds in developing a program that enables the computer to simulate the behavior that is being studied. Cyberneticians therefore often work with computers.

Educational cybernetics studies the behavior of teachers and learners (i.e., teaching and learning processes). It tests its insights (hypotheses) by transferring the functions of the teacher to man-made systems (programmed books, teaching machines, computers, etc.) and observing the changes which take place in the learner when he learns with these. Even the teaching programs developed within the behaviorist school of programmed instruction (on the various schools of programmed instruction, see Bung and Rouse, 1970, p. 179ff.; and Bung, 1976, p. 178ff.) can be interpreted as objectivations of this kind: the objectivation of the *presentation* of information (corresponding to the actual lesson in the classroom). Educational cybernetics (unlike behaviorist-based educational science) has set itself an additional goal, which is even more ambitious. It studies the process of lesson preparation (parallel to that of program development) and seeks ways to simulate it by letting a technical device (the computer) first help in the development of teaching programs and then take over the construction of teaching programs altogether. In very primitive cases (confined to paired-associate learning) this has already been successful (Frank, 1969a, pp. 359–369, and 1969b, pp. 167–176; Bung and Rouse, 1970; examples of such computer-generated teaching programs can be found in Hertkorn, 1970; and Goethe-Institut, 1972).

The difficulties in the way of programming a computer to construct effective teaching programs seem insurmountable, but the long-term research goal is unobjectionable. The aim is to find out what principles/features make a teaching program effective. As long as we cannot get a computer to construct effective teaching programs with a success rate at least as high as that of human program writers, we cannot claim to have "understood"/found the principles in question. The aim must therefore be pursued further. Having such a goal, however utopian it may appear, will lead the researcher to the highest possible standards of precision. It goes without saying that educational cyberneticians, like behaviorist programmers, produce programs not only for research purposes but also for teaching purposes. The number of teaching programs produced in the cybernetic school of programmed instruction is, however, much smaller than those coming from the behaviorist school. On the other hand, even now, computer assistance in the development of teaching programs has so far advanced that it can be of great practical help to program writers.

We have so far listed two features of cybernetics:

1. its object of study: information as such
2. its goal: the creation of devices which simulate the transfer, storage, and processing of information in organisms

The third feature is the *methods* of cybernetics: they are mathematical and quantifying. This distinguishes cybernetics from the humanities and the social sciences as traditionally practiced (Itelson, 1967). The novel feature of cybernetics is that it tries to investigate not only the traditional topics of the natural sciences with mathematical methods but also aesthetics (Fucks, 1957; Frank, 1964a, 1968), literature (Leed, ed., 1966; Gunzenhäuser, 1965), psychology (Attneave, 1959; Frank, 1969a, 1969b; Meyer-Eppler, 1969), and last, educational processes. The mathematical disciplines in question are mainly those of information theory, algorithm theory, automata theory, and conversation theory. These will be discussed below.

Educational cybernetics has thus become, so to speak, a bridge among academic disciplines of widely differing kinds (Frank, ed. 1965a). The need for, and the possibility of creating, such a bridge seems to have been in the air in the birth hour of cybernetics, sometime between 1940 and 1950. When discussing his contribution to the development of computers, Wiener (1961, p. 4) acknowledges the general principle: "These notions were all very much in the spirit of the thought of the time, and I do not for a moment wish to claim anything like the sole responsibility for their introduction. Nevertheless, they have proved useful...." Hermann Hesse made the abstract relations among different disciplines the basis of the world of his novel *Das Glasperlenspiel* in 1943 (English translation: *Magister Ludi*, 1949). The German engineer and physicist Hermann Schmidt lectured and published about the general concept of feedback technology *(Regelungstechnik)* from 1940 onwards. At about the same time, the British psychologist Kenneth Craik anticipated many of Wiener's ideas, interpreting, for instance, the responses of organisms as feedback circuits (1966). In 1948, Norbert Wiener officially launched cybernetics, characterizing it as the science of "control and communication in the animal and the machine." (On the history of the word "cybernetics," see Lang, 1968, and Apter, 1969, pp. 8ff. and 20ff.)

Out of these origins, a variety of widely divergent approaches to cybernetics have organically grown by emphasizing one aspect or other of the original ideas. How divergent these approaches are can be seen by comparing some of the introductory textbooks on cybernetics; e.g., Pask (1961), Ashby (1965), Glushkov (1966), Klír and Valach (1967), Anschütz (1967), Frank (1969a).

Since educational cybernetics began life later than behavioristically inspired educational technology, it was forced initially to set up a sharp contrast between the cybernetic and behaviorist approach to education (Frank, 1966b, p. 70). In fact, the cybernetic model is so comprehensive that it can easily accommodate all that is valid in the behaviorist approach. The essential difference between the cybernetic and the behaviorist approach is that behaviorist investigations of a given system deny that systems have different states, or that these states are a legitimate object of scientific investigation or speculation. The behaviorist approach therefore confines itself to investigating the statistical relations between input and output letters (stimuli and responses) of a system (Rosenblueth, Wiener, and Bigelow, 1943; Pask, 1975a, p. 13ff.) and does not resort to hypothetical "states" in order to make more reliable predictions about the responses of the system. The behaviorist approach is therefore a subset of the cybernetic approach and all results of behaviorist investigations can be interpreted and represented in terms of cybernetic models (but not vice versa). The lack of the concept of "state" (first formalized in 1961 in Glushkov's theory of abstract automata; see Gluschkow, 1963; and Glushkov, 1966) thus leads to serious complications in the expositions of behaviorist-oriented authors, such as Gilbert (1969) and Edney (1972), including some protagonists of the "systems approach."

There are interesting parallels in the development of educational technology away from (or beyond) behaviorism and similar developments in general linguistics. The cybernetic school of educational technology programmatically subscribes to Descartes' method:

1. ...carefully to avoid precipitancy and prejudice, and to comprise nothing more in my judgment than what was presented to my mind so clearly and distinctly as to exclude all ground of doubt
2. ...to divide each of the difficulties under examination into as many parts as possible, and as might be necessary for its adequate solution
3. ...to conduct my thoughts in such order that, by commencing with objects the simplest and easiest to know, I might ascend by little and little, and, as it were, step by step, to the knowledge of the more complex; assigning in thought a certain order even to those objects which in their own nature do not stand in a relation of antecedence and sequence
4. ...in every case to make enumerations so complete, and reviews so general, that I might be assured that nothing was omitted. (cf. Frank, 1965b, p. 17.)

The second Cartesian principle (division of problems) is of central importance. It is neatly matched in Flechsig's (1975) definition of educational technology as the entry of industrial ideology and industrial production methods into the realm of education. Industrial production methods are characterized by objectives, planning, economy of means, *division of labor*, reproducibility of results, evaluation, and systematic improvements. Thus educational cybernetics as a science is dominated by Des-

Figure 19
Educational Cybernetics as Science or Technology

Educational Cybernetics as a	Guiding Principle	Principle introduced by	In
science	division of problems	Descartes	1637
technology	division of labour	Adam Smith	1776

cartes's principle of "division of problems" and as a technology by Adam Smith's principle of "division of labor" (Figure 19).

Inspired by, and in continuous contact with, the cybernetic models described in this article, a cybernetic (Cartesian) approach to programmed language instruction began to develop from 1964 onwards (summarized in Bung, 1975a). This approach kept programmed language instruction a tenable proposition compatible with the methods and findings of modern theoretical linguistics (Chomsky, 1965) and closely adjusted to the inherent requirements of spoken and written language instruction, when programmed instruction of the classical, behaviorist type was already discredited among U.S. linguists not only because of the inappropriate applications of Skinnerian programming techniques to language instruction but also because behaviorist views of the nature of language had been so thoroughly demolished by Chomsky's review of Skinner's *Verbal behavior* (Chomsky, 1959; Skinner, 1957). Strangely enough, Chomsky (*Cartesian linguistics,* 1966) also finds a respectable ancestor in Descartes. Other startling parallels between problems in modern linguistics and educational technology are discussed in Bung (1972). Lest our readers feel uneasy about too neat a set of contrasts and parallels, we should remind them that our learned friends in the behaviorist camp too can claim to have descended from Descartes (Skinner, 1969, p. 3), who first articulated quite clearly the notion of reflex action (Fearing, 1964), so that we are perhaps, after all, all children of one, very prodigious, father.

THE CONSTITUENT MODELS AND THEORIES OF EDUCATIONAL CYBERNETICS

Having characterized the cybernetic applications to education (cf. also Apter, 1969; Frank, 1969a; Frank and Meder, 1971, 1976: Meder and Schmid, eds., 1973ff.),

Figure 20
The Didactic Variables

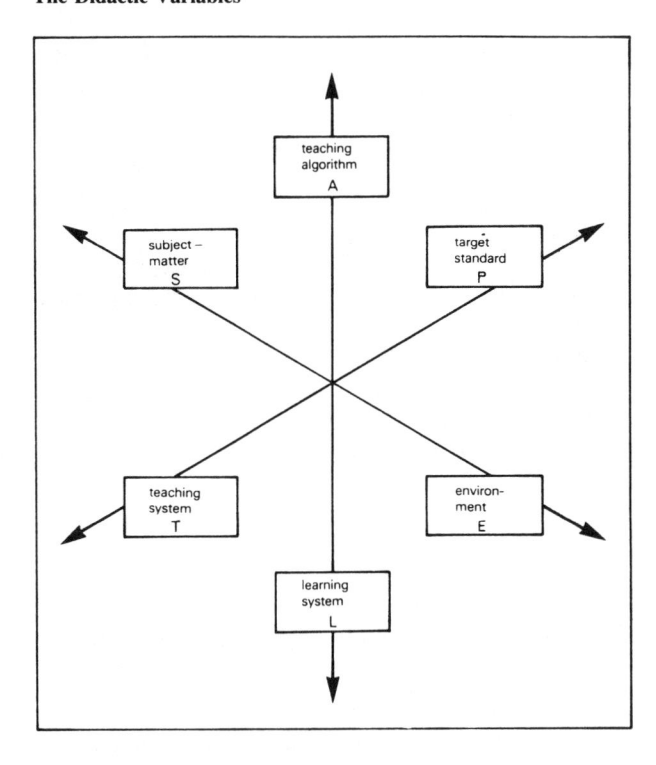

[Figure 20: Diagram showing six didactic variables arranged around a central point with crossing axes: teaching algorithm A (top), subject-matter S (upper left), target standard P (upper right), teaching system T (lower left), environment E (lower right), learning system L (bottom).]

we shall now outline the specific models and theories which are utilized in educational cybernetics.

The Didactic Variables. Each teaching process can be precisely defined by specifying a value for each of the following variables, the so-called didactic variables (Figure 20):

Subject matter: S. Subject matters can be broken down into subject-matter elements, which constitute a partial order of sequential relations (logical support, prerequisite knowledge, etc.). Attempts for finding such partial orders began with Evans, Glaser, and Homme (1960, Ruleg); Mechner (in Glaser, 1962); and Thomas et al. (1963, matrix system). Theoretical investigations into the nature of such structures (and applications to foreign language teaching) are due to Bung (1967b, Delta-Diagram; 1971a, 1973c, 1975a) Pask (entailment structures, 1975a, chap. 7), and Pask, Scott, and Kallikourdis (1973). Other contributions to the theory of sequential relations or their application to specific subject matters can be found in Lánský (1970, concept matrix); Weltner (coherence diagram, 1975a, 1975b, 1975c); Seidel, Kingsley, and Kopstein, (1971); Bink (1975); Pietsch (1971); and Schott and Dierig (1977). Wyant (1972) was apparently the first to use the notation of network analysis, rather than classical graph theory, for the representation of subject matters. System Research Ltd. (1977a, p. 110ff.) lists a few dozen additional authors contributing to the same field. A comparative analysis of the different approaches, analytical techniques, notations, terminologies and their mutual advantages and disadvantages would now be in order.

Target standard: P. Subvariables: percentage of correct responses, accuracy, latency, speed, retention time, etc. (cf. Bung, 1973a, 1975b; Sánchez Carrasco and Bung, 1977). Subject matter and target standard together are covered by the term **"objectives"** (q.v.). Boeckmann (1971) discusses the limitations of specifying "objectives" in terms of subject-matter summary and target standard.

Learning system (learner): L. Subvariables:

—Prior knowledge of subject matter (which may facilitate, or interfere with, learning of subject matter)

—Learning characteristics (the data accumulated by educational psychology: how does the state of the learner change if he receives specific inputs?)

—Learning algorithms mastered by the learner (these enable the learner to process/assimilate larger or smaller chunks of information put out by the teacher, book, or program)

—Degree of willingness to learn (proposed scale of willingness in Bung, 1975b). The degree of willingness determines whether the learner will actually apply any learning algorithms he knows.

Teaching system: T. Umbrella term for animate teaching system (teacher) and inanimate teaching systems (books, machines, tapes, etc.). As will be shown in the discussion of adaptive teaching systems (especially of the Pask type), teaching systems can also be equipped with learning algorithms which enable them to learn about the learning system (See sections below on applications of information theory and educational cybernetics).

Teaching algorithm: A. The teaching algorithm determines how the teaching system is to respond to each move (e.g., error, correct response, interference, etc.) made by the learner. The concept of "teaching algorithm" is closely akin to those of "teaching method," "teaching strategy" (cf. Pask, 1960a, p. 351 and 357; 1976a, 1976c, 1972a; Pask and Scott, 1972, 1973; Pask, Scott, and Kallikourdis, 1973; Pask, 1975c—to be read in that order), and "teaching procedure." A teaching method can be regarded as a set of teaching algorithms which have certain features in common (Bung, 1969a).

Classical programmed instruction raises target standards by developing extremely powerful, often lengthy and detailed, teaching algorithms, minimizing the freedom of the learner (Bung, 1971a). This is an expensive approach, but one necessary as long as the learners do not know sufficiently effective learning algorithms or are not willing to employ those they know (Illich, 1971).

When more effective learning algorithms are used, teaching algorithms can be shortened and simplified and information can be given to pupils in larger chunks (Bung, 1972; Weltner, 1973a, 1973b, 1975c, 1975d).

Environment: E. The environment may facilitate, or interfere with, the predicted effects of the teaching algorithm and must therefore be taken into consideration. The theory of the environment is as yet fairly underdeveloped.

The model of the didactic variables was originated by Helmar Frank following an inspiration by Paul Heimann (1962). Frank formally views each teaching process as a vector specified by the values of the six didactic variables, each of these in turn being specified by vectors of subvariables at various levels of hierarchy. Each teaching process can thus be viewed as a point in an n-dimensional space. These concepts have been explained in simple language by Bung (1972). The original literature about the didactic variables can be tracked down through Bung and Rouse (1970) and Bung (1973a, 1973b, 1973c, 1974, 1975a, 1975b). Frank's own textbook description of the model can be found in Frank (1969a, 1969b) and Frank and Meder (1971, 1976).

The didactic variables have been useful in planning courses, lessons, and programs; in exploring systematically the alternative solutions available for solving a given teaching problem; for making teachers aware of the interdependence of the instruments, actions, goals, etc., at their disposal; and for accommodating isolated research results and fitting them into a comprehensive model (cf. Bung, 1975a, p. 21ff.).

They have also made it possible to define quite clearly and unemotionally various subdisciplines of educational technology. In the most simple terms, each subdiscipline treats one of the didactic variables as its "unknown" and tries to "determine its value" assuming that the values of the other five variables are already determined. In extremely simple cases, such "values" have in fact been "computed" (see Bung and Rouse, 1970), but as a rule it is safer to regard these terms, at least for the time being, as convenient analogies which aid clear and unemotional thinking rather than as computational reality. In particular, "didactics" or "methodology" or "lesson preparation" or "program writing" can be regarded as the search for a teaching algorithm (the unknown variable) when a specific subject matter, target standard, teaching system (book or machine or teacher), learning system (target population with specific prior knowledge, etc.), and environment are given. Or more briefly: given values for S, P, E, L, and T, find a compatible value for A.

At least five more subdisciplines of educational technology (or of educational cybernetics) can be defined in this manner:

1. Find a compatible value for S, given values for the other five variables. This would be a case, for instance, where parents and teachers are trying to determine whether a child is to learn German, Spanish, or mathematics.

2. Similarly, in the search for P, an attempt is made to determine at what level to fix the target standard for each subject-matter element. A computational model has already been developed (Frank and Frank-Böhringer, 1968, 1971) which shows the general criteria to be applied and the calculations to be carried out for very simple cases. Other approaches are discussed by Weltner (1971, 1976).

3. The search for E affects decisions as to whether to build or convert a school and with what facilities, or whether to let pupils study a foreign language abroad, take a child into institutional care, etc.

4. The search for L affects decisions as to whether or not to admit a student to a specific university, send an executive to an advanced management training course, etc.

5. The search for T affects decisions as to whether to teach a subject matter through a live teacher or use a programmed book or a teaching machine or a film, etc.

Establishing the general criteria and procedures for each of these decisions is the task of an existing or potential subdiscipline of educational technology. In reality, the search for the "unknown variable" is usually a little more complicated. Usually less than five variables are rigidly fixed. One is the primary object of search, some can be manipulated within certain limits, and only one or two may be unalterable.

The search for a teaching algorithm, given values for the other variables, has been of particular interest in educational cybernetics. In particular, attempts have been made to get computers to assist as much as possible in the construction of the teaching algorithm (writing of teaching program, lesson preparation). These attempts are described below (see section on application of educational cybernetics).

Among the subvariables of "learning system" are the prior knowledge of the subject matter and of relevant skills and information outside the subject matter. Prior knowledge has to be specified not only in the terms of the subject-matter elements which are supposed to be known at the beginning of the teaching process but also in terms of the "quality of knowledge and skill," i.e., how well each subject-matter element is mastered. In other words, the subvariables of prior knowledge are the same as those of the target standard. We can therefore follow Landa (1968) and simply speak about each pupil's initial state and his final state. It is hoped that the final state is as close as possible to the target state. Final state and target state can be split into two different states, namely, the state reached, or to be reached, at the end of the teaching process (postinstruction state) and that reached, or to be reached, at the end of the desired retention period (postretention period). (The concept of retention period is explained in Sánchez Carrasco and Bung, 1977.) The values of the learner's state drop after the end of instruction, first very rapidly and then with ever-decreasing speed. In order to guarantee a specific postretention state, the teaching process must aim at, and achieve, a postinstruction state with values which are higher than those demanded in the postretention state. The longer the desired retention period and the higher the desired values of the postretention state, the higher the values of the postinstruction state have to be. We can now view the teaching process simply as a transformation of the initial state into the postinstruction state (under the influence of the [teaching system + teaching algorithm] and the environment) and its continued transformation into the postretention state (under the influence of the environment, including the processes of forgetting). The process and the desired, or actual, changes in value can be represented as a matrix (Fig. 21). In our examples of the values, we have confined ourselves to representing the success rate (percentage of correct responses). The model can easily be extended to accommodate the other subvariables discussed in the literature and additional subvariables felt to be desirable for a specific practical purpose.

It is easy to see that the model can be extended by adding a time axis to the didactic variables and specifying desired-state values in relation to specific points on this axis. At least the three states contained in the state matrix (Fig. 21) should be specified, but it may also be of interest to demand that specific intermediate states between the initial state and the postinstruction state should be reached at specific points of time.

Information Theory. The most important concepts of the model of communciation are transmitter, receiver, and channel (Figure 22). The transmitter transmits a message to a receiver through a channel. A message is a sequence of signs, and the basic concepts of the theory of signs are applied to messages. Materially, the signs are represented by signals. We distinguish syntax (formal rules for chaining signs together), semantics (study of the contents of the message) and pragmatics (study of the way the message affects the behavior of the recipient). By investigating the relative frequencies of signs and chains of signs in a language (being a potentially infinite set of messages), one can, according to Shannon and Weaver (1949), define the concept of entropy as the average information (uncertainty, novelty value) per sign. We thus have a measure for the magnitude of messages; i.e., we assign an information value (novelty value) of n times the entropy of the language to a message consisting of n signs. The unit of this measure is called "bit" (*bi*nary dig*it*). If, in such investigations, we take strings of signs rather than simple signs as our elements, we obtain, with increasing length of these strings, a lim-

Figure 21
State Matrix

	Initial state	Postinstruction state		Postretention state	
		Target	Real	Target	Real
Subject-matter element 1	12%	72%	61%	66%	56%
Subject-matter element 2	6%	78%	90%	72%	83%
Subject-matter element 3	9%	86%	98%	79%	90%
etc.					

Figure 22
Communication Model of Information Theory

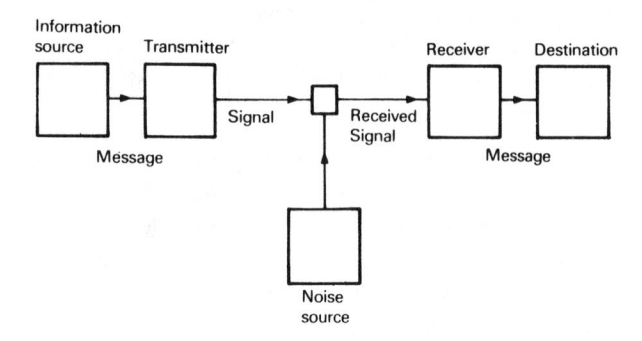

iting value of entropy, which can be used for further applications. Entropy can be interpreted as a measure of the uncertainty which occurs if one tries to guess the next letter (sign) of a message after having been given an initial passage. The basic theorems of information theory refer to the problem of how to transmit messages free of interference when the entropy of the given language and the channel capacity are known. The channel capacity is a fixed feature of the transmission channel, related to the number of signs it can transmit per unit of time.

Information Psychology. One of several models of the learning system (learner) and especially of its learning characteristic developed by Frank (1969b, 1977) and other educational cyberneticians is "information psychology." Learning is regarded as information processing. The human brain works with a pacer (central clock) which is characterized by the "subjective time quantum" (STQ = 1/6 sec). The so-called span of consciousness is about T = 10 sec. Messages are fed into the short-term store (consciousness) with a speed of apperception of C_s = 16 bit/sec = 1 bit/STQ. The storage capacity K_s cannot exceed the size of the product $C_s \times T$ = 160 bit. Learning is an interaction of short-term store and preconscious memory. Preconscous memory is characterized by the so-called learning speed C_p = 0.7 bit/sec. Preconscious memory is divided into short-term memory and long-term memory.

The sample space (i.e., set of alternatives with a probability measure attached) which forms the basis of the concept of (objective) information (uncertainty/novelty value) can differ from the sample space of the recipient. Investigating this individual sample space, one can introduce the analogous concepts of "subjective entropy" and "subjective information." In the information psychological model, learning is based on the process of "informational adaptation." During this process, subjective information approaches objective information and manifests itself in the reduction of the average time of apperception. In this context, one also investigates the processes of forgetting and the curve of learning (in relation to the age of the learner).

Educational Applications of Information Psychology. Inspired by the guessing procedures of Shannon (1951), Weltner (1974a) developed various guessing experiments which enable us to estimate the subjective information of texts whose content is to be learned and to measure the quantity of information ("didactic transinformation") transmitted to, and learned by, a learner during a teaching process. The didactic transinformation is the difference between the subjective information of a subject-matter summary before and after a teaching process.

Anschütz (1970) had the idea to number all new concepts that are introduced in a teaching program and to pair them (in a system of coordinates) with the numbers of the teaching steps (frames). The result is the so-called m-i Diagram. If one knows the subjective information of the concepts, one can use the instruments of information psychology in order to show how best to organize a teaching program into teaching steps, how often and when to revise each concept, etc. (Hilgers, 1976).

Frank (1966b, pp. 109–111) further developed Anschütz's technique and produced the so-called w-t Diagram in order to largely automate this process of program planning. The computer stores the first 1,500 words of the general frequency dictionary of a language (the so-called trivial words). All other words occurring in the subject-matter summary are regarded as nontrivial, i.e., as concepts in the sense of Anschütz's m-i Diagram and are arranged into time spans (10 seconds of 40 syllables each). The number and moments of repetition/revision are determined by the computer.

With these aids, the division of the subject matter into teaching steps can be explained in a less arbitrary way than would otherwise be possible.

Unlike other approaches (Lewis and Pask, 1965; Bung, 1972; or classical programmed instruction à la Skinner, 1969; Crowder, 1963; or Gilbert, 1969), information psychology sets out by establishing a fairly fixed model of the learning system (conceived as the average of a set of learners: target population) and develops the teaching program in advance of the teaching process (program presentation) to suit the model. Pask (1971) sets out with an (adaptive) teaching system that is largely ignorant about the learner, has a learning algorithm which enables it to build up a model of the *specific learner* which it teaches, and adjusts its teaching algorithm (the messages it transmits to the learner) accordingly and minutely (Ballanti, 1974, p. 409). Bung (1967a, 1972, 1975a) equips the learning system with a learning algorithm which enables it to carry out, during the presentation phase, many of the functions which Pask assigns to his adaptive teaching systems instead. Classical programmed instruction (at least in its most radical forms) does not have any model/theory about the learning system at all (Skinner, 1950, 1969; Crowder, 1963; Kelbert, 1964) but develops effective teaching programs by a system that is, at least professedly (cf. Frank, 1966b, p. 72), one of trial and error—(cycles of try-out, improvement, try-out, etc. (Figure 23).

Redundancy Theory of Learning. Entropy (= novelty value = information content), H, would have the highest value in a language in which all signs occurred with the same probability (frequency). The difference between this maximally possible entropy, H, and the actual entropy, B, of a language is called absolute redundancy, R:

$$R = H - B$$

The relative redundancy, ρ, of a language is the proportion of absolute redundancy, R, to maximally possible entropy, H:

$$\rho = R \div H$$

The information content (novelty value) of a message for a specific learner depends on the prior knowledge of the learner and varies from person to person. This information content (seen in relation to a specific message *and* a specific learner) can be determined through guessing experiments of the Shannon (1951) and Weltner (1974a) type. The percentage of signs in a text which a learner fails to guess is the "relative subjective information," i, of the text in respect to this learner. Cor-

Figure 23
Different Ways of Adjusting Content of Instruction to the Learner

Name	School	When adjusted	Homogeneity of learning system (target population)	Teaching sequence selected by	Method of programme development
Frank Lánsky	Cybernetics/ information psychology	Before presentation	Several persons	Teaching system	Each newly constructed teaching step (frame) tested against model of learning system
Pask	Cybernetics adaptive teaching systems	During presentation	One person	ditto	Each newly constructed teaching step tested against concrete learning system
Bung	Cybernetics/ AALP* model	ditto	One person	Learning system	ditto
Skinner, Crowder, Gilbert	Behaviourism	Before presentation	Several persons	Teaching system	Trial and error: complete programme tested against concrete learning system

* 'Adaptive Algorithmic Language Programming'

respondingly, we obtain the "relative subjective redundancy," r, of a text:

r = 100 - i

The redundancy theory of learning (Cube, 1961, 1963, 1965; Cube and Gunzenhäuser, 1961; Lánský and Polák, 1977) defines learning as the process of maximizing the subjective redundancy of the subject matter to be learned (Pask, 1971, p. 309: "... learning is a process that *tends* to *reduce* the subjective uncertainty..."). Cube's theory contains a model of the formation of supersigns during learning processes. Supersigns are either unordered sets of signs or strings of signs. We view an unordered set of signs as a supersign when, for instance, we abstract from the differences among various children and simply call them all "children" or if we abstract from the objective difference of the initial sounds in the words "cup," "cock," and "cool" and treat them all as the phoneme /k/ (Meyer-Eppler, 1969). We view an ordered set (string) of signs as a supersign if we read the word "horse" in "My kingdom for a horse" as one unit rather than as the letter sequence h-o-r-s-e or if we discuss Shakespeare's *Richard III* as one unit rather than as the set of all the sentences (or letters) it contains.

Once we have learned to treat a set of signs as a supersign, the supersign has a lower information value than the set of signs (subsigns) of which it consists. Accordingly, Cube has proposed a formula for the information of supersigns and the corresponding concept of "redundancy of supersigns." Staniland (1966, chap. 16) treats the same phenomena, without reference to Frank and Cube. Lánský (1967a, 1967b) has developed a measure for the information of supersigns in hierarchical stages (see also Stever, 1971, 1973). The experimental results in this field of research have been used by Polak (1973, 1974) as the basis of an algorithm which determines the degree of difficulty of explanations.

Algorithm theory. The term *algorithm,* once only understood and fairly precisely defined by mathematicians, has become quite popular in recent years, but the corresponding concept has lost some of its former precision as a result. We therefore begin by setting out some basic concepts and terms which are needed to define an "algorithm." The set (house, houses) is a set of two elements. Any set of two elements is called a *pair*. The first element of a pair is called its "first coordinate" and the second its "second coordinate." α (below) is a set of pairs, represented in the form of a graph (Figure 24). The arrows indicate which is the second coordinate that belongs to each first coordinate. α is a set of pairs. A set of pairs is called a *relation*. α is therefore a relation. The set of first coordinates of a relation is called its *domain* (or "input set") and the set of second coordinates its *range* (or "output set"). Each element of the domain can be called "input word" and each element of the range "output word." α could also have been written in linear form: α = ([house, houses], [hat, hats], [mother, mothers], ...). Some relations can be given colloquial names such as the "is the singular of" relation (α), or the "is the capital of" (β), "was written by" (γ), "is a place in" (ϵ), "is the author of" (ζ), "is spelled" (η) relations. Others may be purely arbitrary associations (θ). The essential thing about a relation is not the inferences that can be drawn from its colloquial name but the set of pairs actually written out or indicated by a precise formula.

In the relations α, β, γ, δ, η, θ, once the input word is known, it is unambiguously clear which is the corresponding output word. Each input word in these relations is associated with exactly one output word. In the graph representation of a relation this shows itself in the fact that from every element of the domain, exactly one arrow emanates. Such a relation is called a *mapping*. All other relations, such as ϵ and ζ, are nonmappings. Definition: A mapping is a relation whose distinct second coordinates have distinct first coordinates.

Given a mapping and one of its input words, the process of finding the associated output word is called a *transformation:* the input word is transformed into the output word. The transformation can be the result of some fairly general process such as in δ where the input word will be squared and 2 be added to obtain the output word. Or the transformation may be the result of a very specific process where a list has to be consulted in each instance in order to obtain the output word (e.g., θ). Or the process may have a number of parts, some of which are fairly general and others extremely particular, as in the case of α. Such a procedure which assigns the plural to the set of all Spanish nouns (including the so-called exceptions) has been published in Bung (1971b).

A procedure which determines for each input word of a mapping the associated output word (i.e., a procedure which specifies a transformation as defined above) is called a *quasi-algorithm*. Note that quasi-algorithms do not specify the associations in nonmappings. The latter are described by nonalgorithmic or probabilistic procedures.

Quasi-algorithms consist of two types of elements: discriminators, which determine the state of the input word, and operators, which alter it in one or several steps in order to yield the output word. If all discriminators of a quasi-algorithm are confined to determining the presence or absence of certain symbols (letters, digits, etc.) and of certain configurations of symbols in the input word, and all operators of the quasi-algorithms are con-

**Figure 24
Relations**

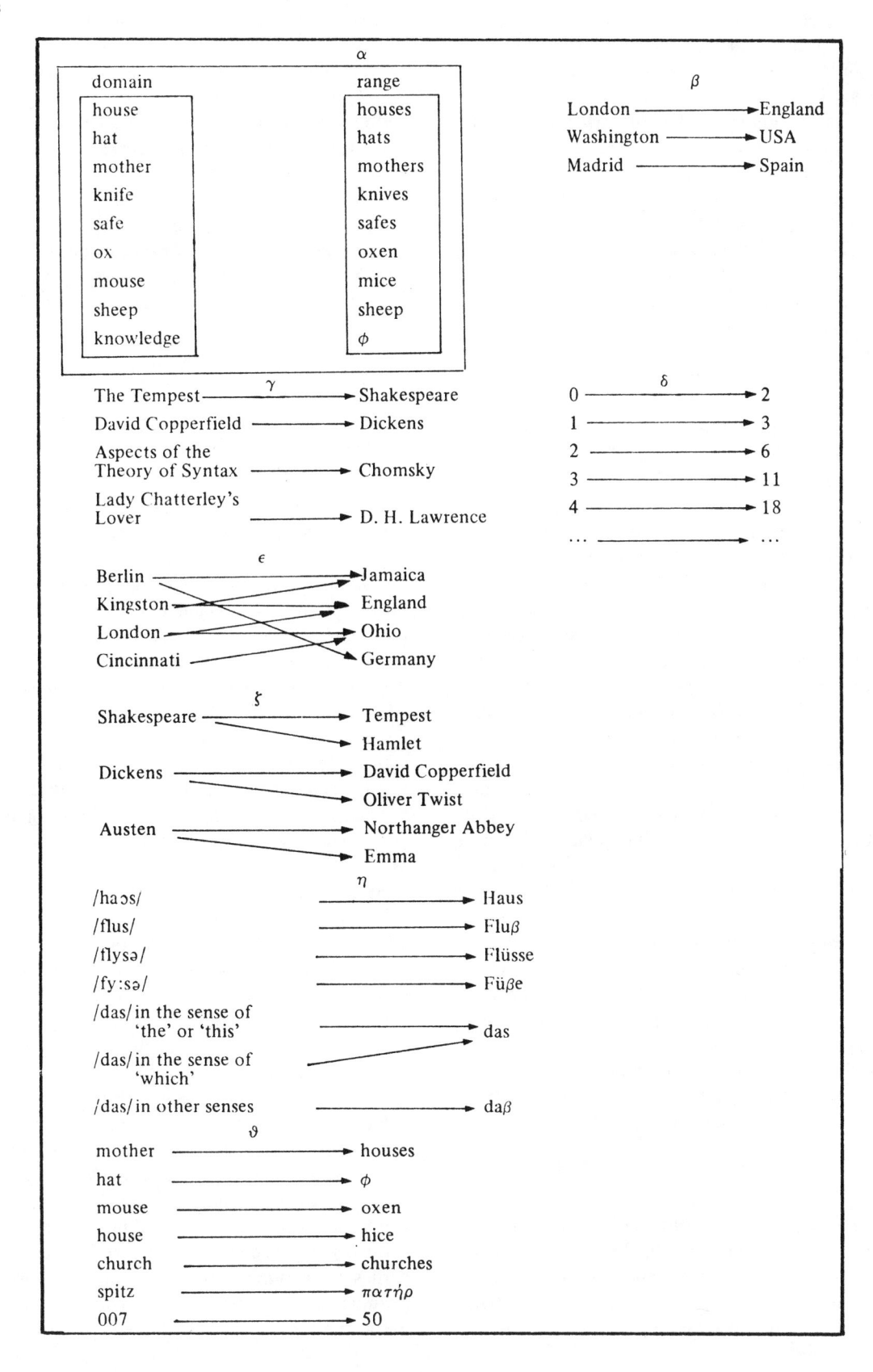

α

domain	range
house	houses
hat	hats
mother	mothers
knife	knives
safe	safes
ox	oxen
mouse	mice
sheep	sheep
knowledge	φ

β

London ⟶ England
Washington ⟶ USA
Madrid ⟶ Spain

γ

The Tempest ⟶ Shakespeare
David Copperfield ⟶ Dickens
Aspects of the Theory of Syntax ⟶ Chomsky
Lady Chatterley's Lover ⟶ D. H. Lawrence

δ

0 ⟶ 2
1 ⟶ 3
2 ⟶ 6
3 ⟶ 11
4 ⟶ 18
… ⟶ …

ε

Berlin ⟶ Jamaica
Kingston ⟶ England
London ⟶ Ohio
Cincinnati ⟶ Germany

ζ

Shakespeare ⟶ Tempest
 ⟶ Hamlet
Dickens ⟶ David Copperfield
 ⟶ Oliver Twist
Austen ⟶ Northanger Abbey
 ⟶ Emma

η

/haɔs/ ⟶ Haus
/flus/ ⟶ Fluß
/flysə/ ⟶ Flüsse
/fy:sə/ ⟶ Füße
/das/ in the sense of 'the' or 'this' ⟶ das
/das/ in the sense of 'which' ⟶ das
/das/ in other senses ⟶ daß

ϑ

mother ⟶ houses
hat ⟶ φ
mouse ⟶ oxen
house ⟶ hice
church ⟶ churches
spitz ⟶ πατήρ
007 ⟶ 50

fined to replacing the given symbols by others or to permutating or deleting them, we say that the quasi-algorithm specifies an *alphabetic* transformation. A quasi-algorithm which specifies an alphabetic transformation is called an *algorithm*.

The quasi-algorithm which specifies η has to determine whether /das/ is used in a certain sense. This cannot be done by determining the alphabetic configurations of the input word. η is therefore no algorithm but only a quasi-algorithm. The quasi-algorithm associated with η (which specifies how to spell the German sound /s/) can be found in Bung (1975a, pp. 161–168).

Every algorithm is a quasi-algorithm but not vice versa. Some quasi-algorithms can be executed by computers *and* humans, and others (nonalgorithms such as η) only by humans. The effectiveness of algorithms is absolute, i.e., given a specific input, they always generate the same output. The effectiveness of quasi-algorithms, however, is relative and can be specified for each set of values of the didactic variables in terms of a percentage, p, where $0 < p < 1$. For any given quasi-algorithm, p depends on the prior knowledge of the learner (and on the other subvariables of the "learning system"). It also depends on the input set to which the quasi-algorithm is applied, i.e., on the subject matter. For instance, a young pupil who uses a subject-matter algorithm to decide which of the words on a given page are nouns and which are not may be 95 percent (p = 0.95) successful if he applies the subject-matter algorithm to a page in a children's primer and only 73 percent successful if he applies the same subject-matter algorithm to a page from a novel by Dickens. Similarly, a subject-matter algorithm designed to have a success rate of p = 0.9 when used by adults of a certain group may show a success rate of only p = 0.35 when used by children. This is the "*p*rinciple of *r*elativity *i*n *q*uasi-algorithms" (PRIQ).

While many algorithms apply to fairly large input sets and either partition these or transform their elements in various other ways, Bung (1971a) has argued that paired-associate learning and copying activities are also algorithmic in character because they differ from the activities traditionally described as algorithmic (or quasi-algorithmic) only in the fact that their input sets are smaller and often restricted to only one element.

Types of Algorithms in Educational Cybernetics.

Teaching algorithms. A vector (Ashby, 1965, pp. 30–41; Landa, 1968, pp. 88–90; Bung, 1972) describing the state of a learner can be viewed stripped of all its semantic connotations and regarded merely as a string of symbols, basically no different from the input and output words occurring in the relations α to Θ (Fig. 22). A teaching process can be regarded as a transformation of the initial vector (input word) into a target vector (output word). A procedure which specifies step by step the changes the initial vector must undergo to turn into the target vector and the operations by which these changes are brought about can be regarded as an algorithm, or, more specifically, as a *teaching algorithm*. From this fairly formal definition of "teaching algorithm" (cf. also Frank, 1964c), we can derive a more popular explanation. A teaching algorithm is a set of instructions to the teaching system which refers to a set of teaching steps (frames) and determines which of these the teaching system has to transmit

(a) to initiate the process of instruction (exactly one "initial teaching step")

(b) as a reaction to any specific response which has come in from the learning system, or learner (example: Landa, 1968, p. 72; Fierli, 1974, p. 492ff.)

Since, at a certain level of abstraction, an algorithm and the (abstract) automaton which executes (embodies) it are identical, the concepts of teaching system and teaching algorithm cannot always be clearly distinguished. Especially in Pask's adaptive teaching systems (see below, applications of educational cybernetics), it is not always easy to assign certain functions clearly to one or the other. Fierli (1974, p. 499) abolished the distinction, while Bung (1975a, pp. 78–81) argued in its favor. Obviously, some open questions remain which must be solved if the general theory of educational cybernetics is to account adequately, as it should, not only for the Frank approach but also for the Pask and other approaches.

Learning algorithms. A set of instructions stored by, and addressed to, the learner and specifying the operations he must carry out in order to assimilate the material transmitted to him during the last teaching step is called a *learning algorithm*. Knowledge or mastery of a learning algorithm may be more or less explicit and more or less conscious. It enables the learner to control his learning activities independently and purposefully until he receives the next teaching step from the teaching system or until he has achieved his objectives.

In a teaching process, defined by a set of compatible values of the didactic variables, there is a trading relationship between teaching algorithms and learning algorithms (Bung, 1972). Other variables being equal, the more effective the learning algorithms used by the learner, the simpler, shorter and less expensive may the corresponding teaching algorithm be. (This principle underlies much current educational work concentrating on learning activities rather than teaching activities.) Similarly, the less efficient the learning algorithm used by the learner, the more complex, detailed, long, and powerful does the corresponding teaching algorithm have to be if a specific target standard is to be reached. (This principle explains the basic response of classical programmed instruction [Skinner, 1954] to unsatisfactory pupil performance.) All failure to learn is due to the learner's unwillingness or inability to apply the required learning algorithms to the subject matter (Bung, 1972; Illich, 1971).

Subject-matter algorithms. Apart from teaching algorithms and learning algorithms, we have a third, quite distinct, type of algorithm, the *subject-matter algorithm*. This specifies procedures which the learner has to master (the "subject matter" to be learned by him) and which are algorithmic in character. They are often loosely referred to as "algorithms" (see special entry **Algorithm** in this encyclopedia). Many subject-matter *algorithms* are in fact only *quasi-algorithms*.

A teaching algorithm can be the vehicle through which a subject-matter algorithm is taught to a learner, and a learning algorithm can facilitate the learning of a subject-matter algorithm. Effective learning algorithms, once discovered or developed, can also be taught. When this happens (e.g., in classes on "study skills"), the subject-matter algorithm *IS* a learning algorithm.

The trinity of teaching algorithm, learning algorithm, and subject-matter algorithm was first conceived as an integrated system in Bung (1969a) and fully set out in Bung (1972). The literature on, and examples of, algorithms of various kinds can be tracked down through Trakhtenbrot (1963), Lewis, Horabin, and Gane (1967), Lánský (1969), Lewis (1970), Bung (1971b, 1972, 1975a, 1977), Lariccia, (1972), Landa (1974), and Sánchez Carrasco (1975).

Automata Theory. The theory of abstract automata, started in the United States by Mealy (1955) and Moore (1956), was synthetized in the USSR by Glushkov (= Gluschkow) and first applied to teaching and learning processes by Kelbert in 1964.

Fundamental concepts of automata theory. The mathematical structure of a system with input, output and a set of states (black box) is called an *abstract automaton* (Gluschkow, 1963; Glushkov, 1966; Starke, 1969). We use the term *sample space* for a vector (A, P) whose components are ordered pairs $(a_i, p(a_i))$ such that $a_i \in A$ is a letter from any alphabet and $p_i \in P$ is a probability associated with a_i, where $0 \leq p_i \leq 1$ and $\sum_i^n p_i = 1$. An abstract automaton, L, is defined as a quintuple (X, Y, Z, δ, λ), whose components have the following meanings. X is the input alphabet (i.e., the set of input letters x_i) which L can distinguish. Y is the set of output letters y_i. X and Y each contain the empty letter, Ø. Z is the set of the automaton's internal states z_i (state alphabet). The automaton functions in discrete time intervals ("instants"), $t = 0, 1, 2, \ldots$. At instant t, the automaton is in state z_t and receives an input letter x_t (which may be the empty letter). The transition function δ maps the pair (z_t, x_t) into a sample space (Z, P), whose components are ordered pairs $(z_{t+1}, p(z_{t+1}))$, where z_{t+1} is a possible state of the automaton at instant $t + 1$ and $p(z_{t+1})$ is the probability that the automaton will move to that state. The sample space (A, P) lists all states z_i of L and associates the probability of $p = 0$ with those states which L cannot assume in the given circumstances. The output function λ maps the pair (z_t, x_t) into a sample space (Y, P) whose components are ordered pairs $(y_{t+1}, p(y_{t+1}))$, where y_{t+1} is a possible output letter of L at instant $t + 1$ and $p(y_{t+1})$ is the probability that L will produce that output letter. Equivalent to the above description of the transition and output function is the following: δ and λ map the Cartesian product of Z and X into the sample spaces (Z, P) and (Y, P) respectively.

If the set P contains only the elements 0 and 1, the sample space (Z, P) is called a deterministic element in L. If L contains only deterministic elements, L is called a *deterministic automaton*. The set of deterministic automata is therefore a subset of the set of probabilistic automata. Any probabilistic automaton which is not a deterministic automaton is called a *nondeterministic automaton*.

Behaviorist programmed learning theory (if there is any) declines any interest in Z and δ, and confines itself to studying the mapping φ which L induces from X to Y. φ maps x_i into a sample space (Y, P) which is characterized as above. φ is called the automaton mapping (Gluschkow, 1963, p. 23). While the triple (X, Y, φ) is uniquely determined by the quintuple (X, Y, Z, δ, λ), the reverse is not the case.

We can now summarize the above definitions:

$L = (X, Y, Z, δ, λ)$

$X = \{x_1, x_2, \ldots\}$

$Y = \{y_1, y_2, \ldots\}$

$Z = \{z_1, z_2, \ldots\}$

$P = \{p_1, p_2, \ldots\} \mid (0 \leq p_i \leq 1, \sum_i^n p_i = 1)$

$δ: Z \times X \rightarrow (Z, P)$

$λ: Z \times X \rightarrow (Y, P)$

$φ: X \rightarrow (Y, P)$

As a rule, transition and output functions are specified in the form of a merged matrix (automaton table) which is composed as follows. The transition function is written as a matrix $T = (t_{ij})$ of the type (m,n) where each row represents an input letter x_i and each column a state z_j. Then t_{ij} represents the state to which the automaton moves

Figure 25
Transition Matrix, T

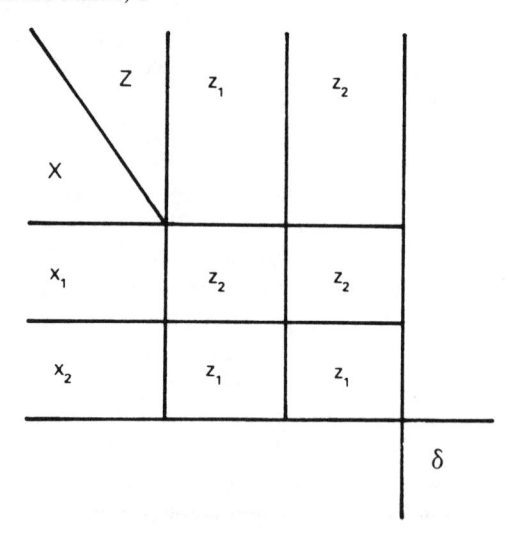

Z \ X	z_1	z_2
x_1	z_2	z_2
x_2	z_1	z_1

δ

when it is in state z_j and receives input letter x_i (see Figure 25).

Similarly, the output function is written as a matrix $O = (o_{ij})$ of the type (m,n) where each row represents an input letter x_i and each column a state z_j. Then o_{ij} represents the output letter which the automaton produces when it is in z_j and receives x_i (see Figure 26).

The transition matrix and the output matrix can be merged into a matrix $M = (m_{ij})$ where rows and columns have the same values as in T and O and (m_{ij}) has the form (δ/λ) where δ represents the new state and λ the output letter (see Figure 27).

The following, very simple, example of an automaton modeling the behavior of a teacher (i.e., modeling a teaching algorithm) has been taken from Fierli (1974).

Figure 26
Output Matrix, O

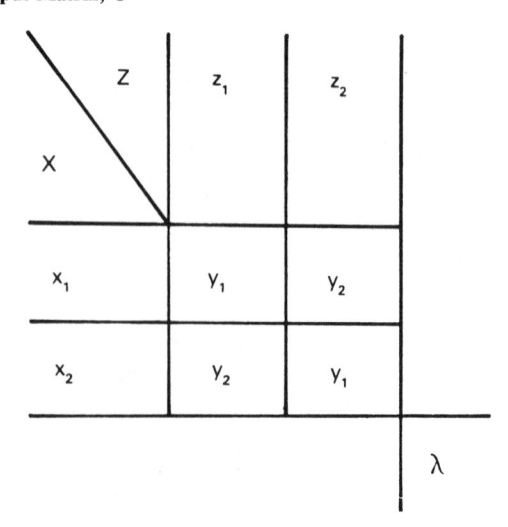

Z \ X	z_1	z_2
x_1	y_1	y_2
x_2	y_2	y_1

λ

Figure 27
Merged Matrix ("Automaton Table"), M

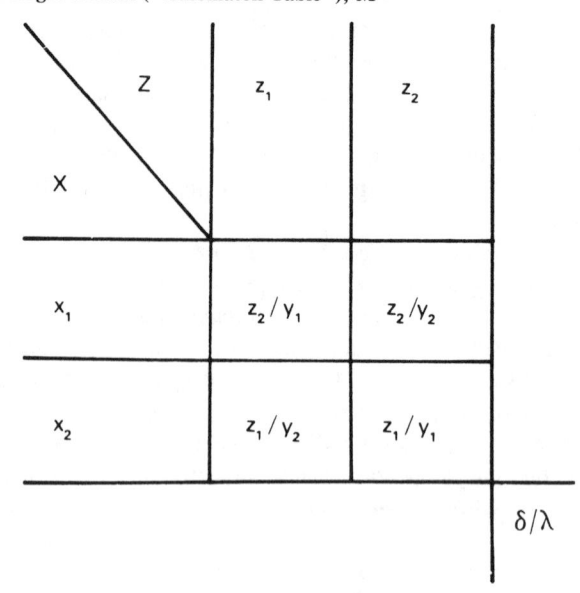

Z \ X	z_1	z_2
x_1	z_2/y_1	z_2/y_2
x_2	z_1/y_2	z_1/y_1

δ/λ

Assume that this teacher confines his activities to presenting his pupil with tasks taken from two sets:

- set d, containing "difficult" tasks, and
- set e, containing "easy" tasks

The corresponding automaton, A, therefore has an output alphabet $Z = (d, e)$. The teacher receives the pupil's responses and marks them

- either "right" (r) or
- "wrong" (w)

A therefore has an input alphabet $X = (r, w)$. The teacher tries to make up his mind on whether the pupil has reached his objectives or not. In this respect, the teacher can be in one of three states of mind:

- "positive" (p)
- "undecided" (u) or
- "negative" (n)

i.e., A has a state alphabet $Z = (p, u, n)$. The teacher behaves in accordance with the following teaching algorithm: when he is in state n and receives a wrong response, he presents the next task from set e and remains in state n. When he is in state n and receives a correct response, he moves to state u (one step toward "positive" = "objectives achieved") but still presents the next task from set e. When he is in state u and receives a wrong response, he moves to state n and presents a task from set e. When he is in state u and receives a correct response, he moves to state p and presents a task from set d. When he is state p and receives a wrong response, he moves to state u and presents a task from

Figure 28
Automaton Table of the Fierli Automaton

X \ Z	p	u	n
r	p/∅	p/d	u/e
w	u/d	n/e	n/e
			δ/λ

set d. When he is in state p and receives a correct response, he decides that the pupil has achieved his objectives and stops presenting further tasks (formally, the automaton puts out the empty letter, ∅, and remains in state p). This teaching algorithm can be unambiguously described through the automaton table in Figure 28.

This example also shows the close link between algorithms and automata. (Another example of a teaching algorithm—how to teach the concept of "circle"—with quite a different kind of notation/presentation can be found in Landa, 1968, p. 72.)

Uses of automata theory. The attempts to describe teaching and learning systems as abstract automata make research and development work in this area easier to integrate. The teaching and learning models which have been conceived in this way are programmed for computers and are particularly suitable for simulating teaching and learning processes and teaching situations in the field of computer-assisted lesson preparation. Automata theory was used by Frank (1964c) for his definition of teaching algorithm. It is also used to make precise descriptions of various learning models. The so-called BETARO-automaton (Lánský, 1972a; Doberkat, 1975) is characterized by having a split input, consisting of a general input and a reinforcement input. By specifying, for any BETARO-automaton, a reinforcement schedule and a set of objectives, the BETARO-automaton becomes a learning automaton (Lánský, 1967b). Its sibling in the interplay of two automata is called *teaching automaton.* The first interpretations of American learning models as probabilistic learning automata were made by Koller (1975a, 1975b). Steinbuch's learning matrix (Steinbuch, 1961a, 1961b, 1965; Steinbuch and Frank, 1961; Steinbuch and Lipp, 1965) and the work of Feichtinger (1968a, 1968b) belong to the same area of work.

Lánský (1970) used automata theory to model the changing states of a learning system as the computer simulates the presentation of a teaching program. The result is a computer program which greatly facilitates the construction of teaching programs. Frank (1966b) used automata theory for similar purposes but modeled the learning system in a different way.

Lánský (1972a) developed a model in which a small group of students and a teaching machine together form a learning automaton. New developments for probabilistic learning models using the theory of dynamic optimization are due to Doberkat (1975).

Bung (1975a) used automata theory in order to construct a model that describes coherently various phenomena occurring in verbal behavior such as understanding, speaking (or writing) one language, understanding without being able to speak/write (dumb illiterate), repeating utterances with or without understanding, speaking two languages without being able to translate, translating, foreign language learning given a grammar, foreign language learning by discovery methods, etc.

Conversation Theory. We shall present this theory informally, by describing a teaching process. All subject matters are relations. Known concepts are brought together to understand new ones, physical objects consist of components which are related, procedures consist of operations which are related, physical operations are used to create new relations or to sever existing ones. Thus everything that may be known or done is interpreted as a relation. Relations may be broken down into constituent relations or combined into higher-order relations. Relations may be presented as graphs (Harary et al., 1965). Each element in a relation can be given a label. This label is called *topic*. The logical presuppositions among the labeled elements in a relation (indicating potential learning sequences) are represented by a (partial order) graph, the so-called entailment structure, $D^1(R)$. Associated with each node in the entailment structure is a specification of the tasks which the node and its label refer to. These tasks can, for instance, be of the following types:

1. Give a description of the topic
2. Build/assemble/dismantle/repair/diagnose the object referred to
3. Carry out the following types of computation, etc.

The task specification is given in canonical form and has minimal redundancy. It may consist of one node or may itself be a partial order corresponding to only one node in the entailment structure. The set of all task specifications corresponding to an entailment structure can be interpreted as a partial order of logical presuppositions and represented as a graph. This graph is called the *task structure*, $D^0(R)$. The task structure includes subject-matter summaries and is sufficiently explicit to allow exercises and tests to be derived from it.

The objective of each teaching process is to enable the learner to *do* something, be it to make an object or to recite a definition or a poem. However, to prove that he will retain what he has learned (that learning was "stable"/effective), the learner must demonstrate that he also knows the theory underlying the task he has successfully carried out. The learner gives this demonstration by explaining and justifying the procedure to the teacher in terms of the topics (procedures) which immediately support it in the entailment structure. These topics in turn have to be explained in terms of their supporting concepts, and so on, until the topic has been traced back to the starting topics (procedures), i.e., those of which the learner was a master at the beginning of the teaching process. Such a demonstration is called *teachback*. The ability to carry out a relevant set of tasks accompanied by relevant teachback is called "understanding" of a relation.

All successful learning leads to the ability to "construct" (= reconstruct = realize = satisfy) relations. We construct a relation if we execute a procedure which, for instance,

1. enumerates instances of the relation (e.g., construct a multiplication table, list the countries ruled by dictators and name the dictators)
2. can decide for any given phenomenon whether or not it is an element of the relation (e.g., underline all adjectives in a given text)
3. prove/demonstrate that a proposition (i.e., relation) is correct
4. construct the physical object that the proposition refers to (e.g., build a car)
5. execute the physical process named by the relation (e.g., drive a car)

A procedure which constructs a relation is called a *concept*. All concepts are interpreted as procedures. For example, a car is not a static entity but something that one makes or drives or dismantles or repairs or paints or writes a poem about or transforms into a work of modern art, etc. All successful learning thus leads to the acquisition of concepts. These concepts, if they are to be concepts, must be stable. A jackass who, by some rare accident, happens to sing, once, the aria of the Queen of the Night does not therefore have a concept of that aria. True concepts are stable and can therefore be recalled (reproduced). Once they have been recalled (or while they are being recalled), they can again be executed. When we recall a concept, we carry out a procedure that is distinct from the procedure denoted by the concept itself. This procedure is called *a memory*. It may be conscious or unconscious (intuitive). Among the conscious procedures are memory aids and the various pegging (mnemonic) systems which enable us to remember associations (relations) between faces and names, names and telephone numbers, or between one operation and its successor in a chain of operations (procedure). Other elements of what we are trying to recall come to us automatically. But the very fact that we may decide to remember something or even make an effort to remember something indicates that viewing memory as a procedure agrees with our intuitions and largely agrees with everyday language. A memory is therefore a "procedure for reconstructing a concept." A concept is a "procedure for constructing a relation." There can be no concept without memory and no memory without concept. Both memory and concept are seen in dynamic rather than static (storage) terms. All successful learning leads to the construction of memories and concepts.

Learning processes (= here "teaching processes") depend on an interaction between individuals (e.g., T and L) which leads to the transfer of relations (procedures) from one individual to the other. For characterizing the learning process it is therefore of vital importance which memories and concepts T and L have. A specification of these is called a psychological characterization of the individual. An individual viewed in these terms is called a "P-individual." It is also possible to characterize an individual by the physical substance and physical configuration (device) which carries out the processes. An individual viewed in these terms is called a mechanically characterized individual ("M-individual"). M-individuals need not be humans but can also be machines, configurations of machines, societies, etc. (cf. the speculative notion of an animate digital computer, whose elements are insects; Frank, 1971, p. 52).

In the following exposition of a learning process, we simplify matters by assuming that there is a clear distinction between the teacher, T, and the learner, L, and that both are human.

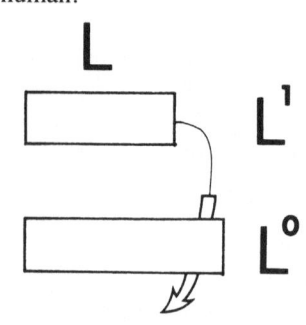

The above figure depicts an arbitrary P-individual, say L, characterized by two sets of procedures, each set represented by a box. The lower box represents the kinds of procedures which typically appear in the task structure. This "level" of the individual is therefore characterized by language L^0. The upper box represents procedures which the individual uses in order to trigger off L^0 procedures. These triggering procedures are carried out in terms of the (cognitive) entailment structure, and this level of the individual is therefore characterized by language L^0. The link from the L^1 box to the L^0 box represents the decision of the individual to carry out tasks associated with a given topic. The decision is one of the procedures in box L^1. The triggering effect of this decision on the appropriate procedure in the L^0 box is "causative" in the physical sense of the word. The causative nature of this coupling is denoted by the bold oblique arrow crossing box L^0. The transaction "Memory recalls a procedure" would also be represented by the same link.

The (mental) procedure (L^0 box) is not identical with the physical action that corresponds to it. The tools, components, and raw materials used for this action are called *modeling facility*. The modeling facility may be a device attached to a computer which allows the learner to make his responses and for them to be registered directly by the computer. Or it may consist of a box of spares out of which the learner is to make a simple radio receiver. Or it may be pencil and paper enabling the learner to write down an essay. The modeling facility is represented by the box at the base (level M) of the following figure. The coupling leading into the modeling facility is causative. The arrows coming out of ⊗ denote feedback.

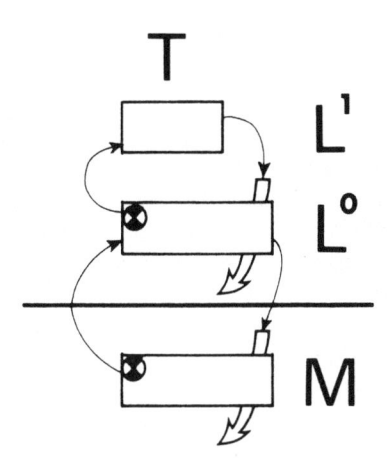

We now couple T with another individual, L, which is structurally identical (see the figure below). The horizontal arrows represent couplings in the form of utterances. Since these couplings are not causative in the physical sense, they are denoted by a symbol (light arrow) that is different from that used for causative couplings. The couplings established by utterances are called *provocative couplings*.

The topics which may be raised during the didactic conversation and their order are restricted by the entailment structure, $D^1(R)$, and the task structure, $D^0(R)$. Circles representing these structures are therefore placed over the interface (vertical broken bar) between L and T.

In the model of a teaching process, T may begin by telling L: "Do such and such" (i.e., construct relation R) (coupling at level L^0). If L cannot do so, T will establish L's baseline in the entailment structure, i.e., which topics he already understands. Once the baseline has been established, L can decide, within the constraints given by the entailment structure, which topics he wants to "aim" at and which subtopics of the aim he wants to make his learning "goal," a "goal" being an *immediate* learning objective. L can opt to make exploratory (superficial) contact with a topic before selecting his aim and his goals.

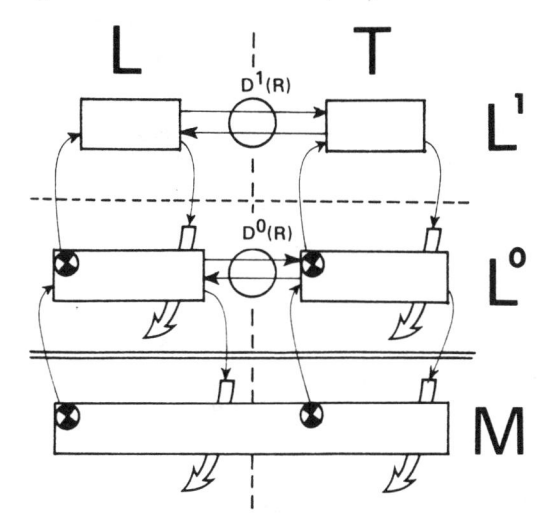

Conversation theory is much more elaborate, in its technical detail, experimental backing, and its present and potential applications, than the rudimentary notions explained here. Its creation is mainly due to Pask, who first formulated it in a paper of 1971 (published as Pask 1975b). Since the publications on conversation theory are highly technical, the following order of reading is recommended: Daniel, 1973, 1974, 1975; Pask, 1976c, 1976a; Systems Research Ltd., 1977a, 1977b; Pask, 1975c, 1975a, 1976b, 1961, 1972a; Pask and Scott, 1972, 1973; Pask, Scott, and Kallikourdis, 1973. *See also* **Conversation Theory.**

Conversation theory provides the foundation for a variety of applications, not only in education.

The strict conversation is a near minimal paradigm from which to start the discussion. But the theory itself applies to all conversations and, given the stricture that a conversation is the minimal unit for psychological observation, all of psychology (including its extrapolation into related areas of education, sociology, social anthropology, and the ecology of sentient beings; for example, architecture, as it deals with cities that are lived in; or information-science, with the rider that information is used whereas data is stored). (Pask, 1975a).

One of the concrete systems built for conducting teaching/learning conversations in accordance with conversational theory is CASTE (Course Assembly System and Tutorial Environment). CASTE provides facilities for

1. the more effective development of courses through a dialogue between a subject-matter expert and an experimenter, linked, aided, and recorded by a computer

2. teaching students various subject matters, especially of a fairly complex cognitive type in a manner which allows them a great degree of freedom in choosing their routes through the entailment and task structures (cf. the very similar notions of Bung, 1971a, 1973b, 1975a, pp. 208–225), thus producing dramatically superior learning results

3. conducting controlled experiments into learning processes covering subject matters of realistic bulk and complexity and extending over longer periods of time, by contrast with the small learning tasks to which behaviorist-oriented investigations have to be confined

In experiments with CASTE, it has been found that learners naturally adopt one of two distinct types of learning strategy and accordingly each learner can be labeled "holist" or "serialist." "The *holist* has many goals and working topics under his aim topic; the *serialist* has one goal and working topic, which may *be* the aim topic.... the holist is assimilating information from many topics in order to learn the 'aim' topic, while the serialist moves on to another topic only when he is completely certain about the one he is currently studying" (Pask, 1976a, p. 130). Teaching algorithms (e.g., courses) can be prepared in holist styles or serialist styles. "If learning takes place in a controlled system... the disparity between matched/mismatched instruction is dramatic. Mismatched students acquire hardly any relevant knowledge" (p. 132). More subtle distinctions have been established in the framework of conversation theory.

APPLICATIONS OF EDUCATIONAL CYBERNETICS

The didactic variables help to define six areas not only of educational research but also of educational development. To all these, educational cybernetics can, in principle, make contributions. In practice, the most important applications of educational cybernetics are in the following areas:

1. the development of special-purpose and universal teaching machines, including computers

2. the development of methods for mechanizing (automating) the construction of teaching programs and other types of teaching material (i.e., automating the process of "lesson preparation"), leading up to the computer-assisted *con*struction of teaching programs

3. the development of computer-assisted (or computer-controlled, etc.) presentation of teaching programs

Of these areas, we shall not discuss (3), as it is fully treated elsewhere in this encyclopaedia.

Development of Teaching Systems. In terms of the didactic variables, (1) is the task of constructing a compatible teaching system, T, given values for the variables, S, P, L, E, A. Such work is treated in general terms elsewhere in this encyclopaedia (see **teaching machines, computer-assisted instruction,** and **language laboratory**). The question arises which teaching systems (including teaching machines) should be regarded as an application of educational cybernetics. All teaching machines, even the simplest, can be interpreted in terms of automata theory; many can be constructed and teaching programs be written for them without automata theory or any of the concepts and techniques of educational cybernetics. However, with increasing complexity *and adaptivity* of the teaching systems to be designed, educational cybernetics becomes increasingly important—and ultimately indispensable for handling the complexities of highly adaptive teaching processes. We confine ourselves here to mentioning some of the more complex teaching systems which can claim to have been the outcome of cybernetic thinking.

Early attempts of designing teaching systems in the framework of educational cybernetics can be studied in various papers in Frank, ed., 1963, 1964b, 1965c, 1966c; see also survey in Meder, 1973). BAKKALAUREUS (Frank, 1969b, pp. 41–59) is a modular system of a variety of acoustic and optic presentation devices and teaching machines, many of which can function on their own or be combined with one another, possibly under the control of a small computer, and is intended to bring about the usual economies of modular systems. It includes a teaching machine for group learning with a general teaching algorithm which encourages cooperative behavior. In one particular configuration, TELE-ALZUDI, it is possible to transmit over post office telephone lines a list of paired associates, which are to be learned together with supplementary information, to a data processing center in a distant town and to receive, within twenty minutes or so, the printout of a linear program which teaches the pairs up to a specified target standard (see below for ALZUDI; Frank 1969b; Bung and Rouse, 1970). The printout is in a format in which it can be inserted into a linear teaching machine without any need for retyping.

A very sophisticated special-purpose machine is the Talking Typewriter (Edison Responsive Environment

Learning System, 1965), designed to teach reading and typing to children and used especially for mentally handicapped children (e.g., Moseley, 1971). The machine has an audio output enabling it to "pronounce" the names of the letter keys or of words or sentences to be typed; a visual output displaying letters, words, and sentences for copying; illustrative slides; and a key-locking device preventing wrong typing responses.

The UNITUTOR from Czechoslovakia (Stejskal, 1971a, 1971b; Meder, 1973) is a multipurpose, computer-independent teaching machine, perhaps the most sophisticated machine of its kind developed in Europe. It can present linear and branching programs, slides, synchronized sound, and moving film sequences. The didactic programmer has unusually great freedom for creating sophisticated branching sequences. Learner responses come through the usual special-purpose push buttons or a complete typewriter keyboard.

Adaptive teaching systems have always been a central concern of educational cybernetics. Various concepts of adaptivity and approaches have been proposed and tried out (Frank and Müller, 1964; Bung, 1967a, 1975a; Bung and Rouse, 1970, p. 186). The most persistent efforts in this field, however, have been made by Pask as from 1953 (Pask, 1960, 1961); Lewis and Pask, 1965). Pask's work in this field mainly led to the construction of machines for teaching psychomotor skills, such as card punching, continuous tracking, etc. The learning and teaching algorithms of his machines can be abstracted from the specific subject matters being taught and the input-output devices required by these. The same algorithms can thus be used "to instruct *any* subject matter that can be broken down into logically tractable stages" (Lewis and Pask, 1965, p. 242). They collect information about the learner's errors and latency (response time) over a span of the learning process and build up a model of the learner. In accordance with this model, they vary the problems, the speed at which fresh problems are presented and the intensity of cuing in such a way that the tasks given to the learner are neither too easy nor too difficult; i.e., the learner is well-motivated and always works at the highest level of his capacity.

The Computer-Assisted Construction of Teaching Programmes. The efforts in this field can be interpreted as the attempt to formalize (algorithmize) (as far as possible) the process of lesson preparation (= program writing, course development, etc.), i.e., to find a compatible "value" for the teaching algorithm, A, when "values" for the other didactic variables are given (Bung and Rouse, 1970). The purpose of this work is not only to make large quantities of teaching programs more quickly and cheaply available but to gain an insight into, and make explicit, the largely intuitive activities of teachers and educational authors and to test the validity of these insights by investigating the effectiveness of the teaching programs constructed through formal procedures.

The search for such procedures began in the field of subject-matter analysis (see references in Bung, 1976, p. 180ff.) The attempts to make the original "methods"/ "approaches" (which tended to be too vague or contradictory; see Lewis and Pask, 1965, pp. 213ff) more explicit lead to the development of semiformal and formal programming algorithms, so-called didactic mappings (German: *Formaldidaktiken),* by Frank and related work by Lánský.

The "manifesto" of all didactic mappings (Frank, 1966b) outlined a procedure, later named COGENDI (Blischke et al., 1968). In COGENDI, the computer is supplied with a minimal-redundancy "subject-matter summary" (set of assertions called "subject-matter elements"). The computer analyzes each subject-matter element, especially to determine its "information content" (degree of difficulty) for the projected target population. It determines the sequence of presentation (within the logical constraints specified by the sequence within the subject-matter summary) and the number of repetitions necessary for the target population with a given initial standard to achieve a specified target standard. The computer also inserts "connectors" (usually multiple-choice questions which lead from one step to the next) in appropriate places. The computer program simulates a *real-life* learning process by addressing a predetermined model of the learner (specified in terms of "information psychology" and with the tools of automata theory), calculating the changes of state within the learner model which information psychology predicts, and comparing these with the specified target state. The same simulation procedure underlies ALZUDI and ALSKINDI.

ALZUDI is a didactic mapping which is fully formalized but had to pay for this by restricting the set of possible subject matters to paired-associate learning. Frank's procedure is described in Bung and Rouse (1970). The computer receives a subject-matter summary in the form of a set of pairs to be learned, a number of interchangeable sentence frames into which the computer can embed these pairs and, for each pair, values for the learners' initial standard and the desired target standard. The computer calculates the information content (difficulty) of each pair, determines the sequence and repetitions of the pairs and, having received a format specification, prints out a linear program in a format ready to be inserted into a simple linear teaching machine.

ALSKINDI (*Al*gorithmic *Skin*ner *Di*dactics) processes a subject-matter summary which must be somewhat more redundant than those of COGENDI and ALZUDI since each sentence in the subject-matter summary is used as it stands in the teaching program to be generated. The computer (having received the summary and initial and target standards for each of its elements) introduces the elements one by one in the order in which they occur in the summary. It calculates the information content of the words occuring in the elements and uses these calculations as a basis for deciding which word to blank out in any one presentation of an element. Elements can be presented repeatedly, with the same or different words blanked out on different occasions. The blanks are to be filled by the learner in the customary Skinner style. The number of repetitions is determined by the same learner model as in COGENDI and ALZUDI and by the given initial and target standards. The printout is in a form ready for insertion into a simple linear teaching machine or for reproduction as a programmed book. It takes 20 to 40 minutes for the computer to generate a teaching program with a learning time of 30 to 45 minutes (Frank, 1969a; Arlt, 1970).

In reviewing didactic mappings and potential future developments, Graf (1973, 1974) notes that they have not satisfied the great expectations which were originally placed in them. One recurrent criticism is their high degree of monotony. However, they have been very important as catalysts to help theoreticians in developing explicit theories about educational processes and to help users (e.g., teachers ''ordering'' ''tailor-made'' computer-generated teaching program) to gain new insights into the nature of their objectives.

VERBAL (Lánský, 1970) exhibits an entirely different approach. It does not try to generate finished teaching programs but only program skeletons, consisting of a list of concepts to be treated in each teaching step including the necessary revisions. The teaching steps are then formulated by human program writers. The teaching program is viewed as a set of definitions, each consisting of one target concept (the concept to be explained) and supporting concepts. The input to VERBAL is a partial order of concepts indicating the logical support relation. For each target concept, the user (e.g., program writer or teacher) *estimates* the degree of difficulty and the initial standard for the target population and specifies a target standard. The learning model contains a function of learning and forgetting. The computer checks the input for flaws such as logical circularity of definitions, ambiguity (two different definitions for the same concept), and incompleteness (a concept not in the learners' initial repertoire has not been introduced as a target concept) and induces the human operator to put these right. The computer then generates a ''Euclidean order'' of concepts (i.e., of the type used in Euclid's ''Elements''), where each supporting concept (axiomatic ones apart) is defined before it serves to support another target concept. Concepts are repeated at optimal places in the list until their target standards have been reached. VERBAL is useful not only for the preparation of teaching programs, but also lectures and course materials of other kinds.

BIBLIOGRAPHICAL NOTE

In order to make the publications of non-English speaking authors accessible, we have referred to English translations or English reports of their work wherever possible. Where translations of German publications do not exist or have not been cited, it is worthwhile to search for related publications by the same authors in English and other European languages (see hints in Bung, 1976). Meder and Schmid (eds., 1973ff.) is an ongoing publication containing all nonbook publications by Frank and his collaborators, including many foreign language contributions. Englert et al., (1966) is useful as a reference work for mathematically minded readers and for the bibliographies attached to most entries. Frank and Hollenbach (1973) is a glossary of technical terms in German with existing or proposed foreign language translations. Seidel (1969) employs many of the concepts discussed in this entry (albeit different terms). Zierer (1970, and numerous other Spanish-language publications of his and his collaborators) applies various techniques of educational cybernetics to the theory of foreign language instruction. Nicklis (1967, 1969) is a fierce critic of educational cybernetics.

Klaus Bung and Miloš Lánský

REFERENCES

Anschütz, H. (1967) *Kybernetik kurz und bündig* (An outline of cybernetics). Kamprath-Reihe kurz und bündig series. Würzburg: Vogel-Verlag.

———. (1970) ''The Distribution of Concepts in Teaching Programmes.'' In *Recall: Review of Educational Cybernetics and Applied Linguistics* 1 (4–5): 122–140.

Apter, M. J. (1969) ''Cybernetics and Its Relevance to Education.'' In *Recall: Review of Educational Cybernetics and Applied Linguistics* (1): 7–24.

Arlt, W. (1970) ''ALSKINDI, eine Formaldidaktik zur automatischen Erzeugung von linearen Lehrprogrammen'' (ALSKINDI, a didactic mapping for the automatic generation of teaching programs). In *Perspektiven des Programmierten Unterrichts,* ed. B. Rollett and K. Weltner. Vienna, Austria: Wissenschaft und Kunst, pp. 237–240.

Ashby, W. R. (1965) *An Introduction to Cybernetics.* London: University Paperbacks.

Attneave, F. (1959) *Applications of Information Theory to Psychology: A Summary of Basic Concepts, Methods and Results.* New York: Holt, Rinehart & Winston.

Austwick, K. and Harris, N.D.C., eds. (1972) *International*

Yearbook of Education and Instructional Technology 1972/73. London: Pitman.

Ballanti, G. (1974) "Istruzione programmata e dispositivi autodidattici." In *Questioni di tecnologia didattica,* ed. R. Titone. Brescia, Italy: Editrice la Scuola, pp. 371–457.

Beishon, J. (1971) *Systems. Technology Foundation Course Unit 1.* Buckinghamshire, England: Open University Press.

The Bell System Technical Journal. Periodical. New York: American Telephone and Telegraph Company.

Bink, W.D.E. (1975) *Zur Sachstruktur des VHS-Zertifikats Mathematik* (The subject matter structure of the VHS certificate in mathematics). Arbeitshiffen für Kursleiter series. Frankfurt/Main, FRG: Pädagogische Arbeitsstelle des Deutschen Volkshocschul-Verbandes.

Blischke, H.; Hilbig, W.; and RuBmann, R. (1968) "Die Halbalgorithmische Formaldidaktik COGENDI" (The semi-formalized didactic mapping COGENDI). *Grundlagenstudien aus Kybernetik un Geisteswissenschaft* 9 (4): 97–110.

Boeckmann, K. (1971) "Basaltext und operationale Lernzieldefinition. Eine vergleichende Betrachtung ihrer Möglichkeiten" (Subject-matter summary and operational specification of objectives. A comparison of their possibilities). In *Fortschritte und Ergebnisse der Unterrichtstechnologie,* ed. B. Rollett and K. Weltner. Munich, FRG: Ehrenwirth Verlag, pp. 26–35.

British Journal of Educational Psychology. Periodical. Edinburgh, Scotland: Academic Press.

Bung, K. (1967a) "A Model for the Construction and Use of Adaptive Algorithmic Language Programmes." In *Problems and Methods in Programmed Learning,* ed. M. J. Tobin. Birmingham, England: National Centre for Programmed Learning, School of Education, University of Birmingham, pp. 108–114.

———. (1967b) *Programmed Learning and the Language Laboratory 2.* Collected papers by Klaus Bung. London: Longmac Ltd., Research Publications Services.

———. (1969a) "Prior Knowledge Analysis for Programmed Language Instruction." *Recall: Review of Educational Cybernetics and Applied Linguistics* 1 (3): 98–117.

———. (1971a) "The Concept of Partial Order in Programmed Language Instruction and the Freedom of the Consumer." *Programmed Learning and Educational Technology* 8: 22–23, 122–124.

———. (1971b) "A Cybernetic Approach to Programmed Language Instruction." *Educational Media International* no. 4: 24–31.

———. (1972) "Teaching Algorithms and Learning Algorithms." Paper presented to the Annual Conference of the Association for Programmed Learning and Educational Technology, held at the University of Bath, Somerset, England, 27–30 March 1972. Mimeographed.

———. (1973a) "Zur Neugestaltung von Helmar Franks didaktischen Variablen" (The redesign of Helmar Frank's didactic variables). In *Fortschritte und Ergebnisse der Bildungstechnologie 2,* ed. B. Rollett and K. Weltner. Munich, FRG: Ehrenwirth Verlag, 406–410.

———. (1973b) *Towards a Theory of Programmed Language Instruction.* Janua Linguarum, Series Didactica, vol. 1. The Hague: Mouton.

———. (1973c) *The Specification of Objectives in a Language Learning System for Adults.* CCC/EES (73) 34. Strasbourg, France: Council of Europe.

———. (1974) "Trends and Problems in the Programmed Teaching of Foreign Languages." In *Le nuove tecnologie educative e l'insegnamento delle lingue,* Milano, Italy: Oxford Institutes Italiani, 67–95.

———. (1975a) *A Theoretical Model for Programmed Language Instruction.* London: Longmac Ltd., Research Publications Services.

———. (1975b) "What Is Educational Technology. 60 Questions and Answers." Mimeographed.

———. (1976) "Educational Technology in Germany and Its European Context." In *International Yearbook of Educational and Instructional Technology 1976/77,* ed. A. Howe and A. J. Romiszowski. London: Kogan Page, pp. 177–206.

———. (1977) "Quasi-algorithms and Their Uses in Industrial and Vocational Training. Questions and Answers." Mimeographed.

———, ed. (1968) *Programmed Learning and the Language Laboratory 1.* Collected papers. London: Longmac Ltd., Research Publications Services. Victoria Hall, Fingal Street, London SE10-ORF, England.

Bung, K. and Rouse, K. (1970) "Introduction to Helmar Frank's Concept of Didactics." *Recall: Review of Educational Cybernetics and Applied Linguistics* 1 (6): 174–196.

Chomsky, N. (1959) "A Review of B. F. Skinner's 'Verbal Behavior.'" *Language* 35:26–58. Repr. in *The Structure of Language: Readings in the Philosophy of Language,* ed. J. A. Fodor and J. J. Katz. Englewood Cliffs, N.J.: Prentice-Hall, 547–578.

———. (1965) *Aspects of the Theory of Syntax.* Cambridge, Mass.: MIT Press.

———. (1966) *Cartesian Linguistics. A Chapter in the History of Rationalist Thought.* London: Harper & Row.

Coulson, J. E., ed. (1962) *Programmed Learning and Computer-Based Instruction.* Proceedings of the Conference on Application of Digital Computers to Automated Instruction, 10–12 October 1961. London: John Wiley and Sons.

Craik, K. J. W. (1966) *The Nature of Psychology. A Selection of Papers, Essays and Other Writings,* ed. S. L. Sherwood. London: Cambridge University Press.

Crowder, N. A. (1963) "On the Differences between Linear and Intrinsic Programming." *Phi Delta Kappan* 44: 250–254.

Cube, F. von. (1961) "Über ein Verfahren der mechanischen Didactick" (About a method of mechanical didàctics). *Grundlagenstudien aus Kybernetik und Geisteswissenschaft,* 2: 7–10.

———. (1963) "Die Redundanztheorie des Lernens und ihre Anwendung bei Lehrmaschinen" (The redundancy theory of learning and its application to teaching machines). In

Lehrmaschinen in Kybernetischer und pädagogischer Sicht 1, ed. H. Frank. Stuttgart, FRG: Ernst Klett Verlag, pp. 45–54.

———. (1965) *Kybernetische Grundlagen des Lernens und Lehrens* (Cybernetic foundations of learning and teaching). Stuttgart: Ernst Klett Verlag.

Cube, F. von and Gunzenhäuser, R. (1961) "Experimente zur Verifikation der Theorie des mechanischen Lernens" (Experiments for the verification of the theory of mechanical learning). *Grundlagenstudien aus Kybernetik und Geisteswissenschaft* 2: 111–119.

Daniel, J. S. (1973) "Serialists and Holist: Vital New Words in the Educator's Vocabulary." *ERM Educational Research and Methods* 6 (1): 24.

———. (1974) *Knowables, Conversations and Learning: A Summary of Recent Work at System Research Inc*. Sainte-Foy, Québec: Télé-université de Quebec.

———. (1975) "Conversations, Individuals and Knowables: Towards a Theory of Learning." *Engineering Education* 65 (5): 415–425. *Die Deutsche Schule*. Periodical. Hannover, FRG: Hermann Schroedel Verlag KG.

Doberkat, E.-E. (1975) "Über Reduktionen in einer Verallgemeinerung von Lánskýs BETARO-Automaten" (Reductions in a generalisation of Lánský's BETARO-automata). *Grundlagen studien aus Kybernetik und Geisteswissenschaft* 16 (3): 77–82.

Edison Responsive Learning System. (1965) *Operational Manual. Edison Responsive Environmental Learning System*. West Orange, N. J.: Thomas A. Edison Laboratory. Marketed by Responsive Environments Corporation, 21 East 40th Street, New York, NY 10016, U.S.

Edney, P. J. (1972) *A Systems Analysis of Training*. London: Pitman.

Educational Media International. Periodical. London: International Council for Educational Media.

Englert, L.; Frank, H.; Schiefele, H.; and Stachowiak, H. (1966) *Lexikon der kybernetischen Pädagogik und der programmierten Instruktion* (Dictionary of educational cybernetics and programmed instruction). Quickborn near Hamburg, FRG: Verlag Schnelle.

Evans, J. L.; Glaser, R.; and Homme, L. E. (1960) "The Ruleg System for the Construction of Programmed Verbal Learning Sequences." *Journal of Educational Research* 55: 513–518.

Fearing, F. (1964) *Reflex Action: A Study in the History of Physiological Psychology*. New York: Hafner.

Feichtinger, G. (1968a) "Eine automatentheoretische Deutung des einelementigen Lernmodells der Stimulus Sampling Theorie" (An automata theoretical interpretation of the one-element learning model of stimulus sampling theory). *Grundlagenstudien aus Kybernetik und Geisteswissenschaft* 9 (1): 13–19.

———. (1968b) "Ein automatentheoretischer Zugang zu Lernprozessen" (An automata theoretical approach to learning processes). *Kybernetik* 5 (3): 85–88.

Fierli, M. (1974) "Le didattiche formalizzate" (Formalised didactics). In *Questioni di tecnologia didattica*, ed. R. Titone. Brescia, Italy: Editrice la Scuola, pp. 481–515.

Flechsig, K.-H. (1975) "Towards a Critical Appraisal of Educational Technology Theory and Practice." Paper read at the 1st Educational Technology Theory and Policy Workshop, Strasbourg, 12–14 November 1975. CCC/TE (75) 23. Strasbourg, France: Council of Europe.

Fodor, J. A. and Katz, J. J., eds. (1964) *The Structure of Language: Readings in the Philosophy of Language*. Englewood Cliffs, N.J.: Prentice-Hall.

Frank, H. (1962) *Kybernetische Grundlagen der Pädagogik. Eine Einführung in die Informationspsychologie und ihre philosophischen, mathematischen und physiologischen Grundlagen* (Cybernetic foundations of educational theory, An introduction into psychology and its philosophical, mathematical and physiological foundations). Kybernetik und Information, Internationale Reihe (International Series of Cybernetics and Information). Baden-Baden, FRG: Agis-Verlag.

———. (1964a) *Kybernetische Analysen subjektiver Sachverhalte* (Cybernetic analyses of subjective phenomena). Quickborn near Hamburg, FRG: Verlag Schnelle.

———. (1964c) "Zur Makrostrukturtheorie von Lehralgorithmen." *Grundlagenstudien aus Kybernetik und Geisteswissenschaft* 5: 101–114.

———. (1965b) "Lehrautomaten für Einzel- und Gruppenschulung" (Teaching automata for individual and group instruction). In *Lehrmaschinen in Kybernetischer and Pädagogischer Sicht 4*, ed. H. Frank. Stuttgart: Ernst Klett Verlag, pp 17–35.

———. (1966a) *Kybernetik un Philosophie. Materialien und Grundriß zu einer Philosophie der Kybernetik* (Cybernetics and philosophy. Materials and outline of a philosophy of cybernetics). Erfahrung und Denken series: monographs to promote the relations between philosophy and individual sciences, vol. 16. West Berlin: Duncker & Humblot.

———. (1966b) "Ansätze zum algorithmischen Lehralgorithmieren" (Towards the algorithmic construction of teaching algorithms). In *Lehrmaschinen in Kybernetischer und padagogischer Sicht 4*, ed. H. Frank. Stuttgart: Ernst Klett Verlag, pp. 70–112.

———. (1968) *Informationsästhetik. Grundlagen-probleme und erste Anwendung auf die mime pure* (Information theory and aesthetics. Basic problems and first application to "mime pure"). 2d ed. Quickborn near Hamburg, FRG: Verlag Schnelle.

———. (1969a) *Kybernetische Grundlagen der Pädagogik. Eine Einführung in die Pädagogistik für Analytiker, Planer und Techniker des didaktischen Informationsumsatzes in der Industriegesellschaft* (Cybernetic foundations of educational theory. An introduction to the science of education for analysts, planners and technicians of the didactic metabolism of information in industrial society), vol. 1, *Allgemeine Kybernetik* (General Cybernetics). 2d ed. Baden-Baden: Agis-Verlag.

———. (1969b) *Kybernetische Grundlagen der Pädagogik. Eine Einführung in die Pädagogistik für Analytiker, Planer und Techniker des didaktischen Informationsumsatzes in der Industriegesellschaft* (Cybernetic foundations of educational theory. An introduction to the science of education for analysts, planners and technicians of the didactic metabolism of information in industrial society), vol. 2, *Angewandte kybernetische Pädagogik und Ideologie* (Applied educational cybernetics and ideology). Baden-Baden: Agis-Verlag.

———. (1971) "Programmatic Note on Organisational Cybernetics." *Recall: Review of Educational Cybernetics and Applied Linguistics,* 2 (1–2): 38–61.

———. (1977) "Derzeitige Bemühungen um Erweiterungen des informationspsychologischen Modells" (Present efforts towards the extension of the model of information psychology). *Grundlagenstudien* 18 (3): 61–72.

———, ed. (1963) "Lehrmaschinen in kybernetischer und pädagogischer Sicht 1" (Cybernetic and pedagogical approaches to teaching machines). Papers presented at the First Nürtinger Symposium about teaching machines. Stuttgart: Ernst Klett Verlag.

———, ed. (1964b) "Lehrmaschinen in kybernetischer und pädagogischer Sicht 2" (Cybernetic and pedagogical approaches to teaching machines). Papers presented at the Second Nürtinger Symposium about teaching machines. Stuttgart: Ernst Klett Verlag.

———, ed. (1965a) *Kybernetik. Brücke zwischen den Wissenschaften.* Frankfurt am Main, FRG: Umschau Verlag.

———, ed. (1965c) "Lehrmaschinen in kybernetischer und pädagogischer Sicht 3" (Cybernetic and pedagogical approaches to teaching machines). Papers presented at the Third Nürtinger Symposium about teaching machines. Stuttgart: Ernst Klett Verlag.

———, ed. (1966c) "Lehrmaschinen in kybernetischer und pädagogischer Sicht 4" (Cybernetic and pedagogical approaches to teaching machines). Papers presented at the Fourth Nürtinger Symposium about teaching machines. Stuttgart: Ernst Klett Verlag.

Frank, H. and Frank-Böhringer, B. (1968) "Zur Rentabilitätsgrenze beim Lernen" (The limits of worthwhileness for learning). *Grundlagenstudien aus Kybernetik und Geisteswissenschaft* 9: 59–64.

———. (1971) "Zur Deduktion quantitativer Lehrziele aus qualitativen Bildungswerten" (Deriving quantitative objectives from qualitative educational values). *Grundlagenstudien aus Kybernetik und Geisteswissenschaft* 12 (4): 101–112.

Frank, H. G. and Meder, B. (1971) *Einführung in die kybernetische Pädagogik* (Introduction into educational cybernetics). Munich: Deutscher Taschenbuch Verlag.

———. (1976) *Introduccíon a la pedagogía cibernética.* Buenos Aires: Editorial Troquel.

Frank, H. and Müller, G. (1964) "Ein adaptiver Lehrautomat für verzweigte Programme." In *Lehrmaschinen in Kybernetischer und pädagogischer Sicht 2,* ed. H. Frank. Stuttgart: Ernst Klett Verlag, pp. 81–87.

Frank, H. and Hollenbach, G. (1973) *Begriffswörterbuch der kybernetischen Pädagogik* (Glossary of educational cybernetics). With English, Russian, Czech, French, Spanish and Portuguese-Brazilian equivalents. Paderborner Forschungsberichte, vol. 1. Hannover: Hermann Schroedel Verlag KG.

Fucks, W. (1957) "Gibt es mathematische Gesetze in Sprache und Musik?" (Are there mathematical laws in language and music?). *Umschau in Wissenschaft und Technik* 57 (2): 33–37.

Gilbert, T. F. (1969) *Mathetics. An Explicit Theory for the Design of Teaching Programmes.* London: Longmac Ltd., Research Publications Services.

Glaser, R. (1962) "Some Research Problems in Automated Instruction: Instructional Programming and Subject-Matter Structure." In *Programmed Learning and Computer-Based Instruction,* ed. J. E. Coulson. London: John Wiley and Sons, pp. 67–85.

———, ed. (1965) *Teaching Machines and Programmed Learning 2: Data and Directions.* Washington, D.C.: Department of Audiovisual Instruction, National Education Association.

Gluschkow, W. M. (1963) *Theorie der abstrakten Automaten* (Theory of abstract automata). Mathematische Forschungsberichte, vol. 19. Berlin: VEB Deutscher Verlag der Wissenschaften.

Glushkov, V. M. (1966) *Introduction to Cybernetics.* New York: Academic Press.

Goethe-Institut. (1972) *Programmierte Instruktion, Zielsprache Deutsch* (Programmed instruction, target language German). Werkheft für technische Unterrichtsmittel, vol. 7. Munich: Goethe-Institut. Contains 12 computer-generated teaching programs for foreign learners of German and a bibliography on the use of formalized didactic mappings for generating teaching programs for foreign language learning.

Graf, K.-D. (1973) "Formale Didaktik und Formaldidaktiken. Ein Überblick über die Entwicklung und Ansätze bis 1971" (Formal didactics and didactic mappings. A survey of developments and approaches up to 1971). *Grundlagenstudien aus Kybernetik und Geisteswissenschaft* 14 (4): 109–120.

———. (1974) "Formale Didaktik und Formaldidaktiken. Ansätze zur Theoriebildung und Ausblick auf notwendige und mögliche Schwerpunkte weiterer Projekte" (Formal didactics and didactic mappings. Approaches towards the development of theories and outlook towards necessary and possible emphases in future projects). *Grundlagenstudien aus Kybernetik und Geisteswissenschaft* 15 (3): 65–74.

Grundlagenstudien aus Kybernetik und Geisteswissenschaft. Periodical. Hannover: Hermann Schroedel Verlag KG.

Gunzenhäuser, R. (1965) "Informationstheorie und Ästhetik. Aspekte einer kybernetischen Theorie ästhetischer Prozesse" (Information theory and aesthetics. Aspects of a cybernetic theory of aesthetics processes). In *Kybernetik. Brücke zwischen den Wissenschaften,* ed. H. Frank. Frankfurt am Main: Umschau Verlag, pp. 285–297.

Harary, F.; Norman, R. Z.; and Cartwright, D. (1965) *Structural Models: An Introduction to the Theory of Directed Graphs.* London: John Wiley & Sons.

Harvard Educational Review. Periodical. Cambridge, Mass.: Harvard University Graduate School of Education.

Heimann, P. (1962) "Didaktik als Theorie und Lehre" (The theory, and the teaching, of didactics). *Die Deutsche Schule* 40: 407–427.

Hertkorn, O. (1970) *Beispiel für Anwendung von COGENDI im Rahmen didaktischer Programmierung. Lehrprogramm aus dem Fachbereich Theologie. Küng: Was ist Kirche?* (Example for the use of COGENDI for the computer-assisted construction of teaching programmes. Teaching programme on theology. Küng: What is Church?). Paderborn: FEoLL.

Hilgers, R. (1976) "Versuch einer mathematischen Analyse des Anschütz-Diagramms" (A mathematical analysis of the Anschütz-Diagram). In *Bericht Über das 10. Werkstattgespräch in Leuven,* ed. G. Lobin and A. Jones. Paderborn: FEoLL, Paderborner Arbeits papiere, Institut für Kybernetische Pädagogik, pp. 46–51.

Howe, A. and Romiszowski, A. J., eds. (1976) *International yearbook of educational and instructional technology 1976/77.* London: Kogan Page.

Illich, I. D. (1971) *Deschooling Society.* London: Calder and Boyars.

Informationen zur Hochschuldidaktik. Periodical. Hamburg: Arbeitsgemeinschaft für Hochschuldidaktik.

International Journal of Man-Machine Studies. Periodical. London: Academic Press.

Itelson, L. (1967) *Mathematische und kybernetische Methoden in der Pädagogik* (Mathematical and cybernetic methods in educational theory). Berlin, GDR: Volk und Wissen Volkseigener Verlag.

Journal of Educational Research. Periodical. Madison, Wisconsin, U.S.

Kelbert, H. (1964) "Kybernetisches Modell der Abarbeitung eines programmierten verzweigten Lehrbuches" (Cybernetic model of a learner working through a branching programmed textbook). In *Lehrmaschinen in Kybernetischer und pädagogischer Sicht 2,* ed. H. Frank. Stuttgart: Ernst Klett Verlag, pp. 49–72.

Klír, J. and Valach, M. (1967) *Cybernetic Modelling.* London: ILIFFE Books Ltd.

Koller, F. (1975a) *Mathematische Lernmodelle und Abstrakte Automaten* (Mathematical learning models and abstract automata). Paderborn: FEoLL.

———. (1975b) *Versuch einer Axiomatisierung der Zusammenhänge zwischen Automaten und lerntheorie* (Attempt at axiomatising the relations between automata and learning theory), trans. from the Czech by V. Polák. Paderborn: FEoLL.

Krohne, R. J., ed. (1975) *Fortschritte der pädagogischen Psychologie* (Advances in educational psychology). Munich: Ernst Reinhard Verlag.

Kybernetik. Periodical. West Berlin: Springer Verlag.

Landa, L. N. (1968) "Algorithms and Programmed Learning." In *Programmed Learning and the Language Laboratory 1,* ed. K. Bung. London: Longmac Ltd, Research Publications Service, pp. 57–135.

———. (1974) *Algorithmization in Learning and Instruction.* Englewood Cliffs, N.J.: Educational Technology Publications.

Lang, E. (1968) "Zur Geschichte des Wortes. *Kybernetik*" (The history of the word *Cybernetics*). *Grundlagenstudien aus Kybernetik und Geisteswissenschaft* 9, suppl.

Lánský, M. (1967a) *On the Subjective Information of the Text Including the Supersigns.* Acts of the Fifth Congress International de Cybernetique. Namur, Belgium.

———. (1967b) "Über ein Gruppierungsverfahren." In *Praxis und Perspektiven des programmierten Unterrichts 2.* Quickborn near Hamburg: Verlag Schnelle.

———. (1969) "Learning Algorithms as a Teaching Aid." *Recall: Review of Educational Cybernetics and Applied Linguistics* 1 (3): 81–98.

———. (1970) "VERBAL: An Algorithm Which Determines the Optimal Distribution of Explanations in a Teaching Programme." *Recall: Review of Educational Cybernetics and Applied Linguistics,* 1 (4–5): 141–168.

Lánský, M. and Polák, V., eds. (1977) *Studien zur Superierung durch Komplexbildung* (Studies about the formation of supersigns through ordered sets and configurations). Paderborner Forschungsberichte, vol. 7. Paderborn: Verlag Ferdinand Schöningh.

Lariccia, G. (1972) "Algoritmi e istruzione Programmata." *Tecnologie Educative* 3 (3): 11–15.

Leed, J. ed. (1966) *The Computer and Literary Style.* Kent, Ohio: Kent State University Press.

Lewis, B. N. (1970) *Decision Logic Tables for Algorithms and Logical Trees.* CAS Occasional Paper, No. 12. London: Her Majesty's Stationery Office.

Lewis, B. N. and Pask, G. (1965) "The Theory and Practice of Adaptive Teaching Systems." In *Teaching Machines and Programmed Learning 2: Data and Directions,* ed. R. Glaser. Washington, D.C.: Department of Audiovisual Instruction, National Education Association, pp. 213–266.

Lewis, B. N.; Harabin, I.S.; and Gane, C. P. (1967) *Flow Charts, Logical Trees and Algorithms for Rules and Regulations.* CAS Occasional Paper, No. 2. London: Her Majesty's Stationery Office.

Lobin, G. and Jones, A., eds. (1976) *Bericht über das 10. Werkstattgespräch in Leuven* (Report about the 10th workshop discussion in Leuven). Paderborner Arbeitspapiere, Institut für Kybernetische Pädagogik. Paderborn: FEoLL.

Lumsdaine, A. A. and Glaser, R. eds. (1960) *Teaching Machines and Programmed Learning.* Washington, D.C.: National Education Association.

Mealy, G. H. (1955) "A Method for Synthesizing Sequential Circuits." *Bell System Technical Journal* 34: 1045–1079.

Meder, B. S. (1973) *Ergebnisbericht über die Untersuchung zur Erprobung neuer Unterrichtsformen in Schule und Hochschule mit dem Besonderen ziel einer Kritischen Würdigung Ausgewahlter Bildungstechnischer Medien.* Paderborner Arbeitspapiere, Institut für Kybernetische Pädagogik. Paderborn: FEoLL.

Meder, B. S. and Schmid, W., eds. (1973ff.) *Kybernetische*

Pädagogik. Schriften 1958–1972 (Publications on educational cybernetics from 1958 to 1972). 5 vols. so far. Stuttgart: Verlag W. Kohlhammer.

Meyer-Eppler, W. (1969). *Grundlagen und Anwendungen der Informationshtheorie* (Foundations and applications of information theory). 2d ed. Kommunikation und Kybernetik in Einzeldarstellungen, vol. 1. West Berlin: Springer-Verlag.

Moore, E. F. (1956) "Gedanken-experiments on Sequential Machines." In *Automata studies*. Annals of Mathematics Studies, vol. 24. 129–153. Princeton, N.J.: Princeton University Press.

Moseley, D. V. (1971) "A Remedial Program for Severely Sub-normal Pupils with and without the Talking Typewriter." In *Aspects of Educational Technology,* vol. 5, eds. D. Packham, A. Cleary, and T. Mayes. London: Pitman, pp 348–353.

Negroponte, N. ed. (1975) *Machine Intelligence in Design.* Cambridge, Mass.: MIT Press.

Nicklis, W. S. (1967) *Kybernetik und Erziehungswissenschaft. Eine kritische Darstellung ihrer Beziehungen* (Cybernetics and the science of education. A critical discussion of their relations). Bad Heilbrunn/OBB: Verlag Julius Klinkhardt.

———. (1969) "Rolle und Funktion der kybernetischen Pädagogik in einer Kritischen theorie des Unterrichts" (Role and function of educational cybernetics in a critical theory of teaching). In *Kybernetik und programmierte Bildung.* Bottrop, FRG: Verlag Wilhelm Postberg, pp. 74–95.

Oxford Institutes Italiani. (1974) *Le nuove technologie educative e l'insegnamento delle lingue* (The new technologies of education and language teaching). Proceedings of Fourth International Conference, held in Milan in 1972. Milan: Oxford Institutes Italiani.

Packham, D.; Cleary, A.; and Mayes, T., eds. (1971) *Aspects of Educational Technology,* vol. 5. London: Pitman.

Pask, G. (1960) "Adaptive Machines." In *Teaching Machines and Programmed Learning,* eds. A. A. Lumsdaine and R. Glaser. Washington, D.C.: National Education Association, pp. 349–366.

———. (1961) *An Approach to Cybernetics.* London: Hutchinsons.

———. (1971) *Organisation and Instruction of Office Skills Involving Communication Data Retrieval and Data Recognition.* Final Scientific Report, October 1970. London: Department of Employment.

———. (1972a) "A Fresh Look at Cognition and the Individual." *International Journal of Man-Machine Studies* 4: 211–216.

———. (1972b) "Anti-Hodmanship: A Report on the State and Prospects of CAI." *Programmed Learning and Educational Technology* 9 (5): 235–244.

———. (1975a) *Conversation, Cognition and Learning: A Cybernetic Theory and Methodology.* Amsterdam: Elsevier Press.

———. (1975b) "Artificial Intelligence—A Preface and a Theory." In *Machine Intelligence in Design,* ed. N. Negroponte. Cambridge, Mass.: MIT Press.

———. (1975c) *The Cybernetics of Human Learning and Performance: A Guide to Theory and Research.* London: Hutchinson.

———. (1976a) "Styles and Strategies of Learning." *British Journal of Educational Psychology* 46: 128–148.

———. (1976b) *Conversation Theory: Applications in Education and Epistemology.* New York: Elsevier Press.

———. (1976c) "Conversational Techniques in the Study and Practice of Education." *British Journal of Educational Psychology* 46: 12–25.

Pask, G. and Scott, B. E. (1972) "Learning Strategies and Individual Competence." *International Journal of Man-Machine Studies* 4(3): 217–253.

———. (1973) "CASTE: A System for Exhibiting Learning Strategies and Regulating Uncertainties." *International Journal of Man-Machine Studies* 5(1): 17–52.

Pask, G., Scott, B.C.E., and Kallikourdis, D. (1973) "A Theory of Conversations and Individuals." *International Journal of Man-Machine Studies* 5(4): 443–566.

Pask, G.; Kallikourdis, D.; and Scott, B.C.E. (1975) "The Representation of Knowables." *International Journal of Man-Machine Studies* 7 (1): 15–134.

Phi Delta Kappan. Periodical. Bloomington, Indiana, U.S.

Philologen-Verband Nordrhein-Westfallen. (1969) *Kybernetik und programmierte Bildung* (Cybernetics and programmed education). Proceedings of the 21st Congress in Gemen, 1969. Bottrop, FRG: Verlag Wilhelm Postberg.

Philosophy of Science. Periodical. Baltimore, Maryland, U.S.

Der Physikunterricht. Periodical. Stuttgart: Ernst Klett Verlag.

Pietsch, E. (1971) "Strukturanalyse eines Lehrstoffgebietes" (Structural analysis of a subject matter area). In *Fortschritte und Ergebnisse der Unterrichtstechnologie,* ed. B. Rollett and K. Weltner. Munich: Ehrenwirth Verlag, pp. 87–92.

Polák, V. (1973) *Modell-Varianten für die Bestimmung des Schwierigkeitsgrades von Explanationen* (Alternative models for determining the degree of difficulty of explanations). Paderborn: FEoLL.

———. (1974) "Zu der Untersuchung des Schwierigkeitsgrades von Explanationen" (Research into the degree of difficulty of explanations). *Grundlagenstudien aus Kybernetik und Geisteswissenschaft* 15 (1): 13–20.

Praxis. (1967) "Praxis und Perspektiven des programmierten Unterrichts 2." Referate des 5. Symposions über Lehrmaschinen 1967 in Berlin. Mit Beiträgen von K Alsleben, H Ankerstein (Praxis and perspectives of programmed instruction 2. Papers read at the 5th Symposium on Teaching Machines 1967 in Berlin). Quickborn near Hamburg: Verlag Schnelle.

Programmed Learning and Educational Technology. Periodical. Journal of the Association of Programmed Learning and Educational Technology. London: Kogan Page.

Psychological Review. Periodical. Washington, D.C.: American Psychological Association.

Recall: Review of Educational Cybernetics and Applied Linguistics. Periodical. London: Longmac Ltd., Research Publications Services.

Rollett, B. and Weltner, K., eds. (1970) "Perspektiven des Programmierten Unterrichts" (Perspectives of programmed instruction). Papers read at the Seventh Symposium of the Gesellschaft für Programmierte Insktruktion, April 1969, Vienna, Austria. Vienna: Österreichischer Bundesverlag für Unterricht, Wissenschaft und Kunst.

———. (1971) "Fortschritte und Ergebnisse der Unterrichtstechnologie" (Progress and results of educational technology). Papers read at the Eighth Symposium of the Gesellschaft für Programmierte Instruktion 1970. Munich: Ehrenwirth Verlag.

———. (1973) "Fortschritte und Ergebnisse der Bildungstechnologie 2" (Progress and results of educational technology). Papers read at the Tenth Symposium of the Gesellschaft für Programmierte Instruktion 1972. Munich: Ehrenwirth Verlag.

Rosenblueth, A.; Wiener, N.; and Bigelow, J. (1943) "Behavior, Purpose and Teleology." *Philosophy of Science* 10: 18–24.

Rubin, M. D., ed. (1971) *Man in Systems*. New York: Gordon Breach Science Publishers.

Sánchez Carrasco, M. J. (1975) *Ein Algorithmus, der Dezimalzahlen in spanische Zahlwörter verwandelt* (An algorithm which converts decimal numbers into Spanish numerals). Paderborner Arbeitspapiere (Institut für Bildungsinformatik). Paderborn: FEoLL.

Sánchez Carrasco, M. J. and Bung, K. (1977) "How to Specify Objectives for Industrial and Vocational Training. 80 Questions and Answers." Mimeographed.

Schott, F. and Dierig, P. (1977) "Entwicklung eines normierten Beschreibungs-verfahrens zur Lehrstoffanalyse" (Development of a normed description procedure for subject-matter analysis). *Grundlagenstudien aus Kybernetik und Geisteswissenschaft* 18 (3): 84–94.

Seidel, R. J. (1969) *Project IMPACT: Computer-Administered Concepts and Initial Development*. Alexandria, Va.: George Washington University, Human Resources Research Office.

Seidel, R. J.; Kingsley, E.; and Kopstein, F. (1971) "Graph Theory as a Meta-Language of Communicable Knowledge." In *Man in Systems*, ed. M. D. Rubin. New York: Gordon Breach Science Publishers.

Shannon, C. E. (1951) "Prediction and Entropy of Printed English." *Bell System Technical Journal* 30: 50–64.

Shannon, C. E. and Weaver, W. (1949) *The Mathematical Theory of Communication*. Urbana: University of Illinois Press.

Skinner, B. F. (1950) "Are Theories of Learning Necessary?" *Psychological Review* 57: 193–216.

———. (1954) "The Science of Learning and the Art of Teaching." *Harvard Educational Review* 24: 86–97.

———. (1957) *Verbal Behavior*. New York: Appleton-Century-Crofts.

———. (1969) *Contingencies of Reinforcement: A Theoretical Analysis*. Century Psychology Series. New York: Appleton-Century-Crofts.

Staniland, A. C. (1966) *Patterns of Redundancy: A Psychological Study*. London: Cambridge University Press.

Starke, P. H. (1969) *Abstrakte Automaten* (Abstract automata). Berlin, GDR: VEB Deutscher Verlag der Wissenschaften.

Steinbuch, K. (1961a) "Schaltungen mit der Lernmatrix" (Circuits for the learning matrix). *Lernende Automaten*, suppl. 2 of *Elektronische Rechenanlagen*. Munich: Oldenbourg.

———. (1961b) "Die Lernmatrix." *Kybernetik* 1 (1): 36–45.

———. (1965) "Adaptive Networks Using Learning Matrices." *Kybernetik* 2 (4): 148–152.

Steinbuch, K. and Frank, H. (1961) "Nichtdigitale Lernmatrizen als Perzeptoren." *Kybernetik* 1 (3): 117–124.

Steinbuch, K. and Lipp, H. M. (1965) "Der autonome Lernmatrix-Dipol" (The autonomous learning matrix dipole). In *Lehrmaschinen in Kybernetischer und pädagogischer Sicht 3*, ed. H. Frank. Stuttgart: Ernst Klett Verlag, 58–62.

Stejskal, B. (1971a) *Producing Programmes for the Unitutor Teaching Machine*, Part 1: *Text*. First pub. in Czech by the Prague School of Economics, 1969. Trans. Till Gottheiner. Prague: Artia, Foreign Trade Corporation.

———. (1971b) *Producing Programmes for the Unitutor Teaching Machine*, Part 2: *Illustrations and Bibliography*. First pub. in Czech by the Prague School of Economics, 1969. Trans. Till Gottheiner. Prague: Artia, Foreign Trade Corporation.

Stever, H. (1971) "Superierung durch Komplexbildung" (The formation of supersigns out of configurations of signs as opposed to sets of signs). Ph.D. diss., Technical University, Karlsruhe, FRG.

———. (1973) "Ein informationstheoretisches Lernmodell" (An information theoretical model learning). In *Fortschritte und Ergebnisse der Bildungstechnologie 2*, ed. B. Rollett and K. Weltner. Munich: Ehrenwirth Verlag, pp. 400–402.

System Research, Ltd. (1977a) *Learning Styles, Educational Strategies and Representations of Knowledge: Methods and Applications*, vol. 1. Progress report 3, 1 May 1976 to 30 April 1977. Richmond, Surrey, U.K.: System Research Ltd.

———. (1977b) *Learning Styles, Educational Strategies and Representations of Knowledge: Methods and Applications*, vol. 2. Progress report 3, 1 May 1976 to 30 April 1977. Richmond, Surrey, U.K.: System Research Ltd.

Technologie Educative. Periodical. Rome: CNITE (Centro Nazionale Italiano Tecnologie Educative).

Thomas, C. A.; Davie, I. K.; Openshaw, D.; and Bird, J. B. (1963) *Programmed Learning in Perspective: A Guide to Programme Writing*. London: Lamson Technical Products Ltd.

Titone, R., ed. (1974) *Questioni di tecnologia didattica* (Problems of educational technology). Brescia, Italy: Editrice la Scuola,

Tobin, M. J., ed. (1967) *Problems and Methods in Programmed Learning*, Part 1. The proceedings of the 1967 APL/NCPL Birmingham Conference. Birmingham, U.K.: National Centre for Programmed Learning, School of Education, University of Birmingham.

Trakhtenbrot, B. A. (1963) *Algorithms and Automatic Computing Machines*. Boston: D. C. Heath.

Weltner, K. (1971) "Lernziele unter dem Aspekt der Informationstheorie" (Learning objectives and information theory). In *Fortschritte und Ergebnisse der Unterrichtstechnologie,* ed. B. Rollett and K. Weltner. Munich: Ehrenwirth Verlag, pp. 26–35.

———. (1973a) "Zur Definition der Begriffe Lernschritt und Lehrschritt" (About the definition of the concepts learning step and teaching and teaching step). *Grundlagenstudien aus Kybernetik und Geisteswissenschaft* 14 (4): 129–136.

———. (1973b) "Leitprogramme als Weiterentwicklung der Lehrprogramme" (Pilot programs as a further development of teaching programs). *Der Physikunterricht* 1: 91–98.

———. (1974a) *The Measurement of Verbal Information in Psychology and Education.* Communication and Cybernetics Series, vol. 7. West Berlin: Springer Verlag.

———. (1975a) "Die Rolle der Informationstheorie und der Graphentheorie bei der Analyse von Lehr- un Lernprozessen" (The role of information theory and graph theory for the analysis of teaching and learning processes). In *Fortschritte der pädagogischen Psychologie,* ed. R. J. Krohne. Munich: Ernst Reinhard Verlag, pp. 30–47.

———. (1975b) "Generation of Optimal Teaching Sequences." Paper read at the UCODI Summer School, Geneva.

———. (1975c) "Zur Förderung des autonomen Lernens. Konzept, Realisierung und Evaluation integrierender Leitprogramme als Studienunterstützungen" (The promotion of independent learning. Concept, realization and evaluation of integrating pilot programs as a study aid). In *Beiträge zur Methodik von Studienunterstützungen,* ed. S. Wittig. Wiesbaden: Bildungstechnologisches Zentrum GmbH, pp. 11–42.

———. (1975d) "Das Konzept des integrierenden Leitprogramms. Ein Instrument zur Förderung der Studierfähigkeit" (The concept of the integrating pilot program. An instrument for promoting the ability to study independently). *Informationen Zur Hochschuldidaktik* 12: 292–305.

———. (1976) "Lehrzielauswahl bei Lernzeitbegrenzung" (Selection of objectives, given a limited learning time). *Grundlagenstudien aus Kybernetik und Geisteswissenschaft* 17(1): 1–8.

Wiener, N. (1961) *Cybernetics or Control and Communication in the Animal and the Machine.* Cambridge, Mass.: MIT Press.

Wittig, S., ed. (1975) *Beiträge zur Methodik von Studienunterstützungen* (Contributions to the methodology of study guides). BTZ-Reihe, vol. 4. Wiesbaden: Bildungstechnologisches Zentrum GmbH.

Wyant, T. (1972) "Knowledge Structure of Graph Theory." In *International Yearbook of Education and Instructional Technology 1972/73,* ed. K. Austwick and N.D.C. Harris. London: Pitman, pp. 100–108.

Zierer, E. (1970) *Elementos de pedagogía cibernética para la didáctica de los idiomas extranjeros* (Elements of educational cybernetics for the teaching of foreign languages). Métodos cibernéticos en la pedagogía, vol. 1. Trujillo, Peru: Departamento de Ciencias de la Educación, University of Trujillo.

EDUCATIONAL INNOVATION. Innovation, significantly, is a relatively recent concept in educational writing. The term came into currency about the mid-1950s and is used to refer to *the process of planned change* in curriculum content, method, and organization. The increasing rate of change in society has created an urgent need for updating syllabi, and the invention of new media of communication and instruction has opened up possibilities of more efficient learning. How to implement innovation remains a major problem: the process of change requires planning if new approaches are to be adopted and developed in education. Consequently, analysis of the process of innovation aims (1) to ensure that proposed reforms are well-designed, soundly field-tested, and properly evaluated; (2) to identify factors which affect implementation, so as to reduce failures and frustration; thus (3) to establish principles for developing efficient teaching and learning systems; and possibly also (4) to allow better management and control of the educational system.

HISTORICAL BACKGROUND

Until about 1950, change in education depended largely on individual initiatives and official reports written in a hortatory and nonspecific style. This process has been described as "unplanned, adaptive drift" (Hoyle, 1969). In the 1950s, projects to reform the science curriculum in schools were set up in the United States, and the concept of "planned change" (Lippitt et al., 1958) emerged. In the 1960s, principally in the United States and Britain, as innovation began to attract public funding, steps were taken to institutionalize the process and to extend it over the whole range of the educational system. Thus, for example, in England the Schools Council was set up in 1964, as an "institution for innovation" (Nisbet, 1980). The study of innovation began in the context of curriculum development (Taba, 1962) and spread to cover the procedures and principles of innovation generally (Havelock, 1969), in order to determine how best to manage and stimulate the process of change. In the 1970s, the focus of interest shifted because of growing concern over the relative failure of new ideas and the disappointing level of take-up. The evaluation of the Schools Council Humanities Project (MacDonald, 1974), for example, suggested that the success of innovation depends more on relationships within a school than on the quality of the innovation itself. (See also Nisbet, 1974, and in a New Zealand context, the Educational Development Conference, 1974.) Subsequent research, however, identified the assumptions and styles of the innovators as crucial factors, and analysis of the process of innovation has become the key to improving the success of new approaches (Bolam, 1975; Dalin, 1978; Fullan, 1982).

MODELS OF INNOVATION

A simple but useful classification (Bennis, Benne, and Chin, 1969) distinguishes three strategies for change: (1) *power-coercive,* persuasion directly by authority or indirectly by control of resources; (2) *empirical-rational,* relying on evidence and rational argument; (3) *normative-reeducative,* resulting from changes of attitudes or values among those who implement the change.

Best known among the early analyses of the change process is Havelock's three-model system (Havelock, 1969, 1970). (1) *Research-development-dissemination,* or R-D-D, is a linear model, in which an idea is uncovered in research, subsequently developed to make it applicable through the creation of appropriate materials or procedures, and then disseminated by publicity and training and the provision of necessary resources. This was the dominant model for innovation in the 1960s, but its weakness is its dependence on an expert group who have to persuade apparently reluctant practitioners to accept the increased work load of unfamiliar procedures. (2) The *social-interaction* model is one in which both the will to change and knowledge of what is on offer are promoted by personal contact: people learn best from other people. In this model, innovators and practitioners interact through intermediary structures (teachers' centers, advisers, animateurs), and there is communication in both directions, so that innovators are more aware of teachers' concerns as well as having a structure for disseminating their own ideas. (3) In the *problem-solving* model, the momentum for change is within the school (or educational institution). The practitioners identify a problem, draw on the help of "change agents" to find and implement a solution, and evaluate to establish further necessary changes in a process of rolling reform.

The contrast among these three approaches can be summarized in terms of a *center-periphery* model and its alternatives (Schon, 1971). Early attempts at curriculum development and innovation (and many later attempts also) proved ineffective because innovation was seen as originating at a center (an expert team, or a government department or committee) and then being disseminated to the periphery (teachers, practitioners). Knowledge and resources, on this model, are concentrated in the center; the problem is to overcome the resistance of those on the periphery. Military metaphors (such as "strategy") are used to describe the task. Teachers' resistance is attributed to conservatism, ignorance, and lethargy, and innovators are puzzled why their gifts are not eagerly accepted. Havelock's problem-solving model reverses the relationship: the practitioners make the decisions and the experts are the servants. Implementation is thus more likely, but control and direction of the whole system is weakened.

These models have been outlined in many texts (for example, Harris et al., 1975; MacDonald & Walker, 1976), and they help to explain a central problem in innovation: the roles of innovator and practitioner and their interaction. Procedures for innovation developed in the 1960s tended to adopt, unquestioningly, the linear R-D-D center-periphery approach. Guba and Clark (1965), for example, describe the process as research, development, dissemination, demonstration, implementation, installation, and institutionalization. The English Schools Council initially adopted a five-stage procedure for its curriculum projects: definition of objectives, development of materials, field trials, dissemination, evaluation. But from the start, the importance of involving teachers in the process was recognized (the normative-reeducative strategy); and shortly before its abolition in 1982 the Council had moved towards a school-based approach (see Nisbet, 1980). An influential text was Stenhouse (1975), who emphasized the need to consider innovation as a process rather than as a product.

BARRIERS TO INNOVATION

Difficulties worldwide in implementing innovation led initially to analysis of resistance to innovation. Many factors were identified: teachers' attitudes, institutional structures, funding policies, and the characteristics of an innovation. Dalin (1976), for example, identified ten categories likely to affect the success of an innovation: centrality (or displacement), complexity, consonance (with accepted goals), competition, visibility, feasibility, support, divisibility (or adoption in part), compatibility (with existing practice), and adaptability. Certain kinds of innovation are more threatening than others. Becher and Kogan (1980) distinguish four varieties: the inexorable, the prescriptive, the radical, and the evolutionary. Or we can distinguish among changes which address problems defined by oneself, changes which are stabilizing, and changes which are disruptive. Clearly, the nature of an innovation is an important element in its acceptability. A key factor, however, is the attitude of those likely to be affected by the change. An Australian report (Karmel, 1973) lists three prerequisites for success: "The effectiveness of innovation . . . is dependent on the extent to which the people concerned perceive a problem and hence realise the existence of a need, are knowledgeable about a range of alternative solutions, and feel themselves to be in a congenial organisational climate."

SCHOOL-BASED INNOVATION

Current trends—in the literature, though perhaps not reflected in official policies—are toward a devolution of as much as possible of the process of innovation. The top-down model clearly does not work; but if innovation were to be left entirely to the classroom teacher, it would probably be slow, limited in scope, and uncoordinated. Where there is a consensus or a power-coercive agreed policy, guidelines issued centrally can give a general direction, and leave the detailed implementation to practitioners to develop in a form which suits local circumstances.

The demand for accountability, for example, calls for the introduction of new procedures for evaluation: these can be introduced centrally in a statewide program of competency testing, or schools and colleges may develop their own programs of self-evaluation (see Adelman and Alexander, 1983; Skilbeck, 1984). The "action research movement" goes further than this, giving teachers the role of researchers, encouraging them to investigate and reflect on their own practice (Elliott, 1981). If schools and teachers are to take a major role in educational innovation, they will require support in developing "organisational health" (Miles, 1975), the capacity to tolerate stress, and also to strengthen their creativity (OECD, 1973), their capacity to "adopt, adapt, generate or reject innovations."

If this shift of focus proves more effective than the previous reliance on centrally initiated change, we may require to reconsider the definition (given in the opening paragraph) of innovation as "the process of planned change." The issue is, whose plan? Who defines the problem which is the starting point for innovation? Innovation is thus a political process as well as a technical procedure. Those who control innovation, if they can do it successfully, are legislators of the future.

John Nisbet

REFERENCES

Adelman, C. and Alexander, R. J. (1982) *The Self-Evaluating Institution: Practice and Principles in the Management Change*. London: Methuen.

Becher, T. and Kogan, M. (1980) *Process and Structure in Higher Education*. London: Heinemann.

Bennis, W. G., Benne, K. D., and Chin, R., eds. (1969) *The Planning of Change*. New York: Holt, Rinehart and Winston.

Bolam, R. (1975) "The Management of Educational Change: Towards a Conceptual Framework." In *Management in Education*, vol. 1, ed. V. Houghton, R. McHugh, and C. Morgan. London: Ward Lock Educational.

Dalin, P. (1976) *Guidelines for Case Studies*. Oslo: IMTEC, University of Oslo (mimeograph).

———. (1978) *Limits to Educational Change*. Toronto: Ontario Institute for Studies in Education.

Educational Development Conference. (1974) *Improving Learning and Teaching*. Wellington: Government Printing Service.

Elliott, J. (1981) "Foreword." *A Teacher's Guide to Action Research*, ed. J. Nixon. London: Grant McIntyre.

Fullan, M. (1982) *The Meaning of Educational Change*. Toronto: Ontario Institute for Studies in Education.

Guba, E. G. and Clark, D. L. (1965) "An Examination of Potential Change Roles in Education." In *Strategies for Educational Change*, Newsletter 2. Columbus, Ohio: Ohio State University.

Harris, A., Lawn, M., and Prescott, W., eds. (1975) *Curriculum Innovation*. London: Croom Helm.

Havelock, R. G. (1969) *Planning for Innovation through Dissemination and Utilization of Knowledge*. Ann Arbor: University of Michigan Institute for Social Research.

———. (1970) *A Guide to Innovation in Education*. Ann Arbor: University of Michigan Institute for Social Research.

Hoyle, E. (1969) "How Does the Curriculum Change?" *Journal of Curriculum Studies* 1: 132–141 and 230–239.

Karmel, P. (1973) *Schools in Australia*. Australian Schools Commission. Canberra: Australian Government Printing Service.

Lippitt, R., Watson, J., and Westley, B. (1958) *The Dynamics of Planned Change*. New York: Harcourt Brace.

MacDonald, B. (1974) *Beyond Evaluation*. University of East Anglia: Centre for Applied Research in Education.

MacDonald, B. and Walker, R. (1976) *Changing the Curriculum*. London: Open Books.

Miles, M. (1975) "Planned Change and Organisational Health: Figure and Ground." In *Curriculum Innovation*, ed. A. Harris, M. Lawn, and W. Prescott. London: Croom Helm.

Nisbet, J. (1974) "Innovation—Bandwagon or Hearse?" *Bulletin of the Victoria Institute of Educational Research* 33: 1–14. Repr. in *Curriculum Innovation*, ed. A. Harris, M. Lawn, and W. Prescott. London: Croom Helm.

———. (1980) "Curriculum Process: International Perspectives." In *Curriculum Issues in New Zealand*, ed. P.D.K. Ramsay. Yearbook of Education, 8. Wellington: New Zealand Educational Institute.

OECD. (1973) *Creativity of the School*. Centre for Educational Research and Innovation. Paris: Organisation for Economic Cooperation and Development.

Schon, D. A. (1971) *Beyond the Stable State*. New York: Norton.

Skilbeck, M., ed. (1984) *Evaluating the Curriculum in the Eighties*. London: Hodder & Stoughton.

Stenhouse, L. (1975) *An Introduction to Curriculum Research and Development*. London: Heinemann.

Taba, H. (1962) *Curriculum Development: Theory and Practice*. New York: Harcourt, Brace & World.

EDUCATIONAL RESEARCH METHODOLOGY.

The domination of educational research by psychologists employing statistical models to test their theories has persisted until so very recently that we have hardly begun to appreciate the contribution that other disciplines and models can make to the study of educational problems and the improvement of educational practice. Yet in only twenty years or so we have moved a long way from the traditional belief that psychometrics would eventually establish a science of education, a best way of organizing and teaching the young in educational institutions with due regard for their inherited characteristics, especially intelligence. A pessimist viewing the present state of research methodology might register disillusionment with psychometrics and other quantitative approaches, dismay at the inability and reluctance of researchers to provide definite answers and solutions, and despair over a chaotic profusion of new and untried methodologies, all competing to become the new orthodoxy. This review will take a more positive line, identifying not just the causes of present discontent but also the developments which seem most likely to help teachers, managers, administrators, and policymakers to understand the issues they have to deal with and to be able to take or share the responsibility for their own solutions.

THE EXPERIMENTAL AND QUANTITATIVE TRADITIONS

Psychometric models of research developed out of two largely simultaneous series of events beginning in the latter part of the nineteenth century. These were (1) the emergence of psychology as an empirical science independent of philosophy and (2) the development of a variety of statistical methods, first in eugenics, then in psychology itself and in other areas of applied science, most notably agriculture, in order to measure relationships such as the heights of father and sons or to test experimentally theories about the influence of one variable, type of fertilizer, say, on another, the growth of seedlings (Hamilton, 1980; Nisbet, 1974 HISTORICAL).

From the period of World War I onwards, one of the main applications of the psychometric approach was the selection of groups according to intellectual performance as measured by large-scale testing, and the prediction of future performance through the investigation of correlated characteristics. This means of identifying talent generated further research into refining selection and predictive techniques in such fields as college entrance in the United States and selection for academic secondary schools in the United Kingdom, and later into the effectiveness of schooling on both sides of the Atlantic. The computer revolution of the 1960s promised to make research in these areas more manageable by making it possible to apply complex statistical techniques to very large data bases. Ironically, however, by this time some of the earlier applications—like selection based on what were now very controversial assumptions about the nature and distribution of intelligence—became a target for social criticism. Research into the consequences of selection had demonstrated that the less than perfect validity and reliability of the tests used for the purpose had led to considerable errors in selection (Vernon, 1957 EXAMPLE) and so, it was claimed, to unhappiness and injustice for many individuals.

Furthermore, reaction against the "numbers game" (Parlett and Hamilton, 1977 BACKGROUND READING) had been growing not only on account of the social consequences, but also because this approach concentrated almost exclusively on the manipulation of numerical data. Meanwhile, the appropriateness of applying eugenics and agricultural paradigms of research to education problems was coming under attack (Hamilton, 1980 HISTORICAL). Again, the statistical underpinning of some American research into the effectiveness of compensatory education programs in areas of urban deprivation and of British research linking pupil progress with teaching styles was shown to be seriously defective (Aitkin, Bennett, and Hesketh, 1981 FURTHER DETAIL). Greater cooperation between researchers and statisticians is essential to prevent similar occurrences in the future.

True empiricism, the setting up of experimental conditions to test the truth of a hypothesis, has been relatively rare in educational research other than in educational psychology, mainly because of the difficulties involved. Many of the possible independent variables likely to be of importance—learner and teacher characteristics and home background, for example—cannot be manipulated (Kerlinger, 1973 JUSTIFICATION OF POINT OF VIEW).

The difficulty can be partially overcome by using ex post facto methods (Cohen and Manion, 1980 DESCRIPTION OF METHODOLOGY). Here the researcher seeks to explain the dependent variable, data on attitudes to school, for example, by studying retrospectively independent variables like ability, sex, and school characteristics (Shanks and Welsh, 1983 EXAMPLE). This approach is not truly experimental since subjects cannot be assigned at random to ability levels or schools as these attributes are already determined. This potential weakness can be at least partially overcome by testing plausible alternative hypotheses which might affect the dependent variable. Their elimination would then strengthen the original hypothesis (Kerlinger, 1973 FURTHER DETAIL). Though undeniably an inferior model in scientific terms, ex post facto research is far more common than experimental research in education and, indeed, more important too, because the issues at stake are more likely to be matters of urgent, general concern.

SURVEYS

A third traditional approach is the survey, which shares some of the characteristics of ex post facto research. Survey implies a breadth of view, and survey methods are designed accordingly to obtain data from as large a number of cases as is economically possible in terms of time, money, and goodwill, consistent always with proper sampling procedures. The usual purpose of surveys in educational research is to measure and compare the attitudes, opinions, behavior, and other attributes of various categories of teachers, parents, pupils, and similar groups. They may be carried out in a variety of ways such as interviewing, where depth is required and answers may need to be followed up by supplementary questions; postal surveys, when the target group is widely scattered and not otherwise accessible; and group-administered questionnaires or inventories, the method most frequently used when the group consists of pupils or students. The preliminary analysis of survey data is invariably quantitative, but it is often considered unnecessary to go beyond the tabulation of frequencies if this will provide an adequate basis for interpretation and discussion. When, however, the survey includes measures of attitudes or opinions resulting in scores, a statistical technique such as analysis of variance is generally employed to test hypotheses of statistically significant differences among groups. Rating scales and yes/no answers to discrete questions can also be treated by appropriate statistical methods (Cohen and Manion, 1980; Moser and Kalton, 1971 DESCRIPTION OF METHODOLOGY).

It might be argued that surveys should be planned on the same lines as experimental research, testing hypotheses formulated in advance of collecting the data. The difficulty, however, is that the data frequently suggest new and unexpected lines of inquiry. Because of the impracticability of revising and repeating large-scale surveys, researchers often test new hypotheses with the data already gathered. This practice is unacceptable in experimental research, but in survey research judicious and cautious snooping among the data may be justifiable, always provided that the project was rigorously planned in the first place (Hays, 1974 JUSTIFICATION OF POINT OF VIEW).

CASE STUDY

The methods mentioned so far assume a detachment on the part of the researcher, who should not permit personal views or enthusiasms to affect the actual conduct of the research. Ideally, given the methodology and research instruments, the outcomes should be identical whoever the researcher and whatever the researcher's wishes about the outcome. With case study, however, we are moving even further away from the scientific ideal of research which can be easily and objectively replicated. It usually takes the form of a systematic study of a single example selected because it is thought to be representative, unique, or otherwise of particular interest. By drawing on several methods of gathering evidence such as interviews, observation of meetings or classrooms, policy statements, and a variety of documentary evidence, the researcher can penetrate more deeply into the workings of a group or institution (Nisbet and Watt, 1978 DESCRIPTION OF METHODOLOGY). In this way the researcher can produce a more rounded interpretation of reality and so illustrate and illuminate general principles more convincingly and appropriately than the more extensive but superficial survey can. Case study can also cope more easily with the unpredictable, and may detect interactions and patterns indiscernible to the researcher using only statistical methods of analysis. The limitations of case study include the qualifications that must attach to generalizing from a single case, and the risks of subjectivity and bias resulting from the researcher's close involvement with the case and from being to some extent his own research instrument.

Awareness of such problems has led to a call for neutrality on the part of the researcher, more openness about methods and procedures, rapid feedback to those whose situation is being studied, and a willingness to leave to them the drawing of conclusions. "The case study worker acts as a collector of definitions, not the conductor of truth" (Walker, 1980 DEFINITION; DESCRIPTION OF METHODOLOGY). The increasing popularity of the method and the emergence of a considerable body of respectable work since the mid-1960s suggest that case study has won a permanent place in research methodology (Reid and Walker, 1975 EXAMPLE).

ACTION RESEARCH

The boundaries between case study and action research are sometimes blurred, and indeed the two may be indistinguishable from one another. The main characteristic of action research is that the researcher has the opportunity to change the situation being investigated at the time. Not all case studies fit this criterion. Objectivity is still required, but may be harder to attain in that the researcher is likely to have a strong commitment to the success of his intervention in solving problems or improving practice. The most ambitious action research program in the United Kingdom (Halsey, 1972 EXAMPLE) sought to improve the education and consequently the life chances of disadvantaged urban children living in what were defined as educational priority areas. The effects of various attempts to improve facilities and involve parents, teachers, and the community could not be adequately evaluated by traditional scientific methods since many of the interventions were unique. Instead, a process of illuminative evaluation was used, in which the researchers kept detailed records of what happened, which problems occurred and how they were dealt with, and how interested parties viewed the success of the actions taken. The outcome of the program was a series of reports evaluating the actions taken in the five EPAs and recommendations for policy to the body sponsoring the research, in this instance a government department. The main report also included a consideration of the principles of action research and their practice in this particular project (Halsey, 1972 THEORETICAL BACKGROUND). Another fruitful field for action research has been that of curriculum development and innovation (Shipman, 1974 EXAMPLE).

THE FUTURE

This account of educational research methodology has concentrated on five distinctive approaches, the experimental and ex post facto, and three examples of methods which are usually used non-empirically, the survey, case study, and action research. There are, of course, many other methods which have had to be omitted, like interaction analysis (Flanders, 1970 DESCRIPTION OF METHODOLOGY), which has been very influential in classroom observation research, and repertory grid analysis (Kelly, 1955 DESCRIPTION OF METHODOLOGY), used for investigating personal constructs and values. The methodology of historical and philosophical research in education lies outside the scope of this entry.

There are fashions in educational as in other research (how much use is made of sociometry now?), but it may not be rash to make two predictions for the future:

1. Continued public and political interest in the accountability and effectiveness of educational institutions will ensure the long-term future of quantitative methods, which will be employed, however, with more awareness of the pitfalls and with greater statistical expertise.
2. Case study, action research, and other methods more akin to the anthropological than to the empirical model will become more extensively used in projects where satisfactory outcomes depend on the quality of the researcher's firsthand knowledge of the world of those whose problems he is studying.

Finally, there is no one best method equally suitable in all situations. The numerous, ever-changing, and unending problems which constitute the field of educational research are more likely to respond to an appropriate combination of diverse methods (Forsythe et al., 1983 EXAMPLE). This is the lesson we are slowly learning.

Derek Shanks

REFERENCES

Background Reading

Parlett, M. and Hamilton, D. (1977) "Evaluation as Illumination." In *Beyond the Numbers Game: A Reader in Educational Evaluation,* ed. D. Hamilton et al. Basingstoke, Hampshire: Macmillan Education, pp. 6–22.

Definition

Walker, R. (1980) "The Conduct of Educational Case Studies: Ethics, Theory and Procedures." In *Rethinking Educational Research,* ed. W. B. Dockrell and D. Hamilton. London: Hodder & Stoughton, p. 58.

Description of Methodology

Cohen, L. and Manion, L. (1980) *Research Methods in Education.* London: Croom Helm, pp. 71–98, 143–157.

Flanders, N. A. (1970) *Analyzing Teaching Behavior.* New York: Addison-Wesley.

Kelly, G. A. (1955) *The Psychology of Personal Constructs,* vols. 1–2. New York: Norton.

Moser, C. A. and Kalton, G. (1971) *Survey Methods in Social Investigation.* 2d ed. London: Heinemann.

Nisbet, J. and Watt, J. (1978) *Case Study,* Rediguide 26. University of Nottingham School of Education. Oxford: TRC-Rediguides.

Walker, R. (1980) "The Conduct of Educational Case Studies: Ethics, Theories and Procedures." In *Rethinking Educational Research,* ed. W. B. Dockrell and D. Hamilton. London: Hodder & Stoughton, pp. 30–63.

Example

Forsythe, D. et al. (1983) *The Rural Community and the Small School.* Aberdeen, Scotland: Aberdeen University Press.

Halsey, A. H., ed. (1972) *Educational Priority,* vol. 1: *EPA Problems and Policies.* London: Her Majesty's Stationery Office.

Reid, W. A. and Walker, D. F., eds. (1975) *Case Studies in Curriculum Change.* London: Routledge & Kegan Paul.

Shanks, D. E. and Welsh, J. M. (1983) "Transition to Secondary School." In *The Rural Community and the Small School,* by D. Forsythe et al. Aberdeen: Aberdeen University Press, pp. 187–198.

Shipman, M. (1974) *Inside a Curriculum Project: A Case Study in the Process of Curriculum Change.* London: Methuen.

Vernon, P. E. ed. (1957) *Secondary School Selection.* London: Methuen.

Further Detail

Aitkin, M., Bennett, S. N. and Hesketh, J. (1981) "Teaching Styles and Pupil Progress: A Reanalysis." *British Journal of Educational Psychology* 51 (2): 170–186.

Kerlinger, F. N. (1973) *Foundations of Behavioural Research*. 2d ed. London: Holt, Rinehart & Winston, pp. 378–394.

Historical

Hamilton, D. (1980) "Educational Research and the Shadows of Francis Galton and Ronald Fisher." In *Rethinking Educational Research*, ed. W. B. Dockrell and D. Hamilton. London: Hodder & Stoughton, pp. 153–168.

Nisbet, J. (1974) "Educational Research: The State of the Art." Inaugural address to the British Educational Research Association. Repr. in *Rethinking Educational Research*, ed. W. B. Dockrell and D. Hamilton. London: Hodder & Stoughton, pp. 1–10.

Justification of Point of View

Hays, W. L. (1974) *Statistics for the Social Sciences*. 2d ed. London: Holt, Rinehart & Winston, pp. 605–607.

Kerlinger, F. H. (1973) *Foundations of Behavioural Research*. 2d ed. London: Holt, Rinehart & Winston, pp. 327–347.

Theoretical Background

Halsey, A. H., ed. (1972) *Educational Priority*, vol. 1: *EPA Problems and Policies*. London: Her Majesty's Stationery Office.

EDUCATIONAL TECHNOLOGY (Journal). A monthly journal covering all aspects of educational technology, with particular emphasis on a systems analysis approach to topics of interest.

140 Sylvan Avenue, Englewood Cliffs, New Jersey 07632, U.S.

EDUCATIONAL TECHNOLOGY. The origins of the term *Educational technology* lie in the problems of categorization which arose during the early 1960s as a result of the burgeoning interest in innovation in educational methods. This interest had been kindled by the seminal publications of Skinner in 1954 and 1958, and brought to fruition by the appearance of Lumsdaine and Glaser's 1960 monumental opus, *Teaching Machines and Programmed Learning* (TMPL).

It was clear that some of the work described in TMPL, such as chemical books, improving marksmanship, etc., could only be incorporated under the umbrella of programmed instruction by in effect discarding the accepted precepts of programming at that time. Similarly, attention was increasingly being focused on the vast array of audiovisual hardware then in existence and in common use in schools and higher institutions. A means, even if only semantic, of bringing all such strands of innovation together was earnestly sought, and thus developed the motherhood title of *educational technology*.

Several definitions have since been advanced as encompassing the spirit and nature of educational technology. The Commission on Instructional Technology considered the essence of educational technology to be "a systematic way of designing, implementing and evaluating the total process of learning and teaching in terms of specific objectives, based on research in human learning and communication and employing a combination of human and non-human resources to bring about more effective instruction," while a British "official" definition is "the development, application and evaluation of systems, techniques and aids to improve the process of human learning."

In spite of, or perhaps because of, such interpretations as these, argument has raged on regarding the degree of reality of educational technology: is the term meaningful in the sense of binding together a set of common elements, possessing some sort of theoretical structure? If so, the theory seems to have successfully eluded those who term themselves educational technologists. Possibly the advent of ubiquitous microcomputer-based education will at last bring forward the necessary common strands which will provide scientific, rather than just convenient, respectability to the concept of educational technology. For the present we can go no further than use the term to conveniently describe a very wide spectrum of educational activity which undoubtedly possesses a number of common elements, but so far defies attempts at rigorous definition. *See* **Audiovisual Media; History of Educational Technology; Programmed Learning.**

Derick Unwin

REFERENCES

Lumsdaine A. A. and Glaser, R. (1960) *Teaching Machines and Programmed Learning*. Washington, D.C.: NEA.

Skinner, B. F. (1954) "The Science of Learning and the Art of Teaching." *Harvard Educational Review* 24: 86–97.

———. (1958) "Teaching Machines." *Science* 128: 969–977.

EDUCATIONAL TELEVISION. *See* **Television, Educational and Instructional.**

EDUCATIONAL TELEVISION ASSOCIATION (U.K.). An agency for bringing together interested bodies and individuals using educational television. Founded in 1967 and now encompassing other media as well as television in its range of interests. The association publishes the *Journal of Educational Television and Other Media* (formerly *NECCTA Bulletin*).

The association was originally called the National Educational Closed Circuit Television Association (NECCTA).

Kings Manor, Exhibition Square, York, U.K.

EFFECT, LAW OF. A law central to instrumental conditioning. Thorndyke suggested that if there is a positive effect shown by an organism to a stimulus, then the probability of this reaction increases. If the reaction (effect) is negative, the probability of learning diminishes.

EFFECTS GENERATOR. A piece of equipment used in television studios to produce electronic wipes and inlay effects. An older term is *special effects generator*.

EFFICIENCY. A term often confused with effectiveness. Many instructional procedures are certainly effective, but their efficiency, expressed as a function of time or money, may be open to question.

EGRULE. A term used to describe the strategy whereby the teacher presents an example of a rule followed by the rule (eg-rule). In more sophisticated situations it may appear as Rule-egrule, with a restatement (often rephrased) of the rule. There is some evidence that teachers who lecture with a high use of this structure are perceived as more effective than those who use other explaining strategies. The method is similar to the inductive method.

EIAJ. Electrical Industries Association of Japan. A body responsible for establishing standards in the field of videotape recording. There are 1/2–inch and 3/4–inch video tape recorder systems based on EIAJ standards.

EIDOPHOR. A device for projecting a television image in which an electron beam builds up an image on a film of oil which is then illuminated by a powerful conventional light source such as an arc lamp to throw an image on a large screen.

EIGHT MILLIMETER FILM. The 8mm cine film format came about when the existing 16mm format was cut in half for amateur use. Roll film for standard 8mm equipment functioned at 16 fps. A redesigned 8mm format with smaller sprocket holes and much more image space available was developed and called super-8. Film for super-8 is usually sold in 50ft (15m) magazines which eliminate film threading in the camera. The magazines also set the meter speed automatically on most cameras. Normal speed for super-8 is 18 fps. Later developments included larger magazines, improved film stock, and the availability of super-8 film with a stripe of magnetic tape for recording sound with a suitable camera or projector. There have been many professional applications of super-8mm film, usually shot and projected at 24fps for improved image stability.

Nowadays, small-format video recording units have largely displaced the 8mm film format for the home movie and institutional market.

EL DISPLAY. See **Electroluminescent Display.**

ELECTRODYNAMIC MICROPHONE. See **Moving Coil Microphone.**

ELECTROLUMINESCENT (EL) DISPLAY. A type of flat-panel display that produces light by electrically exciting solid materials. EL virtues are low power consumption, good contrast and brightness, and ruggedness.

ELECTRON BEAM RECORDING (EBR). A system of transferring television signals to film without using a cathode-ray tube. See **Kinescope.**

ELECTRONIC BULLETIN BOARD. System whereby information—messages, notices, requests, etc.—can be stored on a central computer and relayed to microcomputers or terminals for individuals to read. Various codes can be used to ensure that messages are routed to specific recipients only. See **Teletext.**

ELECTRONIC EDITING. (1) Audiotape editing that is carried out by dubbing recorded material from one tape recorder to another rather than by cutting and splicing the tape (mechanical editing). (2) A form of videotape editing in which material is transferred from one video tape recorder to another via electronic equipment that ensures correct synchronization and compatibility.

ELECTRONIC FLASH. A lighting system for still photography that uses an electrical discharge in a gas-filled tube. Modern electronic flash equipment represents a highly efficient and useful light source for all kinds of still photography. Its advantages are that the flash is extremely intense and of very short duration (usually less than one millisecond), thus "freezing" any movement. The spectral emission of an electronic flash is largely similar to daylight, and it is suitable for exposing daylight-balanced color film without the use of a filter. Small battery-operated electronic flashes are inexpensive and provide a very convenient compact light source. See **Lighting.**

ELECTRONIC MAIL. Systems by which text generated at one terminal of a computer or communication network is electronically transmitted to the terminal of another designated person. See **Teletext.**

ELECTRONIC NEWS GATHERING (ENG). Term applied to modern lightweight plumbicon television cameras which are good enough for educational studio use, but primarily intended as replacements for 16mm film cameras in outside broadcasting. The obvious advantage from the professional standpoint is the instant availability of footage (no processing needed), but educators have greatly benefited from the availability of relatively cheap high-quality equipment. See **Video Recording and Reproduction.**

ELECTRONIC NOTICE BOARD. *See* **Electronic Bulletin Board.**

ELECTRONIC PUBLISHING. The reproduction and distribution of documents using a microcomputer and associated laser printer rather than by conventional printing and publishing methods. *See* **Desktop Publishing.**

ELECTRONIC STENCIL CUTTER. Electronic stencil-cutting device which produces stencils directly from line or tone illustrations, photographs, etc., for duplication on a mimeograph (ink duplicator) machine.

ELECTRONIC UNIVERSITY. An educational telecommunications system inaugurated in 1983 by Tele-Learning Systems, Inc. The system permits the interconnection of students' and instructors' personal computers, unhindered by time or location.

ELECTRONIC VIDEO RECORDING (EVR). A system developed by Columbia Broadcasting System in the mid-1960s that was designed to provide a means of cheap and wide distribution of television recordings that could be played through domestic or educational television monitors. The system used optical images on film. In spite of wide backing from some international enterprises it was never a commercial success. When it was first announced, EVR received wide press publicity as a method of communication that would revolutionize education and home entertainment. The advent of low-cost videotape cassette systems with the ability to record as well as replay was one of the factors that led to the eventual nonviability of EVR.

ELECTROSTATIC COPYING. *See* **Xerography.**

ELECTROSTATIC LOUDSPEAKER. An application of electrostatic principles to loudspeaker design by means of a charged diaphragm (which may be several square feet in area) suspended between two perforated plates.

ELECTROSTATIC MICROPHONE. *See* **Condenser Microphone.**

ELLIPTIC QUESTIONING. A method of questioning much favored in **programmed learning** (q.v.). Instead of posing a direct question, a blank is left for the student to fill in, e.g., ''Acceleration occurs whenever the velocity of a body changes, i.e., a body accelerates if either its———or its———changes.'' *See* **Linear Program.**

EMULATION MODE. By addition of suitable hardware and/or software, a microcomputer of type A can behave as if it were of type B. Thus an IBM-PC can be run in emulation mode as an Apple IIE. Generally, only a more sophisticated computer can emulate a less sophisticated one.

EMULATOR. A program or a hardware device which duplicates the instruction set of one computer on a different computer, allowing, for example, programs developed for an Apple computer to run on an IBM-PC.

EMULSION. The subject of emulsions in **photography** (q.v.) is chemically complex and undergoing constant refinement. Simply put, a photographic emulsion is a combination of light-sensitive crystals, often silver halides, embedded in a carrying agent and coated on plastic or paper base for use. The point is that the crystals react to light in various ways, thus capturing the image in a way that can be chemically processed to produce a visible image. *See* **Developer; Latent Image; Reversal Process.**

ENABLE. A signal condition which permits a specific data processing event to occur. A printer may be switched on, but yet not ready to receive data; the printer must be enabled before use, possibly by pressing a SELECT key.

ENCRYPTION. Encoding of data to protect its privacy, particularly when being transmitted over public circuits or stored in a system such as a microcomputer to which other users have access.

ENCYCLOPAEDIA CINEMATOGRAPHICA. An international collection of 16mm scientific films in biology, anthropology, and technical sciences. The collection was started in West Germany and is of films which portray phenomena that cannot be observed by the unaided human eye (time lapse, high-speed); or they provide a means of comparing phenomena which are rare or are in the process of disappearing from the culture. Archives are located in Germany, the Netherlands, Austria, and Japan; partial archives are maintained in France, Switzerland, Portugal, Turkey, Brazil, Canada, and the United Kingdom.

ENG. *See* **Electronic News Gathering.**

ENIAC. Acronym for Electronic Numerical Integrator And Calculator, the first real electronic digital computer, commissioned at the University of Pennsylvania in 1946. In size it occupied a space 20 x 15 x 10 feet; it consumed 140 kilowatts of power and weighed 30 tons. For all of this bulk, its computing power was less than that of a small home computer today, and of course ENIAC was far from user-friendly. In fact, it has jocularly been referred to as the "first personal computer"—only two people knew how to make it work!

Within twenty years of ENIAC the large digital computer was commonplace in offices, and computer manufacturers such as IBM had become among the most successful corporations in the world. The pace of development has of course been maintained, and the million-dollar computer of the 1960s can now be put onto a chip the size of a match head, and costs only a dollar or two.

ENLARGEMENT. A copy, made by projection printing from a photographic negative.

An **enlarger** (q.v.) is used to produce a larger print of some or all of the negative. The negative is placed in a holder so that light can be shone through it into a lens and thus onto a piece of printing paper. The holder or head of the enlarger can be moved up and down to produce whatever degree of enlargement is suitable. The lens of the enlarger, with or without filters in the light path, produces a sharp image on a base plate. When the part of the negative to be enlarged or "blown up" has been selected and focused, the light from the enlarger is turned off. With the room lights off, and a special safelight on, a piece of coated printing paper is placed so as to capture the image projected from the lens of the enlarger. After an appropriate length of time, the enlarger is turned off and the paper, now holding an invisible positive image of the negative, is processed in suitable chemicals, washed and dried, producing a positive print of the selected size.

Enlarging and printing is a creative and challenging area of photography, particularly now that color prints can be made from color slides or color negatives with relative ease in a home darkroom. *See* **Bromide Print; Latent Image.**

ENLARGER. A device which holds a negative while a light is shone through it to register on a printing surface, thus producing an enlarged image whose size is controlled by the distance between the negative and the photosensitive surface. *See* **Enlargement.**

ENTAILMENT MESH. A representation of knowable topics and their relations; in fact, shared concepts or public concepts as in conversation theory (and thus of entities broader in scope than subject-matter topics, for example, plans; organizations in an educational system). A topic, since it stands for a public concept, has the property of concept-hood (either public or personal) of applicability: it consists of a complementary pair, namely, several procedures (alias a model) which can be applied, often iteratively, to yield some description or a behavior. We may, perhaps, liken this complementary pair to the connotation (and intention) and the denotation of the concept (public or not). At any rate a concept is not just a name, although it usually (perhaps always) has a name.

The relations between topics (concepts) include

(a) Coherence of various kinds: collective, distributive, etc.
(b) Distinctions of various kinds, as revealed by generalizations, analogues, processes, etc.
(c) Applications, which may reveal the character of a mesh of related topics when scrutinized from appropriate points of view or perspectives.

Entailment meshes can be manipulated. In fact, they constitute expressions in a primitive although quite powerful protologic, as in "Protologics are Protolanguage Lp."

One kind of manipulation is an unfoldment of a mesh (authored by one or a team of experts/teachers/students) as an exposition of, for example, some body of subject matter. A variety of unfoldments called "prunings" yield all possible paths through the mesh (for instance, the class of all possible learning strategies that are coherent from a given perspective or perspectives). Another type, called a "selective pruning" under the given pruning, gives one of the usually many learning strategies that are coherent and capable of leading to the selected topics. Other manipulations, some "evolutionary," are noted under Protologic and Protolanguage below.

LEARNING STRATEGIES AND LEARNING STYLES

A learning strategy is a path through an entailment mesh marked by tokens or indicators of what the learner did when dealing with each of the topics encountered (explored, worked on, aimed for as a perspective, tried to understand, did understand). It appears that learning strategies belong to categories (each having several variant forms) which are known as serialist (step by step) and holist (many at once; global and analogize). In general, learning strategies are determined by using a system such as the CASTE (Course Assembly System and Tutorial Environment) of conversation theory or, frequently, by less formal and rigorous interview-like techniques.

Learning styles are dispositions to adopt one or another type of mental operation and may, together with institutional and social constraints, lead to a preference on the part of a learner for specific learning strategies (in terms of efficiency, for an appropriately matched teaching strategy). Styles are determined either by experience and skilled observation or by tests such as the "Spy Ring History" and the "Smuggling Group Development" tests. These constitute lengthy learning (three or four hours) and predictive, selective, and recall experiences (three or four hours). Often more prolonged; hence, not resembling the mental test as a psychometric instrument. Scoring schemes are by no means unique but include "operation learning" (of rules), "comprehension learning" (of descriptions assembled together), "rate learning" (of lists or the like), "versatility" (using both operation and comprehension learning and also extrapolating usefully), "analogy creation" (the construction of analogies, in contrast to the use or selection of those that are given), and a "neutral" score (the neutral score is used for calibration of the differential scores).

The evidence suggests that administration of these tests together with the discussion of the scores (explained, used as discussion promoting feedback) induces "learning to learn." But after a latent interval of between four and eighteen months, "versatility" and "analogy creation" are likely to enhance the likelihood of "learning to learn."

PROTOLOGIC AND PROTOLANGUAGE

The entailment meshes of conversation theory were formed to be manipulable expressions in a protologic which is based on a protologic of which all conversational languages are specified refinements. The protologic Lp manipulation of a protologic is handled, as a matter of convenience (as a matter of fact, as a near necessity), by computer-implemented systems under the general rubric of THOUGHTSTICKER and having the character of epistemological laboratories.

The unfolding operations of "pruning" and of "selective pruning" are noted in entailment meshes. Other operations lead to mandatory construction Lp, legalization of the exposition of experts/teachers/students, and the mesh evolution by promoting information influx from them.

Lp is a primitive logic of coherence, distinction, and process. The author or authors may assert whatever coherencies they desire. But some may not agree with the prior assertions; and incoherent or not Lp legitimate. As part of the authoring process THOUGHTSTICKER checks legitimacy and suggests means of legalizing incoherent expressions. If an author persists in a statement, and if it is illegal, then it is transformed into a legal type; an analogical framework (to be filled in by selecting some or all similarities and refined by adding further destinations) or by creating a generalization (which has the same similarity and difference, form as an analogical framework). In either case, here information is requested and obtained.

Various inference rules also apply. Among these is saturation, the proposal of further coherencies if some are already stipulated, provided that the rule of coherency not losing asserted distinction between topics is respected. *See* **Conversation Theory.**

Gordon Pask

ENTITY. In computer-aided design, an object—such as an arc, plane, or cube—that is a basic building block from which users can construct drawings. Entities may be assigned various characteristics, and users can replicate entities and combine them into more complex objects.

ENTRY SKILLS. The relevant knowledge, abilities, etc., that a student must possess at the commencement of a learning experience.

ENVIRONMENT. The environment in which audiovisual aids are used is usually the classroom or lecture theater. Generally speaking, architectural environment factors such as space, ventilation, temperature, etc., are well standardized, but not so much is known concerning specific audiovisual factors.

Such considerations as, for example, the loudness of television sound, the level of ambient light during film viewing, time of day and period of viewing, have not been the subject of definitive research, although a priori it would seem probable that they are important factors in learning. *See* **Learning Environment.**

EPIDIASCOPE. A device that will project both opaque and transparent pictures. At one time such apparatus was quite common in lecture halls where it was used to project 4.25" x 3.25" lantern slides as well as book illustrations and postcards. It is a large piece of apparatus employing large-scale optics and one or more 1000w lamps.

The advent of the small-format 35mm color slide and the compact slide projector, together with simple means of producing slides from color reversal film, led to the demise of the cumbersome epidiascope, and it is now rarely seen.

EPIE. Educational Products Information Exchange. An organization providing comparative reviews of educational equipment and other supplies.

EPISCOPE. *See* **Opaque Projector.**

EPROM. An abbreviation for Erasable Programmable Read Only Memory. An electronic memory chip whose memory can be cleared by shining ultraviolet light through a built-in window. New contents can be entered by means of an EPROM programmer. Once programmed, the contents of the memory cannot be destroyed or changed except by UV light, so the memory is termed "read only." *See* **ROM**.

ERASE HEAD. The magnetic head in a tape recorder used to erase a magnetic signal from the tape.

ERASING. The process of eliminating previous recordings on magnetic tape. Erasing may be effected by passing a suitable current through the erase head on the tape recorder, or by placing the spool or cassette in the strong magnetic field produced by a bulk eraser.

ERGONOMICS. The science or art of designing the environment to fit man best. Ergonomics draws on such fields as physics, psychology, and cybernetics; a specific example of ergonomic practice is ensuring that 16mm projectors are light enough to be readily portable and have the important operating features logically placed and clearly labeled.

ERIC. The Educational Resources Information Center, which provides reference publications through various centers in the U.S. *See* **Information Systems for Education.**

ERROR MESSAGE. Information displayed by a computer regarding a problem. For example: CANNOT FIND FILE; DISC WRITE-PROTECTED; ERROR TYPE 397. Error messages using plain English are much preferable to those like the last one above.

ERROR RATE. A measure of the success of students undertaking self-instructional sequences. *See* **Gain Ratio.**

ERROR TRAPPING. Computing tactic to handle an unexpected or unwanted action on the part of the user. For example, a CAL question might call for an answer to be A, B, C, or D. If the student presses any other key, an error-trapping routine will ensure that nothing invalid or untoward occurs, and will probably display a reminder on the screen, e.g., "You MUST press one of A, B, C, or D."

In sophisticated user-friendly software a significant proportion of the program will be devoted to error trapping.

ESSAY TEST, EXAMINATION. A test or examination that involves writing essays on one or more topics. It assesses ability to discuss, evaluate, analyze, summarize, criticize, etc., under time constraints.

ESTABLISHING SHOT. The initial shot of a program or of a sequence of related shots. It sets the scene for subsequent action.

ETA. *See* **Educational Television Association.**

ETHERNET. A local data network system development by Xerox, Intel, and Digital Equipment Corporation, it is one of the more popular protocols used on personal computer networks.

EUDISED. *See* **European Documentation and Information System for Education.**

EURODIDAC. The abbreviation of the French translation of the name European Association of Manufacturers and Distributors of Educational Materials = Association EURopéene de Fabricants et de Revendeurs de Matériel DIDACtique. EURODIDAC represents the most important publishers of educational materials and schoolbooks, manufacturers and distributors of means of instruction of all kinds, as well as the leading manufacturers of school furniture. EURODIDAC was inaugurated in 1951 at the first European Educational Materials Fair (the first DIDACTA). Today, EURODIDAC comprises more than 600 members from all European countries with corresponding members in America, Africa, Asia, and Australia.

EURODIDAC organizes the European Educational Materials Exhibition (called DIDACTA), one of the world's largest commercial school equipment exhibitions. The creation of an international market for instruction materials gives educators the opportunity to examine and select the educational materials most suited to their needs.

EURODIDAC, D-7806 Freiburg-Ebnet, Federal Republic of Germany.

EUROPEAN DOCUMENTATION AND INFORMATION SYSTEM FOR EDUCATION (EUDISED). An information retrieval system developed in Europe to cover member countries of the Council of Europe. Standards of bibliographical formats on a multilanguage thesaurus have been produced in English, German, and French. The *EUDISED R & D Bulletin,* published five times per year, presents a broad range of abstracts on ongoing educational research projects. ISSN 0378–7192. *See* **Information Classification and Retrieval.**

EVALUATION. Evaluation is the process of determining value or merit. It consists of methods for the systematic collection and analysis of information with the aim of improving the quality of human services. It is an applied social science which examines the effectiveness and efficiency of these services and enables adaptations to be made to them. The essential features of evaluation as a form of inquiry are its attention to performance or achievement, its use in decision making, and its concern with both ethics and utility.

KINDS OR LEVELS OF EVALUATION FOUND IN EDUCATION

Evaluation in education occurs at several levels. The most global is program evaluation, which includes the evaluation of instruction, curriculum, and learning. In a similar manner, evaluation of the instructional process includes study of the curriculum and of learning. Each kind of evaluation originated in response to different needs, however, and has its own distinguishing characteristics.

Program Evaluation. A program is an operational plan for rendering a service, and the major impetus for the development of program evaluation methods came from the institution of government-funded social programs and the soon-to-follow requirement for accountability of the funds expended on these programs. Social and fiscal responsibility required that proof be given of the need for and effectiveness of programs intended to render service. Two roles of evaluation were distinguished: formative, conducted during the development of a program for its improvement; and summative, conducted at the end of a program to determine its worth (Scriven, 1974 THEORETICAL BACKGROUND). They have been compared in the following manner: "When the cook tastes the soup, that's formative; when the guests taste the soup, that's summative" (Scriven, 1981 BACKGROUND READING, p. 63).

A number of models for program evaluation were developed during the 1970s and became guidelines in the field. One of the first models produced was discrepancy evaluation (Provus, 1973 THEORETICAL BACKGROUND). It consisted of a three-stage process: (1) defining program standards; (2) determining whether discrepancies exist between different aspects of program performance and the standards governing those aspects; and (3) using the discrepancy information either to change performance or to change program standards. The focus of discrepancy evaluation was the match between program goals and performance. In contrast to this model, Scriven's goal-free evaluation (1972 THEORETICAL BACKGROUND) focused on program outcomes, intended and nonintended, with careful regard for side effects. His model was needs-based or consumer-oriented evaluation in contrast with the standard goal-based evaluation.

A third widely used evaluation model is based on the kinds of decisions to be made. In the Context, Input, Process, and Product (CIPP) model, Stufflebeam et al. (1971 THEORETICAL BACKGROUND) defined four different types of evaluation. Context evaluation, which includes needs assessment, serves planning decisions and is characterized by defining the relevant environment, describing actual and desired conditions in the environment, and identifying unmet needs and the reasons for them. Input evaluation serves design decisions; that is, how to utilize resources to meet program goals. It includes the assessment of capabilities of those responsible for a program, the strategies for achieving program goals, and designs for implementing selected strategies. Project proposals are an example of this type of evaluation. Process evaluation is more frequently found in educational settings and consists of monitoring a program to detect and adjust to discrepancies found between program goals and performance. For Stufflebeam et al. this includes monitoring interpersonal relationships, communication channels, resource adequacy, physical facilities, staff, and time schedule. The last type of program evaluation, product evaluation, consists of measuring and interpreting the attainments of the program. It involves devising operational definitions of objectives and defining standards for meeting those objectives, then measuring the achievement of the objectives. The achievement is compared with the standards, and an interpretation is made based on the previously recorded context, input, and process information. A product evaluation thus involves all the types of evaluation.

One last widely recognized model of evaluation breaks the process down into two processes, description and judgment (Stake, 1967 THEORETICAL BACKGROUND). To enable description of a program, Stake recommended the installation of data banks to document the antecedent conditions, transactions, and outcomes, both intended and observed, in educational programs. This data would then be compared to that from another program with similar goals and with the standards of excellence set for the program itself in order to come to a judgment of the program. Stake more recently has stressed the importance of the evaluation process being responsive to the nature of the program and the concerns and values of its constituents (Stake, 1975 THEORETICAL BACKGROUND). Responsive evaluation is organized around observations of activities and interviews with constituents, with a progressive focusing on issues and with frequent reports that illuminate the critical issues. Stake thus brought the focus of the evaluation back to the consumers or concerned constituents of the program. This approach has been further elucidated by Parlett and Dearden (1977 THEORETICAL BACKGROUND) who, in conceptualizing evaluation as illumination, insist on not only technical and intellectual skills on the part of the evaluator but also interpersonal skills.

This review of models allows us to discern important elements of program evaluation.

1. Evaluation is done for a variety of purposes, including accountability, but most frequently for improvement.
2. Evaluation involves the comparison of performance with standards to determine if discrepancies exist and, therefore, changes are needed.
3. Some evaluation models are oriented toward consumers, others toward managers; and some are goal-based, while others attend primarily to program effects. Corollary to this observation is that side or unintended effects of programs should also be weighed.
4. Different types of evaluation—context, input, process, product—focus on different aspects of a program. Different evaluations may involve a number of different types.
5. Evaluation consists of both description and judgment, and requires procedures for data collection and for making judgments.
6. To be effective, evaluation should illuminate the critical issues; it should also respond to the concerns of all parties involved. It therefore requires interpersonal as well as measurement skills on the part of evaluators.

These points reflect the adaptive purpose of evaluation. One set of models that further reflects the use of formal evaluation as a means of interpersonal decision making are the judicial or adversary models (see Owens and Hiscox, 1977 THEORETICAL BACKGROUND). These models use a legal format in which the pros and cons of a program are debated and a judicial decision is made. The process reflects the fact that evaluation is a complex human decision-making process.

Evaluation of the Instructional Process. Although this is a frequent form of process evaluation, it originates in a very different milieu, and the history of its development has had less to do with the monitoring done in process evaluations of programs and more to do with the validity of measuring instruments. The origin of instructional evaluation was in faculties and schools of education where student teachers were observed and rated on their teaching skills. This administrative procedure led to the development of numerous observation checklists, among which Flander's (1965, 1970 DESCRIPTION OF METHODOLOGY) system of interaction analysis is most widely known. In it, categories of teaching behaviors which directly influence (focusing attention, interjecting authority) or indirectly influence students (asking questions, praising students' responses) and student behaviors (responding, initiating) are listed and their occurrence is recorded. Although developed as a research instrument, the system of interaction analysis suggested categories of behavior which later appeared in the rating forms used by leagues of college and university students in evaluating their professors' teaching skills.

Many rating scales have been developed for use in postsecondary institutions. Three of the most widely used are the *Student Instructional Report* (SIR) developed by the Educational Testing Service; the *Purdue Cafeteria System;* and the *Instructional Development and Effectiveness Assessment* (IDEA) System at Kansas State University (see Centra, 1980 RESEARCH). Research on student ratings suggests that different ratings on the same professor correlate strongly whether different forms are used or ratings are taken at different times of the year or over successive years (Murray, 1972 DESCRIPTION OF METHODOLOGY). The use of ratings from five courses of at least fifteen students each has been shown to be a dependable measure of teaching effectiveness (Gilmore, Kane, and Naccarato, 1978 RESEARCH). Ratings tend to vary across disciplines, however. Higher ratings of course value and teacher effectiveness have been found in the humanities than in the social sciences and sciences (Centra and Creech, 1976 RESEARCH). Research productivity does not appear to be strongly linked to teaching effectiveness (Centra, 1980 RESEARCH).

Two trends are appearing in the evaluation of the instructional process. First, there is a move to understand which criteria of good teaching are universally used and which have less general acceptance (Donald, 1984 THEORETICAL BACKGROUND). Organization and clarity, instructor knowledge, and presentation and interaction skills are recognized as important teaching factors (Hildebrand, Wilson, and Dienst, 1971; McKeachie, Lin, and Mann, 1971; Irby, 1978 RESEARCH; Seldin, 1980 DESCRIPTION OF METHODOLOGY). Other criteria such as dynamism or relevant course materials are not as generally accepted (see Seldin, 1980 DESCRIPTION OF METHODOLOGY). The second trend in evaluating teaching is the change from dependence on student ratings to include other forms of evaluation such as colleague and self-evaluation and measures of student achievement (Centra, 1980 RESEARCH; Miller, 1974 THEORETICAL BACKGROUND; Seldin, 1980 DESCRIPTION OF METHODOLOGY). One reason for this is that student ratings do not correlate reliably with student ability, expected grade, or achievement in the course (Abrami, Leventhal, and Perry, 1982; Centra and Creech, 1976 RESEARCH). Measures of course achievement appear to correlate more highly with the amount of course content than with student ratings. The awareness that a teacher has relatively little control over many of the factors affecting learning, including student ability, institutional climate, and course scheduling suggests caution in the use of student achievement data. The additional evidence that approximately 15 percent of the variance in student learning can be judged to be due to instructional method (Walberg, 1978 RESEARCH) introduces a further caution in the use of student achievement data to evaluate instruction. One reasonable solution to the question of the fair use of student achievement data is to ensure that results are used positively, i.e., for improvement or rewards, and not negatively. This brings us full circle to the effective use of student ratings to determine a baseline or set of standards of good teaching. The establishment of such a baseline requires the study of acceptable criteria and ranges of acceptable teaching behaviors agreed upon by the institution or group intending to use them. A set of criteria so developed would provide guidance for teachers and regular feedback on their performance so that necessary adaptations could be made.

Evaluation of Curriculum/Learning Materials. One of the earliest kinds of evaluation done in education was that of curriculum or its concrete representation in learning materials, but it is also an area in which far too little evaluation is done. An analysis of the 60 best-selling textbooks in the United States revealed that less than 10 percent were field-tested before publication (Komoski, 1971 BACKGROUND READING). Programmed instruction materials and television broadcasts had received far less attention. There is no reason to suppose that these figures have changed to any great extent. Curriculum evaluation was first defined by Ralph Tyler (1949 THEORETICAL BACKGROUND) as a process of determining to what extent the educational objectives in a program are actually realized by its curriculum and instruction. This general view of curriculum evaluation emphasized the appraisal of the behavior of students and the fact that it should be a continual process, thus making it the forebear to program evaluation models. For Tyler, evaluation procedures were to provide evidence of how far educational objectives were being met. To do this, he suggested the now-classic two-dimensional analysis which compared the kinds of behavior to be developed with the content to be learned. From the grid produced by such an analysis, the behaviors to be learned in each content area could be located so that situations could be identified in which students could express that behavior, and evaluation instruments could be devised to measure achievement of the objectives. This approach was expanded by Cronbach (1963 THEORETICAL BACKGROUND) when he called for evaluations which would both ascertain what effects a course has and identify aspects of the course where revision is desirable. The intention was to rely not only on tests, but to use a more holistic approach to course improvement.

Curriculum evaluation was given its greatest public impetus in the 1960s in the reaction to the launching of Sputnik, when science and mathematics curricula were revamped and evaluations of them were well-funded. Since educational institutions tend to be consumers of curriculum as it is presented in texts and other media, it is an area in which educators must play the role of judge or quality-control agent. The processes particular to curriculum evaluation are formative and resemble the research and development (R&D) process. Thus one of the tenets of curriculum evaluation is that data are collected on areas that the developers can do something about (Baker, 1974 THEORETICAL BACKGROUND). Baker defines two stages in curriculum evaluation: evaluation of instructional prototypes and operational field-testing. Prototype evaluation proceeds through an internal review of materials which covers the accuracy and range of content, the quality of instructional design, and coordination of materials. If the materials meet standards, they are then tried out on a sample of learners, and student performance and reactions are observed. If the materials are found to be instructionally effective, the evaluation proceeds to the second stage of operational field-testing to determine the feasibility of the product under relatively natural conditions. Attention is then directed toward product utility, access, and integration. Once again, content, instruction, and format coordination reviews are done, but this time to test for fit to the field situation. Data are collected not only on student learning and reactions but also on teacher behavior and satisfaction and on administrator reactions. The number of iterations of these two stages is determined by how well the program works, how much improvement successive revisions have been able to produce, and which resources are available to the developer. Adaptations to meet the needs of different subgroups may lead to further revisions. Thus, materials evaluation must first consider the relationship between the materials and instructional goals, then gauge the effectiveness of the product, then consider adaptability or availability and costs of adoption and use. A major source of information on educational materials is the Educational Products Information Exchange (EPIE; BACKGROUND READING).

Evaluation of Learning. The most fundamental form of educational evaluation, and a measure for the other kinds of evaluation, is that of changes in behavior or performance due to instruction, or learning. The evaluation of learning has a long history in the tests and measurement movement, and the number of standardized tests of ability and achievement is proof of the formidable amount of energy that has gone into the measurement of learning (see Buros, 1972 BACKGROUND READING). The earliest recorded system of written examinations was developed for the Chinese civil service in 2357 B.C. (Ebel, 1972 THEORETICAL BACKGROUND). The first textbook in educational measurement appeared in 1903 and was written by E. L. Thorndike, who provided a new way of thinking about learning as a process governed by laws of readiness, exercise, and effect. Perhaps the most notable landmark in the history of the evaluation of learning was the development of taxonomies of educational objectives in the cognitive, affective, and psychomotor domains (see Bloom, ed., 1956; Krathwohl, Bloom and Masia, 1964 DESCRIPTION OF METHODOLOGY).

The taxonomy of cognitive objectives, the first to be developed, has been used extensively in education but has seen a particular use in categorizing learning objectives and test items developed in reference to them. The hierarchy of increasingly demanding objectives begins with several categories of knowledge, such as knowledge of conventions, of trends and sequences, of methodology, and of theories and structures. The next level, comprehension, includes the abilities of translation, interpretation, and extrapolation. This level is followed by four others: application, analysis, synthesis, and evaluation. The affective domain of educational objectives, which is more difficult to evaluate, contains sections on receiving or attending, responding, valuing, organizing a system of values, and having a philosophy of values (Krathwohl, Bloom, and Masia, 1964 DESCRIPTION OF METHODOLOGY). In the psychomotor domain, seven levels of behavior have been defined: perception, set or readiness, guided response such as imitation, mechanism or habitual response, complex overt response including highly coordinated motor activities, adaptation to fit special requirements, and origination of new patterns (Simpson, 1972 DESCRIPTION OF METHODOLOGY). The taxonomies have been developed with examples of objectives and suggestions for measuring their achievement.

Choice of a test format to measure the achievement of learning objectives depends upon the kind of learning objective, but several general principles guide test construction (see Green, 1975 DESCRIPTION OF METHODOLOGY). The test should be long enough to be valid and reliable but short enough to be usable. Validity and reliability, as well as standardization, are major issues in test construction. Test items should be clear and concise, as should test directions. The preparation and pilot testing of tests to determine their fairness and validity are critical to their utility. Thus, formal tests go through a procedure of (1) careful analysis of objectives and content; (2) administration to a representative sample of the target population; (3) item analysis, editing and revision to eliminate faulty items; and (4) the establishment of standardized scores which represent the levels of performance of the sample or group to whom the test was administered. There are four major test formats that are used to evaluate learning. The first is the objective test, called objective because equally competent scorers can score them independently and obtain the same results. Examples of objective tests are multiple-choice, true-false, short answer, and matching. Three other formats are essay, oral, and performance. A number of texts provide guidance in test construction and validation of these various forms (see Bloom, Hastings, and Madaus, 1971; Green, 1975 DESCRIPTION OF METHODOLOGY; Ebel, 1972 THEORETICAL BACKGROUND).

Two issues in the evaluation of learning have sparked considerable debate: the mastery learning model and criterion- versus norm-referenced evaluation. Mastery learning is based on the premise that most students are capable of mastering a set of learning objectives if given sufficient time. Students are evaluated at each stage of the learning process and are expected to achieve mastery of the objective, often by meeting a standard of 80 or 90 percent of the test questions for that objective. Thus the learning variable becomes time and not grade. The administration of mastery learning must, obviously, be individualized. Evaluation of mastery learning has three phases. First, entering students are tested to determine their level of competence in a diagnostic evaluation. At each stage or unit of learning, formative evaluation provides feedback about how the student is progressing. Finally, summative evaluation provides a record of achievement at the end of instruction. Students thus compete against a criterion rather than their classmates. The advantages include more positive student attitudes and an emphasis on learning rather than grades, but the disadvantages include wider administration time and, potentially, a greater range in student achievement over a defined time period. With the greater use of technology in education, particularly the computer, the administrative disadvantages of the mastery model could feasibly be overcome.

The debate over criterion- versus norm-referenced evaluation rests in whether judgments of learning should be made in comparison with the learning objective or with fellow students. Norm-referenced measurements, for example, most grading systems, are based on an average level of performance and students are graded in relation to that average. Standardized test scores rely upon norms based on representative samples of the relevant population. Criterion-referenced measures, on the other hand, are based on particular abilities or objectives and the degree to which a student has mastered them, as in mastery learning. The disadvantage with criterion-referenced tests, according to Ebel (1972 THEORETICAL BACKGROUND), is that to be generally meaningful, criteria of achievement must represent broad standards, and these are infrequently found in education except where a high degree of skill is developed in a limited set of abilities. One attempt to rectify the lack of specified objectives is the Educational Objectives Bank established at the University of California, Los Angeles (Popham and Ebel, 1978 DESCRIPTION OF METHODOLOGY). The question remains of how readily adoptable the objectives would be in different school regions since abilities and programs differ widely from region to region. A primary disadvantage of using a norm-referenced standard is that it tends to overemphasize competition among students. It does not report what the learner has accomplished or is now able to do. Further, if one is grading according to the normal curve, and a group is not distributed in this manner, the process introduces an invalidity which may translate into an injustice to students. This debate over standards and how relative or absolute they can be and yet still be applied in individual instances is far from resolved. International bodies such as the International Association for the Evaluation of Educational Achievement (IEA), set up through the UNESCO Institute for Education to permit comparisons of educational achievements among nations (Husen, 1979; Peaker, 1975 BACKGROUND READING) may provide insight into how generalizable educational objectives and achievements and their measurement can be.

In conclusion, a review of the kinds or levels of evaluation reveals consistencies on some dimensions and variations on others. The evaluation of learning is necessary for all other levels of evaluation. The fair evaluation of instruction imposes limits on the use of measurements of learning because of the complex of variables influencing learning. Curriculum and program evaluation have in common the goals of education as a paramount consideration although program evaluation procedures and purposes tend to be broader than those of curriculum evaluation. The different levels of evaluation thus have distinct features but are interwoven in their procedures and effects.

EVALUATION METHODS

The methods used in evaluation studies include methods of research design, collection, and data analysis. Different research designs allow for varying degrees of control over the validity of results. The validity of the data is an important criterion in an evaluation study as in any investigation, but in addition, evaluations must meet other standards such as utility and feasibility. One general rule for the use of research design in evaluation is that the design should be as rigorous as possible but should not prevent all critical variables which may affect evaluation results from being considered. For example, the responsive evaluation model calls for the values of the constituents to be considered. Data collection, analysis, and reporting methods suggest solutions to the problem of considering the array of critical variables.

Designs. The methods of research most applicable in evaluation studies are (1) descriptive, case and field study research; (2) correlational research; (3) causal-comparative research; (4) experimental research; and (5) quasi-experimental research. A brief review of these methods will show their complementary functions in the evaluation process.

(1) Descriptive, case and field studies systematically describe a situation or area and are used to collect factual information that describes background and existing phenomena, to identify problems, to make comparisons, and to determine what others are doing with similar problems or situations. These studies act as context evaluations which set the scene for the larger evaluation study (see Isaac and Michael, 1981 DESCRIPTION OF METHODOLOGY).

(2) Correlational designs investigate the extent to which variations in one factor correspond with variations in one or more other factors. Such a design is appropriate where the array of variables is complex, as in most evaluations; it permits the measurement of several variables and their interrelationships simultaneously and in a realistic setting and allows for degrees of relationship rather than an all-or-nothing approach. It has several limitations, including its inability to identify cause and effect, but is important in measuring congruence in evaluation studies.

(3) Causal-comparative research, or modus operandi designs, investigate possible cause-and-effect relationships by observing some existing consequence and searching back through the data for plausible causal factors; for example, the attributes of effective teachers as defined by their performance compared with records over the preceding ten years for extra courses taken or other possible factors which would have affected their performance (see Scriven, 1974 THEORETICAL BACKGROUND).

(4) Experimental research investigates possible cause-and-effect relationships by exposing one or more experimental groups to different treatment conditions and comparing the results to those of a control group not receiving the treatment. This requires rigorous management of the variables and conditions by direct control or through randomization; thus it is less feasible for evaluation studies but yields the most clear-cut results.

(5) Quasi-experimental research designs are intended to approximate the conditions of an experiment in situ-

ations which do not allow the control or manipulation of all relevant variables; for example, to investigate the effects of spaced versus massed practice in the learning of economics in four high school classes without being able to assign students to the treatment at random (see Cook and Campbell, 1979 DESCRIPTION OF METHODOLOGY). To compensate for the absence of control through randomization, the researcher tries to overome threats to the internal and external validity of the project by ascertaining that variables such as the history of the project, maturation of students, or effects of testing, selection, or mortality have not confounded the treatment results. Although quasi-experimental designs are usually the most rigorous designs which can be used in an evaluation, the other designs described here have all been used.

Data Collection. Gathering information requires both measurement and interpersonal skills. The measurement skills fall into two categories: quantitative and qualitative. The difference between quantitative and qualitative measurements rests essentially in the degree to which the measurements have been assigned a number. Experimental designs and behavioral checklists tend to yield quantitative data, while interviews are more likely to yield qualitative data, that is, descriptive data. One general rule is to use multiple measures from multiple sources in a process of triangulation, i.e., attempting to locate or explain a particular variable as precisely as possible through the use of a series of measurements (Anderson et al., 1975 BACKGROUND READING).

Among measurement techniques, the most frequently used are tests and surveys. Tests may be published and standardized, as are those listed by Buros (1972 BACKGROUND READING), or constructed to meet the needs of the evaluation study. They may be criterion or norm-referenced and they may be tests of ability, achievement, aptitude, or perception. They may also be projective; that is, they may present an ambiguous stimulus to which the respondent creates a response revealing his or her own attitudes or thoughts, as in the Rorschach test. Survey methods include questionnaires mailed or used in an interview, telephone surveys, and individual or group interviews which may be structured, that is, follow a well-defined format, semistructured (built around a core of questions with possible branches) or unstructured (with general questions or objectives but otherwise open). The application of these different types of data collection instruments depends upon the evaluation situation and the other instruments being used. Rating scales are often used to measure attitudes or perceptions as is the semantic differential. More recently, emphasis has been put on performance tests, particularly situational tests such as in-basket exercises where identical tasks or problems are presented under identical conditions to different individuals. Data on costs are also collected for efficiency or cost-benefit analyses (see Isaac and Michael, 1981; Posavac and Carey, 1980 DESCRIPTION OF METHODOLOGY; Popham, 1974 THEORETICAL BACKGROUND).

Because of threats to the validity of these methods since they intrude on or change the situation, or evoke responses from the participants, emphasis has also been put on the inclusion of nonobtrusive and nonreactive measures. Three kinds of measures tend to be nonobtrusive: (1) documentation, (2) physical trace, and (3) observation. Documentation involves the collection and study of records such as class attendance, archives, minutes of meetings, or logs or diaries of project events. Physical trace measurements show the use of facilities, such as wear on textbooks or consumption of materials. Observations may be more or less obtrusive. If a one-way mirror is used, observations will be least obtrusive, while introducing an evaluator into the situation as a participant-observer, taking field notes, or using a checklist will be more obtrusive, and taping or videotaping could be disrupting to those being observed.

Since the collection of data frequently requires personal interaction, texts on data collection methods often include sections on learning the language of those being interviewed, establishing rapport, developing relationships, asking questions and probing in interviews, and promoting openness (see Bogdan and Taylor, 1975 DESCRIPTION OF METHODOLOGY). The use of several different kinds of data collection methods is important both for the validity of the evaluation through triangulation and its acceptability and applicability.

Data Analysis and Reporting. Two criteria, at times opposing, guide the analysis and reporting of data. Information must be presented in a format readily understandable by multiple audiences such as sponsors, managers, personnel, recipients, other researchers, and the public at large. At the same time, data will have been collected from a variety of sources under different conditions. This has led evaluators to use a framework or matrix to show which types of data are relevant to the various questions which have been asked (see Baker, 1974; Provus, 1973; Stake, 1967 THEORETICAL BACKGROUND; Borich, 1974 DESCRIPTION OF METHODOLOGY). Where experimental or quasi-experimental designs have been used, the data analysis follows from the design. For other designs, the data reduction process is one of portraying and illuminating in a clear and concise manner a description of the evaluation, the methods used, and the results and recommendations. Descriptive statistics and tables and graphs which are easily read are recommended. Confidentiality must be respected. Suggestions for data analysis which cover analytic procedures such as content analysis, cost analysis, item analysis, various statistical analyses, and tests for validity and reliability can be found in Anderson et al. (1974 BACKGROUND READING); Isaac and Michael (1981 DESCRIPTION OF METHODOLOGY); Popham (1974 THEORETICAL BACKGROUND); and Posavac and Carey (1980 DESCRIPTION OF METHODOLOGY). For illuminative and naturalistic approaches to evaluation, Hamilton et al. (1977 THEORETICAL BACKGROUND) and Guba and Lincoln (1981 DESCRIPTION OF METHODOLOGY) are recommended.

Perhaps one of the most useful aids to identifying the important dimensions that must be explored prior to the final synthesis in an evaluation is the key evaluation checklist developed by Scriven (1981 BACKGROUND READING). (1) Description: what is to be evaluated, described as objectively as possible, with components, their relationships. What are the actual functions, as opposed to intended function or role of what is being evaluated and its dimensions, aspects, or components? What is the delivery system; how does what is being evaluated reach the market; how is it maintained, improved, updated? How are users trained? How is implementation achieved, monitored, improved, and by whom? (2) Client: the person who commissioned the evaluation, distinguished among the initiator of the request for evaluation, the instigator of what is to be evaluated, and its inventor. (3) Background and context: stakeholders in the evaluation, nature of what is being evaluated, expectations of the evaluation, type of evaluation, organization charts, prior efforts. (4) Resources: support system available, including finances, expertise, past experience, technology, and flexibility. (5) Consumer: who is using or receiving what is being evaluated, distinguishing targeted or intended population from true customers or recipients, and the directly or indirectly impacted recipient population. (6) Values and needs: of the impacted and potentially impacted population, including wants, judged or believed standards of merit and ideals, defined goals of a program, and the needs of the instigator, monitor, inventor. Are there preexisting objectively validated standards of merit or worth that apply? Can any be inferred from the checkpoints on client, consumer, function, and needs and values? Can goals be validated as appropriate, legal, ethical? (7) Process: what constraints, costs, and benefits apply to the normal operation of what is being evaluated? For example, to what extent does the actual operation match the stated stipulations or sponsor's beliefs about its operation? (8) Outcomes: what effects are produced by what is being evaluated (intended or unintended)? Scriven suggests a six-dimensional matrix composed of population affected × type of effect (cognitive, affective, psychomotor, health, social, environmental) × size of each type of effect × time of onset (immediate, end of treatment, later) × duration × each component or dimension. (9) Generalizability: to other people, places, or times. This may be labeled deliverability, salability, exportability, durability, and modifiability. (10) Costs: dollar, psychological, personnel; initial and repeated, including preparation, maintenance, and improvement; direct or indirect; immediate, delayed, discounted; by components if appropriate. (11) Comparisons: with alternative options, recognized and not recognized, now available and constructable, leading contenders in the field or critical competitors, identified on the grounds of cost plus effectiveness. (12) Significance: a synthesis of the eleven preceding checkpoints. Scriven suggests the strategy of flexible weighted sum with overrides, although in an earlier document he graphs or profiles a set of checkpoints (Scriven, 1974 THEORETICAL BACKGROUND). (13) Recommendations: may or may not be requested; may follow from the resources checkpoint. (14) Reports: vocabulary, length, format, medium, time, location, and personnel for its or their presentation require scrutiny as does protection, privacy, publicity, and prior screening or circulation of final and preliminary drafts. (15) Metaevaluation: the evaluation itself should be evaluated, preferably prior to implementation or final dissemination of the report, and preferably by an external evaluator after application of the key evaluation checklist.

EVALUATION STANDARDS

The standards which an evaluation should meet have undergone lengthy discussion and have been published by the Joint Committee on Standards for Educational Evaluation (1981 BACKGROUND READING), for use with educational programs, projects, and materials. They consist of four sets of standards, for utility, feasibility, propriety, and accuracy. The intent of the utility standards is to ensure that an evaluation will serve the practical information needs of given audiences. They include audience identification, so that their needs can be addressed, evaluator credibility, i.e., that evaluators should be both trustworthy and competent, and information scope and selection, i.e., that information should address pertinent questions and be responsive to the needs and interests of the audiences. Perspectives, procedures, and rationale for interpreting the findings should be clearly described, and several guidelines for report dissemination are discussed.

The feasibility standards are intended to ensure evaluations that are realistic, prudent, diplomatic, and frugal, and include items on practical procedures that involve minimal disruption of operations, political viability, and cost-effectiveness. For example, an evaluation should produce information of sufficient value to justify the resources expended.

The propriety standards are concerned with ensuring that an evaluation will be conducted legally, ethically, and with due regard for the welfare of those involved in the evaluation, as well as those affected by its results. They include sections on contracting for an evaluation, conflict of interest, full and frank disclosure, the public's right to know, and the rights of human subjects. Evaluators are expected to respect human dignity and worth in their interactions with other persons, to provide an evaluation that is complete and fair in its presentation of the strengths and weaknesses of what is being evaluated, to be responsible in the allocation and expenditure of resources, and to be prudent and ethically responsible.

The accuracy standards apply to the technical adequacy of the evaluation. These include clear identification of what is being evaluated, analysis of the context for its influences on the program, project, or material being evaluated, and a detailed description and monitoring of the purposes and procedures of the evaluation. Sources of information, described in detail so that their adequacy can be assessed; information-gathering instruments and procedures which are valid and reliable; and systematic data control are essential, as is the analysis and interpretation of quantitative and qualitative information. Conclusions should be explicitly justified so that audiences can assess them, and evaluation procedures should provide safeguards to protect the findings and reports from bias or distortion. The standards thus serve as overall guidelines for good evaluations.

In summary, evaluation is a complex process which consists of a variety of methods for collecting and analyzing data for the purposes of adaptivity in human services. It is an evolving field in which emphasis on rigorous data reduction methods vies with the need to make the findings applicable and utilized. The different kinds of evaluation show the wide range of application, and the models and methods suggest the many issues or facets to be considered in an evaluation.

Janet Donald

REFERENCES

Background Reading

Anderson, S. B., Ball, S., and Murphy, R. T. (1974) *Encyclopedia of Educational Evaluation*. San Francisco, Calif.: Jossey-Bass.

Buros, O. K., ed. (1972) *The Seventh Mental Measurements Yearbook*. Highland Park, N.J.: Gryphon Press.

Educational Products Information Exchange Institute (EPIE), Stony Brook, New York.

Husen, T. (1979) "An International Research Venture in Retrospect: The IEA Surveys." *Comparative Education Review*, 23: 371–385.

Joint Committee on Standards for Educational Evaluation of Programs, Projects and Materials. (1981) Hightstown, N.J.: McGraw-Hill.

Komoski, P. K. (1971) "Testimony before the Select Education Subcommittee of the Education and Labor Committee of the U.S. House of Representatives." *Congressional Record*, 11 May.

Peaker, G. F. (1975) *An Empirical Study of Education in 21 Countries: A Technical Report*. International Association for the Evaluation of Educational Achievement (IEA). Stockholm: Almqvist & Wiksell Intl.; Toronto: Wiley.

Scriven, M. (1981) *Evaluation Thesaurus*, 3d ed. Inverness, Calif.: Edgepress.

Theoretical Background

Baker, E. (1974) "Formative Evaluation of Instruction." In *Evaluation in Education: Current Applications*, ed. W. J. Popham. Berkeley, Calif.: McCutchan.

Cronbach, L. J. (1963) "Course Improvement Through Evaluation." *Teachers College Record* 64: 672–683.

Donald, J. G. (1984) "Quality indices for faculty evaluation." *Assessment and Evaluation in Higher Education* 9 (1): 41–52.

Ebel, R. L. (1972) *Essentials of Educational Measurement*. 2d ed. Englewood Cliffs, N.J.: Prentice-Hall.

Hamilton, D., MacDonald, B., King, C., Jenkins, D., and Parlett, M. (1977) *Beyond the Numbers Game: A Reader in Educational Evaluation*. Berkeley, Calif.: McCutchan.

Miller, R. I. (1974) *Developing Programs for Faculty Evaluation*. San Francisco, Calif.: Jossey-Bass.

Nevo, D. (1983) "The Conceptualization of Educational Evaluation: An Analytical Review of the Literature." *Review of Educational Research* 53 (1): 117–128.

Owens, T. and Hiscox, M. (1977) *Alternative Models for Adversary Evaluation: Variations on a Theme*. Portland, Ore.: Northwest Regional Educational Laboratory.

Parlett, M. and Dearden, G., eds. (1977) *Introduction to Illuminative Evaluation: Studies in Higher Education*. Cardiff-by-the-Sea, Calif.: Pacific Soundings Press.

Popham, W. J. (1974) *Evaluation in Education: Current Applications*. Berkeley, Calif.: McCutchan.

Provus, M. (1973) *Discrepancy Evaluation*. Berkeley, Calif.: McCutchan.

Scriven, M. (1972) "Pros and Cons about Goal-Free Evaluation." *Evaluation Comment*. Also in *Evaluation in Education: Current Applications*, ed. W. J. Popham. Berkeley, Calif.: McCutchan.

———. (1974) "Evaluation Perspectives and Procedures." In *Evaluation in Education*, ed. W. J. Popham. Berkeley, Calif.: McCutchan.

Stake, R. (1967) "The Countenance of Educational Evaluation." *Teachers College Record* 68: 523–540.

———. (1975) *Evaluating the Arts in Education: A Responsive Approach.* Columbus, Ohio: C. E. Merrill.

Stufflebeam, D. L. et al. (1971) *Educational Evaluation and Decision-Making.* Itasca, Ill.: Peacock.

Thorndike, E. L. (1903) *An Introduction to the Theory of Mental and Social Measurements.* New York: Science Press.

Tyler, R. W. (1949) *Basic Principles of Curriculum and Instruction.* Chicago: University of Chicago Press.

Research

Abrami, P. C., Leventhal, L. and Perry, R. P. (1982) "Educational seduction." *Review of Educational Research* 52 (3): 446–464.

Centra, J. A., (1980) *Determining Faculty Effectiveness.* San Francisco, Calif.: Jossey-Bass.

Centra, J. A. and Creech, F. R. (1976) *The Relationship between Students, Teachers, and Course Characteristics and Student Ratings of Teacher Effectiveness.* Project Report 76-1. Princeton, N. J.: Educational Testing Service.

Gilmore, G. M., Kane, M. T., and Naccarato, R. W. (1978) "The Generalizability of Student Ratings of Instruction: Estimation of Teacher and Course Components." *Journal of Educational Measurement* 15 (1): 1–13.

Hildebrand, M., Wilson, R. C., and Dienst, E. R. (1971) *Evaluating University Teaching.* Berkeley, Calif.: University of California Center for Research and Development in Higher Education.

Irby, D. M. (1978) "Clinical Faculty Development." In *Clinical Education for the Allied Health Professions,* ed. C. Ford. St. Louis, Mo.: C. V. Mosby.

McKeachie, W. J., Lin, Y., and Mann, W. (1971) "Student Ratings of Teacher Effectiveness: Validity Studies." *American Educational Research Journal* 8: 435–445.

Murray, H. G. (1972) "The Validity of Student Ratings of Faculty Teaching Ability." Paper presented at the meeting of the Canadian Psychological Association, Montreal, Canada.

Walberg, H. J. (1978) "A Psychological Theory of Educational Productivity." Paper presented at the annual meeting of the American Psychological Association, Toronto, Canada.

Description of Methodology

Bloom, B. S. ed. (1956) *Taxonomy of Educational Objectives,* Handbook 1: *Cognitive Domain.* New York: David McKay.

Bloom, B. S., Hastings, J. T., and Madaus, G. F. (1971) *Handbook on Formative and Summative Evaluation of Student Learning.* New York: McGraw-Hill.

Bogdan, R. and Taylor, S. (1975) *Introduction to Qualitative Research Methods.* New York: John Wiley & Sons.

Borich, G. D., ed. (1974) *Evaluating Educational Programs and Products.* Englewood Cliffs, N.J.: Educational Technology Publications.

Cook, T. and Campbell, D. (1979) *Quasi-experimentation: Design and Analysis Issues for Field Settings.* Chicago: Rand McNally.

Flanders, N. A. (1965) *Teacher Influence, Pupil Attitudes, and Achievement.* Washington, D.C.: U.S. Department of Health, Education, and Welfare.

———. (1970) *Analyzing Teaching Behavior.* Reading, Mass.: Addison-Wesley.

Green, J. A. (1975) *Teacher-Made Tests.* 2d ed. New York: Harper & Row.

Guba, E. G. and Lincoln, Y. S. (1981) *Effective Evaluation: Improving the Usefulness of Evaluation Results through Responsive and Naturalistic Approaches.* San Francisco, Calif.: Jossey-Bass.

Isaac, S. and Michael, W. (1981) *Handbook in Research and Evaluation.* 2d ed. San Diego, Calif.: Edits.

Krathwohl, D. K., Bloom, B. S., and Masia, B. B. (1964) *Taxonomy of Educational Objectives,* Handbook II: *Affective Domain.* New York: David McKay.

Popham, J. and Ebel, R. L. (1978) "The 1978 Annual Meeting Presidential Debate—Norm vs. Criterion Referenced Measurement." *Educational Researcher* 7 (11): 3–10.

Posavac, E. and Carey, R. (1980) *Program Evaluation: Methods and Case Studies.* Englewood Cliffs, N.J.: Prentice-Hall.

Seldin, P. (1980) *Successful Faculty Evaluation Programs.* New York: Coventry Press.

Simpson, E. J. (1972) *The Classification of Educational Objectives in the Psychomotor Domain.* The Psychomotor Domain, vol. 3. Highland Park, N.J.: Gryphon Press.

EVALUATION, NATURALISTIC. Evaluation models typically have advance organizers, that is, items of interest around which the data collection and analysis efforts are organized or clustered. So, for instance, there are evaluation models which have as their organizing rubric the *objectives* of a program; the *decisions* which must be made about programs; the *effects,* direct and indirect, of the intervention mounted; or the *political negotiations* surrounding any program. The organizers for naturalistic evaluation, on the other hand, are the *concerns and issues in the minds of stakeholding audiences.* A concern is any matter of interest or importance to one or more parties to the evaluation. A concern may be a perceived threat, the forerunner of an undesirable consequence, or some matter which needs substantiation. An issue is any statement, proposition, or focus that allows for the presentation of different points of view or different values, or any proposition about which reasonable people may disagree.

The roots of naturalistic evaluation are twofold: first, the model grows out of the responsive evaluation model proposed by Robert Stake, where evaluation is responsive to the concerns and issues of those holding a stake in the evaluation; second, the model derives from naturalistic inquiry, a set of axioms for conducting inquiry, which may be contrasted starkly with conventional or rationalistic axioms.

Conventional inquiry paradigms are typically characterized by five axioms including axioms about the nature of reality, the nature of the inquirer-subject relationship, the purpose of the inquiry, the nature of causality, and the role of values in inquiry. The conventional paradigm translates these axioms into the following corresponding beliefs about the nature of the universe: (1) reality is single, tangible, fragmentable (into units and processes which are called variables), and convergent; (2) the inquirer-subject relationship is discrete, separable, and independent; (3) the purpose of inquiry is the generation of generalizations, which are nomothetic and context-free statements of truth that focus on the similarities between objects and events; (4) there are real causes onto which inquiry may converge, and those causes between events and phenomena are temporally precedent or at least simultaneous; and finally, (5) inquiry is, or should be, value-free.

Naturalistic inquiry postulates a substantially different set of axioms, which proceed in the same fashion: (1) reality is multiple, intangible, holistic, indivisible, divergent, and largely constructed in the minds of persons; (2) the inquirer-respondent relationship is interrelated and inseparable; it is characterized by interactivity; (3) the purpose of such inquiry is not generalization, but rather context-bound working hypotheses and idiographic statements which may or may not have transferability to other contexts (a matter for empirical investigation), and the focus is on differences between contexts rather than similarities; (4) explanation is achieved by description not of causality, but rather of webs and patterns of influences and mutual shapers in the environment, best described as feedback and feed-forward; and finally, (5) inquiry is value-bound, appropriately so, in five ways: by choice of the guiding paradigm, by choice of the substantive theory undergirding the inquiry, by choice of the method, by nature of the values which inhere in the context studies, and by virtue of the dissonance or resonance between each of the previous four.

The utility of any axiomatic set may be judged entirely in terms of the fit between its postulates and the nature of the phenomenon under investigation. So, for instance, the choice of whether one uses Euclidian or Lobachevskian geometries depends entirely on whether one wishes to solve problems in earth-sized or interstellar spaces. Naturalistic evaluation as a model contends that the naturalistic axioms exhibit better "fit," or congruence, to social and behavioral phenomena than do the axioms of the conventional or rationalistic paradigm.

The emergent naturalistic paradigm, based as it is on interactive social and behavioral phenomena, necessarily demands new skills of evaluators. Naturalistic evaluation, organized around the concerns and issues of stakeholders, relies heavily on the evaluator as the major data collection and analysis instrument. The reliance on human-as-instrument (rather than paper and pencil instrumentation) tends to demand those methods which represent the strengths of humans: interviewing, observation, and documentary analysis. The point and power of these skills, called qualitative methodologies, is that they allow for the exploration and reconstruction of multiple social realities. These methods are also compatible with other axioms of naturalistic evaluation by (1) taking account of the interactive nature of evaluator-respondent relationships; (2) allowing for the development of working hypotheses and thick description, which in turn allows judgments to be made regarding whether or not findings are transferable; (3) allowing for the webs and patterns of mutual influence to be described and traced; and (4) specifically taking account of multiple, and often conflicting, values and belief systems within a specific context.

Typically, a naturalistic evaluation proceeds in an iterative fashion; that is, steps are repeated and recycled until information becomes redundant and/or expense or decision demands force closure. The evaluation begins by gaining entrée to the site and establishing trust and rapport sufficient to begin data collection. Initial data collection efforts are accomplished by documentary analysis (if documents are available) and open-ended interviews. Initial data analysis begins simultaneously with collection. The analysis proceeds by unitizing the data, or creating single data items; categorizing the data piles by creating titles for the categories; and adjusting and refining the new data set.

Once the new data set is organized, the evaluator conducts "member checks"; that is, he returns to respondents to verify that his constructions of the context and realities match theirs. Member checks allow for refinement of data and additional data collection. All of these activities are recycled; when information becomes redundant, a grounded questionnaire is constructed. This questionnaire for stakeholders validates the concerns and issues unearthed and gives parties to the evaluation the chance to assign priorities to concerns and issues. When priorities are established, additional data may be gathered which address conflicting values inherent in identified issues.

THE TRUSTWORTHINESS OF NATURALISTIC EVALUATION

Because of its unusual axioms and the apparent "softness" of its methods, naturalistic evaluation is often attacked as untrustworthy, in contrast to rationalistic inquiry which has well-developed standards of trustworthiness.

Recently, serious efforts have been undertaken to develop standards which are parallels of those commonly used by rationalists, that is, counterparts to standards of internal and external validity, reliability, and objectivity. Analogous terms have been proposed, to wit, *credibility, transferability, dependability,* and *confirmability,* respectively.

Credibility is seen as a check on the isomorphism between the inquirer's data and interpretations and the multiple realities in the minds of informants. *Transferability* is the equivalent of generalizability to the extent that there are similarities between sending and receiving contexts. *Dependability* includes the instability factors typically indicated by the term "unreliability" but makes allowances for emergent designs, developing theory, and the like that also induce changes but which cannot be taken as "error." *Confirmability* shifts the emphasis from the certifiability of the inquirer to the confirmability of the data.

SUMMARY

Naturalistic inquiry is one of two paradigms currently being used by evaluators within the framework of disciplined research and evaluation. While this paradigm has distinguished antecedents in anthropology and ethnography, it is nevertheless relatively emergent, and not as much is known about its assumptions and procedures as might be desired. Nevertheless, it seems likely that, given several decades in which to develop, the naturalistic paradigm will prove to be as useful as the rationalistic paradigm has been historically.

Yvonna S. Lincoln and Egon G. Guba

REFERENCES

Cook, T. D. and Reichardt, C. I. (1979) *Qualitative and Quantitative Methods in Evaluation Research*. Beverly Hills, Calif.: Sage.

Cronback, L. J. (1975) "Beyond the Two Disciplines of Scientific Psychology." *American Psychologist* 30 (2): 116–127.

Cronback, L. J. and Suppes, P. (1969) *Research for Tomorrow's Schools: Disciplined Inquiry in Education*. New York: Macmillan.

Filstead, W. J. (1970) *Qualitative Methodology*. Chicago: Rand, McNally.

Guba, E. G. (1978) *Toward a Methodology of Naturalistic Inquiry in Educational Evaluation*. Los Angeles: Center for the Study of Evaluation, University of California, Los Angeles.

Guba, E. G. and Lincoln, Y. S. (1981) *Effective Evaluation*. San Francisco: Jossey-Bass.

Scriven, M. (1971) "Objectivity and Subjectivity in Educational Research." In *Philosophical Redirection of Educational Research*, ed. L. G. Thomas. Chicago: University of Chicago Press.

EVENT SAMPLING. A sampling technique used in interaction analysis and systematic classroom observation. Observers record events only when they occur and not at regular intervals (as in time sampling). With event sampling the sequence of elements in interactions can be recorded, but not the duration of individual categories. *See* **Interaction Analysis; Time Sampling.**

EVR. *See* **Electronic Video Recording.**

EXCITER LAMP. In optical sound projectors, a small lamp which is focused on the optical sound track. The sound track modulates the brightness of the lamp as it falls on a photocell, the output of which is amplified to produce the sound for the film.

EXECUTE. To do something, e.g., to perform a specified computer instruction; to run a program.

EXECUTIVE PROGRAM. The supervisory program in computing which controls peripheral transfers, communication, multiprogramming, the interface between the user program and the hardware, store allocation, etc.

EXPANSION SLOT. A connector inside a microcomputer in which a peripheral card (circuit board) can be installed; sometimes called peripheral slot.

EXPERT SYSTEMS. The earliest computers were used for the manipulation of numeric data and for large-scale data processing. Subsequently they were employed not only to store data but also to retrieve and manipulate information. By the late 1960s research was under way in such areas as computer-aided design, systems modeling, and robotics. The increasing sophistication of computing technology was matched by a growth of interest in pattern recognition. The ability of a computer to correlate data held in its memory store with a given situation, or set of conditions, in the way that, for example, a doctor compares a patient's symptoms with his own mental library of patterns and experience, makes the computer a potentially very powerful diagnostic aid. This, in turn, has led to the development of so-called expert systems.

In discussing computer developments it is traditional (and helpful) to think in terms of "generations." Valve-based computers are thought of as first-generation machines, transistors as second, integrated circuits as third, and Very Large-Scale Integration (VLSI) as fourth. Computer technology is currently moving from the fourth- to fifth-generation stage, and with this has come an unprecedented scaling-up of research objectives and financial investment, both on the part of industry and, significantly, national governments. The major research thrust will be in the area of **artificial intelligence** (q.v.) (AI), which Smith (1980) defines as "a branch of computer science which attempts to develop programs to enable computer systems to communicate fluently, to explain why they have taken certain actions, to handle unforeseen situations and to exhibit other signs of intelligent behavior." To date, the most interesting practical outcome of research in AI has been the development of expert systems.

EXPERT SYSTEMS DEFINED

Expert systems have been described in a variety of ways. According to Michie (1980), "an expert system acts as a systematising repository over time of the knowledge accumulated by many specialists of diverse experience. Hence it can and does ultimately attain a level of consultant expertise exceeding that of any single one of its tutors." In Bramer's view (1982), an expert system is "a computing system which embodies organized knowledge concerning some specific area of human expertise, sufficient to perform as a skillful and cost-effective consultant." As Shirley (1983) has noted, expert systems are invariably described in human terms, as being smart, skillful, and friendly. This may, unwittingly, suggest to the layman that expert systems are machines with intelligence. However, when computer or information scientists speak of machines exhibiting intelligent behavior, they are not seeking to imply that the observed cognitive-like behaviors have psychophysiological correlates, as human behaviors and actions do.

Expert systems differ from conventional computer systems in that they emulate human problem-solving strategies. As both the definitions above make clear, expert systems are a means of storing, applying, refining, and optimizing the knowledge and experience of experts or specialists in a particular subject area. To quote Basden (1982), expert systems "imitate methods used in the human mind" in order to represent and process validated knowledge in a given field. Shirley (1983) suggests that an appropriate analogy is with the top-level practitioner. She cites the motor mechanic who can assess the condition of a car engine by listening to the sound it makes as it turns over, and then carries out some fine-tuning. An expert system can similarly carry out a process of assessment and diagnosis, before proposing a particular course of remedial action.

In general terms, expert systems (also on occasion referred to as Intelligent Knowledge Based Systems, IKBS) function as automated consultants in a narrow and clearly defined subject area, performing classes of operations, which, if performed by humans, would be considered to require intelligence. Typically, expert systems are used for planning, diagnosis, prediction, and complex design.

ANATOMY OF AN EXPERT SYSTEM

As a general rule, expert systems are restricted in the following four ways: (1) the knowledge contained in the system is well-bounded; (2) the knowledge base is specialized; (3) the system user is informed about the subject area; and (4) the system has a rule-based architecture (Sparck Jones, 1983). Building an expert system is a complex, expensive, and labor-intensive undertaking, even in a small or well-defined domain. An expert system consists of two elements: a knowledge base and an inference engine, the former comprising a data base of facts and rules, the latter an inference structure to enable the knowledge in the system to be applied to problems arising "in the field."

The knowledge base is quite distinct from the inference engine, which contains the software necessary to link the user's queries with the knowledge base. Answers to queries posed by the system user are provided either by retrieving facts from the knowledge base, or, if an answer is not explicitly stored, by inferring new facts—something conventional computer programming does not permit.

The design of an expert system requires cooperation between two specialists, the subject professional and the knowledge engineer. The task of the knowledge engineer is to elicit all relevant factual information from the acknowledged expert and to determine how it should be structured and represented in the system, i.e., to design the architecture of the inference engine so that the knowledge store can be interactively accessed by the user to answer specific questions. Creating the knowledge base often entails an extended process of cooperation between a recognized panel of experts and the knowledge engineer. In the case of the Hepatitis Knowledge Base (Bernstein et al., 1980), this meant a process of consensus development by a nationally distributed panel of experts. The experts were responsible for identifying and validating the knowledge which was to be embedded in (and added to) the system; the knowledge engineer, for organizing that knowledge in such a way that other specialists' queries could be answered by the system.

Concern has been expressed in some quarters (Bernstein et al., 1980) that this approach may result in selective data input, with only established and approved ideas appearing in such systems. The philosophical and ethical questions which knowledge engineering research has thrown up have not as yet received a great deal of attention in the emergent literature of the field, but there is every reason to believe that this situation will change as the field consolidates.

The knowledge base also contains the rules which are applied to the bedrock of facts. The number of rules in an expert system will depend on the size and complexity of the field in question. Some expert systems contain a fairly small number of rules. PUFF, an expert system used to diagnose lung disorders, consists of 55 rules of the IF...THEN variety, which were formulated by a team of knowledge engineers working alongside an expert over a period of time (Bramer, 1982). One hundred cases, carefully chosen to represent the variety of disease states, were used to extract the 55 rules. To validate the corpus of rules, 150 cases *not* studied during the knowledge acquisition process were tried against the experimental system. PUFF-generated and expert-produced diagnoses were recorded, and agreement was registered in over 90 percent of cases.

The sophistication of an expert system will depend on the number of rules. An expert system capable of playing a good game of chess would need in the order of 500 rules; an expert system capable of defeating a grand master would probably require 50,000 rules (Shirley, 1983). Present-day expert systems typically contain between 400 and 1,600 rules, but with fifth-generation computer architecture systems of 10,000 rules should be feasible.

Because the process of constructing an expert system is painstaking, the design costs are extremely high. It has been estimated that it requires one man-week to generate two finished rules in the average expert system. In due course, it may be possible to overcome this difficulty by using "meta systems" to formulate rules inductively by working from existing examples *(Monitor, 1982)*. In the short term, expert systems research and design will in all probability be the prerogative of subject fields which attract high-level research funding, or industries where the potential return on the initial investment can be considerable (e.g., off-shore oil exploration).

There are two classic control strategies for expert systems, known as forward chaining and backwards chaining. In forward-chaining systems the rules are scanned, searching for one whose conditions match an assertion about the problem/query. This matching process is continued until sufficient congruence obtains for a solution to be proposed. Backwards chaining, on the other hand, begins with the formulation of an hypothesis (e.g., the fault is X; the disease is Y) and then directing specific questions to the system in an effort to determine whether the hypothesis is correct. It may be helpful to think of forward chaining as "analogous to the way in which a theorem appears to be proved in a maths textbook, starting from a collection of axioms and following logically by applying certain rules of inference" and backwards chaining as being "analogous to the way the theorem was probably proved in the first place (by starting from the answer and working backwards)" (Merry, 1983).

In general, backwards chaining is used more often than forward chaining, and seems more acceptable than a random gathering of facts followed by forward deduction. An example of an expert system with a backwards chaining inference structure is MYCIN, which moves from diagnosis to symptoms before suggesting appropriate drug treatment for blood and meningitis infections (Bramer, 1982).

The rules housed in an expert system need not be absolute. Many systems permit inprecise rules, for the good reason that knowledge in many domains is indefinite and evolutionary. This technique is often referred to as inexact reasoning, plausible reasoning, or reasoning with uncertainty. In some systems it may be possible to express the degree of uncertainty as a probability value in the range 0–1 (e.g., "there is suggestive evidence [0.6] that . . . ").

If expert systems are to gain widespread acceptance, then user-friendly design will be essential. An important feature of expert systems is their ability to explain decisions (the "human window" facility) and to make explicit to an uncertain or skeptical user the steps and reasoning employed to arrive at a particular solution or outcome. This interactive facility prevents the system from becoming a "black box" and reduces the likelihood of user alienation.

PRACTICAL APPLICATIONS

Expert systems are being developed for an increasing number of applications in the fields of engineering, medicine, geology, and computer science. Three of the best-known expert systems are DENDRAL, MYCIN, and PROSPECTOR (Bramer, 1982). DENDRAL, the world's first expert system, appeared in 1965 and is now used commercially for the identification of organic compounds by an analysis of their mass spectra. MYCIN, as mentioned already, was designed to diagnose blood and meningitis infections. PROSPECTOR is used to assist geologists in assessing the viability of a particular region for oil deposit exploration. The user, in this case, presents to the system a list of rocks and minerals found in the region in question, and this sets up a dialogue between the system and the user resulting in a probability assessment of a given deposit being located.

In the future, as the technology matures and development costs drop, expert systems will be used for an expanding variety of applications. Colbourn (1983) has, for instance, described an expert system for the diagnosis of reading difficulties in schoolchildren, which could be used by a teacher to establish the nature of a pupil's disabilities. Others have been designed to provide political risk analysis, and IBM recently announced a system which is able to recognize an author's social class and general character merely by scanning a letter *(CTI, 1983)*. High-level research into expert systems has additionally led to the development of expert-systems generators which can be run on inexpensive microcomputers *(Practical Computing, 1983)*.

Any discussion of expert systems also needs to take

account of front-end systems used in on-line searching. In the United States, the National Library of Medicine (NLM) has conducted trials with a system which allows users to run on-line searches on a bibliographic data base without any formal instruction, without the use of a manual, and without the intervention of a trained information intermediary. PAPERCHASE offered a self-service facility to provide access to the medical literature, and proved so popular with medical students and practitioners that more than 60 percent of those who experimented with the system were repeat users (Horowitz and Bleich, 1981). The features common to such systems, several of which are "up and running" (Clarke and Cronin, 1983), include no log-on procedure, automatic data base selection and connection, and acceptance of the user's natural language input.

PRESENT LIMITATIONS OF EXPERT SYSTEMS

Despite recent advances, expert systems research is still in its infancy. Although the spectrum of possible applications is almost limitless, the associated costs are likely to hold back the development cycle. Difficulties may also arise because of the specificity of most expert systems (they only deal with a microscopic area of knowledge) and the knowledge fragmentation which this could cause in the short-term. Michie's (1982) vision of the "integrated reactive library," comprising a battery of expert systems, may prove correct, but it is unlikely to be achieved in the near future.

On a more practical level, stability problems can sometimes arise when expert knowledge in a particular domain continues to grow, and the knowledge base is augmented by a user/subject expert who was not involved in the initial design process. This may sometimes result in the inclusion of dubious or contradictory information in the system. Additionally, there is the possibility that the incorporation of more and more information in the knowledge base will have the effect of making the system incomprehensible to the user. These difficulties are, however, widely recognized, and no doubt will be surmounted in due course.

CONCLUSIONS

Expert systems make it technically feasible to preserve the best of human knowledge and experience in specific subject fields and to ensure that the currency and validity of that knowledge is maintained. They also provide professionals (e.g., engineers, medical practitioners, lawyers, educators, computer scientists, and many others) with a novel decision-support facility, one which should bring about an improvement in the quality, impartiality, and reliability of the advice they offer.

Although the growth of interest in expert systems research will create a demand for knowledge engineers in many specialized fields, the net overall effect of expert systems technology will be to cause a certain measure of de-skilling, at both the technician and professional levels, as machines take over some (or all) of the functions previously performed by the specialist—the classic sting-in-the-tail effect of the new technology.

B. Cronin

REFERENCES

Basden, A. (1982) "What Are Expert Systems?—Towards a Definition." *Newsletter of the British Computer Society Specialist Group on Expert Systems* 6: 10–11.

Bernstein, L. M. et al. (1980) "The Hepatitis Knowledge Base: A Prototype Information Transfer System." *Annals of Internal Medicine* 93 (2): 169–181.

Bramer, M. (1982) "A Survey and Critical Review of Expert Systems Research." In *Introductory Readings in Expert Systems*, ed. D. Michie. London: Gordon & Breach, pp. 3–29.

Clarke, A. and Cronin, B. (1983) "Expert Systems and Library/Information Work: Possible Applications and Implications." *Journal of Librarianship* 15 (4): 277–294.

Colbourn, M. J. (1983) "An Expert System for the Diagnosis of Reading Difficulties." Saskatoon: University of Saskatchewan, Department of Computational Science (unpublished paper).

CTI (Communication Technology Impact) 5 (6) (1983): 17–18.

Horowitz, G. L. and Bleich, H. L. (1981) "Paperchase: A Computer Program to Search the Medical Literature." *New England Journal of Medicine* 305 (16): 924–930.

Merry, M. (1983) "APEX 3: An Expert System Shell for Fault Diagnosis." *GEC Journal of Research* 1 (1): 39–47.

Michie, D. (1980) "Expert Systems." *Computer Journal* 23 (4): 369–376.

———. (1982) *Machine Intelligence and Related Topics: An Information Scientist's Weekend Book.* London: Gordon & Breach.

Monitor 19 (September 1982): 6–7.

Practical Computing 6 (11) (1983): 77.

Shirley, S. (1983) "How Expert Systems Help Experts Decide." *Management Today* February: 33, 36, 38.

Smith, L. C. (1980) "Implications of Artificial Intelligence for End User Use of Online Systems." *Online Review* 4 (4): 383–391.

Sparck Jones, K. (1983) *Report on a Visit to the US, 27.1.83 - 4.2.83.* London: British Library Research & Development Department.

EXPOSURE. The combination of lens aperture and shutter speed that is used in photography to allow the correct amount of light to fall on the film.

EXPOSURE LATITUDE. The range of exposures over which a photographic emulsion will give an acceptable image. It is dependent on the inherent range of the particular emulsion and the brightness range of the subject.

EXPOSURE METER. A device for measuring the quantity of light incident upon or reflected from a scene which is to be recorded on film. Exposure meters use light-sensitive devices, either photocells or photoresistors which give a reading that is combined with the "speed" of the film in use to indicate suitable values for shutter speed and lens aperture.

EXTENDED DEFINITION TELEVISION. This is an approach to the improvement of the quality of the domestic television picture which, while falling short of the radical proposals of HDTV, will improve the definition of pictures received under present-day 525 line/60 Hz (or 625 line/50 Hz) broadcast standards. In general, the enhancement will be achieved by utilizing an increased bandwidth to secure various benefits.

EXTENSION TUBE. A threaded tube or ring enabling a lens to be mounted at a greater distance from a camera than normal. This allows objects to be focused which are closer to the camera than normal. *See* **Close-up.**

F

FACET ANALYSIS. *See* **Information Classification and Retrieval.**

FACILITY INDEX. In item analysis the percentage of the group with the correct answer to an item. *See* **Discrimination Index.**

FACSIMILE. Literally an exact copy. Used to describe, for example, a reproduction of an original document that is as much like the original as possible.

FACSIMILE MACHINE. A device which transmits and receives "printed" information. In fact, the information (chart, text, picture, diagram, etc.) is converted into a suitable form for transmission along a telephone line. At the receiving end the signal is converted back into a facsimile of the original document.

FACSIMILE TRANSMISSION. A system by which documents, photographs, etc., can be transmitted via telephone lines or any other means. In effect, a facsimile of some original material is electronically transferred to a distant location. *See* **Facsimile Machine.**

FACTOR ANALYSIS. Factor analysis attempts to explain the correlations obtained among a large number of variables by variation on a smaller number of underlying or inferred factors. The "orderly simplification" of a number of interrelated measures. An essential tool for researchers who have to reduce large amounts of data.

FACTORING. Videotex fee charged to service providers to cover the cost of billing users for charged information.

FADE. A term used in media production when the active situation is to be gradually reduced to zero. In the case of sound this means the music, conversation, etc., has its volume steadily diminished to silence; while in video the picture is slowly mixed to "black."

FADING. The gradual removal of a prompting stimulus in programmed learning.

FAST FILM. A photographic film with a high film speed; fast film can be used in situations of poor light, or where a very short exposure is required.

FAST MOTION. Motion of film through a cine camera at a speed slower than the standard for that format, which results in action appearing faster than normal when the film is projected at standard rate. *See* **Filming Speed.**

FAX. *See* **Facsimile Transmission.**

FCC. *See* **Federal Communications Commission.**

FEDERAL COMMUNICATIONS COMMISSION (FCC). A government agency responsible for regulating all interstate and overseas communication by television and radio.

Congress has endowed the FCC with wide-ranging powers which include, for example, awarding and withdrawing broadcast licenses, conducting public hearings, enforcing rules concerning the operation of cable television systems, setting technical standards, etc. The FCC is administered by seven independent commissioners who are appointed by the president with Senate ratification. The normal term of office is seven years.

FEEDBACK. A howl or sound from a loudspeaker caused by sound from the speaker entering a microphone connected to the same amplifier that powers the speaker. Also known as *acoustic feedback*.

FEEDBACK CLASSROOM. A special classroom for student performance monitoring. Students' positions are connected to the teacher's desk and responses to multiple-choice questions can be monitored by the teacher. The classroom provides feedback to the teacher about the understanding of the students. There are numerous examples of feedback classrooms, and their use has been widespread in areas where there is extensive use of multiple-choice testing, e.g., motor skill acquisition. A language laboratory is a type of feedback classroom.

FELT BOARD. A visual display device, mainly of interest in elementary education, exploiting the adhesiveness of felt on felt, and in particular the ready way in which items backed with sandpaper will stick to felt or flannel. This permits the easy use of several teaching strategies involving synthesis and analysis on the display board, sometimes making use of commercially available outlines of objects.

FIAC. *See* **Interaction Analysis.**

FIBER OPTICS. Optical fibers have been used as an alternative to conventional electric cables since the late 1970s. To date they have been limited in their channel capacity but have still offered considerable advantages in lack of attenuation and in physical characteristics. Consequently, they have found applications in aircraft, computers, interoffice links, etc. It seems likely that improvements in glass fiber technology in the near future will result in greatly increased channel capacity and even less attenuation, thus dramatically changing the whole cost structure of communications transmission. *See* **Information Technology.**

FIELD. (1) Half a complete television picture. In the case of a nominal 525–line picture, 262.5 lines. These lines span the full screen and successive fields (60 per second NTSC) interlace to give an effective 525 lines 30 times per second (625 lines 25 times per second in the case of PAL). *See* **Frame.** (2) An area for recording a single item of data in a data base or other data recording program. A field can hold a number, a name, a page of text, etc. Conceptually, a field is equivalent to a single-entry box on a paper form.

FIELD TEST. A developmental test carried out under the conditions for which the test is intended, that is, normal-sized groups and live teaching conditions. Also called *operational testing,* i.e., testing under normal operating conditions.

FIFTH-GENERATION COMPUTER. A term applied to the new type of computers currently being developed to act as expert systems. It is hoped that such computers will display advanced **artificial intelligence** (q.v.) of a type that it has not so far proved possible to achieve. *See* **Second-Generation Computer; Third-Generation Computer; Fourth-Generation Computer.**

FILE. A collection of information which a computer data base regards as a single unit. Internally, the data base considers the file to be a collection of records, which in turn are made up of fields.

FILE MANAGER. A limited-function data base program in which the structure of the data is determined by the program that creates and maintains it. Unlike a full data base–management system, it does not make the data and the program independent of each other.

FILESERVER. A hard disk drive that can store and retrieve files for the several microcomputers connected to a network.

FILIAL ROUTING. A simple method of videotext routing from an index frame to appropriate information pages. The page routed (for example, 12347) is related to the page number of the index frame (1234) and the number pressed by the terminal user (7).

FILL LIGHT. A secondary lighting source used to fill in shadow areas. It is usually placed opposite or to the side of the key light, so that it fills in any strong shadows.

FILM CLIP. The term usually refers to a selected section of an available film or videotape incorporated into a presentation in order to illustrate a specific point; also called an "insert."

The term is also used for a physical device which holds a roll of film on a drying line so that its weight keeps the film from curling.

FILM EDITING. The term refers to the process of choosing and combining bits and pieces of a production, which may be created in any sequence, into a finished presentation.

Film is generally edited by working with short lengths of film and cementing them together on a trial basis. Videotape is edited electronically without cutting the tape. Audiotape can be edited in either way. *See* **Moviola.**

FILMED SIMULATION. In many teaching and training situations, it is desirable to produce a visual record of a simulated situation for subsequent analysis and discussion. Examples are simulated interviews, clinical consultations, and classroom situations. As instant playback is often required, such a record is best obtained using one or more television cameras feeding into a video tape recorder. Alternatively, cine equipment can be used, but this has the inherent disadvantage of a compartively long time lag between the initial filming and the recording becoming available.

FILM GAUGE. Cine film is available in the following widths: 70mm, 35mm, 16mm, and 8mm.

The 16mm gauge is the most important in education

as it has an adequate quality margin to give good duplicates. The use of 16mm for television news and documentary filming has meant that there was a wide range of film stock and equipment in this gauge. This situation is changing as ENG video cameras take over from 16mm in many applications.

Eight-millimeter film was mostly used for home movies and has been virtually superseded by video. The 70mm and 35mm gauges are used in the entertainment field.

FILMING SPEED. The rate at which a film is exposed in a cine camera. In normal 16mm applications the camera and projector both run at 24 frames per second (fps), but for special applications the camera rate may be much slower (time lapse) or much faster (high speed) resulting in accelerated or slowed-down motion.

FILM INSERT. Filmed sequence inserted into a television program.

FILM LOOP. A length of cine film spliced into a loop so that it can be projected continuously and repetitively without the need for rewinding. Special 8mm loop projectors make use of plastic cassettes to hold the film allowing it to be inserted into the projector without the need for threading. In 16mm loop projection systems special trays are used to hold the film and feed it to the projector gate.

Apart from allowing the film to run continuously for display purposes, the particular advantage of loop films is that they allow analysis of complicated events by repeated viewing. Videotape units which rewind automatically to the beginning of a selected segment and repeat it seem likely to replace film loops.

FILM PROJECTION. *See* **Film Projector.**

FILM PROJECTOR. A film projector consists essentially of a mechanical film transport mechanism with intermittent movement, an illumination source, and an optical system. To this may be added facilities for playing optical or magnetic sound tracks and sometimes also recording on a magnetic track.

Film projection depends on the phenomenon of the persistence of vision, and it is this that dictates the framing rate. Flicker becomes noticeable at about 48 Hz, and this sets the lower limit at which the light beam must be interrupted by the shutter mechanism. On the other hand, the eye is able to blend intermittent movement into smooth motion at about sixteen pictures per second, provided the movement from one picture to the next is not gross; this determines the slowest framing rate (for cameras also). If a film is to be projected at 16 fps, to avoid flicker it is necessary to use a three-bladed shutter linked to the film transport mechanism so that the film is advanced during one of the three blanking periods. Most 16mm projectors run at 24 fps and have a two-bladed shutter, thus giving a suitable interruption rate of 48 per second.

The sound track capabilities of cine projectors range from optical sound only to optical and magnetic. Magnetic recording is also possible. Such record facilities enable a simple commentary to be added to a completed film on which a magnetic stripe has been placed.

Modern advances in projector design have concentrated on making them simpler to operate. Automatic threading and slot loading now mean that projectors can be used confidently by untrained personnel.

FILM SETTING. A process of setting type for use in some printing systems. Photographic prints are made from negatives of individual letters in the system by an operator using a keyboard. The completed prints can then be combined for the photographic production of the complete printing plate.

FILM SPEED. A numerical value (both ASA and DIN numbers are usually quoted) given to photographic emulsions indicating their degree of sensitivity to light. The speed rating of a film provides a basis for comparison between one emulsion and another and also a value to use in conjunction with an exposure meter.

An increase in film speed always results in an increase in grain size and therefore a decrease in the quality of image obtainable. The speed rating given to a film by the manufacturer may need to be verified under actual working conditions since several factors, particularly the type of development given, can lead to quite wide variations in film speed.

FILMSTRIP. A strip of 35mm film with a series of positive transparencies which may be used in an individual viewer or shown to a group using a filmstrip projector. The individual frames of most filmstrips are half the size of a 35mm slide and, unlike slides, are fixed in the order of production. Filmstrips can be produced on a local level but are usually mass-produced to provide economy. Many filmstrips have an audiotape or disk recording sound track to accompany the visuals. Some machines operate on a synchronization pulse on the prerecorded audiotape so that the frames are advanced automatically at the desired point in the presentation.

FILTER. By superimposing a filter in the path of light reaching a camera, enlarger, etc., changes can be made in the characteristics of the light. For example, it is very common to mount an ultraviolet filter in front of a camera lens to increase the interest of the sky which otherwise would appear as a uniform hue because of the UV present. Other filters can correct for color temperature so that the same film can be used in daylight or tungsten lighting.

FIND (SEARCH) AND REPLACE. Word processor facility whereby a word(s) (or part thereof) can be searched for and then, if desired, replaced by another word(s). Usually the replacement can be on an individual or global (i.e., every occasion) basis.

FIRMWARE. A computer program that is recorded in a storage medium from which it cannot be accidentally erased; also the electronic device containing such a program, e.g., ROM, PROM, or EPROM.

FIRST-GENERATION TAPE. *See* **Tape Generation.**

FISH-EYE LENS. A wide-angle lens with an extremely short focal length and correspondingly wide acceptance angle. It is used for taking very wide-angle shots.

FIXED POINT. The everyday method of expressing numbers, e.g., 1.007413, −334, 4,019,216. Computers, however, often express numbers as powers of 10, especially if the number is large or small. *See* **Floating Point.**

FIXED SATELLITE SERVICE MODE. The satellite provides a two-way link between two defined fixed points. This mode can be used as an alternative to conventional terrestrial microwave or coaxial cable systems.

FIXER. Usually a solution of sodium thiosulfate (hypo) used to remove the unexposed silver salts following development of a photographic emulsion. This ensures that the film or paper is not affected any more by light.

FLAG. An indicator whose state is used to inform a later section of a computer program that a condition, identified with the flag and designated by the state of the flag, has occurred. For example, in a multiple-choice test where the student is only allowed two attempts at a question, the variable (i.e., flag) A would be set at 0 at the start of each question, but changed to 1 after an incorrect attempt. This flag setting would prevent the student being given a third chance.

FLANNEL GRAPH. *See* **Felt Board.**

FLASHBULB. Flashbulbs, whether in bulb, cube, or bar form, provide a convenient form of high-intensity light for photography. They are gas-filled containers which can be used only once. Electronic flash tubes, often called guns or strobes, of various sizes and technical capacity are usually battery-powered and provide a great number of flashes from the rechargeable tube. Both the bulb and gun variety of flash equipment is nearly always color-corrected for use with film designed to work in daylight.

FLASH CARD. An old, established tactic used in the teaching of reading. A word printed on a large card is briefly held up before the students, who are required to read or match it. The tactic is associated with the "look-and-say" method of reading instruction.

FLASH FACTOR (GUIDE NUMBER). Guide numbers, or flash factors, have two main uses in photography. One is to provide a basis for comparison of the output of various electronic flashguns rated for the same film. The second use is in the calculation of the proper aperture for flash photography. With a suitable shutter speed selected, the aperture needed is found by dividing the guide number by the flash to subject distance. Most flashguns incorporate a calculation device to make this easier, and many pieces of equipment solve the problem automatically.

FLAT RESPONSE. The ability of a signal-handling system (especially an audio system or component) to process a full range of frequencies without changing their relative strengths.

FLEXIBLE DISK. A computer storage device made of flexible plastic. *See* **Floppy Disk.**

FLIGHT SIMULATION. The use of simulators as training aids is widely practiced in all armed services, since they allow a trainee pilot, tank driver, gun aimer, etc., to gain proficiency in the use of complicated technical equipment without the danger and expense inherent in the real-life situation. Simulators of this type (originally called "Link Trainers") are particularly valuable in the training of pilots (both military and commercial), where they are used both in basic training and in conversion to new types of aircraft. They are also widely used by commercial airlines for the routine tests which all pilots have to undergo at regular intervals.

FLIP CHART. A set of flip-charts allows the rapid presentation of a series of different charts for a limited period of time. Each chart should have a specific message to communicate and the sequence is not unlike a filmstrip. The commonest way to construct such charts is to mount them by their top edge to a horizontal bar so that the teacher can "flip" the charts over to reveal any one of them to the class.

FLOATING POINT. Computers, like calculators, can only cope with a limited number of digits in a number. In the case of large or small numbers the number is converted to floating-point notation, e.g.,

2.7496301×10^7 (= 27, 496, 301)
7.19×10^{-2} (= 0.0719)

These floating-point numbers will be rounded off to the maximum number of significant digits that the given computer can handle. Note that computers do not use some conventional signs (like $\times$ for multiply), so the two above numbers would be displayed as:

2.7496301E+7   7.19E−2

(E+7 means "times 10 to the power of 7"; E−2 means "times 10 to the power of minus 2.")

FLOODLIGHT. A lamp which produces a wide spread of light. *See* **Lighting.**

FLOOR MANAGER. The person in charge of the set; the person who organizes the presenters, performers, technicians, cameramen, on the floor of the television studio. The floor manager receives instructions from the producer.

FLOPPY DISK. Common storage medium for small computers. There is a larger version, but the usual floppy is 5 1/4" in diameter and capable of storing several hundred kilobytes or more depending on the Disk Operating System in use. Physically the disk is thin, flexible, magnetically coated, and housed inside a nonremovable protective sleeve. The term *diskette* is also used for the 5 1/4" floppy disk.

FLOWCHART. A diagrammatic representation of interrelationships between events or variables in a system. A flow diagram is used specifically in work study or critical path analysis to represent locations of activities and the order of events. *See* **Algorithm; Arrow Diagram.**

FLUTTER. Rapid fluctuation in pitch due to a fault in sound recording or reproducing equipment such as an eccentric drive spindle in a record player.

FLYING SPOT. A device for "reading" (or less commonly, exposing) film. The prime example of this process in action is in the conversion of film images into television signals. Originally this was accomplished by pointing a television camera at a movie screen, but the results were less than good. The flying spot is a very narrow beam of light which scans the film frame by moving back and forth over it while also moving steadily in the vertical direction. The film density and color affect the characteristics of the beam, which in turn is transformed into a varying electronic current for subsequent conversion to a television signal. As the film is advanced frame by frame, so the flying spot scans each of the frames in sequence. *See* **Video Recording and Reproduction.**

FM. *See* **Frequency Modulation.**

F-NUMBER. Technically the f-number is the focal length of a lens divided by the diameter of the lens opening. In practice, f-numbers identify a related range of different-sized openings in a lens so that selected amounts of light may pass. A small f-number identifies a large opening for use in dim light (e.g., f1.8) while a large f-number identifies a small opening for use in bright light (e.g., f16). *See* **Aperture.**

FOCAL LENGTH. The distance from the plane in which a lens forms an image of objects at infinity to the rear nodal point of the lens. The focal length of a lens determines the scale of the image at any given subject camera distance. Sometimes "focus" is used as a synonym, e.g., short focus lens = short focal length lens.

FOCAL PLANE. The plane at right angles to the axis of a lens at which parallel rays of light are brought to a focus. To record a sharp image, the emulsion surface of the film in a camera must be positioned in the focal plane of the camera lens if the object is at infinity (i.e., further away than 30m or so with a standard lens). The focusing of the camera consists of moving the lens forward as the object gets nearer since the image will be in sharp focus behind the focal plane. When the distance from film to lens reaches its maximum, the camera cannot focus sharply on any closer objects.

FOCAL PLANE SHUTTER. A shutter mechanism used mainly in reflex cameras that consists of two blinds of fabric or metal with an adjustable slit between them which moves across and in close proximity to the surface of the film. The particular advantage of a shutter in the focal plane as opposed to a shutter in the lens is that, in reflex cameras, the lens has to be open all the time for viewing and focusing. The focal plane shutter prevents light reaching the film while still permitting through-the-lens composing and viewing.

FOG. An unwanted veil of exposed silver over a photographic image usually caused by accidental exposure to light. With reversal films fog will result in a lowering of density.

FOIL. A term sometimes used to describe a prepared overhead transparency.

FONT. An assortment of printers' type, all of the same typeface and size, consisting of the complete alphabet, numerals, and punctuation marks.

FOOTCANDLE. See **lumen/sq. ft.**

FOOTLAMBERT (FL). A unit of luminance equal to one candela per square foot or to the uniform luminance at a perfectly diffusing surface emitting or reflecting light at the rate of one lumen per square foot. A lumen per square foot is a unit of incident light and a footlambert is a unit of emitted or reflected light. For a perfectly reflecting and perfectly diffusing surface, the number of lumens per square foot is equal to the number of footlamberts.

FOOTPRINT. (1) The surface area taken up by equipment; i.e., how much room it appropriates on your desk. (2) The area on the ground which can receive line-of-sight transmissions from a satellite.

FORCED-CHOICE RESPONSE. A type of multiple-choice question where the subject has to choose from a limited number of responses to a question. Most multiple-choice questions used in testing are forced-choice. The only "free" choice the subject has is not to answer. See **Multiple-Choice Question.**

FORCING. A technique in programmed learning whereby the learner is forced (as a result of thematic or formal prompting) to give a correct response. For example, "Velocity is made up of speed and direction, so velocity will change if either ——— or ——— changes."

FORMAT. (1) The form in which information is organized or presented; or to specify or control the structure of information. (2) To prepare a blank disk to receive information by dividing its surface into tracks and sectors; this process is also known as *initialization*.

FORMATIVE EVALUATION. Evaluation that takes place during the development of a teaching program or course. This evaluation is contrasted with summative evaluation. Also known as *developmental testing*. Formative evaluation takes its name from the way in which it helps establish the form of a course or system. See **Evaluation, Naturalistic.**

FORTH. A computer language particularly strong in its ability to generate and process mathematical functions.

FORTRAN. FORmula TRANslation. A high-level computer programming language used for scientific and mathematical applications. See **COBOL.**

FORWARD ANALYSIS. A term used in critical path analysis. The technique of calculating the earliest event time (EET) in a network. Using forward analysis the critical path through the network can be found. See **Backward Analysis; Latest Event Time.**

FOURTH-GENERATION COMPUTER. A computer based on the technology of integrated circuits. Such computers, which originated in the late 1970s, are much more compact than earlier computers and also have much greater calculating powers than earlier machines of comparable price. See **Second-Generation Computer; Third-Generation Computer; Fifth-Generation Computer.**

FPS. Frames Per Second. The running speed for cine film. See **Film Projector.**

FRAME (VIDEOTEX). One screen full of information. (On the Viatel/Prestel system, approx. 960 characters.)

FRAME. (1) A single image in a series of images on a strip of film. (2) A complete television picture of 525 lines (625 on the PAL system), actually consisting of two interlaced fields. Fields are produced 60 times per second (50 on the PAL system), but the effect is of 30 complete frames per second (25 on PAL). (3) In computerized instruction, usually taken as the material shown at one time on-screen (but note that the term *screen* is also used for this). However, with increasing use of animation and interactive screens, the term may also be used to mean a logical sequence of images treated as a unit in the instructional design. (4) An item in a programmed learning sequence, the term being derived by analogy with the sequential nature of film frames. See **Programmed Learning.**

FRAME ADDRESSABILITY. The ability, as on a videodisc, to refer immediately to any frame without having to pass in sequence through other intermediate frames (as, for instance, with 16mm film).

FRAME SIZE (VIDEOTEX). A Prestel-type frame consists of 24 lines of 40 characters, of which 22 lines (that is, 880 character positions) are available for users to display information.

FREEZE FRAME. A single frame which is displayed while the normal sequence is halted. This is a useful feature found on all videodisc players and many videocassette recorders.

FREQUENCY MODULATION (FM). A method whereby the information in an audio signal is carried on the much higher frequency of a radio wave. The frequency of the audio signal is represented by the rate of change of carrier frequency; audio volume is represented by amplitude of frequency swing. The maximum deviation permitted for FM transmission is set at 75kHz. Transmitter and receiver equipment is engineered to this standard, which is arbitrarily regarded as constituting 100 percent modulation. Overmodulation does not necessarily cause immediate severe distortion (as with AM), and limiters are not needed to avoid overloading transmitter valves. Noise, which appears as fluctuations of carrier amplitude, is strongly discriminated against, though it does produce phase-change effects which cannot be eradicated. Pre-emphasis of top (i.e., prior to transmission), with a corresponding de-emphasis at the receiver, helps to reduce the noise level still further. Unless two carriers on the same wavelength have almost the same strength, the stronger "captures" the area; there is only a small marginal territory between service areas. *See* **Amplitude Modulation.**

FREQUENCY RESPONSE. Range of frequencies or sound vibrations which can be recorded or reproduced. Generally expressed in relation to a stated level of audibility.

FRESNEL LENS. A lens which consists of concentric stepped rings, each of which is a section of a convex surface. It is widely used as a condenser lens in overhead projectors and spotlights.

FRONT-END ANALYSIS. A procedure for determining precisely what the apparent need (problem) is in training or education; the priority (including costs) of solving the need; and the probable cause of the problem. A front-end analysis may result in a solution providing for a training or educational program, course, and so forth, but not necessarily. Any of the following may result:

1. That which appeared at first analysis to be a learning need is really something that did not exist at all.
2. A need exists, but it can effectively be taken care of by a change in the administrative or operational circumstances that surround the persons affected.
3. A need exists, but it can effectively be taken care of by providing or changing motivational circumstances.
4. A need exists, but rather than being resolved by providing an instructional situation or experience, "performance aids" (i.e., algorithms, job aids) may be used by the persons "on the job."
5. A need exists and must be resolved by formalized instructional/learning experience(s).

See **Training Technology.**

FRONT-END PROCESSOR. A separate processing system (such as an analog-to-digital converter) that is used to preprocess signals or data before they are fed into a computer.

FULL DUPLEX. Refers to a communication channel which can simultaneously and independently transmit and receive data. This permits, for example, a printer to advise the computer on its current status while it is receiving data from the computer. *See* **Half Duplex.**

FULL FRAME. Type of filmstrip in which the horizontal axis of the frames is parallel to the length of the film; also known as *double-frame*. *See* **Half Frame.**

FULL FRAME TIME CODE. Also known as "non-drop frame time code," full frame time code is a standardized SMPTE (Society of Motion Picture and Television Engineers) method of address coding a videotape. It gives an accurate frame count rather than the less reliable clock time.

FULL TRACK. System of audio recording in which the entire width of the tape is used to encode the signal. *See* **Half Track; Quarter Track.**

G

GAFFER. The senior lighting technician in film production.

GAIN. The ratio of the output signal level of a system such as an amplifier to the input signal level, usually expressed in decibels.

GAIN RATIO. A statistic designed to put a useful quantitative value on the change between a pretest and a posttest. Many different ratios have been suggested, and there is considerable debate as to the efficacy of the concept in measuring gain. For example:

McGuigan's Ratio = $(m_2 - m_1)/(p - m_1)$

where m_1 is the arithmetic mean of the pretest, m_2 the mean of the posttest and p the maximum score obtainable. The range is 0 to 1.

In fact, there are four important and implicit assumptions made in deriving gain scores:

(a) Scale units are uniform throughout the range of possible gain scores for a given test.
(b) Tests that are used to measure pretest and posttest proficiency can be equivalent.
(c) Observed gain scores rank subjects in the same order as would the best estimate of true gains.
(d) Observed scores are appropriate estimates of true scores.

Generally, not all of these assumptions hold in gain score construction, and thus to some degree it is difficult to make a meaningful interpretation of the scores.

GAME. In an instructional context, any exercise that involves artificial competition (either between participants or against the game system) and rules (arbitrary constraints within which the participants have to operate). A simulation, by contrast, will contain competition only if that is a feature of the real-life situation being simulated.

GAME THEORY. A mathematical theory which serves as a model for decision making. Originally devised for use in macroeconomics to describe the interrelationship of monetary variables. Its use in educational technology is to solve problems relating to strategies in academic games. For example, where one player has a high payoff (numerical value of a game consequence) and another a low payoff, the situation models a real-life game or social situation.

GAMMA. A method of evaluating the contrast characteristics of recording systems. In photographic processes gamma is a measure derived from the slope of the straight line portion of the characteristic curve. Negatives developed to the same gamma should show the same tone reproduction.

A gamma of unity implies that reproduced tones have the same ratio as they do in the original subject.

GANTT CHART. A type of bar chart in which actual performance is plotted against target performance. Such charts are used in the planning and monitoring of projects.

GATE. The part of a cine camera or projector where the film is held stationary during exposure. Part of the gate mechanism is a claw device that advances the film in the gate by one frame at a time. It is important to keep the gate of a projector clean as any dust or particles of film will appear as black shadows on the screen.

GATEWAY. A facility permitting access from one computer network to another. In reference to videotex, this typically involves exchange of information between the host computer and an external, independent computer such as a bank's computer.

GENDER CHANGER. A connector or cable that has two male and two female connectors wired pin to pin, which thus can change a male connector to which it is connected to female or a female connector to male.

GENERATION. A term used in videotape production. The original master film or tape is termed "first-generation," a copy made directly from this is "second-generation," a copy made from this is "third-generation," and so on.

GENLOCK. A device used to lock the frequency of an internal sync generator to an external source, for example, to permit the mixing of signals from a video recorder with those being generated in a studio. Without genlock there will be considerable picture instability whenever unsynchronized signals are joined or mixed.

GEOSTATIONARY ORBIT. A satellite orbit whose speed is arranged to ensure that the device retains a constant position 22,000 miles (35,790 km) above the equator; i.e., it remains fixed over a particular location and appears stationary to an observer.

This is the usual arrangement for communications satellites such as the Intelsat series.

GEOSTATIONARY SATELLITE. See **Geostationary Orbit.**

GEOSYNCHRONOUS SATELLITE. A satellite whose period of revolution precisely equals either the period of rotation of the earth on its axis (i.e., just over 24 hours), or a precise fraction of it: 1/2, 1/3, etc. The result is that the satellite appears at the same place in the sky at the same time every day. See **Geostationary Orbit.**

GHOST. A multiple image on a television receiver occurring because transmission is being received from more than one source. Usually the antenna is picking up not only the line-of-sight signal from the transmitter but also a reflection from a large building, hillside, etc.

GIGABYTE. A thousand million bytes, i.e., 1,000MB. In recent times computer storage has started to be measured in gigabytes, particularly as regards the use of laser-read ROM disks and other type of optical memory.

GLITCH. An error, mistake, or malfunction in a computer program (but in this case usually called a "bug") or computer system. The term is also applied to infelicities in other areas of technology, for example, the erratic picture on a television screen when an uncontrolled edit occurs. See **Pause Edit.**

GLOBAL BEAM. A satellite beam designed to cover all of that part of the earth visible from the geostationary orbit. At the equator this would amount to about one-third of the earth.

GLOBAL VILLAGE. Term coined by Marshall McLuhan to express the view that the advent of modern telecommunications, especially television, has effectively reduced the size of the world community. As in a village of olden days, experiences are witnessed and debated on a common basis around the world.

GLOSSY. A term used to describe photographic paper or other paper with a shiny surface.

GOAL. A general statement of intent or aspiration; virtually synonymous with aim.

GOLF BALL (PRINTER). A printer system (used in typewriters, computer printers, etc.) that employs interchangeable spherical heads each of which carries a particular character set.

GRAININESS. In photography, the tendency of the chemicals in the emulsions of fast films to gather into "clumps" during development, thus reducing the resolution of the final image by producing a pattern of small dots or "grains."

GRAMOPHONE. U.K. term for a record player (archaic).

GRAPHIC DESIGN. Graphic design in educational media, technology, and communications is concerned with the preparation of visual materials, or *graphics,* that are utilized to enhance purposeful communication and learning. A *graphic* is a visual display, most often two-dimensional, that incorporates abstract verbal and pictorial symbols or devices with the intent of improving communication. Common forms of graphics include charts, graphs, drawings and illustrations, posters, and cartoons. These forms have developed with identifying characteristics related to their functional attributes. Strictly speaking, a straight photograph, sometimes called a "study print," would *not* be considered a graphic; but if the photograph were embellished with the addition of some element that has developed meaning through convention (e.g., an arrow, color patch, or outline superimposed on the photograph, having the intent to direct or attract attention), then the pictorial display could be considered a graphic.

A graphic can be used as a discrete communication resource or as an integral component within a program in conjunction with personal presentation or presentation through another medium, such as television, slide set, filmstrip, motion picture, computer, book, etc.

The importance of graphic design correlates with the widespread conviction that of the variety of perceptual stimulus inputs involved in learning, it is the visual system which is dominant (Cobun, 1968 TYPE OF INFORMATION, p. 93). Among the various visual stimuli in instructional settings, materials which are susceptible to graphic design treatment are prevalent. The effectiveness of graphics lies in the graphic designer's ability to judiciously combine complementary verbal and pictorial elements—signs, symbols, and icons—thereby creating a visual stimulus which helps to clarify what might be ambiguous, to simplify what might be overly complex, to organize what may appear to be unstructured, and to form associations between entities that may otherwise appear unrelated.

GRAPHIC DESIGN CONSIDERATIONS

Research, theory, and practice provide the graphic designer with insights that aid in the selection of appropriate graphic forms and their design treatment. Interactive factors which influence graphic design include (1) the type of information to be communicated and the purpose for communicating; (2) the nature of the audience; (3) the impositions of the transmission medium; and (4) the effects of artistic treatments. The graphic designer is apt to utilize principles derived from various social and neurological sciences as well as from the fine and applied arts in order to prepare graphics that are both effectively meaningful and aesthetically elegant.

Type of Information and Communication Purpose. Graphics may be used in a variety of purposeful instructional contexts: to get attention; to arouse interest and motivation; to overview and organize; to provide for participation, practice, and application; to elucidate; to consolidate and review; and to evaluate. In each context and for each particular situation, instructional objectives may include varying degrees of complicity of the three domains of learning—cognitive, psychomotor, and affective. Certain types of graphics and graphic design features appear better suited to obtain desired effects in one domain than another. Charts, graphs, and drawings and illustrations, for example, usually have a substantial amount of data or information which the viewer must refer to or study. Posters and cartoons, on the other hand, generally have a simple, direct message which the viewer should recognize and respond to quickly. Often the former group emphasizes educational outcomes in the cognitive domain, while the latter emphasizes the affective. Humorous graphics may have little informational content, but they can promote a more friendly, relaxed atmosphere that may promote other learning activities.

Travers (1970 TYPE OF INFORMATION) makes reference to the advantages of visual stimuli for *referability* (i.e., the relative durability of the information display for purposes of reference by the receiver), as an alternate when other channels are in use, as well as "when the message is long, when it involves spatial orientation (as in giving directions for getting somewhere), or when the environment is noisy and an auditory message might be lost (as in some classrooms)" (p. 86).

Whether in school or out, an individual's information-handling capacity can be sorely overloaded if the receiving message form and channel are inefficient, especially in this age of increasing knowledge expansion and frenetic information exchange. It has been observed that "Graphic materials serve as a universal shorthand to help readers understand the torrent of information with which they are deluged" (Brown, Lewis, and Harcleroad, 1983 TYPE OF INFORMATION, p. 107).

Within each of the forms of graphics, special types have evolved that serve unique communication functions. Each type has certain characteristics and special conventions that must be recognized for their accurate interpretation. The five forms of graphics and the different types of each form are described below and related to the functions they best serve.

Charts. Charts are particularly useful to illustrate relationships and arrangements. When graphic design is applied to pictorial descriptions of the arrangement of our world, the resultant maps and globes are graphic representations subsumed under the category "charts." Mapmaking, or cartography, has developed to the level of a science in its own right, complete with an elaborate set of conventions. The topic of cartography will not be discussed further (reference to the topic may be found in Lawrence, 1979; Loxton, 1980; and Taylor, 1982 TYPE OF INFORMATION). Other forms of charts are illustrated in Figure 29 and are described in Table 10.

Graphs. Graphs are well suited to pictorially represent statistical data, thus helping in the visualization of comparisons, time trends, and other relationships. The major forms of graphs include bar, line, circle or pie, and pictorial. These forms of graphs are illustrated in Figure 30 and are described in Table 11.

Drawings and illustrations. Drawings and illustrations aid in the conceptualization of objects, processes, and ideas. These graphics are often used in conjunction with verbal or textual information, one complementing or supplementing the other. Drawings for technical purposes, such as blueprints, scale drawings, schematics, exploded views, etc., enable the viewer to appreciate the configuration of physical or operational attributes of an object. Accuracy of content in these graphics is critical—there is little artistic freedom as graphic conventions in technical drawings are of necessity particularly stringent. On the other hand are drawings and illustrations rendered in abstract impressionistic or expressionistic art forms. These forms are more suitable for illustrating the essence of inner, subjective feelings and reactions to situations, situations which would be difficult to describe solely verbally. Also, the abstract form is useful to represent

Figure 29
Types of Charts

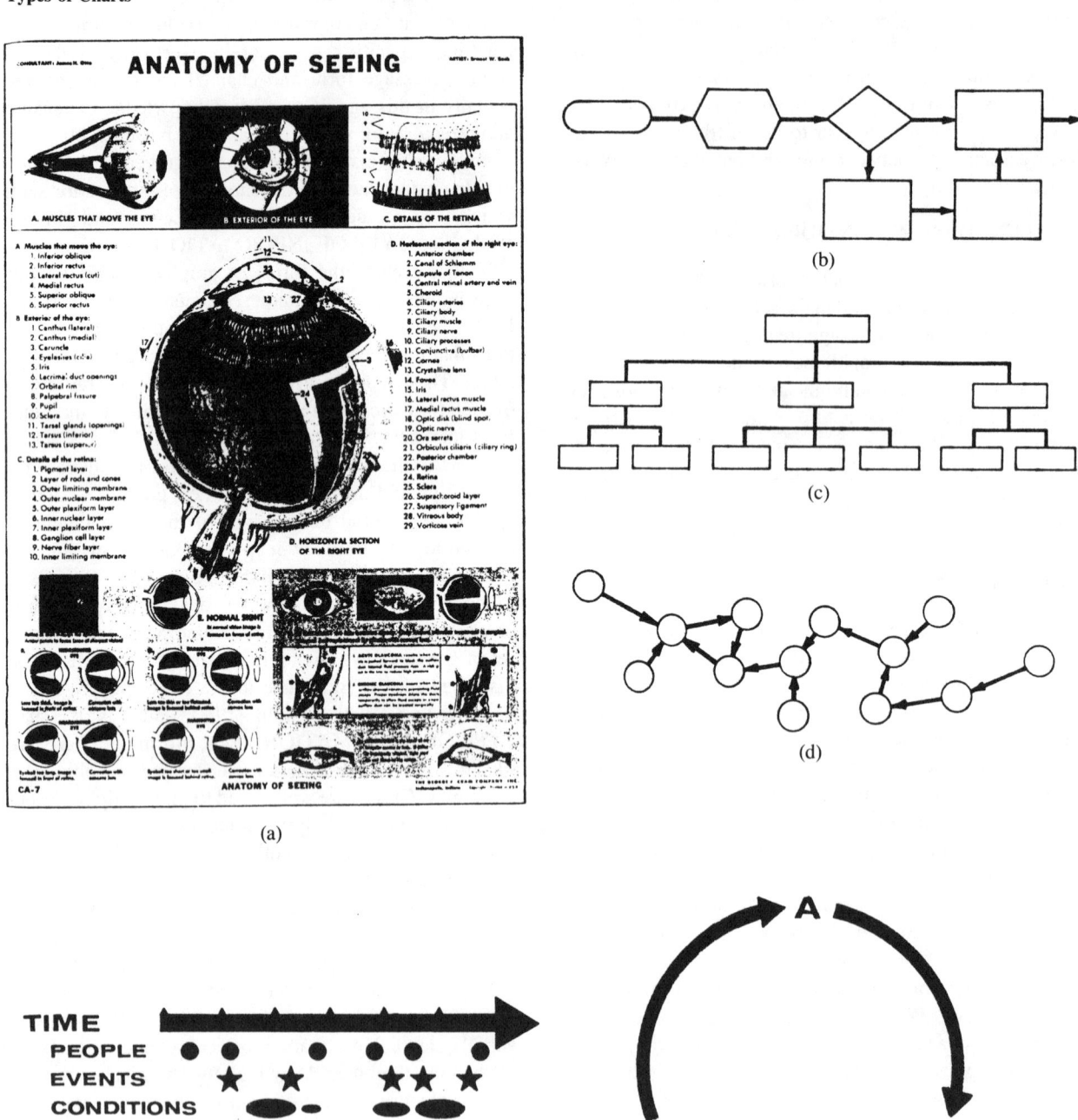

Figure 29 Continued

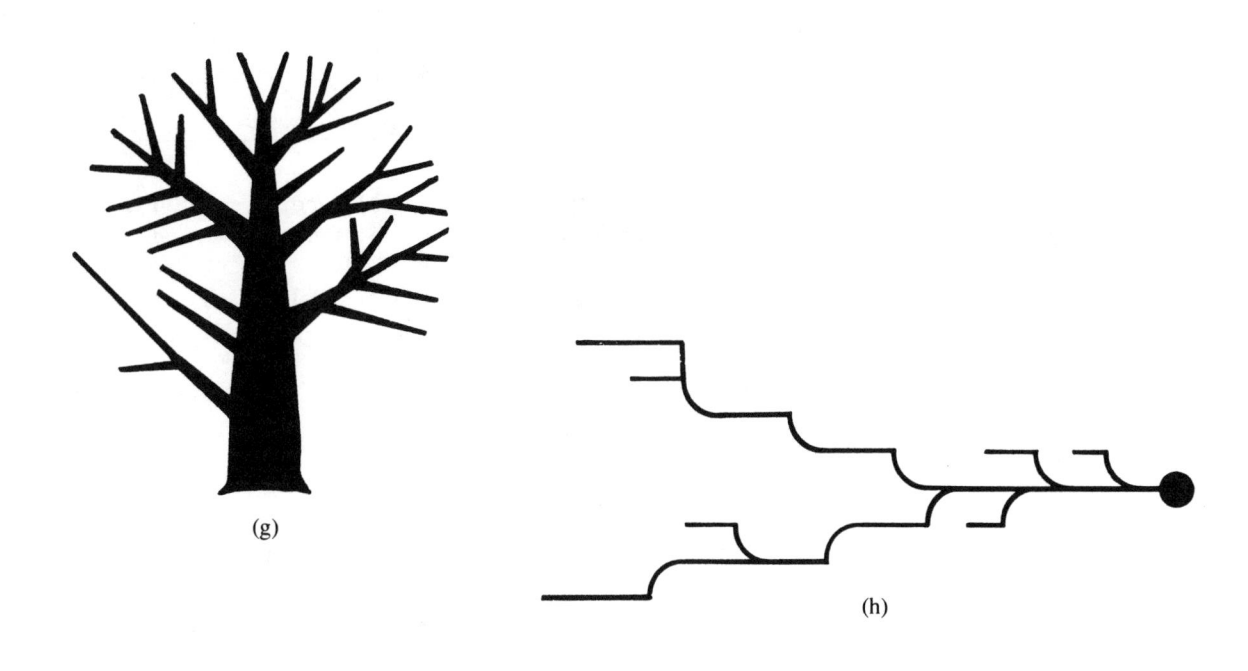

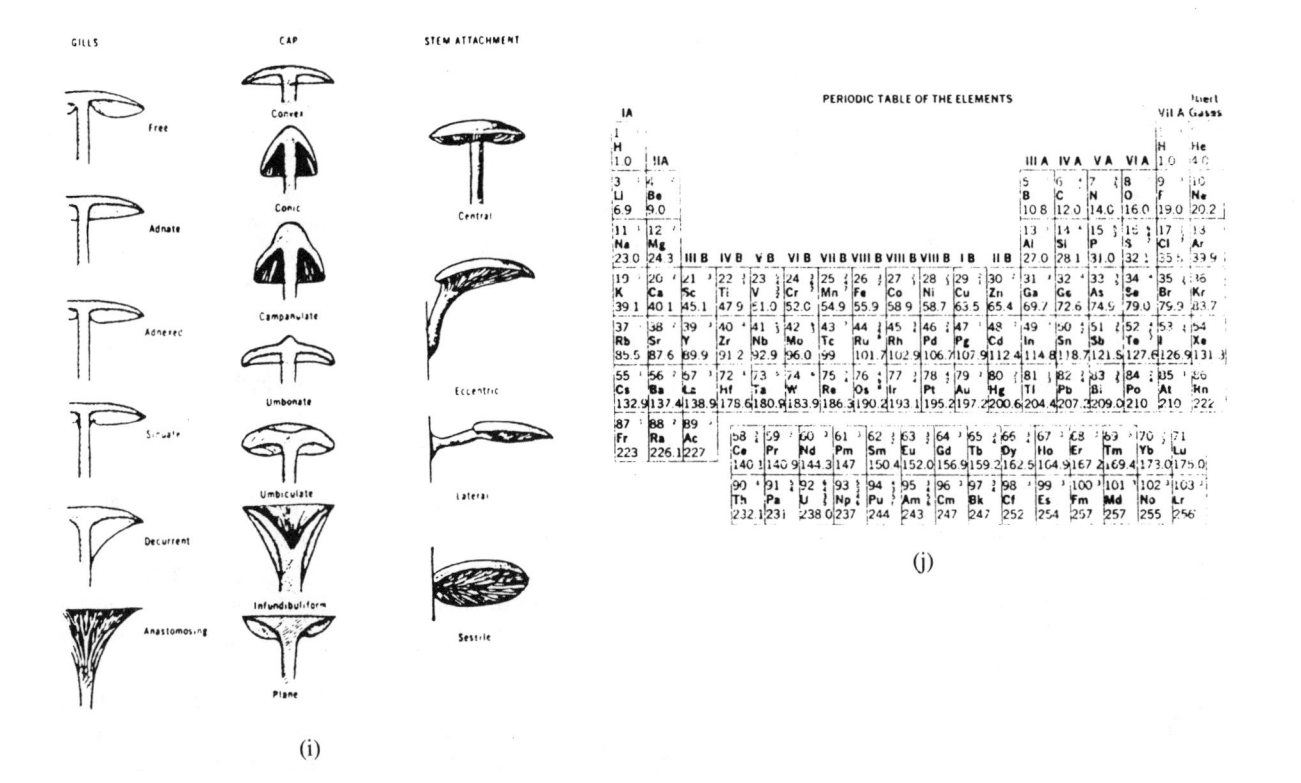

(g)

(h)

(i)

(j)

Table 10
Descriptions of Forms of Charts

	Name of Chart	Type of information particularly well illustrated
(a)	descriptive	associations among pictorially represented items and/or their parts and verbal labels and descriptions
(b)	flow, process, algorithm	sequence of steps in problem-solving or product development; pattern of a real or theoretical process
(c)	organization	linkage of units, especially for management/administrative purposes
(d)	sociogram	web of social relationships
(e)	time line	relationships among labeled historical events
(f)	cycle	sequence of events or stages that are cyclically repetitive
(g)	tree	divergent relationships of development or consequence
(h)	stream	convergent relationships of development or consequence
(i)	classification	taxonomical relationships, generally hierarchical in nature
(j)	tabular	organization of data that group by a common factor, such as schedules, Earth's elements in the Periodic Table, etc.
	flip	progression or buildup to a more complex concept with a series of charts shown one after another

the generality of notions and may arouse in the viewer curiosity and imagination, which in turn can nurture creative thought (Smith and Smith, 1966 TYPE OF INFORMATION). Shown in Figure 31 are contrasting examples of the two types of art forms.

Posters. Posters are characterized by "immediacy"—they are designed to be viewed quickly and their message should be obvious at a glance. The visual elements need to be dynamic, arresting, and simply purposeful. Thus pictorial symbols are often incorporated into poster design. Posters generally are used to elicit "approach-avoidance" behavior—affective domain learning—in contrast to the previously described graphics which emphasize "information"—cognitive domain learning. As the viewer need not keep making reference to the poster for information, the poster should be removed soon after it has made its impact. One example of a poster is shown in Figure 32.

Cartoons. A cartoon is a drawing in which particular features have been exaggerated, caricatured, or satirized to draw attention and make a point. When cartoons are used in education, it is particularly important that the bias, stereotyping, and humorous intent not be misinterpreted by the viewers, particularly youngsters. As with

Figure 30
Types of Graphs

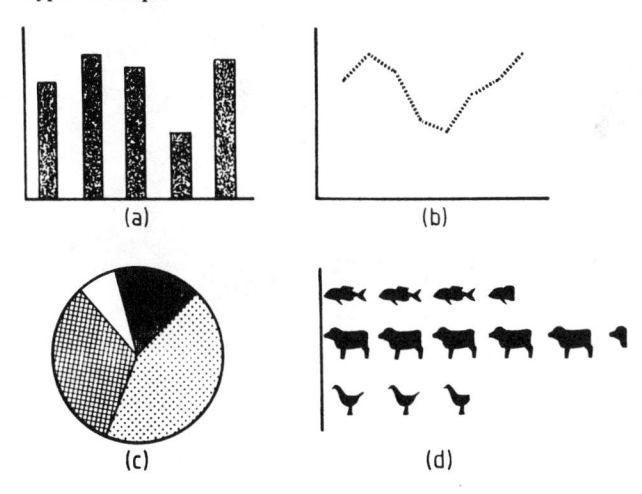

(a) (b)

(c) (d)

the poster, cartoons are most effectively used to achieve affective changes and to promote a more relaxed atmosphere for learning. Figure 33 shows one example of a cartoon.

Nature of the Audience. The graphic designer must appreciate the idiosyncratic decoding ability and personal inclinations of the viewer in order to make effective graphic design decisions. These audience-related considerations for graphic design that are discussed are those relating to visual literacy and acculturation, empathic appreciation, and physiologic constraints.

Visual literacy and acculturation. Even as graphics are able to shortcut and speed up our perceptual grasp, they can do so only by abstracting reality through the conventional use of symbolic codes. If the codes are unknown to the viewer, graphics are dysfunctional. The viewer may not understand and appreciate these codes because of cultural, societal, or personal deprivation or anomalous experiences relative to those of the designer, or the viewer may simply be too immature to grasp the code system (Kennedy, 1974; Vernon, 1971 NATURE OF THE AUDIENCE). In a treatise dealing with the acquisition of symbolic competence, Gross (1974 NATURE OF THE AUDIENCE) cautions:

> There is a level of sophistication necessary for the proper understanding of visual images. Pictures and films often convey misleading impressions of scale, distance, time, and relationship. By overcoming the limitations of space and time they may also fail to communicate the reality and importance of these dimensions. More importantly, perhaps, the images conveyed via these media may be deliberately or inadvertently false. The potential for misleading and dissembling, for confusing fiction and reality, is at least as great with photographs and films as with words and actions, and quite possibly much greater. (p. 77)

The graphic designer must systematically check for decoding debilities in the audience and take corrective measures. The designer must recognize the paradox of both the power and the frailty of graphics in the attainment of desired educational effects because of the visual pictorial symbology characteristic of their design. The graphic designer must be aware that "the meaning extracted from those symbolic systems will be limited to the meaning acquired by the use of that symbol in the referential or experiential world" (Carroll, 1964 NATURE OF THE AUDIENCE).

Table 11
Descriptions of Forms of Graphs

	Name of Graph	Type of relationship particularly well illustrated
(a)	bar	comparisons at fixed-point intervals
(b)	line	trends over time
(c)	circle, pie	comparisons as parts of a whole
(d)	pictorial	as for bar graph, but greater concreteness through the use of units of "universal" symbols; weakness in accuracy when interpreting partial units or if units are size-scaled proportionally

Figure 31
Types of Drawings and Illustrations

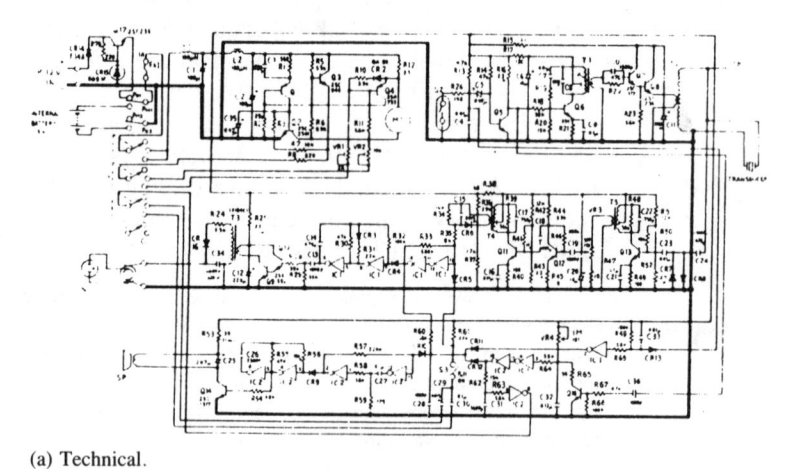

(a) Technical.

(b) Expressionistic.

Figure 32
Poster

BREAKFAST might have helped!

Figure 33
Cartoon

Reprinted by permission: Tribune Media Services.

The visual scanning pattern behavior of an individual is associated with the learned reading pattern. In our culture the norm is left to right, top to bottom. Thus the upper-left quadrant in a display is most apt to be first viewed (Heinich, Molenda, and Russell, 1982; Zimmerman, 1976 NATURE OF THE AUDIENCE). The graphic designer can place important elements in this quadrant of a graphic or incorporate design features that lead the eye to other positions where important information might be located.

The scanning patterns of older and younger viewers differ, with the younger viewers less "disciplined" in attending to "important" details and more likely to regard inconsequential aspects (Mackworth and Bruner, 1970 NATURE OF THE AUDIENCE). The "attention [of viewers generally] is drawn and held by complexity, providing the complexity does not exceed the perceivers' cognitive capacities" (Fleming and Levie, 1978 NATURE OF THE AUDIENCE, p. 22). The graphic designer should note these differences in viewers' characteristics, as preferences for degree of complexity and color change with age.

The effect of color on mood association can influence the predisposition of viewers to learning. For example, the color in graphics can suggest an atmosphere of liveliness or seriousness, of casualness or formality. Cultural variables are considered to be a potent influence on these mood-tone associations (Murray and Deabler, 1957; Wexner, 1954 NATURE OF THE AUDIENCE), as well as on color preferences (Hooke, Youell, and Etkin, 1975 NATURE OF THE AUDIENCE). The graphic designer can employ the suggestive power of color through selective use of color in graphics. A useful summary of color associations, assembled by Birren (1978 NATURE OF THE AUDIENCE), appears in Table 12 below.

Another factor which influences the manner in which information in a graphic is perceived is the cognitive or perceptual style of the individual. As an example of a cognitive style difference, individuals characterized as being "field dependent" are more likely to attend to items in a display that may be considered inconsequential or unimportant. These individuals may consequently rate highly on "incidental" learning (Wolk and Svoboda, 1975 NATURE OF THE AUDIENCE, p. 905), but their attention and cognition directed to more important items are diminished. (For a good review of this cognitive style, refer to Witkin, 1978 NATURE OF THE AUDIENCE. The reader may also be interested in perusing descriptions of a number of cognitive styles and their assessment in Ausburn and Ausburn, 1976 NATURE OF THE AUDIENCE.)

The safe road for the graphic designer, particularly when designing graphics for younger audiences, is to reduce complexity and distractive elements, to incorporate color as an attractive device, and to make the "important" elements as obvious as possible. In so doing, some allowance will be made for chronological differences as well as idiosyncratic cognitive or perceptual styles of viewers.

Empathic appreciation. In addition to the "visual literacy" of the intended audience, there are other graphic design considerations that relate to the attributes of the receiver. How clearly the message is received and how well it is retained are in part due to how personally relevant the message is perceived to be (Gagné, 1970 NATURE OF THE AUDIENCE). This might be referred to as the *empathic* quality of the message, another consideration for the graphic designer. When the viewer observes graphic elements that are familiar and associated with pleasant or successful experiences, these encounters will be connected to the previous experiences with those elements and will be welcomed, at least initially. So use of familiar images of cartoon, television, or performing characters, use of current "in" verbal expressions, and so forth, when tastefully executed, can make the audience more receptive to the whole message and thus make it more memorable.

Physiologic constraints. Other audience-related graphic design factors stem from the physiologic characteristics of the viewers. The resolution of the human eye that has normal visual acuity requires that elements in a graphic need to be a certain minimum size to be clearly distinguished. A simplified rule of thumb concerning verbal symbol legibility is that the smallest letter should be proportionally one inch tall per 32 feet of viewing distance (Kemp, 1980 NATURE OF THE AUDIENCE, p. 118). The graphic designer should allow for this minimal size of verbal material, adjusting the artwork lettering size so that the viewer anticipated to be most distant from the directly viewed graphic or projected image of the graphic will be able to easily distinguish the letters. Other legibility factors such as letter-background contrast, letter style, and line weight are discussed in a following section.

However, not all viewers have normal vision. Visually-impaired individuals may require extra–large-sized graphics or supplemental tactile stimuli incorporated into nonprojected graphics; color-deficient viewers (about 8 percent of men and 0.5 percent of women) may require avoidance of the pairings of particular colors in areas adjacent to each other, especially if the tonal values of the two are similar (Richards and Macklin, 1971). Colors to particularly avoid placing adjacent to each other are listed in Table 13. A brightness contrast of at least 30 percent is recommended so that color-deficient viewers can discriminate adjacent colored areas (Chen, 1971 NATURE OF THE AUDIENCE).

The shape of a graphic is often wider that it is high, particularly if it is designed to be viewed at once, without scanning. This "comfortable" shape, as exemplified by the media of television, motion picture, and CRT displays, is not simply an arbitrary technological choice, but can be related to the physiology of the eye. This horizontally elongated shape coincides with the arrangement of the retinal cells in the eye associated with foveal vision (e.g., Christman, 1971; Polyak, 1941; Schiffman, 1976 NATURE OF AUDIENCE). This vision, according to Travers (1970 NATURE OF THE AUDIENCE, p. 129), is used for detailed analysis, while less important context information surrounding focused vision would fall onto other retinal areas involved with gross analysis. The graphic designer should not design unusually proportioned graphics unless the intended viewers will have sufficient time to survey and study portions of them. The preferred practice in designing the shape of

Table 12
Modern American Color Associations

Color	General appearance	Mental associations	Direct associations	Objective impressions	Subjective impressions
Red	Brilliant, intense, opaque, dry	Hot, fire, heat, blood	Danger, Christmas, Fourth of July, St. Valentine's Day, Mother's Day, flag	Passionate, exciting, fervid, active	Intensity, rage, rapacity, fierceness
Orange	Bright, luminous, glowing	Warm, metallic, autumnal	Halloween, Thanksgiving	Jovial, lively, energetic, forceful	Hilarity, exuberance, satiety
Yellow	Sunny, incandescent, radiant	Sunlight	Caution	Cheerful, inspiring, vital, celestial	High spirit, health
Green	Clear, moist	Cool, nature, water	Clear, St. Patrick's Day	Quieting, refreshing, peaceful, nascent	Ghastliness, disease, terror, guilt
Blue	Transparent, wet	Cold, sky, water, ice	Service, flag	Subduing, melancholy, contemplative, sober	Gloom, fearfulness, furtiveness

Purple	Deep, soft, atmospheric	Cool, mist, darkness, shadow	Mourning, Easter	Dignified, pompous, mournful, mystic	Loneliness, desperation
White	Spatial--light	Cool, snow	Cleanliness, Mother's Day, flag	Pure, clean, frank, youthful	Brightness of spirit, normality
Black	Spatial--darkness	Neutral, night, emptiness	Mourning	Funereal, ominous, deadly, depressing	Negation of spirit, death

Table 13
Color Combinations Inappropriate for Color-Deficient Viewers

Color	Avoid placing adjacent to
blue	dull green, dull purple, blue-purple
blue-green	pink
blue-purple	yellow-green, blue
dull purple	blue
purple	green-blue
green	red, brown, tan
dull green	blue, brown
green-blue	purple, pink
yellow-green	blue-purple
brown	green, dull green
tan	green
red	green
pink	orange, blue-green, green-blue
orange	pink
yellow-green	blue-purple

graphics is to follow the **landscape** (q.v.) format if the pictorial subject is at all amenable to the horizontally elongated composition. In media where the technical requirements do not entirely predicate the composition of the graphics, it is most acceptable to maintain a consistency of format throughout a sequence or set, preferably in the horizontal format, even if there is resultant "waste space" in a limited few graphics. The commonest application of this practice is for projected slide sets, but even so exceptions arise, particularly for wide-screen, multiple-screen, and multiple-image presentations (Eastman Kodak, 1967 NATURE OF THE AUDIENCE).

Impositions of the Transmission Medium. The design of graphics must allow for the peculiarities of the medium in which the graphic will be displayed. Size and shape of graphic, provision of space around the message area, color restraints, contrast range of tonal values, motion in graphics, lettering style and size, and amount of detail possible in graphics are all affected by the capability of the technical system of the medium. Table 14 summarizes a number of graphic design constraints that apply to graphics which are prepared for display through a variety of media.

Size and shape. Specific sizes and shapes of graphics for various media are listed in Table 14. No restriction for size is noted for graphics to be photographed, as camera lenses and accessories can be used to photograph virtually any size of graphic. It is beneficial to work with larger-sized graphics because any imperfection in the artwork will not be magnified as much in the enlarged projected image. However, for economy in material costs and convenience in handling and storage, a smaller-sized graphic is indicated. A compromise in size is required in consideration of the above; typically, graphics to be photographed are prepared in a standard size wherein the message area is about six inches high.

Provision of space. In the preparation of graphics for photographic or television media, a "safe" border should be allowed around the central message-carrying area. This allowance is made to accommodate technical system inaccuracies such as camera viewfinder misalignment and image area lost from the transmitted picture by the television receiver. Important parts of the message should be placed well inside the "message area" to provide a distinct separation between message and edge of viewing screen. This denotes to the viewer that the complete message has been projected and that there is no possibility that parts may have "bled" past the edge of the screen and been lost. The background of the graphic should be

Table 14
Graphic Design Constraints Relative to Display Medium

Graphic Design Constraints

Medium	(a) Message area height to width ratio	(b) Message area size in inches (cm)	(c) Height ratio of minimum sized letter to artwork	(d) Use of color	(e) Amount of detail	(f) Contrast range
Opaque projection	1 : 1	10 x 10 max (25.4 x 25.4)	1 : 50	See Note 1	N.R.	N.R.
Overhead projection[1]	4 : 5 or 5 : 4	7.5 x 9.25 (19.1 x 23.5)	1 : 50	"	N.R.	N.R.
Slide/filmstrip						
35mm full-frame (double frame); European filmstrip	2 : 3 or 3 : 2; 2 : 3	N.R.	1 : 50	"	N.R.	N.R.
35mm half-frame (single frame); N.A. filmstrip[2]	3 : 4 or 4 : 3; 3 : 4	N.R.	1 : 50			
lantern	3.25 : 4	N.R.	1 : 50	"	N.R.	N.R.
Motion picture[3]						
35mm	3 : 4	N.R.	1 : 50	"	not as much detail as still projected pictures	
16mm	3 : 4	N.R.	1 : 50			
super 8mm	3 : 4	N.R.	1 : 50			
Television	3 : 4	N.R.	1 : 25	See Note 2	least detail; use bold lines	limited to 80% full scale

"N.R." signifies "no restrictions."

[1] Overhead projector stage is 10" (25cm) square. Transparency materials generally available in approx. 8½" × 11" (21.6cm × 28cm) sheets; mounts have 8" × 9¾" (20.3cm × 24.8cm) opening.
[2] N.A. filmstrip–North American standard filmstrip
[3] As production of regular 8mm film is obsolete, it is omitted.

Figure 34
Camera Registration for Graphic Artwork

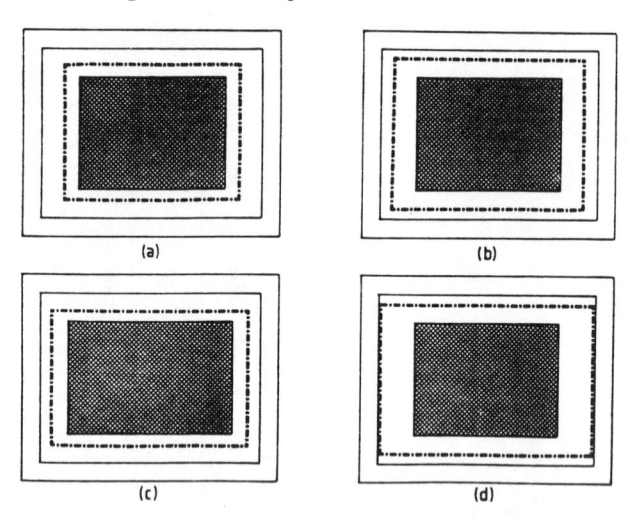

extended, continuing the background artwork, at least 10 percent on each edge for photographic slide preparation, and at least 15 percent on each edge for television. A slide of a graphic to be shown via television needs to incorporate both safety factors. In addition to the camera-ready portion of the artwork, it is advisable that the graphic has extra marginal space for handling purposes. Accommodation for handling is commonly provided by affixing the artwork to an appropriately sized mount board.

There are benefits from standardizing the size of graphics to be photographed for television, slides, and filmstrips: camera work is simplified; graphic materials inventory is reduced; and efficiency of graphic preparation is increased through regularity of application of legibility considerations, etc. One common size for graphic art material is 9″ × 12″ (23cm × 30.5cm), which is affixed to 11″ × 14″ (28cm × 35.5cm) mount board. Figure 34 illustrates recommendations for message area, "safe" border, and extra margin for television and photography graphics. The camera "field" is the rectangular focused plane viewed through a reflex camera viewfinder, corrected for parallax; i.e., the "field" is the focused area to be photographed. The camera field is shown outlined with a heavy broken line; the message area is shaded. Table 15 lists the specific sizes of message areas and camera fields for graphics prepared on the recommended standard-size materials. There is a certain amount of corner cutoff in television screens, so important information should not be placed in the corner areas of television graphics. A large part of the picture area in slides is lost when they are televised. If a considerable number of this type of slide is shot, the photographer may find it convenient to insert over the camera viewfinder screen a transparent mask on which the television scanning and essential message areas are marked. The essential message area should be 0.63″ × 0.84″ (1.6cm × 2.1cm) centered in the viewfinder of a full-frame 35mm SLR camera.

The graphic artist might prepare full-size masks with the message area cut out and the field outlined. Overlaying the mask on the graphic can help the artist position the artwork on the mount as well as guide the photographer in framing the graphic properly in the viewfinder. The mask, of course, would be removed prior to shooting the graphic.

Color restraints. Photographic dyes in color films cannot re-create the brilliance perceived by human vision when fluorescent pigments and art materials are illuminated with a source which has sufficient ultraviolet radiation in it. Thus when one views a photographically filmed image of a graphic which had been prepared with fluorescent markings, those parts will appear to be relatively duller. However, a television image can retain this brilliance if the television camera is trained on the graphic itself rather than on a photographic slide of the graphic.

A monochromatic black-and-white rendering of a colored graphic will show various colors as shades of gray. There are variations in the photographic and electronic derivative processes, and so the graphic designer needs to become familiar with the idiosyncratic nature of system processes in situ; the "color-blindness" of technical systems varies. Wherever possible, the graphic designer should use different tonal values of hues in adjacent areas to facilitate differentiation between them.

Contrast range. The reflectance of materials normally used in the preparation of graphics does not exceed the imaging capabilities of photographic film. It is recommended, however, that television graphics have a reduced scale of reflectance, ranging in the order of about 3 percent for the darkest markings to about 60 or 70 percent for the brightest (Wurtzel, 1979; Zettl, 1976 IMPOSITIONS). The exception is for graphics which are to be used in electronically superimposing images, in which case white is placed on black.

Motion. Media which incorporate motion can make use of graphics and constructions that have moving parts. Cutouts with background slides and masks which are moved during shooting are commonly used to give the impression of "animation," as are "crawls" for extended moving graphics (Zettl, 1976 IMPOSITIONS).

Lettering style and size. Whereas a directly viewed graphic may be closely inspected, a projected or televised image of a graphic is generally viewed under much different circumstances. To facilitate legibility, certain re-

GRAPHIC DESIGN

Table 15
Standard Sizes in Graphics for Camera

Figure 34 Illustration	Medium	Message Area Ratio	Message Area Size, in inches (cm)	Camera Field Size, in inches (cm)
(a)	North American filmstrip; half-frame 35mm slide; 16mm and super 8mm motion picture	3 : 4	6 x 8 (15.2 x 20.3)	7.2 x 9.6 (18.3 x 24.4)
(b)	television	3 : 4	6 x 8 (15.2 x 20.3)	8 x 10.7 (20.3 x 27.2)
(c)	European film strip; full-frame 35mm slide	2 : 3	6 x 9 (15.2 x 23)	7.2 x 10.8 (18.3 x 27.4)
(d)	full-frame 35mm slide for television	3 : 4	6 x 8 (15.2 x 20.3)	8 x 12 (20.3 x 30.5)

All artwork is 9″ × 12″ (23cm × 30.5cm) affixed to 11″ × 14″ (28cm × 35.5cm) mount board.

strictions apply to verbal material appearing in graphics intended for the latter applications.

The size of lettering used in a graphic depends on a number of factors, including the resolving power of the medium, the eyesight of the viewers, the distance of viewers from the image, and so forth. Under normal conditions, it is expected that the eyesight of viewers does not require correction and that the viewers are situated no further away than 8 times the height of the full image projected by motion picture, slide, opaque, and overhead projectors, and 24 times the height of a television receiver picture. Given these assumptions, Table 16 provides a summary of minimum lettering height requirements for graphics intended for those media. The minimum letter heights are based on most distant viewing distances noted above. Two figures are given for the overhead, as both horizontal and vertical format transparencies are commonly intermixed during use. For logistic purposes, though, neither the projector nor the audience are moved during viewing. Thus it behooves the designer to specify a single minimum size for lettering, together with its concomitant maximum distance for viewing, to be used in preparing overhead transparencies in both vertical and horizontal format which are to be screened intermixed at a given session. As a general rule, it is better to use larger letters for the sake of legibility, particularly if the viewing conditions are doubtful.

When selecting letter fonts for graphics, the graphic designer should be aware that sizes of dry transfer letters are given in "points," with about 100 points representing a font in which the uppercase letters are about one inch tall. The point size is historically associated with the actual height of the block on which each letter in a font was carved, thus ultimately limiting the maximum size. Unfortunately for legibility purposes, the point size gives no indication of the lowercase letter height, which may range from one-third to almost two-thirds the height of the uppercase letters, depending on the style of the font.

The selection of style of font affects legibility. Generally, sans-serif styles with normal line weight are preferred (Eastman Kodak, 1974; Kemp, 1980; MacGregor, 1979 IMPOSITIONS). An eye-catching heading or title

Table 16
Minimum Lettering Height* in Graphics

Graphic	Relative height of letter to message area	Message area height, in inches (cm)	Minimum letter height, in inches (cm)
displayed on television	1/25	6 (15.2)	0.36 (9)
all slides, filmstrips, motion pictures	1/50	6 (15.2)	0.12 (3)
opaque projector	1/50	10 (25.4)	0.20 (5)
overhead projector	1/50	7.5 (19.1) / 9.25 (23.5)	0.15 (4) / 0.19 (5)

*This minimum height refers to the height of a small lowercase letter, such as the letter ''a'' when mixed cases are used, or the height of an uppercase letter, such as the letter ''A'' when all uppercase is used. (Uppercase refers to capital letters.)

may employ an uncommon style font, but the use of such styles should be sparing and the style should match the message (e.g., ''SHAKESPEARE'' lettered in an Old English font). A useful reference bibliography on typography has been prepared by Hartley, Fraser, and Burnhill (1974 IMPOSITIONS), updating Herbert Spencer's *The Visible Word* (1969 IMPOSITIONS).

A variety of lettering materials and techniques generally suitable for graphics designed for mediated transmission as well as for direct viewing are available to the graphic designer. Lettering applied freehand or with stencil is relatively inexpensive but requires a certain degree of skill and patience. Cutout adhesive letters can be somewhat costly and are available in limited variety; sufficient quantities need to be on hand for the job. Dry transfer letters have a very attractive appearance and are available in great variety; however, they are relatively costly, require a modest degree of skill in application, and also need to be on hand in sufficient quantity. Photographic lettering machines provide great versatility and high-quality lettering, but are most costly. Reasonably attractive letters can be provided at very low cost and with great speed through use of the typewriter. Although the line weight of typewritten characters is relatively thin, and character spacing is mechanical rather than visual, the ease and speed of preparation and minimal cost outweigh the disadvantages, particularly for low-budget productions. In order to obtain the most suitable lettering for graphics, several guidelines should be followed: an electric typewriter with carbon ribbon should be used; the typeface should be clean; a Gothic or sans-serif letter style is preferable; smooth bond paper and lightweight plate finished bristol or Manila tag are suitable materials on which to type. Because of the ease and economy in doing the lettering, there is a greater than normal temptation which the graphic designer must resist in cramming too much verbal material into the graphic. At least for legibility purposes, the following recommendations should be followed. For opaque and overhead projection graphics, it would be most appropriate to use a large-size typeface, preferably ''primary'' or ''bulletin,'' uppercase only, double-spaced. If the audience is closer than normal to the projected image, lowercase can be used, or uppercase of a smaller type style. For television graphics, typewritten copy should be limited to five lines of uppercase type, double-spaced, each line a maximum of 2 inches long, fitting in a camera field 2″h × 2.6″w. For projection slides, typewritten copy for graphics should be limited to six lines of type, double-spaced, each line a maximum of 3.25 inches long. This provides a full-frame field 2.75″h × 4.13″w, or a half-frame field 2.75″h × 3.7″w. If typed copy is shot with the Ektagraphic Visualmaker, manufactured by Eastman Kodak, the 3″ × 3″ stand should be used. It can accommodate a graphic three inches square with six lines of type, double-spaced, each line a maximum of 2.5 inches long.

Amount of detail. Images made on photographic film can record a large amount of detail—i.e., the magnified image shows distinctions between, or resolution of, fine lines and minute features of the subject. The larger the film on which the image is recorded, the greater the amount of detail. It is generally the *projection* optics which limit and degrade image quality. Even so, commonly available still projection equipment is more than adequate in providing a wealth of detail when standard projection procedures are followed, given the physiologic limit of human vision. Motion picture projection, however, introduces a variation in registration between projected frames. When this is coupled with smaller film size formats, less detail can be distinguished in the image than with still projection. Television introduces yet another limitation—the electronic reconstruction of the image into discrete bits on the television receiver screen, yielding the poorest resolution of pictorial detail. Together with other system effects, fine line detail may be easily lost. Thus graphics for television should have substantial line weight and emphasize boldness of design.

Effects of Artistic Treatments. A good deal of empirical research has been conducted to examine the effects of a variety of artistic treatments that can be applied to the design of graphics. The effects found in the research and the implications of the results are discussed under three general categories: color, detail, and organization. Some of these factors have already been alluded to in other contexts as they relate to viewer motivation and preferences and technical system constraints.

Color. Research which has examined what effects color in pictures and graphics has on learning seems to generally agree that the presence of realistic color is preferred by learners, but does not appear to have any significant beneficial effect on learning unless color is a critical attribute for learning or is used to emphasize learning cues (Dwyer, 1971; Kanner and Rosenstein, 1960; Reich and Meisner, 1976; Rudnick, Porter, and Suydam, 1973 EFFECTS). However, a number of researchers examining the use of color to cue or emphasize found no salutary effect (Gadzella and Whitehead, 1975; Paivio, Rogers, and Smythe, 1968; Webster and Cox, 1974 EFFECTS). In some cases color has been found to be a distractor (Chan, Travers, and Van Mondfrans, 1965 EFFECTS) and false color was found to produce disabling effects on learning (Spaulding, 1956; Travers, 1970; Travers and Alvarado, 1970; Vollan, 1972 EFFECTS). Others have found color to aid certain types of students, usually those with lower ability (Allen, 1975; Booth and Miller, 1974; Dwyer, 1976a; Katzman and Nyenhuis, 1972 EFFECTS).

Although the research about color effects on learning is not totally clear-cut, and the effects of color can be quite subtle, there are some guidelines the graphic designer should follow. It appears that false or unrealistic color should not be used. If color is used for its attractive effects, particularly with younger audiences, it should be realistic color. Color can probably be used to highlight and direct attention, facilitating viewers in comparing, associating, and organizing items. Color can also be used to suggest or provoke a particular feeling or mood to be connected with the message in the graphic and the learning atmosphere.

Detail. It is in the nature of graphics for them to tend to be somewhat abstract, some types more so than others. In illustrations and posters, for example, the designer has quite a degree of freedom in selecting artwork that ranges from simplified line to photograph-like detailed realistic representations, the latter style generally more time-consuming and costly to prepare. The graphic designer should be aware of how the amount of detail in a graphic affects learning. Some research studies have used the degree of detail in the illustrations as an experimental variable. Generally, this research has found that versions of graphics with greatest detail are not necessarily overall the most suitable to achieve learning (Gorman, 1973; Hedberg and Clark, 1976; Moore, 1971; Myatt and Carter, 1979 EFFECTS). There is some research that suggests that *less* detail is not harmful and at times is beneficial to learning (Borg and Schuller, 1979; Franzwa, 1973; Moore and Sasse, 1971; Nelson, Metzler, and Reed, 1974; Smith, Smith, and Hubbard, 1958 EFFECTS). A great number of subjects, in excess of 10,000, have at one time or another participated in experimental research conducted by F. Dwyer, wherein he has varied the graphic treatment of illustrations in a program dealing with the heart and its functioning. Although Dwyer (1976b EFFECTS) is unable to specify that one form of pictorial rendering was found to be conclusively more efficacious than another, an overview of his studies (Dwyer, 1972 EFFECTS) makes apparent that simpler graphics, such as line drawings, were more often reported superior to the more highly detailed versions. In consideration of the above, the graphic designer then, as a rule, might opt for artwork with less detail as long as the detail is not critical for the intended communication.

Organization. Organization, at times referred to as "schemata," involves the composition of elements in a graphic. Pictures have been found to be more memorable if the elements are organized so that meaningful associations are made explicit (Bower, Karlin, and Dueck, 1975 EFFECTS) and, for younger viewers, have fewer elements (Fleming and Sheikhian, 1972 EFFECTS). Organizing elements as they might be expected to be found in real-world scenes also helps to make the elements memorable (Mandler and Johnson, 1976; Mandler and Parker, 1976; Mandler and Ritchey, 1977; Mandler and Stein, 1974 EFFECTS). Adding verbal elements, such as captions or labels, with associated pictorial elements has been found to aid recall (Bahrick and Gharrity, 1976 EFFECTS). The interpretation of a visual display into a figure-ground organization strongly affects memory for the elements, in favor of the figure element (Mitterer and Rowland, 1975 EFFECTS).

The graphic designer should carefully consider the meaningful association—objective, contextual, and metaphorical—of pictorial elements in a graphic, as well as the relationship of accompanying verbal meterial (Davis, 1983). The components of a graphic should be organized so that the structure reinforces the meaningful intent of the information. This can be done through physical proximity and grouping of elements, comparative keying with pictorial symbols or notations, eliminating distractive unessential elements, and emphasizing pictorially the figure (primary information)/ground (contextual information) organization. As an aid to imply a meaningful relationship among elements, the graphic designer should compose the elements to provide the appearance of unification in a graphic rather than apparent disorganization. If some purposeful composition is not apparent, a common practice to alternately achieve the appearance of unification is to arbitrarily compose the elements in a pattern such as the shape of a letter of the alphabet (e.g., letters *X, Y, O,* etc.). A symmetrical "formal" or asymmetrical "informal" balance may be chosen, befitting the information being presented and the type of presentation atmosphere being encouraged.

A caveat. This section has surveyed selected research on artistic treatments in graphics. Certain qualifications of the interpretation and application of the findings need to be made explicit to the graphic designer. Variations in artistic treatment are difficult to compare across research experiments, as there is no standardized hierarchical classification scheme. The classification of degree of detail in a graphic, for example, becomes more complicated when interactive variables, such as color and organization, are introduced. Further complications include the description and measurement of outcome variables—the type and amount of learning, directed and incidental, both cognitive and affective—as well as idiosyncratic viewer factors.

Heidt (1978 EFFECTS) proposes the development of a media classification taxonomy that relates media design variables with cognition. He argues that this sort of scheme would be of inestimable value to researchers in that it could help sort out the maze of interactive relationships and provide a focus for research effort. Until such time that a media taxonomy envisioned by Heidt becomes a workable reality, or an alternate theoretical approach emerges, there will be limitations on the impact research results can have on graphic design practice. This is so because of the contradistinction of the nature of real-life learning experiences compared to the narrow specificity of experimental designs in situ and the necessarily limited scope of description of participants and results. The graphic designer must at this time be content in applying the findings from experimental research, suggested as guidelines for design in this section and elsewhere, knowing that exceptions to the guidelines are to be commonly expected in practice. Nonetheless, graphic design has a great impact on communication and learning processes. The graphic designer should be cognizant of the potential of humans and technology in the communication process as well as their limitations and constraints. The designer must be able to select the artistic treatment that most effectively combines verbal and pictorial symbols in appropriate graphic form. Thus graphics that are designed and used for specific purposes can more certainly and effectively achieve those ends.

Lorne E. Koroluk

REFERENCES

Effects of Artistic Treatments

Allen, W. H. (1975) "Intellectual Abilities and Instructional Media Design." *AV Communication Review* 23: 139–169.

Bahrick, H. P. and Gharrity, K. (1976) "Interaction among Pictorial Components in the Recall of Picture Captions." *Journal of Experimental Psychology: Human Learning and Memory,* 2: 103–111.

Booth, G. D. and Miller, H. R. (1974) "Effectiveness of Monochrome and Color Presentations in Facilitating Affective Learning." *AV Communication Review* 22: 409–422.

Borg, W. R. and Schuller, C. F. (1979) "Detail and Background in Audiovisual Lessons and Their Effect on Learners." *Educational Communications and Technology Journal* 27: 31–38.

Bower, G. H., Karlin, M. B., and Dueck, A. (1975) "Comprehension and Memory for Pictures." *Memory and Cognition* 3: 216–220.

Boyvey, M. R. (1970) "The Relationship of Detail in Visual Illustrations to Effective Learning: An Experiment in Elementary School Social Studies." *Dissertation Abstracts International,* 30: 5335A (University Microfilms No. 70–10,757).

Chan, A., Travers, R. M., and Van Mondfrans, A. P. (1965) "The Effects of Colored Embellishment of a Visual Array on a Simultaneously Presented Audio Array." *AV Communication Review* 13: 159–164.

Davis, R. H. (1983) "AV Graphics: Say It with Symbols." *Audio-Visual Communications* (March): 18, 20, 22, 45, 46.

Dwyer, F. M. (1971). "Color as an Instructional Variable." *AV Communication Review* 19: 399–416.

———. (1972) *A Guide for Improving Visualized Instruction.* State College, Penn.: Learning Services.

———. (1976a) "The Effect of IQ Level on the Instructional Effectiveness of Black-and-White and Color Illustrations." *AV Communication Review* 24: 49–62.

———. (1976b) "Adapting Media Attributes for Effective Learning." *Educational Technology* (August): 7–13.

Fleming, M. L. and Sheikhian, M. (1972) "Influence of Pictorial Attributes on Recognition Memory." *AV Communication Review* 20: 423–441.

Franzwa, D. (1973). "Influence of Meaningfulness, Picture Detail, and Presentation Mode on Visual Retention." *AV Communication Review,* 21: 209–223.

Gadzella, B. M. and Whitehead, D. A. (1975) "Effects of Auditory and Visual Modalities in Recall of Words." *Perceptual and Motor Skills* 40: 255–260.

Gorman, D. (1973) "Effects of Varying Pictorial Detail and Presentation Strategy on Concept Formation." *AV Communication Review* 21: 337–350.

Hedberg, J. G. and Clark, R. E. (1976) "Realism in Pictorial Instruction: What the Research Says." *Educational Technology* (June): 46–47.

Heidt, E. U. (1978) *Instructional Media and the Individual Learner.* New York: Nichols.

Kanner, J. H. and Rosenstein, A. J. (1960) "Television in Army Training: Color vs. Black and White." *AV Communication Review* 8: 243–252.

Katzman, N. and Nyenhuis, J. (1972) "Color versus Black and White Effects on Learning, Opinion, and Attention." *AV Communication Review* 20: 16–28.

Mandler, J. M. and Johnson, N. S. (1976) "Some of the Thousand Words a Picture Is Worth." *Journal of Experimental Psychology* 2: 529–540.

Mandler, J. M. and Parker, R. E. (1976) "Memory for Descriptive and Spatial Information in Complex Pictures." *Journal of Experimental Psychology: Human Learning and Memory* 2:38–48.

Mandler, J. M. and Ritchey, G. H. (1977) "Long-term Memory for Pictures." *Journal of Experimental Psychology: Human Learning and Memory* 3: 386–396.

Mandler, J. M. and Stein, N. L. (1974) "Recall and Recognition of Pictures by Children as a Function of Organization and Distractor Similarity." *Journal of Experimental Psychology* 102: 657–669.

Mitterer, J. O. and Rowland, G. L. (1975) "Picture Memory: Role of Figure-Ground Organization." *Perceptual and Motor Skills* 40: 753–754.

Moore, D. M. (1971) "An Experimental Study of the Value of Size and Type of Still Projected Pictures on the Immediate Recall of Content." *Dissertation Abstracts International* 31: 5041A (University Microfilms No. 71–10,035).

Moore, D. M. and Sasse, E. B. (1971) "Effect of Size and Type of Still Projected Pictures on Immediate Recall of Content." *AV Communication Review* 19: 437–450.

Myatt, B. and Carter, J. M. (1979). "Picture Preferences of Children and Young Adults." *Educational Communications and Technology Journal* 27: 45–53.

Nelson, T. O., Metzler, J., and Reed, D. A. (1974) "Role of Details in the Long-term Recognition of Pictures and Verbal Descriptions." *Journal of Experimental Psychology* 102: 184–186.

Paivio, A., Rogers, T. B., and Smythe, P. C. (1968) "Why Are Pictures Easier to Recall Than Words?" *Psychonomic Science* 11: 137–138.

Reich, C. and Meisner, A. (1976) "A Comparison of Colour and Black and White Television as Instructional Media." *British Journal of Educational Technology* 7 (2): 24–35.

Rudnick, M. R., Porter, M. C., and Suydam, E. L. (1973) "Pictorial Stimulus Variables." *Viewpoints* 49 (2): 21–28.

Smith, O. W., Smith, P. C., and Hubbard, D. (1958) "Perceived Distance as a Function of the Method of Representing Perspective." *American Journal of Psychology,* 71: 662–675.

Spaulding, S. (1956) "Communication Potential of Pictorial Illustrations." *AV Communication Review* 4: 31–46.

Travers, R.M.W. (1970) *Man's Information System.* Scranton, Pa.: Chandler.

Travers, R.M.W. and Alvarado, V. (1970) "The Design of Pictures for Teaching Children in Elementary School." *AV Communication Review* 18: 47–64.

Vollan, C. J. (1972) "Effects of Black and White, Authentic, and Contrived Color on Children's Perceptions of Dynamic Picture Content." *Dissertation Abstracts International* 32: 4435A (University Microfilms No. 72–07,427).

Webster, B. R. and Cox, S. M. (1974) "The Value in Colour in Educational Television." *British Journal of Educational Technology* 5 (1): 44–61.

Impositions of the Transmission Medium

Bretz, R. (1971) *A Taxonomy of Communication Media.* Englewood Cliffs, N.J.: Educational Technology Publications.

Bullough, R. V. (1978) *Creating Instructional Materials.* Columbus, Ohio: Charles E. Merrill.

Eastman Kodak Company. (1971) *Effective Lecture Slides,* pamphlet S-22. Rochester, N.Y.: Eastman Kodak.

———. (1974) *Legibility—Artwork to Screen,* pamphlet S-24. Rochester, N.Y.: Eastman Kodak.

Hartley, J., Fraser, S., and Burnhill, P. (1974) "A Selected Bibliography of Typographical Research Relevant to the Production of Instructional Materials." *AV Communication Review* 22: 181–190.

Kemp, J. E. (1980) *Planning & Producing Audiovisual Materials.* 4th ed. New York: Harper & Row.

MacGregor, A. J. (1979) *Graphics Simplified*. Toronto: University of Toronto Press.

Minor, E. (1978). *Handbook for Preparing Visual Media*. 2d ed. New York: McGraw-Hill.

Minor, E. and Frye, H. R. (1977) *Techniques for Producing Visual Instructional Media*. 2d ed. New York: McGraw-Hill.

Morlan, J. E. (1973) *Preparation of Inexpensive Teaching Materials*. New York: Harper & Row.

Satterthwait, L. (1977) *Graphics: Skills, Media and Materials*. 3d ed. Dubuque, Iowa: Kendall-Hunt.

Spencer, H. (1969) *The Visible Word*. 2d ed. London: Lund Humphries in association with the Royal College of Art.

Turnbull, A. S. and Baird, R. N. (1980) *The Graphics of Communication: Typography, Layout, Design, Production*. 4th ed. New York: Holt, Rinehart & Winston.

Wurtzel, A. (1979) *Television Production*. New York: McGraw-Hill.

Zettl, H. (1976) *Television Production Handbook*. 3d ed. Belmont, Calif.: Wadsworth.

Nature of the Audience

Ausburn, F. B. and Ausburn, L. J. (1976 March-April) "Learning Task Requirements, Cognitive Styles, and Media Attributes: An Interactive Research Model." Paper presented at the annual meeting of the Association for Educational Communication and Technology, Anaheim, Calif. (ERIC Document Reproduction Service, No. ED 118 157).

Birren, F. (1978) *Color Psychology and Color Therapy*. Secaucus, N.J.: Citadel Press.

Carroll, J. (1964) "Words, Meaning and Concepts." *Harvard Educational Review* 34: 178–202.

Chen, Y. (1971) "Visual Discrimination of Color Normals and Color Deficients." *AV Communication Review* 19: 417–431.

Christman, R. J. (1971) *Sensory Experience*. London: Intext Educational.

Eastman Kodak Company (1967) *Wide-screen & Multiple-screen Presentations,* pamphlet S-28. Rochester, N.Y.: Author.

Fleming, M. and Levie, W. H. (1978) *Instructional Message Design*. Englewood Cliffs, N.J.: Educational Technology Publications.

Gagné, R. M. (1970) *The Conditions of Learning*. New York: Holt, Rinehart & Winston.

Gross, L. (1974) "Modes of Communication and the Acquisition of Symbolic Competence." In *Media and Symbols: The Forms of Expression, Communication, and Education,* ed. D. R. Olson. 73d Yearbook, Part 1. National Society for the Study of Education. Chicago: University of Chicago Press, pp. 56–80.

Heinich, R., Mollenda, M., and Russell, J. D. (1982) *Instructional Media and the New Technologies of Instruction*. New York: Wiley.

Hooke, J. F., Youell, K. J., and Etkin, M. W. (1975) "Color Preferences and Arousal." *Perceptual and Motor Skills* 40:710.

Kemp, J. E. (1980) *Planning and Producing Audiovisual Materials*. 4th ed. New York: Harper & Row.

Kennedy, J. M. (1974) *A Psychology of Picture Perception*. London: Jossey-Bass.

Mackworth, N. H. and Bruner, J. S. (1970) "How Adults and Children Search and Recognize Pictures." *Human Development* 13: 149–177.

Murray, D. C. and Deabler, H. L. (1957) "Colors and Mood-tones." *Journal of Applied Psychology,* 41: 279–283.

Olson, D. R. and Bruner, J. S. (1974) "Learning through Experience and Learning through Media." In *Media and Symbols: The Forms of Expression, Communication, and Education,* ed. D. R. Olson. 73d Yearbook, Part 1. National Society for the Study of Education. Chicago: University of Chicago Press, pp. 125–150.

Polyak, S. L. (1941) *The Retina*. Chicago: University of Chicago Press.

Richards, O. W. and Macklin, P. (1971) "Colored Overhead Transparencies: Contrast Gain or Seeing Loss?" *AV Communication Review* 19: 432–436.

Schiffman, H. R. (1976) *Sensation and Perception: An Integrated Approach*. New York: Wiley.

Travers, R.M.W. (1970) *Man's Information System*. Scranton, Pa.: Chandler.

Vernon, M. D. (1971) *The Psychology of Perception*. 2d ed. Baltimore: Penguin.

Wexner, L. B. (1954) "The Degree to Which Colors (Hues) Are Associated with Mood-tones." *Journal of Applied Psychology* 38: 432–435.

Witkin, H. A. (1978) *Cognitive Styles in Personal and Cultural Adaptation*. Worcester, Mass.: Clark University Press.

Wolk, S. and Svoboda, C. P. (1975) "Task Requirements and Field Dependence in Incidental Learning." *Perceptual and Motor Skills* 40: 903–906.

Zimmerman, D. P. (1976) "The Effect of Color on Recognition Memory for Selected Pictorial Material." *Dissertation Abstracts International* 37: 4798–A (University Microfilms No. 77–03,317).

Type of Information and Communication Purposes

Brown, J. W., Lewis, R. B., and Harcleroad, F. F. (1983) *AV Instruction: Technology, Media and Methods*. 6th ed. New York: McGraw-Hill.

Cobun, T. C. (1968) "Media and Public School Communications." In *Instructional Process and Media Innovation,* ed. R. A. Weisgerber. Chicago: Rand McNally, pp. 890–102.

Dale, E. (1969) *Audio-visual Methods in Teaching*. 3d ed. New York: Holt, Rinehart and Winston.

Heinich, R., Mollenda, M., and Russell, J. D. (1982) *Instructional Media and the New Technologies of Instruction*. New York: Wiley.

Kinder, J. S. (1973) *Using Instructional Media*. New York: Van Nostrand.

Lawrence, G.R.P. (1979) *Cartographic Methods*. 2d ed. London: Methuen.

Loxton, J. (1980) *Practical Map Production*. New York: Wiley.

McLuhan, M. (1964) *Understanding Media: The Extension of Man*. New York: McGraw-Hill.

Olson, D. R., ed. (1974) *Media and Symbols: The forms of Expression, Communication, and Education*, 73d yearbook, part 1. National Society for the Study of Education. Chicago: University of Chicago Press.

Richardson, J. A. (1977) *The Complete Book of Cartooning*. Englewood Cliffs, N.J.: Prentice-Hall.

Roth, A. (1977) *Cartooning Fundamentals*. New York: Stravon Educational Press.

Smith, K. U. and Smith, M. F. (1966) *Cybernetic Principles of Learning and Educational Design*. New York: Holt, Rinehart and Winston.

Taylor, D.R.F., ed. (1982) *Graphic Communication and Design in Contemporary Cartography*. New York: Wiley.

Travers, R.M.W. (1970) *Man's Information System*. Scranton, Pa.: Chandler.

Williams, C. M. (1968) *Learning from Pictures*. 2d ed. Washington, D.C.: Department of Audiovisual Instruction/National Education Association.

Wittich, W. A. and Schuller, C. F. (1979) *Instructional Technology*. 6th ed. New York: Harper & Row.

GRAPHICS. *See* **Graphic Design.**

GRAPHICS SCREEN. A computer display mode in which the output directed to the screen is composed of small blocks called *pixels*. Each pixel can be "on" or "off," and may be of various colors according to the type of monitor. Graphic shapes of all sorts can be assembled using the pixels as building blocks. Clearly, the resolution of the graphics depends on the size of the pixels, or as more usually expressed, the number of pixels available on the screen.

The standard IBM-PC color display offers 640 × 200 pixels, whereas the enhanced graphic display increases this to 640 × 350. It is possible to display text on the graphics screen by composing each letter as an individual graphic; this is in fact done by some word processors, resulting in a trade-off of speed for the benefit of SWYG (seeing different fonts, underlining, etc., on the screen pretty much as they will appear in the printout). *See* **Pixel; Text Screen.**

GRAPHICS TABLE, TABLET. A surface over which a drawing device can be moved by hand in order to draw graphics and shade or fill in spaces. The graphics tablet will be connected to a computer via a communications port.

GRAPH PLOTTER. A device for drawing lines according to coordinate values supplied by a computer.

GRAY SCALE. Variations in value from white, through shades of gray, to black on a television screen. The gradations approximate the tonal values of the original image picked up by the television camera.

GREEN SCREEN. Many monochrome (one-color) monitors use green phosphor, displaying light-green characters on a greenish-black background. Operators prefer this color combination to white-on-black or black-on-white images, but the origins of green screens lie in the special requirements of electronic instrument displays.

GROUPROGRAM. An audio-based teaching strategy devised by S. T. Tiagarajan. The audiocassette, as well as providing a structure and input, provides a timing device for the activity of the group. *See* **Audio Instruction.**

GRUNDYTUTOR. A branching teaching machine which enjoyed some success in Britain in the 1960s, particularly in the context of industrial training. Essentially, the machine was an Autotutor look-alike, requiring the student to press buttons in response to frames and questions displayed on a rear-projection screen. The name is derived from that of the president of the manufacturing company. *See* **Autotutor; Teaching Machines.**

GUESSING. One of the commonest objections to multiple-choice tests is that they allow the student to guess. Many formulas have been developed to correct scores achieved by students in order to eliminate chance success due to guessing. For example:

$S = R - W/(K-1)$

S = score corrected for guessing

R = number of correct responses

W = number of incorrect responses

K = number of choices offered in item.

Another strategy is to increase the number of distractors (i.e., wrong alternatives) from, say, three to five, thus decreasing the chance of achieving a correct guess. A further strategy adopted is to have a penalty marking system (countermarking). The number of incorrect answers is deducted from the number of correct answers to give the corrected score. *See* **Objective Test.**

GUIDE NUMBER. *See* **Flash Factor.**

GUN MICROPHONE. A highly directional-sensitive microphone in which a long tube is used to eliminate all sounds other than those emanating from the precise direction in which the tube is pointed. Also called a *rifle microphone* or *shotgun microphone*.

H

HACBSS. Homestead And Community Broadcasting Satellite Service. Receive-only earth stations located in remote areas of Australia, designed to receive satellite broadcasting services at individual homesteads and small communities.

HALE REPORT (U.K.). In 1961 a committee under the chairmanship of Edward Hale was appointed by the U.K. government to study university teaching methods. The committee, which reported in 1964, gave an enthusiastic discussion of programmed learning but left the main task of dealing with audiovisual aids to the Brynmor Jones Committee. The Hale report was based on oral evidence and four surveys; it concentrated on universities and "other interested bodies." Regarding programmed learning it said: "This form of teaching seems to us to be sound in principle . . . but the preparation of a program is a most exacting and time consuming process. . . ." See **Brynmor Jones Report; Hudson Report.**

HALF DUPLEX. Refers to a communication channel which can receive and transmit, but not simultaneously. Compare a walkie-talkie ("Can you hear me? Over!") with a telephone. See **Full Duplex.**

HALF-FRAME. A term applied to a filmstrip in which the horizontal axis of the frames is perpendicular to the length of the film; also known as *single-frame*. See **Full Frame.**

HALFTONE. A halftone visual is one comprised of printed dots which, viewed at the proper distance, produce the impression that there is a continuous range of tones from white to black. Photographs printed in newspapers are a convenient example. Halftones are necessary for printing press use since printing plates can only imprint ink with uniform density, thus the illusion of a range of tones is produced by the size and spacing of the dots. When viewed close up, the seemingly solid image can be clearly seen as an arrangement of dots. See **Halftone Screen.**

HALFTONE SCREEN. Halftone screens are used over a continuous tone visual, such as a photographic print, to convert the original to an arrangement of dots which can be used on a printing press. During the process of "screening," the light from the original passes through the dot pattern of the screen and is thus recorded as dot patterns on the printing plate.

Different halftone screens produce a variety of sizes for particular printing processes. Screening for color printing has become much more common in newspapers through technological developments.

HALF TRACK. (1) A position between the concentric magnetic circle patterns on which disk drives normally store data. Because the computer can control the stepper motor directly, it can have the head positioned between tracks. Recording on the half tracks is one component of many copy-protection methods. (2) An audiotape with two separate recordings on it, each using a track approximately half the width of the audiotape. The recordings usually run in opposite directions on the tape so that one may be played at a time (monaural), the tape having to be flipped to play the other side. Alternatively the tracks may run in the same direction with two channels of a stereophonic recording or with two separate monaural tracks for language instruction applications. See **Language Laboratory; Quarter Track.**

HANDSHAKING. Computer term for the exchange of information which is an essential preliminary to the mutual cooperation of two pieces of equipment. For example, before the computer can send data to a printer the computer must "initialize" the printer, and the printer must inform the computer of various settings and conditions. This handshaking takes only a fraction of a second to occur, but is nonetheless an absolutely necessary first step.

HARD COPY. Photographs on paper or written documents that can be physically handled and evaluated as opposed to projected images or coded information.

HARD DISK. A magnetic storage device consisting of a rigid circular metal base coated with a ferrite material. Contrast **floppy disk** (q.v.), whose base consists of a thin mylar, hence floppy, material. The storage capacity of a hard disk is measured in megabytes, ten or more times as great as that of a floppy disk.

HARD-SECTORED. Disks that use extra holes around the inner ring or outer track to keep track of where information is stored.

HARDWARE. In computing, the term applied to all the physical equipment making up the computing system. By derivation, a term also used to describe audiovisual equipment. *See* **Software.**

HAWTHORNE EFFECT. A situation where improvement in learning apparently brought about by the use of a novel technique is wholly or largely due to the increased interest and motivation that are induced by the new technique rather than to the intrinsic properties of the technique itself.

HDTV. *See* **High-Definition Television.**

HEAD. (1) A component of an audiotape recorder or video tape recorder, that is used to transfer a signal to or from the tape or to erase an existing signal. (2) A component of a compact disk player or videodisc player used to scan the signal carried on the disk. (3) A device used to read data into or out of a data storage medium such as a disk.

HEAD ALIGNMENT. *See* **Alignment.**

HEADPHONES. A pair of small listening devices held to the ears by a headband. Any communication system that requires that messages be transmitted without interference to microphones or other people requires the use of headphones.

In television, headphones enable personnel in a studio to hear sound signals which must not be picked up by the studio microphones. In learning resource centers, students studying audiovisual material use headphones so that they do not distract students studying in adjacent carrels.

HEADSET. A device for individual listening to an audio source. The headband incorporates a small receiving transducer, and optionally a microphone for two-way communication. Headsets may be connected by wire to the sound source, or may be wireless, in which case some sort of radio receiver will be incorporated. The terms *headset*, *headphone(s)*, and *earphone(s)* tend to be used interchangeably.

HECTOGRAPH (SPIRIT DUPLICATOR). A duplicating process that uses a master prepared on paper in contact with a ''carbon'' transfer sheet. In the duplicating machine the master is brought into contact with sheets of paper which have been moistened with a solvent, resulting in part of the carbon image on the back of the master being printed onto the paper. Up to 200 or so legible copies can be made from one master depending on the quality and color of the transfer sheets. The advantage is that the machinery involved is simple and the copies are very cheap to produce. Purple is the usual color of transfer sheets, but red, green, and blue give good results if only a small number of copies, say, 50, is required.

A master sheet can have several different colors on it and the multicolored copies are produced in one pass through the machine. A useful convenience is that master sets are available which permit masters to be made on a thermal copier. Otherwise, the masters must be typed or drawn with ballpoint pen.

HELICAL SCAN. A common system of video recording in which the tape is wrapped helically round a fixed drum while the recording head or heads rotate within a slot in the side of the drum. The helical path of the tape round the drum means that the recording head scanning path is diagonally across the tape.

HERTZ. Unit of frequency. An internationally agreed alternative for cycles per second. One hertz (Hz) is equal to one cycle per second (c/s).

HEURISTICS. A name given to what is also called the *discovery method*. Work is arranged in a series of topics chosen so that the learner ''discovers'' for himself rather than learning directly from a teacher. *See* **Educational Cybernetics.**

HEXADECIMAL. A number system which uses the ten digits 0 through 9 and the six letters A through F to represent values in base 16. Each hexadecimal digit in a hexadecimal number represents a power of 16. Hexadecimal numbers are often preceded by a dollar sign, thus $0E is 14, $12 is 18.

HIERARCHY. An ordered sequence of events that ensures that events occur in order of importance in relation to achieving an objective. Each event is subordinate to the next higher rank. Many motor skills can be broken down into a hierarchy. The knowledge of event 1 is assumed in event 2, and likewise for all events. *See* **Algorithm.**

HI-FI. *See* **High Fidelity.**

HIGHBAND. Video recorders are referred to as highband if they are capable of working with the normal frequencies of the color subcarrier. In other words, their electronics have a high bandwidth and a high price. The common VCR is not a highband device, and the color information has to be modified before it is recorded; such lowband machines are not suitable for originating broadcast television signals. However, the signal from a lowband machine can be converted to broadcast standards by use of sophisticated electronic techniques.

Originally, highband recorders were always 2–inch format, but highband U-matic (0.75–inch) machines are now available.

HIGH-CONTRAST FILM. Photographic film used for reproducing line drawings or similar materials. As its name implies, it gives high contrast between the dark and light parts of the resulting image.

HIGH-DEFINITION TELEVISION (HDTV). The "quality" of a television picture depends in part on the number of lines which go to make up the picture, and the number of times per second the picture is updated. Two systems are common: 525 lines at 60 frames per second (U.S.) and 625 lines at 50 frames per second (Europe). (*See* **NTSC; PAL.**) The definition (i.e., degree of viewable detail) provided by these two existing standards is acceptable only for general purposes on domestic-sized receivers.

If larger screen sizes are sought, or if definitions as good as those associated with cine film are required, then it is necessary to go to high-definition television. International standards for HDTV are still evolving, but systems utilizing, for example, 925 lines are in course of development; conceivably the sorts of television pictures thus enabled would be indistinguishable in quality from projected film.

It seems inevitable that HDTV will become a commercial reality in the near future with notable potential for educational use, especially for classroom viewing of video material and in association with computer graphics. *See* **Extended Definition Television.**

HIGH FIDELITY (HI-FI). An inexact term used to imply a high degree of faithfulness in a sound reproducing system.

HIGH-LEVEL PROGRAM LANGUAGE. A computer language in which instructions correspond to several machine code instructions. Examples are BASIC, Pascal, FORTRAN, LISP, etc. *See* **Assembler Language; Machine Code.**

HIGHLIGHTS. The maximum brightness of a television picture, occurring in regions of highest illumination. Undesirable highlights can appear on performers' noses, bald heads, jewelry, etc.

HIGH-RESOLUTION GRAPHICS. Imprecise term for a computer graphics display in which the pixels are sufficiently small that a graphic cannot be readily resolved into the individual pixels. This would require a screen containing about 500 x 375 pixels which would provide reasonably good curves and at least a first approximation to pictorial composition. In fact, several common microcomputers claim to possess a high-resolution graphics capability, even though they can only muster a screen of, for example, around 280 x 210 pixels.

HIGH SIERRA GROUP. Industry association concerned with the development of proposals for a standard CD-ROM logical file structure.

HIGH-SPEED CAMERA. These are specialized cine cameras designed to capture images of objects moving very quickly so their behavior can be examined. Conventional film transport mechanisms with sprocket holes can attain some 500 frames per second. More elaborate equipment can produce more than a million frames a second. This is fast enough to freeze such things as bullets in flight, which cannot be caught by cameras with the usual speed range. *See* **Filming Speed.**

HISTORY OF EDUCATIONAL TECHNOLOGY. This entry is designed to provide a broad perspective of the historical background and development of educational technology in American education. Because of space limitations, we must be highly selective.

One of the primary difficulties in developing a comprehensive history of educational technology is to arrive at an acceptable definition or to draw some precise boundaries so that a historical analysis may be made with a greater degree of accuracy. Certainly the past years have generated a motley array of statements and definitions concerning educational technology. I have discussed elsewhere two persistent conceptions of educational technology (the physical-science-media and the behavioral science concepts), two viewpoints which are often antagonistic but can be complementary as well (see Saettler, 1978 BACKGROUND READING). The dominant traditional or media concept of educational technology has been manifested in the empirical findings which have consistently shown *"no significant differences"* in improved learning when experimental comparisons of different treatments, such as film versus print versus live teachers were made. Although over half a century of both theoretical and applied research has produced these results, there is widespread sentiment that *"technology can make education more productive, individual and powerful, make learning more immediate; give instruction a more scientific basis, and make access to education more equal"* (see Tickton, 1970 BACKGROUND READING, p. 7). Yet media research to date forces us to the conclusion that we know neither how to measure the psychological effects of media nor how to adapt them to the goals and functions of education.

The alternative behavioral science conception of educational technology has not been tied to particular media or devices, but rather to a broader conception of the educational process. In this sense, the history of educational technology is viewed as the development of the science of instructional design rather than a product form. This view is also congruent with my definition of educational technology as the systematic application of the knowledge of the behavioral sciences or other relevant knowledge (i.e., insights and implications flowing from the humanities and/or the arts) to the problems of learning and instruction.

With the foregoing as background, we now turn to the central task of this entry, namely, that of providing an overview of the development of educational technology.

HISTORICAL ROOTS

The historical roots of educational technology constitute two major clusters. One cluster lies in educational thought and practice; the other cluster lies in the developing behavioral sciences.

Educational technology is basically the product of a great historical stream consisting of trial and error, long practice and imitation, and sporadic manifestations of great individual creativity and persuasion. Most important changes in educational aims and instructional practices can be attributed to particular social, political, and economic influences. For example, the transformation of Athens in the fifth century B.C. from an agricultural society into the leading maritime power brought with it a great expansion of trade, a new class of wealthy merchants, and a new attitude toward government. These changes led to a demand for an education that would prepare young men to practice business and politics, a demand soon met by the Elder Sophists, who taught what they called *"the art of living."* They can be considered the true ancestors of modern educational technology because they laid the groundwork for the first prototype of educational technology by their systematic analysis of subject matter and by their design and organization of instructional materials. They were also well acquainted with the problems associated with human perception, motivation, individual differences, and evaluation. Moreover, they realized that different instructional strategies were required for various behavioral outcomes. What is particularly significant is that they viewed technology, or *techne* as the practical art of using knowledge to solve problems of learning and instruction.

Throughout the centuries, many educators have made important contributions to the growth and development of educational technology. For example, the growth of knowledge in the seventeenth century led Johann Comenius (1590–1670) to envision a system of instruction whereby learners could be led inductively to generalized knowledge by working with natural objects and studying practical things.

Before the nineteenth century, instruction was essentially that of strict recitation of matters learned entirely by rote. This was in accord with the dominant theory that children were innately evil and that their natures had to be broken and brought into complete subjugation. However, there were forerunners of contemporary educational technology whose theories and concepts were far ahead of prevailing educational practices of the time. Such men as John Locke (1632–1704), Johann Pestalozzi (1746–1841), Frederick Froebel (1782–1852), and Johann Herbart (1776–1841) viewed instruction in more systematic terms, and cognitive elements came into central focus in the instructional process (see Saettler, 1968 HISTORICAL).

In the early years of this century, American educators looked to the development of a science of instruction. Edward Thorndike (1874–1949) was the exemplar of what could be accomplished by empirical-inductive means. John Dewey (1859–1952) also rose to eminence during this period and contributed to educational technology through his conception of instruction in terms of scientific method (see Dewey, 1932 BACKGROUND READING). The coming of the machine age and the realization that not all who went to school could enter white-collar jobs stimulated the growing demand for more practical curricula and more functional methodologies. Evolving slowly were ideas concerning the best use in instruction of new media, such as the museum exhibit, the photograph, the projected still picture, charts and globes, and the motion picture.

It took time to bring about widespread changes in content and methodology. In the early decades of this century, small groups of educators in the United States formed associations which featured the words *visual in-*

struction or *visual education*, stressing the pictorial content as opposed to the verbal emphasis of lectures and books. An early abstract-concrete continuum designed to serve as a guide to instructional strategies appeared in 1910 (see Adams, 1910 BACKGROUND READING). However, this conceptual framework, followed later by others, appears to have been introduced more as post hoc rationalizations for using visual media or visual instruction (later called *audiovisual instruction*) than as a direct influence on the design and development of instructional materials. It is clear, for example, that the development of motion pictures and television occurred almost entirely without reference to education or learning theory. Historically, audiovisual materials have been used primarily for group or mass presentation without explicit regard to individual differences in learning ability. What is more, instructional films have traditionally been seen as *aids* to teaching rather than as self-contained sequences of instruction.

One factor which characterized general overall thinking about the use of media in the early decades of this century was specialization in the production and administration of instructional media. At the outset, following the turn of the century, commercial interests producing media for school purposes centered on one or two media. Certain companies made blackboards, others produced slides, some produced motion pictures, others concentrated on maps and models, one focused on sets of slides and stereographs, others produced slide films, and some specialized in recordings.

Parallel with specialization by producers of media there was specialization in the administration of media for instruction. For example, New York State's Division of Visual Instruction collected and distributed lantern slides only. The St. Louis Educational Museum concentrated on exhibits and the distribution of object materials. The University of California Department of Visual Instruction in Berkeley distributed motion pictures only. In a number of universities, the department of visual instruction was in charge of the distribution of motion pictures and another department was charged with radio instruction. At one point during the 1930s, there was a national association of "visual educationists," a national association of educators specializing in school excursions, and a national association of those in charge of education by radio. As time went on, there were those who administered "audiovisual materials" under one central unit and who tried to develop a rationale for the value and place of each medium or device in instruction.

The relationship between the behavioral sciences and educational technology was somewhat tenuous during the early years of this century, but connections began to take a firmer hold as the century progressed. As we have seen, Edward Thorndike was the precursor of the modern behavioral science concept of educational technology. Thorndike in turn influenced the work of W. W. Charters, Douglas Waples, and Franklin Bobbitt, men who laid much of the groundwork for a behavioral science technology of instruction. Meanwhile, a significant early development which brought about a closer relationship between the behavioral sciences and educational technology was the emergence of programmed instructional techniques in the early years of this century. Although Sidney L. Pressey is usually given credit for pioneering the programmed instruction movement, it was actually Maria Montessori who devised the first self-correcting devices as early as 1912 (see Saettler, 1968 HISTORICAL). By the middle of the century, programmed instruction was further developed and refined for computer uses (see Crowder, 1960; Skinner, 1968 BACKGROUND READING).

Another important influence on the development of a behavioral science educational technology came from the cybernetics tradition. Shortly before and during World War II, it became increasingly apparent that the exploration of control problems in devices held a particular significance for the development of man-machine systems. The application of cybernetic principles to instruction was first systematically developed by Gordon Pask with the introduction of his so-called adaptive teaching systems in England in 1953. This was the first of many steps toward a computer-assisted instructional system. Other influences on modern educational technology from cybernetics are gaming and simulation.

It is clear that the trend in the 1980s is away from a machine thing object orientation to a technology of instruction rooted in cybernetics and systems analysis, instructional design and behavioral engineering, as well as decision theory, simulation, and operational research. Today the dominant term has become either educational or instructional technology despite the fact that some still resist this approach and feel that the words *communication and learning* or *learning resources* are essential to the concept of educational technology.

INSTRUCTIONAL DESIGN AND MEDIA SELECTION

Since the beginning of early instructional media research dating back to 1912, it is clear that no single medium is superior in all respects in any instructional situation (see Saettler, 1978 HISTORICAL). However, it is also apparent that any medium can make a viable contribution to almost any learning task. Nevertheless, recent research can offer only limited or incomplete guidance to the instructional designer in the selection and use of media for instruction. This need has been evident for a long time, and even now, there is hardly an adequate solution to the problem. At a more theoretical level, research has been seriously hampered by the absence of a theory of the structure of the symbol systems that constitute such an important part of our environment, the media that transmit these symbols, and the cognitive transformations that take place in those exposed to them. Media research, without this framework, has reflected this limitation.

Some time ago, this author stated that *"an urgent need exists for a taxonomy of instructional media which can provide a systematic approach to the selection and uses of media for educational purposes"* (Saettler, 1968 THEORETICAL BACKGROUND). Since then, important work has been done, but the need still exists. For example, after an extensive review of the research in the hope of finding some source of help on this matter, Campeau concluded that to date, media research has not provided *"decision makers with practical, valid, dependable guidelines for making these choices on the basis of instructional effectiveness"* (1974 JUSTIFICATION OF POINT OF VIEW).

It is clear from the Campeau study and later studies that a comprehensive analysis is required both of the types of learning tasks and instructional events that make up teaching and of the media of instruction so that their characteristics and uses can be incorporated into a design that includes the total learning situation. Moreover, such an analysis must include data concerning individual differences and the classification of different learning conditions.

Gagné's *The Conditions of Learning* (1970 THEORETICAL BACKGROUND) made a stronger connection between learning theory and the design of instruction. Other notable attempts have been made in recent years to provide a guide to instructional design and media selection. Briggs et al. developed a procedure for the design of multimedia instruction (1967 DESCRIPTION OF METHODOLOGY).

Unfortunately, the present state of the art does not solve the persistent problem of instructional design and media selection. As Heidt says, *"Most classification systems claim to be applicable to the solution of practical problems of media design and instruction. Such pretensions, however, prove to be illusory as soon as a media designer or teacher attempts to use them for one of his everyday problems"* (1976 THEORETICAL BACKGROUND, pp. 37–38).

The development of differential learning psychology in recent years has resulted in a particular learning research known as "aptitude-treatment interaction" (ATI) or "trait-treatment interaction" (TTI) research, which considers the connections between personality traits of the learner and variables of the instructional situation. Consequently, the introduction of modern media into instruction and learning has offered an opportunity to take into account the treatment of **instructional design** (q.v.) and media as part of the learning environment.

A provocative approach to instructional design and media use has been offered by Salomon (1974 DESCRIPTION OF METHODOLOGY). According to Salomon, when one chooses a medium for instruction, one should analyze what is to be taught, then search for the symbolic coding system and the method of presentation that best fits the key elements of the information to be transmitted.

Numerous educators and psychologists have contributed to the development of a taxonomy of educational objectives. Three domains have been considered: cognitive, affective, and psychomotor. Discussions of these three domains and related taxonomies are available from a variety of original and secondary sources (see, for example, Brooks and Friedrich, 1973; Kibler, Barker, and Byers, 1970 DESCRIPTION OF METHODOLOGY). Although the objectives were originally written in general terms, some writers (e.g., Mager, 1962; and Vargas, 1977 DESCRIPTION OF METHODOLOGY) have explained how to make them behavioral. Probably the most significant research implication concerns the use of behavioral objectives as a specific message design so as to cue the learner to attend to relevant information (e.g., Kaplan and Rothkopf, 1974 THEORETICAL BACKGROUND). Jean Piaget's approach (1970 THEORETICAL BACKGROUND), which focuses on both the psychomotor and cognitive domains, has several implications for the instructional designer.

Researchers have not to this time characterized instructional tasks and medium potentials precisely enough to reach any definitive conclusions about which medium is better suited to which educational objective. As Schramm (1977 JUSTIFICATION OF POINT OF VIEW) concluded after a comprehensive review of the research, instructional media may be equally useful for most educational tasks. However, the quality of media research is probably the real issue. It appears likely that more quality research will be conducted in the next decades for the purpose of determining the total effects of a given medium or combination of media in particular learning situations. Probably the crucial question will focus on the question of whether or not individual learners process information more effectively via print, visual, or audio media. Moreover, it is clear that educational technology can no longer afford to remain isolated from the fields of developmental psychology, differential psychology, and neuropsychology (Wittrock, 1978 JUSTIFICATION OF POINT OF VIEW).

SYSTEMS APPROACHES TO INSTRUCTION

One of the significant advances in educational technology in recent years has been the development of systems approaches to instruction. During the 1950s and 1960s educational technology became increasingly focused on language laboratories, teaching machines and programmed instruction, multimedia presentations, and the use of the computer in teaching. Out of this development came a systems approach, or an effort to design a complete program or develop a course of instruction to meet specific needs and objectives. This movement obviously paralleled those in the military and business worlds, and the procedures were similar. Instructional goals and objectives were precisely defined, the various alternatives were analyzed, the instructional resources were identified and/or developed, a plan of action was devised, and the results were continuously evaluated for possible modification of the program.

Many instructional systems approaches or instructional designs have evolved with their various flowcharts and lists of steps to be followed. One of the clearest models was developed in the early 1970s (see Kemp, 1971 DESCRIPTION OF METHODOLOGY).

A focus on the design of entire instructional systems provides a clear distinction of educational technology in contrast to traditional instructional approaches. Gibson (1971 DESCRIPTION OF METHODOLOGY) has described this approach as "the systematic application of people, ideas, materials, and equipment to the solution of educational problems. The process by which the modes of communication are designed, and arranged in the learning environment, and the strategies by which human and non-human resources are utilized to improve the efficiency and effectiveness of education is *educational technology*" (pp. 1–2).

Educational technology not only includes problems of instructional design and management of learning, but must also involve development and management of diverse educational systems where instruction and learning can take place.

Conceptual Contributions to Systems Approaches. There have been many distinct discipline areas which have made important conceptual and methodological contributions to systems approaches in educational technology. These are general systems theory, cybernetics and the resulting management information and control devices and techniques (i.e., program evaluation and review techniques [**PERT**], (q.v.) and **GANTT charts** [q.v.], critical path method [CPM], **cost-benefit analysis** [q.v.], simulation techniques, and operations research strategies), and psychological systems which purport to study man's psychological state (system) as a function or product of a variety of interrelationships.

Programmed and Computer-Assisted Instruction. Conceptually and methodologically, programmed instruction and **computer-assisted instruction** (q.v.) can be viewed as minisystems. In the early 1960s, definitions of programmed instruction usually described various formats, such as small frames, requirements for responses, and the like. In more recent years, programmed instruction has come to be widely accepted as "validated instruction" or is considered to be a systematic development process in which the developer or instructional designer assumes complete responsibility for student learning.

Computer-assisted instruction (CAI) has been defined in many ways through the years. One definition views CAI as "an interaction between a student, a computer controlled display, and a response-entry device for the purpose of achieving educational outcomes" (Bunderson and Faust, 1976 THEORETICAL BACKGROUND, p. 47). Without question, CAI offers a new science and technology of instruction whose potential has hardly been probed. Perhaps it will someday constitute the main thrust of a behavioral science–oriented educational technology.

The programmed instruction movement reached its peak during the early 1960s. Unfortunately, the claims of programmers far exceeded their skill, and school storehouses began to be filled with unused teaching machines and programs. By the late 1960s and early 1970s, publishers had drastically retrenched and there came to be a realization that effective programmed instruction must involve a systematic and empirical development process. Meanwhile, the middle 1960s marked the beginning of the boom in CAI. Again, as with the programmed instruction movement, computer companies were merging with publishing companies and there were great expectations for profits in the educational market. Federal aid for research and development provided much of the impetus for CAI, and many projects were begun. However, by the 1970s, federal funding began to diminish, and the new educational market had not materialized. Computer companies and publishers began to withdraw from the field and a new decline set in. Mistakes of the programmed instruction movement had been repeated once again because CAI's complexities of hardware, software, and courseware as well as cost involved had not been sufficiently understood.

A notable number of CAI programs have been developed. One of the earliest, the **PLATO** (q.v.) project begun at the University of Illinois in 1959, had a great influence on CAI development because it shared ideas and materials, conducted research, and provided a training ground for the next generation of CAI developers and users. Another important influence came from the **TICCIT** (q.v.) (Time-shared Interactive Computer-Controlled Information Television) Project in the 1970s. In recent years, Gordon Pask in Great Britain has developed an instructional approach to CAI which is radically different from earlier procedures. Pask's method is based on a comprehensive cybernetic theory which involves a conversation between two or more participants on a series of topics that form a conversational domain. One participant is the subject; the other may be a machine or a person serving in the role of the experimenter's agent. Because of the complexity of this cybernetic learning environment, it usually involves some type of complex electronic equipment. Pask's work (1975 THEORETICAL BACKGROUND) is still not widely known or understood, but it appears likely that it may have significant influence on future approaches to instructional design and provide a theoretical framework for those working on **artificial intelligence** (AI) (q.v.) systems for CAI.

It appears that the greatest progress in educational technology during the remainder of this century will be seen in the development of increasingly sophisticated CAI instructional systems. Indeed, it does not seem overly optimistic to predict that a historical breakthrough will be made in the design and development of highly individualized systems before the end of this century. These systems will be capable of diagnosing individual differences, providing for continuous feedback for the revision and improvement of programs as well as providing for self-pacing, practice, and conversational procedures between learner and programmer involving problem-solving situations. Moreover, future systems promise day-to-day instructional design possibilities which would allow teachers to become instructional developers for computers without the necessity of learning computer programming. Just as solid-state technology has made calculators widely available, so the microcomputer revolution promises to make CAI terminals readily accessible in homes, schools, and learning centers.

DEVELOPMENT OF MEDIA TECHNOLOGIES FOR INSTRUCTION

The development of media technologies for instruction has exerted an immense impact on educational technology during the latter years of this century. One important developmental process is reflected in the emergence of simpler, more practical video recorders, cassettes and disks, and low-cost television equipment. An even more recent development, sometimes called cellular communications, may even render obsolete many present radio, telephone, television, and navigation systems.

New media technologies for the future point in the direction of both macro and micro technologies. At the macro level, where broadcasting was once confined to terrestrial transmission, the development of communications satellite technology has made the idea of a **global village** (q.v.) a reality. Also, as an alternative to open broadcasting, broadband communications or cable systems involving direct video and audio signals have important implications for educational broadcasting. At the micro level, an increasing miniaturization of equipment, or what has been called "microelectronics," has meant that media can be used more extensively. Micro technologies include such developments as the portapak video camera, the videocassette, and electronic films. As distinguished from photographic film, electronic films are delicate masses of electronically active material condensed, for the most part, from hot vapors onto cold, hard insulating surfaces such as glass. Depending on the materials used, such films, called either thin or thick, are often ten times thinner than an ordinary soap bubble. These films may eventually lead to a television camera only half an inch square, a hand-held battery-operated computer, a form of computer that could store a quarter million bits of information on a glass slide half a foot square, a new type of videotape which could store pictures optically for later readout by an electron beam, and a revolutionary type of integrated circuitry for application in all forms of electronic equipment.

The application of new media technologies for instruction has occurred in a number of ways in recent decades. One of the more notable applications in the industrialized world was that of the Open University in Great Britain. This system involved multimedia combinations of radio, television, films, and programmed materials. Similar systems have been developed in other regions of the world, notably, the Long Distance Studies Institute in West Germany, and the Project Sun system in the United States. Moreover, telecommunications satellite systems have been developed for experimental purposes in various parts of the world for educational purposes (Saettler, 1978 BACKGROUND READING). In terms of the future applications of satellites for instruction and information, it can be stated with assurance that future developments will intensify and expand in this field. Additional experimental communications satellites are in the planning stage.

Communications satellites used for broadcasting as well as telephony unquestionably present opportunities unparalleled by more traditional media technologies, but they lack the kind of interactive communication which the traditional media do provide. For example, posters, filmstrips, films, maps, charts, etc., may more effectively meet such needs as mobility and low cost. The potentials of radio, with its easy accessibility, relatively low cost, and its possibilities for two-way interactive communications, have not been fully realized in the industrialized nations. In contrast, too much attention tends to focus on such big, prestigious media as television, computers, and communications satellites. Neither so-called big media or little media are necessarily better or more effective in instructional situations. It is clear, however, that the increasing diversity and development of media technologies will require serious decisions about a rapidly expanding range of strategic alternatives that will be appropriate for specific educational objectives.

PROBLEMS OF EDUCATIONAL TECHNOLOGY

The potential of educational technology is revolutionary, but this potential is not likely to be realized in any reasonable time unless a number of serious problems are solved. These problems involve public policy issues, technical stategies, research and evaluation, as well as the problems associated with the development of a behavioral science–oriented educational technology.

An integrated approach to educational planning and research is needed. The great advances of media technologies and their rapid expansion in recent decades call for a new type of research typified by the works of Katz and Wedell (1977), Parker and Mohannadi (1977), and Oettinger (1977 BACKGROUND READING). An integrated approach to the problem of educational policy and planning would have to focus on message content, intent, production, distribution, and evaluation. Also, since most media research in the United States has followed the Shannon-Lasswell paradigm of the communication process called S-M-C-R-E—a source (S) sends a message (M), via certain channels (C), to the receiver (R), who responds or reacts to this stimulus with an effect (E)—it is time that media researchers adopt new, more fruitful paradigms. The prevailing model assumes a mechanistic and atomistic approach to the communication process and focuses on the effects of the source, message, or the channel on change in knowledge, attitude, and overt behavior of the receiver—as if he or she were passive and lived in social isolation. Therefore, some researchers have reversed the question of media effects to ask, rather, what uses and gratifications the receiver brings to the media.

It appears abundantly clear that educational technology cannot reach its full potential until research discovers more about the learning process and how it varies in each individual with different instructional treatments. Although media research shows no significant difference in achievement than control groups taught by a teacher, Oettinger and Zapol (1973 JUSTIFICATION OF POINT OF VIEW) point out that

Learning is largely independent of the details of means, hence—issues of policy and technology, on the one hand, and of learning method and content, on the other hand, are essentially independent. No-significant-difference findings, therefore, leave alternatives to the accepted ways of schooling wide open, alternatives that might, according to public preferences, achieve lesser costs, greater individualization, or some other personal or social benefit without, at the very least, making any difference so far as measurable learning performance is conceived. These benefits are neither all equally attractive to everyone nor unequivocally measurable. Preferences and priorities keep changing. Acceptable strategies for making technology responsive to learning must therefore permit continuing and diverse public choices; decisions about ends and means must be reserved as matters of public policy and not left unattended to experts. The strategic question of how technology affects control over the means of learning must take preference over pedagogical nits to assure that public preferences—or significant differences, if some are ever found—will be accommodated and not dictated by how technology is deployed. (pp. 6–7)

One of the basic problems confronting the American educational system is that it is not in fact treated as a system. It has been generally fragmented and broken down into discrete functions. Moreover, educators for the most part have resisted the ideas of operational research and systems analysis. As a consequence, little or no consideration has been given to the total learning environment. Until all the theories of learning are synthesized and brought together in one system, there is not likely to be an effective way to unify the structure and process of instruction. In addition, any systems analysis must take into account the timetable for bringing about instructional change as well as determining the probable costs. Very little has been done to define what instructional priorities should be established and how educational technology can be implemented to realize these goals. I am convinced that the most exciting contribution of educational technology in the future will have to be in instructional systems rather than media.

In the years ahead, instructional units will probably be more flexible than they presently are, and each unit or instructional system may involve the learner in designing various aspects of the program. While some may view the systems approach as depersonalized and inhuman, it is important to point out that educational technology has the potential of developing a humanized system as well. A systems approach does not depersonalize education unless it is designed for that purpose. The essential problem of educational technology is that it has been restricted to media when the real need is a new conceptualization of instruction as a system.

PROSPECTS

In terms of media technology, the future promises many communications marvels. For example, it is likely that a portable terminal/display "carrel" may be developed whereby the user could have immediate access to practically all of the printed or audio-video information stored anywhere in the world. This electronic carrel would contain a video monitor, a photocopier to instantaneously reproduce any material desired, a fiber-optic laser terminal that would provide potential access to thousands of information channels, and a series of operational modes which could give the learner access to computer-based instructional programs or instructional materials in every "viewing" or "listening" mode. Meanwhile, the home itself may be transformed into an instructional resource or learning center by means of a television wall screen connected to videotapes, facsimile printers, and minicomputers which can be activated to transmit any type of stored information or instructional program available. By means of two-way communication, the learner will also be able to send messages as well as receive them. A real breakthrough in man-computer communications will come with the development of speech interfaces for computers. Through this capability and the universally available telephone system, as well as radio and cable communications with computers, computer capability will be opened to almost everyone who has access to a telephone. With this development the possibility of extensive instructional computer networks is likely to materialize in the future.

Speculations about the technical possibilities of the future are relatively easy because most of the hardware components have already been worked out theoretically or in a practical sense. However, the difficult predictions for the future of educational technology focus on the process itself. As indicated in the previous section, the real problem of educational technology is that of instructional design. For example, John Goodlad (1974 JUSTIFICATION OF POINT OF VIEW) concluded:

> Many of the changes we have believed to be taking place in schooling have not been getting into classrooms; changes widely recommended for the schools over the past fifteen years were blunted on school and classroom door. Chances are, most teachers seeking to teach inductively, to use a range of instructional media, to individualize instruction, to nongrade or team teach, have never seen any of these things done well, let alone participated in them to the point of getting a "feel" for them on how to proceed on their own. We simply do not have in this country an array of exemplary models displaying alternative modes of schooling, in spite of assumed local control and diversity. (p. 103)

A look into the future sees the realization of a new conceptualization of instruction as a system. However, this development promises to be evolutionary rather than revolutionary. There is an obvious lag between our ability to establish the level of the behavioral change we desire and our ability to determine whether the change has occurred. This problem will have to be solved if a true systems approach is to be developed. Moreover, it has rarely been pointed out or recognized as a problem that information and knowledge are not identical or synonymous, as it is frequently assumed. For example, computer information systems are not just objective recording devices. They also reflect concepts, hopes, and attitudes. Thus, the communications revolution has within it the poison seeds of the past. Instead of creating a "new future," modern communications may mask the underlying forces of politics and power.

It is the particular futuristic bias of this writer that educational technology can generate humanistic experiences. Thus, a system designed specifically for that purpose will synchronize the goals, methods, means, and evaluation so as to bring about an effective and humane system. However, unless some basic conceptual, methodological, and political changes occur within the foreseeable future, the glowing expectations for educational technology may not be realized before the end of this century. Let us hope that educational technology in A.D. 2001 will develop into something far more exciting and creative than we now have.

Paul Saettler

REFERENCES

Background Reading

Adams, J. (1910) *Exposition and Illustration.* New York: Macmillan.

Crowder, N. A. (1960) "Automatic Tutoring by Instrinsic Programming." In *Teaching Machines and Programmed Learning: A Source Book,* ed. A. Lumsdaine and R. Glaser. Washington, D.C.: Department of Audiovisual Instruction, NEA, pp. 286–298.

Dewey, J. (1932) *How We Think.* Boston: Heath.

Katz, E. (1977) *Social Research on Broadcasting: Proposals for Further Development: A Report to the BBC.* London: BBC.

Katz, E. and Wedell, E. C. (1977) *Broadcasting and National Development.* Cambridge, Mass.: Harvard University Press.

Oettinger, A. G. and Zapol, N. (1973) "Will Information Technologies Help Learning?" In *Content and Context: Essays on College Education,* ed. Carl Kaysen. Carnegie Commission on Higher Education. New York: McGraw-Hill, pp. 293–358. Also available as an ERIC document (chapter preprint: ED 064 902).

Parker, B. and Mohannadi, A. (1977) "National Development Support Communication." In *Communication Policy for National Development,* ed. M. Tehranian, F. Hakimzada, and M. L. Vidale. London: Routledge and Kegan Paul, pp. 167–201.

Saettler, P. (1978) "History of Educational Technology." In *Encyclopaedia of Educational Media Communications and Technology*, ed. D. Unwin and R. McAleese. London: Macmillan, Limited, pp. 366–378.

Skinner, B. F. (1968) *The Technology of Teaching*. New York: Appleton-Century-Crofts.

Tickton, S. (1970) *To Improve Learning. A Report to the President and the Congress of the United States by the Commission on Instructional Technology*. Washington, D.C.: U.S. Government Printing Office.

Description of Methodology

Briggs, L. J., Campeau, R. L., Gagné, R., and May, M. A. (1967) *Instructional Media: A Procedure for the Design of Multimedia Instruction, A Critical Review of Research and Suggestions for Future Research*. Pittsburgh, Pa.: American Institute for Research.

Brooks, W. D. and Friedrich, G. W. (1973) *Teaching Speech Communications in the Secondary School*. Boston: Houghton-Mifflin.

Gibson, C. D. (1971) "Future Directions in Educational Facilities Design." Paper presented at the Conference on Instructional Technology and the Planning of School Plants, Los Angeles, California, 26 February.

Kemp, J. E. (1971) *Instructional Design: A Plan for Unit and Course Development*. Belmont, Calif.: Fearon Publishers.

Kibler, R. J., Barker, R. E., and Byers, J. P. (1970) *Behavioral Objectives and Communications Instruction*. Boston: Allyn and Bacon.

Mager, R. F. (1962) *Preparing Instructional Objectives*. Belmont, Calif.: Lear Siegler.

Salomon, G. (1974) "What Is Learned and How It Is Taught: The Interaction Between Media, Message, Task, and Learner." In *Media and Symbols: The Form of Expression, Communication, and Education*, ed. D. R. Olsen. 73d Yearbook of the National Society for the Study of Education, Part 1. Chicago: University of Chicago Press.

Tosti, D. T. and Ball, J. R. (1969) "A Behavioral Approach to Instructional Design and Media Selection," *AV Communication Review* 1: 5–25.

Vargas, J. S. (1977) *Behavioral Psychology for Teachers*. New York: Harper & Row.

Historical

Saettler, P. (1968) *A History of Instructional Technology*. New York: McGraw-Hill.

Justification of Point of View

Campeau, P. L. (1974) "Selective Review of the Results of Research on the Use of Audio-Visual Media to Teach Adults," *AV Communication Review* 22 (1): 5–40.

Goodlad, J. I. (1974) *Looking Behind the Classroom Door: A Useful Guide to Observing Schools in Action*. Worthington, Ohio: Charles A. Jones.

Schramm, W. (1977) *Big Media, Little Media*. Beverly Hills, Calif.: Sage Publications.

Wittrock, M. C. (1978) "Education and the Cognitive Processes of the Brain." In *Education and the Brain*, ed. J. S. Chall and A. F. Mirsky. 77th Yearbook of the National Society for the Study of Education, Part 2. Chicago: University of Chicago Press.

Theoretical Background

Bruner, J. S. (1966) *Toward a Theory of Instruction*. New York: Norton.

Bunderson, C. V. and Faust, G. W. (1976) "Programmed and Computer-Assisted Instruction." In *The Yearbook of Teaching Methods*. 75th Yearbook of the National Society for the Study of Education, Part 1. Chicago: University of Chicago Press, 44–90.

Gagné, R. M. (1970) *The Conditions of Learning*. New York: Holt, Rinehart and Winston.

Heidt, E. U. (1976) *Instructional Media and the Individual Learner*. New York: Nichols Publishing.

Kaplan, R. and Rothkopf, E. Z. (1974) "Instructional Objectives as Directions to Learners: Effect of Passage Length and Amount of Objective Relevant Content," *Journal of Educational Psychology* 66: 614–622.

Lesser, G. S. (1974) *Children and Television*. New York: Random House.

Pask, G. (1975) *Conversation, Cognition, and Learning: A Cybernetic Theory and Methodology*. New York: Elsevier.

Piaget, J. (1970) *Science of Education and the Psychology of the Child*. New York: Viking.

Saettler, P. (1968) "Design and Selection Factors," *Review of Educational Research* 38: 115–128.

HOLOGRAPH. A method of storing photographic images using the interference patterns of laser-generated light. Holographs have been proposed as a powerful data storage medium, but as yet practical difficulties remain to be overcome. *See* **Holography.**

HOLOGRAPHY. Wave-front reconstruction, or holography, was invented by D. Gabor in 1948 as a method of improving the resolution in the images of electron microscopes by recording the unfocused diffraction pattern of the subject and recalling its image from this diffraction pattern. A coherent source of illumination is required for the process, and at the time of Gabor's invention, the only sources available were of very low intensity. Despite this, Gabor was able to demonstrate the technique with visible coherent illumination.

Sources of higher intensity coherent light became available in 1962, by which time laser devices had been developed and laser holography became possible. Two centers in the United States were developing lasers and simultaneously began to work with laser holography; at Stanford Research Institute pulsed laser development took place, and at the University of Michigan applications of the gas laser were studied as extensions of radar research. At that time, the laser power available was restricted to one or two milliwatts (about the same as a candle at a meter distance), and as a result the type of subject which could be used in the production of a hologram was limited in size and complexity.

The basic diffraction pattern of a subject is produced by recording the interference pattern produced between a reference light wave and the light backscattered from the subject using a common source for both waves. The recording medium commonly used is a photographic emulsion. Pulsed lasers produce their energy in a very short period of time (typically 30 nanoseconds) which is fast enough to freeze motion in photographic terms. The output from a gas laser is continuous and restricts work to subjects which will stay stationary long enough to give sufficient energy from the backscattered light for correct exposure of the photographic emulsion. Holography with continuous lasers is generally easier to perform than pulsed laser holography because the continuous laser can be tuned more easily to give the narrow bandwidth of illumination required for the formation of the diffraction pattern. Most of the early work in holography was based on the use of the continuous laser operating on a mixture of helium and neon to give light at a wavelength of 0.6328 micrometers.

The hologram stores information as to the intensity of light backscattered from the subject and of the phase of this backscattered light relative to the coherent reference wave. The phase information is related to the position of the subject, and it is this which provides the three-dimensional properties of a reconstructed holographic image. Early holograms used metallic subjects, such as toy cars, which gave adequate backscatter to expose the recording emulsion, were small and stable, and exhibited easily recognizable three-dimensional facets to give realism to the holographic reconstruction. These early holograms have now become classics and the impact of the early work was enough to merit a paper in *Scientific American* (212, no. 6 [1965]: 24).

Scientific uses of holography developed from these early beginnings. The first was discovered by accident when two workers in the University of Michigan, Powell and Stetson, made a small hologram of a metal can, using a laboratory near the air-conditioning plant. The resulting hologram exhibited interference fringes which were identified as a contour map of a vibration mode of the can. After mathematical analysis it became clear that this accident had established a new method for viewing vibration modes, and the technique became known as *time-averaged holography*. The recorded hologram contains two images representing the positions of a subject at the two stationary states of a resonant sinusoidal motion; these two images interfere with one another to produce contours in the reconstruction representing the amplitude of vibration.

The ability to produce two holograms of a single subject in the same photographic emulsion gave rise to further uses of holography in the science of metrology. The two images formed on reconstruction could be made to interfere and produce fringes if a small displacement was given to the subject between the two exposures. These fringes gave a measure of the displacement of the subject between exposures. Because there is a finite time between the two exposures forming the hologram, this process is known as *lapsed-time holography*. If the hologram of a subject is replaced in the original recording position after processing, then the image from the hologram interferes with the wave front scattered from the subject to produce an interference pattern as the subject is deformed. This process is known as *real-time holographic interferometry*. Applications of laser holography to metrology have developed in detail and now form a major application of holography known as holographic metrology.

The recording of multiple images on one hologram has been extended, and as many as 50 individual images have been recorded on a single hologram, permitting them to be reconstructed simultaneously. Interference between such reconstructions is prevented by separation, and the process has been used to compound a complete scene from picture parts. For example, in medical work a number of two-dimensional X-ray negatives can be compounded to give a three-dimensional X-ray picture of a subject. This process can be extended into the field of display and education where a combination of photographs can be displayed complete with correct relative depth. Holograms of a subject can be made for exhibition purposes or a hologram can be used to show the assembly of a complex machine.

Holograms consist of an interference pattern on a minute scale which cannot be seen by the eye. Suitable recording materials need to resolve some 3,000 lines per millimeter, and while a number of sensitized media will respond to this, the photographic plate is the most widely used. The main reason for this is that photographic emulsions can combine high resolution with modest recording light levels, a desirable feature when using expensive laser light.

In photographic terms, the information recorded in a hologram initially appears as an indistinguishable fog. To improve the reconstruction efficiency for display purposes, the emulsion is often bleached, leaving the plate apparently completely transparent. The bleaching process converts the photographic fog into a phase-modulating medium capable of forming an image from laser illumination. The reconstructed image is viewed by illuminating the plate with laser light from the back at a suitable angle. The image is viewed by looking through the plate along a direction roughly perpendicular to its surface, and the image is then seen situated in the space behind the plate. In effect the plate acts as a window with the observer in front and the image behind, a form of holography known as *transmission holography*. This "virtual" image cannot be projected onto a screen, but reversing the optical arrangement allows the image to be formed on the same side of the hologram as the observer, and it is then possible to place a screen through this "real" image. Since the image is in three dimensions in space, any screen placed through it will show only sharp features for the plane in the image with which the screen coincides. Due to the focusing properties of the optical system used in the recording, the real image is defocused so that it cannot be seen by the unaided eye, and a lens is needed to make it visible. For display purposes a specific form of reference wave is used in the recording process so that the real image is formed in parallel or collimated light, thus having the effect of making it visible to the unaided eye. The real image observed in this way is, however, inside-out, or "pseudoscopic." For display purposes this problem is overcome by using a double holographic method where an ordinary hologram of the subject is produced first, and a second hologram is made from the reconstructed image of the first hologram. This second hologram will thus produce a true real image which stands out in space and can be observed in front of the holographic plate.

In what has been discussed so far, holograms are produced using a coherent light source to give a reference wave and light backscattered from the subject, both of which illuminate the recording emulsion from the same side of the photographic plate. The holograms so produced require coherent light to produce a reconstruction. In 1962 Yu N. Denisyuk described a hologram produced by passing the reference wave through the recording emulsion before illuminating the subject. In this way the light backscattered from the subject reaches the emulsion from one side while the coherent reference wave arrives from the other side, producing a different form of interference pattern to that occurring in ordinary holography. Development of this technique has led to the use of separate waves from the same source for reference and subject illumination. In addition to recording the intensity and phase of light from the subject, a multilayer interference pattern between reference and backscattered light is recorded, causing stratification of the emulsion. Illumination of the processed hologram, using a small incoherent white light source from the same side as the original reference wave, produces a reflected wave of single color due to this stratification, and this reflected monochromatic wave forms an image of the subject. The development of "white light" holography has proceeded along similar lines to that of ordinary holography, and it is now largely used for display purposes. It is not so easy to deduce information of scientific use from a white light reflection hologram, and ordinary transmission holograms are preferred for this purpose.

The process of forming an image from a hologram is similar to the refracting action of a lens which collects light and forms an image. Holographic optical elements can be produced, and a hologram made from a lens will exhibit the properties of that lens with the restriction that it will work only in the narrow band of illumination by which it was produced. Holographic optical elements can be used as correcting devices added to ordinary lenses, and holograms can be produced to generate optical elements such as diffraction gratings or to provide complex wave shapes as required for metrology. The phase and amplitude of the interfering radiation used to produce a hologram can also be described numerically and the interference pattern calculated by computer. The resulting computer output can then be plotted and photographically formed into a hologram of the correct scale, which, when illuminated by coherent light, generates an image of a subject which exists only in the form of a mathematical equation.

The hologram is recorded as an interference pattern whose features are closely spaced (typically one micron). Ordinary photographic emulsion exhibits no directional sensitivity, and it is possible to record on the order of 10^7 elements of information per square millimeter. Thus a very small hologram can store a large amount of information. A whole page of a book, for example, can be stored on a square millimeter of photographic plate. This large storage capacity of holograms has been examined for possible use as a data store in computers, and as a data retrieval system on interplanetary missions.

F. N. Birkett

REFERENCES

Butters, J. N. (1971) *Holography and Its Technology*, IEE Monograph Series, No. 8. London: Peregrinus.

Collier, R. J., Burckhardt, C. P., and Lin, L. H. (1971) *Optical Holography*. New York: Academic Press.

Dainty, J. C. et al. (1975) *Laser Speckle and Related Phenomena*. Heidelberg: Springer Verlag.

Denisyuk, Y. N. (1962) "On the Reproduction of the Optical Properties of an Object by the Wavefield of Its Scattered Radiation." *Soviet Physics-Doklady*, No. 7, p. 543.

Gabor, D. (1949) "Microscopy by Reconstructed Wavefronts." *Proceedings of the Royal Society*, Series A, 197 (1051): 454–487.

Kock, W. F. (1975) *Engineering Applications of Lasers and Holography*. New York: Plenum Press.

Leith, E. and Upatnieks, J. (1965) "Lensless Photography." *Scientific American* 212 (6): 24–35.

Stetson, K. A. (1969) "A Rigorous Treatment of the Fringes of Hologram Interferometry." *Optik* 29 (4): 386–400.

Stroke, G. W. and Labeye, A. E. (1966) "White Light Reconstruction of Holographic Images Using the Lippmann-Bragg Diffraction Effect." *Physics Letters* 20 (4): 368–370.

HOME EXPERIMENT KIT. A package sold or given to students so that they can perform practical experiments at home. Traditionally, a microscope and slides, or a skeleton, was a home experiment kit. The Open University (U.K.) has pioneered the use of such kits to overcome the problems of teaching at a distance. *See* **Open University.**

HORIZONTAL FREQUENCY. The number of lines per second in a video signal. The standard television frequency is approximately the same for both PAL and NTSC signals, at around 15,700 Hz.

HORIZONTAL PANEL BOOK. A programmed textbook in which pages are divided into panels which are read in a sequence across the book for the length of a chapter. That is, the student starts at the top of page 1, then goes to the top of pages 3, 5, and so on until he reaches the end of the section, when he returns to the second "strip" on page 1, etc.

At one time in the 1960s such a format was popular on account of its preventing accidental cheating, since the answer to each frame was to be found only after turning the current page. An interesting historical instance of this type of book is J. G. Holland and B. F. Skinner's *The Analysis of Behavior* (New York: McGraw-Hill, 1960). *See* **Programmed Text; Scrambled Text; Vertical Panel Book; Zigzag Book.**

HOT KEY. (1) Where a microcomputer is connected to a mainframe computer, a hot key allows the user to switch between the micro's function as a local terminal of the large computer and its role as a personal computer. Some, but not all, mainframe communications packages provide this capability, usually as a software command. (2) A key (or often a combination of two keys such as CONTROL-Z) on a microcomputer which brings a resident program into play. For example, calling up "Sidekick" while using a word processing package.

HOUSEKEEPING (ROUTINES). The software responsible for the processes by which a computer keeps track of all relevant information regarding addresses, availability of memory, etc.

HOUSE STYLE. A set of rules for writing frames that ensure the consistency of frame design in a videotex system.

HUDSON REPORT (U.K.). A U.K. government committee was set up in 1971 "to recommend new central arrangements for promoting educational technology... to advise the Government whether a National Centre for Educational Technology is required... and what its functions and structure should be." The committee, under the chairmanship of J. A. Hudson, reported in 1972. The report largely carries on from the **Brynmor Jones Report** (q.v.), in particular in its concentration on a National Centre for Educational Technology. The essence of the report was a structure for the new national organization, consisting of a council (Council for Educational Technology); a Steering Committee for Development and Innovation; a Review Committee for Sector Requirements; and a "special consultative relationship" with "accredited consultative bodies."

HYPERCARDIOID. A type of microphone with response intermediate between figure-of-eight and true cardioid. *See* **Microphone Characteristics.**

HYPERFOCAL DISTANCE. With a lens set at infinity, the hyperfocal distance is the distance between the lens and the first point of the zone of sharp focus (depth of field). For adjustable focus cameras, the point of using the hyperfocal distance is to obtain a greater depth of field so that the photographer can concentrate on events which may occur so rapidly that there is no time to focus by the usual methods. For example, with a lens focused at infinity, assume that the zone of sharp focus (depth of field) begins at 50 feet and goes to infinity. If we refocus the lens to this hyperfocal distance of 50 feet, we find that the depth of field now begins at a point 25 feet from the camera rather than 50 feet away. The usefulness of this procedure varies with the aperture setting of the lens. *See* **Depth of Field.**

HYPNOPAEDIA. From the Greek "education in sleep." Learners are purported to learn in a hypnotic state in order to avoid the usual difficulties of absorbing information while awake. Wild claims have been made with regard to hypnopaedia, and although it is possible to establish experimentally that retention and recall of learned events is possible, there is no direct evidence that meaningful learning can take place in one's sleep.

I

ICAI. *See* **Computer Nomenclature.**

ICEM. *See* **International Council for Educational Media.**

ICON. A pictorial symbol that represents an operation, file, program, peripheral device (such as a printer), or disk.

IDIOT BOARD, SHEET. Colloquial names for a teleprompter.

IEC. International Electro-Technical Committee. *See* **Standards in Audiovisual Technology.**

ILLUMINATIVE EVALUATION. A modern approach to evaluation which is concerned with description and interpretations within the total context of an innovation rather than with the attainment of certain prespecified criteria. *See* **Evaluation, Naturalistic.**

IMAGE GRAPHICS. *See* **Vector Graphics.**

IMAGE INTENSIFIER. A device coupled by fiber optics to a television image pickup tube to increase sensitivity.

IMAGE ORTHICON. One of the first television camera tubes widely used for studio work. It was capable of giving excellent quality pictures. Most broadcast monochrome television cameras used this type of tube, but it was always too expensive for educational applications. *See* **Plumbicon; Vidicon.**

IMAGE PROCESSING. The use of a computer to restore (e.g., remove signal noise), enhance or transform (e.g., increase contrast or accentuate a boundary), and analyze a picture. The technique is particularly important in surveying and mapping.

IMPACT PRINTING. A term applied to all printing systems in which images of characters are produced by hammering an inked ribbon onto the paper using a hard die, as in a typewriter.

IMPEDANCE. The opposition presented by a circuit or a component to the flow of an electric current. The term is used to describe one of the characteristics of the input and output of electronic devices so that when interconnections are made, components are used which match and do not upset the balance of the circuits involved. Impedance is of particular importance when applied to microphones, as it is essential that a microphone match the input impedance of the amplifier it is used with; otherwise serious distortion or lack of signal strength will result. Impedance is measured in ohms.

IN-BASKET TECHNIQUE. The in-basket, or in-tray, technique was originally used in business simulations to introduce items of the type that might come to the attention of an executive during the course of a normal working day. However, the technique has found much wider applications and is now used as a method of introducing problems into simulated situations of many different types. For example, in-basket techniques are now extensively used in teacher training, where they help student teachers learn to cope with different classroom situations as and when they arise. The technique can also be used to control the inflow of information into a simulation, since it allows such inflow to be regulated in terms of both timing and distribution.

INDEPENDENT ACCESS. Access to a system or resource that is not dependent on the fulfillment of some prior criteria, e.g., the entries in this work, the books on the shelf of a library, the tracks on a phonograph disk. The term is analogous to RAM in a computer. *See* **Sequential Access.**

INDEPENDENT BROADCASTING AUTHORITY (IBA) (U.K.). This authority was created in 1954 as the Independent Television Authority to provide a comprehensive television service additional to that of the BBC. Under terms of the Sound Broadcasting Act 1972, the authority was renamed the Independent Broadcasting Authority, and its functions were extended to cover the provision of local commercial radio.
70 Brompton Road, London SW3, U.K.

INDEPENDENT STUDY SESSION. An element in the audio-tutorial method where learners work on their own with learning resources. *See* **Individualization of Instruction.**

INDEPENDENT VARIABLE. In experimental work, research studies, etc., a variable which is controlled or selected by the researcher, and which is deemed to be causally related to the dependent variable. For example, if we wish to investigate the relationship between height and mathematical ability, we would measure the heights of large numbers of students (the independent variable) and compare the results with the students' scores in an appropriate test (the dependent variable). *See* **Dependent Variable.**

INDEX. A set of pointers that connect logical values with the location where the applicable data is stored. In some data base programs you can have only one index per data base; others allow you to have several. The index functions much like a card catalog in a library: it is much faster to look up a topic in the index and then go directly to the correct location on the shelf, rather than combing through all the books.

INDEX FRAME. A videotex frame listing a number of items of information available. Users can select the item to be viewed by pressing the appropriate number (in the range 0 to 9). *See* **Routing.**

INDIVIDUALIZATION OF INSTRUCTION.

WHY INDIVIDUALIZE?

"Students are a lot like people." This seemingly trite statement embodies a philosophy that is having considerable impact on instructional design since the 1960s and will play an even greater role in the future. The idea that students are people (individuals) and that the objective of teaching is to help individuals learn is not a new one. Many good teachers throughout the history of education have been dedicated to the primary purpose of helping people learn. However, through the years, the number and kinds of people seeking education have increased phenomenally, and with the increase, educational activity has become more and more institutionalized. It has become a business, a big business, and as big business practices have been applied to education, the needs of the individual have received less consideration. The number of concerned teachers has been diluted by many whose primary concerns are their own welfare. Students have been forgotten as the focus of instruction, and in the minds of many teachers and administrators, students are merely subjects to be processed at so many dollars per head.

The fantastic world in which we live has been unified through communication technologies undreamed of just a few short years ago. Many people living today, who in their earlier years never anticipated the possibility of television, now, in the comfort of their living room, watch events happening all over the world at the very moment of their occurrence. The opportunities to see how other people live have caused rising aspirations for people everywhere. Many people in the past who were content to occupy their niche are now seeking further development of their own intellectual capacities. Patricia Cross (1976) has suggested that we have reached our goal of education for all, and we now must turn our attention to providing education for each. Virginia B. Smith (1974) lists five pressures that have led to the adoption of individualized, self-paced instruction: (1) heterogeneity of the student body; (2) a growing commitment to lifelong learning; (3) a desire to experiment with new methods of delivery of education; (4) the potential for greater efficiency and effectiveness; and (5) growing support for dispersed learning centers. It is true, as Virginia Smith suggests, that there is an increase in diversity among students seeking education. This trend is not limited to the United States. Many other countries such as Australia, Britain, and Canada have instructional programs specifically designed to accommodate the change in composition of student populations. In the United States, for example, college-level study is being made available to every citizen who wants it, especially through the development of community colleges. Many nontraditional types of institutions have been developed to accommodate this trend such as the **Open University** (q.v.) in Britain and the extensive correspondence programs in Australia and South Africa.

The new groups of learners who are now going to school have had a major impact on the nature of the school itself. Curricula are being changed to include applied sciences and mechanical arts, and many schools are including occupational subjects. The "campus without walls" concept is an attempt to serve a full spectrum of learners who may have very little in common. Many schools that take in unlikely candidates for a college degree must develop systems that will permit students to grow at their own pace and yet maintain standards that will have respectability in the academic world. The important point is that attempts must be made to provide individuals of all types with an opportunity to exploit their potential to the fullest extent.

Why individualization? Because students are a lot like people, and people are individuals. As individuals they have diverse characteristics, needs, interests, and capacities. These variations are not accommodated in a system where information is delivered to all individuals alike and all are expected to proceed at the same pace. Statements made by Smith (1974) are just as true in 1987 as in 1974:

> In the past, we have assumed some degree of uniformity of preparation and, while we recognize some differences in speed of learning, for the most part, we assume these differences were operating within a relatively small range. Working on these assumptions, we saw no disadvantage in holding time constant, scheduling many elements of an instructional program on a basis that would require each student to reach the same point of preparation at that time. We did, however, recognize differences in the amounts of content that students may have mastered within the constant time—indeed we used those differences in content to sort out the students and assign them grades of ability. For the heterogenous student body we are recognizing what a great loss is involved in the assumption of relative uniformity of speed of learning. The scheduled demonstration—or the pre-scheduled discussion group or the set of series of lectures—may add little to the understanding of the learner if he has not yet arrived at the point in his understanding that would permit him to make use of the scheduled event.

Cross (1976) says that

> it is now apparent that higher education tends to serve the full spectrum of learners—rich and poor, black and white, male and female, old and young, the able and not so able, the mobile and not so mobile. It also appears that colleges intend to offer the full range of the subject matter—classical, applied, vocational, and avocational. And it is clear that students can be campus residents, commuters, or people who never set foot on a campus.

Therefore, the reasons and the needs are clear, and in a great many schools the implementation has begun. But the need is not limited to students in the typical educational setting. Many industries have taken over the task of teaching their employees a great variety of subjects for improving the quality of their work as well as the quality of their lives. Judy A. Capraro and Stephen E. Cline (1983) comment on these problems as follows:

> Those involved in training and retraining are faced with a special challenge. They must close the gap that exists between current competency levels and the skills required of the new technologies. To do so in the most cost-effective manner will require a well-targeted training effort, consisting of five important steps: (1) establishing clear-cut objectives; (2) assessing trainees' individual needs; (3) designing programs flexible enough to accommodate diverse individual needs; (4) selecting delivery systems best suited to achieving the desired results; and (5) providing for evaluation of the trainee's program and overall program effectiveness.
>
> Because companies have different training requirements, and trainees have different competency levels, training programs should be built around each individual's instructional needs, if they are to be efficient. Given the time and money constraints involved with training employees, it becomes all the more critical to focus on what is required.

Clearly there is a widespread need for individualized instruction.

WHAT IS INDIVIDUALIZATION?

Individualization is not a simple matter of providing all people access to an instructional program or merely introducing new technology into the classroom. J. G. Sherman (1982), in a recent issue of the *Individualized Instruction Newsletter,* points out that what we are all about is effective teaching. Individualization is a very complex and demanding process involving the identification of the wants and needs of individuals and helping them to acquire the knowledge and skills that will satisfy these wants and needs. It assumes that the conventional educational system does not accomplish these ends. It is important to note here, however, that the conventional system does satisfy the wants and needs of a segment of our population. Many of us who are on the bandwagon for individualization must be aware that the term connotes the concern for *all* individuals rather than a certain few. This is the basis for the whole trend to the individualization movement. The destruction or elimination of conventional teaching should not be the goal of supporters of individualization. The nature of individualization would require an acceptance of conventional instructional techniques as being appropriate for some students who are served best by this approach. The need is to produce additional learning alternatives that will serve the population whose needs are not met by conventional lectures and laboratories.

As pointed out earlier, much of the basis for conventional instructional design was a delivery system of information which treats all students as if they were equal. Instruction is cut off and grades are given through some kind of examination program associated with norm-referenced evaluation. This practice does not provide for individual differences in capacity, background, or interest of students but treats them all the same. Thus the educational system becomes a screening device for those who operate most effectively within the system. Talented individuals as well as slow learners may be eliminated because of the system rather than ability. Many students and teachers are challenging this philosophy.

In the early 1960s Robert Mager and others made visible an old idea, that of specifying objectives. This concept, which Mager elucidated so well in his book *Preparing Instructional Objectives* (1962), provides a whole new approach to instructional design. In contrast to the norm-referenced evaluation, objectives permit the use of criterion-referenced evaluation. Bloom (1956) indicates that more than 90 percent of the students he tested could learn if the subject matter was held constant and time of study was allowed to vary. This approach frees the learner to use any and all available instructional materials, and the efficacy of these materials can be carefully evaluated. Student learning styles can be matched with procedures and media useful in providing a successful experience for the learner. It is clear that no single instructional system will accommodate all students in all situations and for all subject matter.

Cross (1976), writing of the United States, suggests that we must take a hard look at the three sacred cows of education: the semester, the credit hour, and the grading system:

These sacred cows are measures of learning and they are woefully inadequate. The semester represents mass education at its worse. Under a bind of a semester we batch people of vastly different backgrounds and ability, to do what we can for them in the time available. It is as though the Ford Assembly Line batched cars that were almost complete with cars that were barely started and did what they could for each car in the time available for each station. Imagine conscientious workers, comparable to a faculty, working hard to get the first wheel on some cars and the last one on others. Predictably, at the end of the line there would be cars unable to run because they have only one wheel, cars lurching on three wheels, cars riding smoothly on all four wheels. Noting these obvious differences Ford might compound the original error by grading within batches. The cars with three wheels will rate an A if it appears in a batch lacking four wheeled cars, but it will receive a B if it passed through the line with some four wheeled cars. Quality control may note with some dismay that the average Ford car has only two wheels, but management will point out that after all each car has been through the standard eight stations and by definition eight stations equals one car much as eight semesters equals one degree.

It is true that much of our instructional system is somewhat analogous to the assembly line Cross describes. The question is whether alternative systems can be developed that will provide effective and acceptable adjustments for individual differences. Is it possible to assist those individuals that are analogous to the two-wheeled car with opportunities to acquire the additional two wheels? Self-pacing appears to provide a partial answer.

However, individualization must go further than merely providing self-paced learning. Provision must be made for variation in learning styles and in kinds and levels of content. Further, it must be recognized that differences in capacities may make it impossible to bring all people to the same level of competence. In the true sense of the term *individualization*, the system must recognize this impossibility and accept it as one of the alternatives in the individualization process. In our zeal for implementation of new and innovative methods of self-pacing and other techniques designed to provide for variation in individuals, we must maintain an appreciation of excellence and preserve standards of high-quality learning throughout the individualization movement.

What is individualization? It is an attempt by certain educators to develop instructional systems that will provide alternatives to the conventional instructional system with the hope that these alternatives along with the conventional instructional system might provide opportunities for all persons to pursue their educational goals commensurate with their interests, backgrounds, and capacities.

HOW CAN INDIVIDUALIZATION BE ACHIEVED?

Koerner (1977) says,

Work with the technologies of instruction takes place on the basis of many assumptions about learning that are difficult or impossible to verify, and it takes place in close relationship to other kinds of pedagogical experimentation. Every where that educational technology is found, its natural collaborator, self-paced instruction, is found. The **audio-tutorial** (q.v.) method of self-paced instruction as well as the **Keller Plan** (q.v.) (named after the psychologist, Fred K. Keller), and many variants of both methods provide the framework for most of the instructional materials associated with educational technology.

While these two instructional strategies and their variations are based on the philosophy of individualization, they represent only small steps in the direction of individualizing instruction. The technology of providing education for each is in its theoretical stages, and evidence of its effectiveness and efficiency is just beginning to be accumulated (Brewer, 1977; Fisher, 1976; Kulik and Kulik, 1975; Nance, 1973).

Much more thoughtful and creative effort is still needed to modify educational practices to be consistent with educational theory. Communication technologies such as computers, videotapes, audiotapes, and satellites are far ahead of our ability to use them effectively and efficiently in an instructional design. Even simple things such as recognition of achievement may have to be reexamined and new mechanisms developed for their acceptance. For example, Nolfi (1976) says,

Finally, a set of competency-based credentials at all levels should be created and awarded independently to the existing instructional and school structure. This action would give thousands of adults the opportunity to obtain credentials based on what they know, rather than on how or where they learned it. Not only would this procedure restore some equity and legitimacy to learning in diverse settings, it would also provide an important incentive for those who have and can earn credits to continue in traditional degree programs for adults.

Individualization requires that attitudes of all people associated with education must be changed including that of administrators, the public, the teachers, and the students themselves. It is too much to expect that this major shift in instructional design can be done quickly and with smooth transition, especially in view of the fact that conventional instruction accommodates well the individuals who are especially adapted to it. All of us have been so conditioned over the many years of the lectures/laboratories approach that we tend to equate this procedure with learning itself. Our administrative methods are adapted to this practice, and our facilities are designed to accommodate it. Even minor shifts from the customary instructional activities create concerns for a full array of people associated with the educational process. Many teachers have difficulty in expressing teaching in terms other than the words *lecture* and *laboratory*. Despite this, the time is ripe for change to occur and it is well underway.

Many movements have contributed greatly to the potential for individualization, such as the use of objectives, mastery learning, improved communication technology, some new understanding in the ways in which learning must take place, and the modularization of content into minicourses. The communication technology (hardware) is advanced well beyond our ability to use it constructively; however, much effort is being put forth and some of the potential is described in the following paragraphs.

Computer. Perhaps the computer is one of the most promising education technologies at present and probably will be in the future. The first IBM 1500 instructional system was completed in July 1966, and installed at the Brentwood Elementary School in East Palo Alto. This pioneering step, while fraught with many frustrations, was a valuable experiment which has led to many subsequent ones. A very successful CAI program is the **PLATO** (q.v.) system at the University of Illinois. The system is interactive, analyzes the learners' needs, and is a true application of instructional technology. Its potential seems almost unlimited, except for some restrictions in the physical capacity and the rate at which it can be expanded. It is impossible to include a comprehensive review of the great number of CAI, or **computer-assisted instruction** (q.v.) activities generated during the last few years. Several teachers have championed this effort, such as Ted Crovello at Notre Dame University, who enthusiastically shares his expertise with fellow teachers in many workshops and publications.

The constant improvement of technology seems destined to open up totally unexplored possibilities for making instruction available to all individuals. At this early stage of development and the current status of the software, it is impossible to assess the potential quality and quantity of instruction that can be done by this method. Many skeptics feel that the present expense of developing software and providing the necessary hardware is wasted and that much of what is being done can be done very well using conventional media. Currently, much CAI is of the drill-and-practice nature and merely relieves the instructor of some of the tiresome teaching activities. It assists in the identification of students' weaknesses and helps diagnose their future needs.

A few clever individuals like Ann Piestrup see the computer as a way to structure "environments" that allow children to discover the intricate concepts of Venn diagrams, three-dimensional graphs, and Boolean logic. The programs give the children a positive experience and are self-pacing, nonviolent, errorless, and easy to implement. The computer can record massive amounts of data on students to assist in managing and matching their learning styles with the content needed to help them achieve their goals. Presently, much of the value of this tool has been in mathematics, where the student can have access to immense amounts of information and manipulate it in a number of ways to attain answers that physically and intellectually would be almost impossible without computer assistance. Instructional designers have just begun to explore the potential of the computer for games and simulation activities that may replace much study that is now done in laboratories and much more laboriously. Computers can search for bits of information and, in very short time, supply these to students who otherwise could not spare the time for conventional methods of acquiring this content. Large-scale operations and sharing instructional programs may ultimately make computer-assisted intruction a very cost-effective means for individualization.

Television. While television has been available since the 1930s, it still has not replaced conventional instructional programs as many predicted in its early use in education. Advances in television technologies, such as color, videodiscs and slow-scan television, have provided some new tools for individualization. These and other variations of television technology have not yet been carefully examined for their potential use in education. Further, the cost of television cameras, the use of portable cameras, and improved mechanisms for producing instructional programs all combine to make many new instructional procedures possible. Hundreds of lessons have already been produced in projects such as the Open University in Britain, many in the United States and several other countries as well, and are now available. These can be used in a great variety of contexts as the technology expands. Software is being developed at a tremendous rate and much redundant material is being produced, partially because of lack of communication about what is already available, partially because of teacher ego, and partially because of adaptation requirements to local needs and interests. Full exploitation of video merely awaits greater acceptance, production of some additional software, and the administrative techniques to provide credit to those students who have demonstrated achievement. The ultimate use of television cannot occur until a better understanding of its potential and improved mechanics for instruction through television are more thoroughly explored.

The development of the videodisc has considerably improved the possibilities for a home video system which will herald a whole new era in home learning. The videodisc is similar to a phonograph recording, and with the use of an adapter device, it can be viewed through the home television set. The videodisc combined with a small computer may revolutionize individualized instruction in the future. The potential is well illustrated by the description of ActionCode given by Judy A. Capraro and Stephen E. Cline (1983):

ActionCode consists of optical laser videodisc, a video monitor with touch screen, a scanning wand, a specially designed microprocessor circuit, and encoded workbooks. ActionCode has eliminated the dependence on a keyboard interface.

Entirely "user friendly," the system is activated when a trainee runs the scanning wand over bar codes printed on the workbooks. The simple bar scanning process activates the videodisc player, bringing the specified material to the video screen. Video sequences highlight, illustrate, and expand the textual information. Through push-button controls, the user can stop the video, reverse, or advance it.

Because ActionCode combines the familiarity and portability of text material with the demonstration power of video, retention of transfer-of-learning is enhanced. The touch screen capability allows learners to control lesson progress and gets them directly involved with realistic demonstrations of tasks and procedures. Full color and sound add to the realism of the learning experience. The text material may be studied before and/or after the ActionCode. The specially encoded workbooks clearly show course organization and allow the learner to review any part of the lesson, with instant access to video segments.

There is no wear and tear on the record, and the disc will contain around 54,000 tracks which roughly are comparable to the grooves on a phonographic record. This device can use materials transferred from films, videotapes, filmstrips, transparencies, microfilms, printed text, audiotapes, and phonograph records. The density of information that can be coded on a videodisc is so great that the storage of video information will no longer be a problem. The user has full control of the system and is not bound to the linearity of ordinary television. Coupled with the computer, the videodisc will then become a completely interactive system, giving the student the advantages of both computer-based instruction and user-controlled video reproduction. This appears to approach the ultimate in technology. The major problem is the availability of software. The low cost of a home model disc player, relatively low cost of the videodiscs, and low cost of microcomputers may eventually provide education at the learner's convenience and at much reduced cost over the current expenses of attending college on campus.

Other Technology. A great many additional devices, perhaps not as exciting as the video and computer but still important, have a great deal of potential for individualization. Among these is the radio, which has been used for quite a few years now, but not as extensively as it merits. Perhaps this is due, in part, to the fact that commonly it is a one-way presentation and there is lack of control of the pace by the learner. The Open University has used radio effectively, as has the Radio School of the Air at Broken Hill in Australia. The Open University has specific listening times for its widely scattered students and can communicate announcements and other pertinent information to them by this means. The School of the Air in Australia involves a two-way exchange between the teacher and student(s). Each has a transmitter-receiver device. The teacher and students (students are dispersed over a large territory, up to 350 miles away from the teacher) at a prescheduled time use their radios to communicate with each other. Students may recite or sing in unison or separately, and all students have an opportunity to participate. The teacher calls them by name and is aware of their presence or absence in the discussion. It is important to note that one of the big benefits of this program is the opportunity for the students to identify with the teacher and with each other even though they are miles apart and must rely on sound. The program strongly implies that, even though learning must be done individually, a good learning system must include group interaction. The major limitation is that only trivial information is easily transferred by audio. Involved information is much more readily transferred by a combination of audio and printed materials.

Audiotapes have the same potential as radio, except for the broadcast nature, and they provide students the possibility of controlling rate and an unlimited amount of review. The audiotape has become more and more extensively used in recent years and, in many cases, as some variation of the audio-tutorial system (Postlethwait, 1981). Audiotape can store explanation, information, discussions, and sound effects to be used in combination with a variety of visuals, tangible items, and a study guide. The programmer can sequence learning activities to suit the subject matter and the needs of the student (Kahle, 1978). Many learning programs can be changed significantly by simply making alternate audiotaped programs. This simple instructional arrangement is useful for study in a variety of locations such as learning centers, home study, or any other appropriate location. It is gradually being accepted in a great many disciplines and is likely to be more widely used in the future as the educational community becomes more adaptable with lecture and laboratory.

The **microfiche** (q.v.) is a low-cost device which is growing in use and can be combined with other technology such as the computer, audiotape, and videotape. It is possible to store large quantities of information on an extremely small 12.5cm X 10.0cm plastic card. The greatest problem with this device is psychological and, perhaps, the inconvenience of a special projection device to read the highly miniaturized photographs.

A very important and often overlooked medium for individualized instruction is a device that has been with us for a great many years, the book. Its value is often ignored, especially in this present age of more elaborate technical devices for storing information. Conventional instruction has been centered on the lecture and laboratory as the instructional tool; however, it is likely that these two instructional strategies have had little real impact on the learning that has occurred. Books probably have contributed most to the learning process and in many systems are probably the only real source of most learning. Laboratories and lectures have merely provided motivation and, in an informal way, helped the student to determine which information was important.

One can add other devices such as filmstrips, slides, movies, etc., to the above. These can be combined in a variety of ways to facilitate learning, and a great many teachers are using various combinations of these to aid in the individualization process.

Parallel with the development of individualization has been considerable progress in investigating how the learning process occurs. Joseph Novak of Cornell University in his book *A Theory of Education* (1977) critically examines several theories of learning and the basis they provide for developing instruction. He suggests that Ausubel's theory is a practical basis for development of instructional programs and that it will enable us to design learning sequences for more effective use of instructional devices. This book merits careful study by all teachers.

The division of subject-matter into small units has provided an opportunity to individualize content with increased resolution for needs of students. The larger conventional units, called *courses,* do not permit the flexibility of curriculum organization required by the new education. *Module* is a term currently popular, but *minicourse* might be more appropriate. These units of subject matter are indeed small courses, and the concept should not be confused by relating them directly to any specific instructional strategy. These small courses provide students with subject-matter packets which can be used with a great deal of flexibility. Minicourses can be organized into a great variety of patterns consistent with different approaches or themes. Students can have freedom in adjusting study time and subject-matter content to their individual needs and particular interests. Failures can be pinpointed to specific subject matter and subsequently remedied in a minimum of time and effort. This is in contrast to conventional procedure, which requires a student to complete an entire term of course work. Inadequate achievement can be identified at each critical step in the student's progress. Information can be mastered before the student is forced to proceed to subsequent studies. The habit of thorough and positive approaches to learning is thus encouraged. Instructional materials for many minicourses are portable and easily made available in a variety of locations. This provides the possibility of interchange among schools for updating in-service training of teachers and improving instruction of off-campus students. Some basic subject matter may remain the same for many years; however, subject matter which is constantly changing can be updated without a major revision of all study materials. Diagnosis and prescription can be arranged more effectively. Several instructional programs can be designed for a single minicourse, and students may utilize any one or more of these to help them master the objectives for the unit of subject matter. Minicourses provide advantages listed above, yet they can be organized into conventional course units compatible with our present instructional system.

SUMMARY

John Hinton (1977), the editor of *One-To-One,* a newsletter of the International Congress for Individualized Instruction,* defines individualized instruction as

having no absolute quality or quantity; it is, simply, the learning act which has been developed to best meet the needs of each individual learner, his needs for a content which is presented in a way that is appropriate to be learned effectively, a content which when possible is relevant to him as a person with unique qualities, expectancies and potentials.

Hinton further states,

---

*In 1972 there was established an organization called the International Congress for Audiotutorial Instruction. Later it become the International Congress for Individualized Instruction. In 1982 several organizations merged with it under the name International Society for Individualized Instruction.

in order to understand the activities which may be manipulated to best meet the needs of the individual let us consider the three major constants which are found in most learning situations.

1. The student is an individual with a particular learning style, expectancies, motivations and levels of competency for the learning situation.
2. The teacher is an individual with a particular teaching style and understanding of the learning act and his role in it.
3. A defined content for a subject which includes all of the knowledge, skills and attitudes appropriate for the instructional situation.

The present attitude of many educators and students and the high level of proficiency of communication technology combine to provide a situation conducive to *individualization*. The great diversity of people now desiring an education demands the attention of all associated with the educational process. How can we provide each individual with an opportunity to achieve the full limit of his or her capacity? There is no one way or one procedure that can make available the variety of learning conditions necessary to accommodate all individuals. A multiplicity of approaches must be made available and in a multiplicity of ways. The technology is currently available and new technology will be forthcoming that can make individualization feasible for almost anyone who wishes it. The greatest deterrent is the attitude of people associated with the process of education. Ideas have become stereotyped over a very long span of exposure to lecture/laboratory, and many consider this procedure to be the only mode to learning. A break from the conventional format will require much time, and progress will be accomplished very slowly. The concepts of **mastery learning** (q.v.), **objectives** (q.v.), improvements in **communication engineering** (q.v.), use of **minicourses** (q.v.), and new understandings of the learning process have provided tools that have enabled us to make great strides in the process of individualization. We are far from the ultimate in *helping students learn* as effectively and efficiently as desirable, but a great many people are accepting the fact that *students are a lot like people* and are trying to do something about it.

S. N. Postlethwait

REFERENCES

Bloom, B. S., ed. (1956) *Taxonomy of Educational Objectives, Handbook I: Cognitive Domain.* New York: David McKay.

Brewer, J. (1977) "SIMIG: A Case Study of the Innovative Method of Teaching and Learning." *Studies in Higher Education* 2: 1.

Capraro, J. A. and Cline, S. E. (1983) "ActionCode: The Latest in Videodisc Technology." *Individualized Instruction* 3–4.

Cross, K. P. (1976) "The Instructional Revolution." In *Accent on Learning: Improving Instruction and Reshaping the Curriculum.* San Francisco, Calif.: Jossey-Bass.

Fisher, K. M. (1976) *A-T Science Teaching: How Effective Is It?* Arlington, Va.: BioScience.

Healy, T. S. (1976) "The CUNY Experience." In *Individualizing the System,* ed. D. W. Vermilye and William Farris. San Francisco, Calif.: Jossey-Bass.

Hinton, J. R., ed. (1977) "Excerpt from NOTICIAS on Individualizing Instruction." *One-to-One Newsletter* 3: 8, 10.

Kahle, J. B. (1978) "A-T Instruction: A Perspective and a Prediction."*American Biology Teacher* 40: 17–20, 42.

Keller, F. S. (1968) "Goodbye, Teacher . . . ." *Journal of Applied Behavior Analysis* 1: 79–89.

Koerner, J. D. (1977) *The Present and the Future in Educational Technology.* New York: Alfred P. Sloan Foundation.

Kulik, J. A. and Kulik, C.L.C. (1975) "Effectiveness of the Personalized System of Instruction." *Engineering Education* 66: 28–33.

Mager, R. F. (1962) *Preparing Instructional Objectives.* Palo Alto, Calif.: Fearon.

Nance, J. B. (1973) *Operations Research Analysis of Audio-tutorial Systems.* Englewood Cliffs, N.J.: Educational Technology Publications.

Nolfi, G. J. (1976) "The Case for Selective Entitlement Vouchers." In *Individualizing the System,* ed D. W. Vermilye and William Farris. San Francisco, Calif.: Jossey-Bass.

Novak, J. (1977) *The Theory of Education.* Ithaca, N.Y.: Cornell University Press.

Postlethwait, S. N. (1981) "A Basis for Instructional Alternatives." *Journal of College Science Teaching* (September): 44–46.

Sherman, J. G. (1982) "PSI: Another History." *International Society for Individualized Instruction Newsletter* 82 (1): 2.

Smith, V. B. (1974) "Individualized Self-paced Instruction." In *Personalized Instruction in Higher Education, Proceedings of the First National Conference,* 5–6 April. Washington, D.C.: Georgetown University Press, p. 182.

INDIVIDUALIZED LEARNING. See **Individualization of Instruction.**

INDUCTION LOOP. Audio teaching system in which a classroom is surrounded by a loop of wire. Any student inside the loop can hear via wireless headphones the signals passed into the loop from a tape recorder or microphone. This technique has been used successfully for sports teaching in arenas as well as for the more obvious classroom applications.

INFORMATICS. The study of information: the way in which it is created, processed, and used.

INFORMATION CLASSIFICATION AND RETRIEVAL. This entry examines the general aspects of the classification and retrieval of educational information used in teaching and instruction.

INTRODUCTION

The act of classification forms one of the most basic of all mental processes; without an ability to classify we should not be able to survive, for we should never know in our daily life what to expect next. Classification is essential to our identification of the events we observe in the world around us, yet only in recent years have psychologists begun to unravel the highly complex nature of the process (Bruner, 1960; Joynson, 1974; Luria, 1979 BACKGROUND READING; Guilford, 1968; Inhelder and Piaget, 1964 THEORY). Bruner, for example, has commented: "Perhaps the most basic thing that can be said about human memory, after a century of intensive research, is that unless detail is placed into a structured pattern, it is rapidly forgotten."

The importance, if not the full complexity, of the process has been recognized since antiquity: for Plato, to know things meant to place them in their correct classes, and the traditional theoretical basis of classification derives from the logic of Aristotle, in which an object was to be identified by enumerating its several characteristics and determining which of them were like, and which unlike, the characteristics of other objects whose identity—the class they belonged to—was already known. The simplest example of this type of classification is the separation of a set of objects into two groups: those which possess a specific characteristic, and those which do not. The schedule of terms which results from a series of such separations constitutes a scheme of classification. Such a scheme exhibits the relations between genus (class) and species (individual instances of the class) and between coordinate species of the same class.

As this type of analysis is basic to our understanding, it follows that a similar procedure ought to be of value in communicating information, and in schemes for the systematic arrangement of documents containing information. If we look at education in terms which have achieved widespread acceptance through the development of **educational technology** (q.v.), that is as a *system,* an important element in it is the input and flow of information. Information acts, indeed, as part of the energy input necessary to keep the system functioning at full efficiency.

The subsystem in which the channels through which information passes form the primary network comes into operation when a set of concepts formed in one human mind begins to be transferred to other minds. One way of doing this is to make an oral communication—a lecture, a chat at the bar—and it is well-known that this is one of the most important ways of information gathering. Another way is to make use of the system of publication through books, journals, and the various forms of audio-visual media; this system launches the information on a voyage of many destinations, and in order that the progress of the voyage may be controlled, we also establish systems for collecting and disseminating the information, in much the same way that ports are systems for receiving and distributing goods from abroad. We call these systems libraries, or resource centers, and in them we find subsystems for classifying and then retrieving the information coming in, so that it reaches those who may need to use it. Classification and retrieval are two facets of the same process: the aim of classification is to effect retrieval, and efficient retrieval cannot be effected by bad classification.

DECIMAL CLASSIFICATION (DC)

Modern thought and practice in library classification schemes began with Melvil Dewey, who published the first edition of his *Decimal Classification* in 1876, while he was librarian at Amherst College. It at once became, and remains, the most popular of all such schemes; an abridged edition has been produced by the School Library Association, and the nineteenth edition has been published from an office now in the Library of Congress.

Dewey's great achievement was really twofold: first, he realized that the systematic arrangement of information in libraries could be achieved only by allocating places to *subjects,* and not to specific books, as had been the common practice; second, he realized that *relative location* of subjects could be symbolized and mechanized by giving them a decimal fraction notation. Such a notation would not only display the subdivisions from genera to species but would also allow for the insertion of new subjects that had to be accommodated between two existing subjects.

599	Mammals
599.8	Primates
599.88	Apes
599.884	Gorillas

In the above sequence, each term on the right is a species of the preceding term, and the steps in the hierarchy are accurately represented by the addition of another digit to the notation to show the increasing specificity. The latest, nineteenth, edition has no heading or index entry for educational technology, but the following is part of the schedule for "audio and visual materials for teaching":

371.33	Audio and visual materials for teaching
371.333	Audio materials and devices

371.335	Visual and audiovisual materials and devices
371.335 2	Pictures
371.335 22	Slides and filmstrips
371.335 8	Television
371.335 84	Teaching methods
371.335 87	Administration
371.335 89	Production of programs and specific programs

The alphabetical index, much expanded in the nineteenth edition, includes the following references to this schedule:

Audiovisual
  aids *see* Audiovisual materials

  materials
art appreciation use	701.1
bibliographies	011.37
spec. kinds	012–016
ed. use	371.335
s.a. spec. levels of ed.	
library trmt	025.177
technology	621.380 44

The classified array at 371.335 gives the systematic arrangement of terms used in this part of the field, while the alphabetical index points to the other places in the scheme where they are also relevant.

It will be clear, however, that the terms in this schedule do not, as in the first extract, form a true hierarchy. The terms "teaching methods" and "administration" are not *species* of television, but the notation presents them as though they were. In fact, any term has of course the potential of being subdivided by more than one characteristic; as Inhelder and Piaget have shown, children organize concepts into matrices, or multiplicative classifications, at about the same age as into additive classifications, or single hierarchies. Dewey himself realized this, and provided for synthesis of numbers by adding notations from the history and geography sections; additional tables included from the eighteenth edition onwards provide for subdivision of any subject by area, language, literature, and ethnic groups. This form of synthesis of notations gives considerable economy and flexibility in making schedules, and has been taken to much greater lengths in the Universal Decimal Classification.

UNIVERSAL DECIMAL CLASSIFICATION (UDC)

The UDC was originally based on Dewey's DC, but was expanded by the addition of many auxiliary schedules in order to make possible the classification of very specific subjects such as are found in periodical articles. This scheme has proved very popular in Europe, particularly for science and technology, and is in process of publication, in fascicles, by the British Standards Institution. The more commonly used auxiliaries are:

+	Plus	Connection of nonconsecutive numbers
/	Stroke	Connection of consecutive numbers
:	Colon	Relation (a very general notion)
(1/9)	Brackets	Place
(=)	Brackets equals	Race and nationality
" "	Inverted commas	Time

In spite of this extensive facility, the subject schedules themselves continue to exhibit a mixture of cross-classifications, as this extract from Class 37 Education shows:

37.018	Fundamental forms of education
37.018.2	School education
37.018.26	Attitudes of parents to school
37.018.263	Parent-teacher relations

As in the DC extract above, although the notation is still hierarchical in form, the series of terms is not a true hierarchy; the later terms are not species of the preceding, and are in fact subjects compounded of several different concepts. This fixing or binding of concepts into compounded subjects is now called *precoordination,* because it is done in the schedule of terms before any documents have actually been classified.

FACET ANALYSIS

The aim of a classification scheme is to arrange documents and information in a way which makes sense to users, and hierarchical genus-species classifications certainly made sense in the nineteenth century, especially in the classificatory sciences. They still do when we are dealing with single entities or classes, such as "primates"; we do not have to abandon this essential intellectual technique because it does not provide the complete answer, and indeed such a classifying or grouping process remains central to all learning. Today, however, the usual contents of a document describe relations between a number of concepts, often drawn from several different contexts. "Attitudes of parents to school" clearly relates terms from three contexts—"attitudes," "parents," "school"—which are easily distinguishable from each other, and each belongs to a different set of groups or classes.

The part played by category formation in the learning process has exercised philosophers since Aristotle, and from recent work we may cite that of Hirst (1966 THEORY), Bloom (1956, 1964 THEORY), Bernstein (1971 THEORY), Rescorla (1981 SIMILAR RESEARCH), and Luria (1979 BACKGROUND READING) among those who have studied the problem in philosophy, psychology, and sociology. Luria, for example, says that "categorical thinking is not just a reflection of individual experience, but a shared experience that society can convey through its linguistic system." A classification scheme has exactly this function, of helping to convey information by means of what could be called an artificial language of ordinal numbers.

As a justification for his taxonomy, Bloom clearly relates category formation to systematic organizing of information:

The provision of major categories as well as sub-categories in the taxonomy enables the user of the taxonomy to select the level of classification which does least violence to the statement of the objective. Further, the hierarchical character of the taxonomy enables the user to more clearly understand the place of a particular objective in relation to other objectives.

Unfortunately, Bloom's taxonomy is very much influenced by behaviorist psychology, and the subjectivity of his approach and the doubtfulness of its suitability for use in a retrieval system are shown by the very mixed collection of subjects he cites to illustrate each category. His category 2, "Responding," has as one of its subdivisions, 2;2 "Willingness to respond," and his examples include these subjects:

—Practises the rules of good health, particularly with reference to rest, food and sanitation

—Responds with consistent, active and deep interest to intellectual stimuli

—Cooperates in the production of a room or school newspaper or magazine

—Performs simple experiments relating to biological or physical science

Experience indicates that anyone searching a documentation system for information on these topics would not expect to find them in the same place or category. Nevertheless, Bloom's taxonomy continues to interest and influence both theory and practice, and Furst (1981 HISTORICAL) has provided a review of the discussions over philosophical and educational issues since its publication. The *Journal of Verbal Learning and Verbal Behavior, Journal of Child Language,* and *Child Development* all contain records of research studies on the role of category formation in the development of logical thinking and classification. Lauer and Baltig (1972 SIMILAR RESEARCH) specifically compare the retrieval efficiency of classified and alphabetical indexes, and state that "one major finding of this experiment was the consistently greater effectiveness of taxonomic category than first-letter communality among words, both with respect to free-recall performance and output organization."

In order to reflect a logical structure, modern schemes for indexing compound subjects should consist of sets of simple, or elementary, terms in categories which are derived from the main subject or class by a series of characteristics which are each logically distinct from the others, and which can be clearly seen to be based on the logic inherent in the main subject. This process of division is called *facet analysis,* the name given to it by S. R. Ranganathan (1960 FURTHER DETAIL), who was the first to apply the technique of analysis into such logical categories to a scheme of documentary classification. Precoordination is kept to a minimum and should be applied only to true hierarchies; the main process in classifying a document is therefore in a postcoordinate mode, that is, deciding on the terms which actually represent the subject and assembling those terms from the different facets of the scheme, together with their notation symbols. The schedules of the scheme should themselves provide a display of terms in their logical relationships, which will aid users to find their way into the collection of documents.

LONDON EDUCATION CLASSIFICATION (LEC)

The LEC (Foskett and Foskett, 1974 FURTHER DETAIL) was the first scheme to apply facet analysis to the subject of education, and has been in use in the Library of the University of London Institute of Education since 1965. It starts from the notion that the basic process of education is the acquiring of information, understanding, and mastery of skills from sources of these by those who do not yet have them. For this it is necessary to have a learner, for without a learner there can be no education; the primary facet is therefore the educand, or learner. Some critics of the LEC have preferred to give primary place to the *curriculum,* and it is true that, for many users of educational documentation, a curriculum subject is the first point of approach. But we do not set up an educational system in order that we shall all know more about any particular subject; every subject has some educational value, but no subject is the basic reason for establishing an educational system. We set up such a system in order to produce educated people, and from this point depend all the other facets of the subject education. Ranganathan has called this the "wall-picture" principle: one cannot hang a picture until one has a wall on which to hang it.

Given the notion of educand, we can proceed to enumerate a logical sequence of ideas, each of which depends on what has gone before. What does the learner study? The curriculum facet. How do the learners study? The teaching methods facet. How do they learn? Psychology facet. Who teaches? Where do they teach and learn? What are the principles and philosophy of education? And so on.

From a detailed examination of the literature of education, the second edition of LEC included the following facets:

Educands
Educational institutions—schools, colleges, etc.
Curriculum
Teaching methods
Teaching aids, audiovisual media
Students' work
Psychology of education
Human biology, health and hygiene
Management of education
Personnel in education
Teaching profession
Buildings, services, equipment
History of education
Comparative education
Planning and economics of education
Sociology of education
Philosophy of education

Several problems have emerged from the construction of this scheme. For example, some of these subjects are not "core" areas of education; that is, they are very relevant to many other subjects as well. A facet such as the curriculum might well include every subject known to us, since all of them may be taught and learned. In any special classification such as this, a compromise has to be arranged; it usually takes the form of borrowing from another existing scheme of a more general character, or else listing only a selection of the terms that would be necessary in a complete scheme.

The notation of LEC departs radically from the numerical system of DC and UDC, and consists of letters grouped in three and occasionally four. Many of these groups are pronounceable, which gives them a mnemonic character; a number of articles in the *Journal of Verbal Learning and Verbal Behavior* supports the theory that this quality of pronounceability helps to improve memory and recall, which is useful in referring from a catalog to the shelves of a library. Some LEC notations are highly mnemonic:

Bon	Inspectorate
Bux	Documentation
Fab	Teaching profession
Ror	Choir school
Ruf	"Outward Bound" school
Tef	Deaf children

These symbols are constant; that is, they always have the same meaning. To classify a document, one simply analyzes its subject, finds the proper terms in the schedules, and puts their notations together. Thus the subject "Curriculum development in science in colleges of education" would be classified as Sef Mabb Mob, where

Sef = colleges of education
Mabb = curriculum development
Mob = science

Using a scheme like this, where the several facets are clearly distinguished, makes it easy to construct an index for retrieval purposes: an entry is made for each facet of every document's subject, so that although a document may be found in only one place in a library, an index entry for it will be found in as many places as there are facets in its subject.

BIBLIOGRAPHIC CLASSIFICATION

Early in this century, H. E. Bliss improved on DC by making a still more systematic attempt to provide a matrix type of scheme, and his Bibliographic Classification, first published in outline in 1910, is used in a number of university and other education libraries. An abridged version has been published by the School Library Association. Bliss provided 45 Systematic Auxiliary Schedules and a number of Alternative Locations by which a subject might be placed in one of several different schedules according to the interest of the library. A new edition, known as the second, is in course of compilation under the direction of J. Mills at the Polytechnic of North London. The active Bliss Classification Association meets regularly to ensure continued support for the scheme, which is being published in fascicles by Butterworths.

Class J, Education, was the first class to be published (Mills and Broughton, 1977 FURTHER DETAIL). Early publication was possible because Class J is largely founded on the faceted LEC and uses a very similar structure:

J	EDUCATION
JA	PRINCIPLES, THEORY
JB	ADMINISTRATION OF EDUCATIONAL SYSTEM
JE	PSYCHOLOGY OF EDUCATION
JH	TEACHERS & TEACHING
JI	Teaching methods & aids
JK	CURRICULUM
JL	EDUCANDS, PERSONS TAUGHT

Bliss's principle of Alternative Locations is preserved:

JW	(Teaching aids)
	*Alternative to JI
JY	(Curriculum)
	*Alternative to JK

THESAURUS

Following the lead of Melvil Dewey, each scheme of classification has since provided an alphabetical relative index, in which each term is listed in all the contexts in which it appears in the schedules of the scheme. Several similar lists of subject headings for use in alphabetical, or dictionary, catalogs have been published, with lists of related terms under each heading linked by cross-references. A "see" reference means that the term at which it appears should not be used at all, but entries made under the term to which the reference is directed; this takes care of synonyms and aims to avoid inconsistency in indexing the same subject on different occasions. A "see also" reference means that entries will be found under both headings.

In spite of all the research, particularly in the United States, proving the superiority of classified over alphabetical structures in retrieval performance, the introduction of computers for information storage and retrieval led many to conclude that there was no further need for classification schemes, since the computer gives random access and does not display a systematic arrangement of subjects or documents. Nevertheless, practical experience showed that some set of authorized terms was still necessary to ensure consistency; and the name "thesaurus" was introduced to define such vocabularies. Several thesauri were compiled by the schools taking part in the Schools Council Resource Centre project carried out at the London Institute of Education Library (Beswick, 1975 BACKGROUND READING). The well-known *Thesaurus of English Words and Phrases* by Peter Mark Roget consists of terms arranged and classified into a set of categories based on abstract notions like Existence, Quantity, Form, Matter, Intellect; these are followed by an alphabetical index which, like that of DC, brings together under each word references to all the different contexts in which that word may be used.

Most modern thesauri, however, began in the American tradition as alphabetical lists with little or no category structure. But they did set out to refine the structure of cross-references beyond the simple "see" and "see also" references. There are some variations, but most have adopted the following set of conventional symbols:

(Term Heading)

SN	Scope note	This is used where the term heading is not self-explanatory, as a definition of the term's meaning in this context.
USE		Reference from a term not used to its synonym, which should always be used for both terms. Equivalent to "see" reference.
UF	Use for	The reciprocal of USE.
BT	Broader term	Reference to the next more general heading.
NT	Narrower term	Reference to more specific heading(s).
RT	Related term	Reference to other headings, not BT or NT, under which relevant entries may also occur.

BT, NT, and RT are more clearly distinct types of "see also" reference, and if one term is listed as NT under another term, the latter should also be listed as BT under the former.

In education, the LEC provided the first faceted structure, similar to Roget. Another similar set was also used by Barhydt and Schmidt (1968 FURTHER DETAIL) in their *Information Retrieval Thesaurus of Education Terms,* which was intended to be used in the Educational Resources Information Center of the U.S. Office of Education, known as ERIC or ERIST, a number of "centers of excellence" given the responsibility for indexing and abstracting the current literature of their fields. That thesaurus was not used; instead, another first draft was produced as an alphabetical list. Subsequent editions, nine so far, have progressively introduced categories called "Descriptor Groups". These have no apparent logic of selection or structure, and lack both clarity and consistency, which makes the ERIC *Thesaurus* (1982) difficult to use with confidence. The sets of terms under such headings as "Ability" or "Cultural" defy analysis, and the vast proliferation of entry headings in the ERIC indexes testifies to the excessive reliance on the computer which serves to excuse the haphazard selection of terms for entry into the thesaurus.

The fact is that any set of words not based on some systematic structure is bound to be haphazard, since we think in terms of structure and not in terms of alphabetical order. The second edition of the LEC demonstrates how to compile a thesaurus using a faceted classification as the foundation. Because the logic of the subject is built into the facet structure, it automatically becomes reflected in the alphabetical array of terms, and the process of construction is extremely simple (Foskett, 1973 THEORY). In a faceted classification, the choice of terms for each facet is straight-forward, because once we have chosen facets called "Educand," "Curriculum," and so on, the enumeration of terms in the facet follows readily enough, since we are concentrating our minds on this particular aspect of our subject. The USE/UF combination and the BT/NT combinations are drawn from the same section of the classified schedule; but RT need not be confined to the one schedule, and may well be drawn from several other facets according to how terms appear related in the literature to be classified.

In LEC, educational technology is treated as a separate heading at the end of the "Teaching methods" facet, because this is a developing area of knowledge, and it would not be correct to confine its meaning to audio and visual materials, as in DC. The thesaurus entry reads as follows:

Educational Technology		Lvb
SN	Systems approach to the teaching process	
BT	Teaching	
RT	Audiovisual aid	
	Broadcasting and television	
	Teaching aid	
	Teaching machine	

If we now turn to the symbol Lvb in the classified section, we find the term "Educational Technology" at the end of the facet, of which the subsections are clearly defined by cross-headings such as "Teaching Methods Identified by Name of Innovator" (for example, "Pestalozzian," "Montessori"), "Aids provided by Mass Media," "Aids for Self-Instruction," among others. The schedule under "Aids provided by Mass Media" includes

Lop	Film, Cinema
Loq	Filmstrip
Lor	Broadcasting and Television
Los	Radio
Lot	Television
Lou	Electronic video recording
Lov	Closed-circuit television

Thesaurus entries can be easily made from such an array, because the indentation of the schedule displays those terms which are in genus-species relation to each other, those which are coordinate species of the same genus, and those which are synonyms.

Film		Lop
SN	As teaching aid	
UF	Cinema	
BT	Teaching aids	
NT	Filmstrip	
RT	Projector	

Television		Lot
BT	Broadcasting and television	
NT	Closed-circuit television	
	Electronic video recording	
RT	Film	
	Radio	
	Records and recording	

Thus not only does a thesaurus based on a classification scheme display a systematic structure, but the two in combination provide a guide for users in both indexing documents and searching for information. Whichever word a user chooses to begin a search, the thesaurus should lead to the correct facet in the schedules; there, that entire area of the subject is laid out in a sequence which makes sense. The user quickly comes to understand the system and so can learn to use it easily and effectively.

This technique has been adopted by Jean Aitchison (1977 FURTHER DETAIL) in her *UNESCO Thesaurus*, which borrows much of its material from Bliss and LEC; it has a similar structure, illustrated by the following:

J	EDUCATION
J10	Educational philosophy, policy and development
J20	Educational planning and administration
J45	Educational psychology
J55	Teaching materials and equipment
J60	Curriculum
J60.10/99	Curriculum subjects
J70	Educational systems and institutions
J70.07	Schools
J90	Students

There has, indeed, been a great deal of activity in thesaurus-making in Europe. UNESCO's International Bureau of Education (1973 FURTHER DETAIL) produced its own scheme early on, and the Council of Europe has brought out several versions of its multilingual thesaurus for its project EUDISED (Viet, 1974 FURTHER DETAIL). For several years, this thesaurus followed LEC main structure of facets, with alphabetical subdivision within facets, but a retrograde step appears to have been taken lately. Another working group, latest in a long series, is undertaking a revision of the structure, and the first fruit is a computer-printed *Alphabetical List of Descriptors* (Council of Europe, 1982 FURTHER DETAIL). A useful, though somewhat superficial, comparative study of thesauri has also been published by the Council of Europe (Pennells, 1983 SIMILAR RESEARCH), in pursuit of "a multilingual terminology data base for education."

DOCUMENTATION IN EDUCATION

The advent of computers made possible the storing in small spaces of very large quantities of data, and ready access can be provided by indexing these data with an efficient thesaurus. Of course, this is only part of the retrieval story: the next step is to supply the documents found in a search. Many document supply systems have sprung up round the world; in Britain, the British Library Document Supply Centre is the center for the project known as Universal Availability of Publications. Both the United States and the USSR have set up systems at the national level, with some significant differences. As might be expected, more control and authority is vested in central bodies in the USSR than is found in Washington at the headquarters of ERIC at the National Institute of Education. The Soviet Academy of Pedagogical Sciences has a Central Research Institute of General Pedagogy, which exercises control of documentation through its Department of Scientific and Pedagogical Information, DSPI.

The function of ERIC is to provide a bibliographical resource in machine-readable form, covering published and unpublished (report type, or "gray") documents. The two major indexes are *Current Index to Journals in Education* (CIJE) and *Resources in Education* (RIE). Another useful tool, *Current Contents,* is produced by the Institute for Scientific Information in Philadelphia, which also publishes *Social Science Citation Index,* a very detailed and intricate guide to a large range of journals, including some important journals in education.

In the United Kingdom, the Librarians of Institutes and Schools of Education (LISE) formed a voluntary association to promote interinstitute cooperation. This has taken many forms over the years, including a union catalog of books and journals, union lists of holdings on foreign countries, and an extensive interlibrary lending scheme. For many years, these librarians cooperated to publish the *British Education Index,* which provides an easily used record of the British journal literature for over 30 years. BEI has now become the responsibility of Leeds University and is computer-produced using a thesaurus of educational terms now being constructed with the aid of a grant from the Leverhulme Trust.

Centralization of documentation activities has been most complete in the socialist countries, beginning with the Soviet VINITI early in the 1950s. The DSPI stands at the head of a nationwide system, with regional subsystems in the several republics, and the Ushinsky Library of Pedagogical Sciences in Moscow is at the head of a parallel network of libraries. The DSPI is very active in the collection and processing of data, as well as carrying out research on techniques of abstracting, indexing, and dissemination. It forms direct relations with authors, encouraging them to make abstracts and reviews of their own work and giving them guidance on selection of descriptors and the compiling of abstracts.

This example has been followed by other socialist countries. Some, like the German Democratic Republic, have systems based on an academy of pedagogical sciences; others, like Czechoslovakia, within the Ministry of Education. The Institute of Educational Information in Prague has sponsored a series of international conferences, known as EDICO, with the cooperation of UNESCO and attended by representatives from most of the countries of Europe. The latest took place in Prague in 1980 (EDICO-3, 1980 BACKGROUND READING).

The pattern is by no means confined to socialist countries. The Institut National pour la Recherche et Documentation Pédagogiques in Paris now has similar functions, and they also figure in the programs of the International Bureau of Education in Geneva. These are based on "centralized decentralization"; the initial unit is a national center or network, linked to regional centers which help to organize and coordinate the work of the national bodies. One of these, the European Documentation and Information System for Education (EUDISED), covers the countries of the Council of Europe. This has published several technical studies, surveys of national educational research, and two important instruments for computerized indexing and retrieval: the multilingual thesaurus and a set of standards for bibliographical formats.

The present stage of EUDISED consists of applying these two instruments to indexing research projects, usually in machine-readable form. A regular *EUDISED R & D Bulletin* contains abstracts of research projects submitted through the national cooperating institutions; the projects are grouped and cross-referenced according to the facets and subfacets of the EUDISED thesaurus, with author and subject descriptor indexes. In the United Kingdom, the National Foundation for Educational Research (NFER), the Scottish Council for Research in Education, and the Northern Ireland Council for Educational Research all cooperate in the project, and the NFER has published four large volumes of the *Register of Educational Research in the United Kingdom* (NFER, 1976 FURTHER DETAIL). This *Register* contains abstracts of research work sent in by members of universities, colleges, local education authorities, and individual persons and institutions. The abstracts are arranged in order of institutions, with an author and a very detailed subject index based on an updated version of the LEC.

CONCLUSION

Information classification and retrieval systems in education require efficient techniques soundly based on the logic of the subject and the ways in which specialists approach their subjects, plus a network of libraries and documentation centers which can rapidly supply the documents which the inquirers identify from the indexes as relevant to their work. Some have considered that the techniques of facet analysis and thesaurus construction go to extreme lengths in their complexity, but it must be remembered that education itself, as a subject, has almost infinite ramifications, as shown by the NFER *Register*. It is highly desirable that the results of research should be widely disseminated, on an international level, and therefore the tools for classifying and indexing are bound to be complex themselves. Like all tools of high quality, however, once understood they are simple to use and produce high-quality results.

D. J. Foskett

REFERENCES

Background Reading

Beswick, N. W. (1975) *Organising Resources*. London: Heinemann.
Bruner, J. S. (1960) *The Process of Education*. New York: Vintage Books.
EDICO-3. (1980) *The Establishment of Information Systems for the Use of Educational Systems*. Prague: Institute of Educational Information.
Joynson, R. B. (1974) *Psychology and Common Sense*. London: Routledge and Kegan Paul.
Luria, A. R. (1979) *The Making of Mind*. Cambridge, Mass.: Harvard University Press.
Ranganathan, S. R. (1973) *New Education and School Library*. Delhi: Vikas Publishing House.

Further Detail

Aitchison, J. (1977) *UNESCO Thesaurus: A Structured List of Descriptors for Indexing and Retrieving Literature in the Fields of Education, Science, Social Science, Culture and Communication*.Paris: UNESCO.
Barhydt, C. C. and Schmidt, C. T. (1968) *Information Retrieval Thesaurus of Education Terms*. Cleveland: Case Western Reserve University.
Bliss, H. E. (1976 onwards) *A System of Bibliographic Classification*. London: Butterworths.
Council of Europe. (1982) *EUDISED Multilingual Thesaurus 1982: Alphabetical List of Descriptors*. Strasbourg:, Council of Europe.
Dewey, M. (1979) *Decimal Classification*. 19th ed. Lake Placid, N.Y: Forest Press.
ERIC. (1982) *Thesaurus of ERIC Descriptors*. 9th ed. New York: CCM Information Corporation.
Fédération Internationale de Documentation. (1965) *Universal Decimal Classification: Special Edition for Education (FID 374)*. The Hague: FID.
Foskett, D. J. and Foskett, J. A. (1974) *The London Education Classification*. 2d ed. University of London Institute of Education Library.
Mills, J. and Broughton, V. (1977) *Bliss Bibliographic Classification: 2 e Class J Education*. London: Butterworths.
NFER. (1976 onwards) *Register of Educational Research in the United Kingdom*, Vols. 1 to 4. Windsor: NFER*Nelson.
Ranganathan, S. R. (1960) *Colon Classification*. 6th ed. London: Asia Publishing House.
UNESCO: IBE. (1973) *The UNESCO: IBE Education Thesaurus*. Paris and Geneva: UNESCO, IBE.
Viet, J. (1974) *EUDISED Multilingual Thesaurus for Information Processing in the Field of Education*. Paris: Mouton.

Historical

Furst, E. J. (1981) "Bloom's *Taxonomy of Educational Objectives for the Cognitive Domain:* Philosophical and Educational Issues." *Review of Educational Research* 51 (4): 441–453.
Mathies, L. M. and Watson, P. (1973) *Computer-based Reference Service*. Chicago: American Library Association.

Similar Research

Lauer, P. A. and Baltig, W. F. (1972) "Free Recall of Taxonomically and Alphabetically Organized Word Lists as a Function of Storage and Retrieval Cues." *Journal of Verbal Learning and Verbal Behavior* 11: 333–342.
Pennells, D. L. (1983) *An Investigation into the Feasibility of Establishing a Multilingual Terminology Data Base for Education*, DECS/Doc (83) 12. Strasbourg: Council of Europe.
Rescorla, L. A. (1981) "Category Development in Early Language." *Journal of Child Language* 8 (2): 225–238.

Theory

Bernstein, B. B. (1971) "On the Classification and Framing of Educational Knowledge." In *Knowledge and Control*, ed. M.F.D. Young. London: Collier-Macmillan.
Bloom, B. S. et al. (1956, 1964) *Taxonomy of Educational Objectives*. 2 vols. London: Longmans.
Foskett, D. J. (1973) *A Study of the Role of Categories in a Thesaurus for Educational Documentation*, DECS/Doc (73) 8. Strasbourg: Council of Europe.
Guilford, J. P. (1968) *Intelligence, Creativity and their Educational Implications*. San Diego, Calif.: Robert R. Knapp.
Hirst, P. H. (1966) "Educational Theory." In *The Study of Education*, ed. J. W. Tibble. London: Routledge and Kegan Paul.
Inhelder, B. and Piaget, J. (1964) *The Early Growth of Logic in the Child*. London: Routledge and Kegan Paul.

INFORMATION EXPLOSION. A term used to denote the unprecedented rapid increase in knowledge that has taken place in the second half of the twentieth century and the consequent problems of information exchange, storage, and retrieval.

INFORMATION MAPPING. A system for improving the layout of information in a book. The procedures are designed to assist information retrieval, reduction of reading material, and the logical development of information in texts. The method may be applied to the production of self-instructional books or even the organization of CAI. The principal unit of writing is the information block, replacing the paragraph in a textbook. It has the following features:

1. Information is presented in blocks.
2. Labels identify the type of information in a block (Introduction, Procedure, etc.).
3. Functional and uniform headings allow for easy scanning of the text.
4. Indices at the foot of maps provide page numbers for guide location of selected topics.

INFORMATION OWNER. Information provider (videotex).

INFORMATION PROVIDER (INPUT PROVIDER). A person or agency which supplies material for the U.K. Prestel videotex system. IPs may be commercial data sources (e.g., travel agents), educational institutions, etc.

INFORMATION SYSTEMS FOR EDUCATION. Educators who require information to meet a variety of needs use a variety of information systems. Even though individuals often create their own files and establish personal contacts to meet local needs, more comprehensive information systems offer extended opportunities to acquire new facts and opinions.

In the field of educational technology, a professional would likely have access to this encyclopaedia, the *Educational Media and Technology Yearbook* (Ely et al., 1988 BACKGROUND READING) and the *International Yearbook of Educational and Instructional Technology* (Osborne, 1986 BACKGROUND READING) as comprehensive and specialized sourcebooks.

In the field of education, information systems are larger, more sophisticated, and more comprehensive than one or two published references. There are three established information systems in education which serve the profession. Their scopes include educational technology but are broader than this one specialized field. The systems include (1) Documentation Centre, International Bureau of Education; (2) Educational Resources Information Center (ERIC); and (3) European Documentation and Information System for Education (EUDISED). Other information systems in education exist but are usually limited to one country or region. Each of the three discussed here are international and serve educators worldwide.

ELEMENTS OF INFORMATION SYSTEMS

Each of the three systems has several common elements: (1) information is collected from a variety of sources; (2) information is reviewed to determine its suitability for the system; (3) bibliographic data and abstracts are prepared; (4) controlled vocabulary is used; (5) publications are announced to subscribers; and (6) information analysis publications are written and distributed.

ACCESS TO THE SYSTEMS

Individuals who use the systems usually go to libraries that subscribe to information services. Libraries and other information centers often use computer-based searching to gain access to each system (Ely, 1983 FURTHER DETAIL). Specific aspects of each system are outlined below.

IBE Documentation Centre. Located in Geneva, Switzerland, IBE Documentation Centre operates two programs; the International Network for Educational Information (INED) and the International Educational Reporting Service (IERS). INED includes more than 11,500 specialists and some 1,200 institutions throughout the world and provides them with bibliographic abstracts on innovations in education with special supplements focusing on lifelong learning and educational technology. IBE's data bases, IBEDOC and IBECENT, use English, French, and Spanish key words for indexing, recording, and retrieving data and are published in the *UNESCO IBE Education Thesaurus*. IBEDOC contains bibliographic data and abstracts on lifelong education and documentation of the International Conference on Education. IBECENT contains institutional data on national, regional, and international centers of educational documentation, information, adult education, and research. In order to facilitate cross-cultural research and development, IBE also publishes multilingual glossaries of terms.

Educational Resources Information Center (ERIC). Based in the United States, ERIC consists of a central office, which establishes policy and monitors the system; sixteen subject-oriented clearinghouses, which acquire and analyze the educational literature; a central editorial and computer facility, which maintains the data base and prepares the abstract journal *Resources in Education;* a central document reproduction service, which prepares microfiche and paper reproductions; and a commercial organization which publishes *Current Index to Journals in Education* and the ERIC *Thesaurus*.

ERIC indexes and abstracts educational documents that are not usually available from commercial sources such as research and technical reports, monographs, speeches, curriculum materials, conference papers, statistical compilations, and other literature which does not get into the mainstream of education. ERIC also indexes over 750 journals in education. The *Thesaurus of ERIC Descriptors* (10th ed., 1986) contains 9,288 terms. The data base of educational documents and journal citations from 1966 to 1986 contains over 600,000 citations. The ERIC Clearinghouse on Information Resources at Syracuse University specializes in educational technology, and library and information science.

European Documentation and Information System for Education (EUDISED). Located in Strasbourg, France, EUDISED publishes abstracts of educational research and development which is either in progress or recently completed. The fourteen member states, Greece, and Portugal, supply information which meets predetermined selection criteria. The information abstract is published in the *EUDISED R & D Bulletin,* which is distributed to more than 400 subscribers in 33 countries. The published abstracts comprise the EUDISED data base, which numbered over 2,000 items in 1980. The latest revision of the multilingual thesaurus (Dutch, English, French, German, and Spanish) was published in 1982.

D. Ely

REFERENCES

Background Reading

Ely, D. P., Wood, R. K., and Broadbent, B.B. (1988) *Educational Media and Technology Yearbook 1988.* Littleton, Col.: Libraries Unlimited.

Osborne, C. W., ed. (1986) *International Yearbook of Educational and Instructional Technology 1986/87.* London: Kogan Page.

Further Detail

Ely, D. P. (1983) "Computers and the Handling of Information." In *Computers and Education,* ed. J. Megarry et al. London: Kogan Page.

Documentation Centre, International Bureau of Education, Route des Morillons, 1218 Grand-Sacconnex, Geneva, Switzerland.

ERIC Processing and Reference Facility, 4833 Rugby Avenue, Suite 303, Bethesda, MD 20014 U.S.

ERIC Clearinghouse on Information Resources, School of Education, Syracuse University, Syracuse, NY 13244-2340 U.S.

EUDISED, Council of Europe, Documentation Center For Education in Europe, BP 431 1R6, F 67006 Strasbourg, France.

INFORMATION TECHNOLOGY.

TECHNOLOGY AND INFORMATION

Information technology is the technology for storing, transferring, or processing information. Information may be defined as one or more pieces of idea or perception. Technology may be defined as the means by which a person, organization, or society does things.

Information and technology can each range from being very simple to very complex. Examples of information technology, in rough historical progression, are gestures, grunts, speech, drawings, symbols, writing, printing, telegraphy, photography, telephony, radio, moving pictures, sound recording, television, and computers. This list omits the development of mathematics and music and nonhuman information.

Information can be classified in many ways, a fair coverage being

—Form of expression (e.g., words, pictures)
—Manner of representation (e.g., writing, oral speech, recorded speech)
—Technology of representation (e.g., ink on paper, magnetic tape in a word processor)
—Quantity (e.g., number of words, number of ideas, number of bits)
—Coherence (e.g., raw data, conclusions)
—Acceptance (e.g., believed, doubted—"error-free" or "corrupt")
—Precision (e.g., exact approximate)
—Process (e.g., stored, being transmitted)
—Permanence (e.g., recorded, transient)
—Use (e.g., entertainment, action-oriented)
—Participants (e.g., private, broadcast)
—Presentation (e.g., structured, unstructured)

There is always an interaction between the technology and each of these distinctions. However, there is usually an element of subjectivity in the classification of information.

In a similar manner, technologies can be classified in many ways, a fair coverage being

—Complexity (e.g., simple, complex)
—Scientific basis (e.g., electronics, optical)
—Physical size (e.g., nationwide system, discrete device)
—Process (e.g., storage, transmission)
—Capacity (e.g., large quantity of information, small quantity)
—Permanence (e.g., record, transient)
—System type (e.g., wires, radio)
—Configuration (e.g., switched, broadcast)
—Mode of representation (e.g., analog, digital)
—Type of information (e.g., words, pictures)
—Fidelity (e.g., exact, approximate)
—Robustness (e.g., resistant to interruption and interference, susceptible)
—Ease of use (e.g., requires skill and training, "even a child can do it")
—Method of control (e.g., automatic, requires manipulation)

There is always an interaction between the information and each of these distinctions, as can be seen by the appearance of similar pairs of examples in the two lists. When choosing a technology for a particular purpose, it may be worthwhile to use these two lists to make a checklist of the characteristics needed in the particular applications.

It is often easy to ignore the meaning of information when considering the technology. Expressions of truth or falsehood are equally well conveyed over the telephone. Love songs are no more easily borne over the air waves than propaganda of hate; and the computer just as readily calculates a loss as a profit. However, the particular technology employed does appreciably impact on the meaning that is meant to be conveyed.

While information that is stored, transferred, or received is always only a selection of what was available, the particular technology employed plays its characteristic role in the selection. This role is often unnoticed, especially with technologies that we are very familiar with. This and other aspects of the interaction between technology and meaning are discussed below in the section Technology and Understanding.

FUNCTIONS OF INFORMATION TECHNOLOGY

Information technology performs one of three functions, namely, storage, transfer, or processing, or a combination of them. Obviously there are overlaps between the functions. A store of information is useless if it does not contain the means of transferring. Indeed, it would be impossible to recognize a store that was unable to transfer. Similarly, transferring must involve some processing, in order for the information to be identified.

There are subdivisions of two of the functions. Transferring can be "active," i.e., a receiver of the information actively seeks it out, or "accesses" the information from the store. Also, it can be "passive," in which case the receiver needs to take action not to receive it, for example, the unduly loud music next door.

CURRENT TECHNOLOGIES

Physical Content of Different Forms of Information. Information technologies need to be able to represent the forms in which information is produced or accepted by human beings. These are as follows:

Writing	Symbols in a complex sequence.
Numerals	Symbols, such that a distinguishable symbol or sequence of symbols exists for every conceivable (or allowable) rational number. The representation of numerals is not a subset of symbols for writing speech, but an intersecting set. It has some additional characteristics required for computation.
Speech (and other sounds)	Mechanical vibrations, which contain a highly complex combination of three characteristics, namely; strength (or volume or amplitude); frequency (i.e., number of vibrations per second); crude directionality, based on the human process of binaural perception.
Pictures	Light, i.e., electromagnetic vibrations, arranged in a very complex manner with respect to three characteristics, namely; strength (i.e., brightness or darkness); frequency, or, more subjectively color; an extremely precise directionality (resolution).
Three-Dimensional "Pictures"	Essentially an extension of pictorial representation to satisfy the human binocular process of three-dimensional perception.
Moving Pictures	A succession of still pictures with the rapidity of succession being sufficient to induce a perception of smooth motion. Each successive picture must appear and disappear, rather than move into and out of view.
Other	Smoke signals, tom-toms, semaphore, heliograph, flag signals, messages from outer space, and augury almost fit into one or more of the above, but are not considered further here.

Technologies for Writing. Technologies for writing must satisfy two requirements; the presentation of distinguishable characters and the preservation of a given sequence of characters. The characters must be distinguishable not only from each other but also from extraneous "noise." Writing is itself a technology, in the broadest sense of that word, and has the following characteristics: sequential, i.e., one idea at a time; randomly accessible, i.e., possible to select any piece of information without starting at the beginning and going through each element in sequence. The technologies used are books, microfiche, magnetic tape and disk, and microelectronics (including optoelectronics).

Analog and Digital. The terms *analog* and *digital* refer to ways of representing quantities, in particular quantities that are continuously changing. As an example, consider sound vibrations in air. At a particular point, the pressure of the air is continuously increasing and decreasing at a very rapid rate. For example, a pure middle C would cause an increase from "normal" pressure to some maximum value, followed by a decrease to and below the normal value, and back to normal again at a rate of about 260 times a second. This is often shown in diagrams as a sine wave, with the horizontal axis representing time and the vertical axis representing pressure.

Such a diagram is occasionally seen displayed on video screens in demonstrations, and for speech sounds presents an extremely jagged pattern. There is a continuously variable range of values in this pattern. A pictorial representation such as this is an analog representation. If this wave were "frozen," a copy of it could be drawn by placing a grid of squares over it and marking where the wave crossed the squares. A digital representation could be obtained by quoting in sequence the height of each square crossed. The faithfulness of the digital representation would depend upon the fineness of the grid. A coarser grid would give a representation with less information content, perhaps insufficient for the speech to be intelligible.

To compare analog and digital, consider the magnetic tape on which the sound is recorded. If it is an analog recording, there will be a continuously changing amount of magnetization at each point bearing a direct relationship to the corresponding amount of sound pressure. If, for example, the sounds were sampled 8,000 times a second, then there would have to be 8,000 symbols stored in the length of tape that passes the pickup head in one second, if it were a digital recording.

Technologies for Numerals, and Binary Codes. Although numerals are symbols, and are often given the same form of representation as letters of the alphabet, they have an additional requirement: they need to be capable of processing for computation. There are no rules for performing arithmetical functions on letters of the alphabet, unless they are used as numerals, in which case they are no longer representations of speech.

Numerals on paper are expressed in Arabic, Roman, Chinese, or other similar notation that contains systematic rules for performing arithmetic functions. Computers, being currently based on two-state technology, can recognize only two symbols, 1 and 0. From these symbols is built the system of binary notation, in which:

$1 + 1 = 10$

$1 + 10 = 11$

$1 + 11 = 100$, etc.

A little experimentation will show that 7 is 111 in binary.

Binary notation can be tedious for human manipulation. Thus 256 (= 2^8) is 100000000 in binary, i.e., 1 followed by eight zeros, and 511 (= $2^9 - 1$) is 111111111 in binary. To make the handling easier we often use octal notation, i.e., after 7 the next number is expressed as 10. Thus, by dividing the binary for 511 into three segments,

511 (decimal) = 777 (octal)

Similarly a hexadecimal notation is also used, based on segments of 1111 (binary) which = 16 (decimal).

The digits 1 and 0 are called *binary digits*. The smallest piece of information that can be represented is one binary digit. This is like a guessing game where the only answers allowed are "yes" and "no." One bit of information is defined as the information content of one binary digit.

Computers are able to perform arithmetic functions on numerals in binary form. They are also able to recognize patterns of 1s and 0s, and to count the number of bits received or handled.

Information theory provides a way of treating written or spoken language as a series of bits of information, and of measuring the content in bits. The number of bits is usually so great that larger units are used. A kilobit (k bit) is one thousand bits (or often $1024 = 2^{10}$ bits). Similarly, one million bits = one megabit (M bit), one thousand million bits = 1 gigabit (G bit).

Bits are often grouped into sequences of eight or nine, for example, to represent the characters of a typewriter or computer keyboard (with a few extra bits thrown in for error detection, etc.). Such a group is called a *byte*. Accordingly, we have kilobytes, megabytes, and gigabytes.

Information theory provides a way of measuring the information content of a particular sample. It looks at a language as if it is an instrument for handling information, without considering the meaning of the content. As an example, the written word *cat* in English contains three symbols presented in a given order.

The total range of symbols from which these three are selected is 26 (or greater number if the set contains capital and small letters, numerals, punctuation marks, etc.). To store or transmit the written word *cat* it is necessary to identify their order, i.e., not *act*. The minimum number of elements of information measured in "bits" required for this complete identification is about fifteen, five for each character. It is necessary, of course, that the receiver already have the required information to understand the particular language employed. A teleprinter machine (which transmits bits of information as either the presence or absence of a pulse of electricity) would send or receive fifteen bits to represent the word *cat*. However, to represent the sound of the spoken word *cat* would need many more bits, depending on the required clarity of the speech, whether intonation was to be expressed, and whether any identifiable characteristics of the individual speaker were to be retained. To transmit the spoken word *cat* by telephone or to record it would require at least a few hundred bits of information. In practice, because of redundancies in speech sounds, more than a thousand bits would usually be used.

If a series of five binary digits (which gives 32 possible sequences) can represent the letters of the alphabet, a series of seven (128 sequences) can represent all the letters, uppercase and lowercase, the numerals 0 to 9, with accommodation for punctuation marks, mathematical symbols, etc. International codes have been developed for use in telex transmission and computing, based on a series of bits. Additional bits may be added for various purposes such as error detection and "start of character," etc. Some well-known codes or "alphabets" are **ASCII** (q.v.) (American Standard Code for Information Interchange), the Teletype code, and the baudot code. Computers are programmed to recognize the patterns of bits for each character and to respond by, for example, printing the character in roman type or converting it into the binary equivalent of the numeral represented, for the purpose of computation.

When text is stored in magnetic or microelectronic form, a convenient technique is to employ an appropriate binary code. In fact these media can store text and numeric data with equal ease. Moreover, if speech or other sound (and indeed, video) is presented in digital form, the quantities can be expressed in binary form, i.e., as a series of bits. This is the principle of **pulse code modulation** (q.v.) (PCM). Storage media for sound or video are used also for text, and a single device, e.g., a disk, can contain the equivalent of thousands of pages of print.

Technologies for Storing Speech and Other Sounds. Sound is by its very nature nonpermanent. That is, it consists of vibrations, which are continuous changes in the mechanical condition of the material that is carrying it. The vibrations can be represented, for storage, by any permanent medium that varies in accordance with the sound vibrations. Thus the amount of blackening along the transparent edge of a movie film, or the strength of magnetization along the length of a cassette tape or the depth of indentation in the groove on the surface of a disk record, can be varied in such a way that a sensing device can re-create the original sound, to a greater or lesser degree of fidelity.

Any sound can be analyzed into a combination of "pure tones" or "sine waves". Each tone may vary in strength, both absolutely and with respect to the other tones, and this variation usually occurs very rapidly. It is the changes, in fact, that convey most of the information. In speech, the different speech sound elements, or "phonemes," are produced by different combination of tones (timbre), different overall perceived frequency of the tones (pitch and intonation), differences in volume of the sound (stress), and sudden starts and stopping of the sound (plosives and stops).

The human ear can hear sounds in the frequency range of from about 20Hz (i.e., about 20 vibrations per second) to about 20kHz (i.e., about 20,000 vibrations per second), the range decreasing at both the high and low ends as the person gets older.

For good reproduction of music, a frequency range of at least 50Hz to 15kHz is generally regarded as necessary, and a "dynamic range," i.e., the difference between softest and loudest sounds of at least 40db. For intelligible speech a frequency range of about 500Hz to 1kHz is adequate, depending on the nature of the voice, and for telephonic communication there is an international standard of 300Hz to 3.6kHz, which gives intelligibility and recognition of the voice. There is therefore no point in insisting on a hi-fi recording of the voice that provides the telephone service that tells you the time. Each storage medium must be capable of meeting the required degree of fidelity for its application, but in most cases higher fidelity means higher cost. The main technologies used for storage sound are shaped grooves in disks, for either mechanical or optical reading; magnetic tape and magnetic disk; and microelectronics.

There are techniques employing the incorporation of sound in the rim of movie film. Systems such as player piano rolls and music boxes are mechanically coded systems, not stores of sound as such.

Decibels. In discussions of sound (or noise) and of radio and telephone transmission, the term *decibel*, or db, is used in describing the power level of sound, or radio wave, electric wave, or optical signal. A decibel is one tenth of a bel. A bel is a ratio of ten to one between two power levels. A wave whose power level is 10 watts is 1 bel or 10db above a wave of 1 watt. Similarly, a wave of 5,000 watts is 10db above a wave of 500 watts. A wave of 5,000 watts is also 20db above one of 50 watts and 30db above one of 5 watts, and so on. That is, the scale is logarithmic. A power ratio of two to one is very close to 3db, and twenty to one to 13db.

Technologies for Storing Pictures, Including Three-Dimensional Pictures. The technologies for storing still pictures are very well-known. Pictures can be drawn, printed, or photographed using the same methods as for writing.

Three-dimensional or stereoscopic pictures consist of pairs of pictures of the same subject such that each represents what would be seen separately by each eye of the person viewing the subject. The pair of pictures is presented to the viewer so that the left eye sees only the "left eye view" and the right eye only the "right eye view." This presents a three-dimensional appearance to people with stereoscopic vision.

Technologies for Storing Moving Pictures. Because the representation of motion is by a rapid succession of stills, the associated equipment must be capable of presenting each successive picture, holding it motionless during the time it is visible, presenting "nothing" during the changeover to the next picture, and so on *(see* **Movie***)*. Television is less simple. There are

—two media: videotape and videodisc

—two standard sizes of videotape (in cassettes), and two types of videodisc

—differences in the number of frames per second and lines per frame in the standards employed by different countries -three standard ways of adding the color signal onto the basic information of the monochrome picture.

Just as a magnetic tape for sound recording is produced by converting the sound to its electrical representation, which is then used to magnetize the tape, so a television recording on videotape is produced by an electrical representation of the picture, and the tapes are technically very similar.

Television pictures are built up as a series of lines from top to bottom of the picture and slope down slightly from the left-hand side. The camera sweeps across the scene, recording the line as a series of blobs of varying degrees of light and dark, then switches off until it returns to the left-hand side for the next line, and so on to the bottom. It then repeats the procedure but the second set of lines interleaves the first. The common standard numbers of lines per picture are 525 and 625.

The degree of detail that can be obtained in a standard television picture is not determined by the size of the screen. In the vertical direction, the fineness of detail is limited by the number of lines per picture. In the horizontal direction, the number of discernible "dots" is limited by the number of cycles of electrical or magnetic energy that can be fitted into a line.

This is determined by the time allowed for each line and the limitations placed on the frequency band of the resultant video signal. Since this frequency is about 6MHz, the horizontal resolution works out to about the same as the vertical, when allowance is made for the *aspect ratio* (q.v.) of the picture (i.e., width to height), and extra control information such as that needed to keep the picture in synchronism. The accompanying sound recording and the three colors of a color picture are also included in the same band of frequencies, and all recorded as a single track on the tape or disk.

Videodiscs (which are similar to the smaller "compact disks" used in sound recording) operate by the deflection of a laser light beam from a shiny metal (aluminum) surface. The degree of deflection is determined by the shape of the metal surface. The metal surface of the disk is recorded as a track, as with a gramophone disk, but the playing head, which consists of a laser and a light-sensing device, can move over the radius of the disk to precisely determined locations as the disk spins at high speed. It is therefore possible to read from a programmed series of locations on the disk, as with a hard magnetic disk in a computer. It is also possible to read the same piece of track continually, thus producing a still as well as a moving picture. The playing machines contain microprocessors, and so allow the presentation of different programs consisting of movies, stills, and voice from the one disk.

The disks are recorded on both sides, and each side can contain up to 60 minutes of movie film. The disks are about 350mm in diameter. The metal surface is covered with a protective coating of clear plastic, which makes the disk fairly robust. It can be played without damage or appreciable distortion and will usually not break or be damaged if dropped. The disks must be factory-produced, and are copied from videotape.

TRANSMISSION OF INFORMATION

Apart from the physical transporting of books, films, tapes, etc., the transmission of information is by telecommunications, which involves the conversion of the information into some electrical form, and transmitting it by wire, radio, or optical fiber. This involves conversion either direct from the source or from a storage medium. The conversion for transmission is essentially the same as conversion for storage.

As well as the type of information transmitted there are other factors that affect the type of transmission technology used:

—amount of rate of information (e.g., a telex message is transmitted at 50 to 300 bits per second, a television program at 6 to 7 megahertz, or if in digital form, about 140 megabits per second)

—allowable technical impairment (e.g., incorrect letters or figures in a telex message, noise or muffled sound in a telephone call, or distortion patterns in a television picture)

—distance and terrain

—stationary or mobile senders and/or receivers
—broadcast or transmission only between selected persons or points
—one-way, two-way, multiway (conferences)
—security from disruption and/or overhearing

Transmission technology contains three elements, namely, the transmission medium and the sending and receiving equipment.

Radio. Radio transmission is used at an enormous range of frequencies, from a few thousand hertz up to tens of billions of hertz. Below 300kHz, only special applications, notably military, are employed. For convenience of description the radio frequency spectrum is divided into bands, each band being ten times the frequency of the one below it, and each having a somewhat typical set of characteristics.

Medium Frequency or Medium Wave (300kHz to 3MHz). Typically used for broadcasting of sound (but not FM). The wave travels along and around the surface of the earth, particularly at the lower frequencies, and also through the air, being reflected from the ionosphere, particularly at the higher frequencies. The ground wave and the reflected sky wave interact, limiting the useful range of distance.

High Frequency (HF) or Short Wave (3MHz to 30 MHz). Typically used for long-distance broadcasting of sound and telephonic communications to sparsely settled and remote areas. Such communications are readily able to be overheard by anyone with an HF receiver. The wave travels through the air and is reflected by the ionosphere, and the reflected wave is again reflected by the earth. It is therefore possible, and common, for HF to travel right around the earth. However, the changing characteristics of the ionosphere, diurnally, throughout the sunspot cycle and during magnetic storms, severely reduce the reliability and consistency of HF transmission.

The upper end of this band is used in some countries for short-distance citizens band (CB) radio communications, using radio hand phones, which can transmit and receive on some twenty channels. The communications can be heard and answered by anyone within the range who has a compatible CB radio set.

HF radio is used in sparsely settled areas of Australia for educational purposes, with members of a class in the School of the Air being spread over thousands of square kilometers.

Very High Frequency (VHF) (30MHz to 300MHz). Used for

—television broadcasting—each television channel occupies about 7MHz of the frequency band
—FM sound broadcasting, which is less subject to atmospheric noise—each (stereo) FM channel occupies about 30kHz of the frequency band
—mobile radio, e.g., for taxis and other vehicle fleets
—single-channel and up to six-channel point-to-point telephone systems
—networks for emergency services
—ground-to-aircraft communications

VHF propagation, particularly at the higher frequencies, is regarded as requiring a line-of-sight path between transmitter and receiver. However, at the lower frequencies the wave can "creep around corners" to some extent, and at the higher end can be reflected from significant surfaces such as large buildings, often resulting in the reception of more than one signal from the same source (hence "ghosts" on television pictures).

Ultrahigh Frequency (UHF) (300MHz to 30GHz). Used for

—UHF television broadcasting (ten times more bandwidth available, so each channel uses a smaller proportion of the UHF than of the VHF)
—low, medium, and high capacity (up to about 900 telephone channels) point-to-point telecommunications links
—mobile radio for taxis and other vehicle fleets
—radio telephone services, including mobile services connected to the public telephone network and providing individual connections
—networks for emergency services
—ground-to-aircraft communications
—links between satellites and earth stations (at the higher end of the frequency band)

UHF propagation is strictly line-of-sight, but subject to reflections, particularly from bodies of water, buildings, etc. Except where coverage of a geographical area is required, the wave is directed as a narrow beam. The radio paths need to be carefully surveyed to avoid obstructions, surfaces that could cause a reflected ray to interfere with the direct ray, and paths being directly in line with other similar transmission paths (including satellites). Long-distance radio routes are built up of individual links, each being of up to about 35km in length, with a change of frequency at each repeater.

Super High Frequency (SHF) and Extremely High Frequency (EHF). (3GHz to 30GHz and 30GHz to 300GHz). The lower end of the SHF up to about 15GHz is used for similar transmission as the upper UHF. Beyond that frequency, propagation is affected by rain, dust, and other atmospheric characteristics, each effect being of particular significance at particular ranges of frequencies.

Communication Satellites. Artificial satellites fitted with radio receivers and transmitters and power supply equipment can be used to form communication links to a large part of the earth's surface. Most such satellites are now placed in a geostationary orbit; that is, their orbit circles the equator and they travel at such a speed and direction that when seen from the earth they appear to remain in the same point in the sky. The height above the surface of the earth for such an orbit is about 36,000km, which is determined by the earth's mass and speed of rotation. In such an orbit a satellite can be seen from, and can "see" about a third of the surface of the earth, and this constitutes its maximum area of coverage using (line-of-sight) radio transmission. There are other types of satellites that circle the earth at different heights and in different directions, and relay back information detected by television cameras, for example, geographical or military information.

The function of a **communications satellite** (q.v.) is to transmit back to earth stations the information sent up from other earth stations. The transmission being from one earth station to another, the cost of transmission is independent of the terrestrial distance between them. Satellite transmission therefore has advantages over terrestrial transmission over long distances or difficult terrain.

Satellites can provide very wide distribution of television programs to low-cost receive-only earth stations, and have been used for this purpose in India to communal television sets in villages, in Canada to remote settlements, in the United States for relay to pay-TV programs on cable television networks, and in Australia to television transmitting stations serving rural townships and communities. Other uses of satellites require two-way transmission, i.e., the earth stations must both transmit and receive, which requires a much more costly installation. The cost of the earth segment of a sophisticated satellite network can be very great, and well-developed two-way terrestrial systems can often operate at lower cost for all but the longest distances.

One important characteristic of a satellite communication is the time it takes the radio wave to travel from earth to satellite and back to earth—about a quarter of a second. This means that in a conversation a reply is delayed by half a second. In what would be the extreme case, an international connection with a satellite employed in each of the national systems and also in the international link, this would add up to one and a half seconds. The delay is of no consequence in any form of broadcasting. It has some effect, which can be compensated for, on the transmission of data between computers. However, appreciable delays also occur on long terrestrial connections.

Cables. Virtually every country has a network of telecommunications cables radiating from telephone exchanges to customers' premises. These cables contain pairs of copper wires, insulated with paper or plastic, and twisted together. Cables contain from one pair of wires to several thousand. Generally, one pair of wires serves one telephone, i.e., it carries a band of frequencies of up to about 4kHz.

In many cities of the world there are also cable television (CATV) networks, carrying twenty or more television programs. Subscribers to the system are "tapped" into the cable, and receive a larger range of programs and/or a better quality picture than is available by direct radio reception. The cables used are **coaxial cables** (q.v.), i.e., a central conductor supported along the center of a tubular outer conductor. The whole cable is about 1cm in diameter. The cables may carry frequencies of up to 400MHz and may need amplification at intervals of less than 300m.

Optic fiber cables have been used as an alternative to electrical cables since the late 1970s. With present technology information is developed in electrical form and then inserted into the end of the fiber in the form of light by a laser or a light emitting diode (LED). The fibers are a fraction of a millimeter in diameter and are of very pure glass which has had controlled amounts of additional material added so as to give a difference in refractive index between center and periphery. Attenuations below 1db per kilometer are achievable in practice, and this allows distances of tens of kilometers without amplification. Dispersion within the glass is a limiting factor to capacity. The present (1986) limit is about 8,000 speech channels per pair. However, new developments will give very much higher capacities on fibers that will transmit over distances of hundreds of kilometers without amplification.

Optical fibers are used on aircraft, inside computers, within offices, as cable television links, and as intracity and intercity telecommunications links. The costs of transmission using optic fibers are generally very much lower than with electrical cables, particularly over longer distances.

Submarine cables, laid on the bed of the sea or ocean, have been used to provide international telecommunications for over a hundred years. Present-day cables carry hundreds of telephone and similar circuits and are an alternative to satellites. Their main advantage over satellites is the much shorter transmission time, i.e., the time between sending the signal and its receipt at the distant end. Although transmission over cable is somewhat slower than radio propagation, the much greater path length to and from a satellite results in an appreciable difference in transmission time. Optic fiber submarine cables are now being used, and they have very much greater capacities and lower transmission delays than their predecessors.

Sending and Receiving Devices. Sending and receiving transducers, i.e., devices that turn the information source into electrical energy, or vice versa, come in two main kinds; those for sound and those for pictures.

Sound. Sound is picked up by microphones, which contain a component that vibrates in tune with the sound vibrations that impinge on it. The vibration of this element is converted into electrical vibrations by one of several methods, such as by varying the resistance of a component of an electric circuit, or by moving in a magnetic field thus generating electric currents, or by moving in an electrostatic field. Each method has specific advantages and disadvantages. The variables are cost, sensitivity to low levels of sound, power outputs, frequency range, allowable amount of introduced distortion or noise, and directivity.

Many types of microphones need to be associated with an amplifier to compensate for their intrinsic characteristics. Sound is produced from electrical signals by devices known variously as loudspeakers, speakers, receivers, or earphones. In almost all cases these consist of an electromagnet which causes a diaphragm to vibrate in accordance with the incoming electrical vibrations. This is structurally the same as one type of microphone, and speakers can be used as microphones.

Pictures. For recording and transmission, pictures are divided into horizontal lines and each line into a series of elements (picture elements, or "pixels"). The sensing device, whether video camera or facsimile machine, scans the field, line by line. It sends a signal to mark the end of each line, so that receiving equipment can respond correctly. As it scans each line the sending device produces an electric current whose strength varies in accordance with the lightness or darkness of the elements along the line. The degree of fineness of the picture depends on the amount of area "looked at" any instant by the scanning device and on the closeness of the lines.

Facsimile machines are designed to send and receive images of pages of documents over telephone lines. There are different types of machine capable of transmitting one A4 size page in from six minutes, down to about two seconds. There is virtually no standardization in the slower machines, and machines from one manufacturer often will not work with those of another manufacturer. The faster machines, intended to be universally compatible, have a range of computer-controlled facilities and capability of text processing.

Modern facsimile machines can have automatic paper feed and automatic dialing and answering for use after normal office hours or when lower telephone rates apply.

PROCESSING

Processing consists of changing some aspect of information in accordance with set rules, to make it more suitable for some purpose. The set of rules, which may be extremely complicated because it must include every necessary logical step and precaution, is the *program*. Programs perform several different types of functions; for example, they

—identify patterns of characters

—select out sequences that conform to given patterns

—arrange items in accordance with some predetermined rule or sequence

—count items

—perform logical functions

—perform substitutions

—perform arithmetic functions

Up to the 1950s programs were performed manually or by mechanical systems (abacus, cash register, electromechanical telephone exchange). Electronic computers have enormous processing power compared with earlier technologies.

Computer programs typically contain all or many of the above functions, and depending on which functions predominate, the program (and computer) may provide any of the following capabilities:

—data processor (routine sorting of large quantities of data with fairly simple arithmetic processing)

—word processor (has rules for page formats, recognition of words and substitution of words, phrases, and paragraphs)

—management system (has complex rules for sorting and comparing, in accordance with a wide range of possible conditions and management requirements, and presentation in the form of spreadsheets, graphs, charts, etc.)

—environmental control (simple recognition of conditions that warrant action, and either an alarm or process control function

—process control (sequence of actions that are to be performed, with accompanying criteria on when each action starts and stops, and means of activating each step, e.g., computer-controlled manufacturing, telephone exchanges)

—simulation (mathematical representation of some process, with the ability to vary the simulated conditions by inputting different quantitative information)

—calculations (as, for example, in calculators)

—pictorial representation (automated engineering design, buildup or enhancement of images (CAT scans), movie film animation

—expert systems (making judgments by applying sets of rules to the specific facts of individual cases as in medical diagnosis, geological exploration)

—special-purpose devices (optical scanners, voice recognition, simulated voice and music robots)

In each of these there are several elements, namely, the computer (hardware), the built-in instructions, the specific program to do the job in hand (software), the input, and the output. The input might be from a telex machine or other keyboard equipment, another computer or computer memory, an information storage device, or a sensing device. Sensing devices can be measures of pressure, voltage, etc., or television cameras or microphones. The output equipment might be a printer, a cathode-ray screen, a microfiche, a loudspeaker, or a device that controls some other mechanical or electrical equipment. Input and output equipment might be part of the computer hardware or quite remote, even in outer space. In virtually every case, communication between these devices ("peripherals") and the computer is by streams of digital signals.

Computer systems suffer from the following logical problems:

—inconsistencies, omissions, or logical errors in structuring the system or writing the program

—errors in the input data, or misunderstandings concerning input data

—faults in the hardware or power supply

—errors in the actual processing or transmission of data

SYSTEMS AND NETWORKS

Types of Networks. Equipment for storing, sending, transmitting, receiving, and processing information is combined into networks which become the nervous system of society. Networks consist of distribution systems that serve individual users, switching systems that connect users together, and trunk systems that join together all the switching systems throughout a country or around the world.

The most universal are the telephone and telex networks, which connect virtually all countries together. Internationally accepted standards prescribed by the CCITT (International Consultative Committee for Telephone and Telegraphy), CCIR (International Consultative Committee for Radio), ISO (International Standards Organization), IEC (International Electro-Technical Committee) ensure compatible interworking throughout.

The predominant manufacturer of computers, IBM, has also imposed quasi-standards on the industry, and so, to a lesser extent, have other manufacturers.

Other national and international networks exist for carrying data (i.e., computer-associated information); for connecting broadcast radio, television, and cable television programs; and for military purposes. These may use the transmission facilities of the telecommunications administrations, or privately owned facilities, including satellites, or a combination of both. Two well-known networks are Timenet and Telenet in the United States, which allow subscribers worldwide access at a price to computers that supply information stored on data bases, or special-purpose processing, or both. Most advanced countries have public data networks, which allow users to make various types of computer connections, either fixed point-to-point or switched.

Switching allows customers of a network to be connected to other customers at will. Most networks employ circuit switching; i.e., there is a transmission path established between the calling and the called parties, and this path remains intact until cleared down at the end of the interaction. This is typical of telephone and telex networks, where two-way communication is normal. In message switching, a message sent from the originating end may be stored within the network before arriving at its destination. This is typical of telegrams.

In a still-developing technique, packet switching, the message is divided into "packets" of about one thousand bits each, and the packets are "labeled" with the address of the destination, and consigned by the most appropriate route through the network. This has the advantage of avoiding the ineffective transmission time in circuit switching when the "listening" end is not sending. Packet-switching networks contain many added facilities, including error detection and correction. It is interesting that the newly emerging service **teletex** (q.v.), which connects together communicating word processors (CWPs), is proposed in some countries to operate over packet-switched networks, in others over circuit-switched data networks, and in others over the telephone network. Teletex will operate at almost 50 times the speed of telex, but connections to the telex network and other text services (with buffers to accommodate the speed difference) have recently been produced.

Other Text Services. Another text service is **videotex** (q.v.), which uses a domestic television set (or in some cases a special terminal with a television screen) in conjunction with the telephone in order to access a large data base of commonly used information. The information is supplied by "information providers" in the form of "pages" of 24 lines of 40 characters each and simple graphics. The information may be timetables, advertising, encyclopaedia-type facts, and some systems have facilities for electronic mailbox theatre reservations, catalog shopping, and access to computer programs. Access to the different pages and facilities is obtained by a calculator-type keypad with guidance from the system as to what number to press to get what facility. The user pays the telecommunications authority for access to the system and the information providers for the information accessed.

There is virtually no limit to the number of pages that this service can contain. A similar, but strictly limited, service is **teletext** (q.v.)—(not to be confused with Teletex)—in which the pages are included as part of the signal in a television channel. By using a suitably modified television set, it is possible to access the information free of charge.

Electronic mailbox services enable (registered) users, with a great variety in allowable terminal equipment, to send messages to others' electronic mailboxes. The messages are read by connecting to the system and inserting the correct name of the mailbox and the (secret) password associated with that box. Messages can be answered (i.e., a reply sent to the originator's mailbox); forwarded to other mailboxes, with added comments if desired; filed in the user's storage space in the system; or edited. There can be closed user groups; i.e., certain users can send and receive only to other members of the group, who are identified by name and password only. The mailboxes may also be able to send and receive messages of other text services, e.g., telex or teletex.

Mobile Services. There are two types of mobile service, paging and mobile telephone. Paging is essentially a one-way communication of a small amount of information to a small receiver carried in the pocket or on the belt of the user. The pager gives an audible, visual, or vibratory signal when called, and may display short messages on a small screen. The signals are sent from one or more radio transmitters that provide general coverage of the service area, often activated automatically over the telephone system. There are typically pockets of poor reception, e.g., in or behind large steel framed buildings.

Mobile telephones provide two-way communication, are almost entirely in motor vehicles, and may be in private networks, e.g., taxis or delivery fleets, or connected to the telephone network, in which case they make and receive calls like any other telephone service. Technical developments are leading to a very great increase in the number of mobiles in use, and the mobile telephone itself now can be small and portable (e.g., carried in a briefcase).

TECHNOLOGY AND UNDERSTANDING

Any piece of information is always a selection. The selection is partly made by choice and partly imposed by the nature of the technology.

A picture can present many ideas all at once; speech and writing must present one idea at a time. Photographs and particularly film and television carry an implication of truth and unambiguity; drawings, particularly caricatures and cartoons, imply interpretation and often ambiguity.

Television news, because of its potential similarity to humdrum life and the price of viewing time, is forced to concentrate on the spectacular. Radio news can be more selective and add description, while newspapers can afford to be reflective. Similar comments apply to advertisements over the three media.

By the use of expressive and emotional inflection, speech can make illogicalities sound convincing. Writing, which by contrast has no inflection but allows time for thinking, leads to greater logical rigor. Symbolic representation is capable of very great rigor. However, because the symbols are easily dissociated from the concepts they represent, the "meaning" is easily and often distorted. Slogans and newspaper headlines suffer the same kind of distortion.

Studies show that because a telephone conversation has different types of information transfer to face-to-face communication, it has very different effects. It allows more intimate or daring things to be said (like talking to someone in the dark), it removes threatening gestures and grimaces, and it tends to reduce the effect of difference in status. Studies into the reasons why video telephones were not accepted suggest that, in addition to the very great price differential, the absence of visual information is important for some types of communication.

The technology also has effects on perceptions of knowledge. Illiterate people are said to have much better spatial and aural perception and conception than literate people. "Gutenberg Man" is said to have been constrained by the written medium into thought patterns, based on sequential logic, that give a reductionistic view of reality. People brought up on television rather than on reading are said to be more impressionistic and holistic.

The way information is presented to the user also gives an impression of the complexity of knowledge. An encyclopaedia in book form gives a more complex conception of the nature of knowledge than a videotex system whose pages consist of 24 lines of 40 characters on a television screen. A computer data base that is accessed in terms of key words, and which may contain hundreds of references to a particular topic, many of them conflicting, gives another impression. Each particular information technology therefore exerts a very powerful influence over the whole thinking pattern and concept of the nature of knowledge.

THE FUTURE

The rate of accumulation of knowledge over recent years has been immense. The ability to accumulate depends on technologies for storing and retrieving information. Finding new knowledge is enormously assisted by ready access to and analysis of existing information. Research of all kinds and the developments of information technology have been mutually stimulating.

In virtually every field of information technology it is possible to see how further great increases in capability are possible. Moving holographic pictures that are truly three-dimensional, wrist radio telephones and television sets, **artificial intelligence** (q.v.), and instant access to all the world's information are now all technologically feasible. Optic fibers, complex molecules that will replace the silicon chip, very high-level computer languages, and new radio techniques will provide the means. Apparently disparate technologies have amalgamated in the past, and it has been postulated that information technology may amalgamate with biotechnology. Such developments may seem astounding, thrilling, frightening, liberating, or destructive. A hundred years ago the same would have been said of the bulldozer, the airplane, the radio, or the atomic bomb.

Graeme Lindenmayer

REFERENCES

Brookes, D. A. (1986) *Intelligent Information Systems for the Information Society*. Amsterdam: Elsevier.
Campbell, J. (1984) *Grammatical Man: Information, Entropy, Language, and Life*. London: Pelican.
Cannon, D. L. and Leucke, G. (1985) *Understanding Communications Systems*. Dallas: Sams.
Dordick, H. S. and Williams, F. (1986) *How to Manage Smarter Using the New Telecommunications: A Guide to Applications and Products*. New York: Wiley.
Jones, B. (1982) *Sleepers, Wake*. Melbourne: Oxford.
Lamberton, D. M., ed. (1974) *The Information Revolution*. Philadelphia: American Academy of Political and Social Science.
McLuhan, M. and Frove, Q. (1967) *The Medium Is the Massage*. Harmondsworth: Penguin.
Martin, J. (1978) *The Wired Society*. Englewood Cliffs, N.J.: Prentice-Hall.
Page, E. S. and Wilson, L. B. (1978) *Information Representation and Management in a Computer*. Cambridge: Cambridge University Press.
Pool, I. S., ed. (1977) *The Social Impact of the Telephone*. Cambridge, Mass.: MIT Press.
Storrs, G. (1986) *The Telecommunication Revolution*. Aruntel, Sussex: Bookwright Press (Illustrated, Juvenile, Grades 4 to 6).

INFORMATION THEORY. The theory associated with the transmission of information by technical and pedagogic systems. The theory is mostly concerned with quantitative measures which relate the various processes of information transmission, reception, and storage to each other. *See* **Communication Engineering; Educational Cybernetics.**

INITIAL BEHAVIOR. The behavior of the subject or organization at the start of instruction. Initial behavior is important in that it establishes a base criterion for performance assessment.

INK JET PRINTING. Computer printing technology offering low-priced dot matrix output with a reasonably high resolution. A particular attraction is the very quiet operation of ink jet printers.

The technology involves vaporizing a drop of ink into a bubble which bursts through a nozzle onto the paper. The ink is drawn from a collapsible rubber reservoir which forms part of a completely disposable print cartridge, including the printhead.

INLAY. A process whereby some part of a television picture is cut out electronically and is replaced with part or all of another picture. *See* **Chroma-Key.**

INNOVATION. *See* **Educational Innovation.**

INPUT. Information transferred into a computer from some external source, such as the keyboard, a disk drive, or a modem; or the act or process of transferring such information.

INPUT PROVIDER. *See* **Information Provider.**

INSERT. A video editing procedure wherein video and/or audio sequences are electronically "dropped" into a master recording. These inserts can be as short as a single frame or as long as desired. Typical educational applications include the lecture delivered directly to the camera with the subsequent insertion of captions, photographs, location shots, etc., to produce a final version which appears to be a balanced presentation with plenty of visual materials.

INSITE PROJECT. Instruction Systems in Teacher Education—a project developed by the Indiana University School of Education (U.S.). The project uses simulation in preparing student teachers and makes use of slides and audiovisual media. Its basic concern is with decision making in the classroom.

INSTANT LETTERING. Rub-down self-adhesive letters which are transferred from a plastic carrier sheet to artwork. Instant lettering is available in an ever-increasing range of typefaces and sizes as well as many special symbols and characters. Translucent colored letters, symbols, lines, and shapes are available for making overhead transparencies. Manufacturers of instant lettering also manufacture self-adhesive tints, color, or shading sheets for applying texture, color, or tone to artwork. *See* **Graphic Design.**

INSTANT REPLAY. Instant replay of televised events is accomplished using a specially designed disk recording device. Segments of 30 seconds or so of video are stored on the disk and can be replayed normally or in slow motion, as required.

INSTRUCTIONAL DESIGN. The design of instructional materials has been variously described as an art, a science, or a totally intuitive process. Attempts to prescribe recipes for successful design first came into prominence in the period of programmed learning's greatest popularity, and it was possible at that time to follow several fairly precise methods of attaining supposedly "correct" finished products. Inevitably, as with painting by numbers, the instructional materials so generated suffered from an arid and mechanistic rigidity.

Today it is generally accepted that although there are numerous precepts or guidelines useful in the construction of good learning packages, there is no golden road to success. The skilled designer will pay heed to considerations arising from several disparate fields, and in the end will also have to rely heavily on his/her own inspiration and creativity. *See* **Assessment; Course Design; Curriculum Design; Motivational Design; Resource-Based Learning.**

INSTRUCTIONAL INNOVATOR. The former name of *TechTrends,* a publication of the Association for Educational Communications and Technology.

1126 Sixteenth Street NW, Washington, D.C. 20036, U.S.

INSTRUCTIONAL SCIENCE. Journal published quarterly.

PO Box 211, 1000 AE Amsterdam, Holland.

INSTRUCTIONAL TELEVISION. *See* **Television, Educational and Instructional.**

INSTRUCTIONAL TELEVISION FIXED SERVICE. A low-powered and limited-range television system much cheaper to run than the conventional broadcast systems. Twenty ITFS channels are available (U.S.), all in the microwave frequency range of 2,500 to 2,690MHz. ITFS is dedicated to instructional purposes but participating institutions are able to attract fees by providing specially designed courses for outside agencies.

INTEGRATED CIRCUIT. An electronic device which is composed of thousands of individual miniaturized components and circuits (hence, integrated). Such devices are also known as "silicon chips" and are manufactured using **large-scale integration** (LSI) (q.v.) techniques.

INTELLIGENT COMPUTER-ASSISTED INSTRUCTION. An amalgam of CAL with the concept of expert systems. Effectively, very high-quality computerized teaching material which emulates the style of an expert teacher. *See* **Computer Nomenclature; Expert Systems.**

INTELLIGENT (SMART) TERMINAL. A computer terminal which can be used to perform data processing itself, without having to make use of the central processing unit to which it is connected. Such terminals are, in effect, microcomputers.

INTELLIGENT TUTORING SYSTEM. *See* **Computer Nomenclature.**

INTELSAT. The fifth Intelsat geostationary **communications satellite** (q.v.) was launched in 1983; it utilizes 27 transponders and can carry over 25,000 voice circuits at a cost per circuit per year of around $200. This compares with a figure of $23,000 per circuit per year for the 240 circuits on Intelsat I ("Early Bird") launched in 1965.

INTERACTION ANALYSIS. A type of classroom observation system devised by N. A. Flanders. It has been used both as a research methodology and as an aid to the training of teachers. It involves the capturing of behavioral events followed by translation into a code for subsequent analysis. The "capturing" can be accomplished by either tape recording (usually video) or by the presence of a trained observer; both systems have their deficiencies. *See* **Classroom Observation.**

INTERACTIVE. A mode of operation with a computer in which the user and the program interact in a conversational type of communication: the user answers questions, selects alternatives, requests help, etc.; the computer reacts to these prompts just as a human tutor would.

INTERACTIVE COURSEWARE DEVELOPMENT. A technique whereby the teacher plans, writes, and evaluates a computer-based course from a computer terminal. For example, in the PLATO system the teacher uses interactive courseware development in an author language called TUTOR.

INTERACTIVE VIDEO. Interactive video has emerged as a promising instructional delivery system for educators. An offspring of the computer and video technologies, interactive video has the potential to revolutionize learning via electronic media.

THE INTERACTIVE VIDEO PROCESS

Interactive video combines the visual impact of television with the computer's speed in processing information. A typical interactive video program introduces new concepts or skills through a combination of video and computer text presentations. Interactivity takes place when the learner is required to respond to questions or problems that appear at strategic points in the program. If necessary, the learner is branched to a new or repeated segment for remediation. The power of an interactive video program lies in the fact that active participation is required. Either by responding to questions and problems or by selecting segments to be viewed, the learner becomes part of the instructional process.

Interactive video is to be regarded as more than just a fusion of the video and computer technologies. It is a medium that has taken on some unique characteristics from each of its principal parts. Video itself is capable of incorporating other media as well, and the strengths of all should be assessed, together with the content and the ability, level, and style of the learner. The most appropriate combination of audio, visual, and textual cues should then be selected. In a study involving the U.S. 7th Army, soldiers completed an interactive program on electrical equipment designed with the factors mentioned above (DeBloois, 1982 FURTHER DETAIL). Significant learning resulted, and more important, soldiers felt that the instruction matched their reading and reasoning abilities.

THE TECHNOLOGY OF INTERACTIVE VIDEO

There are four basic hardware components in an interactive system: a computer, an interface unit, a video player, and a video monitor (Floyd, 1982 FURTHER DETAIL). The components are purchased either as an integrated package or individually in order to build a system in phases or to complement equipment already on hand.

The Computer. Although minicomputers are sometimes used in larger systems, the microcomputer is central to most interactive systems because of its widespread availability and diminishing costs. Learners interact with the program using the keyboard, or in some systems a keypad, touch-sensitive screen, or light pen. The microcomputer processes the learner's inputs and produces the corresponding video or text display. The computer also performs diagnostic and record-keeping activities.

The Interface Unit. The interface unit is a communication link between the computer and video player. It enables the computer to control the video player by encoding and then locating spots on the video for playback. Most interactive systems use an internal interface card that plugs into a peripheral slot in the computer. External interface units which are compatible with any computer equipped with a serial communications board are also available. A variety of interface units are on the market at this time, and one should consider cost, compatibility with computer and video player, control features, and reliability (Schwartz, 1985; Wilson, 1983 FURTHER DETAIL).

The Video Player. There are two types of media on which video can be stored and retrieved: laser videodisc and videotape. There are advantages and disadvantages to both media (Nave and Zembrosky-Bardin, 1985; Schaffer, 1985 FURTHER DETAIL). The potency of the videodisc lies in its enormous capacity to store 54,000 frames of information on each side and its ability to rapidly locate specific frames on the disc. Videodisc information may be displayed as single frames of pictures or text, as linear video in either slow-motion or real-time sequences, or more likely a combination of all. Two audio tracks can accompany the video for playback in stereo or of independent audio programs such as for a bilingual application. The videodisc is impervious to wear because a laser beam is used to pick up digital signals from the disk, thus no surface contact is made. Once a master is produced, it is inexpensive to duplicate disks in large volume. However, the cost of producing a master disk is high and material typically must be sent outside for mastering. Unlike videotape, the videodisc is a playback-only medium and cannot be edited for revisions or updating (Currier, 1983; Fort, 1984 FURTHER DETAIL).

The videotape is a viable medium for interactive video

applications in schools and small training departments where wide dissemination is not a factor. Videotape is a record/playback medium that can be locally produced and duplicated on already available video tape recorders. Tape is cheaper and quicker to produce than the videodisc. Intended as a linear medium, videotape has its drawbacks because access time to video segments includes searching by fast-forwarding or rewinding the tape. Videotapes naturally deteriorate over time and use and are sensitive to the environment.

The Video Monitor. In an interactive system the video monitor displays visual information generated by the computer and video player. The video monitor also amplifies audio signals from the video player. A color monitor is necessary if color video and graphics are used.

DEVELOPING INTERACTIVE PROGRAMS

Although a thorough understanding of the hardware is necessary, many other important skills are involved in designing and producing interactive video programs (Call, 1983; Gayeski and Williams, 1980; O'Bryan, 1982; Price and Marsh, 1983; Troutner, 1983 FURTHER DETAIL). These skills may be grouped into four categories: instructional design, computer programming, content expertise, and video production. A small-scale and low-budget project can be produced by one person. However, for most projects, a team approach is more efficient and ensures a better-quality product. Since many of the skills overlap, close cooperation among team members is critical.

Instructional Design. **Instructional design** (q.v.) principles specifically for interactive video have not yet been established, but some tentative guidelines have been proposed (Hannafin et al., 1985 FURTHER DETAIL) and a number of models for designing **computer-assisted instruction** (q.v.) appear especially appropriate for interactive video (Gagne, Wager, and Rojas, 1981; Walker and Hess, 1984 BACKGROUND READING). However, the application of fundamental principles for effective instruction is essential in developing an interactive learning process (Gagne and Briggs, 1979 BACKGROUND READING). As required in designing instruction for other media, instructional design activities should include (1) documenting why an interactive program is needed, (2) analyzing specific characteristics of the target users, (3) writing instructional objectives, (4) writing test items to assess learning, (5) developing and sequencing the content to be presented, (6) developing practice and feedback items, (7) writing a script, and (8) designing a program evaluation.

Computer Programming. A computer program is written to electronically piece together the interactive process. Authoring software (on a diskette) simplifies the programming process. Most interface unit manufacturers offer an authoring system or authoring language with their units. Authoring systems are menu-driven and may be used by nonprogrammers to write interactive video lessons. **Authoring languages** (q.v.) offer more programming flexibility than authoring systems and are intended to assist those who have more programming experience but do not have the time or skill to write a lesson using a programming language such as BASIC or Pascal (Gayeski and Williams, 1982; Kearsley, 1984 FURTHER DETAIL). A crucial activity in programming an interactive lesson is in developing instructional flowcharts. The flowchart diagrams the instructional process in a sequence of learning events. The events may be associated with video, audio, computer text, and any other medium necessary for instruction. Test items are indicated at strategic points during and/or after learning events. For each possible response to a test item, a branch to another part of the program is indicated on the flowchart. Branching leads to a new instructional segment, or to segments that clarify, expand, review, or remediate the original content.

Content Expertise. Experts who are knowledgeable in the content to be presented need to be closely involved in the instructional design process. The experts provide valuable resource information for developing the instructional objectives, test items, content, practice and feedback items, script, flowchart, and remedial items. Content experts should also be involved in program evaluation activities to help determine whether users are really learning what they are supposed to.

Video Production. Technical production for an interactive program consists of translating the design of the program into a completed videotape or videodisc (Nave and Zembrosky-Bardin, 1985; McEntee, 1982 FURTHER DETAIL). Video segments with accompanying audio should be edited to match the sequence of learning events. If videotape is used, branching segments should be edited in close proximity to minimize the time required to reposition the tape. Computer text can be used to cover any videotape delay time. Videotapes, usually 3/4–inch or 1–inch, may be sent to a number of videodisc companies for mastering and duplication (Schwartz, 1985 FURTHER DETAIL). Each company has special requirements for technical quality of the tape, digital dumps, and special encoding.

INTERACTIVE VIDEO APPLICATIONS

Interactive video is a relatively new technology. An interactive program on biology developed by the World Institute for Computer-Assisted Teaching

(WICAT) in 1977 is recognized as the first microcomputer-based interactive video program (Floyd, 1982 FURTHER DETAIL). Since then, WICAT has conducted interactive video projects for different levels of education, government, and industry with diverse content such as engine repair, science education, missile maintenance, medical education, and banking (Bunderson, 1983 FURTHER DETAIL). The descriptions below are a small representation of other successful interactive video applications.

Education. At a planetarium in Chicago students sit at a space station, select an interplanetary destination, blastoff into space, and land at their selected planet. As a video segment appears, students view their trip through space and on the planet. A narration provides information about their exploration. After the video portion, questions appear on the screen. Answering the questions correctly permits another space journey. An incorrect answer brings additional information on the screen. This interactive video program brought another dimension to learning about astronomy (Waldrop, 1982 FURTHER DETAIL). A comprehensive interactive video system known as CAVIS was developed at the West Sussex Institute of Higher Education for a wide range of subject matter. CAVIS was developed to improve the effectiveness and efficiency of the educational facilities. A needs analysis identified nine key requirements for the interactive system (Copeland, 1983 FURTHER DETAIL). Junior high school students learned about decision making through an interactive program. Vignettes depicting important concepts were followed by questions to test comprehension. The video segments of the program were obtained from a professionally produced television program and adapted for use on an interactive system (Troutner, 1983 FURTHER DETAIL). In a mathematics project, students were introduced to key mathematical concepts by viewing social situations. Mastery of concepts was determined by student responses to interactive problems. Students were then branched to further video sequences and interactive exercises on related concepts or were presented with help or review sequences. Completion of the module resulted in a computer display of the student's performance and encouragement to practice the concepts in a module workbook (Karwin, Landesman, and Henderson, 1985 FURTHER DETAIL).

Business and Industry. Training departments in business and industry have found varied applications for interactive video. At a bank, automation training required bank employees to become familiar with a new computer system. An interactive program was designed to simulate actual procedures on the new computer. Employees controlled their own training program according to their own pace and learning style (Handshaw, 1982 FURTHER DETAIL). A CPR (cardiopulmonary resuscitation) training program compared their interactive learning system against live instruction. Students receiving interactive video instruction registered three times as many passing scores as those receiving live instruction. The interactive program used a variety of features such as a light pen to register responses on the screen, high-resolution graphics, and a manikin wired to a computer to provide feedback on hands-on performance (Hon, 1983 FURTHER DETAIL). A flight training program identified two advantages in using interactive video. It enabled efficient training through the individualized and branching capabilities of the interactive format; the added visual impact increased student interest and motivation. A ten-step model was developed and used to produce the interactive flight programs (Girod, 1982 FURTHER DETAIL). In addition to training, interactive video has experienced recent success in retail sales applications. Interactive point-of-sale systems enhance customer service by providing product information and demonstrations. Consumers' requests are made from display menus, and the corresponding video and/or computer segment is presented. Point-of-sale systems are also used to process credit card purchases and hotel reservations and to conduct simulations that dramatize the benefits of various products or services such as life insurance, health insurance, and retirement plans.

THE FUTURE

Part of the future of interactive video lies in the hands of the electronic industry. As technological advances continue to occur, lower prices and improved features are foreseen. For the videodisc to be practical in education, local recording and duplicating capability needs to be developed. Several companies are working on read/write videodisc systems, and projected costs appear to be feasible. The continued development of such input devices as voice recognition and touch-sensitive screen could eventually lead to a different level of interactivity. The improvement of authoring software will allow broader applications of interactive video. The integration of **artificial intelligence** (q.v.) techniques with authoring will facilitate a deeper level of understanding about the way in which students learn and a more sophisticated method for tutoring. The incompatibilities among computers, interfaces, and software appear to be industry's biggest challenge for wider acceptance of interactive video. An eventual standardization of the technology would clear the way for a better system for disseminating interactive programs.

A big part of the future also lies in the hands of those who are responsible for developing interactive video programs. The application of the technology unfortunately does not automatically improve with advances in hardware. Big strides in research and development need to be taken in finding more practical and effective applications for this new technology. It is clear that interactive video holds the answer to many educational and training problems. The potential rests not only in technology but also in educators' grasp of the opportunity which interactive video presents.

Curtis P. Ho and Geoffrey Z. Kucera

REFERENCES

Background Reading

Gagné, R. and Briggs, L. (1979) *Principles of Instructional Design*. New York: Holt, Rinehart and Winston.

Gagné, R., Wager, W., and Rojas, A. (1981) "Planning and Authoring Computer Assisted Instructional Lessons." *Educational Technology* 21 (9): 17–26.

Walker, D. and Hess, R. (1984) *Instructional Software*. Belmont, Calif.: Wadsworth.

Further Detail

Bunderson, C. (1983) "A Survey of Videodisc Projects at WICAT." *Performance and Instruction Journal* 22 (9): 24–25.

Call, D. (1983) "Basic Principles for Doing Interactive Discs." *EITV* 15 (10): 98–105.

Copeland, P. (1983) "An Interactive Video System for Education and Training." *British Journal of Educational Technology* 14 (1): 59–65.

Currier, R. (1983) "Interactive Videodisc Learning Systems." *High Technology* 3 (11): 51–59.

DeBloois, M. L. (1982) *Videodisc/Microcomputer Courseware Design*. Englewood Cliffs, N.J.: Educational Technology Publications.

Floyd, S., ed. (1982) *Handbook of Interactive Video*. White Plains, N.Y.: Knowledge Industry Publications, pp. 15–41.

Fort, W. (1984) "A Primer on Interactive Video." *AV Video* 6 (10): 39–41.

Gayeski, D. and Williams, D. (1980) "Program Design for Interactive Video." *EITV* 12 (12): 31–34.

———. (1982) "How 'Authoring' Programs Help You Create Interactive CAI." *Training* 19 (8): 32–34.

Girod, J. (1982) "First Union Bank of North Carolina: Branch Automation Training." In *Handbook of Interactive Video*, ed. S. Floyd. White Plains, N.Y.: Knowledge Industry Publications, pp. 147–150.

Handshaw, D. (1982) "First Union Bank of North Carolina: Branch Automation Training." In *Handbook of Interactive Video*, ed. S. Floyd. White Plains, N.Y.: Knowledge Industry Publications, pp. 141–145.

Hannafin, M., Garhart, C., Rieber, L., and Phillips, T. (1985) "Keeping Interactive Video in Perspective: Tentative Guidelines and Cautions in the Design of Interactive Video." In *Educational Media and Technology Yearbook*, ed. E. Miller and M. Mosley. Littleton, Colo.: Libraries Unlimited, pp. 13–25.

Hon, D. (1983) "The Promise of Interactive Video: An Affective Search." *Performance and Instruction Journal* 22 (9): 21–23.

Iuppa, N. (1984) *A Practical Guide to Interactive Video Design*. White Plains, N.Y.: Knowledge Industry Publications.

Karwin, T., Landesman, E., and Henderson, R. (1985) "Applying Cognitive Science and Interactive Videodisc Technology to Precalculus Mathematics Learning Modules." *Technological Horizons in Education Journal* 13 (1): 57–63.

Kearsley, G. (1984) "Instructional Design and Authoring Software." *Journal of Instructional Development* 7 (3): 11–16.

McEntee, P. (1982) "Producing Interactive Video Programs." In *Handbook of Interactive Video*, ed. S. Floyd. White Plains, N.Y.: Knowledge Industry Publications, pp. 85–106.

Nave, G. and Zembrosky-Bardin, P. (1985) *Interactive Video in Special and General Education: A Development Manual*. Eugene, Oreg.: International Council for Computers in Education.

O'Bryan, K. (1982) "Instructional Strategy and Evaluation." In *Handbook of Interactive Video*, ed. S. Floyd. White Plains, N.Y.: Knowledge Industry Publications, pp. 67–83.

Price, B. and Marsh, G. (1983) "Interactive Video Instruction and the Dreaded Change in Education." *Technological Horizons in Education Journal* 10 (9): 112–117.

Schaffer, L. (1985) "Is Interactive Video for You?" In *Educational Media and Technology Yearbook*, ed. E. Miller and M. Mosley. Littleton, Colo.: Libraries Unlimited, pp. 26–34.

Schwartz, E. (1985) *The Educators' Handbook to Interactive Videodisc*. Washington, D.C.: Association for Educational Communications and Technology.

Troutner, J. (1983) "How to Produce an Interactive Video Program." *Electronic Learning* 2 (4): 70–75.

Waldrop, H. (1982) "A New Technology Blasts Off." *Electronic Learning* 2 (3): 72–74.

Wilson, R. (1983) "Interactive Video: What Makes It Work?" *Performance and Instruction Journal* 22 (9): 26–27.

Suggestions for Further Reading

Bennion, J. (1976) *Authoring Procedures for Interactive Videodisc Instructional Systems*. Provo, Utah: Brigham Young University, Institute for Computer Uses in Education.

Burke, R. (1982) *CAI Sourcebook: Background and Procedures for Computer Assisted Instruction in Education and*

Industrial Training. Englewood Cliffs, N.J.: Prentice-Hall.

DeBloois, M., Maki, K., and Hall, A. (1984) *Effectiveness of Interactive Videodisc Training: A Comprehensive Review.* The Monitor Report Series. Falls Church, Va.: Future Systems.

Fleming, M. and Levie, W. (1979) *Instructional Message Design.* Englewood Cliffs, N.J.: Educational Technology Publications.

Landa, R. (1984) *Creating Courseware: A Beginner's Guide.* New York: Harper and Row.

INTERCUTTING. This occurs in television or film when two shots are repeated one after the other again and again, e.g., in conversation between two people where there is no need for a change of camera angle.

INTERFACE. The connection between two computer peripherals. The term arises because of the necessity for both pieces of equipment to "talk the same language." Very often special provision has to be made in order that the connection is properly established. Interfaces may be either serial or parallel. In the case of parallel transmission information is transmitted byte by byte using a number of wires to carry the data elements simultaneously; serial transmission needs only one wire each way as the signal is sent as a sequence of bits. *See* **Bit; Byte; Handshaking.**

INTERLACE. Broadcast television systems (NTSC and PAL) put half the scanning lines on the screen in one field, then in the next field the other half of the lines are interlaced, thus giving the illusion of 525 (PAL 625) lines on the television screen. *See* **Field.**

INTERNATIONAL COUNCIL FOR EDUCATIONAL MEDIA (ICEM). ICEM seeks to encourage and facilitate international cooperation in the audiovisual field through exchanges of information and audiovisual materials, coproduction activities, and various joint projects.

ICEM, Office Français des Techniques Moderns D'Éducation, 29 Rue d'Ulm, Paris, France

INTERPRETER. A computer program which controls the execution of another program which has not previously been compiled or assembled. The procedure is slow since the translation into machine code instructions has to be done one line at a time.

INTRINSIC MOTIVATION. Motivation based on the satisfaction obtained by the performance of a task rather than from external reinforcers.

INTRINSIC PROGRAM. Another name for branching program (in programmed learning). The originator of the branching mode, Norman Crowder, preferred the description "intrinsic," but it achieved little general usage. *See* **Programmed Learning.**

INVERTED FILE. A type of file frequently used in data bases. In such a file, the attributes of items are identified by index terms, which are then collected in so-called inverted files that list all items possessing that particular attribute.

I/O. Input/Output; the transfer of information into and out of a computer.

IONOSPHERE. A layer of the earth's atmosphere some tens of kilometers thick, and starting at about 40km above the surface, which contains a high percentage of ionized gases. It is very reflective to some frequencies of radio waves, thus permitting broadcasting without line of sight.

IP. *See* **Information Provider.**

IRIS. *See* **Aperture; F-number.**

ISAM. An acronym for indexed sequential-access method. IBM pioneered this method of organizing a data base when magnetic tape was the principal means of storage.

ISO. International Standards Organization. *See* **Standards in Audiovisual Technology.**

ITEC. Information Technology Education Centre. U.K. arrangement whereby unemployed youth can be given crash training in such skills as word processing at a convenient location, i.e., an ITEC.

ITEM ANALYSIS. A set of related statistical and mathematical techniques that are used to analyze test items in multiple-choice tests. Item analysis has three aspects: (1) item validity, (2) item difficulty, and (3) item selection.

1. Item validity (the power to discriminate) is determined by the extent to which the given item discriminates among subjects who differ sharply in the function measured by the test as a whole. Point Biserial Correlations are usually computed. Cross-validation should be undertaken by computing the item validity with a different sample from that used in the original test.

2. Item difficulty can be computed in a variety of ways:
   (a) By experts who rank the items in order of difficulty
   (b) By how quickly an item can be solved

(c) By the number of subjects in the sample who get the item correct

3. The selection of test items can be aided by statistics, but essentially it is a skill the test constructor must develop. When items are stored in an item bank, i.e., a collection of validated test items, selection is relatively easy, as long as the test constructor has a clear set of objectives.

The basic principle that item analysis attempts to establish is the construction of meaningful tests. This will require several trials and the initial selection of more items than required for the test (approximately two times the number). Many computer programs have been written which undertake item analysis. Their main advantage is that they can very rapidly compute various indices for items, and this can be useful when the trials are made on a large sample.

ITEM BANK. A large collection of validated objective items from which sets of items may be selected as required in order to make up a particular objective test. Also, an alternative name for a data bank or data base.

ITFS. *See* **Instructional Television Fixed Service.**

ITS. *See* **Computer Nomenclature.**

ITV. (1) Instructional television. (2) Independent Television: generic name for the commercial television broadcasting system that operates in the United Kingdom.

J

JACK PLUG. Small connector used for many low-voltage applications in the communications industry. The most common type of plug is used for headphones. A "standard" jack plug is 0.25 inches in diameter but miniature versions are in common use.

JANET. Joint Academic NETwork. U.K. computer network linking higher education institutions.

JOB AID. Any form of aide-mémoire facilitating either the learning or performance of a task.

JOURNAL OF EDUCATIONAL TELEVISION. See **Educational Television Association (U.K.).**

JOURNALS. Journals fulfill an essential role in any field of study. Notwithstanding the increasing importance of nonprint-based (e.g., electronic) information exchange, journals are still the best way researchers and practitioners have to disseminate their findings, experiences, and concerns. However, nowadays it is practically impossible to keep pace with all that is published even in one specific area: a conservative worldwide estimate of journals related to educational technology, communications, or media puts the figure in excess of 600. Thus, interested professionals have to resort to one or more of the following strategies: reading regularly a few general, broad-perspective publications; restricting their reading to specialized journals in a particular subfield; or concentrating on publications relating to a geographical region. Implied within these strategies is indeed the possibility of losing (i.e., not reaching) important information.

In order to find out what are considered to be the most important journals in the field, the writer conducted a survey among researchers and practitioners from different countries. As expected, it was found that little agreement exists, although there was some degree of consensus about the following English language journals:

American Educational Research Journal (U.S.)
British Journal of Educational Technology (U.K.)
Computers and Education (U.K.)
Educational Communications and Technology Journal (U.S.)
Educational Media International (U.K.)
Educational Technology (U.S.)
Instruction Science (Holland)
Journal of Instructional Development (U.S.)
Performance and Instruction (U.S.)
Programmed Learning and Educational Technology (U.K.)
Review of Educational Research (U.S.)
Simulation/Games for Learning (U.K.)
Teaching at a Distance (U.K.)
TechTrends (U.S.)

Clearly there is no such thing as a general, international forum to expose ideas; but could there, and should there, be one? Presumably, with the increasing importance of electronic information exchange, such a forum could be composed by the ensemble of several data banks, from which particular pieces of information could be added or retrieved by anyone linked to the system/network. In such a scenario, though, the only way to cope with the enormous amount of otherwise indigestible information would be by means of indexes and searches. A good example of a system already accomplishing those functions (although on a somewhat restricted data base) is provided by the *Current Index to Journals in Education* (CIJE).

Jesus Vazquez

JOYSTICK. An analog device for inputting data to a computer. Usually used for playing computer games but also suitable for graphic purposes. Physically, a joystick is a two-dimensional pointer, allowing the user to indicate direction and/or position through a 360–degree arc. See **Paddle.**

JUMP. An instruction which, when executed, can cause the computer to fetch the next instruction to be executed from a location other than the next sequential location. For example:

670 GET U$
680 GOSUB 2000
690 PRINT U$;" IS ";Y$

On reaching line 680 the program will always jump to the subroutine at line 2000.

JUSTIFICATION. In printing, typesetting, etc., arrangement of the characters and spaces so as to produce text lines of equal length, thus producing justified text.

K

K. In common parlance 1,000, but amended in computerese to mean 2 to the tenth power, i.e., 1,024; for example, 64K equals 64 times 1,024, or 65,536.

KELLER PLAN. A name given to a type of individualized learning strategy. It gets its name from F. Keller. The Keller Plan, or PSI (Personalized System of Instruction), is mainly characterized by the replacement of lectures by written material. Assignments consisting of sections from conventional texts, articles, and specially prepared material are combined with study instruction and questions. After completing a unit, the student takes a quiz. This quiz is scored by a proctor who tutors the student if there are errors. The quizzes are mastery tests, and only when a test is answered completely does the student move on to the next unit.

Four characteristics describe the essence of the Keller Plan:

1. Mastery of concepts before progress
2. Self-pacing
3. Eclectic teaching methods
4. Proctors used to test and tutor

The method has achieved its greatest success in the teaching of science.

KEY. The part of a record that is the identifier when indexing or sorting records. In the telephone book, for example, the key is the subscriber's name. In a data base, it is often the order or transaction number, date, a name, zip code, etc. Some data bases allow duplicate keys; others require that the key fields be unique.

KEYBOARD TRAINER. A training device for students of typewriting. A large screen portrays a keyboard, and an audiotape synchronizes a sound commentary with illumination of various keys on the screen.

KEYER. An electronic device which enables one picture to be clearly superimposed over another. A common use is to superimpose a title over another picture.

KEY GRIP. Key grip has primary responsibility for moving and safeguarding the camera. He/she is also the leader of a team of technicians, or "grips," who do the various manual jobs on the set.

KEY LIGHT. The principal light illuminating the central subject in a set or scene.

KEYPAD. A set of numeric keys, similar to those on a calculator. Some cheaper computers do not possess a keypad, relying instead solely on the numeric keys along the top row; this is a disadvantage if there is a need for much numerical input from the keyboard.

KEYPUNCH. A machine formerly used to manually punch cards or paper tape for computer input.

KEYSTONING. The nonrectangular image produced on a screen when the axis of a projection lens is not perpendicular to the screen. If a projector is pointing up at a vertical screen, the result is a picture that is wider at the top and is of keystone shape.

KEY WORD. In indexing, a significant word selected from the text of a document for use as an entry in a key word index, an alphabetical index of such key words designed to help locate sections that deal with specific topics. Also referred to as a *descriptor*.

KILOBYTE. A unit of data size or data storage capacity equivalent to 1,024 (i.e., 1,000 to all intents and purposes) bytes. *See* **Gigabyte; Megabyte.**

KILOWATT. A unit of electric power equal to the expenditure of 1,000 joules of energy per second. Lighting units used in television studios and for some film applications will often consume power in kilowatts, e.g., a 2kw floodlight would be quite common.

KILOWATT-HOUR. The usual unit in which electrical energy consumption is measured and charged for. Consumption is calculated by multiplying power in kilowatts by time in hours. That is, units consumed = (power of appliance in kilowatts) × (time in hours that the appliance is in use)

So if a 2kw lamp is in use for 4 hours, 8 units of electricity will be used.

KINESCOPE (TELERECORDING). Early technique for converting television into cine film. The usual method was to display the television image on a high-quality cathode-ray tube and film it using a cine camera with a specialized rapid pull-down mechanism. In addition, special circuits were used to ensure that the two systems were running at the same framing rate. If telerecording was attempted using a conventional cine camera, some of the television picture information was lost and the shutter in the camera caused a "bar" to appear on the image. Although the ability to record on videotape has reduced the kinescope process to historical interest, it is becoming increasingly common to convert video into film for use in theaters generally. This has been made possible by the use of a laser beam to "transform" video into film.

In practice, color separation negatives are made by exposing the film with a laser modulated by the video signal. Vertical fluctuations of the beam are induced to remove the horizontal lines from the finished product, which is of comparable quality to film exposed by conventional means. *See* **Video Recording and Reproduction.**

KIT. A package of learning materials and/or equipment designed for use in a particular teaching or learning situation.

L

LACING. The U.K. term for the process of feeding a tape or film into an item of equipment such as a recorder, player, or projector by threading its leader through the appropriate path. The equivalent U.S. term is *threading*.

LAMBERT. Unit of brightness as applied to both reflecting surfaces and light sources. One lambert is equal to a rate of reflection or emission of one lumen per square centimeter.

LAMINATING FILM. A transparent acetate or mylar film for laminating with the aid of a dry mounting press or thermal copying machine. It provides a useful means of protecting documents that are likely to receive a lot of handling.

LAN. Local Area Network. A collection of microcomputers and peripherals linked by a short-range, common communications path. It allows users to share files such as data bases and spreadsheets, and peripherals such as hard disk drives and printers. *See* **Local Area Network.**

LANDSCAPE. Rectangular framing (e.g., a visual display unit) in which the long dimension is horizontal. The alternative vertical mode is termed *portrait*.

LANGUAGE. *See* **Programming Language.**

LANGUAGE LABORATORY. A language laboratory is a classroom or other area sometimes designed specifically for the purpose, in which each student's place is fitted with a headset consisting of microphone and earphones connected to a central teacher's console, and used, as the name suggests, in the teaching of languages. Specifically designed lesson material is broadcast from a tape recorder on the console to the students who work upon it in isolation from each other.

DEVELOPMENT OF THE LANGUAGE LABORATORY

The first language laboratories properly speaking were installed in the early 1950s in the United States (Hocking, 1964; Leon, 1966 HISTORICAL). The first to be installed in Britain was at Ealing Technical College in 1960. Since then, progress in electronics has aided the rapid development of improved types of laboratory installation. Modular construction, solid-state electronics, the introduction of the compact cassette, and consequent miniaturization have reduced costs while maintaining a high standard of reliability. In some countries, notably in the United States, some very large and sophisticated installations were to be found in colleges and universities in the 1960s (Forrester, 1966 HISTORICAL). The technical advance represented by the hardware, however, was not on the whole paralleled by a similar breakthrough in software. To the contrary, the close association in the early years of language laboratories with a now widely discredited view of the psychological processes involved in learning a language provoked misgivings about the assumptions that led to their widespread adoption in schools and their cost-effectiveness (Strevens, 1971 FURTHER DETAIL). The resulting skepticism has slowed down or halted development, while leading to a greater diversification in the use of language laboratories in language teaching.

TYPES OF LANGUAGE LABORATORIES

The two principal types of language laboratories commonly distinguished are the **Audio Active (AA)** (q.v.) and the **Audio Active Record (AAR)**, also known as **Audio Active Comparative (AAC)** (q.v.). The AAR laboratory will be described first here, the AA laboratory being identical save for the absence of certain important features.

The average-size laboratory contains about 30 student positions with a separate tape recorder for each position. These student positions are usually isolated in booths made of wooden partitions with some soundproofing, and each student wears a headset consisting of earphones and microphone, designed to exclude outside noise. The students' tape recorders can be controlled in all or some of their functions both by the student and by the teacher, who sits at a central console. The lesson material is relayed to all the students' tape recorders and recorded there, either before the class, or, more usually, in the first part of the hour, from a program source which will usually be a master tape recorder on the teacher's console. During the laboratory session, the teacher can communicate with the class as a whole or with any individual student or group of students over an intercom. By a switch on the console the teacher can monitor, that is to say, listen to any student position without the students being interrupted or even knowing that they are being listened to. The teacher can also usually, if necessary, take control of the students' machines from the console, as well as advising or correcting their work. The students are in complete isolation from the rest of the class and, except while being monitored, from the teacher. They are alone with the lesson material and, to a varying degree, can work at their own pace upon it, rewinding their machines to make sure of something that they have not understood fully or to repeat an exercise that they did not do very well.

The students' tape recorders, whether tape or cassette, are specially designed for language laboratory working. They are twin-track, or rather dual-track, machines, on which both tracks may be recorded on and played back simultaneously. The lesson material relayed from the console is copied onto the master track, usually the upper one on the tape, on the student's machine. The student records on the student track, and can do this while listening to the master recording. This means that though the students may speak at the same time as hearing the master recording, they cannot erase the lesson material. And they can work over the same tape a very large number of times without any danger of damaging the master recording. Whether the students are recording or merely responding or repeating in the air, so to speak, their headsets are, in almost all models of laboratory, audioactive. This means that as the students speak, the signal from their microphones is amplified into the earphones with the effect that they hear their own voices as others hear them, i.e., from "outside," and not by conduction through the bones of the skull.

In an AA laboratory, earlier known as a broadcast laboratory, the essential difference from the installation described above is that the students' positions do not have individual recorders. The lesson material is broadcast from the program source on the teacher's console to the students' audioactive headsets. This means that though the students hear their own voices as they speak into their microphones, they do not have the capability of recording their voices and comparing their utterances with the model on the master recording. The usefulness of this facility has, however, been called in question (Perelle, 1975 ILLUSTRATION; Higgins, 1969 AUTHORITY). The principal disadvantage of an AA laboratory, as compared with the full AAR type, is therefore not so much that the students cannot record their voices, but that they are obliged to work together all at the same rate, and the advantage of individual working is lost. The advantages of an AA laboratory are, first, that it is evidently very much cheaper to purchase, to install, and to maintain, costing usually rather less than half as much as a full AAR model. A second advantage is its greater adaptability. An AA laboratory can be installed in an ordinary classroom: audioactive systems are available in which the hardware, headsets, teacher's console, and master recorder can be unplugged from the furniture and stored away in a cupboard. In one type, the Audio Loop system, the material is broadcast on a radio frequency from a loop of wire around the room to the students' headsets, which each contain a full battery-powered receiver, thus avoiding the need for cabled connections. Full accounts of the basic types of language laboratory can be found in Turner (1965 FURTHER DETAIL), Hayes (1968 AUTHORITY), Department of Education and Science (1968 FURTHER DETAIL), and Chatterton (1972 FURTHER DETAIL).

In some installations, particularly in universities and institutes of further or higher education, there is no central console, the students treating the language laboratory as a library, selecting a tape from the stock and working on it on their own. The tape material for this type of working is usually more or less closely structured. Another type of library mode installation uses a **dial access information retrieval** (q.v.) system (Cressman, 1970 FURTHER DETAIL). Here there is a central program source or set of sources which is constantly broadcasting a large number of sets of material, or programs (the word is often very loosely used in the language laboratory context). The student sits down at a position and dials the number of the tape wanted, which is immediately relayed to him or her. It will be seen that this is a type of AA laboratory in that the students have to work in lockstep with the program source which they cannot control. Costly and of uncertain cost-effectiveness, dial access systems have not found favor outside the United States (Hoffmann, 1976 FURTHER DETAIL).

LANGUAGE LABORATORY EQUIPMENT

Three features are essential to all equipment for a language laboratory: high acoustic quality, robustness, and simplicity of operation.

The acoustic requirements are different from those of, for example, a hi-fi stereo designed for playing music. Though it is true that many people with good hearing can perceive audio signals of 20,000 cycles per second, it is thought that the most useful auditory frequencies for listening to speech and for which it is therefore necessary to have the best possible reproduction is from 150 cycles per second to about 8,500 ± 2db. This is, of course, a very much wider range than is normally considered necessary for the recording of speech when dealing with a familiar language in everyday applications. Absence of distortion and noise is even more important than range of frequency response (Hayes, 1968 AUTHORITY), and to this end frequencies above 8,500 should be attenuated rapidly. There also must be as high a signal to noise ratio as possible (>40db) and an absence of switch noises, mains hum, and other such interference. Tape speed of the students' machines, and above all of the program source, must be constant. Nowadays it is customary for tape machines to work at three inches per second (ins/sec) and cassettes at one in/sec, and slow fluctuations of speed (known as *wow*) and rapid ones (known as *flutter*) must not exceed 0.25 percent of this.

This high level of acoustic quality has to be maintained week in and week out; equipment must therefore be robust. In particular, because of the way it is used, with frequent stopping and starting and rewinding, the electromechanical parts must be specially designed, and it is for this reason that machines adapted from domestic tape recorders are unsuitable. Knobs, switches, headsets, etc., must also be designed to stand up to being used by a large number of not always careful people. The controls must be simple to operate and laid out in such a way as to be easy to learn and to remember for the student, but above all for the teacher. The more switches that have to be touched for each operation, the more opportunities there are for time wasting mistakes.

Choice of a language laboratory should above all be dictated by the three considerations above. Facilities which it may be an advantage to have are the following.

More Than One Program Source. This makes it possible to have students at different levels, or using different materials, in the same class.

Fast Copy. A very useful facility, found only on cassette laboratories, by which it is possible to transfer a tape from the console to the student positions at, usually, four times normal speed, thus enabling a teacher to copy a twenty-minute recording in five minutes, the interval between two classes.

Slow Rewind, or Recap. This is a button on the students' machines which greatly simplifies the movements needed to rewind and repeat or listen to a short section of recording.

Tape Counters on Student Machines. Some installations have the students' machines rack-mounted at the side of the room or in a different room altogether. This allows easy maintenance but means that the students have no way of knowing where they are on a tape, which may be inconvenient when using some self-instructional materials.

Conference Mode and Pairing. A switch which puts selected students with or without a teacher in communication with each other. It can be used for dialogues or discussions without disturbing the other student positions.

Tape Repeater. A machine for the intensive study of linguistic material. It is basically a tape recorder within a tape recorder, the second recorder containing a continuous loop of tape onto which the material on the main machine is constantly being recorded and erased. At any moment, by switching the loop mechanism to playback and stopping the main machine, one can hear the last few words (or sentences according to the length of the loop) being repeated over and over again. There is currently no tape repeater on the market; university language centers are obliged to construct their own.

Quarter-inch tape, either standard or medium play on five-inch spools is normally used on the master machines. The student positions may be fitted either with reel-to-reel recorders taking quarter-inch tape, or compact cassette machines. In recent years cassette laboratories have replaced reel-to-reel almost universally. The cassette machines are cheaper, and the cassettes themselves of course cost very much less than five-inch spools of tape. However, the tape transport system of cassette machines is less well suited to the heavy use of a language laboratory unless very carefully designed, and the tape is also more liable to stretch, producing deformations of the recorded material. In a large installation working in the library mode, storage of tapes must be specially provided for. Master tapes in particular must be protected from magnetic influences (by wooden shelving) and must be run through periodically to guard against magnetic print-through, the layers of closely wound tape producing ghost echoes on each other if left too long undisturbed.

The fullest technical account of language laboratory equipment is to be found in Hayes (1968 AUTHORITY). Other useful authorities are Department of Education and Science (1968 FURTHER DETAIL) and the Ministry of Technology (1969 FURTHER DETAIL).

USING THE LANGUAGE LABORATORY

The organization of the students' work in a language laboratory is as much dependent on the design and the arrangement of the hardware as it is on the level of the students' linguistic proficiency and the type of instruction being given (Dahms and Cicerau, 1976 FURTHER DETAIL). In the library mode, where the students are working in isolation and usually without supervision, the structure of the laboratory session is almost entirely dictated by the design of the taped lesson material on which they are working. Where students are working together, however, in a classroom laboratory, under the supervision of a teacher, the type and design of the laboratory itself imposes certain patterns of working upon the class. In an AA laboratory, which is dependent upon a single program source, the group is obliged to work in lockstep. Normal practice with this style of laboratory is for the class to work through the material several times, the teacher correcting, encouraging, or commenting on the performance of individuals, groups, or the class as a whole. The possibility of individuals monitoring is usually very limited, since short of stopping the work of the class as a whole, the teacher can only talk to individual students by preventing them from hearing the lesson. Ways have been suggested of getting round this (Van Abbé, 1968 ILLUSTRATION; Parker, 1973 FURTHER DETAIL).

In an AAR laboratory, work is usually divided into two phases. In the first phase the laboratory is used as an AA laboratory; the material is broadcast from the teacher's console and recorded on the students' machines. During this transfer phase the teacher will listen to individual students but will not interrupt them. If there is a fast-copy facility, this first phase can be dispensed with. In the second or individual working phase, the machines are rewound to the start, and students are given control of them and work through the material a second time, this time with freedom to stop, start, rewind, or repeat an exercise. It is in this phase that monitoring from the teacher is most effective.

A class of students in a language laboratory constitutes a series in the Sartrian sense, as distinct from a group, since even when addressing all the students together over the intercom, the teacher is in a one-to-one relation with each individual. A quiet person-to-person style of speaking is therefore required (the teacher's mouth is after all the equivalent of a few inches from each student's ear), which makes the language laboratory more suited to encouraging what is positive in the student's performance than to nagging him or her about errors. However, the possibilities of monitoring are severely limited by the time available, and it is rarely possible to monitor effectively more than a dozen or so students in an hour, if one allows for listening to what each student is saying. The situation may be improved if the transfer phase can be avoided by organizing a type of supervised library mode working (Farrington, 1974 FURTHER DETAIL). Whether supervised or not, students make the best use of a language laboratory when they can work independently of each other, which makes the laboratory particularly suitable for older, more advanced, and relatively highly motivated students who can study alone. For this,

self-instructional programmed materials which are, as far as possible, teacher-independent are needed (Bung, 1967; Howatt, 1969; Farrington and Richardson, 1977 ILLUSTRATION).

Earlier writers insist on the importance of relating the language laboratory session to classwork. Where the language laboratory session consisted mostly of drills (see below), this was imperative because of the meaningless nature of the drill material (Howatt and Dakin, 1974 AUTHORITY). This type of working tends to be avoided now, and where fully contextualized or notional material is used, it is much less important. It may not be a coincidence that more self-instructional materials are appearing at the same time as linguists are becoming more concerned with communicative competence. (See below for an explanation of these terms.)

For a fuller account of the general methodology of the language laboratory see Stack (1966 HISTORICAL), Turner (1968 FURTHER DETAIL), and Bennett (1967 AUTHORITY).

MATERIALS FOR THE LANGUAGE LABORATORY

The effectiveness of the language laboratory depends almost entirely on the linguistic materials used. This can be easily vitiated by monotony, a defect which language laboratory material is particularly prone to. A wide variety of activities have been devised for the laboratory (Turner, 1968 FURTHER DETAIL; Higgins, 1969 AUTHORITY; Campbell, 1976 FURTHER DETAIL), and there is nowadays little excuse for allowing the laboratory to bore the students. A criticism leveled at much standard, commercially available language laboratory material is that it is not varied or challenging enough (Pill, 1971 FURTHER DETAIL). What is more, the possibilities of the instrument cannot be fully exploited by a teacher who simply takes it, and a set of commercially produced materials, for granted (Harper, 1975 FURTHER DETAIL). The teacher must be prepared, and trained, to produce his own materials. The following are the principal types of activities which may go on in a language laboratory.

Listening. The simplest, if not perhaps the most obvious, activity is direct, unmediated listening to recordings in the foreign language, preferably of spontaneous speech at normal or near normal speed. The opinion of an increasing number of writers is that this is the most useful thing that can be done in a laboratory (Dakin, 1973; Howatt and Dakin, 1974 AUTHORITY). What programming, or structuring, of the activity there is may be found on the printed material accompanying the exercise. Listening is not simply a receptive skill, and exercises can be devised which give training in its several aspects (Hughes, 1974 FURTHER DETAIL).

Repetition. Another very simple language laboratory exercise is that in which a student is given a passage or set of sentences to repeat, usually as practice in pronunciation. The material is usually "exploded," that is to say, a gap is inserted in the master recording after each intonation group so that the student may repeat the passage group by group. The student relies on mimicry to help in articulating the sounds of the foreign language, the audio-active headset aiding. Intensive monitoring is needed in work of this type to teach students to recognize their own errors (Léon, 1966 AUTHORITY). Parallel or simultaneous repetition is an exercise in which the student repeats either from memory or from a written transcript in unison with the master recording. This gives practice in listening for noticing and reproducing intonation and stress patterns. It can be used to effect also in the study of poetry.

Drills. Drills, sometimes called *structural drills* or *pattern practice,* used to be the principal activity carried on in language laboratories. The loosely used expression "language laboratory methods" usually refers to an intensive use of drills. The commonest type of drill (Stack, 1966 HISTORICAL) consists of four phases:

Phase 1: Stimulus (e.g., *John speaks French*)
Phase 2: Student's attempt *(John does not speak French)*
Phase 3: Correct response *(John doesn't speak French)*
Phase 4: Student's repetition of correct response *(John doesn't speak French)*

As can be seen, the stimulus presents students with a piece of language which they have to process in a predetermined way. Drills of this type have been much criticized (Hilton, 1973 ILLUSTRATION) for "turning the Language Laboratory into an electronic grammar grindstone," and it has been pointed out (Dakin, 1973 AUTHORITY) that the absence of any relation to meaning makes it possible to do the exercise faultlessly without understanding a word of it. As a result, the learner's performance in real language situations may be only marginally improved by hours of drilling.

Drills in which an element of meaning is included are more interesting and relate better to the way in which language actually works. Such drills are described as contextualized (Buckby, 1967 FURTHER DETAIL).

Other activities may include, for example,

Dialogue. The student is given alternate halves of a dialogue on the tape and has to invent the other role. By using recorded performances of plays, this exercise can be used to study the expressive uses of language, erasing the role of one actor for the student to replace.

Translation, consecutive and simultaneous. For the latter it is necessary to be able to switch off the top (master) track so as to assess the student's work (Henderson, 1975 FURTHER DETAIL).

Oral testing. The students' answers can be recorded from their machines to the console recorder for assessment (McKinstrey, 1973 FURTHER DETAIL).

For advanced students these basic activities can be adapted in a variety of interesting ways (Hilton, 1967; Ager, 1970; Dickinson, 1970 FURTHER DETAIL).

VISUAL MATERIAL IN THE LANGUAGE LABORATORY

It is uneconomic to use the language laboratory for the presentation of the visual part of an audiovisual course, which can be as efficiently done in an ordinary classroom. However, there can be advantages in using the intercom system of the language laboratory when showing video material if the audio can be relayed through the students' headsets and recorded on their machines, because of the considerable gain in acoustic quality.

The main purpose in using visual material in language laboratory exercises is to give a context, to add a dimension of meaning to an activity that is too often meaningless (Dakin, 1973 AUTHORITY). Where the visuals are presented in the simplest form, on cards or pages in a book, the representational possibilities are limited, but the main advantage of the language laboratory is retained in that the students can work individually at their own pace. Where more elaborate visual presentations are used, CCTV or film, this advantage is lost, and the laboratory must be used like an AA laboratory, with the class in lockstep. In spite of this, however, where CCTV is available it is possible to devise interesting exercise material which exploits the facility offered by the combination of language laboratory and television to present sound and image separately (Smith, 1969; Sherrington, 1973 FURTHER DETAIL). It is probable that the development of satellite television, and the consequent availability of, for example, Russian or Arabic video material off-air will lead to increased experimentation in this area.

A possible solution to the problem of lockstep working is the replacement of the students' recorders by video recorders or the addition of a video recorder to each booth. It is excessively costly, however, both in installation and in use, because a videotape can be used only a very limited number of times as compared with audiotape. What is more, the fact that students cannot interact with a VTR any more than with an ordinary tape recorder means that the language skills practiced are largely limited to aspects of listening comprehension, and the study of the communicative use of language is restricted largely to receptive skills. However, interesting possibilities are being explored (Riley 1976, 1981; Harding-Esh, 1982 FURTHER DETAIL).

LANGUAGE LABORATORIES AND LINGUISTIC THEORY

To the structural linguists of the 1940s and 1950s language was a form of behavior. Language learning could be compared (Skinner, 1957 BACKGROUND) to the process by which one learns a physical skill such as swimming or riding a bicycle, namely, by obliging one's body to go through certain movements until they became automatic, habitual. The audio-lingual method (Brooks, 1964; Rivers, 1968 HISTORICAL) by which language is learned inductively, by analogy rather than analysis, was the application of this view to language teaching. The language laboratory was ideally suited and rapidly adopted as an instrument for this purpose. In the early 1960s, language laboratories were being installed in schools on a large scale, first in the United States and later in Britain and other countries. At the same time the theoretical basis for the audio-lingual method of language learning was beginning to be seriously challenged.

The view of language as verbal behavior was in particular attacked by Noam Chomsky (1959 AUTHORITY), who, pointing out the inconsistencies inherent in seeing language as a habit structure, said that it is rule-governed and the product of an innate cognitive mechanism, a set of processes unique to human beings. At the same time it became increasingly clear to psycholinguists that the view of language as behavior was an oversimplification and that (Miller, 1965 BACKGROUND) if a language were to be learned simply as behavior, i.e., by stimulus and response techniques, it would take more than a lifetime to learn one. Subsequent developments in linguistics have all tended to see language as cognition rather than behavior, and, consequently, the learning of a language as a set of problem-solving operations rather than as the formation of habits. The audio-lingual method has in recent years to some extent been replaced by what is known as the code cognitive approach (Carroll, 1968 BACKGROUND), which is deductive and analytical, in direct contrast to the audio-lingual method (Lugton and Heinle, 1971 BACKGROUND). But it would be truer to say that the audio-lingual method has been replaced by a healthy skepticism regarding all methods claiming to offer a general solution. It will not be clear how much of language is cognition and how much is behavior until more is known about the psychology of language learning. Until then it may be wiser to see it as something of both (Wilkins, 1972 AUTHORITY).

Chomsky's term "grammatical competence" is that knowledge of language which enables a native speaker to produce well-formed sentences, but as other linguists have pointed out, this is not all his knowledge: he not only knows how to say something, he also knows when to say it, who to, and indeed even what to say and whether to speak at all. In other words, he has not only grammatical competence but communicative competence (Hymes, 1968 BACKGROUND). Recent thinking in the field of applied linguistics has been toward paying greater attention to meaning in language—in particular situational, communicative, or functional meaning—with an aim to giving the learner communicative competence. It can be seen that the artificial, mechanical nature of language laboratory materials, the fact that the student can only interact with the machine in a most limited way, and in a highly unreal, untypical situation, makes the instrument less than essential to a teacher who adopts a communicative, or, as it is sometimes called, notional approach. It is for this reason that listening is now seen by some as the most useful language laboratory activity (Riley, 1974 FURTHER DETAIL).

For an account of developments in linguistics as they concern language learning, see Roulet (1975 BACKGROUND), Wilkins (1972 AUTHORITY), and Allen and Widdowson (1975).

EFFECTIVENESS OF THE LANGUAGE LABORATORY

A number of research projects have been carried out into the effectiveness of language laboratories in schools, the two largest and best known being those described in the Keating report (1963 BACKGROUND) and the Pennsylvania Project (Smith and Baranyi, 1968 BACKGROUND). A full account of these and other investigations may be found in Forrester (1975 FURTHER DETAIL). The results of this research can be interpreted in more than one way, but the fact remains that it has not been possible to demonstrate clearly that the language laboratory is effective as a teaching instrument in school. Much of the research suffers from the difficulty, common to all large-scale research projects in education, of isolating the variable under investigation and holding all others constant. The York Project (Green, 1975 BACKGROUND), which covered three years and examined the effectiveness of the language laboratory as it is actually used in most British schools, was more conclusive. It found that such use of the laboratory constituted an "ineffective . . . exploitation of costly equipment."

In the light of such conclusions and of the linguistic considerations described above, it is evident that the day of "language laboratory methods" is over. This is certainly a good thing, since what has fallen out of favor is not the instrument but a use that had been made of it. As a means of vastly increasing a learner's exposure to a foreign language, the language laboratory is not in question. It may be that the essential instrument is not the complex of student positions and console but rather the individual dual-track tape recorders housed together, for technical and geographical convenience, in a center. Future developments seem likely to lie in the way of greater diversification and the development of equipment more adaptable to a variety of differing needs (Forrest, 1976 FURTHER DETAIL). The laboratory has been shown to be highly effective in specific areas of specialized linguistic instruction, for example, with advanced students (Freedman, 1969 ILLUSTRATION), and in relation to particular, narrowly defined linguistic skills such as listening comprehension, described above. Another line of development is towards more individual working and self-instructional methods (Ross, 1975 ILLUSTRATION; Ingram et al., 1975; Bullivant, 1979 FURTHER DETAIL). This again is more suited to advanced or older students, and mostly it is in universities that such developments have taken place. Roeming (1971 FURTHER DETAIL) describes one such university installation and presents arguments for its cost-effectiveness. Jalling (1971 FURTHER DETAIL), describing research in Sweden which showed the effectiveness of individualized instruction using language laboratory tape recorders, concludes that the likely future is a multimedia computer-controlled language laboratory. The appearance of computer-controlled tape recorders as in the Tandbeg AECAL system, which permit not only computer-assisted learning in the language laboratory but, more interestingly, the study of the interface between speech and writing, opens up perspectives which are yet to be explored (Fujimura, 1971; Last, 1983 FURTHER DETAIL).

B. Farrington

REFERENCES

Authority

Bennett, W. A. (1967) *Aspects of Language and Language Teaching*. London: Cambridge University Press.

Chomsky, N. (1959) "Review of B. F. Skinner: 'Verbal Behavior.'" *Language* 35 (1): 26–58.

Dakin, J. (1973) *The Language Laboratory and Language Learning*. London: Longman.

Hayes, A. S. (1968) *Language Laboratory Facilities*. Oxford: Oxford University Press.

Higgins, J. J. (1969) *Guide to Language Laboratory Material Writing*. Oslo: Universitetsforlaget.

Howatt, A. and Dakin, J. (1974) "Language Laboratory Materials." In *The Edinburgh Course in Applied Linguistics 3*, ed. J.P.B. Allen and S. P. Corder. London: Oxford University Press.

Leon, P. R. (1966) *Laboratoire de langues et correction phonétique: essai méthodologique*. Paris: Didier.

Wilkins, D. A. (1972) *Linguistics in Language Teaching*. London: Edward Arnold.

Background

Carroll, J. B. (1968) "The Contributions of Psychological Theory and Educational Research to the Teaching of Foreign Languages. *Modern Language Journal* 49: 278.

Farrington, B. (1969) "The Place of a Language Laboratory in a University French Department." *Audio Visual Language Journal* 8 (1): 19–24.

Green, P. S. (1975) *The Language Laboratory in School*. Edinburgh: Oliver and Boyd.

Hymes, D. H. (1968) "The Ethnography of Speaking." In *Readings in the Sociology of Language*, ed. J. Fisherman. The Hague: Mouton.

Keating, R. F. (1963) A study of the effectiveness of language laboratories, summarized in *IAR Research Bulletin* (Columbia University), 3: 3.

Lugton, R. C. and Heinle, C. H., eds. (1971) *Towards a Cognitive Approach to Second Language Acquisition*. Philadelphia: Center for Curriculum Development.

Miller, G. A. (1965) "Some Preliminaries to Psycholinguistics." *American Psychologist* 20: 15–20.

Roulet, E. (1975) *Linguistic Theory, Linguistic Description and Language Teaching*. London: Longman.

———. (1975) "Théories grammaticales et pédagogie des langues." *Language Teaching and Linguistics Abstracts* 9 (4): 197–211.

Skinner, B. F. (1957) *Verbal Behavior*. New York: Appleton-Century-Crofts.

Smith, P. D. and Baranyi, H. A. (1968) *A Comparison Study of the Effectiveness of the Traditional and Audio-lingual Approaches to Foreign Language Instruction Utilizing Language Laboratory Equipment*, USOE Project 7–0133. Harrisburg, Pa.: State Department of Public Instruction.

Further Detail

Ager, D. E. (1970) "Advanced Students in the Language Laboratory." *Visual Education* (May): 13–15.

Buckby, M. (1967) "Contextualisation of Language Drills." *Modern Languages* 47 (4): 165–70.

Bullivant, D. B. (1979) "Games People Play in the Language Laboratory—or 'The Punch and Judy Show.'" *System* 17 (2): 117–124.

Campbell, A. (1976) "Preparation of Materials for the Language Laboratory." *Modern Languages in Scotland* 9: 17–41.

Chatterton, D. J. (1972) *Language Laboratories*. Barnet, U.K.: Print & Press Services.

Cressman, D. M. (1970) "The Current State of the Remote Access Audio Video Information System." *Audiovisual Instruction* (September): 20–23.

Dahms, R. G. and Cicerau, E. J. (1976) "Effective Utilisation of the Language Lab: Planning, Evaluation, Procedures." *Canadian Modern Language Review* 33 (1): 32–38.

Department of Education and Science. (1968) *Language Lab-*

oratories, Education Survey 3. London: Her Majesty's Stationery Office.

Dickinson, L. (1970) "The Language Laboratory and Advanced Teaching." *English Language Teaching* 25 (1): 32–42.

Farrington, B. (1974) "A University Language Laboratory." *Modern Languages in Scotland* 3: 39–45.

Forrest, R. (1976) "Five Uses of the Language Lab with Advanced Students." *English Language Teaching* 30 (4): 332–339.

Forrester, D. L. (1975) "Other Research into the Effectiveness of Language Laboratories." In *The Language Laboratory in School*, ed. P. S. Green. Edinburgh: Oliver & Boyd.

Fujimura, O. (1971) "Technological Development for Language Learning." In *Applications of Linguistics*, ed. G. E. Perren and J.L.M. Trim. Selected Papers of the Second International Congress of Applied Linguistics, Cambridge, 1969. Cambridge: Cambridge University Press.

Harding-Esh, E. (1982) "The Open-Access Sound and Video Library of the University of Cambridge." *System* 10 (1): 13–28.

Harper, D. (1975) *Orientation and Attitude Formation in the Language Laboratory*. ELT Documents no. 1. London: British Council.

Henderson, J. A. (1975) "Design and Use of the Language Laboratory for the Teaching of Interpreting." *Audio Visual Language Journal* 13 (2): 101–109.

Higgins, J. J. (1975) "Problems of Self-Correction in the Language Laboratory." *System* 3 (3): 145–156.

Hilton, M. (1967) "Language Laboratory Exercises for Post A-Level Students." *Modern Languages* 48 (4): 151–156.

Hoffmann, N. (1976) "Information Retrieval Systems Retrieved? An Alternative to Present Dial Access Systems." *Audio Visual Language Journal* 14 (1): 9–15.

Hughes, G. (1974) "Aspects of Listening Comprehension." *Audio Visual Language Journal* 12 (2): 75–79.

Ingram, R. et al. (1975) "A Programme for Listening Comprehension." *Slavic and East European Journal* (Urbana, Ill.) 19 (1): 1–10.

Jalling, H. (1971) "Preliminary Recommendations of the Swedish Research Project on Language Laboratories in University Teaching: An Interim Report." In *Applications of Linguistics*, ed. G. E. Perren and J.L.M. Trim. Selected papers of the Second International Congress of Applied Linguistics, Cambridge, 1969. Cambridge: Cambridge University Press.

Last, R. W. (1983) *Computer-Assisted Language Learning*. London: Blackwells.

Lindsay, P.C.S. (1973) "Language Laboratories: Some Reflections after Ten Years." *English Language Teaching Journal* 28 (1): 5–10.

McKinstrey, R. (1973) "Large Scale Testing in the Language Laboratory." *Audio Visual Language Journal* 11 (1): 57–61.

Ministry of Technology. (1969) *Report of the Assessment of Language Laboratories*, RAF Farnborough Technical Report, No. 69100. RAF Farnborough, Hants, U.K.

Parker, K. (1973) "Language Laboratories: Which System?" *Audio Visual Language Journal* 11 (1): 7–11.

Pill, G. (1971) "How to Use the Language Laboratory without Actually Feeling Guilty." *NALLD Journal* (Athens, Ohio) 5 (4): 35–42.

Riley, P. (1974) *The Language Laboratory: Implications of the Functional Approach*. Nancy: Centre de Recherches et d'Applications Pédagogiques En Langues, Université de Nancy, pp. 53–64.

———. (1981) Viewing comprehension: "L'oeil écoute." ELT Documents Special, no. 1. London: The British Council, pp. 143–156.

Riley, P. and Zoppi, C. (1976) *The Sound and Video Library: An Interim Report on an Experiment*. Nancy: Centre de Recherches et d'Applications Pédagogiques En Langues, Université de Nancy, pp. 125–143.

Roeming, R. F. (1971) "A New Concept of the Language Laboratory and Its Application to Research and the Development of Proficiency in Language Learning." In *Applications of Linguistics*, ed. G. E. Perren and J.L.M. Trim. Selected Papers of the Second International Congress of Applied Linguistics, Cambridge, 1969. Cambridge: Cambridge University Press.

Sherrington, R. (1973) *Television and Language Skills*. London: Oxford University Press.

Smith, R. W. (1969) "Closed Circuit Television in the Language Laboratory." *Times Educational Supplement*, no. 2801 (24 January): 253.

Strevens, P. (1971) "Where Has All the Money Gone?" In *Applications of Linguistics*, ed. G. E. Perren and J.L.M. Trim. Selected Papers of the Second International Congress of Applied Linguistics, Cambridge, 1969. Cambridge: Cambridge University Press.

Turner, J. D. (1965) *Introduction to the Language Laboratory*. London: London University Press.

———. (1968) *Programming for the Language Laboratory*. London: London University Press.

Historical

Brooks, N. (1964) *Language and Language Learning: Theory and Practice*. New York: Harcourt Brace.

Forrester, D. L. (1966) "A Look at American Labs." *Audio Visual Language Journal* 3 (3): 147–148.

Hocking, E. (1964) *Language Laboratory and Language Learning*, DAVI Monograph 2. Washington: National Educational Association of the United States.

Léon, P. R. (1966) *Laboratoire de langues et correction phonétique: essai méthodologique*. Paris: Didier.

Marty, F. (1960) *Language Laboratory Learning*. Roanoke, Va.: Audio-Visual Publications.

Rivers, W. M. (1968) *Teaching Foreign Language Skills*. Chicago and London: University of Chicago Press.

Stack, E. M. (1966) *The Language Laboratory and Modern Language Teaching*, rev. ed. New York: Oxford University Press.

Illustration

Bung, K. (1967) *Programmed Learning and the Language Laboratory I & II*. London: Longman.

Farrington, B. and Richardson, C. (1977) "A Self-Instructional Language Laboratory Course in French for First Year University." *Audio Visual Language Journal* 15 (2).

Freedman, E. S. (1969) "An Investigation into the Efficacy of the Language Laboratory in Foreign Language Teaching." *Audio Visual Language Journal* 7 (2): 75–95.

Hilton, J. B. (1973) *Language Teaching: A Systems Approach*. London: Methuen.

Howatt, A.P.R. (1969) *Programmed Learning and the Language Teacher*. London: Longman.

Perelle, I. B. (1975) "Level II vs. Level III Language Laboratories: An Investigation of Their Relative Efficiencies." *System* 3 (3): 157–163.

Ross, L. (1975) "Self-Instructional Language Laboratory Reading Courses Based on Auditory Perception." *System* 3 (2): 106–190.

Van Abbé, D. (1968) "Differences between Audio-Active and Audio-Active-Comparative Language Laboratories." *Audio Visual Language Journal* 6 (1): 22–24.

LANGUAGE MASTER. A teaching machine developed by Bell & Howell which used software in the form of large cards on the base of which was a strip of magnetic tape. Thus a word could be printed on the card and the sound of the word recorded on the tape. The card could be inserted into the machine, which would then read out loud whatever was recorded on the tape.

The Language Master is typical of a number of educational inventions which appeared in the 1960s, in that the hardware was much more ingenious than the courseware made available to go with it.

LANTERN SLIDE. A large-format slide for projection. Historically, such slides were associated with medical illustration, and their size (4 1/4" x 3 1/4") permitted wax pencil annotations on the slide itself. However, such teaching innovations were necessarily restricted by the vast quantities of heat generated by the very high wattage lamp required to obtain a bright picture on the screen.

LAPEL MICROPHONE. Another name for a clip-on microphone.

LARGE-SCALE INTEGRATION (LSI). High-density integrated circuits for complex logic functions. LSI circuits can range up to several thousand transistors on a square millimeter silicon chip.

LASER. An electronic device that produces an intense, coherent, monochromatic beam of light using the process of *L*ight *A*mplification by *S*timulated *E*mission of *R*adiation. Such devices are increasingly being used in audiovisual and information technology systems, e.g., for decoding the stored information on compact disks and optical videodiscs, and in laser holography and laser printers.

LASER DISK. *See* **Video Disk.**

LASER DISK PLAYER. An electronic device which reads information from a disk by scanning with a laser. Each side of a standard disk can hold up to around 50,000 tracks (actual number depends on whether PAL or NTSC), giving a continuous playing time of approximately 30 minutes, or 50,000 still pictures, or combinations of both. Laser disks are also being used as ROM, in which case the storage capacity per side is about 1,000 Mbytes. *See* **Constant Angular Velocity; Constant Linear Velocity.**

LASER HOLOGRAPHY. *See* **Holography.**

LASER PRINTING. A laser printer operates in a manner comparable to an electrostatic photocopier. That is, the output from a computer modulates a laser beam, which thus causes an image to be built up on a selenium drum. By use of toner, heat, etc., this image is transferred to paper and "fixed."

The laser beam moves in a television-like raster and the process is extremely fast. Output quality is comparable to electronic typewriting.

LASER VISION. The trade name for an optical videodisc system developed by a consortium of companies including Philips, MCA, Pioneer, and Sony. The system encodes television signals in the form of a continuous spiral track on either surface of a plastic disk 300mm in diameter; each track consists of a series of pits of varying length and separation that are read by reflected light from a laser beam.

LATENT IMAGE. The invisible change caused by the action of light on the silver halide crystals in a photographic emulsion. A visible silver image is produced from the latent image only when the emulsion is developed.

LATEST EVENT TIME. The latest possible time at which an event can occur in an arrow diagram. *See* **Critical Path Analysis; Earliest Event Time.**

LAVALIER MICROPHONE. *See* **Neck Microphone.**

LCD. *See* **Liquid Crystal Display.**

LEADER. (1) A protective length of film, which is used to thread the projector so none of the actual picture is lost in threading. The leader may have pertinent information on it, such as title, laboratory information and name of distributor. It may have "count-down" cue numbers. Two such leaders, developed by the Society of Motion Picture and Television Engineers and by the Academy of Motion Picture Arts and Sciences, are denoted as SMPTE and Academy leader respectively. (2) The length of uncoated tape at the beginning of a spool of audiotape.

LEARNING-BY-APPOINTMENT. A system in which individual learners can reserve access to instructors, tutors, self-instructional materials, instructional hardware, etc., as and when they need them by making appropriate appointments.

LEARNING CONTRACT. An agreement between an individual learner and an instructor, department, institution, or organization which specifies some or all of the educational objectives to be attained, the method of instruction, and the way in which the eventual performance of the learner will be assessed. *See* **Contract-Based Learning.**

LEARNING ENVIRONMENT. The learning environment is not a neutral given in education. There is a strong relationship between environment and the behavior of individuals and groups. This relationship is complex and needs to be considered in social and psychological terms. In recognition of this, it is common to find social scientists contributing to the planning and the design of environments for learning in collaboration with architects and engineers.

The purpose of this entry is to draw together ideas and evidence from a diversity of sources and to illustrate how these ideas might be related to the design of the learning environment. Examples will be drawn mainly (but not exclusively) from higher education in Western society. Two major questions are posed as a basis for the discussion which follows. These questions are, Why should the learning environment be designed? How can the learning environment be designed?

DEFINITION OF CONCEPTS

Environments for learning are shown diagrammatically in Figure 35. This figure shows that the learning environment is part of a hierarchy and that this environment has two major parts: learning space and campus space. Learning spaces include classrooms, libraries, and laboratories. At this level, learners and teachers respond to the design of the space, its furnishings and fittings, and to other occupants of the space. Learning spaces are part of campus space. Campus space includes all learning spaces, buildings, open areas, roads and pathways, and

Figure 35
Model of Environment for Learning

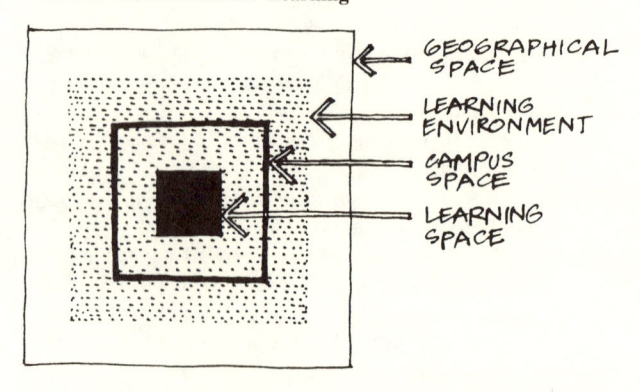

the relationships that exist between these. Campus space is one part of the learning environment within which learners and teachers work and which has an important influence upon the process of teaching and learning. The learning environment is part of geographical space which is worldwide in scale. (Because the learning environment has infinite physical size and varying boundaries, it is depicted in Figure 35 by the shaded area.)

Man's attempt deliberately to influence or modify his environment will tend to be most effective at the smaller scales of learning and campus space. This process of deliberate influence can be conceived of as a process of design, a process of establishing desirable characteristics for the learning environment and then using the best available means to achieve them. This process of design has become increasingly complex because educational goals and the means of achieving them have become more diverse and because they are also in a constant state of change. For example, **tertiary education** (q.v.) has become less elitist, and a steadily growing proportion of the population has enrolled for tertiary courses. This surge in enrollments has had an influence on types of courses offered in tertiary institutions and on teaching methods. Courses are more varied, and this has created demands for specialized learning spaces. Changes in methods such as the spread of individualized learning have also created demands for different kinds of spaces. At the primary and secondary levels of education there has been a trend toward open education. This trend is reflected in modern school design, which is often characterized by open-space areas and an absence of the traditional "box-like" classroom.

WHY SHOULD THE LEARNING
ENVIRONMENT BE DESIGNED?

There is little direct information on *how* the environment affects learning. However, it is known that environment *does* affect student behavior (including learning) and that, in turn, educational theory and practice influence the environment in which learning takes place. This interaction between learning and environment is of interest to designers whose task it is to create the most suitable settings for learning to take place.

A case for designing suitable learning environments can be made under the following two headings: (1) arguments based on man-environment interaction and (2) developments in the curriculum and in educational technology.

Arguments Based on Man-Environment Interaction. The learning environment provides a setting within which students and teachers work. Environment does not necessarily *determine* behavior, but it does influence and make possible, or impossible, certain patterns of behavior. Conversely, man is capable of exerting considerable influences on the environment around him. The more we understand the consequences of this man-environment interaction, the more we shall be capable of designing environments which meet our educational goals. Studies of man-environment interaction have been conducted at various scales and have had their origins in several disciplines, such as geography and psychology.

Schofer (1975 REVIEW) reviewed several studies which show how the geographical location of universities and colleges can be a critical variable in their success or failure as institutions. Studies have shown how distance and institutional character are major variables in what is referred to as "institutional drawing power". Schofer suggests that the failure of nine out of every ten colleges founded in the early years of the United States may have reflected a problem of geographical location as much as educational policy or practice.

The potential utility of location models (which take account of student preferences and institutional drawing power) for planning campus locations has not been widely recognized, as Abercrombie's account of nine new British universities illustrates (Abercrombie et al., 1974 REVIEW). Major factors influencing location decisions taken by the responsible University Grants Committee included application for a university from local authorities, the cost of sites, and the size of sites. Criticisms of the resulting suburban and rural locations of the new universities have been based on arguments of the relationship between the university and the community. The separation between town and gown has created feelings of physical and social isolation among students (Marris, 1964 RESEARCH). Others have argued for the greater degree of interaction between the university and its community that is best in central urban locations.

The case for a closer campus-community relationship is argued by Whisnant (1971 THEORY). Considerations of location and use of campus space are of profound importance in understanding community attitudes to universities and the behavior of individuals towards the campus:

The insular campus, first of all, serves as a ready focus for the hostility of the surrounding community. The intellectual and psychological (and usually economic) distance between town and gown is reinforced when each can locate the other in mutally exclusive and jealously guarded spaces. . . .

Second, spatial fragmentation on the campus itself leads to internal conflict: rivalry between departments, schools and colleges is virtually guaranteed when each isolates itself physically and psychologically in its own private space.

Environmental psychologists also recognize that the physical environment has meaning for people. Techniques for measuring this meaning have been applied (Wools and Canter, 1970 RESEARCH METHOD). However, the environment consists of more than purely physical variables (such as structures, pathways, and boundaries).

Ittelson et al. (1974 THEORY) have identified other variables which include

—affective variables (beauty, comfort, order)

—functional variables (the suitability of an environment for its task)

—cognitive variables (the meanings implicit in an environment suggesting certain uses and interpretations)

—social variables (environmental cues for the behavior of groups)

Whisnant (1971 THEORY) stresses the neglect of the cognitive and social variables in his attack on traditional campus planning and use. He concludes that "we must be less pious about the use of physical facilities, accept pluralism of architectural style as an item of policy, integrate traditionally separate spaces and function to a much greater degree and abandon the insular campus model." Buildings which integrate a diversity of facilities such as student residences, administrative offices, learning spaces, and cafeterias are suggested as a means of achieving this.

Some of the basic assumptions underlying the design of learning spaces have been challenged. For example, de Carlo (1974 THEORY) asks and discusses the following questions: "Is it really necessary for contemporary society that educational activity be organized in a stable and codified institution?" and "Must educational activity take place in buildings designed especially for that purpose?" Ways of designing and using "alternative" learning environments (which may be suggested by considering these questions) are drawn together in a thought-provoking collection of papers edited by Coates (1974 THEORY).

Documents of various kinds have been published to help campus planners and designers. One of the most comprehensive of these documents was published by UNESCO in 1975 (DESIGN GUIDES). This publication gives detailed advice on all major procedures in planning and design (policy formulation, planning, briefing, and implementation) and includes an extensive bibliography cross-referenced to each step in the procedure.

The 1960s witnessed a period of remarkable expansion in campus construction. Several appraisals of the work completed have been undertaken (Schmertz, 1972; Birks, 1972; Brawne, 1967 REVIEW). Much of this work is architectural in orientation. Social factors (including education) have received comparatively little attention.

Other evidence of man-environment interaction is provided in studies of space belonging to the field of inquiry known as environmental psychology. These studies have useful descriptive value and implications for the design and use of all learning spaces. Studies of learning spaces as behavior settings have suggested that the location of an individual in the space is a likely influence on that individual's interaction with the space and with other occupants of the space. A pioneering study found that in a circular seating arrangement persons seated opposite tended to interact more than those seated side by side (Steinzor, 1950 RESEARCH). A later study by Hearn (1957 RESEARCH) suggested that the "Steinzor effect" was operative in groups with minimal leadership but the effect diminished as direction and control by a leader increased. Howells and Becker (1962 RESEARCH) found that seat location was an important factor in determining leadership emergence and communication patterns.

Among the studies of interaction in larger discussion groups are those of Sommer (1967 RESEARCH) and Adams and Biddle (1970 RESEARCH). Both showed that interaction rates are highest among people seated up front and in the middle of typical row and column classroom layouts. What these studies did not answer is the question, Does the location determine interaction or do the more vocal students select these locations? Koneya (1976 RESEARCH) addressed himself to these questions and found that students categorized as "high verbal interactors" chose central seats to a significantly greater degree than did "low verbal interactors." Koneya suggests that low verbalizers may deliberately seek seats with a low potential for interaction after having ⋅ le a preliminary appraisal of the situation they are a⌃ ⌄t to encounter. This explanation is also advanced by Canter (1970 RESEARCH). Koneya found that seat location was a determinant of verbal interaction rates among a group designated as "moderate verbalizers." Centrally seated moderate verbalizers produced significantly higher verbalization rates than did non–centrally seated moderate verbalizers. The relative position of the teacher also influences patterns of student seating behavior. Canter discovered that the "near" or "far" position of a tutor had a marked influence on seating patterns in a formal row arrangement of classroom furniture.

Much, if not all, of the available learning spaces in universities can be described as "hard": chairs are arranged in straight rows or around rectangular tables, the floors are tiled, and color schemes are drab. Sommer and Olsen (1980 RESEARCH) report an experiment which transformed such a typically hard classroom into a "soft" environment. Hexagonal lounge-style seating, carpet, adjustable lighting, and decorative items were added. The outcomes included a positive attitude to the room among students who used it and increased verbal participation. The authors point out, however, that the room did not suit all groups of students due to differing curriculum demands. The same problem exists, of course, for all general-purpose rooms, regardless of whether they are "hard" or "soft."

The impact of the careful design of learning spaces on behavior has also been demonstrated at the other end of the educational spectrum—in kindergartens. Nash (1981 RESEARCH), for example, has shown how the deliberate design and arrangement of classrooms contributed positively to a number of specific learning outcomes.

The library as a learning space has been studied by Sommer (1966, 1968 RESEARCH). The earlier study (1966) showed that about half of a surveyed group of university students preferred to study in large public reading areas and the other half in semiprivate areas such as tables in the book stacks or study carrels. On this finding Sommer writes:

The ideal library would not be one with all individual study rooms or all open areas but, instead, would contain a diversity of spaces that would meet the needs of introvert and extrovert, lone studiers, browsers and daylong researches. *It is a serious mistake to assume that all people have the same spatial needs.* (emphasis in original)

It would also be a mistake to assume that library users go there to use the collection. Sommer (1968b, 1970 RESEARCH) reports that most readers (up to nine-tenths of them) are using their own materials rather than the collection. These findings have important implications for learning space designers as well as administrators.

A variety of other settings are, of course, used by studiers. These settings include the student's place of residence, cafeterias, empty classrooms, and outdoor areas. Sommer concludes that "it is an illusion to think in terms of an ideal study environment. . . . What is needed is a variety of study situations that can appeal to students with particular interests'' (1970 RESEARCH).

Space designers have badly neglected the outdoor ares of campus space. Sommer's studies show that students often have positive reasons for working out of doors rather than in a library or at home (1970 RESEARCH). These reasons include the pleasantness of the surroundings and proximity to other activities (such as a lecture theater or laboratory). However, many opportunities for outdoor study are lost through sheer neglect or poor design, such as badly constructed seating, absence of windbreaks, lack of privacy, and inadequate landscaping.

The design of student residences has also been examined for their influence on student behavior. Here again, architectural influences are apparent (Wilcox and Holahan, 1976 RESEARCH).

What are the implications for learning space designers of man-environment interaction findings? First, it is clear that the environment is not neutral in teaching and learning. Studies of classroom layout and libraries show that a strong relationship exists between layout, perception of classroom activity, position of tutor, student characteristics, interaction patterns, and use of space. This suggests that designers ought to give close attention to each of these variables. Second, what takes place within learning spaces is a highly complex psychological, sociological, and physical interaction. It follows from this that social scientists have significant contributions to make to the design of learning spaces. Third, student choice of study space and classroom location is influenced by a wide variety of factors, including personality traits. Thus, no one design will suit the needs of all individuals; therefore, a variety of types of learning spaces ought to be provided. Fourth, the arrangement of physical facilities at all scales (geographical to learning space) has a strong communicative power that should not be ignored by designers and teachers.

Anthropometrics establishes statistical averages for the anatomical measurements of different populations. Data prepared from these averages are often used as a basis for the design of spaces, equipment, and furniture and the basis of building codes. Some are published in architectural handbooks such as the *AJ Metric Handbook* (Sliwa and Fairweather, 1970 DESIGN GUIDES) or in anthropometric guides (Dreyfuss, 1967 DESIGN GUIDES). When applied to specific work tasks (such as the school, office, or factory), these data come within areas known variously as human engineering, biomechanics, engineering psychology, or ergonomics. These areas consider the problem of fit between man and machine, and standards such as lighting, temperature, and acoustic levels. Valuable sourcebooks in this area are Woodson (1981) and Woodson and Conover (1973 DESIGN GUIDES). Rapoport and Watson (1967–1968 RESEARCH) have shown that supposedly ''hard'' data (relating to lighting, temperature, etc.) need to be used with some caution. They observe that anthropometric standards vary considerably between societies and within a society. These standards also vary over time. Evidence suggests that practical limits to this data may be determined by the *social* context rather than by physical or biological factors. This is true for furnishings, temperature, noise, and light. For example, a comparison between recommended maximum levels of artificial light for learning and office spaces shows a range of 300 lux for Sweden, 700 for Australia, and 5,000 for the United States (1 lux = lumen square meter, S1 Units).

Developments in Curriculum and Educational Technology. Educational research has underlined the importance of variety in teaching and learning and of the different needs and characteristics of the student population. In recognition of this, one trend has been toward individualized instruction (at school, college, and university) and to open education (at school level). Among the concepts associated with the philosophy of individualized instruction that have spatial design implications are diagnosing the needs of each learner; providing alternative modes of instruction; and providing a rich and diverse curriculum. These concepts imply a need for space in which to counsel students, space for learners to study alone or in groups of varying sizes, spaces for modes of instruction independent of direct personal contact with a teacher and spaces for specialized areas of the curriculum such as languages, science, and crafts.

These concepts are recognized in the expansion of open education at the school level. Stephens (1974 THEORY) describes open education as ''an approach to education that is open to change, to new ideas, to curriculum, to scheduling, to use of space, to honest expression of feeling between teacher and pupil and between pupil and pupil and open to childrens' participation in significant decision-making in the classroom.'' Schools designed by this philosophy are generally known as ''open plan'' schools. A helpful review and study of this concept in practice is provided by Bennett et al. (1980 RESEARCH). Open plan schools are characterized by a general absence of partitioning into standard-size classrooms, a variety of area sizes (divisible if necessary by screens or flexible partitions), and a variety of attractive furnishings and fittings. Not all children learn effectively in an open environment, however, and in some open plan schools pupils have been transferred to traditional classrooms (Thompson, 1972 RESEARCH). Gill (1977 RESEARCH) was unable to find evidence that the architectural change from conventional schools to open plan schools *necessarily* resulted in changes in teacher-pupil activity. These experiences underline findings—typical of the classroom studies discussed previously—that not all students have identical needs for instructional mode, space, or contact with others. Increasing variety in the curriculum is also reflected in the provision of special educational facilities for ethnic minorities, handicapped students, and those participating in **distance education** (q.v.) programs.

A development concurrent with the philosophical and curricular changes has been the evolution of educational technology. In its widest sense, educational technology has meant the exploitation of available knowledge about teaching and learning to meet the demands of educational goals. In its narrowest sense, it has meant the use of audiovisual media in education. In both senses, it has had an important impact on the design of learning spaces. This impact is most clearly reflected in the design of some lecture theaters (Taylor, 1967 DESIGN GUIDES) and the design of new libraries, or resource centers (Thompson, 1972 RESEARCH).

The development of educational technology has, according to Green (1970 THEORY), led to conflicts between the educational philosophy of schools and space and facilities. Conflicts have evolved from

1. A narrow concept of educational technology that has resulted in a failure to provide facilities for both large-group teaching and individual learning
2. A lack of a definitive role for educational technology, often leading to the purchase of (educationally) inappropriate equipment and materials
3. Failure to discover available and appropriate options in equipment and to consider the impact of these options on building design
4. Inadequate accommodation for equipment with concurrent problems of space layout, screens, and relationships with other media and methods
5. Failure to anticipate changes in educational technology
6. A neglect of planning for equipment access and transport of facilities between spaces
7. Failure to provide all the facilities needed to support educational technology such as production, service, and library facilities

According to the Carnegie Commission (1972 THEORY), experience with educational technology (compared with early hopes) is showing that it is costing more, developing more slowly, and adding to, rather than replacing, older approaches. However, the commission states: "Nevertheless, by the year 2000, it now appears that a significant proportion of instruction in higher education on campus may be carried on through informational technology—perhaps in the range of 10–20 per cent." New buildings, according to the commission, should be built with adequate electronic components. These buildings would be necessary to accommodate the technologies which will come into common use by around the year 2000.

The wider view of educational technology has equally important implications for learning space design. Examples include the educational (as well as spatial) integration of a variety of methods and media, use of off-campus teaching facilities, and the evaluation of teaching and learning which could conceivably result in constant modification of learning spaces as well as the modification of teaching and learning.

HOW CAN THE LEARNING ENVIRONMENT BE DESIGNED?

In answering this question, emphasis will be placed on the design of learning spaces, especially those spaces intended for use in higher education. A common approach to learning space design has been for the architect to follow some kind of carefully sequenced steps. Smith (1974 DESIGN GUIDE) has produced additions to this approach by formulating checklists of questions for the client, user, and architect. These checklists have been developed from research into the use of educational technology in primary and secondary schools and are directed specifically to these levels of education.

Learning Spaces. Teaching and learning are often restricted because of the design and use of available learning spaces. One important consideration is the design of spaces to accommodate educational technology. Green (1970 THEORY) reached the following conclusion in his discussion of guidelines for the use of technology:

When accommodating technology seek the simple solutions, the solutions that are educationally sound but which require the least commitments in terms of facilities. Above all, don't first plan a school for instructional technology; rather plan a school for people.... A school building that is good for people is about as good as a school can be and chances are it will also be good for instructional technology....

Principles to guide designers in the planning of educational technology for schools have been suggested by Green (1966 DESIGN GUIDES; 1970 THEORY). Following are some of the more important of these principles:

1. *Centrality of learning.* The planning and design of learning spaces must create an environment which encourages and in no way interferes with learning. This principle has im-

plications for lighting, climate, color selection, seating, acoustics, and equipment.

2. *Variety of spaces.* A variety of spaces will be necessary to meet the requirements of schools. The effective use of media will require a system of spaces composed of

   - learning spaces for individual students and different sized groups of students
   - spaces for the production, maintenance, storage, and distribution of equipment and materials

3. *Flexibility.* Flexibility is desirable to accommodate different group sizes, teaching methods, and media. An analysis of learning spaces in terms of function may help to establish appropriate flexibility. The analysis may reveal a need for

   - spaces for interchangeable functions, such as rooms equally suitable for tutorials and for individual private study
   - spaces for specific functions but multidisciplinary use, for example, lecture theaters
   - spaces for specific discipline use, for example, engineering laboratories, which would be quite unsuitable for other uses

4. *Media.* Media should be potentially available in every learning space. This may mean the provision of cables or conduits and an array of display surfaces such as chalkboards and screens. Mobile trolleys, equipped with a variety of media, could be housed within an area and moved from space to space as necessary (see, for example, figure 40).

5. *Age level.* Learning spaces should not be rigidly geared to one age level but should be capable of reassignment to other age levels as required. This principle recognizes a trend toward greater community use of school facilities.

6. *Changes in technology.* Technology should not necessarily be built into the fabric of the building. New equipment can more readily replace the old if this advice is followed. Self-contained, portable equipment may be a more satisfactory way of providing facilities for technology.

These guidelines tend to place emphasis upon the media aspects of educational technology. A more encompassing view considers three questions in designing for technology: (1) How will information be presented to students, or presented by students? (2) What kinds of interaction will there be between students and teachers? (3) What other kinds of activity (e.g., practical work) will students be required to engage in? (Cannon, 1976 THEORY). The answers to each of these questions will help in planning physical facilities that will have to be provided in each learning space.

Learning Spaces for the Presentation of Information. The lecture is still a common method used to present information to learners (especially in higher education). Reviews of research into lecturing include the following generalizations, which have implications for space designers:

1. Lectures are as effective as other methods of imparting information (but not more so).
2. The uninterrupted 50–minute lecture is a poor method for learning. Lecture effectiveness may be improved if there can be student participation, application of what is learned, feedback to the learner, and variety in presentation of information and in interaction (Bligh, 1972 RESEARCH).

Among the implications of these generalizations are that lecturing (as a teaching method) is likely to continue but that variety in presentation is desirable. One way of achieving variety is to use audiovisual media. Factors influencing the design of spaces for audiovisual media are summarized in Table 17.

Lectures are often delivered in spaces capable of accommodating several hundred students and in other spaces (perhaps more appropriately called lecture rooms or classrooms) with a capacity for about forty students or less. Possible groupings and layout of lecture spaces are indicated in Figure 36.

The lecturer-dominated pattern is only one of several possible interactions that can occur. Other interactions that might be desirable to achieve increased attention and learning are described below. The implications of these interactions for the learning space are also described.

Buzz groups, or small subgroups of students in a lecture, can discuss a problem for two to five minutes and perhaps report to the whole group. The main requirement for buzz groups is to create an arrangement of seating and writing surfaces that enable students to face each other. Such an arrangement at the Sydney University Law School is illustrated in Figure 37.

Feedback systems (or student response monitors) allow a lecturer to evaluate understanding or the effectiveness of a presentation immediately. These systems consist of a response unit of four or five buttons to each student position connected to a computer and display screen at the lecturer's bench. The computer can analyze data and display it within seconds. In planning such a system it is necessary to know the number and location of student positions and to provide conduit for wiring.

It is possible to set problems for students to solve individually in lectures. This enables new knowledge to be applied immediately and provides a test of understanding. During problem solving the lecturer may wish to move around and help students having difficulty. Space for movement between rows of students thus needs to be provided. Alternatively, small groups of students may be able to gather around the lecturer's bench to witness a demonstration. When numbers prevent this,

Table 17
Some Factors Influencing the Design of Spaces for Audiovisual Media

Factor	Maximum Criteria for Effectiveness	Space and Design Considerations
Lecturer	a. Audible	a. Acoustic design and speech amplification system
	b. Visible to all students	b. Lines of sight and internal geometry of space
	c. Able to conduct and control demonstrations	c. Suitable lecturer's bench and working surfaces for demonstrations
	d. Able to control audiovisual media and lighting system	d. Controls on or adjacent to lecturer's bench. Proximity and ease of operation of overhead projector, display boards, screens, and lights
Display boards (including one or more of the following in combination: chalkboard, whiteboard, pinboard)	Visible (i.e., not blocked from view by other facilities or by students). Ease of use, cleaning, manipulation (i.e., of roller and sliding boards	Arrangement of boards at front of space (or in a corner). Position and height of boards Relationship between display boards, screens, and lecturer. Location of mobile boards
Maps and charts	Visible Ease of manipulation	Availability of display surface (could be on pinboard or on magnetic chalkboard with magnetic devices); or fixtures on which to hang charts; or fixed rollers to store and to display frequently used maps or charts
Screens (for slide and film projection)	a. Correct size for location	a. Screen width—one-sixth of the length of the teaching space
	b. Accurate reflection (or transmission of light if rear projection is used)	b. Alternate screen types are translucent (for rear projection); matte white, aluminized; beaded; lenticular

348

		c. Viewing angle depends on screen type. For the common matte white screens the horizontal viewing angle should not exceed 60°
		d. In large spaces the bottom edge of the screen should be about 2m from the floor. Screens may be placed across a corner of the space
Multiple screens (usually two or three adjacent screens for comparison of simultaneously projected slides)	c. Picture satisfactory over as wide a viewing angle as possible	As for Screens above
	d. Visible and correct position for type of room	
Overhead projector screen	Visible (may also be adjustable for slide and film projection)	Screen should be high and tilted forward at the top to avoid keystoning (a projected image being wider at the top than at the bottom)
Audio aids (i.e., tapes, cassettes, radio broadcasts)	Audible	Amplification and distribution system. Location of speakers. Tape and cassette players may be permanently installed or provision may be made at lecturer's bench to plug into the system provided
	Ease of use and control	Radio reception facilities
Film projector	Projected images visible	Location of projector for either front projection or rear projection
	Sound audible	Control of projector
	Ease of use and control	Choice of lens appropriate to type of film, size of screen, and location of projector

Table 17 (continued)

Factor	Maximum Criteria for Effectiveness	Space and Design Considerations
Film projector (continued)		Location of speakers and/or provision to plug into sound system Suitable room darkening and light control facilities
Video	Video images visible Sound audible Ease of use and control	Depends on nature of video system in use, i.e., a. Closed circuit video system to relay demonstration at lecturer's bench to lecture theater will require camera and camera stand; connections to video system; suitably located monitors on movable stands or fixed to ceiling; or video projector system b. Video and broadcast distribution system will require off-air reception facilities; videocassette player(s); suitably located monitors (either color or black and white) (Note: Institution's video system needs to be able to cope with a variety of software formats (i.e., monochrome videotapes and color videocassettes)
Slide projector	Projected images visible Ease of use and control	Location of projector in readily accessible position (the projector may require its own movable table or trolley) Suitable room-darkening and light-control facilities
Computer	Displays visible Accessible computer terminal or computer display outlet	Computer terminal and/or display monitors (may be integrated with closed-circuit video system)

350

Figure 36
Grouping and Layout of Lecture Theaters

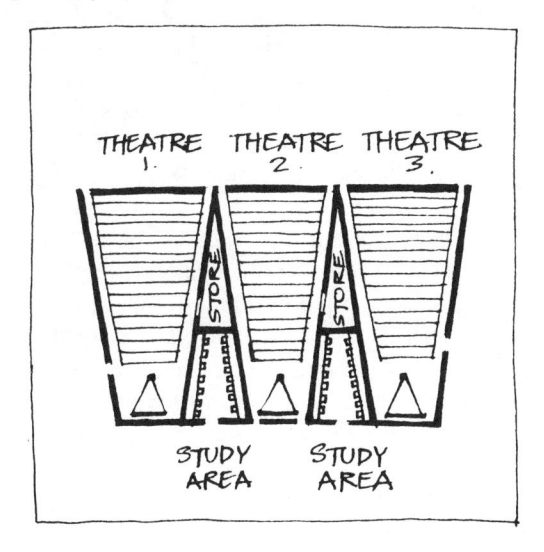

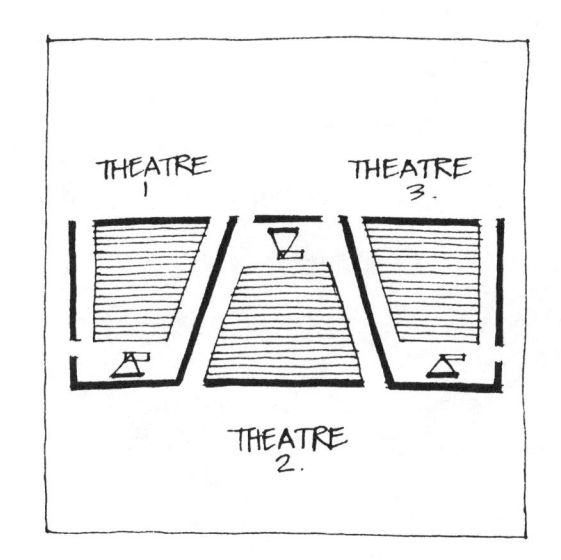

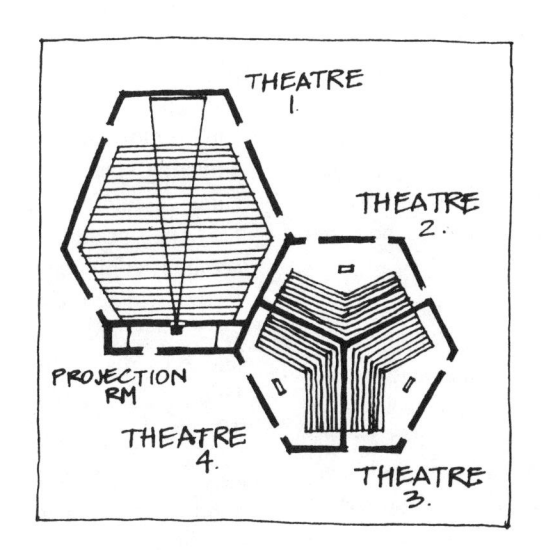

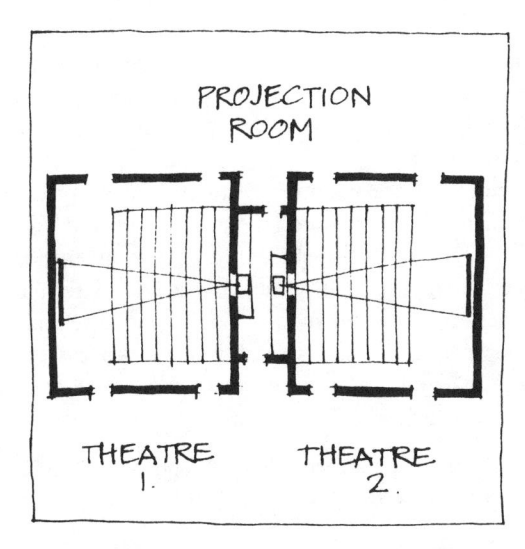

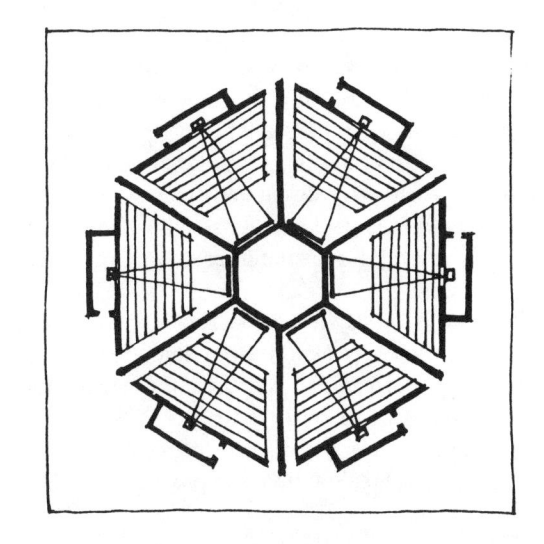

351

Figure 37
Design of a Theater at Sydney University

demonstrations can be displayed using closed-circuit video. Although interactions of these kinds can be used in lecture theaters, some of them are more suitable for smaller groups. The needs of small groups can be better met in smaller spaces such as classrooms.

Learning Spaces for Interaction between Teachers and Learners: Seminars, Conferences, and Small Group Methods in Education. Spaces for seminars and conferences should give people the opportunity of facing each other for discussion. Although there must also be reasonable facility for the presentation of information, there will need to be provision for a high degree of interaction between all participants and for flexibility in the arrangement of furnishings, fittings, and audiovisual media. The major consideration is to design a space in which the dual purposes of presentation and discussion can be achieved comfortably. Figure 38 presents some alternative arrangements within these types of spaces.

Figure 39 shows how a series of conference and small group teaching rooms (for discussion) may be usefully grouped adjacent to a larger lecture space. Such grouping is particularly useful for conferences involving large numbers of people.

One difficulty is to establish an ideal size for a seminar or small group room. We know from studies of small groups that a group size of five is optimal for meaningful discussion to take place (Hare, 1976 RESEARCH). However, this number is clearly too small for most seminars and for conferences. One solution is to provide a number of spaces of varying capacities as shown in Figure 39. Another is to divide a larger area with suitable screens to reduce the effective size of the area and make it seem reasonably "full" with comparatively small numbers of people and to discourage dispersed seating patterns. Small group spaces can be used for a diversity of purposes, as illustrated in Figure 38. These purposes may include simulations, role-play, debates, and workshops.

Flexible arrangements, such as those illustrated, require movable furniture and fittings, including chairs, tables, screens for projection, screens for dividing up spaces, benches, equipment trolleys, chalkboards, and display boards. Flexibility of this kind can be valuable in overcoming the built-in formality of fixed furnishings or of standard column and row arrangements of furniture. Because there may be a high degree of movement and considerable noise, it is important to plan for the acoustic difficulties that will be encountered. Curtains, soft floor coverings, and sound-absorbing screens will be useful for this purpose. (Curtains can serve the additional purpose of providing blackout to windows.)

A character conducive to informality and interaction can be introduced in learning spaces through the use of carpeting, the careful selection of furnishings and, in some cases, facilities for the preparation of coffee and tea. Appropriate facilities for using audiovisual media in seminar, conference, and tutorial rooms may be chosen by referring to Table 17. However, it is unlikely that each small group teaching room will be equipped with audiovisual aids. In this case, equipment trolleys that can be moved from room to room will be most useful (Figure 40).

Learning Spaces for Other Activities. Space requirements for the implementation of individualized learning depend on the nature of the aims and on the content of courses offered using these methods. Space requirements could range from a single carrel for one student working from a programmed text to whole rooms full of equipment, laboratory benches, carrels, discussion rooms, and private studies.

Some of the common features of each type of individualized learning are an emphasis on student activity; the opportunity for students to work independently at their own pace or in groups of various sizes; the use of a variety of media such as books, models, real objects and specimens, slides, audio and video cassettes, and film. The design implications of these three features are listed below.

1. There will be a need to provide appropriate working areas to meet the requirements of these varied activities. These

Figure 38
Alternative Arrangements for Furnishings in Seminar Rooms

Figure 39
Grouping of Different Size Learning Spaces

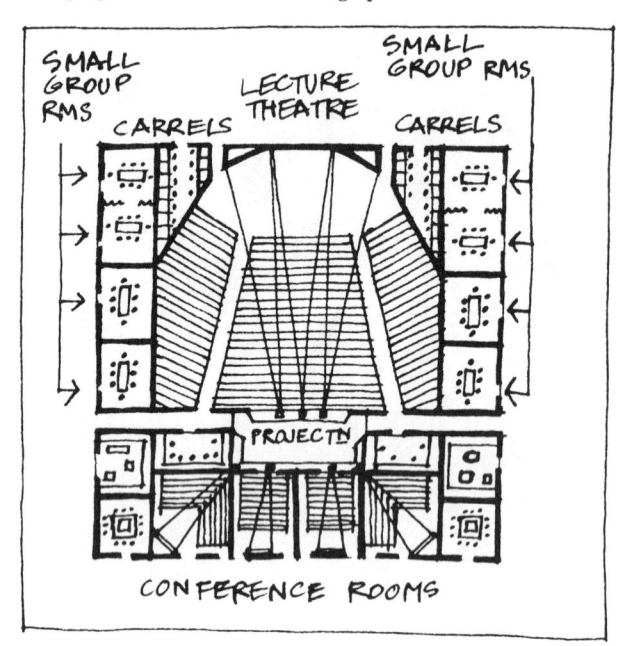

work areas could include access to laboratories, workshops, carrels, or group discussion rooms.

2. Some students will require a place to study independently free of the distractions surrounding them.
3. Facilities for media will need to be provided on an individual basis as well as on a group basis. Where media are used, storage and supervision of equipment and materials need to be considered. Teaching materials (slides, tapes, specimens)

Figure 40
Trolley for Audiovisual Equipment

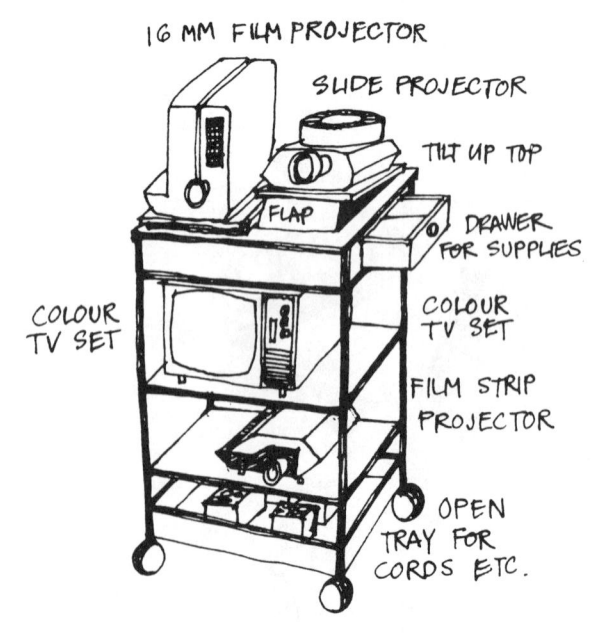

Figure 41
Space for Individualized Instruction

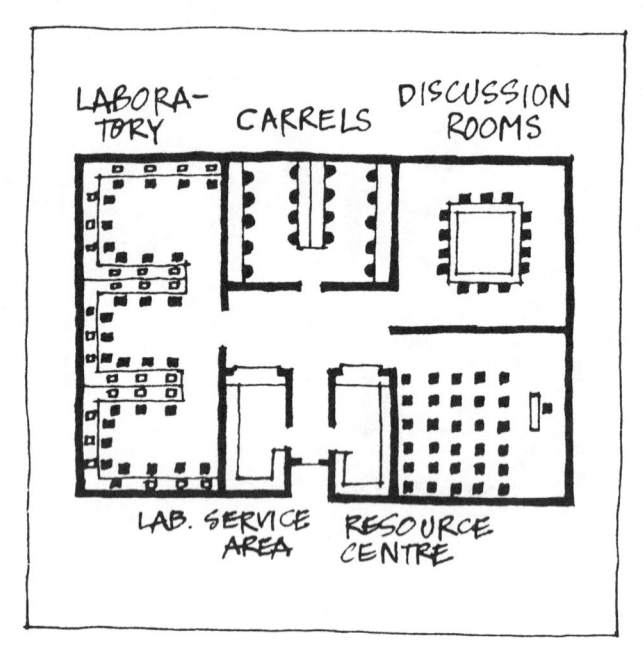

may be stored and issued from a service area within the learning space. Computing facilities will also be needed.

Spaces for individualized learning frequently need to be grouped together. Figure 41 illustrates one arrangement for a subject in which laboratory work is associated with materials prepared for individual study. In this arrangement carrels are grouped together so they can share common facilities such as lighting, acoustics, furnishings, and service areas. Group facilities are provided where these are an integral part of the course, and these can be used for discussion, project work, testing, and student counseling.

In other courses it might be undesirable to separate functions so discretely. Postlethwait et al. have described the physical facilities used for a botany course at Purdue University taught by the audio-tutorial method (1972 DESIGN GUIDES). These facilities include a learning center (comprising service area, bulletin boards, carrels, display tables, study table, and reference library), an adjacent workroom and preparation room, a lecture theater, small group rooms, and a greenhouse. These facilities for individualized learning are indicative of the special curriculum requirements (in this case, botany). Carrels will vary in design but will generally include some provision for using audiovisual media. Special-purpose carrels may include wiring for audio and video programs from a remote control room, and gas, water, air, and electrical services. However, most carrels will not need these services except for power outlets. In determining the number of carrels needed for a particular learning area, it is important to take account of each of the following: the number of students who will use the area, the estimated number of carrel hours per week, and the number of hours per week the learning area will be open to students.

Practical work within particular curriculum areas usually presents the designer with a unique challenge. Much has been published on the design of science laboratories (Purvis, 1973; Ferguson, 1973 DESIGN GUIDES). Generally, these publications focus on physical questions of layout and equipment, reflecting the paucity of knowledge about human factors in laboratory design. One exception is Kendrick's paper (1975 RESEARCH) describing laboratories for building science courses. This paper gives close attention to ergonomic considerations in chair, table, and equipment layout. The basic furniture module in the laboratory is based on a cube of size 700mm (including castors). This module is available in a modified configuration for writing and for laboratory equipment of various dimensions.

The library as a learning space is considered in several of the studies previously described. Langmead and Beckman (1970 DESIGN GUIDES) outline an approach to academic library planning which considers technological considerations equally with purely library and architectural ones.

The variety of methods of teaching and learning depends on the provision of certain minimum physical facilities for their effective implementation. These physical facilities are embodied in spaces which reflect careful consideration of lighting, acoustics, climatic control, and furnishings, and which make provision for educational technology. Opportunities to alter the spatial relationships between learners, teachers, and some of these physical facilities are often desirable to help achieve certain aims in teaching, especially those aims best achieved by varying group size.

Lighting systems need to be suitable for all the activities which occur in the learning space. These activities need to be carefully identified at the planning stage. Activities may include notetaking; the projection of slides, films, and overhead transparencies; the viewing of television; displays of various kinds (charts, maps, chalkboard); discussion; and certain kinds of practical work. Appropriate levels of illumination (for given activities) on screen and display surfaces, working surfaces (desks or tables), and surroundings need to be considered. During the projection of film or slides, students' writing surfaces should be adequately lit to facilitate note taking. In larger spaces, such as lecture theaters, supplementary lighting should be provided on chalkboards, display surfaces for charts and maps, and demonstration areas. An appropriate means of controlling the lighting system, and any natural light sources, needs to be provided. However, controls should be as simple as possible. If lights are arranged in banks in lecture theaters, it is essential to be able to switch them on and off in rows across the ceiling paralleling the seating rows. This arrangement facilities projection of films or slides and at the same time enables a sufficient level of illumination to be provided for note taking. A common error is to place bright room lighting immediately in front of overhead projection screens. This gives a "washed-out" image on the screen and makes the projected image difficult, if not impossible, to read.

Good acoustic qualities are essential in all learning spaces. Acoustic considerations include the distribution of sound within the space, the passage of sound between spaces, and levels of background noise. Acoustic design may sometimes include the installation of amplification systems for recorded sounds, film, and television in lecture theaters. However, acoustically well-designed lecture theaters should need no speech reinforcement system, provided there is no interference from outside noise. Learning spaces should also be comfortable in terms of temperature, humidity, and ventilation.

Furnishings include seating, writing and work surfaces, lecture benches, room dividers, storage units, curtains, and floor coverings. Furnishings should meet functional, aesthetic, and ergonomic criteria. These criteria need to be identified early in the planning stages since furnishings are an important part of the total facility for teaching and learning, and have been shown to influence learner behavior (Sommer and Olsen, 1980 RESEARCH).

Seating can be fixed, movable, or combined. Fixed seating has the advantage of assuring that every occupant is in the proper relationship to display surfaces and screens but has limitations in flexibility. Fixed seating is possibly most appropriate in lecture theaters. Movable seating permits flexibility in arranging rooms to meet particular requirements but can sometimes result in disorder of arrangement if not suitably controlled. Combined seating consists of movable seats arranged behind fixed writing surfaces. Some commercially available seats have their own tablet arms for writing, but these arms are often far too small for student needs. Where movable seating (without tablet arms) is provided, it is desirable to have a flexible arrangement of tables which can be used for seminar or discussion groupings. Alternative arrangements of rectangular and trapezium tables are illustrated in Figure 42 to show how this might be achieved. The modular writing unit described by Kendrick (1975 RESEARCH) is a very useful innovation, especially for certain kinds of laboratories.

A movable lecturer's bench is illustrated (see Figure 43) which overcomes some of the difficulties of size and

Figure 42
Alternative Arrangements for Rectangular and Trapezium Tables

6 TABLES – 8 PERSONS

2 TABLES – 6 PERSONS

Figure 43
A Movable Lecturer's Bench

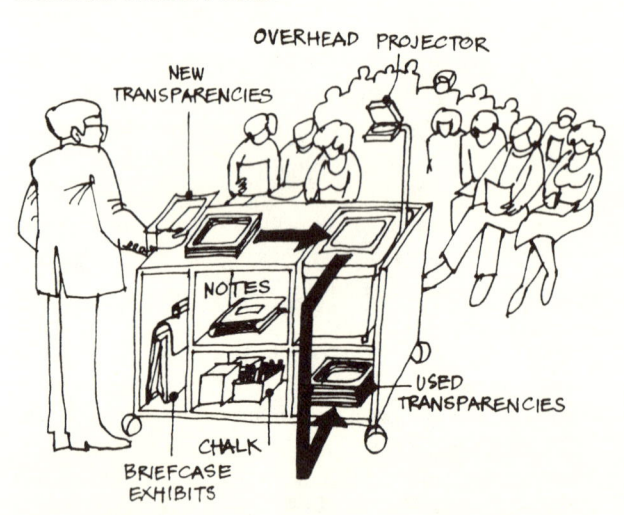

OVERHEAD PROJECTOR
NEW TRANSPARENCIES
NOTES
USED TRANSPARENCIES
CHALK
BRIEFCASE EXHIBITS

inflexibility so often found in theaters. The bench provides reasonable storage for notes, books, the lecturer's coat and bag and is designed to afford easy use of the overhead projector. The same kind of bench (but of different dimensions) could be used in other spaces such as class or conference rooms.

Movable screens are useful to break up larger rooms into small work areas. These screens can often be used as display surfaces and as projection screens or chalkboards.

Guidelines for planning media facilities have already been listed. Such facilities need to be provided to assist in the presentation of information and to allow for appropriate variations in presentation. Traditionally, the teacher and the chalkboard have been major sources of information for students. Modern learning spaces should provide facilities for a wide range of audiovisual media such as projection, television, and sound distribution systems. A list of these media, together with design considerations, is given in Table 17. The information in Table 17 can be applied to learning spaces of various sizes in a diversity of institutions.

The arrangement of the space and its facilities should permit easy access and circulation of people within it. Problems include the arrival and departure of learners and access to seating between aisles. Whenever possible, access should be through doors placed at the back of the learning space (especially lecture theaters) to avoid distractions to teachers and other learners. There will also be fire and safety regulations to consider in providing access that will have to be considered by the designer.

Outdoor Study Areas. It is known that students have positive reasons for studying outdoors (Sommer, 1968 RESEARCH). Ways of facilitating this study activity include the provision of outdoor facilities in the campus space such as windbreaks and sound-deflecting walls; tree and shrub plantings to give privacy; comfortable outdoor seats (not the backless park bench type); tables, arbors, and perhaps sitting walls, some of which have been constructed to facilitate face-to-face contact for those who want it; and rotundas (for small group work). Experience with landscaped outdoor spaces in schools in South Australia reveals two major deficiencies in design. One is a scale inappropriate to the needs of young children; the other is lack of privacy. Privacy is now being solved by dense plantings of shrubs and small trees.

CONCLUSION

Discussion of "how can the environment be designed?" raises the inevitable question of "who designs the learning environment?" In discussing learning spaces, Smith (1974 DESIGN GUIDES) refers to contributions from architects, users, and clients. This team approach is also evident in the design advice offered to those responsible for library spaces (Langmead and Beckman, 1970 DESIGN GUIDES) and for open plan schools (Bennett et al., 1980 RESEARCH). However, studies suggest that there may be an important lack of congruence between the perceptions of the architect (as reflected in the design) and those of the user for whom the design was intended. This can lead to serious difficulties in the team approach to design (Canter, 1969 RESEARCH). On this problem, Manning (1970 THEORY) writes:

Few educators can visualize suitably innovative building solutions to educational needs and, unfortunately, but not unreasonably, the average architect is really in no position to advise his client at the crucial stage of programming.... in this problem of determining and describing user-needs a major demarcation problem exists and the boundary is rarely joined. Having hired his consultant the client feels he is entitled to be told what he should have, so that he may say "yes" or "no." The architect though, expects his client should know more about his (the client's) business than he, the architect, does. As yet the skills and techniques required to bridge this gap hardly exist.

Part of the solution, according to Manning, lies in the education and training of architects and the architectural education of the administrator, teacher, and others. On the latter he suggests nonvocational university courses in architecture. Such a program is now being offered by the University of Adelaide. In concluding their study of open plan schools in Britain, Bennett and his colleagues were critical of the frequent failure of architects to evaluate the effectiveness of their buildings, so that future designs would be improved. They also suggest that architects should explain the design principles of their creations to users (Bennett et al., 1980 RESEARCH). This may overcome the apparent lack of conscious awareness and sensitivity to space use by teachers and learners (Durlak and Lehman, 1974 RESEARCH). Other solutions may lie in the training of teachers and in the communication of spatial awareness to learners through sensitive and varied use of physical space in schools. Kendrick (1975 RESEARCH) expressed the hope that his carefully planned laboratories would communicate something about space use to his architecture students who would then be able to apply their understandings in professional practice.

R. A. Cannon
Illustrations by Zig Kapelis

REFERENCES

Design Guides

Dreyfuss, H. (1967) *The Measure of Man: Human Factors in Design*. 2d ed. New York: Whitney Library of Design.

Ferguson, W. R. (1973) *Practical Laboratory Planning*. London: Applied Science Publishers.

Green, A. C. et al., eds. (1966) *Educational Facilities with New Media*. Washington, D.C.: National Education Association in Collaboration with the Center for Architectural Research, Rensselaer Polytechnic Institute.

Langmead, S. and Beckman, M. (1970) *New Library Design—Guidelines to Planning Academic Library Buildings*. Toronto: Wiley.

Postlethwait, S. N., Novak, J., and Murray, H. T. (1972) *The Audio Tutorial Approach to Learning*. 3d ed. Minneapolis: Burgess.

Purvis, J. M. (1973) *Laboratory Planning*. Baltimore: Williams and Wilkins.

Sliwa, J. A. and Fairweather, L., eds. (1970) *AJ Metric Handbook*. London: Architectural Press.

Smith, P. (1974) *The Design of Learning Spaces*. London: Council for Educational Technology.

Taylor, J. (1967) *The Science Lecture Room*. London: Cambridge University Press.

Thompson, G. (1977) *Planning and Design of Library Buildings*. 2d ed. London: Architectural Press.

UNESCO. (1975) *Planning Buildings and Facilities for Higher Education*. London: Architectural Press.

Woodson, W. E. (1981) *Human Factors Design Handbook: Information and Guidelines for the Design of Systems, Facilities, Equipment, and Products for Human Use*. New York: McGraw-Hill.

Woodson, W. E. and Conover, D. W. (1973) *Human Engineering Guide for Equipment Designers*. 2d ed. Berkeley, Calif.: University of California Press.

Research

Adams, R. S. and Biddle, B. (1970) *Realities of Teaching: Explorations with Video Tape*. New York: Holt, Rinehart and Winston.

Bennett, N., Andreae, J., Hegarty, P., and Wade, B. (1980) *Open Plan Schools: Teaching, Curriculum, Design*. Windsor: NFER.

Bligh, D. A. (1972) *What's the Use of Lectures?* Harmondsworth: Penguin.

Canter, D. V. (1969) "An Intergroup Comparison of Connotative Dimensions in Architecture." *Environment and Behaviour* 1: 37–48.

———. (1970) "Should We Treat Building Users as Subjects

or Objects?'' In *Architectural Psychology,* ed. D. V. Canter. London: RIBA Publications.
Durlak, J. T. and Lehman, J. (1974) ''User Awareness and Sensitivity to Open Space: A Study of Traditional and Open Plan Schools.'' In *Psychology and the Built Environment,* ed. D. Canter and T. Lee. London: Architectural Press.
Gill, W. M. (1977) ''Classroom Architecture and Classroom Behaviours: A Look at the Change to Open Plan Schools in New Zealand.'' *New Zealand Journal of Educational Studies* 12: 3–16.
Hare, A. P. (1976) *Handbook of Small Group Research.* 2d ed. New York: The Free Press.
Hearn, G. (1957) ''Leadership and the Spatial Factor in Small Groups.'' *Journal of Abnormal and Social Psychology* 54: 269–272.
Howells, L. T. and Becker, S. W. (1962) ''Seating Arrangements and Leadership Emergences.'' *Journal of Abnormal and Social Psychology* 55: 148–150.
Kendrick, J. F. (1975) ''Some Design, Planning and Ergonomic Considerations for Building Science Laboratories.'' *Architectural Science Review* 18: 26–34.
Koneya, M. (1976) ''Location and Interaction in Row and Column Seating Arrangements.'' *Environment and Behaviour* 8: 265–282.
Marris, P. (1964) *The Experience of Higher Education.* London: Routledge and Kegan Paul.
Nash, B. C. (1981) ''The Effects of Classroom Spatial Organization on Four- and Five-Year-Old Children's Learning.'' *British Journal of Educational Psychology* 51(2): 144–155.
Rapoport, A. and Watson, N. (1967–1968) ''Cultural Variability in Physical Standards.'' *Transactions of the Bartlett Society* 6: 63–83.
Sommer, R. (1966) ''The Ecology of Privacy.'' *Library Quarterly* 36: 234–248.
———. (1967) ''Classroom Ecology.'' *Journal of Applied Behavioural Science* 3: 489–503.
———. (1968a) ''Going Outdoors for Study Space.'' *Landscape Architecture* 58: 196–198.
———. (1968b) ''Reading Areas in College Libraries.'' *Library Quarterly* 38: 249–260.
———. (1970) ''The Ecology of Study Areas.'' *Environment and Behaviour* 2: 271–280.
Sommer, R. J. and Olsen, H. (1980) ''The Soft Classroom.'' *Environment and Behaviour* 12(1): 3–16.
Steinzor, B. (1950) ''The Spatial Factor in Face to Face Discussion Groups.'' *Journal of Abnormal and Social Psychology* 45: 552–555.
Thompson, J. (1972) ''Augmented Classroom and Open Space.'' *South Australian Teachers' Journal* 4: 7.
Wilcox, B. L. and Holahan, C. J. (1976) ''Social Ecology of the Megadorm in University Student Housing.'' *Journal of Educational Psychology* 68: 453–458.

Research Method

Wools, R. and Canter, D. (1970) ''The Effect of the Meaning of Buildings on Behaviour.'' *Applied Ergonomics* 1: 144–150.

Review

Abercrombie, N., Cullen, I., Godson, V., Major, S., and Timson, L. (1974) *The University in an Urban Environment.* London: Heinemann.
Birks, T. (1972) *Building the New Universities.* Newton Abbott, U.K.: David and Charles.
Brawne, M., ed. (1967) *University Planning and Design.* London: Architectural Association.
Schmertz, M. F., ed. (1972) *Campus Planning and Design.* New York: McGraw-Hill.
Schofer, J. P. (1975) ''Determining Optimal College Locations.'' *Higher Education* 4: 227–232.

Theory

Cannon, R. (1976) ''Learning Spaces for Higher Education.'' *PLET* 13 (1): 13–24.
Carnegie Commission on Higher Education. (1972) *The Fourth Revolution: Instructional Technology in Higher Education.* New York: McGraw-Hill.
Coates, G., ed. (1974) *Alternative Learning Environments.* Stroudsburg, Pa.: Dowden, Hutchinson and Ross.
de Carlo, G. C. (1974) ''Why/How to Build School Buildings.'' In *Alternative Learning Environments,* ed. G. Coates. Stroudsburg, Pa.: Dowden, Hutchinson and Ross.
Green, A. C. (1970) ''Instructional Technology and School Buildings—Influences, Conflicts and Guidance.'' In *To Improve Learning, an Evaluation of Instructional Technology,* vol. 1, ed. S. G. Tickton. New York: Bowker.
Ittelson, W. H., Proshansky, H. M., Rivlin, L. G., and Winkel, G. H. (1974) *An Introduction to Environmental Psychology.* New York: Holt, Rinehart and Winston.
Manning, P. (1970) ''The Wider View.'' *Canadian Architect* (June): 143–147.
Stephens, L. S. (1974) *A Teacher's Guide to Open Education.* New York: Holt, Rinehart and Winston.
Whisnant, D. E. (1971) ''The University as a Space and the Future of the University.'' *Journal of Higher Education* 42: 85–102.

LECTURE. An instructional activity in which a teacher or trainer gives a systematic oral presentation of facts or principles (often supported by illustrative material) to a class, with the students generally being responsible for taking notes on the material covered.

LED. Light Emitting Diode: the familiar display of digital clocks and a whole variety of instruments. LEDs have relatively high power requirements and are only used where mains power is available.

LENS. *See* **Achromatic; Close-up; F-number; Photography; Projection Lens; Telephoto Lens; Wide-Angle Lens.**

LETTERPRESS. The system of printing which uses a raised surface to carry the ink which is transferred by pressure to the paper. Letterpress is used for the printing of the majority of books although offset litho methods are being used increasingly. Letterpress blocks and halftone blocks are used for letterpress printing.

LETTER QUALITY PRINTER. A printer that produces output of similar quality to a standard typewriter. Such printers usually have golf ball or daisy wheel printing heads and can print onto single sheets of paper.

LEVEL (VIDEODISC). Several levels of sophistication have been identified for videodiscs, ranging from the basic consumer model (level 1) with freeze frame, frame addressability, chapter stop, right up to levels permitting interfacing with a computer and other peripherals.

LIBRARY ASSOCIATION (U.K.). Professional body in the U.K. for all grades of librarians.
7 Ridgemont Street, London, WCI 7AE, U.K.

LIGHT BOX. Internally illuminated box with ledges or other arrangement to hold rows of 35mm slides for inspection, editing, etc.

LIGHTING. Lighting, combining elements of the mundane, the artistic, and the scientific, is crucial to photography. The implications of the nature, psychological impact, and manipulation of light are too broad to cover in any one book. Simply put, however, there are three main concerns for the photographer. The first is to ensure enough light so that a particular film can register a usable image. Modern developments in film technology for the amateur have resulted in a range of readily available films designed to work in situations ranging from extremely bright daylight all the way down to the glow from a single candle. Thus the first choice is to pick a film capable of satisfactory results in the expected lighting conditions.

The second choice is whether to use the existing light alone, in combination with portable lighting, or to rely only on portable light. If a simple recording of an object is the point of the photograph, then one need only meter and set the camera accordingly. This is rarely satisfactory since most objects persist in existing where there is too much light on one part of the scene and too little on other parts. Fortunately, light can be directed into the shadowed area by adding light from an additional source or by diverting some of the strong light into the dark area using a reflecting board. This can often achieve a mildly lit area roughly half as bright as that lit by the main light source. A flash unit can be used to flood the area, producing a flat light which lacks dimension. It is worth noting that simple flash units are effective to about twelve feet. If the flash-to-subject distance is greater, more sophisticated units are required. A flash unit may, with appropriate calculations, be used to fill in only the shadowed area without washing out the bright area. Then, too, it may be possible to move the object in question into a more suitable area of existing light.

The third concern for the photographer of three-dimensional objects to consider is the modeling effect of light. Briefly put, the idea is to use one light source as a key light, a second light source, half to one-third as bright, as a fill light to wash out the strong shadows cast by the key light while leaving some shadows to give depth to the image. A third light is carefully aimed at the back of the object from behind to highlight upper surfaces, thus increasing the illusion of depth and separating the object from the background. Additional light sources may be used to light the background. This multipoint lighting is often achieved by using photographic flood lights or spotlights with film balanced for tungsten light. It can also be achieved with multiple flash units balanced for daylight film. These are connected to a single trigger at the camera. Flash units have many advantages if the subject will be moving during the session. In either case, the lights must be carefully positioned to achieve the desired ratio between the key light and the others. Colored filters are often used over the lights for specific effects. Close-up photography and highly reflective surfaces pose special problems for which specialized lights and techniques have been developed.

Conventional wisdom suggests that light from above eye level at about 45 degrees is the most flattering for human subjects. Light from below eye level creates a special impact often called "monster lighting." Light directly from eye level produces a very flat effect with no shadows to model the dimensions of depth. At best this is unflattering; at worst it often results in making people appear more plump than they are. This familiar flat lighting is usually imposed on the subject from a flash unit mounted on the camera for convenience. If the flash is mounted too close to the center of the lens, the light may bounce back from the retina of the eye, producing the dreaded red-eye effect. This can be avoided in a number of ways, the most familiar being to separate the flash from the camera. Many camera-flash combinations are designed with an appropriate distance to avoid red eye. Another solution is to bounce the light from the flash off a nearby ceiling, wall, or portable reflector so that the light falling on the subject is diffused. This bounce lighting is very flattering, but requires aperture adjustment since the amount of light reaching the subject falls off sharply because the distance traveled while bouncing is greater than it would be in a direct line from flash to subject.

An impressive array of filters has been developed to

fit over the camera lens to achieve particular effects by influencing the light as it passes through the filter into the lens. One of the most common is the ultraviolet or skylight filter which enhances cloud effects and reduces atmospheric haze while protecting the lens surface. A polarizing filter can be used to cut down glare and reflection by being rotated in its mounting on the front of the lens. Filters also exist which can be used to achieve a reasonable match when the photographer is forced to use a film balanced for one kind of light in another. *See* **Aperture; Artificial Light; Backlight; Color Cast; Flashbulb; Flash Factor.**

LIGHTING CONSOLE. A control panel whereby the lighting in a studio, set, etc., can be remotely controlled once the desired arrangement of light units has been set up.

LIGHTING GRID. A construction of metal frames housed in the roof of a television or film studio from which the lanterns are suspended.

LIGHT PEN. A photoelectric device used as an adjunct to a computer's cathode-ray tube display. It detects images displayed on the screen when it is passed over the surface and can be used to activate the computer to change or modify the images, for example, on the basis of a selected answer (selected by touching the light pen to an answer box on the screen). *See* **Communication Engineering.**

LINE AMPLIFIER. An amplifier for audio or video signals that feeds a transmission line.

LINEAR PROGRAM. Arising out of the work of B. F. Skinner in the 1950s, the linear program appeared as a new instructional device. In theory, all students worked sequentially through every frame (i.e., item), although at their own individual speed. Mastery learning was implicit; that is to say, the fact that a student had reached a certain frame number implied that the student had adequately learned all the material dealt with up to that point. The behavioral antecedents of the linear program created a quite rigid prescription for the construction and use of such programs; very short items, behavioral objectives, self-pacing, constant reinforcement, etc. In practice, it was found that few of these rules appeared to possess much validity. Thus after the first psychology-based explorations with linear programs, there came about a period of rapid change and evolution, such that the writing of programs became a confused and esoteric art.

Various attempts were made to codify the concept of a "program," that is, to isolate those factors which could be considered to impart a programmed ingredient to teaching materials. Ten features were usually agreed upon:

1. The materials are constructed according to a predetermined scheme.
2. The aims of the course are stated in measurable or objectively identifiable terms.
3. The materials have been validated, i.e., they have been tried out and revised according to results.
4. A pretest is provided, or the required initial behavior is stated.
5. A posttest is provided.
6. The materials are arranged in steps of appropriate size.
7. The student is required to respond actively (not necessarily overtly).
8. Arrangement is made for immediate confirmation of responses.
9. The teaching medium is appropriate for both students and subject matter at all stages.
10. The materials are self-paced or presented in a controlled manner.

It can be clearly seen that these ten attributes have nowadays come to be accepted as desirable features of any set of teaching materials. Thus, although the linear program per se cannot be considered to have had the success its originators hoped for, nonetheless much of the philosophy underlying the construction and use of modern teaching materials arose out of early work with such programs.

Derick Unwin

LINEAR TEACHING MACHINE. A device that displayed linear programmed materials. Most such machines were essentially devices for presenting instruction frame by frame. Some early versions incorporated arrangements for their students to record their answers on a paper roll in the machine, in the hope that this would prevent cheating (i.e., looking at the answer before responding to the question). Needless to say, human nature generally overcame any such cheat-proof devices. *See* **Teaching Machines.**

LINE BLOCK. A photomechanical printing plate of a line drawing or diagram which has no gradation of tone but is made up of areas of black and white only.

LINE DRAWING. Any drawing in which there are no middle tones and which shading (texture), if any, is obtained with black and white lines or with screen overlays.

LINE PRINTER. A high-speed printing machine employed as a peripheral to a mainframe computer. Such a printer is capable of printing several thousand characters per second.

LINK TRAINER. The link trainer, a type of flight simulator first developed by E. Link during World War II, is probably the best-known example of the use of mechanical simulation as a training aid. It was particularly useful in training pilots to fly at night or in bad weather. The company founded by Link (Link-Miles Flight Simulators) still supplies simulators to most of the world's air forces.

LIP SYNC. Short for lip synchronization, the recording of speech in a film so that it precisely fits the lip movements associated with it when the speaker's face is seen. The term is also used to designate any exercise where precise synchronization of picture and sound is maintained.

LIQUID CRYSTAL DISPLAY (LCD). The flat panel technology of watch displays and numerous portable computer displays. The most common colors are the familiar black characters on a light gray background, but a variety of color LCDs are becoming available. LCDs use little power and are ideal for portable applications, but they are difficult to make in large sizes, and the electronic circuits for driving detailed displays are complex. Thus, a display large enough for a computer screen is still more expensive than a video monitor. *See* **Super-Twisted Birefrengence Effect.**

LISP. An abbreviation for LIST PROCESSING. It is a powerful interpretive language used to develop higher-level languages, and often utilized for **artificial intelligence** (q.v.) systems. LISP is the grandfather of languages such as Logo.

LIST. To display on a monitor, or print on a printer, the contents of the computer memory or of a file.

LITH FILM. Short for lithography film, a high-contrast film originally used for making plates for lithography printing but also useful for many other photographic applications where extreme contrast is needed. For example, lith films can be used for making white-on-black line slides where the extreme contrast will give clear letters on a solid black background; further processing can then produce slides with any colored letters on a colored background. *See* **Graphic Design.**

LITHOGRAPHY. A printing process based on the mutual antipathy of grease and water. Originally, slabs of limestone were used on which drawings were prepared using greasy crayons. The modern version of the process uses thin aluminum plates on which the ink-accepting image is produced photographically. *See* **Offset Lithography.**

LOAD. To transfer information from a peripheral storage medium (such as a disk) into main memory for use; for example, to transfer a program into memory for execution.

LOCAL. In reference to connections between large computers, terminals, etc., this term means connected directly by wire rather than via a communications link and modem.

LOCAL AREA NETWORK (LAN). A connection among multiple computers intended to allow the individual stations to share resources and exchange files within an office, building, or group of buildings employing direct connections. LANs can be classified by how they encode data for transmission (baseband and broadband), how they regulate the flow of data (carrier sense, with or without collision detection, or token), and their topology (star, ring, or bus).

LOG. As applied to computerized instruction, a record of student responses to lesson material (and, as a verb, to create the record). A logging facility can help a lesson author identify those sections giving students trouble and in need of improvement, or it can help a teacher spot problems a student may be having that the computer cannot help with. Authoring languages and systems often offer logging facilities.

LOGGING IN (ON), LOGGING OUT (OFF). The procedure by which a user initiates or terminates a particular session of on-line interaction with a computer. It is usually abbreviated to log in (on), log out (off).

LOGIC. The basic principles and/or actual connection of circuit elements for computation in computers.

LOGISTICS . The art of moving and quartering troops *(Oxford English Dictionary)*. Nowadays generally applied to systems for organizing the distribution and use of hardware and software.

LOGO. (1) A computer language created to help children learn how to use a computer. It is especially noted for its "turtle graphics" which lets users draw shapes by giving simple commands to an imaginary turtle. Along with turtle graphics, Logo also comprises a programming language with good text-handling capabilities. Both the graphics and programming parts are extensible, meaning that one can define new routines (as chains of existing commands) and then use these "macros" just as if they were part of the Logo language. See **Logo Language.** (2) Abbreviation for logotype, an identifying symbol designed as a trademark of an institution, organization, firm or product.

LOGO LANGUAGE. Logo is a general-purpose programming language sometimes misleadingly described as a language for children. It was designed to allow a beginner to do significant projects without having such mathematical prerequisites as the x of algebra. This and other features enable children to find a route into Logo far more easily than into BASIC or any other commonly available language. Hence its popularity as a language in the elementary schools. But it is not a toy language. Indeed, it is more sophisticated and modern than BASIC.

Logo borrows from LISP, and advanced list-manipulating ability. An example of how this is used is the fact that Logo programs are represented as lists of lists. As a result, a Logo program is a legitimate Logo object which can be manipulated (constructed or changed) by another Logo program. Another important modern feature of Logo is its procedurality: new commands can be defined by the user and then used just like those that are built-in. In other words, Logo is an extensible language.

Most implementations of Logo have a well-developed graphics system including the turtle graphics which was developed along with Logo by the team around Seymour Papert at MIT. Most Logo versions offer traditional Cartesian graphics as well, and some of them offer control over dynamic screen objects of the kind used in video games.

Logo was first implemented on large machines, typically the PDP-10 and the PDP-11 from about 1968 until 1978. The first microcomputer to carry Logo was the TI 99/4, followed by the Apple. Logo is now implemented on all the widely used microcomputers including the IBM PC and PCjr, the Atari series, the Commodore 64, the French Thompson, the British Sinclair Spectrum, and the Japanese Fujitsu, NEC, Hitachi, and JVC machines.

Seymour Papert

REFERENCES

Abelson, H. and diSessa, A., (1980) *Turtle Geometry*. Cambridge, Mass.: MIT Press.
Papert, S. (1980) *Mindstorms: Computers, Children and Powerful Ideas*. New York: Basic Books.

LONG-TERM OBJECTIVE. A type of behavioral objective where the expected outcome is not in the current teaching period. An objective not achieved immediately.

LOOP PROJECTOR. A projector, usually 8mm, for use with film loops, enabling continuous and repetitive showing of a film sequence. The facility of easy operation and loading led to the use of loop projectors as a simple means of using film in the classroom or for self-instruction. See **Film Loop.**

LOUDSPEAKER. The final link in the chain of audio reproduction, and frequently the link which determines the quality of perceived sound. Speakers are a relatively expensive part of a sound system, and as such are often not capable of giving the full potential of the other components of the system if costs have been cut in this area.

LOUD-SPEAKING TELEPHONE. An arrangement which allows the telephone to be used for conferences or for class teaching. Each station is equipped with a loudspeaker and a microphone (possibly voice-activated), and the participants sit around a table with the equipment in the center. In some applications this process is enhanced by the use of **videotex** (q.v.) to provide visual support. See **Teleconferencing.**

LOWBAND. See **Highband.**

LOWERCASE. Small letters like, a, b, c, etc. The corresponding capitals A, B, C, etc., are described as uppercase.

LOW-LEVEL PROGRAMMING LANGUAGE. A computer programming language which requires the programmer to specify his/her program in minute detail, but which provides access to more specialized facilities of the hardware. It also results in programs which are much more rapidly executed than those written in a high-level language (e.g., BASIC) because they are closely related to the machine code instructions that actually make the computer operate. Low-level languages are usually specific to a particular make or range of machines, and are generally much more difficult to learn and tedious to work with than high-level languages.

LOW-RESOLUTION GRAPHICS (LOW-RES GRAPHICS). A form of computer graphics in which shapes are composed from relatively large blocks. Bar charts, simple diagrams, and many unsophisticated games can be programmed using low-res graphics.

LSI. *See* **Large-Scale Integration.**

LUMEN. The unit of luminous flux. It is equal to the flux through a unit solid angle (steradian) from a uniform point source of one candela or to the flux on a unit surface of which all points are at a unit distance from a uniform point source of one candela.

LUMEN/SQ FT. A unit of incident light. It is the illuminance on a surface one square foot in area on which a flux of one lumen is uniformly distributed, or the illuminance on a surface all points of which are at a distance of one foot from a uniform source of one candela.

LUMINANCE. (1) The component representing brightness in a video signal. (2) An objective, quantitative measure of the luminous intensity of a surface due to reflection, self-luminous emission or transillumination. The SI unit of luminance is the candela (unit of luminous intensity) per square meter. *See* **Screen Brightness.**

LUX. The SI unit measuring the amount of illumination falling on a surface. One lux is the illumination produced by one lumen of light falling on one square meter of surface.

M

MACHINE CODE (LANGUAGE). Coded information (usually in some form of binary representation) which can be directly accepted and used by a computer. This language is composed of instructions, addresses, and data. The instructions are those for which the machine has been designed to operate. Every different model of computer has its own machine language, hence machine language programs are not transportable between different models of machines. High-level languages such as FORTRAN or BASIC require translation to machine code before they can work, generally with the aid of compilers and interpreters.

MACRO. A subroutine or sequence of actions which accomplish a particular event when invoked. One example is in computer graphics where a set of sequential screens may be combined together into a macro forming part of an animated display; it is common for word processing programs to allow for the use of macros to perform a multitude of tasks such as instantly typing out form letters, searching for headings and printing them out as a separate document, etc.

MACROPHOTOGRAPHY. The term is used to identify photographs producing a bigger view than is generally possible with "normal" lens equipment. While there is some debate about the actual limits, macrophotography is considered to be in a range where the image on the film is the same size as the object or actually bigger than the object itself. When the image is bigger than the object by a factor of roughly 10, then specialized techniques are required, usually termed *photomicrography*. Many **zoom lenses** (q.v.) are now equipped with a special "macro" setting which enables them to produce very usable extreme close-ups even though they may not be "macro" in a technical sense.

MAGAZINE. A light-tight container for holding cine film or film for still cameras which can be inserted into or attached to a camera in daylight. Also used to describe a holder for 35mm slides for insertion into an automatic slide projector. *See* **Cassette.**

MAGNETIC BOARD. A steel or magnetically treated presentation board to which objects may be attached with magnets. Magnetic boards are used as a means of providing quick, changeable visual displays or demonstrations. Magnetized "string" and "tape" are available, as is a whole range of magnetized symbols, etc.

MAGNETIC DISK STORE. A computer store in which the magnetic medium is on the surface of one or more rotating disks. The access time to a disk is relatively short by comparison with the earlier mass-storage system; magnetic tape.

MAGNETIC INK CHARACTER RECOGNITION (MICR). A system whereby characters, written or printed in special ink, can be detected by a machine and the encoded data either recorded or relayed. *See* **Optical Character Recognition.**

MAGNETIC RECORDING FILM. Sprocketted 35mm or 16mm wide recording tape on which the sound track of a film is recorded independently of (but in synchronization with) the picture film. The magnetic film and the picture are edited together in complete synchronization and eventually the sound track is transferred, as either an optical or a magnetic track to the release prints of the film.

MAINFRAME COMPUTER. A large computer system usually equipped with a central processor capable of addressing a large amount of main memory and often having the ability to communicate with many terminals and other satellite computers. Such systems usually provide very significant storage facilities through subsystems of hard disk and magnetic tape drives.

MAIN MEMORY. The memory component of a computer system that is built into the computer itself and whose contents are directly accessible to the computer.

MAJOR CITY EARTH STATION (MCES). Each capital city in Australia has a MCES for receiving and transmitting radio, television, data, and telephone signals to and from satellites.

MANAGEMENT BY OBJECTIVES. A formalized procedure involving the agreed establishment of targets for every employee, including managers, with the identification of key results areas for each job position. The total integration of individual targets hopefully ensures the accomplishment of organizational objective(s).

MANAGEMENT GAMES. Management games have a long history of use in the training of executives, managers, and administrators of all types. Such exercises generally involve a written or filmed description of an actual or fictional situation, and are usually presented in some detail. Management games may deal with a total enterprise or with a problem occurring within a specific area, such as marketing or personnel. Others may be concerned with universal problems such as organization, communication, or participation, often in the form of role-play.

Management games vary enormously in sophistication and length. Some may consist of a few pages and can be completed in a hour or so, while others may last several days. A computer is an essential component in many games.

MANPOWER SERVICES COMMISSION (MSC). Body set up under the U.K. Employment and Training Act 1973 to operate public training and employment services which were previously a part of the Department of Employment. The MSC is officially an independent organization, but most MSC staff are established civil servants, and management links to government are close. MSC is used by government to intervene in the labor market to protect and create jobs (job creation). It is responsible for Jobcentres, Industrial Training Boards, the Training Opportunities Scheme (TOPS), etc.

MARK SENSE. *See* **Optical Character Recognition.**

MARRIED PRINT. A cine film carrying both picture and sound. During production the picture and sound track are recorded separately and are "married" in the final stages of production to produce a print for projection.

MASK. A pattern for checking data being entered into a data base to make sure it has the right form for entries in that field. For example, a mask might specify five digits for a zip code, or the form MM/DD/YY for the date.

MASTER. Original cine film which has been exposed in a camera and from which prints are made. It is extremely important that master film is handled with the utmost care, as any marks or scratches will be reproduced on prints. For this reason a master should never be projected.

MASTERY LEARNING. A term that refers to the type of instruction where students must meet a criterion of competence on a unit before progressing to the next unit. Such a criterion is often 90 percent success on a multiple-choice test. Among the components of mastery learning that are common are (1) pretest of competence; (2) specification of behavioral objectives; (3) formative or diagnostic evaluation; (4) remedial instruction; and (5) criterion-referenced summative evaluation.

The main advantages claimed relate to teaching basic skills and low-order cognitive outcomes. It may be useful with slow learners and students unable to work independently without close supervision. It has been suggested that the main defect of mastery learning is that it holds back the able students who cannot go beyond the prespecified behavioral objectives—a criticism that can of course be applied to objectives-based instruction in general.

MATHETICS. A method of information presentation. A series of sheets of paper contain a demonstration of content, prompts, and a release sheet (test sheet). A variety of presentation sequences are used, with backward chaining (q.v.) being common. The procedure at one time attracted considerable notice, especially because of its axiom that each act of learning should be fulfilled, i.e., should result in the completion of the task in hand. A concrete example would be teaching a child to tie up his/her shoelaces: the first step in the training should be the final act in the task—the completion of the bow.

MATRIX. A rectangular array (table) of numbers or characters. A dot matrix is a two-dimensional array of dots that make up, for example, the letter A. *See* **Array.**

MATT. A term applied to a surface with a dull, nonreflecting finish, especially matt photographic paper.

MATTE. (1) Used in "split-image" techniques in filmmaking to allow, for example, an actor to appear with himself. The matte is a mask used during printing to enable two separate images to be printed in succession on different areas of the same film. (2) A card or metal mask placed in front of a camera to give such effects as looking through binoculars, through a keyhole, etc. The masks are placed in a matte box which is secured to the front of the camera.

MCES. *See* **Major City Earth Station.**

MDS. *See* **Multipoint Distribution Systems.**

MECHANICAL MOUSE. A mouse that depends solely on moving internal parts to relay signals about the positioning of the device. The advantage of this type of device is that it can be used on most surfaces, so no special pad or plate is needed.

MEDIA CLASSIFICATION. Instructional media are not ends in themselves; they are means intended to serve a specific instructional purpose or function. Since nowadays there is a wide range of such means from which to select the "best" or "most appropriate" medium, one of the main questions for every educator is: What are the criteria to decide which will be the best or most effective medium for my purpose?

A number of authors have tackled the problem of media selection by analyzing media and constructing corresponding media taxonomies. These classification systems try to bring the different media into a clearly arranged order, which is to facilitate the choice for the teacher in a specific instructional situation and to enable a more systematic media research, especially the experimental assessment of the most appropriate use of different media.

This entry is concerned with the question: Where, in what features, really lie the differences between different media with respect to their potential instructional usage? After a look into what the research has said so far and what seems to be the present state of the art, I shall describe some of the attempts to analyze and classify media and then draw some conclusions as to the most promising directions for future efforts.

A SUMMARY OF RESEARCH SURVEYS

The Overall Result. Experimental research studies into media exist in abundance; most of them compare two or more media in order to assess their relative effectiveness. All attempts, however, to extract generalizable conclusions from these studies have failed so far: either it was impossible to detect significant differences or the results were contradictory. It may suffice to refer the reader to some of the more important media research surveys of the last 25 years: Lumsdaine (1963), Campeau (1966), Twyford (1969), Allen (1971), Levie and Dickie (1973), Campeau (1974), and Jamison, Suppes, and Wells (1974 RESEARCH SURVEY).

Although no general and fundamental differences between the various media and teaching methods could be detected, one conclusion can be drawn from the otherwise inconsistent results of media research: not only may most media be used effectively for the attainment of a great number of different objectives, but most objectives may also be achieved through any of a variety of media. This conclusion at least partly qualifies the present approach to media in instruction, which often gives the impression that the attainment of a certain objective would depend upon the use of a certain medium or that the use of an expertly selected medium could guarantee a positive learning outcome. The experiences of the preceding centuries, however, have shown that a literate public can be taught all subjects with the help of illustrated textbooks. Nevertheless, researchers as well as media practitioners agree that there are differences between different types of media, that these are, however, only relative and of a more subtle kind than hitherto expected. Thus previous researchers in general tried to answer the wrong questions; i.e., they generated irrelevant hypotheses and employed inadequate methods and research designs.

Although most reviewers draw attention to serious methodological flaws with respect to basic principles of sound empirical research, this defect is—at the present stage—of secondary importance only, since the best formal experimental design does not help as long as one does not ask the right research questions. As for generating more relevant hypotheses, several surveys agree in particular on the following points which, although dealt with separately in the next paragraphs, are clearly interrelated.

The most fundamental criticism concerns the *theoretical foundation* of previous media research, or rather the lack of it. This led to such a haphazardness in the selection of variables and in the investigation of possible correlations that we are today confronted with a mass of fragmentary and isolated research results, which can hardly be interpreted on their own and from which it is impossible to draw any valid generalizations. What is needed, therefore, is an at least tentative theory about the functions media may fulfill in the instructional process, especially how they may influence human learning. Such a theoretical framework is a necessary prerequisite for the definition of the most promising variables, the generation of sound and relevant hypotheses, and the subsequent interpretation of research results.

Critical Variables. First among the independent variables of past research, the selection of which is heavily criticized by now, rank the *media categories* themselves. Most research studies use terms like *film, television, textbook, audiotape, slide,* etc., to specify the different media they are going to compare as to their instructional effectiveness. Each of these terms, however, covers a great variety of actual items. One has, for example, only to look at the number of textbooks all entitled "Introduction to Educational Psychology" to realize how different they are in reality with respect to the basic methodological approach to the topic, the sequencing and structuring of the presentation, the employment of special typographic techniques, the use of illustrations, etc. The use of only the term *textbook* to define each of these various items tends to conceal the real differences between them. Since the same applies, of course, to films, audiotapes, and all other generic media concepts of the kind mentioned above, Levie and Dickie (1973 RESEARCH SURVEY) concludes "Hundreds of studies have been conducted to compare the effectiveness of one medium with another without having carefully defined what is being compared" (p. 860).

As a consequence of these considerations it has been suggested that media variables should be defined in a terminology of specific attributes, which describe in detail the capabilities of that medium. The attribute of a medium is thus "any structural component which has an influence on the *kind* of material one can present, the *arrangement* of the material with relation to other materials, or the *way* the material is presented" (Salomon and Snow, 1968 THEORY, p. 230). Examples for this kind of analytical variable are the capacity to show motion, to present separate or simultaneous visual and auditory stimuli, to manipulate temporal and spatial dimensions, etc. (a more comprehensive listing is given by Allen, 1970 RESEARCH SURVEY). These attributes, then, should be taken as variables for experimental studies so that different learning results, e.g., are no longer ascribed to the medium "film," but to the media attribute "presentation of a continual motion." Such a result gives as yet no information about the technical realization of this attribute. In this case it could be a film as well as a videotape, a transparency with special effects, etc.

Such a definition of media in terms of their attributes, however, is a first step only toward a more appropriate specification of relevant variables. This becomes evident in those sections of the general media research reviews of Lumsdaine (1963 RESEARCH SURVEY) and Levie and Dickie (1973 RESEARCH SURVEY) which deal with this kind of media attribute, or in the special surveys on the motion variable (Allen and Weintraub, 1968; Spangenberg, 1973 RESEARCH STUDY), on the effect of color (Webster and Cox, 1974 RESEARCH SURVEY), or on different kinds of television variables (Chu and Schramm, 1967 RESEARCH SURVEY; Anderson, 1972 THEORY). They all suggest that no media attribute bears an inherent general advantage. Neither motion (as against still visuals) nor color (as against black and white) nor any other attribute has produced a significant overall positive effect on learning. Their relative value depends upon the specific *learning task*. Thus Spangenberg (1973 RESEARCH STUDY) summarizes that the use of motion appears to be effective only "when the particular content to be learnt consists of the movement itself and its characteristics, or where the content is enhanced and differentiated by the cues provided in the action of the movement" (p. 435). The same applies to all other attributes: they may enhance learning only when they are not just an additional embellishment of the presentation but an instructional function with regard to the specific learning task.

Finally, research critics mention a third group of variables, the inadequate specification of which is seen as another main reason for the overall result of "no significant differences," and that is the *learner* or the group of learners taking part in the experiment. Although one of the central problems in everyday instruction has been how to pay regard to the individual differences between learners by choosing appropriate educational and instructional measures, educational researchers in general and media researchers in particular attempted to tackle this problem by studying collective manifestations of cognitive principles. In the majority of these studies the learning individuals were reduced to an "average learner," and individual differences were not taken into account. If, however, through the use of undifferentiated averages a virtually heterogeneous group is treated as a homogeneous entity, all eventual differences between individuals are cancelled out in the overall result. Snow and Salomon (1968 THEORETICAL BACKGROUND) very aptly worded the criticism of that kind of media research: "almost all of the research evidence accumulated to date applies to some generalized 'average student,' and thus to no one" (p. 341). In order to make research more relevant and its results applicable to instructional practice, it becomes necessary to acknowledge the importance of individual differences in the conception and design of experiments. Since different students in reality may react differently to the same sort of instruction, the use of a specific item of instructional media may be effective for a certain type of learner but ineffective or even disadvantageous for another learner with other characteristics. Researchers therefore should concentrate on investigating the effectiveness of different kinds of media for different individuals or well-defined types of students. Consequently, the learners in media studies must be carefully specified with regard to their aptitudes, in particular their special intellectual abilities, their learning styles, motivation, and other similar personality variables.

A Suggestion for Future Research. One may sum up the survey of media research reviews by stating that they agree that the question so characteristic of most previous research —"Which medium (e.g., film or textbook) or which media attribute (e.g., color or black and white) is better and more efficient than the other?"—has proved unproductive and therefore should be abandoned. They suggest replacing it by studies of the type "What *media attributes* are relevant for learners with what *personality characteristics* for what kind of *learning tasks?*" This reorientation does not just mean a more precise specification of relevant variables, which then might be dealt with separately. The different variables are rather supposed to interact, and this must be taken into account in the theoretical framework, which should serve as a basis for the design and interpretation of media research. This development is quite in keeping with a general shift of emphasis from research into the main effects of isolated sets of variables to research into the complex totality of the teaching-learning process. The general implication for the domain of instructional media has been stated by Levie and Dickie (1973 RESEARCH SURVEY): "The medium through which instruction is presented is but one aspect of the teaching-learning situation, and a theory of media selection would be subsumed by a theory of instruction" (p. 877). It would then seem necessary to analyze media within a coherent though tentative theoretical framework in terms of those attributes that can fulfill an instructional function with regard to specific learning tasks and specific learners.

On the basis of the results of this survey the next section will deal more directly with the problem of media classifications and taxonomies.

THE CONSTRUCTION OF CLASSIFICATION SYSTEMS

General Considerations. The generic term *classification* as used in this entry covers the concept of "order" on the one hand and that of "taxonomy" on the other. An order works with categories which permit the formation of separate classes of things or concepts. A taxonomy in addition brings a fixed structure to such an order by putting the classes into a sequence according to a single rule or to several interconnected principles. Thus it represents not just a complete as possible accumulation of isolated classes but gives some information about the relation of the phenomena it classifies. Instances of such taxonomies from other sciences are the periodic table in chemistry, and Linnaeus's system in biology. Meredith (1965 THEORETICAL BACKGROUND) warned against the frequent misconception that such classifications are revealing the true order of nature:

man himself contributes significantly to the structure of his taxonomic systems. He imposes an order on things which can be arranged in many alternative orders. He should have a rational basis for the particular type of order he selects. And since in educational media we are dealing with systems which are largely man-made, the idea that there is any one objective, "natural" classification is somewhat absurd. (p. 379)

This comment stresses two important points: first, there may be several relevant taxonomies of educational media; second, the relevance of a classification system depends not only on its internal logic, its formal consistency, but upon its usefulness for a specific purpose. A classification, e.g., of media with regard to the quantity of sensory cues they transmit, may already be relevant for a researcher in the field of information theory and cybernetics, and a classification of audio and video equipment with respect to the number and mode of transistors and integrated circuits used may be meaningful for an engineer. These systems, however, are insufficient for both the educational researcher, who deals with the question of how media interact with other variables of the instructional process, and the biology teacher, who wants to use audio and video equipment in class.

A relevant—and that means useful—criterion for a classification cannot be logically deduced from the phenomena to be classified in the sense of just exposing the underlying ordering principle. The criterion for any particular arrangement is externally chosen, thereby normative, and its relevance is determined by the intention of the taxonomist or of the subsequent user. With respect to educational media, the development of taxonomies has been attempted in particular by two groups with different intentions. To begin with, there are the scholars and researchers in the field of educational technology. For them, as Meredith (1965 THEORETICAL BACKGROUND) puts it, "the function of a good taxonomy is not merely to order materials but to order people's thinking about the material" (p. 380). It must be in accordance with some theoretical framework which allows the generation of meaningful hypotheses and the interpretation of subsequent empirical research results. The other group consists of the producers and users of instructional media. Their intention is to develop handy instruments which help to facilitate the selection of appropriate instructional media for specific learning situations. The intentions of both groups are, of course, interrelated since the researcher hopes that his experiments in the end will provide practically valid guidelines, and the practitioner tries to base his selection decisions on empirical research evidence. The fundamental difference, however, is that the researcher aims at an accurate and proper description and explanation of instructional media, their unique functions and effects, in order to find generalizable relations, while the practitioner intends to design and control educational systems in the most effective way. Efforts to develop a taxonomy for the latter purpose do not exclude more ambitious attempts like the one formulated at the end of the previous survey section. It permits, however, to take up in addition other principles of classification which are important for the practical management of instructional systems, but which do not necessarily refer to unique features of instructional media—e.g., financial, technical, and organizational criteria.

The crucial problems, then, for any media taxonomy are, first, to select a principle of classification that seems promising for the intention of media research and/or media selection; second, to choose and label the instances of the class of phenomena one wants to classify, thus distinguishing media from nonmedia and one medium from another. As to the latter question, one can from the outset identify at least two subclasses of instances to be classified in a media taxonomy. They may be labeled the hardware and the software component of a medium. The *hardware* is the technical equipment or device; the *software* is the specific kind of information or material which can be recorded and transmitted by the respective hardware.

Examples of Previous Classification Systems

R. Bretz. The present literature on the subject rather frequently mentions the classification system of Bretz (1971 EXAMPLE) (Figure 44). In his *Taxonomy of Communication Media* he classifies various technical communication devices on two dimensions.

First, he distinguishes seven classes of media with respect to the kind of information they are capable of presenting: audio or visual, still or motion. As additional determinants for his classification in the visual field he uses the categories picture, line graphic, and print. He considers picture and print as two ends of a visual continuum, which ranges from highly realistic photographs in motion to static alphanumeric symbols with line graphics somewhere in between. Although he suggests that the audio sector can be subclassified as well with regard to the categories of the human voice, natural or artificial sounds and noises, and music, he does not use these subdivisions in his taxonomy but treats sound as a single element. On the second dimension he divides communication media into two groups: telemedia, which can transmit programs across distance in real time, and recording media, which can record programs, store them, and play them back at later times.

The principle behind the arrangement of the seven classes of media into a taxonomic structure seems to be the quantity of different informations a medium is capable of recording or transmitting. A medium of class I (e.g., sound film) is capable of representing all kinds of audio or visual information, while a medium of class VII (e.g., Teletype) can present information only in the form of alphanumeric characters. The final taxonomy, however, is open to several critical comments. Why, e.g., are audio-still-visual media grouped in class II and motion-visual media in class IV, since both of them are capable of transmitting four different kinds of information? The same question applies to classes V and VI; here the three different kinds of information of still-visual media are due to the further subdivision of the visual field. If Bretz had realized his mentioned subdivision of the audio field as well, one would get three different kinds of audio information in class VI. In both cases the quantitative principle of classification appears to be unconsciously supplemented by a qualitative valuation of the author. A second point is that the grouping of different instances of media into one class without further subdivision tends to conceal existing and relevant differences, like the obvious ones between a talking book and a recorded still television (both in class II) or between a video file and a printed page (both in class V).

In addition to these open points as to the internal formal consistency, it is difficult to realize the instructional relevance of this classification of hardware in terms of software capabilities. Bretz gives no explanation why he chooses to specify media in terms of hardware, the listing of which might not—as he has to admit—be as complete as he intended in the beginning, nor does he hint at any concealed relevance, which might justify the specific order of the seven classes. For an educational researcher the taxonomy provides no starting point for the generation of any relevant hypothesis with regard to instructional problems; it does not yet order our thinking about media in an obviously meaningful way. Although Bretz himself states that his work is directed "more toward media users and professional practitioners than towards scholars or researchers in the field" (p. ix), there is no possibility for a direct application of this taxonomy to more practical problems of media development and selection. What is still missing is specified exactly in Bretz's promise for the future: a discussion of "the uses to which instructional media are being put and the criteria which determine their appropriateness to the various uses" (p. 141).

C. J. Duncan. Several of the research surveys discussed in the first section of this entry show that instructional media are used extensively, that selection and usage decisions, however, are not based on established evidence of instructional effectiveness. As media research has failed to provide the desired valid guidelines, media selection decisions have

Figure 44
The Communication Media

TELECOMMUNICATION	Sound	Picture	Line Graphic	Print	Motion	RECORDING
CLASS I: AUDIO-MOTION-VISUAL MEDIA							
	X	X	X	X	X	Sound film
Television						Video tape
	X	X	X	X	X	Film, TV recording
	X	X	X	X	X	Holographic recording
Picturephone	X	X	X	X	X	
CLASS II: AUDIO-STILL-VISUAL MEDIA							
Slow-scan TV	X	X	X	X		
Time-shared TV						Recorded still TV
	X	X	X	X		Sound filmstrip
	X	X	X	X		Sound slide-set
	X	X	X	X		Sound-on-slide
	X	X	X	X		Sound page
	X	X	X	X		Talking book
CLASS III: AUDIO-SEMIMOTION MEDIA							
Telewriting	X		X	X	x	Recorded telewriting
CLASS IV: MOTION-VISUAL MEDIA							
		X	X	X	X	Silent film
CLASS V: STILL-VISUAL MEDIA							
Facsimile		X	X	X		Printed page
		X	X	X		Filmstrip
		X	X	X		Picture set
		X	X	X		Microform
		X	X	X		Video file
CLASS VI: AUDIO MEDIA							
Telephone	X					Audio disc
Radio						Audio tape
CLASS VII: PRINT MEDIA							
Teletype				X		Punched paper tape

Source: R. Bretz, *A Taxonomy of Communication Media*. Englewood Cliffs, N.J.: Educational Technology Publications, 1971, p. 66.

been based on considerations of cost, equipment availability, individual preferences, and administrative and organizational requirements. Consequently, the only reliable and in general undisputed kinds of media taxonomy are those which use such pragmatic determinants as criteria for a classification. An example for this type of taxonomy, which as a rule does not claim to be of relevance for research purposes, is the hierarchical order (Figure 45) of selected audio-visual instrumental media proposed by Duncan (1969 EXAMPLE).

In his one-dimensional array he proceeds from the simplest to the most complex media. As to the principle of arrangement, he explains:

As we descend the order, the unit costs and generality increase while the ease of use, flexibility, and economy decrease. The simpler and cheaper the aid, the more specific it will generally be to the selected audience and the task. This is not so much on technical as on economic grounds. If great cost and complexity are involved... the base will in general be broadened and the argument diluted or blunted to make the material and vehicle more suitable for a wider audience and thus allow the high costs to be recovered with more certainty. (p. 14)

Figure 45
A Hierarchical Order of Selected Audiovisual Instrumental Media

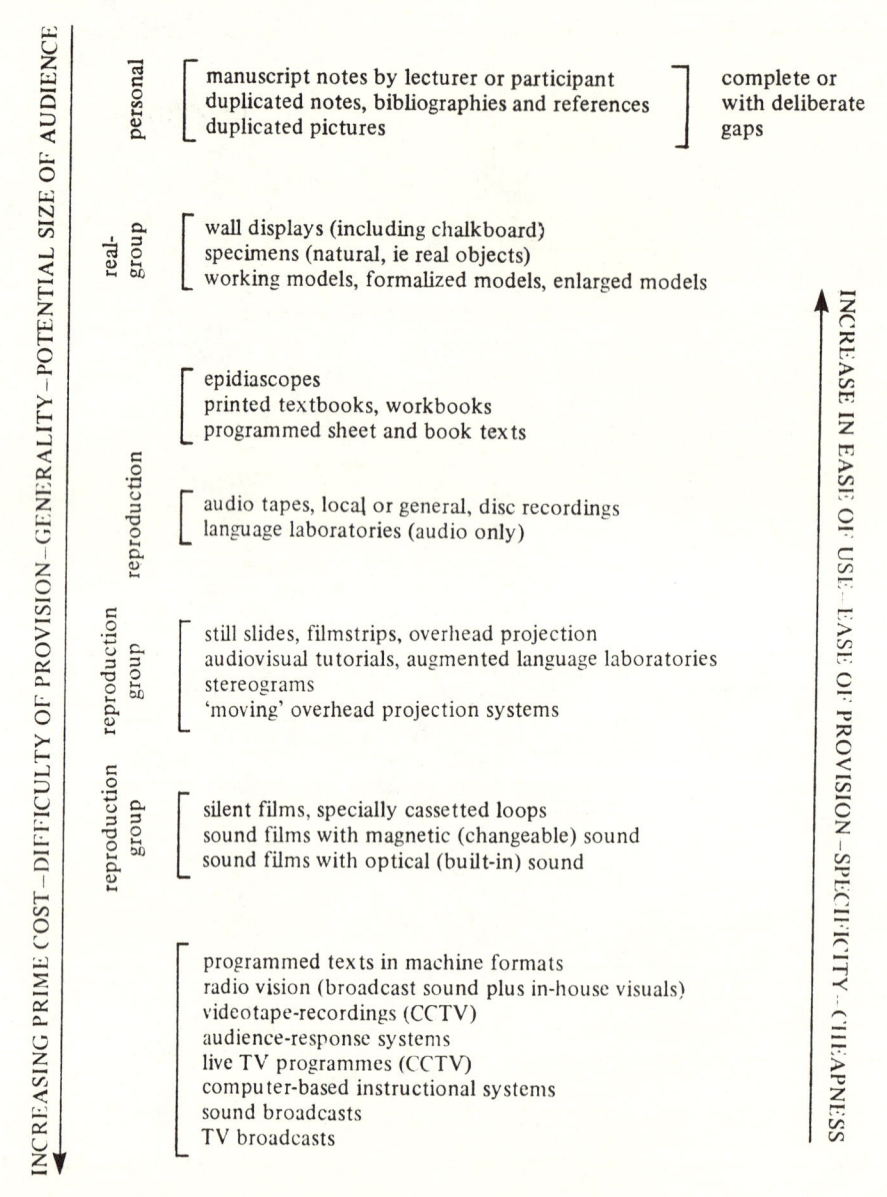

⬆ INCREASING PRIME COST – DIFFICULTY OF PROVISION – GENERALITY – POTENTIAL SIZE OF AUDIENCE ⬇

personal:
- manuscript notes by lecturer or participant
- duplicated notes, bibliographies and references
- duplicated pictures

complete or with deliberate gaps

real-group:
- wall displays (including chalkboard)
- specimens (natural, ie real objects)
- working models, formalized models, enlarged models

reproduction:
- epidiascopes
- printed textbooks, workbooks
- programmed sheet and book texts

reproduction:
- audio tapes, local or general, disc recordings
- language laboratories (audio only)

reproduction group:
- still slides, filmstrips, overhead projection
- audiovisual tutorials, augmented language laboratories
- stereograms
- 'moving' overhead projection systems

reproduction group:
- silent films, specially cassetted loops
- sound films with magnetic (changeable) sound
- sound films with optical (built-in) sound

- programmed texts in machine formats
- radio vision (broadcast sound plus in-house visuals)
- videotape-recordings (CCTV)
- audience-response systems
- live TV programmes (CCTV)
- computer-based instructional systems
- sound broadcasts
- TV broadcasts

⬆ INCREASE IN EASE OF USE – EASE OF PROVISION – SPECIFICITY – CHEAPNESS

Source: C. J. Duncan, "A Survey of Audiovisual Equipment and Methods." In *Media and Methods: Instructional Technology in Higher Education,* ed. D. Unwin. London: McGraw-Hill, 1969.

Duncan himself points to the problem of considering audiovisual media in isolation. He thinks it a necessary requirement from an analytical point of view, however, before media can be seen appropriately in the total educational context. He emphasizes that there are a number of at least equally important factors to be taken into account, first among which rank the professional pedagogic considerations. Only when the instructor has defined the aims of the learning task, identified the audience in specific terms, and selected the method to be used on pedagogic principles, can he on the basis of these previous considerations devise or choose the appropriate medium. Duncan's purpose is "to set out the various methods and their instrumentation in an orderly way so that the process of selection, realisation, and integration can be made educationally effective" (p. 16). He warns against considering his hierarchy as a rigid prescription table and points out that there might be a considerable overlap between simple instances of one media type and complicated examples of another, which makes the order rather tentative. Also there are other factors, like permanence, cost of storage, and ready availability, which have to be taken into account but do not correlate too well with the order given. Thus Duncan's comments in the text, which accompanies the taxonomy, underline the problematic nature of all attempts to condense the complex relationship between media and the other factors of the instructional situations into a one-dimensional array. Because of the many mental restrictions, one has to bear in mind, when using such a hierarchical order, that the applicability to specific practical selection problems is rather reduced. It was mentioned above that this taxonomy is not intended to serve any research purposes.

R. M. Gagné. In his well-known book *The Conditions of Learning* (1965 EXAMPLE) Gagné tries to relate classes of instructional media directly with instructional functions. In describing the instructional situation he identifies eight different component functions which "represent the ways in which the learner's environment acts on him" (p. 271). One of the most important tasks for the instructional designer is to select from among the many means available the most appropriate one to fulfill the desired functions, thereby establishing optimal external learning conditions. Gagné then mentions seven classes of media of instruction which may be employed to perform these functions and discusses their characteristics in detail. He summarizes his considerations as to which media are appropriate or inappropriate for which instructional functions in a diagram (Figure 46). The ratings within his matrix are to indicate the suitability of each class of media to fulfill each of the seven functions.

Gagné gives no reason why he chooses just these seven classes of media out of the great variety of possible means. His selection is not made on a systematic basis but casually follows a general discussion of traditional and newer media. Thus the list of media appears to be somewhat arbitrary; e.g., the modern technical audio media (record, tape) are omitted completely, while the field of visual media is sufficiently represented. The reduction of the live teacher to "oral communication" seems as problematic as the category "teaching machines," which serves—this is obvious from the preceding description—merely as a label for the principle of programmed instruction. In spite of the above quotation, the list of eight instructional functions is certainly not complete. Proof of this is that in the second edition of Gagné's book there appear nine partly modified, partly new functions.

The effort to classify media according to instructional functions, however, poses an even more fundamental problem. Instructional functions as specified by Gagné and most other authors are just formal labels which become instructionally relevant only in relation to a particular learning task. A teacher, for example, usually does not want to present an arbitrary stimulus, but one required for the learning task in hand. What the teacher tries to find is a medium which is most appropriate to present just this particular stimulus. In the same way an instructor does not direct the intention of his learners without an aim. He may want to direct it to certain features of an object, the crucial point in a philosophical problem, etc. The decision about which medium may be most appropriate therefore always depends on the content and the objective of the particular learning task. The same is true for all other instructional functions. Without such a reference to a particular learning task, one may at the same time devise examples of instructional situations which support the use of a particular medium for one of the instructional functions and other examples which show that the use of the same medium for the same function is inappropriate.

Another problem is that some of the ratings in the matrix are self-evident, others not. Without further information it is not plausible that printed media should have only a limited value for presenting the stimulus in comparison to still pictures, since Gagné himself states in the preceding text that printed media include still pictures in the form of illustrations. A main reason for this is that the rating categories—"yes, limited, no"—are too comprehensive and often conceal the differences between the various classes of media. This is in particular true of the category "limited." Here it would be interesting to learn why and how the medium is limited for the particular instructional function. It is also difficult to relate the class of media selected to the actual hardware and software decisions in a practical instructional situation. Not only is the whole audio field missing, but a category like "still pictures" neglects the instructionally relevant differences between an illustration in a book, a slide, and an overhead transparency. Because of all these open questions and critical points Gagné's taxonomy provides hardly an adequate instrument for media selection decisions nor a basis for media research.

D. T. Tosti and J. R. Ball. A rather differnt approach to the problem is chosen by Tosti and Ball (1969 EXAMPLE), who see the main reason for the unsatisfactory situation of educational media research and instructional design practice today in the fault to distinguish between the actually relevant classes of factors and in the confusion of presentational, content, and gross media variables. The most significant feature of their model, therefore, is the distinction between medium and presentation form, both of which are to be considered independent of content. The following example should illustrate the difference: the picture of an elephant in a book and the verbal description of an elephant by a teacher are different in both medium and presentation form. However, the picture of the elephant in the book

Figure 46
Instructional Functions of Various Media

Function	Objects: Demonstration	Oral Communication	Printed Media	Still Pictures	Moving Pictures	Sound Movies	Teaching Machines
Presenting the stimulus	Yes	Limited	Limited	Yes	Yes	Yes	Yes
Directing attention and other activity	No	Yes	Yes	No	No	Yes	Yes
Providing a model of expected performance	Limited	Yes	Yes	Limited	Limited	Yes	Yes
Furnishing external prompts	Limited	Yes	Yes	Limited	Limited	Yes	Yes
Guiding thinking	No	Yes	Yes	No	No	Yes	Yes
Inducing transfer	Limited	Yes	Limited	Limited	Limited	Limited	Limited
Assessing attainments	No	Yes	Yes	No	No	Yes	Yes
Providing feedback	Limited	Yes	Yes	No	Limited	Yes	Yes

Source: R. M. Gagné, *The Condition of Learning.* New York: Holt, Rinehart and Winston, 1965, p. 284.

and another one on a slide are delivered by two different media but have the same presentation form. Finally, the picture of the elephant in a book and the printed verbal description of it in another book use the same medium but differ in presentation form. Tosti and Ball argue that "a student does not learn from the media. He learns from the presentation form. Media do little more than deliver the information to be learnt in whatever presentational form previously decided upon" (p. 9). Since they hold the presentational variables to be primary in learning research and instructional design, they aim at identifying and classifying the relevant dimensions and the corresponding categories. They distinguish stimulus, response, and management, each of which is again subdivided with regard to *form* and *duration or frequency*. Thus the six dimensions of presentation are (1) stimulus encoding form (environmental structure, pictorial, symbolic, and verbal); (2) stimulus duration (length of time the presentation remains intact, from persistent to transient); (3) response demand form (covert, selective, constructed, vocal, motor, and affective); (4) response demand frequency (from sparse to frequent); (5) management form or purpose (need, attainment, prescriptive, enrichment, motivation, and systems support management); (6) management frequency (frequency of decision to change presentation, from sparse to frequent).

Only after the decisions with respect to all dimensions of the presentation form have been made does one proceed to the consideration of the most appropriate medium to carry it. This involves a specification of media with regard to the different dimensions of presentation. For a complete analysis of media selection possibilities, a six-dimensional matrix would have to be used. Since this would be too complicated, Tosti and Ball suggest a series of two-dimensional matrices, of which they give two illustrations (see Figures 47 and 48).

Such an analysis will often result in a list of two or more apparently adequate media. Tosti and Ball argue

Figure 47
Media Classified by Encoding versus Duration

Environmental	Demonstration	Laboratory Field Trip	Object
Pictorial	Film Video	Slide	Photograph Illustrated Text Painting
Symbolic	Animation	PI-workbook Flashcard	Diagram Blackboard
Verbal	Conversation Lecture		Text Manual
		Flashcard PI-workbook	
		Group Discussion	
	Tutor		
	Transient		Persistent

Encoding Dimension (vertical axis)
Duration Dimension (horizontal axis)

Source: D. T. Tosti and J. R. Ball, "A Behavioral Approach to Instructional Design and Media Selection." *Audiovisual Communication Review* 1 (1969): 22.

Figure 48
Media Classified by Encoding versus Response Demand

Environmental	Demonstration Field Trip	Item Sort			
Pictorial	Film Video Slide Painting Photograph	Multiple Choice Teaching Machine		Illustrated PI-text	Laboratory
Symbolic	Blackboard Diagram	Card Sort	Flashcard		Diagram
Verbal	Lecture Audiotape	PI-workbook	Conversation Role-playing Audiotape		
	Text	Tutor	Tutor	Tutor	Tutor
	Covert	Selective	Vocal	Constructed	Motor

Encoding Dimension (vertical axis)
Response Dimension (horizontal axis)

that the final choice should not be made on the basis of media advantages. They instead propose a negative selection procedure: all those media are eliminated from the list which do not fit the requirements of the presentation form. Since several media may meet the requirements of the presentation form but have different limitations, they consider their procedure as more than just the reverse of selecting media on the basis of their advantages. They finally also include cost, availability, and market or user preference as decision determinants.

The model of Tosti and Ball is one of the most coherent and comprehensive efforts among previous classifications. It emphasizes the important argument that the selection of media cannot consist in a simple matching of instructional functions or similar criteria on the one hand with the medium as the complex technical equipment on the other. Thus they suggest the introduction of a connecting link, the presentation form. The illustrative matrices show that the subcategories suggested for the different dimensions of the presentation are really an equivalent of media attributes, which play such an important part in present research recommendations. They also suggest basing the specifications of the presentation form on an analysis of task and student variables. Although they combine their classification system with a flowchart which specifies the necessary steps of the decision process, one of the most crucial questions is not yet satisfactorily answered: given a particular learning task and a particular group of learners, *why* is the stimulus to be encoded in, e.g., a pictorial or a symbolic form, and *why* again is the response demand form to be selective or constructed? *How* do student and task variables enter the decision on the most appropriate presentation form? Considering the present state of the art, Tosti and Ball's simple direction does not solve the problem but just puts the question in another form: "Deduce the presentation factors which produce the desired behavioral effect *employing established evidence in learning*" (p. 8, italics mine). The survey of media research has shown that what is missing is exactly any "established evidence" of such correlations.

Summary and Conclusions. The analysis of these four media classifications, which are representative of many more attempts, has shown that the principles of analysis and arrangement were different in each case. Media were classified as to the sensory channels involved (audio or visual), their application in a usage system (transmitting or recording), and visual media were further subdivided as to their capability to convey different kinds of visual information. Other authors took as distinguishing criteria economic and organizational factors, instructional functions, or differences in the presentation form, which different media are most apt to carry. This is only a small selection from the many possible principles of classification, which could be supplemented very easily by taking into account further attempts at taxonomic development. Since they point to the great number of angles from which media may be viewed, each approach may be considered as an at least partially useful contribution to the discussion of instructional media. One should, however, always be aware that each attempt can take into consideration only a single or at best a few of the many relevant instructional factors. The interrelation of instructional media with other components of the instructional situation is too complex to be covered appropriately by a single taxonomy, and even the six-dimensional matrix of Tosti and Ball falls short in that respect. Since most of them pick out only isolated factors of a rather formal or abstract level, the applicability of the taxonomies analyzed here to practical instructional problems is quite limited despite the express claims to the contrary.

Though each of the criteria of classification may in principle be of consequence for a particular problem, none of the earlier attempts resulted in a comprehensive and conclusive classification of instructional relevance for research or selection purposes. The multiplicity of aspects used for bringing media into an order rather emphasizes that the central problem is not to find out *if* media can be classified at all within a consistent order, and to construct some sort of corresponding taxonomy. The crucial question is *which* principle of classification and *which* categories are instructionally relevant.

At this point one may clearly recognize the direct consequence of the lack of a theoretical foundation—which has been mentioned in the above research survey—for developing media taxonomies; and it affects in particular the classifications for research purposes. Although some researchers hold that a media taxonomy would provide the reference system for a theory of educational media, it seems to me that—quite the contrary—such a theoretical framework constitutes the precondition for an instructionally relevant classification. It has been explained above that the relevance of a classification system depends not only on its formal consistency but on its usefulness in a specific context. Lest a selection of chance categories lead to a formally correct but irrelevant or inadequate classification and thus impede the appropriate perception of the phenomena under investigation, one should at least have the outline of a tentative theoretical conception about the important factors and their interrelations.

AN ALTERNATIVE APPROACH

Instead of the usual approach of just selecting and labeling instances of media in the hope that the classification thus developed will in the end prove instructionally relevant, another approach is suggested here. I shall take an instructional theory as my starting point, accordingly select and label relevant task and learner categories, and finally propose to analyze and classify media in terms directly related to task and learner variables.

Aptitude-Treatment Interaction (ATI). A fundamental contribution to the problem under discussion has come

Figure 49
Media Taxonomy Cube

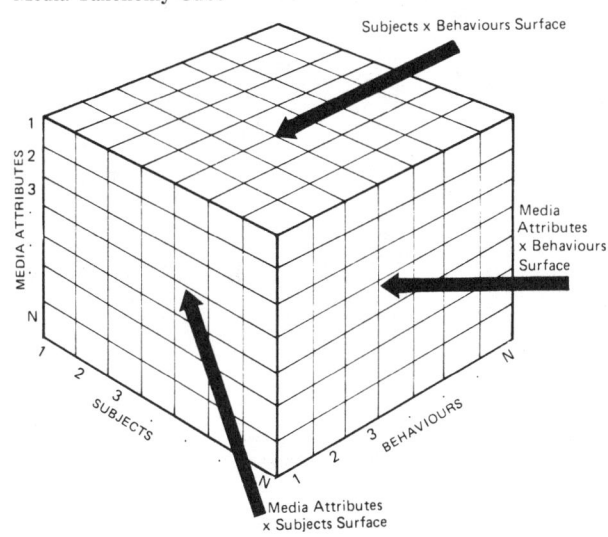

Source: P. E. Clark, "Constructing a Taxonomy of Media Attributes for Research Purposes." *Audiovisual Communication Review* 2 (1975): 209.

from the field of differential psychology, in particular from the aptitude-treatment interaction approach (ATI). In ATI research the instructional situation is seen as a complex system of interacting elements or subsystems. Thus learning results cannot be explained by looking only at the instructional measures or treatments. The effects of learning in a particular instructional situation must rather be interpreted as the result of *interactions* between specific features of the treatment, in particular of instructional media, and specific aptitudes or traits of the learning individual. Since most ATI studies took a mere trial-and-error approach towards the selection and investigation of potentially interacting variables, only very few significant interactions have been experimentally proved to date. This absence of conclusive empirical evidence has resulted in increased efforts to develop a theory about *how* media and learner variables interact in an instructional situation, thus providing a basis for a more systematic way of research (Cronbach and Snow, 1976 THEORETICAL BACKGROUND).

With that end in mind Clark has put forward the proposal of "Constructing a taxonomy of media attributes for research purposes" (1975 THEORY). He is particularly concerned with the question of how to validate a list of potentially relevant media attributes. He suggests the construction of a three-dimensional matrix (Figure 49) which includes media attributes as one of the dimensions. The other dimensions are subjects and behaviors. After a large-scale study has provided the record of the behavior associated with each media attribute for each subject, it would be possible to collapse the matrix across each of the three factors in turn and factor the intercorrelations. When the matrix is collapsed across subjects, one can compute the correlation between each of the pairs of media attributes and perform a factor analysis on the intercorrelation matrix: "A high correlation between two media attributes would imply that they elicit similar behaviors. A factor, thus, represents a group of functionally similar media attributes that tend to evoke the same behaviors" (p. 209). Clark's approach, therefore, has the general advantage of stressing the functional rather than the nominal similarity of media attributes.

Although I consider Clark's taxonomy an important contribution to the methodology of media research in an ATI context, it is evident that a major problem still has to be tackled prior to the suggested validation of the list of media attributes. I think it vital that the preliminary list of media attributes, aptitudes, and behaviors, which is to be put to the test of the proposed large-scale study, should already be based on thorough considerations of potential interactions between instances of the three classes of variables. Otherwise, research would start from an arbitrary accumulation of isolated instances and blind guesses and be confronted with an unnecessary amount of work in separating a great deal of chaff from a small amount of wheat by means of a complicated and time-consuming method.

Supplanting Mental Operations. One of the most convincing theoretical models about potential aptitude-treatment interactions, which pays special regard to instructional media, has been developed by Salomon, (1972 THEORY; 1979 THEORETICAL BACKGROUND). From the observation that different learners often respond to the same information in quite different ways, he argues that the crucial point in the reaction of a learner is not the overt and observable behavior but the internal operations in processing the stimulus, the information. As the most important function which media can fulfill with respect to internal learning operations, he identifies the function of *supplantation*. By this he implies that media can be designed deliberately in such a way that they explicitly present, and thereby supplant, what otherwise the learner would have to do himself internally, based on our assumptions about the mental operations required for a particular learning task. Media now may differ with regard to the *nature* of the process supplanted and with regard to the *amount* of supplantation provided. Some media can show continual transformations; others show only situations or steps of a transformation. Some media can present only auditory information, while others have the potential for visual and iconic information. These *structural* media attributes can be compiled in a single list. It is, then, necessary to develop a list of *functional* media attributes "which contains only those attributes having a unique psychological effect on the viewer" (Salomon and Snow, 1968 THEORY, p. 231ff). This latter list is a flexible subset of the former. As the function of a structural attribute depends upon the intended learning process, i.e., the task in hand, each change in the learning task causes—at least potentially—a change in the functional valence of the structural attributes. Thus the same attribute can be functional, neutral, or even dysfunctional in different instructional situations. This again stresses the importance of the particular learning task for statements about the suitability and effectiveness of media. These considerations imply that learner characteristics must be described in terms of internal operational abilities. Learning tasks, then, must be specified with reference to the internal operations they require. Finally, media must be described with respect to the different degrees of supplantation they can provide for these operations.

In order to describe the intellectual aptitudes of learners in a more systematic way, I take Guilford's structure of intellect model (1967 THEORETICAL BACKGROUND) as a terminological frame of reference. Guilford has constructed a model which comprises 120 intellectual abilities or factors. He uses a three-dimensional model to organize these factors into a system. The three dimensions with the corresponding subcategories are the kind of mental *operation* (cognition, memory, divergent production, convergent production, evaluation), the kind of *content* of information (figural, symbolic, semantic, behavioral), and the kind of *product* (units, classes, relations, systems, transformations, implications). Each intellectual ability is defined by one category in each of the three dimensions. Thus, e.g., the ability "visualization" is defined by the categories "cognition, figural, transformations," and the ability "expressional fluency" is specified by "divergent production, semantic, systems." Guilford's system comprises not only the different mental operations in great detail, but with its content and product categories refers to stimulus characteristics which are in any case of great relevance when dealing with instructional media. For the time being I shall leave out of consideration other nonintellectual personality domains.

Specifying Media Attributes. The appropriate categories for the specification of media attributes must be directly related to the categories of the personality trait domain. They must take up the definitions of the internal learner operations and give information about which kind of internal process can be supplanted to what degree by a particular medium. While the learning task in hand de-

Figure 50
The Three Levels of the Stimulus Encoding Dimension

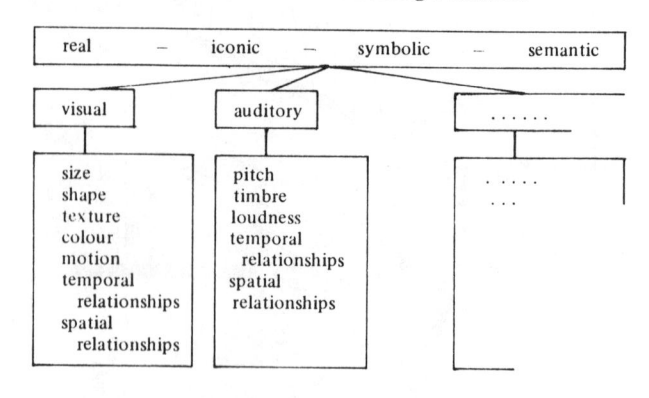

| real | — | iconic | — | symbolic | — | semantic |

visual	auditory	......
size shape texture colour motion temporal relationships spatial relationships	pitch timbre loudness temporal relationships spatial relationships	......

termines to a large extent the *nature* of the learner operation to be supplanted, the *amount* of supplantation required depends upon the degree of the availability of the respective operational ability by the learner. Taking Guilford's structure of intellect model as a frame of reference, it is evident that the total "content" dimension of this model can be adopted without any modification as a description of a similar dimension of media attributes. In order to get a more accurate instrument of specification, it is necessary, however, to supplement Guilford's level of categories "real, iconic, symbolic, semantic" by two more levels, the first of which covers the sensory modalities, while the second comprises those elements through the modification of which the medium can be adopted to the different personality traits. I suggest calling this three-level dimension, with reference to Tosti and Ball, the "stimulus encoding dimension" of the presentation form. In Figure 50 I confine myself to the visual and auditory domains. The possibility of including other sensory modalities is indicated by the empty frame.

In the same way, the category "transformations" of Guilford's product dimension can be related to another dimension of Tosti and Ball's presentation form. It corresponds to the media attribute "stimulus duration dimension," which describes the degree to which a stimulus or certain of its attributes can be modified during presentation. While the attributes of the stimulus encoding dimension and the stimulus duration dimension serve as the basic vocabulary, the operation and product categories of Guilford's model provide the syntactic instructions, which specify in which way which of the elements of the vocabulary are to be put together.

It should have become evident (in particular during the analysis of Tosti and Ball's model) that the identification of categories for an appropriate description of instances is only a first step toward the analysis and classification of media. What is needed further is a method or procedure which shows how these categories

Figure 51
Identifying Functional Media Attributes

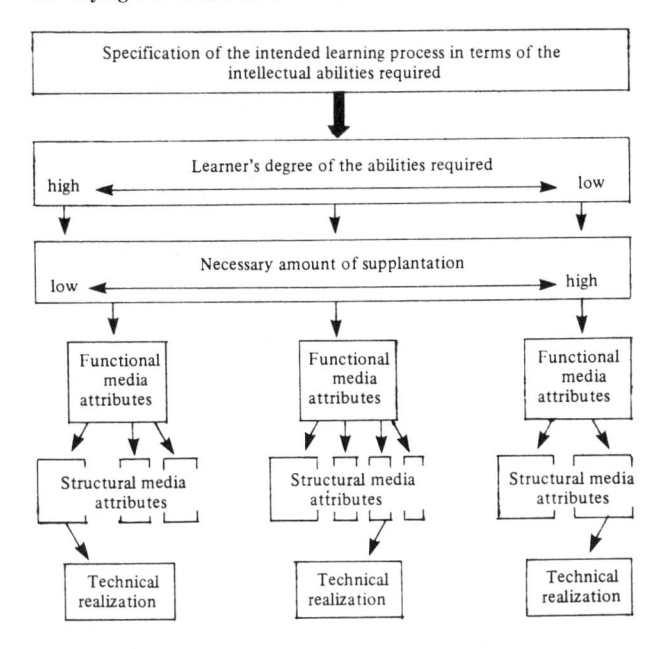

```
┌─────────────────────────────────────────────────┐
│ Specification of the intended learning process  │
│   in terms of the intellectual abilities required│
└─────────────────────────────────────────────────┘
                        ↓
┌─────────────────────────────────────────────────┐
│        Learner's degree of the abilities required│
│  high ←─────────────────────────────────→ low   │
└─────────────────────────────────────────────────┘
       ↓                 ↓                 ↓
┌─────────────────────────────────────────────────┐
│            Necessary amount of supplantation    │
│  low  ←─────────────────────────────────→ high  │
└─────────────────────────────────────────────────┘
       ↓                 ↓                 ↓
  ┌─────────┐       ┌─────────┐       ┌─────────┐
  │Functional│      │Functional│      │Functional│
  │  media  │       │  media  │       │  media  │
  │attributes│      │attributes│      │attributes│
  └─────────┘       └─────────┘       └─────────┘
       ↓↓↓              ↓↓↓↓             ↓↓↓
  ┌─────────┐       ┌─────────┐       ┌─────────┐
  │Structural│      │Structural│      │Structural│
  │  media  │       │  media  │       │  media  │
  │attributes│      │attributes│      │attributes│
  └─────────┘       └─────────┘       └─────────┘
       ↓                 ↓                 ↓
  ┌─────────┐       ┌─────────┐       ┌─────────┐
  │Technical│       │Technical│       │Technical│
  │realization│     │realization│     │realization│
  └─────────┘       └─────────┘       └─────────┘
```

may be utilized in an instructionally relevant way by the researcher and/or the practitioner. In the following I shall try to explain the steps to identify the functional media attributes (Figure 51) with regard to a particular learning task and a specific learner.

First, on the basis of the learning task in hand, the intended learning process is described with categories of the required intellectual abilities, using Guilford's model as a frame of reference. Thus the *nature* of the learning process to be supplanted is identified. Second, the appropriate *amount* of supplantation is determined depending upon the degree to which the learner has at his command the required operational abilities. Third, on the basis of this information the necessary *functional* media attributes are specified. They are described with categories corresponding to those of Guilford's model and refer to sensory modalities, to the encoding form, and the duration dimension of the stimuli required. The identification of these functional attributes is the crucial step within this approach and should always result in the same categories no matter who performs the analysis. The next steps, however, from the functional and structural attributes, and further on to the technical realization, leave ample room for the creative mind of the skillful media designer. The *structural* attributes of media are those which can be used in the sense of the functional attributes defined before. They include the whole scope of design techniques and can already be regarded as the features of specific software/hardware configurations. In most cases there will be several alternatives, several structural attributes, which can be employed in the sense of a single specific functional attribute. Finally, one must decide which kind of *technical equipment* meets the structural specifications best. It has been illustrated elsewhere (Heidt, 1977; 1978 THEORY) how the suggested model can be set to work in actual research and design projects.

FINAL COMMENT

Most current surveys of media research and media selection models support the view that it is not media per se which make a difference in learning outcomes but that future research should focus on method, task, and aptitude variables (Clark, 1983 RESEARCH SURVEY; Heidt, 1985 SURVEY). This view, which leads to more complex and sophisticated research designs, is hardly reflected in classification systems for practical media selection problems, most of which still aim at the identification of media in gross categories like television, film, books, etc. The survey of media research to date and the discussion of a number of classification systems have made it quite clear that the search for the single media taxonomy, the handy instrument which provides the direct help required for the many purposes of media producers, teachers and researchers alike, is an attempt at squaring the circle. The suitability and effectiveness of instructional media depend upon many interacting factors, first among which rank task and learner variables. On account of the complexity and diversity of instructional situations and educational problems, many authors have warned against simple rules for media classification and selection and have even considered a deductive procedure, a sequence of logical steps to identify the best medium for a given situation, as not feasible. Considering the use of psychologically defined personality characteristics of the learner as factors for media selection, it has to be admitted that, although the ATI approach opens promising ways for future media research, its relevance for the media practitioner seems to be rather limited. What is necessary, therefore, is a careful and thorough analysis which takes into consideration the particular requirements of the specific situation. For this effort different classification systems and selection models may fulfill a heuristic function, and even the most sophisticated taxonomy cannot do much more.

E. U. Heidt

REFERENCES

Example

Bretz, R. (1971) *A Taxonomy of Communication Media.* Englewood Cliffs, N.J.: Educational Technology Publications.

Duncan, C. J. (1969) "A Survey of Audiovisual Equipment and Methods." In *Media and Methods: Instructional*

Technology in Higher Education, ed. D. Unwin. London: McGraw-Hill.

Gagné, R. M. (1965) *The Conditions of Learning.* New York: Holt, Rinehart & Winston.

Tosti, D. T. and Ball, J. R. (1969) "A Behavioral Approach to Instructional Design and Media Selection." *Audiovisual Communication Review* 1: 5–25.

Research Study

Allen, W. H. and Weintraub, R. (1968) *The Motion Variable in Film Presentation: Final Report.* Los Angeles, Calif.: University of Southern California Press.

Spangenberg, R. W. (1973) "The Motion Variable in Procedural Learning." *Audiovisual Communication Review* 4: 419–436.

Webster, B. R. and Cox, S. M. (1974) "The Value of Colour in Educational Television." *British Journal of Educational Technology* 1: 44–61.

Research Survey

Allen, W. H. (1970) "Categories of Instructional Media Research." *Viewpoints Bulletin of the School of Education Indiana University* 5: 1–13.

———. (1971) "Instructional Media Research: Past, Present and Future." *Audiovisual Communication Review* 1: 5–18.

Campeau, P. L. (1966) "Selective Review of Literature on Audiovisual Media of Instruction." In *Instructional Media: A Procedure for the Design of Multi-Media Instruction,* ed. J. L. Briggs et al. Pittsburgh: American Institutes for Research.

———. (1974) "Selective Review of the Results of Research on the Use of Audiovisual Media to Teach Adults." *Audiovisual Communication Review* 1: 5–40.

Chu, G. C. and Schramm, W. (1967) *Learning from Television: What the Research Says.* Stanford, Calif.: Stanford University Press.

Clark, R. E. (1983) "Reconsidering Research on Learning from Media." *Review of Educational Research* 53 (4): 445–459.

Jamison, D., Suppes, P. and Wells, S. (1974) "The Effectiveness of Alternative Instructional Media: A Survey." *Review of Educational Research* 1: 1–67.

Levie, W. H. and Dickie K. E. (1973) "The Analysis and Application of Media." In *Second Handbook of Research on Teaching,* ed. R. M. Travers. Chicago: Rand McNally.

Lumsdaine, A. A. (1963) "Instruments and Media of Instruction." In *Handbook of Research on Teaching,* ed. N. L. Gage. Chicago: Rand McNally.

Twyford, L. C. (1969) "Educational Communications Media." In *Encyclopedia of Educational Research,* ed. R. L. Ebel. 4th ed. London: Macmillan.

Survey

Heidt, E. U. (1985) "Instructional Design: Media Selection." In *International Encyclopedia of Education: Research and Studies,* ed. T. Husen and T. N. Postlethwaite. Oxford: Pergamon Press, pp. 2548–2553.

Reiser, R. and Gagné, R. (1982) "Characteristics of Media Selection Models." *Review of Educational Research* 52 (4):499–512.

Theoretical Background

Cronbach, L. J. and Snow, R. E. (1977) *Aptitudes and Instructional Methods.* New York: Irvington.

Guilford, J. P. (1967) *The Nature of Human Intelligence.* New York: McGraw-Hill.

Meredith, P. (1965) "Toward a Taxonomy of Educational Media."*Audiovisual Communication Review* 4: 374–384.

Salomon, G. (1979) *Interaction of Media, Cognition and Learning.* San Francisco: Jossey-Bass.

Snow, R. E. and Salomon, G. (1968) "Aptitudes and Instructional Media." *Audiovisual Communication Review* 4: 341–357.

Theory

Anderson, C.M. (1972) "In Search of Visual Rhetoric for Instructional Television." *Audiovisual Communication Review* 1: 46–63.

Clark, R. E. (1975) "Constructing a Taxonomy of Media Attributes for Research Purposes." *Audiovisual Communication Review* 2: 197–215.

Heidt, E. U. (1977) "Media and Learner Operations: the Problem of a Media Taxonomy Revisited." *British Journal of Educational Technology* 1: 11–26.

———.(1978) *Instructional Media and the Individual Learner.* London: Kogan Page.

Salomon, G. (1972) "Heuristic Models for the Generation of Aptitude-Treatment Interaction Hypotheses." *Review of Educational Research* 3: 327–343.

Salomon G. and Snow, R. E. (1968) "The Specification of Film Attributes for Psychological and Educational Research Purposes."*Audiovisual Communication Review* 3: 225–244.

MEDICAL EDUCATION. This entry examines the impact of educational media on medical education.

HISTORICAL DEVELOPMENT

Medicine is the art and science of caring for human beings as they grow, mature, age, and die. Caring has to take account of the individual, his family, the society, and the environment in which he works and lives. Students of medicine must thus master a wide range of facts, concepts, principles, and skills. They receive their basic education at the university, they specialize while they continue their training in a hospital or in the community, and they continue their training for the rest of their professional life, truly a lifetime of learning. Medical illustrations have been used for many centuries to foster understanding, memory, and familiarity with the appearance of disease and aspects of techniques. Artists were the earliest illustrators, and the anatomical drawings of Leonardo da Vinci (Bearn, 1963) are still admired for their beauty and accuracy. Cheselden is credited with the application of the camera obscura (Gernsheim, 1961) to ensure precision of perspective and detail of the human body. Towne created his wax models of dissections, facial expressions, and manifestations of numerous diseases in the first half of the nineteenth century (Everall, 1976). His carefully preserved collection at Guy's Hospital Medical School in London bears witness to a craftsman who has not been equaled even by present-day artists working with modern plastics.

The discovery of photography was soon put to such good use that Professor Jean Martin Charcôt found it necessary to establish a special department of medical photography at the Hospice de la Salpêtrière, Paris, in 1874, and a journal, the *Inconographie Photographique de la Salpêtrière,* was published between 1876 and 1880. Cinematography, too, was still in its infancy when Marey (1888) in France employed it in physiology, the study of function of the body. Early in the present century portrait photographers were called on to make paper prints from glass X-ray negatives and occasionally to photograph patients in some of the major teaching hospitals (Gernsheim, 1961). However, it was not until World War II that departments of clinical photography were established in earnest. Since then the meteoric developments in audiovisual technology, coupled with the renaissance of medical education, have altered the emphasis from clinical recording to the preparation of audiovisual aids and, more recently, to emphasis on audiovisual communication and educational technology.

These developments in recent years are mirrored not only in the changing designation of the original hospital departments of clinical photography to departments of medical illustration and departments of audiovisual communication. It can also be traced in the growing interest shown by major organizations concerned with medicine. For example, the Department of Audio Visual Communication at the British Medical Association became the British Life Assurance Trust Centre for Health and Medical Education in 1976, and the World Health Organization created a section on Educational Communication Systems in its Division of Health Manpower Development.

Numerous societies have also played an active role in this evolution. In Great Britain the Medical Groups of the Royal Photographic Society and of the Institute of Incorporated Photographers, and the Medical Artists Association of Great Britain were created to advance medical photography and illustration through conferences, exhibitions, award of qualifications, and publications. More recently an amalgamation of interests has led to the formation of the Institute of Medical and Biological Illustration, which has taken over the British Medical Association's quarterly journal *Medical and Biological Illustration,* now renamed the *Journal of Audiovisual Media in Medicine*. In the United States Eastman Kodak has published *Medical Radiography and Photography* since before the last war. Of the same vintage is the *Journal of the Biological Photographic Association.*

Another significant development of the 1970s was the creation of the Health Sciences Communications Association in North America. This has brought together those who are concerned with the production of audiovisual aids and those academics who are interested in the planning, design, and application of educational materials for the health professions. Its conferences and its publication, *The Journal of Biocommunication,* have an important role to play in developing educational technology in the health sciences.

The emergence of this wide spectrum of activities is based not only on advances in technology; it has also been encouraged by increasing pressures for improved acceptability, effectiveness, and efficiency of medical education. The conferences of organizations such as the Association of American Medical Colleges in the United States and the Association for the Study of Medical Education in the United Kingdom, and their respective journals, the *Journal of Medical Education* and *Medical Education,* show evidence of awareness of the potential importance of audiovisual communication and educational technology for the improvement of medical education. The British Medical Association, through the publications, research, and assessment activities of the BLITH Centre for Health and Medical Education, and the National Library of Medicine in the United States make major contributions at the corporate level. The latter supports the development of **computer-assisted instruction** (q.v.) by a number of American medical schools. It is actively exploring continuing education through **communication satellites** (q.v.) for isolated professionals in areas such as the north of Alaska. It includes citations from the literature on educational technology and audiovisual communication in its worldwide computer reference service MEDLARS. The National Library of Medicine also had a subsidiary organization in Atlanta, Georgia. This, the National Medical Audiovisual Center, has produced useful bibliographies (1969) and two collections of relevant papers from the literature (1967, 1969); it assisted medical teachers in the planning and design of packages for individual learning; and it organized the assessment and cataloging of existing audiovisual learning materials. Materials judged to be of adequate educational standards are included in the computer system of the National Library of Medicine. This information is then made available on an on-line basis through Avline in North America. In Britain, a similar assessment system is operated by the BLITH

Centre for Health and Medical Education (Engel, 1969), and the Council for Educational Technology for the United Kingdom publishes a computer catalog on medical audiovisual materials entitled *Helpis-Medical*. The World Health Organization has expressed its concern that such evaluation information should be made available on a worldwide basis (WHO, 1974).

The organization of audiovisual communication and educational technology services within individual institutions varies considerably. Britain can be justly proud of the technical excellence of its medical illustration services and the teaching films produced by small film companies. However, it has yet to develop units that can assist in medical education at a really sophisticated level. The units of medical education at the universities of Dundee and Southampton are unique in Britain, while many North American medical schools enjoy the assistance of departments that provide both educational and technical expertise and research functions. Even so, such units have usually been created as an adjunct to the existing structure of long-established medical schools and are sometimes regarded as the icing on the cake. It is, therefore, worth noting that the University of Newcastle in Australia from its inception incorporated medical education in the administrative structure of the medical faculty by establishing a discipline of medical education, as well as disciplines in the traditional basic and clinical sciences.

Training and career structures are still in an early stage of evolution. The only thorough investigation and recommendation in relation to the staffing of resource centers in the United States stem from the University of California (Merrill and Drob, 1974). In Britain a joint University Grants Committee and Department of Education and Science (1965) inquiry made only brief reference to these matters, although Duncan (1964) had submitted an extensive report on these aspects. Since then the Council for Educational Technology in the United Kingdom (Wright, 1973) has discussed recruitment and training of technical staff. However, only the World Health Organization (WHO) has concerned itself specifically with training for medical education (for example, WHO, 1973). A number of regional teacher training centers have been established with the brief to train medical teachers so that they can build up national centers where local medical academics can become familiar with present-day methods of medical education and educational technology. In the United States the University of Illinois and Michigan State University offer master's degrees in medical education, and the Rochester Institute of Technology provides courses in medical photography. In Britain artists and photographers of the London medical schools combined to offer outstanding training to students who have already qualified in graphic art or photography respectively. British medical schools accord lecturer or senior lecturer status to lay heads of their audiovisual departments, and readerships (equivalent to associate professorship) to the very few medically qualified heads of such departments. North American universities are more liberal in their award of academic rank, and heads of departments of medical education usually have the rank of full professor.

PRESENT DEVELOPMENTS

The increasing application of the systems approach in medical education (Engel, 1971) has led to a number of developments that run parallel to similar advances in other fields of higher education. Growing emphasis on small group, individual and independent learning (WHO, 1972), and problem-based learning (Barrows and Tamblyn, 1980) has begun a silent revolution. There is less emphasis on teaching through lectures and set laboratory exercises in favor of a more flexible management of learning. This trend, coupled with a shift toward the integration of the basic and clinical sciences, is creating a demand for specially designed study materials. In response a number of collaborative ventures have emerged. For example, the Health Sciences Consortium, based at the University of North Carolina, is now supported financially by more than one-third of the medical schools in the United States, and its catalog lists a sizable volume of contributions from its member universities. Individual medical schools, such as St. Bartholomew's Hospital in London, produce numerous series of audiotapes with sets of 35mm transparencies. In Britain the Graves Audiovisual Library has established the Medical Audiotape Slide Producers' Association in order to coordinate and rationalize the production and distribution of such materials in medical schools and teaching hospitals. Increasing sophistication in the assessment of students has created a demand for assessment instruments that will test for specific types of objectives at the higher levels of the cognitive, psychomotor, and affective domains respectively (Feletti et al., 1983). While multiple-choice questions (Lennox, 1974) are no longer accepted uncritically, the modified essay question (Knox, 1975) is being explored for its potentially more flexible application (Engel et al., 1980).

Videotape cassettes are rapidly replacing motion picture films. The videodisc is no longer confined to patent specifications but is the subject of active experimentation, particularly in combination with microcomputers (Leveridge, 1980). Computers, large and small, are making their presence felt and are forcing producers to design more sophisticated programs which take account of present-day understanding of adult learning and clinical reasoning. The general acceptance that medical education is a continuum—from undergraduate to postgraduate and continuing education—ensures that new communication technologies are applied to all three phases of medical education.

AIDS TO LEARNING AND TESTING

The opening paragraphs touched on the venerable history of audiovisual aids in medical education; indeed, an overhead projector, marked 1905 and complete with gas fitting and lime mantle, is a permanent installation in the physics theater demonstration bench at Guy's Hospital Medical School in London. Medicine has not rested on its laurels but has continued to play a pioneering role in the development of communication media. The first continuous two-hour color television broadcast in Britain took place between Alexandra Palace and Broadcasting House, London, in 1957 (Engel and Warwick, 1958) in order to demonstrate to university teachers the potential advantages of educational television in color. Since then the University of London has established a regular program of postgraduate medical education through television (Bowen, 1981).

The following paragraphs will outline practices and trends in relation to each of the media. An alphabetical order has been adopted to avoid the risk of appearing to rank the media in order of priority. Apart from the specific characteristics of a medium that makes it especially useful for a particular education task, application in medical education will usually depend on its relative complexity. The simpler and more flexible it is in the hands of teachers and students, the more frequently it is likely to be used. A case can be made for providing teachers and students with the means for producing and using their own simple audiovisual records without the interface of producers and technicians (Engel, 1962, 1974a).

Audiotapes. Audiotapes have been used extensively to provide access to lectures in recorded form. Drs. John and Valerie Graves established the Medical Recording Service Foundation, now the Graves Medical Audiovisual Library, soon after the last war, so that isolated general practitioners could meet in each other's homes and discuss the views and evidence presented by experts (Graves, 1962). More elegant presentations have since been produced by illustrating the lecture with 35mm transparencies, frequently synchronized with the recording. These illustrated talks were modified to include questions for students to answer, followed by the correct answer. This approach has been found particularly useful for students who prefer to work with peers in small groups (Harden et al., 1969), and a more elaborate set of programs for groups was produced by Squire et al. (1972) for the study of radiographic appearances. The group is encouraged to point to special features and produce diagrams to check their understanding of the appearances that have been demonstrated. The audio-tutorial method has been adapted for biochemistry at the University of Dundee, where students can study by listening to a recorded tutorial and instructions, read texts, and observe, as well as undertake laboratory experiments (Macqueen et al., 1976).

A loose adaptation of programmed learning led the BLAT Centre for Health and Medical Education, London, to experiment with illustrated booklets for integrated use with audiotape cassettes (Engel, 1972). The booklet can be retained by the student. It can include a list of content, learning objectives to be achieved through the use of the program, prerequisites, as well as pretest and correct answers. The main body of the booklet carries illustrations and additional information on each left-hand page which is linked with the commentary. Each right-hand page is left blank for the student's own notes or for answers to questions or problems posed by the tutor's commentary. At the end of each program the student is encouraged to answer questions or to solve problems that will indicate to what extent he has attained the objectives. By placing the correct answers and reasons for the answers on the tape, the student can check and amend his responses. He is given repetition without being bored, and he has an opportunity to correct anything he may have misheard or misunderstood. Once the script has been approved from an educational point of view, it is deliberately transcribed into the spoken language, so that the student will hear the tutor speaking to him, not lecturing or reading at him. At the same time attempts are made to minimize the disadvantages of learning by listening. Sentences are shortened. Indirect references are replaced by the appropriate noun, and the conjunction is placed at the end of the sentence. This approach has been tested successfully for its acceptability, effectiveness, and efficiency (BLAT, 1971; Clarke, 1975; Engel et al., 1972, 1974) at undergraduate and postgraduate levels, as an alternative to the lecture, preparation for clinical responsibilities, integration of theory and practice in a laboratory setting (Jolly and Poland, 1975), and a guide to revision. Acceptability and effectiveness are not affected by the voice of the commentator, whether the commentator is the student's own tutor, another subject specialist, or someone else, so long as more than one speaker is used to record a series of programs (Wakeford, 1972). A simple modification of inexpensive cassette players makes it possible to direct the student to skip a segment of the recording by letting the tape run fast forward until he comes to an audible signal. This device can add further flexibility to the use of audiotape cassettes with booklets (Fewings and Wakeford, 1974). The Board of Studies in Physiology, University of London, has adopted this approach, as each participating institution can readily adapt the booklets and written scripts for its own needs before making its own recordings and duplicates. Mention should also be made of the use of audiotapes as straightforward records of heart and other sounds and of interviews with patients. Such records can be used for individual study and as illustrations during a lecture (Russell, 1966).

Computer-Assisted Instruction and Assessment. Computer-assisted instruction and assessment is beginning to emerge from simulating programmed texts and from presenting students with multiple-choice questions (Folk et al., 1976). De Dombal et al. (1974) were among the pioneers to explore more sophisticated applications. Present-day programs explore clinical decision-making processes, as well as data gathering and evaluation in the context of real-time changes in the physiological changes taking place in the simulated patient. The same program may also prevent access to data of tests which would not be immediately available in real life (Skinner et al., 1983). Similar programs are also being tested in the basic sciences (Pagliaro, 1981). The use of acoustic-coupled terminals to link the student by telephone line to the main computer (Dugdale and Chandler, 1977) and similar devices are virtually out of date as microcomputers come into universal use. Computer graphics (Clark, 1980) and microcomputers for teaching slide retrieval (Gibson and Collins, 1982) are breaking new ground in medical education.

Films. Films in the British National Film Archive include an impressive collection of medical titles, and the early achievements in the field of medical cinematography are ably described by Michaelis (1955). Medical education has made prolific use of motion picture film as illustrated lectures, to introduce or summarize a topic, to illustrate complex abstract concepts, and to provide standard test situations for examinations (Hubbard, 1971; Langsley and Ayerigg, 1970). The concept film was adopted by medical educators very early (MacKeith, 1954; Collard and Engel, 1954), but videotape has replaced film to train students in observation, comparison, discrimination, deduction, and decision making. Numerous organizations, for example, the British Medical Association and the International Scientific Film Association, have fostered the production and use of films through annual competitions and the award of prizes. The British Medical Association and the British Industrial and Scientific Film Association produced a document for medical users and producers of films (Engel, 1975) in order to further the educational effectiveness of medical films. The use of fiberscopes has made it possible to record movement in virtually all parts of the human body (Morton, 1982).

Microfiche. Microfiche is being used for random access problem-based learning (Hartwig and Watson, 1981) and to provide a compact catalog for visual scanning of large collections of illustrations (McArthur, 1980). Since production techniques have been perfected (Renner et al., 1976), color microfiche has become readily available, and suitcase-type readers make it possible for students to use microfiches as universally as the printed word.

Models and Specimens. Models and specimens, initially in wax and more recently in plastics, play an important role in the understanding of anatomical and structural relationships and the recognition of abnormal appearances. Medical artists continue to develop new techniques for the creation of accurate, lifelike models of organs and external features (Neave et al., 1976). Others have concentrated on embedding methods, so that actual tissues can be preserved and handled (Bridgman and Humelbaugh, 1963). Tompsett (1970) has perfected methods of injecting plastics into organs, so that vessels such as arteries and veins and other structures—for instance, the air spaces of the lungs—can be made visible after removal of the surrounding tissues. Students are also encouraged to reconstruct anatomical structures, for example, by building up muscles, nerves, veins, and arteries on a skull by using different-colored plasticine (Herbertson, 1969). Biochemists, in particular, have devoted a great deal of attention to simple three-dimensional devices to assist students in their understanding of complex molecules (Yon, 1974).

Simulation Devices and Simulators. Simulation devices and simulators have been developed to an advanced stage of sophistication, and the use of special clinical skills laboratories has been investigated (Penta and Kofman, 1973). Biran and his colleagues (1976) have experimented with a model and simulated eyes in order to allow students to acquire the skills of ophthalmoscopy, the examination of the back of the eye. Harley (1976) and Sajid et al. (1977) confirmed earlier results by McGuire et al. (1964) that practice with a heart sound simulator helps students acquire skills of auscultation, distinguishing heart sounds, and to transfer these diagnostic skills when examining patients. Even more elaborate equipment has been devised by Abrahamson and Wallace (1980) where the model is linked to a computer so that the effects of administered anesthetic agents on blood pressure, heart action, pulse, etc., can be measured.

Human simulators were first trained and used by Barrows and Bennett (1972) in order to investigate the mental processes of the doctor when he examines a patient to arrive at a diagnosis. Barrows (1971) has also perfected the simulated patient for the teaching and examining of students. Since then many others, for example, Maguire (1976), have used simulated patients in educational experiments and in the medical curriculum (Neufeld and Spaulding, 1973).

More recently, problem-solving card games (Barrows and Tamblyn, 1977), problem boxes, and sophisticated kits have been developed particularly at McMaster University in Canada and at Michigan State University, United States, to provide students with patients' histories, radiographs and other diagnostic evidence, prescription forms, and other educational materials for learning problem solving and patient management.

Static Displays. Static displays tend to be neglected in the literature as a worthy subject for educational research, yet they can be relatively inexpensive and most useful for individual study. The British Medical Association, the British Life Assurance Trust for Health Education, and the Council for Postgraduate Medical Education in England and Wales (1973) assembled a comprehensive booklet on type and purpose of displays, their planning, design, and evaluation. Dwyer (1971) and Netter (1967) are among the many artists who have attempted to promote the visual arts as a useful aid in medical education. Poster displays have become an integral part of most medical conferences, and Simmonds (1980) has made a major contribution with his guide to simple but effective graphics.

Telecommunication. Telecommunication by telephone and radio has been used extensively in the United States particularly for continuing medical education. Live or recorded lectures are broadcast by a local radio station, and participants at scattered hospitals can comment and ask questions by telephone. Such a "confraphone" system allows all participants to hear questions and answers wherever they are (Evans and Mobley, 1972). More recently, radiographs and electrocardiograms have been transmitted over the telephone lines, both for teaching and for consultation (Peter et al., 1973). The telephone is also used to allow medical practitioners to listen to a selection of short audiotape recordings on topics of current interest (University of Dundee, 1976). Williams (1972) compiled a useful survey which outlines present and potential uses of telecommunication in medicine.

Television. Television, broadcast or closed circuit, live or recorded, has been a familiar medium since its introduction for entertainment (Engel, 1963). The Open University uses the medium for its continuing medical education program (Gale, 1983), and the University of London has perfected its use for both postgraduate and continuing education (Bowen, 1981).

Live television is frequently employed for demonstration and guiding a large group of students in laboratory observation and procedures (Olson, 1970). The advent of videotape cassettes has greatly accelerated the use of television instead of film to record events, phenomena, and techniques. In particular, it has led to the recording of students while they interview a patient, undertake physical examination, or perform a diagnostic or therapeutic procedure. These records are then used for self-assessment, for peer group evaluation (Anderson et al., 1970), or for discussion with a tutor. Investigation has established that reliable scoring from videotapes with the use of a detailed schedule can be achieved with nonexpert staff. As the study of psychiatry demands close observation of both verbal and nonverbal messages, it is no surprise that this branch of medicine makes prolific use of television (Berger, 1970; Onder, 1970). The availability of high-quality, small-scale color cameras and video recording equipment has led to a proliferation of videocassette programs for interactive learning and for trigger material to stimulate discussion (Engel and Clarke, 1979). Videodisc is the subject of intense experimentation as an ideal rapid, random access audiovisual extension of self-instructional computer programs (Leveridge, 1980; Bryce and Stewart, 1983).

Textbooks. Textbooks have been used for centuries, but little has changed except, perhaps, more lavish illustrations and cost. The University of Dundee has taken a fresh look at the format of the printed text and has evolved a loose-leaf book where each page carries both basic and more advanced text, so that the student can decide how far he wishes to go in any one topic. The illustrations are so arranged that the printed word can be amended without the costly resetting of color separation blocks. Many other improvements are possible and should be adopted, from evidence provided by experiments in programmed learning. Learning objectives and prerequisites for each chapter, questions, problems and exercises with correct answers interspersed with the text, and end-of-chapter self-testing exercises with correct answers should be incorporated. Sample questions of the type that students can be expected to ask—for example, what does this word mean, what is the underlying principle, what additional information is available?—could be set in the margin with a reference to a companion text. This would provide the student with additional material as and when he needs it and would thus make the book more flexible for a wider range of students. It is interesting to note that **information mapping** (q.v.) (Horn et al., 1969) is seldom if ever applied in the writing of textbooks. Perhaps authors should write for their students and not for their reviewers. Color offset lithography has become sufficiently versatile to be used for in-house printing of booklets for students and for patients (Siwek and Chessell, 1981), but the most promising development is the "add-on" journal *Medicine,* which publishes up-to-date chapters in its monthly issues and thus represents a textbook which renews itself at regular intervals.

TRENDS

Fundamentally, the concept of using illustrations in one form or another to enhance the understanding and experience of students is not new. Comenius (1728) developed in the mid-eighteenth century an illustrated text for schoolchildren to stimulate their interest, to make learning relevant, and to build on previous experience: "Now there is nothing new in the understanding, which was not before in the sense. And therefore to exercise the senses well about the right perceiving the differences of things, will be to lay the grounds for all wisdom, and all wise discourse, and all discreet action in one's course of life."

Educators and educational technologists are assuming a new role (Engel, 1974b). They will pass on to teachers and students the distillate of what has been proved to be educationally sound (Jason, 1968). Blackman et al. (1976) are among a growing number of authors who report on the educational and administrative advantage of helping students to prepare their own learning materials. The World Health Organization (1972) has emphasized the need to support teachers in the creation of materials for individual and small group study. In the United States the Medical Audiovisual Center in Atlanta and in Britain the BLITH Centre for Health and Medical Education accept as a priority the task to assist teachers in the design and production of educational programs. The advent of the videodisc and the microcomputer, as well as access to satellites, makes professional guidance increasingly essential in the appropriate application of our growing knowledge of adults' learning and the way doctors solve and resolve problems.

C. E. Engel

REFERENCES

Abrahamson, S. and Wallace, P. (1980) "Using Computer-Controlled Interactive Manikins in Medical Education." *Medical Teacher* 2: 25–31.

Anderson, J., Day, J. L., Dowling, M.A.C., and Pettingale, K. W. (1970) "The Definition and Evaluation of Skills Required to Obtain a Patient's History of Illness: The Use of Videotape Recordings." *Postgraduate Medical Journal* 46: 606–612.

Barrows, H. S. (1971) *Simulated Patients (Programmed Patients).* Springfield, Ill.: Charles C. Thomas.

Barrows, H. and Bennett, K. (1972) "The Diagnostic Problem Solving Skill of the Neurologist." *Archives of Neurology* 26: 273–277.

Barrows, H. S. and Tamblyn, R. M. (1977) "The Portable Patient Problem Pack: A Problem-Based Learning Unit." *Journal of Medical Education* 52: 1002–1004.

———. (1980) *Problem-Based Learning: An Approach to Medical Education.* New York: Springer.

Bearn, J. G. (1963) "Leonardo da Vinci and Movements of the Forearm." *Medical and Biological Illustration* 13: 250–254.

Berger, M. M., ed. (1970) *Videotape Techniques In Psychiatric Training and Treatment.* New York: Brunner/Mazel.

Biran, L. A., Wakeford, R. E., Harden, R. McG., Porteous, I., Haining, W. M., and Jolly, B. C. (1976) "Self-instruction and Simulation in Training Users of Diagnostic Instruments." In *Aspects of Educational Technology* 10, ed. J. Clarke and J. Leedham. London: Kogan Page.

Blackman, J. G., Teather, D.C.B., Milan, D. M., and Redshaw, N. R. (1976) "Student Participation in the Production of Learning Materials." *Medical and Biological Illustration* 26: 223–225.

BLAT Centre for Health and Medical Education. (1971) *Final Report to the Nuffield Foundation: The Development and Evaluation of Audiotape with Illustrative Material for Individual Learning in Medical Education 1968–1971.* London: British Medical Association.

Bowen, P. (1981) "The Early Days of Postgraduate Medical Television in London." *Journal of Audiovisual Media in Medicine* 3: 134–135.

Bridgman, C. F. and Humelbaugh, F. A. (1963) "Plastic Embedded Specimens in Medical Teaching." *Medical and Biological Illustration* 13: 265–272.

British Medical Association, British Life Assurance Trust for Health Education, and Council for Postgraduate Medical Education in England and Wales. (1973) *Static Displays—Posters, Wallcharts, Exhibits—in Medical Education.* London: BLAT Centre for Health and Medical Education.

Bryce, C.F.A. and Stewart, A. (1983) "Videodiscs in Medical Education." *Medical Teacher* 5: 57–59.

Clark, D. R. (1980) "Computer Graphics in Medical Illustration." *Journal of Audiovisual Media In Medicine* 3: 140–141.

Clarke, R. M. (1975) "Replacement of Class Instruction in Histology by Audiotape and Booklet Self-instruction Sessions." *British Journal of Medical Education* 9: 34–37.

Collard, P. and Engel, C. E. (1954) "The Short Film and Its Automatic Projection in Medical Teaching." *Lancet* 2: 406–407.

Comenius, J. A. (1728) *Visible World, or a Nomenclature of all the Chief Things That Are in the World, and of Mens Employments Therein,* trans. Charles Hoole. Little Britain: John and Benjamin Spring.

de Dombal, F. T., Leaper, D. J., Horrocks, J. C., Staniland, J. R., and McCann, H. P. (1974) "Human and Computer Aided Diagnosis of Abdominal Pain: Further Report with Emphasis on Performance of Clinicians." *British Medical Journal* 1: 376–380.

Dugdale, A. E. and Chandler, D. (1977) "Teaching Diagnosis and Treatment with an Interactive Computer Terminal." *Medical Journal of Australia* 1: 145–149.

Duncan, C. J. (1964) *The Recruitment and Training of Staff for University Departments of Teaching and Research Services*. Report to the UGC Committee on the use of audio-visual aids in institutions of higher education. Newcastle-upon-Tyne: University of Newcastle.

Dwyer, F. M. (1971) "Adapting Varied Visual Illustrations for Optimum Teaching and Learning." *Medical and Biological Illustration* 21: 10–13.

Engel, C. E. (1962) "Who Should Press the Button?" *Guy's Hospital Gazette* 76: 608–611.

———. (1963) "Television in Medical Education." *Nature* 200: 725–728.

———. (1969) "Central Information, Reference and Circulation: The Role of the BMA." *Medical and Biological Illustration* 19: S57–S58.

———. (1971) "Educational Technology, a Systematical Approach to Teaching." *Annals of General Practice* 16: 121–124.

———. (1972) "Tape Recordings for the Individual Student." In *Visual Media in Chemistry*. London: British Universities Film Council.

———. (1974a) "Medical Illustration in the New Health Service: Broadening the Base." *Medical and Biological Illustration* 24: 174–176.

———. (1974b) "Educational Assistants." *Lancet* 2: 573–575.

———, ed. (1975) *Film in Medical Education—Production and Use*. London: Councils and Education Press.

Engel, C. E. and Clarke, R. M. (1979) "Medical Education with a Difference." *Programmed Learning and Educational Technology* 16: 73–87.

Engel, C. E., Feletti, G. I., and Leeder, S. R. (1980) "Assessment of Medical Students in a New Curriculum." *Assessment in Higher Education* 5: 279–293.

Engel, C. E., Irvine, E., and Wakeford, R. E. (1972) "Report on the Transferability of an Individual Learning System." *British Journal of Medical Education* 6: 311–316.

Engel, C. E., Lowe, G.D.O., Marshall, P. B. and Wakeford, R. E. (1974) "Teaching Basic Pharmacology to Medical Students, An Experimental Self-instructional Approach." *Medical and Biological Illustration* 24: 130–134.

Engel, C. E. and Warwick, R. (1958) "Colour Television in University Teaching." *Nature* 181: 91–92.

Evans, B. B. and Mobley, J. E. (1972) "Tele-lecture-conference: A Teaching Method." *Journal of the American Medical Association* 219: 500–501.

Everall, J. D. (1976) "Three Dimensional Clinical Models." *Medical and Biological Illustration* 26: 209–210.

Feletti, G. I., Saunders, N. A., and Smith, A. J. (1983) "Comprehensive Assessment of Final-year Medical Students Performance Based on Undergraduate Programme Objectives." *Lancet* 2: 34–37.

Fewings, M. J. and Wakeford, R. E. (1974) "Adaptive Programmes on Audiotape: Branching Tape." *Medical and Biological Illustration* 24: 18–21.

Folk, R. L., Griersen, J. V., Beran, R. L., and Camiscioni, J. S. (1976) *Individualizing the Study of Medicine*. New York: Westinghouse Learning Corporation.

Gale, J. (1983) "An Open University Pilot Course for Doctors." *Medical Teacher* 5: 18–24.

Gernsheim, A. (1961) "Medical Photography in the Nineteenth Century." *Medical and Biological Illustration* 11: 85–92, 147–156.

Gibson, C. C. and Collins, J. M. (1982) "Use of Microcomputers in Departments of Medical Illustration for Retrieval of Clinical Teaching Slides." *Journal of Audiovisual Media in Medicine* 5: 130–134.

Graves, V. (1962) "The Use of Sound in Medicine." *Medical and Biological Illustration* 12: 98–104.

Harden, R. McG., Lever, R., and Donald, G. (1969) "Audiovisual Self-instruction in Medicine." In *Aspects of Educational Technology* 3, ed. A. P. Mann and C. K. Brunstrom. London: Kogan Page.

Harley, A. (1976) "Evaluation of a Heart Sound Simulator in Teaching Cardiac Auscultation." *Journal of Medical Education* 51: 600–601.

Hartwig, N. G. and Watson, C.R.R. (1981) "Microfiche-based Exercise in Clinical Microbiology—A Valuable Assessment Technique for Teachers and Students." *Journal of Audiovisual Media in Medicine* 4: 26–28.

Herbertson, J. E. (1969) "Technic to Aid in the Teaching of Human Anatomy." *Journal of Dental Education* 33: 493–499.

Horn, R. E., et al. (1969) "Information Mapping for Learning and Reference." *U.S. Air Force Systems Command*. Belford, Mass.: USAFSC.

Hubbard, J. P. (1971) *Measuring Medical Education*. Philadelphia: Lea & Febiger.

Jason, H. (1968) "Evaluation of Audiovisual Methods of Medical Teaching." *Canadian Medical Association Journal* 98: 1146–1150.

Jolly, B. and Poland, J. (1975) "The Use of Self-instructional Materials in Veterinary Pathology." *Medical and Biological Illustration* 25: 111–114.

Knox, J.D.E. (1975) *The Modified Essay Question*, Medical Education Booklet No. 5. Dundee: Association for the Study of Medical Education.

Langsley, D. G. and Ayerigg, J. B. (1970) "Filmed Interviews for Testing Clinical Skills." *Journal of Medical Education* 45: 52–58.

Lennox, B. (1974) *Hints on the Setting and Evaluation of Multiple-choice Questions of the One from Five Type*, Medical Education Booklet No. 3. Dundee: Association for the Study of Medical Education.

Leveridge, L. L. (1980) "Experience in Educational Design for Interactive Videodisc and Quadrasync Presentations." *Journal of Educational Technology Systems* 8: 221–230.

McArthur, J. R. (1980) "The American Society of Hematology Slide Bank." In *Hematology, Hematologic Transfusion*. Montreal: American Society of Hematology.

McGuire, C., Harley, R. E., Babbott, D., and Butterworth, J. S. (1964) "Auscultatory Skills: Gain and Retention after

Intensive Instruction." *Journal of Medical Education* 39: 120–131.

MacKeith, R. (1954) "Teaching Medical Diagnosis: the Use of Films." *Lancet* 2: 404–406.

Macqueen, D., Chignell, D. A., Dutton, G. J., and Garland, P. B. (1976) *Biochemistry for Medical Students: a Flexible Student-oriented Approach*. Dundee: Association for Medical Education in Europe.

Maguire, P. (1976) "The Use of Patient Simulation in Training Medical Students in History-taking Skills." *Medical and Biological Illustration* 26: 91–95.

Marey, E. J. (1888) *Comptes Rendu Hebdomadaire des Stances de l'Académie des Sciences* 107: 677.

Merrill, I. R. and Drob, H. A. eds. (1974) *Criteria for Planning the University Learning Resources Center*. San Francisco: University of California.

Michaelis, A. R. (1955) *Research Films*. London: Academic Press.

Morton, R. (1982) "Photography through the Fibrescope." *Journal of Audiovisual Media in Medicine* 5: 137–140.

National Medical Audiovisual Center. (1967, 1969) *Part I, Part II Toward Improved Learning: a Collection of Significant Reprints for the Medical Educator*. Atlanta, Ga.: U.S. Department of Health, Education, and Welfare.

National Medical Audiovisual Center, formerly part of National Communicable Disease Center. (1969) *Training Methodology. Part I Background Theory and Research, Part II Planning and Administration, Part III Instructional Methods and Techniques*. Atlanta, Ga.: U.S. Department of Health, Education, and Welfare.

Neave, R.A.H., Barson, A. J., and Percy, S. (1976) "Models for Medical Teaching." *Medical and Biological Illustration* 26: 211–218.

Netter, F. H. (1967) "The Role of Illustration in Medical Education and Medical Progress." *Journal of the Mount Sinai Hospital, New York* 34: 396–400.

Neufeld, V. R. and Spaulding, W. B. (1973) "Use of Learning Resources at McMaster University." *British Medical Journal* 2: 99–101.

Olson, I. A. (1970) "Advantages and Disadvantages of Closed-circuit Television in the Teaching of Large Classes in Preclinical Medicine." *British Journal of Medical Education* 4: 312–315.

Onder, J. J. (1970) *The Manual of Psychiatric Television: Theory, Practice, Imagination*. Michigan: Maynard House.

Pagliaro, L. A. (1981) "Analysis of Computer Assisted Instruction in Pharmacology." *Proceedings of the Western Pharmacology Society* 24: 113–115.

Penta, F. B. and Kofman, S. (1973) "The Effectiveness of Simulation Devices in Teaching Selected Skills of Physical Diagnosis." *Journal of Medical Education* 48: 442–447.

Peter, T., Harper, R., Luxton, M., Pring, M., McDonald, R., and Sloman, G. (1973) "Personal Telephone Electrocardiogram Transmitter." *Lancet* 2: 1110–1112.

Renner, W. E., Kulmann, R., Lepp, G., Marr, K., and Woo, S. W. (1976) "New Improvements in Production Techniques of Self-instructional Color Microfiche." *Journal of the Biological Photographic Association* 44: 123–126.

Russell, J. K. (1966) "Sound and Visual Teaching Aids in Obstetrics and Gynaecology." *Medical and Biological Illustration* 16: 218–222.

Sajid, A., Magero, J., and Feinzimer, M. (1977) "Learning Effectiveness of Heart Sound Simulator." *Medical Education* 11: 25–27.

Simmonds, D. (1980) *Charts and Graphs: Guidelines for the Visual Presentation of Statistical Data in the Life Sciences*. Melbourne: MTP Press.

Siwek, R. and Chessell, G. (1981) "In-house Color Offset Lithography for Medical Education: Development and Applications." *Journal of Audiovisual Media in Medicine* 4: 40–44.

Skinner, T. B., Knowles, G., Armstrong, R. F., and Ingram, D. (1983) "The Use of Computerized Learning in Intensive Care: An Evaluation of a New Teaching Program." *Medical Education* 17: 49–53.

Squire, L. F., Blotnick, V., and Becker, J. B. (1972) "Self-instruction in Radiology for Medical Students." *Radiology* 105: 681–684.

Tompsett, D. H. (1970) *Anatomical techniques*. Edinburgh: E. and S. Livingstone.

University Grants Committee, Department of Education and Science and Scottish Education Department. (1965) *Audio-visual Aids in Higher Scientific Education*. London: Her Majesty's Stationery Office.

University of Dundee. (1976) "Dial a Medical Education Service." Mimeo issued by the Centre for Medical Education, University of Dundee, Dundee.

Wakeford, R. E. (1972) "Preparing Audiotape Recordings for Individual Study: Notes on Relative Acceptability of Different Speakers." *Medical and Biological Illustration* 22: 13–14.

WHO. (1972) *Implications of Individual and Small Group Learning Systems in Medical Education*, WHO Technical Report Series No. 489. Geneva: World Health Organization.

———. (1973) *Development of Educational Programmes for the Health Professions*, Public Health Papers No. 52. Geneva: World Health Organization.

———. (1974) *Selection of Teaching/Learning Materials in Health Sciences Education*, WHO Technical Report Series, No. 538. Geneva: World Health Organization.

Williams, E. (1972) *Telecommunications and Medicine: Impact and Effectiveness*. University College, London: Communications Studies Group, Joint Unit for Planning Research.

Wright, A. (1973) *Training for Educational Media Design*, Working Paper No. 9. London: Council for Educational Technology for the United Kingdom.

Yon, R. J. (1974) "A Large Polypeptide-chain Model Capable of Realistic Folding." *Biochemical Education* 2.

MEGABYTE. One million bytes. That is, computer storage equivalent to approximately 1,000,000 characters (letters, numbers, etc.). *See* **Hard Disk.**

MEGAHERTZ. Unit of frequency equal to one million cycles per second.

MEMORY (COMPUTER). The part of the computer where the programs and data are stored.

A program to be run by a computer must reside in its memory. Each instruction is fetched from memory and implemented in the central processor. If some of these instructions need data, this too is fetched from the memory to the processor. The amount of the memory installed in a computer determines how much data or how large a program the machine can accommodate. The amount of memory in a computer is measured in units of "thousands of words," or "Ks," where each word is composed of 8, 16, or 32 bits (binary digits) depending upon the word size of the computer. Some manufacturers specify their memory size in kilobytes. This is thousands of 8-bit words (bytes).

Since the memory contains the instructions and data of a program, the speed at which a program can be executed or run to completion depends upon how fast the processor can fetch the instructions and data needed to implement them. Notwithstanding the speed of the actual processor, one of the limiting factors on the time to run a program is the memory "access time." It is, in effect, how long it takes to find an address in memory, knock on the door, open the door, secure the data, close the door, and get the data back to the processor. Access times are usually in the order of tenths of microseconds.

The amount of memory that can be addressed in a computer is limited to the bit width of the registers in the central processor and the address "buses" of the system. As an example, an 8-bit machine can normally only address 64K (more accurately 65,536) words. Additional memory can only be addressed by switching to other 64K "pages."

One major difference between types of memory is their ability to retain their data, even though the electric power used to operate them has been removed. Memories with this ability are termed nonvolatile. Magnetic storage is an example of nonvolatile memory. Individual magnetic spots on a magnetic disk can be polarized and will maintain this polarity for long periods of time, without the need of electric power. Data is often stored off-line in magnetic disks, spool to spool tapes, cassettes, and cartridges because of their cost-effectiveness. This type of memory is termed *mass* (for great amount) *memory*.

Earlier computers utilized magnetic "cores" as their main memory. Core memory has now been superseded by semiconductor memory. This memory comes in a volatile form called Random Access Memory (RAM), whose data becomes scrambled when power is lost. Often a battery supply is provided to hold the data in RAM memory in the event of a power loss. Nonvolatile semiconductor memory is available in the form of Read Only Memory (ROM) and Programmable Read Only Memory (PROM). Neither of these devices can have its contents changed easily. Hence ROMs and PROMs are used as memory for instructions and fixed data only.

ROMs are used when many copies (thousands) of a program are needed. If only a few copies of a program are needed, it is stored in a PROM. ROMs are less expensive in large quantities than PROMs; the programs for stand-alone video games, for instance, are stored in ROM memory.

Tom McHale

MEMORY CHIP. A semiconducting device which stores information in the form of minute electrical charges.

MENU. A list of choices presented by a program from which the user can select.

MENU DRIVEN. Computer software in which users select their requirements from a menu. This is an algorithmic process, requiring the furnishing of simple responses which inevitably lead users to their goal.

MEP. *See* **Microelectronics Education Program.**

MICR. *See* **Magnetic Ink Character Recognition.**

MICROCOMPUTERS IN EDUCATION.

INTRODUCTION

With the advent of the widespread media enthusiasm for computer and information technology, the general public has expected the educational arena to quickly come to terms with this relatively new force in technology. The focus most primary and secondary educators have taken has been computer awareness, keyboarding skills, and programming, as these appeared to be the most vital issues of this new resource. It has only been recently accepted that the use of this technology has numerous more far-reaching effects within education, especially in schools. Many educators have gone through the exercises of selecting hardware and software and trying to get the optimum economic and technical "fit" for their purposes. They would now be considered "enlightened" users by the information technology industry as they can make reasonably objective decisions without undue influence from the hype and gloss of advertising and salesmanship.

IMPACT OF TECHNOLOGY

The technology of computers is expanding at a brisk pace even when viewed from within the industry. In the early days of computing, schools were equipped with machines and software of minimal resources, and the operation often required a high level of computer awareness by the students and staff alike. Also, because of the rather minimal configurations of memory, CPUs, and mass storage, the authors of educational software packages required significant programming as well as creative and motivational skills. As a result, few good quality products emerged during this generation.

We now have more powerful processors, able to compute more quickly, more addressable memory for the storage of larger programs and data sets, and larger and less expensive mass memory for the on-line storage of gigabytes of data. Eight-bit processors are now being replaced by 16- and 32-bit versions which, when combined with more advanced computer graphics hardware and laser compact disk technology, offer the developer of educational applications powerful computational engines. Software development tools such as programming and authoring languages are also advancing at a considerable rate, and the advent of **artificial intelligence** (q.v.) tools is having a significant impact on the simulation of natural systems for educational uses.

COMPUTING APPLICATIONS IN EDUCATION

The use of computer technology within educational institutions can be classified in the following areas:

(a) Administration and management
(b) The teaching of computer technology subjects
(c) The teaching of subjects impacted by computer technology
(d) Educational aids
(e) Computer-assisted learning and simulation
(f) Exploitation of software packages, such as data bases and spreadsheets, designed for other markets

Administration and Management. The administration of educational institutions benefits from the same productivity aids that information technology offers most small- to medium-sized businesses. These applications are well defined, and packages are available which can operate on hardware configurations affordable by most schools. Some of the applications which the administration of schools could utilize are these:

(a) a simple bookkeeping package
(b) an inventory control system for equipment and consumable supplies
(c) a student data base and inquiry system
(d) a statistical package for the analysis of student results
(e) a scheduling package for personnel, classes, and resources
(f) a desktop publishing system for newsletter and notes production

Often some of these applications can be satisfied by the use of generalized data base and spreadsheet products.

The Teaching of Computer Technology Subjects. The most obvious and popular use of computers in schools was originally for the teaching of computing-related causes. This trend has now reversed with the availability of products for other subjects and administrative activities. The teaching of computer technology subjects requires either several small but powerful workstations or terminals connected to a main computational processor which can time-share several users at one time.

Courses involving the development of software using either high-level languages or packages for data base development, etc., require access to significant computing resources such as fast processors, considerable RAM memory, megabytes of mass memory, and preferably fast hard-copy printout devices.

It is generally agreed that all other factors being equal, students learn computing skills at a optimal rate when given considerable access to the computing resources. In addition, while users are on the computer, "reasonable" response time is required for them to get rapid feedback on the effectiveness of their designs during the development stages.

The Teaching of Subjects Impacted by Computer Technology. Computer technology has impacted several different areas of study in schools. As a result, the exploration of these subjects requires access to appropriate resources to learn and practice the required skills. The most obvious area of this kind would be secretarial skills. Word processing has in a few years required all schools teaching in such career areas to provide their students with at least the basic understanding of word processing. In addition, areas such as journalism, accountancy, management, and librarianship now heavily rely on computing resources.

Subjects involving mathematics, science, and engineering have always fallen in this category and until recently were the major users of resources in most institutions.

Educational Aids. The computer has provided the educator with a tool which can

—compute, sort, and compare at a far greater speed than most humans;
—store and give access to large amounts of both text and graphic data;

—present graphics in reasonable resolution and color;
—be programmed with fairly complex rules;
—allow student interaction via keyboard text, screen locations (cursor control), and voice.

Computer-Assisted Learning (CAL) and Simulation. CAL facilities have taken the onus off teachers to become computer experts in order to utilize the advantages of the computer. Authoring languages now provide the infrastructure to design activities with all the benefits of automatic connections, retesting, and tracking of progress.

Some phenomena in biology, physics, chemistry, economics, etc., are often expensive, dangerous, morally difficult, or tedious to demonstrate to students. For example, the simulation of chemical reactions, dissection of animals, and fiscal policy provides students with individual interaction with systems which may otherwise have been impossible to experience. These simulations often allow control of time progression to either slow down or speed up the natural system to ascertain the results of various scenarios.

Exploitation of Special Course Packages. The availability of data bases and inquiry procedures on subjects such as geography gives students the opportunity to develop and investigate relationships between various parameters which they could not otherwise do without much time and significant printed resources. These data bases are often updated and distributed on a regular basis by a central agency so that students are using the best available information at all times.

Similarly, spreadsheets offer unique opportunities to analyze topics as diverse as history, philosophy, nutrition, and citizenship. Programs of immense power are cheaply available.

Word processors provide a very special tool for use in the study of language and literature, as well as providing the student with the means for effective and efficient editing of her/his own work.

Games. The computer games industry has given birth to programs which can be roughly classified as either simulations or hand-eye coordination tests. These simulation games often test logical deduction processes, strategy development, and rapid computational skills.

Some games have been especially developed to motivate the students to become heavily involved in the simulated process, thereby making it almost inevitable that learning will occur. Computer games have also been effectively used to introduce novices to particular computer systems. The game often introduces keyboarding, data formatting, and operating system skills with the minimum of tedium and frustration.

CONCLUSION

With the advance of relatively inexpensive data communication facilities and the improvement in computational skills of both educators and students, the microcomputer will be playing a larger role in education. Data communication facilities allow access to other resources both public and private. The technology of computers is combining with the technologies of television, telephone, and satellites to provide rapid transfer of data (pictures and text) to virtually any location on earth. The educational global village is quickly shrinking.

Tom McHale

See **Authoring Languages; Computer-Assisted Instruction; Computer Graphics.**

MICRODRIVE. Computer storage device (Sinclair Research plc) using a continuous loop of tape about 40mm wide and 5m long. Storage capacity is up to 128K. Access time can be around one minute. An earlier similar system, known as a "stringy floppy," had little success.

MICROELECTRONICS. *See* **Integrated Circuit.**

MICROELECTRONICS EDUCATION PROGRAMME (U.K.). The Microelectronics Education Programme (MEP) was announced in March 1980. Its dual aim was to promote the study of microtechnologies in schools and to encourage the use of those technologies to enhance teaching and learning in other subjects. The directorate, headed by Richard Fothergill, was established between November 1980 and April 1981. Originally budgeted at $16 million, MEP was extended to end in April 1986, with a total budget of $30 million from the Departments of Education for England and Northern Ireland and the Welsh Office. The director estimated that MEP attracted an added value of $120 million from other sources for all its activities.

MEP operated both nationally and regionally, through groupings of local education authorities, with twelve regions in England and one each for Northern Ireland and Wales. Most of its Regional Information Centers (RICs) opened for business by January 1982, providing a service of information, guidance, training, and advice and a resource center of hardware and software for education advisers and teachers. Each week the RICs together handled some 3,000 visits and substantial inquiries. The RICs made extensive use of electronic mail and word-processing publishing systems to interrogate nationally and regionally compiled data bases in order to respond to inquiries and to publish information sheets and regional newsletters.

MEP ran short in-service courses for teachers in each region in electronics and control technology, the use of the computer as a device (including computer studies), computer-based learning, and communications and information systems. In addition, MEP has developed and provided training materials to every LEA, school and teacher training college in the United Kingdom in support of Department of Trade and Industry schemes to subsidize the purchase of microcomputers. Finally, the **Open University** (q.v.) produced for MEP a distance-study course on microcomputers in schools. In the first year alone MEP courses and materials trained 40,000 teachers. A national Primary Project was established at the end of 1983 to provide training for the estimated 750 primary sector teacher trainers and advisers in the country.

MEP funded curriculum development for new classroom and training materials in most areas of the secondary and primary curriculum. This included electronics, computer studies, craft design and technology, office and clerical studies, and CBL developments in the sciences and humanities. Development projects funded included those in each region (an average of eight to ten projects each region per year), and national development centers for software and devices, including Chelsea College Computers in the Curriculum Project, the ITMA project at Plymouth and Five Ways Software. The emphasis was on innovations which were teacher-initiated and teacher-led and targeted on the broader range ability bands.

Products were disseminated through commercial publishers and manufacturers, through the RICs where certain categories of materials could be freely copied and copyright-protected materials might be sampled, and by electronic publishing through telesoftware on **teletext** (q.v.) and **viewdata** (q.v.) systems. MEP established a reputation abroad for innovation, and its products are licensed and sold extensively overseas. In the field of special (disadvantaged) education MEP funded four Special Education Resource Centres (SEMERCs) to provide information, resource selection advice and training. Some 18 percent of curriculum development funds went to special education development projects.

John S. A. Anderson

REFERENCE

Fothergill, R. and Anderson, J.S.A. (1981) "Strategy for the Microelectronics Education Programme (MEP)." *Programmed Learning and Educational Technology* 18 (3): 121–129.

MICROFICHE. A type of microform consisting of a sheet of film 12.50cm × 10.00cm that contains images of up to 140 pages of normal-sized text. Microfiches are increasingly used in libraries for interlibrary loans, cataloging, etc.

The advantage of the microfiche over several other forms of information storage is that it is a practicable compromise between extreme reduction (microdot) and microfilm which is relatively large and bulky. Special microfiche readers are available which allow random access to individual pages on the fiche. Like other forms of enlarging readers, they are simple to operate but tiring to use, due to the brightness and contrast of the projected image. The Educational Resources Information Center (ERIC) reproduces its documents on microfiche.

Ultrafiche is a high reduction ratio form of microfiche, with one fiche easily containing up to 3000+ images. Ultrafiches are produced by proprietary equipment, and because of the high level of magnification are very susceptible to scratches, dust, etc., which can severely limit their readability.

MICROFILMING. The process of producing miniature photographic copies of documents or books on rolls or sheets of film for filing and storage. *See* **Microforms.**

MICROFILM READER. A projection device which enlarges microfilm images to a readable size. They are available in many designs with varying degrees of sophistication. The more expensive models have automatic film advance, and some have the capability of producing paper prints of selected frames.

The introduction of simple inexpensive readers has contributed to the wider use of microforms especially in education.

MICROFORMS. Microform is best defined as "the generic term for any form, usually film, which contains micro images" (ISO, 1980). In the same international standard that carries this definition, one will find micrographics defined as "the general term for techniques associated with the production, handling and use of microforms" (ISO, 1980). Microform material is simply information—textual, illustrative, or tabular—stored in reduced size on photographic film. Libraries have computer output microform catalogs and growing collections of microform publications. The history and practice of microform librarianship is outlined in a standard text (Teague, 1985). Microforms are a vital educational resource.

The film can be either black and white (monochrome) or full color. It is similar to the film in one's own camera, except that it does not have sprocket holes. Thus a greater area of film is actually usable. The modern films are "safety" base films, being made of polyethylene terephthalate or cellulose ester, and are difficult to ignite, slow in burning, and produce very low emission of toxic oxides in burning. A microform may be positive or negative.

TYPES OF MICROFORM

Microforms are produced in three formats; film, fiche, and card. Within these formats they will be in one of several standard sizes and carriers.

Microfilm. Microfilm is either 35mm or 16mm wide; 35mm is normally on open reels with 30m of film per reel, and 16mm is normally housed in cassettes or cartridges. A cassette has two spools within it, one spool to take up the film from the other when in use on a microform viewer. A cartridge has one spool within it, and the microform viewer needs to be designed with built-in take-up spool especially for cartridges. The 35mm film is used for microform storage and retrieval of large originals such as newspapers and maps; 16mm film is used for microform storage and retrieval of standard periodical publications and learned journals.

Microfiche. Microfiches are flat sheets of film measuring 105mm × 148mm cut from 105mm roll film. Each fiche carries either 98 or 60 frames of images in rows and columns and is headed with an eye-legible title strip. Thus a book or other publication of 98 or fewer pages can be miniaturized on one microfiche at a reduction ratio of up to 1:24.

Ultrafiche. Ultrafiches are microfiches produced at very high reduction ratios, 1:150 being typical. Basically, they are microphotographs of microphotographs. The object is to attain even greater space economy by packing more onto the fiche. However, as the viewing equipment is more costly, for a very limited advantage, it is unlikely that ultrafiche usage will develop in the way that microfiche has.

Computer Output Microform. A computer can have an output device interfaced with it, a COM recorder that involves displaying the output data on a cathode-ray tube and microfilming it. The computer microform output can be in any standard format, that is to say, 35mm or 16mm microfilm, microfiche, or aperture cards (see below). Computer output microfiches have reduction ratios of either 48:1, giving a 270–frame fiche, or 42:1, giving a 208–frame fiche. They thus need a microfiche viewer that provides the appropriate magnification, and modern equipment usually has switchable lens capability for reading ordinary microfiche and COM.

Microfilm Jackets. Jacketed microfiche is a flexible medium in which the microfiche is made up of slots or channels into which short strips of exposed 16mm or 35mm microfilm, or a combination of each, can be inserted, depending on the design of the jacket used. This provides for revision and updating of material.

Aperture Cards. Aperture cards are based on standard punched cards, that is, cards that are machine-sortable by the holes punched in them. They measure 82.5mm × 187.25mm and the apertures on them can house one or more frames of 35mm or 16mm microfilm or a combination of each. They can bear eye-legible details and can be mechanically or hand-sorted.

Micro-Opaques. There are two opaque microformats likely to be encountered, Microprint and Microcard, both proprietary products. Microprint are 152mm × 229mm cards produced by offset lithography, and Microcards are photographically produced 76mm × 127mm cards. Being opaque, they need a special viewing apparatus, based on reflected light, rather like the epidiascope. Like ultrafiche, the micro-opaque format is not a developing medium.

Microforms in Color. Microforms are predominantly black and white but can be in full color. There is a growing application in medical education, and in art and literature (e.g., reproducing illuminated manuscripts). Color film stock is not archival.

VIEWING EQUIPMENT

Microforms need to be read with the aid of viewing equipment, for, by definition, they are not legible to the unaided eye. A microform viewer is an optical projection device either incorporating its own screen or projecting onto the table or onto a suitable wall surface. The screen may be either translucent, in the case of rear-projection optical systems, or opaque, in the case of front-projection optical systems. Because of the design problems involved, microform viewers normally deal with one type of microform only. Microfiche viewers are of simple design and relatively cheap, while microfilm readers should be motorized and thus more expensive.

Modern microform equipment is designed with due regard to aesthetic and ergonomic factors as well as safety. The basic requirements are that it bring back the original to full size on the screen, precisely focused, without glare, and with variable luminance to suit differing eyesight needs. The British Standards Institution has produced specifications that encourage production of good equipment (BSI, 1983). The National Reprographic Centre for documentation at Hatfield Polytechnic is an independent, but government-financed, organization, that gives objective assessments of equipment (NRCd, 1982).

The environment in which the reading of microforms takes place is important, and lighting capable of local control is desirable.

COPYING FROM MICROFORMS

Plain paper reader printers from which a user may readily obtain a copy of a frame or frames of text from the microform are now available. However, in most countries there are substantial copyright restrictions to protect the rights of authors and publishers *(see* **Copyright [U.K.]; Copyright [U.S.]**). Even for the purposes of research and study there may be fees payable or limits set to the extent of the copying.

COMPUTER-ASSISTED RETRIEVAL

The only viable means of keeping up-to-date and publishing certain major reference books in the near future will be to assemble author-produced camera-ready copy, microfilm it, store it in an automated retrieval device, and collect payment from on-line users, either directly or indirectly through such services as **Videotex** (q.v.). Computer-assisted retrieval devices can retrieve and display a particular frame on a microfiche or film and, thus, the precise page of a book as required. They are much used in government, industry, and commerce for large-scale data devices.

MICROPUBLICATIONS

Optical disk technology notwithstanding, there is a growing future role for micropublishing. Micropublications trickled into libraries in the 1930s but became a stream in the 1970s. Space economy and conservation of originals are now, in the 1980s, matters of pressing importance because of the cost of space and the fact that books printed since the 1860s on machine-made paper are decaying at an alarming rate in all our libraries. Silver halide microform will last for hundreds of years; it is of archival quality. Other factors of recent influence are the ability to publish material in microform that could not be published at an acceptable price in any other format; the ability to make collections of material in great libraries and archives available for academic purposes in microform copies worldwide; the ability to buy complete back sets of any journal in microform; the advent of the fiche-book, which has a small book format with printed introduction, together with the main text on microfiches housed in envelopes bound as a book; and, of course, above all, the advent of the microfiche itself, so easy to handle and use. There is a growing body of specialist micropublishers, worldwide, and particularly in America and Britain. These are listed, together with a guide to the subject areas of the microforms they publish, in a book by Teague (1985).

EDUCATIONAL APPLICATIONS

A major application of microforms is for storage and retrieval of educational records. Student, staff, financial, and committee documents can conveniently be converted to microform. **Aperture cards** (q.v.) can include a photograph of each student.

In aid of research, original documents such as unpublished diaries, account books, and drawings and personal papers of an engineer, for example, can be microfilmed and a copy purchased by a researcher's own college or university library.

In teaching, one can photograph the occasions when experiments actually work perfectly, when microscopes actually show what is supposed to be happening, and put the results on microfiche. Jacket microfiche can be used by teachers at all levels to produce their own updatable background material for a course. Teaching packs of source material can be converted to microform to include items of diverse sizes and formats, selected passages of key texts, and specimen typed solutions to mathematical problems, all reduced to one microfiche.

A holistic approach to teaching is made possible at acceptable cost by, for example, supplying historical, geographical and geological maps of a district, its census returns, rating records, enclosure applications, railway and road planning schemes, copies of local diaries, portraits, wills, newspapers, and copies of previously unpublished computer-produced sociological data in order to provide a completely rounded picture of the life of a district at a given point in time. In art teaching and appreciation, microfiche in color can add a dimension with, say, 60 pictures per fiche and each student having a copy to study. To all these microform educational aids audiotaped instruction can be related, as required.

That the microform medium has a continuing role in education is certain. While new publications can be produced by the authors on word processors and published in various ways using computers, it is not economically feasible to convert the vast existing resources of our libraries to computerized format. Neither will it be economically feasible, during this century, to copy whole libraries onto videodisc. Film-based microforms are the medium for copying the decaying records of our heritage into a lasting format (Gray, 1987).

S. John Teague

REFERENCES

British Standards Institution. (1983) *Measuring the Screen Luminance, Contrast and Reflectance of Microform Readers.* BS 6354. London: BSI.

Gray, E. (1986) "To Film, or Not to Film." *International Journal of Micrographics and Video Technology* 5 (3/4): 177–183.

International Standards Organization. (1980) *Micrographics Vocabulary. General Terms.* ISO, 6196/1. Geneva: ISO.

National Reprographic Centre for Documentation. (1982)

Group Evaluation of Full Size Microfiche Readers. TER 82/3. Hatfield, U.K.: NRCd.

Teague, S. J. (1985) *Microform, Video and Electronic Media Librarianship.* Butterworths.

MICRONET. A satellite network connecting universities and community colleges in several Pacific islands including Hawaii.

MICRO-OPAQUE. A type of microfiche that uses an opaque support. Also known as microprints or microcards, they are read using a viewing device that illuminates the card by reflected light and projects an image on to a viewing screen.

MICROPHONE CHARACTERISTICS. As microphones are used in many different situations they are designed for specific applications. The directivity pattern of a microphone is represented by a polar diagram. Directivity patterns are in three main forms (see Figure 52):

1. *Omnidirectional.* Such a microphone is equally sensitive in all directions.
2. *Bidirectional.* The polar diagram for this type of microphone is a figure eight, indicating that it is sensitive from two sides only. Ribbon microphones are usually of this type.
3. *Unidirectional.* Often referred to as *cardioid* due to its heart-shaped polar curve. Microphones of this type are particularly useful for recording a single speaker or announcer, as they are sensitive on one side only and therefore are able to discriminate between a sound source placed on the sensitive side and unwanted ambient noise coming from other directions.

An important characteristic of microphones is their **impedance** (q.v.). Generally, microphones have either a high (50 kilohm) or low (30 ohm) impedance output. The advantages of high impedance microphones is that they are usually of high sensitivity and they can be coupled straight into amplifying equipment without a transformer. However, a long cable on such a microphone acts as a capacitor and attenuates the signal. For this reason microphones with low impedance output characteristics are used for most audio applications. It is essential that the impedance of a microphone is always matched to the input impedance of the amplifier to be used.

MICROPHOTOGRAPHY. The production of microscopically small photographs of objects or drawings by extreme optical reduction. Microphotography is used in the production of miniaturized printed circuits. Not to be confused with photomicrography.

MICROPIT. The storage mechanism on a laser videodisc. The reflections of the laser from the successive micropits reconstitute the stored information.

MICROPROCESSOR. An integrated circuit which provides in one chip all those functions which are required in the central processing unit of a computer. The microprocessor receives and executes instructions and may also be capable of arithmetical functions.

MICROPROJECTOR. A microscope with a very intense light source and special eyepiece and prism device used for projecting microscope sections onto a screen for teaching purposes. Unfortunately, the amount of light required to give a reasonable size image with high-power objectives is often such that it will bleach the dyes used to stain the histological preparation. For this reason it is usually preferable for teaching purposes to use photomicrographic transparencies.

MICROSLEEP. A term for a type of short attention break that a learner periodically experiences during a lecture or other learning activity that lasts longer than his/her attention span.

MICROTEACHING. A range of techniques used in training teachers and others concerned with interpersonal communication in specific skills in simulated teaching situations. A typical microteaching session would involve a trainee teaching a lesson to a few students with his/her performance being recorded on videotape for subsequent discussion and analysis.

MICROWAVE LINK. A radio system used for the point-to-point transmission of a television signal, thus avoiding long lengths of cable. Microwave links are limited to line-of-sight situations. They operate in the 7GHz and 11GHz bands (1 gigahertz = 10^9Hz). It is possible to link points as far apart as 50 miles (80 kilometers) using microwaves.

Figure 52
Microphone Characteristics (Shaded Area Indicates Area of Sensitivity)

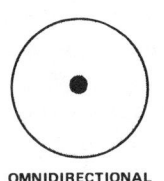

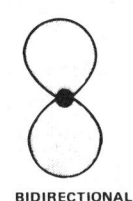

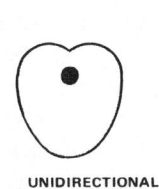

OMNIDIRECTIONAL   BIDIRECTIONAL   UNIDIRECTIONAL

MIDAS. An international data transmission service operated by OTC Australia. MIDAS allows computers in Australia to be interfaced with worldwide data base and other computing resources. Access to the system is either direct or via AUSTPAC.

MIDWEST PROGRAM ON AIRBORNE TELEVISION INSTRUCTION (MPATI). During the period 1961–1967 educational television programs were transmitted in parts of the United States from a cruising airplane. More recent developments in communications have rendered such schemes as MPATI obsolescent. *See* **Tethered Communications Satellite.**

MILITARY TRAINING. This entry will attempt to provide an overall view of military training rather than deal with the specific features of the subject as it relates to a particular country or armed forces. It represents not an official view but the personal opinions of several workers in military training.

THE SIGNIFICANCE OF MILITARY TRAINING

The strength of any organization depends very much upon the skill, knowledge, and attitudes of the personnel which it employs. Military organizations are no exception, and it is significant that effective defense systems are manned extensively by personnel who are designated as requiring special skills. Training in the military context is therefore of vital importance.

In their operational functions military organizations are unique in that only on rare occasions may they be called upon to plan real campaigns and fight actual battles, the purpose for which they are created. Thus military training must not only develop skills but maintain them by means of exercises which are a significant feature of peacetime operations. This artificiality of operations means that it is extremely difficult to produce reliable performance data to indicate whether training does actually confer the military effectiveness that is expected of the man-machine systems under true battle conditions (Nelson, 1971; de Leon, 1977; Augustine, 1982 BACKGROUND READING).

Allied with the requirement to ensure effectiveness is the need to conserve the performance life of military equipment and its consumables, e.g., fuel, ammunition, and missiles. Military equipment is acquired for fighting, and its excessive use in training and exercises reduces operational life, resources, and therefore battle readiness. A conjoint factor is the reluctance to employ situations in which death or injury as a result of training occurs on the same scale as that of true battle. In addition to the constraints imposed by the need to safeguard equipment and personnel, there is frequently a limitation on training arising from the requirement to protect the environment and the inability to actually undertake the fullest exploration of the outcomes of potential offensive and defensive strategies (Wanstall, 1982 FURTHER READING). Consequently, for reasons of this kind, military training requirements have been a significant driving factor in the development of training simulators.

A major influence on the development of military training is the pace of technological development. The impact of this is that the frontline service life of any equipment may be very short or may be extended by the modification and improvement of the equipment and its operation. The consequent implication for training is that it must be able to adapt quickly to requirements and be capable of leading the introduction of new systems. Problems arising from this source extend from the operational into the maintenance areas of military activities. Here also training must be provided, but frequently the actual equipment itself may be too costly or totally unsuited to be used as a means of developing and maintaining a skill.

Therefore, military training deserves special consideration because requirements created by the armed forces have been instrumental in the development and application of methods of analyzing training requirements, initiating training methods, and evaluating means of determining the final effectiveness of the training provided.

The uniqueness of military training having been identified, it must also be pointed out that there is an interdependence with the civilian world. In most countries the armed forces are a major employer relying on the civilian educational system for the source of its recruits. However, the military can also play an important role in providing skilled training for personnel who subsequently return to the civilian world.

THE MILITARY CONTEXT

The nature of any armed service is influenced by those external factors which constitute its environment, including international relations; national—political, social, and economic—issues; and technological developments. Military training likewise will respond to such factors. The scale and purpose of military training will depend upon the nature of perceived threat; the pattern of training will depend upon national trends in education and in employment. Social values will determine whether the force is volunteer or conscript. All of these factors will influence the nature of military training.

Whether the manning of the armed forces should depend upon volunteers or conscription is a political decision, outside the influence of the military system itself, but the chosen system will have a direct influence on the design and scale of military training. With a volunteer force the entrants must be selected in competition with other employers: those who are selected should fit the job requirements more accurately and should give a longer period of service so that extended specialist training can be provided with a reasonable return of service.

The shorter period of time spent in service by conscripts makes the balance between the length of time spent in training and the time remaining for productive service more critical so that it may not be cost-effective to provide training to high levels of skill. It may be necessary to change the nature of many jobs so that less training is necessary, allowing the individual to perform effectively but within a more limited area of competence.

The relative merits of a volunteer force against a conscript force are considered in more detail in Van Doorn (1975 BACKGROUND READING).

Military training contains within its bounds two distinct stages. The first is the conversion of a civilian into a responsive member of an armed force. It consists of developing the long-established skills and attitudes associated with the profession of arms. Training in military discipline, physical fitness, drill, and weapons proficiency are essential features of this initial training.

The second stage is the conversion of the proficient soldier, sailor, or airman into the skilled specialist. How these kinds of training will be provided is also defined by the military context. In the past the armed services generally fulfilled all of their training needs, for both initial and specialist training. However, with a developed educational sector the services can utilize civilian training resources either by recruiting entrants with high educational qualifications or by sending trainees to external schools and colleges.

The high level of technology in military operations and the accompanying support services required for the maintenance of equipment have created extensive training requirements. In armed forces throughout the world this has resulted in the creation of specialist commands or organizations whose sole responsibility is the provision of training. The range of specialist training courses in a modern military organization is extensive, and courses vary in length and in the range of skills given. For example, in the United Kingdom the basic training organization within the Royal Air Force provides training for airmen and airwomen in more than sixty major specializations ranging from electronic engineering to catering and clerical support.

This two-stage pattern of training will be the same for both officers and other ranks although the points of entry, duration, and content of training will be different.

These, then, are the factors which have led military training to a unique position in the forefront of innovation and evaluation in relation to training. For a more extensive examination of the context of military training, see Downey (1977 FURTHER DETAIL).

THE DESIGN AND MANAGEMENT OF MILITARY TRAINING

Most Western military organizations now follow a criterion-based systematic approach to training called by names such as Instructional Systems Design (ISD) in North America and Systems Approach to Training in Britain. These systems have the following concepts in common: (1) operational requirements, (2) task analysis, (3) training objectives, and (4) evaluation. The crucial first step in a systematic training scheme is to specify precisely and unambiguously the operational requirement, the ultimate training goal. A detailed examination of this topic is outside the scope of this entry; however, those interested in this aspect are referred to Chatelier (1979 METHODOLOGY).

Next follows the task analysis, which not only seeks to describe the task which the student will have to perform but specifies the required actions, identifies the conditions under which those actions occur, and determines performance criteria. An immense amount of literature has been generated on task analysis (see Duncan, 1972 BACKGROUND READING; McCornichi, 1976 FURTHER READING). One can discern two general approaches: one is classificatory, or taxonomic; the other is structural, where the structure of skilled performance is usually assumed to be hierarchical. For a useful literature review of military work on task analysis and task taxonomies, as well as for examples of the procedures and recording formats, see Folley (1964a, 1964b BACKGROUND READING).

Since the early 1970s military institutions have tended to move away from the relatively complicated taxonomic approach to task analysis in favor of hierarchical methods. In particular, the influence of the work of Mager and Beach (1967 METHODOLOGY) is widespread. The Mager and Beach method employs job description, task listing, and task detailing. The job description is written in such a way as to focus attention onto the task objective rather than the particular activity being performed. Task analysis provides the basic information for defining the training objectives, the training strategy, and the course content.

Mager's (1962 METHODOLOGY) threefold guide for objectives is now extensively used by the armed forces. It comprises

(a) Specification of the kind of performance which is acceptable as evidence of successful instruction

(b) Statement of the conditions under which the performance is to occur, e.g., whether a translation is to be performed with or without a dictionary or whether a repair task is to be supported by a fault location guide

(c) Specification of performance standards, usually concerned with accuracy and speed

This approach challenges the effectiveness of training objectives, even existing objectives, which have been formulated without explicit reference to operational or field performance. It contrasts sharply with Bloom's approach (1956 METHODOLOGY), which takes existing curriculum statements and attempts to develop post hoc logical classifications of objectives.

The impact upon the organization of this kind of systematic review of training objectives should not be underestimated. It has influenced not only the training system itself—by providing a more purposeful and more economic use of resources, and by reshaping the pattern and style of instruction—but it has also challenged many of the basic assumptions about military life and behavior.

A more detailed level of task analysis, looking at the components of individual skills and the kinds of feedback required for skilled response, can also be used to define the precise content and style of instruction. (See Duncan and Annette, 1967; Duncan, 1972; Duncan and Sheperd, 1980 BACKGROUND READING.)

A surprising feature of education and training programs generally is that, even today, they are not subject to anything approaching evaluation in the sense of objective assessment of their effectiveness. On the other hand, military training systems are subject to continuous and critical evaluation, costly though this procedure may seem to be. Because of rapidly changing technology in the armed forces, trainers have to be aware that a training procedure, no matter how well designed initially, can rapidly become ineffective if it is not reviewed constantly.

It is convenient to classify the evaluation of training into three parts; internal validation, external validation, and evaluation. Internal validation focuses on the process of training, determining how effectively the instruction meets the objectives which have been specified. Measures used for this purpose may include trainee opinions, examinations and performance tests, or the time taken to achieve a specified standard. External validation is concerned with the relevance of the training objectives to the job. Assessments given by recent trainees and their superiors are used to determine job performance. Clearly, training based on **task analysis** (q.v.) is likely to show up well on an external validation. Evaluation, in terms of some relevant objective criterion, is much less common; it is sometimes particularly hard to use in a military context, and military exercises and full battle scenarios therefore have a particular importance. However, evaluation within the military setting is rigorously pursued where novel equipments or procedures are developed.

The significant feature of the military's formalized management of training is its organization as a self-correcting system. Structures and procedures have been developed which continuously review operational requirements and the suitability of training arrangements (Travis, 1983 BACKGROUND READING).

TRAINING TECHNIQUES AND SPECIALIST SKILLS

The armed forces use training techniques and principles to be found elsewhere; however, because of their specialized training requirements they rely on some particular techniques such as simulation (see **Simulation and Gaming**) and **computer-assisted instruction** (q.v.). These are often associated with the more complex specialist skills such as operating tasks, command and control, equipment maintenance, and leadership.

Simulation and Training Devices. Simulation and training devices are used to create situations in which students can be trained on a replica of the operational situation that is sufficiently like the "real thing" to provide positive transfer of training. One of the advantages of a training device over the real environment is that it provides the opportunity to augment the environment—to vary the content, order, repetition, and timing of the training elements—in order to enhance learning. However, this training advantage may often be seen as secondary when compared with the reduced costs, greater safety, and additional capabilities which are feasible with a simulator rather than the actual equipment. Such considerations have been a significant driving factor in the development of training devices (Hartley 1981, FURTHER READING).

Simulators first found military applications in teaching skills relating to the operation and handling of aircraft, tanks and ships. The most familiar example of these is the flight simulator (*See* **Flight Simulation**). These devices have been subjected to extensive evaluation for both their training- and cost-effectiveness; the results show that the simulator has distinct advantages for a range of training tasks (Orlansky and Chatelier, 1983; Rolfe and Waag, 1980 REPORTED RESULTS). Subsequent developments have extended the use of simulation into areas where the size of the student team is increased and where skills relating more to tactical command and control than to psychomotor performance predominate. Examples are simulators of air traffic control and military operations rooms. In parallel with these developments there has been an increase in simulators for maintenance training. This requirement has been brought about by the arrival of complex and expensive systems for which it would be impossible to justify the acquisition of a full system for training purposes (Orlansky and String, 1981 REPORTED RESULTS).

Two questions are of principal concern to trainers using simulation and training devices. The first is how to define the features required in a training simulation. It is often assumed that because a simulation has high training device fidelity—i.e., it looks, feels, and behaves like the real equipment—it must be an effective training device. This need not be so. For example, if the aircraft is a poor learning environment for some tasks, then a device that simulates this environment exactly will incorporate the same disadvantages. It is therefore crucial to identify the features necessary for effective learning, a task which is itself difficult and complex and can call upon the skills of a range of expertise. For example, in an attempt to identify simulator fidelity required for pilot training, the disciplines of engineering, psychology, and physiology must all be brought into play (Agard, 1980 BACKGROUND READING).

The procedures contained in the Systems Approach to Training or Instructional Systems Development are valid for making decisions about the features required in a training device (Houston, 1976; Knight and Sharrock, 1983 REPORTED RESULTS). The specification of a training device should follow a task analysis and take into account its relationship to the total training system (Andrews, 1983 BACKGROUND READING). However, in an examination of the application of ISD in the USAF, Miller, Swink and McKenzie (1978 BACKGROUND READING) concluded that a premature commitment to a particular training medium frequently results in the device dictating the training requirement rather than vice versa. Eddowes (1974 METHODOLOGY) attempted to apply cognitive principles to the acquisition of flying skills and subsequently developed a concept based on "least-cost, sequenced, multi-media training." The objective is to match the students' level of discriminative/cognitive/organizational readiness with the complexity and representativeness—or fidelity—of the training task environment. It is based on the observation that a significant portion of flight instruction can be presented more effectively in places other than the cockpit and that almost any other instructional medium can be more cost-effective.

The second question is how to determine the actual training value of a simulator. This problem is not unique to simulation as it applies to other forms of training devices as well, however much research effort has been devoted to the problem especially in relation to flight simulation. Three measures have been frequently used: user opinion, the degree of realism, and the use of the simulation. However, these are highly suspect measures (Rolfe and Caro, 1982 BACKGROUND READING).

The legitimate model for the evaluation process is seen by military researchers as that of the transfer of training experiments with stated objectives, pretest and posttest measures, and adequate control groups. One such measure is the Training Effectiveness Ratio (TEO) derived by Roscoe (1980 REPORTED RESULTS). This measure relates the amount of training effort required to meet the objectives without the aid of simulation to the amount of training effort required with the simulation. The results of a number of studies using the TEO are reported in Orlansky and String (1979 REPORTED RESULTS).

Computer-Assisted Instruction. Computer-assisted instruction (CAI) embodies many of the techniques introduced with **programmed learning** (q.v.). The principles common to both systems would include individualized instruction, with self-pacing, conditional branching to provide remedial exercises where necessary, prompt feedback and reinforcement, continuous review and consolidation of learning, progressive development, and integration of knowledge and skills. This provides a common standard of skill acquisition—usually indicated by criterion testing—and the possibility of distance learning.

Computer-assisted instruction extends the scope of individualized instruction. Where **teaching machines** (q.v.) would be limited to one remedial routine in response to any incorrect answer to a question, computers have the flexibility to provide a range of remedial routines and to relate these to particular kinds of student response. Computer display facilities can provide dynamic, interactive graphics which have made possible training for new perceptual, procedural, and control skills with part-task trainers (Knight and Sharrock, 1983 REPORTED RESULTS). Mass storage facilities can support a variety of new student/instructor aids such as visual playback and freeze, the monitoring of student responses, and more sophisticated analysis in terms of reaction times, degrees of error, etc. As programmable machines, computers allow instructors much greater freedom to develop, present, and modify their materials.

Computers are widely used as the controlling element in other systems, as the basis for simulators or part-task trainers. In this kind of application the key features of the learning situation—the control of stimuli and the reaction to student responses—are pre-empted by other features of the system. Interest in CAI centers on projecting the organizing principles and concepts which underlie the task, but this distinction is difficult to maintain. For example, microcomputers have been interfaced with operational keyboards to present lesson materials and simulated graphics in response to realistic keyboard procedures.

In maintenance training an important part of fault-finding skill is conceptual, e.g., learning to search efficiently so as to maximize information gained as to the whereabouts of a fault, and this requires little interaction with the equipment. It is now widely accepted that these conceptual skills can be acquired by generalized procedures trainers and that minimal simulation fidelity is required. This has stimulated the development of training using flat-panel techniques (i.e., the two-dimensional screen representation of equipment layouts, control panels, etc.). Where hands-on practice with complex operational equipment is required, CAI invariably offers cost savings. In the support areas, the division between training and performance of the task will become less distinct. This will be brought about by the introduction of more sophisticated military systems including embedded training and task aiding. Operating and maintenance personnel will receive on-the-job training and have available to them aids to prompt and guide them when actually performing their tasks. Many of the savings attributed to CAI projects stem from reduced individual training times. To get the best out of CAI therefore also requires modifying timetabling procedures and organizational constraints (Orlansky and String, 1979 FURTHER READING).

Artificial intelligence (q.v.), the development of stochastic reasoning patterns in computer systems, has been applied in two main areas within the military training context. First, it is being used in the development of **expert systems** (q.v.) producing teaching devices which try to embody the probabilistic elements of a skilled operator's judgment. Unlike conventional CAI systems, expert systems are not limited to a finite set of prescribed solutions and do not automatically identify these with specific student responses. The important feature of this kind of teaching device is not its ability to incorporate a pattern of highly skilled operation but its ability to reflect and respond to the intermediate patterns of skill which trainees must develop but which eventually become redundant as trainees reach the highest levels of performance (Gregory, 1980 FURTHER READING). Secondly, it is being used to produce high-level decision-making aids, principally in the areas of command and control, and of fault finding in technical systems. Working examples in the defense sector are difficult to cite; more accessible examples are to be found in the civilian context such as the MYCIN program to advise on medical diagnosis (Boden, 1977 BACKGROUND READING).

Operating Tasks. The classical work of Craik (1948 METHODOLOGY) identifying the human operator as a control element in man-machine systems provided the foundation for early work on performance in complex, dynamic tasks. However, the nature of the essential skills in these tasks is changing in the military from continuous perceptual and psychomotor skills to serial or discrete information-processing and decision-making skills. Technical developments have displaced the primacy of the senses. Sensors can now detect more acutely, can analyze more thoroughly, and can respond more quickly than the human operator, whose role is to direct, select, classify, and decide.

Flying and driving tasks have become dominated by information-processing requirements: monitoring several activities, handling high information work load, assigning priorities, time-sharing, and decision making. Models of cognitive function have concentrated on the limits to information-processing capacity; consequently, performance problems are tackled by raising selection standards or redesigning equipment. Training strategies are few, reduction of work load by overlearning being the dominant practice. Developing ways to teach information-handling skills is the primary challenge facing military trainers today. In a similar way, while signal detection was once important, in radar operation, for example, the present requirement is for the development of search strategies and classification skills in the management of radar and sonar sensors (Cook et al., 1983 REPORTED RESULTS). For unaided target recognition, classification systems based on pattern recognition were developed (Beard, 1983 METHODOLOGY). However, this model is inappropriate for the classification of coded/representational displays derived from electromagnetic sensors; here, analysis and decision-making **heuristics** (q.v.) are more appropriate.

With the development of automated tracking and control systems, the need for skills in detection and control has been overshadowed by the higher levels of cognitive skill needed to be able to manage the equipment. Research on training typically concentrates on areas of inadequate performance in order to develop training procedures to obviate these. Some awareness of the need for teaching information-handling and cockpit management skills has been stimulated by investigation of aircraft accidents (Jensen, 1982; Telfer, 1982 FURTHER READING).

Equipment Maintenance. In its efforts to ensure national security, the military makes technological innovations faster and more extensively than does industry or commerce. Equipment maintenance skills need to be revised accordingly. During the 1960s and 1970s a substantial effort was directed toward improving the serviceability of complex equipment. From the point of view of manpower use, efforts were mainly directed toward improvements in training, particularly for the nonroutine maintenance tasks, i.e., for fault-finding or troubleshooting tasks. A review of the research by Wallis, Duncan, and Knight (1967 BACKGROUND READING) identified the three main areas of theoretical development: functional context training, cue-response analysis, and generalized fault-finding strategies.

Functional context training concentrates on teaching the relatively gross cause-effect relationships between functions and parts and between faults and symptoms. Circuit layouts are typically presented in schematic, functional terms rather than in terms of physical layout or conventional wiring diagrams (Garland and Stainer, 1970 REPORTED RESULTS). Cue-response analysis attempts to make routine the fault-finding aspects of maintenance by the provision of detailed job aids for specific equipment. Derived from observation of the malfunctions which occur in a particular equipment, these would indicate for each set of symptoms (or cues) the general area to be examined (response). The aids, or fault-finding guides, would specify what tests to carry out and would direct the maintainer to an identification of the component to be replaced, adjusted, or repaired (Foley and Camm, 1972 FURTHER READING). The development of generalizable fault-finding strategies concentrates on teaching the logic of making efficient checks within systems (i.e., the half split technique) and ways to modify that logic in terms of the likelihood of faults occurring in a component and the cost in terms of accessibility and in time required to check the different parts of the equipment (Parker and Knight, 1976 REPORTED RESULTS).

Changes in the design of modern equipment have substantially altered the skill requirements for maintainers. For example, the widespread use of solid-state circuits has dramatically increased the inherent reliability of much equipment; standardization has increased the physical and constructional similarity of electronic systems; modular design principles simplify fault location and allow for repair by replacement. Considerable efforts have also been made to improve serviceability by the provision of built-in test equipment (BITE) and automatic test equipment (ATE). Fink and Shriver (1978 BACKGROUND READING) consider the implications of these changes for maintenance training and conclude that training philosophies which concentrate on a functional understanding of systems, on fault-finding strategies, and on the provision of job aids will be especially appropriate. They also forsee the possibility of a corresponding polarization of maintenance jobs—less skilled, short-service technicians handling the automatically diagnosed faults, and more highly skilled, extensively trained technicians dealing with the small proportion of faults outside the scope of the test equipment.

The increased reliability of new equipment makes possible the introduction of "distance servicing" whereby nonroutine maintenance is carried out by less skilled men on the spot who interact with, and are prompted and instructed by, remote computer-based maintenance aids (Klass, 1982 REPORTED RESULTS).

Leadership. There has always been an extensive commitment to leadership training in the military; and while training programs have responded to the findings of contemporary studies, they have always placed the primary emphasis on social skills, stressing the interpersonal behavior considered appropriate to leaders of the time. Early studies—mainly historical and political—concentrated on the personalities of recognized leaders. Functional analyses of leader behavior stressed the nature of the task and the relevance of differences in leadership styles, e.g., task-oriented and person-oriented behaviors (Bales, 1953 METHODOLOGY). Fiedler's more formalized contingency theory (1967 METHODOLOGY) considered leadership effectiveness as the function of a number of variables and identified (1) leader-group relations, (2) the openness or structured nature of the task, (3) the power inherent in the leader's position, and (4) feelings of stress as the key determinants of effectiveness. Fiedler argued that leadership behavior was difficult to change and that reassigning groups and leaders or restructuring the task were easier. Others such as Adair (1968 FURTHER READING), working in a military context, have stressed that leaders need to become sensitive to these situational variables and must learn to adapt their behavior accordingly.

The distinction between leadership as a social skill (making the most of one's men) and as command, or decision-making capacity, has been underlined by the increased importance of telecommunications. Beaumont (1983 FURTHER READING), for instance, argues that Command Control and Communication systems require quite different and conflicting leader characteristics. Numerous studies have been conducted into the way that officers evaluate and respond to intelligence information, particularly how they assign probabilities to written reports and how they integrate the slow buildup of information before making their decisions. One of the more accessible summaries of this work is given by Watson (1978 BACKGROUND READING). Training in the principles of information handling, which was based on computer models but presented in the form of simple reference cards, produced demonstrable improvements on maneuvers and in real-life exercises (Olson, 1969 REPORTED RESULTS).

One aspect of leadership often overlooked by theorists is following behavior (Hollander, 1955 REPORTED RESULTS, is a notable exception). Military institutions, however, pay equal regard to this factor in early training and in the organization of the system of rewards and punishments. The studies of Hollander and of Nelson (1964 REPORTED RESULTS) are relevant to military leadership situations but are qualified by the fact that they dealt with leaders and followers in situations where personal liking was a common feature.

These studies have significantly influenced training programs by providing more relevant definitions of leader behaviors and of the factors related to military effectiveness. Notably fewer studies, however, have been aimed directly at improving procedures for military leadership training. Goldstein (1980 BACKGROUND READING) highlights the contribution of Bandura's social learning theory and of behavioral role modeling to leadership training, with its emphasis on learning some points or principles, observing a model that utilizes the principles, rehearsing the behaviors by role-playing, and receiving reinforcement from the trainer and group members. For enlisted personnel, prompt compliance with orders and a strict adherence to service norms are the leadership aspects given greatest stress; for officers, an awareness of basic responsibilities and the elementary skills needed to direct the efforts of others are emphasized.

Lectures usually provide the principal medium for presenting the theory of leadership. Discussions, films, case studies, and role-playing exercises are used to present leadership problems and examples of model behavior. Basic training typically includes a wide range of practical leadership situations—giving lectures, briefs, solving problems, commanding fellow trainees, and role-playing exercises such as disciplinary boards. These exercises are founded on active participation, carrying out the required behavior, accompanied by extensive feedback through peer ratings, debriefs, formal assessments, etc., and with a strict observance of procedures and performance standards. The example set by the instructors and the responses required of the trainees, as followers, are a significant feature of the training pattern. Secondary duties, or asssignment to some form of community service, are a requirement commonly used to provide another source of leadership experience.

Closely related to the topic of leadership training is that of attitude formation. Military leadership is firmly based on a set of values and beliefs, not solely on a consideration of behavior and actions. Developing the appropriate attitudes is a key aspect of the initial training. Standards of discipline and the codes of behavior required of trainees are especially rigorous and are generally quite unrepresentative of later experiences. Festinger's theory of cognitive dissonance (1957 METHODOLOGY) has provided the stimulus for numerous models of attitude change and together with Bem's (1967 METHODOLOGY) analysis provides a rationale for many features of the military training environment. Sarason and Novaco (1982 REPORTED RESULTS) examined the effectiveness of marine drill instructors and found that the most effective instructors developed within their platoons the feeling that the recruits' own efforts and activities could influence their own outcome and rewards. This process was enhanced with the introduction of other media (i.e., videotape modules) to help develop these attitudes.

DEVELOPMENTS IN MILITARY TRAINING

In many respects changes in military training follow the pattern of technological innovation in industry. There are improvements or innovations in training research and theory, and there is a period of development or controlled application before new ideas and techniques are adopted by the military organization. Academic research (often funded by the military) or in-house research may provide ideas and techniques for changes to the pattern of military training, but these will ultimately be implemented by service personnel.

While the armed services have successfully developed and applied procedures to the design and management of training, and to the development of new training technologies, there has not been an equal degree of attention paid to the training process itself (e.g., to instructional technique, to learning styles, etc.). This aspect of training may show the greatest changes in the future. For example, research on information-processing models of performance on intelligence tests is providing new insights into the range and effectiveness of individual strategies of problem solving (Sternberg, 1977; Hunt, 1979 METHODOLOGY) and suggests the kinds of learning skills that might be enhanced through training and educational interventions. Equally, research on the differences between experts and novices in knowledge structure and cognitive processes is being used to suggest techniques for developing decision-making skills. This procedure is also used to identify the knowledge requirements for training courses to develop classification aids and to produce the decision-making "rules" for expert systems. For individual skills such as those required by aircrew and other frontline weapons operators, there are programs underway to develop improved techniques for training in information-handling skills. Elsewhere attention is centering upon improving training methods for the development of command and control effectiveness in battle and strategic operations. Developments in interface technology, i.e., voice recognition and voice synthesis equipment, will be a key issue while the creation of effective personal training aids will be a major source of research effort.

CONCLUSIONS

This entry has sought to describe the context in which military training takes place and the special requirements of the military task which have led to the adoption of innovative and objective strategies for training. Duncan and Wallis (1978 BACKGROUND READING) aptly assessed military training as "on the one hand the combination of technological sophistication and scientific rigour and on the other accountability." However, these authors expressed their concern that these features were not widely found in public education and industrial training.

The view of the present contributors is that this position has altered. Technological innovation, particularly that provided by the microcomputer, is now readily available and at a cost which is within the means of public education. At the same time, industrial training is making fuller use of new interactive audiovisual aids for training. In some aspects of training these developments may be in advance of military thinking. However, in both public education and industrial training it can be argued that there is still some reluctance to undertake the assessment of the effectiveness of the training obtained along the rigorous lines practiced by the military.

J. M. Rolfe, N. M. Hardinge, C. C. Elshaw, J. L. Robinson, and D. A. Sharrock

REFERENCES

Background Reading

AGARD. (1980) *Fidelity of Simulation for Pilot Training,* AGARD Advisory Report No. 159. Paris: NATO, Advisory Group for Aeronautical Research & Development.

Andrews, D. H. (1983) *Important Differences between Simulators and Training Devices.* Proceedings of IEE International Conference on Simulators. London: Institution of Electrical Engineers.

Augustine, N. A. (1982) "Air Munitions: The Missing Link?" *Military Electronics and Countermeasures* (April): 33–43.

Boden, M. (1977) *Artificial Intelligence and Natural Man.* Brighton: Harvester Press.

de Leon, P. (1977) *The Peacetime Evaluation of the Pilot Skill Factor in Air-to-Air Combat.* The Rand Corporation, Santa Monica Report R-2070-PR.

Duncan, K. D. (1972) "Strategies for Analysis of the Task." In *Strategies for Programmed Instruction: An Educational Technology,* ed. J. Hartley. London: Butterworths.

Duncan, K. D. and Annette, J. (1967) "Task Analysis and Training Design." *Journal of Occupational Psychology* 41: 211–221.

Duncan, K. D. and Sheperd, A. (1980) "Analysing a Complex Planning Task." In *Changes in Working Life,* ed. K. D. Duncan et al. New York: Wiley.

Duncan, K. D. and Wallis, D. (1978) "Military Training." In *Encyclopaedia of Educational Media Communications and Technology,* ed. D. Unwin and R. McAleese. London: Macmillan.

Fink, C. D. and Shriver, E. D. (1978) *Simulators for Maintenance Training,* AFHRL-TR-78-27. Texas: Air Force Human Resources Laboratory, Brooks Air Force Base.

Folley, J. D. (1964a) *Development of an Improved Method of Task Analysis and Beginnings of a Theory of Training.* NAVTRADEVCEN 1218 26. New York: U.S. Naval Training Device Center.

———. (1964b) *Guidelines for Task Analysis,* NAVTRADEVCEN 1218 22. New York: U.S. Naval Training Device Center.

Goldstein, I. L. (1980) "Training in Work Organisations." *Annual Review of Psychology* 31: 229–272.

Miller, R. M., Swink, J. R., and McKenzie, J. F. (1978). *Instructional Systems Development (ISD) in Air Force Flying Training,* AFHRL-TR-78-59. Phoenix: Williams Air Force Base.

Nelson, P. D. (1971) "Personnel Performance Prediction." In *Handbook of Military Institutions,* ed. R. W. Little. Beverly Hills, Calif.: Sage Publications.

Rolfe, J. M. and Caro, P. (1982) "Determining the Training Effectiveness of Flight Simulators: Some Basic Issues and Practical Developments." *Applied Ergonomics* 13 (4): 243–250.

Travis, R. C. (1983) "The Principles of the Systems Approach to Training and Systems Approach to Training Experience in NATO." *RAF Education Bulletin,* no. 21.

van Doorn, J. (1975) *The Soldier and Social Change.* London: Sage Publications.

Wallis, D., Duncan, K. D., and Knight, M.A.G. (1967) *A Review of Electronic Training Research in the British Armed Services.* London: Her Majesty's Stationery Office.

Watson, P. (1978) *War on the Mind: The Military Uses and Abuses of Psychology.* London: Hutchinson.

Further Reading

Adair, J. (1968) *Training for Leadership.* London: Macdonald.

Beaumont, R. A. (1983) "The Paradoxes of C^3." In *Military Leadership,* ed. J. H. Buck and L. J. Korb. Sage Research Series on War, no. 10. Beverly Hills, Calif.: Sage Publications.

Downey, J.C.T. (1977) *Management in the Armed Forces: An Anatomy of the Military Profession.* London: McGraw-Hill.

Foley, J. P. Jr. and Camm, W. B. (1972) *Job Performance Aids Research Summary.* Dayton, Ohio: Air Force Human Resources Laboratory, Wright-Patterson Air Force Base.

Gregory, R. (1980) *APU Man-Computer Studies Group,* Seminar Proceedings 1 Memo AMTE(E)TM 80/09. Teddington: Applied Psychology Unit, Admiralty Marine Technology Establishment.

Hartley, D. A. (1981) "Simulators for Military Training." In *Perspectives on Academic Gaming and Simulation 6,* ed. B. Hollinshead and M. Yorke. London: Kogan Page.

Jensen, R. S. (1982) "Pilot Judgement: Training and Evaluation." *Human Factors* 24 (1): 61–73.

McCornichi, E. J. (1976) "Job and Task Analysis." In *Hand-*

book of Industrial and Organisational Psychology, ed. M. D. Dunnette. Chicago: Rand McNally.

Orlansky, J. and String, J. (1979) *Cost-Effectiveness of Computer Based Instruction in Military Training,* IDA Paper P-1375 (AD A073 400). Arlington, Va.: Institute for Defense Analysis.

Telfer, R. (1982) "Cockpit Resource Management: A New Emphasis." Paper presented to the Annual Conference of the General Aviation Association of Australia, November.

Wanstall, B. (1982) "Tactical flying in Europe: Realism versus environment." *Interavia* 9: 924–926.

Methodology

Bales, R. F. (1953) "The Equilibrium Problem in Small Groups." In *Working Papers in the Theory of Action,* ed. T. Parsons, R. F. Bales, and E. A. Shils. New York: The Free Press. Cited in *Leadership,* ed. C. A. Gibb. Harmondsworth, Middlesex, Eng.: Penguin Books Ltd., 1969.

Beard, C. B. (1983) "Armoured Fighting Vehicle Identification Training System." *RAF Education Bulletin,* no. 21.

Bem, D. J. (1967) "Self-Perception: An Alternative Interpretation of Cognitive Dissonance Phenomena." *Psychological Review* 74: 183–200.

Bloom, B. S., ed. (1956) *Taxonomy of Educational Objectives.* New York: Longmans.

Chatelier, P. (1979) "UUSDRE, Fletcher J D, DARPA and Orlansky J, IDA, Front End Analysis of Emerging Systems—R&D Requirements." Report on a workshop held in Santa Fe.

Craik, K.J.W. (1948) "Theory of Human Operator in Control Systems: II." *British Journal of Psychology* 38: 142–148.

Eddowes, E. E. (1974) *A Cognitive Model of What is Learned during Flying Training,* AFHRL-TR-74–36. Phoenix: Flying Training Division, Air Force Human Resources Laboratory, Williams Air Force Base.

Festinger, L. (1957) *A Theory of Cognitive Dissonance.* New York: Harper & Row.

Fiedler, F. E. (1967) *A Theory of Effective Leadership.* New York: McGraw-Hill.

Hunt, E. (1979) "Intelligence as an Information Processing Concept." Arlington, Va.: Office of Naval Research. Contract N00014–77–C-0225.

Mager, R. F. (1962) *Preparing Instructional Objectives.* San Francisco, Calif.: Fearon.

Mager, R. F. and Beach, K. M. (1967) *Developing Vocational Instruction.* San Francisco, Calif.: Fearon.

Sternberg, R.J. (1977) "Component Processes in Analogical Reasoning." *Psychological Review* 84 (4): 353–378.

Reported Results

Cook, J. R., Haydon, D. P., and Sharrock, D. A. (1983). *Maritime Reconnaissance—A Microcomputer-Based Simulation for Training Air Electronics Operators.* Proceedings of IEE International Conference on Simulators. London: Institution of Electrical Engineers.

Garland, D. J. and Stainer, F. W. (1970) *Modern Electronics Maintenance Principles.* London: Pergamon Press.

Hollander, E. P. (1955) *Emergent Leadership and Social Influence.* Cited in *Leadership,* ed. C. A. Gibb. Harmondsworth, Middlesex, Eng.: Penguin Books Ltd., 1969.

Houston, R. C. (1976) *Individualized Instruction Techniques.* Dallas, Texas: American Airlines, Training Center.

Klass, P. J. (1982) "Technique Benefits Novice Technicians." *Aviation Week & Space Technology,* October 11.

Knight, M.A.G. and Sharrock, D. A. (1983) *Simulators as Training Devices: Some Lessons from Military Experience,* Research Note 5/83. RAF Brampton, Cambs: Research Branch, HQRAFSC.

Nelson, P. D. (1964) "Similarities and Differences among Leaders and Followers." *Journal of Social Psychology* 63: 161–167.

Olson, H. C. (1969) *Improvement in Performance on a Leadership Game as a Result of Training on Information Handling,* HumRRO Professional Paper 24–69 (cited in Watson, 1978 BACKGROUND READING).

Orlansky, J. and Chatelier, P. R. (1983) *The Effectiveness and Cost of Simulators for Training.* Proceedings of IEE International Conference on Simulators. London: Institution of Electrical Engineers.

Orlansky, J. and String, J. (1979a) *Cost Effectiveness of Flight Simulators for Military Training.* Proceedings of 1st Interservice/Industry Training Equipment Conference. Orlando, Fla.: NTEC Report IH-316.

———. (1981) "Cost Effectiveness of Maintenance Simulators for Military Training." Report issued by the Institute of Defense Analyses, IDA Paper P-1568.

Parker, G. R. and Knight, K.R. (1976) "Can Computer Assisted Learning Reduce the Cost of Equipment Training?" *RAF Education Bulletin* 13.

Prophet, W. W. and Boyd, H. A. (1970) *Device-Task Fidelity and Transfer of Training: Aircraft Cockpit Procedures Training,* HumRRO Technical Report 70–10. Fort Rucker, Ala.: Human Resources Research Organization, Division No. 6.

Rolfe, J. M. and Waag, W. (1980) "Flights of Fancy: Simulators for pilot training." In *Perspectives on Academic Gaming and Simulation,* No. 7, ed. L. Gray and E. Waitt. London: Kogan Page.

Roscoe, S. N. (1980) *Aviation Psychology.* Ames, Iowa: Iowa State University Press.

Sarason, I. G. and Novaco, R. W. (1982) *Stress and Coping in Recruit Training: Roles of the Recruit and the Drill Instructor.* Office of Naval Research.

MIMEOGRAPH (INK STENCIL). A method of producing duplicate copies, usually of typewritten matter, using a system whereby characters are cut into a thin waxed paper or plastic sheet which is then mounted on a machine to allow ink to penetrate through the letters and be transferred onto sheets of plain paper. Stencil duplicating is a widely used inexpensive system for producing multiple copies.

Methods of cutting the stencil range from the conventional technique where a typewriter is used, usually with the ribbon removed, to electronic stencil cutters which scan the master document and, by using a high voltage spark, cut a duplicate image into the stencil. It is also possible to scribe on the stencil with a stylus. The main disadvantage of stencil duplicating is that it can be a messy process. The use of plain paper copying has supplanted the stencil to a considerable extent.

MINERVA. An electronic mail service operated by OTC Australia. Minerva is linked to similar networks in the United States, the United Kingdom, etc., and offers a full range of features such as text editing, reply requested, filing, and so on.

MINICOMPUTER. A general term used to describe small (but bigger than micro) computers. In this sense small usually implies both the computer's physical size and its memory size. Most minicomputers are designed with a 16–bit word size, but sizes from 8– to 32–bit have been produced.

MINICOURSE. A self-instructional package used in teacher training. Teaching skills are practiced as in microteaching; however, there is no supervisor present and the student teacher works at his/her own pace following an individualized multimedia package.

MINIFLOPPY. A 3 1/2" diameter diskette, offering greater robustness than floppy disks and the ability to store up to 720KB or more per disk.

MINITEL. Strictly speaking, the name of the terminal used in the French videotex system, but popularly used to refer to the system generally.

MINOR SERVICE PROVIDER. Viatel term for service provider with a small number of frames of information.

MIXER. Device for combining together two or more signals. Audio mixers permit the balancing of microphones, appropriate input (such as music or sound effects) from phonograph records, tapes, etc. In the case of video mixers, usual inputs include several cameras, videotape, character generator, telecine; these inputs can be superimposed, or switching (cutting) can be performed between any two inputs.

MNEMONIC. A system that serves as an aid to memory, e.g., use of an easily remembered phrase such as "Richard Of York Gave Battle In Vain," to recall the colors of the spectrum in correct order.

MODEL. (1) A realistic representation, often to scale, of a real object, e.g., a model building used in demonstrating wind resistance characteristics in a wind tunnel. (2) A conceptual organization of variables that describes their interdependence, e.g., a learning theory model. (3) A pattern of events to be copied, e.g., a demonstrated technique for learners to emulate. *See* **Paradigm.**

MODEM. An abbreviation for the term *modulator-demodulator*. The modem is a device which can translate or demodulate telephone line signals into digital signals compatible with computers and translate or modulate computer digital signals into signals which can be transmitted over telephone lines and networks.

MODULAR COURSE. A flexible course that allows individual learners to select the particular components which will combine together to make up the most desirable course for them.

MODULAR SYSTEM. Any instructional package which is composed of self-contained elements, such that each can be studied as a complete unit.

MODULATION. The process of modulating a carrier wave with a signal. This is usually done because the electronic circuits in use are able to work more efficiently at the higher frequency of the carrier wave. Most domestic television receivers are capable of responding only to a VHF or UHF modulated signal; thus the output from a home computer has to be suitably modulated in order for the computer to drive the television set. Some microcomputers have a built-in modulator for this purpose. *See* **Amplitude Modulation; Frequency Modulation; Monitor.**

MONAURAL. Sound with only one channel (mono), as opposed to stereophonic sound (stereo).

MONITOR. A device for displaying television pictures, usually in a studio or other professional environment. Monitors differ from ordinary television receivers in that they are constructed to higher standards and are incapable of receiving broadcast signals; i.e., they are only sensitive to unmodulated video input. Some conventional receivers are modified to accommodate both types of input, and these are designated receiver-monitors.

MONO (MONOPHONIC SOUND). Sound heard from a single channel. This is defined by the form of the recording or transmission, and not by the number of speakers. A number of microphones may be used and their outputs mixed; several loudspeakers may be used, and their frequency content varied, but this is still mono unless there is more than one channel of transmission.

MONOCHROME. This term applies to monitors with only one shade of phosphor. The most popular monochrome monitors use green screens, but amber and black-and-white screens are also common.

MONTE CARLO TECHNIQUE. A simulation technique employing statistical data to which probability theory is applied within defined limits for a number of random occurrences. Used in operations research projects, particularly to model queuing and games (chance) situations.

MOTION DECOMPOSITION. Videodisc term describing the facility to break motion right down into individual frames, stepped backwards and forwards, slow motion, etc.

MOTIVATION. *See* **Motivational Design.**

MOTIVATIONAL DESIGN. Motivational design is an aspect of instructional design which refers specifically to strategies, principles, and processes for making instruction appealing. This adds another dimension to the traditional definition of instructional design as being the process and technique of producing efficient and effective instruction. *Efficiency* refers to economy in the use of instructional time, materials, and other resources. It is not generally viewed as relating to the motivational aspects of instruction.

Effectiveness, however, is sometimes regarded as including motivation. The argument is that instruction cannot be effective if it is not appealing to people. But in practice, instructional designers tend to use effectiveness to refer to how well people *can* learn from an instructional event *given* that they *want* to learn (see Keller, 1983 RESEARCH SYNTHESIS). The desire to learn in a given instructional setting may not come from the instruction itself; it may come from long-range goals, institutional requirements, or many other sources. Instruction, like a trip to the dentist, can be very effective without being at all appealing, but the experience will be avoided unless absolutely necessary. In contrast, motivational design strives to make instruction more intrinsically interesting.

At the other extreme, instructional materials can be very appealing without being effective, especially when their appeal comes purely from their entertainment value. We have all heard variations of the following dialogue:

Child: Boy, that textbook had a lot of good cartoons in it.
Teacher: Yes, it did. What was the book about?
Child: I don't know.

Thus, motivational design is concerned with how to make instruction appealing without making it *purely* entertaining.

One additional distinction of importance is that of motivational design versus behavior modification. When instructional developers or teachers begin to talk about motivation, they have a strong tendency to identify students with severe problems. This leads into behavioral diagnosis and change strategies, and it includes such things as counseling, psychological education, and even psychotherapy. This is outside the boundaries of motivational design, even though motivational design draws upon many of the same supporting concepts and theories, and good motivational design can lead to improved motivational profiles for some students. However, motivational design is concerned primarily with improving the appeal of instruction for groups of students who fall within normal boundaries of readiness to learn provided the instructor neither bores them excessively nor overexcites them.

MOTIVATIONAL DESIGN MODELS

As established by J. M. Keller (1979 THEORETICAL BACKGROUND; 1983 RESEARCH SYNTHESIS), there has been very little work on developing models of motivational design, and many of the following models are not, strictly speaking, motivational design models. They combine mixtures of behavioral change and instructional design strategies. However, they are included because they represent the state of the art from which new and improved motivational design models will emerge.

Motivational design models can be categorized into four groups. The first three are grounded in psychological theories of human behavior. They can be classified as person-centered theories, environmentally centered theories, and interaction theories. The fourth group has a more pragmatic origin and includes omnibus models that incorporate both instructional design and motivational design strategies. These models tend to grow out of solutions to specific kinds of instructional problems.

Person-Centered Models. These models postulate that people have innate drives, potentials, values, and motives that influence personal motivation and development. They assume that the primary impetus for psychological growth and development comes from within the individual. Relevant psychological theories include the work on curiosity and sensation seeking (e.g., Berlyne, 1965; Zuckerman, 1971 THEORETICAL BACKGROUND) and the work on human motives and self-fulfillment by a succession of people such as Maslow, Herzberg, and Rogers (see Weiner, 1980 TEXTBOOK).

The primary contributions to person-centered models of motivational design in this area have come from McClelland (1965 MODEL DESCRIPTION), Alschuler (1973 MODEL DESCRIPTION), and Simon, Howe, and Kirschenbaum (1978 MODEL DESCRIPTION). McClelland published a model for bringing about change in the motive profile of an individual. Used in many workshops, McClelland's model was at the heart of the system developed by Alschuler, who focused on the problem of increasing achievement motivation among school children. His approach, called "psychological education," was concerned with changing behavior rather than simply making instruction more appealing.

Similarly, Simon et al. concentrated on developing strategies for helping children to be more articulate about their values, more self-aware, and more analytical. His model is not a true motivational design model as it concentrates on behavioral change, but both his model and Alschuler's are fruitful sources of examples and ideas that can be used in a motivational design model to help make the instruction relevant to the students' needs and desires.

Environmentally Centered Models. These models assume that behavior can be adequately explained in terms of environmental influences, that the reinforcement contingencies in the environment exert powerful controls on human volition. Many people are associated with this school of thought, but one of the most important is B. F. Skinner, who applied his concepts to education (1968 THEORETICAL BACKGROUND). The primary result of his work became known as programmed instruction, which is a combination instructional design and motivational design model. It uses the motivational principle of positive reinforcement following correct responses, and it requires that instruction be structured to ensure correct responses to the fullest extent possible (see Markle, 1969 TEXTBOOK, for a review and explication of this approach).

Skinner's instructional design approach was expanded by F. S. Keller (1968 MODEL DESCRIPTION) into a plan for teaching whole courses of instruction. Called the **Personalized System of Instruction** (q.v.) (PSI), or the **Keller Plan** (q.v.), it has many of the features used in programmed instruction. It is a complete instructional management system, and it is grounded in a set of motivational design strategies based on conditioning principles.

In a different approach, Sloane and Jackson (1974 TEXTBOOK) provide a model which describes how basic concepts of conditioning and reinforcement can be used to control the motivation of students. The model also attempts to describe how to move the students from an external reinforcement system to an intrinsically rewarding condition. However, as Deci and others (see Lepper and Greene, 1978 THEORETICAL BACKGROUND) have shown, intrinsic motivation can be decreased by extrinsic reward systems, and can be very difficult to establish initially, or reestablish after being diminished.

Interaction-Centered Models. These models assume that neither the personal nor the environmental assumptions provide an adequate basis for understanding or explaining human motivation. In this approach, sometimes called "social learning theory," or "expectancy-value theory" (see Keller, 1983 RESEARCH SYNTHESIS), human values and innate abilities are seen to both influence and be influenced by environmental circumstances. Currently, interaction-centered models are probably the most widely used in the study of human learning and motivation in an educational context. DeCharms and Muir (1978 RESEARCH SYNTHESIS) and Hunt (Hunt and Sullivan, 1974 THEORETICAL BACKGROUND) have offered theories and reviews of motivational research that focus on the interactions of individual traits with environmental influences on behavior. Environmental influences can include social factors such as teaching style and the manner of using praise (Brophy, 1981 RESEARCH SYNTHESIS).

Working within the general context of expectancy-value theory, deCharms (1968 MODEL DESCRIPTION) developed an applied model with two major variables: achievement motivation representing the value component, and personal causation representing the expectancy component. DeCharm's model is patterned after the work of McClelland and Alschuler, but by including the concept of personal causation, it becomes an interactive model. It is concerned primarily with changing individual behavior to help students feel more confident and more in control of their destinies, and it includes many motivational strategies that can be used in a general instructional design process.

Wlodkowski (1978 MODEL DESCRIPTION) provides one of the first comprehensive, applied approaches to motivation. He includes a large number of motivational factors including both humanistic and behavioral principles, and he divides motivational strategies into six categories: attitudes, needs, stimulation, affect, competence, and reinforcement. He puts these into a process model which specifies things to do at the beginning, during, and at the end of a lesson or module of instruction. His model has many excellent strategy selections, and is of primary benefit as an aid to classroom teachers.

J. M. Keller (1983 RESEARCH SYNTHESIS) has developed a motivational design model that is grounded in expentancy-value theory and has four categories of motivational variables: attention, relevance, confidence, and satisfaction (ARCS). These were derived from a comprehensive review of motivational concepts and research studies. The ARCS model is a problem-solving model which helps a designer identify and solve motivational problems related to the appeal of instruction. It includes strategies related specifically to the design of materials, style of teaching, and overall design of a course (Keller, 1984; Keller and Dodge, 1982 MODEL DESCRIPTION).

Omnibus Models. These models are best described as complete solutions to given instructional goals. They are not motivational design models, but they are included here because they offer excellent examples of motivational strategies in situ. The models sometimes have a theoretical underpinning, but their primary basis is pragmatic in that they incorporate a complete system of teaching and instructional management that is designed to accomplish a specific type of instructional purpose. Motivational strategies are embedded in the totality of these models but are not usually highlighted or labeled as such. Instead, they are listed under the functional category they serve. These might include such things as "getting attention," "clarifying values," "monitoring progress," or "rewarding achievement." These models are helpful to instructional designers concerned with motivation.

Joyce and Weil (1972 MODEL DESCRIPTION) provide the best compilation of these models. They use a consistent format to present sixteen different teaching models which are grouped under one of four categories depending on whether the primary purpose of the model is social interaction, information processing, personal growth, or behavior modification. In three subsequent books (e.g., Weil and Joyce, 1978 MODEL DESCRIPTION) the authors provide more detailed examples of the models in use and instructions for learning to use them.

OBSTACLES TO MOTIVATIONAL DESIGN

There are many problems related to developing a formal approach to the study and practice of motivational design, but two are of particular interest. The first concerns the unstable nature of motivation and is related to the difficulties in establishing a useful theory of motivation. Unlike ability, which is a fairly stable and predictable human characteristic, motivation includes many factors which range from highly transitory states of arousal to reasonably enduring preferences for given types of activities. Furthermore, the intensity of these factors can vary tremendously over short periods of time, and they generally have a nonlinear, "inverted U-curve" relationship to performance. As motivation or arousal increases, the quality and quantity of performance increase to an optimal level. Beyond that, performance begins to deteriorate as motivation continues to increase. This is comparable to moving from a state of boredom through a state of optimal arousal to a state of anxiety. Performance is less than optimal at either end of the curve.

Another aspect of this problem is the multiplicity of motives and goal orientations of individuals. At one level, people tend to have fairly stable orientations and motive profiles. That is, a person with a high need for achievement will tend to prefer predictably different kinds of activities from a person high on need for affiliation. Yet both of these motives can be overridden by a motive, such as the need for physical security, that assumes a higher priority in a given situation. This variability is a challenge to anyone who tries to develop models of motivational design.

The final problem, which is that of measurement, is closely related to the preceding. Just as it is difficult to obtain a functional theory of motivation, it is difficult to measure the important elements of influence and change in motivational design. There are four, and probably more, sets of variables that have to be considered in motivational design. First are the human characteristics that pertain to motivation; second are the design strategies intended to influence motivation; third are the social and environmental conditions that might influence the effectiveness of the motivational strategies; and fourth are consequences, which present special problems. All too often, changes in achievement are used as the dependent measure for motivational studies. It is better to use measures of effort, such as time on task, intensity of effort, or latency of response, because these are direct measures of motivation. Achievement is an indirect measure that is influenced by many nonmotivational factors such as ability, prior knowledge, and instructional design factors. For a more comprehensive discussion of available measures and measurement problems, see Keller (1983 RESEARCH SYNTHESIS), and Keller, Kelly, and Dodge (1978 TEXTBOOK).

CONCLUSIONS

There is little doubt that there is a growing interest in the problem of motivation, both in relation to understanding learners and in relation to motivational design. There are professional organizations in the United States, the Netherlands, and perhaps other countries, that are concerned exclusively with problems of motivation in education, and the number of articles on motivation in educational research journals is growing.

Despite this increased activity, there is still very little work on the specific problem of motivational design. Wlodkowski (1978 MODEL DESCRIPTION) has developed an effective program for helping teachers learn how to help unmotivated students, and Keller (1979 THEORETICAL BACKGROUND; 1983 RESEARCH SYNTHESIS; 1984 MODEL DESCRIPTION) has developed a more theory-based, generic model for identifying motivational strategy needs and options. His model is intended for instructional designers, trainers, and teachers. However, all of this work will benefit from an increase in the number of people who are developing and testing alternative approaches.

The ability of educational designers to create instructional systems that are effective for students who *want* to learn has grown tremendously in the last several decades. Yet there is a lag in knowing how to systematically develop effective motivational components of instruction. Because motivation appears to be a major problem in many school systems, it is likely to receive more research and development in the future.

J. M. Keller

REFERENCES

Model Description

Alschuler, A. S. (1973) *Developing Achievement Motivation in Adolescents: Education for Human Growth*. Englewood Cliffs, N.J.: Educational Technology Publications.

deCharms, R. (1968) *Personal Causation*. New York: Academic Press.

Joyce, B. and Weil, M. (1972) *Models of Teaching*. Englewood Cliffs, N.J.: Prentice-Hall.

Keller, F. S. (1968) "Goodbye Teacher." *Applied Behavior Analysis* 1: 78–79.

Keller, J. M. (1984) "Use of the ARCS Model of Motivation in Teacher Training." In *Aspects of Educational Technology*, ed. K. Shaw. London: Kogan Page.

Keller, J. M. and Dodge, B. (1982) *The ARCS Model of Motivational Strategies for Course Designers and Developers*. Fort Monroe, Va.: U.S. Army Training Developments Institute.

McClelland, D. C. (1965) "Toward a Theory of Motive Acquisition." *American Psychologist* 20: 321–333.

Simon, S. B., Howe, L. W., and Kirschenbaum, H. (1978) *Values Clarification*. New York: Hart Publishing.

Weil, M. and Joyce, B. (1978) *Information Processing Models of Teaching*. Englewood Cliffs, N.J.: Prentice-Hall.

Wlodkowski, R. J. (1978) *Motivation and Teaching*. Washington, D.C.: National Education Association.

Research Synthesis

Brophy, J. (1981) "Teacher Praise: A Functional Analysis." *Review of Educational Research* 51: 5–32.

deCharms, R. and Muir, M. S. (1978) "Motivation: Social Approaches." *Annual Review of Psychology* 29: 91–113.

Keller, J. M. (1983) "Motivational Design of Instruction." In *Instructional Design Theories and Models: An Overview of Their Current Status*, ed. C. M. Reigeluth. New York: Lawrence Erlbaum.

Textbook

Keller, J. M., Kelly, E. A., and Dodge, B. (1978) *Motivation in School: A Practitioner's Guide to Concepts and Measures*. Syracuse, N.Y.: Syracuse University, ERIC Clearinghouse for Information Resources.

Markle, S. M. (1969) *Good Frames and Bad: A Grammar of Frame Writing*. 2d ed. New York: Wiley.

Sloane, H. N. and Jackson, D. A. (1974) *A Guide to Motivating Learners*. Englewood Cliffs, N.J.: Educational Technology Publications.

Weiner, B. (1980) *Human Motivation*. New York: Holt, Rinehart and Winston.

Theoretical Background

Berlyne, D. E. (1965) "Motivational Problems Raised by Exploratory and Epistemic Behavior." In *Psychology: A Study of a Science*, vol. 5, ed. S. Koch. New York: McGraw-Hill.

Hunt, D. E. and Sullivan, E. V. (1974) *Between Psychology and Education*. Hinsdale, Ill.: Dryden Press.

Keller, J. M. (1979) "Motivation and Instructional Design: A Theoretical Perspective." *Journal of Instructional Development* 2 (4): 26–34.

Lepper, M. R. and Greene, D., eds. (1978) *The Hidden Costs of Reward*. Hillsdale, N.J.: Lawrence Erlbaum Associates.

Skinner, B. F. (1968) *The Technology of Teaching*. New York: Appleton-Century-Crofts.

Zuckerman, M. (1971) "Dimensions of Sensation Seeking." *Journal of Consulting and Clinical Psychology* 36: 45–52.

MOTOR SKILLS. Skills that require the body to move, e.g., walking, chewing gum, lathe operation, painting. Bloom, in his taxonomy of objectives, calls these skills "psychomotor." See **Bloom's Taxonomy.**

MOUNTING. See **Dry Mounting; Photography.**

MOUSE. An input device to a computer. As the device is moved around a worktop (e.g., office desk), so a cursor moves around the screen. When the cursor is in the desired position, such as a response square, a button on the mouse is pressed. A similar effect is generally realizable by pressing appropriate keys.

MOVIE. Originally a slang term for cine film, "moving film," now most often used to describe equipment and materials used by amateur filmmakers.

MOVIE MAP. A videodisc which depicts very large numbers of scenes of, e.g., a town, an engine, the human body, etc., thus permitting the student to visually explore the item in question. Interactive use (under computer control) of movie maps allows the user to simulate actual movement to obtain varying views and perspectives.

MOVING COIL MICROPHONE (DYNAMIC MICROPHONE). A microphone in which a signal is generated by a coil moving in a magnetic field. The coil is mounted on a diaphragm between the poles of a permanent magnet. Moving coil microphones are robust and can be made extremely small. They have many applications in all aspects of sound recording. The output **impedance** (q.v.) of moving coil microphones is low. *See* **Microphone Characteristics.**

MOVIOLA. A brand name (now generic) for a picture-viewing device used for film editing. The film moves horizontally between two spools on a table, passing through the optical element which rear-projects the frames onto an angled screen. The speed of movement is under the control of the operator, and facilities for marking and cutting the film are incorporated. *See* **Film Editing.**

MPATI. *See* **Midwest Program of Airborne Television Instruction.**

MSC. *See* **Manpower Services Commission.**

MS-DOS. A microcomputer operating system devised by Microsoft Corporation, widely used especially with IBM-compatible configurations.

MULTIACCESS. The mode of computer use enabling many users to have independent access to a single computer installation at the same time, each one being able to act through her/his remote terminal as if (s)he had the entire machine at her/his disposal. In fact, the machine will only deal with one ''client'' at a time, but theoretically any delays will be very short and hopefully unnoticeable (in practice many such systems are overloaded and delays may reach unacceptable levels).

MULTI-IMAGE. Two or more projected images viewed simultaneously. The intention is to increase the impact and/or aesthetic value of the presentation. *See* **Multiscreen.**

MULTIMEDIA KIT. An inexact term referring to any instructional package not consisting solely of one format. This to say, a book is definitely not a multimedia kit; a film strip with accompanying notes may be.

MULTIPLE-CHOICE QUESTION (MCQ). A question to which there is more than one forced choice. MCQs are used in objective testing, and they can be constructed to test recall, synthesis, or evaluation of concepts. Usually MCQs have four or five possible answers and incorporate distractors, i.e., wrong but plausible answers. *See* **Item Analysis.**

MULTIPLEXER. (1) Part of a telecine arrangement with movable mirrors or prisms set up in such a way as to direct slide and film images into a television camera. (2) Any device permitting several sources to be interfaced with one receiving device, as with the connection of terminals to a mainframe computer.

MULTIPOINT DISTRIBUTION SYSTEMS. A (U.S.) low-powered limited-range television system, offering common carrier facilities in the 2,500 to 2,690MHz frequency range.

MULTISCREEN. Presentation system for film or slide projection in which several projectors are used, each making its own contribution via one of several screens. The technique can provide highly spectacular shows but calls for very sophisticated control equipment (often computerized) so as to ensure appropriate synchronization of the various projectors. *See* **Projection.**

N

NAEB. *See* **National Association of Education Broadcasters.**

NAPLPS. The North American Presentation Level Protocol Syntax. The official North American Videotex Standard approved by ANSI and the CCITT.

NATIONAL ASSOCIATION OF EDUCATIONAL BROADCASTERS. An organization founded in 1925 to serve the professional needs of individuals interested in telecommunications and related fields. Membership now consists of individuals who provide a service in the areas of professional development, information and publications, research and planning. The association supports a wide range of educational broadcasting activities and sponsors a major convention of public telecommunications professionals.

1346 Connecticut Avenue, N.W., Washington, D.C. 20036, U.S.

NATIONAL BEAM. Satellite term referring to a broadcast beam which reaches all of a country; although in the case of a small country this would be referred to as a "spot" (narrowly directional) beam.

NATIONAL CENTRE FOR PROGRAMMED LEARNING (U.K.). A government-financed research unit which operated at the University of Birmingham, United Kingdom, to investigate all aspects of the use of programmed methods. The Centre, under the leadership of G.O.M. Leith, produced a large number of reports and informative papers during the approximate period 1965–1970. By comparison with later official investment in the more glamorous field of computer-assisted learning, the National Centre for Programmed Learning was never funded to an extent which would have permitted it to influence U.K. developments to a significant degree.

NATIONAL COMMITTEE FOR AUDIOVISUAL AIDS IN EDUCATION (U.K.). The U.K. National Committee for Audiovisual Aids in Education (NCAVAE) was established in 1946 by local education authorities with the following terms of reference: (1) the planning of a visual education policy; (2) the collection, collation, and dissemination of information; (3) advice on the supply, selection and maintenance of apparatus; and (4) the training of teachers in the use of visual aids. These terms of reference were later enlarged to include audio and audiovisual aids. The National Committee is composed of representatives of local government and teachers organizations, and close liaison is maintained with the Department of Education and Science and with the teaching profession.

The Information Department is responsible for disseminating information concerning audiovisual equipment and materials.

The Demonstration Center houses a collection of over 200 pieces of audiovisual equipment, constantly updated by the manufacturers and distributors. Comparisons between different products and evaluation of potential usefulness can be made by teachers and lecturers visiting the department.

The Resource Center contains over 10,000 audiovisual items including filmstrips, slides, tapes, records, cassettes, multimedia packages, wall charts, etc. Different storage methods are employed so that visitors can browse and evaluate materials and compare methods of storing them.

The Experimental Development Unit tests for performance, construction, and safety, and reports all significant contributions by manufacturers to the variety of audiovisual equipment available. It cooperates with similar bodies in Germany and France to ensure international acceptance of certain standards and give wider coverage to the equipment tested. The unit's Technical Reports are sent directly to all U.K. education authorities' offices and are also available on subscription to other organizations.

254 Belsize Road, London NW8 4BY, U.K.

NATIONAL DEFENSE EDUCATION ACT (NDEA). The success of the Soviet Union in launching its Sputnik satellite in 1957 had a profound effect on American education. In particular, Congress passed in 1958 the National Defense Education Act, which released immense funds for educational research. Very many of the significant developments in educational technology can be traced directly to the impetus provided by the NDEA.

NATIONAL DEVELOPMENT PROGRAMME IN COMPUTER-ASSISTED LEARNING (U.K.). A government-funded R & D program carried out in the 1970s.

NATIONAL EDUCATIONAL CLOSED CIRCUIT TELEVISION ASSOCIATION (NECCTA) (U.K.). *See* **Educational Television Association.**

NATIONAL SOCIETY FOR PERFORMANCE AND INSTRUCTION (NSPI). Founded in the 1960s as the National Society for Programmed Instruction, the society seeks to advance education and training through the collection, development, and diffusion of information concerned with the process of developing instructional materials. A journal *(NSPI Journal)* is published.

NSPI, 1126 Sixteenth Street NW, Washington, D.C. 20036, U.S.

NATIONAL TECHNOLOGICAL UNIVERSITY. School providing master's degrees to remote students via satellite links to workplaces. NTU is based in Fort Collins, Colorado, and utilizes faculty from all around the United States.

NATIONAL TELEVISION SYSTEM COMMITTEE (NTSC). The body that sets standards for the television signals used in the United States and some other countries. In particular, the initials NTSC are frequently used to denote the system of color television in use in North America, Japan, and elsewhere, which is incompatible with the PAL and SECAM systems. In the NTSC format, each picture has two fields of 262 1/2 lines (525 lines to a frame), with 30 frames transmitted per second. Color information is provided by the phase (timing relationship) of a color signal added at 3.58MHz above the bottom of the video signal. *See* **PAL.**

NBC. National Broadcasting Company, a major U.S. broadcasting organization.

NCAVAE (U.K.). *See* **National Committee for Audiovisual Aids in Education.**

NCET (U.K.). *See* **Council for Educational Technology.**

NDEA. *See* **National Defense Education Act.**

NDPCAL (U.K.). *See* **National Development Programme in Computer-Assisted Learning.**

NECCTA (U.K.). *See* **Educational Television Association.**

NECK MICROPHONE. A microphone on a neck halter so that it can be positioned near the mouth. The technique of providing a speaker or group of speakers with neck microphones allows a good signal level to be obtained without interference from ambient sounds. It allows a lecturer the freedom to move around which would not be available with a fixed-stand microphone.

In recent practice, small clip-on microphones have come to be preferred.

NETWORK. An interconnection of microcomputers and peripheral devices (e.g., a printer, a hard disk), each remote from the others, exchanging data and sharing facilities as necessary to perform the specific function of the network.

NETWORK ANALYSIS. A management technique used and devised originally by the U.S. Polaris Missile Project. It was used to schedule, plan, and organize the complex items in the missile project. It has applications in curriculum development and the planning of syllabi. *See* **Critical Path Analysis; Information Mapping.**

NEUTRAL DENSITY FILTER. An optical device. A light filter that reduces the intensity of light without changing the spectral distribution of the light.

NEW TECHNOLOGY AND EDUCATION. The new information technologies have the potential to improve many problems inherent in the traditional model of education, and the development of sophisticated instructional devices may be an essential step in industrial countries' emerging transformation to a knowledge-based economy. Clarifying how these technologies can best be used and exploring implementation strategies such as "educational information utilities" will be key steps in the adoption process. Over the next two decades, promising technologies include intelligent machine-based tutors and coaches, "cognition enhancers" incorporating **artificial intelligence** (q.v.) approaches, interactive videodisc, and computer-telecommunications synthesis devices. As with any powerful technology, careful attention must be given to potential side effects and to overcoming barriers to implementation.

TECHNOLOGY AND EDUCATIONAL REFORM

Educational practices have changed little over the past century, despite massive shifts in other aspects of civilization. During the last three decades, public concern about instructional quality has increased as the gap between what schools produce and what advanced industrial societies need has steadily widened. As a variety of studies have documented (National Commission on Excellence, 1983 EXAMPLE), the traditional educational paradigm is plagued by the following problems:

1. Only a small percentage of pupils develop higher-order thinking skills, and most adults remember few of the facts they learned as students. A significant proportion of students leave school functionally illiterate in the skills needed to be productive workers and citizens.
2. Schools are held accountable for the accomplishment of all instructional outcomes; society's other educational agents (families, communities, workplace, and media) have few responsibilities. Without the involvement of these other educational agents, schools cannot succeed in transmitting the complex skills and knowledge needed for economic and cultural development.
3. Instruction is labor-intensive; improvements in classroom outcomes can occur only through slow, politically difficult, and expensive reforms such as upgrading teacher qualifications or halving class sizes.
4. Attracting and keeping quality teachers is hard because of low salaries, poor working conditions, and lack of respect from society.

Many nations have become increasingly dissatisfied with the results of the traditional educational approach, and innovations to improve the cost-effectiveness and quality of schooling are continually being attempted. Since World War II, when people became aware of the power of technology, many reform movements have involved substituting an instructional device for some part of the teacher's duties. For example, in the late 1950s educational television was seen as the solution to problems with pupil motivation and achievement; a decade later, programmed instruction using computer terminals was thought to be a "teacher-proof" way to improve student outcomes. Through the 1970s, technological innovations in education were characterized by sweeping claims, low cost-effectiveness, and rapid disillusionment. (Of course, the same discouraging statement could be made about nontechnological attempts at educational reform!)

Now, advocates of microcomputers in classrooms are struggling to avoid repeating this cycle. At the same time, the new information technologies are transforming manufacturing and office work, and fluency in using these devices is becoming an essential skill for many types of occupations. Forecasts indicate that the power-cost ratio of computers will increase for another two decades, that the coming fusion of telecommunications and computers will produce devices with powerful new attributes, and that the advent of software based on **artificial intelligence** (q.v.) will give machines another dimension of useful capabilities (OTA, 1985 BACKGROUND READING).

As the information technologies continue to evolve and to reshape society, will a technology-intensive educational approach emerge that could resolve the problems of the traditional model of schooling? Given the failures of instructional technology historically, what attributes would these educational devices need to be successful? Which new technologies seem likely candidates to have these necessary characteristics? What side effects and hidden consequences might result from adopting an approach which heavily utilizes instructional devices? What types of barriers may prevent a technology-intensive educational model from being implemented?

These are important questions, but a deeper issue must be examined before these other concerns can be addressed. Two decades from now, when many aspects of the developed nations have been reshaped by advanced information technologies, will what society needs from schools necessitate the use of educational technologies? For example, are instructional devices essential to preparing students for a future in which most jobs will require expertise with sophisticated information tools?

THE PROMISE OF INSTRUCTIONAL TECHNOLOGY

Historically, the major reason used to argue for instructional devices has been increased efficiency in accomplishing traditional educational goals. For example, those in favor of **computer-assisted instruction** (q.v.) have drawn analogies to how other institutions have used technology to increase productivity (Willett, Swanson, and Nelson, 1979 EXAMPLE). Compared to the impacts of automation in factories or word processing in offices, innovations targeted to improving teachers (rather than substituting machines) have produced only small gains in the cost-effectiveness of schooling. Hence, many believe, the primary challenge for instructional technologists is to create devices and courseware which can fit easily into the standard classroom, raise test scores, and lower per pupil expenditures.

Microcomputers using computer-assisted instruction (CAI) courseware may have the potential to accomplish this mission—if difficulties with funding, teacher training, the availability of quality software, curriculum integration, and resistance to adoption can be resolved. Thus, advocates of CAI are claiming that additional resources to resolve these problems are all that is needed to perfect a technology-intensive educational model, while others argue that small computers and CAI software will fail and fade as have previous waves of instructional technology.

However, a more fundamental issue is whether productivity gains in achieving traditional instructional goals are the major promise and optimal usage of educational technology. The problems of the current schools go much deeper than issues of efficiency; an ideal educational device would

1. promote mastery of higher-order cognitive skills and increase the usage in adult life of knowledge learned in school;
2. facilitate the participation of parents, community, workplace, and media in education;
3. increase the cost-effectiveness of instruction;
4. enable schools to be more responsive to the changing needs of society; and
5. improve the working conditions and status of teachers.

If gains in cost-effectiveness for teaching descriptive knowledge and lower-level cognitive skills are all that advanced instructional devices can offer, then a technology-intensive educational reform movement is likely to fall short even if its innovations are successful.

As will be discussed later, many believe that artificial intelligence–based devices which combine the capabilities of telecommunications and computers can accomplish all the goals above (Wenger, 1986 EXAMPLE). Intelligent machine-based tutors and coaches are more capable of tailoring their interactions with learners than CAI software, which is limited by the large number of screens of information which must be prepared and linked to teach complex subjects in an individualized manner. However, even a technology-intensive approach targeted to a wide range of the traditional educational model's problems would not encompass the most important reason why new instructional technologies may transform education.

Both the "increased efficiency" and the "overall improvement of schools" rationales for instructional technology make the assumption that the goals of education are likely to remain static over the next few decades. However, a growing group of economists, business leaders, and educators believe that such a future is unlikely. As will be discussed below, the developed nations seem to be moving from an industrial economy centered on standardized, automated manufacturing to a knowledge-based economy focused on customized, value-added products created by partnerships between skilled workers and intelligent information tools (Ayres, 1984 BACKGROUND READING).

That this evolution will occur is a matter of debate; some economists and educators see instead a coming intensification of automation and a gradual decline in the skills prospective workers need (Carnoy and Levin, 1985 CONTRADICTORY RESEARCH). Preparing for such a future would require few changes in educational systems, and a transformation to a technology-intensive instructional model would be unlikely. While this "intensive automation" scenario is plausible (especially in developing nations building a strong industrial base), most experts believe that a value-added economy is the next step in the evolution of the developed countries.

In a knowledge-based economic future, the fundamental definitions of educational efficiency, effectiveness, and quality would shift as the outcomes society needs from schools alter. For example, as sophisticated workplace tools become sufficiently "intelligent" to assume many job roles now performed by people, a new definition of human intelligence might emerge based on what machines could not do. This would have enormous implications for instructional goals and the role of technology in education.

Education is intrinsically future-oriented, especially the schooling of young children; the skills elementary school students learn today will not be used in occupations until the next century. Thus, determining the best goal for the evolution of educational technology requires forecasting the instructional outcomes that the developed nations will want formal education to produce a generation from now. (Developing countries will likely retain industrial age educational goals and methods for several more decades.) As industrial nations have matured, the goals of schools have not greatly changed from generation to generation compared to the transformation that occurred with the shift from agricultural to industrial economies. Will the next two decades produce such sweeping changes in developed countries that another transformation in educational outcomes will be needed?

SHIFTS IN SOCIETY'S GOALS FOR EDUCATION

Since the advent of industrialization, the predominant goal of instruction has been mastery of descriptive knowledge and rote problem-solving skills. Progress toward this goal is assessed by pupil performance on standardized multiple-choice tests; pedagogical methods rely heavily on group exposure to concepts followed by exercises to build low-level cognitive processes. Some societal dissatisfaction with the performance of graduates is due to the inadequacies of schools in building these basic skills, but increasingly nations are recognizing that a deeper type of intellectual development is also needed to produce productive workers and citizens.

In the developed countries, a massive shift may be beginning from an industrial economy to a knowledge-based workplace built on cognitive partnerships between people and information tools. Such an evolution would be driven by the global marketplace now emerging; in this new economic "ecology," each nation is seeking a specialized niche based on its financial, human, and natural resources. Developed countries which no longer have easily available natural resources and cheap labor cannot compete with rising Third World nations in manufacturing standardized industrial commodities; the advent of biotechnology will only intensify this erosion of economic strength (Reich, 1983 BACKGROUND READING). However, a nation with considerable technological expertise, an advanced industrial base, and a relatively educated citizenry might seek to develop an economy which uses sophisticated workers and information tools to make customized, value-added products.

One way of understanding this contrast is to compare how information technology has changed the job roles of the supermarket checker and the typist. Many supermarkets now have bar code readers; rather than finding the price on each item and punching that into the register, the checker needs only to pass the goods over the scanner. Efficiency and productivity have increased, but the food you buy tastes the same as before, and fewer skills are needed to do the job.

In contrast, substituting a word processor/information networking device for a typewriter completely alters a secretary's function. To use the information tool to its full capability of customizing data to the individual needs of a variety of recipients, the clerical role must shift from "keyboarding" to utilizing data base, text manipulation, communications, and graphics applications. The job now demands higher-order cognitive skills to extract and tailor knowledge from the enormous information capacity of the tool.

With the evolution of artificial intelligence, job performance tools will begin to include embedded models of skilled performance, such as expert "coaches" which can suggest better strategies for accomplishing a task. For example, a word processor might contain a machine-based coach which would understand the full range of formatting commands available and would monitor user actions, examining to see whether the best approach to structuring the document is being utilized. When these expert decision aids are available, the thinking skills required of the human role in the partnership will become even more sophisticated to tap the full power of the intelligent tool (Dede, 1987 BACKGROUND READING).

Current work in cognitive science suggests that computers and people have complementary intellectual strengths; each can supply what the other lacks. For example, advanced information tools are adept at standardized problem solving because of their large short-term memory and rapid symbolic manipulation speed. As a result, intelligent devices are beginning to replace human workers in accomplishing complex but well-structured tasks. People, however, are more adept than artificial intelligence devices at recognizing and solving unusual problems in unstructured situations, due to their superior ways of storing and reasoning about knowledge.

Complex work roles involve a mixture of structured and unstructured decisions, and partnerships between people and intelligent tools seem likely for jobs which create value-added, customized products and services. Current trends in office and factory automation (as well as national problems with debt and balance of trade) make the emergence of economic development policies which would promote a knowledge-based workplace a plausible alternative future. What occupational characteristics would a nation with such an economy expect its educational agents to develop in learners?

CHANGES IN INSTRUCTIONAL OUTCOMES

These person-tool partnerships would require more worker intelligence than present occupations, since the human cognitive strengths in the partnership involve skills such as creativity, flexibility, decision making given incomplete data, complex pattern recognition, information evaluation/synthesis, and holistic thinking. Such higher-order mental attributes might become a new definition of human intelligence, as basic cognitive skills would increasingly shift to the intelligent tool's portion of the partnership.

Future workers would still need fundamental knowledge—one cannot master higher-order skills without a foundation of lower-order processes—but the goal of teaching basics would shift from performance fluency to providing a cognitive underpinning for sophisticated problem recognition and unusual problem solving. Methods of educational assessment would shift from charting mastery of descriptive knowledge to evaluating attainment of higher-order skills.

The changes required in educational effectiveness would go beyond shifts in cognitive skills; the transition to a knowledge-based workplace would also alter the affective and social goals of schools. For example, in countries beginning to implement person-tool partnerships, employers are finding that workers hired on the basis of their skills in creativity, flexibility, and decision making given incomplete data do not like blindly taking orders. These employees apply their cognitive skills to the organization of power and responsibility within the workplace and resent hierarchical authority structures. As a result, in Japan, companies are implementing "Theory Z" management styles; in Europe, unions are focusing on "economic democracy"; and, in the United States, organizational development experts are experimenting with alternative models of transhierarchical power distribution (Ouchi, 1981 ILLUSTRATION OF A POINT).

Whatever the resolution chosen, workers must have

skills of cooperation, compromise, and group decision making to operate in authority systems that combine the speed and accountability of hierarchy with the decentralization and democracy of knowledge-based organizational action. In a future of person-tool partnerships, the development of these affective and interpersonal attributes would be an important measure of educational effectiveness and would require altered classroom organizational structures and goals.

AN ALTERNATIVE, TECHNOLOGY-INTENSIVE EDUCATIONAL MODEL

If society demands increasingly more complex instructional outcomes from its educational agents, how can this be accomplished? Already, the traditional model of instruction is severely stressed; in what ways can schools be altered and other educational agents linked to meet these emerging challenges? A partial answer may be found in the technological changes discussed earlier which are creating new definitions of school effectiveness.

Into the next century, five major themes in the development of instructional information technologies will be:

Individualization. The evolution of narrowcasting, interactive videodisc, and **videotex** (q.v.) all indicate rapidly growing capabilities for tailoring information to user needs. Over time, the passive, spectator role for students will be increasingly replaced by opportunities for directed response to queries, for exploration (e.g., "surrogate travel/experience" via interactive videodisc), and for creative interchange with artificial intelligence software. Simultaneously, networks capable of interconnecting all users and transmitting huge amounts of information among them will gradually appear.

Intermixing. The growing shift to use of digital code will allow the increasing synthesis of data, video, audio, and software signals. The Tower of Babel problems now prevalent with incompatible devices will gradually diminish, and telecommunications will become the unifying medium for all information technologies. Combining the attributes of the computer, television, radio, videodisc, copier, telephone, and printing press will produce new tools with great power for facilitating learning. Because of this synthesis of technologies, the struggle for control of the information economy will intensify among corporations marketing computers, telecommunications devices, and radio/television/hi-fi equipment.

Quality. Capabilities never before possible are becoming economically feasible because of advances in processing power, memory storage, and delivery systems. Very high resolution; freeze-frame, zoom, and multiple images; freedom from electromagnetic interference; and portability all will combine to enhance the power of the medium to educate students. Just as talkies, stereo, and color expanded the experience of users, so will these new attributes contribute to the motivational and instructional force of programming.

Cost Decreases. In contrast to most technologies, information tools have become less expensive year by year for equivalent power. For example, the amount of information which can be processed by computers has been doubling every two years per unit cost and time for the past four decades, and this trend will likely continue until the year 2000. Fiber-optic cable is cheaper than copper cable, smaller, lighter, more reliable and secure, immune to electromagnetic interference, and has much greater capacity. Optical scanners which two years ago cost $2000 (U.S.) now retail for $7 (U.S.). Because of these and other technical advances, the proportion of the population which can afford access to high-quality information services is steadily expanding.

Multiple Options. The range of technologies by which users can choose to receive a service is growing rapidly. For example, in the near future educational programming will be deliverable by broadcast, one-way cable, two-way cable, **direct broadcasting satellite** (q.v.), **instructional television fixed service** (q.v.) (ITFS), low-power television, **high-definition television** (q.v.) (HDTV), digital television, videotape, and videodisc. Manufacturers, suppliers of services, and consumers alike are confused by this plethora of alternatives and uncertain as to how to invest their resources.

An "ecology" of information technologies is emerging, in which each tool has its own niche determined in part by cost, attributes, installed base, and the availability of quality programming. The size of the total "information ecosystem" is growing, as expenditures on information technologies continue to rise faster than overall personal consumption. The shape of each niche is shifting, both as new technologies with greater capabilities or lower costs cut into the market share of older technologies and as the boundaries between technologies increasingly blur. Instructional telecommunications/computing will be on the cutting edge of all five of these shifts.

One type of evolution takes place when quantitative changes in capabilities result in a qualitative shift in attributes. When slides could be flashed on the screen quickly enough, the illusion of motion was created, and the "movie" became a new medium. Automobiles added an order of magnitude of speed to horses, then airplanes added another order of magnitude; these quantitative gains led to qualitative leaps in the structure of civilization. The themes discussed above describe quantitative advances, but a different type of evolution is also occurring based on completely new attributes from artificial intelligence. Educational devices incorporating AI would "understand" what, whom, and how they were teaching and could therefore tailor content and method to the needs of an individual learner without being limited to a repertoire of prespecified responses, as is CAI.

Now, limitations on the power of the computers that schools can afford and on our knowledge of how to program instructional devices restrict their usefulness to simple educational tasks (e.g., drill and practice, tutorial, simulation, demonstration). However, as the speed and memory of inexpensive computers increase and as advances in computer science, cognitive psychology, and artificial intelligence allow the development of intelligent courseware, the role that instructional devices can play in schools will greatly expand. In particular, five types of "cognition enhancers" may emerge in the next decade:

1. intelligent tutors (which use the Socratic method and understand what, whom, and how they are teaching);
2. intelligent coaches (which provide a model of expert performance in a learning-by-doing situation, intervening based on a pedagogical strategy of hints and "frontier" knowledge);
3. "idea processors" (which facilitate building and manipulating a sophisticated, nonlinear web of interconnected concepts);
4. "microworlds" (which create limited alternative variations of reality [e.g., a universe in which the force of gravity alters in different ways at the learner's option] as a means for developing an understanding of complex phenomena); and
5. "empowering environments" (e.g., intelligent word processors, data bases, spreadsheets, graphics tools, music construction sets).

In combination, these instructional functions are powerful enough to extend significantly the capabilities of teacher and learner (Brown, 1985 FURTHER DETAIL).

In this new model of schooling, the curriculum would be divided into two parts: *training* and *education*. Material which has a limited range of right answers to questions is *training* (e.g., basic arithmetic operations [just one right answer to 7 × 9] or decoding words [only one correct spelling, perhaps two or three possible meanings and pronunciations]). The beginning portions of most subjects and the advanced parts of some (e.g., accounting) are predominantly training. In contrast, *education* is the portion of the curriculum in which a question could have many possible right answers, or the correct answer is not known, or the question is not meaningful in terms of "right" and "wrong" responses. The advanced parts of many subjects are education; some fields (human relations, creative writing, citizenship) are predominantly education.

Emerging information tools have no significant potential for stand-alone education; the range of right answers is too wide to be recognized, and the device does not itself have the cognitive strengths requisite for the new definition of intelligence. The education portion of the curriculum would be taught in a teacher-tool instructional model much as now (groups of students sharing and building knowledge with the facilitation of an expert educator). However, information tools would add to the teacher's capabilities to present and develop concepts. For example, as a means of promoting involvement and individualization, the interactive videodisc could be used for "surrogate travel" (e.g., a student could "walk" through an art museum, choosing which paintings to see and the order, angle, and duration with which they are viewed). Also, "cognition enhancers" such as "idea processors," "microworlds," and intelligent "empowering environments" could aid pupils in refining complex cognitive skills.

However, the training portion of the curriculum would be done primarily by intelligent tutors and coaches. Instructional devices will never surpass the abilities of a skilled educator working one-on-one, but are becoming increasingly efficient and cost-effective compared to a teacher attempting to train 20 to 30 pupils simultaneously. Training is best done in an individualized and interactive manner, and intelligent information technologies can recognize a limited range of right answers and provide guidance on how to correct common mistakes. By using a combination of teachers and tools, schools can more effectively accomplish both training and education: instructional devices providing the basic skills; and teachers building a mastery of complex occupational, citizenship, and ethical concepts on this foundation.

Over the next decade, advances in information technology will change other aspects of schooling as well. Administrator-tool partnerships will allow policy setting based on more detailed data, and knowledge-based computer systems may give site decision makers the ability to consult "mechanized experts" as competent on specialized problems as international authorities. Direct broadcast satellites and read-only-memory compact optical disks will greatly increase educators' capabilities for low-cost dissemination of instruction and information. When coupled with the trend toward transhierarchical decision-making structures, all these innovations would allow each person associated with the educational process—parent, teacher, employer, administrator, learner

—more data and increased communication to use in shaping instructional outcomes.

Of course, research advances in artificial intelligence and cognitive science are crucial to achieving the sophisticated instructional devices discussed above (Dede, 1986 FURTHER DETAIL). Investing the resources needed to move beyond CAI to intelligent computer-assisted instruction (ICAI) is essential to achieving this future, nor will some technology-peripheral improvement of the present educational model be sufficient to sustain a knowledge-based economy. Development of the higher-order cognitive skills needed for partnerships between people and intelligent tools can be achieved only through sophisticated, individualized instruction (Bloom, 1984 THEORETICAL BACKGROUND), which CAI cannot provide. No variation of the traditional model of education could achieve this goal either, both because of expense (much higher teacher salaries and teacher-pupil ratios would be needed) and because students need to develop cognitive partnerships with information technologies early on if they are to develop fluency in using these devices.

If a technology-intensive paradigm for instruction were to be implemented, what types of new delivery systems for educational services might evolve? Major information technology corporations are competing to devise packages for the education market which combine hardware, courseware, information tools, and data. A development which seems to be emerging is the concept of a "utility" for instructional services (Dede, 1985 FURTHER DETAIL).

EDUCATIONAL INFORMATION UTILITIES

Some companies specialize in decentralized delivery of information: newspaper publishers, television stations, and phone companies are information "utilities." Information utilities have a more complex market than corporations delivering physical products. Everyone wants pure water; but individual consumers have widely varying preferences about the proportion of news, sports, weather, or recipes they desire in the local paper. Determining whether the electricity being delivered meets basic standards of voltage and cycles per second is fairly easy; monitoring the quality of television news for bias, inaccuracy, or even its contribution to informed citizenship is much more difficult and controversial. Yet clients of information utilities need protection as much as do consumers of natural gas.

Now, as the developed countries move toward knowledge-based economies, information is increasingly becoming a marketable commodity; and new technologies capable of great economies of scale in delivering data to consumers are being developed. One possible "mutation" in the "ecology" of information tools would be a utility—comparable to the electric, gas, or water company—which would supply clients with equipment and software to access enormous amounts of information in the form of data bases, computer programs, electronic mail networks, and the like. Such a utility might use any one of a number of delivery methods (e.g., optical disks, videotex, dedicated satellite channels, and subcarriers on radio or television broadcasts with a phone modem backlink from user to sender).

In our rapidly changing society, people need ways quickly to filter information from data, knowledge from information, wisdom from knowledge. Essential to this process are two factors: access to a wide variety of data, and tools/training for screening out "meaning" from "noise." An information utility would supply both of these commodities on a decentralized basis to clients (in this case, to educational institutions). Access to a wide variety of data bases would give clients of such an educational utility many possible sources of detailed information, ranging from historical copies of newspapers to compilations of research, from stock market results to publishers' listings. This aspect of the service would be analogous to an electronic library.

However, users could also download computer programs into their terminals; these would span a spectrum of applications from computer-assisted instruction to management software, from "empowering environments" (such as sophisticated word processors) to computer languages like PASCAL or Logo. This facet of the utility would be similar to having a storehouse of cognitive tools.

Finally, educational information utilities could offer limited interactive services among users, depending on what type of backlink (phone, modem, cable) between client and distribution center was used. For example, electronic mail could be sent from a campus to the state education agency; this feature of the utility would be like a telegraph service.

Any educational information utility, regardless of its delivery system or degree of service aggregation, should offer its clients two fundamental benefits: convenience and cost cutting. As with other types of utilities, one advantage to consumers is major economies of scale; if many institutions are part of an educational utility, their collective negotiating power for discounts on machines and courseware licenses becomes considerable. The more turnkey the services that the utility provides, the larger the savings to consumers—assuming that the utility passes on its purchasing advantages to clients rather than accumulating excess profits (as other types of utilities have been known to do).

Also, rather than worry about potential hardware incompatibilities, the possible collapse of information technology manufacturers, or the acquisition of site copying rights for courseware, sites can simply pay a monthly fee and let the utility handle these concerns. An indirect benefit of aggregating the currently fragmented education market is that more hardware manufacturers and software vendors may be willing—given a predictable purchasing base—to produce products specialized to instructional needs. Moreover, to the extent that clients of an educational utility have little incentive for software piracy (so long as usage billings are reasonable), expensive and controversial methods of courseware copy protection may become outmoded.

All this suggests that information utilities may be a very positive innovation in education. However, educational information utilities could conceivably have considerable disadvantages and risks. One problem is lack of flexibility: hardware purchased from turnkey services will only work when subscribing to that utility, forcing consumers to use its services even if quality declines. Once schools have made a substantial, locked-in investment in equipment, training, and curriculum modification, monthly prices for utility services could potentially be raised to the point that what once appeared a bargain would become a financial liability.

Moreover, institutions have direct access only to whatever data and computer programs their utility provides. Not all information is equal, and some very useful software might not be available via a particular educational utility, making its integrated usage problematic for that site. Particularly in the start-up phase, when its installed base is small, a utility might find that convincing all the best courseware companies to participate would be a difficult task.

Also, being on the cutting edge of any innovation carries inherent risks. The costs to early subscribers to an educational utility could be high until a critical mass of clients is reached. If multiple, alternative utilities vie for market share, one is likely to dominate eventually; and consumers who used the unsuccessful competitors may face an expensive and frustrating conversion process.

Overall, educational information utilities seem a promising idea which could alleviate many current problems with technological delivery of instructional and library services. Moreover, usage of data bases and electronic networks in educational settings will help to prepare students for similar tools in the future workplace. A decade from now, one of the major corporate markets for schools could well be an information utility.

However, what technology educational information utilities will use for delivering data and courseware to classrooms and how turnkey their services will be are still open questions. Also, the early attempts by corporations to market these utilities illustrate the tension between optimal uses of instructional technology and maximum profits from selling these devices. Implementing any technology-intensive model may create unforeseen side effects if the institutional implications of the new approach are not examined carefully in advance.

LIKELY CONSEQUENCES OF A TECHNOLOGY-INTENSIVE APPROACH

The two most common errors made in technological forecasting and assessment are to overestimate the speed of diffusion of an innovation and to underestimate its eventual consequences and side effects. What unintended impacts might result from implementing a technology-intensive educational model?

One probable outcome from the growing use of information technologies throughout society is a shift in the attributes of students. Today's youngsters are the first generation to have information technologies as part of their environment from earliest childhood, as previous generations had the telephone or the automobile or the airplane. Long range, the effects of sophisticated telecommunications and computers on cognitive style, personality characteristics, and social skills may be profound; the best historical analogy to document this assertion is the impact of television. Three decades after the television first became a part of family life, individual values and social interaction have been dramatically altered because of its influence. Many of these shifts have pathological aspects, indicating the subtle and unintended power that a frequently used entertainment/education device can exert.

For example, numerous studies have shown that children's attitudes and expressions of violence are affected by the television programs that they watch. In young people especially, television plays a major role in socialization. Norms for successful and acceptable behavior are gained not only from peers and parents but also from the dramas portrayed on frequently watched programs. The level of violence in most cartoons and police shows has been criticized by many groups, who feel that sociopathic and deviant responses may develop in some children (especially given that many youngsters spend more time viewing television that attending school, playing with friends, or interacting with adults).

Also, television has altered the interpersonal dynamics of families. Time that was once spent in group discussion now is lost sitting as isolated spectators at a common entertainment. Some of the pathologies in families that have increased over the last three decades (high divorce rates, teenage pregnancies, drug use, physical abuse) may stem in part from these reduced interaction patterns—or at least may be worsened by them.

Cognitive style may be altered by the information technologies as well. Teachers report that this generation of children has a very short attention span and expects a continual mixture of entertainment with learning. The speed with which people can process incoming information seems to have increased as the information technologies have become more sophisticated: contrast the pace of action in silent movies to that of television shows today.

Thus, the television has altered intellectual and interpersonal dynamics. It seems probable that computers and sophisticated telecommunications will also have significant impact on individual values and familial dynamics as these devices become commonplace. Interactive information tools allow the user to be a participant, shaper, creator. This opportunity to design and control one's own universe is very seductive to most people, especially given that many feel as if they have little power over their lives and their interactions with others (Turkle, 1984 BACKGROUND READING).

Preliminary studies indicate that home microcomputers have a greater range of impacts than the television; depending on how the computer is used, family interaction can increase or decrease. In some households, the computer is used primarily by one individual (usually male) in an isolated setting; in others, the machine is centrally located, used by several people simultaneously, and bridges generation and gender gaps (Dede and Gottlieb, 1985 FURTHER DETAIL).

This flexibility is likely to be characteristics of the next generation of information technologies; computers and telecommunications devices will be "double-edged swords" capable of shaping user attitudes towards extroversion or introversion, socialization or deviance, creativity or conformity, depending on their design. The challenge for corporations, information technology manufacturers, software developers, educators, and parents is to promote a type of usage by children, students, families, and workers which increases individual human potential and collective well-being. As discussed earlier, building skills of cooperation, compromise, and group decision making will be particularly important.

A second type of consequence which will flow from adoption of a technology-intensive educational model is shifts in institutional roles, such as changes in the school library. No longer will learning resource centers be predominantly depositories of books, films, and other forms of data; with emerging storage media, any student can have thousands of volumes on a few optical disks, including unified indices which allow very rapid key-word searches for specific information.

Instead, the role of the library will become to teach students how to filter knowledge from multiple information sources (rather than how to find data). Personnel will model how to create effective cognitive partnerships with intelligent data bases, simulations, tutors, and other empowering environments. As discussed earlier, a gradual divergence in instructional role may occur, with teachers increasingly responsible for education and learning resource centers for training.

Also, an "applied educational science" could emerge from the advances in the quality of educational research discussed earlier. Cognitive psychology, ergonomics (studies of human-machine partnerships), and educational research all would benefit greatly from detailed empirical knowledge about teaching/learning, which could be synthesized from data collected by instructional technology. Comparable gains in educational theory using information collected solely from human instruction would be prohibitively expensive; thus, the emerging information technologies offer the promise of a fundamental breakthrough in understanding the workings of the mind.

Other types of side effects which might occur with the implementation of a technology-intensive educational approach include

—a centralization of educational financing and courseware production

—a decentralization and decredentialization of the learning environment

—a privatization of the educational enterprise

—new diagnostic, assessment, and evaluation strategies

—a different type of person attracted to the various educational professions

—a revolution in teacher training and certification

If new approaches are implemented without careful thought, the undesirable side effects from the changes mentioned above could outweigh the benefits (Dede, 1981 FURTHER DETAIL). For example, if the advantages of instructional technology are distributed unequally to students, educational equity may be decreased rather than enhanced. Decisions made now, when use of these technologies is just beginning, will be very influential in shaping consequences later when habit and tradition are well established. (Of course, this discussion is assuming that a technology-intensive model of instruction could be implemented, despite the resistance to change which has kept the traditional educational paradigm stable for so long.)

BARRIERS TO EDUCATIONAL EVOLUTION

Historically, the use of information technologies in schools has been restricted by three factors (other than the very limited capabilities these devices have had in the past). Attempts to innovate with information technology have been less successful than expected because:

1. Teachers were often not trained to use new instructional devices; as a result, educational applications were unsophisticated and sometimes counterproductive.
2. Courseware was often of low quality and seldom capable of achieving complex instructional objectives.
3. Academic reward systems were not geared to encouraging teachers' use of technology; institutional funding formulas were not directed toward promoting productivity through machine-based delivery of services.

All three of these remain potential traps for educational institutions seeking to pioneer in instructional applications of the new information technologies, and parallel problems exist for administrative applications.

An analogy can be drawn between historical utilization of instructional devices by teachers and the failure of the post-Sputnik science curricula to achieve significant usage in the American public schools. The U.S. government spent hundreds of millions of dollars in the late 1950s and early 1960s developing improved elementary and secondary school curricula in physics, chemistry, biology, earth science, and engineering as a means toward reducing a perceived gap between American and Soviet technical manpower. However, after some initial success in incorporating these new programs into public schools, teachers quickly returned to their previous instructional methods and materials. The new curricula were effective, but "teachers teach as they were taught," and insufficient staff development had been done to prepare them for the new approaches.

Similarly, teachers learn, by example, to use noninteractive technologies such as overhead and movie projectors; but their training in instructional devices has been insufficient to prepare them for using microcomputers, interactive telecommunications devices, or videodiscs. Established insights in the application of information technology to education have not been systematically communicated to teachers; as a result, the new methods have been perceived as threatening, time-consuming to learn, and of insufficient value to warrant their usage. Certainly, instructional devices do not work well if used in ways similar to conventional teaching (e.g., the "talking heads" approach to instructional television). Corporations have found that the investment required for staff development in technology utilization is more than justified in productivity returns, but educators have often failed to follow this successful model.

Once programming is developed, delivery systems for large-scale dissemination of instruction to students must be in place; otherwise, the costs of courseware development will not be recovered and new capital to create more materials will not be generated. Historically, some schools have tried small-scale, limited applications and found them to be too expensive; the successful innovation projects have been those in which the size of the client population was sufficiently large that production costs could be distributed over many students. Fortunately, through such innovations as information utilities, dropping hardware costs and increasing power are making large-scale access to interactive instructional devices an attainable goal for education.

CONCLUSIONS

Typically, new information technologies have their impact on societal institutions in four sequential stages:

1. The new technology is adopted by an institution (e.g., a school) to carry out existing functions more efficiently.
2. The institution changes internally to take better advantage of these new efficiencies. Schools which have not utilized the innovation are less cost-effective and lose ground; in consequence, the technology is widely adopted.
3. Schools develop new functions and activities made possible by additional capabilities of the technology; other institutions (e.g., business) compete with education for dominance in this new role.
4. The original role of the institution (school) may become obsolete, be displaced, or be radically transformed as new functions dominate the institution's activities.

Long term, the stage 4 impacts tend to be the most profound; early assessment of these hidden consequences for an institution is crucial. As Isaac Asimov once said, "The important thing to forecast is not the automobile, but the parking problem; not the income tax, but the expense account; not the television, but the soap opera."

The leading-edge colleges and universities implementing instructional technology are now in early stage 2, and the phase of widespread adoption of CAI and telecommunications is just beginning. Of course, as the information technologies continue to evolve, new stage 1 devices will emerge (such as ICAI). Stages 3 and 4 will probably begin by the mid-1990s for existing CAI and telecommunications approaches; artificial intelligence approaches will probably not reach these latter stages of impact until the twenty-first century.

The new information technologies have the potential to improve many problems inherent in the traditional model of education, and the development of sophisticated instructional devices may be an essential step in industrial countries' emerging transformation to a knowledge-based economy. Clarifying how these technologies can best be used and exploring implementation strategies such as educational information utilities will be key steps in the adoption process. Over the next two decades, promising technologies include intelligent machine-based tutors and coaches, "cognition enhancers" incorporating artificial intelligence approaches, interactive videodisc, and computer-telecommunications synthesis devices. As with any powerful technology, careful attention must be given to potential side effects and to overcoming barriers to implementation.

Christopher Dede

REFERENCES

Background Reading

Ayres, R. U. (1984) *The Next Industrial Revolution*. New York: Ballinger.

Dede, C. J. (1987) "Artificial Intelligence Applications to High Technology Training." *Educational Communications and Technology* (Fall).

Reich, R. B. (1983) *The Next American Frontier*. New York: Penguin.

Turkle, S. (1984) *The Second Self*. New York: Simon and Schuster.

U.S. Congress. Office of Technology Assessment. (1985) *Information Technology R & D: Critical Trends and Issues*. Washington, D.C.: U.S. Government Printing Office.

Example

National Commission on Excellence in Education. (1983) *A Nation at Risk: The Imperative for Educational Reform*. Washington, D.C.: U.S. Government Printing Office.

Wenger, E. (1986) *Artificial Intelligence and Tutoring Systems: Computational Approaches to the Communication of Knowledge*. Los Altos, Calif.: Morgan Kaufmann.

Willett, E. J., Swanson, A. D., and Nelson, E. A. (1979) *Modernizing the Little Red Schoolhouse: The Economics of Improved Education*. Englewood Cliffs, N.J.: Educational Technology Publications.

Further Detail

Brown, J. S. (1985) "Process Versus Product: A Perspective on Tools for Communal and Informal Electronic Learning." *Journal of Educational Computing Research* 1 (2): 179–202.

Dede, C. J. (1981) "Educational, Social, and Ethical Implications of Technological Innovation." *Programmed Learning and Education Technology* 18 (4): 204–213.

———. (1985) "Assessing the Potential of Educational Information Utilities." *Library Hi Tech* 3 (4): 115–119.

———. (1986) "Review and Synthesis of Recent Research in Intelligent Computer Assisted Instruction." *International Journal of Man-Machine Studies* 24 (4): 329–353.

Dede, C. J. and Gottlieb, D. (1985) "The Long Term Influence of Home Microcomputers on Family Interaction Patterns." *Futurics* 9 (1): 10–18.

Illustration of a Point

Ouchi, W. (1981) *Theory Z: How American Business Can Meet the Japanese Challenge*. New York: Addison-Wesley.

Theoretical Background

Bloom, B. S. (1984) "The Two Sigma Problem: The Search for Methods of Group Instruction as Effective as One-On-One Tutoring." *Educational Researcher* 13: 3–16.

Contradictory Research

Carnoy, M. and Levin, H. M. (1985) *Schooling and Work in a Democratic State*. Stanford, Calif.: Stanford University Press.

NEWTON'S RINGS. A pattern of colored rings which is sometimes apparent when glass-mounted slides are projected. It is caused by optical interference which occurs because of multiple reflections between two flat surfaces which are not completely parallel over all their surfaces. Slide holders with slightly roughened glasses are available to prevent Newton's rings appearing.

NODE. A connection or switching point in a network. It may be a workstation, a dedicated server, or a connection point for routing messages. Most networks are limited in the total number of nodes that can be connected.

NOISE. This is generally defined as unwanted background to a signal. It includes such things as acoustic background sounds, electrical hiss, rumble, hum, electromagnetic interference, etc. In all electronic components and recording or transmission media the signal must compete with some degree of background noise and it is vital in recording work to preserve an adequate signal-to-noise ratio at every stage. In general, noise consists of all frequencies or a band of frequencies rather than particular frequencies (hum is an exception to this). **White noise** (q.v.) contains all frequencies in equal proportion. Noise is also used as a general term meaning unwanted useless information.

NOMINAL GROUP TECHNIQUE. A way of organizing groups which enables individuals to express personal views without being identified. It is so named because individuals act (i.e., speak, write) on their own behalf, so that such a group is only "nominally" a group. However, the nominal group reports as a group, thus preserving the individual anonymity.

NOMINAL SCALE. A type of scale where the class categories are neither measurable one against the other (i.e., not a ratio scale like the height of a population) nor capable of being ranked in order (as with an ordinal scale like racing results). One example of a nominal scale is FIAC, a scale used in coding classroom behavior. Other examples would be eye color, sex, or nationality.

NONPARAMETRIC TEST. A statistical test which is not based on the concept of normal distribution. By contrast, a parametric test assumes normality of distribution and, where a comparison of two or more populations is considered, equal variance. Nonparametric tests make no such assumptions and are commonly used where interval data is not normally distributed and for nominal and ordinal measures.

NONVOLATILE. Generally refers to computer random access memory which is not erased when power is disconnected. This facility is achieved by using CMOS memory chips and providing power from a battery or other independent source to maintain memory in the absence of the main power source. Bubble memory is also nonvolatile. *See* **Bubble Memory; CMOS.**

NORMAL DISTRIBUTION. A normal or Gaussian curve is a symmetrical bell-shaped curve which represents the normal or expected distribution of naturally occurring phenomena.

NORM-REFERENCED TEST. Test designed to measure an individual's achievement in comparison with other individuals who have taken the same test. *See* **Criterion-Referenced Test.**

NOTICE BOARD. *See* **Bulletin Board.**

NSPI. *See* **National Society for Performance and Instruction.**

NTSC. *See* **National Television System Committee.**

NULL MODEM. A small connection box for hooking up two computers, each of which is to be linked up through a modem. In addition to crossing the main data wires so that one computer's output is the input to the other, it also connects the proper hardware-control lines to simulate the signals that a modem would provide if a complete connection had been made.

NYBBLE. Half a byte.

NYSERNET. A project connecting fourteen New York universities and the Brookhaven National Laboratory in a computer network.

O

OBJECT CODE. The machine language program with which the computer actually deals, obtained by translation from a high-level language (the source code, e.g., a BASIC program), either by the computer itself at run time or via a compiler program.

OBJECTIVES. Clear statements of intended action or behavior. Distinguished from aims by being written in more precise terms. *See* **Behavioral Objectives.**

OBJECTIVE TEST. Strictly, a test requiring no judgment on the part of the marker. In practice the term is synonymous with multiple-choice test in which the testee selects from the presented alternatives. Usually one choice is correct and all the others wrong, but this is not necessary: different scores can be allocated to different answers, or more than one answer may be correct. In all cases however, there can be no dispute over the score to be allocated, irrespective of who marks the test. *See* **Assessment.**

OBSERVATION INSTRUMENT. A specially designed form for recording classroom behavior. The act of observation is made up of three phases: detecting the presence of an observable event; encoding the observed behavior or behaviors based on a specified set of categories; and recording or writing down (usually in shorthand notation) the observed and encoded event. A variety of observation instruments are possible depending on whether the sampling is **time sampling** (q.v.) or **event sampling** (q.v.). Verbal, nonverbal, and spatial activities need coding in a variety of different ways. In the context of classroom observation, an observation instrument does not measure an event or a behavior; it simply records its presence or absence. *See* **Interaction Analysis.**

OCR. *See* **Optical Character Recognition.**

OEM. Original equipment manufacturer, i.e., equipment as supplied by the manufacturer.

OFF-AIR RECEIVER. A television set which has a tuner as part of its circuit, such as a standard domestic television set. Receivers are not able to accept video signals, e.g., from a camera, without modification. The term *receiver-monitor* is sometimes used for such a modified instrument. *See* **Monitor.**

OFF-LINE. Pertaining to those machines or operations which are part of a data processing system in a computer but are not directly controlled by the central processor, e.g., a card punch may be off-line if it is preparing cards for subsequent input.

OFFSET LITHOGRAPHY. The most common form of lithographic printing system in which the greasy ink image from the printing plate is transferred to a nonabsorbent rubber blanket, and is then transferred to the paper.

OHP. *See* **Overhead Projector.**

OMNIDIRECTIONAL MICROPHONE. *See* **Microphone Characteristics.**

ON-BOARD DATA PROCESSING. A facility to be offered by future geostationary satellites. It will enable satellites to transmit information on the basis of stated requirements, for example, by calling up the appropriate data base to satisfy an inquirer's needs. On-board data processing is an essential step in the drive towards a worldwide information network.

ON-BOARD SWITCHING. The facility allowing a satellite to switch transponders to different beams by command from the ground.

ON-LINE. (1) Pertaining to peripheral equipment connected to and controlled by the central processor of a computer. (2) A computer terminal is said to be on-line when it can send/receive data directly to/from the central processor.

OPAQUE PROJECTOR (EPISCOPE). A device for projecting opaque pictures (as opposed to transparencies). As an episcopic system depends on the use of reflected light, it is impossible for it to give a bright projected picture unless the room is totally blacked out and the projection lamp is very high-powered. In spite of this restriction, many teachers make good use of the opaque projector, often to display items from newspapers and magazines, or from reference works. Opaque projectors are bulky machines, and require mounting on a wheeled trolley.

OPEN COLLEGE OF THE AIR (U.K.). Distance learning institution set up in the United Kingdom for the training and retraining of adults. The Open College, sponsored by the Manpower Services Commission, is intended to be the technical and vocational equivalent of the Open University.

OPEN LEARNING. A development from distance learning, this term describes flexible learning systems which are student-centered, seeking to allow people to study so far as possible at their own pace, where and when they want.

OPEN REEL. Tape recording system in which the tape travels from one reel to another. The threading has to be carried out by the operator, and normally the tape is removed only after it has been totally wound to one end or the other. For most educational audio and video purposes, open reel machines have been superseded by those using cassettes, but some professional-quality machines still use open reel.

OPEN TECH (U.K.). An MSC initiative, originally intended to fill apparent gaps in the provision of technician training and retraining in the United Kingdom, and to make existing courses more accessible through the use of open learning methods depending on new information technology.

OPEN UNIVERSITY. This entry discusses media employed by the Open University in its system for teaching students at a distance, mainly in their own homes. It identifies some of the problems that have arisen through use of educational technology on a large scale in a university that served over 120,000 students in 1986.

PRINT

Print is the principal medium through which Open University students learn. They spend about 90 percent of their study time reading and writing, except in some science and technology courses containing practical (experimental) work.

Printed materials prepared by the university fall into three main categories: course units; readers and other specially prepared texts; and tests, notes, and other supplementary materials. All students buy for each course certain texts published by commercial publishers and available from bookshops.

Course units are printed in what is known as "magazine" format, with well-designed covers and plenty of illustrations. The actual exposition is laid out in various ways, depending on the course, but always with plenty of space for students to make their own notes alongside the text. Each unit takes about a week to study, part-time, together with related readings and written work.

Most of the units begin with a set of objectives. These are not perfectly molded behavioral statements that would meet Mager's criteria (1962 DEFINITION); problems in using this approach have been fully discussed by MacDonald-Ross (1973 THEORETICAL BACKGROUND). Instead, the objectives provide a guide to course writers, students, and tutors regarding content and offer a foundation for developing examination questions.

The text within many of the units is in semiprogrammed form. That is to say, it has been "chunked," each chunk being followed by self-assessment questions or by student activities, requiring students to read, collect data, calculate, or make notes. Sample answers are included elsewhere in the unit. Students are thus involved actively and helped to acquire some confidence in what they do. The text may also refer students to other media. For example, integration of text with broadcast media is very tight in some courses. In other courses, students may have to work at a computer terminal for a while, or undertake fieldwork, before continuing their reading.

Thus, in some weeks students are asked to read considerably more than is in the units. They read regularly parts of the course reader, usually published specially for the course and consisting of a collection of papers in a particular field.

There is no doubt that students in the Open University are provided with far more reading than most can hope to master. They have to learn selective negligence, or drop out. The university's norms for work load related to print are still exceeded by many course teams, although not as much as in the 1970s. Reading speed studies show that the number of words students are expected to read each week is too great. The majority of students staying in the system tell the university that they exceed the norm of twelve hours of study a week, for all media combined, for a full-credit course. Other feedback does not reflect much correlation between time taken and student performance, however, and there is some evidence to support the view that conceptual density must be taken into account: for some students, shorter texts are much harder to master because of the high density of the prose.

Much can be done to help students gain access to ideas contained in print. The Open University's Institute of

Educational Technology offers advice to course teams regarding use of print and conducts a program of research (see MacDonald-Ross and Smith, 1981; Waller, 1979, 1980; Waller and Lefrere, 1981 RECENT RESEARCH).

BROADCASTING

Before the Open University was actually established, the Planning Committee responsible for it had succeeded in concluding a provisional agreement with the British Broadcasting Corporation (BBC) for production facilities for television and radio, and for transmission times on the BBC's national networks (mainly BBC-2 for television, plus Radio 3). This unique partnership between the Open University and the BBC has proved very profitable, and during the decade from 1972 to 1982 some 300 television programs (24 minutes each) and about the same number of radio programs (15 minutes) were made annually. Since all these programs were recorded, the stock and the number available for transmission rose considerably over the decade. Most were repeated once the same week, and at the peak of transmission, in about 1979, well over 30 hours of television and nearly as much radio were transmitted. At first, these hours included many in the early evening on weekdays.

It is impossible to list all uses made of broadcasts in the Open University (Bates, 1975b EXAMPLES), but it is worth quoting a few examples if only to show that the "talking head" is seldom used on television, and that that talks and discussions are not the only use made of radio. For instance, in a geology course the television camera's flexibility is capable of helping students to identify minerals, as hand specimens, in the field or as thin slides (sections). The camera can show rocks in situ, zoom in on specimens, and later be attached to a petrological microscope. In their home experiment kit, students have a microscope fitted with a polarizer and analyzer and use techniques demonstrated on television to examine their own specimens and slides from the kit. Television can also provide primary source material for students of education, in the form of pictures of what happens in classrooms. After they have read the printed material, students are asked to observe the children very closely. The radio program may follow this up with a discussion about the children observed, enabling students to check their own observations.

Programs are spread over a large number of courses, and from the individual student's point of view, television and radio do not loom very large. On average, students use rather less than 5 percent of their time for the broadcast media. Bates (1975a RESEARCH RESULTS) showed that most Open University students in the early 1970s had easy and regular access to both broadcast media, and that for the average course they watch about two-thirds of television broadcasts and listen to about half the radio, but these figures have declined recently (Grundin, 1983 RESEARCH RESULTS). In fact, two considerable problems now face the university over its use of broadcast media. First, airtime is shrinking, particularly on radio, for a number of reasons relating more to the BBC's view of itself than to the university. Unfortunately, alternative delivery systems do not equal broadcasts in cost-effectiveness for large numbers of students. Second, the relationship between the Open University and the BBC is being placed under some strain by shrinking airtime and cuts in the university's government-provided budget.

In the university's 1975 evidence to the Annan Committee on the future of broadcasting in Great Britain it was pointed out that the university needed at least twice as much airtime as it then had. The reason was simple: only half the full repertoire of courses was then available, yet already many students were being expected to view and listen at times that were inconvenient. Forecasts of airtime needed by the university in the mid-1980s were clearly too high, however, for the BBC to agree to provide so much, in competition with other BBC internal requests for airtime. In fact, the time available to the university has declined sharply for radio, while for television the early evening hours have gone, leaving the weekends in the daytime as the main Open University time.

The university has naturally turned to examine alternative delivery systems (see Bates, 1978 EXAMPLE). The cost to the university of open-circuit transmission is not high, since it is marginal cost, not true cost (see Eicher et al., 1982 DISCUSSION). Even for low-enrollment courses, with 300 students a year, open-circuit transmission may be cost-effective for the university compared with **videocassette recorders** (q.v.). The latter have an initial capital cost still too high for the university to expect students to obtain their own or for the university to supply one to each student; therefore, the recorders can at best be placed only in study centres, where they are not very accessible. Further, the cost of supplying tape, prerecorded or not, is still high. The cost of providing sound-only recorders and tape is much lower, needless to say. Faced with decreasing airtime, the university has in fact established a service which provides thousands of video- and audiocassettes to students on request, for use on their own or borrowed machines. This service supplements, rather than replaces, broadcast programs.

As the government has cut back the university's budget each year since 1979, so the demand from academics for less money to be spent on the BBC contract has become louder. This demand is now backed up by figures that show the decline in student viewing. Broadcasting's status is slipping among students and staff alike, for different reasons. Academics see it as a very expensive portion of the instructional package, and one that is far from easy to use well. Students rate television as less important than print, and radio as less important than television, although they give higher ratings to programs made available on cassette.

Against this background, there has been talk of changes in the partnership or even its collapse, despite the transfer to Milton Keynes, to the Open University campus, of all production following completion of the university's fine new studio block, operated now by the BBC. These bleak prospects may be an illusion, however, because low-cost technology could change the picture within a few years. In the meantime, the university is applying stricter criteria for allocating broadcasting time and making ever increasing use of cassettes (see Bates, 1979; Dickinson, 1980 RESEARCH RESULTS; Hawkridge and Durbridge, 1983 DISCUSSION). Feedback from students is employed to assist the allocation process, amid protests from some staff. Previously, financial and logistical considerations dominated, with some courses getting more on a rule-of-thumb basis (Hawkridge, 1973 HISTORICAL).

HOME EXPERIMENT KITS

The Open University has not pioneered scientific and technological kits for carrying out experiments at home, but it has certainly produced the largest range for higher education. The university's kits are integrated closely with other media and material for the courses to which they relate and are learning media as much as print or broadcasts.

A typical kit contains 20 to 40 experiments to be carried out at the rate of three or four a month. All necessary apparatus is provided, except for items commonly found in the home. Chemicals, electrical and electronic apparatus, glassware, and other potentially dangerous material may be included; one even contains a sheep's brain for dissection. Students pay only a small deposit, although some kits are worth hundreds of pounds.

The science and technology faculties in particular have tackled the problem of teaching students experimental aspects of their disciplines by trying to identify what is essential. They have questioned the approach used in other universities, where students frequently spend many hours undertaking routine laboratory work, sometimes using obsolete equipment and acquiring skills they will never use again. Instead, the faculties have used kits for three reasons: to teach manipulative skills, to teach difficult concepts that are made clearer through experimental work, and to acquaint students with certain items of apparatus. Moreover, experimental method and design is part of theory, and students benefit from applying the theory.

The kits replace laboratory practicals only to a limited extent, because Open University students do practical work at summer schools held in other British universities and view television programs that emphasize the experimental side by demonstrating complex apparatus and by taking students into experimental situations they would not otherwise experience.

What good do students get out of kits? That is hard to tell precisely. Evaluation of students' use of kits is problematical in distance teaching. Some kits are returned unopened, yet students who do not trouble to carry out the experiments do not necessarily fail. Few course teams make the kits compulsory, though all believe the practical work based on them is important. Most students seem to like doing the experiments and say they find them helpful, but not as useful as the print and television. Malfunctioning apparatus puts off some students. Difficult home conditions hinder others. Course teams continue to develop and revise kits with little evidence about what works (Kaye, 1973; Maskill, Morgan, and Moss, 1974 EVALUATION).

COMPUTING

The university's main administrative computer is used in many ways to run the university, but not for instruction. The nearest it comes to instruction is in marking tests and recording the results. On the other hand, the university's Academic Computing Service offers students opportunities to learn computing or to carry it out (say, for computing statistics) within their courses. Terminals located in over 200 study centers are linked to a mainframe computer in Milton Keynes. A very limited amount of computer-assisted learning is also available, particularly on terminals located at summer schools (see Lockwood, 1980 EVALUATION).

Although the service's network is an important one, what is really required is a terminal in every (computing) student's home or, better still, a fairly powerful microcomputer for each one. On a very small number of courses, the university is already supplying computing devices as part of the teaching materials (Calder, 1981 MARKET RESEARCH).

Computers, particularly microcomputers, seem destined to become much more important in the university's teaching system, but the development costs of programs remain very high (Hawkridge, 1983 AUTHORITY).

OTHER MEDIA

Print, broadcasting, home experiment kits, and computing all require heavy investment by the university, running into millions of pounds a year. Other media, including much cheaper ones, must be kept under review.

The university has been keeping in touch with teletext developments such as Ceefax and Oracle, and videotex (Prestel), but has not found a cost-effective way to use these other than to advertise its courses (on Prestel) and to operate an internal communication system (Optel) available to students at some summer schools. **Interactive video** (q.v.), using videocassettes or videodiscs in conjunction with microcomputers, is being explored (Laurillard, 1983 EVALUATION). Loud-speaking telephones are used for telephone tutorials (Turok, 1973 EVALUATION). Slides and filmstrips meet special requirements in science and art history. Gramophone records carry music, drama, and poetry. Audiocassettes are used in conjunction with print (audiovision). There have been some experiments with telephone tutoring, and the university has developed Cyclops, a prototype electronic blackboard system that uses telephone lines to transmit **slow-scan television** (q.v.) pictures plus voice.

CONCLUSION

The Open University claims to make good use of the tools provided by modern technology for higher education. It is developing more courses using more media than ever before. Evaluation of its success in using a particular medium is difficult, since specific effects cannot be detected. Instead, the overall success of the university stands as testimony to the ability and dedication of its students as well as the quality of its staff and its media, there being by December 1987 in excess of 70,000 graduates.

The most sophisticated media in education are worthless without careful design of the content they carry. In the Institute of Educational Technology, we are naturally interested in the media as media for education, including new information technology, but our primary interest is in how to teach the content well. This may be the principal contribution educational technology can make at the university level, a contribution of considerable interest to other distance teaching institutions (Kaye and Rumble, 1981 AUTHORITY).

D. Hawkridge

REFERENCES

Authority

Hawkridge, D. G. (1983), *New Information Technology in Education*. London and Baltimore: Croom Helm and Johns Hopkins University Press.

Kaye, A. R. and Rumble, G. (1981) *Distance Teaching for Higher and Adult Education*. London: Croom Helm.

Definition

Mager, R. (1962) *Preparing Instructional Objectives*. San Francisco: Fearon.

Discussion

Eicher, J. C. et al. (1982) *The Economics of New Educational Media*, Vol. 3. Paris: UNESCO.

Hawkridge, D. G. and Durbridge, N. (1983) "Video in Education and Training." *Intermedia* (October): 16–19.

Evaluation

Kaye, A. R. (1973) "The Design and Evaluation of Science Courses at the Open University." *Instructional Science* 2: 2.

Laurillard, D. (1983), "The Problems and Possibilities of Interactive Video." In *New Technologies for Distance Education*, ed. T. O'Shea. Brighton: Harvester Press.

Lockwood, F. (1980) "CICERO: Computer-assisted Learning Within an Open University Course." *Teaching at a Distance* 17: 57–63.

Maskill, R., Morgan, A., and Moss, D. (1974) "Practical Teaching, the Media and the Open University." In *Aspects of Educational Technology* 8, ed. G. H. Jamieson et al. London: Pitman.

Turok, B. (1973) *Teaching by Telephone*. Milton Keynes: Regional Tutorial Services, The Open University.

Example

Bates, A. W. (1975b) "The Use of Television and Other Audiovisual Media in the Open University." In *Enciclopedia della Scienza a Tecnica*. Milan: Mondadori.

———. (1978) "Options for Delivery Media." In *Alternative Routes to Formal Education*, ed. H. Perraton. Baltimore: Johns Hopkins University Press.

Historical

Hawkridge, D. G. (1973) "Media Taxonomies and Media Selection." In *Aspects of Educational Technology* 7, ed. R. Budgett and J. Leedham. London: Pitman.

Market Research

Calder, J. (1981) *Buyers and Users and the Learning Package Microprocessors and Product Development: a Course for Industry*. Milton Keynes: Institute of Educational Technology, The Open University.

Recent Research

MacDonald-Ross, M. and Smith, E. (1981) *Language in Texts: A Bibliography*. Milton Keynes, Institute of Educational Technology, The Open University.

Waller, R. (1979) "Four Aspects of Graphic Communication." *Instructional Science* 8: 3.

———. (1980) "Typographic Access Structures for Educational Texts." In *Processing of Visible Language 1*, ed. P. Kolers et al. New York: Plenum Press.

Waller, R. and Lefrere, P. (1981) "New Technologies in Academic Publishing: Implications for the Open University." *Teaching at a Distance* 19: 32–39.

Research Results

Bates, A. W. (1975a) *Student Use of Broadcasting*. Milton Keynes: Institute of Educational Technology, The Open University.

———. (1979) "Whatever Happened to Radio at the Open University?" *Educational Broadcasting International* (September): 119–123.

Dickinson, R. (1980) *An Evaluation of Use of Videocassette Machines in the Regions*. Milton Keynes: Institute of Educational Technology, The Open University.

Grundin, H. (1983) *Audio-visual Media in the Open University: Results of a Survey of 93 Courses*. Milton Keynes: Institute of Educational Technology, The Open University.

Theoretical Background

MacDonald-Ross, M. (1973) "Behavioural Objectives: A Critical Review." *Instructional Science* 2: 1.

OPERANT CONDITIONING. A term associated with B. F. Skinner. He argued that as behavior operates on the environment to achieve reinforcement, there is a distinct difference from classical conditioning. Operant or respondent conditioning depends on observing the behavior of the organism and reinforcing desired behavior. Early experiments with such reinforcement often used pigeons as subjects: to condition the pigeon to peck at a black door in a trial box, any movement towards the black door is rewarded, and the behavior of the bird is shaped toward the desired end. A spin-off from this work has been the adoption of the techniques for animal training of all kinds; however, its application to human learning has not been so universally accepted. *See* **Programmed Learning.**

OPERATING SYSTEM. *See* **Disk Operating System.**

OPERATIONAL DEFINITION. A description that is testable and verifiable. Often theoretical statements are "operationalized" in order to test them. In educational technology, learning can be operationalized by having adequate descriptions of the observable learner characteristics.

OPERATIONAL GAMING. Applying the technique of operational gaming to a given sphere of activity involves creating a situation that is composed of a number of points of reference, each of which will serve as a focus for feedback from participants (including the controller). An example would be one of the many classroom simulations in which participants are immersed in some dramatic situation (e.g., a natural disaster) and required to "act out" a role.

Operational gaming is distinguished from a computerized simulation of a situation based on mathematical models by the fact that it relies on human decision makers reacting at a given point in time to a particular combination of circumstances. Thus, it not only allows for irrational or inconsistent patterns of behavior to dominate a situation, but also allows for behavior to change in the light of experience.

OPERATIONAL RESEARCH (OR). The use of mathematical methods of analysis to solve pratical problems. *See* **Educational Cybernetics.**

OPTICAL CHARACTER RECOGNITION (OCR). An OCR machine can recognize conventional letters or numbers and either record or relay such data. OCR is often used to input data to computers, and increasingly to input typescript to printing machinery. As yet only characters of certain type styles and quality are easily recognized: handwriting and print pose problems still to be overcome (1986). *See* **Magnetic Ink Character Recognition.**

OPTICAL MEMORY. Digital data encoded on an optical disk: such a system is capable of providing vast quantities of storage. Over a gigabyte of memory can be provided on an optical disk; by comparison, magnetic storage is very limited. *See* **CD-ROM; Optical Storage and Retrieval.**

OPTICAL MOUSE. A mouse that senses its movement by reading light patterns reflected from a light-emitting diode or lamp into a photocell. Most models must be used on glass or metal plates printed with special grid patterns.

OPTICAL POINTER. A battery or transformer-powered "flashlight" which projects a small arrow or spot of light for use as a pointer for images on a projection screen. Such a device avoids the screen damage which could be caused by a rigid pointer.

OPTICAL SOUND TRACK. The sound track which runs down the edge of a cine film and which, by modulating the light reaching a photocell from the "exciter" lamp reproduces the film's sound track. Optical tracks are printed by the film laboratory from a master negative track. Optical tracks can be played on all 16mm sound projectors. *See* **Magnetic Sound Track.**

OPTICAL STORAGE AND RETRIEVAL. Conventionally optical images have been stored on film or videotape. Although these media are still dominating educational practice there are various new systems coming to the fore. In particular, the next decade is likely to witness a massive increase in the use of videodisc, holographic images, and microfiche. Each of these techniques offers very cheap mass storage, random access retrieval, and possible enhancement in image quality.

See **CD-ROM; Holography; Videodisc; Video Recording and Reproduction.**

ORACLE. A U.K. version of **teletext** (q.v.).

ORGANOGRAM. A cybernetic model or diagram of the way an organization or body processes information. *See* **Educational Cybernetics.**

ORPHAN. *See* **Widow.**

ORTHOCHROMATIC. Black-and-white photographic emulsion which is sensitive to blue and green light only. *See* **Panchromatic.**

ORTHOGRAPHY. Reserch in comunications tecnology wil eventualy make posibl a tremendus breakthru in comercial, sientific, and privat afairs, with the increse in qantities of vewdata availabl for milions of peple. Th dificult botlnek that could stil be opend up is obviusly English spelling.

Research in communications technology will eventually make possible a tremendous breakthrough in commercial, scientific, and private affairs, with the increase in quantities of viewdata available for millions of people. The difficult bottleneck that could still be opened up is obviously English spelling.

Education has a double concern with literacy, which is both a subject for teaching and the medium for all other learning through the printed word.

The earliest **information technology** (q.v.) is the writing system itself. It has developed historically from picture symbols, to ideographs and syllabaries, to alphabets in which each symbol theoretically represents one sound—although never perfectly in practice, and there is no reason to assume that pure phonemic representation must be the ultimate in written language. Writing often began as a sacred script, then extended to the upper classes, but today mass literacy is needed to operate modern technological societies, and difficult spelling is now a public problem, not a matter for elitist pride.

Orthography is literally "correct writing." What defines correct? English spelling was only gradually standardized following the invention of printing, which made uniformity more desirable, but the criteria of precedent and etymology that were used to establish "correct" English spelling by dictionary just over two hundred years ago would not be acceptable today. Like "correct" manners of the time, "correct" spelling was elaborate and time-consuming. It performed the social function of a quick screening test to distinguish the more cultured, intelligent, or industrious from the vulgar mob. It has even been considered a moral discipline for the young.

The premise of English spelling is alphabetic "spelling as you speak," but it has become a "psycholinguistic guessing game" (Goodman, 1970 FURTHER DETAIL) through historical accidents and expedients, its diverse linguistic inheritance, pronunciation shifts in spoken language, and modifications by semantic links and grammatical markers. A modified Latin alphabet of 26 letters with 5 vowel symbols must cope with an Anglo-Saxon language with around 42 identified sounds (phonemes) including about 19 vowel sounds. There are some prevailing sound-symbol relationships, but altogether up to 658 different ways to represent the 42 phonemes have been listed (Pitman and St. John, 1972 FURTHER DETAIL). The Chomsky claim (N. Chomsky, 1970; C. Chomsky, 1970 THEORETICAL BACKGROUND) that English spelling is "optimal" because it has an underlying lexical basis or "deep structure" through the sharing of similar spellings by related words—e.g., *nation/national*—has been disproved by the weight of contrary evidence—e.g., *fly/flies/flight*.

Most users of English today are not native speakers, and this majority is rapidly increasing, but the international advantages of the English language through its simple grammar, rich vocabulary, and concise expression are counterbalanced by a spelling that has had no updating in the past hundred years, unlike every other major language except French.

English readers have assumed, along with most English spelling reformers, that any change in spelling must be so radical that everything now in print would be obsolete, and everyone now literate forced to relearn horribly. There may well be some future revolutionary solution for written communication, made possible perhaps by computerized printing of logographs which can cross language barriers, with alphabetical representation of local grammars. In the meantime, there may be radical developments in using **computer graphics** (q.v.) and **interactive video** (q.v.) to teach present spelling to humans, while dictionaries are built into computers to correct continuing human error. Conceivably, however, English spelling could be improved to retain its advantages without its disadvantages.

Instructional design now finds more effective ways to present information through textual layout, "readability," and textual cohesion—but spelling is still omitted from its brief. This lag has had three consequences in education. The dilemma in schools is to allocate a disproportionate time to repetitive rote learning to read and spell, or to produce many poor readers and worse writers. Anglo-Saxon rates of functional illiteracy are high relative to educational expenditure for many reasons, but complicated by orthography difficult to learn. To compensate for consequent reading difficulty, there is a trend to oversimplify and reduce reading content, vocabulary, and syntax, begun at primary level, with a flow-on to secondary and even tertiary texts.

The ease with which pupils acquire "computer literacy" raises questions about the inevitability of their long struggle for "book literacy." Information technology values are efficiency, economy, logic, consistency, speed in processing, and mass access. Its "human engineering" principle is that tools are adjusted to people if people cannot adjust to the tools. We come to the concept of a "user-friendly" spelling too.

In schools, the most publicized attempts at easier initial spelling for learners have been the initial teaching alphabet (i.t.a.) of the 1960s (Warburton and Southgate, 1969 FURTHER DETAIL) and the U.S. Writing to Read project of J. H. Martin, funded by IBM in the 1980s.

The conviction that present spelling is unalterable or ideal is further loosened by "advertising spelling," with its tendency to shorten brand names for faster reading and a broader mass readership as well as for novelty impact (Jaquith, 1976 ILLUSTRATIVE RESEARCH), and even literacy kits given labels such as Rediguides and Pik-a-pak. American and English spellings increasingly coexist without comment, the extending international vocabulary of exported English words is usually respelled more economically by foreigners, and mastery of "correct" spelling is now shaky even in the prestige press. As another way of narrowing the gap between spoken and written English, there is also a trend for pronunciation to come closer to spellings (Kerek, 1976 ILLUSTRATIVE RESEARCH).

Research in orthography formerly concentrated on the nature of present spelling and the defects of failing learners, but now extends to the major issues that must be understood if spelling and its teaching are to be improved. Human abilities to read and spell are studied through cross-cultural research (Kavanagh and Venezky, 1980 ILLUSTRATIVE RESEARCH) and investigation of human and machine processes for pattern recognition, short- and long-term memory storage and retrieval (Frith, 1980; Henderson, 1982 ILLUSTRATIVE THEORY AND RESEARCH). With understanding of how skilled readers integrate visual, phonological, semantic, and lexical factors in reading, writing, and learning, their techniques can be externalized to aid the less skilled. Human visual processes in reading are shown not to be merely photographic, and flexibility of "spelling set" when systems are consistent may be as possible as automatic adjustment to different scripts, type, and lettercase.

Orthography, or "correct writing," could be redefined to mean the most effective system of visible language that can be devised by research in cognitive psychology, linguistics, and information technology to meet the practical needs of users as well as learners, readers as well as writers, machines and humans, native and foreign speakers, mass access and elite proficiency, while maintaining backwards compatibility with present spelling.

Valerie Yule

REFERENCES

Background

Scragg, D. G. (1974) *A History of English Spelling*. Manchester: Manchester University Press.

Further Detail

Goodman, K. S. (1970) "Reading, a Psycholinguistic Guessing Game." In *Theoretical Models and Processes of Reading*, ed. H. Singer and B. Ruddell. Newark, Del.: International Reading Association.

Pitman, J. and St John, J. (1972) *Alphabets and Reading*. London: Pitman.

Warburton, F. W. and Southgate, V. (1969) *i.t.a.: An Independent Evaluation*. London and Edinburgh: Murray & W & R Chambers.

Illustrative Research

Jaquith, J. R. (1976) "Digraphia in advertising." *Visible Language* 10 (4): 295–308.

Kavanagh, J. F. and Venezky, R. L., eds. (1980) *Orthography, Reading and Dyslexia*. Baltimore, Md.: University Park Press.

Kerek, A. (1976) "The Phonological Relevance of Spelling Pronunciation." *Visible Language* 10 (4): 323–338.

Illustrative Theory and Research

Frith, U., ed. (1980) *Cognitive Processes in Spelling*. London: Academic Press.

Henderson, L. (1982) *Orthography and Word Recognition in Reading*. London: Academic Press.

Theoretical Background

Chomsky, C. (1970) "Reading, Writing and Phonology." *Harvard Educational Review* 40 (2): 287–309.

Chomsky, N. (1970) "Phonology and Reading." In *Basic Studies on Reading*, ed. H. Levin and J. P. Williams. New York: Basic Books.

OUTPUT. Information transferred from a computer to some external destination, such as the display screen, a disk drive, a printer, or a modem; or the act or process of transferring such information.

OUTTAKES. Discarded film footage after the editing process, i.e., that which is "left on the cutting room floor." In professional filming the outtakes may amount to very much more film (eight times or more) than is actually used.

OVAC (U.K). Overseas Visual Aids Centre. *See* **Center for Educational Development Overseas.**

OVEREXPOSURE. In photography or reprography, exposure of sensitive material to light or heat at too great an intensity or for too long a time, thus producing a degraded image. *See* **Underexposure.**

OVERHEAD PROJECTOR. A still projector for large-size transparencies (10″ × 10″ or A4) or diagrams drawn on transparent sheets. These are placed on a horizontal illuminated panel and projected onto a screen behind the operator via a lens and mirror mounted above the transparency platform.

The overhead projector, apart from providing a means of showing large transparencies (which can be made with elaborate overlays), also acts as an alternative to the chalkboard and enables the teacher to face the class while writing. Due to the large size of the transparency, high screen brightness is obtainable and room lights can be left on.

OVERHEAD TRANSPARENCY. Several methods exist for making transparencies for use on overhead projectors. The simplest is, of course, to write on a sheet of acetate with a felt pen. Plain paper copiers have superseded to a large degree the use of thermal machines since they can make transparencies from quite finely drawn originals and are not particularly fussy about the color of the original.

Irrespective of what method of production is used, the commonest fault is to include too much information on the one transparency.

OVERLAY. (1) The superimposition of one transparency onto another. This may be done for photographic or graphic purposes, and is often encountered in connection with overhead projection, where it permits objects, tables, processes, etc., to be built up or broken down highly effectively. In any overlay situation it is important to achieve accurate register of the component parts. (2) A videotex technique that allows the contents of a frame to be overlaid on top of a frame that is already displayed. An overlay frame can continue for up to 25 frames (frames B to Z). *See* **Register.**

OVERSTRIKING. Substituting one character for another on a visual display unit screen.

OVERT RESPONSE. A response by an organism that is observable. In programmed learning, overt responses are those that the subject makes by saying, writing, or in some way consciously and openly responding. Overt responses, as opposed to covert responses, have generally been favored in programmed learning. *See* **Programmed Learning.**

P

PACED TRAINING. Training on an increasing speed basis to achieve performance levels related to the pace of either a production line or a specific machine.

PACKET. A group of binary digits (bits) including data and control information which is switched as a composite whole. The data and control information are arranged in a specific format. Typically, a data packet may contain up to 1,024 bits of user data.

PACKET SWITCHING. Technique of data transmission in which a message is divided into packets of around 1,000 bits, each packet being labeled with an address, i.e., destination. The packets are routed by computer to the destination in the optimum manner, and various error-correcting routines are incorporated. This technology, as typified by AUSTPAC, offers several advantages over other means of data transmission, especially for the small to medium user. A useful analogy is the postal service: no dedicated transmission lines are required by the user—the packet is just "thrown" into the collection agency and automatically delivered to the addressee. *See* **Teletex.**

PADDLE. Device usually associated with computer games. A paddle is a handset which contains a rotating knob and a switch button; the knob is used to position something (spacecraft, racing car, frog, etc.) on the screen; the switch initiates a course of action (fires phasor, eats butterfly, etc.). In fact, paddles act as an analog input to the computer and can also serve such purposes as graphic design, responding to computer tutoring, etc. *See* **Joystick.**

PAGE (VIDEOTEX). The logical unit of access to the pagestore. Every page is associated with a unique page number, which is used to access the page. Each page can consist of up to 26 frames. The originator of a hierarchy of pages is termed an *information owner* or *information/service provider*. Pages may be free or chargeable to users depending on the provider's choice.

PAGESTORE. The data base containing videotex information; the unit of access to the pagestore is known as the page. The pagestore is a disk file and can be spread over more than one physical disk volume. There is no practical limit to the size of pagestore, other than the limit imposed by the maximum page number, typically 100,000,000,000.

PAL. A system for encoding color information in television broadcasting, recording, and reproduction. The PAL system is standardized in Western Europe (except for France), Australia, and many other parts of the world. The U.S. NTSC and French SECAM systems are incompatible with PAL and with each other, even though PAL is essentially a variant of NTSC.

PAN. (1) To move a camera in a horizontal plane. Usually the camera will be on a tripod or dolly and the panning amounts to a horizontal rotation of the camera. It is important to pan a camera very slowly, otherwise an unpleasant visual effect is obtained. The corresponding vertical movement is called *tilt*. (2) To move the displayed part of a drawing from side to side or up and down. The image translates (moves) in space. The panning motion in computer graphics and CAD is not the same as a pan in film and video, where a pan is a rotation from a single point rather than a translation in space.

PANCHROMATIC. Black-and-white photographic emulsion which is sensitive to the whole of the visual spectrum. *See* **Orthochromatic.**

PANTOGRAPH. A precision-made drawing instrument consisting of a metal or wood frame with adjustable joints. Used to make enlargements or reductions of original artwork by movement of the tracing point actuating a pencil point held in contact with a drawing surface for the reproduction.

PAPER SIZE. In the early 1970s international standardization of the size of paper used in photography, reprography, and the graphic arts was introduced in an attempt to provide a rationalized system. Known as A sizes, the range is from A1 (841mm × 594mm) to A6 (148mm × 105mm). Each A size is the same format as, but half the area of, the previous size.

A sizes in millimeters
A1 841 × 594
A2 594 × 420
A3 420 × 297
A4 297 × 210   (Contrast USA standard 280 × 216 mm)
A5 210 × 148
A6 148 × 105

Outside North American A4 has become the standard paper size for normal documents, letters, reports, etc. Standard North American size is slightly wider and shorter at 11" × 8 1/2".

PAPER TAPE. A narrow strip of paper on which holes are punched in patterns which represent characters for subsequent "reading" by a computer. This form of data storage and retrieval is now outmoded.

PAPER TAPE PUNCH. Obsolescent device taking two forms:

1. An output device on-line to a computer, which punches patterns of holes into paper tape thus allowing data to be stored for subsequent input.
2. An off-line device operated manually for preparing paper tape from source documents, for subsequent input to the computer.

PARADIGM. Strictly speaking a paradigm is a unique example. It is, however, taking on a wider meaning in education. Usage is permitting *paradigm* to mean an operational model; that is, an attempt to organize a set of variables or events into some order that will allow their interrelationships to become apparent and to permit limited predictions to be made. One can refer, for example, to paradigms of teaching, that is, interrelationships between teachers, learners, and the context.

PARALLAX. The difference between the picture seen through the viewfinder lens and the image recorded by the camera lens, due to the lens and viewfinder being in different positions. Parallax increases as the subject is brought nearer the camera. No parallax problems arise with single-lens reflex cameras as the same lens is used for viewing and taking.

PARALLEL TRANSMISSION. *See* **Interface.**

PARITY CHECK. A method of checking the correctness of binary data after that data has been transferred from or to storage. An additional bit, called the *parity bit*, is appended to the binary word or character to be transferred. The parity bit is chosen so as to maintain either an odd (odd-parity) or an even (even-parity) number of 1s in each word. This ensures that the loss of significant data is unlikely to go undetected.

PARTICIPANT CLASSROOM OBSERVATION. A classroom research strategy that, in contrast to systematic **classroom observation** (q.v.) has the observer taking part in the activities being observed. Observers attempt to get closer to the meaning of the classroom and therefore increase the validity of their observations. There are two problems that participant observers encounters: lack of observational distance and effect on the activities they are observing. However, both of these are encountered in other forms of observation to some degree. *See* **Interaction Analysis.**

PARTITION. To reserve an area on a hard disk for a program or operating system, or the area so reserved.

PASCAL. A computer language originally designed to be a teaching medium for students of computing. It is highly structured and encourages good programming practice in all areas of application; because of this, Pascal has come to be widely used as a general programming language in spite of the didactic intentions of its inventor, Nicklaus Wirth.

Inevitably with such general use, various dialects have evolved, often with conflicting features, thus somewhat denigrating the original purpose. A common version, referred to as UCSD Pascal, evolved at the University of California, San Diego.

Pascal is not an acronym so is not capitalized. It is, in fact, named after the mathematician Blaise Pascal (1623–1662).

PATCH. In programming, a program statement, or statements, intended to debug a program or to add a modification or enhancement to some portion of the program.

PATCH PANEL. A panel where circuits are terminated and facilities provided for interconnecting between circuits by means of jacks and plugs.

PATH (NAME). Method by which disk operating systems identify a file. A path is a sequence of file names that specify the path to be taken from directory to directory in order to get to a certain file. For example, C:/wp/ms/eemcat/final/output7.pq is a path indicating that the file "output7.pq" is stored in a directory called "final" which is itself a subdirectory of a directory called "eemcat" which is a subdirectory of.... on drive C:. See **Disk Operating System.**

PAUSE EDIT. A video edit of the sort obtained by using the PAUSE key (or even the STOP key) on a VCR to eliminate, for example, a television commercial. A similar procedure is often followed when using a portable video camera: the tape is paused between scenes. Such edits will always produce a glitch on replay, i.e., the picture will break up momentarily. This is because the pause has introduced a discontinuity into the synchronization signal which is also being recorded.

Glitches like this tend to get worse on dubbing, and it is generally considered essential to use electronic editing when copying is to take place, or indeed wherever professional results are desired. Nonetheless, for many valuable educational purposes tapes edited in this manner are quite satisfactory, and of course pause editing is quick and needs no special skills.

PAVLOVIAN CONDITIONING. A name often applied to classical conditioning.

PAY-CABLE. *See* **Cable Television.**

PAY-TV. *See* **Cable Television.**

PCM. *See* **Pulse Code Modulation.**

PEACESAT. Pan Pacific Education and Communication Experiments by Satellite. An "intercontinental laboratory to develop improved communication methods of education, health, and community sciences in the Pacific and a base for long-range planning." PEACESAT has been operating since 1971, using a NASA ATS-1 satellite. *See* **ALOHA.**

PEAK-TO-PEAK. The amplitude (voltage) difference between the most positive and the most negative peaks of an electrical signal.

PEDAGOGY. Educational science, i.e., the study of classroom methodology and educational techniques.

PEL. Abbreviation for picture element. The term is often used interchangeably with *pixel* but should preferably be reserved for reference to the smallest picture element available in the current mode, rather than the absolute smallest possible element, i.e., a pixel.

PERCEPTUAL MOTOR SKILLS. Human skills which depend upon the coordination of hand and eye, the eye providing feedback information which brings about constant adjustment of the work of the hand.

PERFORMANCE ANALYSIS. Also termed *performance appraisal*. Seeks to determine the level of existing performance, normally of an individual by a systematic examination of elements of the job. From the analysis, training needs are established and potential for development determined. The intended purpose is to maintain a continued improvement in performance.

PERFORMANCE-BASED INSTRUCTION. An inexact term for instruction that is based on mastery criteria. That is, a student must be successful in one unit before (s)he progresses to the next. It is argued that successful performance is necessary before a learner can properly move on to a hierarchically related unit. *See* **Keller Plan; Mastery Learning; Programmed Learning.**

PERFORMANCE OBJECTIVES. Objectives relating to performance, stated in behavioral terms. *See* **Behavioral Objectives.**

PERIGEE. The closest point of a satellite's elliptical orbit to the surface of the earth.

PERIPHERAL EQUIPMENT (PERIPHERALS). A collective term referring to devices such as printers, card readers, and magnetic tape decks, which are or can be connected to and controlled by the central processor of a computer.

PERSISTENCE. The time taken for an image (or its subjective impression) to die away after the signal or stimulus giving rise to it is removed. Both motion pictures and television rely on the persistence of vision occurring in the human eye to produce a subjective impression of continuous movement using a succession of still pictures.

PERSONAL COMPUTER. A term commonly applied to microcomputers, especially those priced for the domestic market. *See* **Microcomputers in Education.**

PERSONALIZED INSTRUCTION. Personalized Instruction, or Personalized System of Instruction (PSI), is a technique for individualizing teaching devised by Fred Keller. It lays great stress on tutorials and performance on mastery-based progress criteria. *See* **Individualization of Instruction; Keller Plan.**

PERSONALIZED SYSTEM OF INSTRUCTION (PSI). A generic name given to individualized instruction systems of the Keller Plan type. *See* **Individualization of Instruction; Keller Plan.**

PERSONNEL TRAINING. A term used in industry to mean measures which make up the vocational or in-service training of employees. *See* **Training Technology.**

PERT. Program Evaluation and Review Technique. A system of network analysis designed to trace the critical path and to predict effects of any redeployment of resources.

PHONEME. Phonemes are speech sound elements produced as a result of different combinations of tone, pitch, volume, and other factors. *See* **Information Technology.**

PHONOGRAPH. Also known as *record player* or *gramophone*. Development of the long-play record in the late 1940s gave an enormous boost to the quality and hence popularity of this form of sound reproduction. Despite the widespread advent of tapes and tape cassettes, the phonograph has held its own to a considerable degree, but the introduction of such techniques as the Dolby system of enhancing tape recording and the use of laser-scanned audio disks inevitably point to the gradual demise of the phonograph.

PHOSPHOR. The chemical compound on the inside of the CRT screen that emits light when struck by electrons. Phosphors differ in color, persistence (how long they remain lit after the electrons stop), efficiency (how much light for a given flow of electrons), and burn resistance (how well they can withstand a steady image without permanently showing that pattern).

PHOTOCOPYING AND DUPLICATING. Until the 1960s, photocopying and duplicating could be clearly delineated: machines which produced a few facsimile copies by direct photographic or other means were copiers, while machines that produced longer runs using an intermediate master were duplicators. In recent years, however, large copiers (xerographic/electrostatic) have become viable for much longer runs, both on output and economic grounds). Meanwhile, duplicators using low-cost, quick-change masters can economically be used for runs of ten copies or even fewer. For the purpose of this entry, we shall retain the technical demarcation, even if it must be ignored when making economic comparisons.

The four principal methods of copying documents are described below. They are not in order of importance but of chronological order of development.

PHOTOGRAPHIC

An adaptation of conventional photography in which an image is created by the action of light on a silver halide emulsion. The light forms a latent image, which is subsequently rendered visible by the action of a developer and made permanent by a fixer which renders the unused chemicals soluble so that they can be washed away, leaving a negative image (laterally and tonally reversed) consisting of minute specks of metallic silver in gelatin. To produce a positive image, the process is repeated using the negative as the original. Exposure can be by projection, now almost obsolete, or by the reflex (contact) method.

In the chemical transfer process (typified by Agfa Copyproof materials) the negative is developed while in contact with a receiving sheet to which the image transfers in seconds. The two sheets are peeled apart and the negative discarded. It was the advent of CT (or diffusion transfer, as it was then known) about 1950, employing small combined exposure and development units, that started the boom in photocopying.

Another, more recent, variant of the process is stabilization, in which the developer is incorporated into the emulsion, processing being effected by a liquid activator followed by a stabilizer to render the unused chemicals inert. The best-known trade name for these materials is Agfa Rapidoprint. Stabilized prints are not archivally permanent and will eventually discolor.

The high cost of silver and the relative slowness of the processing made these processes obsolete for office copying, although chemical transfer and stabilization are still used for high-quality copying (such as photographs), or in graphic arts application.

DIAZO

A process (also called dyeline, and called whiteprinting in the United States to distinguish it from blueprinting, which it replaced) in which a translucent original is exposed to high-intensity ultraviolet light in contact with paper coated with diazonium salts. The effect of the light is to decompose the diazonium salts in the background areas, the image (having been protected by the lines of the original) then being developed to create a visible dye image. Development is usually by ammonia gas (loaded in liquid form and vaporized by heat) or by a liquid developer, although in some machines development is achieved by heat or an activator applied under pressure.

Because of the need for a translucent original and because the images fade, especially if exposed to sunlight, the process is mainly used for engineering drawings.

THERMOGRAPHIC

Thermographic (also called *heat* or *infrared*) copiers produce an image by exposing the original, in contact with a sheet of heat-sensitized paper, to infrared emission. With some copiers, a sheet of transfer paper (similar to carbon paper) is used to create the image. One disadvantage of the heat process is that it will only copy images with a carbon or metallic content, so that writing inks and most colored printing inks will not reproduce. Heat copiers, however, can be used to make transparencies for overhead projectors and masters for spirit duplicators, or to laminate covers or notices with a transparent protective film.

A variant of the heat process (introduced to overcome the limitation on copying colors) is dual spectrum, in which the original is first exposed to tungsten light in contact with a flimsy intermediate sheet, this latter sheet then being exposed to heat in contact with a sheet of copy paper. The additional exposure obviously slows down the speed of copying, but quality is slightly higher. The main advantage of the dual spectrum process is that the capital cost of the copiers is very low, so that they can be installed in low-volume copying situations where no other copier would be economically viable. Dual spectrum machines can also be used to make overhead projector transparencies. Thermographic copiers have a high wastage rate and low copy quality, so the process is now rarely used.

ELECTROSTATIC

In this process, now used for nearly all office photocopying, an image is formed by the action of light on a photoconductive surface, that is, a material which can retain an electrostatic charge in the dark but not in the light. The subsequent development of the image depends on which of the two types of the electrostatic copier are used, transfer or direct, better known as plain paper or zinc oxide respectively.

PLAIN PAPER COPIERS

Once the preserve of Xerox machines, there is now a bewildering array of plain paper copiers to choose from. In a typical machine, an image of the original is projected through a lens onto a revolving drum coated with selenium (the photoconductor) which has been given an electrostatic charge by a corona unit. The charge is immediately dissipated in the background areas, but remains in the image areas, where no light has fallen on the drum. As the drum continues to revolve, oppositely charged toner powder (carbon black and resin) mixed with fine glass or metal beads to act as a carrier, is transferred to it, usually by a magnetic brush. The toner adheres to the image areas and is transferred (by reversing the charge) to a sheet of bond paper which then passes through a heat fuser section in which the resin is melted, bonding the image into the fibers of the paper to form a permanent image. Excess toner is cleaned off the drum and the machine then stops, or if more copies are required, repeats the cycle.

Some machines use other photoconductors such as cadmium sulfide and some use a belt or sheet instead of a drum. Monocomponent toners (avoiding the use of a carrier) are becoming more common, and are claimed to produce better-quality copies. Most current machines have a stationary glass platen on which the original is placed, and for book copying this is more satisfactory than a traversing platen.

Many copiers are now fitted with zoom lenses, typically providing reduction and enlargement from about 60 percent to 140 percent. The typical speed of the smaller desktop copiers is 10–20 copies per minute, but machines designed for high-volume copying operate at up to 70 copies per minute. Even faster machines are available, but these are designed as electrostatic printers rather than copiers. On-line sorters are among the useful features provided on these machines, and the quality of copy can equate with offset litho printing.

The early plain paper copiers required an 80 gsm (grams per square meter) bond paper with a closely defined moisture content. Recent machines are more tolerant in the range of stock that can be used, and most of them will copy onto self-adhesive labels and transparent material for overhead projectors.

In liquid toner transfer copiers, now rarely used, the charged toner particles are held in suspension in a volatile fluid (the dispersant), avoiding heat fusing. The copy paper for these machines has to be alkaline paper with a smooth finish; ordinary bond paper will adversely affect the toner/dispersant, resulting in poor copies.

ZINC OXIDE COPIERS

The basic difference between transfer and direct electrostatic copiers is that in the latter the photoconductor (in this case, zinc oxide) is coated onto the surface of the copy paper. This paper is charged and an image of the original projected onto it. Development can be dry or liquid, and if dry toner is used, pressure fusing is sometimes used instead of heat, eliminating the possibility of a sheet being burned in the fuser section. However, zinc oxide paper has a less pleasant "feel" than bond paper, is easily marked by paper clips, and is not available in colors. Consequently, this process has largely been superseded by plain paper copiers.

SPECIAL COPIERS

Many copiers can be fitted for coin-operating, and magnetic cards for this purpose are also being developed.

A range of facsimile machines (more commonly called "fax") is now available, enabling the facsimile of a document to be transmitted over a telephone line and reproduced at the receiving end.

Several of the major copier manufacturers have produced machines for making copies in full color. However, such copiers are very expensive both to purchase and to use, so that they are mainly found in the larger instant-print or copy shops.

We now examine the duplicating processes.

STENCIL

A duplicating process in which a stencil (a sheet of long-fiber paper with a coating of cellulose or wax) is cut on a typewriter or manually, and then mounted on a rotary machine. Ink is forced through the image areas of the stencil onto absorbent paper between the stencil and an impression roller.

Some machines use a perforated drum, into which the ink is loaded. Others have twin cylinders around which a "silk" carrier runs, and the ink is fed by a pump onto oscillator rollers which distribute it onto the underside of the carrier.

Single-drum machines have the advantage that a color change is easily effected (by keeping a spare drum), while two-cylinder machines can offer ink control by being able to feed the ink to selected areas. Single-drum machines use less ink (because it is much thinner) and copies are less liable to "set off" (images transferring to the back of the adjacent sheet) but more liable to "show through" (images being visible through the back of the sheet) than twin-cylinder machines.

Another method of preparing stencils is to use an electronic stencil cutter. This is a machine in which the original and an electronic stencil are fastened to a drum side by side. As the drum revolves, a photoelectric cell scans the original, the signals activating a stylus which makes minute holes on the stencil in the image areas.

Short-run (paper) and long-run (plastic) stencils are available, and some machines have a variable scanning pitch (or rate of lateral travel) so that a finer result is possible at the expense of taking longer.

SPIRIT

Masters for the spirit duplicating process are formed by placing a sheet of hectographic carbon against a sheet of art paper (paper with a glossy china clay coating) and typing or writing on the other side of the paper to create a reverse-reading dye image. This master is fastened to the cylinder of a rotary machine, and with each revolution it is damped with a highly volatile spirit and some of the image transferred to a sheet of smooth (preferably cream wove) paper.

Since the master must contain sufficient dye for all the copies, it follows that this is a short-run process and copy quality rapidly falls off as the master becomes exhausted. The possible maximum can be considered as less than 50, although with a good-quality master and machine, it could be more than 100.

One major advantage of this process is that copies can be run off in up to seven colors at one time, simply by using differently colored hectographic carbons at various stages of making the master. It is this advantage, coupled with simplicity of operation, that makes this process so popular in schools, despite the well-known finger-staining properties of the hectographic carbon (or ink) and the relatively weak images that are formed.

OFFSET LITHO

A process that depends on the mutual antipathy of grease and water, so the master must consist of a greasy image on a water-receptive surface. This master is clamped to a cylinder on a rotary machine, and with each revolution the whole master is both dampened and inked. Since the greasy image areas will only accept ink and the dampened areas will only accept water (or fount solution, which is mainly water with a trace of glycerin), it is possible to transfer a layer of ink to a rubber blanket on an adjacent drum and from there onto paper as it is fed between the blanket cylinder and an impression cylinder.

It is the use of a rubber blanket that enables a right-reading master to be used, and distinguishes offset litho from direct lithography, a process now only used to produce prints, the artist drawing the original in reverse.

Even the smallest tabletop machines are relatively expensive and more operator skill is required than with other processes, to maintain the correct ink and water balance. However, the advantages are considerable. Copy quality can be very high indeed, masters can be made by several methods, and paper of almost any weight and surface can be used—in some machines from air mail to six-sheet card.

It is possible to make masters for offset litho duplicating by typing with a special greasy ribbon (since it is the grease content and not the visible image that will attract the printing ink) on direct-image paper masters. However, masters are now more commonly made on electrostatic platemakers. In some cases these were originally designed as copiers but were later adapted for platemaking; in others they are adaptations of small vertical process cameras.

The CT (chemical transfer) process is used for making litho plates, as is the conventional photolitho process (involving a film negative of the original, which is "printed down" to an aluminium plate using ultraviolet light), but in both these cases one is in the realm of printing rather than duplicating because of the cost and skill involved.

FINISHING

Completed copies often need making into sets or books. This may involve collating (gathering separate pages into sets); sorting (distributing a page at a time onto sets); stapling (using a device that pushes an angled piece of wire through the set and turns over the ends); stitching (using a machine that forms the staples from a reel of wire and clenches them flat), or other means of binding.

Binding methods available include adhesive binding (using either cold PVA adhesive or a hot glue, according to the equipment), slide-on plastic spines, plastic comb binding (a length of curved plastic inserted into a series of square holes punched along the binding edge), or of course, loose-leaf folders and binders necessitating punching or drilling two or more holes in the copies.

F. C. Crix

REFERENCES

Crix, F. C. (1979) *Reprographic Management Handbook*. 2d ed. London: Business Books Limited.
Tyrell, A. (1974) *Basics of Reprography*. London: Focal Press.

PHOTOFINISHING. The name given to that part of the photographic trade which deals with the developing and printing of films.

PHOTOFLOOD. A type of lamp which is of higher luminance than normal for its wattage. This is accomplished by running the filament at a higher temperature. The gain in light efficiency is at the expense of lamp life, and photofloods last only a short time.

PHOTOGRAMMETRY. The technique of determining the dimensions of objects by accurate measurements taken from stereoscopic photographs. A common use for the technique is in making topographic maps from aerial photographs.

PHOTOGRAPHIC LETTERING. There are several ways of producing lettering photographically. Black transfer lettering on a cel may be used as a negative and contact printed onto photographic paper to produce white letters on a black background.

Several types of machines are available with master negatives on a disk. The operator dials the required letters, and they are printed onto strips of photographic paper which can be pasted up and used as television captions or as originals for platemaking. Many of the machines print only black letters on a white ground, which in the television context is limiting unless it is possible to reverse-phase the caption camera. *See* **Graphic Design.**

PHOTOGRAPHY. Photography is clearly the most popular hobby in the world. Miles and miles and miles of film of various types is cheerfully consumed by amateurs all over the world. While much of this is of the "Aunt Martha standing in front of the Eiffel Tower" (and blocking the view) type, clearly there is more appeal to the hobby than just documenting a trip, family occasion, or the one special thorn in a garden of roses. "Professional" images of various types loom out at us in advertising, television, magazines, books and newspapers. The impact of the one right image in the right place to persuade us to buy, to vote, to take a trip, or to support a cause is now a common part of our world's experience. Professional image making is easy to accept. But why do so many of us seem compelled to take pictures for our own uses?

One school of thought suggests that we need to prove to ourselves, and our long suffering family and friends, that we exist. Somehow in a world of earthquakes, famine, nuclear missiles and other more mundane threats to our existence, we feel a need to document our presence, to record something of our personal experience to leave behind us. One need only consider the centuries of initials and graffiti spread all around the globe to support this view.

Another school of thought suggests that each of us needs to feel creative in some way, to make something unique that expresses something about the way in which we view the world. It may be everybody's sunset, but our photograph makes it somehow our personal experience. The current explosion of handcrafts of all sorts in a world of plastic and microchip mass production supports this view.

Another view suggests that practicing the art/science of photography enables us to feel a part of the otherwise overwhelming world of science and technology—that pushing the button, perhaps even doing the rest ourselves, proves that we understand and can handle some part of the technological mysteries by which we are surrounded. A related view suggests that it is that very technological aspect of all the gadgets which bolt, screw, or clip on which attracts us in the first place. We feel that if only we had that new lens, that bigger and better flash unit, or that particular set of trick filters we could really win friends and impress people with that elusive perfect photograph. Certainly we seek status, real or imagined, in trendy ways in other areas.

Perhaps all of this is a part of an answer. The best answer to why do we do it may well be the obvious one. Without further analysis and self-examination, photography is, with all of its disappointments and "if-onlys," clearly an enjoyable activity. It is fun! We like it or we wouldn't do it at all, let alone do it at the rate which keeps inventors, manufacturers, and merchants as busy as they are.

Aside from the hobby aspects, some of which are serious attempts at art, photography has an impressive number of practical applications. For the educator, the photograph, whether teacher-made or commercially prepared, has all the obvious advantages involved in bringing dangerous or impractical parts of the subject under study to the classroom. Whether study print, filmstrip, slide, kit, wall poster, film or video, the selected image has a unique communications role. For the pupil, the image presents an opportunity to learn more about what is being presented that is difficult to surpass. The learning potentials inherent in the pupil's using photography to explore, experiment, and present an individual point of view have been amplified by such developments as instant films, automatic cameras, and reusable video.

For the scientist, photography has become an invaluable tool for both research and the related task of communicating the findings to a wider audience. These uses can only be described as fascinating. Photographs taken inside the human body contrast with photographs taken outside the earth's atmosphere and beyond. Photographs taken through electron microscopes have revealed the incredibly tiny as clearly as extremely high-speed cameras have stopped the incredibly fast for our observation. Photographs obtained by emulsions sensitive to invisible light wavelengths and heat compare neatly with photographs of, and from, space which are rendered more clearly for us by computer enhancement. When one considers the possibilities of video and film as means of observation and communication, the continuing role of photography in science is awe-inspiring. (Military and police applications produce other reactions.)

For the artist, attempting to record, create, or manipulate reality, photography has become not only a tool, but a medium in itself. As a vehicle for expression, the flexibility of the photograph and the enormous range of emotional reactions which that photograph can produce seem at least as challenging and as stimulating as the traditional media of blank paper, new wood, or rough stone.

The impact of the moving photograph, whether captured on motion picture film or electronic recording devices, has done more than provide us with a tool for accurate memory of things past. By combining light, color, movement, sound, the dance, and the drama into one communication package, the movie changed the way we viewed the world and our place in it. Television, the most intimate of moving photographs, has a unique ability to captivate us with live events as they happen somewhere else. While it has brought the motion picture into our homes for a closer personal contact, it has also insinuated its own qualities into our lives.

Whether we permit all this photographic technology to go to waste in mundane content or whether we can divert some of its potential into higher levels of expression remains an open question. Certainly the motion picture has proved itself to be a format worthy of serious artistic consideration—for many of us, the jury is still out on commercial television.

HISTORICAL SKETCH

When Louis Daguerre and Isidore Niépce sold their photographic process to the French government, which announced it to a joint meeting of the Academies of Science and Fine Arts in Paris on August 19, 1839, they were capitalizing on a long series of technical developments and experiments which had preceded their work.

To begin with, the idea of producing an image on something by letting light shine through a hole in an otherwise opaque surface had been around since somebody noticed what happened on one wall of a tent when a small hole had been torn in a facing wall. Da Vinci seems to have been working on the idea before 1500. By 1558 Giovanni della Porta had observed an inverted image on a white wall produced by a small hole in a dark room. He set about designing a system of lenses which would turn the image right side up. This "camera obscura" idea soon became a common portable drawing aid for artists working on problems of perspective. These portable tents developed into a prismatic device called the "camera lucida." This prism-on-a-stick enabled the artist to see the subject and trace the image on a horizontal surface at the same time, thus removing the need to transport a dark space. While these were tracing devices, the search for some way of recording the image without drawing it was an obvious challenge.

Physicists, chemists, and a number of amateur scientists in many countries contributed bits and pieces of the puzzle. For example, by 1802, Thomas Wedgwood had developed a process of exposing paper coated with nitrate of silver to produce images on glass. Unfortunately, the process could not be controlled, and the image disappeared as the silver went all the way to solid black.

The three men generally credited with producing a

durable image we call a photograph were Joseph Niépce, Louis Daguerre, and William Fox Talbot. There is considerable debate over who thought of what first and who actually deserves the credit.

By 1829 Joseph Niépce was able to produce a lasting image on a metal plate. Daguerre and Niépce, and later Niépce's son Isidore, worked together on the principle of controlling the image produced by the tendency of silver to turn dark when exposed to light. Working with silver-coated copper plates which were exposed to iodine vapor, they used a system of long exposure (20 minutes), and subsequent treatment with mercury vapor and sodium hyposulfite which developed the image and then stopped the process at a desired degree of darkness, thus fixing the image.

Henry Fox Talbot had been working on a different process for many years. Talbot had been printing on paper which had been treated with salt and silver nitrate. He then fixed, not quite so completely, the developing image in potassium iodide. It seems that Talbot first learned of Daguerre following a January 7, 1839, lecture. At any rate, he presented his work to the British Royal Society on January 31, 1839.

Both of these systems drew considerable attention, particularly from Sir John Herschel, an astronomer who had discovered, in 1819, that hyposulfite of soda dissolved silver salts. His work with this approach produced reliable and effective fixing of photographic images.

Talbot's system was essentially the production of a negative from which large numbers of positive prints could be made. Unfortunately, his process required longer exposures and the fiber marks of the negative were transferred to the prints. Daguerre types were more expensive and of better quality. They were single images made in the camera and could not be used to produce multiple copies. They were extremely popular and were the major type of photograph available until the 1850s.

Improvements on both processes produced many variations. The most common were the ambrotype collodion negatives transferred to dark glass. The cheaper tintype produced a positive image on varnished mild iron when viewed at the correct angle. An interesting variation was the carte de visite which produced eight collodion negatives at one exposure. These were cut and mounted for use as a type of calling card. The calotype (or Talbotype) was an improvement based on a shorter exposure with the negative being chemically retreated and printed on silver chloride paper for mounting.

All of these processes were replaced by the wet plate which was superior because it used clear glass, which did not interfere with printing quality, coated with a sensitive emulsion. The glass negatives were invented by an English sculptor, Frederick Scott Archer, in 1851. Coated with collodion (a solution of gun cotton, alcohol, and ether), the plates were dipped, still wet, into a solution of silver nitrate salts. The wet plates were placed in a camera, exposed, then rushed into a developing bath of pyrogallic acid. All this required a light-tight tent, or wagon, very close to the camera, so that the plates did not dry. Aside from the massive technical support and long exposure times, the processes produced clear and effective images from which prints, or woodcuts for early printing processes, could be made.

One example of the possibilities of the new process was the work of Roger Fenton, who became the first official war photographer in 1855 when he covered aspects of the Crimean War with five cameras, a darkroom, four horses, and some seven hundred glass plates. His 300 glass negatives of landscapes, fortifications, and still formal portraits, forced by the long exposure times, provide a fascinating view of the events. Perhaps the most famous use of the process is that of a former pupil of Samuel Morse, a photographer before he developed the telegraph. Matthew Brady had become a famous portraitist in New York and Washington. Lincoln is said to have given major credit for his political victory to a Brady portrait used in the campaign. Brady's coverage of the Civil War with a fleet of darkroom wagons and large staff of cameramen is well-known. He is less well-known for another first in professional photography. He took credit under his own name for the photographs produced by his staff.

The use of the process continued all over the world, with strong and adventurous photographers hauling huge cameras, some using plates as large as 20" × 24", into inaccessible places, bringing back powerful images. An interesting sideline was the use of steroscopic photography which used two photographs of the same scene which, when viewed through an eyepiece holder, produced a startlingly effective three-dimensional image. These became a fixture all over the world. The range of artistic, travel, geography, and current event photographs was immense.

By 1864 dry emulsion plates which were easier to use had been developed. A major breakthrough occurred in 1871 when Richard Maddox used gelatin, instead of collodion, as an emulsion. Maddox, a physician, is said to have made the discovery because he disliked the smell of the ether used in the wet plate process. His procedure enabled images to be made at exposure times in the range of 1/25 second.

The next revolution in photography was brought about by a manufacturer of dry plates in Rochester, New York. By 1899 George Eastman had invented roll film by using a strip of nitrocellulose plastic as a base for the photographic emulsion. His first consumer cameras, named

Kodak, supposedly an attempt to imitate the sound of the shutter, were box cameras sold with factory-supplied film. After pushing the button for the 100 negatives, the photographer sent the camera back to the factory, receiving a reloaded camera and the negatives and round prints in return. At the factory the film was processed, prints were made from the negatives, mounted, and returned to the consumer by the enormous and sophisticated support system. Roll film, also being used for the new motion pictures being developed by Edison and others, was easy to use, produced stable images of high quality, and was reasonably inexpensive. Thus by the early years of the century, photography was available to an enthusiastic mass market, as well as the professional.

Gelatin emulsion and roll film led to improvements in the chemistry of printing paper and the ability to enlarge small negatives by shining electric light through them into a lens and thus produce enlargements instead of same-size contact prints. During a period of intense scientific activity in many areas, the art/science of photography benefited from improvements in lens capability. Shutter speeds and lens openings were more or less standardized, and film of various types became more sensitive and reliable. For example, Kodachrome color slide film was introduced for the mass market in 1935, Kodacolor print film in 1942.

In 1924, following some interesting wartime use of photography such as cameras built into briefcases and aerial scouting and observation, the world received the first practical 35mm camera. Oskar Barnack, a microscope maker in Germany, had developed the first Leica camera from his 1913 prototype. Using the widely available film size developed for motion pictures by Edison, it had a 50mm collapsible lens with an aperture of 3.5. Changeable lenses, better films, low-light shutters, and related technical achievements reduced the weight and size of cameras and made possible the taking of "candid" photographs without the need for elaborate studios and controlled lighting. Erich Salomon, a German, is generally credited with starting this continuing trend during the 1930s. The documentation of man's varied activities has developed into photojournalism. Improvements in printing processes occurred at a parallel rate, thus by the late 1930s, mass-circulation photo magazines had become a major influence. *Life* magazine is a convenient example of the impact of photography combined with printing, but there were many others all over the world. (Television and film photojournalism is the current state of the trend of bringing a particular version of the world to your door, not an unmixed blessing.)

Technical advances during the last few years have concentrated on film and related chemistry, the use of electronic circuits in the camera to measure light, adjust shutter speeds, and even control the focus of the lens. While many of these developments have concentrated on the 35mm format, similar changes have been incorporated into other formats. Indeed, two new formats have been introduced in the last few years. The miniature 110 size print and slide films and cameras have had an impact on the amateur market with a range of small, convenient cameras which go from extremely simple to quite sophisticated. Another format recently introduced utilizes a disk-type mounting for the film and incorporates a number of technical innovations, most of which are in the automation category. Manufacturers of the 35mm format are currently rushing newer models and technical changes into the marketplace.

Another interesting format is the instant print camera, where the chemistry required for the development of the image is incorporated into the film when it is manufactured. This produces a usable image in minutes. The process, invented by Edwin Land in 1947, has spread into a number of camera and film sizes, some of which can be used in attachments for medium- and large-format cameras. A competing and incompatible process has been marketed by Kodak and manufactured under license by several firms. The Land corporation is now marketing a 35mm slide film which can be used in a standard camera and processed very rapidly on the spot, producing a usable slide in a few minutes. It is logical to expect additional formats of this type.

Parallel to the rapid changes in film and camera sophistication has been the invention of portable light sources. Interestingly enough, Henry Fox Talbot received a patent in 1851 for a process using a high-speed electrical spark as a photographic light source. A more practical device was the flashbulb. This was a single-use glass container which typically contained a bit of magnesium foil in a combustion supporting gas. When triggered by the shutter release mechanism, the bulb fired, producing a blast of light which varied with the size of the bulb. The time from ignition to the full light output was about 1/25 second. With the shutter open for a related length of time, the light could travel a medium distance, illuminate the subject, and bounce back to the film before the shutter closed. Used either off or on the camera, this burst of light enabled the photographer to capture images otherwise unavailable.

A related development, which has almost replaced the flashbulb format, is the electronic flash unit, often called a "strobe gun." During the 1930s and 1940s, Harold Edgerten of MIT perfected a reusable flash tube which produced strong light for fractions of a second. Unlike the bulb, which required a lot of time to build up to the full light, the flash tube produces a full flash duration in about 1/2000 second. This requires the shutter to open, the light to flash out and back, and the shutter to close again at a rapid rate. Thus cameras with focal plane shutters require a synchronized shutter speed. This is usually 1/60, 1/90, or 1/125 second. Using a speed faster than the synchronized "X" setting will not work satisfactorily. Improvements in rechargeable batteries, storage for the required electrical charge, and automatic light-sensing devices have combined to make the modern electronic flash tube a convenient, responsive, and very versatile light source capable of reaching impressive distances. These flash units are usually color corrected for use with daylight film and can be used on or off the camera, singly or in groups. A variety of devices have been developed to enhance their artistic uses. They have the additional advantage of being able to freeze very rapid action for an instant so it can be photographed, for example, a bullet leaving the barrel of a gun.

It is always difficult to make a summary statement on a rapidly changing area of technology such as photography which embodies aspects of so many scientific fields. Two prophecies seem safe. First of all, the rapid developments in video cameras and recording devices have made this electronic recording of a visual image certainly better, smaller, and less expensive. It can be assumed that the trend will continue.

The second most obvious change will likely occur in new ways of recording a still image. Several manufacturers are reportedly working on a film-like device which, instead of capturing light, will translate it into stored digital signals which can be erased, shown, changed, and manipulated by electronic means. It has been a long road from the camera obscura to the laser beam, but we will still be drawing with light which, in more than one way, is what photography is all about.

HOW PHOTOGRAPHS HAPPEN

Video photographs happen when light is focused in a controlled manner through a lens onto a sensitive surface in a pickup tube which releases electrons in a pattern directly related to the pattern of the light hitting the surface. The pattern of electrons is more or less stored magnetically on tape or disk or can be transported to a receiver. A picture is formed in the picture tube when the stored pattern of electrons is thrown against a sensitive surface, producing a pattern of light which is directly related to the pattern of the electrons hitting its surface. For a number of technical reasons, using a narrow, rapidly moving electron beam pattern to trace a picture with what is, in effect, a rigidly controlled dot of light, has become common. The tracing is done very rapidly, producing a more or less complete picture every 1/60 second. What the viewer sees as a smoothly changing picture is not composed of a rapid series of still photographs with small changes between them, as is the case with motion picture films; rather it is formed by that rapidly shifting light pattern. It is worth noting that while scanning patterns vary within three major systems in the world, the principle remains the same.

Color television pictures are formed from a mix of three colors of light: red, green, and blue, each in a separate electron source in a camera or picture tube. The reliable transmission of color signals, which must also work successfully on a black-and-white television receiver, is a remarkable technical advance which we now take for granted.

Nonvideo photographs happen when light is focused in a controlled manner onto a surface which has been treated with a chemical mix which reacts to light in predictable ways. Most photographs happen in a camera where the light-sensitive surface is stored in the dark so that it can react only to the light controlled by the lens. The light-sensitive surface consists of a mix of chemicals and holding agents called the *emulsion*. The emulsion is coated on a convenient carrier such as a strip or single sheet of plastic.

In its simplest form, black-and-white photography is possible because silver, particularly in a silver bromide form, reacts to light by turning black as the action of the light creates dark silver. The relation between the amount of light and the amount of silver produced is predictable and can be controlled in a variety of ways. Simply put, the image of light and shades of light is translated by the chemical action to a pattern of silver and shades of silver. Thus dark areas of the original scene are recorded as free of silver and light areas of the original scene as black with silver, with shades between the two extremes. This is obvious in the tonal reversal of the traditional black-and-white negative.

If light is passed through the same negative in a controlled situation and allowed to fall on an emulsion-coated piece of paper, the light and dark patterns will be recorded on the emulsion of the paper in a reversed, or normal, light and dark pattern. Following the rest of the processing, the result is a positive print with the correct tonal relationships. This is the familiar negative/positive system.

Color negative/positive systems work in much the same way. The emulsions involved are, however, more complex. Color emulsions incorporate "couplers," which are substances which react with the development chemicals to form colored dyes which are related to the extent and location of the silver involved. The dyes involved are the primary hues of cyan, magenta, and yellow. The emulsion has a layer of chemicals for each. The composite result of shining light through a color negative onto color printing paper is a positive color print with tone and color close to that of the original. A different, yet related, system exists for producing a positive color print from a positive color slide.

Positive color slides, or reversal transparencies, are provided in a related way. Again, silver and couplers are used in the emulsion, but the film that goes into the camera is processed differently so that it becomes a positive during the process. When that same film is processed, cut and mounted, it is a positive; that is, when light is shone through it onto a screen, the tonal relations and colors are acceptable.

There are many variations, including "instant" films, but photographs are possible because of the way light can produce changes on chemically treated substances. These changes can be controlled, manipulated, and enhanced for particular purposes. The principle is simple, the variations are complex, but the end result for the photographer is reliable, convenient, and relatively inexpensive.

G. R. McNutt

REFERENCES

Benedict, J. (1976) *Creative Photography: Darkroom and Camera Manual*. Tempe: Audio Visual Services, Arizona State University.

Carroll, J. S. (1977) *Photo-Lab Handbook*. New York: American Photographic Publishing.

Desilets, A. (1979) *Taking Photographs*. Toronto: Macmillan (Habitex).

Gernsheim, H. (1965) *A Concise History of Photography*. London: Thames and Hudson.

Gouland, P. (1975) *Electronic Flash Simplified*. New York: Amphoto.

Jacobs, M. and Kokrda, K. (1977) *Photographs in Focus*. Chicago: National Textbook Company.

Langford, M. J. (1976) *Visual Aids and Photography in Education*. London: Focal Press.

Rhode, R. B. and McCall, F. H. (1971) *Introduction to Photography*. New York: Macmillan.

(The reader is cautioned to note dates of publication of books and to consider Kodak publications, the Time-Life Series on *Photography*, the Focal Press Series, and many magazines and guides as useful and perhaps more up-to-date sources.)

PHOTOGRAVURE. "Gravure" and "intaglio" are terms used to identify a printing process where the image is transferred from ink-filled depressions in a printing plate rather than from inked raised patterns on a plate. High-quality printing of continuous tone paintings, illustrations, and photographs can be produced by a photographic process used in making a gravure plate. While the quality of the results is high, photogravure is expensive and reserved for special purposes. The process is less satisfactory for the reproduction of typescript.

PHOTO-MECHANICAL PROCESSES. Any process of printing or duplicating images using photographically prepared printing plates.

PHOTO-TYPESETTING. A technique of setting type for printing that uses photographs of type characters recorded on photographic film from which lithographic printing plates are made. *See* **Film Setting.**

PICI (U.K.). *See* **Programmed Instruction Centre for Industry.**

PICTURE PRESTEL. A development of videotex which permits a high-resolution format. A television-quality color picture can extend over one quarter of the display.

PICTURE TUBE. The cathode-ray tube in a television monitor or receiver on which the pictue is produced by variation of the beam intensity as the beam scans the raster.

PIE CHART, DIAGRAM. A graphical representation of data consisting of a circle divided into sectors whose angular sizes are proportional to the relative sizes of the quantities represented.

PILOT. An authoring language developed for writing computer-assisted instruction (CAI) programs. The language uses simple commands to present material (including graphics and sound if required), solicit responses, and then match the student's responses against the "correct" answers. Thus, writing computerized lessons in PILOT is easier than it would be in a general-purpose language such as BASIC. Numerous versions of PILOT are available to suit almost all microcomputers.

PILOT TONE. A control signal recorded alongside a film sound track to enable the sound track to be synchronized with the picture.

PINCUSHION DISTORTION. Distortion of an image whereby straight lines, parallel to the edge of the field, curve outward at their ends. *See* **Barrel Distortion.**

PIP. Acronym for programmed individual presentation, a projection system introduced by the Phillips Company in the early 1970s. The system used a combination of a super-8mm film cassette and a standard audiocassette.

Both cassettes clipped into a portable viewing unit with a daylight viewing screen, a built-in speaker and provision for two headsets. With the dual cassette system, electronic pulses on the audiotape controlled a variable speed film frame advance mechanism, maintaining sound and vision in synchronization. This meant that while the sound program continued at a constant speed, the film could be programmed to hold a single frame for any length of time, run at any speed up to 24 fps, or skip past frames completely if required.

In the normal way, 50 feet of super-8mm film running at a constant film speed of 24 fps has a program time of just over two and a half minutes. With PIP, making use of variable speed projection for both live action and animation and utilizing single frames for all nonmoving visuals such as titles, maps, and diagrams, program times of half an hour or longer could be achieved. The existence of an independent sound source enabled a single PIP film to present in an appropriate form all the required information for varying interests and levels of detail. Thus multilingual, multilevel, and even multipurpose programs were possible.

PIXEL. An abbreviation for *picture element,* the smallest spot that can be turned on or off on a display. In microcomputers the resolution of the graphics facility can be measured by the number of pixels the screen can contain: the greater the number (and hence the smaller the pixels), the better the resolution. As with screened printing, large dots (as in newspapers) give a poorer picture than small dots (as in magazines).

Cheap microcomputers commonly have a graphics screen with around 240 × 180 (= 43,200) pixels, enough for games and schematic diagrams, but of limited use for pictorial illustration. A useful parallel is an NTSC television receiver which can be considered to have around 525 × 700 (= 367,000) pixels. *See* **High-Resolution Graphics.**

PLANETARY CAMERA. A microfilming camera that is positioned vertically above a baseboard and is designed for microfilming large documents and books. Also known as a *flatbed camera.*

PLATE CAMERA. Originally a camera that used glass plates to carry the photographic emulsion. Although glass plates have now been replaced by cut film, the term is still used for all large-format cameras that use single sheets of film. *See* **Photography.**

PLATED DISK. A type of hard disk that has been coated with a metal alloy instead of the more common iron-oxide material. Drives using plated media are good for packing more data into smaller spaces and are better for portable use because of greater robustness.

PLATEN. (1) The flat glass surface or platform in an overhead projector or opaque projector on which the material to be projected is placed. (2) The surface bearing the force of striking print elements in typewriters and printing presses.

PLATO. PLATO is an acronym for Programmed Logic for Automatic Teaching Operations. This is a computer-based teaching system which provides a means of individualizing student instruction. The teacher designs the instructional material and stores it in the computer, which then presents it to the students while monitoring and evaluating their performance. Students can work at their own pace with access to special information and help when problems arise. Teaching strategies that are available include drill and practice, tutorial, simulation, inquiry, and dialogue. Student interaction with the computer is used to provide information on lesson effectiveness.

Development of the system began in 1960 (PLATO I) at the University of Illinois, U.S. Since then, various versions of the system have been developed, and it has grown from a single to a large multiuser system (PLATO IV). At present there are many hundreds of terminals attached to the network. These are to be found not only on the University of Illinois campus but also at locations throughout the United States and in a number of overseas institutions.

A special CAI author language called TUTOR is used for the construction of PLATO courseware. Authoring is done interactively at the terminal, and an author can switch in a few seconds from authoring the lesson to testing it as a student and then return to writing and correcting it. The system's responsiveness in rapid transition from author to student mode and back again is extremely useful in lesson creation. PLATO lessons are written to accommodate individual rates and styles of learning as well as to provide acceptance of student-constructed answers, immediate feedback for student responses, and remedial or advanced instructional material. PLATO has been used in public school, community college, and university undergraduate and graduate-level courses covering over 100 subject disciplines.

The PLATO IV terminals are connected and controlled by a CDC computer system. Output from the computer to the terminals is achieved by means of a single TV channel. Input from the terminals to the central computer system is by telephone lines. The terminal which the student uses is based upon a plasma display panel. In combination with the technique of back-projection it is capable of showing simultaneously, computer-generated graphic material and computer-selected photographic color slides. The slide store (microfiche) which is housed in the terminal has a capacity to hold 256 slides, all of which can be accessed within 0.2 second. The screen of the terminal is touch-sensitive thereby allowing students to interact with the computer by touching the images of objects that are displayed on the screen. Audio effects can be produced by means of a magnetic audiodisk which can be attached to the terminal. The disk can store more than 4000 random access messages (totaling up to 23 minutes in length), the average access time of which is 0.5 second. A wide range of other more specialized peripherals can also be attached to PLATO terminals.

PLATTER. The actual thin round disk on which a computer hard-disk drive stores data. Drive may incorporate several platters, according to their capacity.

PLAYING TIME FOR AUDIO TAPE.

Spools

Length (feet)	(meters)	Playing time per track in minutes (3.75 ips)	(1.875 ips)
300	91	16	32
600	183	32	64
900	274	48	96
1200	366	64	128
1800	549	96	192
2400	732	128	256

Cassettes

C60 : 30 minutes per track
C90 : 45 minutes per track
C120 : 60 minutes per track
C180 : 90 minutes per track
C240 : 120 minutes per track

PLAYING TIME FOR CINE FILM.

16mm (at 24 fps)

100ft (30.5m) plays for 2 minutes 46 seconds

Super-8mm (at 18 fps)

100ft (30.5m) plays for 6 minutes 40 seconds

PLAYING TIME FOR VIDEOTAPE. Larger and older formats (e.g., 1 inch reel-to-reel, 1/2–inch reel-to-reel or cartridge, 3/4–inch U-matic) commonly have maximum playing times of one hour. The modern cassette systems (Beta, VHS) are available with up to several hours playing time, and there are also long-play (half-speed) options which can extend playing time to around eight hours. *See* **Video Recording and Reproduction.**

PL/1. A computer language designed by IBM. The intention was to combine together the best features of FORTRAN and COBOL; thus the new language would have excellent facilities for file handling as well as computation. PL/1 is highly regarded as a programming language which offers these features, but it is difficult for nonprofessionals to use and consequently not commonly encountered in educational applications.

PLOTTER. A visual display or computer output device where the values of one variable quantity are automatically plotted against those of another. *See* **X-Y Plotter.**

PLUMBICON. The commonest type of sensing device found in television cameras. The cheapest cameras, such as those used for surveillance, utilize **vidicon** (q.v.) tubes, and these were formerly used in educational television cameras. However, in more recent times the plumbicon tube has demonstrated its superiority and enjoys general acceptance.

POINTER. A number that tells where to find some item of data. Most data bases use an indexed system to keep track of where data is stored on a disk. In these systems, you use a "key" to request a data record; the system then searches a table for the key and reads the associated pointer to find the location on the disk of the applicable record. *See* **Key.**

POINT SYSYEM. A system for measuring type height, one point being equal to 1/72 inch (0.351mm); thus type 1 inch high is described as 72 point type.

POLARIZING ATTACHMENT (FOR OVERHEAD PROJECTOR). A device using polarizing filters which, when combined with specially prepared overhead transparencies, gives an illusion of movement.

POLAROID PROCESS. A camera system utilizing a proprietary diffusion transfer process which after exposure gives a finished print in a matter of seconds. In addition to the common black-and-white and color print film, a number of specialized technical films are marketed, including, for example, one which produces a monochrome negative simultaneously with a print.

In 1983 Polaroid introduced a self-developing transparency film which does not require the use of a special camera, thus making possible instant 35mm color slides.

POLITICAL GAMING. Political gaming is a form of role-play that simulates the process of decision making at local government, national, or international level. Political games vary enormously in length and complexity, ranging from small-scale "public inquiry" situations dealing with purely local issues to highly sophisticated simulations of international relations that can last for several days. Both real and hypothetical situations are used as the basis of such games.

POLL. Mode of operation of facsimile (fax) machine whereby one master machine calls up documents at a predetermined time from several peripheral fax machines.

POP-UP. Computer menus which erupt from the bottom of the screen upon demand.

POP-UP MENU. A set of choices that is presented when its title or icon is selected.

PORT. An output/input socket on a computer. Printers and other peripherals must be connected to a port in order to communicate with the computer. *See* **Interface.**

PORTABILITY. The ability of a computer program to run on various machines. This does not relate to the medium of storage (e.g., disk) but to the actual software. Most forms of BASIC are not compatible, and a BASIC program prepared for one computer will often need substantial rewriting before it will run on a different make of computer.

PORTAPAK. Originally a Sony trade name (c. 1970), the term is now used generally to describe any lightweight portable television recording kit. Components include a video camera and recorder, power supply, and usually some form of microphone—often incorporated into the front of the camera. *See* **Video Recording and Reproduction.**

PORTRAIT. Rectangular framing (of, e.g., a visual display unit) in which the long dimension is vertical. The alternative horizontal mode is termed "landscape."

POSTERIZATION. Reproduction of a photographic or video image using only a few specific tones or flat colors, with most of the tonal gradation and detail suppressed.

POSTPRODUCTION. The activity required to put together a finished production, after shooting has finished. Usually this means editing (both vision and sound), perhaps incorporating graphics and post-sync sound.

POSTPRODUCTION PREMASTERING. A videodisc production term also referred to as video processing, this is the process of editing, assembly, evaluation, revision, and coding of intermediate materials. The resulting premaster is a fully coded videotape, ready for the final stage of cutting the master disk.

POSTTEST. A test carried out after a unit of instruction. Posttests are designed to measure change from an original state. *See* **Evaluation; Gain Ratio.**

PREAMPLIFIER. An amplifier, the main purpose of which is to increase the output of a low-level source in order that the signal can be further processed without additional deterioration of the signal-to-noise ratio.

PREBOOT. A special program that permits a microcomputer to read a nonstandard disk or to use unusual peripherals. The preboot is loaded and then the nonstandard disk is booted. Many copy-protected software packages require a preboot for use on hard disks or with special display cards.

PREKNOWLEDGE. The knowledge that a subject has before a unit of instruction. Preknowledge forms the base for measurement of change. *See* **Evaluation; Gain Ratio.**

PREPRODUCTION. A term used in connection with the production of films, videotapes, videodiscs, etc. In general, it refers to all those tasks which have to be performed prior to the actual production, e.g., flowcharting, making up a storyboard, scriptwriting, and so on.

PRESTEL. A videotex system developed by British Telecom, originally known as Viewdata. *See* **Videotex.**

PRETEST. A test carried out before an experiment to ascertain preknowledge. Pretests are designed to measure the baseline in measuring change. *See* **Evaluation; Gain Ratio.**

PREVIEW. A term applied to a television monitor in a control room which is usually placed beside the transmission monitor. It is used to check the composition of a picture before it is transmitted or recorded.

PRIMARY COLORS. Color television utilizes the colors red, blue, and green to achieve all required hues and shades. If all three are mixed together in equal proportions, the result is white.

PRINTER. A peripheral computer device which produces printed output. Cheap printers are usually of the dot-matrix type; daisy wheel or thimble printers offer typewriter quality and easily changeable type heads for different type styles, but are more expensive and usually slower than dot-matrix ones. Mainframe computers use very fast line printers.

Newer types of printer such as ink-jet and laser printers, for example, enable faster and/or superior printing to be obtained at economic prices, and with the great benefit of almost silent operation. Dot-matrix and laser printers are capable of producing graphic output.

PRINTOUT. Printed pages produced by a computer.

PRINT SPOOLER. Mechanism by which one or more documents can be sent to a printer while other computer functions take place concurrently. Effectively, a print spooler permits time-sharing between the printing process and some other activity. A simpler version of this facility is a buffer store, which permits slabs of output to be fed to a printer from the buffer with concurrent computer usage.

PRINT-THROUGH. The transfer of magnetism from one layer of tape to another layer while the tape reel is stored. Naturally this results in some degradation of the stored information.

PROCESS CAMERA. A large precision camera used for making negatives of flat copy (e.g., pasteups) for subsequent printing or display purposes.

PRODOS. An Apple operating system designed to support hard disks as well as floppy disk storage.

PRODUCER. As used in television this term refers to a role very similar to that of director in a film production. The producer is head of the production team and responsible for the artistic and creative standards. Even in the simplest in-house educational production, someone has to decide what pictures are to be recorded; i.e., someone has to be effectively a producer.

PROGRAM. A set of instructions describing actions for a computer to perform in order to accomplish some task; while conforming to the rules and conventions of a particular programming language.

PROGRAMMED INSTRUCTION. *See* **Programmed Learning.**

PROGRAMMED INSTRUCTION CENTRE FOR INDUSTRY (U.K.). A government-financed unit which operated for a time at Sheffield University, Sheffield, U.K., to carry out research and development activities into industrial training applications of programmed methods. Some of the work of the center continues at the Instructional Technology Unit at Sheffield Polytechnic, England.

PROGRAMMED LEARNING. Programmed learning can be defined as the study of carefully prepared material in a step-by-step procedure which is accompanied by immediate knowledge of results and the possibility of taking different pathways through the instruction according to one's knowledge or mistakes.

ORIGINS

Programmed learning was mainly a phenomenon of the 1960s. There was some prehistory, as we shall see below, and there is a legacy. However, to appreciate this legacy we must first trace the origins of programmed learning.

It is conventional to begin a discussion of programmed learning and teaching machines with the work of Sidney Pressey in the 1920s. However, it is important to observe that there have always been machines and devices to aid teaching and learning for as long as there has been recorded history. Nonetheless, Pressey is usually accorded the first place in the annals of programmed instruction because he was one of the first psychologists to embody the laws of learning as they were then formulated into instructional devices. The modern objective test procedure, which was being developed at that time, suggested to Pressey the building of a simple scoring device which could test a learner's achievement after he had been taught something (Pressey, 1926 HISTORICAL). Pressey developed a series of mechanical devices which presented **multiple-choice questions** (q.v.) to learners after their instruction and which gave them immediate knowledge about the correctness (or not) of their choice of answers. Pressey discovered that such testing after instruction led to improved recall scores on subsequent examinations.

The work of Pressey received little attention until the era of programmed learning began properly in the 1950s, particularly with the work of B. F. Skinner. Skinner was often called "the father of programmed learning," probably because of his enormous influence in this field, and because his views were the most prestigious (and the most controversial) of all the figures to be discussed. In 1954 Skinner delivered the now-famous address entitled "The Science of Learning and the Art of Teaching" (1954 HISTORI-

CAL). In this paper Skinner analyzed what for him were some of the basic limitations of the American educational scene at that time, and his answers to them. He argued that in a conventional classroom situation there were four major limitations:

1. Educational control was mainly aversive. The student learned in order to escape from negative evaluations, threats, and punishments.
2. There was a lack of skillful programs which moved the learners forward through a series of progressive or successive approximations to the final complex behavior required.
3. The contingencies of reinforcement were far from optimal: it was not physically possible for one teacher to reinforce each student in a class each time a correct response was made. Reinforcement arrived too long after a response had been produced.
4. Reinforcement was relatively infrequent. This was seen as the most serious failing of current instruction. (By reinforcement Skinner meant providing some event or stimulus that served to strengthen behavior. In other words, reinforcement makes that behavior's recurrence more probable.)

Skinner's linear teaching program (and its associated linear teaching machine) represents, like Pressey's devices, a solution to these limitations based upon a then-current theory of learning. An example from a linear programmed text is shown in Figure 53. In it are demonstrated the principles that Skinner was aiming at:

1. Educational control is not aversive. Learners learn because they want to, under no threat of punishment or failure.
2. There is a skillful program which moves the learner one step at a time from simple to more complex behavior.
3. The contingencies of reinforcement are (in Skinner's terms) optimal: learners work at their own pace and receive reinforcement as soon as they make a response.
4. The reinforcement for responding (in the form of the feedback given for each correct response made) is frequent.

A further principle, which Skinner did not stress at that time, was that a teaching program itself should first be tried out and tested in order to see if, in fact, it works. As learners work through a program, they leave a residue of responses—to each item and to the interim and final tests. Analyzing these responses from a group of students can indicate sources of difficulty in a program. By revising weak sections of a program it can be improved until (by repeated testing and revision) one can fairly well guarantee the success of a program in doing a particular job with a particular group of learners. Research workers advocated that 90 percent (or more) of the learners should obtain 90 percent (or more) on the final test of a successful program.

Several machines were constructed in the 1960s with the purpose of giving individual learners step-by-step self-paced reinforcement. Inspection of the written material shows, however, that it was the writing of the program rather than its mechanical presentation that provided the difficulties, for the subject matter to be taught required painstaking analysis. The machines, by contrast, were often little more than paper roll devices.

Such machines, nonetheless, did help control the learning process. They ensured that items were presented individually, that learners could not move on until they had made a response, that the correct answer was not available until the learners had made their own, and that the learners worked through the program in the way intended by the author. Furthermore, the machine format was intrinsically motivating: most people enjoyed turning the paper on, and the bulk of what had to be learned could be hidden so that the learners did not feel that the size of the task was beyond them. These advantages of machine presentation were not present to the same extent in the more common programmed textbooks.

However, there were many objections to **linear programs** (q.v.)—not least that "overprogrammed" texts provided a boring and monotonous way of learning—and the principles of programmed learning outlined by Skinner were subjected to much research and detailed criticism (see, e.g., Hartley, 1974; Mackie, 1975 RESEARCH REVIEWS). In the early days Norman Crowder was often presented as a challenger to Skinner's theories—as indeed he was—but it is important to note that originally Crowder's work was carried out independently of Skinner's. Crowder was not particularly interested in theories of learning: he was interested in whether or not material was communicated successfully (Crowder, 1960 HISTORICAL).

In a Crowder-type branching program, learners were usually presented with a paragraph of information and then asked a question about it. A number of alternative responses or answers were supplied with each question, only one of which was correct. In the machine system the learners were then asked to press a button which indicated which response they had chosen. The program moved on. If the learners were correct, the next item told them why and then gave them fresh information. If, however, an error had been made, the nature of the error was explained, and the learners were directed back to the initial question. If a serious error had been made, then the learners might be sent along a special remedial sequence.

The most well-known machine using this technique in the 1960s was the Autotutor, and textbook presentations of the same material were also available, although these

Figure 53
An Extract from a Typical Early Linear Program

	A second important condition for efficient learning is the presentation of subject matter in a series of *small logical* steps. The learner must master Step A before he can grasp .... B. 20
Step 20	An ancient Greek fable tells us that Milo was able to lift his full-grown bull because he had lifted it daily since it was a calf. Since the animal had *small* increases in weight daily, Milo's weight-lifting "program" progressed through a series of many .... steps. 21
small 21	Unfortunately, under usual classroom conditions it is difficult for the instructor to present subject matter in steps which are sufficiently .... in size. 22
small 22	A later item in this program – to which you probably cannot yet respond correctly – reads "Another condition is that each response is followed by . . .". That item is a large step beyond the present one. However, after being led through many .... steps, you will later be able to .... correctly. 23
small respond 23	This program may seem annoyingly simple. But the merit of a step-by-step presentation of subject matter is shown by the fact that you have made few, if any, incorrect .... to the statements or stimuli of this program. 24
responses 24	

Source: Ohmer Milton and Leonard J. West. Copyright © 1961 by Harcourt Brace Jovanovich, Inc. Reproduced with permission.

were often very bulky. A typical item from such a program is shown in Figure 54.

This kind of programming was called "branching" to contrast it with Skinner's "linear" one. Its advantages were (1) that it allowed more for individual differences in knowledge and comprehension and (2) that it was more suitable for dealing with more complex subject material.

DOES PROGRAMMED LEARNING WORK?

Considerable research effort was spent in the 1960s and 1970s in making comparison studies between the different systems of programming discussed above, and of course, between programmed instruction (of whatever kind) on the one hand and conventional instruction (whatever that is) on the other. A typical study is that reported by Touq and Mokbel (1977, EXAMPLES). Because the results of such specific comparisons are not generalizable, the present author pooled the results of 112 such studies to see if any generalizations did emerge. The results are summarized in Table 18. These results speak clearly for themselves. Although doubt may be expressed about the scientific rigor of many of the studies, there was evidence that in many cases programmed instruction could be as effective as, or better than, conventional

Figure 54
A Typical Frame from a Branching Program on Electronics

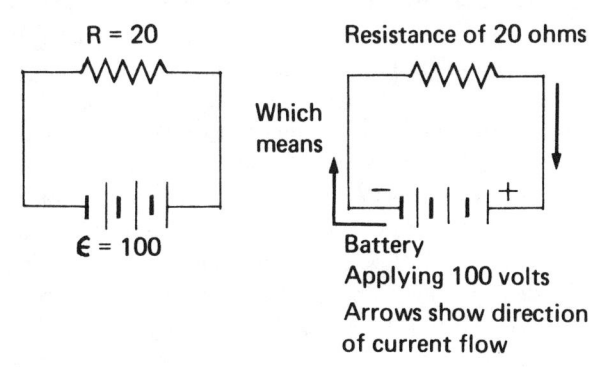

Source: R. J. Hughes and P. Pipe, *Introduction to Electronics*. Copyright © 1961 by English Universities Press, Ltd. Reproduced with permission.

instruction. Perhaps of more interest, however, were the results of comparison studies in which an instructor working with a program was compared with an instructor working alone or with a program alone. Of twelve studies reviewed by the author (Hartley, 1972 RESEARCH REVIEWS), eleven concluded that the instructor with the program was the best system. A later study by Hughes and Reid (1975 EXAMPLES) was of interest here: in this study the teacher did best, after first memorizing the program.

Many people, of course, said that even if programmed learning worked, it could only teach facts, not encourage independence of thought or creativity. Certainly there was an emphasis on mathematical, scientific, and so-called factual subject matter in this area of endeavor. However, even if it is accepted that this is the sole area in which programmed learning can apply—a proposition not accepted by all—then this would certainly not imply that programmed learning should be dismissed. There is a severe shortage of science and mathematics teachers worldwide and programmed learning can still be actively exploited here. Programmed learning allows the achievements of effective teachers to be disseminated widely.

A different approach to the argument about independence of thought and creativity is to ask people who say that programmed learning cannot teach these things to explain what in fact they mean by these terms. If such terms are explainable, if these concepts can be measured, then surely, in principle they can be taught? It is perhaps important to note here that modern approaches to programming (see below) can allow for contrasting opinions in answers just as easily as (and perhaps even more than) conventional teachers can (and these opinions are open to inspection). Even if it is accepted that we cannot teach creativity or independence of thought in itself, we might well be able to use a program to increase pupils' already existing abilities in this respect, and several researchers have taken this approach (see, e.g., Williams, 1977 EXAMPLES). Furthermore, it is important to remember that students may be able to develop further if they have a better grasp of the basic issues.

WIDENING THE APPROACH: THE LEGACY OF PROGRAMMED LEARNING

In the early days of programmed learning, there was much discussion concerning the relative merits of the different systems outlined above—linear versus branching, multiple-choice questions versus written response,

Table 18
The Results of 112 Studies Comparing Programmed with Conventional Instruction

		Programmed Instruction Group		
Measures recorded	Number of studies recording these measures	Significantly superior	Not Significantly different	Significantly worse
Time taken	90	47	37	6
Test results	110	41	54	15
Retest results	33	6	24	3

Note: Figures in the first column differ because not all three measures are recorded for every one of the 112 studies.

large steps versus small steps, and so on—and compromise solutions appeared (e.g., see Kay and Sime, 1963; Markle, 1978a EXAMPLES).

What is important to note here about the early systems, and even the compromise ones, is that in those days the instructional programs were machine-dominated rather than student-oriented. In other words, if one was producing a linear program, the material had to be arranged in segments in order to fit into a linear machine. Similarly, if one was constructing a branching text, the material had to be written in such a way that a multiple-choice question could be asked at the end of every page. In other words, a program's format was more controlled by its method of presentation than by considerations of what it was appropriate for learners to be doing at a particular time.

More modern approaches to designing programmed materials began to concern themselves with problems raised by this latter question. When is it appropriate to ask a multiple-choice question? When might a careful linear exposition in short steps be most appropriate? Do we need the student to make a response to every item? Do we always have to provide a correct answer? Can this point best be made with an appropriate illustration? Is it more appropriate to use lengthy prose passages (with adjunct questions) at certain times? Can learners work in groups on this topic? When is it better for learners to control their own sequences of questions? And so on. Modern programs are therefore much more flexible than the traditional ones which appear to be better known (e.g., Markle, 1978a EXAMPLES).

By the late 1960s it had become clear that the psychology that had sustained programmed learning up to that time was to some extent restrictive (Annett, 1973; Hartley, 1985 ILLUSTRATIONS). The emphasis in programmed learning began to change from examining what the learner did to examining what program writers did in constructing programmed materials. In the early 1970s the essence of programmed instruction appeared to lie in working through four interrelated steps:

1. Specifying the objectives (knowing where you were going)
2. Analyzing the learner's task and selecting appropriate teaching methods and media (trying to get there by the best means possible)
3. Evaluation (assessing whether you had got there successfully)
4. Revision (using the results from the assessment to improve the teaching in step 2)

Within this broader framework programmers began to use a variety of methods in step 2 (including conventional programs of the kind described above) while maintaining the other stages. This wider thinking allowed programmers to escape from thinking limited to machines and texts alone, and to think in terms of larger systems: of programmed instructional packages rather than single programmed textbooks; of packages which might contain tapes, slides, audiovisual aids, programmed and conventional instruction materials; and of whole courses which lasted a complete term or year, instead of single lessons. As long as the objectives were clear, the achievement of these objectives assessed, and feedback used to improve the system, then such packages and courses were said to be programmed. One development which is typical of this approach is that of the Keller Plan, or personalized instruction (Keller, 1968 EXAMPLES).

However, the massive amount of necessary clerical work in such systems hastened development in the direction of computer-managed or computer-assisted learning. Researchers in the field of programmed learning grasped the fact that teaching and learning was a complex business, and began to move more and more into computer-assisted learning. This shift was accompanied by a considerable general debate about the function and role of objectives, **task analysis** (q.v.) and related teaching strategies, presentation methods, and evaluation (e.g., see Hartley and Davies, 1978 RESEARCH REVIEWS; Knapper, 1980 ILLUSTRATIONS).

In one sense, we could say that programmed learning (as it is usually thought of) has been and gone. Nonetheless, it has left a legacy (Markle, 1978b; Stones, 1981 SIMILAR VIEWS). The idea has become much more widespread that in order to instruct well, one should specify one's aims in advance, one should analyze what is required, one should attempt to evaluate one's success, and one should use feedback in order to improve the instruction. These features are essential if we are to provide well-constructed instructional programs for the microcomputers which are now emerging in our schools.

J. Hartley

REFERENCES

Examples

Hughes, D. C. and Reid, N. A. (1975) "Programmed Learning and Conventional Teaching." *Educational Research* 18 (1): 54–61.

Kay, H. and Sime, M. E. (1963) "Survey of Teaching Machines." In *Mechanisation in the Classroom,* ed. M. Goldsmith. London: Souvenir Press.

Keller, F. S. (1968) "Goodbye teacher. . . . " Repr. in *Contributions to an Educational Technology,* ed. J. Hartley and I. K. Davies London: Kogan Page; New York: Nichols, 1978.

Markle, S. M. (1978a) *Designs for Instructional Designers*. Champaign, Ill.: Stipes.

Touq, M. S. and Mokbel, M. S. (1977) "The Effectiveness of Programmed Instruction in Teaching English at Secondary School Level." *Programmed Learning and Educational Technology* 14 (4): 289–293.

Williams, R. E. (1977) "Programmed Instruction for Creativity." *Programmed Learning and Educational Technology* 14 (1): 50–64.

Historical

Crowder, N. A. (1960) "Automatic Tutoring by Intrinsic Programming." In *Teaching Machines and Programmed Instruction,* ed. A. A. Lumsdaine and R. Glaser. Washington, D.C.: NEA.

Pressey, S. L. (1926) "A Simple Apparatus Which Gives Tests and Scores—and Teaches." Repr. in *Teaching Machines and Programmed Learning,* ed. A. A. Lumsdaine and R. Glaser. Washington, D.C.: NEA, 1960.

Skinner, B. F. (1954) "The Science of Learning and the Art of Teaching." Repr. in *Teaching Machines and Programmed Learning,* ed. A. A. Lumsdaine and R. Glaser. Washington, D.C.: NEA, 1960.

Illustrations

Annett, J. (1973) "Psychological Bases of Educational Technology." In *Aspects of Educational Technology* 8, ed. R. Budgett and J. Leedham. London: Pitman.

Hartley, J. R. (1985) "Some Psychological Aspects of Computer-Assisted Learning and Teaching." *Programmed Learning & Educational Technology* 22 (2): 140–149.

Knapper, C. (1980) *Evaluating Instructional Technology*. London: Croom Helm.

Research Reviews

Hartley, J., ed. (1972) *Strategies for Programmed Instruction*. London: Butterworths.

Hartley, J. (1974) "Programmed Instruction 1954–1974: A Review." *Programmed Learning & Educational Technology* 11: 278–291.

Hartley, J. and Davies, I. K. (1978) *Contributions to an Educational Technology,* vol. 2. London: Kogan Page; New York: Nichols.

Mackie, A. (1975) "Programmed Learning—a Developing Technique." *Programmed Learning & Educational Technology* 12 (4): 220–228.

Similar Views

Markle, S. M. (1978b) Preface to *Designs for Instructional Designers*. Champaign, Ill.: Stipes.

Stones, E. (1981) "Programmed Learning Revisited: a Case Study." *Programmed Learning & Educational Technology* 18 (1): 7–10.

PROGRAMMED LEARNING & EDUCATIONAL TECHNOLOGY (Journal). *See* **Association for Educational and Training Technology.**

PROGRAMMED TEXT. An instructional manual formatted in accordance with one or other scheme of programmed learning. Those following the tenets of "branching" required readers to move in nonsequential order around the book, according to their responses to questions. Such a system was less common than the "linear" text, in which short teaching items ("frames") were arranged in strips down the pages, or in a few cases across the book. Most frames posed a question, and the geometric arrangement of frames was intended to allow learners to avoid accidental sighting of the answer before they made their own attempt. *See* **Scrambled Text.**

PROGRAMMER. A person who formulates, from the system documentation prepared by a systems analyst, a set of instructions written in a suitable language, which enables a computer to process data in the manner required.

PROGRAMMING LANGUAGE. A set of rules or conventions for writing programs. *See* **BASIC; FORTRAN; Pascal.**

PROJECTION. In all cases, projection consists of three essential elements: an illuminated object (e.g., a film frame), a projection lens, and an image. The general aim of projection is to obtain a clear, bright, large image in full view of the audience. Several factors will determine the extent to which this aim is realized:

1. The object to be projected must be brightly lit—this is much easier with film than with opaque materials.

2. The lens needs to be of good quality, and of a focal length to match the screen size and distance.

3. The environmental conditions must be good, i.e., appropriate blackout, suitable screen, clear sight-lines.

See **Projection Lens; Projection Screen.**

PROJECTION LENS. Unlike a camera lens, a projection lens is usually of fixed aperture: the quantity of light it passes is not adjustable. In most cases, too, the focal length is fixed, although **zoom lenses** (q.v.) are in use, particularly for 8mm projection.

If the screen is suitably sized for the auditorium, then a standard lens (focal length 50mm [16mm film]; 85 or 100mm [35mm slides]) will fill the screen if the projector is at the rear of the room. Different lenses need to be fitted if the screen is small and the projector cannot be brought nearer the screen. In any event, for optimum viewing the picture width should be at least equal to one-sixth of the throw.

PROJECTION SCREEN. Many different materials are in use for front-projection screens, and indeed it is perfectly feasible to project onto a white wall with satisfactory results. However, most applications call for a fabric screen of some sort, possibly coated with glass beads. In general, the use of special coatings will enhance the image brightness for viewers near the axis of projection, but will demonstrate a notable falling off in quality as the angle subtended at the screen increases. It is important that the size of image is appropriate for the particular auditorium, and the screen size must permit this, and of course allow for wide-screen format if such films are to be screened. (A rule of thumb is that screen width should be at least one-sixth of the distance from screen to back row.) Rear-projection is almost always onto a plastic translucent screen, which offers exceptional convenience but usually is accompanied by some sacrifice of image quality.

PROJECTION TELEVISION. Display systems in educational television usually depend on conventional monitors or domestic-type receivers. However, large screen displays are possible using one of two systems:

1. By projecting the image of a specially bright cathode-ray tube using mirror optics. Such projectors for color television use this system in triplicate, the images (red, blue, green) from each tube being superimposed on the screen.
2. The **Eidophor** (q.v.) system uses an oil-film light-valve. This produces a very bright image suitable for a large screen but is expensive and may require specially trained operators.

The quality of the projected image may be noticeably inferior to the conventional television screen, and in particular varies from one viewing position to another.

PROM. Programmable Read Only Memory. In effect, a blank ROM which can be written to just once and then it becomes like a normal ROM. However, some PROMs can be erased using ultraviolet light (through a provided window) and then reprogrammed as before—these are termed **EPROMs** (q.v.). *See* **Memory; ROM.**

PROMPT. To remind or signal the user that some action is expected, typically by displaying a distinctive symbol, a reminder message, or a menu of choices on the display screen.

PROPORTIONAL SPACING. In typesetting, lettering, etc., spacing characters in proportion to their width. Thus "i" occupies less space than "m" and so on. This is the normal mode of operation with letterpress, but is less common with typewriters and computer printers.

PROTECTION SYSTEMS. Several systems are in use to prevent piracy of computer software. An early procedure was to modify the disk operating system (DOS) so that some sectors of the disk were unreadable unless the modified DOS had been loaded into the computer. No opportunity then existed for the user to LIST or SAVE the program. Inevitably, both hardware and software devices have become available to circumvent the various protection schemes. "Nibble" copy programs seek to analyze the disk contents byte by byte, whereas firmware copiers wait until the required program has been loaded into memory and then break in and send a copy to a disk. In turn, these developments are leading to ever more sophisticated protection schemes, including, for example, the use of special disks with mechanically encoded data.

It has been suggested that if software houses took a more enlightened attitude to the making of backup copies, and provided more in the way of updating documentation and programs, the piracy problem would be much diminished. At time of writing (1987) this tendency is becoming discernible, with several leading software houses abandoning protection schemes.

PROTOCOL. A set of rules governing the way information is exchanged over a computer network. Microcomputer networks generally use simple protocols meant originally for teletypewriters or various protocols included in proprietary software packages. Although they are directly incompatible with mainframes, personal computers can be hooked up to large computers with protocol-converter units.

PSI. *See* **Personalized System of Instruction.**

PSTN. Public Switched Telephone Network.

PSYCHODRAMA. The dramatic presentation of personal conflict or crisis for diagnostic or therapeutic purposes. It is related to sociodrama and is therefore one of the routes to simulations. Psychodrama is often associated with J. L. Moreno.

PSYCHOMOTOR DOMAIN. One of the three fields into which educational objectives are divided according to the ideas of Bloom and his coworkers. The psychomotor domain contains all those attributes associated with the coordination of mind and body in carrying out psychomotor activities, e.g., playing squash, scratching foot, etc.

PULL-DOWN MENU. A menu (one that shows all the choices only when you select its title) that comes down from the top line of the screen. *See* **Pop-Up Menu.**

PULSE CODE MODULATION. The expression in binary form of audio and video signals.

PUNCHED CARD. A card of defined dimensions on which data is represented as a pattern of holes in specified positions; a standard card can represent a maximum of 80 characters. The cards are used for input to a mainframe computer using a card reader.

PUNCHED TAPE. A tape on which information is recorded by means of a pattern of punched holes. It was once a common input/output medium for computers but is now obsolescent.

PUZZLE BOX. A box used by early experimenters in conditioning (e.g., Thorndike) to investigate the learning of animals. Animals attempted to open a trapdoor in the box in order to obtain food.

Q

QUADRAPHONIC. A sound recording or sound reproduction system that makes use of four discrete sound tracks or channels, employing two loudspeaker units placed in front of the listener (as in stereophonic systems) plus two behind, to increase the realism of the sound.

QUADRATURE (QUADRUPLEX). A system of video recording used for many years in broadcast standard recorders. The name derives from the four magnetic heads. Quadrature recorders have largely been rendered obsolescent by developments in helical-scan video recording. *See* **Video Recording and Reproduction.**

QUANTIZED. The quantum theory of physics states that there is not a continuous range of amounts of energy, but only a discrete number of energy states, which are determined by fundamental physical laws. In some forms of digital representation of varying levels of energy, e.g., speech, there are arbitrarily assigned levels, and each sample represented is considered to be equivalent to one of these levels. The samples are then said to be "quantized."

QUARTER-TRACK. The system used in four-track audiotape recording. The record and playback heads have two pole pieces which cover the first and third quarters of the tape. The second and fourth quarters are recorded/played by flipping the tape, which brings those strips of tape into contact with the heads.

QUARTZ-IODINE LAMP. *See* **Tungsten Halogen Lamp.**

QUERY BY EXAMPLE. To ask for information from a data base system by defining the qualifications for selected records on a sample record, rather than describing a procedure for finding the information.

QUEUING THEORY. A mathematical technique borrowed from operational research where allocation of limited resources is planned on the basis of a model of the flow of facilities into the system. Applications in educational technology are restricted due to the lack of models relating variables together. However, the use of a library, a computer, or a self-service facility are applications which have been studied.

QWERTY KEYBOARD. A keyboard in which the keys are laid out in the same way as on a standard typewriter. The name is derived from the top row of letters, which go Q W E R T Y from the left. It is often stated that this arrangement is a historical accident and that much more efficient systems, such as the Dvořák keyboard, should be used.

R

RADIO FREQUENCY (RF). Electromagnetic waves having frequencies in the range used to carry radio or television signals, i.e., between 0.5MHz and 3,000MHz. *See* **UHF; VHF.**

RADIO MICROPHONE. Microphone connected to a small radio transmitter that can be placed in a performer's pocket. The signal is picked up by a suitable amplification system for recording or replay through loudspeakers. Thus a teacher may address a large class without having to stay close to a fixed microphone, and yet not have the inconvenience of trailing wires. Also known as a *wireless microphone*.

RADIOVISION. A media facility devised by the British Broadcasting Corporation, in which a filmstrip is matched to an educational radio transmission. Users are expected to record the radio program and to subsequently play it to a class while also projecting the synchronized pictures. The filmstrip has to be purchased from the BBC. *See* **Audiovisual Media.**

RAGGED RIGHT. Text that is not aligned on the right-hand side of the page, i.e., is unjustified. Also termed *ranged left*.

RAM. Random Access Memory. A computer memory which allows information to be stored as well as retrieved. Normally, RAM is used to hold information only temporarily; permanent storage is provided on magnetic disk or tape. The power of a microcomputer is commonly measured by the number of kilobytes of RAM it contains. *See* **Memory; ROM.**

RAMDISK. Memory chip(s) which emulate disk storage. Thus all disk commands will be carried out (SAVE, LOAD, etc.), but the transfer of data will be very rapid. Unlike a conventional disk the data in a RAMdisk will be lost if power is disconnected, so it is necessary to store all data onto disk at the end of a working session.

RANDOM ACCESS. This term refers to a storage or memory system from which any individual piece of information may be retrieved immediately without searching through a lot of intervening items. For example, RAM computer memory enables retrieval of material stored in it once the "address" of the item has been specified.

Random-access slide projectors permit computer-controlled or manual selection of particular slides without having to work through intervening items. On the other hand, a particular section of audiotape can only be reached from any other section by searching sequentially either backwards or forwards.

RANDOM INTERLACE. A technique for scanning that is often used in cheaper television systems where there is no fixed relationship between adjacent lines in successive fields. It offers reduced precision by comparison with the interlacing employed in commercial broadcast services.

RANDOM SAMPLE. A sample where every member of the population has an equal chance of being included. In experimental research, use is often made of tables of random numbers to ensure that selection procedures are unbiased, for example, in choosing survey respondents from a telephone directory.

RANGED LEFT. Text that is aligned on the left side of the page only, i.e., ragged right or unjustified.

RANGE FINDER. An attachment to, or system incorporated in, a camera that measures the distance from camera to subject. Usually the lens focus will be automatically adjusted according to the reading of the range finder.

RANK ORDER CORRELATION. A nonparametric correlation technique where the ordering of the elements of the variables is used for computation. For example, a correlation could be determined between subject preference and performance.

RAPID READING. Various means of increasing speed of reading are in use. Generally speaking, these involve some type of scanning procedure in order that the reader may absorb the essentials of the book or paper, ignoring all redundant material. The value of rapid reading is clearly related to both the purposes of the reader and the density of information in the material.

RASTER. A predetermined pattern of scanning lines on a picture tube which provides substantially uniform coverage of an area, or the area of a picture tube scanned by the electron beam. A computer normally only synchronizes the timing of the raster and turns the beam on and off; the monitor makes the raster itself. Having the computer supply information for a standard raster produces much cheaper displays than having the computer control the placement of every line (such an arrangement is called *vector graphics*).

RATING SCALE. A scale that attempts to quantify the degree to which a subject has a particular characteristic. There is a considerable body of opinion and fact about such scales and how they should be used. In general, ratings are easy to make but difficult to interpret. Each scale has individual characteristics of reliability and validity. The main source of error variance is the rating, not the scale.

RATIO SCALE. The most complete form of classification. Its units of measurements are constant, and it has an anchor point (absolute zero). It is therefore possible to say, since height is a ratio scale, that subject A is 1.07 times as tall as subject B. Whereas we cannot meaningfully say that subject X (of IQ 120) is 1.2 times as intelligent as subject Y (of IQ 100).

REACTION TIME. The time taken by a subject in responding to a stimulus. For example, the time to complete a frame in a programmed learning sequence.

REACTIVE INHIBITION. The tendency of every reaction to cause in an organism a state opposed to the recurrence of the reaction. This inhibition is not unlike fatigue. It is therefore a negative impulse and is associated with conditioned responses.

READ. To transfer information into computer memory from a source external to the computer, such as a disk drive or modem.

READABILITY. A measure of the appropriateness of reading material for the ability of the reader. Several readability formulas are available. *See* **Cloze Technique; Textbook Design.**

READ ONLY MEMORY. Memory whose contents can be read (i.e., retrieved) but not written to. *See* **ROM.**

REALIA. Term for real objects as distinct from software, e.g., an actual tarantula, dead or alive, rather than a photograph of one.

REAL-TIME PROCESSING. The computer processing of data as it arises so that the information obtained can be of immediate use in analyzing or controlling external events happening concurrently. For example, the computer control of automatic bank tellers.

REAR PROJECTION. *See* **Back Projection.**

RECEIVER. Term applied to devices capable of receiving broadcast television signals. This contrasts with a monitor which is only capable of utilizing a video frequency input (e.g., from a camera) and may have no sound-reproducing facility. Receiver/monitors are available which can accept both types of input.

The advent of microcomputers has sharpened the distinction between receivers and monitors. The basic output from the computer is a video signal, which has to be passed through a modulator before it can be viewed on a receiver. The quality is necessarily inferior to that on a monitor, an important consideration where text or data is to be read.

RECEIVER/MONITOR. A television receiver that is also capable of being used as a television monitor; it is equipped to handle both broadcast signals received via an antenna or VCR and video signals fed in by cable from a camera or ITV system.

RECORD. The collection of information about a single person, item, or transaction in a data base that moves as a unit when the data base is sorted or reordered. A record is analogous to a card in a card index, with several fields containing information.

RECORD HEAD. The part of a tape recorder that imparts the signal to the tape. It is an electromagnetic device which consists of a ring-shaped metal core broken at a gap. Coils wound on either side of the ring energize the head during recording. During replay the same head is usually used to pick up the magnetic fields on the tape and transform them into electrical currents for subsequent amplification.

RED TAPE. Administrative information associated with each videotex page and frame. For example, title and routing information.

REDUCTION PRINT. The print of a cine film made from a large format master, for example, an 8mm print from a 16mm master. In the production of 8mm films for teaching, it was usually advantageous initially to make the film with 16mm film stock and equipment, as this ensured the best possible quality.

REDUCTION RATIO. The degree to which a copy is smaller, in linear dimensions, than the original from which it was made, e.g., 1:4 reduction of a diagram 120mm × 160mm would give a copy 30mm × 40mm.

REDUNDANCY. The repetition of material in teaching. The topic lacks clarity in the human learning situation because of the difficulty of defining a ''unit'' of teaching or presentation. In general it is true to say that multiple repetitions, i.e., a degree of redundancy, enhance learning.

REEL-TO-REEL. A term describing a process or machine in which tape or film moves from one open reel to a separate open take-up reel during processing, recording, playback, projection, etc.

REFLEX CAMERA. *See* **Single-Lens Reflex Camera; Twin-Lens Reflex Camera.**

REFRESH. To repeat a display on a visual display unit which would otherwise fade. *See* **Refresh Rate.**

REFRESH RATE. The number of images displayed per second. On a CRT display, too low a refresh rate causes flicker; on an LCD display, a low refresh rate causes smear and ghosting. Standard NTSC video refresh rate is 60 fields per second (PAL 50 fields per second).

REGISTER. In many graphic and photographic applications it is necessary to secure total alignment between two or more elements, such as transparent overlays or successive exposures on the same negative. This process is referred to as achieving register, and there are a number of devices and techniques in use to ensure that these elements are maintained in register. Often these rely on mechanical features such as register pins which physically hold sheets of film in correct juxtaposition, but there is an increasing dependence on electronic support using microprocessors to ensure register. *See* **Graphic Design.**

REGISTRATION. Locating slides, artwork, etc., in the *precise* position required for lining up (i.e., registering) with other visuals. Specialist cameras and easels are equipped with registration pegs and calibration markings to ensure accurate registration for such purposes as animation, color printing, etc.

REGULAR 8. Alternative name for the obsolescent standard 8mm cine film format.

RELATIONAL DATA BASE. A data base whose basic organization is modeled after a table, with rows containing the individual records and data stored in a series of columns.

RELEASE PRINT. A cine film in its final form suitable for projection. *See* **Answer Print.**

RELIABILITY. A term used variously to mean

1. That part of a result derived from nonerroneous effects
2. The accuracy with which a measurement technique (e.g., a rating scale) measures a characteristic

A test that is reliable will have stable scores on repetition, parallel stability with a similar test on the same subjects, and internal consistency as measured by a consistency formula.

RELOCATABLE. Object programs that can reside in any part of computer memory. The actual starting address is established at load time by adding a relocation ''offset'' to the previous starting address.

REMEDIAL FRAMES. A single frame or a series of related frames in a programmed learning sequence that covers a teaching point again. In a branching program, a loop that takes learners back over material that they do not understand. *See* **Programmed Learning.**

REMEDIAL INSTRUCTION. In a branching programmed learning sequence, remedial instruction is (or may be) provided to students selecting an incorrect response.

REMOTE TERMINAL. A computer terminal situated at a distance from a central computer, i.e., not physically forming part of the central facility.

REMOVABLE DISK. A type of hard-disk drive where the disk itself is constructed as a cartridge that can be taken out of the drive. This kind of drive is relatively expensive but combines the speed and capacity of the hard disk with the floppy-like advantages of security and flexibility.

REPLENISHER. Solutions added to a photographic developer or other processing bath to compensate for the exhaustion of the active constituents that takes place in the course of processing.

REPORT (DATA BASE). An on-screen display or printed listing showing selected information extracted from a data base (and, as a verb, the act of generating this listing). Most data base systems allow you to design report formats, and some allow quite extensive editing and mathematical processing.

REPROGRAPHY. General term for printing, photocopying, mimeographing, etc. In recent years the introduction of highly versatile photocopiers has revolutionized this field, allowing for the cheap reproduction of high-quality educational materials in several colors, different magnifications, and so on. Desktop publishing seems destined to carry this tendency further, bringing sophisticated reprographic facilities within the grasp of students as well as teachers. *See* **Desktop Publishing; Photocopying and Duplicating.**

RESIDENT. A program stored in **ROM** (q.v.) and consequently always available as soon as the computer is powered up. This is the situation with BASIC in some microcomputers.

RESIN COATED PAPER. *See* **Bromide Print.**

RESOLUTION. An indication of the detail shown in a picture. Movie film and color slides give a high resolution (how high depends on the quality of the optics and other physical factors). In the case of video displays the resolution is indicated by the number of lines the screen displays. Many television sets can barely reproduce 250 lines; a low-resolution monitor should do better than 350. A medium-resolution monitor may manage up to 550, and an expensive system designed for vector graphics can do better than 4,000. *See* **High-Resolution Graphics; Pixel.**

RESOLVING POWER. The ability of an optical or electronic system to reproduce fine detail. *See* **Definition; Resolution.**

RESOURCE-BASED LEARNING. Any discussion on resource-based learning requires a prior consideration of terminology and some recognition of the breadth of the implications associated with its introduction. Three questions come to mind in this context. First, what are "resources"? Second, what are the aims and implications of basing educational and instructional activities on resources? Third, what are the implications of laying stress on learning through the use of resources as opposed to teaching with or without the extensive provision of aids? The first question concerns the nature of "resources." Resources can be grouped under three heads: human, environmental, and material. This entry is mainly concerned with material resources, that is, learning materials and the means whereby they are made available. Their use, however, clearly has implications for those who introduce them and the places in which they are employed, and these will not be ignored. The second and third questions relate to aims and implications.

Reliance on resource-based learning assumes that different outcomes are anticipated from those arising from traditional instructional methods. The move toward resource-based learning has taken place with, until recently, increasing pace throughout the last twenty years and reflects the growing concern for education and instruction to be centered more on the learner than on the teacher. The theoretical justification for such a development is not difficult to formulate. The practical import is, however, less easily understood and expressed and has resulted in resource-based learning frequently becoming yet another educational bandwagon. This entry will indicate briefly the history of its development, and some of its basic principles; its aims; and the implications of its introduction for staff, accommodation, and resource provision in the shape of learning materials and related equipment facilities.

In a paper presented to the British Association, Josleyn Owen (1975) succinctly expressed what is, for this entry, an apt introduction:

Perhaps the mystery of the resources should be diminished. An esoteric language has already developed far enough to bring confusion to the world of libraries, in-service training and school loan services of various types.... Everything that money is spent on, even in school meals and transport, forms a resource for learning. It is extremely expensive: lines should be clear about where and why the money goes.

A BRIEF HISTORY OF RESOURCE-BASED LEARNING

There is little doubt that the launch of the first Sputnik in 1957 came as a shock to the Western world. Before that date it seems reasonably certain that, west of the Iron Curtain, the immense strides made in technological development by the Communist bloc were not truly appreciated. The outcome of this remarkable achievement by a country until then considered to be relatively backward in technological development resulted in the setting up of numerous commissions of inquiry all charged with the remit of, first, considering how it was that the Russians had been able to overtake the Western democratic nations in the promotion of aerospace engineering and, second, of making recommendations for action designed to remedy past failings.

As so frequently happens, it was the educational system which had to bear the brunt of the blame for not preparing people with sufficient technological expertise and drive to continue the momentum achieved during World War II. Among the main criticisms leveled were that too much attention was paid to the needs of the teacher and too little to those of the learner and that the educational process was far too concerned with content and factual knowledge at the expense of the development of skills and conceptual understanding of the foundations of knowledge structures. Recommendations followed which led to the setting up of teams of specialists charged with the task of modifying the existing curricula and developing new curricla. The specialists were drawn from many disciplines but mainly from the sciences including mathematics. Most teams included one or more psychologists, a significant development in the search for improved educational programs.

The accent in the late 1950s and throughout the 1960s was on the need to develop learning theories and teaching methodologies, hence the reliance placed on the psychologists. Professors Piaget, Skinner, and Bruner provided much of the theory on which the curriculum development teams based the design and trials of materials. Programs for various disciplines were prepared and disseminated by the teams; most, if not all, making far greater use of learner-centered activities than had been the case in the past, many relying heavily on specially prepared resources or learning (as opposed to teaching) materials generally available and low in cost.

The ten years following World War II had seen quite significant increases in the availability of instructional aids. These were mainly "hardware" presentation devices of the filmstrip/slide projector and early audiotape recorder types of equipment. Some ready-made "software" filmstrips, slides, and prerecorded audiotapes existed, but much was of doubtful potential in the schools' situation and production expertise among teachers was not widespread. Such aids can be interpreted as being "additive" resources, that is, they are "used to extend the range of experiences offered by the teacher. If they were not available, the lesson would still continue" (Walton, 1975). The development in the late 1950s and throughout the 1960s was, however, much more concerned with the "integrative" resource. In contrast to the "additive" resource, the integrative resource forms an essential part of the teaching-learning process. The learner participates through its use to a much greater degree, and its removal would be critical to the nature of the learning.

The 1970s have seen further developments in the use of resources. In the previous ten years in the United Kingdom, several programs financed by the Nuffield Foundation had provided a curriculum development model which relied on a small team of specialists drawn from areas throughout the United Kingdom. Their contribution to a project was for a period of a few years, thereafter the team dispersing, presumably in the expectation that their activities would have been sufficiently well publicized for significant and successful implementation to have taken place widely throughout the school system. Teachers' resource centers were created to support such programs, and some teachers attended regularly to discuss problems and approaches associated with the various developments. Unfortunately, such a curriculum development model was not as successful as had been anticipated, and today, the move is towards much more locally inspired change with the concomitant need for high levels of in-service training of teachers. This in turn brings about yet another need for the intensive development of resources since, in the United Kingdom and generally throughout the Western world, such massive training programs can only be undertaken by some form of learning at a distance as finance is not available to support teacher attendance on large-scale university and college-based courses. Further, even the worth of the latter type of courses is now being questioned. The belief is growing that concurrent implementation of developments in the classroom alongside the training program is far more likely to result in significant curriculum change taking place. This has led in the 1980s to a broadening of the focus of resource-based learning to encompass the wider area of "open" learning. This recently introduced term contains the resource center model *and* learning at a distance where materials, instead of being housed in an institution, are delivered to students via the post or by television or radio broadcasts. Although distance learning has a considerable history (e.g., British **Open University** [q.v.] and correspondence courses) it is only in fairly recent times that it has become accepted in "mainstream" education.

That then, in brief, is the history of the development of resource-based learning. There have always been resources for learning—teachers, plant, materials, and books. The change has been towards resources as learning, the resources themselves being essential to the process, and designed to meet very specific and explicit aims.

THE AIMS OF RESOURCE-BASED LEARNING

The last twenty years have seen much confusion in the educational world. The great debate about the aims of general education has ranged from considerations of highly prescriptive curricula based on the use of such methodology as the **systems approach, critical path analysis, programmed learning,** and **educational technology** (q.v.) (defined as a systematic approach to learning implying that any course is based on the achievement by the learner of specific goals) to the writings of Illich and his advocacy of a deschooled society (Illich, 1973). While it is probably true to say that at some time proponents at each point in the range have advocated the use of resources as learning, their introduction is intended to cater to the needs of the individual learner, who will thereby gain skills related to and mastery of any appointed task rather than accumulate a store of factual knowledge and model problem-answering techniques. Bruner (1967) has argued that "We teach a subject not to produce little living libraries on that subject but rather to get a student to think mathematically for himself, to consider matters as a historian does, to take part in the process of knowledge-getting. Knowing is a process, not a product."

Most curriculum development projects have had as a main aim the development of a radically new approach to learning in a discipline, an increase in the student population able to benefit from such learning, or the growth of interdisciplinary studies previously somewhat ignored. Some have been all-embracing and were deemed to have all of these aims.

Professor P. H. Hirst (1967) asserts that we have no need for a "radically new pattern of the curriculum. As I see it, the central objectives of the curriculum are developments of the mind.... No matter what the ability of the child may be, the heart of all his development as a rational being is, I am saying, intellectual. Maybe we shall need very special methods to achieve this development in some cases."

Bruner (1960) in a much-queried but often-quoted statement has said "that any subject can be taught effectively in some intellectually honest form to any child at any stage of development." These educators and many more imply an ever-increasing need for resources as learning since such resources cater to the needs of the learner. They allow the individual to satisfy his own interests, to progress at his own pace, in his own time and, frequently, at his own base. A variety of resources fulfills various needs at the same time. They allow greater levels of active participation by the learner, greater possibilities of interaction between tutor and pupil, and the use of a wider range of media for communication. Pupils or students with different abilities and background knowledge can study, each at his own level, or conversely, achieve a common level ready for further progress. It was the Nuffield 5–13 Mathematics Project which resurrected the old Chinese proverb: "I hear and I forget, I see and I remember, I do and I understand." Resources allow greater freedom to hear and to see but above all to do and so to satisfy the spirit of inquiry which permeates constructive and purposeful curriculum development based on meeting the needs of an ever-increasing proportion of the population. Traditional classroom teaching methods can never satisfy the needs of a modern industrial society whose members require an education fitting them for a working life, the principal characteristic of which is likely to be a need for flexibility of achievement and of approach to career problems.

The benefits arising from the use of resources as learning can then be summarized in two senses, first, for the teacher and the course he designs and, second, for the learner. The teacher using resources as learning has access to a wide range of instructional methodology which, at least in theory and certainly in well-implemented practice, can improve the quality of learning since, by definition, the learner will be much more actively involved in the process. Traditional teaching methods result in passivity on the part of the learner. Resource-based learning increases manifold active participation with the intended consequences of greater understanding of knowledge structures and the more certain growth and control of intellectual and dexterous skills, and the development of attitudes and personal values.

Resource-based learning increases the variety of the teaching methods which can be employed. Resources can be used for demonstration purposes with mass audiences but, to generalize, they are much better employed when manipulated by the learner. This is true, not only of structured material in whatever medium but also of the media themselves since a wide range at the disposition of the teacher greatly increases his effectiveness when retrieval and control is in the hands of the individual learner. This is even more true when such teaching methods can be backed up by face-to-face contact in tutorials.

The possibility of providing learning situations for individuals or small groups enables the teacher to cater more readily to the slow learners and the more able. Timetables can be liberalized as indeed they must be if the full potential of resource-based learning is to be realized. The benefits of tutorials have been mentioned: resource-based learning increases both the need for and the possibility of increased teacher-learner interaction. Finally, resources as learning, well used, are highly motivating. The motivation is intrinsic to their use, always a bonus for any component of an educational program.

Reference has already been made to the benefit of active participation in the learning process for the learner who has access to resources as learning. Much more responsibility is placed on him for achievement than in the conventional group teaching situation. While not all students respond positively to this advantage, nevertheless most do, and many researchers have established the widespread acceptance of a move toward individualized or small group learning based on the use of resources. While resources can be used to achieve similar goals to those of traditional teaching, they open up practical activities and pursuits uncatered to by formal methods. Skills of observation and recording; the use of reference sources and other research skills; the competent handling of equipment and materials; the ability to follow instructions; the gaining of experience in interpreting, classifying, and evaluating evidence; the making of independent judgments; and communicating fluently and accurately are all gains which arise from well-designed learning activities based on the use of resources.

THE IMPLICATIONS OF RESOURCE-BASED LEARNING

A decision to use resources as learning as a significant component in any educational or instructional course can only be successfully implemented if a major appraisal of all the implications is undertaken. Such a study can be, and is likely to be, based on three questions: (1) What is to be achieved? (2) How is it to be achieved? (3) How is achievement to be assessed?

This section of this entry will, first, briefly consider the implications of answering these questions as they relate to academic staff, courses, nonacademic staff, and accommodation. Later, the implications for production and retrieval facilities will be considered.

The Implications for Academic Staff. Any use of individualized and self-instructional materials on a course is bound to result in some change of role for the teachers involved. In the main, this will be brought about in two ways: first, it is likely that any major use of such materials will require at least some of its preparation by the staff and, second, its management will greatly differ from that of the traditional teaching situation. While such a change is no doubt appreciated in many innovative developments, its extent frequently becomes clear to most of those involved only as an innovation progresses. It is, therefore, highly desirable that the person with overall responsibility for the change should be well experienced in educational development both as a producer and a manager. He or she, at least, should have an insight into the likely nature of the development, and the needs that will arise for academic and nonacademic staff, for equipment and for services.

Relatively few teachers are authors, yet the skills relating to authorship are those that will be of supreme importance to staff preparing manuscripts for learning materials. The skills of an author in the general and conventional sense are those of communication, but in the preparation of learning materials, supplementation of these skills is essential. An author always has an aim, as does a teacher, but the teacher preparing learning materials must have as the major concern the results following their use. Such results should be made explicit in terms applicable to the learner, not as the aims of the teacher. Much teaching is carried out on an intuitive basis, often with aims of a highly specious nature, the achievement of which is virtually impossible to assess. In my opinion, a move from intuitive instruction to learning based on objectives, stated in terms of the learners' behavior on completion of a course of study, is essential if the use of resources as learning is to achieve significant success, and this is particularly true in the case of distance learning authorship. An entry of this nature does not allow development of any argument in support of the use of behavioral objectives, but the interested reader is referred to the works of Benjamin S. Bloom et al. (1965) covering the classification of educational goals in the cognitive (knowledge) and affective (attitudes and emotions) domains. The taxonomies of objectives categorize learning into various levels. In the cognitive domain, of six levels the three highest are those of analysis, synthesis, and evaluation. Resource-based learning is rather more likely to lead to the development of abilities in these aspects of learning than is conventional teaching since, to achieve success with intellectually demanding material, the learner is constantly having to apply these skills. Since teachers do not normally perceive their activities in terms of learner behavior (as opposed to achieving their own aims, e.g., covering the content of a syllabus), this is a need, first, of which they must be made aware and, second, in which they must themselves be trained. Occasionally, textbooks include revision or summary paragraphs but frequently they do not. On the other hand, all self-learning materials must regularly include such sections in some form providing information (feedback) to the student so that he is aware of the progress he is making.

Application of the principle of feedback is inherent in all good self-instructional material, but some methods make rather more use of it than others. Some courses are designed around the use of resource-based activities which must be "mastered" in turn before progression to the next takes place. One such method is called the **Keller**

Plan (q.v.) (Keller, 1968), or **personalized system of instruction** (PSI) (q.v.).

Specialized educational and instructional methodologies such as those highlighted above make it essential for staff development to be of prime concern for any institution involved in change. One of the functions, therefore, of the person responsible for the innovation must be that he or she recognizes and is able, usually personally, to meet the training need. Producers of materials need to be made aware of what constitutes acceptable forms of learning packages; the principal elements of self-instructional materials, including statements of aims and objectives; use of feedback both to student and to lecturer for purposes of evaluation; the means of production; the characteristics of media; learning theories; the characteristics of individual learners; methods of assessment; their own rights in their material and those of others, including performers; and of sources of materials produced outside their own institutions.

Teachers must also be able to analyze curricula and to modify courses to make effective use of resources. Implicit in such use is the ability to enable students to profit further from experience already gained from self-study activities. To be able to perform these tasks effectively, in addition to training, teachers will need appropriate accommodation for tutorials and a range of supporting services adequately staffed.

Consideration of the question, "What is to be achieved?" leads not only to the implications for academic staff but also to those for courses. As already indicated, resource-based learning is intended to achieve different ends from traditional teaching, so it is likely that courses too will differ from the conventional model. The use of resources allows greater flexibility in the course structure and also in content. Given that students are aware of the expected outcomes, they can use whatever resources enable them to achieve their goals. When these are conceptual, it is possible that specific content is not important, and so a range of resources can be used to meet the same need. Since resource-based learning enables students to work at their own pace, in their own time and, often, in a place of their own choosing, it might also be possible for them to work at their own level, especially if they are considerably more able than their peers. Resource-based learning also provides for students to be profitably engaged without the presence of a teacher who can be otherwise engaged in discussions with an individual or a small number of students.

The use of resources can, therefore, allow a course with given content to be studied by students with a wide range of ability since they can work in circumstances which suit the individual. On the other hand, their use can allow the development of a range of courses (or a range of options within a course) since students can be gainfully employed using media as information carriers and controls for their activities.

Implications for Nonacademic Staff and Accommodation. The production of learning materials using the possible media of print, photography, audio recordings, computer programs, and moving pictures, either as film or television, will need staff with skills not normally widely found among academics. Specialized equipment and accommodation will also be required and while mention will be made later of equipment, accommodation requirements and staff should be considered together.

Any institution producing significant amounts of learning materials using a variety of media will have the problems normally associated with a publishing house. Given that the teaching staff can and do produce the original manuscripts, an editing service must be provided which can also be responsible for supervising the passage of the material through the production processes. Some of these processes should be close together. The reprographic facilities, composition, graphics, print, and photographic units need to be in close proximity of each other since their functions are often related to the output of a single product. On the other hand, audio and television facilities require at least acoustic isolation from other activities of the institution and acoustic internal treatment so that clear and interference-free recordings can be made. This isolation also relates to the film production facilities, since sound synchronizing and transfer can be a very disturbing influence on other activities, especially when a measure of concentration is essential.

Most media facilities and especially the electronic services require staff with very highly specialized skills. Such personnel may well command salaries at least commensurate with those of their academic colleagues, and it is certainly a false economy to attempt to staff or equip an essential technical service at a level where reliability cannot be almost fully guaranteed.

One study of the needs of an institution developing a significant component of resource-based learning in its courses can be read in the feasibility study prepared for the Dundee College of Education (Clarke, 1978). The events leading up to the preparation of this study and the opening of the college are detailed in a history prepared for the **Council for Educational Technology** (q.v.) for the United Kingdom (Lickley, 1977).

The Implications for Production and Retrieval of Learning Materials. Consideration of the question, "How is learning based on the use of resources to be achieved?" leads to the implications for the production and retrieval services.

Technological developments in the 1970s and 1980s

have been very much in favor of the institution wishing to implement resource-based learning. Three developments in particular have assisted the process: in printing, in television, and in computers. The need of commerce for cheap in-plant offset printing services has brought about the very rapid growth of an industry supplying equipment capable of speedy and good-quality output of printed material including photographic material as halftones. Plates, adequate for about 1,000 impressions, are produced on paper-backed material at very low cost, and the printing machines using such material are robust, generally reliable, and capable of being operated by technicians who can quickly be trained on the job. Easy access to a servicing agency for the printing equipment is desirable, but highly qualified operators are not essential.

The second development concerns television. Videocassette recorders and players are now commonplace in educational and training institutions. Color video programs can therefore be produced at modest cost. Maintenance and repair of such equipment, ideally, requires staff on the premises. Complex electronic machines tend not to be fully reliable when operated by a large number of users, and constant attention is essential. The same general argument applies to microcomputers.

The production of multimedia learning materials necessitates a retrieval system which is highly reliable and readily available. Questions of security arise as well as of distribution, maintenance, and repair of equipment. There is nothing more injurious to motivation either of the teacher or the learner than equipment which is constantly breaking down or malfunctioning, or is not available when required. Much thought went into the design of a carrel (study booth) system in the Dundee College of Education (Clarke, 1978) to achieve security of equipment, reliability of operation, ready availability to the students, and ease of maintenance and repair. Standard items readily available are used in the construction of the furniture. For its assembly only a mallet or hammer is required when the pieces are supplied cut to size. The basic unit is made up of three walls which support a working surface and a shelf. To save time and effort for the users and the need to provide further storage space for the equipment, all projectors are housed in compartments, incorporating working surfaces, which can replace the standard working surfaces. Audio players and projectors control equipment are housed in the shell. Video replays can be obtained from other carrels containing videocassette players. A description of the system can be found in Clarke (1974a, 1974b). This is a very brief description of a system, custom built to conform to the main principles of reliability and constant availability. Many other solutions are possible and, indeed,

have been found, but the essential considerations are that, whatever provision for retrieval is made, the system including classification and indexing must fully conform to the criteria stated above.

When provision is made by an institution for activities based on the use of resources or for a carrel system such as that just described, it is often to be found in a resource center. Ideally, this will be the library. This is the normal storage point for resources such as books, records, audio and videotapes, computer programs, slides, filmstrips, microfiche, etc. Resource-based learning carried out in the library resource center, however, is often an academic, theoretical, or vicarious exercise. Many resources are used in laboratories, workshops, art studios, music rooms, or, astonishingly, as in the case of the implementation of some resource-based programs, corridors. Clearly, the provision of suitable and adequate accommodation for resource-based learning activities must be considered when plans are prepared for its implementation. In many cases this provision is very thorough and examples are well-documented, one account being related specifically to the carrels described in this article (Gill, 1975). Again, the question of staffing arises. In the past many librarians have viewed with considerable apprehension the invasion of their domain by technical wizardry and nonbook resources, respectively incompatible with the normal library atmosphere and systems of classification and indexing. If the library is to be developed as or changed into a resource center with comprehensive retrieval facilities for multimedia materials and, possibly, their production, the library staff must at least be sympathetic to the aims to be achieved and, with great advantage, skilled and experienced in the management of resource-based learning.

THE PURPOSE OF ASSESSMENT IN RESOURCE-BASED LEARNING

No study of resource-based learning can be complete without some thought being given to the question, "How is achievement of success in learning based on the use of resources to be assessed?" There are many facets to the assessment of success in learning and the evaluation of learning materials, but the problem can basically be related to the eventual purpose for which assessment is being carried out. At an early point in this entry, the need for an expression of aims and objectives related to resource-based learning activities was discussed. Assessment of the success of such activities is essential both for the teacher and the learner, for the teacher because he wants to know if the activities themselves are effective, for the learner because he needs to know his successes and the areas in which he has failed. Such assessment is "formative" in that it assists with the revision both of the materials (the presentation) and of the work (the student's course). On the other hand, in time the use of proven learning materials might be assessed on a continuous basis and contribute to the "summative" or overall measurement of the learner's achievement.

Resource-based learning, often in the form of individualized or small group activities, however, is normally associated with **mastery learning** (q.v.). In such cases, assessment of mastery is used as a measure indicating the readiness, or otherwise, of the learner to proceed to the next task. Much traditional assessment is carried out in the form of oral or written examinations regardless of the nature of the skills and competences supposedly learned. There are many forms of **assessment** (q.v.), each appropriate for measuring achievement in a range of learning tasks. Statements of objectives take account of the goals to be achieved by the learner, and it is important that both the anticipated outcomes and measurement of achievement are stated and carried out consistently. In other words, if an objective states that learners will be able to *do* something, measurement of their achievement will be directly concerned with their carrying out the activity, not in describing how to do it.

This very brief summary of the functions and nature of assessment serves to indicate yet another probable area of need for producers of learning materials. Detailed knowledge of the forms of assessment; the relationship to the use and selection of presentation media; and their effect on staff-student relations frequently related to the uses made of the results of assessment suggest that some time needs to be spent on staff development courses discussing the complex nature of assessment procedures. This will be time well spent especially by those engaged in the development of activities based on the use of resources. In a learning system making extensive use of aids outside the direct control of the teacher the need to measure the success of the learning and to evaluate the worth of the materials for the benefit of both learner and teacher is paramount. See **Component Resources**.

T. W. Fyfe

REFERENCES

Bloom, B. S. et al. (1956) *Taxonomy of Educational Objectives*, Handbook 1. *Cognitive Domain*. London: Longmans.

Bruner, J. S. (1960) *The Process of Education*. Cambridge, Mass.: Harvard University Press.

———. (1967) *Towards a Theory of Instruction*. Chicago: Belknap Press.

Clarke, J. (1974a) *A Carrel System for an Institution of Higher Education*. Dundee, Scotland: Dundee College of Education.

———. (1974b) "A Carrel System for an Institution of Higher Education." In *Aspects of Educational Technology, 8*, ed. J. P. Baggaley, G. H. Jamieson, and H. Marchant. London: Pitman.

———. (1978) *Learning Resources for an Institution of Higher Education: A Feasibility Study*. Dundee, Scotland: Dundee College of Education.

Gill, B. H. (1975) "Educational Technology in the Academic Library." *PLET* 12 (3): 151–62.

Hirst, P. H. (1967) *The Educational Implications of Social and Economic Change,* Working Paper No. 12. London: Schools Council.

Illich, I. D. (1973) *Deschooling Society*. Harmondsworth: Penguin.

Keller, F. S. (1968) "Good-bye Teacher. . . ." *Journal of Applied Behavior Analysis* 1: 78–89.

Lickley, A. (1977) *Towards Individualized Learning for Teacher Education: Dundee College of Education Case Study*. London: Council for Educational Technology for the United Kingdom.

Owen, J. G. (1975) "Resources for Learning: The Role of the Local Education Authority." Paper delivered to British Association Annual Meeting.

Walton, J. (1975) *Resources as Learning*. London: Ward Lock Educational.

RESOURCE CENTER. A library facility where resources used in resource-based learning are held. Resource centers are used by both teachers and students. *See* **Learning Environment; Resource-Based Learning.**

RESOURCES. *See* **Component Resources; Resource Based Learning.**

RESPONSE CARD (SHEET). A printed card or sheet specially designed to facilitate multiple-choice testing. The student indicates selections by marking printed "boxes" with a pencil; generally, the actual scoring will be accomplished using automatic machinery.

RESPONSE PAD. Push-button device for viewers to send information or indicate a response in two-way **cable television** (q.v.) or **videotex** (q.v.) systems.

RESPONSE TIME. The time between the initiation of an operation from a computer terminal and the receipt of results at the terminal. Response time includes transmission of data to the computer, processing, and transmission of results to the terminal.

RESPONSE WHEEL. A type of feedback device devised by D. Langdon. A circle of cardboard is divided into segments and used by the students to indicate their choice of response. The wheel is rotated on a card holder and a mark indicates the response. A very simple and cheap device. *See* **Cosford Cube; Feedback Classroom.**

RESTRICTED RESPONSE. Where the response to a question has finite elements, it is a restricted response. Either in terms of choosing a response from, say, five, or in terms of the number of missing letters, or words in a prompted answer. *See* **Multiple-Choice Question.**

RETENTION. What is remembered, as opposed to what is forgotten. The ability to remember varies, therefore, retention of facts, etc., varies as well. In general, "forgetting" sets in very soon after an item or fact has been learned, and we can expect retention to show a very definite reduction as time passes.

REVERBERATION TIME. The time taken for sound to die away in an acoustic environment such as a television studio. Technically, reverberation time is defined as the time taken for the sound intensity to fall by 60 decibels.

REVERSAL PROCESS. The system whereby a positive image photograph is produced by special processing techniques. The process has three steps: (1) develop negative image; (2) reexpose remaining silver halide image; (3) redevelop. This process, or a modified form, is used in all color reversal processes to produce color transparencies.

REVIEW ITEMS. Items or frames in a programmed learning sequence that cause the learner to repeat or review material. Review items are used to reinforce learning or to summarize points learned.

RF. *See* **Radio Frequency.**

RGB. An acronym for red-green-blue, the three color signals that make up a color video image. Monitors that accept input as these three separate signals allow more precise control of the color signals than do composite-video monitors and therefore generally offer better resolution.

RIBBON CABLE. A type of flat cable made of individual insulated wires joined side by side. It is inexpensive to manufacture and physically flexible. Many connections inside microcomputers use ribbon cable, but because it is difficult to shield and regulations against radio interference have become more stringent, it is less common for connections between devices.

RIBBON MICROPHONE. An electromagnetic microphone that consists of a thin strip of metallic foil held between the elongated pole pieces of a magnet. The ribbon acts as a diaphragm and a current is produced along its length as it vibrates. Ribbon microphones have a bi-directional polar diagram and give extremely high-quality results. They are, however, rather delicate and are used for studio work only. *See* **Microphone Characteristics.**

RIGID DISK. *See* **Hard Disk.**

RING. A network layout that arranges all connections in a circle. All signals pass through each station on the network in turn. *See* **Local Area Network; Token Ring.**

ROLE-PLAYING. Role-playing is a technique whereby participants in a simulation or game take on the roles of other people (e.g., a conservationist, industrial chemist, or social worker) and act out these roles in a simulated situation of some sort.

Examples of exercises in which role-play is important are simulated interviews and consultations, **management games, war games, sociodramas** (q.v.), and political games (*See* **political gaming**). One reason why the technique is used so widely is that it almost invariably produces a high level of motivation and involvement on the part of the role-players; in addition, it is claimed that it generally leads to increased sympathy and tolerance.

ROLL. A loss of vertical synchronization which causes the picture to move up or down on a receiver or monitor.

ROM. Read Only Memory. Computer memory in which information is permanently stored, usually at the time of manufacture of the computer. For example, the operating system is often provided in ROM in microcomputers. *See* **EPROM; Memory; PROM; RAM.**

ROMAN. The standard form of typeface, vertical as opposed to the slanting form of italic typefaces.

ROSTRUM CAMERA. A film or television camera mounted vertically so that it can shoot material placed directly beneath it. Used for graphics and particularly animation.

ROTARY CAMERA. A microfilming camera used for making microcopies of single-sheet documents. The exposure is made while the document and film are moving, in synchronization, within the machine.

ROUGH CUT. In film or television editing, the initial assembly of shots in their intended order.

ROUTING (VIDEOTEX). The method of providing a path from an index frame to the appropriate information pages. There are two principal routing facilities: filial routing and free routing.

ROUTING AND LOCATION STUDIES. Studies concerned with the logistics of the physical distribution of products from manufacturer to final consumer and the provision and routing of services, e.g., delivery of films and tapes, equipment maintenance services. Normally such studies seek to minimize costs using a range of operational research techniques.

RS232. An electronics industry standard (actually RS232C) for serial interfaces (serial refers to the eight bits—equal to one character—successively sent down one wire) used by most computers, modems, and printers. Minor variations in the way various devices interpret the standard often make the successful connection of equipment a matter of some complexity.

RULEG. A term used in teaching to describe the technique of associating an example with a rule. In a lecture the points are exemplified in the form:

Rule - Example; Rule - Example; etc.

A variation of the original idea is Egruleg. That is,

Example (of the Rule) - Rule - Example (further example).

There is evidence that the frequency of complete Ruleg units in lecturing is positively associated with effectiveness as perceived by students. *See* **Egrule.**

RUMBLE. Low frequency noise originating from the turntable system of a phonograph.

RUNNING HEADING, TITLE. A heading that is printed at the top of each page (or facing pair of pages) in a document, giving the document title and/or the chapter or section title.

RUN TIME. The time required to complete a single uninterrupted execution of a program.

RUSHES. These are quickly produced prints of material shot during the production of a film. They are not required to be of the same quality as a finished print of the same material would be since they are used only as a check during production. They are usually produced on a daily basis. Videotape is often used for this purpose as well.

S

SAFELIGHT. A light in a photographic darkroom whose color and intensity allow light-sensitive materials to be handled safely without unwanted exposure. In the case of some color materials there is no suitable safelight and work must be carried out in darkness.

SAGSET (U.K.). *See* **Society for the Advancement of Games and Simulations in Education and Training.**

SAGSET JOURNAL. *See* **Simulation/Games for Learning.**

SAKI. *See* **Self-Adaptive Keyboard Instruction.**

SANDWICH COURSE. U.K. term for cooperative education, in which the learner or trainee alternates between periods of full-time study at college and work experience on the job.

SANS SERIF. A typeface without serifs, i.e., the ascending and descending strokes of letters finish cleanly without small cross-lines.

SATCOM. U.S. domestic satellites operated by RCA.

SATELLITE INSTRUCTIONAL TELEVISION EXPERIMENT (SITE). An experiment, started in 1975 in India, to bring to a wide audience television programs on specific aspects of science and technology, agriculture, health and hygiene, and family planning. The satellite used was made available by NASA for a period of one year.

Reports on the outcome of the experiment have provided encouraging information about the relevance of such research as a means of economical education in developing countries.

SATELLITE TECHNOLOGY. *See* **Communication Satellites.**

SATURATION. The degree to which a color is "undiluted" with white light, i.e., the vividness of a color, described by such terms as bright, deep, pastel, pale, etc. Saturation is directly related to the amplitude of the chrominance signal.

SBE. *See* **Super-Twisted Birefringence Effect.**

SCAN LINE. One line on a television picture. The NTSC system has 525 lines to a complete picture, PAL and SECAM 625.

SCANNER. A device which translates a page of text or a picture/diagram into a computer file. The mechanical operation of the device consists of a light source which tracks over the page in a **raster** (q.v.) fashion, reporting to the computer on the nature of each point of inspection, i.e., light or dark. Software of considerable complexity is required to interpret the information thus received. Different models of scanner vary in their resolution and in the number of typefaces they can read.

SCEDSIP (U.K.). *See* **Standing Committee on Educational Development Services in Polytechnics.**

SCENARIO. Background information relating to an educational activity such as a simulation or role-play.

SCET. *See* **Scottish Council for Educational Technology.**

SCHOOL OF THE AIR. Name given to facilities for providing teaching by radio. For example, in the United States institutions at all levels engage in this form of instruction using normal broadcast transmissions; in Australia the term is reserved for special arrangements for very remote children of school age, the transmission is two-way and serves to back up correspondence classes. *See* **Distance Education.**

SCOOP. Floodlight used in photographic, film, or television work to illuminate large areas close to the camera.

SCOTTISH COUNCIL FOR EDUCATIONAL TECHNOLOGY (SCET) (U.K.). The council was founded more than forty years ago as the Scottish Film Council, the Scottish arm of the British Film Institute. One of the first services to be set up was the Scottish Central Film Library aimed at supplying film for schools. Alongside the use of film in schools, the council was able to foster an interest in the development of a wide range of audiovisual aids through close contact with enthusiastic teachers. The Hudson Report on the future of educational technology in the United Kingdom contained the recommendation that there should be a Scottish Council for Educational Technology, and the Scottish Film Council was chosen as the basis for this new organization.

The Scottish Council for Educational Technology carries out its work through a wide range of activities including publication, production, fieldwork, conferences, seminars and working parties, stimulating innovation, and by linking people to people and projects to resources. Some of the work arises as special projects but a large part results from the many inquiries that are received each year and are catered to through the services of the council.

The Information Service has built up a set of data bases covering audiovisual hardware, nonbook materials, audiovisual services, courses in educational technology, reference material, and a cross-reference file of manufacturers, publishers, and distributors of both hardware and software.

The Advisory Service deals with inquiries from any sector of education, industry, or training. The advisory staff interact in the field with teachers groups, etc. This role is in many cases that of an intermediary, placing inquirer in touch with sources of expertise and resource.

The Scottish Central Film Library now distributes about 7,000 titles (30,000 prints) including holdings of other collections such as COI, Royal Anthropological Institute, and the Higher Education Film Library. Distribution of films, though mainly in Scotland, covers the whole of the United Kingdom.

The Preview Service acts as an extension of the SCFL providing viewings of new films around Scotland and the chance for educationists and trainers to select films for integration into their programs. A new development has been the holding of nonbook materials, other than film, on short-term loan as a "current awareness service."

The Scottish Educational Media Association, formerly the Scottish Educational Film Association, is a voluntary organization for teachers funded by SCET providing a grass-roots point of contact and a feedback mechanism to the council on teachers' needs and opinions.

Other areas serviced by the council include Regional Film Theaters, the Scottish Association of Amateur Cinematographers, and film societies in Scotland.

R. Tucker

SCOTTISH MICROELECTRONICS DEVELOPMENT PROGRAMME (S.M.D.P.). An officially funded R&D program in the educational use of microcomputers, run in parallel with the U.K. Microelectronics Education Programme. These British programs sought to establish a microcomputer environment in schools and colleges, and within their limitations achieved reasonable results. In 1984 the S.M.D.P. was absorbed into the activities of the Scottish Council for Educational Technology. *See* **Microelectronics Education Programme (U.K.).**

SCRAMBLED TEXT (BOOK). A text in which the reading sequence is not in page order, but whose sequence is determined by learner responses to questions. A type of branching program. *See* **Programmed Learning.**

SCREEN. CAI term referring to a frame or page of instructional information, i.e., that which appears at one time on the display screen.

SCREEN BRIGHTNESS. The luminance of a projection screen when there is no film or slide in the gate. It depends on the reflectivity of the screen as well as the light output of the projector. It is usually expressed in candelas per square meter; for example, the BSI standard for 35mm motion picture projection is in the range 27 to 55 candelas per square meter. *See* **Projection Screen.**

SCREEN DUMP. A printout of the entire contents of a computer display, text, graphics, or whatever. A useful facility associated with dot-matrix printers.

SCROLL. To move all the text on a display upwards to make room for more at the bottom.

SCSI. Short for Small Computer System Interface, an industry-standard interface between computers and peripheral device controllers used by some microcomputers. SCSI offers a facility for fast data transfer, i.e., of the order of a megabaud. Conventional interfaces, e.g., RS232, are unable to handle communication at such speeds.

SECAM. The system of encoding color television signals used in France, Brazil, and the Soviet Union. SECAM programs are not compatible with the PAL or NTSC system.

SECOND-GENERATION COMPUTER. A computer of the type built during the 1960s, using transistor technology. *See* **Third-Generation Computer; Fourth-Generation Computer; Fifth-Generation Computer.**

SECOND GENERATION TAPE. *See* **Tape Generation.**

SECTOR. An arc-shaped section of the magnetic track pattern on a disk, or the data that is recorded in that section. In Apple DOS, for example, it is equivalent to 256 bytes. Apple DOS (version 3.3) divides each track into 16 sectors.

SELF-ADAPTIVE KEYBOARD INSTRUCTION (SAKI). A historic piece of educational hardware. The machine was designed by Gordon Pask to train punch card operators. It presented data to be punched together with learning prompts in the form of a simulated keyboard where appropriate keys would light up. As learning progressed, the simulated keyboard was generally withdrawn and the rate of new material presented speeded up. In programming language there were three key elements to SAKI: the speed of presentation, the content, and the amount of visual prompt. *See* **Conversation Theory.**

SELF-INSTRUCTION. Generally independent study, but the term implies a form of study in which students make use of programmed material such as a tape/slide program and work on their own. Self-instructional techniques are seen as an important part of individualizing instruction as they enable students to learn in a way that suits their own needs. *See* **Individualized Learning; Keller Plan.**

SEMIOTICS. The study and general theory of linguistic signs. *See* **Communication Engineering.**

SENSITIVITY ANALYSIS. An area of sensitivity training, also referred to as *group dynamics, T-group,* and *group relations training.* It examines the complex of relationships which exist within a group and the effect these have on the operational performance of the group.

SENSORY STIMULI. Stimuli received by the peripheral receptors and sensory nerves. For example, a ring from a bell, an electric shock, or a flash from a lamp.

SEPARATION NEGATIVES. Negatives made through red, green, and blue filters of a color original, in photomechanical work, from which printing plates are made for color printing.

SEPMAG. Short for separate magnetic. A magnetic sound track recorded on a separate sprocketted tape, not on the edge of the picture film.

SEPOPT. Short for *separate optical.* An optical sound track on a separate film from the picture film.

SEQUENTIAL. Information that is stored as a list. Sequential organization is efficient for searching or retrieving in the same order as that in which the information is stored, but it is inflexible and hard to update. Most data base systems use alternative direct-access methods. *See* **Sequential Access.**

SEQUENTIAL ACCESS. Access to items or information that depends on passing through a predetermined position or series of positions. For example, an audiotape presents sequential access to the listener as, when it is playing, the "first" item appears before the "second" item, and so on. A gramophone record presents random access as the stylus can be started at any point and very rapidly moved back or forward, without traveling through unwanted passages.

Information retrieval can be characterized as being either random or sequential access. *See* **Random Access.**

SERIAL FILE. A file in which items are entered in alphabetical or numerical order; they are searched for sequentially. *See* **Inverted File.**

SERIAL TRANSMISSION. A method of data transfer between a computer and a peripheral device in which data is transmitted for input to the computer (or output to the device) bit by bit over a single circuit. *See* **Interface.**

SERIF. A typeface with small cross-lines finishing off the ascending and descending strokes of letters.

SERVER. A LAN station that handles special duties such as disk storage, printing, or communications. A dedicated server handles only one function. In other cases, a microcomputer can be used as a server while still being accessible as a workstation.

SERVICE PROVIDER. An information provider/owner: anyone who rents space on a videotex system and offers information to users as a service or for a charge.

SEVENTEL (SEVENTEXT). A teletext system operated in Australia by the Seven television network. *See* **Teletext.**

SHADOW MASK. The system of producing a colored television picture where a perforated metal screen is set slightly back from the red, green, and blue phosphor dots on the inner surface of the tube face. It ensures that each electron gun excites only the appropriate phosphor dots.

SHAPING. The gradual modification or alteration of behavior using reinforcement techniques. Often used in a pejorative way when referring to behavior modification or behaviorism. *See* **Operant Conditioning.**

SHEET FILM. *See* **Cut Film.**

SHIELD. A foil or braided wire covering for a cable that prevents excessive noise pickup or radiation.

SHOT. In film or television production, a scene or sequence that is photographed or video recorded as one continuous action.

SHOTGUN MICROPHONE. *See* **Gun Microphone.**

SHUTTER. Device in a camera to prevent light from reaching the film except when required. In the case of still cameras, two types are used: focal plane or diaphragm. Focal plane shutters are common in 35mm SLR cameras and consist of a blind which moves rapidly across the face of the film; the different shutter "speeds" are obtained by the blind having a slit of variable width. In the nature of this type of operation there can be considerable distortion in the photographic image, depending on the direction of travel of the slit relative to any motion in the picture. A classic example of this phenomenon is the long-held view that golf clubs flexed significantly backwards during the downswing, a totally mistaken view based on a famous series of photographs showing the celebrated golfer Bobby Jones in action, taken with a focal plane shutter. Had the camera been held upside down it would have shown the club flexing forwards!

The diaphragm shutter, on the other hand, consists of a diaphragm which opens and shuts within the actual lens element. It does not suffer from the distortion problems inherent in the focal plane mode, but it does result in additional expense if interchangeable lenses are to be used. Also, the focal plane shutter can provide shorter exposure times than are possible with the diaphragm type.

SIGNAL. Technically, information encoded for transmission. Flags (semaphore), Morse code, smoke signals, and satellite transmissions are all examples of signals. Modern technology is increasing greatly the use of digitally encoded signals, in effect electronic Morse code. *See* **Digital Recording.**

SIGNAL-TO-NOISE RATIO. In all electronic components and recording or transmission equipment, wanted signals must always compete with some degree of unwanted background noise. In every situation a good signal-to-noise ratio is desirable.

SILK SCREEN PRINTING. The process of printing that uses silk or similar closely woven fabric stretched on a frame. A stencil is laid on the screen and paint or greasy ink is squeezed through the open mesh areas onto a receiving surface. The stencils are often produced as an integral part of the screen using photographic processes, shellac, gum, or gelatin. Silk screen printing is a very versatile process whereby an image can be printed onto almost any flat surface. The process is used for commercial printing of leaflets and posters and for printing textiles of all descriptions. *See* **Graphic Design.**

SIMULATION AND GAMING. The last two decades have seen a great increase in the production and use of simulations and serious games—serious in the sense that these games have an explicit and carefully thought-out educational purpose and are not intended to be played primarily for amusement (Abt, 1971). While some simulation/games have been devised solely for research or planning purposes, most are for educational use. The quality of published simulation/games varies, but well-designed simulation/games can often involve the players more deeply than can conventional teaching methods. Some see simulation and gaming as "a powerful new form of communication, particularly suited to conveying *gestalt*" (Duke, 1974). Certainly, the educational use of simulation/games forms part of a major contemporary shift in the pattern of teaching and learning which is occurring throughout our educational systems—a shift "towards heuristic, active, individual and small group learning, away from received authority, passivity and class teaching" (Taylor, 1976).

SIMULATION AND GAMING FROM DIFFERENT STANDPOINTS

Simulation can be all things to all men; it can be a game without external threats, it can be a serious approximation to reality which may determine acceptance for, or rejection from, a specific career, e.g., British War Office Selection Board Procedures. Simulation can range from a simple interface between one man and a machine, the "Link Trainer" of the Second World War is a useful example, to war games involving many procedural patterns. (Jamieson, 1973)

Berger et al. (1970) have gone so far as to identify the ability to simulate as an essential defining characteristic of the human species.

The playing of games is also a universal human attribute, though the design and use of serious games for teaching and research purposes have become widespread only in recent years. Wilson (1970) points to several centuries of development of war games, but dates the first politico-military game from 1929. Serious interest in business games is usually associated with the success of the American Management Association's *General Management Business Simulation* in 1957, though the idea of business and management education through simulation/games was being developed before 1939 (Thomas, 1957). Simulation/games for social science purposes did not emerge in their own right until the early 1960s (Duke, 1974), while simulation/games were introduced into many schools in the late 1960s through the work of curriculum reform projects such as the Social Studies Curriculum Project, directed by J. S. Bruner, and the American High School Geography Project (Fitzgerald, 1969).

The 1960s and 1970s witnessed a great increase in interest in the serious use of simulation/games.[1] Megarry (1984) describes the current situation as follows:

By the early 1980s most developed countries had a rapidly growing literature on the subject; most had national organisations devoted to its spread. Currently there are half a dozen periodicals on simulation and gaming in the English language alone [Coombs, 1980], directories listing thousands of simulation/games, conferences on the subject somewhere almost every month, even an International Simulation and Gaming Association (founded in 1970). The movement is something of an invisible college whose membership spans conventional divisions between subjects, age groups and institutions.

Simulation/games provide such an incredibly rich tapestry, reflecting many spheres of human activity, that it is not surprising that workers from a diversity of backgrounds have been attracted to the field. Duke (1974) lists several perspectives from which those involved attempt to explain gaming and simulation:

1. *Systems exposition*—an extension of operations research that views the primary purpose of gaming as the representation of some complex system in abstract form, usually through simulation, in a man-machine interaction.
2. *Game-theoretical*—an attempt to describe and understand games as an extension of the mathematical theory of games.
3. *Educational technique*—the view that a game is a classroom technique, the modern equivalent of colored paper and paste.
4. *Correlation with societal process*—an emphasis on role-playing and on the duplication of social interaction.
5. *Hyphenated disciplinary technique*—political science gaming, or war gaming, or business gaming, or urban gaming, or social science gaming, and so on.
6. *Crowd-pleasers*—the widespread and sometimes indiscriminate use of games for the primary purpose of obtaining an enthusiastic player response.

Duke acknowledges the virtues of each of these perspectives in the appropriate context. But claiming that they do not, individually or in combination, provide a satisfactory explanation of gaming, he goes on to develop a "unifying perspective on the nature of gaming-simulation . . . which combines a game specific language and appropriate communication techniques with the multilogue[2] interaction pattern." While Duke does succeed in providing a useful perspective on simulation games as a form of communication, and in focusing attention on those patterns of interaction which typically occur within urban planning, political and business simulation games, his analysis is more difficult to relate to some of the wide variety of classroom activities which are commonly placed under the simulation/games umbrella.

After recounting some attempts as defining games and simulations, the remaining sections of this entry will concentrate largely on educational applications of simulation/games. The treatment will not rigorously follow through one particular theme (as, for example, did Goodman's [1973] excellent treatment of the field from a game theoretical standpoint) but will rather present a collage through which the potential richness and diversity of simulation and gaming as an educational medium will become apparent.

ATTEMPTS AT DEFINITION

In the early literature on simulation and gaming, different authors used the terms *simulation* and *game* in different ways. Some use them interchangeably, while other distinguished between them merely on the basis of prestige. Some treated gaming as a subset of simulation, others the reverse. While any arbitrarily chosen jargon may enable cognoscenti to communicate with each other, the often conflicting use of basic terms did nothing to increase either the understanding or the sympathy of the much greater number of potential simulation/game users.

More recently, the terms *game* and *simulation* have been used with less ambiguity. Bloomer (1973) provides a useful and now widely accepted perspective, conceptualizing the relationship between simulations and games as between two overlapping sets, each defined by distinct but not incompatible properties. She cites Abt's (1968) definition of games and Guetzkow's (1963) definition of simulation:

Game—any contest (play) among adversaries (players) operating under constraints (rules) for an objective (winning, victory or pay-off).
Simulation—an operating representation of central features of reality.

Any activity which combines the properties of a game (competition, rules, players) with that of a simulation (operational representation of reality) is a simulation game and belongs to the intersection of the two sets (Figure 55).

For the purpose of this entry we will use the above definitions, and also the shortened form "simulation/games" which is gaining currency as an all-inclusive term to denote any or all of the three categories: game, simulation, or simulation game. Guetzkow's definition of simulation, emphasizing its *ongoing* nature, excludes static analogues such as maps and graphs which would be admitted by some other definitions. In connection with Abt's formal definition of games, it is worth noting that game rules may be of two distinct types: those that govern the moves which may be made and those that govern the termination of a play (and specify what the outcome of the play is for each player). Abt qualifies his definition when he points out that, in some games, players *cooperate* to achieve a common goal. He then offers the more general definition of a game as: "an *activity* among two or more independent *decision-makers* seeking to achieve their *objectives* in some *limiting context*" (Abt, 1971).

Shirts (1975) introduces a third basic category on a par with "simulations" and "games," namely, that of "contests." The essence of a contest is competition. Elections, competitions between rival firms, and man's struggle against his environment are examples of contests. For Shirts, as for Abt (1971) and many other writers, games do not have to be competitive. He cites the Opies' observation, in *Children's Games in Street and Playground* (1969), that when confined to schoolyards, children tend to play competitive games with winners and losers (what Shirts calls "contest-games"); but when they are not confined by the school boundaries and can roam at will in the streets and in the fields, they tend to play non-competitive games which aim to create laughter, physical exercise, and body contact. Shirts classifies many of the encounter games, where the purpose is to create an open climate of trust, many of the theater games and much of what is generally referred to as "play" as noncompetitive, nonsimulation games.

From his three basic categories, simulations, games, and contests, Shirts (1975) derives four further categories by combination (Figure 56) and provides definitions and examples of each. Other authors, impressed by the range of case study techniques, have made this into another overlapping category, some showing case studies as a subset of simulations, others as intersecting with all simulation/games. While such classification schemes have merit as a basis for conceptualizing the field, the descriptive terms which result (e.g., simulation game contests) are not in common use.

THUMBNAIL SKETCHES OF THREE SIMULATION/GAMES

Toreside Comprehensive School (Ferguson, 1977) is a simulation game designed to encourage trainee teachers, who have been trained as subject specialists prior to taking up teaching appointments in secondary schools, to think about the relationships between various subject disciplines—including the assumptions which underlie their own future positions as subject teachers. In the simulation game they are required to assume the roles of teachers

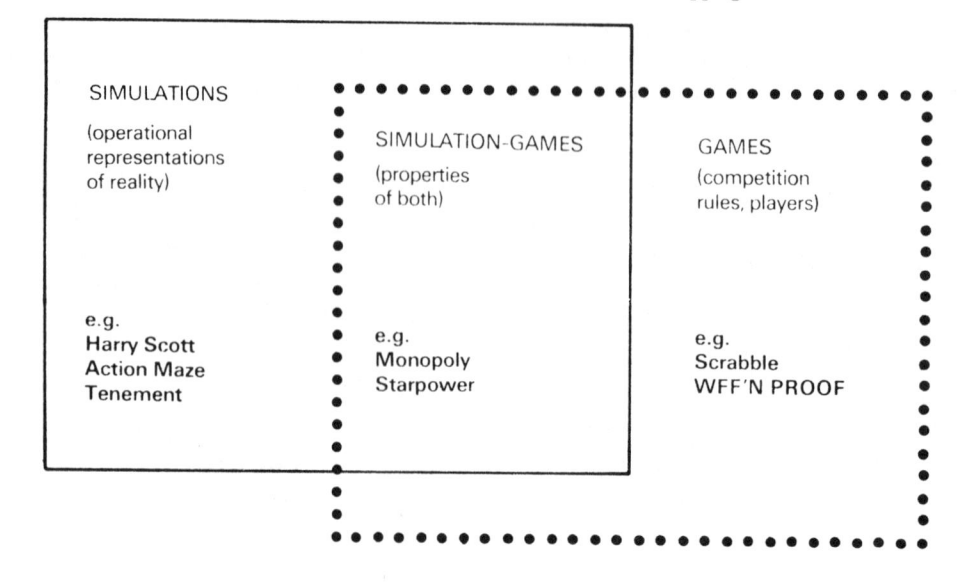

Figure 55
Diagrammatic Representation of Relationship between Simulations and Games: Two Overlapping Sets

```
┌─────────────────────────────────┬·················································
│  SIMULATIONS                    ·                                                ·
│  (operational                   ·  SIMULATION-GAMES                              ·
│  representations                ·  (properties                    GAMES          ·
│  of reality)                    ·  of both)                       (competition   ·
│                                 ·                                 rules, players)·
│                                 ·                                                ·
│                                 ·                                                ·
│  e.g.                           ·                                                ·
│  Harry Scott                    ·  e.g.                           e.g.           ·
│  Action Maze                    ·  Monopoly                       Scrabble       ·
│  Tenement                       ·  Starpower                      WFF'N PROOF    ·
│                                 ·                                                ·
└─────────────────────────────────┴·················································
```

Figure 56
Diagrammatic Representation of Relationship between Simulations, Games, and Contests: Three Overlapping Sets

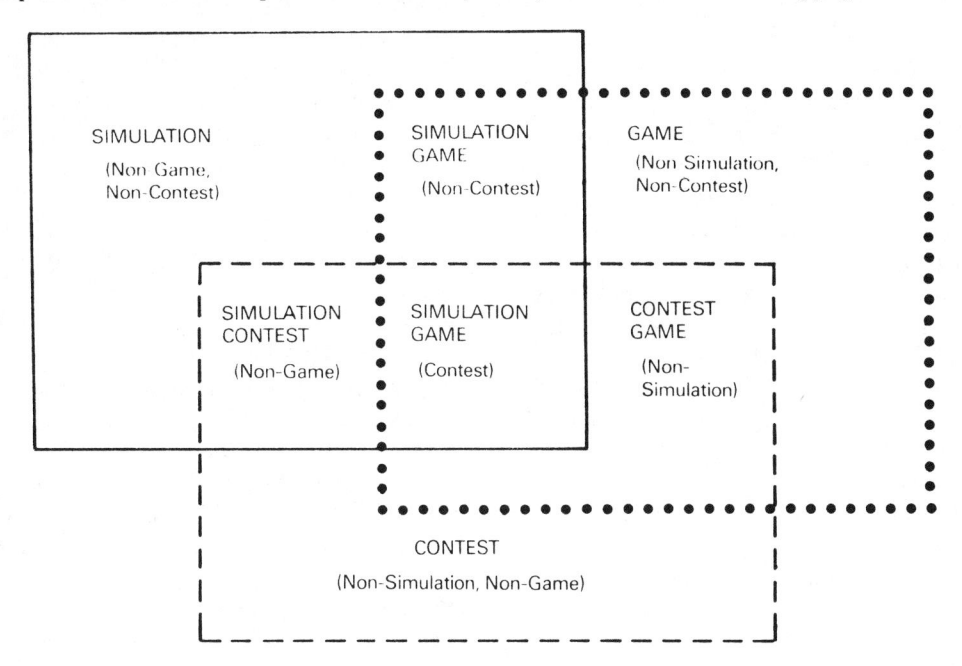

```
┌─────────────────────────────────────────┐
│                    ·······················
│  SIMULATION     · SIMULATION  ·  GAME       ·
│  (Non Game,     ·   GAME      · (Non Simulation,·
│   Non-Contest)  · (Non-Contest)·  Non-Contest)  ·
│                 ·              ·              ·
│        ┌────────·──────────────·──────┐       ·
│        │ SIMULATION· SIMULATION · CONTEST│       ·
│        │ CONTEST   ·   GAME     ·  GAME  │       ·
│        │           ·            │  (Non- │       ·
│        │ (Non-Game)· (Contest)  │ Simulation)│    ·
│        │           ·            │        │       ·
│                    ·······················
│        │           ·            │        │
│        │         CONTEST        │        │
│        │  (Non-Simulation, Non-Game)     │
│        └────────────────────────────────┘
```

of their own disciplines. In a simulated staff room setting, the "headmaster" precipitates a crisis by announcing that teaching of the first-year classes will no longer be subject-based but will require an integrated curriculum. He requires the various departments to work out plans for cooperation. After the headmaster's announcement, the staff disperses to departmental rooms to discuss the problem. The participants have two hours in which to reach agreement.

After 80 minutes, in one play of the simulation game, the headmaster was observed leaving the science department staff room:

The immediate reaction [to the headmaster's comments] was silence then uproar vented against the headmaster. The Head of Department tried to get proposals [from his staff] but unanimity was impossible. Unable to solve their own problems they resolved to make contact with the Geography Department and follow up their suggestion that Geography could serve as a focal point for interdisciplinary studies. However, lack of trust in each other prevented them from finding a suitable representative from among their number. They decided, therefore, that they would go as a group. . . . Unknown to the Science Department all other Departments were already meeting together and, in a calmer atmosphere, they were struggling with the difficult problem. . . . [When the Science group entered] the surprise on the faces of the Science staff revealed their failure to anticipate that others might not be in the same impasse. (Ferguson, 1977)

The high level of involvement illustrated by this extract can be sustained over time. At a country house in mid-Wales, students of politics from the University College of Wales, Aberystwyth (the first British university to use international politics simulation gaming as a teaching device), and young officers from the army and RAF are playing out an international crisis, having been assigned the roles of national governments. In response to a scenario, a plausible narrative describing a sequence of events leading up to an international crisis set some months in the future, the players have to discuss the implications of the crisis, develop policies, and take decisions on behalf of the states they represent. This simulation game is structured into a number of well-defined move periods, each lasting two to three hours in real time but representing anything from a day to a week in game time, during which interteam communications and negotiations take place. At the end of each move all the participants come together in a plenary session to explain their policies and the actions they have taken. The position reached forms the starting point for the next move.

At the end of one play of the simulation game, one participant was asked whether he found it an exhausting experience. He replied,

I found myself suffering a very strange emotion at the end of the first evening. I was tired having had to drive from home at 5 o'clock in the morning anyway, but I felt terribly disillusioned and disappointed that the operations of the day had been suspended so abruptly. When I got back to my hotel I found myself quite involuntarily thinking about the next move. This was true of my feelings at the end of every day—that it is so horribly false to just stop in any form of crisis that one is led to sympathise with the politicians who have to do it 24 hours a day. (Baylis et al., 1972)

Aberystwyth's *Crisis Games* run for three days. By no means are all educational games so time-consuming. *Circuitron* (Megarry, 1977; Ellington et al., 1981) is a science game designed as a follow-up to practical work with electric circuit boards. The game avoids real-life problems, like run-down batteries and loose connections, that can so easily provide an initial obstacle to learning. Bulbs, cells, and other components of electric circuits are represented by their symbols on pieces of card. Pupils draw a "hand" of pieces, and each tries to make a circuit on a special board. Their objective is to put down as many pieces as possible to form a complete circuit which is valid, i.e., obeys the laws of physics. Pupils then look for mistakes in each other's circuits, with the teacher as final arbiter. If the circuit is valid, points are scored according to the color of the pieces incorporated in the circuit; these colors were chosen according to how difficult it would be to use the pieces correctly—ammeters are worth most, connectors worth least. Pupils play the game in pairs, with two pairs round each board. The members of each pair help each other to score maximum points from their pieces, but the two pairs are in competition. By varying the number of pieces dealt, and by varying the rules (e.g., introducing ammeters to make the game quantitative), the level of difficulty of the game can be adjusted to the abilities of the pupils. Megarry remarks that pupils show enormous enthusiasm for learning about electricity by means of the game.

WHAT IS MEANT BY THE "EDUCATIONAL USE" OF SIMULATION/GAMES?

These examples illustrate educational uses of gaming and simulation. In all three cases the designer has created a simulation/game environment in order that the *players* gain new insights. One can differentiate this kind of use of simulation/games from other uses—as when, for example, the urban planner invites public participation through a simulation/game format in order to gather data relevant to planning decisions; when war or politico-military simulation games are played as aids to policy formation; or when a social psychologist studies participants' actions in a game in order to relate these to theories of group dynamics.

Coplin (1970) takes the view that the distinction between "research" and "teaching" purposes of man-computer simulations "has more to do with *who* is learning than anything else." Coleman (1968) points out, however, that while both children and professional sociologists can learn from the same social simulation game (simulation games which abstract from life some elements of social relations or social organization), what is meant by learning in the two cases is quite different. While children are learning to incorporate the experience into their own lives, learning to recognize the dominant aspects of the social environment of the game so that they can respond appropriately to them when they meet such an environment in their own lives, the professional sociologist is learning how to describe in general terms the functioning of the abstract system of relations, learning to fit the system of relations to an abstract conceptual scheme.

Clearly, many simulation/games can serve more than one purpose, but in this entry, emphasis is on the use of simulation/games for educational purposes. These can be defined as uses in which the intention is *to communicate skills and insights previously acquired by the simulation/game designer to the players through the medium of the simulation/game*. This does not, of course, exclude the possibility of players making insights during the simulation/game which are novel both to them and to the designer. Nor should we overlook the fact that the simulation/game designer (who may often be the teacher of a group of players) may learn, by observing the simulation/game being played, not only more about the simulation/game itself, but also more about the skills and insights which he or she intends to communicate.

The growing use of simulation/games is in accord with a major change in the pattern of teaching and learning which is occurring throughout our educational systems, "towards heuristic, active, individual and small group learning, away from received authority, passivity and class teaching" (L. C. Taylor, 1976). J. L. Taylor and R. Walford (1972) identify three major attributes of simulation (which they take to include gaming) that seem to them significant in relation to modern trends:

1. Simulation is a technique oriented towards *activity* in the classroom, and in such activity both teachers and pupils participate. It represents an informal and corporate approach to the understanding of a situation.

2. Simulation is usually *problem-based* and therefore helpful in the development of interdisciplinary approaches to learning. It also frequently involves the use of social skills which are directly relevant to the world outside the classroom.

3. Simulation is a technique which is fundamentally *dynamic*. It deals with situations that change, and which demand flexibility in thinking and responsive adaptation to circumstances as they alter.

CHANGED ROLES FOR TEACHERS

The trend which L. C. Taylor identifies is not without its ramifications outside the classroom, but within it it requires, among other things, a change in balance between different aspects of the teacher's role. On different occasions in a conventional classroom the teacher may lecture, ask questions, discuss work with individual students and, among many other activities, perhaps show film. While a film is being shown, the teacher has effectively handed over the class to another instructor—the one who made the film—although the teacher would do well both to prepare students in advance of the screening and to capitalize on it afterwards. So with a simulation/game. During the successful play of a simulation/game much of the authority in the classroom resides in its rules:

> The role of teacher as judge or disciplinarian no longer exists when a simulation is in progress. There is no question of disciplinary problems. True, there is a lot of movement and a high level of talk on occasions, but there is no person who is constantly disrupting the class, for if he did this would be interfering with his peers' enjoyment and they would not permit it. Nor does the teacher have to evaluate and declare a winner, for the winner is declared within the framework of the rules. (Tansey and Unwin, 1969)

Shirts (1976) points out that the natural inclination of most teachers to help their students whenever possible can be counterproductive in a simulation/game context. During the play the teacher will often have to repress the desire to explain in order to allow students to learn from the feedback mechanism of the simulation/game itself. Again, at the end of the simulation/game the temptation may be to interpret, explain, and lecture on the meaning of the experience rather than to assist the students to interpret and derive meaning from the experience themselves. These points notwithstanding, there will also be occasions during play when the teacher will have to intervene quickly and decisively should the rules of the simulation/game prove inadequate to cover unforeseen circumstances. Megarry (1984) provides useful guidelines for teachers intending to use simulation/games in the classroom.

CHANGED ROLES FOR STUDENTS

Students, like teachers, must adjust to new roles. Duke (1974) suggests that players go through three stages in their perception of a simulation game:

1. Initially, the player is put off by the complexity and by the array of information being presented.
2. The player enters into a stage where he is in control of, or at least at ease with, the environment and during this time will explore with ingenuity a variety of options that come to mind within the context of the game.
3. The player develops a sophistication which exceeds the limits of the game and withdraws voluntarily from further participation.

While some aspects of this sequence will apply neither to all simulation/games nor to all players—not all players will be put off by their initial encounter nor will the end point in a classroom situation always be voluntary—it is a useful general description. Clearly the sequence implies role changes for students. For example, in some simulation/games they will need to cope with uncertainty, to learn to experiment without the fear of censure, to derive meaning from their own experience, and to marry this meaning with information from more traditionally accepted sources, such as textbooks.

ROLE-PLAYING: A VITAL ELEMENT IN MANY SIMULATION/GAMES

Role-play is such an important element in the effective educational use of many simulation/games that it merits special consideration (Milroy, 1982; van Ments, 1983). For Taylor and Walford (1972) role-play, when used alone, has little formal structure: "All that is required is for the participant to accept a new identity, step inside someone else's shoes, and act and react as appropriately as he is able." When role-play is incorporated into a simulation/game, however, the way in which players may interpret their roles is restricted by the rules. To play a role is, in the words of Goodman (1973), "to make specific choices within a range of choices." The concept of role does not define the range of choices with the same precision as do the rules governing the moves in a game.

Goodman (1973) gives the following illustration:

> A father in a given instance (in real life) may choose to play his role in a number of ways.... But a person playing the role of father in a simulation game must compare the choices open to him according to the move rules with the choices he is aware of in terms of his understanding of the role of father, the choices which would be open to him if he were *not* limited by the game rules.

Simulation/games incorporating role-play attempt to relate vague rules about the role to precise rules governing the way in which the role can be played in the simulation/game. They may force players to take actions which they might not choose to take in real life. Simulation/games permit players to experiment with roles, and these "experiments" can be analyzed in terms of the information available to the players, the choices they make, and the consequences which follow.

What learning results from such an exercise will depend not only on the rules of the simulation/game but on the understanding which the players have of their roles. Some simulation/games, e.g., *Ghetto* (Nelson, 1970), are specifically structured to increase the participants' role awareness during play; others depend more heavily on the understanding of their roles which players bring to the simulation/game. The *Toreside Comprehensive School* simulation game, outlined above, falls into the latter category, and Ferguson (1977) used several devices to build players' role awareness before the start of the simulation/game itself. These included

1. A role pro forma (Figure 57). This defines selected aspects of the role but allows players a free choice of other aspects. The fact that the pro forma is issued well before the start of the game—and has to be completed by players—forces them to think about their roles in advance of the game itself.

2. Pregame meetings of small groups of players to whom similar roles have been assigned. At these meetings the players, with the aid of their completed role pro formas, discuss their intended interpretation of their roles.

In *Toreside Comprehensive School* the players (trainee teachers) were required to play roles (of experienced

Figure 57
Role Pro Forma Used by Players in the Toreside Comprehensive School Simulation-Game

---

Role Pro forma

Please complete this form in *duplicate*. Retain one for yourself and hand the other to the controller prior to the first staff meeting.

Role name:*
Age:*
Post at Toreside Comprehensive:*
Department:*
Years at Toreside:
Previous teaching post (if any).
    where?
    what dates?
    what taught?
Teacher training (if trained).
    where?
    what dates?
Higher education.
    where?
    what dates?
    what studied?
Secondary education.
    type of school?
    what dates?
Other work experience:
Other school responsibilities:
Marital status:
How many children?
Where do you live relative to the school?
What are your outside interests?
Political affiliation:**
Attitudes:** Do not write these out unless you want to, but think about your attitudes to: capital punishment, corporal punishment, long hair, school uniform, non-streaming, public schools, discipline.

* These role attributes are specified for each player by the game controller. All other attributes are specified by the individual player.

** These categories are intended to provoke the role player into considering the underlying values and attitudes of the individual he is playing.

Source: S. Ferguson (1973), "Toreside Comprehensive School: An Account of a Simulation-Game for Teachers in Training." *SAGSET News* 3: 51-63.

teachers) with which they could readily identify. To the extent that the players do not bring relevant role experience to the simulation game, the operation of the rules should guide, and if necessary dictate, appropriate choices. If the rules alone do not suffice, other mechanisms can be used. For example, in Aberystwyth's *Crisis Games* referred to above, the final arbiter as to whether a choice of action made by players is permitted or not is the control team. This team comprises experienced staff acting the role of omniscient "God and Nature" (Baylis, 1977). If, in the opinion of the control team, a particular choice would, in the real world, be beyond either the state's physical or constitutional power, the choice is disallowed, and a new, more plausible choice has to be made by the players concerned.

The suggestion that some forms of role-play might be inadequate for useful learning to occur is made by Clayton and Rosenbloom (1968) and results from their experience in the design and evaluation of social studies simulation/games in which the players are required to play quite unfamiliar roles. They suggest that schoolchildren interacting with each other in such simulation/games do learn something about human behavior, but what they learn is how other schoolchildren respond to an unfamiliar simulation/game—not how those whose roles they play would respond in real life.

Difficulties of a different kind occur when players are *too* familiar with the corresponding real-life roles, or (expressing the same idea in a different way) when the degree of sophistication demanded by the rules is significantly less than that possessed by the players. Shirts (1976) quotes an example of a simulation game in which the players were faced with the problem of deciding the political, educational, and tax boundaries of a fictitious metropolitan area. Field-tested with school and citizens' groups and found to be satisfactory, this simulation game was viewed as a gross oversimplification when played by a group of politicians who, as it happened, had been deeply involved in trying to solve a problem quite similar to that being simulated.

SERIOUS GAMES DESERVE SERIOUS PREPARATION

To be used successfully, serious games need to be treated seriously. This is not to say that they should not be enjoyed—indeed they should—merely that they should not be viewed as Friday afternoon diversions. A colleague with wide experience of observing the use of simulation/games in New Zealand schools remarked that the biggest single factor causing disillusionment arises from the failure of teachers to prepare and plan their use adequately. Taylor and Walford (1972) claim that using simulation/gaming as a technique in the classroom is a demanding skill which requires considerable effort to be rewarding, while a survey conducted by Zuckerman and Horn (1970) on 400 simulation/games then available in the United States about which these authors obtained detailed information, revealed that between one and five hours are required to become familiar with rules, materials, and flow of play. (Note that over 60 percent of the simulation/games cited were for college or continuing education use.)

Shirts (1976) suggests that simulation/games be used sparingly, and clearly a decision to use a simulation/game at all needs to be related to the total program of work. Only if there are objectives in this program which can best be met by playing a game, and then only if a suitable game is available, should it be used. Pregame briefings may be necessary, as may a session, or sessions, for analysis and discussion after the game. The time needed for playing will differ from game to game. Aberystwyth's *Crisis Games* were run twice a year as three-day residential courses, capitalizing on the more traditional course work which had occurred during the remainder of the year. Business management simulation/games, such as the *EDIT 515 Management Game* sponsored by the *Scotsman* newspaper, involving teams from a number of centers throughout the country, may extend over several months. One can readily envisage how such an extended period of play, a few hours per week but spread over many weeks, lends itself to linkage with concurrent course work of a more traditional kind. Many social science and geographical simulation games used in schools may be played in one sitting, though not infrequently the school timetable may need to be amended to accommodate them. Too many published accounts of gaming and simulation, however, taking social science simulation games as the norm, omit to mention the quite different logistic requirements for games in other fields. Megarry (1975) makes the point that the ideal use of many science, mathematics and language games—designed to provide practice, revision, and consolidation of previously learned material—is in frequent, short spells interspersed with other kinds of activity. At the tertiary level several different kinds of simulation/games may be integrated into a total program, as in the teacher education program at the Canberra College of Advanced Education (Hughes and Traill, 1975); in other cases specialized facilities, such as the patient simulation laboratory in the University of Illinois Medical Center, Chicago (Sajid et al., 1975), may be set up.

EVALUATION AND RESEARCH: WHAT BASIS DO THEY OFFER FOR DECISION MAKING?

The appropriate integration of a simulation/game with other teaching is often crucial to one of the major benefits of this technique, namely, increased student motivation. If a social studies simulation/game is followed up with related materials, such as case studies on similar themes, maximum benefit is likely to be derived. There is no doubt that the motivating power of a well-run simulation/game can be very great, and comments such as "students did not walk to meetings—they ran" (Cowan, 1973) are not at all unusual.[3] Other benefits claimed for simulation and gaming as an educational technique are, however, less widely accepted. There is little *generalizable* data on the ability of simulation/games to improve learning, foster critical thinking, effect attitude change, and facilitate the achievement of other desirable goals (see, e.g., Garvey, 1971; Greenblat, 1973; Rosenfeld, 1975). This lack of hard evidence has been used by some (e.g., Scarfe, 1971) to disparage the use of the technique, despite the fact that the use of more traditional techniques (which by implication are preferred) has no better empirical justification.

There is, however, a profound difference between the kinds of evidence that different groups of educators find acceptable. Tansey and Unwin (1969) point out that if simulation/games motivate children to the extent that they want to come to school and enjoy the classroom experiences, that is measure enough for the teacher. Others regret that what is known after years of research and development in simulation/gaming is not known "in the sense that most professionals would prefer—answers backed by hard research data" (Shirts, 1976). The middle ground is taken by Taylor (1974), who anticipates "a growing acceptance of systematized subjective judgements of experienced observers"—the equivalent for simulation/games of the well-established practice of specialist review panels for films.

Because of the likely magnitude of intervening variables in the classroom situation—not least the attitude and ability of the teacher—the judgments of review panels need to be supplemented by the results of the class teacher's own evaluation of the use of simulation/games; for such evaluations are conducted with the teacher's own pupils under constraints similar to those likely to be encountered in future plays of the simulation/game. The case for small-scale classroom-based research has been argued elsewhere (Teather and Whittle, 1971).

SOURCES OF FURTHER INFORMATION ON SIMULATION/GAMES

Some years ago I remarked that the pattern of use of simulation/games in secondary and **tertiary education** (q.v.) probably owed as much to the chance meeting of individuals as to the nature of what is taught. But nowadays, for those seeking information on what simulation/games are available, there are a number of sources. Directories (Gibbs, 1974; Stadsklev, 1975; Horn and Cleaves, 1980) are particularly useful, especially when they include—as does Horn and Cleaves—evaluative comments in addition to descriptions of individual simulation/games.

The journals *Simulation and Games* (U.S.), *Simgames* (Canada), and *Simulation/Games for Learning* (U.K.), in addition to articles, also include reviews, usually based on the reviewer's personal experience in playing or observing the play of the simulation/games being reviewed. While most reviews consider one or at most two or three simulation/games, some deal with a series in a particular subject area, for example Greenes' (1975) review of mathematics games and Megarry's (1975) review of science games. Lists and sometimes reviews of simulation/games occasionally appear in subject publications and the Society for the Advancement of Games and Simulations in Education and Training (SAGSET) publishes lists of resources about simulation/games in mathematics, chemistry, business and management training, economics, health education, education management, teaching English as a foreign language, geography, music education, human relations, and on the design and evaluation of simulation/games.

DESIGNING YOUR OWN (AND MODIFYING OTHER PEOPLE'S)

According to the acknowledgment on the cover, *The Trans-South American Highway Game* was "Adapted by J. Rapley, Secondary Division, Christchurch Teachers College, from J. Pepper's *The African Railway Game* itself an adaptation of *The Railway Pioneer's Game* in *Games in Geography* by Rex Walford, Longmans, 1969." I doubt if Walford would object, for in the first published account of his eminently successful *Railway Pioneers,* he said: "The best use of operational games in the classroom will come not if particular games are taken up and then played to exhaustion, but if teachers themselves use such games as ideas for better ones. The best game will be that devised to suit the needs of one's own pupils and syllabus" (Walford, 1969).

Modifying existing simulation/games is not difficult, particularly if one accepts Cowan's (1974) contention, expressed in a short and convincing paper, that

1. The essential features of any game are those which are virtually unrelated to the subject matter.
2. Standard game forms can be readily changed from one subject field to another, with a minimum of creative effort.
3. The suitability for transfer of a standard form from one field to another depends on the compatibility of the educational objectives in both fields.

While all simulation/games can be analyzed to expose their basic structure, some, known as "frame games," are deliberately designed to be content-free. They are evaluated by Thiagarajan and Stolovitch (1979). Their use raises similar issues to those raised by the use of computer software which is said to be "content-free."

With the growing availability of computer hardware, many existing simulation/games have been modified for use on a computer. A game like *Circuitron* may be successful in manual form, but it may nevertheless benefit from the use of a computer to relieve participants of the game's routine administration—keeping scores, generating random "hands" of pieces, adjusting levels of difficulty, and so on. Indeed Megarry (1984) states that the computer version of *Cicuitron* was found to be more effective educationally than the manual version, and attributes this to the fact that the computer was able to give faster and more consistent feedback than was possible from teachers or peers. Walker and Graham (1979) consider the contribution of the microcomputer to simulation/gaming.

Designing educational simulation games is time-consuming. It usually involves the initial formulation or adoption of an idea and the construction of a pilot version which is then successively modified by feedback from playing sessions. The literature on simulation/game design is burgeoning—the SAGSET resource list (Gibbs, 1982) cites 87 articles and books relevant to the topic—and a number of authors have published flowcharts purporting to give a systems approach to simulation/game design. But Megarry (1984) points out that there is little if any evidence that designers operate in the highly structured way that such schemes suggest. She concludes, "after 15 years of research, we know much more about how not to design a game than how to do it well," and lists twenty common mistakes in simulation/game design.

One important feature which sets apart educational simulations from simulations for research purposes is especially worth noting in connection with their design. Shirts (1976) makes the point when he remarks that the purpose of an educational simulation is to teach, not to represent reality. There are many times when a designer may wish to exaggerate, distort, grossly oversimplify or make the world seem more complicated than it really is in order to communicate a particular idea, fact, or relationship. And he gives the example of a cross-cultural simulation game for primary pupils in which the participants in one of the artifical cultures (dreamed up by the designer) must stand at least one arm's length away from all other members of that culture at all times. While there is no real-world culture which has a similar requirement, this particular rule draws attention to and dramatizes the importance people of various cultures put on personal space.

SOME POSSIBLE FUTURES FOR SIMULATION AND GAMING

Quite a number of writers have attempted to portray not only the current state of the art but also future prospects for gaming and simulation. Shirts (1976) sees a continuation of the work of enthusiastic individuals and small groups, from a wide variety of disciplines, conducting workshops, researching the most readily available problems, and developing new simulation/games. He predicts that although outstanding new simulation/games will be sparse, methods of presenting and using existing simulation/games will improve considerably, thus making them easier to use and more acceptable to more teachers. Any trends towards freeing up school and college timetables will ease logistic problems facing teachers wishing to use those simulation/games which demand considerable playing time and will thus encourage their wider adoption.

Abt (1971), with what may yet prove to be a prophetic insight, sees an increasing use of simulation/games in the classroom as schools seek additional ways to make learning active, relevant, and exciting for students and teachers. He states, "It is not difficult to imagine a school of the future as a 'laboratory school'—a school making massive use of educational simulation games, laboratory activities, and creative projects—a school in which almost everything to be learned is manipulated, physically and mentally." Teachers highly skilled in the use of interactive techniques will be needed, but will not be available unless such techniques are regularly *used*— not just demonstrated or discussed—in pre- and in-service teacher education programs (Megarry, 1980).

Perhaps Abt's vision may seem unreal to many classroom teachers, faced with present-day realities of shrinking education budgets. But the view of simulation and gaming as just another educational technique, to be used as an optional extra in the teaching of parts of the syllabus, would be regarded by some as conservative. Duke (1974), for example, regards gaming simulation as a communication form *uniquely appropriate* as a means of enabling students to understand the complex relationships of modern society. Criticism is widespread that our schools are too often concerned with single-discipline teaching toward examinations with little practical relevance. Too often they fail in preparing school leavers with the insights and skills which they need in order both to reach personal fulfillment and to contribute adequately to the complex postindustrial society in which they live. Gaming simulation is seen as a communication form which can play a major part in rectifying this situation in the schools, and in providing for adults the means through which they are enabled both to understand and to participate more fully in community decision-making processes.

David C. B. Teather

NOTES

I wish to thank Jacquetta Megarry for making available hitherto unpublished material which has been used in the updating of this entry.

1. At least, outside the military field. The use of gaming techniques by the military is difficult to document, though the size of the establishment concerned with war-gaming is reputedly very great—estimated by Wilson in 1968 at between 15,000 and 30,000 officers and scientists in America alone.

2. Multilogue = many dialogues, focused on the same topic, being conducted simultaneously. "Multilogue is the primary interaction pattern in gaming-simulation. This pattern . . . is central to the game's ability to display *gestalt*" (Duke, 1974).

3. This should not be taken to imply, however, that all games will motivate all players. One of the perennial problems associated with international politics crisis games is how to involve sufficiently those players who are assigned the roles of countries peripheral to the crisis.

REFERENCES

Abt, C. C. (1968) "Games for Learning." In *Simulation Games in Learning,* ed. S. S. Boocock and E. O. Schild. Beverly Hills, Calif.: Sage Publications.

———. (1971) *Serious Games.* New York: Viking Press.

Baylis, J. (1977) "Aberystwyth's Experience with Crisis Gaming." In *Aspects of Simulation and Gaming,* ed. J. Megarry. London: Kogan Page, pp. 90–99.

Baylis, J., Lewis, J., and Teather, D.C.B. (1972) *Crisis Gaming.* 16mm film. Liverpool: Centre for Communication Studies, University of Liverpool.

Berger, E., Boulay, H., and Zisk, B. (1970) "Simulation and the City: A Critical Overview." *Simulation and Games* 1: 411–428.

Bloomer, J. (1973) "What Have Simulation and Gaming Got To Do with Programmed Learning and Educational Technology?" *Programmed Learning and Educational Technology* 10 (4): 224–234.

Clayton, M. and Rosenbloom, R. (1968) "Goals and Design: Games in a New Social Studies Course." In *Simulation Games in Learning,* ed. S. S. Boocock and E. O. Schild. Beverly Hills, Calif.: Sage Publications.

Coleman, J. S. (1968) Preface. In *Simulation Games in Learning,* ed. S. S. Boocock and E. O. Schild. Beverly Hills, Calif.: Sage Publications.

Coombs, D. H. (1980) "Simulation/Gaming Journals: A Review of the Field." *Simulation/Games for Learning* 10 (2): 60–66.

Coplin, W. D. (1970) "Approaches to the Social Sciences through Man-Computer Simulations." *Simulation and Games* 1: 391–410.

Cowan, J. (1973) "Confessions of a Recent Convert: A Construction Site Simulation." *SAGSET News* 3: 44–47.

———. (1974) "Identification of Standard Game Forms with Definable Objectives." *Programmed Learning and Educational Technology* 11 (4): 192–196.

Duke, R. D. (1974) *Gaming: The Future's Language.* New York: Wiley.

Ellington, H. I., Addinall, E., and Percival, F. (1981) *Games and Simulations in Science Education.* London: Kogan Page.

Ferguson, S. (1977) "Toreside Comprehensive School: A Simulation-Game for Teachers in Training." In *Aspects of Simulation and Gaming,* ed. J. Megarry. London: Kogan Page, pp. 148–159.

Fitzgerald, B. P. (1969) "The American High School Geography Project and Its Implications for Geography Teaching in Britain." *Geography* 54: 56–63.

Garvey, D. M. (1971) "Simulation: A Catalogue of Judgements, Findings and Hunches." In *Educational Aspects of Simulation,* ed. P. J. Tansey. London: McGraw Hill, pp. 204–227.

Gibbs, G. (1982) "Designing Games and Simulations (References)." *Simulation/Games for Learning* 12 (2): 88–91.

Gibbs, G. I., ed. (1974) *Handbook of Games and Simulation Exercises.* London: Spon.

Goodman, F. L. (1973) "Gaming and Simulation." In *Second Handbook of Research on Teaching,* ed. R. M. W. Travers. Chicago: Rand McNally.

Greenblat, C. S. (1973) "Teaching with Simulation Games: A Review of Claims and Evidence." *Teaching Sociology* 1: 62–83.

Greenes, C. E. (1975) "A Review of Mathematical Games." *Simulation and Games* 6: 408–422.

Guetzkow, H. (1963) *Simulation in International Relations: Developments for Research and Teaching.* Englewood Cliffs, N.J.: Prentice-Hall.

Horn, R. E. and Cleaves, A., eds. (1980) *The Guide to Simulations/Games for Education and Training.* 4th ed. Beverly Hills, Calif.: Sage Publications.

Hughes, P. W. and Traill, R. D. (1975) "Simulation Methods in Teacher Education." *Australian Journal of Education* 19: 113–126.

Jamieson, G. H. (1973) "Simulation: Some Implications of Skill Theory." *Programmed Learning and Educational Technology* 10 (4): 239–247.

Megarry, J. (1975) "A Review of Science Games: Variations on a Theme of Rummy." *Simulation and Games* 6: 423–437.

———. (1980) "Selected Innovations in Methods of Teacher Education." In *World Yearbook of Education 1980: Professional Development of Teachers,* ed. E. Hoyle and J. Megarry. London: Kogan Page.

———.(1984) "Simulation and Gaming." In *International Encyclopedia of Education: Research and Studies,* ed. T. Husén and T. N. Postlethwaite. Oxford: Pergamon Press.

Megarry, J., ed. (1977) *Aspects of Simulation and Gaming: An Anthology of SAGSET Journal.* London: Kogan Page.

Milroy, E. (1982) *Role-play: A Practical Guide*. Aberdeen: Aberdeen University Press.

Nelson, L. W. (1970) "Simulation Review: Ghetto." *Simulation and Games* 1: 341–345.

Opie, I. and Opie, P. (1969) *Children's Games in Street and Playground*. Oxford: Clarendon Press.

Rosenfeld, F. H. (1975) "The Educational Effectiveness of Simulation Games: A Synthesis of Recent Findings." In *Gaming-simulation: Rationale, Design and Application*, ed. C.S. Greenblat and R.D. Duke. New York: Wiley.

SAGSET. (various dates) Society for the Advancement of Games and Simulations in Education and Training, Centre for Extension Studies, Loughborough LE11 3TU, U.K. Publishes specialized resource lists, annual conference proceedings, quarterly journal *Simulation/Games for Learning* (formerly *SAGSET Journal*).

Sajid, A., Lipson., L. F., and Telder, T. V. (1975) "A Simulation Laboratory for Medical Education." *Journal of Medical Education* 50: 970–975.

Scarfe, N. V. (1971) "Games, Models and Reality in the Teaching of Geography in School." *Geography* 56: 191–205.

Shirts, R. G. (1975) "Notes on Defining 'Simulation.'" In *Gaming-simulation: Rationale Design and Application*, ed. C. S. Greenblat and R. D. Duke. New York: Wiley.

———. (1976) "Simulation Games: An Analysis of the Last Decade." *Programmed Learning and Educational Technology* 13 (3): 37–41.

Stadsklev, R. (1975) *Handbook of Simulation Gaming in Social Education, Part 2: Directory*. Institute of Higher Education Research and Services, University, Ala.: University of Alabama.

Tansey, P. J. and Unwin, D. (1969) *Simulation and Gaming in Education*. London: Methuen Educational.

Taylor, J. L. (1974) "Preliminary Observations on Improving the Performance of Environmental Simulation Systems in Higher Education." *Programmed Learning and Educational Technology* 11 (4): 197–203.

Taylor, J. L. and Walford, R. (1972) *Simulation in the Classroom*. Harmondsworth: Penguin.

Taylor, L. C. (1976) "Educational Materials: Their Development, Supply, Use and Management." In *Materials for Learning and Teaching*. London: Commonwealth Secretariat.

Teather, D.C.B. and Whittle, S. J. (1971) "Classroom-Based Research for Teachers in Training." *Education for Teaching* 86: 24–31.

Thiagarajan, S. and Stolovitch, H.D. (1979) "Frame Games: An Evaluation." *Simulation and Games* 10 (3): 287–314.

Thomas, C. J. (1957) *The Genesis of Operational Gaming*. Baltimore: Operations Research Society of America.

van Ments, M. (1983) *The Effective Use of Role-play*. London: Kogan Page.

Walford, R. (1969) "Operational Games and Geography Teaching." *Geography* 54: 34–42.

Walker, D.R.F. and Graham, L. (1979) "Simulation Games and the Microcomputer." *Simulation/Games for Learning* 9 (4): 151–158.

Wilson, A. (1970) *War Gaming*. Harmondsworth: Penguin.

Zuckerman, D. and Horn, R. (1970) "What Is It You Want to Know?" *Media and Methods* (October): 42–44.

SIMULATION/GAMES FOR LEARNING (JOURNAL). Formerly called *SAGSET Journal*. See **Society for the Advancement of Games and Simulations in Education and Training.**

SIMULATION SOFTWARE. Software that presents the user with a set of facts concerning a particular situation or event, requires inputs about what to do next, and then demonstrates the results of the user's decisions. Simulations are extensively employed in industrial and commercial training and increasingly in educational software.

SINGLE CONCEPT FILM LOOP. As 8mm loop systems allow quick and extremely easy projection, it is possible to separate concepts in a teaching film into single loops allowing each concept to be shown separately and repeatedly until fully understood.

SINGLE DENSITY. Floppy disk as used on some personal computers. The maximum available number of tracks is 40, but the number used in a particular application will depend on the operating system in use. See **Double Density.**

SINGLE-LENS REFLEX CAMERA (SLR). A camera which has a 45° mirror within the camera body so that the scene to be photographed is projected into the camera viewfinder. The mirror hinges out of the light path while the picture is taken. The SLR is the most common form of camera design for 35mm and professional roll-film cameras. The many advantages of the design include the ability to aim and focus the camera with extreme accuracy and to assess exposure automatically with a high degree of accuracy by use of light sensors built into the viewfinder.

SINGLE SYSTEM SOUND. See **Edge Stripe.**

SITE. See **Satellite Instructional Television Experiment.**

SIXTEEN MILLIMETER FILM (16mm). Narrow-gauge cine film introduced in the 1920s for amateur filmmakers, widely used for educational and scientific filmmaking but under increasing threat from video. See **Electronic News Gathering; Film Gauge.**

SKILLS. A set of behaviors that constitute a recognizable operation or complex behavior are referred to as a *skill*. For example, "the ability to add," "the ability to swim," or "the ability to teach."

Skills vary greatly in their complexity and are frequently taught using specially designed training techniques. For example, **microteaching** (q.v) is used in the training of teachers: individual skills are isolated and practiced until some criterion of performance is achieved.

SKILLS ANALYSIS. Sometimes confused with job analysis, of which it is strictly a part. In general, the systematic process of analyzing knowledge and physical skill required to perform a nonsupervisory task in industry or commerce to form the basis of a training program. Specifically for manual and similar skills, to identify and record the mental and physical characteristics of adequate performance.

SKINNER BOX. A container named after B. F. Skinner and used for experiments with animals in **operant conditioning** (q.v.). Usually a lever, when depressed by the subject, releases a pellet of food.

SKIP BRANCHING. A programmed learning technique where not all the frames are worked on. A student, on successful completion of one frame, may be "skipped" ahead, missing out repetitive material. *See* **Programmed Learning.**

SLEEP TEACHING. *See* **Hypnopaedia.**

SLIDE DUPLICATOR. A photographic device for the automatic or semiautomatic copying of 35mm slides. Usually a photoelectric sensing element is used to determine the required intensity of a built-in electronic flash, and various filters can be incorporated to achieve the desired color balance.

SLIDE-TAPE. An instructional program in which material is presented by audiotape with accompanying 35mm slides. The projection (often rear-projection) of the slides may be under the control of the student but is often synchronized by pulses on the sound track.

SLOT. A socket inside a microcomputer for the installation of peripheral device cards such as printer interfaces.

SLOW MOTION. A process which slows down the speed of movement on the screen for study or dramatic effect. It is achieved by running the film at a faster than normal speed in the camera during shooting. Rather crude slow motion in video can be achieved by slowing down the speed of the tape during playback, but to achieve superior quality, as in replays of sporting incidents on broadcast television, it is necessary to use advanced tape or magnetic disk recording systems. *See* **Filming Speed.**

SLOW SCAN TELEVISION. It is possible to transmit television signals as telephone messages or modulated radio transmissions. This is done by restricting the bandwidth and taking very much longer to process the pictures; this is slow scan television. The technique is used for facsimile transmission, especially of documents, charts, etc.

SLR. *See* **Single-lens Reflex Camera.**

SMALL ASSEMBLY SESSION. A stage in the audio-tutorial method where the learners gather in small groups to discuss the learning material.

S.M.D.P. *See* **Scottish Microelectronics Development Programme.**

SME. *See* **Subject-Matter Expert.**

SMPTE. *See* **Society of Motion Picture and Television Engineers.**

SNOOT. A conical hood which restricts the width of the beam emerging from a light source.

SNOW. A random pattern of white dots in a television picture indicating a low signal-to-noise ratio.

SOCIETY FOR THE ADVANCEMENT OF GAMES AND SIMULATIONS IN EDUCATION AND TRAINING (SAGSET) (U.K.). Former name (until 1983) of the **Society for the Advancement of Games and Simulations in Education and Training** (q.v.). SAGSET is a U.K.-based international organization founded in 1970 to promote the use of simulations and games in schools, colleges, universities, and training establishments. Its activities include the publication of a quarterly journal *(Simulation/Games for Learning)*, the provision of a comprehensive information service to members and the organization of an annual conference.

Center for Extension Studies, Loughborough University, Loughborough, Leicestershire, U.K.

SOCIETY OF MOTION PICTURE AND TELEVISION ENGINEERS (SMPTE). The SMPTE is a U.S. organization which promotes the interests of persons working in the technical and engineering areas of film and television. The society concerns itself with technical and professional standards.

Annual conventions and equipment exhibitions are held, and a monthly journal is published.

SOCIODRAMA. Sociodrama is the use of role-playing as a means of seeking a solution to a social problem of some type. The problem may be one extracted from the real world, or it may be one specially designed to present a particular situation for solution. In both cases, the role-players (or actors) are required to devise an acceptable solution to the situation with which they are confronted. Sociodrama differs from role-playing only in the objective which is sought. Whereas role-playing seeks to provide competence or understanding in a particular role for the person playing the role, sociodrama seeks to utilize the role-playing as a means of devising a solution to a prescribed problem situation. *See* **Role-Playing.**

SOFT. Adjective used in computer and related applications to denote an action or phenomenon which either has an aspect of impermanence or does not destabilize an existing situation. Thus a soft hyphen is one used to split a word at the end of a line; a soft exit (from a computer mode) is one which leaves a language or operating system intact.

SOFT ERROR. A temporary error in reading a disk that does not recur when the disk is reread. Typically, the specifications of a hard disk call for an error rate of not more than one soft error in 10^{10} reads, and even this one-in-ten-billion read error will almost always be caught by the controller.

SOFT FOCUS. The deliberate production of an image with reduced sharpness, in order to achieve an artistic effect.

SOFT FONT. A system for improving legibility of NTSC video pictures. A major gain is the ability to use a display with 80 characters per line on a color television receiver.

SOFT-SECTORED. Disks on which each individual section of data within a track is marked by a magnetic address pattern, rather than by a physical timing hole in the disk. Because locations are denoted by magnetic patterns, these patterns must first be written on the disk before it can be used, a process called *initializing* or *formatting* the disk.

SOFT SWITCH. A switch which can be operated under program control, as distinct from having to make a physical operation.

SOFTWARE. In computing, the term used to describe the program material. By derivation, a term used to describe learning materials. In the classic definition of educational technology (hardware, software, systems), software are those items used by or in hardware, e.g., film, paper, videotape.

Confusion can exist between what might be termed the actual material of the software, e.g., film, paper, etc., and the message it may be carrying, i.e., the instructional content. The term **courseware** (q.v.) can be used for this latter purpose.

SORT. A function performed by a data base management program; items in a data file are arranged or rearranged in a logical sequence designated by a key word or field in each item in the file.

SOUND MIXER. A device for combining audio signals from different sources into a single combined signal. The mixer will usually have facilities that allow the relative strengths and tonal characteristics of the various sounds to be controlled and modified before mixing occurs.

SOUND PAGE. *See* **Talking Book.**

SOUND SYNCHRONIZATION. The process of recording sound in accurate step with moving pictures. In the case of video or cameras using edge-striped film, this is accomplished automatically. However, most 16mm and larger-format movie cameras require special synchronizing devices to be used to ensure that the sound and pictures remain in step throughout filming and the subsequent editing process. *See* **Lip Sync.**

SOURCE CODE. Program material not written in machine language. Before the computer can use the program, it has to be transformed into object code, e.g., by means of a compiler or interpreter.

SPECIAL EFFECTS (SFX). In television production, visual effects such as split screens, wipes, inlays, and superimpositions that are produced using a (special) effects generator.

SPECIAL EFFECTS GENERATOR. An electronic device which can combine and/or modify video signals in order to produce special effects. Commonly referred to as an *effects generator*.

SPEECH COMPRESSION. A procedure which speeds up the reproduction of speech but without raising the pitch (as would be the case if one merely replayed a tape at a higher speed than the recording speed). The absence of the "Donald Duck" effect permits the listener to understand speech at very much faster speeds than normal.

SPEED READING. *See* **Rapid Reading.**

SPIN STABILIZATION. The design of satellites calls for the body (or "drum") of the satellite to rotate. This spinning motion provides gyroscopic stability, but the communications antennas are despun and remain pointed towards the coverage zones unique to each.

SPIRAL BINDING. A form of mechanical binding in which the sheets of a document are held together by a helical wire passed through holes along the edges of the pages. *See* **Comb Binding.**

SPIRIT DUPLICATOR. *See* **Hectograph.**

SPLICE. In the editing process film is cut and spliced so as to bring the frames into the required sequence; either glue or adhesive tape is used to make the join. Broken and damaged film can also be cut and spliced for reuse.

Audiotape can be satisfactorily spliced, but a splice in videotape would cause damage to the rapidly rotating video head(s), thus editing of videotape has to be accomplished by electronic means. *See* **Edit (Video and Film).**

SPLIT SCREEN. Modern effects generators are capable of showing input from two sources at once by dividing the screen into two areas. The areas may be equal vertical halves, a cutout circle, or whatever.

Important educational applications include, for example, showing a teacher together with student reaction, two views of a mechanical process, etc.

SPOOLER. *See* **Print Spooler.**

SPOT BEAM. A satellite beam designed to cover a particular part of the earth's surface, usually a relatively small segment. For example, AUSSAT 1 has national beams covering the entire Australian continent, and several spot beams including one directed at Papua New Guinea.

SPOTLIGHT. A lamp which produces a narrow beam of light.

SPREADSHEET. Microcomputer software exemplified by Lotus 1–2–3. In effect, the user constructs a table or matrix relating to his or her interest. The program will calculate values for each "cell" (i.e., intersection of row and column) depending on supplied values and formulae.

A simple example is a sales chart showing sales by salesmen A, B, C, etc., for each month of the year. The spreadsheet can be instructed to calculate the cumulative totals for A, B, C; yearly totals or monthly totals for all salesmen, etc. One of the most fruitful uses is probably in forecasting, e.g., "What would happen if——— ?" Surprisingly, spreadsheets turn out to be useful in the teaching of many subjects, from algebra to home economics.

SPRITE. A graphic design which comprises a programmable entity on a computer display. For example, a spaceship, frog, Pac-Man, General Custer—all can be composed in advance and then used in a program by referring to the composed sprite. Additionally, many personal computers contain sprites in **ROM** (q.v.), often consisting of "building" blocks for graphic designing. Sprites can move across the screen as complete units and thus greatly simplify graphics programming and permit rapidly changing displays.

SPSS. Statistical Package for the Social Sciences. A very celebrated statistics program available for most large computers. Virtually all the statistical procedures used in educational research are available in SPSS.

STABILIZATION PROCESS A rapid processing system for photographic paper which employs a roller processor and special printing paper incorporating a developing agent. Development is induced by an activator, and this is followed by a stabilization bath in place of fixing and washing. The print emerges from the processing machine in about fifteen seconds and is virtually dry.

Stabilization prints will not last for long without discoloring unless they are subsequently fixed and washed, so the advantage of the system is confined to materials needed for more or less immediate use. The process is most often used in situations where the time saved in meeting a deadline is worth more than the expense involved.

STACK. A sequential data list held in computer memory, having special provisions for program access from one end or the other. Storage and retrieval of data from the stack is generally performed automatically.

STAFF DEVELOPMENT. The various mechanisms (both systematic and incidental) whereby teaching staff develop their skills and expand their knowledge—e.g., through attending courses, seminars, and conferences; carrying out research and consultancy; engaging in professional activities, etc.

STANDARDS IN AUDIOVISUAL TECHNOLOGY. The word *standard*, like many other English words, has many meanings, from a flag to rally around to an inferior cut of beef. It may also refer to a once-common phonograph needle and record speed.

Standards in audiovisual technology have been selected, adapted, or created for a number of specific purposes by both national and international standards-making and dissemination bodies. Among them are the following.

1. Standards for units of measurement. Descriptors such as "whisper quiet," "light as a feather," "brightest," and "hi-fi" have no definite meanings that can be used for specifications or comparisons. Many projectors have been purchased with "500 watt illumination" when the accepted units for light on the screen are lumens, which have a definite and agreed-upon definition. Most of the technical world today uses the International System of Units which is abbreviated SI from the French original. This system is often called the metric system. The United States is the only technological nation that still resists "going metric," but the move is underway and inevitable. In audiovisual technology we have traditionally referred to 8, 16, and 35 millimeter films, but often referred to their length in feet. The following SI quantities are often used in audiovisual technology:

frequency	hertz	Hz
force	newton	N
power	watt	W
magnetic flux	weber	Wb
length	meter	m
luminous flux	lumen	lm
illumination	lux	lx
sound ratio	decibel	db
temperature	celsius	°C

2. Standards for fit. The slide, film, or tape and its cartridge, reel, or cassette must interface or mate with the machine necessary to reproduce it. A good example is 16mm film and the reels to mount or hold it. Due to standardization of all necessary dimensions, any 16mm film has been usable on any 16mm projector anywhere in the world for over fifty years. Many improvements in film, reels, and projectors have been made without sacrificing compatibility. We take for granted that lamps will fit the socket, batteries will fit the compartment, cassettes will fit the recorder, etc. But we also have had enough frustrations and problems with fit to know that standards should not be taken for granted. They are the work of many competent and dedicated standards engineers over a long period of time.

3. Standards for interconnection. Much media use involves connecting one device to another. A microphone is needed for a public address system, an audio recorder, and a video recorder. A variety of impedances, voltages, and connectors makes choices or substitutions difficult or impossible. Adapters or special connecting or patch cords are often needed. One audio or video recorder is often connected to another. A computer output needs to be connected to a monitor or distribution system. Much standards activity is directed toward making such interconnections possible, safe, easy, and inexpensive.

4. Standards for performance. Good, better, and best are no longer satisfactory for specifying or describing the performance or quantity and quality of the visual and/or acoustic output of equipment with its software or materials. Due to standards work, it is now possible to specify optical characteristics such as screen lumens, center to corner ratio, resolution, and contrast with no question about meaning. It is also possible to measure and report the quantity and quality of electrical signals delivered to the loudspeaker or headphones. Unfortunately, we have not yet succeeded in making standards for the actual sound delivered to the audience or students.

5. Standards for safety. Use of the device must not be a hazard to the operator or audience under any expected conditions of use. It must be recognized that in order to do their jobs effectively, audiovisual machines must use mechanical, electrical, and optical devices that could tear, shock, burn, or dazzle someone under some adverse circumstances. Many countries now test audiovisual equipment for safety and demand a unique national approval. A new committee (IEC 61G) has been formed to prepare one worldwide standard for projector safety to obviate the need for all of the separate and redundant national tests. Safety also involves the materials used with the equipment. The film, slides, tapes, etc., must not be damaged or unduly worn by going through the mechanism.

6. Standards for vocabulary. The terms used to describe a device and the materials to go with it must have the same meanings for everyone. From several meanings,

a cassette now means a container with two spools, and a cartridge now means a container with one spool. Most standards committees now have a working group on vocabulary.

7. Standards for symbols and labels. Space on controls, rating plates, sockets, lamps, etc., is so limited that symbols and abbreviations are necessary. Much equipment made in one country is used in another with a different language. A major problem in developing countries is the matching of equipment to various electrical supplies without damaging it.

8. Standards for life testing. Most equipment and materials wear out in time, but some will last much longer than others. This is a particular problem with projection lamps. To determine average life, a rigorous test has been devised that is valid and repeatable.

9. Standards for control placement and layout. Ergonomics has recently become a major concern. Standards for placement, order, movement and operation of various controls are under consideration. A similar confusion with automobile controls resulted in standardization some years ago, much to the relief of drivers who use more than one model.

10. Reference standards. Test materials such as slides, films, and tapes of known technical quality have been painstakingly made to check the performance of machines. Machines of known technical quality have been made or selected to check the quality of materials. These are particularly important in comparing competitive products.

11. Standards for acceptability. These are usually minimum performance levels for a particular application. They may also include safety approval, maximum weight, and compatibility with other equipment or materials.

Audiovisual standards work in the United States has for fifteen years been primarily done by PH7 of the American National Standards Institute (ANSI) and sponsored by the National Association of Photographic Manufacturers, the National Audio Visual Association, and the Association for Educational Communications and Technology. Subcommittees are working on standards for performance characteristics and standard test methods, safety, image characteristics, electroacoustical characteristics, magnetic recording equipment and software, consumer interest in audiovisual characteristics, reading apparatus, and connectors and hardware. Several other ANSI committees have prepared or are working on standards for projection lamps, acoustics, motion pictures, optics, etc., of interest to audiovisual technology. Liaison among committees is assured.

International audiovisual standards were for ten years the primary responsibility of International Electrotechnical Commission (IEC) Subcommittee 60C. It had working groups on symbols and identification, electrical and mechanical matching, electronic control of learning systems, safety, audio recording systems, video recording systems, and methods for measuring and reporting the performance of AV equipment and systems. IEC SC 60C has recently been combinbed with IEC SC 29B to form a new technical committee, TC 84, for equipment and systems in the field of audio, video and audiovisual engineering. Several other IEC committees prepare standards related to audiovisual technology and constant liaison is maintained. The International Standards Organization (ISO) is concerned with nonelectrical standards and its technical committee 36 on cinematography and 42 on photography regularly work on needed standards with constant liaison.

Even though much work has been done, there are many glaring examples of the lack of standardization. Eight millimeter films might have been popular if a standard cartridge or cassette had been agreed on. Every AV center has a confusing array of connectors, adapters, and patch cords. Television tapes come in almost countless formats or configurations. Acoustical output (noise and sound) is not available or meaningless. We have hundreds of projection lamps instead of a few.

Some important lessons have been learned from more than fifteen years of work on technical standards for audiovisual equipment and materials:

1. Standards must be made with the participation and consensus of those who manufacture or produce, those who distribute or sell, and those who buy or consume the products.

2. The standards process takes much time. There is no good way for rapid standards production.

3. National and international standards should be the same or at least compatible.

4. Developing countries have particular needs for standards, and they currently do not participate in their preparation.

5. Consumers or users of educational technology need to be much more active in the standards field. Few of them currently feel technically competent to do the needed work, and even fewer have financial backing for the travel and meeting expenses needed.

6. The current division of international standards between IEC and ISO makes no sense for educational technology, which makes use of both electric and nonelectric devices in many combinations.

7. Standards must not hinder the development of truly better products. If we had standardized on 78 RPM, we would not have LP records. If we had stuck to reels, we would not have audio cassettes. On the other hand, we have been plagued with a proliferation of slightly better or only different products that were not compatible with another.

Many professionals in audiovisual technology, who are absolutely dependent on equipment and machines, seem to have little or no interest in or knowledge of the technical standards that make them usable. Participation in national and/or international standards work is much needed and most welcome. Nearly every country has a national standards organization with many committees or working groups to address specific areas needing standards. The American National Standards Institute includes PH7 for Instructional Audiovisual Systems Standards, and it can be reached through its secretary, Richard Hittner, National Association of Photographic Manufacturers, 600 Mamaroneck Avenue, Harrison, New York, 10528. International Electrotechnical Commission TC 84 can be reached through its secretary, A. J. G. van Kuijk, Product Standardization, ELA/EMB, N.V. Philips Gloeilampenfabrieken, 5600 MD, Eindhoven, The Netherlands. The International Standards Organization can be reached at 1 Rue de Varembe, Geneva, Switzerland.

Raymond Wyman

REFERENCES

Alden, A. (1979) "The Role of Standards in Technological Progress." *Educational Media International* 4: 13–14.
Central Secretariat of the ISO. (1979) "The Role of the International Standards Organization." *Educational Media International* 4: 18–19.
Crocker, A. H. (1979) "Standardization—An Overview." *Educational Media International* 4: 4–11.
Greetfeld, H (1979) "Standardization of Audio-Visual Equipment in Education." *Educational Media International* 4: 2–4.
Koeter, W. (1979) "The Work of the International Electrotechnical Commission." *Educational Media International* 4: 15–19.
Lebas, G. (1979) "Aspects of Audio-Visual Equipment Standardization." *Educational Media International* 4: 14–15.
Tham, W. (1979) *Standardization of Educational Materials in Western Europe*. Eurodidac Publications, No. 2. Basle: Eurodidac, Jagerstrasse 5, CH-4058.
UNESCO Report. (1980) *Standardization of Educational Audio Visual Equipment*. Belgrade: Yugoslav Commission for Cooperation with UNESCO.
Wyman, R. (1968) "The Need for Performance Specifications for Overhead Projectors." *Journal of the SMPTE* 77: 1048–1050.
———. (1970) "Mediaware Specification Guidelines." *Audiovisual Instruction* (June-July): 106–108.
———. (1975) *International Standards for Educational and Training Equipment*, No. 1: 2–9.
———. (1979a) "Safety Standards for Projectors." *Audiovisual Instruction* (March): 48.
———. (1979b) "Standards for a Non-Standard World." *Educational Media International* 4: 12–13.
———. (1980a) "Buying Better Can Cost Less." *Instructional Innovator* (January): 44.
———. (1980b) "How Efficient is your Audiovisual Equipment?" *Instructional Innovator* (May): 43–46.
———. (1983) "How to Write Better Specifications for Record Players." *Instructional Innovator* (March): 38–40.

STANDBY. A condition of electronic equipment when all circuits are energized except for the prime operation. For example, a video recorder will be "warmed up," merely awaiting a key to be depressed for recording, playing, etc.

STANDING COMMITTEE ON EDUCATIONAL DEVELOPMENT SERVICES IN POLYTECHNICS (SCEDSIP) (U.K.). An organization founded in 1974 with the aim of improving the effectiveness of educational development services in British polytechnics (i.e., institutions offering university-type courses but often with a vocational bias). Bulletins and occasional papers are published, as is a register of educational development provision in polytechnics.

Center for Educational Services, Bristol Polytechnic, 20 Coldharbor Lane, Bristol, U.K.

STAR. A network layout that connects all stations to a central computer. All signals pass through the central point.

STENCIL DUPLICATOR. See **Mimeograph.**

STEPPER. A type of microcomputer disk drive that uses a motor that moves in fixed increments to push the read/write head in and out. Although not as fast as some other types, stepper drives are inexpensive and reliable.

STEP SIZE. A term that refers to either (1) the length of time to complete a frame in programmed learning, (2) the number of words in a frame, or (3) the "amount of information" in a frame.

Many different values have been computed for "ideal" step size. In linear programs steps are shorter than in branching programs. See **Programmed Learning.**

STEREOPHONY (STEREO). Sound systems which use more than one microphone to record two or more separate channels that are played back through separate speakers, thus creating sound with "depth."

STILL FRAME. A single picture on a film, videotape, or videodisc. Line drawings, photographs, etc., can each be presented as a still frame.

STILL FRAME AUDIO. Proposed technique for providing a few seconds of audio during the display of a freeze frame on a videodisc system.

STILLITRON. An electrical response device invented by G. Stillit. The Stillitron consisted of a printed circuit board which was slipped under a page of a specially printed book. The student responded to multiple-choice questions by pressing a stylus on the indicated "boxes" on the pages. According to the correctness of the student's response, a green or red light was illuminated.

Teacher-prepared materials were used with the Stillitron by means of special hecto masters.

STOP. *See* **Aperture.**

STOP MOTION. The technique of exposing one frame at a time in a cine camera for time lapse or animation work.

STORYBOARD. A process of preparing sketches or photographs to illustrate all, or parts, of an accompanying script for use during the planning process of a production. Often done on individual cards for ease in revisions of the program, the sketches are presented on a board (often several walls), for discussion. Storyboarding, or comic strip sketching, has other uses in education, particularly when the manipulation of sequence elements of a story is important for an individual child.

STREAMER (STREAMING TAPE). A mass-storage device for microcomputers. The streamer records all the contents of a hard disk by writing to a continuously moving tape cassette. The process is slow (perhaps 30 minutes to store 20MB) so is only used for backup purposes.

STREAMING CARTRIDGE. A type of cartridge tape drive that records whole tracks at one time. The mechanism is less expensive than incremental (start-stop) recorders and can hold more data per cartridge.

STRINGY FLOPPY. *See* **Microdrive.**

STRIPED FILM. Cine film that carries a narrow strip of magnetic oxide down one edge on which a sound track can be recorded. *See* **Edge Stripe.**

STROBOSCOPE. (1) A variable frequency flashing light used to measure the frequency, or to freeze the motion of rotating or vibrating systems. (2) Any pulsating device used to produce an illusion of stationary motion, or to produce effects occuring as a result of intermittent flashing of light.

STRUCTURAL COMMUNICATION. A technical term for a type of communication which purports to be more than the transfer of data. Structural communication implies an act of judgment in which two or more people share knowledge or seek instructions or strive for a common understanding. It is based on a study unit that causes the learner to be challenged: it attempts to "stretch" the capabilities of learners toward new goals.

STRUCTURED PROGRAMMING. A programming practice which is generally favored in that the program consists of clearly labeled and distinct sections, each of which performs a unique task. Languages such as Pascal are designed to support and encourage a structured approach to programming. *See* **Pascal.**

STUDIO. A specially designed or adapted area used for artistic, graphic, or photographic work, or for the production of audio programs, television programs, films, etc. Studios are characterized by open areas unimpeded by fixed furniture; good lighting, either natural or (much more commonly) via floods and spotlights; and dedication to a special purpose.

SUBCARRIER. NTSC (and its derivative PAL) color television is essentially a monochrome signal with color added (thus permitting use of B/W receivers, and allowing color receivers to access B/W material). This is accomplished by generating a waveform, the subcarrier, which carries the color information only, and using this subcarrier to modulate the luminance signal which carries all other picture and synchronizing information.

SUB-IP. A subsidiary information (input) provider on a videotex system. The sub-IP buys pages from an IP for their own use, or indeed for further sale. The application usually arises because many providers wish to take fewer than the minimum number of pages offered by the operator.

SUBJECT-MATTER EXPERT. The person who supplies or checks the content for computer-assisted instruction (CAI) lessons or artificial intelligence (AI) expert systems. In most cases, the SME works in a team with experts in instructional design or AI and perhaps with a programmer, researcher, and graphic artist to create the lessons.

SUBROUTINE. Computer term referring to a set of instructions frequently accessed by a program. For example, an educational drill program in arithmetic may use a subroutine to continually generate new numbers for a student to add together. Much of the power of computers derives from their ability to repeatedly call up subroutines.

SUBSERVICE PROVIDER. Anyone who rents space on a videotex system from a service provider. *See* **Sub-IP.**

SUNSPOT CYCLE. A periodic (about eleven years) increase and decrease of the activity at the surface of the sun, during which there are changes in the intensity of particles given off by the sun. These changes affect, among other things, the condition of the ionosphere, and hence the quality of electromagnetic communication.

SUPER. To superimpose captions onto a film or video, possibly for didactic purposes (e.g. to label an object) but often for credits and/or titles.

SUPER-8. *See* **Eight Millimeter Film; Film Gauge.**

SUPER-TWISTED BIREFRINGENCE EFFECT. An LCD technology which gives a blue-on-white display of superior readability.

SURVEY ANALYSIS. A procedure for establishing connections between census-type data characteristics, e.g., size of class, number of teachers in a school, salaries, etc. Typically, these linkages are expressed in terms of correlation coefficients.

SWIG. "See What I'm Getting." Same as SWYG.

SWITCHER. The person who operates the vision mixing desk in a television production. Also known as the *vision mixer*.

SWYG (SWIG). "See What You Get" or "See What I'm Getting." A characteristic of certain word-processing programs in that the final appearance of the print is previewed on the screen, including refinements such as justification, boldface, underlining, etc.

SYMBIONICS. It will soon be possible to build sophisticated intelligence amplifiers significantly more powerful than present-day computers and connect them directly or indirectly to the human brain for both input and output. These brain prostheses will amplify and strengthen all the intellectual abilities we now take for granted as comprising intelligent human activity. They have been called "symbionic" minds (derived from the words symbiotic + bionic) because of the close, interdependent relationships that will almost certainly exist between them and humans, and because they will make human beings, to some degree, bionic (Cartwright, 1980a, 1980b ORIGIN).

Symbionics refers to the design and development of such brain-computer interfaces. Symbionics will be the principal outcome of a merger among a number of currently independent research areas, including (but not restricted to) (1) emgors, (2) brain pacemakers or cerebellar stimulators, (3) biocybernetic communication and neurometrics, (4) artificial intelligence, and (5) biotechnology.

The first of these is the development of emgors (electromyogram sensors), which are now used to enable amputees to control artificial limbs in an almost natural manner. The aim of the research is to create artificial limbs that respond to the will of the patient by finding in the stump of the severed limb the brain's own natural impulse called the myoelectric signal, or electromytogram (EMG), improving it through amplification or other means and using it to control electromechanical devices in the prosthetic appliance. An obvious use would be to have it control an artificial limb called a myoelectric arm. In the future, the same principles may be used to benefit everyone by allowing us to control mentally an extensive assortment of useful devices.

The second area is the development of brain pacemakers or cerebellar stimulators. These followed the creation of cardiac pacemakers and are based on much of the research involving the electrical stimulation of the brain. Cerebellar stimulators have been implanted in spastic children to help them achieve some measure of control over their muscle functions. Such mental pacemakers are now being used to prevent patients from falling into deep depressions, to avoid epileptic seizures, and to reduce intractable pain. Several patients who suffer from psychosis, and for whom chemotherapy has failed, have already been fitted with brain pacemakers to help them on the path to normal behavior. The controversial technique has been used with neurotics, schizophrenics, and others who have experienced the feelings of extreme anger often associated with psychosis or violent behavior (Heath, 1977 AUTHORITY). Other cerebellar stimulators have been implanted as brain pacemakers to minimize the spasticity and athetosis associated with cerebral palsy (Cooper et al., 1976 AUTHORITY). Somewhat related to cerebellar stimulation is the experimental work on electrical muscle stimulation which permits electrical impulses to be fed directly to inactive muscles paralyzed by injured spinal cords (Petrofsky, Phillips, and Heaton, 1984; Petrofsky, Phillips, and Stafford, 1984; Phillips and Petrofsky, 1984 AUTHORITY). The mere existence today of simple versions of such devices as cerebellar and muscle stimulators to help alleviate specific medical conditions points the way to a potentially bright future for the more complex models of tomorrow.

In the third area of development, biocybernetic communication and neurometrics, experimental work is underway in an attempt to interpret brain wave patterns to link them to specific thoughts. At Stanford University, researchers were able to have a subject hooked to a computer screen move a white dot about simply by thinking about it (Pinneo et al., 1975 AUTHORITY).

In the area of neurometrics, the study of evoked-response potentials (EPs) in the cortex has produced interesting results. These are achieved by measuring minute voltage changes that are produced in response to a specific stimulus like a light, a bell, or a shock, but which are of such small amplitude as to not show up on a conventional electroencephalogram (EEG). An averaging computer sums the responses over time to make them stand out against background noise. Since the background noise is random, it tends to be cancelled out.

Through the use of this technique, it has now been established that the long latency response known as the P300 wave (positive potential, 300 millisecond latency) is usually associated with decision-making activity. Though the wave appears after each decision, it is often delayed when a wrong decision is made. Theoretically, then, it should be possible to construct a device to warn us when we have made a bad decision, to alert us when we are not paying attention (a boon to air traffic controllers), or to monitor general states of awareness.

It is also possible using EPs to distinguish motor responses from cognitive processes, and decision-making processes from action components (Taylor, 1979 BACKGROUND READING). As its objectivity (patient cooperation is not needed) and noninvasiveness come to be appreciated, more and more clinical applications of EPs are beginning to appear (Ziporyn, 1981a, 1981b, 1981c BACKGROUND), and it is likely that the number of nonclinical applications will also rise.

One obvious goal of such a technological development as biocybernetic communication would be to use thought to control a wide variety of appliances. For example, it may be possible to harness thought to facilitate a broad assortment of human activities from controlling simple pocket calculators to complex machinery like army tanks (Cartwright, 1981 FURTHER DETAIL). The utility of a pocket calculator would be greatly enhanced if one could operate it by just thinking about the numbers rather than pushing corresponding buttons. In fact, almost any device which now exists would be intrinsically more useful were it under the direct control of the human brain. The extension of this kind of research might eventually result in mental communication between individuals and machines, and even between individuals, in a manner similar to telepathy, but based on proven scientific principles and sophisticated technology.

The fourth area is that of artificial intelligence, which includes the study of pattern recognition, problem solving, and speech comprehension with a view to reproducing these abilities in computers.

Less well-known is the work in the fifth area of biotechnology. In small laboratories, scientists are now at work in an attempt to use genetic engineering principles to construct tiny biological microprocessors of protein or "biochips" ("Futuristic Computer Biochips," 1981; Posa, 1981; "Whatever Happened to Molecular Electronics" 1981 FURTHER DETAIL). The advantage is that by using the techniques of recombinant DNA, very small devices (VSDs) can be assembled with great precision.

As unbelievable as it may sound, such biochips may even be designed to assemble themselves. If biochips can be successfully constructed, it is likely they will have higher density and higher speed, and will consume less power than conventional chips. This in itself will be no mean achievement because of the continuing reduction in circuit size to the point where some are now below the size of a living cell. Successful though the silicon chip is, new circuits the size of molecules are already being envisioned which could significantly damage the silicon chip industry and ultimately lead to the creation of a molecular computer.

Biochips would have a greater probability of successful implantation in the cortex due to their higher degree of biocompatibility. One company in America has already received a grant from the National Science Foundation for a feasibility study of the creation of a direct interface between the central nervous system and an integrated circuit. Their initial plan called for increasing the number of effective electrodes from an 8 × 8 platinum array currently used in clinical trials to an array with 100,000 electrodes. The development of such technology will depend heavily on the use of an implanted integrated circuit and state-of-the-art microfabrication techniques. The actual device is expected to consist of electrodes connected to an interface of cultured embryonic nerve cells which can grow three-dimensionally and attach themselves to mature nerve cells in the brain (EMV Associates, 1981; "The Next Generation...," 1981 AUTHORITY). Ultimately, the provision of the appropriate set of genes could enable such a chip to repair itself, DNA codes could be used to program it, and enzymes used to control it ("Biotech..." 1981 FURTHER DETAIL). Already under development as a first step is a device called an "optrode" consisting of a polymer waveguide with a photovoltaic tip capable of photon electron conversion. Research is underway to study the feasibility of using such a tiny, photoconducting microelectrode to record the firing of a single neuron, or perhaps even cause it to fire (McAlear, and Wehrung, n.d. AUTHORITY).

Though the immediate medical goal is to produce a more effective visual prosthesis, the perfection of such a technology has much wider implications.

THE BIRTH OF SYMBIONICS

These five areas have much in common. For the most part, they deal with the brain directly, with thought processes individually, and with intellectual activity primarily. They are steadily converging. Once a merger is effected culminating in a routine way of interfacing with the brain, either directly by using implanted electrodes or indirectly by picking up brain waves with external sensors, the symbionic mind will have been born.

The symbionic mind may thus be defined as any apparatus consisting of some useful device, interfaced with the human brain, capable of intelligent action. The most difficult task in its creation will be the design and construction of the interface unit required to link these devices to the human cortex. Such a complex interface will no doubt represent the major component of the symbionic mind, and the creation of a wide range of standard and optional accessories to attach to it will probably prove to be a comparatively easy task.

Such auxiliary brain prostheses, or symbionic minds, will be used for appliance control, computation, monitoring of particular body functions, problem solving, data retrieval, general intelligence amplification, and inter- and intra-individual communication. The ultimate revolutionary advance may even be the direct, electronic transmission of human thought.

While no such symbionic minds yet exist, technological progress in the five component areas suggests that such interfaces to the human cortex, using sensors and/or direct implants, coupled with microprocessor technology, may become a reality in the future.

SYMBIONIC FUNCTIONS

The most obvious use for a symbionic mind would be to improve human memory. It is easy to see how people with failing memories might benefit from supplementary aids—in this case, tiny mind prostheses or "add-on" brains with extra memory storage and better retrieval.

Symbionic minds will do more than just improve memory, but as yet one can only speculate as to their full range of uses. Because the symbionic mind will be able to interpret our thoughts, our very wishes will become its commands. Thus it will be able to take dictation directly from our thoughts, improve them through editing, and like the word processors of today, rearrange whole paragraphs, perform spelling checks, and supervise the typing of final documents.

To some degree, the human brain may be limited by its small number of input senses. But a symbionic mind connected to the brain, to amplify its abilities, improve its skills, and complement its intelligence, could be used to handle additional sensory inputs and to make low-level decisions about them, discarding irrelevant data and passing on more important information to the brain itself. In the future, it may be possible to build into the symbionic mind totally artificial senses and connect them directly to the brain. These artificial senses would simulate most of our existing senses but would bypass currently available receptor organs. For example, television pictures may be able to be received directly without the aid of a conventional television set. Conventional television sets are really only converters: they convert the broadcast signals we are unable to receive in our natural state into visual signals which can be input through our eyes. From the eyes, the signals are converted to electrochemical impulses to be sent to the visual cortex for analysis.

Imagine a small device which could receive television signals, but instead of displaying them on a video screen, could channel them directly to the human cortex. The sensation of "seeing" the pictures would still exist, but one's eyes would be freed for watching other things. Such devices would not be limited to television but might include radio and telephone reception as well. In all these instances, the normal sensory inputs of eyes and ears would be bypassed. Already, preliminary work in this direction has been undertaken at the University of Florida to find ways of implanting up to 100,000 miniature photovoltaic cells to stimulate previously unused parts of the retina in cases of retinal blindness. In the auditory domain, patients at the Los Angeles Ear Research Institute have been fitted with electronic ear stimulators to stimulate auditory nerves in an attempt to improve hearing.

The immediate goal is to develop medical prostheses, but the result is that this kind of research represents the beginning of the creation of a direct interface with the brain, and perhaps even the eventual development of artificial senses of use to everyone. Some of these might include components of our existing five senses; others will be totally new, and the line distinguishing one sense from another may become increasingly blurred. Exactly what these new senses will be and the uses to which we shall put them must remain, for the moment, in the realm of speculation, but one example might be a totally new sense to detect currently invisible hazards like harmful levels of radiation or pollution in our immediate environment.

The symbionic brain will provide a sophisticated interface between us and a wide variety of household gadgets. The symbionic mind will provide a "thought switch" to enable us to control appliances merely by thinking about them. The symbionic brain will turn lights on and off for us, activate television devices and switch channels (feeding the signal directly to the brain), answer telephone calls and initiate them, and keep household inventories. It will guard us from a number of dangers and protect us in a wide variety of situations. At a party it will monitor our blood alcohol level and warn us when we have had too much to drink. It will keep an eye on other bodily functions including digestion and blood sugar levels, and warn us of impending illness, undue stress, or possible heart attacks. It will guard us while we sleep, listening for prowlers, and sensing the air for smoke. It will attend to all household functions and perhaps will ultimately direct the activities of less intelligent household robots which are sure to have come into existence by that time. It will share with us its vast memory store and its ability to recall information virtually instantly—information we thought we had forgotten. It will do math calculations, household budgets, business accounts, and even make monthly payments for us automatically. It will update its own information daily by scanning a number of information sources, perhaps listening to its own information channel, perhaps digesting local newspapers, sifting for information which it feels it should bring to our attention, helping us make sense of the world around us. It will provide a whole new dimension of living to quadraplegics, allowing them to perform many of the routine daily tasks essential to life and restoring to them some measure of control over their lives.

It will change the entire realm of communications as we know it today. Merely thinking of someone you wish to talk with by telephone will initiate a search by the symbionic mind to locate that person anywhere in the world and establish direct contact. Though physical telephones will be avoided, the two symbionic minds will be in direct communication over the regular telephone network, and thoughts will flow between beings in seemingly telepathic fashion; indeed this may be the closest we will ever come to true telepathy.

The symbionic mind will not be a truly separate brain but will be an extension of us, of our very being. It will not seem to be foreign to us in any way, nor will it pose to us any kind of threat by trying to take us over any more than would our own brain. The symbionic mind will be as much a part of us as a hand or an eye, and it will seem to us simply our own brain doing the thinking. It will be transparent to us. We will not be aware of any separate entity, nor of any other change except an increased ability to perform those intellectual tasks we have always performed, and a new capability to accomplish those which were previously impossible. The new symbionic mind will act purposefully and willfully, but always on our behalf and at our direction. It will be our constant companion and friend, conscience and alter ego. The development of the symbionic mind and the study of symbionic effects may well mark the next significant step in the evolution of our species to a higher plane of existence, and the dawn of a new era.

Glenn F. Cartwright

REFERENCES

Authority

Cooper, I. S., Riklan, M., Amin, I., Waltz, J. M., and Cullinan, T. (1976) "Chronic Cerebellar Stimulation in Cerebral Palsy." *Neurology* 26: 744–753.

EMV Associates. (1981) "Brain/Computer Direct Link Subject of NSF Grant." Press release. November 1, Rockville, Maryland.

Heath, R. (1977) "Modulation of Emotion with a Brain Pacemaker." *Journal of Nervous and Mental Disease* 165 (5): 300–317.

MacAlear, J. H. and Wehrung, J. M. (n.d.) *Photoconducting Electrode Prosthesis*. Rockville, Md.: Gentronix Laboratories.

Petrofsky, J. S., Phillips, C. A., and Heaton, H. H. (1984) "Feedback-Control System for Walking in Man." *Computers in Biology and Medicine* 14: 135–149.

Petrofsky, J. S., Phillips, C. A., and Stafford, D. E. (1984) "Closed-loop Control for Restoration of Movement in Paralyzed Muscle." *Orthopedics* 7: 1289–1302.

Phillips, C. A. and Petrofsky, J. S. (1984) "Computer-Controlled Movement of Paralyzed Muscle—the Medical Perspective." *Artificial Organs* 8: 390.

Pinneo, L. R., Johnson, P., Herron, J., and Rebert, C. S. (1975) *Feasibility Study for Design of a Biocybernetic Communication System*. Menlo Park, Calif.: Stanford Research Institute (August).

"The Next Generation of Microprocessors: Molecular 'Biochips' Instead of Silicon Wafers?" (1981) *Biotechnology Newswatch* (September 21): 7.

Background

Taylor, G. R. (1979) *The Natural History of the Mind*. London: Secker and Warburg.

Ziporyn, T. (1981a) "Evoked Potential Emerging as a Valuable Medical Tool." *Journal of the American Medical Association* 246 (12): 1287–1291.

Ziporyn, T. (1981b) "Evoked Potentials Give Early Warning of Sensory and Behavioral Deficits in High-Risk Neonates." *Journal of the American Medical Association* 246 (12): 1288–1289.

Ziporyn, T. (1981c) "Add EPs to List of Intraoperative Monitors." *Journal of the American Medical Association* 246 (12): 1291, 1295.

Further Detail

"Biotech Breathes Life into Microchips." (1981) *Engineering Today* (November): 11.

Cartwright, G. F. (1981) "Toward a New Level of Awareness: Symbionic Consciousness." Paper presented at the annual meeting of the American Association for Social Psychiatry, New York City.

"Futuristic Computer Biochips: New Market for Synthesized Proteins." (1981) *Genetic Technology News* 1 (9): 9.

Posa, J. G. (1981) "Bioelectronics to Spawn Circuits." *Electronics* 54 (18): 48–50.

"Whatever Happened to Molecular Electronics?" (1981) *IEEE Spectrum* (December): 17.

Origin

Cartwright, G. F. (1980a, July) "Symbionic Minds: The Advent of Intelligence Amplifiers." Paper presented at the First Global Conference on the Future, Toronto, Canada.

Cartwright, G. F. (1980b) "And Now for Something Completely Different: Symbionic Minds." *Technology Review* 83 (1): 68, 70.

SYMBOLS. A synonymous term, to all intents and purposes, for signs. Signs and symbols rely on shared conventions by users. The main uses of such "icons" in educational technology are (1) shorthand notation, and (2) unambiguous and universal labeling.

Manufacturers of equipment are notorious for their confusing, nonstandard, and often illogical use of symbols to indicate functions of controls and facilities. The U.K. Council for Educational Technology has produced a most useful USPEC, USPEC 19, on "Symbols for Use on Audio/Visual Equipment." Their symbols are based on the International Electro-Technical Commission Publication 417, "Graphic Symbols for Use on Equipment."

It is hoped that the CET USPEC will become internationally accepted, thus conferring these important benefits:

1. Users of audiovisual equipment in differing parts of the world would be able to interpret line diagrams and instructions without ambiguity.
2. Symbols can be combined to give more complex symbols (see Figure 58). For example, television video, loudspeaker, and television camera can be combined to show a self-confrontation analysis system.

See **Standards in Audiovisual Technology.**

Figure 58
Examples of Audiovisual Symbols

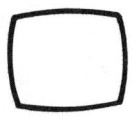

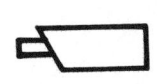

Video Display   Television Camera   Loudspeaker

SYNC. Short for *synchronization,* and refers to the part of a video signal that carries timing information. Also used as a general descriptor for matched or mismatched signals, e.g., the output from a video recorder will not be in sync with output from a camera unless a **genlock** (q.v.) device is in use.

SYNC GENERATOR (SPG). Short for *synchronizing* pulse generator, the equipment used in television camera chains to produce pulses which coordinate the scanning circuits in the cameras so that they work in synchronism. Unless all cameras are "driven" from such a source, mixing the signals from different cameras is not possible without serious disturbance to the picture.

SYNCHRONIZED SOUND. *See* **Sound Synchronization.**

SYNCHRONIZING PULSE. *See* **Sync Generator.**

SYNCHRONOUS COMMUNICATION. Signal transmission where all devices on a network are operating on a common timing system, all being strictly in phase with each other—for example, television transmission.

SYNCHRONOUS SATELLITE. *See* **Geosynchronous Satellite.**

SYNTAX. The structure of instructions in a given computer language. If a syntax mistake is made in entering an instruction, the computer will generate the message SYNTAX ERROR, usually at run time but in some cases as soon as the offending line is entered.

SYSTEMATIC CLASSROOM OBSERVATION. The group of techniques that collectively describe the process of observing, encoding, and decoding classroom interactions. Systematic implies, although does not guarantee, that prespecified categories are used to describe the observed events. The main advantage of this research strategy is to allow monitoring of innovations by looking at the hour-to-hour, day-to-day processes that often explain the success or failure of an innovative project. An assumption made in this research is that the observer or observers in no way interact with the classroom participants. They may, however, affect the "normal" stream of events by their presence. *See* **Interaction Analysis.**

SYSTEM PROGRAM. A program that makes the resources and capabilities of the computer available for general purposes, for example, an operating system or a language compiler. *See* **Application Program.**

SYSTEMS ANALYSIS. The study of new (and hopefully better) ways of doing things based on a close analysis of all the factors and systems involved. Out of this organizing activity have developed the modern sciences of organization and methods, work study, systems engineering, and other similar techniques.

Systems analysis now refers specifically to the use of computers in handling the vast amounts of information involved in analyzing complex activities.

SYSTEMS APPROACH. Loose term intended to suggest a minutely planned, systematic framework for the design of learning materials.

SYSTEMS THEORY. This term refers to a systematic approach to the planning and design of educational materials. Typically, knowledge is applied from all relevant fields on the basis of a detailed analysis of purpose and requirements.

T

TALK-BACK. A voice intercommunicator; an intercom.

TALKING BOOK. A device incorporating pages of books and a machine that plays a disk or tape relaying the contents of each page. Used in audiovisual reading schemes.

TALKING HEAD. A term, usually used in a derogatory manner, describing a common form of televised instruction. That is, the presenter delivers what amounts to a lecture, and the video consists of pictures of the presenter's head and shoulders.

TAPE. Magnetic recording medium consisting of a ferromagnetic coating on a plastic base. Different widths of tape are used for different applications. Videotape is used in 1″, 3/4″, 1/2″, and 8mm widths while sound recording tape is generally 1/4″ or 1/8″. The thickness of the plastic base will determine the length of tape it is possible to accommodate on a spool. Thinner tape is more susceptible to print-through and more easily broken.

TAPE CASSETTE. A plastic cassette containing tape to allow easy placement and removal from a tape recorder. In sound recording the universally standard tape cassette is the "compact" cassette. In television the use of cassettes is complicated by the existence of several incompatible systems. In education, three systems are widely used: Beta, U-Matic, and VHS. Generally speaking, the use of the U-Matic is confined in educational applications to situations where a particularly high quality is required, especially mastering. For distribution purposes the half-inch formats offer substantial advantages of cost and convenience.

At all levels of education tape cassettes are used extensively as their ease of operation means that they can be used by students and teachers, no technical skill being required. *See* **Tape.**

TAPE DECK. The actual mechanical parts of a tape recorder, i.e., the transport mechanism, together with those electronic components needed to read or write to the tape. Amplification and other processes may be accomplished elsewhere.

TAPE GENERATION. An original recording, video or audio, is referred to as a first-generation tape. Copies (often edits of several first-generation segments) made from the first-generation master are second-generation tapes, and so on. In the case of videotape there is often a noticeable reduction in quality after the second generation.

TAPE RECORDER. Although any recorder that uses magnetic tape may be called a tape recorder, the term is generally taken to refer to machines that are used for recording sound. In essence, the principle on which a tape recorder works is to apply a sound signal to a recording head which produces a varying magnetic field through which a tape coated with magnetic material is passed. The signal is recorded as a magnetic pattern on the tape. The tape is made of ferric oxide coated on a thin plastic base. Recordings may make a single track on the tape or, by a special arrangement of recording heads, two or four tracks may be recorded.

The tape transport mechanism must draw the tape at a constant speed past the recording head, and a heavy flywheel is attached to the tape drive capstan to achieve this. Higher tape speeds give a better frequency response; the advantage of slower speeds is that they are very economical on tape and give good enough quality for general purposes.

Professional machines usually have three heads, one for record, one for replay, and one for erase. On cheaper machines the record and replay functions are carried out by one head. One particular advantage of separate record and replay heads is that the signal on the tape can be monitored at the same time as it is recorded. The function of the erase head is to remove any previous recordings by demagnetizing the tape.

TAPE-SLIDE PROGRAMS. *See* **Slide-Tape.**

TAPE-SLIDE SYNCHRONIZATION. The system used in tape-slide presentations to link the tape to the slides mechanically and electronically so that the slides are changed automatically by pulses (usually silent) on the tape.

TAPE SPEED. *See* **Playing Time for Audio Tape; Playing Time for Video Tape.**

TARGET POPULATION. The population that the teaching material is designed for.

TASK ANALYSIS (ACTIVITY ANALYSIS, JOB ANALYSIS). A detailed analysis of tasks or operations to identify subelements or components. Task analysis identifies areas of difficulty and may be used in the construction of **behavioral objectives** (q.v.). *See* **Training Technology.**

TASK HIERARCHY. The ranking of tasks (jobs) into three main levels; motor, or simple repetitive; procedural, those within a sequential progression; and fault finding, tasks demanding integration of information and the making of decisions.

TAXONOMY. A conceptual organization of interrelated variables. Often a taxonomy is hierarchical (as in biological classification or book classification), but in media taxonomy the organization is often more akin to an input-output table. *See* **Bloom's Taxonomy.**

T-COM. *See* **Tethered Communications Satellite.**

TEACHER EDUCATION. The need for adequate training of teachers in the use of media and technology has long been recognized. In 1924 F. D. McClusky (1923) stated that "the movement for visual education will progress in direct proportion to the number of teachers who are trained in the techniques of visual instruction." In 1935 Pennsylvania became the first state to insist that all teachers "shall be required to present evidence of having completed the approved course in visual and sensory techniques" (Saettler, 1968).

Since those early days it has come to be universally accepted that teachers require to be trained in the use of all manner of visual aids, including modern media such as sound recording and television. Not only is training needed in the physical use of hardware and software, but even more essential is an understanding of effective ways of exploiting them for teaching purposes. Ironically, recent developments in microcomputers have occurred so fast that it can no longer be asserted that teacher education is capable of meeting its obligations in this direction. In fact, educators are now confronting a situation in which school students, compared with their teachers, are more familiar with and have greater expertise in what is arguably the single most important development of the second half of the twentieth century. Governments in many countries have shown an eager willingness to equip schools with computing hardware, but only belatedly does it become apparent that the provision of hardware merely scratches the surface of the problem, and that training of teachers and the provision of software are both more difficult and vastly more expensive.

At the time of writing (1987) this dilemma seems unresolved. Much of the hardware is used at best for a cursory degree of familiarity with computers; in some cases the machines are gathering dust or being used for games or with unimaginative educational software of a quality which would not be tolerated in other media.

The extent to which teacher education is upgraded to give all teachers familiarity, and many teachers expertise, will determine the degree to which the microcomputer challenge is met and exploited for the good of future generations.

Derick Unwin

REFERENCES

Gage, N. L. (1963) *Handbook of Research on Teaching.* Chicago: Rand McNally.
Lewis, R. (1983) "Teachers, Pupils and Microcomputers." *Technological Horizons in Education* 10: 81–87.
McClusky, F. D. (1924) "Comparisons of Different Methods of Visual Instruction." In *Visual Education,* ed. F. N. Freeman. Chicago: University of Chicago.
Saettler, P. (1968) *A History of Instructional Technology.* New York: McGraw-Hill.
Travers, R.M.W. (1974) *A Second Handbook of Research in Teaching.* Chicago: Rand McNally.
Zuckerman, R. A. (1983) "Computers and Teacher Training." *AEDS Journal* 16: 123–130.

TEACHING EFFECTIVENESS. The effectiveness of any or several teaching methods. Research in teaching goes back to the early years of this century (some would argue much earlier). There is no one set of agreed characteristics that go to make up effective teaching. Educational technology is concerned with improving teaching effectiveness, but only cultural and philosophical views will ultimately define what is "good teaching."

TEACHING MACHINES. Mechanical teaching devices, formerly known as automatic tutors or auto-instructional devices, intended to assist or replace the teacher where he/she is functioning as a giver of information or a tester of performance. Programmed learning or teaching machines contain programmed software.

DEVELOPMENT

It is impossible to say who built the first teaching machine. As early as 1866 Halcyon Skinner patented a spelling machine (Skinner, 1866). Ordhal and Ordhal (1915) working with mentally subnormal children devised a simple machine to teach serial skills. It was, however, Sidney L. Pressey, working at Ohio State University, who can be considered the father of the teaching machine. His first paper on teaching machines was not published until 1926 (Pressey, 1926). However he wrote in 1915 of his "continuous choice-reaction apparatus"—a testing machine (Pressey, 1915). The theoretical progenitor of the machine age must surely be Edward L. Thorndike. Thorndike, a prime figure in the development of the reward theory and accredited with the "law of effect," saw a rosy future for teaching machines: "if, by a miracle of mechanical ingenuity, a book could be so arranged that only to him who had done what was directed on page one would page two become visible and so on, much that now requires personal instruction could be managed by print" (Thorndike, 1912).

Pressey and his students worked through the 1930s on teaching-testing machines (Peterson, 1931; Little, 1934). The early machines were crude, both in construction and in their rigid application of S-R theory. Some of Pressey's machines actually gave sweets or biscuits as rewards! Later writers were no less enthusiastic for the behavioristic philosophy. Skinner (1961) in a "popular" account of teaching machines wrote that their "purpose is to teach rapidly, thoroughly and expeditiously a large part of what we now teach slowly. . . . Some of the machines also hold the promise to teach behavior of a kind and subtlety that until now has seemed beyond the reach of explicit teaching methods." Although much of the groundwork for programmed learning was done by Pressey in the 1930s, educational writers did not acknowledge the contribution of a reward theory or mechanical aids until the 1950s. McKeown and Roberts (1940) and the seminal Dale (1947) made no acknowledgment of teaching machines. While Dale recognized Pressey's psychology, he did not see the imminent advent of the "machine age."

The first teaching machine in the postwar era mentioned by Skinner was the Slider Machine (Skinner, 1954). This was rapidly followed by the Disk Machine, and by 1958 IBM had assembled an IBM 650 Digital Computer with a typewriter in order to teach binary arithmetic (Rath et al., 1959). A rather appropriate subject matter for the program! All the initial machines had linear programs. The largest and most expensive noncomputer teaching machine was the Mark 1 Auto Tutor developed by Norman Crowder for US Industries Inc. The Mark 2 AutoTutor and later in the United Kingdom the GrundyTutor was a simpler device. The original Auto Tutor used microfilm and could handle up to 10,000 frames. The Mark 2 had some 1,500 frames. Apart from its size, the Auto Tutor was a new step in that it incorporated Crowder's intrinsic or branching programs.

The main influence from Britain came from Gordon Pask (1958), who developed an adaptive teaching machine, SAKI. The **Self-Adaptive Keyboard Trainer** (q.v.), or in the United States the Psychomotor Skills Trainer, was developed by Systems Research Ltd. in Britain and the Rheem Califone Conferation in California. The Rheem Califone Conferation had a unique place in the development of **programmed learning** (q.v.) in the United States of America not only because of its machines but because it "supported" what seems to be the first specialist programmed learning journal, *Automated Teaching Bulletin* (1959). This journal was distributed free of charge to interested individuals (471 in 1960, including 3 in the United Kingdom and 453 in the United States); the journal was edited by Lloyd Homme in this instance and subsequently by Rheem Califone personnel; it was an important "academic" support to that manufacturer's hardware.

The electronic computer was not left out of the development for too long (Rath et al., 1959). Coulson and Silberman (1961) adapted a Bendix G-15 computer into a sophisticated branching teaching machine. Further developments like SOCRATES and **PLATO** (q.v.) moved the teaching machine into the separate world of computer-assisted learning (Suppes, 1966).

CONCEPTUALIZATION

By the mid-1960s it was possible to identify three types of machines:

Type 1 Linear machine (e.g., ESA Tutor; Leedham and Unwin, 1965)

Type 2 Partially adaptive/branching (e.g., Grundy Tutor; Leedham and Unwin, 1965)

Type 3 Adaptive machine (e.g., SAKI; Pask, 1958)

Each of these types can be shown to have common characteristics and unique features. Stolurow (1961) in an attempt to conceptualize teaching machines identified nine parameters that were critical requirements both for engineering design and application of theory.

With the advent of the second and third generation of computers, all these functions could easily be accommodated into one system, the visual display unit providing the learner with display, response, and feedback, and the functions incorporated into the mainframe of the computer. Further analysis of teaching machine paradigms can be found in Smallwood (1962) and Buter (1973).

DECLINE

During the early 1960s international enthusiasm kept the teaching machine industry flourishing. Inevitably, the

United States led the market. Machine sales in the United Kingdom were buoyant until the end of the decade. By 1972, Romiszowski was able to quantify the decline in machines available. Figures for the United Kingdom show 30 machines available in 1969, 18 in 1972, 16 in 1974, and only 13 by 1976 (Howe and Romiszowski, 1974, 1976). At the same time a comparison of Foltz (1961) and Hendershot (1968, 1973) show that in the early 1960s over 100 American companies were actively involved in machine manufacture, but by 1973 only some 70 machines were still available. Of these machines a considerable number were only marginally programmed learning machines.

Many reasons have been suggested in order to explain the failure of teaching machines (Leith, 1969; Biran, 1972; Beck, 1969; Romiszowski, 1972). Five problems can be identified in general terms:

Hardware standardization. In the mid-sixties the British Standards Institute was investigating problems of compatibility between formats. Lamb (1967) suggested that without cooperation, the standarization of machines was going to be difficult to achieve. Impossible, as it turned out. Commercial interests ensured that different formats were produced. It would be wrong to criticize manufacturers for independence: on the other hand, it is inevitable that without standardization, there had to be many machines going to the wall.

Software. Some argue that software was the main problem. Not necessarily the number of programs available, although this must have contributed, but the difficulty of user preparation of software. Again, this is perhaps not a direct reflection on the machines, but on the theory of programmed learning and the adaptability of teachers to using "commercially" produced teaching software.

Computers. These threatened tooled and polished machines; the limitations of storage capacity and speed of feedback or programming capacity were serious drawbacks. The mainframe and later the small computer made individual machines redundant.

Man-Machine Relationships. Many early machines were cumbersome and required the manual dexterity of a concert pianist and the single-mindedness of a diver in a minisubmarine. There was little consideration for the ergonomics of learner-machine interactions. It has not been until recently (Cook, 1974) that such considerations have been examined in detail.

Theory. The theory of programming and the philosophical and pedagogical objections leveled at programmed learning adversely affected the status of the machine. By the late 1960s in the United Kingdom fewer studies were being undertaken into machines or programmed learning, and the total systems approach to instruction was emerging.

Some might argue that it is a pity that the rosy future predicted by Thorndike has not happened. Perhaps this is so, but it is salutory to the proponents of heavy technology that the machine itself is only transitory, and that without a sound theoretical base, no technology-based innovation will survive. All along, the designers and manufacturers of teaching machines were ahead of the theoreticians. It is a commonplace in educational technology that there are many more technical answers than educational problems. The Type 1 Linear Machine and Type 2 Partially Adaptive Machine were answers to problems that were not well formulated. The Type 3 Adaptive Machine may yet have a place in educational technology (e.g., artificial intelligence), but only time will tell.

Ray McAleese

REFERENCES

Beck, J. E. (1969) "A Survey of Problems Encountered by a Number of Industrial and Commercial Users of Programmed Instruction." In *Aspects of Educational Technology 3*, ed. A. P. Mann and C. K. Brunstrom. London: Pitman.

Biran, L. (1972) "The Role and Limitations of Programmed Instruction." In *Yearbook of Educational and Instructional Technology 1972/1973*, ed. A. J. Romiszowski. London: Kogan Page.

Buter, E. M. (1973) *Educational Technology: The Selection and Design of Teaching Learning Situations*. Holland: Alphen.d.d. Rijn.

Cook, U. (1974) *The Human Factors Aspect of the Student/Terminal Interface in CAL Systems*, NDPCAL Technical Report No. 7. London: National Development Programme in Computer Assisted Learning.

Coulson, J. E. and Silberman, H. F. (1961) *Results of Initial Experiments in Automated Teaching*. Santa Monica, Calif.: Systems Development Corporation.

Dale, E. (1947) *Audio-visual Methods in Teaching*. London: Harrap.

Foltz, C. I. (1961) *The World of Teaching Machines: Programmed Learning and Self-instructional Devices*. Washington, D.C.: Electronic Teaching Laboratories.

Hendershot, C. H. (1968) *Programmed Learning and Individually Paced Instruction Bibliography*. 1st ed. Bay City, Mich.: Hendershot Publications.

———. (1973) *Programmed Learning and Individually Paced Instruction Bibliography*. 5th ed. Bay City, Mich.: Hendershot Publications.

Howe, A. and Romiszowski, A. (1974) *Yearbook of Educational and Instructional Technology, 1974/1975*. London: Kogan Page.

Howe, A. and Romiszowski, A. J. (1976) *International Yearbook of Educational and Instructional Technology, 1976/1977*. London: Kogan Page.

Lamb, R.T.B. (1967) *Aids to Modern Teaching: Short Survey.* London: Pitman.

Leedham, J. and Unwin, D. (1965) *Programmed Learning in the Schools.* London: Longmans.

Leith, G.O.M. (1969) *Second Thoughts on Programmed Learning,* Occasional Paper No. 1. London: NCET.

Little, J. K. (1934) "Results of Use of Machines for Testing and for Drill upon Learning in Educational Psychology." *Journal of Experimental Education* 3: 164–182.

McKeown, H. C. and Roberts, A. B. (1940) *Audio-visual Aids to Instruction.* New York: McGraw-Hill.

Ordhal, L. E. and Ordhal, G. (1915) "Qualitative Differences between Levels of Intelligence in Feeble Minded Children." *Journal of Psycho-Asthenics,* Monograph Supplement 1 (2): 3–50.

Pask, G. (1958) "Electronic Keyboard Teaching Machines." *Education and Commerce* 24: 16–26.

Peterson, J. C. (1931) "The Value of Guidance in Reading for Information." Repr. in *Teaching Machines and Programmed Learning: A Source Book,* ed. A. A. Lumsdaine and R. Glasser. Washington, D.C.: Department of Audio-Visual Instruction, 1960.

Pressey, S. L. (1915) "Continuous Choice-Reaction Apparatus." *American Journal of Psychology* 32: 347.

———. (1926) "A Simple Apparatus Which Gives Tests and Scores." *Teachers, School and Society,* 23: 373–376.

Rath, G., Anderson, N. S., and Brainerd, R. C. (1959) "The IBM Research Center Teaching Machine Project." In *Automatic Teaching: The State of the Art,* ed. E. Galander. New York: John Wiley.

Romiszowski, A. J. (1972) *APLET Yearbook of Educational and Instructional Technology 1972/1973.* London: Kogan Page.

Skinner, B. F. (1954) "The Science of Learning and the Art of Teaching." *Harvard Education Review* 24: 86–97.

———. (1961) "Teaching Machines." *Scientific American* 205 (5): 91–102.

Skinner, H. (1866) Improvements in Apparatus for Teaching Spelling. Washington, D.C., Patent 52758, U.S. Patents Office.

Smallwood, R. D. (1962) *A Decision Structure for Teaching Machines.* Research Monograph. Cambridge, Mass.: MIT Press.

Stolurow, L. M. (1961) *Teaching by Machine.* Cooperative Research Monograph No. 6. Washington, D.C.: U.S. Department of Health, Education and Welfare.

Suppes, P. (1966) "The Use of Computers in Education." *Scientific American* 210: 64–82.

Thorndike, E. L. (1912) *The Psychology of Learning.* New York: Macmillan.

TEACHING METHOD. A set of characteristics that, taken in conjunction, define the limits of one style of teaching. There are probably as many teaching methods as teachers; however, certain characteristics of individuals can be grouped and an agreed method defined. For example, authoritarian, didactic, lecture method, or resource-based, each being defined on the basis of differing sets of criteria. A useful term in general speech, but of restricted usefulness in describing teaching.

TEACHING PROBLEMS LABORATORY. A set of simulation materials devised by D. R. Cruikshank and his associates. A very realistic school setting is created through the medium of films, faculty handbooks, and other resources. Participants are required to solve problems presented on film and to take part in role-play.

TEAM TEACHING. Team teaching is a systematic instructional arrangement where two or more teachers organize, for a specified group of students, learning situations that improve the knowledge, skills, and techniques of the members of this student group. The team organizers concentrate on the overall curriculum, but a single subject area may become the focus especially at the implementation of a team project. Team organization and planning are the essential components of team teaching. Decisions are made that enable the team of teachers to achieve more effective instructional situations. By planned cooperative organization, team teaching becomes a viable reality. The factors associated with team teaching are teaching cooperatively and joint planning with a view to appropriate use of audiovisual aids, computer devices, etc.

The term *cooperative teaching* can be used synonymously with "team teaching." This method of teaching has occurred more frequently in elementary schools because ever-increasing numbers of teachers at this level are using new educational approaches such as individualized instruction, different patternings of groups for instruction, continuous progress learning, and open concept schooling.

Because of various successful experiments at this level of instruction more and more serious undertakings are being trialed at higher levels. As an educational idea, team teaching is flourishing despite the lack of attention in journals and forums.

HISTORICAL BACKGROUND

It is impossible to identify accurately the origin of team teaching, but it would seem that "departmentalization" (or subject teaching) had some of the ingredients of the modern concept of team teaching. It was not until the early 1960s that any detailed treatment of the theory and practices involved with team teaching was made available. Trump and Baynham (1961) and Anderson (1966) were early advocates of the more structured approach to team teaching. Their ideas were broadly accepted although it was the Lexington Plan as outlined by Blair and Woodward (1964) that caught the imagination of the pedagogical world. It is this model that was followed more closely in structure than any other. The slogan adopted by this pioneering team teaching school was "most of the teachers in the teams will teach most of the subjects most of the time." As this idea was widely accepted, it did not increase the degree of specialist teaching in the school, but rather the teacher with "expert" knowledge made a specialist contribution to the team by planning the instruction for a particular subject. Goodlad (1963), another innovator in this modern development in teaching strategies, does not accept the fact that team teaching can exist without a hierarchical structure, and it does seem reasonable to assume that all forms of team teaching have leaders. These individuals may evolve from the situation rather than be a deliberately placed element in the original structural arrangement of the team.

STRUCTURAL FORMS

The disparate capabilities, leadership abilities, and personalities of the individual members of a teaching team ensure that no two groups will ever be identical. The methods adopted may be similar, but the various formal and informal structures that are possible are endless. Some examples of the formalized arrangements are the following:

1. "Master teach" plan. This implies a hierarchy of personnel and involves a master teacher giving an introductory lesson which is then followed up by lessons prepared by other teachers in the team who act in a tutorial capacity.
2. "Wedges of cheese" plan. This plan is used more by the subject specialist teachers or in a situation where there is a clear division of units of separated material. The instruction of each section does not necessarily relate to and is not dependent upon knowledge obtained from other individual sections of work.
3. The "cut pie" plan. Here each teacher shares the work load as with the "wedges of cheese" plan. Each teacher is responsible for a section of instruction, but there is no formal pyramid-type structure. Greater cooperation is involved, however, as each section of work is closely associated and a merging of ideas becomes necessary for greater understanding to occur. Cooperation is the keynote to this plan of instruction.

ESSENTIALS FOR A TEAM

Suggestions that have been made indicate that team teaching is a technique that should not be undertaken unless there is a common philosophical ground. Some observers have signified that it is desirable that even two years of planning must go into the establishment of this commonality of ideas. Once there is agreement upon this philosophical base, it is most likely that skills associated with group leadership will be the ultimate consideration when it comes time to make provision for the actual personnel structure of the team. The team must act as a whole, and it must be understood that there is joint responsibility to be shared for the *total* population of pupils under the control of the team: at no time should individual members assume "subgroup" accountability alone. If this latter situation does occur, the fragmentation of ideas could be the forerunner to the collapse of the team teaching concept.

PRACTICAL APPLICATION

The size of the school and the educational philosophy adopted will determine the type of teaching team for a particular school. Individualized instruction has been a prominent feature of moves toward catering to the unique needs of each child. The emphasis has shifted from the *teaching* of a subject to *learning*. Methods are being utilized that help the pupil discover and understand concepts rather than the mere remembering of facts. This recognition of the individual differences of pupils has been paralleled by a realization that teachers also vary in their knowledge, skill, aptitude, and motivation with regard to certain subjects, their use of particular instructional methods, and their preferences for groups of mixed or specific age/sex groups. When consideration is being given to the membership of teaching teams, these variations must be taken into account.

Team teaching has often been allowed to degenerate into a glorified rotation system: some thematic or project-type methods especially tend to lead to this. Careful planning is needed before embarking upon any form of team teaching whether it be of the specialist teaching type or a fully integrated interdisciplinary approach. Groups of equal size can be used, but studies have shown that larger groups can learn from a teacher equally as well as smaller groups. If a teacher is proficient in using instructional aids, there are good reasons why this teacher should in fact be encouraged to instruct more pupils. Remedial instruction groups become a possibility if there is a work plan involving groups of varying sizes. Accordingly, depending upon the pupils' learning speed and maturity, a greater proportion of school time can be utilized using combinations of horizontal (more of the same subject or grade level) and vertical (advanced subjects) enrichment.

RESEARCH FINDINGS

Effectiveness is the measure of the endeavors of any team teaching program, and recent research is proving that planning and vigilant evaluation are the price of effective teaching. Studies that have been carried out on team teaching procedures are no exception. Although most of these studies are descriptive, usable data can be obtained using various observational techniques that are defining the methods that any teacher can use to maintain a "learning environment." If all cooperative teaching situations can be maintained, effective team teaching does exist. Where there have been failures of team teaching, such as some "Trump Plan" models, writers have noted that the main contributing factor for this is staff turnover and the lack of proper training for the replacements. Convincing research findings are few because of the difficulty of categorizing the forms of team teaching, so much so that it is almost impossible to compare statistically the results obtained from such diverse methods of instruction.

ADVANTAGES

Observation and reports indicate that the quality of instruction of both experienced and inexperienced teachers rises as a direct result of teaching in a team. Morale generally rises and favorable attitudes toward their participation in this style of teaching has been noted in almost all cases. Where there are reservations these generally stem from lack of organizational and administrational skills within the team. There is a much more effective distribution of learning materials, and because of the flexibility of teaching strategies an optimal use of space is achieved. Groups vary in size and structure and this helps the interaction between groups, and where individualized instruction is deemed necessary, students receive teacher contact time as is found necessary.

Members of a teaching team have found that they have more opportunity to improve their professionalism. This occurs because of the times available for team members to observe the style and methods used by their colleagues in the team.

DISADVANTAGES

Just as it is difficult to obtain empirical knowledge about the favorable aspects of team teaching, it is difficult to cite convincing data that can indicate any of the disadvantages that are inherent in this particular instructional technique. Probably the argument that is most frequently used against team teaching is that the child lacks the security of a close contact with a parent-teacher image.

Whatever method is used, instruction can be influenced by poor scheduling techniques, but this is more likely to be detrimental to learning in the team teaching situation. Reporting and assessing procedures have tended to be more difficult with team teaching, but with experience it has been found that eventually more knowledge is obtained about a pupil by this method because of the increase in the number of observers. As with other factors, if there have been problems, these are more often attributed to a lack of administrative experience than to the system of instruction.

A more important factor and sometimes an almost insurmountable difficulty is the interpersonal interaction of the team members. A scheme can easily fail because of problems arising out of emotional tensions and antagonisms brought on by the informal power relationship. Lack of communication can also cause gross misunderstanding. These problems should ideally be overcome by selecting teachers who *wish* to take part in a teaching team as partners. Planning is the essence for such a scheme, and the grounding of an educational philosophy must be common before any team is formed.

Neil Doherty

REFERENCES

Anderson, R. H. (1966) *Teaching in a World of Change*. New York: Harcourt, Brace & Jovanovich.
Basett, G. W. (1970) *Innovation in Primary Education*. London: Wiley-Interscience.
Blair, M. and Woodward, R. G. (1964) *Team Teaching in Action*. Boston: Houghton Mifflin.
Goodlad, J. J. (1973) *Speaking of Team Teaching*. New York: McGraw-Hill.
Shaplin, J. T. and Olds, H. F. (1964) *Team Teaching*. New York: Harper and Row.
Trump, J. L. and Baynham, D. (1961) *Guide to Better Schools*. Chicago: Rand-McNally.

TECHNICOLOR. The color cine film process, first introduced in 1915, by which color cine films are made. Since the introduction of the process, it has been changed and improved and is now used mainly as a technique for producing release prints from film shot on color negative stock.

TECHNOLOGY LEARNING FACILITY (TLF). Concept evolved by the Queensland State Government (Australia), whereby new information technology such as computer-based learning, satellites, etc., is exploited to provide a centralized learning resource. At present (1987) TLFs are still in the planning stage.

TECHTRENDS. Commencing March 1985 the semimonthly journal of the Association for Educational Communications and Technology was renamed *TechTrends*. It was formerly titled *Instructional Innovator*.

TELECINE. The process used to show cine film on television. The equipment used converts the film image into a television image. Two techniques are used; the simpler uses a normal film projector mechanism and projects the image onto the camera tubes. (At a very basic level, it is perfectly feasible to project onto a screen and point a television camera at the projected picture. There will necessarily be some loss of quality in such a procedure.)

A more sophisticated technique is to use a "flying spot" device where the light used to illuminate the film comes from the face of the cathode-ray tube and is converted by a photo-multiplier into a television signal. Telecine is the opposite process to kinescope recording where a television signal is transferred to film. *See* **Kinescope.**

TELECONFERENCING. Conference arranged so that the delegates are connected to an open circuit telephone system. A special telephone is often used which contains a loudspeaker and sensitive microphone, so that several people can take part at any desired location. Also called *telephone conferencing.*

TELEMEMO. A computer-based message exchange service first offered by Telecom Australia in 1986. The system has much in common with electronic bulletin boards, plus a number of sophisticated filing and editing facilities, and interconnection with the telex and teletex networks, thus giving a vast field for communication.

TELENET. Computer network providing subscribers with access to a large data base and other facilities. *See* **Videotex.**

TELEPHONE CONFERENCING. *See* **Teleconferencing.**

TELEPHONE TUTORING. Connecting tutor and a student over a telephone link is called telephone tutoring. One common use of such a system has been by the U.K. **Open University** (q.v.).

TELEPHOTO LENS. Although used to describe all long-focus lenses the term refers specifically to lenses that are designed in such a way that the nodal points lie in front of the lens system. This means that the distance between the lens and the film plane is considerably shorter than would otherwise be the case and results in smaller, more compact designs.

TELEPRINTER. A machine with a typewriter-type keyboard and printing mechanism that is used to send and/or receive electric telegraph signals, for example, telegrams and telex messages.

TELEPROMPTER. A device which allows a presenter to look directly into the lens of a television camera and read from a prepared script. Various mechanical and optical devices are available, but in each case the print appears to scroll up on a reflective arrangement which is invisible to the camera but easily read from in front.

TELERECORDING. *See* **Kinescope.**

TELESOFTWARE. *Telesoftware* is the term used to describe a means of storing and distributing computer programs through a **viewdata** (q.v.) or **teletext** (q.v.) system.

DESCRIPTION OF VIEWDATA TELESOFTWARE

Viewdata systems can be used to store and transmit computer programs as well as pages of text. Suitably equipped microcomputers are used to receive and store programs transmitted by telesoftware, and the process whereby a microcomputer receives and stores such programs is known as "downloading." Most microcomputers can be used with a downloading package to access viewdata systems to obtain programs via telesoftware.

A downloading package for a microcomputer consists of a suitable adapter or modem, downloading software and a lead to connect the adapter or modem to the microcomputer. When the downloading software is loaded and the telephone connection to the viewdata system has been established using the adapter or modem, the microcomputer functions as a viewdata receiver with alphanumeric capability. In a typical use of telesoftware, a viewdata system is likely to hold a library of programs which are loaded onto the system from a microcomputer. Remote users can then access the viewdata system and browse through the library, reading viewdata pages which describe the programs until they select one which is suitable. One command from the keyboard allows the microcomputer to retrieve the selected program from the viewdata system, and it can then be stored on cassette or disk for later use. Any transmission errors (due to "noise" on the telephone line) are detected and corrected by retransmission of those sections of the program which were incorrectly received. Telesoftware can also be used to transmit program documentation as a text file. After it has been transmitted and stored on the microcomputer, it can be printed out to provide hard copy to accompany the program.

The time taken to download a computer program or text file is dependent on the size of the program or text file and on the speed of transmission. For viewdata systems which are Prestel compatible, the speed of transmission from the viewdata system is 1,200 baud, which allows 1K of program or 140 words in a text file to be downloaded in approximately 10 seconds. Programs or text files in telesoftware format are stored on several viewdata frames with 1K program or 140 words in a text file occupying one viewdata frame. Thus the only necessary cost to the user of telesoftware distribution from a viewdata system is simply the telephone charge, which is based on the time connected, the time of day, and the distance of the user from the viewdata system. To receive programs in telesoftware format from a viewdata system, a microcomputer user must of course have a downloading package and such packages are now available in the United Kingdom at prices under £100.

Conventional methods of distributing computer programs involve the distributor in heavy staff, material, and postage costs since disks, cassettes, and documentation have to be produced in multiple copies centrally and sent to users. Distribution of a program by telesoftware reduced the central costs to those involved in loading the programs and documentation once onto the viewdata system, and the major costs of obtaining the program automatically fall on the users who retrieve the program onto their microcomputers.

When a program and its documentation are improved or upgraded, distribution of the upgraded version by conventional methods involves the distributor in the same heavy costs as the original distribution. Using telesoftware, the upgraded program and documentation are loaded onto the viewdata system, and a message is sent to all users (via the user-to-user message facility) advising them that the program has been upgraded and that they should download it again to obtain the most recent version. The central costs involved in the original distribution of programs and in the distribution of upgrades by telesoftware are low in comparison to the costs of conventional distribution. Thus viewdata telesoftware is an attractive method of software distribution which allows users to obtain programs and information about programs in a cheap and convenient way.

Microcomputers are now being installed in schools and colleges throughout the world, and in the United Kingdom every secondary school and many primary schools have at least one microcomputer, purchased with the help of a central government subsidy. The widespread availability of microcomputers in schools and colleges provides teachers and lecturers with new opportunities for teaching, and pupils and students with new learning opportunities. However, the education system is only beginning to tackle the problems of training teachers in the use of microcomputers and of developing and distributing suitable software. Viewdata telesoftware is likely to play a major part in helping to overcome the problems of software distribution.

DESCRIPTION OF TELETEXT TELESOFTWARE

Teletext systems can be used to store and transmit computer programs as well as pages of text. Suitably equipped microcomputers are used to receive and store programs transmitted by teletext telesoftware; microcomputers can be used with a downloading package to obtain programs via telesoftware transmitted as pages from a teletext system.

A teletext telesoftware downloading package for a microcomputer consists of an adapter which accepts the ordinary broadcast signal, downloading software, and a lead to connect the adapter to the microcomputer. When the downloading software is loaded and the adapter is receiving the broadcast signal, the microcomputer functions as a teletext receiver. A teletext system is likely to hold a small number of programs (due to the overall restriction on data storage on teletext systems) which are loaded onto the teletext system from a microcomputer. Remote users would be able to select a program, and as in the case of viewdata telesoftware, one command from the keyboard will allow the microcomputer to retrieve the selected program from the teletext system, and it can then be stored on cassette or disk for later use. Transmission errors (due to interference on the broadcast signal) can be detected and corrected by retransmission of those sections of the program incorrectly received. Text files can be transmitted as well as computer programs using teletext telesoftware.

Due to the cyclical transmission of teletext pages, it usually takes significantly longer to transmit programs using teletext telesoftware than by using viewdata telesoftware. However, since no telephone charges are involved, there is no cost to the user in receiving programs via teletext telesoftware. Teletext telesoftware downloading packages can be purchased in the United Kingdom for less than £200.

Teletext telesoftware and viewdata telesoftware are compared in a similar way to the general comparison of teletext and viewdata. Since teletext communication is in one direction only, response frames and user-to-user messages cannot be implemented in connection with teletext telesoftware. The major disadvantage of teletext telesoftware at present is the limited data storage available; and the fact that control of data transmission is likely to be with broadcasting authorities and cannot readily be devolved to local education authorities or other educational organizations. Although teletext is usually a free service without direct user charges, the fact that it is a public broadcast service creates difficulties over access to software. Thus if an educational organization wished to make programs available free of charge to schools but not to commercial organizations, this could be implemented using viewdata telesoftware by restricting access to the viewdata system by issuing access passwords only to schools. However, such restricted access cannot readily be achieved with teletext telesoftware. In some cases, the system operator might wish to charge users for downloading programs from the system. Again this charging can be readily achieved with various charging mechanisms available in a viewdata system, but charging cannot be used with a teletext system.

Thus while teletext telesoftware has an interesting educational application, further technical developments are required to allow it to be as useful and flexible as viewdata telesoftware.

D. Daly

TELETEL. A videotex system operated by the French national Posts & Telecommunications Department. By far the largest and most successful videotex operation in the world, it is unique in that the terminals are provided free to customers. This has led to the situation where in four years over two million Minitels (the terminals) are in use; this contrasts with the United Kingdom, where after a decade of Prestel there were still less than 75,000 terminals.

Teletel usage includes telephone directory inquiries, message exchange, electronic shopping, information services, games, etc.

TELETEX. System for interconnecting communicating word processors (CWPs) using packet switching. Transmission by teletex will be very much faster than telex (which can be considered a primitive forerunner to teletex), but arrangements for a mixed telex-teletex system are proposed. Teletex terminals may be microcomputers or memory typewriters as long as they meet certain requirements.

TELETEXT. Teletext is the generic term for noninteractive information services which generally use the broadcast television signal to communicate information from a central computer to users having suitable terminals. These terminals are usually television sets or microcomputers which also have a teletext facility.

DESCRIPTION OF TELETEXT

Teletext shares certain basic features with **viewdata** (q.v.). Text, in a similar format, is transmitted to a display screen. Pages are selected by means of a hand-held or an integral numeric keypad. (Where a combined viewdata-teletext terminal is in use, a single keypad may serve both systems.) The pages are continuously updated. There is also a telesoftware option.

Teletext pages can provide text on the whole screen, replacing the usual television picture, or can provide subtitles on a normal television picture. This latter use allows the deaf to follow an ordinary television program since the subtitling provides a limited amount of text superimposed on the ordinary picture.

Teletext magazines are provided on different broadcast channels and typically include information on news, weather, entertainment, travel, and business. Teletext magazines can be considered as comparable to electronic newspapers in terms of range and depth of information provided.

To receive teletext, an ordinary television receiver with a decoder, either built-in or attached, is required. Teletext signals are broadcast as part of the normal Television signal in continuous cycles of (typically) 100 pages. Operation of the keypad instructs the receiver's decoder which page to display on the screen from those being continuously received. The decoder acts as a "page grabber," which intercepts and stores the requested page when it next comes round in the cycle.

COMPARISONS OF TELETEXT AND VIEWDATA

Teletext and viewdata are significantly different in a number of ways, these differences deriving from the different modes of transmission. The major differences are as follows:

(a) In the case of teletext the communication is in one direction only. Therefore, viewdata facilities such as response frames cannot be implemented in a teletext system.

(b) Compared with most viewdata systems, the current teletext data bases are very small, being determined by the mode and speed of transmission.

(c) With teletext, the user has to wait some time between requesting a page and the requested page being displayed. This waiting time varies according to the point in the cycle at which the user requests a particular page and is of course dependent on the number of pages in the cycle and the speed of cycle transmission. In the United Kingdom, the maximum delay in a 100–page magazine is presently 16 seconds. By contrast, access to viewdata pages is virtually instantaneous. This advantage is slightly lessened, however, by the fact that a viewdata page usually "builds" on the screen more slowly than a teletext page.

(d) Since teletext is transmitted as part of the normal broadcast signal, it is available only during broadcasting times (including transmission of test cards). In practice this means that the service is not available in the United Kingdom for some 7 hours each night. Viewdata systems, on the other hand, may operate 24 hours a day.

(e) Since the data storage capacity of a viewdata system is large, it is usually neither difficult nor expensive for any organization or private company to communicate information using viewdata. By contrast, the data storage capacity of a teletext system is usually small, and it is often the case that the broadcasting authorities are the sole providers and controllers of teletext information.

(f) Since there are usually no direct user charges for receiving normal television programs, teletext is also generally free of such charges.

(g) Whereas the number of simultaneous users of a viewdata system is determined by the number of computer access ports provided, the number of simultaneous users of teletext is not subject to any such restriction and is unlimited.

EDUCATIONAL APPLICATIONS

Because teletext has no interactive capability, it is generally accepted that its educational uses are relatively limited.

Computer programs can be stored on teletext pages and can be transmitted using the broadcast signal from a central computer to a microcomputer with an attached broadcast telesoftware adapter. In the United Kingdom, an educational **telesoftware** (q.v.) service is already available on teletext.

A second use of teletext is to relate pages to educational television programs, providing backup and additional information related to the programs.

The third use of teletext is the provision of subtitles on normal television pictures for the deaf and hard of hearing.

Teletext, like viewdata, is developing its educational potential and further applications may be identified in time.

D. Daly

TELETYPEWRITER. Typewriter with an electronic communications facility, thus permitting digital signals to be transmitted to other equipment. Computer terminals and telex machines are common examples.

TELEVISION, EDUCATIONAL AND INSTRUCTIONAL.

INTRODUCTION

A U.S. Focus. Although the use of television for educational purposes is a worldwide phenomenon, this entry will largely be limited to events and applications in the United States. Nevertheless, in many senses, the U.S. experience can be expected to be representative, and hence well worth close examination.

HISTORY

The Early Years. Educational television has its roots in the rise of the use of audiovisual equipment in schooling as well as in the development of broadcasting, which obviously began as radio. Indeed, educational institutions are credited with being among the first experimental radio stations on the air in the United States. Thus, the University of Wisconsin started 9XM as an experimental station in 1917 (this later continued as WHA, one of the leading U.S. university stations), and a university in Salt Lake City obtained a regular broadcast license in 1921, only a year after KDKA went on the air. Although mostly started as engineering demonstration projects, many of the university radio stations devoted considerable effort to providing educational programming. By 1925, some 50 percent of the university stations formed the Association of College and University Broadcasting Stations to represent its interests. Although its growth was inhibited by lack of funding, the comparative glamour of commercial radio, and the general slump in the economy resulting from the depression, educational broadcasting did grow slowly, especially in the Midwest where stations offered sorely needed programming in agricultural extension to relatively isolated farm listeners.

In spite of repeated requests for favored treatment by regulatory agencies, educational broadcasters' requests for channel reservations were rejected in favor of commercial broadcasters. This trend stopped with the significant 1945 FCC reservation of twenty channels in the new FM radio spectrum solely for noncommercial use. Now educators were assured that a group of broadcast frequencies would be permanently set aside for them and protected from commercial dominance.

The other basis for the educational development of television was the increasing use in schools of educational film and other media (e.g., lantern slides, phonograph recordings) leading the National Education Association to recognize its significance by establishing in 1923 its Division of Visual Instruction which later evolved into the Division of Audiovisual Instruction (DAVI), once electronic tape recordings had become a part of school materials. Later DAVI split off to establish itself as the Association for Educational Communication and Technology (AECT), which presently is the leading association for educational media people, including school users and producers of television.

The First Involvements of Education in Television. Several midwestern universities experimented with teaching programs for the early scanning disk televisions in 1932 and 1934. Between 1932 and 1939 W9XK experimentally broadcast nearly 400 educational programs from the Iowa State University. Although little progress was made in television development during the war years, television was used in New York City for air raid warden training.

Following World War II, commercial television expanded explosively, and had it not been for the freeze imposed by the FCC on continuing channel allocations, educators might not have succeeded in persuading regulators to reserve any channels for educational use. However, following the FCC's "Sixth Report and Order" of 1952, noncommercial broadcasters were set aside 242 of the 2,053 channels allocated. Since then the FCC has allocated over 650 channels for noncommercial broadcasters, of which almost 300 have been activated. The first noncommercial station, KUHT, activated by the University of Houston, led the establishment of bona fide educational television stations in the United States. However, since the institution of noncommercial allocations was a delayed one, most of the noncommercial allocations were in the UHF band, which has always remained less accessible to viewers.

Finding External Financial Help. As with radio, educational television operations had been largely linked with schools and universities, and as always, their lack of resources had been a critical hindrance to significant development. It was thus that educational broadcasters had to seek financial assistance from alternate sources.

Involvement of the Ford Foundation. Help for educational television turned up surprisingly from an artifact of big business. When, on the death of car manufacturer Henry Ford, the Ford Foundation expanded, its appointed panel decided to focus its munificence on the education of the population at large and established in 1950 two funds to channel its grants. Educational broadcasting over the years received some $300 million in grants for a series of useful demonstration projects and for a number of research panels which made essential recommendations for helping educational television to thrive. Ford funds helped in the lobbying effort to get the FCC's channel allocations; to set up the National Citizens Committee for Educational TV (NCCET), which helped set the pattern for community television stations; and funded innumerable crucial instructional demonstration projects in the 1950s and 1960s. Above all, it provided the wherewithal for lobbying efforts with federal and state granting agencies.

Federal Funding Begins. Two sources of federal funding provided a great stimulus to the growth of educational television. The first of these was the passage of the 1957 **National Defense Education Act** (q.v.) created to stimulate technical education in response to the launch of Sputnik. Two titles of that act supported the acquisition of media hardware and research into use of instructional technology, both of which served educational television. This act also supported the eventual development of instructional television libraries. The second source of federal support was the Educational Television Facilities Act of 1962, which provided ongoing funding for station construction and improvement. Within two years of the passage of this act, there had occurred a 40 percent increase in the number of stations on the air.

Outcomes of Some Representative Programs. The NCCET, mentioned above, stimulated the development of community television stations nationwide. The significance of these is measured by the impact of the "flagship stations" that arose in seven major metropolitan areas of the United States, namely WQED (Ch. 13) in Pittsburgh, KQED (Ch. 9) in San Francisco, WGBH (Ch. 2) in Boston, all of which were on the air by 1955, followed by WTTW (Ch. 11) in Chicago, WNDT which became WNET (Ch. 13) in New York, KCET (Ch. 28) in Los Angeles, and WETA (Ch. 26) in Washington. These stations succeeded in raising substantial funds within their communities and provided the example of the nonschool-based station that was geared toward broad educational or enrichment goals rather than being obligated primarily to the dissemination of instruction, which by the mid-1960s was incorporated into the curricula of thousands of schools.

Another Ford Foundation supported project, the National Educational Television and Radio Center (NETRC) led the way to the conceptualization of a working network of stations. When, in 1963, the foundation decided to cut back its support, the radio aspect was separated and the resulting organization, National Educational Television, or NET, became the precursor for public television in the United States. This, in effect, set the stage for important events to follow shortly.

Three instructional projects, stimulated by Ford Foundation support, have stood out because they greatly influenced future developments. The first of these was the 1956 Hagerstown, Maryland, closed-circuit television linkup of a large number of public schools. The success of this program pointed to the eventual establishment of similar educational television networks statewide—such as the one in South Carolina—and probably helped in the arguments for the FCC to authorize the establishment of **Instructional Television Fixed Service** (q.v.) (ITFS). This, even now (although in a somewhat curtailed form), offers educators one of the most convenient methods for the closed-circuit, broadcast dissemination of educational programming. The second program, also in 1956, was the Chicago TV College, which gave the impetus for numerous community colleges to develop telecourse programs. Thus, systems like Coast Telecourses, the Southern California Consortium for Community College Television (SCCCCT), the systems of the Miami-Dade Community College, and of the Dallas County Community College are representative among others. The third project of great significance was the 1961 initiation of the **Midwest Program on Airborne Television Instruction** (q.v.) (MPATI). In this plan six states joined in the production of "courseware" (programming for instruction) and cooperated in launching two high-flying transmitters abroad DC-6 aircraft to broadcast instruction on two UHF channels. The program was operational for over six years and demonstrated the feasibility of interstate cooperative projects, pointing the way for future successful satellite-based systems. To some extent the current cooperative libraries—the Agency for Instructional Television (AIT) and the Great Plains Instructional TV Library (GPNITL) as well as recent satellite networks such as the Appalachian Community Service Network (ACSN)—have been beneficiaries of the MPATI project.

The End of Infancy for Educational Television. The above precursors all indicated the promise of what educational television could offer. The Ford Foundation had played its role of midwifery, and it was time to find a long-range source of funding. In the winter of 1965 the Carnegie Commission on Educational Television was convened with the blessings of President Johnson to study this question. Its 1967 report, "Public Television: A Program for Action," conceptualized the idea of "public broadcasting" and set the stage for federal involvement in its financing. Under Johnson's guidance Congress acted promptly and by that fall Johnson signed into law the Public Broadcasting act. This set the stage for the establishment of the Corporation for Public Broadcasting, the Public Broadcasting Service, National Public Radio, and for federal support of the enterprise. This system has survived to the present with only the funding levels starting to decrease during the early 1980s.

THE BROADCAST/NONBROADCAST DUALITY OF EDUCATIONAL TELEVISION

Broadcast television was established long before the invention of video recording, and consequently the concept of nonbroadcast television is a more recent development. Indeed, the affordability and reliability of video recording equipment with the advent of videocassette recorders (VCRs) has radically increased the utility of producing video programs which are never intended for wide-scale dissemination. Dissemination itself also differs, depending on whether the channel used is for open or closed circuit transmission. It is important to remember that not all closed circuit systems are based on the **coaxial cable** (q.v.). The aforementioned ITFS approach is for practical purposes closed circuit and so are some of the recently demonstrated light carrier systems using an infrared beam. Typically, programs on closed circuit systems tend to have more relaxed production values.

Indeed, what is broadcastable, or of broadcast quality, is a moot point. Anything captured on videotape that is newsworthy we are finding to be broadcastable (with perhaps some control track enhancement by the broadcaster), no matter how roughly the original was produced. On the other hand, network producers would scoff at the quality of material produced at small local commercial stations. Nevertheless, three "layers" of extensively overlapping production quality have become delineated—all of which are used by producers of educational television. Most of these criteria are tied to recording formats and to the cost and concurrent quality of equipment used. *Broadcast quality* is usually associated with work produced using the three-tube cameras in $20,000+$ range and recorded on 1-inch or 2-inch tape (although the latter is presently being phased out due to the bulkiness and weight of the equipment and cost of magnetic media). Indeed, nowadays the broadcast quality 1/2-inch cassette formats such as Sony's Betacam and Panasonic's M II systems are becoming the chief recording format in some forward-looking systems. The next lower step in quality is termed *industrial*. Typically the recording technique used here is the 3/4-inch U-Matic videocassette format (although Sony's "industrial Beta" 1/2-inch cassette format has also made significant inroads here), and cameras are either of the lower priced three-tube or the higher priced single-tube type selling for $3000+$. Programs produced using both of the preceding "standards" are distributed extensively. At the bottom lies *consumer quality* with its Beta, VHS, and 8mm recorders and cameras that may sell for as little as $400. Nevertheless, acceptable programs that are very useful to educators can be produced with such equipment.

Examples of Nonbroadcast Uses. Because of the recent proliferation of truly inexpensive videocassette recorders (VCRs), a lot of programming can be produced solely for direct playback of the cassettes rather than for distribution as a television signal directed to remote viewers. The cost of producing duplicate cassettes is now so low in comparison to production costs that this form of dissemination is cost-beneficial. Hence, producing programs which may be "published" in less than a dozen copies can be justified. Although such programs may not enjoy the production values associated with widely distributed programming, they need not be casually executed. For such limited editions, productions involving expensive equipment may be entirely inappropriate, yet using television may be essential to successfully conveying the message.

Audiovisual ("Noncourseware") Applications. Although one always thinks of television in terms of produced programs, namely **courseware** (q.v.), a term coined to yield a parallel to *software,* there exist numerous crucial roles for television in which no program is produced for retention. Typical here is the use of television to disseminate live events over an area, be that to adjacent rooms to accommodate overflow audiences or to nearby cities. Indeed, most of the programming distributed by ITFS is of such a live category and may be as bad or as good as are any live presentations. Other obvious uses are for image magnification with macro lenses or attached microscopes for viewers who may be only feet from the object viewed. Other, less obvious uses capitalize on the modern camera's ability to produce acceptable images in very low light levels (e.g., showing classes the behavior of nocturnal animals in darkened enclosures), of being small enough to be inserted into locations where human viewers don't fit (e.g., to provide close-up views inside automotive engine housings), or being either sturdy enough or inexpensive enough to permit their use in dangerous settings where human viewers cannot or should not risk being present. All of these are uses that are appropriate in education. What is worth noting is that the audiovisual-courseware gap is easily bridged. Should an instructor choose to record a microscope dissection rather than repeat it live in the next class, an "instructional module" has been created, and courseware, no matter how casually conceived, now exists.

Microteaching. Occasionally it is valuable to produce recordings while still not seriously thinking in terms of doing a "production" with all its appropriate planning and care. Microteaching is such a prime use of television in teaching. The use of television in this instance is for feedback to a learner practicing either a teaching technique or any of several psychomotor skills (e.g., tennis serves) which are best learned by delayed (and perhaps repeated) scrutiny of the performance, either alone or under supervision. Film, and now television, has thus been used for decades in conducting postgame evaluations in team sports.

Broadcast Programming. With the institution of National Educational Television (NET) setting the stage for the public television of today, much programming without an instructional focus started to appear. However, it was still fundamentally distinct from commercial program fare. The criteria used were that the programming offer an alternative to commercial programming as well as something that is decidedly informational and culturally enriching. Also, in the case of community stations, a strong commitment to meeting the interpreted needs of the community was emphasized. Although commercial broadcasters also attended to some of these concerns, their prime concern had to be meeting the needs of advertisers, and thus when the Ford Foundation–supported TV-Radio Workshop offered the very well-produced cultural program "Omnibus," essentially free to commercial broadcasters, they were unable to air it continuously and at the same time stay in business.

A problem with which educational broadcasters had to deal during the early years was that of informational programming offered as sequential series. Early programming had been designed to teach in a consecutive manner to bring the learners progressively to more sophisticated knowledge built on prerequisite learning. This seriously inhibited viewers from starting into programs midstream and lost potential audience for educational television. Currently, even telecourses offered for college credit are so structured that the sequential learning is borne by accompanying texts, and the televised segments are fairly well able to be viewed as independent segments. This assures that casual viewers will still benefit from contact with the programming.

BASIC PRINCIPLES OF ETV PROGRAM DESIGN

Principles of Instructional Design. Because of the fact that designing good instructional television programming is about the most expensive form of development of educational materials (i.e., compared to **textbook design** [q.v.] or even the development of professional workshop series), it requires the best planning possible. Probably the finest examples of such approaches are productions of the Children's TV Workshop (CTW) such as "Sesame Street" and "The Electric Company," among others. Nothing was produced until extensive preliminary research and design had been completed.

This instructional design cycle has come to be known under the heading of instructional technology, not so much for its involvement of technology as for its **systems approach** (q.v.) in emulating the industrial development model. Perhaps the most concise definition is the one quoted from *To Improve Learning: A Report to the President and the Congress of the United States* by the Commission on Instructional Technology (Washington; USGPO, 1970):

Instructional technology is . . . a systematic way of designing, carrying out, and evaluating the total process of learning and teaching in terms of specific objectives, based on research in human learning and communication, and employing a combination of human and nonhuman resources to bring about more effective instruction. (p. 19)

Numerous schemes for delineating the instructional design process have been offered, ranging from a few steps to dozens. Suffice it to say that they all involve a planning stage, including needs and audience analysis leading to the establishment of a series of precisely stipulated objectives. This is followed by a research, scripting, and production stage, involving careful assessment of costs and benefits, the incorporation of some schemes for progress management, and the inclusion of steps for ongoing evaluation and revision as well as the allocation of resources to ancillary concerns. All instructional design schemes culminate in an evaluation step leading to successful validation, revision, or rejection of the outcome. If too many of these steps are overlooked, successful programs emerge consistently only as a matter of luck or innate talent in which the designers probably have internalized the process without acknowledging its use.

Options for Program Formats. Viewers used to watching interminable hours of medium shots of talking faces have come to disdain much educational television as only that. Indeed, good program formats exist that range into a variety of options. Typically, the best programs offer a wide variety, including that "talking head." Some of these alternatives are the following: (a) illustration of a lecture with stills, motion visuals, and audio examples; (b) demonstrations, whether these be in a lab setting or in a naturalistic setting; (c) interviews with experts or with learners; (d) panel discussions involving varied people; (e) staged dramatizations of points being made; (f) either short segments recorded in the field for inclusion or longer documentary footage; and (g) astute use of either interspersed or superimposed text or graphics—easily and attractively accomplished with modern character generators. If these various techniques are intelligently combined, well-designed educational programming will have little to fear from commercial competition, as has been well illustrated by popular successes such as "Cosmos" or more tried and true series like "The Ascent of Man."

Considerations of ETV Use. All audiovisual materials, including educational television (ETV) programs, can serve at various levels. To some extent these depend on the scale and scope of the program, but also on user choices. Thus an instructional television program can be made to provide all the instructional content that will be offered the learner—a form of total teaching. This places great responsibility on the learner and is consequently used infrequently. More typical uses are those where the television programs structure the learning sequence and pacing but do not carry the full teaching burden—a characteristic of telecourses discussed further on. The most popular use of ETV programs is either as a major resource incorporated into classroom teaching or as supplemental programming used to augment lectures.

In any of these settings it is crucial not to ignore the role of the in-class teacher or training administrator. The attitude and skill of this person are important in assuring maximization of learning from media. The classroom teacher must assure the "three-Rs" of ETV use: before-viewing readiness (i.e., being told what to attend to); acceptable reception (e.g., use of a properly tuned receiver); and adequate reinforcement of what was learned (i.e., immediate application of content). These skills are not obvious, and not including planning for sound administration of program implementation can assure failure for the best of ETV programs.

PURPOSES AND DIRECTIONS TAKEN

Educational and instructional television can be divided into three broad categories by the purposes for which it is used. These are public television, television used for formal schooling, and corporate television. Although corporate communication has become a force in non-commercial television only in the past decade, it presently has more resources at its disposal than the other two facets mentioned above.

Public Television. When one thinks of public television, one thinks first of the Public Broadcasting Service (PBS) and the large community stations mentioned earlier. Although membership in the PBS is well-nigh universal for educational television stations, not all of them devote a substantial segment of their airtime to the type of cultural enrichment fare characteristic of the PBS.

The passage of the 1967 Public Broadcasting Act established the Corporation for Public Broadcasting (CPB), a nonprofit corporation, as the intermediary between the federal government and educational broadcasters, which had now become "public" broadcasters. The CPB was not to be involved in any operational aspects, but was to disseminate federal funding to the broadcasters. To actually handle the interconnect between the stations, PBS and later, National Public Radio (NPR), were created. PBS replaced the predecessor NET since it was felt best not to continue a strong central network with unified program origination but to establish a mutual type interconnect. Only NPR was authorized to originate programming.

Between 1971 and 1973 a series of events put the relationship between the CPB and PBS through a crisis. PBS programming was criticized by the Nixon administration for excessive liberal bias, and the CPB was criticized for excessive centralization. Funding for the CPB was vetoed by President Nixon; this was followed by protest resignations and eventually by compromises that somewhat changed the roles of the two organizations, assured further decentralization, and finally reestablished equilibrium and long-term federal funding.

Following the decentralization thrust, PBS member stations have been sharing in program production through the Station Program Cooperative (SPC) wherein a substantial percentage of PBS fare is annually presented at a "program fair," and then bid upon in a series of computer-assisted decision steps leading to a package buy by the membership. Although the entire cost of program production is not borne by the stations, nevertheless programs tend to get selected either for their price or popularity with viewers. Consequently, programming acquired through the SPC is criticized for not often enough representing the kind of incisive and controversial programming decision making that earlier had brought on the presidential criticism. Many feel that this tendency toward "safer" programming represents a loss to the viewing audience.

Although the federal funding represented a significant boost in resources for PBS, it has by no means been its prime fiscal source, representing in the early 1980s roughly a quarter of the income. Depending on the type of station, substantial funding comes from community support through subscriptions and drives, from state support either directly or through its university systems, or from local public school districts. All along, PBS has relied on corporate underwriting to support program production and recently, with severe cutbacks of federal funding, both PBS and the stations have experimented with alternative sources of funding. Prime among these have been leasing production studio space, extensively experimenting with on-air commercials (termed "enhanced underwriting"), leasing time and access on satellite transponders, transmitting teletext (especially of the "silent radio" variety) on the television stations (or SCA programming by the NPR members), and even considering pay-TV transmissions of first-run cultural programming during selected hours. All in all, public broadcasters are looking into entrepreneurial ventures for financing.

Not everything that PBS stations present is geared toward adult enrichment programming. Many stations devote only a few hours daily for such fare, and most are in some ways involved with programming for preschool children. Typically PBS stations also attempt to offer some coverage of local issues and news and air in-class television and telecourses, the latter typically for college credit.

It was indeed with a concern for schooling that educational television began, and it still remains its primary, if not most visible, aspect. Educational television stations can be differentiated into four categories. These are the aforementioned community stations, airing primarily PBS cultural and informational programming, and three kinds of school-oriented categories. This brings us to the next category.

Television for Formal Schooling. The largest percentage of educational television stations have been state-owned. These stations are members of about two dozen state-funded education-oriented networks. State networks are primarily clustered in the South, with the most noteworthy being found in South Carolina, which operates a network of ten ETV stations, six FM stations, ITFS systems, and cable systems. Next come the university-operated stations that were instrumental in launching the movement and account for about a quarter of all the stations. Last in number are stations operated by individual school districts. These stations primarily serve the classroom needs of the district and only secondarily attempt to provide PBS cultural fare during the late afternoon and evening hours.

The Consortium Movement. Because quality program production is so expensive, individual efforts at program origination have yielded only minimally satisfactory results even when funded by large districts. Consequently, astute producers have turned to the development of consortia to broaden the baseline of users and funders. In this, U.S. educational broadcasters have attempted to emulate the perceived success of the British **Open University** (q.v.) with its broad base of coverage and indeed one of the U.S. consortia with the widest range, the National University Consortium (NUC), established during the early 1980s and now called the International University Consortium, was a direct outcome of applying some of the techniques and courseware of the Open University to United States needs. Other similar consortia have emerged from cooperation between community college television production groups which have ranged over regional areas like the aforementioned Southern California Consortium or nationwide as is the loosely knit group called the Telecourse People. College-level telecourses are offered through universities for home use by students enrolled, or enrolled through extension solely for the telecourse or a remote learning degree program. The latter was the protocol of the NUC. Most telecourses are offered as a package with a text, access to a consulting professor available by telephone, term papers to be mailed in for grading, and examinations taken collectively under supervision. As such, telecourses offer course credit parallel to that offered by the administering college.

The Program Library and the Agency. Telecourses are the primary form of instructional television for schools. Some telecourses remain highly sequential, building information in steps and presuming prior knowledge for the understanding of advanced episodes. Most are essentially self-sufficient although building a specific body of knowledge; some are simply a loosely knit group of informative programs on related topics. As mentioned earlier, the development of telecourses received its impetus during the MPATI demonstration, and on its close the existing complement greatly expanded the collection that is presently the Great Plains National Instructional Television Library, known simply as the GPN. Even though the MPATI materials have now been largely retired, the GPN collection is a formidable one. Programs in this collection range from 4 to 52 episodes each and were produced by stations nationwide. However, GPN typically doesn't participate in the production decisions. It acquires programming from producers attempting to recoup their production costs through wider distribution.

A different tack is taken by the Agency for Instructional Television (AIT). It is a true consortium in the sense that AIT has participated in the development of courses from start to finish, compiling a diverse basis of participation, involving numerous state (and Canadian provincial) departments of education, large school districts, and major PTV stations. These agencies cooperate in funding, needs analysis, and content standardization for such a diverse audience, establishment of objectives, scripts, etc., and finally in "farming out" the production segments to numerous producing stations. This helps to distribute the benefits of having work to as many participating stations as possible. Programs in the AIT catalog are first available to those participating in its production and ultimately to all ETV facilities for broadcast to schools. The series from AIT and GPN can also be rented by individual schools and are carried on the educational satellite networks for use by participating districts. Most of the AIT and GPN telecourses are for in-class use in the primary grades and a few for high school use; some are suitable as general information programming for television viewers at home. GPN also offers some college telecourses through its catalog.

The Satellite Networks. With the 1974 launch of NASA's Applications Technology Satellite No. 6 (ATS-6), educational uses of satellite technology became obvious. As a demonstration project it clearly showed the way for relatively inexpensively reaching learners in remote areas as well as the value of making programming available for very large numbers of viewers. ATS-6 was devoted exclusively to educational uses and served time over the Rocky Mountains, the Appalachian area, and later over India in a series of different projects. The Appalachian demonstration led to the follow-on program of the Appalachian Community Service Network (ACSN) which continued to serve the region's hard-to-reach valleys with educational programming transmitted by leased transponders on commercial satellites. Its success paved the way for the ACSN to distribute telecourses nationwide as the "Learning Channel." Meanwhile, PBS had initiated a satellite-based interconnect nationwide and experimented with dividing its programming service into three groupings, PTV-1, -2, and -3. PTV-3 (now the Adult Learning Service) is devoted to educational and children's programming and serves as a distribution system. In addition, there have existed other satellite networks such as the Interregional Program Service and some independent educational program distributors, like Western Instructional Television, have leased satellite time from any source on a need basis.

Nonbroadcast Uses. As discussed earlier, a great deal of television uses are independent of any formal distribution plan and in some cases do not even require recording of the televised activity. An example would be needing a record of an interview or demonstration for playback to a single class where only the original recording is ever needed. Such use represents an ever-increasing educational application for television as the cost of minimal production equipment (recorder and camera) have dropped below $1,000 and tape prices are substantially less than $1 per hour (in the slow speed). Indeed, now highly portable 1/2–inch single-unit "camcorders" (encompassing a recorder and a camera) are occasionally sold for around $1,000. This points to the need for regular classroom teachers to become minimally competent as television field producers since the cost of any personnel to help with the videotaping will outstrip costs of materials and equipment amortization for such miniproductions. It is in this field of nonbroadcast video production that industrial users overlap educational television.

Another interesting implication of the inexpensive 1/2–inch cassette manifests itself in a new alternative to broadcast telecourse distribution through videocassette rental. Learners rent lessons from a video store, buy the text from a college bookstore, and enroll in the telecourse for credit through either a local or distant college.

Corporate Video. It is estimated that as of the mid-1980s some 8,500 corporate video producers in the United States annually produce far more different programs (approximately 55,000 hours of programming) than do the other production agencies, both commercial and noncommercial, combined. Many of these nearly ten thousand corporate and institutional producers are working for firms that can, and do, afford the very finest production facilities—comparable to the networks themselves. Included in this grouping is industry, public service (e.g., hospitals), and many governmental agencies. This category of "private television" has been growing extremely rapidly in the past decade and can be expected to continue to grow for some time. Because of its needs and resources, much of the innovative in applications for informational television can be expected to emerge from these private sources.

In-house Systems. Although setting up an in-house production facility can cost a firm handsomely, tying up funds, space, and personnel, there are secondary benefits beyond the possible cost savings in producing programs in-house. Among such benefits are control over the security of the program content, ability to schedule productions at will, and to a lesser extent, the prestige of such ownership. Consequently, many corporations will install television production facilities even as they routinely farm out productions to commercial production facilities or else have their own personnel produce programs in rented commercial facilities.

Typically, corporate production facilities are outgrowths of personnel departments which produced their own training programs, at first on film, then as the costs of video equipment plummeted, almost exclusively on television. Skills training programs probably still rank first in numbers if not in budgets. (Employee orientation programs are now running a close second.) Much of what is produced now is targeted for various interactive individualized learning schemes and equipment manufacturers are offering numerous systems (tied to ever more sophisticated computer systems) to allow learners to interact with and control the training programs.

Private television also produces numerous corporate sales programs for its sales forces and a variety of "corporate image pieces" to promote the organization at conferences and sales meetings. Another category of programming, less demanding of sophisticated production values, is the video memo introducing branch organizations to various employee groups and the increasing production of in-house news programs that show the executives presenting the information pictorially directly to the employees rather than as distributed printed memorandums. Into this latter category also fall numerous presentations prepared for use with video teleconferences that have become an ever more affordable alternative to business travel.

Training Development Firms. Just as there are a few independent instructional television production firms for public education, there are numerous independent training firms serving the industrial market. They are noteworthy because their product is frequently exemplary of the best in media-based instruction that money can buy and because they are frequent employers of educational specialists. It is worth noting that firms with in-house capability will frequently turn to such professionals just as they almost always go to commercial firms for slick television commercials, rather than using their extensive in-house facilities for such work. These specialist firms usually provide the know-how and packaging for major products for which the client firms have neither the personnel nor inclination.

Teleconferencing. As with program production, teleconferencing based on video transmission is also split between the in-house and service bureau approaches. If need for the security of information content warrants it, large corporations are setting up quite expensive facilities for satellite video teleconferencing. Installations can cost up to a million dollars each and involve state-of-the-art television equipment. Such systems incorporate two-way video transmission, often with a second slow-scan transmission for still graphics and automated multicamera setups to cover the participants. Many are using quite expensive digital data compression systems based on "codecs" (encoders/decoders) that allow the two-way transmission of a somewhat degraded moving image while using a fraction of the video bandwidth.

However, equally popular may be corporate reliance on several nationwide teleconferencing networks that set up the business conferences, locate and acquire the satellite transponder time, set up the feeds, and even plan the menus for those in attendance. Typically, such teleconferences are set up in hotels (e.g., the systems promoted by hotel chains such as Hilton and Holiday Inn) and offer video transmission in only one direction with audio-only talk-back. These are one-time setups, as distinguished from permanent installations, but typically they are cheaper. Since the prime presentation is in video, most such teleconferences rely heavily on the incorporation of preproduced informational television presentations.

THE NEWER TECHNOLOGIES

Besides a nearly constant reduction in the weight, bulkiness, fragility, and cost of video equipment, there have also appeared numerous technological devices that have a direct bearing on the educational user. Prime among these have been the consumer-oriented systems, videodisc players, and assorted devices for making television interactive with its users. Lastly, the inexpensive microprocessor itself has had an impact as have the large mainframe computers in the form of computer-assisted instruction (CAI) as well as with the still-unrealized promise of computer-driven videotex.

Affordable Video Recorders. Only a few educational program producers could have afforded access to the original

2-inch video recorders; and the early versions of the 1-inch recorders left a lot to be desired. It was the introduction of the 3/4-inch U-Matic cassette system that finally provided educators and corporate users with affordable and reliable equipment. Versions of the 3/4-inch format appeared that provided a signal quality acceptable for broadcast and first permitted reasonable editing at a low cost. For educational broadcasters, the more recently introduced Type C 1-inch format, although not inexpensive, also afforded more flexibility and economy, compared to the 2-inch recorders.

Accompanying the development of affordable recorders was the development of color video cameras that were both compact and progressively lower priced. Within the past year prices of cameras suitable for professional use have dropped below $3,000, and cameras acceptable for use with consumer recorders have appeared for under $500.

Indeed, it was the development of the "consumer line" of videocassette recorders (or VCRs) that probably constituted the most significant breakthrough for low-budget television producers. Over the past several years both versions of the half-inch format, the Beta and VHS formats, have been greatly improved, and editing equipment has been made available, to the point that for non-broadcast, limited-use purposes, television production has become accessible to everyone. This not only provides the means for educators to produce needed programs at will but also facilitates the development of more meaningful television literacy among users of television for learning. The more recent introduction of the 8mm video format has introduced affordable compactness, to the point where corporate distribution of programs in the 8mm format is being widely anticipated.

Videodisc Systems. Although videodisc players were announced over a decade ago, it has been only in the past several years or so that many of the promised benefits of the technology have emerged reliably and routinely. Several formats were introduced, but only one seems to have emerged successfully in the United States, namely, the laser, or optical, videodisc. The capacitive, or CED, format had a short, fairly successful run with some very promising developments, but was aborted by its developer as it seemed about to take off. The optical system, however, does appear to be ideal for interactive educational uses.

Optical Videodisc Systems. The optical, or laser vision, players appear to have been successfully standardized and are presently being produced for the U.S. market by two different manufacturers, Sony and Pioneer, each with differing, yet more or less compatible features. The composite video and audio information is encoded beneath the transparent protective surface in the form of tracks of micropits which are reflectively "read" by an ultrafine laser beam. Each concentric track represents one frame of video information. In the "constant angular velocity" configuration there are 30 minutes (54,000 frames) of programming on a side. Since the disk spins at a constant angular velocity (or rotation rate), the laser can be quickly (within less than two seconds) located to any track on the disk and can scan it as a steady still frame indefinitely. This permits the disk to be used as a storage system for a mix of motion sequences and still images—indeed, enabling the storage of 54,000 still pictures on one side—any of which could be randomly accessed in seconds. With the recent introduction of the still-frame audio capability by several firms, thousands of still pictures with short accompanying audio passages (totalling to tens of hours) can now be accessed from one side of an optical videodisc.

It is this ability to randomly access program segments on the disk that has made the optical system such a promising tool for developers of educational television programs who have been seeking methods to permit the process of branching with complex visual programming. *Branching* is a term introduced in programmed instruction, meaning the offering of choices in response to steps taken by individual learners during their work through the program. This is the essence of the "interactive" instructional design mentioned above, but prior to the introduction of the videodisc, such interactive systems could not easily access large numbers of good quality visuals. Interactive design for laser disks has been described as taking place in a number of levels ranging from simply stopping the program periodically to take some action to one where, with the assistance of either an integrated or add-on microcomputer, the implications of the user's actions are sensed and the computer command tracks individual users through any possible pathways programmed by the designer. This last type of design is fully feasible with the current equipment but presents some substantial design challenges. Consequently, only sophisticated demonstration prototypes tend to be produced. The bulk of interactive systems tend to fall between the two extreme levels.

Following years of discourse, videodisc developers have settled on designations based on three levels of interactivity. Level 1 is essentially used for linear programs either that are played through without stops or that allow each user its control over the program directly by advancing or backing the disk to specific frame numbers or "chapters." Level 1 does not depend on computer assistance. Level 2 makes use of an industrial videodisc player's built-in microprocessor for automatically selecting the pathway through a program on the basis of learner choices. Level 3 incorporates substantial external computer power both for control and to generate text and overlaid displays as well as incorporating features such as touch-sensitive display screens and external sensors. One such was used with the American Red Cross's interactive videodisc-based training program on cardiopulmonary resuscitation which was based on a touch sensitive human model called the ResusciAnnie. Different manipulations of the dummy by the learner are sensed by embedded electronic sensors which inputs are interpreted by the external computer and then elicit a variety of corrective instructions and video demonstrations from the computer controlled videodisc.

Although the constant angular velocity mode of operation is ideal for the random access needs of interactive users, the half-hour per side capacity is limiting for longer motion video programs. To permit playback of longer recordings, laser disks can also operate in a constant linear velocity mode wherein the rotational velocity of the disk changes during the playback. This, however, deactivates the rapid random access feature. In this mode, laser video players offer an hour per side, suitable for lengthier entertainment programming.

Capacitive Systems. In an effort to circumvent the inherently high cost of the laser systems needed in the optical videodisc players, RCA developed the Capacitive Electronic Disk, or CED system, which sold for about half the cost of the least expensive optical players. The disks played an hour per side, cost about the same as the laser disks, and offered equivalently excellent image quality. The system was progressively improved to allow stereo sound, a modified still frame, and random access to "chapters" but failed to become a commercial success as VCR prices plummeted and videocassette rentals became popular. Although software for the CED continues to be available, the players are now off the market. An analogous, but even more flexible, capacitive system called Video High Density, or VHD, was introduced and successfully marketed in Japan but never materialized in the United States.

Recording Versions. Because of the cost of videodisc players, and the constantly dropping price of VCRs, many buyers who never objected to the LP record's inability to record sound, do take offense that the videodisc is only a playback format. That has served to limit its popularity. Second, production of videodiscs is a far costlier and more complicated process than is the mastering and pressing of an LP record. Also, videodisc production was a time-consuming process until the 3M Company and some other firms started to offer same-day turnaround. This also limited the acceptance of videodiscs.

Thus there has always existed considerable pressure on the manufacturers to offer a recording disk format. Several versions have been shown experimentally, a few that permit rerecording on the same disk (as is done with magnetic media); most of the others have been limited to single recordings on fresh blanks. So far only one more or less portable system has been offered commercially (by Panasonic) and the price of the unit and the recording blanks seems prohibitive for most users. Other systems suitable for large production facilities have come on the market that allow the production of single laser disks while the client waits. These enable production of about a half-hour disk for just a few hundred dollars. Last, for big facilities, an incompatible optical system allowing quick mastering is being offered by one of the big U.S. aerospace firms. With ongoing development, some further significant breakthroughs can be expected.

Interactive Systems. For years the only interactive instructional systems were those built around large mainframe computers; these did not involve the use of video recorded information. With the recent advent of the inexpensive microprocessor, interactive instructional systems have been built specifically for use with VCRs and videodisc players. Numerous firms sell ancillary interface "cards" (to be plugged into personal computer expansion ports) that connect to the control terminals of video equipment which allow the integration of personal computers and video players, either tape or disk.

Programmable Search Controls. Both Sony and Panasonic introduced some time ago (for the industrial Beta and VHS formats respectively) controls that allow the programmer to take an existing videocassette and develop a step-by-step pathway through the content so that it can be viewed in any preset sequence. In effect, that allows an educational user to produce a raw tape and play it back as if it had been edited into a desired sequence. This preserves the quality of first-generation recording and eliminates the need for costly and time-consuming editing. The playback so attained can, however, be full of annoying delays and start-stop points are not necessarily frame accurate. Along the same lines, VCR manufacturers have also developed interactive keyboards for limited student interactivity directly with a programmed videocassette. Most of the current generation of videodisc players have substantial on-board computers enabling the direct interactive playback of extensively programmed presentations.

Interactivity through Microcomputer Interfaces. In an effort to permit more extensive programming of branching and interaction between instructional video recorded lessons and the individual user, several manufacturers have released the aforementioned interface cards for personal computers such as the Apple II. With appropriately programmed software these allow the computer to take control of the movement of the information and to determine on which frames the program is to stop. This applies either to the tape in a VCR or to the positioning of the laser in a videodisc player. It also allows the computer to "read" digitally encoded information from these sources. With such systems, the skilled programmer may economically develop interactive programs on as limited a scale as may be needed; if necessary, individualizing a particular videocassette for any specific instructional purpose. Many of these systems are priced for the low-budget educational user.

Educational Uses of Videotex. Although teletext and its variants have many demonstrable commercial uses, they have been shown to be also effectively usable for enhancing telecourses. In a demonstration by KCET-TV, the French-designed Antiope system was integrated with in-school telecourses so that at the end of a lesson students could be quizzed via teletext. Using the "reveal" function (which permits a "page" of teletext to be revealed in two stages), the answer could be temporarily withheld and then revealed upon completion of the student response. Similarly, teletext can be used independently for both the informational content and the self-tests to follow. However, the initial cost of teletext decoders coupled to the cost of high-resolution RGB type receivers needed for optimum teletext display have all worked against successful adoption of this technology in the United States.

Two-way videotex as a communication source for personal computers linked to television sets is an obvious educational use for television. Networks such as The Source and CompuServe can be used for information-gathering purposes; but where these overlap into computer-assisted instruction (CAI) lie the most challenging uses for digital communication.

CAI Systems and Television. Two major CAI projects have a well-established history in the United States, namely, the **TICCIT** (q.v.) and **PLATO** (q.v.) systems. The former was initially conceptualized for cable-based delivery to television receivers, whereas PLATO initially used a plasma display, quite radically different from a television set. However, recent demonstrations have shown the feasibility of offering PLATO courseware via cable television for reception on a television set. Also, both the TICCIT and PLATO systems have been restructured to run on personal computers (PCs), and as these become ever cheaper with ever greater memory capabilities, more and more corporate training is being offered on PCs. Demonstrations have also been offered to show that the otherwise digitally presented instructional content of CAI, usually originating from large mainframe computers, can be profitably integrated with analog graphic or motion video material from a videodisc. Such systems point the way for the most sophisticated integration of television into educational programs.

CONCLUSION

Although educational television in the United States has had a turbulent history plagued with funding problems and perhaps occasionally excessively high expectations, it continues to serve well both public education and industry. New technological breakthroughs promise even more, and the integration of television and microprocessor technology points to the possibilities for successfully providing the best in totally individualized instruction, and doing so economically.

A. Arvo Leps

REFERENCES

Ackerman, J. and Lipsitz, L. (1977) *Instructional Television.* Englewood Cliffs, N.J.: Educational Technology Publications.
Bensinger, C. (1982) *The Video Guide.* 3d ed. Santa Fe, N.M.: Video-Info Publications.
Brush, J. M. and Brush, D. P. (1977) *Private Television Communications: An Awakening Giant.* Berkeley Heights, N.J.: International Television Association.
———. (1981) *Private Television Communications: Into the Eighties.* Berkeley Heights, N.J.: International Television Association.
———. (1986) *Private Television Communications: The New Directions,* The Fourth Brush Report. Cold Spring, N.Y.: HI Press, in association with ITVA.
Carnegie Commission. (1967) *Public Television: A Program for Action.* New York: Bantam Books.
———. (1979) *A Public Trust.* New York: Bantam Books.
Cartwright, S. R. (1986) *Training with Video.* White Plains, N.Y.: Knowledge Industry Publications.
Dordick, H. S. et al. (1979) *ITV: A User's Guide to the Technology.* Washington: Corporation for Public Broadcasting.
Gayeski, D. M. (1983) *Corporate & Instructional Video: Design & Production.* Englewood Cliffs, N.J.: Prentice-Hall.
Gordon, G. N. (1970) *Classroom Television.* New York: Hastings House.
Marsh, K. (1974) *Independent Video.* San Francisco, Calif.: Straight Arrow Books (Simon and Schuster).
Purdy, L. N., ed. (1983) *Reaching New Students Through New Technologies: A Reader.* Dubuque, Iowa: Kendall/Hunt.
Wood, D. N. and Wylie, D. G. (1977) *Educational Telecommunications.* Belmont, Calif.: Wadsworth.
Zigerell, J. (1986) *A Guide to Telecourses and Their Uses.* Costa Mesa, Calif.: Coast Community College District.

TELEVISION PROJECTOR. See **Projection Television.**

TELEVISION RECEIVER. A display device capable of receiving broadcast television signals by means of an antenna. Receivers can be used in combination with a modulator as a display device for a microcomputer, and this is often done in the home where the major requirement may be to display video games. However, if the viewing of text or numbers is important, then it becomes necessary to use a video monitor which gives a better resolution.

TELEX. Long-established communication system using telephone lines to transmit messages between subscribers. The operating device is a teletypewriter which is used to address and send messages, and to type out incoming communications. Telex is widely used in commerce, and most corporations and many other institutions around the world have telex facilities and their own unique telex address. Modern developments have pointed the way to much faster alternatives to telex, and its importance can be expected to wane in the years ahead. See **Teletex.**

TELIDON. The name of the Canadian coding scheme for alphageometric graphics which can be used in either videotex or teletext systems. Telidon is now the same as NAPLPS. The name is based on the two Greek words "to see" and "distance." See **NAPLPS; Videotex.**

TELSTAR. The first communications satellite, built for AT&T and launched in 1962. Telstar opened up the new age of global communications: it was capable of simultaneously transmitting and receiving, and was used for data transfer as well as television and telephone purposes. Telstar's orbit was very elliptical and its output power was only 3w (compare 1,000w for Intelsat V), but it must be ranked as one of the most significant of technological advances.

TERMINAL. A typewriter-like device for receiving or sending information to a computer. Terminals commonly incorporate a television-screen but this is not essential, and the computer output may be typed on paper. Large and medium-size computers may have anything from a few up to hundreds of terminals, all operating on a time-sharing basis.

TERTIARY EDUCATION. The importance of educational technology in teaching at university level is clearly evidenced by the almost universal provision of centralized audiovisual facilities. The advent of the microcomputer has resulted in a rekindling of interest in various forms of computerized learning, and it seems likely that this will become a significant element in tertiary courses.

TESTING MACHINES. Machines designed to test the learner. Early teaching machines were also testing machines, and the distinction between the two was not always clear.

Various arrangements are available for the automatic scoring of multiple-choice tests. These operate on a mark-sense basis, i.e., the machine (which is often a computer peripheral) senses pencil marks made by students and is able to rapidly score the test. Other information is frequently provided relating both to the students (e.g., mean score, variance) and to the test (e.g., measures of reliability).

TEST PATTERN. A chart especially prepared for checking overall performance of a television system. It contains various combinations of colors, lines, and geometric shapes. The camera is focused on the chart, and the pattern is viewed at the monitor for fidelity.

TETHERED COMMUNICATIONS SYSTEM (T-COM). A proposal of the 1960s to provide educational television services by using an inflated balloon as a transponding mechanism.

TEXTBOOK DESIGN. It is interesting to reflect that books are probably the greatest source of information for learners (more than 500,000 book titles are issued in the world every year—a new book every minute), yet only a limited amount of space has been allowed for an entry on textbooks in this encyclopaedia. Why should this be so? Why is the ubiquitous textbook often neglected in discussions of educational media? One answer might be that textbooks, like teachers, are too varied and too complex to make generalizations about them. Another might be that textbooks are ignored because of their very commonplaceness. The present writer would maintain, however, that the unnoticed deserves respect. It is the unnoticed that sets the context for the unusual.

There have been a number of useful articles and books about textbooks in general (e.g., see Whipple, 1931; Cronbach, 1956; Buckingham, 1960; Hilton, 1969; Barker and Escarpit, 1973 RELATED READING). Most of these concentrate on three main areas of concern about textbooks: their aim and function, their production and marketing, and their selection and evaluation. Recent textbooks, however, focus more on their design (e.g.,

Jonassen, 1982, 1985; Duffy and Waller, 1985; Hartley, 1985 ILLUSTRATIONS).

In this entry four design issues are discussed:

— the choice of page size;
— the spatial arrangement of the text on that page size;
— the use of typographic cues to accentuate aspects of the text; and
— the use of "access structures" to help readers find their way around a text.

The issue of the language of the text—its suitability—is not discussed here. (Interested readers may consult the texts by Duffy and Waller, 1985 ILLUSTRATIONS; and Gilham, 1986 RELATED READING.)

The purpose of the following discussion is not to provide a set of guidelines based upon research; this has been done elsewhere (see Hartley, 1981 ILLUSTRATIONS). The aim of this entry is to inform readers about some of the choices open to them, and about the possible effects of making particular choices. Limitations of space unfortunately prevent the inclusion of any illustrations of these effects, but illustrations may be found elsewhere (e.g., see Rehe, 1974; Reynolds and Simmonds, 1981; Hartley, 1985 ILLUSTRATIONS).

CHOICE OF PAGE SIZE

Most people expect a review of textbook design to begin by considering issues such as type size, typeface, and line length, and reviews of this literature are available (e.g. Tinker, 1965; Watts and Nisbet, 1974; Hartley, 1986 RESEARCH REVIEWS).

However, it is important to realize that the choice for each of these variables is already constrained by an earlier one, that of deciding on what size page to print the text. Clearly one does not expect to find a large type size in a pocket dictionary, or a single column of print in a daily newspaper. These examples are extreme, but they illustrate a point. Text is printed on a page size which is appropriate to its use, and page size constrains what can be done.

The choice of appropriate page size is not always easy. Often large sizes are preferred because of the need to present detailed illustrations and tabular materials. But factors such as cost, ease of use, and what page sizes are available all have to be taken into account. (In Europe the choice of page size is made somewhat easier because there is a set of standard page sizes—those recommended by the International Organization for Standards—see Hartley, 1985 ILLUSTRATIONS.)

The choice of page size is crucial because it forms the baseline from which the remaining decisions are made. Once the size of the page is decided on then it is possible to choose the layout for that page, the width of columns, the typeface and type sizes to be used, and the interline spacing. Following these decisions come related ones about the positioning of illustrations, running headlines, page numbers, and so on (see Hartley, 1985 ILLUSTRATIONS).

THE SPATIAL ARRANGEMENT OF TEXT

Unlike the prose of a novel—or even much of this encyclopaedia—instructional text often contains a wide variety of components. For example, there may be headings and subheadings, hierarchically developed and numbered arguments, lists of information, diagrams, tables, illustrations, captions, footnotes, appendixes, etc. Furthermore, much of this material will not be read continuously. A learner's focus of attention often ranges from a place on the page to somewhere else—to the teacher, to the task in hand, to other learners, and back again to the place on the page. The spatial arrangement of the text must support this situation by providing a consistent frame of reference, which the learner can move to and from without confusion.

Yet if one inspects many school textbooks it is hard not to come to the conclusion that these are often composed page by page during production, on a sort of "let's put this here" basis. Such a procedure produces inconsistency from page to page, particularly in terms of spacing the different components. The argument of this entry is that the layout of the text must be planned in advance of production if the instructional materials are to provide a consistent frame of reference for the reader.

One helpful device for doing this is the typographic reference grid. Such a grid "maps" the information area of the page horizontally in units of the type size chosen and vertically in units of line feed, or interline space (see Hartley, 1985 ILLUSTRATIONS). The amount of space to leave between the components in the text is determined in advance, and this spacing is used consistently throughout when proofs are pasted onto the grid. Typographic grids are becoming more common in textbook production, and although subject to some debate, the more complex the text the more useful they seem to be. Indeed, some producers of mathematical and computer-based texts insist that authors submit their copy on preprepared grids. Readers may examine illustrations of the effectiveness of consistently spacing text in several "before" and "after" examples provided by Hartley (1985 ILLUSTRATIONS).

TYPOGRAPHIC CUING

The first two sections of this entry have concentrated on problems of layout. There are, of course, additional devices that writers, designers, and printers use to draw the reader's attention to specific points or important issues in the text. Such devices are generally known as "typographic cues." Typical examples of such cues are

—underlining (especially in typescript)
—italics
—capital letters
—color

Hartley et al. (1980 RESEARCH REVIEWS AND EXPERIMENTS) considered over 40 studies on underlining and came to the conclusion that underlining did no harm and was sometimes useful, but that the conditions in which it was useful were not well-known. In particular, and this seems true of all work on typographic cuing, the cues only work when the reader knows what they signify. Furthermore, the research suggests that children have to learn to use the typographic cues that adults take for granted.

There has been little research on the effectiveness of using italics or capital letters for emphasis, possibly because of the effectiveness of early studies which showed that passages set in italics and capitals were harder to read than passages set in lowercase letters (Hartley, 1986 RESEARCH REVIEWS).

Color has been used in the printing of instructional materials for different purposes. Color has been used functionally, to aid instruction, or aesthetically, to attract readers. Waller et al. (1982 RESEARCH REVIEWS), in a brief review of the problems, point out that it may be useful to employ a second color:

—where pointer lines linking labels to diagrams might be confusing if only one color is used
—where a colored grid might be superimposed over a black-and-white illustration to indicate, for example, some sort of grouping
—in situations where there might be two or more levels of text running in parallel (e.g., study guidance for mainstream subject matter)

One difficulty with cuing systems is that the same cues are often used for different purposes. Boldface, for example, can be used to indicate that a word will be defined elsewhere in a glossary, or to emphasize an important concept, or to indicate a heading. Similarly, italics can be used to draw attention to a technical term, to emphasize a point, to indicate a heading, or to signify a book title. It would probably be more helpful to the reader if a single cue were used for a single purpose.

ACCESS STRUCTURES

In addition to typographic cues for emphasis, there are other devices which authors and designers use to orient readers and to help them find their way around a text. Typical examples of such "access structures" would be

—contents pages
—titles
—summaries
—headings and subheadings
—numbering systems
—references and bibliographies
—indexes

Contents pages, reference lists, bibliographies, and indexes are characterized by the fact that each of these devices is a list structure, that is to say, each one consists of a string of main elements all of which contain a number of subelements. Thus a contents page for an edited textbook will contain a list of authors, titles, and page numbers. Similarly, a set of references will contain a list of authors, titles, and dates and places of publication. The task of the designer is to display each main element and each subelement clearly because different people will want to use the list in different ways. The research in this area suggests that a key feature in the design of a list structure is its spatial arrangement. While users like a combination of spatial and typographic cues to indicate the function of each element in a list structure, when given a choice between a spatial arrangement without typographic cues or a run-on display with typographic cues, then users typically prefer the spatially arranged text (Hartley and Guile, 1981 RESEARCH REVIEWS AND EXPERIMENTS).

The research suggests that summaries can aid the recall of salient facts, although there is some debate about whether they do this better if they are placed at the beginning or the end of a piece of text (see Hartley and Trueman, 1982 RESEARCH REVIEWS AND EXPERIMENTS). Many authors, of course, distinguish between and use different kinds of summaries. Thus overview summaries presented at the beginning provide a description of what is to follow in general terms, interim summaries sum up the argument so far, and review summaries placed at the end summarize what has gone before—often using the more technical terminology introduced in the text itself.

Research on the effectiveness of headings and titles suggests that these features can aid the recall of salient facts. Headings can also help readers find and retrieve information from the text (Hartley and Trueman, 1985 RESEARCH REVIEWS AND EXPERIMENTS). There is some debate about the value of the frequency of headings, their length, position (marginal or embedded), style (e.g., questions versus statements), and quality (poor headings can mislead).

Numbering systems are often used to help sequencing in text. Headings and sections in technical materials are frequently numbered 1.00, 1.01, 1.02, 2.00, etc. However, some numbering systems which are designed to aid retrieval can in fact be confusing, especially if there are references in the text to other numbering systems—page numbers, chapter numbers, section numbers, table numbers, and so on. Waller (1977 ILLUSTRATIONS) provides an illuminating example.

Finally, we may note here that there has been very little attempt to inquire into different ways of typographically presenting access structures. Summaries, for instance, may be set apart from the main text, printed in different typefaces and type sizes, and so on. But the effectiveness of these strategies has not been adequately researched. Similarly, how one denotes headings typographically (especially if they are hierarchically ordered) has still to be examined (see Twyman, 1981 ILLUSTRATIONS).

CONCLUSIONS

The information explosion makes text increasingly important as an educational medium—be it printed or electronic. At one end of the educational ladder, newly literate readers depend on text to reach higher levels of reading skill. At the other end, already literate adults rely on text to reach higher levels of knowledge. Making the presentation of text more effective consequently deserves the increase in research attention that it is currently enjoying. Much has been achieved, but there is still a great deal to do.

J. Hartley and George R. Klare

REFERENCES

Illustrations

Duffy, T. and Waller, R., eds. (1985) *Designing Usable Texts*. Orlando, Fl.: Academic Press.
Hartley, J., ed. (1980) *The Psychology of Written Communication: Selected Readings*. London: Kogan Page; New York: Nichols.
———. (1981) "Eighty Ways of Improving Instructional Text." *IEEE Transactions on Professional Communication* PC-24 (1): 17–27.
———. (1985) *Designing Instructional Text*. 2d ed. London: Kogan Page; New York: Nichols.
Jonassen, D. H. ed. (1982) *The Technology of Text*, vol. 1. Englewood Cliffs, N.J.: Educational Technology Publications.
———, ed. (1985) *The Technology of Text*, vol. 2. Englewood Cliffs, N.J.: Educational Technology Publications.
Rehe, R. F. (1974) *Typography: How to Make It Most Legible*. Carmel, Ind.: Design Research International.
Reynolds, L. and Simmonds, D. (1981) *Presentation of Data in Science*. The Hague: Martinus Nijhoff.
Twyman, M. "Typography without Words." *Visible Language* 15(1): 5–12.
Waller, R.H.W. (1977) "Notes on Transforming No. 4." Repr. in *The Psychology of Written Communication: Selected Readings*, ed. J. Hartley. London: Kogan Page; New York: Nichols, 1980.

Related Reading

Barker, R. and Escarpit, R., eds. (1973) *The Book Hunger*. Paris: UNESCO.
Buckingham, B. R. (1960) "Textbooks." In *Encyclopaedia of Educational Research*, ed. C. W. Harris. London: Macmillan.
Cronbach, L. S., ed. (1956) *Text Materials in Modern Education*. Urbana: University of Illinois Press.
Gilham, B., ed. (1986) *The Language of School Subjects*. London: Heinemann.
Hilton, E. (1969) "Textbooks." In *Encyclopaedia of Educational Research*, ed. R. Ebel. London: Macmillan.
Whipple, G. M. ed. (1931) *The Textbook in American Education*. National Society for the Study of Education. Bloomington Ill.: Public School Publishing Company.

Research Reviews

Hartley, J. (1986) "Planning the Typographical Structure of Instructional Text." *Educational Psychologist* 21 (4): 315–332.
Tinker, M. A. (1965) *Bases for Effective Reading*. Minneapolis: University of Minnesota Press.
Waller, R., Lefrere, P., and Macdonald-Ross, M. (1982) "Do You Need That Second Colour?" *IEEE Transactions on Professional Communication*, PC-25 (2): 80–85.
Watts, L. and Nisbet, J. (1974) *Legibility in Children's Books*. London: National Foundation for Educational Research.

Research Reviews and Experiments

Hartley, J., Bartlett, S., and Branthwaite, J. A. (1980) "Underlining Can Make a Difference—Sometimes." *Journal of Educational Research* 73: 218–224.
Hartley, J. and Guile, C. (1981) "Designing Journal Contents Pages: Preferences for Horizontal and Vertical Layouts." *Journal of Research Communication Studies* 2: 271–288.
Hartley, J. and Trueman, M. (1982) "The Effects of Summaries on the Recall of Information from Prose: Five Experimental Studies." *Human Learning* 1: 63–82.
———. (1985) "A Research Strategy for Text Designers: The Role of Headings." *Instructional Science* 14: 99–155.

TEXT EDITOR. A word processing typewriter which confines itself to memory editing of text. The text may be stored in memory or often on disk as well, and generally the text-handling facilities will be quite powerful. However, the device normally stands alone, and has no capability of communication with other machines.

TEXT SCREEN. A computer display mode specially configured for the display of ASCII characters. It is not possible to show graphics on a text screen, except in so far as the required graphics can be assembled from the available ASCII character set, e.g., boxes, borders, and the like. Most microcomputer text screens offer 25 lines of text, each of which can contain 80 characters.

T-GROUP. A group technique wherein members study their own social interactions and try to improve their interpersonal and social skills.

THERBLIG. An iconic representation for various movements. Therbligs (the word is an anagram of Gilbreth, its inventor) are used in time and motion studies.

THERMAL COPIER. A document copying system that uses a heat-sensitive paper (or transparent film). The system uses infrared radiation to produce an image in the copy paper which is placed in contact with the original. The copy does not require "processing," but it remains heat-sensitive. The main use of the process is to make overhead transparencies.

THERMOFAX. Trade name (3M Corporation) for a thermal copying system.

THESAURUS. Originally, a list of words with cross-reference to other words associated with the same or similar meaning. Peter Mark Roget's *Thesaurus of English Words and Phrases* groups words into categories based on fundamental concepts such as existence, quantity, number, time, space, matter, etc., with an alphabetic index. After the introduction of computers into the field of information storage and retrieval, many specialized thesauri have been designed in order to provide a controlled vocabulary for information classification and retrieval.

In education, those already published include the *ERIC Thesaurus* (U.S.); the *UNESCO-IBE Education Thesaurus* (IBE, Geneva); the *EUDISED Multi-Lingual Thesaurus* (Council of Europe, Strasbourg); and the *London Education Classification/Thesaurus* (University of London Institute of Education).

THIMBLE. Printhead device for a computer printer, directly comparable to a daisy wheel or "golf ball." Numerous fonts are available at moderate cost. Although thimbles are constructed of plastic, they are guaranteed for millions of impressions.

THIRD-GENERATION COMPUTER. A computer that uses silicon chips as its main components. Such computers started to be built during the early 1970s. *See* **Second-Generation Computer; Fourth-Generation Computer; Fifth-Generation Computer.**

THIRD WORLD. *See* **Developing Countries.**

THOUGHTSTICKER. *See* **Entailment Mesh.**

THREADING. Feeding film or tape along the indicated path in a projector, tape recorder, etc. Also called *lacing*.

THREE-TWO (3–2) PULLDOWN. A means of transferring film shot at 24 frames per second (fps) into video (30 fps). The first film frame is actually exposed on three video fields, and the next film frame is exposed on two fields. Thus two film frames take up five video fields which equals 2.5 video frames, in both cases accounting for one-twelfth of a second of elapsed time (2/24 = 2.5/30). The technique is completely unnoticeable to the viewer.

TICCIT. An acronym for Time-shared, Interactive Computer-Controlled Instructional Television. This is a computer-aided instructional system that was originally developed by the MITRE Corporation in conjunction with the University of Texas CAI Laboratory and the Brigham Young University Instructional Research and Development Department. The system was originally based upon small computers, color television sets, and typewriter-like keyboards (all "off-the-shelf" items) to provide individualized instruction for as many as 128 students simultaneously.

The student terminal (a combination of a normal, unmodified television set and an input keyboard) enables students to see, hear, and respond to instructional materials which take the form of rules, examples, and practice exercises. These are displayed to the students on their television screen and include computer-generated alphanumerics, graphics (in seven different colors), supplementary videotapes and audio via a special audio-response unit. The keyboard of the terminals which contains special keys labeled EASY, HARD, HELP, ADVICE, etc., is ergonomically designed for the learner. A rule or practice item is displayed on the television screen only when the student depresses the appropriate key. The complexity level of the displays that are to be produced can be controlled by the student who, if necessary, can obtain step-by-step explanations of any troublesome item.

TICCIT has been used both in regular curricula and in evaluation projects in the following general application areas: university and community college courses, in-house training within the MITRE Corporation, and for teaching handicapped children.

In Amherst, Massachusetts, TICCIT has successfully been used for learning purposes in conjunction with interactive cable television.

P. G. Barker

TILT. To move a camera in the vertical plane, as opposed to panning, which is movement in the horizontal plane.

TIME BASE CORRECTOR. The output from a video recorder is not in synchronization with camera and other signals, and is also inherently unstable. A time base corrector locks together and stabilizes all frequencies with the result that the signal quality is vastly improved. Moderately priced units are now available for educational installations and can provide the means to achieve near-broadcast standards of picture.

TIME-COMPRESSED SPEECH. A technique which speeds up the presentation of the spoken word. The simplest method is to replay recorded speech at a faster speed than it was recorded at, but better results are obtained using computers and a sampling technique. The main application of time-compressed speech is in "audio books" for the blind. Speech can be satisfactorily speeded up to almost three times normal rate. *See* **Audio Instruction.**

TIME-EXPANDED SPEECH. Recorded speech whose characteristics have been changed by slowing down the presentation of words, pauses, etc. *See* **Audio Instruction; Time-Compressed Speech.**

TIME LAPSE. The technique of taking a series of exposures on cine film at intervals, to record changes that take place slowly with time. The technique is used in two ways, first as a means of speeding up an event that takes place extremely slowly. Changes that are imperceptible to the eye can be readily seen and analyzed in a time lapse record; the growth of plants is a typical example.

Another way in which time lapse techniques are used is in the analysis of situations with complex patterns of movement, where each frame of the film is studied separately. Time lapse is used in this way in classroom analysis.

TIMENET. Computer network providing subscribers with access to a large data base and other facilities. *See* **Videotex.**

TIME SAMPLING. A sampling technique used in interaction analysis and systematic classroom observation. The observer codes the behavior observed at regular timed intervals. For example, in coding classrooms using the Flanders system for categorizing the verbal interaction of the teacher and pupils, about twenty codings are made per minute (i.e., about every three seconds).

In order to record the sequence and duration of interactions, regular timed sampling allows the observer to code from a complicated system at a steady pace. Timing rates ranging from one second to perhaps five minutes are used, measurement being by means of a metronome, stopwatch, etc. Regularity of coding is more important than precision of timing. *See* **Event Sampling; Interaction Analysis.**

TIMES EDUCATIONAL SUPPLEMENT (TES). The *TES* and its sister publication, the *Times Higher Education Supplement,* are weekly publications which provide wide news coverage of the educational field in the United Kingdom. Developments in media and technology are fully reported.

New Printing House Square, Gray's Inn Road, London WC1X 8EZ, U.K.

TIME-SHARING. A mode of computer usage whereby a number of users can interact simultaneously with the machine, each having the illusion of having the whole system to himself. This is accomplished by the computer actually dealing with each "customer" in turn, the actual processing being so fast that the users are not inconvenienced by this sharing.

In practice it is not uncommon for systems to be overloaded, with consequent adverse effects only too clear to the user. One of the attractions of single-user microcomputers is the lack of time-sharing delays.

TIME-SHIFT RECORDING. The use of tape recording to allow for making use of broadcast radio or television programs at times other than those chosen by the broadcasting agencies. This is one of the most significant uses made of home video recorders.

TLF. *See* **Technology Learning Facility.**

TOKEN RING. A type of local area network in which stations are connected so that signals pass through each station in turn; a special circulating signal tells the individual stations when the network is open for them to pass a message into the network.

TONER. The powder that is used to produce the image in electrostatic copying. Toner used to be black only, but various colors are now available.

TOPOLOGY. The arrangement of pathways, and therefore the flow of information, on a network. The most common are rings (where messages pass through each station in turn), stars (where messages pass through a central node), and buses (where each message is presented to all nodes).

TOUCH-SENSITIVE SCREEN. A VDU with the capacity to detect where on its screen it is being touched. This permits several useful teaching strategies; for example, young children can match words and pictures, locations in maps and diagrams can be readily identified, alternative answers can be selected, and so on. Unfortunately, this facility is not easily or cheaply provided. *See* **PLATO.**

TRACK. One of the concentric magnetic patterns on a disk used for storing data. Floppy disks have 35–80 tracks, hard disks many more. *See* **Double Density; Sector; Single Density.**

TRACKING. An adjustment on a video recorder to "fine-tune" the read head to the precise line of the recorded track on the tape. Unlike audio recording, video utilizes elaborate paths on the tape, and the head must be accurately aligned with the track.

TRAINING. As applied to computerized instruction, training generally refers to lessons aimed at a specific task-related skill; education, on the other hand, is often concerned with general instruction in broader topics. Commercial and industrial training is one of the largest applications for CAI, CML, etc. *See* **Training Technology.**

TRAINING DESIGN. The design of training with particular reference to industry. Industrial training distinguishes itself from other sectors in many ways, in particular from higher education where the training (teaching) forms an integral part of the output of the system. In industry, training is mostly a means to an end, not an end in itself.

TRAINING TECHNOLOGY.

INTRODUCTION

The principles of educational technology remain the same whether the context of their practice is within education or in industrial training. It is not, therefore, the purpose of this entry to reexamine the basic ideas behind the name "educational technology," but rather to describe the nature and extent of their application within industry, where, under the name of "training technology," the educational technology approach has become widely accepted over the last twenty years.

ACCEPTANCE OF TRAINING TECHNOLOGY

The reasons for the relatively ready acceptance of educational technology principles in industry, as against education, are not far to seek. In many ways the practical, objectives-oriented approach of educational technology appeals a good deal more to those responsible for training in industry than it does to educators. On the whole, the aims of trainers are relatively short-term and well-defined; the nature of their responsibilities is narrower—they have to equip adults to do defined jobs in a specific environment, not to equip children for "life," whatever life may bring; and the demands made on training departments by companies are more precise and less subject to inconsistent social and political pressures. All this is to say that the system within which the trainer operates is much better defined, and easier to relate to, than the system within which the educator operates. However ill-defined may be the aims of a company or government department, they are easier to relate to than are those of society as a whole.

In less general terms, the implications of change within the training department of an industrial organization are much less threatening than they are within an educational establishment. Training is a relatively minor activity within an industrial organization. Innovation may alter the structure of the training department, but it does not change the character of the organization as a whole. Most people, for example, do not think of the leading banks, British Telecom, or Kodak as *primarily* characterized by their use of advanced training methods. In educational institutions, teaching and learning are the essential activities, so that fully to adopt new methods and approaches implies adopting a new character for the whole organization—most people do think of the **Open University** (q.v.) as primarily characterized by the way it teaches. It is obviously easier for an organization which produces goods or services to change one of its ancillary activities than it is for an educational institution to change the way it carries out its major function. The difficulties and implications of innovation in an education context have become a major object of study among academic educational technologists; trainers are, of course, concerned with the allied problems of obtaining resources and equipment, but the organizational and attitudinal problems associated with "innovation in education" rouse little interest in training circles.

NATURE OF INDUSTRIAL TRAINING COURSES

Again, even within education, innovation has proved much easier in the context of new courses and new subject material. Within established courses, new teaching and learning problems can be incorporated into curricula using traditional methods, and any failures in performance can be attributed to a number of causes, among which teachers tend to rank shortage of time high and inferior teaching methods low. The Open University was able to introduce new teaching methods partly because the courses were being devised from scratch, partly because they were being devised to meet types of teaching and learning problems which were new in the context of tertiary education. Industrial training courses are much shorter than educational courses. Three months is a long time for a training course. It is thus relatively easy to rethink and remodel such a course incorporating new methods. It is also true that whereas an academic subject may not change very much over quite a long period, industry is continually faced with new problems or newly identified ones, and it is clear that this context, of a relatively frequent demand for new, short courses, has favored the development of new approaches and methods within industry.

Another contributory factor is perhaps the fact that educational technology has frequently been presented and accepted as a matter of the use of more or less advanced hardware as a medium for education or training. Similar considerations apply to the adoption of new methods, particularly for individualized training. In general, the hardware approach has had little appeal to teachers. Trainers have been readier to find the will and the means to experiment with new equipment and have found the hardware less of a barrier to the adoption of educational technology at a more serious level. In some industrial contexts training takes place on the job or in the job environment, presenting the providers of training with considerable problems of logistics. In such contexts the use of portable training materials (programmed instruction, audiotapes, television, etc.) often offers a welcome and necessary solution to real difficulties.

Another, more basic reason for the relatively good acceptance of educational technology within industry lies in the nature of the types of problems to which it has been called upon to provide solutions. Most problems tackled by training departments involve comparatively simple knowledge structures (Cowan, 1976 AUTHORITY) or physical skills, or an understanding of relatively simple processes (including the processes involved in the development of interpersonal skills). Very early in the development of programmed instruction as an applied technique, the question of whether the programmer should be a subject matter expert cropped up. The implied problem was whether the tools available to educational technology were powerful enough to enable the programmer to structure *any* system of knowledge, however complex. This question was explored by MacDonald Ross (1972a, 1972b AUTHORITY), who expressed "a certain dissatisfaction with the generalists' rather poverty-stricken tool-kit, consisting of the behavioral objective and the systematic approach to course design." After he showed that these tools had not been adequate to structure a complex system of knowledge for students at tertiary level, educational technologists within the academic world tended to abandon the "hard-line" educational technology approach.

While retaining the basic ideas of educational technology they turned their attention to problems of innovation and management of change within institutions, and of staff and student development. While the combination of recession and the availability of computer time has revived interest in the possibilities of media-based learning, few would now claim that educational technology offers a total solution to the needs of education. In training, a high proportion of problems in practice are concerned with comparatively much simpler and more restricted knowledge structures, so that the limitations have not presented the same difficulties to trainers as they have to educators.

INTERPRETATIONS OF "TRAINING TECHNOLOGY"

In training, however, as elsewhere, "training technology" has different levels of meaning. At one level, it is possible to perceive the technology as a system in itself, which draws on a number of different disciplines for knowledge and techniques to use in the solution of education and training problems. This view of the subject is not very common among trainers, who tend to see it as a way of doing things rather than as a subject of academic study and development. Even in this sense there are several ways of looking at educational technology. It may be seen as essentially a systems approach in which the training department, itself part of a larger system, shares the task of identifying problems to which training is an appropriate solution, and devises the most elegant possible solutions to these problems. Although there is considerable support in theory for this sort of role for training departments, it is not very common in practice. (Training Services Division of the MSC, 1968 EXAMPLE). In general, training departments do not have the kind of influence in their organization that would make easy the adoption of a proactive role in determining what should and should not be regarded as a training problem. They are much more likely to be in the position of reacting to requests from management to produce courses on matters which have been identified elsewhere as demonstrating the need for training. A systems approach, using the "performance problem analysis" or "front-end analysis" techniques advocated by Mager and Pipe (1970 AUTHORITY) and Romiszowski (1981 AUTHORITY), not infrequently reveals that problems which have been assumed to be appropriately dealt with by training may in practice be better solved by other means. For example, failure to observe safety regulations may be caused not by unfamiliarity with the regulations or inability to observe them, but by attitudes which make people unwilling to observe them, or reward systems which ensure that it does not pay to carry them out. The kind of attitude change required needs active development from management within the relevant departments; the new reward system is an organizational matter; neither is properly the responsibility of the training department, whose role in this kind of approach is to assist in the decision about the proper solution to a particular problem, rather than simply to provide training at the request of other departments.

THE SYSTEMATIC APPROACH

In the majority of organizations, however, training is seen as a relatively lowly service department, there to provide courses as required. In such contexts the contribution of training technology is to provide trainers with a systematic way of structuring, implementing, and evaluating their courses. As such, it is relatively widely accepted, to the extent that it is uncommon to find a professional training officer who does not claim to use the approach. The degree of sophistication with which educational technology principles are applied varies very much according to the size of the organization, the nature and extent of its training activity, and the kind of knowledge and skills being purveyed to the trainees. In some large organizations (the banks, the Dutch railways, many of the special projects devised for the U.N. organizations like WHO, ILO, etc.) genuine and extensive applications of educational technology principles have resulted in the development of instructional systems based on thorough analysis and refined by detailed evaluation. At the other end of the spectrum, the approach has been diluted to the point where a few behavioral objectives have been extracted from existing course outlines, and evaluation is represented by a "happiness sheet" circulated, if the trainer remembers, among the trainees at the end of the course.

There are, of course, also still some trainees who regard training or educational technology as meaning simply the use of hardware in a training context. A survey of the take-up of educational technology in this restricted sense was made more than ten years ago by Romiszowski and Ellis, who found that the use of audiovisual media was well established among respondents, 50 percent of whom also reported using techniques such as the then-fashionable programmed instruction, management games, training by objectives, role-play, etc. (Romiszowski and Ellis, 1974 AUTHORITY). There is little reason to doubt that industry is still comparatively well-equipped and comparatively ready to experiment with new methods and media as they become available, though the emphasis is now heavily on the development of applications for the computer within training.

EFFECTS OF THE SPREAD OF COMPUTERS

The training world is much subject to fads; that for programmed instruction is the most obvious but not the only example of a technique that roused enormous interest in its heyday and is now completely out of fashion. Some observers take the view that computer-based training is destined for a similar fate. It is certainly true that some of the applications currently envisaged for the computer as a training medium seem unlikely to become a permanent feature of the training scene, at least in the present state of the art. Computer-based learning does not seem to have much to offer, for example, as the medium for an induction course, but current predictions about the impact of the computer in all aspects of life suggest that its availability and use are certain to increase, and if this is the case, it is hard to avoid the conclusion that it is most unlikely to disappear from the training scene.

At present computer-based training materials are not, on the whole, particularly impressive, tending to be slight in import and conventional in pedagogic method. Most of them have been designed by computer experts with little knowledge of training, or by trainers with little knowledge of computing, and their deficiencies are only too obvious. At present, after an initial honeymoon with BASIC, many trainers are turning to authoring systems which simplify the process of producing material, though some of them tend to facilitate the production of relatively unsophisticated material, similar to, if not identical with, branching programmed learning materials. But this is only the beginning. It is possible to foresee the widespread development of effective simulation techniques in many training applications and, in the slightly longer term, of powerful systems based on the use of computer-controlled video; some excellent examples are already in existence, notably the videodisc on car maintenance produced by Thorn EMI (not on the market, but exhibited, for example, at Brighton Polytechnic's 1983 Conference on Interactive Video/Computer-based Training).

Hitherto, those who have thought of educational technology in terms of the use of hardware have been able to concentrate on slickness of presentation (as in many, though by no means all, commercially produced video and slide-tape materials), rather than devoting at least an equivalent effort to solid analysis and thorough evaluation of their materials. The advent of the computer as the principal item of educational hardware must in the long term change this situation for the better. At present, there is, naturally enough, a heavy concentration on the problems of presenting learning materials on the computer screen; after all, no amount of careful instructional design will get the student past the problem of not understanding how to get to the next screen and being unable to interpret the graphics (Haines, 1983 AUTHORITY). However, it is not possible to design any but the most trifling piece of computer-based material without adopting some sort of systematic approach (Dean and Whitlock, 1983 EXAMPLE), and it is to be hoped that not too much effort will have to be devoted to rediscovering the wheel before the educational technology approach is fully appreciated and applied by those involved with computer-based training.

APPLICATIONS OF TRAINING TECHNOLOGY

Although, as has been said, an educational or training technology approach is well established among professional trainers, it is not true that most or much training takes the form of "educational technology materials" in the sense of prepared self-learning materials in various media forms. In most training departments the "live course" is the standard medium of instruction, and the influence of educational technology is revealed in the analysis and design of these live lessons. However, training in industry presents a number of administrative and logistic problems which often make it difficult to provide live courses exactly when and where trainees need them; very typical of these difficulties are the situations where training has to be provided for a number of employees located at different branches of an organization, or where there is a continual intake of small numbers of new employees, perhaps one or two at a time, who need training but may have to wait for it until the number of potential trainees is large enough to justify the setting up of a course for them. Although industry as a whole does not show much sign of turning to individualized or packaged learning methods as the *preferred* means of instruction, they have many obvious advantages to organizations faced with the types of problems described, and many of the most successful applications of educational technology in training have been devised to meet such situations. The development of computer-based training on an increasing scale is making it easier and more attractive to bring the training to the trainees, in this sort of way. This is partly because the materials look deceptively easy to prepare, but a more important consideration is the substantial reductions in cost that organizations can reasonably expect to achieve by training in this way.

The cost of computers is coming down all the time; the cost of transporting and accommodating people on training courses is going up all the time, and the conclusion is obvious (Fielden and Pearson, 1977 AUTHORITY). In order to achieve these economies, organizations must be prepared to make a considerable investment in resources, of which the cost of equipment is a relatively small proportion, compared to the cost of developing materials. This initial investment often appears frighteningly high, and it is not a simple matter to estimate the cost-effectiveness of the new methods taking into consideration the costs, the level of training efficiency achieved, and the number of trainees. High development costs may render the cost per trainee hour apparently very high, particularly where the target populations are small.

It is clearly to the advantage of industrial concerns if they can buy in and use ready-made materials. In many training applications this is simply not possible because the training requirement is peculiar to the organization, for example, training in the manipulation of an organization's particular paperwork (like bank forms, insurance company forms, etc.), in knowledge relating to particular products (many sales training applications), the operation of special plant and machinery, and even induction courses. If materials for these sorts of applications are required, there is seldom an alternative but to create them for the organization. However, a substantial amount of technical training in particular is peculiar not to individual organizations but to groups of specialists. For example, nearly all large organizations need specialists in health and work safety laws; all these specialists need approximately the same sort of training and updating, and there are not very many of them in any one organization. In such instances it makes sense for organizations to think of sharing or buying in materials instead of having them specially prepared. Commercial producers do something to meet this kind of need, but the current hope is that the **Open Tech** (q.v.) will become the clearinghouse for materials which can be used in this way, and that MARIS will provide the central source of information about them.

NATURE OF TRAINING PROBLEMS

The point needs to be clarified that a substantial proportion of the training requirements of industry are met, not by industrial organizations themselves, but by colleges and increasingly through the agency of the **Manpower Services Commission** (q.v.). Except for some remaining apprenticeship schemes, knowledge, and skills required for various types of employment are generally acquired outside the employing organization, and most in-house training effort is directed to the acquisition of organization-specific knowledge or building on existing background to equip trainees to change or enlarge their present skills. The range of teaching and learning problems tackled by industry as a whole is extremely wide, including the updating of highly qualified experts in the latest developments of their subjects, down to the training of packers in how to construct and label the appropriate containers for a range of lethal chemicals.

APPLICATIONS OF TRAINING TECHNOLOGY

The main areas in which different educational technology practices have been applied in industry include the following:

Conceptual Knowledge. For example, the knowledge of medical topics required by pharmaceutical representatives; the knowledge of accounting procedures required by managers not directly involved in dealing with accounts; the knowledge content, often quite limited, required in jobs like those of the packers mentioned above. Nearly all job training contains some elements of conceptual knowledge, though this may be and often is a small proportion of the necessary training.

Physical Knowledge. Craft, technician, and operator skills all have substantial elements of physical skills content.

Process Understanding. The understanding of processes at different levels is an important background to many different types of jobs, not only to process operators but also to managers, clerks, supervisors, and other people whose work involves decision making at different levels and in different contexts.

Interpersonal Skills. Skills in dealing with other people are an important component of job training throughout industry, for any trainees whose work involves them with dealing with other people—that is, practically everyone. Traditionally, training in interpersonal skills used to be regarded as a problem of "attitude" change. Romiszowski (1984 AUTHORITY) takes the view that interpersonal skills are skills of control over one's own and other people's behavior. While this is a helpful approach, it leaves some questions unanswered, and another approach is to regard these skills as the outcome of the understanding of the special kind of process represented by personal interactions. Interpersonal skills are particularly important in management personnel and sales training, in which contexts a good deal of attention has been devoted to them in recent years.

Role Definition. In some jobs it is relatively easy to train people in the knowledge and skills that analysis shows them to need, yet the training is often unsatisfactory even when the trainees can demonstrably do all the defined tasks. This kind of dissatisfaction is quite common in clerical and supervisory training in particular, and occasionally also in management training. It arises because to train people in what they are supposed to *do* within an organization does not necessarily make it clear to them what their role in the organization implies in organizational or interpersonal terms.

ANALYSIS PROCEDURES

Most jobs contain elements of each of these types of knowledge and skill, which are sometimes not self-evident to managers or even to jobholders themselves. Much of the success of the educational technology approach in training has been the result of the development and application of analytical procedures to discover the actual training requirements in particular situations. No one model of training needs analysis is universally accepted or universally applicable, but four characteristic stages can be identified.

Front-end, or Performance Problem Analysis. Training is proposed as a way of enabling or persuading employees to do something or do it in a particular way. The lead question at this level of analysis is, "Is training the most efficient way of achieving this end result, or could it be achieved more simply by other procedures—redesigning the job, changing the reward structure, recruiting different types of employees?"

Job Analysis. The analyst then proceeds to examine the problem and all possible means of solving it, looking to training only when it is clear that no simpler or less expensive solution will be appropriate. Once the decision to train has been made, the analyst proceeds to examine the job to discover what is involved in the training task. What are the different tasks which together make up the trainees' daily job? What is the relative frequency with which the jobholder carries out each of these tasks; what is their relative difficulty, and their relative importance?

Task Analysis. Only when he or she has a clear picture of what the job entails does the analyst start examining individual tasks in detail. What is the exact procedure for carrying out each task? What knowledge and skills does the trainee need? Analysis at this level can be developed in great detail, so that every step in a particular procedure is identified, together with the appropriate method of carrying it out. This kind of very detailed analysis has proved particularly useful in the training of physical skills (Seymour, 1968 AUTHORITY; Willoughby and LeHunte, 1968 EXAMPLE) but is not invariably required for all tasks.

Analysis of the Target Population. What can trainees be expected to be able to do already? In many cases recruits are selected because of their knowledge and experience in the skill areas required by the job. Some of the identified tasks will require little or no training; in other cases trainees may have to undergo retraining to learn new ways of carrying out tasks of a familiar general type.

Target population analysis should also reveal something about the personal characteristics of the trainees—their ages, interests, and so forth—so that training presentations can be as motivating and attractive to them as possible.

The degree of importance of each of these stages of analysis, and the types of information which turn out to be important in developing a solution to a specific training problem, vary between different training situations. In some types of jobs, particularly those involving a substantial proportion of physical skills, the tasks can be relatively easy to identify and require extremely detailed analysis using skills analysis or mathetics techniques. Once a complex physical skill has been correctly analyzed, the training problem may be essentially cracked. But in other types of jobs, the real problem facing the analyst is correct identification of the nature of the job and the role the trainee plays in the organization. Much clerical training, in particular, has been less than satisfactory because managers and trainers have made incorrect assumptions about the nature of the job and have then proceeded to sometimes excessively detailed analysis of specific tasks, leaving the trainees very well trained in discrete elements of their jobs and wholly lacking understanding of the overall processes and of their place within the organization. Again, some trainees, for example, technical representatives, require a detailed knowledge base. In such cases the burden of the analytical work will lie in the structuring of the knowledge content, though it would be unusual to find that this was the whole content of the training.

Although it is possible to make some generalizations about the types of knowledge and skills that are likely to be important in specific types of job, in practice, training problems of any job can turn out to be full of surprises, and the value of the analytical procedure is that it allows the trainer to approach each situation with a fresh eye. It is precisely because of this that it is difficult to devise a detailed model for analysis. Once the process is under way, answers to one set of questions will provide the analyst with his next set, and the analysis may take a wholly unexpected course.

TRAINING METHODS AND MEDIA

The completion of the analysis leaves the training technologist with a clear and sufficiently detailed outline of the objectives of training and the instruction the trainee is going to need to meet them. In training, the variety of knowledge and skills required is often so great that there is a corresponding variety in the methods in common use in the implementation of training.

There are other reasons for this variety. Logistic problems account for much use of individualized learning in various forms. A good deal of training involves the operation of dangerous or expensive machinery and equipment, and in such cases it is common to find that considerations of safety or of cost have suggested the use of particular media—demonstrations on video, or practice in operating through the use of simulators are examples of methods frequently adopted for these reasons. Again, training courses are often very intensive, and the trainer may feel that a change in the nature of learning activity may be a good thing in itself, and will deliberately introduce a new learning mode simply to add variety to the course.

Sometimes, of course, new methods are adopted in a spirit of experimentation or because they are in fashion. Such experiments have not always had entirely happy results, and training technologists are rightly wary of agreeing to decisions about the media of instruction before analysis has indicated what the problems are going to be, but the general willingness to explore new possibilities in training has on the whole been productive rather than otherwise, and has offered training technologists valuable opportunities to discover the possibilities and limitations of new ideas and methods.

It is unusual to find that a single approach to teaching and learning methods will be adequate for the whole training for any job. Selection of methods and media is nearly always limited by considerations of time and cost, and the availability of equipment or space. But within these limitations trainers can and do select from a wide range. Learning tasks involving conceptual knowledge may be approached in fairly conventional ways, through lectures, reading, and seminars, or through the use of individualized media. Much of the experience with such methods as information mapping and structural communication is virtually limited to their use in industrial training contexts, and considerable efforts are currently being devoted to the development of computer-based training for various applications. Similarly, the training of physical skills is often tackled in conventional ways, through demonstration and practice, but where appropriate, more adventurous techniques include the use of simulators, video, and audiotape (in noisy environments, or where the trainer needs both hands free).

Industry's need for training in the understanding of a very wide range of processes, including interpersonal transactions, has led to the development and use of a number of techniques of varying sophistication. At one end of the scale simulators are used to show the effects of various actions on physical plant and machinery. The paradigm of the physical simulator is the flight or driving simulator in which the learner is able to operate a simulacrum of the machine in highly realistic surroundings, obviating the risks implied in gaining practice on the real machine. In some applications of this idea the realism of the simulation is less crucial, and models of plant and machinery which indicate the effect of various actions in a purely symbolic way are often perfectly adequate for training purposes. It is predictable that the spread of computers will extend their use. Computers, too, are a useful basis for simulations designed to train in financial decision making and in various other kinds of planning skills, where they offer the advantages that trainees can examine the consequences of their decisions without risk in the real world, and that the decision-making process and its probable results can be telescoped in time, where learning from real life would be an unproductively extended process.

Training problems relating to interpersonal processes have attracted a substantial effort, particularly in the 1960s and 1970s, when there was a general, if not very coherent, effort within industry to change the pattern of work relationships, especially through changing management styles. Techniques used to train in this area include a number drawn from various aspects of the human relations movement, like sensitivity training, transactional analysis, and so forth, but the fashion for these seems to be dying away. The most effective approaches to these problems seem to be those which assist trainees both to analyze transactions by giving them an adequate terminology, and to develop their responses in the desired direction by giving them frequent and copious feedback. Appropriate terminologies vary according to the kind of transactions being examined, but there is little doubt that video replay techniques provide the best way of giving feedback for this group of skills (Reckham and Morgan, 1977 AUTHORITY).

EVALUATION

In theory the criterion of successful training is the performance of the trainee on the job. In some cases, where the job and the training are of a limited and highly specific nature, it is possible to evaluate training on this criterion alone, but in practice the issue is usually complicated by any of several factors. In the first place, unless the trainees are going to perform the tasks trained for, and only those tasks, immediately after they leave the course, a number of factors can interfere with the effects of training to modify their performance of the tasks in question. The most obvious of these is time—if we train people to program in Pascal in January, and they start writing their first programs in September, the trouble they are going to have is not necessarily or even probably due to faulty training. Another common source of interference is the attitudes and practices of others; we may train someone to observe safety precautions but he or she will soon abandon them if no one else follows the same procedures. Experience can also, and usually does, improve job performance, so that inadequately trained persons can often develop on the job the skills in which their training left them deficient. Few situations provide the chance for realistic evaluation of training solely on the basis of job performance, and it is often difficult to reach an accurate assessment of the effects of interference, both positive and negative. In practice, therefore, other criteria of evaluation are used in the assessment of training, just as they are in education. Apart from formal and informal testing during and at the end of the course, the most widely relied-on source of evaluation data is the expressed opinions of the trainees themselves. This kind of opinion gathering takes quite sophisticated forms, particularly in management training courses, where trainees are frequently asked to keep diaries and notes of their reactions throughout the course, and to fill in more or less detailed questionnaires at the end of it. This kind of information can be extremely valuable, and it is often practical politics to collect and react to it, but the importance of evaluation at this level does always need to be qualified by reference to the assessed performance of the trainees. Whatever they think of the course, the question that matters is whether they can achieve the objectives, and whether, when they return to their jobs, these objectives turn out to be correct, that is, to include all the items they need, and little or nothing that is superfluous. Thus evaluation procedures for training need to cover questions not only about the success of the training procedures—whether the trainees have met the objectives—but also about the nature of those objectives—whether trainees who have met the training objectives can carry out the job in practice. But job needs tend to change all the time, as new factors enter the work situation. The evaluation process in training thus becomes a continuous one; the trainer, correctly to evaluate the objectives for each course, needs to be aware of the processes of change within the job so that he can adjust training objectives to keep them up-to-date. The appeal of educational technology in training applications is that it provides a framework for doing this and in doing so makes the process of course analysis, implementation, and evaluation explicit, manageable, and adaptable to the changing needs of the individual organization.

Anne Howe

REFERENCES

Authority

Cowan, J. (1976) "Must Self-instructional Materials Be Firmly Structured and Directed towards Lower Level Objectives?" In *Aspects of Educational Technology 10,* ed. J. Clarke and J. M. Leedham. London: Kogan Page.

Fielden, J. and Pearson, P. K. (1977) *The Costs of Learning with Computers.* London: CET.

Haines, J. (1983) *Strategies for CAI: Screen Design.* Marlborough, Mass.: Digital Press.

MacDonald Ross, N. (1972a) "Behavioural Objectives and the Structure of Knowledge." In *Aspects of Educational Technology 6,* ed. K. Austwick et al. London: Pitman.

———. (1972b) "Should the Programmer be a Subject Matter Expert?" In *Aspects of Educational Technology 6,* ed. K. Austwick et al. London: Pitman.

Mager, R. F. and Pipe, P. (1970) *Analyzing Performance Problems.* Belmont, Calif.: Fearon.

Reckham, J. and Morgan, T. (1977) *Behaviour Analysis in Training.* London: McGraw-Hill.

Romiszowski, A. J. (1981) *Designing Instructional Systems.* London: Kogan Page.

———. (1984) *Producing Instructional Systems.* London: Kogan Page.

Romiszowski, A. J. and Ellis, P. (1974) "The Use of Innovative Techniques and Media in Industrial Training." *PLET* (January): 39–50.

Seymour, W. D. (1968) *Skills Analysis Training.* London: Pitman.

Background Reading

Anderson, R. H. (1976) *Selecting and Developing Media for Instruction.* New York: Van Nostrand Reinhold.

Ashby, W. R. (1956) *An Introduction to Cybernetics.* London: Chapman and Hall.

Banathy, B. H. (1973) *Developing a Systems View of Education: The Systems-Model Approach.* Belmont, Calif.: Fearon.

Belbin, E. and Belbin, R. M. (1972) *Problems of Adult Retraining.* London: Heinemann.

Block, J. H. (1971) *Mastery Learning: Theory and Practice.* New York: Holt, Rinehart and Winston.

Bloom, B. S. et al. (1956) *Taxonomy of Educational Objectives, Handbook 1: Cognitive Domain.* David McKay. New York: Reprinted in paperback; New York and London: Longmans, 1972.

Boydell, T. H. (1973) *A Guide to Job Analysis.* London: British Association for Commercial and Industrial Education (BACIE).

Bretz, R. (1971) *A Taxonomy of Communication Media.* Englewood Cliffs, N.J.: Educational Technology Publications.

Briggs, L. J. (1970) *Handbook of Procedures for the Design of Instruction.* Pittsburgh, Penn.: American Institutes for Research.

Briggs, L. J., Campeau, P. L., Gagné, R. M., and May, M. A. (1966) *Instructional Media.* Pittsburgh, Penn.: American Institutes for Research.

Broadwell, M. M. (1976) "Classroom instruction." In *Training and Development Handbook,* ed. R. L. Craig. New York: McGraw-Hill.

Butler, F. C. (1972) *Instructional Systems Development for Vocational and Technical Training.* Englewood Cliffs, N.J.: Educational Technology Publications.

Davies, I. K. (1971) *The Management of Learning.* London: McGraw-Hill.

Davies, I. K. and Hartley, J. (1972) *Contributions to an Educational Technology.* London: Butterworths.

Gagné, R. M. and Briggs, L. J. (1974) *Principles of Instructional Design.* New York: Holt, Rinehart and Winston.

Gane, G. P., Horabin, I. S., and Lewis, B. N. (1966) "The Simplification and Avoidance of Instruction." *Industrial Training International* 1 (4): 160–166. Repr. in *Contribution to an Educational Technology,* ed. I. K. Davies and J. Hartley. London: Butterworth.

Gilbert, T. F. (1961) "Mathetics: The Technology of Education." *Journal of Mathetics,* Vols. 1 and 2. Repr. as supplement No. 1 of the *Review of Educational Cybernetics and Applied Linguistics.* London: Longman, 1969.

Hartley, J. (1978) *Designing Instructional Text.* London: Kogan Page.

Holmberg, B. (1977) *Distance Education.* London: Kogan Page.

Horn, R. E. (1973) *Introduction to Information Mapping.* Lexington, Mass.: Information Resources.

Industrial Training Research Unit. (1975) *CRAMP: A Guide to Training Decisions—Users' Manual.* ITRU Research Paper TR1. University College, London: Industrial Training Research Unit.

Krathwohl, D. R., Bloom, B. S., and Masia, B. B. (1964) *Taxonomy of Educational Objectives,* Handbook 2: *Affective Domain.* New York: David McKay.

Landa, L. N. (1976) *Instructional Regulation and Control: Cybernetics, Algorithmization and Heuristics in Education.* Englewood Cliffs, N.J.: Educational Technology Publications.

Langon, D. G. (1973) *Interactive Instructional Designs for Individual Learning.* Englewood Cliffs, N.J.: Educational Technology Publications.

Lewis, B. N. and Wollfenden, P. J. (1969) *Algorithms and Logical Trees: A Self-Instructional Course.* Cambridge, England: Algorithms Press.

Mager, R. F. (1962) *Preparing Objectives for Programmed Instruction.* Repr. as *Preparing Instructional Objectives.* Belmont, Calif.: Fearon, 1975.

———.(1968a) *Goal Analysis.* Belmont, Calif.: Fearon.

———.(1968b) *Developing Attitude Toward Learning.* Belmont, Calif.: Fearon.

———.(1973) *Measuring Instructional Intent.* Belmont, Calif.: Fearon.

Mager, R. F. and Beach, K. H. (1967) *Developing Vocational Instruction.* Belmont, Calif.: Fearon.

Mager, R. F. and McCann, J. (1961) *Learner Controlled Instruction.* Palo Alto, Calif.: Varian Associates.

Markle, S. (1969) *Good Frames and Bad: A Grammar of Frame Writing.* New York: Wiley.

van Ments, M. (1983) *The Effective Use of Role Play.* London: Kogan Page.

Pask, G. (1976) "Conversational Techniques in the Study and

Practice of Education." *British Journal of Educational Psychology* 46. Rep. in *Contributions to an Educational Technology 2*, ed. J. Hartley and I. K. Davies. London: Kogan Page, 1978.

Romiszowski, A. J., ed (1970) *The Systems Approach to Education and Training*. London: Kogan Page.

———.(1974) *Selection and Use of Instructional Media: A Systems Approach*. London: Kogan Page.

Rushby, N. J. (1983) *Selected Readings in Computer Based Learning*. London: Kogan Page.

Seymour, W. D. (1968) *Skills Analysis Training*. London: Pitman.

Simpson, E. J. (1967) "Educational Objectives in the Psychomotor Domain." *Behavioural Objectives in Curriculum Development,* ed. M. B. Kapfer. Englewood Cliffs, N.J.: Educational Technology Publications.

Stradsklev, R. (1974) *Handbook of Simulation Gaming in Social Education*. University, Ala.: Institute of Higher Education Research and Services, University of Alabama.

UNESCO. (1975) *A Systems Approach to Teaching and Learning Procedures: A Guide for Educators in Developing Countries*. Paris: UNESCO.

Wellens, J. (1974) *Training in Physical Skills*. London: Business Books.

Wheatcroft, E. (1973) *Simulation for Skill*. London: McGraw-Hill.

Winfield, I. S. (1979) *Learning to Teach Practical Skills*. London: Kogan Page.

Woodcock, J.A.D. (1972) *Cost Reduction Through Operator Training and Retraining*. London: Kogan Page.

Wyant, T. G. (1974) "Network Analysis." In *APLET Yearbook of Educational and Instructional Technology 1974/75*, ed. A. Howe and A. J. Romiszowski. London: Kogan Page.

Example

Dean, C. and Whitlock, Q.(1983) *Handbook of Computer Based Training*. London: Kogan Page.

Training Services Division of the MSC. (1968) *Training of Trainers*. First Report of the Training of Trainers Committee, MSC. London: Manpower Services Commission.

Willoughby D. and LeHunte, D. (1968) "The Application of Mathematical Analysis." In *Aspects of Educational Technology 2* ed. W. R. Dunn and C. Holroyd. London: Methuen.

Further Sources of Information

Much useful material relating to training technology is published only in journals or in the publications of advisory or consultancy organizations, some of which also hold information about packaged learning materials in various forms. These organizations include

British Association for Commercial & Industrial Education, 16 Park Crescent, London W1N 4AP, U.K.

CITAR (Computers in Training as a Resource) Imperial College, Exhibition Road, London SW7, U.K.

Council for Educational Technology, 3 Devonshire Street, London W1N 2BA, U.K.

CET Open Learning Unit, Rooms 24–27, Prudential Building, Above Bar Street, Southampton SO1 OSG, U.K.

The Industrial Training Research Unit, Lloyds Bank Chambers, Cambridge, U.K.

MARIS (Materials & Resources Information Service), Bank House, 1 St. Mary Street, Ely, Cambs CB7 4ER

Training Services Division, Manpower Services Commission, Moorfoot, Sheffield, U.K.

Journals

Educational Communication and Technology: A Journal of Theory, Research and Development (formerly *AV Communication Review*). Articles on research aspects of educational technology, research, and book reviews. Association for Educational Communication and Technology, 1126 16th St. NW, Washington, D.C. 20036, U.S.

Education: The Digest for Vocational Education and Training. Guildford Educational Services Ltd, 164 High Street, Guildford GI1 3HW, U.K.

Improving Human Performance. The official research journal of the NSPI. Editor Philip Tiemann, NSPI. 1126 Sixteenth Street, NW, Suite 315, Washington, D.C. 20036, U.S.

Industrial and Commercial Training, The Management of Human Resources. Monthly. All aspects of training and manpower development. Wellens Publishing, Guilsborough, Northants NN6 8PY, U.K.

Journal of European Industrial Training. MCB Publications, 198–200 Keighley Road, Bradford, West Yorkshire, BD9 4JO, U.K.

NSPI Journal. Short articles and news items on instructional and performance technology. Editor Harold Stolovitch. 1126 Sixteenth St. NW, Suite 315, Washington, D.C. 20036, U.S.

Programmed Learning and Educational Technology. Official journal of the Association for Educational and Training Technology. Quarterly. Kogan Page Ltd, 120 Pentonville Road, London N1 9JN, U.K.

Simulation/Games for Learning. The journal of SAGSET (formerly entitled *SAGSET Journal*). Quarterly. Kogan Page, 120 Pentonville Road, London N1 9JN, U.K.

Training. Official journal of the Institute of Training and Development. Monthly. Pitman Periodicals Ltd, 41 Parker Street, London WC2, U.K.

The Training Officer. Monthly. Marylebone Press Ltd, 25 Cross Street, Manchester M2 1WL, U.K.

TRANSACTIONAL ANALYSIS. A method of analyzing teaching situations, conversations, negotiations, etc., that involves identifying each initiation, response, etc., in terms of a particular role (e.g., teacher, student).

TRANSCRIPTION UNIT. U.K. term for high-quality record playing unit.

TRANSDUCER. A device which converts information from one form into another, in particular into an electrical signal, as in the case of a microphone which converts variations in air pressure (i.e., sound waves) into variations in an electric current.

TRANSFER LETTERING. *See* **Dry Transfer Process.**

TRANSFER RATE. The amount of data that can be read from or written to a disk in one second. It is primarily a function of how fast the disk turns and how closely together the bits can be packed on the disk surface.

TRANSFORM. *See* **Kinescope.**

TRANSISTOR. A semiconducting device which during the 1950s began to supplant the thermionic valve for reasons of cheapness, size, and reliability. In its turn the transistor has itself been largely superseded by integrated circuits, which may contain the equivalent of many thousands of transistors on one chip. All such devices basically act as either switches or amplifiers.

TRANSMISSION MONITOR. The television monitor which shows the picture being recorded or shown to the viewers. It is the final link in the chain.

TRANSPARENCY. Term which can be applied to any example of a sheet of transparent material with printing or drawing upon it. However, the commonest use is in regard to overhead projection. *See* **Overhead Transparency.**

TRANSPONDER. An amplifying device, especially in satellites, which caters for both transmitted and received signals. That is, a transponder receives a signal in its capacity as a relay station, amplifies it, then transmits it forward.

TRANSPORTABLE. Computer software which runs on more than one type of machine.

TRUTH TABLE. A listing which presents all possible input and output states of a logical function.

TTC & M GROUND STATIONS. Tracking, telemetry, command and monitoring stations which control the position and performance of a satellite in orbit.

TTL. Transistor-transistor logic. Integrated circuits operating to certain electrical standards. *See* **TTL Voltage Levels.**

TTL VOLTAGE LEVELS. Signals that are carried as voltages between 0 and +5 volts (the levels needed for a type of integrated-circuit technology known as transistor-transistor logic). TTL devices may become damaged if accidentally connected to voltages outside that range.

TUNER. That part of a radio or television receiver which separates the required signal from all the other frequencies collected by the antenna. Some applications make use of a stand-alone tuner but usually the device is an integral part of the receiver.

TUNGSTEN-HALOGEN LAMP. A lamp used extensively for studio lighting and in projectors. The distinguishing feature of the lamp design is that a trace of iodine and/or bromide vapor in the envelope combines with the tungsten evaporated from the filament, preventing it from depositing on the envelope (it is redeposited onto the filament). Such lamps give about 25 percent more output at constant color temperature for twice as long as a similar lamp without halide. The envelopes are usually made of high melting-point glass rather than quartz although the term QI (quartz-halogen) still persists. *See* **Lighting.**

TURNKEY. Turnkey installations are computer systems sold as complete and ready to go; e.g., a library circulation system, a motor retailer spare parts inventory system.

TURTLE. The cursor used in Logo, an educational computer programming language. By moving the representation of a turtle around the screen, the user is able to perform various tasks, including graphics. *See* **Logo.**

TWEETER. A small loudspeaker designed to handle only the top part of the audible spectrum.

TWIN-LENS REFLEX CAMERA. A camera that uses two lens systems geared together one above the other. The top is used to form an image via a 45-degree mirror on a ground glass screen for viewing and focusing, while the other is used for exposing the film. This design of camera was very popular in the past but has now been largely superseded by the ubiquitous single-lens reflex camera. *See* **Camera.**

TWISTED PAIR. Two wires that have been wrapped around each other, thereby lessening any tendency to pick up electrical noise. Shielded twisted-pair wiring is popular for LAN use, offering greater noise resistance and higher data rates.

TYPOGRAPHY. *See* **Graphic Design; Textbook Design.**

U

UHF. Ultrahigh frequency. The part of the frequency spectrum used for some television transmission. The frequencies used for broadcasting are divided up into five groups or bands by Article 5 of the International Radio Regulations of the International Telecommunications Union. Bands 4 and 5 ranging from 470MHz to 860MHz are known as UHF.

ULTRAFICHE. *See* **Microforms.**

ULTRAMICROFORM. *See* **Microforms.**

U-MATIC. Trade name (Sony Corporation) for a video recording system using 3/4–inch tape housed in a cassette. *See* **Tape Cassette.**

UNCAL (U.K.). An acronym for "understanding computer-assisted learning"—an evaluation project carried out by a team of evaluators based at the University of East Anglia for the National Development Program in Computer Assisted Learning. The three-year study, costing about $150,000, was completed in 1977.

UNDEREXPOSURE. Exposure of film or other material to light or heat at too low an intensity or for too short a time to produce a properly formed image. Underexposure is hard to compensate for because detail is actually missing, whereas in overexposure it is often possible to produce a satisfactory result. *See* **Overexposure.**

UNESCO. UNESCO, the United Nations Educational, Scientific and Cultural Organization, is a specialized agency of the United Nations (U.N.) family, established in 1946. Its purpose is to contribute to world peace in education, science, culture, and communication.

An intergovernmental agency which has its own constitution, UNESCO is made up of 160 member states at present. Its budget and its program are voted biennially by its General Conference in which each member state has one vote. In addition to this regular budget of some $430 million, UNESCO, in order to develop operational assistance to member states draws also on funds from other U.N. agencies, especially the Development Program and the World Bank, and on voluntary contributions from member states.

Between sessions of the General Conference, the Executive Board is the governing body. The Secretariat has its headquarters in Paris and is administered by a director general elected by the General Conference for a term of six years. The director general (1987) is Mr. Amadou Mahtar M'Bow, from Senegal, who was reelected in 1980. He is assisted by a deputy director general and one assistant director general for each of the main sectors of activity: education, natural sciences, social and human sciences, culture, communication, cooperation for development and external relations, studies and programming, and program support and administration.

Several member states are represented by permanent delegates to the Secretariat. In most of the member states, National Commissions for Cooperation with UNESCO try to promote and contribute to the development of UNESCO's programs. Furthermore, UNESCO cooperates with international institutions called "nongovernmental organizations," such as the International Council for Social Sciences and the International Film and Television Council, who have their secretariats at UNESCO headquarters.

EDUCATION SECTOR

The present structure of the education sector was set up by the Nairobi General Conference (1976) and comprises eight divisions: educational policy and planning; financing of education; equality of educational opportunity and special programs; structures, content, methods and techniques of education; science, technology and vocational education; higher education and training of educational personnel; literacy, adult education and rural development; and an operational programs division which is in charge of all extrabudgetary financed projects.

There are also four regional offices for education, in Bangkok, Beirut, Dakar, and Santiago de Chile. The International Bureau of Education in Geneva and the International Institute for Educational Planning in Paris are also parts of the education sector.

In 1976, the director general outlined the scope of UNESCO's program in education as follows:

UNESCO's programme in education is designed in the vast area of the promotion of human rights and the strengthening of peace and more specifically, in connection with the renewal of educational systems, to enable education to make a more effective contribution towards the solution of the major problems of mankind today. Activities are centred around the concept of overall, lifelong education, the object of which is the complete fulfilment of the individual's potential and his effective participation in the life and progress of society (*Learning to Be*— the UNESCO Press).... In many cases, what is needed is new types of educational action which will make good the shortcomings of traditional systems and which, far from implying opposition between school and out-of-school education, are based on their complementarity and make it possible to meet the needs of the least privileged groups more effectively, or to contribute towards the solution of certain problems which are partly educational and partly socio-economic in nature.

EDUCATIONAL TECHNOLOGY AT UNESCO

The unit responsible for educational technology is the section for methods, materials, and techniques of education, which is part of the division of structures, content, methods and techniques of education. Its principal task is to promote, develop and update the use of educational technology in order to favor the expansion and improvement of both in-school and out-of-school educational systems in the member states. Other units also dealing with development of educational technology are within the communication sector, and are the Division of Free Flow of Information and Communication Policies, which is concerned with international circulation of educational materials, and the Division of Development of Communication Systems, which concerns itself with the aspects of the development of communication through radio, television, and the press.

In the natural science sector, the Division for Scientific Research and Higher Education deals with educational technology insofar as training and retraining of university science teachers are concerned. It is also concerned with the development of informatics and the strengthening of national research, training and application of programs in informatics, particularly through the development of regional and international cooperation.

PRINCIPLES OF ACTION IN EDUCATIONAL TECHNOLOGY

In the field of educational technology, UNESCO's action is based on the assumption that the application of new methods and the use of new techniques should be sustained by a general concept of education which reflects the overall view of the educational process and its ultimate concerns. Curriculum reform and the use of new methods and techniques are seen as a component of a general effort to renew and modernize educational systems. Furthermore, the improvement of content seems inseparable from the improvement of the methods whereby it is communicated; experience in recent years has shown that the educational process can be made substantially more efficient through the contributions of modern technologies and data processing. This, however, does not necessarily mean giving up certain well-tried teaching methods, which have lost none of their relevance and in fact lend themselves to adaptation. The use of educational technology must be guided by a science of teaching which it cannot, in any case, claim to replace. Studies are therefore required to show how to rationalize the use of methods by adapting a number of current methods and/or adopting new, more efficient methods which are educationally more suitable. Thinking about the theory of learning in its relationship with the various ultimate aims of education and the characteristics of the various groups concerned has an important place in any action aimed at improving and modernizing educational methods. The diversification of methods according to specific subjects, the particular objectives in view, and the needs and the sociocultural and psychological characteristics of the various groups of pupils, students and adults, together with the elaboration of new systems for organizing learning, particularly on the basis of self-teaching, correspond to areas of increasing concern.

For the next six years, the activities concerning improvement of educational methods will aim to enrich the sum of knowledge and disseminate experience in the improvement of educational methods. It will help to strengthen the national capacity of member states in respect to the formulation, development, and evaluation of educational methods and to promote regional and international cooperation in this field. Particular attention will be paid to the adaptation to education of the new communication and data processing technologies, to training in the skills required for their utilization, and to the evaluation of their impact and their potential.

MAIN AREAS OF ACTIVITIES

Normative Action. As part of its ongoing program, UNESCO participates in different actions of a normative nature concerning educational technology. The most important is the promotion of the free circulation of educational materials which is favored by the Agreement on the Importation of Educational, Scientific and Cultural Materials, adopted by the General Conference in Florence in 1950. This agreement was amended in 1976 by an additional protocol extending its application to visual and auditory materials of an educational, scientific, or cultural character, such as videotapes, videodiscs, materials for programmed instruction, slides and multimedia kits, etc.

Important concerns are also the promotion, in cooperation with the International Standardization Organization (ISO), the International Council of Educational Media (ICEM), and producers of educational media organizations such as EURODIDAC, of a better harmonization of audiovisual equipment and improvement of the information on educational software provided by producers and distributors in their catalogs.

Organization and Management. UNESCO's program also focuses on management and economics of educational technology. After publishing a handbook on the systems approach at micro level, *Systems Approach to Teaching and Learning Procedures: A Guide for Teachers in Developing Countries* (2d ed., revised and expanded, UNESCO, 1981), the Secretariat is carrying out this program through seminars, related studies, and the development of training materials. A large program dealt with the costs of educational media and has led to the publication of *The Economics of New Educational Media* (Vol. 1, 1977; Vol. 2, 1980; Vol. 3, 1982). The third volume offers a coherent and unified analysis of cost, effects, and cost-effectiveness of technology used in education.

In the field of management, UNESCO has published *Organizing Educational Broadcasting* (London: Croom Helm, and Paris: UNESCO Press, 1982). In cooperation with the International Council of Educational Media, UNESCO has analyzed procedures and regulations developed in different countries for the management of educational materials and equipment—"The Administrator of Education and the Educational Media" (Paris: UNESCO Press, 1984).

Development of Educational Industries. With a view to increasing the production of educational materials and equipment so as to keep pace with the growth of educational systems, UNESCO cooperates with member states in order to improve the present conditions in which educational materials are produced and distributed by fostering a keener awareness of the educational and economic implications of technical options available and of the methods of organization adopted in connection with the design, production, and distribution of certain types of materials, including school textbooks, reading materials, audiovisual materials, and computer software. Activities will also foster the creation of infrastructures for the large-scale production and distribution of educational materials and equipment, especially in Africa, Latin America and the Caribbean, and the Arab States.

Advanced Techniques. UNESCO seeks to contribute to the promotion of worldwide thinking on the possible use and limitations of new communication and data processing technologies for educational purposes. Studies are focused on the possibilities offered by the advances in communication technologies (distribution satellites, videotex, teletext, etc.) for improving educational methods, for developing self-instruction and home-based education, for the extension of educational services to disadvantaged population groups, and for organizing distance teaching systems, particularly with a view to the further training of educational personnel and postsecondary training. The program also convenes regional and international meetings in order to examine the various uses of computers in education, particularly as a means of managing educational systems and the educational process, as a subject of general and technical education and the popularization of technology, and as a tool for research and learning at various levels.

Development of International Cooperation. As a tool for international understanding in educational technology, UNESCO, in cooperation with the International Council for Educational Media, has published a multilingual glossary—English-French and English-Spanish—of some 1,700 terms related to educational technology (UNESCO-IBEDATA, 1984). Other versions, with Russian and Arabic, will be prepared. Intellectual cooperation between member states is furthered through the development of regional and subregional networks of institutions contributing to educational innovation in Asia, Africa, the Arab States, the Caribbean, and Southeastern Europe. Within the framework of the European subregional network, UNESCO is supporting the AVINTER system, which was set up for the exchange of information and audiovisual programs between member states of Central and Southern Europe and to hold educational film weeks with a view to facilitating the exchange of educational materials in Europe. National case studies are launched by the member states participating in the European subregional network on ways and means of preparing teachers for the use of modern teaching techniques. Other training activities deal with the identification of national needs for specialists in educational methods and techniques, including the determination of possible sequences of study and training programs, and the launching in 1985 of training courses for specialists in national services responsible for programming and managing educational materials and equipment in which special attention is given to forecasting of needs, monitoring of quality on the basis of educational, cultural, and economic criteria, and the organization of distribution.

Eteinne Brunswic

UNIDIRECTIONAL MICROPHONE. See **Microphone Characteristics.**

UNIVERSAL DECIMAL CLASSIFICATION. A system of classifying books and other publications whereby main classes are designated by a three-digit number and subdivisions are shown by numbers after a decimal point. Also known as Dewey classification after its inventor. *See* **Information Classification and Retrieval.**

UNIVERSITY OF THE AIR. A term inaccurately associated with the U.K. Open University. The concept is of tertiary courses conducted entirely via the broadcast media. *See* **Distance Education.**

UNIX. A computer operating system originated at Bell Laboratories. UNIX is closely associated with the C language, and is transportable between many different computers. Claimed advantages for UNIX include power, flexibility, and simplicity of use.

UPDATE (DATA BASE). To change information in a data base, or to fill in information in an existing record.

UPLEG. Uplink.

UPLINK. The communications path from a transmitter to a satellite.

UPLOAD. To send a file from a small computer to a larger computer. Uploading depends on the computer at the sending end knowing how to format the material and the system at the receiving end knowing how to receive and store the data. Popular uses include the uploading of data to bulletin boards or for onward transmission to other personal computers.

UPPERCASE. In printing, lettering, etc., a term applied to normal-sized capital letters like A, B, C, D, as opposed to lowercase, or small capitals.

USER-FRIENDLY. Software or hardware designed to be easily used by naive users. Special precautions are incorporated to ensure that mistakes on the user's part are caught and remedied by the system. "Help" routines are usually made available, and an algorithmic structure may lead the users to their requirements via a series of menus.

Although the term originally applied to microcomputers and their software, there would seem to be no reason why it should not be applied in other areas, e.g., audiovisual technology such as videodiscs.

USPEC (U.K.). User specification. A term used to describe a series of guides issued by the U.K. Council for Educational Technology to assist in the standardization of audiovisual material and equipment. Uspecs have been produced on such topics as 8mm cassette systems, synchronized tape-sound systems, overhead projectors, cassette audiotape recorders and playback units, combined filmstrip/slide projectors, plugs and connectors, VHF radio receivers, microform readers, synchronized tape/vision operating practice, headphones, symbols for use on audiovisual equipment, focus on safety, selection of microcomputers, etc.

USPNET. Satellite network based on the Suva campus of the University of the South Pacific, Fiji. Extension centers in several other Pacific island nations receive instructional materials via satellite transmission.

UTILITY PROGRAM. Program allowing a microcomputer user to rename, copy, format, delete, and otherwise manipulate files. Also, programs which provide useful additional facilities relating to general computer use, e.g., clock displays, screen appearance, calendars, notebooks, etc.

V

VALIDATION. Trying out teaching materials on appropriate students to check that they work effectively; originally a programmed learning technique, now commonly associated with CAL, etc. Full validation tests whether students have actually learned the material; program validation simply checks whether the flow of lesson screens is bug-free.

VALIDITY. A test is valid when it actually measures what it purports to measure.

VBI. *See* **Vertical Blanking Interval.**

VCR. Originally a trade name (Philips Corporation) for a videocassette recorder using 1/2–inch tape housed in a cassette, now a generic name for the various formats such as VHS and Beta. The VCR system was the first to eliminate tape handling.

VDU. *See* **Visual Display Unit.**

VECTOR GRAPHICS. Computer graphics mode wherein the computer not only varies the intensity and color of the projected spot (as in common graphics) but also controls the horizontal and vertical movement of the electronic beam. Thus, pixels can be placed at any point on the screen. Vector graphics calls for very high-resolution monitors, and may put an effective 2,000 or more lines on the screen. Naturally all this costs a great deal of money, for computer, monitor, and software. *See* **Raster.**

VERIFAX. A Kodak trade-name for a "wet" copying system.

VERTICAL BLANKING INTERVAL. A number of lines on a television picture are not seen by the viewer. These lines can be utilized for such purposes as teletext, or in the case of videodiscs, for the encoding of frame numbers, chapter stops, white flags, etc.

VERTICAL FREQUENCY. In a video image, the number of times per second the electron beam travels from the top to the bottom of the screen. In North America the standard vertical frequency for video signals is 60Hz. In Europe it is 50Hz.

VERTICAL PANEL BOOK. A programmed textbook in which pages are divided vertically into panels. *See* **Programmed Text.**

VHD. *See* **Capacitance Disk.**

VHF. Very high frequency. The part of the frequency spectrum used for television and FM radio transmission. The frequencies used for broadcasting are divided up into five groups or bands by Article 5 of the International Radio Regulations of the International Telecommunications Union. Bands 1 to 3, ranging from 41MHz to 230MHz, are known as VHF.

VHS. One of the two common videocassette recorder formats, the other being Beta. The two systems are indistinguishable in performance but are of course quite incompatible.

VIATEL. Videotex system marketed by Telecom Australia, based on the British Prestel system.

VIDEO. A medium for transmitting information in the form of images to be displayed on the screen of a cathode-ray tube.

VIDEO CARTRIDGE. Obsolescent storage device for videotape wherein the tape is gradually unwound during play or recording and taken up in the recorder. The tape consequently has to be completely rewound before the cartridge can be removed from the recorder.

VIDEOCASSETTE. Storage device containing two spools; during recording or play a loop of tape is withdrawn into the recorder, but the tape is actually wound and unwound entirely within the cassette. Cassettes can be removed from the recorder at any point once the loop has been extracted from the machine.

VIDEOCASSETTE RECORDER (VCR). A videotape recorder that uses tape in cassettes. *See* **VCR.**

VIDEODISC. A disk on which sound and pictures are recorded. Several types of disk are available, but the important common feature for education is the ability to randomly address individual frames or sequences. High-quality interactive video has become feasible with videodisc. *See* **Capacitance Disk; Laser Disk.**

VIDEO EDITING. A process in which portions of prerecorded videotapes are electronically combined and arranged on another tape without physically cutting the original material. The quality of the new recording varies with the equipment used. Video editors permit vision and/or sound to be edited in two distinct ways: assemble and insert. Both techniques are of value in the production of instructional video sequences. *See* **Assemble; Insert.**

VIDEO HIGH DENSITY. *See* **Capacitance Disk.**

VIDEO MONITOR. A television display device that will accept only a video signal (i.e., one which is unmodulated because it has come direct from a television camera, video recorder, or computer). A genuine monitor may give a higher quality picture than a regular television set, and often has no facility for sound. Educational receiver-monitors are capable of performing as monitors but also function as off-air receivers. *See* **Television Receiver.**

VIDEO PROJECTION. *See* **Projection Television.**

VIDEO RECORDING AND REPRODUCTION. Few areas of educational technology have seen such rapid development as video recording and reproduction during the last twenty years. The leapfrogging of achievement by one company or another and one country or another has meant an almost bewildering array of choices available to the professional educator, choices which have possibly become outdated within months of equipment being ordered or delivered.

A basic appreciation of some of the problems involved is important to follow the history and development of the process. For example, to achieve a video recording quality comparable with normal off-air programs, equipment needs to be able to record or play back information at the rate of 5 million hertz (cycles per second). This compares with 20,000 hertz for what is regarded as high-quality sound. Not only does information need to be handled at this rate, but it must also be organized in a manner that is useful to the television receiver or monitor. For instance, to reproduce high-quality color a stability in the timing of the signal to less than 5ns (.000000005 seconds) is required.

HISTORICAL DEVELOPMENT

Broadcasting. The late 1940s in the United States saw a boom in the sale of television receivers, culminating in 7.5 million being sold in 1950. This boom in receiver sales brought on an upsurge in activity in station programming, which until this time had been either live or by means of film recording and subsequent replay over telecine. The early 1950s saw a number of organizations responding with intense research and effort to the problem of instantaneous television recording. The major thrust was to extend audio magnetic tape recording to video bandwidth.

Bing Crosby Enterprises, in late 1951, used a multiple-track longitudinal approach for their solution. General Electric in 1953 demonstrated an experimental, multiple-track video recorder. RCA followed with a five-track color recording system. In this period, the BBC began work on their VERA (Vision Electronic Recording Apparatus). This machine used two tracks for video and one for audio, running at very high speed and taking very large reels of tape. Even so, this gave only a short recording time, and the project concluded in 1958. None of the early longitudinal recording systems went into production.

Meanwhile, Charles Ginsberg of Ampex Corporation in California headed a young design team aiming to produce a commercial video recorder. Work began in 1951, and in March 1956, CBS agreed to purchase the first available units at a demonstration. The unveiling of the first commercial video recorder was on 14 April 1956 at the National Association of Radio and Television Broadcasters Convention in Chicago. Ampex had achieved what many other larger companies had failed to do. The difference in their machine was that it did not employ multiple tracks in the longitudinal motion. RCA's machine, for example, ran at over 900 centimeters per second. This was later reduced but still remained a very high speed. Even at the reduced speed, more than 2,000 meters of tape was required for a fifteen-minute recording. The Ampex machine recorded its video information in a single track laid down transversely, or across the width of the tape. This was accomplished by using four recording heads mounted on a rapidly rotating drum. Each head successively scanned across the tape. Sound information was recorded on a longitudinal track, with control signals on a second longitudinal track to enable the rotating head to scan that part of the information required at that particular time. This method of transverse recording using a so-called quadruplex head reduced the linear speed required for 2–inch tape to a modest 38 centimeters per second. To ensure good low frequency response on the tape an FM recording system was used, resulting in a bandwidth with a capability of broadcast quality signals.

On 30 November 1956, the first videotape program was broadcast from the CBS station at Television City in Los Angeles. These first video recorders were monochrome machines. They rapidly made their presence felt by providing improved picture quality at much lower operating cost than film techniques.

The earliest application of video recorders in the broadcasting field was for the time delaying of programs originating on the American East Coast for replay on the West Coast. Rapidly, television producers came to regard videotape as a useful day-to-day production tool. Some broadcasters even in these early days, installed videotape machines with suitable cameras and microphones in small mobile vehicles that could rush to a location to record a news story at the scene.

The early years also saw problems of compatibility of video tape recorders. In some instances a situation arose in which video heads were actually shipped with videotapes for replay on machines in another location. Under the sponsorship of the Society of Motion Picture and Television Engineers, a committee was formed in 1958 to look at standards and interchangeability. With the full cooperation of the two manufacturers of machines, standards problems soon reduced to zero.

The first color video recorder was demonstrated by RCA in 1957, and in 1958, of the 42 videotape machines installed and operating, 8 were color machines. These numbers may seem very small, but by the end of 1960 the total number of machines delivered was almost 1,000. In 1976, estimates placed the number of reel-to-reel quadrature head machines at over 10,000 worldwide.

Almost every year since the first appearance of quadrature video recorders, a succession of developments has provided ever increasing refinements in both operational ease and quality of signal handling. Today, we have in the broadcasting field the situation of "intelligent" video recorders; that is, machines controlled by microprocessors monitoring throughout the machine the signal quality and standard, as well as operational controls to ensure that the highest quality of signal possible is delivered to the station transmitter. There are also other methods of video recording used to provide broadcast quality signals, the most significant of these being helical machines which have undergone a recent rapid development as described in the following section.

Helical Video Recording. As early as 1960, Toshiba had shown impressive results using a helical scan format machine using 15mm-wide tape moving at 38 centimeters per second. The helical scan machine differs from the quadrature machine in that the tape moves around a rotating head to achieve the high head to tape speed necessary to produce the required information rate.

There are two broad types of helical machines: those recording a full television field on one scan of the head; and those segmenting the television field with several scans being required for each field. Ampex and others in 1961 and 1962 introduced machines on this concept for closed-circuit applications, and development continued, with many manufacturers producing machines, all of which were incompatible with those from another manufacturer. Companies saw the potential market available and jostled vigorously to capture the maximum share of the market with the machine they respectively felt was best designed to do the job. The 1960s saw many formats developed and superseded, and also, perhaps more important, many items of equipment were purchased with the intention of solving any or all audiovisual problems, but lack of reliability and complexity of use left equipment sitting idle, and the educators sadly disillusioned. If some worthwhile materials were produced, very often they would be useless for loan to another institution because of conflicting formats. The first real attempt at standardization came with the 1/2–inch EIAJ monochrome open-reel format, which became very common for educational use in the 1970s.

The late 1960s and early 1970s saw a worldwide boom in the sales of color television, and consequently an increased demand for a cheaper, easily operated color video recorder. Some companies modified black-and-white machines in ways which again presented compatibility problems, but in 1972, Sony released its U-Matic format color videocassettes based on 3/4–inch tape. Meanwhile in Europe, the Philips Company was busy producing its VCR format based on 1/2–inch tape, again in cassette format. The U-Matic machines were first released as NTSC machines and the VCRs as PAL machines. Because of this, each rapidly achieved a dominance in their own respective market. The U-Matic sales were aimed primarily at the institutional and advertising markets and achieved very significant penetration in the United States. Broadcasters, especially after the release of a portable version, found the performance of these machines acceptable for much news work. With the development of lightweight color cameras, their acceptance as an electronic news-gathering (ENG) system came into being.

The year 1977 saw the culmination of development at the other end of the helical range, i.e., the emergence of true broadcast-quality helical video recorders. While U-Matic machines were being very widely used for news broadcasting in the United States, most European broadcasters were reluctant to commit themselves to extensive use of U-Matic format for news reporting because of the lower quality available in the PAL system. Spurred on by requests from both European broadcasters for news gathering and American broadcasters for economic reasons, manufacturers showed at the International Television Symposium in Switzerland, in 1977, three 1–inch based formats for broadcasting purposes. Two by Sony and Ampex, not interchangeable, used full field recording. The other format using segmented scanning was by Bosch of Germany. It seemed that the closed-circuit battle of the 1960s was about to be reenacted in the broadcast field in the late 1970s.

The Society of Motion Picture and Television Engineers again elected committees to investigate standardization, and this resulted in two accepted formats: type B for a segmented format and type C for a unified nonsegmented scan format. These two formats, with the type C machines showing significant sales supremacy, have almost totally eclipsed quadrature format sales. A full broadcast-quality portable recorder is now available weighing under 5 kilograms, a far cry from the 200 or more kilogram monster required to achieve a much lower standard of performance twenty years earlier.

The domestic market, and increasingly the institutional market, has settled down to quite spectacular sales of video recorders utilizing 12.5mm tape in two major formats, Beta, initiated by Sony, and VHS originating from the Japanese Victor Company. The ubiquitous nature of VHS and Beta recorders has been the major factor in the vast expansion of the use of video in education and training.

Digital Recording. The handling of video signals in digital form has many advantages. While the information rate required is much higher, there exists a capability of better performance especially for multiple generations. As yet, digital video recording is not accessible to the education market.

Refinements and Accessories. Producers of audiovisual programs are generally conversant with the idea of stopping and starting, or cutting audiotape in the assembly of these programs. They very quickly encountered a limiting problem when working with videotape: because of the necessity of providing the stored information in an ordered sequential manner, correctly timed, it was not possible to stop and start a videotape recording for scene changes and so on. Early quadrature recordings were actually cut and spliced as with audiotape, but the stability of the spliced signals was not good, and most often unreliable. In 1962 electronic video editing for quadrature recorders was introduced, followed fairly rapidly by similar capabilities on helical machines for the low-end market. All of these electronic editors necessitated cuing or parking the machines at some time before the edit point and a roll-up and subsequent switch electronically from playback to record at the editing point. Today, much of this preroll timing is done either by small desktop editors controlling a number of machines, or alternatively by microprocessors actually built within the latest generation of "intelligent" video recorders, even in domestic machines.

Another problem that became evident in low-cost video recorders was their inability to play back pictures fully synchronized with cameras for mixing or inserting into special effects pictures. The larger broadcast machines had very complicated servo systems to give highly stable pictures that were fed into time-variable delay lines to ensure constant timing output. Consolidated Video Systems, in 1972, released a time-base corrector using digital techniques to enable cheaper, nonbroadcast video recorders to have their signals time-stabilized and processed. This improved dramatically the capabilities of such machines as U-Matics, VCR, and others in their applications in both broadcasting and institutional production. No longer was the additive timing error in doing duplications a problem. And no longer was there a problem in dissolving from tape to titles in postproduction work.

The early 1980s witnessed the start of digital manipulation of pictures with time-base correctors using a full frame of memory enabling freezes, zooms, pans, etc., of the played-back signal. The rate of development seems to be constantly accelerating, and every year sees exciting new techniques being used to help producers achieve the quality and style of communication they desire.

Other Video Recording Methods. Four different types of videodisc became available in recent years. The Teldec and RCA systems utilized a contact stylus to read information from a disc in a similar way to a phonograph, with attendant wear and associated problems. The system from JVC utilized variable capacitance with longer inherent life, and the system developed by Philips and marketed by them and others has videodiscs being scanned by very fine laser beams. In the event the laser disk stood the test of time, and has been the focus of production of some very fine educational materials.

The laser disk is stamped out in a similar process to the manufacture of phonograph records. This system has practically zero wear because of no contact and can be used for long-term still-frame display. While the laser scan videodisc is as yet incapable of instantaneous recording, it does provide the video equivalent of the phonograph—an easily achieved, mass-produced information storage medium that is relatively cheap and could be universally available. It is a device allowing tens of thousands of still frame "pages" to be stored on one disk produced for a cost very little more than that of a 12-inch audio disk. The ability to address or access individually any of these frames constitutes a revolution in information storage and retrieval of enormous significance to educators.

Yet another recent innovation in video recording is the storage and retrieval of very large numbers of television stills, exploiting magnetic or optical storage technology from the computer industry. Systems with broadcast quality and the ability to access any of over 100,000 stills within one second are now available and being used.

Conclusion. Methods of recording video signals have grown rapidly in the thirty years video recording has existed, and this rapid growth is continuing. We will see in the near future many fruits of research growing to reality as commercial products, providing even further advances in video recording, help the educator or entertainer fulfill his calling.

Bruce Window

REFERENCE

Brush, J. M. and Brush, D. P. (1986) *Private Television Communications: The New Directions.* Cold Spring, N.Y.: HI Press/ITVA.

Gross, L. S. (1983) *The New Television Technology.* Dubuque, Iowa: W. C. Brown.

Owen, D. (1982) *The Complete Handbook of Video.* London: Penguin.

Pensinger, G. (1983) "Black Boxes That Provide Better Pictures." *EITV* (April): 31–32.

Thomas, L. M. (1983) "Television Summary of Advances." *SMPTE Journal* (April): 407–410.

VIDEO SIGNAL. The unprocessed composite signal containing picture and scanning information produced by a television camera or video tape recorder.

VIDEOTAPE. The magnetic tape used for television recording.

VIDEO TAPE RECORDER (VTR). A machine for recording video and audio signals on magnetic tape. The original machines used two-inch tape and were priced well beyond the educational market. During the early 1960s relatively cheap one-inch machines became available, and for the first time educators were able to make use of this extremely valuable facility. Nowadays the cost of machines and tape has become relatively insignificant. *See* **Video Recording and Reproduction.**

VIDEO TELEPHONE. An abortive experiment to provide a television picture of the speakers taking part in a telephone conversation. Apart from the considerable expense of this extra facility, there is also reason to believe that the absence of visual information is one of the strengths of the telephone, at least for some purposes.

VIDEOTEX. System using telephone lines to connect subscribers to a central computerized data base. A keyboard and domestic television receiver are all that are required in addition to the videotex interface. Great promises have been made for videotex, but the U.K. Prestel system, for example, is years behind its projected take-up targets. Several videotex systems are in use, including Viatel (Australia), Telidon (Canada), and Prestel (U.K.). Common features are the use of the public telephone network to access a computerized data base. Videotex is interactive, and users can send messages and carry out transactions such as the purchase of goods, banking operations, etc. The information available may be charged for at rates from zero up to several dollars for a "page."

Access to public videotex systems is relatively slow, with communication to the system being carried out at the rate of only 75 baud; however, actual input from subscribers usually consists only of a few digits, so the speed is of little concern. A greater limitation is the coarseness of the display, which consists of 25 lines, each with a maximum of 40 characters. Each character position can be allocated as a graphic block consisting of six pixels, thus providing an extremely "chunky" appearance to videotex graphic displays.

Most videotex terminals are in fact microcomputers, which gives the opportunity to download and store material from the central data base. This facility is used, particularly in the United Kingdom, to provide computer software by videotex. Such a procedure is probably only justified in the case of short programs likely to be in great demand.

Videotex has been described as an interesting technology without any obvious purpose: the passing of time has not yet belied this judgment. *See* **Viewdata.**

Derick Unwin

REFERENCES

Byte. (1983) Seven articles on videotex. 8(7): 40–129.

Fleming, J. (1983) "NAPLPS: A New Standard for Text and Graphics." *Byte* 8 (2,3,4,5)

Godfrey, D. and Chang, E., eds. (1981) *The Telidon Book.* Toronto: Press Porcepic Ltd.

Grecsei, J. (1983) *The Architecture of Videotex Systems.* Englewood Cliffs, N.J.: Prentice-Hall.

Helliwell, J. (1983) "Exploring Graphics with NAPLPS." *PC Magazine* (July): 316–327.

Tydeman, J., Lipinsky, H., Alder, R. P., Nyhan, M., and Zwimpfer, L. (1982) *Teletext and Videotex in the US: Market—Potential, Technology Public Policy Issues.* Menlo Park, Calif.: Institute for the Future.

Woolfe, R. (1980) *Videotex: The New Television/Telephone Information Services.* London: Heyden & Son Ltd.

VIDEO TYPEWRITER. Name now preferred to *caption generator*. A device for inserting captions and other graphics into a television signal.

VIDICON. A television camera tube. Vidicons are simple tubes used in inexpensive equipment. They are characterized by good sensitivity and resolution but are slow to respond to changes of light intensity at low lighting levels. This results in a smearing effect in which objects leave a trace as they move across the television screen. In education vidicon tubes have mostly been replaced by plumbicon tubes (generally marketed under exotic names, Supercon, Megacon, and similar clones), which give more acceptable results and are often more compact. *See* **Plumbicon.**

VIEWDATA. In the United Kingdom, this term is used to cover both *viewdata* and *teletext*. However, it should be noted that CCITT has assigned the term *videotex* only to viewdata services. CCITT is the Comité Consultatif International Télégraphique et Téléphonique—the International Telegraph and Telephone Consultative Committee—which is part of the International Telecommunications Union, an agency of the United Nations. The term *videotext* is sometimes used instead of *videotex* but it has no official recognition.

DEFINITION OF VIEWDATA SYSTEM

Viewdata is the generic term used for interactive information services which use cable links to communicate information between a central computer and a user's terminal. At present, the cable link is usually the ordinary telephone network, but in the near future other cable systems capable of handling two-way data communications (e.g., fiber-optic cable) will become increasingly common. The user's terminal is a modified television receiver or microcomputer which is used to display pages of information (text and graphics) selected from a large store held on the central computer.

DESCRIPTION OF VIEWDATA SYSTEM

To communicate data over the telephone network, a modem (modulator-demodulator) is required. Purpose-built viewdata receivers have a built-in decoder and modem and use a domestic television display. Viewdata adapters provide the necessary modification to an ordinary television receiver as a separate piece of equipment, connected to the television receiver via its aerial socket. It is also possible to connect a modem or viewdata adapter to a microcomputer (rather than a television receiver) and use the screen of the microcomputer to display the pages of information. A microcomputer is most commonly used for viewdata in **telesoftware** (q.v.) applications. The viewdata receiver, adapter or modified microcomputer, is usually connected to the telephone network very simply using a jack plug and socket, although in some cases an acoustic coupler is used.

In order to use a viewdata system, the remote user must first establish the link with the central computer, and a small keypad (about the size of a pocket calculator) is usually used for this purpose. If the cable link used is the telephone network, the user simply presses a button on the keypad and the viewdata terminal automatically dials the appropriate number and establishes the link with the central computer. Apart from the viewdata "call" key, the keypad includes keys for the numbers 1 to 9 plus zero and the symbols * and #. Some viewdata terminals (e.g., modified microcomputers) have full alphanumeric keyboards.

The user accesses the required pages of information by keying in the numbers of the pages if known. Such page numbers are usually found in printed directories, published by the viewdata system operator or by the providers of information to the viewdata system. Alternatively, the user can search the information indexes of the computer by keying in numbers as prompted.

There are (at least) four technically different viewdata standards currently being used throughout the world. The major differences between standards are in the display of text and graphics to the user and in the speed of transmission of information between the central computer and the user's terminal. Viewdata was invented in the United Kingdom in the early 1970s and most viewdata systems currently in use are technically compatible with Prestel, British Telecom's pioneering public viewdata service. For Prestel-compatible viewdata systems, each page (or frame) contains about 90 words of text in a format of 24 lines of 40 characters per line. Text can be displayed in seven different colors on eight background colors, and the system allows simple graphics to be displayed using alphamosaic techniques. In some viewdata systems which are not Prestel-compatible (e.g., the Canadian Telidon system) alphageometric techniques are used to allow high-resolution graphics to be displayed.

Information on viewdata systems is usually organized in a "tree structure" of pages in which a menu of up to ten routes is offered to a user on any page, and progress to the other pages offered on the menu is by keying a single number. By keying a number corresponding to a choice on a number of successive menu or index pages, the user can be led quickly and easily to the information required.

The use of the domestic television receiver for display of text and graphics and the simple input from the user which allows him to obtain the required information are the important features which distinguish the use of viewdata systems from more sophisticated information retrieval systems.

EDUCATIONAL USES OF VIEWDATA SYSTEMS

Prestel, British Telecom's viewdata service, was originally conceived as a public information system holding information provided by a large number of organizations. Public viewdata services are now being developed and made available in many countries throughout the world. In addition, many private viewdata systems have been established with information typically provided by one organization or private company for use by its staff or agents. While many viewdata applications are for commercial users in the private sector, both public and private viewdata systems are currently being used by teachers, lecturers, librarians, and others in education.

INFORMATION ABOUT EDUCATION

When information is held in electronic form on a viewdata system, it can be changed instantly and distributed cheaply. By comparison, it is slow and expensive to publish and distribute information in printed form. Viewdata systems are presently being used to store information about courses, including local availability and course vacancy. Viewdata systems are also being used to provide up-to-date information and guidance to pupils on career opportunities, and detailed information on qualifications and awards.

ELECTRONIC MAIL

An important feature of a viewdata system is its interactive capability which allows the user to send information back via the computer to a provider of information or to another user of the system.

A viewdata response frame can be regarded as the electronic equivalent of a mail order coupon, with the important distinction that the sender's name, address, telephone number, and date and time of sending can be automatically completed on a response frame by the computer. Response frames are designed by providers of information to the viewdata system and they are preformatted in such a way that the user can input numbers (or text if he has an alphanumeric keyboard) at places in the response frame predetermined by the information provider (IP). An IP can also design a free-format response frame leaving a substantial part of the response frame blank to allow a user with an alphanumeric keyboard to key in a text message. Completed response frame messages are received by the IP when he next accesses the viewdata system. A user-to-user message facility is available on most viewdata systems. This facility allows any user of the system to send a message to any other user, with the sender "addressing" the message by keying in the recipient's user number. Senders of messages select from a number of preformatted and free-formatted message pages, and a directory gives the names and user numbers of all users registered on the system. Messages are sent and received in the same way as response frame messages, but in this case, recipients of messages can be any system user and are not restricted to IPs.

By combining response frame and user-to-user message facilities, a simple and inexpensive electronic mail capability is provided, and these facilities are already being used by teachers. Typical uses are to allow teachers and headteachers to send messages to other schools and to the local education offices, arranging for teachers to attend courses, ordering supplies, requesting the hire of tapes, books, etc. Investigations are currently being carried out into the feasibility and costs of communicating information electronically using a viewdata system between schools and education offices, and a number of pilot projects have been started.

TELESOFTWARE

A major educational use of viewdata systems is telesoftware, the storage and transmission of computer programs rather than pages of text. (This application is fully described elsewhere in the encyclopaedia). Telesoftware may well become the major use of viewdata systems in education.

INTRODUCTION TO ELECTRONIC INFORMATION SYSTEMS

Since electronic information systems are becoming increasingly common in the public sector and in the commercial world, it is important for schools and colleges to train pupils and students to use these systems. Viewdata offers a suitable introduction to the use of electronic information systems since it uses familiar equipment (television and telephone); the running costs involved in using viewdata are relatively low; and the skills and techniques employed in the use of viewdata are transferable to more sophisticated information retrieval systems.

PROGRAMMED LEARNING SEQUENCES

The way in which information is structured in a viewdata system makes it easy to implement simple programmed learning sequences. The learner can be presented with information on pages, a question can be posed, and the learner can be presented with up to ten possible answers in multiple-choice format. The learner keys the number corresponding to his assessment of the correct answer and is given feedback on the choice of answer. A number of multiple-choice questions can be combined with pages of instructional text to produce a programmed learning sequence with remedial loops. The use of color can provide an attractive display, and information can be color-coded (e.g., yellow for instructional text and answers, white for questions, blue for text in remedial loops). Use of the conceal/reveal facility offers some advantages for viewdata over print and paper for implementing programmed learning sequences. Response frames on viewdata systems can be used by learners to give the designer of the instructional sequence feedback on its effectiveness.

Since the telephone line is in use when a learner is connected to the viewdata system and working through such a programmed learning sequence, it is likely that any extensive use of viewdata for this purpose will be made during off-peak periods when telephone time is cheaper. Some experimental use of programmed learning sequences on a viewdata system has already been made in the United Kingdom for the in-service professional education of doctors in a distance learning context, and similar use for other professional groups is being investigated.

QUIZZES, GAMES, AND TESTS

Quizzes and games are already popular on public viewdata systems. Simple word games, logical games, and travel games can be implemented on viewdata systems, and made informative as well as entertaining. Quizzes on geography, history, science, and other subjects have been provided on viewdata systems, and they may be of some educational value.

Simple tests can also be made available on a viewdata system, but it may not always be feasible to determine a user's score in tests administered on a viewdata system since the system may not "remember" the user's responses to questions.

D. Daly

VIEWPOINT. CAD term for on-screen windows (sections of the screen showing different programs or different aspects of the data).

VIGNETTING. A cutting off of the edges of a picture, either accidentally or deliberately.

VIRTUAL DISK. A section of memory treated as a disk drive through the use of special driver software. A virtual disk allows programs that would otherwise have to wait for the relatively slow mechanical operations of a disk drive to run at electronic speeds. Of course, material stored on a virtual disk is subject to the same vulnerability as any other RAM storage, should there be a power failure, for example. *See* **Cache.**

VIRTUAL MEMORY. Storage that is actually provided on a disk drive or other mass-storage device but appears to programs to be part of the main memory of the computer. Thus, the programs seem to use more main memory than is actually provided.

VISION MIXER. An electronic controller for combining separate video signals into a synchronized composite signal. A central feature of a television production control room.

VISUAL DISPLAY UNIT (VDU). An input/output terminal for a computer giving a visual display of data by means of a cathode-ray tube. Black-and-white displays have given way to green or amber screens in applications where operators spend long periods working at the VDU.

VISUAL EDUCATION. The official magazine of the U.K. National Committee for Audiovisual Aids in Education, published monthly.
254 Belsize Road, London NW6 4BY, U.K.

VISUALIZER. A kind of art aid camera which is used simply to view artwork at different scales of magnification and allow a copy to be traced at a different scale from the original.

VISUAL LITERACY. Traditionally, the concept of literacy has been applied to verbal skills, that is, the ability to interpret verbal symbols (reading) and to communicate with them (writing). The term *visual literacy* was coined by John Debes to describe a variety of theoretical and practical considerations relating to visual communication. The new term emerged as a response from a group of educators who felt that the importance of the development of specific skills related to the interpretation and production of visual messages. The first conference on visual literacy was held in March 1969 in Rochester, New York. The International Visual Literacy Association grew out of that first conference.

In subsequent years following the first conference, the term has grown beyond education. It has stimulated research from different disciplines as well as many curriculum projects concerned with visual communication.

DEFINITION

Many definitions of visual literacy have been proposed (Debes, 1970; Hattersley, 1976; Ausburn and Ausburn,

1978; Braden & Hortin, 1982; Heinich, Molenda, and Russell, 1982). One of the most clear and straightforward definitions was offered by Ausburn and Ausburn: "Visual Literacy can be defined as a group of skills which enable an individual to understand and use visuals for intentionally communicating with others" (p. 291). This definition contains the two basic elements of the visual literacy concept: intentional communication through visual symbols (Ausburn and Ausburn, 1978), and the notion that a visually literate person can both understand and communicate visual language.

RATIONALE

Flory (1978) pointed out the basic assumptions that support a rationale for Visual Literacy:

1. A visual language exists.
2. People can and do think visually.
3. People can and do learn visually.
4. People can and should express themselves visually.

The idea of a visual language is central to the concept of "visual literacy." Proponents of visual literacy have drawn parallels between verbal and visual language. Like verbal language, visuals can be used to make statements by the use of elements such as color, size relations, angle of view, light and shadow, and so on. Children develop a visual vocabulary prior to a verbal one (Debes, 1968; Ausburn and Ausburn, 1978; Cochram, 1982); that is, "visual languaging" ability is the foundation for learning and communicating. It is also assumed that the development of the visual skills has a beneficial effect on verbal and numerical skills. Furthermore, mastery of visual communication skills is crucial in modern society because modern communication technology is heavily visually oriented. Media such as film, television, and pictorial advertising dominate today's society. Dondis (1973) suggested that visual literacy is as necessary today as print literacy. The person who understands the conventions of the visual media is able to understand technology and is less likely to be controlled or mystified by it.

AREAS OF CONCERN

Debes (1970) conceived visual literacy as a broad field of study. The sources that "feed" visual literacy, he maintained, can be found in many different fields such as linguistics, philosophy, technology, and art. All of these disciplines, he suggested, can contribute to the understanding of how humans communicate through visual symbols.

This very open model has stimulated contributions from people from many different disciplines. Pett (1980) has summarized the most frequently referred to areas by people concerned with visual literacy. These are

1. Areas that relate to the individual involved in the communication process: visual perception, hemispheric lateralization of the brain; mental imagery; cognitive styles.
2. Areas that relate to visual signs: sign systems, visual languaging, image variables, image analysis.

Several authors have expressed the need to specify the parameters of visual literacy. Levie (1978) proposed that visual literacy should not be concerned with vision as a sensory modality but mostly with the symbolic codes of visual media. He suggested that instructional research on visual literacy should concentrate on the study of these symbolic codes. Cochram et al. (1980) have advocated a cognitive approach for future research on visual literacy. Braden and Hortin (1982) proposed a classification schema in order to clarify the relationship between visual literacy and other disciplines. They proposed three types of relationships: (a) areas of concern which are totally subsumed by visual literacy such as visual language; (b) areas with overlapping concerns such as linguistics; and (c) areas where the differences between fields of study are fairly clear such as fine arts. The authors offered an extensive list of references classified according to this schema.

The conclusions from research on visual literacy have been summarized by Hortin (see Hortin, 1982 for supporting references); these are

1. Perception involves the active processing of information by the individual.
2. An important aspect of perception is the ability to understand visual elements.
3. Visual elements and their composition are thought to be analogous to verbal language elements such as letters and syntax, justifying the use of the term *visual language*.
4. Visual language is a means to visual thinking through the study of symbolic systems, dual coding, mental imagery, and visualization.
5. Visual literacy is understanding visual language.

Cassidy and Knowlton (1983) strongly questioned the value of using literacy as a metaphor to describe visual skills. The authors concluded "there is little cross-cultural or developmental literature to substantiate the contention that people need to be taught how to interpret pictures" (p. 89).

Sless (1984) argued that Cassidy and Knowlton's article takes a narrow empiricist point of view. He claims that the visual literacy movement has placed too much emphasis on experimental psychology, ignoring other valuable sources of knowledge such as the cultural history of visual thought and the understanding of the professions dealing with visual communication. More than a "failed metaphor," Sless claims, visual literacy has been "a failed opportunity."

EDUCATIONAL CONCERNS

Proponents of visual literacy have emphasized the need to develop visual communication programs. These programs, they maintain, should not only be the concern of art teachers but they should be an integral part of the curriculum. As Hutton (1978) pointed out, "seeing and visual thinking are complex processes with enormous potential across the curriculum" (1978, p. 72).

The visual literacy movement has stimulated the development of many curriculum projects at all educational levels. There is no clear agreement about what specific skills a visual literacy program should include. Different programs emphasize different skills. Some of the most frequent educational goals are to understand and relate the elements of a visual; to analyze, critique, and appreciate the content of visual communication; and to learn to appreciate, critique, and produce visual media. Most visual literacy programs encourage students to present their message through a visual language. It is assumed that in the process of creating visuals, students will develop a better understanding and appreciation of visual media.

An example of the forementioned programs is the Australian Visual Education Curriculum. This is one of the most comprehensive visual literacy programs in existence. This project was founded by the Curriculum Development Centre in Canberra and directed by Deanne Hutton at Salisbury College, South Australia. The basic abilities that this program attempts to promote are (a) to observe objects and to translate this visual information into pictorial form, (b) to interpret and use visual analogies, (c) to translate numerical and verbal information into pictures and vice versa, (d) to employ mental imagery in solving problems, (e) to search for and to evaluate the visual information in such media as television, films, books, magazines, and newspapers (Hutton, 1978).

This is just one example of the many visual literacy programs that have been developed. Burbank and Pett (1982) have offered a summary of eight successful programs developed in the United States, Canada, England, and Australia. The annual proceedings of the Visual Literacy Conferences also include a variety of papers dealing with curriculum projects.

Mariela Tovar

ASSOCIATION

International Visual Literacy Association, P.O. Box 5622, Bloomington, Indiana, 47401, U.S. Publications:

(a) *Visual Literacy Newsletter* (monthly)

(b) *Journal of Visual Verbal Languaging* (twice a year)

(c) Proceedings from annual conference

(d) *Contributions to the Study of Visual Literacy*. Edited by L. Burbank and D. Pett. IVLA, 1983.

REFERENCES

Ausburn, L. J. and Ausburn, F. B. (1978) "Visual Literacy: Background, Theory and Practice." *PLET* 25 (4): 291–297.

Braden, R. A. and Hortin, J. A. (1982) "Identifying the Theoretical Foundations of Visual Literacy." In *Television and Visual Literacy*, ed. R. Braden and A. Walker. Readings from the 13th Annual Conference of the International Visual Literacy Association. Bloomington: Indiana University Press.

Burbank, L. and Pett, D. (1982) "Eight Dimensions of Visual Literacy." *Instructional Innovator* (January): 25–27.

Cassidy, M. F. and Knowlton, J. Q. (1983) "Visual Literacy: A Failed Metaphor?" *ECTJ* 31: 2.

Cochram, L. M. et al. (1980) "Exploring Approaches for Researching Visual Literacy." *ECTJ* 28 (4): 241–265.

Cochram, L. M. (1982) "Visual Literacy: The Most Basic Skill." In *Television and Visual Literacy*, ed. R. Braden and A. Walker. Readings from the 13th Annual Conference of the International Visual Literacy Association. Bloomington: Indiana University Press.

Debes, J. L. (1968) "Some Foundations for Visual Literacy." *Audiovisual Instruction* (November): 961–964.

———. (1970) "The Loom of Visual Literacy—An Overview." In *Proceedings of the First National Conference on Visual Literacy*, ed. C. M. Williams and J. L. Debes. New York: Pitman.

Dondis, D. A. (1973) *A Primer of Visual Literacy*. Cambridge, Mass.: MIT Press.

Flory, J. (1978) "Visual Literacy: A Vital Skill in the Process of Rhetorical Criticism." Paper presented at the Annual Meeting of the Southern Speech Communication Association, Atlanta, Georgia, April. ERIC Document No. ED155 772.

Hattersley, R. (1976) "What Is Visual Literacy?" *35mm Photography* (Summer): 6.

Heinich, R., Molenda, M., and Russell, J. (1982) *Instructional Media and the New Technologies of Instruction*. New York: John Wiley.

Hortin, J. A. (1982) "Experimental Phenomenology and Visual Literacy." In *Television and Visual Literacy*, ed. R. Braden and A. Walker. Readings from the 13th Annual Conference of the International Visual Literacy Association. Bloomington, Ind.: Indiana University Press.

Hutton, D. W. (1978) "Seeing to Learn: Using Visual Skills Across the Curriculum." In *Proceedings from the Tenth Annual Conference on Visual Literacy*, ed. W. Armstrong. Bloomington, Ind.: International Visual Literacy Association.

Levie, H. W. (1978) "A Prospectus for Instructional Research on Visual Literacy." *ECTJ* 26: 25–36.
Pett, D. W. (1980) "Visual Literacy: Theory and Practice." *Mediagram* (Virginia Educational Media Association) 5 (3): 11–15.
Sless, D. (1984) "Visual Literacy: A Failed Opportunity." *ECTJ* 32: 4.

VISUAL NOUNS. A term used to describe basic media elements which can be incorporated into various schemes of instruction or learning. For example, a slide depicting a bulk ore carrier; a short audio tape of street noises. *See* **Component Resources.**

VLSI. Very Large-Scale Integration: a technology achieving the increased miniaturization of microelectronic components.

VOICE-COIL. A type of hard-disk read/write mechanism that moves from track to track very quickly.

VOICE-OVER. Off-camera voice on sound track of film or television program. Voice-over is usually added at the postproduction stage.

VOLATILE. Refers to computer random access memory which depends on normal power supply being connected. That is to say, if the power switch is turned off, all information in memory is lost. *See* **Nonvolatile.**

VOLUME. A region on a hard disk with its own directory.

VTR. Video Tape Recorder. *See* **Video Recording and Reproduction.**

W

WALL CHART. A large sheet of paper, exhibiting information in graphic or tabular form, designed to be attached to a wall for display purposes.

WAR GAMES. War games, the name given to simulations of conflict situations, have been used for many decades in military training. Although such games as "military chess" were used before the eighteenth century, it was not until around 1870 that their great potential as a legitimate and worthwhile method of training officers, developing tactics, etc., was really accepted by the armed forces. Following the Boer War, however, there was a lack of activity in the development of war games for about 50 years.

The past 30 years has seen a resurgence of war-gaming, although the new war games are finding more use as an instrument for research than an aid to planning or training. The reason is twofold: there was a growing need to study new forms of warfare (e.g., nuclear warfare) of which there was little practical experience; and there was an awareness that a great deal of the weapon assessment that had been carried out since World War II was based on simplifications with regard to terrain and tactics which were no longer tenable. What developed was a sort of "experimental war" in which new tactics could be tried out, hypothetical weapons examined, and so on. Several hundred such research games, representing operations at various levels and also air and sea warfare, have been developed.

WARM START. The process of restarting a microcomputer with the power already on, without reloading the operating system into main memory and hopefully without losing the program or data already in memory.

WATT. Unit of electrical power equal to a rate of consumption of energy of one joule per second. Many physical characteristics are related (although not linearly) to the power, or wattage, of a piece of equipment: for example, the brightness of a lamp, the maximum volume of sound from a loudspeaker, the strength of a radio or television broadcasting station.

WEB OFFSET. An offset lithography printing system in which the paper is in a continuous roll and passes from a reel, through the printing press or, in the case of color, a set of presses, to the delivery end. *See* **Reprography**.

WEIGHTING. A statistical procedure for valuing certain scores higher or lower than others. For example, in a test certain questions may be considered harder to answer than others, and these may therefore carry a higher weighting. If each question is marked out of 10, then the marks for Q2, say, may be multiplied by 3 if this question is deemed to be three times as difficult as the others.

WHITEBOARD. A marker board with a white surface for use with dry marker felt pens.

WHITE FLAG. A videodisc code that identifies a new film frame. The purpose is to ensure that in freeze frame mode the two fields being continually read are taken from the same film frame. Because of the technique necessary to transfer film to video, it will often happen that adjacent fields on the disk are taken from dissimilar film frames, i.e., at the point of a cut. *See* **Three-Two Pulldown**.

WHITE NOISE. Random noise unbiased toward any particular frequency.

WIDE-ANGLE LENS. A lens of short focal length with an angle of field of 60 degrees or more. Such lenses have many uses, both practical and artistic. The wider the angle the closer the lens will focus and the greater the field of view, but these benefits are obtained at the expense of increasing distortion, with objects closer to the camera appearing disproportionately large. Thus people appear to have big noses, and so on.

WIDOW. "Widows" and "orphans" are printing terms without precise meaning. However, it is common to use "orphan" to refer to a single word forming the last line of a paragraph; whereas a "widow" occurs when the last line of a paragraph spills over to a new page. More sophisticated word processors can eliminate widows and orphans.

WILD CARD. A wildcard character is used to represent any character or group of characters when specifying a filename in a microcomputer program. For example, a file called PIG.DOC could be accessed by searching for PI?.* where ? is a wild card standing for one character only, and * is a wild card standing for any number of characters; however, note that there may be other files whose names will also fit, such as PIN.DOC, PIT.MS, etc.

WILD SOUND. Recorded sound which is not accurately synchronized with film; the lack of synchronization becomes apparent if the lips of speakers come into view. *See* **Lip Sync.**

WINCHESTER DISK. Term now largely supplanted by the generic *hard disk*. The origin is alleged to be that the early IBM specification called for both a 30MB fixed disk and a 30MB removable disk, thus the project was referred to as "30–30" and hence Winchester after the celebrated rifle of that name. *See* **Hard Disk.**

WINDOW. Computer term describing the ability to designate part of the viewing screen for the purpose of inspecting new data, while still preserving some or most of the original display. Thus in a word-processing program we might create a window to view a calculator in order to enter the result of a financial formula without leaving the word processor.

WIPE. A television special effect in which a new picture appears to push the existing picture off the screen. Wipes can be vertical or horizontal, or may take more sophisticated forms such as an expanding circle.

WIRELESS HEADSET. Headset with no physical connection to the audio system. *See* **Headset.**

WIRELESS MICROPHONE. Another name for a radio microphone. *See* **Radio Microphone.**

WORD. *See* **Memory.**

WORD PROCESSOR.

GENERAL CONSIDERATIONS

Along with the spreadsheet the word processor is probably the most obvious example of the innovations made possible by the advent of the cheap microcomputer. At its very basic a word processor is a computerized typewriter. When a key is struck, the symbol is not printed on paper—it is stored in computer memory. All corrections and amendments are carried out in memory, and only when the document is perfect need it be printed out—generally at high speed. The document is also usually stored on magnetic disk so that it can be retrieved again and again if required.

Suppose a long document (say ten pages) was keyed in, printed, and stored. Subsequently, a glaring omission is discovered on the first page, requiring the addition of some fifteen words or so. The document can be retrieved, the fifteen words inserted, and a new printout obtained, all in the space of a few minutes. All wording below the correction will have been moved down and rearranged perfectly. Contrast this with the prospect of retyping the whole document on a conventional typewriter: up to an hour's typing with every chance of introducing new mistakes. Additionally, if more copies, or variants, of the document are required now or later, it will take only a few minutes to obtain each one.

Other great conveniences include the "find and replace" facility whereby a word or phrase can be automatically searched for and replaced, corrected, etc.; the incorporation of dictionary software to eliminate misspellings; a great variety of formatting commands to allow documents to be printed with any desired margins, spacing, and justification.

The skills required for word processing consist of those associated with normal typing, together with an ability to think clearly about what is actually happening in the machine. It is particularly important to adopt a very disciplined approach to correct procedures, because the very convenience of the machinery makes it only too easy to perpetrate major disasters requiring work to be repeated all over again.

Many word processors offer sophisticated facilities such as merging, where a list of names, addresses, etc., is held in the machine and on command an identical letter can be printed for each individual, including "personalizing" features—"Dear Bruce," "Give my love to Sue-Ellen and the kids," etc. Again, word processors can act as communications devices, sending/receiving messages to/from other word processors.

EDUCATIONAL IMPLICATIONS

Inevitably, within a few years the conventional typewriter will have become a rarity in most offices. At the very least the average typist will be expected to use a simple word processor *(See* **Text Editor**). This has obvious vocational implications for schools. However, a much wider challenge and opportunity is offered by the potential for language teaching. It has always been possible to edit writing with an eraser, but this is slow and laborious, and the end result is visually unattractive. With word processing students of all ages can be given the opportunity to fine-tune their creative writing, to gain insights into syntax and grammar, and to have the fruits of their work in a form which they can share with others unhindered by the usual disincentive of most handwriting.

Teachers have not been slow to appreciate the significance of word processing, and software such as the Bank Street Writer has been specially developed to allow microcomputers to act as word processors for teaching purposes.

EQUIPMENT

We can distinguish three categories of word processor:

1. Stand-Alone, Dedicated, Expensive. Such machines are likely to be found in larger offices. They may also have communications facilities to other similar machines. The future of such machines seems doubtful.
2. Text-editing Typewriters. In this case the basic machine costs no more than a conventional electric typewriter, but it has a small internal memory allowing for easy correction. Facilities such as centering, automatic indent, etc., are available. These machines will continue to be in demand in situations where the convenience of typewriting is required for certain tasks, e.g., small insertions, form filling, etc.
3. Using Computer Software. Even a very basic personal computer system is capable of word processing. However, such an arrangement is unlikely to appeal if the purpose is to produce conventional documents. Nonetheless, for educational uses this proviso may not apply.

Using a microcomputer as a word processor for office work will require a minimum configuration of

—80–column display on a high-quality monitor
—substantial RAM: 64K would be an absolute minimum for even simple purposes since the RAM has to accommodate both the word-processing program and the user's document. In fact, most top-selling word processors for IBM-PCs require over 200K RAM just for the program
—disk drive
—a letter-quality printer

Given such facilities, a microcomputer can serve as an excellent word processor, depending of course on the quality of the chosen software. In fact, outstanding word processing packages are available at very low prices.

CONCLUSIONS

Word processing offers enormous advantages in speed, accuracy, reproducibility, and convenience. Conventional typewriters represent outdated technology and will not endure, at least in the commercial environment.

The technique offers exciting and rewarding opportunities for teaching, and will assist in restoring the written word to an important role at all levels of elementary and secondary education. *See* **Teletex**.

Derick Unwin

WORD SIZE. A computer concept related to the power of the microprocessor in use. An 8–bit microprocessor uses 8–bit words called *bytes,* and one byte is capable of representing any ASCII character. A 16–bit microprocessor deals with 16–bit words which can represent two ASCII characters, and so on. The greater the word size, the faster and more powerful the processing.

WORDSMITH. One who fashions documents by use of word processing, spell-checking, and other tools. The new technology equivalent of an author.

WORK MEASUREMENT. One of the two principal components of work study, it involves the application of techniques designed to establish the time for a qualified worker to carry out a specified job at a defined level of performance. The main methods used are direct time study with a stopwatch, synthetics, predetermined motion time system, and analytical estimating.

WORM. Write Once Read Mostly. A type of CD-ROM under development (1987) which permits the user to copy data to the disk once only. Also referred to as *CD-PROM* (i.e., programmable).

WOW. The unwanted rise and fall in the pitch of reproduced sound caused by mechanical deficiencies in the recording or replay apparatus. Similar distortion occurring at high frequency is called **flutter** (q.v.).

WRITE. To transfer information from the computer to a destination external to the computer, such as a disk drive, printer, or modem.

WRITE ENABLE NOTCH. The square cutout in one edge of a microcomputer disk jacket that permits information to be written on the disk. If there is no write-enable notch, or if it is covered with a write-protect tab, information can be read from the disk but not written onto it.

WRITE-ON SLIDE. A slide with a translucent matt surface on which information can be written or drawn by hand.

WRITE PROTECT. To protect the information on a microcomputer disk by covering the write-enable notch with a write-protect tab, thus preventing any new information from being written onto the disk. Other methods are available to safeguard individual files, but write protecting is the only absolutely secure procedure.

X

X-AXIS. The horizontal axis of a graph, oscilloscope, plotter, etc. This is the axis along which the independent variable of a system is usually plotted. *See* **X-Y Plotter; Y-axis.**

XEROGRAPHY. A positive-to-positive electrostatic process developed by the Xerox Corporation and utilizing a light-sensitive, selenium-coated plate or drum which carries a positive electrostatic charge. When exposed to light, the charge is dissipated, leaving a latent image to which negatively charged black powder is adhered. The powder image is then transferred and fused to other positively charged surfaces such as paper or metal printing plates.

Recent years have seen many other corporations producing electrostatic copiers with a variety of claimed advantages. Certainly the real cost of copying has been steadily reducing over the years. *See* **Photocopying and Duplication.**

X25. CCITT Recommendation X25 establishes certain standards for connections to data networks. Thus, to make use of AUSPAC, for example, X25 data terminals and X25 interfaces must be provided.

X-Y PLOTTER. A plotting device in which the two variables are plotted along a horizontal x-axis and a vertical y-axis.

Y

YAGI. A directional antenna array named after its Japanese designer. An example of a YAGI antenna is the conventional domestic television antenna.

Y-AXIS. The vertical axis of a graph, oscilloscope, plotter, etc. This is the axis along which the dependent variable is usually plotted. *See* **X-axis; X-Y Plotter.**

Z

ZERO-SUM. Situation where one party must lose if another is to win; e.g., poker, baseball, lawsuits, etc.

ZIGZAG BOOK. A scrambled text in which pages are divided into cut sections which can be turned forward or backward independent of each other. *See* **Programmed Text; Scrambled Text.**

ZIMDEX. An audiocuing technique. Numbers or pulses are put on the bottom track of an audiocassette to mark (i.e., index) the content of the top track. *See* **Audio Instruction.**

ZOOM. An effect obtained by varying the focal length of a lens. What is observed is an apparent magnification or diminution of the observed picture, thus "zooming in" or "zooming out" have the effect of appearing to move closer to or further away from the subject. *See* **Zoom Lens.**

ZOOM LENS. A lens of varying focal length. Zoom lenses are more common (because they are cheaper and smaller) with smaller formats such as television and 16mm than with still cameras. In all cases they operate over a stated range, e.g., 20–200mm, and are primarily intended to supply a choice of focal lengths rather than the ability to vary the focal length during a shot. It is noteworthy that whatever the focal length, only objects at a certain distance will be in focus at a particular lens focusing setting.

Index

This index is intended to guide the user to topics that they would not be able to find easily using the alphabetical listing of terms. The encyclopaedia has many topics covered in the macro and micro entries. In general the reader will find topics using the alphabetical listing. In addition, entries have a limited amount of cross-referencing using the q.v. convention. **Bold** page numbers indicate macro entries.

Acculturation, 263–265
Action research, 225
Activity-based learning, 170
Adult literacy, 192–193
Aesthetics, 158
Affordable video recorder, 518–519
Algorithm, 199–200, 201, 204, 206, 207
Analysis procedures, 532–533
ANIK, 99
Answer analysis, 58
Aperture card, 393, 394
Aptitude-Treatment Interaction (ATI), 284, 376–377
ARABSAT, 99
Artificial intelligence, **10–19**, 243–246, 286, 320. *See also* Expert systems
Assessment, **20–27**
Assessment, formal, 182
Assessment, oral, aural, and practical, 23–25
Attainment test, 22
Audio-active comparative language laboratories, 333
Audio-active language laboratories, 333
Audio indexing, 37
Audio instruction, **29–38**
Audio-tutorial, 296. *See also* Keller Plan
Audiotape, 383–384
Audiovisual media, **39–52**
Audiovisual aids, 39–52
Audio workbook, 33–34
AUSSAT, 99
Authoring languages, **53–62**, 323
Automata theory, 207–209
Automatic tutors, 502
Autotutor, 451–452

Backtracking, 12
Backward chaining, 34, 245

Behavioral objective, 30–31, 156–157. *See also* Bloom, Benjamin
Berne Convention, 122–123
Big media, 41
Binary code, 88
Biochips, 496
Bit, 81–92, 201
Bloom, Benjamin, 105, 146–147
Brain-computer interface, 495–499
Branching program, 503
British Broadcasting Corporation, 169, 188–189
Broadcasting, 427–428
Broadcasting, educational, 544–545. *See also* Educational Broadcasting
BUGGY, 12, 15
Buzz group, 347
Byte, 81–92

Cartoons, 262
Case study, 225
Cassette. *See* Audiotape; Videocassette
CASTE, 212. *See also* Conversation theory
CCIR (International Radio Consultative Committee), 96
CCITT (International Telephony and Telegraphy Consultatative Committee), 97
Channel capacity, 84, 92–93
Charts, 259
Chicago TV College, 178
CIPP model, 233
Classification of media, 367–380
Code, binary, 88
Communication engineering, **81–97**
Communication satellites, 94, 97–102, 381
Communication theory, 81–92
Community media, 172
Component resources, **103–106**

Computer Curriculum Corporation, 108
Computer-assisted instruction, 10–19, **107–116**, 285, 384
Computer-assisted instruction, authoring languages, 53–62
Computer-human interaction. *See* Human-computer interaction
Computer interface, 88–92. *See also* Human-computer interface
Computer program, 317
Cone of experience, 39, 42
Conference television, 90
Context evaluation, 233
Continuing education, 181
Continuous assessment, 21. *See also* Assessment
Contrast range, 270
Conversation theory, 122–123, 209–212
Cooperativre teaching, 505–507
Copyright (U.K.) **122–125**
Copyright (U.S.), **125–127**
Copyright Act (1956, U.K.), 123–124
Copyright Revision Act (1976, U.S.), 125
Corporate video, 517–518
Cost-benefit analysis, 128–130
Cost-effectiveness, 46, **128–130**
Council for Educational Technology (U.K.), 124, 130–131
Course design, **131–135**
Courseware, 514
Coursewriter, 53, 56, 59
Crisis games, 480
Criterion-referenced evaluation, 236
Crowder, Norman, 283, 503
Cultural analysis, 157
Cultural map, 158
Current Index to Journals in Education (CIJE), 307

Curriculum, 137–151. *See also* Curriculum design
Curriculum design, **137–152**
Curriculum development, school-based, 145–146
Curriculum theory, 137, **152–161**
Cybernetics, educational, 194–221

DAIR. *See* Dial access information retrieval
DAL, 55, 58, 60
Data, 82
Decimal classification, 301–302
Delphi Technique, **165–166**
Design models, 132–133
Developing countries, **167–175**
Dewey, Melvil, 139–142, 157, 301, 304
Dial access information retrieval, 334
Diazo document copying, 438
Digital recording, 546
Digital speech, 113
Discrepancy evaluation, 23
Discrimination index, 23–24
Distance education, 45, 99–100, 172–173, **177–184**, 345
Downloading, 508
Drawings, 259
Drill and practice, 11, 337

Educational broadcasting, **187–194**
Educational cybernetics, **194–221**
Educational evolution, 420–421
Educational goals, 138
Educational information utilities, 418–419
Educational innovation, **221–223**
Educational Products Information Exchange, 235
Educational reform, 412–413
Educational research methodology, **223–227**
Educational technology, **168–173**. *See also* History of Educational technology
Educational technology, history of, **281–289**
Educational television, 171–172, 173, 187–194. *See also* Educational broadcasting
Effectiveness of media, 368
"The Electric Company," 190
Electronic mail, 99, 319, 549
Electrostatic document copying, 439
Empyries, 158
Encoding, 83
Entailment mesh, 121–122. *See also* Conversation theory

Entropy, 201, 203
ERIC, 304–307, 309–310
Essays, 22. *See also* Assessment
Ethics, 158
EUROSAT, 99
Evaluation, **232–241**
Evaluation, naturalistic, **241–243**
Examinations, norm-referenced, 24–25
Examinations, open book, 23. *See also* Assessment
Expert systems, **243–246**, 400

Facet analysis, 302–303, 304
Facility index, 23–24
Facsimile machine (FAX), 317, 318, 440
Feedback, 195, 211
Film, 39, 43–45, 384
Film loop, 44–45
Filmstrip, 42
Flight simulation, 398–399
Formative assessment, 20–21
Forward chaining, 245

Gagné, Robert M., 373
Graphic design, **258–277**
Graphs, 259
Grouprogram, 34
GUIDON, 15. *See also* Expert systems

Hagerstown project, 189–190
History of educational technology, **281–289**
Hologram. *See* Holography
Holograph. *See* Holography
Holography, **289–292**
Home experiment laboratory, 428
Human-computer interaction, 88–92, 322, 491–493
Human-computer interface, 88–92
Humanities Curriculum Project (HCP), 149

Illuminative evaluation, 226, 239
Illustrations, 259
Independent Broadcasting Authority, 188–189
Individualized instruction, **294–300**
Industrial training, 528–536
Inference engine, 244–245
Information, 82–83, 195; types of, 259
Information classification and retrieval, **301–308**
Information systems for education, **309–310**
Information technology, **310–320**

Information theory, 81–84, 210, 320
Innovation, barriers to, 222–223
Innovation, models of, 222
Innovation, school-based, 223
Instruction, effectiveness of, 406, 413–414
Instruction, efficiency of, 406, 413–414
Instructional design, 33–34, 283–284, 323
Instructional effectiveness, 40
Instructional film, 43–44
Instructional outcomes, 415–416
Intelligent terminal, 96
Interactive video, **322–326**
Intrinsic program, 503
IPS, 55
ISO, 97, 392, 491–493
ITU (International Telecommunication Union), 97

Job analysis, 532

Keller Plan, 110–111, 296, 467–468
Knowledge, forms of, 139, 152–157
Knowledge, personal, 158. *See also* Synnoetics
Knowledge acquisition, 11. *See also* Expert systems
Knowledge base, 244–245. *See also* Expert systems
Knowledge engineer, 244–245

Landa, Lev, 200
Language laboratory, 45, **333–341**
Laser, 289–292
Leadership training, 401–402
Learning, 202
Learning environment, **342–358**
Learning spaces, 346–347
Learning theory, 203, 207
Linguistic theory, 338
Link trainer, 476
Liquid toner transfer, 439
LISP, 10
Little media, 41
Logic Programming, 17
Logo, 15
London Education Classification (LEC), 303

Mager, Robert, 295–296
Management by objectives (MBO), 146–148
Management games, 483
Man-environment interaction, 343, 504. *See also* Human-computer interaction

Man: A Course of Study (MACOS), 149
Mastery learning, 236
Media attributes, 368–369
Media classification, **367–380**
Media, types of, 41
Media selection, 47, 283–284
Medical education, **380–388**
Medical illustration, 380–388. *See also* Medical education
MEDLAR, 381
Memory, 210–211
Message, 81
Metabook, 39
Meta-evaluation, 239
Microcomputers in education, **389–392**
MICRO-PROLOG, 17
Microfiche, 299, 384, 393
Microfilm, 393
Microforms, **392–394**
Micro–opaques, 393
Micropublications, 394
Microwave, 98–99
Midwest Program on Airborne Television Instruction (MPATI), 513
Military training, **396–404**
Minicourse, 299–300
Moderation, 22
Modulation, 86–87
Morse code, 83
Motivational design, **406–409**
Moving pictures, 42–43
MYCIN, 15, 245. *See also* Expert systems

NATAL, 55, 62
Naturalistic evaluation, 239, 241–243
Natural-language interpretation, 10
Natural-language processing, 113
Network, linear, 95
Network, mesh, 94–95
Network, ring, 94–95
Network, star, 94–95
Network representation, 13
Networks, 94–96, 317
Neuristics, 400
New technology and education, **412–422**
Noise, 84–85, 87–88
Norm-referenced evaluation, 236
Normalization, 25

Objective-type test, 21, 23–24
Objectives, educational, 20
Observations, teaching, 225
OECD, 143
Offset litho copying, 441

Open University, 100, 157, 178, 294, **426–430**, 528–529
Optical fiber, 94
Orthography, **431–432**
OSI (International Standards Organisation), 97
Overhead projector, 41–42

Page size, 523
Papert, Seymour, 15–17
Pask, Gordon, 122–123, 198, 202, 283, 503
Performance problem analysis, 532
Photocopying and duplicating, **438–441**
Photographic document copying, 438
Photography, 438, **441–446**
Piaget, Jean, 284
Picture, 317
PILOT, 54–55, 61
Pitman, Isaac, 178
Pixel, 317
PLANIT, 53, 56, 61
PLATO, 53–54, 59, 197, 285, 447–448
Posters, 259
Postlethwait, Samuel N., 33
Precis, 307
Pressey, Sidney L., 283, 450, 503
Print media, 426–427
Product evaluation, 233
Production rule, 14–15
Program evaluation, 233–234
Programmed instruction. *See* Programmed learning
Programmed learning, 147, 197, 399, **450–455**, 502–504
PROLOG, 17
PSI (Personalized System of Instruction), 110–111, 468. *See also* Keller Plan
Psychometric model, 224
Public television, 515–516
PUFF, 244–245. *See also* Expert systems
Pulse code modulation, 88

Radio, 172
Rand Corporation, 165
Raster, 90
Rating scale, 225
Readability, 431
Reading, rate of, 431–432
Rear projection, 44
Redundancy, 84
ReGIS, 60
Reliability of assessment, 21–22
Resource-based learning, **464–470**

Resources, component, 103–106
Resources, flexible, 105–106
Resources in Education (RIE), 307
Rolemap, 34
Rule-based system, 244–245

SAKI, 503
Satellite, communication, 286–316
Satellite broadcasting, 172
Satellites, 517. *See also* Communication satellites
Schema, 158
SCHOLAR, 13
Schools Council (U.K.), 143
Science Education Project (Australia), 141
"Sesame Street," 190
SHRDLU, 13–14. *See also* Expert systems
Sign, 201, 204
Signal, 81, 84–86, 201
Simulation and gaming, **476–487**
Simulators, 384–385
SITE, 191
Skinner, B. F., 198, 283, 450–451
Skinner, Halcyon, 502
SMALLTALK, 16–17
Social Education Materials Project (SEMP), 149
SOCRATES, 503
SOPHIE, 14. *See also* Expert systems
Sound, recorded, 45
Speech, 83
Speech compression, 29, 36–37
Spelling, 431–432. *See also* Orthography
Spirit copier, 440
Standards in audiovisual technology, **491–493**
Stake, Robert, 241
Static displays, 385
Stencil copier, 440
Still pictures, 41–42
Summative assessment, 21
Summative evaluation, 236
Surrogate travel, 417. *See also* Interactive video
Survey research, 225
Symbionics, **495–499**
Symbolics, 158
Symbol-manipulated machine, 10
Synnoetics, 158
Synoptics, 158
Synthetic speech, 89
Systems behavior, 195, 285–286
Systems theory, 131

TAL, 55, 57
Tape-slide presentation, 42, 45–46

Task analysis, 398, 532
Taxonomy, 236
Taxonomy of media. *See* Media classification
Teaching machines, 399, **502–505**
Team teaching, **506–507**
Teleconference, 518
Teleconferencing, 99
Telesoftware, **508–510**, 548, 549
Tele-teaching, 101
Teletex(t), 318, 319
Teletext, 193
Television, educational and instructional, **517–521**. *See also* Educational broadcasting
TELSTAR, 99
TenCore, 54
Textbook design, **522–525**
Textbooks, 385–386
Text editing, 556–557
Text processing, 556–557
Thermographic, document copying, 439
Thesaurus, 304–306, 309, 526
Thorndyke, Edmond L., 282, 503

TICCIT, 54, 59, 61, 286
Time-compressed speech, 36–37
Training skills, 398–399
Training technology, **528–536**
Trait treatment interaction, 284
Trigger film, 45
TTI, 284
Turtle geometry, 15–16
TUTOR, 53, 62
Tyler, Ralph, 146, 235
Typographic cuing, 523–524
Typography. *See* Textbook design

Ultrafiche, 393
UNESCO, 145, 172, 173, 177, 179, **539–541**
Universal Copyright Convention, 122
University of the Air. *See* Distance education

Validity, construct, 22
Validity, face, 21
Validity of assessment, 21–22
Videodiscs, 46, 115, 298, 519–520

Video recording and reproduction, 544–547
Videotape, 43–45
Videotex, 521
Videotex(t), 46, 318, 394
Video typewriter, 105, 548. *See also* Character generator
Viewdata, **548–550**
Visual language, 551
Visual literacy, 40–41, 263–265, **550–553**
Visual tutorial, 46
VLSI, 243

Weiner, Norbert, 195
Whitford Committee (U.K.), 124–125. *See also* Copyright (U.K.)
WHO, 382
World Book, 167–168

Xerography, 439

ZIMDEX, 34, 35, 563
Zinc oxide copier, 439–440

R 371.3303 U62e
The Encyclopaedia of education
0 1901 0046135 8
Carson Library, Lees-McRae College